DRAMA
CRITICISM

Guide to Gale Literary Criticism Series

For criticism on	Consult these Gale series
Authors now living or who died after December 31, 1959	*CONTEMPORARY LITERARY CRITICISM (CLC)*
Authors who died between 1900 and 1959	*TWENTIETH-CENTURY LITERARY CRITICISM (TCLC)*
Authors who died between 1800 and 1899	*NINETEENTH-CENTURY LITERATURE CRITICISM (NCLC)*
Authors who died between 1400 and 1799	*LITERATURE CRITICISM FROM 1400 TO 1800 (LC)* *SHAKESPEAREAN CRITICISM (SC)*
Authors who died before 1400	*CLASSICAL AND MEDIEVAL LITERATURE CRITICISM (CMLC)*
Authors of books for children and young adults	*CHILDREN'S LITERATURE REVIEW (CLR)*
Dramatists	*DRAMA CRITICISM (DC)*
Poets	*POETRY CRITICISM (PC)*
Short story writers	*SHORT STORY CRITICISM (SSC)*
Black writers of the past two hundred years	*BLACK LITERATURE CRITICISM (BLC)*
Hispanic writers of the late nineteenth and twentieth centuries	*HISPANIC LITERATURE CRITICISM (HLC)*
Native North American writers and orators of the eighteenth, nineteenth, and twentieth centuries	*NATIVE NORTH AMERICAN LITERATURE (NNAL)*
Major authors from the Renaissance to the present	*WORLD LITERATURE CRITICISM, 1500 TO THE PRESENT (WLC)*

ISSN 1056-4349

Criticism of the Most Significant and Widely Studied Dramatic Works from All the World's Literatures

VOLUME 10

Lawrence J. Trudeau, Editor

DETROIT • SAN FRANCISCO • LONDON • BOSTON • WOODBRIDGE, CT

STAFF

Lawrence J. Trudeau, *Editor*

Debra A. Wells, *Assistant Editor*

Maria Franklin, *Permissions Manager*
Kimberly F. Smilay, *Permissions Specialist*
Kelly Quin, *Permissions Associate*
Sandy Gore, *Permissions Assistant*

Victoria B. Cariappa, *Research Manager*

Michele P. LaMeau, *Research Specialist*
Julie C. Daniel, Tamara C. Nott, Tracie A. Richardson,
Norma Sawaya, Cheryl L. Warnock,
Research Associates

Mary Beth Trimper, *Production Director*
Cindy Range, *Production Assistant*

C. J. Jonik, *Desktop Publisher*
Randy Bassett, *Image Database Supervisor*
Michael Ansari, Robert Duncan, *Scanner Operator*
Pamela Reed, *Photography Coordinator*

Library of Congress Catalog Card Number 92-648805
ISBN 0-7876-2017-3
ISSN 1056-4349

Printed in the United States of America
Published simultaneously in the United Kingdom
by Gale Research International Limited
(An affiliated company of Gale Research Inc.)

10 9 8 7 6 5 4 3 2 1

Contents

Preface

Drama Criticism (*DC*) is principally intended for beginning students of literature and theater as well as the average playgoer. The series is therefore designed to introduce readers to the most frequently studied playwrights of all time periods and nationalities and to present discerning commentary on dramatic works of enduring interest. Furthermore, *DC* seeks to acquaint the reader with the uses and functions of criticism itself. Selected from a diverse body of commentary, the essays in *DC* offer insights into the authors and their works but do not require that the reader possess a wide background in literary studies. Where appropriate, reviews of important productions of the plays discussed are also included to give students a heightened awareness of drama as a dynamic art form, one that many claim is fully realized only in performance.

DC was created in response to suggestions by the staffs of high school, college, and public libraries. These librarians observed a need for a series that assembles critical commentary on the world's most renowned dramatists in the same manner as Gale's *Short Story Criticism* (*SSC*) and *Poetry Criticism* (*PC*), which present material on writers of short fiction and poetry. Although playwrights are covered in such Gale literary criticism series as *Contemporary Literary Criticism* (*CLC*), *Twentieth-Century Literary Criticism* (*TCLC*), *Nineteenth-Century Literature Criticism* (*NCLC*), *Literature Criticism from 1400 to 1800* (*LC*), and *Classical and Medieval Literature Criticism* (*CMLC*), *Drama Criticism* directs more concentrated attention on individual dramatists than is possible in the broader, survey-oriented entries in these Gale series. Commentary on the works of William Shakespeare may be found in *Shakespearean Criticism* (*SC*).

Scope of the Series

By collecting and organizing commentary on dramatists, *DC* assists students in their efforts to gain insight into literature, achieve better understanding of the texts, and formulate ideas for papers and assignments. A variety of interpretations and assessments is offered, allowing students to pursue their own interests and promoting awareness that literature is dynamic and responsive to many different opinions.

Each volume of *DC* presents:

- 5-10 entries

- authors and works representing a wide range of nationalities and time periods

- a diversity of viewpoints and critical opinions.

Organization of an Author Entry

Each author entry consists of some or all of the following elements, depending on the scope and complexity of the criticism:

- The **author heading** consists of the playwright's most commonly used name, followed by birth and death dates. If an author consistently wrote under a pseudonym, the pseudonym is listed in the author heading and the real name given in parentheses on the first line of the introduction. Also located at the beginning of the introduction are any name variations under which the dramatist wrote, including transliterated forms of the names of authors whose languages use nonroman alphabets.

- A **portrait** of the author is included when available. Most entries also feature illustrations of people, places, and events pertinent to a study of the playwright and his or her works. When appropriate, photographs of the plays in performance are also presented.

- The **biographical and critical introduction** contains background information that familiarizes the reader with the author and the critical debates surrounding his or her works.

- The list of **principal works** is divided into two sections, each of which is organized chronologically by date of first performance. If this has not been conclusively determined, the composition or publication date is used. The first section of the principal works list contains the author's dramatic pieces. The second section provides information on the author's major works in other genres.

- Whenever available, **author commentary** is provided. This section consists of essays or interviews in which the dramatist discusses his or her own work or the art of playwriting in general.

- Essays offering **overviews and general studies of the dramatist's entire literary career** give the student broad perspectives on the writer's artistic development, themes and concerns that recur in several of his or her works, the author's place in literary history, and other wide-ranging topics.

- **Criticism of individual plays** offers the reader in-depth discussions of a select number of the author's most important works. In some cases, the criticism is divided into two sections, each arranged chronologically. When a significant performance of a play can be identified (typically, the premier of a twentieth-century work), the first section of criticism will feature **production reviews** of this staging. Most entries include sections devoted to **critical commentary** that assesses the literary merit of the selected plays. When necessary, essays are carefully excerpted to focus on the work under consideration; often, however, essays and reviews are reprinted in their entirety.

- As an additional aid to students, the critical essays and excerpts are often prefaced by **explanatory annotations**. These notes provide several types of useful information, including the critic's reputation and approach to literary studies as well as the scope and significance of the criticism that follows.

- A complete **bibliographic citation**, designed to help the interested reader locate the original essay or book, precedes each piece of criticism.

- The **further reading list** at the end of each entry comprises additional studies of the dramatist. It is divided into sections that help students quickly locate the specific information they need.

Other Features

- A **cumulative author index** lists all the authors who have appeared in *DC* and Gale's other Literature Criticism Series, as well as cross-references to related titles published by Gale, including *Contemporary Authors* and *Dictionary of Literary Biography*. A complete listing of the series included appears at the beginning of the index.

- A **cumulative nationality index** lists each author featured in *DC* by nationality, followed by the number of the *DC* volume in which the author appears.

- A **cumulative title index** lists in alphabetical order the individual plays discussed in the criticism contained in *DC*. Each title is followed by the author's name and the corresponding volume and page number(s) where commentary on the work may be located. Translations and variant titles are cross-referenced to the title of the play in its original language so that all references to the work are combined in one listing.

A Note to the Reader

When writing papers, students who quote directly from any volume in *Drama Criticism* may use the following general formats to footnote reprinted criticism. The first example pertains to material drawn from periodicals, the second to materials reprinted from books.

[1]Susan Sontag, "Going to the Theater, Etc.," *Partisan Review* XXXI, No. 3 (Summer 1964), 389-94; excerpted and reprinted in *Drama Criticism,* Vol. 1, ed. Lawrence J. Trudeau (Detroit: Gale Research, 1991), pp. 17-20.

[2]Eugene M. Waith, *The Herculean Hero in Marlowe, Chapman, Shakespeare and Dryden* (Chatto & Windus, 1962); excerpted and reprinted in *Drama Criticism,* Vol. 1, ed. Lawrence J. Trudeau (Detroit: Gale Research, 1991), pp. 237-47.

Suggestions are Welcome

Readers who wish to suggest authors to appear in future volumes of *DC,* or who have other suggestions, are cordially invited to contact the editor.

Acknowledgments

The editors wish to thank the copyright holders of the excerpted criticism included in this volume and the permissions managers of many book and magazine publishing companies for assisting us in securing reproduction rights. We are also grateful to the staffs of the Detroit Public Library, the Library of Congress, the University of Detroit Mercy Library, Wayne State University Purdy/Kresge Library Complex, and the University of Michigan Libraries for making their resources available to us. Following is a list of the copyright holders who have granted us permission to reproduce material in this volume of *DC*. Every effort has been made to trace copyright, but if omissions have been made, please let us know.

COPYRIGHTED ESSAYS IN *DC*, VOLUME 10, WERE REPRODUCED FROM THE FOLLOWING PERIODICALS:

American Theatre, v. 11, October, 1994. Reproduced by permission.—*The Drama Review,* v. 19, June, 1975. Copyright © 1975, *The Drama Review.* Reproduced by permission of The MIT Press, Cambridge, MA./ v. 30, Spring, 1986. Copyright © 1986 by New York University and the Massachusetts Institute of Technology. Reproduced by permission of The MIT Press, Cambridge, MA./ v. 21, December, 1977 for "I Write These Messages That Come" by María Irene Fornés. Copyright © 1977, *The Drama Review.* Reproduced by permission of The MIT Press, Cambridge, MA and the author./ v. 22, March, 1978 for an interview with Dario Fo by Luigi Ballerini and Giuseppi Risso. Copyright © 1978, *The Drama Review.* Reproduced by permission of The MIT Press, Cambridge, MA and Luigi Ballerini.—*The Explicator,* v. 55, Winter, 1997. Copyright 1997 by Helen Dwight Reid Educational Foundation. Reproduced with permission of the Helen Dwight Reid Educational Foundation, published by Heldref Publications, 1319 18th Street, NW, Washington, DC 20036-1802.—*Forum Italicum,* v. 20, Fall, 1986. Copyright © 1986 by *Forum Italicum.* Reproduced by permission.—*The French Review,* v. LVII, December, 1983. Copyright 1983 by the American Association of Teachers of French. Reproduced by permission.—*Harvard Library Bulletin,* v. XXVI, October, 1978 for "Theatrical Censorship in France, 1844-1875: The Experience of Victor Séjour" by Charles Edwards O'Neill. Reproduced by permission of the publisher and the author.—*Ideologies & Literature,* v. III, January-March, 1981. Reproduced by permission.—*International Journal of Women's Studies,* v. 5, March/April, 1982 for "Women's Work—Trifles? The Skill and Insights of Playwright Susan Glaspell" by Beverly A. Smith. Reproduced by permission of the author.—*The Kenyon Review,* v. XIX, Summer-Fall, 1997 for "Notes about Political Theater" by Tony Kushner. Copyright © 1997 by Kenyon College. All rights reserved. Reproduced by permission of the author.—*Modern Drama,* v. XL, Winter, 1997; v. XLI, Spring, 1998; v. XXXI, March, 1988; v. XXXII, December, 1989; v. XXXIII, March, 1990; v. XXXIX, Spring, 1996. © 1997, 1998, 1989, 1990, 1996 University of Toronto, Graduate Centre for Study of Drama. ALL reproduced by permission.—*The New Republic,* v. 208, May 24, 1993; v. 209, December 27, 1993. © 1993 The New Republic, Inc. Both reproduced by permission of *The New Republic.*—*New York,* Magazine, v. 26, May 16, 1993; v. 26, December 6, 1993. Copyright © 1993 PRIMEDIA Magazine Corporation. All rights reserved. Both reproduced with the permission of *New York* Magazine.—*The New York Times,* May 5, 1993; November 24, 1993. Copyright © 1993 by The New York Times Company. Both reproduced by permission.—*The New Yorker,* v. LXIX, May 31, 1993 for "Angels on Broadway" by John Lahr.; v. LXIX, December 13, 1993 for "Earth Angels" by John Lahr. © 1993 by the author. All rights reserved. Reproduced by permission of Georges Borchardt, Inc. for the author.—*Newsday,* May 5, 1993; November 24, 1993. © Newsday, Inc., 1993. Both reproduced with permission.—*Nineteenth-Century French Studies,* v. 1, February, 1973. © 1973 by *Nineteenth-Century French Studies.* Reproduced by permission.—*Partisan Review,* v. LI, 1984 for "The Un-American Satire of Dario Fo" by Joel Schecter. Copyright © 1984 by *Partisan Review.* Reproduced by permission of the author.—*Performing Arts Journal,* v. VIII, 1984. Copyright © 1984 *Performing Arts Journal.* Reproduced by permission of The Johns Hopkins University Press.—*PMLA,* v. 113, January, 1998. Copyright © 1998 by the Modern Language Association of America. Reproduced by permission of the Modern Language Association of America.—*Raritan: A Quarterly Review,* v. 13, Winter, 1994 for "Roy Cohn in America" by Ross Posnock. Copyright © 1994 by *Raritan: A Quarterly Review.* Reproduced by permission.—*Theater,* v. 10, Spring, 1979. Copyright © 1979 by Yale Drama School. Reproduced by permission of Duke University Press./ v. 24, 1993 for"Angels in America, Devils in the Wings" by Gordon Rogoff. Copyright © 1993 by Yale Drama School. Reproduced by permission of the Duke University Press and the author.—*Theatre Journal,* v. 44, May, 1992; v. 45, October, 1993; v. 47, May, 1995. © 1992, 1993, 1995, University and College Theatre Association of the American Theatre Association. Reproduced by permission of The Johns Hopkins University Press.—*Theatre Quarterly,* v. 5, March-May, 1975 for "The Agitprop Pilgrimage of Luis Valdez and El Teatro Campesino" by John Harrop and Jorge Huerta. Reproduced by permission of Jorge Huerta and the Literary Estate of John Harrop.

List of Playwrights Covered in *DC*

Volume 1
James Baldwin
William Wells Brown
Karel Capek
Mary Chase
Alexandre Dumas (*fils*)
Charles Fuller
Nikolai Gogol
Lillian Hellman
Christopher Marlowe
Arthur Miller
Yukio Mishima
Richard Brinsley Sheridan
Sophocles
Thornton Wilder

Volume 2
Aristophanes
Albert Camus
William Congreve
Everyman
Federico García Lorca
Lorraine Hansberry
Henrik Ibsen
Wole Soyinka
John Millingon Synge
John Webster
August Wilson

Volume 3
Bertolt Brecht
Pedro Calderón de la Barca
John Dryden
Athol Fugard
Langston Hughes
Thomas Kyd
Menander
Joe Orton
Jean-Paul Sartre
Ntozake Shange

Volume 4
Pierre-Augustin Caron de
    Beaumarchais
Aphra Behn
Alice Childress
Euripides
Hugo von Hofmannsthal
David Henry Hwang
Ben Jonson
David Mamet
Wendy Wasserstein
Tennessee Williams

Volume 5
Caryl Churchill
John Pepper Clark
Adrienne Kennedy
Thomas Middleton
Luigi Pirandello
Eugène Scribe
Lucius Annaeus Seneca
Sam Shepard
Paul Zindel

Volume 6
Amiri Baraka
Francis Beaumont and
    John Fletcher
Ed Bullins
Václav Havel
Clifford Odets
Plautus
Tom Stoppard

Volume 7
Frank Chin
Spalding Gray
John Lyly
Emily Mann
Pierre Carlet de Chamblain de
    Marivaux
Peter Shaffer
Terence
Ivan Turgenev
Derek Walcott
Zeami

Volume 8
Aeschylus
Jean Anouilh
Lonne Elder III
John Ford
Brian Friel
Oliver Goldsmith
Charles Gordone
Larry Kramer
Marsha Norman

Volume 9
Anton Pavlovich Chekhov

Volume 10
Dario Fo
Maria Irene Fornes
Susan Glaspell
Tony Kushner
Edmond Rostand
Victor Séjour
Luis Valdez

Dario Fo
1926-

INTRODUCTION

Nobel Prize-winning playwright, director, and actor Dario Fo is one of the most controversial figures in Italian theater. Through his avant-garde comedic stage productions—the spirit of which has been likened to that of such diverse artists as German plawright Bertolt Brecht and American comedians Lenny Bruce and the Marx Brothers—Fo reacts against injustice, discredits symbols of authority, and espouses a progressive left-wing political theory. Although his works were banned and censored in both Europe and the United States for years, by the mid-1980s Fo gained prominence as one of the most widely produced contemporary Italian playwrights outside of his native country.

BIOGRAPHICAL INFORMATION

Fo was born in San Giano, Lombardy, Italy, the son of Felice (a railroad stationmaster) and Pina Rota Fo. Young Fo began refining his animated method of storytelling as a child, listening to the tales told by the locals in San Giano. After leaving Milan's Academy of Fine Arts without earning a degree, Fo wrote and performed with several improvisational theatrical groups. He first earned acclaim as a playwright in 1953 with *Il dito nell'occhio* (*A Finger in the Eye*), a socially satiric production that presented Marxist ideas against a circus-like background. His 1954 attack on the Italian government in *I sani de legare* (*A Madhouse for the Sane*), in which Fo labeled several government officials fascist sympathizers, resulted in the cutting of some material from the original script and the mandated presence of state inspectors at each performance of the play to insure that the country's strict libel laws were not violated. Also in 1954, Fo married the actress Franca Rame, with whom he began to collaborate. The couple established a touring company and appeared on Italian television in a popular comedy revue.

By the 1960s Fo and Rame were censored for the explicit political content of their routines, and Fo vowed to "stop playing the jester of the bourgeoisie." Amid the social and political turmoil in Europe in 1968, the couple formed a new troupe, *Nuova Scena*, under the sponsorship of the Italian Communist Party. Fo first performed *Mistero Buffo*, generally considered his greatest and most controversial play, in 1969. Fo's criticism of the Communist party bureaucracy soon led to a split with *Nuova Scena*, and Fo and Rame formed *Il colletivo teatrale la comune* in 1970. Fo's best-known works come from the early years of this

group, whose explicit goal was to raise the consciousness of the working classes and encourage the overthrow of the bourgeois state to bring about a socialist government. Fo's strong sense of justice prompted him to compose the absurdist play *Morte accidentale di un anarchico* (*Accidental Death of an Anarchist*) in response to the 1969 death of anarchist railway man Giuseppi Pinelli. The play was a smash hit in Italy, playing to huge crowds for more than four years. When officials pressured a theater in Bologna to halt plans for production, the work was alternatively staged in a sports stadium for an audience of more than six thousand people.

In 1980 and 1984 Fo and Rame were denied visas to the United States because of their alleged involvement in fund-raising activities for an Italian terrorist organization. The couple dismissed the accusation and maintained their innocence. Through the efforts of civil libertarian and cultural groups in Europe and the United States, Fo and Rame ultimately received visas, and *Mistero Buffo* finally opened in New York in the spring of 1986. Throughout his career Fo has been the recipient of numerous prizes, including the Sonning Award, Denmark (1981), an Obie Award (1987), and a Nobel Prize in Literature (1997).

MAJOR WORKS

Fo's artistic style draws on the venerable Italian traditions of the medieval *giullari*, itinerant street entertainers, and the more polished ensemble *commedia dell'arte* of the Renaissance to stage polemical works rooted in Marxist ideology. His signature piece, *Mistero Buffo*, first produced in 1969, consists of a series of skits that satirize Italy's institutions of power, including the government and the Pope, as well as farcical inversions of traditional folk tales and biblical morality lessons. Broad international acclaim came with *Morte accidentale di un anarchico* in 1970. This was Fo's first play to be produced in both England and the United States. The work concerns the death of the railway worker Guiseppi Pinelli. The death was apparently connected to efforts by right-wing extremists in Italy's military and secret service agencies to discredit the Italian Communist party by staging a series of seemingly leftist-engineered bombings. The railway worker was implicated in the worst of these bombings, the 1969 massacre at Milan's Agricultural Bank. While being held for interrogation, Pinelli fell—it was later shown that he was pushed—from the fourth-floor window of Milan's police headquarters. In his play Fo introduces a stock medieval character, the maniac, into the investigation of the bombing to illuminate the truth. Fo's other works include *Non si paga, non si paga* (*We Won't Pay! We Won't Pay!*), a farce lampooning consumer economics, and *Clacson, trombette e pernacchi* (produced as *Trumpets and Raspberries* in England and *About Face* in the United States) a reworking of the Aldo Moro kidnapping into a satire on capitalist/worker relations. Since the 1980s Fo has increasingly collaborated with Franca Rame, and their productions have featured Rame's feminist perspective while focusing on male/female relationships. Fo explained the more personal focus of these works when he said, "In the face of the failure of revolutionary ideals, the basic problem is how people relate to one another." Because all of Fo's works rely so heavily on improvisation and audience interaction, each production bears only a general similarity to its published text.

CRITICAL RECEPTION

In bestowing the 1997 Nobel Prize for Literature on Fo, the Awards Committee said, "He if anyone merits the epithet of jester in the true meaning of that word. With a blend of laughter and gravity he opens our eyes to abuses and injustices in society and also the wider historical perspective in which they can be placed." The Committee's award is one of the most controversial decisions in the history of the Nobel Prize. While his broad farce, wild slapstick, and earthy irreverence have made him one of the world's most widely produced contemporary playwrights, Fo's political ideology has earned him the enmity of the rich and powerful objects of his satires. His style has also deeply divided critical response to his work along political lines. The Swedish Academy addressed this aspect of his work as well: "Fo is an extremely serious satirist with a multifaceted oeuvre. His independence and clear-sightedness have led him to take great risks, whose consequences he has been made to feel while at the same time experiencing enormous response from widely differing quarters." Such divergent groups as the Italian government and police, the Italian Communist Party, the Vatican, and the U.S. State Department have all denounced and sanctioned Fo.

In its zany humor and slapstick exaggeration, Fo's work has been compared with that of Charlie Chaplin, the Marx Brothers, and Monty Python. His biting satire and scatological humor have led many to liken him to Lenny Bruce. Some critics have praised Fo's abilities as both writer and performer. "Imagine a cross between Bertolt Brecht and Lenny Bruce, and you may begin to have an idea of the scope of Fo's anarchic wit," said Mel Gussow in *The New York Times* in 1983. Responding to Fo's receipt of the Nobel Prize, Italy's best-known theater director, Giorgio Strehler, said, "With Dario Fo, we feel honored as Europeans and as men of the theater." Fo's own response to receiving the award bears no trace of his onstage jester persona: "I'm flabbergasted," he is reported to have said. "I'd be a hypocrite if I told you that I counted on it. I didn't. I didn't expect it at all."

PRINCIPAL WORKS

PLAYS

Il dito nell'occhio [*A Finger in the Eye*] 1953

I sani da legare [*A Madhouse for the Sane*] 1954

Ladri, manachini e donne nude [*Thieves, Dummies, and Naked Women*] (four short plays) 1958

Comico finale [*Comic Finale*] (four short plays) 1958

Gli arcangeli non giocano a flipper [*Archangels Don't Play Pinball*] 1959

Aveva due pistole con gli occhi bianchi e neri [*He Had Two Pistols with White and Black Eyes*] 1960

Storia ver di Piero d'Angera: che alla crociata non c'era [*The True Story of Piero Angera, Who Wasn't at the Crusades*] 1960

Chi ruba un piede è fortunato in amore [*He Who Steals a Foot Is Lucky in Love*] 1961

Isabella, tre caravelle, e un cacciaballe [*Isabella, Three Sailing Ships, and a Con Man*] 1963

Settimo: rub un po' meno [*Seventh Commandment: Thou Shalt Steal a Bit Less*] 1964

La colpa è sempre del diavolo [*Always Blame the Devil*] 1965

La Signora è buttare [*The Lady Has to Be Thrown Away*] 1967

Grande pantomima con bandiere e pupazzi piccoli e medi [*Grand Pantomime with Flags and Small and Medium-Sized Puppets*] 1968

Mistero Buffo [*Comic Mystery*] 1969

L'operaio conosce trecento parole, il padrone mille. Per questo è lui il padrone [*The Worker Knows 300 Words, the Boss 1000. That's Why He's the Boss*] 1969

Legami pure che tanto io spacco tutto lo stesso [*Go Ahead, Tie Me Up, I'm Going To Break Everything Anyway*; produced in English as *The Boss's Funeral*] 1969

Morte accidentale di un anarchico [*Accidental Death of an Anarchist*] 1970

Tutti uniti! Tutti insieme! Ma scusa quello non è il padrone? [*United We Stand! All Together Now! Hang On, Isn't That the Boss?*] 1972

Fedayn 1972

Pum, pum! Chi é? La polizia! [*Knock, Knock! Who's There? Police!*] 1972

Guerra di popolo in Cile [*The People's War in Chile*] 1973

Non si paga, non si paga [*We Won't Pay! We Won't Pay!*] 1974

Il Fanfani rapito [*Fanfani Kidnapped*] 1975

La giullarata 1975

La marijuana della mamma è la più bella [*Mother's Marijuana Is the Best*] 1976

Tutta casa, letto e chiesa [*All House, Bed, and Church*] (with Franca Rame) 1977

†*Diario di Eva* [*Eve's Diary*] 1978

La storia di un soldato [*The Soldier's Tale*] (adaptor; from a chamber opera by Igor Stravinsky) 1978

Storia della tigre et altre storie [*The Tale of a Tiger and Other Stories*] 1978

Clacson, trombette e pernacchi [*Trumpets and Raspberries*; also produced as *About Face*] 1981

L'opera dello sghignazzo [*The Opera of Guffaws*] (adaptor, with Rame; from John Gay's *The Beggar's Opera*) 1981

Il fabulazzo osceno [*The Obscene Fable*] (with Rame) 1982

Coppia aperta, quasi spalancata [*The Open Couple—Wide Open Even*] (with Franca Rame) 1983

Quasi per caso una donna: Elisabetta [*A Woman Almost by Chance: Elizabeth*] 1984

Hellequin, Harlekin, Arlechino 1985

Una giornata qualunque [*An Ordinary Day*] 1986

Il ratto della Francesca [*The Kidnapping of Francesca*] 1986

La parte del Leone 1987

Lettera dalla Cina 1989

Il papa e la strega [*The Pope and the Witch*] 1989

Zitti! stiamo precipitando! 1990

Johan Padan a la escouverta de le Americhe [*Johan Padan and the Discovery of the Americas*] 1991

Parliamo di donne: L'eroina—grassa è bello [*Let's Talk about Women*] (with Rame) 1991

Il diavolo con le zinne [*The Devil with Boobs*] 1997

TELEVISION SCRIPTS

Chil'ha visto? [*Who's Seen It?*] 1962

Canzonissima 1962

Parliamo di donne [*Let's Talk about Women*] 1977

Buona sera con Franca Rame 1979-80

Manuale minimo dell'attore [*The Tricks of the Trade*] 1985

Trasmissione forzata [*Forced Transmission*] 1988

Una lepre con la faccia da bambina (with Rame) 1989

Parti femminili 1989

Promessi sposi 1989

Coppia aperta [*The Open Couple*] (with Rame) 1990

Settimo: ruba un po' meno [*Seventh Commandment: Thou Shalt Steal a Bit Less*] 1991

Mistero Buffo 1991

OTHER MAJOR WORKS

Poer nano et altre storie [*Poor Dwarf and Other Stories*] (radio series) 1951-52

Lo svitato [*The Screwball*] (screenplay) 1956

Manuale minimo dell'attore [*Basic Handbook for the Actor*; translated as *The Tricks of the Trade*] (essays) 1987

Dialogo provocatorio sul comico, il tragico, la follia e la ragione [*Provocative Dialogue on the Comic, the Tragic, Folly and Reason*] (interviews; with Luigi Allegri) 1993

*This work was not published until 1981, and not staged until 1984.

†Written in 1978, this work was not staged until 1984.

AUTHOR COMMENTARY

Dario Fo Explains (1978)

SOURCE: "Dario Fo Explains: An Interview" by Luigi Ballerini and Giuseppi Risso, in *The Drama Review*, Vol. 22, No. 1, March 1978, pp. 34-48.

[*In the following, Fo discusses influences on his work in the theater.*]

At the Rai Studios in Milan, Dario Fo is just finishing the editing of a series of shows to be aired in the Spring of 1978. We are at a delicate moment in the comedy **La signora e da buttare** (**The Lady Has To Be Thrown Away**), a satire of bourgeois imperialism. At this moment, parts of the dialog are being "reinforced." Dario's finger is pointed at the technician: "Here!" At his command, applause and laughter mingle artfully with the murmur of the audience.

The monitors reflect several sequences of Dario Fo's mocking face. He is a man of 50—actor, singer, dancer, mime, writer, impresario, choreographer, political activist, and a personality both feared and opposed, like one of the characters in the farces he realizes onstage: opposed by government, politicians, the church, and the petty bourgeois. He is the only actor in Italy who can boast of performances attended by 25,000 spectators; the only one whose visibility, in the history of postwar Italian theatre, can be compared with that of Eduardo DeFilippo and Strehler.

On the monitors, we watch a few scenes from the comedy that takes place under the tent of a 19th-century circus:

We hear a violent knocking at the window of the caravan. . . . The window opens and a vulture appears, evidently stuffed, its wings flapping. The clown Bob enters the scene.

BOB: Here it is again—the vulture (*pointing to the bird that opens its wings in the classic pose of the American Eagle*).

Other clowns enter noisily to watch the scene.

CLOWN DARIO: (*moving toward the caravan*) Away! Away! Filthy animal! Damn beast! Your food isn't ready yet. . . . The old lady isn't dead yet . . . And even if she was dead a week and well tenderized—we wouldn't even give you a bite. . . . Everything to the hyena. Get it? *Voice of the old lady from behind the tent.*

OLD LADY: So who is it that's well tenderized?

The telephone, hanging from the caravan, rings. The nurse speaks into a hose which also serves as the source of oxygen for the old lady. Dario answers the phone.

NURSE: Hello. Who's the idiot making all this fucking noise?

DARIO: The idiot is me. The noise is over.

NURSE: You managed to wake the old lady up.

DARIO: It wasn't me, it was the vulture; (*to the vulture*) you filthy creep. But now, I'm gonna make you pay for it, over and out. (*He hangs up the phone and moves rapidly toward the caravan. He goes in. The vulture reenters from the window through which we can catch a glimpse of a violent fight between Dario and the vulture.*) Come here, sweetie. I've got to talk to you. . . . Ah! You turn on me!? Ouch! What a beak you've got! I'll pluck all your feathers out! Get this . . . all the feathers from your ass . . . and may you catch a nice cold on the above mentioned . . . and drop dead!

Squealing and croaking from the vulture. Dario comes out of the caravan cooling himself with a feather-fan.

OLD LADY: (*barely audible*) Who's crying? Who makes my animals weep?

NURSE: It's nothing, Madam! Don't get excited. Go to sleep. Sleep. La la la la la la. . . .

Lullaby.

CLOWNS: (*in chorus*) La la la . . . (*gathered at center stage, the clowns sway*).

Preceded by a loud honking, a three-seater scooter with 3 passengers rushes onstage from the right. It runs over

some of the clowns who fall pirouetting. The scooter, proceeding carelessly, exits.

DARIO: Murderers, schmucks, bastards!

The old lady peeps out from the canopy of her bed holding a huge rifle, typical of the pioneers.

OLD LADY: Injuns! Injuns! Quick—round up the wagons!

NURSE: No, no. It's not the Indians.

OLD LADY: No. Well then, I guess I'll sleep. (*She disappears behind the canopy.*)

One reel is finished. Dario Fo comes to meet us.

* * *

[Luigi Ballerini and Giuseppi Risso]: *Your name is known throughout the world as an actor and an author of political satires.* ("*Now my plays are being performed in an incredible number of German, Swedish, Norwegian, Danish, Belgian and French theatres. My latest plays are being staged above all in West Germany, while those written thirty years ago are being given especially in East Germany, Poland, Bulgaria and the Soviet Union.*") *It is curious to note that his more extreme political productions have found a forum in many so-called western democracies, while in the countries of Eastern Europe more emphasis is given to his early generically social satires, and perhaps solely to them.*) *In the U.S. are known, above all, the works that you have written in the last five or ten years. Would you briefly describe the development of your career, so as to give a more complete picture of your work, starting with your first experiences in cabaret. . . .*

[Dario Fo]: That's inexact. . . . I've never done *cabaret*, but rather a form of theatre tied to popular traditions; if anything, in the framework of *avanspettacolo*. (A kind of variety theatre performed between two movie showings. It was very much in vogue in Italy between 1930-40.) All our comics, from Petrolini himself, to Ferravilla and Scarpetta have all contributed to this type of theatre.

When, for example, we did **Il dito nell'occhio (*The Finger in the Eye*)** with the Piccolo Teatro (twenty years ago), the ambience was not that of a cabaret—the space itself, 700 seats, the stage being twelve to thirteen yards wide, the complete set, the number of people acting (there were twelve of us), and finally, the concept of the piece, which, yes, was a string of sketches, but had a logical continuity of its own. **Il dito nell'occhio** was based upon a story whose origins go back to the goliard tradition, but mixed with elements from *commedia dell'arte* and modified by my experience with the theatre of Strehler, who, at that time, was truly revolutionary. It had little to do with the French or German tradition in *cabaret*. That is, it was something better than *cabaret*, which forces one to adopt a certain unnatural format: a café performance requires a very private and intimate form of speaking. With us, instead, everything was flung out: the action, the amount of physical expression inherent in our way of acting—a pantomime learned not from the tradition of the white mime (Pierrot) but from commedia dell'arte. In short, we had with us Lecoq who had worked with Moretti (the famous Arlecchino in *Arlecchino servitore di due padroni*, staged by Strehler in 1947. Lecoq was a pupil of Moretti), whose experience went back to Paduan theatre; De Bosio (theatre and movie director best known for his staging of Ruzanti), the works of Ruzante, Zanies, Harlequins and so forth. We were working along these lines. Moreover, there was a popular element that consisted of the storyteller's visual narration, and this element we used rather explicitly and directly.

The source of my work before *Il dito nell'occhio*, is in fact that of the storyteller. I started twenty-five years ago. Then, also, I recaptured the jester's tradition. The storyteller and the jester are two fixed points, the former going back to the 17th-18th century, while the latter, the jester, is medieval. But the key is the same; they have the same dimension. I had learned it from the storytellers of the north shore of Lake Maggiore, where I was born and where I lived. It is a tradition that has disappeared, like the balladeers are disappearing in Sicily and the mountebanks or the "poets," as they say in Tuscany (both storytellers and jesters). I learned this lesson early in life from the storytellers who told their stories not in the squares but in taverns or along the lake while people were fishing. There were those who told their stories to children, to the common folk who gathered around them, and one might say they were paid in kind.

Another influence has been the puppet theatre—hand puppets, not marionettes. Finally, I was acquainted with a popular form of epic theatre staged by traveling players, who performed plots based on 15th-century stories such as *Romeo and Juliet* (not the Shakespearean version but the Lombard one), *Othello*, melodramas with enticing titles such as *Sin Avenges Sin*. The players would stay for a month or so and then move on to another village.

At that time, right after the war, I got involved in the birth of the Piccolo Teatro, which meant an enormous change in the general conception of theatre and of the role of the actor. In my town, I was considered as one who had mastered the teachings of the storytellers. Little by little, I had collected many traditional tales, and others I had invented myself. They all had either Biblical motifs or were based on the clichés of a melodramatic tradition or inspired by sensationalist news items of the day, which I obviously rendered in a satirical way. . . .

My decision, then, to do theatre was not traumatic, instead, it was a natural development. I was a student of architecture and I really started for fun: first in my home town, Luino, then in Varese; eventually I also did something in Milan. It was then that I met Franco Parenti (among the first actors of the Piccolo Teatro), with whom I put together shows that were fragmentary and a little amateurish. Finally, still with Parenti and the Nava sisters (Pinuccia, Diana and Lisetta Nava, famous Italian soubrettes of the 1950's), I

did a variety show in which my role was really that of a storyteller. It was a show with chorus girls, skits, and it was there that I learned to dance, sing, etc.

Who wrote the texts?

In the beginning I wrote my own texts, then in collaboration with Durano (author and actor, active in variety theatre and radio programs. His early success has considerably slackened after the days of his collaboration with Fo and Parenti), with whom I worked for about a year after the experience with the Nava. Soon after, Parenti, Durano, Lecoq and I staged *Il dito nell'occhio*. which caused a huge stir. The scene was more or less fixed as in the Elizabethan theatre. There were no costumes. There were simply props, a platform, etc., and we wore nothing but black leotards. It ran for a whole summer at the Piccolo Teatro in Milan—a real shock, especially because of the amount of pantomime and the great precision of the improvisations. The performance was always changing, adjusting, modifying itself according to the reactions of the public.

How were these texts realized—at your desk or through experimentation onstage?

At the beginning, the text was constructed directly on the stage. Actually, every time I tried to stage a text that I had written, read, and reread, we always arrived at a crisis point during rehearsals, so that we had to elaborate and rewrite. Then, we would try it out on an audience, and I would continue to rework it. This holds true for the duration of my experience within a conventional theatrical framework.

Later, things became even more complicated. Many texts result from downright investigations. Once the investigation is completed, we read the text to our public or, better yet, to those people who directly support our work: laborers, students, workers on strike, members of cultural and political organizations. Texts are discussed; then rewritten; then rehearsed first without, then with, our public; staged a third time only to be questioned all over again. Certain plays, like *Pum Pum qui e la polizia* (*Bam Bam! It's the Police*), *Pinelli*, or *Si paga non si paga* (*To Pay or Not To Pay*) have been completely rewritten three or four times. There are three different versions of *Pum Pum qui e la polizia*. . . . the texts are torn apart, composed and recomposed all the time. For example, the original *Grande Pantomima per pupazzi piccoli e medi* (*Great Pantomime for Small and Medium-Sized Puppets*) was transformed, after two years, into something completely different. Even the title was changed.

The public, then, plays an essential role in your productions. . . .

Generally speaking, theatre today is still an intellectual product consumed by the public. There is, however, a *public* that attends only that type of performance capable of involving it because it is directly related to political actions. Let's take an example: some of our performances were born and died in the course of two or three days. Let's say that we would give a performance in support of someone being tried in court, as in the case of the Marini trial (young activist of the leftist movement). There, we did an outdoor performance with the townspeople, recounting, in a grotesque and satirical way, the trial itself and, along with it, certain events that had taken place a century earlier in that very same place. We told them about the rebellion of "bandits," who were no other than the peasants from the hinterland of Salerno. We wanted to show that the symptoms of rebellion, oppression, and repression were constant features analogous to those that marked the trial that was now taking place. This performance we gave only twice.

It happened, also, in Pescara. . . . There was a trial against fifty rebellion prisoners . . . and we staged a counter-trial. I could give you countless examples. There is a kind of theatre that we call "Immediate Intervention" and, indeed, in this case, we must act rapidly. Three days after the bombing incidents in Brescia (one of the many Fascist acts of terrorism that have plagued Italian life in the last decade. The bombs exploded during a political rally. Many people died and many more were wounded), we performed in the same square where these events had taken place, with 5,000 to 10,000 people overflowing into the adjacent square because it was larger.

Are these texts of Immediate Intervention based on documentation of facts?

We begin with an inquiry. For instance, we went to Brescia and we asked for people's versions of the events . . . the performance included excerpts from previous work, though they were adapted through improvisation to a new format. The performance for Chile was one that changed from place to place, because of the various ways in which the audience participated. I don't know if you know this, but since many of our performances had been raided by the police, we decided to plant our own policemen led by a commissar—all imposters—who would interrupt the show. Some of our people would be carried off to the police station to be arrested . . . we provoked our audiences and there was always a great tension . . . people's anger was on the verge of exploding every minute. Some went so far as to pull out knives and assault the commissar.

At the beginning of your theatrical work what political party did you identify with?

With the communist party. We were immediately spotted. We had to contend with Scelba's police (a Christian Democrat. Minister of the Interior. His name is linked with one of the darkest moments in the history of the Italian police force), censorship, innumerable difficulties. Our performances were boycotted all the time. It was a real persecution.

Did the communist newspaper follow your activities? Did it back you up or keep you under surveillance?

It backed us up, but the timing was always late. The first ones to act were the students, then the leftist intellectuals, then the laborers; finally, the communist party . . . but then again, they never did very much for us . . . the PCI always felt a reverence for the official culture. Our work was accepted, above all, by the rank and file, but there were also some intellectuals who were supportive. Togliatti (The famous secretary of the communist party, which he had founded with Antonio Gramsci in 1921) for example, liked many of our works. I remember seeing him in the audience once. He was still bandaged after an assassination attempt on his life. Actually, a year had already passed . . . and he had a bodyguard. He came to see us at the Piccolo Teatro at the end of the season—toward September . . . he was enthusiastic.

There were always debates over the type of theatrical philosophy that we espoused. Many intellectuals, however, didn't make any effort to understand. One who did understand immediately and even wrote an important article on us was Vito Pandolfi. But it's well known the party never considered Pandolfi orthodox . . . in short, a large part of the masses supported us and also the more intellectually sophisticated segment of the bourgeosie. At the same time, certain critics like D'Amico (founder of the Italian Academy of Dramatic Art) could not stomach a theatre with a clearly defined political basis and one so obviously opposed to the elitist type of theatre that they loved and promoted. Then there was the problem of verbal texts versus mime and the art of physical gesture . . . not that we went overboard with gesture, but it certainly was the first time that gesture was treated on an equal basis with words. All this, while the prevailing mentality still extolled the written, not the spoken, word.

* * *

A new interruption. The scenes on the investigations of President Kennedy's assassination from the comedy *La signora e da buttare* are on the monitors.

CLOWN BOB: We've got proof!

CLOWN ARTURO: What Proof? Tell me what I shot her with.

C. BOB: With this. (*He puts a gun in Arturo's hand.*) You can all testify that we caught him with the weapon in his hand.

C. ARTURO: What are you talking about? It's a water gun! (*To demonstrate, he turns to the clown closest to him and squirts some water in his face.*)

C. DARIO (*in the fashion of a town crier*): Exactly. In fact, the old lady drowned.

CLOWNS (*in chorus*): That's right.

C. VALERIO: Let's not exaggerate. How could she have drowned?

C. DARIO: You're right. We've exaggerated just a bit. Actually, how did she die?

C. VALERIO: The truth is—the murderer used a technically advanced weapon of the greatest precision: an Italian model '91 with a sight. Here it is. (*He shows them the gun.*)

C. DARIO: Where is the sight?

C. VALERIO: Here. (*He slides a pair of spectacles along the barrel of the gun.*)

CLOWNS (*in chorus*): Amazing!

C. VALERIO: With one bullet?

C. BOB: Just one.

C. VALERIO: . . . he managed to hit the old lady three times plus the chauffeur and a stray dog, not to mention the back-right tire of an ice-cream cart.

ALL THE CLOWNS: Unbelievable! How did he do it?

C. VALERIO: Quiet. Listen to the ballistics expert. How *did* he do it? (*A blackboard is brought onstage. It is covered with lines and diagrams. Dario will use it to give a scientific demonstration of the ballistic puzzle. The clowns follow him as he moves along the complicated trajectory of the bullet, which he physically describes from one end of the stage to the other.*)

C. DARIO: It's extremely simple. As we can clearly see on the blackboard, the old lady's murderer was here at point A, that is to say, on platform #1; there he is. An amateur would have aimed directly at point B, where the old lady was. But we are dealing with a specialist. He aims exactly in the opposite direction, at platform #4. The bullet hits the post; bounces back and goes to hit, for the first time, the old lady at point B. It goes through her and strikes the bell of the telephone we see here at a point which we will call Alpha. A new rebound; the bullet lands here with an angle of 116 degrees in the direction of the lamppost, on top of which a stray dog is perched. God knows what it's doing there at the top instead of being at the bottom where he should be, according to the rules. The investigation will clarify this.

C. BOB: Naturally.

C. DARIO: The bullet rebounds—not the stray dog, that remains in his place. As we were saying, the bullet rebounds and travels in the direction of the shooter, who, with a baseball bat in hand, sends it once again (*with extreme precision*) back to the old lady. It hits the old lady a second time, goes through her again, and again hits the telephone bell. The impact on the bell, this time, as we can clearly deduce from the markings at point Beta, causes no longer, as before, a rebounding linear trajectory, but a curvilinear one which, moving in the opposite direction describes a type of parabola known in technical language as Archimede's Protoparabola. A new impact on the ground and a new rebound toward the lamppost on which, in the meantime, has climbed the rescuer of the stray dog: the old lady's chauffeur. The chauffeur, with the bullet in his mouth, bounces toward the shooter who, with a baseball bat, hits him on the back of the head forcing him to spit out the bullet, which then moves along the above-mentioned trajectory and goes through the old lady a third time.

The bullet would have run its course ad infinitum had it not been for the fact that the tire of the ice-cream push cart found itself in its path. It was this tire, then, that literally brought to an end the mad race of the bullet. Stop. We'll return after a brief message.

* * *

Let's go back for a second to what you were saying about a theatre with a clearly identifiable political base—that is, if I'm not mistaken, to a theatre understood as a place where not only the conflict between destiny and its modifications is defined, but also where one proposes a physical model of willpower capable of excluding, overcoming, or redeeming the censorship implied by any established truth. . . .

This is the basis of all theatre, the fundamental key to everything . . . They've always told us that classical theatre is above everything and everyone, that it has nothing to do with class struggle. No, classical theatre is fundamentally a class theatre, planned, written, and developed by one social class to defeat another. You can talk as much as you want about Shakespeare, about the moon and the purity of poetry, etc. Shakespeare's themes reflected class problems. At one moment he sides with power and at another he doesn't, according to the political events of his time. You cannot take Shakespeare out of context with what happened to other poets and writers such as Marlowe, Ford, etc., who were subjected to indirect or even direct repression or death. Men such as these were burned at the stake or met with horrible ends one way or another.

Or else, to point out interpretations that normally are not even mentioned, let's take the theme of *Alcestis*. Let us ask ourselves what is the meaning of a woman's role in a society where she can only sacrifice herself for someone? For her husband, for the male who stands for an entire history, for humanity itself. She can reach the maximum of her glory only by renouncing her own life, thus enabling the male to continue with his.

It isn't an accident that these themes were dealt with. Think of the reactionary dimension of those writers who exploited and reversed popular tradition. Aristophanes, for example. It's more than evident in the way in which they antagonized women. There were feminist movements in those days compared to which today's movement is almost laughable: feminist communism, women fighting for their own rights. How else would one want to read the official comedies of the satirists, if not as a testimony of the attempt to destroy these extraordinary thrusts coming from the popular movement.

Don't you think, however, these thrusts should be nourished not only by antagonistic *investigation, but in a truly "tragic" way by a sense of ulteriority and by a courage capable of reconnecting the proponents of those thrusts to the* agonistic *areas of life, that is, those areas where existing and being reflect on one another: the world of enigma, for example—the course of a truth understood as a "wonder" or "awesomeness" and not as "revelation" or "accommodation" to a deduction?*

I would put it in simpler terms. As far as my, our, experience goes, I would have to say that when I started to have a sense of theatre and my role in it, I realized that there were two fundamental aspects of it that I then found aptly formulated by Brecht, Meyerhold, the theorists of epic drama. What were they? They were what in correct terminology I could today call the "literary" concept of theatre on the one hand and, on the other, the concept of the "situation," which is fundamental.

What do I mean by literary concept? The text first and above all. This notion belongs to a precise social class, that which controls the power.

Opposed to it, there is another theatric lexicon composed of text, pause, rhythm; a lexicon in which, many times, the word is dependent upon an action or a situation. "Situation" means thrusting ahead the conflicts that exist between people; it is *this* conflict that occupies the stage. It even precedes the literary text.

In order to liberate the actor from this pseudo-responsibility of having to represent an other, Molière, in the tradition of *commedia dell'arte*, resorted to the construction of a proscenium, an *avantscène*, forcing the actor to step out of the frame. In this way, he practically destroys the scene, that is to say, the atmosphere, the physical box within which the actor was belittled by the very things that were to support him; voices, sounds, and above all, the physical dimensions of the stage. Without a supportive dimension, Molière said, the actor must himself be the scene, the sound, etc., and Meyerhold added that when an actor needs the tweet-tweet of the birds to create an atmosphere of dawn, this means that he does not have enough power to create it through his gestures, voice, rhythms, tempo. He is the dawn, not the spotlights dimming or brightening, producing cold rather than warm light, and so forth. Molière eliminated all scenic effects. This means that the actor must be the exclusive renderer of whatever happens, that he does not have to wear a robe to become a character, but to become a mask.

So, what is this mask? The mask is the dialectical synthesis of conflicts, whereas a character carries with him conflicts without ever achieving their synthesis. He thus tries to be himself, that is, to identify completely with his role and to recount his own *trippe*, as Molière said, the disturbances of his own self. So the actor is an individual entity, while the mask is collective, because it tells of a general concern. In still other words, it is the voice of the story, not the means of acting it out. It is not I who identify with what I present onstage. Rather, I can criticize, suggest conflicts, contradictions, hypocrisies, and comment under any circumstance. This is the epic fact, the estrangement. The estrangement gives the actor the same possibilities that the puppets give the puppeteer. This is theatre's fundamental ideological condition. And this is drama.

In a basically literary theatre . . . Chekhov, a fundamental pivot . . . also, our more recent authors (Pirandello, for instance) did nothing but perpetuate the notion of actor as self-actualizer. Identification. And so, what happens? The spectator is reduced to a voyeur: someone who is there to steal a naturalistic event that is proposed time and again as if it were real life. Even the time sequence is that of a real action . . . more or less. Agreed, it is shortened, synthesized—but it is presented as if it were real.

The other kind of theatre, instead, destroys completely the notion of historical time because events are not modelled on it, there is only the time of the narration—the synthesis of the telling. The very fact that Chekhov and Pirandello eliminate the prolog is no mere accident. The prolog, in fact, reveals everything, takes away the possibility of unforeseeable events, the suspense.

Indeed, in classical tragedy, the whole fact is known ahead of time.

Of course. It is all told in advance. Also, in the theatre of the late 18th century, everything is unfolded prior to the action. What counts is the manner of the unfolding, the special machinery reinvented each time on a known theme. How it ends is not important at all; it is a literary degeneration that allows you to capitalize on irrational emotivity and on a sequence of tricks.

It is a form of cultural terrorism: I know how it ends, you don't. Therefore . . . There is, however, something else that I would like you to clarify. We have this pseudo-theatre, then a theatre that describes approximately, your area of activity: counter-information set off by fact. How do you evaluate that third type of theatre that we could call "formalistic" theatre; one dedicated to the search for a new theatric language and also, really, a new word language in theatre. Artaud comes immediately to mind.

The new language . . . you see, I read Artaud in a different way. . . . He is important to me because he gave me the courage to reutilize the *grammelot*—the newest language and the oldest of them all, buried in literature because it cannot be rewritten. It must be reinvented every time because it depends so much on the relationship created with the audience. The pace is determined by their laughter, their stillness, the magical mood. I do mean magic, especially when speaking about Artaud, which is not coercion, but the play of the imagination, of the imaginary reconstruction of the world. I think we have worked in the direction of a new language. Take, for example, certain Italian singers' mode of performing: before they begin to sing they know that the song is a pretext to speak, to tell, to invent, etc. These singers are in the *grammelot* tradition, in the storyteller's tradition. Once, it was possible to say "And now a song from Maestro Angelini (conductor. Some of his tunes were extremely popular during the 1940's and 1950's) and his orchestra . . ."; today, that's no longer done. Instead, singers talk, chat, narrate, in short, they have rediscovered the prolog. Many times, the songs themselves don't matter much . . . as I said, they are a pretext. . . .

Let's go back to your experience with the Piccolo Teatro.

Yes, there we were able to create a rapport between literary and grassroots theatre . . . My experience with Il Piccolo was very important . . . Above all because of the mimes I worked with: Covelli and those two very good actresses Galvani and Ridoni, Franca, Tairanti, who later married Parenti, and others. (Dario Fo mentions the names of actors who did not become very well known, with the exception, that is, of Franca (Rame), his wife. She is the daughter of a traveling player and is extremely gifted in satirical roles and caricatures. She is also politically involved and heads "Soccorso rosso" (Red Aid), a leftist organization created to assist imprisoned political activists by providing lawyers, etc.)

I remember Strehler used to come and lend us a hand with the lights. He always came to our rehearsals—he would hide among the seats not to disturb us. It was a meaningful working relationship.

Were you guests of the Piccolo Teatro, or were you part of it?

Well, half and half. We were guests, but we also belonged there. We were not there as a group who had rented the theatre. Our technicians were the same as those of the Piccolo, the scenes were designed at the Piccolo Teatro school for stage designers, even the costumes were provided by the Piccolo.

Then came the parting of the ways between Parenti and myself. It occurred mainly for ideological reasons. He wanted to stage a socially inclined type of theatre, but not one as directly involved with politics as that I had in mind. In fact, eventually he ended up doing Ionesco. I could not possibly bring myself to agree with his choices. So after the two years of our collaboration, I moved to Rome.

Actually the split was also a consequence of the great repression to which we were subjected. Guess who was "Ministro dello Spettacolo" at the time? Andreotti (a Christian Democrat, Italy's present prime minister), and then Scelba as Minister of the Interior, and then the E.T.I. (Ente Teatrale Italiano.), a residue of the Fascist regime, which it is, to some extent, even today. Repression took on the usual forms: we were boycotted, forced to move here and there, etc. Times were really bad.

In Rome I worked as a scriptwriter together with Pietrangeli, Zarattini, Age and Scarpelli, and Pinelli, Fellini's scriptwriter. That was also a great experience. I worked also with Lizzani both as scriptwriter and codirector of *Lo svitato* (*The Screwy One*), then with Pietrangeli on other films.

So you were still associated with a Communist milieu?

Yes, Pietrangeli had worked with Visconti and Rossellini from the very beginning. After a while, however, Franca and I decided to give up everything and go back to grassroots theatre.

We started again with eight farces. We worked again at the Piccolo for a whole summer when we staged **Ladri, manichini e donne nude** (***Thieves, Store-Dummies and Naked Women***). We even realized some of Franca's scripts. One was called *La comica finale* (scripts from the collection of Franca Rame's father). Some of these farces are being performed now in Milan. . . . But they have also been staged all over Europe. Many groups in Sweden, Norway, Denmark and Eastern Europe would choose one of our one-act plays and perform it together with works by Adamov, Beckett, Genet: the big names. This diffusion began right away, practically the year after we had done the pieces. They have also been performed in off-Off theatres in the States and in Canada.

Two years later we did **Gli arcangeli non giocano al flipper** (***Archangels Do Not Play Pinball***). It was quite a success, but censorship was still around, and, above all, Scelba was still around. He became even tougher the following year. Our satire of bureaucracy, common man, power, ministries, and the State, hit him where it hurt.

Another play **Aveva due pistole con gli occhi bianchi e neri** (***He Had Two White-and-Black-Eyed Guns***) satirized latent Fascism. It was the story of a bandit whose two-sided character was portrayed through the use of doubles, in the tradition of Greek and Roman theatre. Censorship had become just about intolerable, and we almost ended in jail for having refused to submit the text for approval by the authorities, knowing that permission could be obtained only after they mutilated the work beyond recognition.

Subsequently we did **Chi ruba un piede è fortunato in amore** (***He Who Steals a Foot is Lucky in Love***), an allegorical play which, again, hit hard upon bourgeois morality, the art of cheating, etc. It was the year of Tambroni (a Christian Democrat. His short-lived government fell as the result of what was on the verge of becoming a popular insurrection. Right after this experience, the first Center-Left government was formed: it included a number of Socialist ministers and brought about substantial democratic reforms).

This all ended with the first Center-Left government . . .

Right, Tambroni fell from power, and we were asked to do *Canzonissima*. (A very popular TV show. Dario Fo's and Franca Rame's participation in it was suddenly revoked before the expiration of their contract. Their performances were considered politically unacceptable. They have only recently returned to work for the state-controlled channels of the Italian TV network.) You know what happened. The trial that lasted for fourteen years just ended. The Rai-TV sued us for something like $350,000. I think we ended up by paying about $8,000.

After *Canzonissima* we were completely ostracized from the studios. We went back to the theatre with **Christoforo Colombo** and **Isabella, tre caravelle e un cacciaballe** (***Christopher Colombus***; ***Isabel, Three Caravels and a Bullshitter***) which dealt with intellectual opportunism.

Settimo: ruba un po' meno (*Seventh: Steal a Little Less*), which we did afterwards, was also quite a violent critique. Censorship was finally beginning to slacken.

It was more or less at this time, however, that you decided to break away completely from official theatrical circuits . . .

We broke away from bourgeois theatre. And started again at the *Case del popolo* (literally: "houses of the people." Communist social and cultural centers). There were about forty of us. We ourselves built the stage, the sound and lighting equipment, etc. We staged *L'operaio conosce trecento parole, il padrone mille. Per questo è lui il padrone* (*The Laborer Knows Three Hundred Words, the Boss One Thousand, That's Why He's the Boss*) and also two one-act plays: *Il funerale del padrone* (*The Funeral of the Boss*) and *Legami pure che tanto spacco tutto lo stesso* (*Go Ahead, Tie Me Up, I'm Going To Break Everything Anyway*). The first was a story based on an investigation of child labor and other illegal forms of employment. The other dealt with the birth of political awareness among workers who had taken over a factory that the owner had closed down.

But even the *case del popolo* were not ideal places for us. The P.C.I. did not find our performances agreeable. Pajetta and Berlinguer intervened. (Pajetta: one of the most outspoken members of the communist party. Berlinguer: present secretary of the P.C.I. and principal promoter of today's Eurocommunism.) For a while we banged our heads against the party organization, then we realized that there was nothing else to do but to withdraw.

We started all over again, in movie houses, dance halls, places where no one had ever seen a play before. For the most part we performed in small towns. In Torino we stayed only four days and each day staged a new show. Bourgeois newspapers would not review us, although, I must say, there were two notable exceptions: Monticelli and Blandi. (Theatre critics of *Il Corriere della sera* and *La stampa*, two of the largest Italian daily papers.) The P.C.I. either avoided talking about us or gave us devastating reviews. Then we rented a space, *Il capannone di via Colletta* [A warehouse type of space situated in a Colletta (Milan)] where we resumed *Mistero buffo* (*Mystery-Bouffe* by Mayakovsky), under the auspices of A.R.C.I. (Cultural association affiliated with the P.C.I.), and put together a work called *Vorrei morire anche adesso se sapessi che non è servito a niente* (*I Would Want to Die Now if I Knew that It Didn't Mean Anything*). It was a series of stories from the Resistance narrated by partisans themselves—victorious moments in the history of class struggle and the conflicts those moments created in the very men who lived them. Then we did *Morte accidentale di un anarchico* (*Accidental Death of an Anarchist*) which had an enormous success.

By then there were two groups of players: one headed by Franceschi with fifteen people and our group of twenty. But we grew even larger and had to form three companies

(fifty people). We were more numerous than the company of any major Italian theatre and operated on a budget of a few thousand dollars. We all received the same amount of money: about twelve dollars a day.

We began to tour and could count everywhere on enormous audiences: at the *Palazzo dello sport*, in Milan, for instance, not to speak of outdoor performances. And all the time we were defending ourselves from aggressions and what not. We were registered as a private association and were not obliged to deposit our scripts with anyone. The police could not enter our premises; we managed to block them every time they tried. At Reggio Emilia, however, they arrested many comrades, and since I was officially liable for all three companies, I ended up with forty indictments. So far I have won all the trials that have taken place.

During this period, Franca and I worked in *Tutti uniti tutti insieme, ma scusa, quello non è il padrone?* (*All Together, All United, But Excuse Me, Isn't This Guy The Boss?*). Then we did *Feddajn,* in which Franca Rame played with real Feddajns who spoke only in Arabic. And took up again *Pum pum qui è la polizia. Mistero buffo* had by then split into three different shows.

Unfortunately, at this point our cell divided into a majority and a minority group which could not agree on such strategic issues as political alliances with this or that organization or segment of the Movement. The gap soon turned into a feud. The majority group, with which I had not sided, seized everything, including records and books (we sell a lot of texts on class struggle, government crime and so forth). They really took everything. We were back to zero once again. To top it all off I was arrested. Franca was assaulted in a movie house in Quarto Oggiaro, a suburb of Milan. (Franca Rame was sequestered by a band of fascists who attempted to rape her and kill her. Fortuitous circumstances alone prevented a tragic ending.)

To pull us out of this situation, there arrived an invitation to perform at the French Téâtre National. We went and were received enthusiastically. Upon our return, we expropriated the Palazzina Liberty, where we have been performing ever since. Others have followed our example: some young people in need of performing space took over a deconsecrated church, etc. Even without counting the Molotov cocktails thrown at my house, the bomb at the Palazzina, the innumerable court trials that await me, I feel that during this last decade we have lived at least two hundred years.

OVERVIEWS AND GENERAL STUDIES

Franca Rame (essay date 1975)

SOURCE: An introduction to *Dario Fo Plays: Two*, Methuen Drama, 1994, pp. xix-xxx.

[Rame is Fo's wife and collaborator. In the essay below, which was written in 1975, she recalls their early years working together.]

There are many people who seem to think—perhaps because it is easier and more exciting—that our transition (I mean Dario's and mine) from the traditional theatre to that in which we now work, occurred suddenly, almost overnight, as a consequence of a sort of mystical crisis, as though we had been overcome by the 1968 wave of students' protest and workers' struggles. As if one fine morning we woke up saying: 'That's enough, let's wrap ourselves up in the red flag, let's have our own cultural revolution!'

In fact our true turning point, the point that really mattered, we took at the very beginning of our journey, twenty-two years ago, when with Paventi, Durano and Lecoq we staged for the first time **The Finger in the Eye.** Those were the days of Scelba and his 'subculture', of Pacelli (the pope) with his civic committees, the days of total censorship. Police superintendents, ministers, bishops and cops understood it immediately: we were 'a company of communists' and we were making 'red propaganda'. Every night there would be an inspector in the auditorium checking our words one by one against the script and the Ministry for Entertainment would obstruct our touring arrangements, while the most reactionary theatre-owners would refuse us their buildings and the bishops would ask the police to tear our programmes from the walls of their cities.

The Finger in the Eye was underlined everywhere we went, among the shows 'advised against' in the parish bulletins. This hounding of 'the communist enemy of civilisation and of Holy Mary' went on for many years with all our shows. However, the workers, the students and the progressive bourgeoisie were supporting us, thereby allowing us to move on and make ourselves known, despite the lack of any prizes.

On more than one occasion we were almost prevented from performing our plays. The opening of **He Had Two Guns,** a play about the collusion between fascism and the bourgeoisie, and between political power and organised crime, was halted by the extremely severe interference of censorship which literally butchered our script. We decided to take no notice of the cuts and get on with the play. There was a trial of strength between us and the Milan prefecture which threatened us with immediate arrest, but in the end the Ministry, worried about a possible scandal, lifted the cuts. The script of the **Archangels** was taken away from us because of the many unauthorised jokes we had added to it during the performance. For the same show we collected 'reports' to the police superintendent of every single town we visited. I was reported for making a remark against the army in a play about Columbus. While running the same **Columbus** we were assaulted by fascists outside the Valle Theatre in Rome, just at a moment when, by a strange coincidence, the police had disappeared. Dario was even

challenged to a duel by an artillery officer, for having slighted the honour of the Italian army, and, crazy as he is, he even accepted the challenge on condition that the duel should be fought barefoot as a Thai boxing match, of which he boasted being regional champion. The artillery officer was never seen again. However, there weren't just funny incidents. Though we were operating inside the 'official' theatre, we were beset by endless troubles and difficulties. The reactionaries and the conservatives could not swallow the kind of 'satirical violence' present in our scripts. Dozens of critics accused us of debasing the stage by introducing politics at every step and they went on proposing the usual, worn out model of 'art for art's sake'.

Our theatre was becoming increasingly provocative, leaving no room for purely 'digestive' entertainment. The reactionaries were getting furious. On more than one occasion there were brawls among the audience, provoked by the fascists in the stalls. The Chief of Siena police had Dario taken in by two 'carabinieri' at the end of a show, because he had offended a foreign head of state (Johnson). Whatever the criticism of our work, it must be recognised that our theatre was alive—we spoke of 'facts' which people needed to hear about. For this reason and for the direct language we used, ours was a popular theatre.

Audiences increased at every performance. From 1964 to 1968 our box-office takings were always the highest among the major companies in Italy and we were among those who charged the lowest prices. Yet it was just at the end of the 1968 season (a true record in terms of takings) that we arrived at the decision to leave the traditional structures of the official theatre. We had realised that, despite the hostility of a few obtuse reactionaries, the high bourgeoisie reacted to our 'spankings' almost with pleasure. Masochists? No, without realising it, we were helping their digestion. Our 'whipping' boosted their blood circulation, like some good birching after a refreshing sauna. In other words we had become the minstrels of a fat and intelligent bourgeoisie. This bourgeoisie did not mind our criticism, no matter how pitiless it had become through our use of satire and grotesque technique, but only so long as the exposure of their 'vices' occurred exclusively within the structures they controlled.

An example of this rationale was offered by our participation in a TV programme, *Canzonissima*. A few months earlier we had done a show, *Who's Seen Him?*, for the second TV channel which had only recently become operative and was still the privilege of the well-to-do. On that occasion we had been allowed to do a socio-political satire of rather unusual violence, at least by TV standards. Everything went well, without great hitches. Indeed the reviews were totally favourable and we were 'warmly' applauded by the 'selected' audience. However, when we tried to say the same sort of things before an audience of over 20 million people and in the most popular programme of the year (which *Canzonissima* certainly was), the heavens fell. The same newspapers that had applauded our earlier show now unleashed a lynching campaign. 'It is infamous,' they would say, 'to feed such wickedness, worthy of the basest political propaganda, to an audience as uneducated and easily swayed as the great mass of TV viewers.' Consequently the TV governors, urged by civic committees and by the most backward centres of authority, imposed cuts and vetoes of unimaginable severity. Our scripts were being massacred. It was a return to Scelba's censorship. We were forced to abandon the programme and faced four law suits. For eighteen years now we haven't set foot in the TV studios. Thirteen years of 'banishment' and 200 million lire in damages, plus 26 million to pay. Authority does not forgive those who do not respect the rules of *its* game.

It's the usual story. The great kings, the potentates who understand such things, have always paid fools to recite before a public of highly-educated courtiers, their rigmaroles of satirical humours and even of irreverent allusions to their masters' power and injustices. The courtiers could exclaim in amazement: 'What a democratic king! He has the moral strength to laugh at himself!' But we well know that, if the fools had been impudent enough to leave the court and sing the same satires in the town squares, before the peasants, the workers and the exploited, the king and his sycophants would pay them back in a different currency. You are allowed to mock authority, but if you do it from the outside, it will burn you. This is what we had understood. In order to feel at one with our political commitment, it was no longer enough to consider ourselves as democratic, left-wing artists full of sympathy for the working class and, in general, for the exploited. Sympathy was no longer sufficient. The lesson came to us directly from the extraordinary struggles of the working people, from the new impulse that young people were giving in the schools to the fight against authoritarianism and social injustice and for the creation of a new culture and a new relationship with the exploited classes. No longer could we act as intellectuals, sitting comfortably within and above our own privileges, deigning in our goodness to deal with the predicament of the exploited. We had to place ourselves entirely at the service of the exploited, become their minstrels. Which meant going to work within the structures provided by the working class. That is why we immediately thought of the workers' clubs.

The workers' social clubs (*case del popolo*) in Italy represent a peculiar and very widespread phenomenon. They were set up by workers and peasants at the turn of the century, when the first socialist cells began to appear. The fronts of these first buildings used to bear the following inscription: 'If you want to give to the poor, give five coppers, two for bread and three for culture', and culture does not only mean being able to read and write, but also to express one's own creativity on the basis of one's own world-view.

However, by working in these places, we realised that the original need to study and produce culture together, which inspired workers and peasants to build their own clubs, had been completely dissipated. The clubs had become nothing more than shops, selling more or less alcoholic drinks, or dance halls or billiard rooms. I'm not saying that drinking, dancing and playing cards or billiards is unimportant. The trouble is that nothing more went on there. There were almost no discussions. Some documentary films or little shows were put on, but only as a recreational activity. The working class parties had failed to follow up the needs for creative expression that had been manifested so powerfully among workers and peasants. This failure was based on their persuasion that it is useless to stimulate the development of a proletarian culture, since this does not and cannot exist. 'Only one culture exists'—is what those 'who know' say—'and it is above all classes. Culture is one, as one is the moon or the sun that shine equally for all those who want and can take advantage of them.'

Naturally we soon found ourselves fighting against this unity of classes theory. In the arguments that followed we often quoted the example of the Chinese revolution, where the Party had shown a very different faith in the creativity of the masses and in their ability and willingness to build a different language and a different philosophy of human relationships and social life. Above all we pointed to the great, truly revolutionary determination of the Chinese leaders to urge the intellectuals towards active political participation beyond any personal artistic interest. The intellectuals were asked to commit themselves totally to class struggle, with the aim of studying the culture of peasants and workers and learning about their needs in order to transform them *together* into artistic expression. These ideas drove the Party bureaucrats furious. They would cling to the usual cliché that 'we must move on gradually, starting from the lowest levels, avoiding any flight forward'. They also evinced a certain mistrust of the workers' intelligence and ability not only to express but also to invent a particular cultural world of their own. In fact the workers' clubs' audiences not only listened but actively participated in our debates and our work.

Now, as I read the proofs of those early plays, I remember our first show at the Sant' Egidio club in the suburbs of Cesena. We had decided to go there for our main rehearsals four or five days before the opening. We were assembling the scaffolding for the stage with the help of the lads in the organisation (ARCI) and a few workers and students. However, the club members went on playing cards at the other end of the hall, looking at us now and again, but with diffidence. Clearly for them we were a group of intellectuals, mildly affected perhaps by the populist bug, stopping over for a few days to refresh our spirit among the proletariat and then away again to where we had come from. What took them by surprise was actually seeing us working, working with our own hands, lifting boxes, carrying steel tubes, fixing nuts and bolts, setting up the stage lights. What? Actors, both male and female, slogging away? Incredible!

In the meantime a rather serious problem had arisen: voices reverberated too much in the hall. We wouldn't perform in those conditions. We had to first arrange some cables underneath the ceiling and to hang a few acoustic panels. We decided to use egg-boxes, the kind made of cardboard. But it was necessary first to tie them together with string, a job which I took on myself together with two other women comrades. We started stringing the boxes together with the help of some upholstering needles, but it wasn't at all easy. After swearing for a couple of hours trying to get the needles through the cardboard, we noticed that the comrades from the club had interrupted their games and were looking at us, following our work with interest but in complete silence. After a while an old comrade muttered, as though talking to himself: 'One would want a much longer needle for that job.' Then, silence again for a few more minutes. Then someone else said: 'I could easily make one with a bicycle spoke.' 'Go!' they all said. In a moment the comrade was back with ten very long needles. Then everybody started to help us to get the string through the boxes and hang them, climbing on step-ladders, like jugglers, cracking jokes, laughing as though it were a big game. A few hours later there were so many people in the hall that we could hardly move. Even the most stubborn billiard players had come to help us and some women too, who had just come to get their husbands back home.

The ice was broken and their diffidence entirely overcome. We had won their sympathy by showing that we too could work and sweat. In the late afternoon, after work, they would come to help us and when we started rehearsing, they would sit at the opposite end of the hall looking at us very quietly. The old men would silence the young ones, who burst out laughing at our jokes: 'You mustn't disturb,' they would say. Then little by little they all loosened up. At the end of our rehearsals we would ask for their views, whether they had any criticism to make. At first they wouldn't unbutton, saying that they knew nothing about theatre, but later they became less shy and began to make critical remarks and give us some advice too, which invariably was as unassuming as it was pertinent and to the point. When we finally got to the opening night, the show didn't just belong to 'The New Stage': it was our show in the sense that it belonged to all of us in that hall, who had built it together. Later on, when we moved to other clubs in the vicinity, those comrades followed us and introduced the show to the local comrades. They went out hanging posters and were always the first to speak in the debates. They supported us, we were their team.

In that first year we performed in more than 80 workers' clubs, indoor bowling alleys, occupied factories, suburban cinemas and even in some theatres. We performed before 200,000 and more spectators, of whom 70 per cent had never before seen a play. The debates that followed our shows were always lively, going on till very late at night. Everyone spoke—women, boys, grown-ups and old people. They all talked about their experiences—the Resistance and their struggles—and they told us what we could put on the stage in future: their history.

We drew new themes and plots from those debates, and we found above all a new, direct language without rhetoric

or sophistication. For this reason we were accused of populism, but populists are those who parachute down to the people from high above, not those who are up to their necks inside the world of the people and who do their utmost to learn about the struggles of everyday men and women. And by living with the people we have also been able to verify for ourselves the great truth expressed by Brecht when he said: 'The people can say deep and complex things with great simplicity; the populists who descend from above to write for the people say with great simplicity hollow and banal things.'

However, the debates, the polemics and especially the shows that resulted from them, began to annoy the clubs' managers, not to mention those of ARCI, the organisation within which we all were operating. We held on for a while, but in the end were forced to give up. The tension was causing real rows and all sorts of outbursts against us, in oral and written form—in polemical articles in the *Unità*; and the Party's cultural journals. Sometimes we reacted without much dialectical sense, in a confused and fanciful manner. We had very little experience of political subtleties nor did we know how to be restrained and accommodating. Nevertheless today, if we look back objectively, while recognising how sectarian we sometimes were and admitting our mistakes, we must say that we could do nothing else. Had we stayed within those structures, we wouldn't have made a single step forward, we would have been ensnared by a thousand compromises.

The separation with ARCI didn't come easily. There was a further division within us too. More than half the company chose to continue working within the ARCI structures and kept calling themselves 'The New Stage'. We called our group 'The Commune'. We had come through a great crisis, but it had been a crisis towards growth and clarity. Basically there had always been a conflict in the company between two fundamentally different ways of looking at our roles as actors. What were we, militants at the complete service of the working class or, more simply, left-wing artists? The dilemma kept emerging. The latter point of view meant accepting more or less correct compromises, veering towards opportunism, renouncing any vigour not only in respect of our own criteria, but also of our collective and individual behaviour both inside and outside the activity of the group. Moreover, there was among ourselves a sort of self-defeating democraticism that was the first cause of arguments, conflicts and division. Dario and I, while trying to avoid acting as managers, made the opposite mistake. We didn't provide any direction at all for the group. What is worse, we allowed some ambitious individuals who were after 'power', to organise political factions to the point of endangering our autonomy. Therefore, two years ago, at the time of the last break-up, Dario and I found ourselves with only four other comrades, completely alone and bereft of everything—the lorry, the vans, the electrical equipment, including our personal stage equipment—we had put together during twenty years' work and which, on leaving the official theatre, we brought to the company.

Whether those comrades were correct in bringing about the split can perhaps best be judged from the fact that in less than one year their productions have achieved only indescribable failures. They have been cutting each other's throats, they have broken up again, wasted money, sold or abandoned all the equipment. And now they have broken up for good, they don't exist any more. This disaster does not give us any pleasure at all. It only makes us very sad, as we realise how many comrades, with the ability and the quality of good actors, how many who could have continued working for our common aim, can have been so easily undone by the deleterious ideology which time and again emerges like a tumour inside every company: individualism, the struggle for personal power and all the evils that go with it. But we learned one thing, that this mistake can be fought and overcome only if we tie ourselves even more closely to the working class and their struggles, if we let the workers direct our activity and put ourselves entirely at their disposal and service with the utmost confidence. It is because of this principle that the mood inside our group has entirely changed: there is no more tension, no more personal arguing.

Well, despite all the problems, rows, conflicts and splits, the positive thing is the result of these seven years' work—the millions of people who have seen our plays, our intervention with purpose-written scripts in occupied factories and cities where political trials were being held (as was the case with **Accidental Death of an Anarchist,** performed in Milan during the Calabresi-*Lotta Continua* trial; or with **Bang Bang, Who's There? Police!,** performed in Rome for the Valpreda trial; or our interventions on behalf of Giovanni Marius in Salerno and Vallo della Lucania, in Pescara during the trial of fifty prisoners who had rebelled in the city's jail in Mestre to help the Marghera workers; and many other shows in other cities, when the total takings went to support the striking workers of Padua, Bergamo, Asti, Varese, Turin and for a long period, Milan; or the sale of 10,000 glasses from an occupied Milanese factory carried out at the Palazzetto dello Sport of Bologna, which was an incredible event, every comrade, every spectator carrying a glass in his hands.)

The fact that Dario, despite so many internal and external worries (trials, assaults, arrests, attempts on his life), managed to write and produce something like three scripts every year (not to mention all the emergency sketches) seems amazing even to me, though I have personally lived through all these ordeals.

At this point I should say something about Dario's craft as a writer, or, I should say, as a maker of scripts for the stage. Why a maker rather than writer? Because, when he writes, Dario needs to think out and build a stage or, preferably, a sequence of scenic spaces and planes on which the dramatic action can take place. It is also a question of the-atrical construction rather than simple writing because his theatre is not based on characters, but on *situations*. The characters become masks, i.e. emblematic pretexts at the service of a situation. The stage moves on by virtue of an action, just as the actor moves by virtue of his gestures and his words. Even the stage props therefore become part of an action. This demands great open-mindedness at the level of stage management. Therefore Dario can allow himself to bring on to the stage puppets and marionettes, masks and mannikins, actors with natural or painted faces. And all this he joins together from the inside with the songs, the jokes, the coarse shouting, the use of noisy instruments, the pauses, the exasperated rhythm—though never overdone, because his style is rigorous even when everything seems haphazard and accidental. Only superficial people can in fact think that Dario's theatre is 'handmade'. On the contrary, it is all reasoned out in advance, written, rehearsed, rewritten and rehearsed again and always in a practical relationship to and with the audience. It must be remembered that Dario studied as an architect and that, besides being an actor and a writer, he is also a choreographer. He always sees the stage (and he insists on this) as 'plan, elevation, foreshortening and perspective'. Personally, coming from a family of actors, I've seen, since I was a child, all kinds of shows being prepared and written, but I have always been struck by Dario's method. He has a constant inventiveness and is always lively and young, never banal and obvious. His scripts are always technically perfect, never boring or tiresome. What amazes me most of all is that when he writes, he always keeps the structure of his text entirely open, he doesn't build in advance a complete framework. He invents dialogue based on a paradoxical or a real situation and goes on from there by virtue of some kind of natural, geometric logic, inventing conflicts that find their solutions in one gag after another in correspondence with a parallel political theme, a political theme which must be clear and didactic. You are moved and you laugh, but above all you are made to think, realise and develop your understanding of everyday events that had before escaped your attention.

This is what I think of Dario Fo as playwright. Many others have talked about Dario as writer-director-actor. I can add something about Dario's behaviour as an actor on the stage. He is always alert, ready to catch the mood of an audience with inimitable timing. For the comrades who work with him he is a comrade up until the end of every show. He regrets his success when it compromises that of other actors and he does his utmost to make sure that each one achieves adequate personal satisfaction. If a comrade misses a burst of laughter, he goes on working at it and isn't satisfied until the colleague gets it back.

About Dario the man and partner I am reluctant to say anything, except that his honesty and his inner beauty can be seen better on his face as he grows older. He is getting more gentle, nice and calm, humble, generous and patient. I don't know anybody with so much patience, especially with those who pester him, and God knows how many of them we have met in these years. Moreover, he is generous and stubborn. Nothing depresses him, I've never heard him say 'let's give up'. Even the hardest ordeals, such as my kidnapping by the fascists, or the 1972 split, he has overcome by reasoning with his usual strength, confident that he would make it, trusting the support and the respect of the comrades who have followed us by the thousands. What would you say? Do you think that I am quite 'crazy' about Dario? That I admire him a lot? Too much? Well, I say that yes, I admire him, but even more, I respect him. I was so lucky to meet him! If I hadn't already done it, I'd marry him now.

Suzanne Cowan (essay date 1975)

SOURCE: "The Throw-Away Theatre of Dario Fo," in *The Drama Review*, Vol. 19, No. 2, June 1975, pp. 102-13.

[*In the following essay, Cowan traces Fo's career and delineates the essential characteristics of his works.*]

In Western Europe, where Brecht's plays have by now become standard fare for bourgeois audiences and where political theatre remains, by and large, the domain of students and middle-class intellectuals, the work of Dario Fo stands out as an anomaly. He is a gifted poet and playwright, as well as an actor, director, and full-time cultural activist; but, although his plays are known throughout Italy and numerous other European countries, they are usually discarded after a few months' performance. His company does not consider itself avant-garde, and eschews formal experimentation for its own sake, yet it has incorporated many innovative techniques both in the dramatic structure of its productions and in its mode of organization. Although his group does not perform agit-prop or guerrilla street theatre, it is small, flexible, mobile, and militant. Fo has definitively renounced the commercial stage and dedicates his energies to serving the revolutionary movement in Italy; yet he continues to enjoy enormous popular support. His theatre company receives no financial backing from either the state or any major left-wing political parties, but it has a mass national following and attracts more than half a million spectators annually. Its audiences include serious drama scholars, students, middle-class left-wing intellectuals, small shopkeepers, and, above all, workers.

In order to explain how a radical theatre group can command so much attention and support, it is necessary to look both at the role of culture in Italian left-wing politics and at Fo's own professional background. To begin with, Italy has the largest organized leftist movement of any Western country today. (We include in the loose term "movement" all those forces of political opposition to the left of the ruling Christian Democratic Party, ranging from Catholic Socialists to the mass-based, powerful Communist Party, to the far-left "extra-parliamentary" groups.) In no major Capitalist nation does the left exercise stronger ideological influence and cultural hegemony than in Italy. Since the end of World War II, the notion of "cultural work" has been a central focus in the organizing strategies of every movement and party of the left. The Communist and, to a lesser extent, Socialist parties have long been engaged in a campaign to use cultural products—including

theatre—as tools for the political education of the working class.

Fo was born into an anti-fascist, proletarian family. From his first experience in theatre during the early Fifties, he was interested in its potential as a means of heightening class-consciousness. By 1962, he had achieved a considerable reputation as comedy-writer and actor in cabarets, small urban theatres, and the famous Piccolo Teatro of Milan, as well as on the national radio and television network. Although his early comic pieces did not have an explicitly political content, they usually involved satirical jibes aimed at common aspects of middle-class life in Italy: the pursuit and adulation of privilege, cult of the hero, religious mystification, blind obedience to established authority. His most prolific production of dramatic works came out of his "rediscovery" of popular farce of the *commedia dell'arte* tradition and of popular culture in general. He composed numerous comedies in the style of 17th Century popular theatre, heavily weighted with social satire. In 1966, his research into folk culture led him to direct the first in a series of three spectacles of popular and work songs set to dramatic pantomime, entitled *Io ci ragiono e canto* (*I Think Things Out and Sing About Them*), using the talents of a number of folk singers and musicians, many of whom were virtually unknown at that time. (This was Fo's first experience at introducing the protagonists of popular culture themselves into a show, an initiative he was to repeat in later productions.)

Between 1959 and 1967, Fo wrote and performed a number of comedies along with his wife, the actress Franca Rame. Although these shows continued to play in small theatres patronized mainly by the urban middle class the growing radicalization of the Italian political climate that occurred during the late Fifties and early Sixties encouraged Fo to adopt a more direct political content. With the formation of the first center-left coalition government in 1962, he and Rame gained access to the State-controlled television network, appearing in leading roles in the popular TV series, *Canzonissima*. In recent years, this show has regularly claimed about 25 million viewers—roughly half the population of the country—and although this number was smaller in 1962, it is still safe to say that Fo's comic sketches, performed on *Canzonissima*, received as wide a public exposure as any form of entertainment may ever hope to attain in Italy. This is significant, because later, when they abandoned commercial theatre and the mass media altogether, Fo and Rame were able to attract enormous numbers of people to their shows not only, or not merely, on the basis of their performances' intrinsic political and theatrical value, but also on the drawing-power they enjoyed as highly successful, popular comedians—a fact which continues to haunt them and which has no doubt had its negative effects on their ability to project a purely political image, free of distortion by residual television-personality glitter.

Nevertheless, even on *Canzonissima* they violated many established norms, performing hilarious and outspokenly political sketches directed against the Catholic hierarchy, industrial bosses, and particularly the Mafia. This was too much for the Italian State television network: the shows were censored, and Fo and Rame clamorously terminated their involvement with the mass media. A few years later they removed themselves entirely from the bourgeois theatrical circuit, forming a new company, *Nuova Scena*, under the auspices of the Communist Party's large cultural and entertainment organization. The greater flexibility and freedom afforded by this "alternative circuit" led them to experiment with new forms of planning and organization, new materials and dramatic techniques. In 1969, Fo presented his most thoughtful and, perhaps, his most theatrically original work, *Mistero Buffo* (*Comic Mystery*). More than a play, it is actually a series of dramatic monologs taken from medieval religious sources, re-written and re-interpreted as socio-political satire. Its emphasis is on the spontaneous genius of popular culture, which used religious drama and parable as metaphors for illustrating, in a cruelly comic vein, the oppression of the poor by the ruling classes, particularly the ecclesiastical hierarchy and nobility. *Mistero Buffo* represents the culmination of Fo's research into forms of the popular theatre of the Middle Ages; it is one of the few plays that he continues to present year after year, adding new material and improvising on the original text.

The other productions that came out of this period were based primarily on contemporary political problems. For example, *Legami pure che tanto spacco tutto lo stesso* (*Tie Me Down; I'll Bust Up Everything Just the Same*) portrayed the exploitation of "piece-workers" who operate small machines in their own homes, a form of labor still widespread in Italy; *Il funerale del padrone* (*The Boss's Funeral*) dealt with the daily sacrifice of industrial factory workers; and *L'operaio conosce trecento parole, il padrone mille: per questo lui è il padrone* (*The Worker Knows 300 Words; The Boss Knows a Thousand: That's Why He's the Boss*) examined the primary role of culture and education as ideological weapons in the class struggle.

Nuova Scena's work met with resounding success. Its performances drew unprecedented numbers of working-class people in cities and towns all over the country. Collaboration with the Communist Party cultural organization went well, as long as the plays limited their attacks to the more blatantly oppressive institutions of the bourgeois state. But soon their political criticism began to touch the party itself, and in some highly sensitive spots, particularly its reformist strategy and bureaucratic structure. In raising such issues, *Nuova Scena* was not isolating itself completely from the left in Italy, but simply reflecting a position that had become increasingly widespread since 1968. At any rate, it was undoubtedly the threat of erosion of its mass base, just as much as the content of the criticisms leveled against it, which caused the party to react so bitterly to the line taken by *Nuova Scena*. For it was clear that the company was able to command its own public, outside of the control of the orthodox left, and that it could provide its audiences with a vehicle for open political and

ideological debate, completely free of bureaucratic or institutional restrictions. The party reacted by denouncing *Nuova Scena*. It threatened to close off its access to labor halls and other meeting-places, and, finally, boycotted its performances. The cultural and recreational organization withdrew support, and in 1970 Fo and Rame formed their present company: *Il Collettivo Teatrale La Comune*.

* * *

The fact that immediately strikes a spectator at one of *La Comune*'s performances, and which stands out even more clearly on reading Fo's plays, is that they make no pretense of being great, or even good theatre. Little attention is paid to formal structure, or expressive language; a play may appear to be slapped together: a series of scenes, rather than an organically constructed whole, which maintains its internal unity mainly by revolving around the central axis of a particular political problem or situation. Fo writes his plays down in a great hurry; while he writes, the company discusses the subject, outlines the main characters, and begins to improvise the scenes. This improvisation continues even after the text is all down on paper, so that a scene or piece of dialog may be considerably altered from one performance to the next. Sometimes, after several months or a year, a play is resuscitated, keeping the same characters and parts of the dialog, but with a totally different political theme. Entire scenes may be shifted around, rewritten, or added at the end; the result is that what one sees performed on stage rarely corresponds exactly to the version of the play printed in the edited text.[1] Since most of the plays deal with contemporary events and situations, they are given a certain run—usually a few months—and then discarded. History moves too fast, *La Comune* would say, for theatre pieces which require a lengthy job of interpretation, careful, laborious construction, staging, and rehearsal. New political issues are constantly arising, and the theatre has to keep up with them.

This is not to say that Fo's plays resemble agit-prop or guerrilla street theatre. They are too long, too involved for that. If the nature of guerrilla theatre is to give a quick, encapsulated statement of an issue, or to motivate spectators to take swift action on a particular problem, or—as in the case of groups like the Bread and Puppet Theatre—to present a general statement about social and political problems through the use of a kind of Surrealistic allegory, it is not an apt vehicle for in-depth treatment of historical or political questions. As jerry-built as Fo's plays often seem to be from a formal point of view, when it comes to content they cover the ground they set out to explore with painstaking thoroughness. For example, the subject of *Morte accidentale di un anarchico* (*Accidental Death of an Anarchist*) is the death of Giuseppe Pinelli, who allegedly threw himself out of the fourth-story window of the Central Police Headquarters in Milan during an interrogation in 1969. The play goes into the case in exhaustive detail, including in the script lengthy citations from the official police report presented as testimony during the inquiry into the circumstances of Pinelli's death. ***Pum pum, chi è? La polizia! (Knock Knock, Who's There?—Police!*)** deals with the case of Pietro Valpreda and two other anarchists who were arrested and held in prison for several years, having been falsely accused of setting bombs which exploded in a downtown Milan bank in 1969, killing fourteen people. The enormous complexity of this case—one of the most sensational political-judicial events to occur in Italy during the postwar period—is explored in depth by the play. It starts with Valpreda's arrest and proceeds through all the relevant documentary and circumstantial evidence until responsibility for the coverup of Fascist involvement in the crime is finally laid in the lap of the Prime Minister himself. The printed text of the play[2] is preceded by a 112-page "historical-political chronology on the 'State massacre' from 1969 to January, 1974," and is followed by a 55-page appendix containing several documents pertaining directly to the case. ***Tutti uniti! Tutti insieme! Ma scusa quello non è il padrone?*** (***All United! All Together! Hey, Wait a Minute, Isn't That the Boss?***), a play about Italian working-class struggles from 1911 to 1922, is published with an introduction in the form of a "Historical chronicle of the Socialist movement and the class struggle, from the formation of the Socialist Party to the birth of the Communist Party of Italy (1892-1921)," followed by the transcription of an address delivered by the historian Massimo Salvadori to the *La Comune* group of Milan in 1971, entitled "Fascism, Anti-Fascism, and Class Struggle," and finally a bibliographical note consisting of forty volumes "consulted for the preparation of the show."[3] These are only a few examples, but whether the plays are based on general problems and conditions, or on a single specific incident or historical period, they incorporate a great deal of research and documentation. It may seem paradoxical that plays which make such wide use of slapstick can be at the same time valid educational experiences. The fact is that most of Fo's plays are packed with information, and any spectator who doesn't already possess a fairly good working knowledge of Italian history and social and political institutions will find them difficult to understand.

But they are, and are meant to be, entertaining. In the course of a debate following the performance of ***Tutti uniti! Tutti insieme!*** in Bologna in 1971, Dario Fo remarked:

> What are those laughs that we put in there? We could take them out, if we wanted to. But they provide breathing space, to make the audience pay attention. An audience which isn't used to following a continuous discussion with no pauses, would grow bored after a while and lose its contact with the topic being discussed. So you invent comic solutions, special effects, grotesque situations. Like a key, and this is the point, for "screwing" (that's a very old term. Molière used it) the behind (he called it something else) to the seat. . . . The problem is to adopt all means, the best there are, to arrive at the topic, which is what interests us. As long as the means are theatrical, because in the long run we are still interested in delivering our point by

means of theatre. Otherwise, as Mao Tse-Tung said. "if you can't express yourself through art, this means that it's better for you to express yourself through a public meeting. Otherwise you do a disservice both to the public meeting and to art."[4]

Fo insists on the importance of the comic-grotesque element in theatre, both as part of the patrimony of genuine popular culture and as a basic tool for raising political consciousness. Like Brecht, he was always fascinated by popular theatre, incorporating all its comic-dramatic tricks into his plays: double-takes, mistaken identities, scurrilous language and behavior, mimicry, characters hiding behind curtains and pieces of furniture, blips and buffetings on the head and kicks in the rear—the entire panoply of popular belly-laugh technique.

The dialog, too, is ridiculously funny, again in the manner of the popular theatre or TV routine. Here is an example, from ***Il Funerale del padrone*** (first performed in November, 1969):

> PROFESSOR: (*Grabbing the hand of the dead man.*) Where is the patient?
>
> WIDOW: You're holding his hand, Professor.
>
> PROFESSOR: Oh, really? (*To the cadaver*): Good for you! Get living! (*To the others*): The first rule is always to give the patient a sense of confidence . . . (*To the cadaver again*): You'll see it's nothing serious. (*Takes his pulse.*) Have you taken his temperature?
>
> INDUSTRIALIST'S LOVER: No, Professor.
>
> PROFESSOR: Very bad!
>
> LOVER: But he's dead!
>
> PROFESSOR: So, what of it? And anyway, who told you he was dead?
>
> WIDOW: But his heart has stopped beating!
>
> PROFESSOR: Ah, because you still hold on to that medieval notion that the heart is the determining organ. No, it's the brain . . . that's the thing which must beat . . . palpitate . . . live! And in fact, this brain . . . is dead.
>
> EVERYONE: Dead?
>
> PROFESSOR: Yes, but that's not important. Have you given him an enema? (*The Professor asks if there is a terminal patient who could donate his heart in order to save the industrialist.*)
>
> DOCTOR: Well, yes, there is a patient, but he has heart disease; in fact, he is dying of a heart attack . . . we should give *him* a heart transplant, but he's a welfare patient . . . you understand.
>
> PROFESSOR: Hm, yes, of course, the ones on welfare can't be saved. But I understand this man is an industrialist; therefore it seems to me impossible, with all the workers he has, that at least one of them hasn't suffered a serious injury in the last twenty-four hours!

WIDOW: But you see, Professor, these scoundrels are out on strike, and if they're not working, they won't die . . . the bastards!

WORKERS: Pardon us!

PRIEST: Let's try phoning the National Association of Manufacturers.

LOVE: I've just phoned this minute . . . the information office. They said there were a lot of accidents, as usual, but all minor cases. (*She reads off the list.*)

WIDOW: But that's preposterous . . . no death? Why, how can that be; according to statistics one industrial death occurs every two hours . . .

LOVER: In fact, there have been quite a few. But the first in the series was a welder who fell from a height of 120 feet. They scraped him up with a teaspoon. The second fell into a sausage making machine, and since that was a total manufacturing and assembly unit, he came out uniformly stuffed and distributed into twenty-five two-pound salamis, which were, as usual, given to his widow. The third one, who worked at a fuel depot, got blown up. The fourth . . .

WIDOW: That will do. Really! You might show a bit of good taste! It's true we're standing before a corpse, but to come here and talk about people dying in such a vulgar manner!

Just as important as the comic dialog in Fo's plays is his frequent use of dialect: an aspect of Italian life whose importance cannot be overestimated. Since the vast majority of working-class people have always spoken some form of dialect which is quite different from the official Italian used in schools and the media, the question of language has for centuries been strictly connected with issues of class, politics, and culture. Dialect is correctly seen, by Fo and other artists, as a precious heritage of Italian popular culture and a fundamental element in the struggle for working-class hegemony. Fo has devoted years of research to popular dialects, going back to the Middle Ages. His *Mistero Buffo* is entirely recited in 15th Century dialect of the Po Valley. In *Vorrei morire anche stasera se dovessi pensare che non è servito a niente* (*I Would Be Willing to Die This Very Night if I Thought All That Had Been for Nothing*), a play based on documentary testimonies of participants in the Italian anti-Fascist, anti-German Resistance Movement, Fo lets the participants "speak for themselves" through the mouths of the actors, in their own dialects. One monolog, taken from the testimony of a woman who fought with a partisan group in the Veneto region, is recited in a very ancient northern Italian dialect, a cross between the popular languages of Veneto and Ferrara. Although most of Fo's plays are written and performed mainly in Italian, they all contain a liberal sprinkling of dialect as well as popular regional slang.

In addition to monologs and solo "sketches," the plays almost invariably incorporate music—a few verses, or entire songs[5] accompanied by guitar, harmonica and other light instruments. The songs are used as satirical commentaries

to a scene, or, like Greek choral recitations, to emphasize and comment upon some aspect of the issue being acted out on stage. The folk music spectacles *Io ci ragiono e canto* I, II, and III have already been mentioned; one of the principal performers, a Sicilian former bricklayer named Ciccio Busacca, has remained as a regular member of Fo's collective. Busacca first gained a reputation as an outstanding *cantastorie* (a singer who composes narrative ballads around some event in past or contemporary history; usually, but not always, an occurrence in the history of a single town or region), and performs his compositions in many of *La Comune*'s shows. Musically, the songs used in the plays are not terribly sophisticated, although they have great rhythmic energy. They are not usually intended to focus attention on themselves as much as to complement the dramatic action taking place; they can stand alone, in performance, but are better appreciated as part of the larger context of the play.

Given the mobile nature of *La Comune*, and the fact that most of its performances are not held in regular theatres, the props and equipment are kept at a modest level. There are banners, posters, and simple costumes, but little else. It seems that Fo has decided to abandon the puppets, marionettes, backdrops, and flamboyant costumes used in some of the early productions of the *Nuova Scena* group. Instead, current productions owe their visual interest to the extraordinary verve with which the characters move about on stage. The direction—which is in part done by Fo and Rame, in part worked out collectively—stresses physical movement and group interaction, which must be rapid and dynamic. This is especially necessary because, with the exception of Fo himself and sometimes Franca Rame, the individual actors are not particularly important. There are no "characters," in the psychological sense, only types or personifications—the madman, policeman, politician, union bureaucrat, worker, the bourgeoisie, and so forth. Actors can, and often do, change roles in the middle of a play. Dario Fo usually plays the part of several different characters—in *Morte accidentale di un anarchico,* for example, he is a madman pretending to be a psychiatrist, who subsequently assumes the roles of a police commissioner, a Supreme Court judge, a captain of the Scientific Division of the Police Department, and a Catholic bishop. Any character functions basically as a personification of a certain political problem, and as such can change roles the moment his or her function on stage is to articulate an issue different from one that was treated a few minutes before.

A similar observation can be made for the "plots," such as they are, of Fo's plays. It is nearly impossible, after seeing one, to give an account of "what happened," since there is rarely a linear sequence of events. Rather, there is a series of episodes that illustrate certain political or historical situations and comment upon them. What starts off as one plot may turn into a different one, reverse itself and go off in an unexpected direction, or break down entirely with a surprise ending. In the historical plays, there is frequent use of flashbacks. *Tutti uniti! Tutti insieme!* begins and ends in 1923, with the major part of the action taking place between 1911 and 1922. It proceeds through a series of chronologically organized episodes that revolve around the same characters, but there is no central story-line. *L'operaio concace trecento parole* opens in a workers' recreation center, where several volunteers are restoring a long-unused library; as they take each volume down from the shelf to dust it off, the books "come to life" and their subjects are enacted on stage. These separate situations form the main body of the play.

Fo never attempts to hide the make-believe element of theatre behind a naturalistic screen; on the contrary, theatrical "artifice" is emphasized wherever possible. An actor will frequently step outside of his character and address himself directly to the audience; some productions utilize a "play-within-a-play" format and end with the actors discarding their roles altogether and initiating a debate with the public. Surprise endings are frequently employed to illustrate political points and throw them, as it were, directly "into the lap" of the audience. For example, *Il funerale del padrone* ends with a live goat about to have its throat cut onstage by one group of actors, while on the other side of the stage a second group, playing an efficient and machine-like "death squad," pantomimes the garroting of a nameless worker—one among the thousands who die each year from work-related illness and industrial accidents. The issues of police harassment and official crackdowns on the left are dramatically stated at the close of *Guerra di popolo in Cile* (*People's War in Chile*), when several actors, who have not appeared on stage during the play, enter the hall pretending to be police officers in search of certain left-wing activists allegedly seated in the audience. They announce that these individuals must be brought down to police headquarters for "routine questioning," and demand to read the militants' names aloud, after which everyone will be permitted to leave the theatre. Tension mounts steadily as Fo and Rame deliver "impromptu" statements on the repression of the bourgeois State, and members of the audience attempt to shout down the reading of the list of names. The charade is broken only when it looks as though actual physical violence may break out, at which time the "policemen" climb on stage and join the rest of the troupe, and the audience, in singing the "International."

There is nearly always an impassioned political debate at the end of the collective's performances. The nature and subject of discussion depends both on the content of the play and the type of audience in attendance. When the group performs in a primarily working-class area, there are often many older people present, as well as veterans of various political and labor struggles, and not infrequently former combatants in the Resistance Movement. Among such audiences, comments about Fo's attitude toward the "parliamentary left," Communist Party, and labor unions tend to be sharply critical. Audiences mainly composed of students and middle-class left-wing intellectuals readily discuss the formal, esthetic elements of the productions as well as their political content. Whether a play deals with contemporary issues or historical struggles, with Third-World liberation

movements (such as *Fedayn*, a show presented by members of the Palestine Liberation Movement and directed by Fo) or factory conditions in industrialized capitalist countries, the debates almost invariably cover certain basic issues: the historic and present role of the Italian Communist Party, the world and domestic economic situation, the crisis of the Italian bourgeoisie and ruling political party, weaknesses and strengths of the "extra-parliamentary left," the situation of the industrial working class and the problems of southern Italy. Although literally dozens of topics may arise in the course of a post-performance debate, these seem to be the most common.

The *Collettivo Teatrale La Comune* perceives its role to be that of engaging in militant cultural work, using each performance as an instrument of counter-information, consciousness-raising, and political growth. Its activity is part of a larger movement working to strengthen all those forces which struggle to bring about the eventual overthrow of the bourgeois state and the construction of Socialism. As such, this cultural activity appears as directly connected to political organizing. The collective therefore involves itself in active struggle whenever and wherever its participation is requested: during strikes, factory occupations, demonstrations, public meetings; in old theatres, schools, workers' recreation centers, union and labor halls, agricultural co-operatives, open areas outside factory gates, city parks and village squares. Its contact with the authorities is nearly always abrasive, and the group is constantly obliged to take extreme precaution against attacks or harassment by Fascist gangs, provocateurs, and police. Before each performance, spectators' purses and parcels are checked at the entrance for explosives: an annoying but necessary measure, considering the enormous hostility with which the group's activities are regarded by the right wing. Last year, in Rome, Franca Rame was abducted and roughed up by a group of Fascists. Police arrested Fo in Sassari (Sardinia) and held him for several days at the orders of the chief, who claimed that the members of the collective were illegally using the local cinema—which had been rented to them quite straightforwardly and, for once, without undue financial complications—to perform their show.

One of the most clamorous cases of harassment and obstruction of *La Comune*'s work by public authorities occurred last spring (1974), when the City Council of Milan attempted to stop the group from restoring an old building which it intended to use as a permanent base, as well as opening it to the entire surrounding community for a theatre, meeting hall, child care center, and library. The ornate old "Palazzina Liberty" had been falling to ruin for years due to neglect, and the collective had repeatedly applied to the City Council for permission to take over one of the many abandoned buildings close to the center of the city. These requests were systematically ignored. When its formal application to restore the Palazzina met with the customary silence, a group of neighborhood volunteers decided to begin work on the building along with members of the collective, in hopes that this concrete action would achieve the results that years of petitioning had been unable to accomplish. Christian Democratic city leaders instead responded by having a fence put up all around the building and drawing up a court order making it illegal to work on or use the Palazzina. This action immediately aroused a violent reaction among residents of the area, who rallied unanimously to the defense of the collective, and overnight the case became a national *cause célèbre*. Thousands of leaflets were distributed showing a picture of the fenced-in building and bearing the slogan *I topi ringraziano la DC*—"the mice say thanks to the Christian Democrats" (since the Palazzina, like many other unused structures around the city, attracted rats and mice, the work of internal reconstruction initiated by the volunteers provided a hygenic as well as a social and esthetic service to the community). Months of mobilization followed: the building was occupied, rallies and meetings were held on the grounds surrounding the building, and crowds of up to 10,000 people turned out for performances put on by the collective in order to raise money and support. The court order was subsequently appealed and the troupe began its long, tedious march through the legal system. At this writing, a final court decision on the future status of the "Palazzina Liberty" has not been reached.

* * *

In the meantime, Fo and the *Collettivo Teatrale La Comune* continue to improvise, write down, and perform new plays. This fall and winter they have been presenting a show entitled ***Non si paga, non si paga*** (***We Won't Pay, We Won't Pay***), based on the explosive "civil disobedience" movement to reduce gas, water, electric bills, and public transportation fares, which was instigated by rank-and-file union members and immediately picked up by working people throughout the country. The troupe plans other productions about the prison system, women's rights, and the struggle over abortion. Every major political issue, every important national or international event, creates the need for a new play; and every new play pinpoints new contradictions in the system, giving rise—dialectically, one might say—to a higher, more advanced stage of debate and organization.

To be sure, there are certain fundamental problems in the work carried out by Fo and the theatre collective, problems which *La Comune* itself seems frankly too busy and harassed to deal with, but which cannot be overlooked by any critical observer. Apart from the theoretical question of the ability of theatre—or, for that matter, any other cultural medium—to profoundly influence political reality in advanced capitalist society, there is the more concrete difficulty of organizing theatrical work in a truly collective manner when the key figures in the group have the personal prestige, overwhelming talent and energy of Fo and Rame. It is unfortunate, but perhaps unavoidable, that many of the estimated 700,000 spectators who attend their performances every year, come not to see the results of the collective work of their company, but to see them. (This observation can be verified by simply comparing

the size and loyalty of *La Comune*'s audiences to the relatively small following commanded by the numerous other political theatre groups currently active in Italy.) In the past, this situation has led to considerable tension between Fo and members of the companies he has helped to organize; turnover among performers tends to be quite high. Of course, without Fo, the theatre collective would be reduced to virtual insignificance, he could always gather a new group of people and turn it into an important cultural-political force. Nevertheless, this hardly compensates for the lack of a truly unified, egalitarian spirit and mode of organization in a company firmly committed to overturning old forms of privilege, hierarchy, and authority in society as a whole.

Furthermore, as intensely involved in political work as the troupe is at all times, one cannot avoid the feeling that its effective communication with the masses of working people is to some extent obstructed and overshadowed by the presence of a great performer. No matter how democratic, how sincerely "anti-status" he may be, a Star must in some ways inhibit the performance of mundane, everyday political tasks. And it is only through such unglamorous organization work that political change can, in the last analysis, take place. Revolutions nearly always have their flamboyant heroes, moments of pageantry, theatrical climaxes. But revolutions are not *theatre*. At times Fo seems to lose sight of this distinction, and tends to upstage both the working people who make up the majority of the mass movement of which his theatre is a part, and the members of his own company. These difficulties may be overcome as the people of the collective continue to work together and participate in daily political tasks along with working men and women in one neighborhood (hopefully, that of the "Palazzina Liberty"). To the extent that Fo and *La Comune* are able to perceive the limitations of the role that they can and should play in the wider movement, and if they can maintain a balance between raising of critical consciousness and acting as direct protagonists in the organizational work of the left, they will continue to occupy a vital place in the revolutionary movement in Italy.

NOTES

[1] So far there have been four major editions of Dario Fo's plays:

Compagni senza censura (Teatro politico della Associazione Nuova Scena), Milano, Mazzotta, 1970, V. 1. This volume contains several of the political plays written and directed by Fo when he worked with the *Nuova Scena* company. Volume 2 (Il Collettivo Teatrale La Comune), published in 1973, contains the major plays performed by *La Comune* up to that date. Both volumes contain photographs, documentary materials and texts of debates held after performances. *Testi del Colletivo La Comune*, Vernoa, Bertani editore. Bertani has published a series of separate editions of plays written by Fo for *La Comune*. Each volume contains documents and notes to the text. Bertani also plans to publish an edition of Fo's complete works starting in 1975.

Le Commedie di Dario Fo, Torino, Einaudi, 1974, 2 vols. This edition contains a selection of short comedies written during the years 1959-1967.

Dario Fo: Teatro Comico, Milano, Garzanti, 1971. A single-volume pocket edition of Fo's early comedies.

[2]*Pum, pum! Chè? La poliziu!*, Vernoa, Bertani editore, 3a. edizione, gennaio 1974.

[3]*Tutti uniti! Tutti insieme! Ma scusa quello non è il padrone?*, Verona, Bertani editore, aprile 1972.

[4]*Compagni senza censura*, Milano, Mazzotta, 1973, Vol. 2, pp. 112-113.

[5]Much of the music for songs written between 1970 and the present was composed by Paolo Ciarchi, a member of *La Comune*. An edition of Fo's complete poems, songs, and ballads is scheduled for publication by Bertani in 1975.

Joel Schechter (essay date 1984)

SOURCE: "The Un-American Satire of Dario Fo," in *Partisan Review*, Vol. LI, No. 1, 1984, pp. 112-19.

[*In the following, Schechter emphasizes the political satire in Fo's work.*]

Dario Fo received official recognition as a subversive comedian in May 1980, when the United States government refused to let him perform in New York. The Italian satirist and his wife, actress Franca Rame, were denied entry visas by the State Department. Comic monologues performed by the couple in Italy, England, France, Germany, Canada, Peru, and China for over a million spectators could not be seen in America. While the State Department kept the performers out, their satire has recently entered the country in the form of dramatic texts. One of Fo's plays, *We Can't Pay, We Won't Pay!*, was staged in San Francisco, Los Angeles, Seattle, New York, and Detroit during the past three years. Another satire, *Accidental Death of An Anarchist,* had its American premiere in January 1983, at the Mark Taper Forum in Los Angeles. A third political satire, *About Face,* opened at the Yale Repertory Theatre a few months later. If the State Department feared that Fo and Rame's sense of humor would attract a following, its fears were not wholly unfounded.

He may be Europe's leading political satirist and the most influential political playwright since Brecht, but Dario Fo is only beginning to be known in America. Not only has he yet to arrive here in person, over thirty of his plays remain unstaged, untranslated, and unpublished in the United States, despite the recent productions. The loss is more ours than Fo's. Neglect of his plays, and our government's refusal to let Fo and Rame perform here, betray cultural impoverishment and political biases that are peculiarly American.

Fo himself once observed that when politically uninformed actors appear in his plays, "a learning process is set in motion." The political content of the satires—which concern inflation, anarchism, terrorism, police interrogation, and other humorous subjects—has to be understood before actors can perform them accurately; this obstacle alone may explain most of the delay in America's reception of

Fo. Also, directors and actors in the United States tend to be box office conscious, even at subscriber-supported, nonprofit institutions; this militates against strong, political satire and politically biased presentations that might unsettle the settled, paying sector of the public.

A few American theaters became interested in staging *Accidental Death of An Anarchist* after it proved to be a box office success in London. The play, performed by a socialist theater group called Belt and Braces, transferred to London's West End and ran there in 1980 through 1981 for over five hundred performances. Suddenly Dario Fo was discovered by the English-speaking world. It seems he has commercial potential despite his politics—or perhaps because of them.

Fo has encountered success before. In 1968 he declared he would no longer be a "jester of the bourgeoisie," and he gave up a steady, handsome income as a creator of middle-class comedies in order to start over again. Since then he and his wife have performed for factory strikers, students, working class audiences—rarely for the wealthier sectors of society. Fo's popularity continues today, as he performs new plays and a one-man show, *Mistero Buffo,* for audiences of thousands who fill the stadiums, assembly halls, and circus tents on his tour circuit. His comedy as playwright and actor extends the traditions of Italian folk comedy and minstrelsy by using them for topical social commentary.

Born in 1926 in a small town in Lombardy, Fo comes from a working class family (his father was a railroad worker). He studied painting and architecture in Milan, and began writing satirical sketches in the 1940s. Since then he has created plays with Franca Rame, and with several collectives, the most recent of which is *La Comune*, based in Milan. His satires have won Fo enemies as well as friends. The Italian Communist Party ended two years of support for him in 1970 because he ridiculed it along with other venerable institutions such as the Catholic Church, the Christian Democrats, and the CIA. In 1973 an Italian fascist group abducted and raped Franca Rame. Fo himself has often been subjected to police harassment and censorship. He once noted that *Accidental Death of An Anarchist* was so successful in its exposure of state repression that it "produced a violent reaction in the centers of power. . . . We were subjected to provocation and persecution of all kinds, sometimes more grotesque and comical in their repressive stupidity than the very farce we were performing."

Evidently the United States Department of State wanted to play a role in this continuing farce. The official reasons it offered for Fo and Rame's visa denial in 1980 had to do with their membership in Soccorso Rosso (Red Aid), a group slightly to the left of Amnesty International. Their legal aid for political prisoners in Italy hardly amounts to the support of terrorism of which the State Department accused them. Fo may be a heterodox Marxist, but he is not an advocate of terrorist violence or kidnapping;

he condemns and ridicules such actions in his plays. Admittedly, his reasons for opposing terrorist violence are not the same as the State Department's; he objects to terrorism because it serves the state, providing the government with an excuse to increase its repression and control over dissenters.

The folly of terrorism is one subject of Fo's recent play, *Klaxon, Trumpets and Raspberries* (1981). A terrorist failure to kidnap Fiat owner Gianni Agnelli results in a grotesque farce of mistaken identities and Keystone Kops routines. Agnelli is rescued from a burning car by one of his workers, Antonio, but his face is disfigured and his memory is temporarily lost. Hospital surgeons remodel their unknown patient's face to match a photograph of Antonio, who has fled for fear of arrest. When Agnelli leaves the hospital, Antonio's wife assumes the recuperating amnesiac is her husband and takes him home. For a time Agnelli lives a worker's life, complete with exposure to assembly line work and police surveillance. In Milan, Dario Fo played the roles of both Agnelli and Antonio, a virtuoso doubling which suggested that if not for their faces, their property, and armed force, all men might be equal.

Fo's decision to portray a wealthy industrialist and one of his workers in this play is symptomatic of a comic, consciously practiced schizophrenia that pervades his satire. He embraces class enemies as collaborators in farce, presses them into his service, impersonates them, and articulates their contradictory roles with immense humor. In *Accidental Death of an Anarchist,* one of his most frequently produced plays, Fo himself performed the roles of maniac, police inspector, high court judge, and bishop. He kept disowning or temporarily exchanging one persona for another, so that the maniac's opening confession in the play might well be Dario Fo's personal testimony; he claims to suffer from a psychic disorder, "histromania," a compulsion to play multiple roles.

This disorder is not new, of course. Fo traces his performance and playwriting styles back to the storytelling of medieval minstrels. His characters continually tell one another stories, and impersonate their subjects as they describe them. Besides its continuation of the minstrel tradition, Fo sees in his theater an affinity with Brecht's epic style; Brecht asked actors to present roles "in the third person," narrating their story at the same time they enacted it, and Fo's plays too call for epic acting insofar as they require narrative techniques from actors.

Discussing the connection between his work and Brecht's in a 1974 essay on popular culture, Fo noted that spectators accept the fourth wall convention and identify with the actor's representation of a single character in bourgeois theater. In popular and Brechtian theater, instead of seeing isolated individuals on stage, the audience sees a "chorality." When any role taken by an actor becomes a pretext for his speaking of, as, and to many people, the imaginary fourth wall, the "delegated space" between audience and

actors, is destroyed. The audience, like the actors, cannot remain isolated individuals or voyeurs under these circumstances.

As Fo's characters accumulate stories, superstitions, words, and phrases from one another, and mimic one another in retelling stories or events, they reveal a collective aspect of character; one character's gestures and words are frequently stolen or learned from another. Fo's theater further destroys the "delegated space" of actor and audience in the sense that his plays resist notions of character and language as private property. The plays portray redistribution of property—consumer goods in *We Can't Pay,* and the intellectual property of state secrets in *Accidental Death of an Anarchist*—a central action which parallels the redistribution of individual characters' language and gestures.

Invention of an alibi by the police in *Accidental Death of an Anarchist* becomes a collective act of character creation; the story of the anarchist's death is retold and reenacted many times with variation by men at a Milan police station. The play, written in 1970, is based on an actual occurrence in which an Italian anarchist accused of terrorism was said to have jumped to his death from the fourth floor of a Milan precinct station. We now know, and Fo suspected as much when his collective first performed the play, that the anarchist, Giuseppe Pinelli, was pushed to his death by the police.

The subject may not sound like promising material for a farce, but Fo turned it into a political satire that was extremely topical when it opened. In a preface to the play, Fo calls it "an exercise in counterinformation." He notes that all references to the death are based on authentic documents—transcripts of investigations carried out by judges as well as police reports. Now that the case is over a decade old and Pinelli's innocence has been proven, the facts are not so urgent or controversial. However, the play still functions as a complex, comic statement on state secrecy and abuse of power. While it was once a political act, a rallying point for opponents of state repression, and was seen as such by over half a million Italians, Fo's play remains popular in other countries because it suggests that forms of law and power are based on controlled information—state secrets which lose force once they are revealed, shared, and consequently "democratized."

The play's central character, a maniacal buffoon originally acted by Fo himself, parodies the state's control of information by pretending to be a high court judge. He is the epitome of a "documentary clown," turning state evidence around, so it testifies against the state. In his disguise, the buffoon encourages police officers to compose their alibi against accusations that they murdered Pinelli. In 1970 the state issued different reports that contradicted one another and offered specious conclusions, thereby inadvertently exposing its manipulative control of information. Parodying this process to expose it more fully, Fo juxtaposes the contradictions of different official reports for comic effect.

By impersonating different authorities, using different alibis, encouraging the policemen to speak lines and lies he gives them, confusing them so they don't know which thoughts are theirs and which are the impostor judge's, Fo literally turns the police alibis about the murder into charades. In doing this he intimates that state power itself may be one long series of charades, cover-ups, and manipulations of facts that abusive power requires for its perpetuation.

The capacity of Fo's buffoon to impersonate policemen, anarchists, judge, and bishop fosters a comic, carnivalesque vision of society where, as Bakhtin said of the carnival in Rabelais's world, people become interchangeable in their mass body. Fo becomes a one-man carnival, and amply represents the collectivity, in one scene in **Mistero Buffo** where he portrays fifteen different characters by himself; they are the spectators watching the miracle of Lazarus's resurrection, and through gestures alone, Fo expresses their varied responses to the event. Fo's ability to perform crowd scenes solo may be one reason that French critic Bernard Dort praised the "ubiquity" of this "epic actor." Writing about Fo's performance in **Mistero Buffo**, Dort regarded it as the opposite of a personal display; Fo was not on stage to show himself, but rather to show many others.

The ubiquitous acting style is also evident in Fo's playwriting, where characters alter society, at least temporarily, by transforming themselves and creating new personae. Given the proper words and gestures, Fo's characters can change from factory owners into factory workers, and from policemen into anarchists. The first act of **Accidental Death** ends with the police singing a favorite hymn of anarchists, because the buffoon convinces them it will make them look more human and sympathetic to the public. "I beg of you! For your own good . . . so the investigation will turn out in your favor . . . Sing!" And they sing:

> The whole world is our homeland.
> Our law is liberty.
> And through our thought
> This world of ours shall finally be free.

The grotesquery of the situations in which Fo's characters find themselves is almost Rabelaisian. Bakhtin noted that in Rabelais's world, the grotesque "discloses the potentiality of an entirely different world, of another way of life . . . a return to Saturn's golden age . . . [requiring] bodily participation in the potentiality of another world." The policemen who sing an anarchist song briefly enter another world—that of their victim. But far more grotesque transformations occur in other scenes by Fo. A police officer appears to experience an hysterical pregnancy in **We Can't Pay, We Won't Pay!**. In the same play several women stuff boxes of pasta and vegetables under their coats, so that they look pregnant; their husbands almost instantly accept the roles of worried, expectant fathers. The play is based on actual events in Milan, where massive "proletarian shopping" (shoplifting) began after grocery prices skyrocketed in 1974. In Fo's satire the women try to hide their stolen goods from husbands and policemen. The resulting farce offers a vision of urban Saturnalia, where instead of Rabelaisian monks, pilgrims, or scholars, we see housewives, factory workers, and police officers undergo illegal or bizarre transformations in body, and in their relations to nature (vegetables, birth) and private property (unaffordable groceries). Two wives choose to participate bodily in "another world" when a policeman discovers that their bulging bellies are actually bags of salad. Antonia and Margherita claim a miracle has occurred. The police inspector searching for stolen groceries has to accept their word or risk sacrilege:

> INSPECTOR: Oh yes? The cabbage miracle. Where are the roses?
>
> MARGHERITA: Who can afford roses? They're very expensive.
>
> ANTONIA: In hard times, one makes what miracles one can. With the veg you've got handy. Anyway, miracles aren't illegal, you know. Also, there's no law that says a person can't carry a mixed salad on their belly.

The satire here ridicules religion in an age of consumer capitalism, an age of democracy where "miracles" can be purchased in any grocery store; the greatest miracle is that one can afford to pay the bill. In **We Can't Pay, We Won't Pay!** the humor is less exotic than, say, the episode in Rabelais where Gargantua eats six pilgrims in a salad because they had hidden under lettuce in a garden to escape their enemies. Rabelais's grotesquery has given way to antic transformations more suitable for an age of inflation, shoplifting, and miracle salad dressing.

Fo's utopian satire allows us to witness small miracles, to see policemen turn into anarchists, and unborn children turn into food; but Fo also knows his satire cannot achieve larger miracles. One speech in **Accidental Death of an Anarchist** questions the play's efficacy as social corrective, and inadvertently explains the play's success at box offices twelve years after it was written. Having revealed Italian political scandals, the buffoonish impostor in the play informs us that:

> The average citizen doesn't stand to gain anything from the disappearance of dirty deals. No, he's satisfied to see them denounced, to see a scandal break out so that people can talk about it. For him, that's real freedom and the best of all possible worlds.

If Fo knows the limits of his art, he also knows the source of its appeal. The buffoon in **Accidental Death of an Anarchist** tells us that his hobby is "the theater of reality, so my fellow artists must be real people, unaware that they are acting in my productions, which is handy, as I've got no cash to pay them." The law officers who hear him, and the audience offstage, willingly become this masterful charlatan's coconspirators, his "fellow artists," as he winks at both groups in turn, confides his impostures and scandals to listeners, and asks them to approve of his disguises. His need for audience acceptance is complemented by his listeners' (on and offstage) desire to be part of a political conspiracy, to hear secrets of state whispered aloud. The spontaneous and intimate sense of conspiracy between the satirist and his audience cannot be achieved by him as easily on electronic media as on stage, in person, especially if the person is Dario Fo.

While Fo's plays allow the audience to eavesdrop on dirty political deals or parodies of them, the playwright resists passivity and voyeurism in spectators. He too uses "real people" as his "fellow artists." To do this he involves the audience and actors in playwriting, by incorporating their suggestions into works-in-progress. Plays such as **Accidental Death of an Anarchist** have acquired several different endings as a result of Fo's exchanges with the audience. Other plays, such as **The Boss's Funeral,** contain an "unwritten" last act; instead of finishing the story, Fo and his cast discuss the play and its political issues with the audience. In this way he allows spectators to "enter" (his word) the performance and modify it; they too become agents of change.

"In this way his performance becomes a discussion (about social conditions) with the audience he is addressing," Brecht wrote of an epic actor's technique; and this can be said of Fo's performance style too, although his style differs markedly from Brecht's epic theater in its factually based, documentary satire. And while both playwrights have tried to break through the fourth wall with techniques that allow them to address the audience directly, Fo has gone one step further "out of character." He leaves his personae behind, to become Dario Fo, listener, conversationalist, debater, political organizer. When he engages in democratic, postperformance dialogues, there is no need for that perpetual outcast and renegade, the political satirist.

Ron Jenkins (essay date 1986)

SOURCE: "Dario Fo: The Roar of the Clown," in *The Drama Review*, Vol. 30, No. 1, Spring 1986, pp. 172-79.

[*In this essay, Jenkins argues that "Fo has developed a modern style of epic performance that speaks to his audience with the immediacy of a newspaper editorial, shifts perspectives with the fluidity of cinematic montage, and pulsates with the rhythmic drive of a jazz improvisation."*]

The intellectual complexity and bacchanalian passions of Dario Fo's epic comedy are usually reduced in translation to the flatness of a political cartoon. Even successful productions like Rennie Davis' version of **We Won't Pay, We Won't Pay** leave the audience with the impression of Fo as a clever satirist whose work can be comfortably categorized as political theater. This limited view ignores the subtler dimensions of Fo's talents. In their original versions Fo's plays are dense with poetic wordplay, visual references to medieval paintings, and sophisticated rhythmic structures that are lost by translators and directors who focus singlemindedly on Fo as a political clown.[1]

Of course, there is a fundamentally political dimension to all of Fo's work, which includes mocking references to police brutality, government fraud, and social injustice. His recurring theatrical allusions to current events reflect Fo's commitment to a theater that is politically relevant, but during the three months that I travelled with him and his company, he rarely spoke explicitly about politics. Rehearsals, seminars, and casual mealtime conversations revolved around topics like the theatricality of regional dialects and the actor/audience relationship. Artistic concerns like these are linked to political issues, but Fo manages to make the connections without waving flags as blatantly as do some of his adaptors abroad. An actress in the New York production of **We Won't Pay** referred to it as a "spoon waving" version of the play, because she was directed to play the role of a housewife by standing on the edge of the stage and waving a spoon at the audience as she lectured them on the evils of capitalism.

Fo's outrage against political and social injustice emerges more obliquely, as in the moment at the dinner table when the company's electrical technician asked him if he believed that people spoke regional dialects because they were too ignorant to speak "proper Italian." Fo responded with a spirited defense of the inherent beauty of the dialects and an attack on the Italian school system's policy of branding the variations as inferior. In his plays Fo uses a poetic blend of regional dialects, and it is clear that the choice reflects his commitment to the celebration of working class popular culture. What Fo's audiences hear onstage, however, is not a didactic manifesto about the "language of the people," but a magnificent cascade of coarse poetry that is an indirect tribute to the lyricism of the dialects spoken in Italy's village markets.

Fo's fusion of subversive politics and poetic slapstick is exemplified in his portrayal of Harlequin. Having been sent by his master to fetch a love potion, Harlequin uses it himself in a visit to a prostitute. When he returns home, Harlequin's disobedience is betrayed by the fantastic and uncontrollable growth of his penis. Using his mimetic talents, Fo creates the illusion that his organ has become almost as big as Harlequin himself. To avoid detection he wraps it in a blanket and pretends it is a baby. All the women in the neighborhood coo and stroke it, resulting in a great comic situation. The focus of the comedy is ostensibly erotic, but at the heart of the piece is the servant's revolt against his patron, the refusal of the impoverished Harlequin to submit to the master's repressive rules. The humor is generated by the tension between Harlequin's fear of his tyrannical master and his pleasure over his enhanced potency. Fo's performance is an allegory of rebellion camouflaged behind a mask of crude buffoonery. The politics are clear, but they never overwhelm the piece's exquisite slapstick poetics.

Fo blends politics and art with an effortless eloquence that makes him a Brechtian clown. Frequently describing the style of his theater as "epic," Fo borrows Brecht's terminology, but his points of reference go back to the medieval town jesters (*giullari*) and the commedia dell'arte players who were the originators of Italy's epic comedy tradition. Looking to these models for inspiration, Fo has developed a modern style of epic performance that speaks to his audience with the immediacy of a newspaper editorial, shifts perspectives with the fluidity of cinematic montage, and pulsates with the rhythmic drive of a jazz improvisation.

A good example of Fo's epic clowning can be found in his play about the relationship between Shakespeare and Queen Elizabeth, *Elisabetta: Quasi per Caso una Donna.* Shakespeare never appears on stage, but Fo, playing a maidservant, acts out the entire plot of *Hamlet* for the head of Elizabeth's secret police as he explains that it is a veiled satire of the Queen's regime. Playing all the parts himself, Fo uses gestures and gibberish to re-enact the high points of Shakespeare's tragedy in less than two minutes, as if the action were unfolding on high-speed film. The police captain is totally bewildered, and Fo has structured the episode so that the audience identifies the official's dullness with the thickheadedness of modern Italian police investigators. Angered by the abusive mockery of her policies, Elizabeth tries to prevent Fo from recounting his second-hand Hamlet, but the clown is unstoppable. When she grabs his left hand, he continues miming the story behind his back with his right hand, and when she manages to tie up both his arms, he continues gesturing with his feet. The comedy of the scene is rooted in the muscular rhythms of Fo's performance. The Queen's clumsy attempts at physical censorship are no match for the irrepressible satiric impulses of the clown.

This style of densely-layered comedy appears frequently in the plays that Fo writes for his theater ensemble, but the simplest way to isolate the essential techniques of Fo's epic clowning is to look at examples drawn from his solo comic performances. In one-man plays like *Mistero Buffo, Fabulazzo Osceno*, and *Storia della Tigre* Fo demonstrates most clearly his genius for creating theater that unites art and politics in a seamless comic blend. Among the key elements that give Fo's performances their distinctive power are his musically orchestrated rhythms, his montage-like use of multiple perspectives, and the intimately immediate quality of his relationship with his public.

RHYTHM

When Fo directs rehearsals of his plays or critiques the work of his students, he always stresses the importance of rhythm. Fo is a musician as well as a playwright, and his theater flows with a dynamic musicality that is generated by the basic emotional impulses of the situations he enacts. For example, his portrayal of a starving man in *The Grammelot of the Zanni* is structured around the rhythms of hunger as experienced by a 14th-century peasant.

The hungry Zanni is so famished that he begins to eat his own body, popping his eyeballs into his mouth and slurping up his disemboweled intestines as if they were pasta in a bowl. The action could easily become mired in infantile grotesquerie, but Fo makes it comic by cannibalizing himself with the rhythmic joy of a big band leader in full swing. The body parts are devoured with tempos of building excitement that culminate in percussive burps or climactic sighs of contentment. Although the piece is extremely funny, there is nothing frivolous about the mood Fo's rhythms evoke. There is never any doubt that the man is in pain, that he suffers not only a hunger for food but also a hunger for dignity and justice.

After consuming himself, the peasant challenges the complacency of God and the audience by threatening to eat them next, but he gets sidetracked by the dream of cooking a feast in an overstocked kitchen. His delirious fantasies are accompanied by the syncopated sounds of gurgling stews and sizzling oils. Fo creates all the effects himself with musical vocalizations that resemble a jazz singer scatting his way through a song. The piece concludes when the famished man wakes up from his dream and satisfies his cravings by eating a fly. He sucks the juice off the wings and savors each morsel of the insect with a primal howl of delight. Fo's performance is comparable to Chaplin's classic routine of eating a boiled shoe in *The Gold Rush*.

Fo's rhythmic pantomime is antithetical to the style of a performer like Marcel Marceau. There is nothing refined, delicate or quiet about a performance by Dario Fo. It is full of crude sounds and coarse gestures expressing human desires and needs. Marceau's technique of pure mime calls attention to itself as something apart from everyday gesture. Fo submerges his technique in a flurry of sounds and movements. He seems to have just come off the subway and invented it all on the spot. Fo is full of passions, obscenities, odors, growls, and desires that could not exist in the rarified world of classical mime. These irrepressible urges give Fo's performances their inner pulse. The comic cadences of the hungry Zanni's actions are inseparable from his struggle to survive.

MONTAGE

The earthy rhythms of Fo's style are complemented by his ability to present a story from several perspectives successively rather than from a single point of view. In the enactment of the Zanni's hunger, for instance, Fo first offers the grotesque fantasy of the man eating himself, then shifts to the pleasurable dream of a giant kitchen, and concludes with the stark portrait of a starving man eating a fly. All of this is presented in the context of a political/historical explanation for the man's hunger presented by Fo in his introductory prolog.

The shifts of perspective are intentional. Like Brecht, he wants his audience to see a situation from a variety of viewpoints so they can reflect on its multiple aspects, instead of simply losing themselves in empathy for a single point of view. In describing the way his epic style of characterization differs from traditional acting, Fo uses the analogy of a sculptor carving a statue. As a performer he circles a situation the way a sculptor circles an unfinished statue, examining the way the lights and shadows are formed when viewed from different directions.

Fo's technique of shifting perspectives is equivalent to cinematic montage. One of the most vivid examples of Fo's multiple-perspective storytelling is his satire of the attempted assassination of the Pope. Alone on the stage without props, Fo recreates the scene of the Pope's arrival in Spain. Fo becomes the people shouting their greetings in the welcoming crowd. Fo becomes the Pope's airplane, advertising its sacred passenger with a giant papal cap on top of its wings. Fo becomes one of the peasants explaining to another that the magnificently attired plane is not the Pope, but that the Pope is inside the plane. Images and characters appear and dissolve with a rapidity that gives the audience the impression of watching a televised news report of the event, with the camera angles changing every few seconds.

The Pope emerges from the door of the plane. Fo both portrays and describes him, presenting the scene in first and third person simultaneously. After showing the Pope in all the splendor of his jewels and colored robes, Fo slips out of the story completely to recount a newspaper article he had read recently that criticized the Pope's taste for opulence as the opposite of Christ's renunciation of material pleasures. Fo then quotes the Bible story in which Jesus was tempted by the devil with the power to fly all over the world. "Jesus said no to the devil," quips Fo, "but the Pope says 'yes'." Continuing to mock the Pope's incessant world travels, Fo jokes that "God is everywhere, but the Pope's already been there."

Moving back to the newsreel images of the Pope, Fo portrays the gunman, the Bulgarian agents with walkie-talkies directing the gunman, the police asking the gunman what he is doing with the bullets, and the gunman replying that they are a new kind of rosary bead. He says a prayer as he loads each one into the chamber, and the guards leave him alone. Fo then resumes the role of narrator to wonder aloud why no one was able to stop the gunman, given that so many photographs were taken of him in varying phases of preparation for the assassination. Fo becomes a series of still photographs leading up to the gunshots, and he then acts out the fall of the wounded Pope, the television commentators announcing that the Pope has been shot in the sphincter, and the outraged Vatican spokesman who refuses to acknowledge that the Pope has a sphincter, insisting instead that the Pope's bowels should be referred to as a divine conduit.

Fo's looney tune version of the shooting leads to another quick change of perspective, this one more drastic, taking the audience to the twelfth century and the Papacy of Pope Boniface VIII. Fo's story is a 12th-century illustration of the 20th-century newspaper column describing the Pope as the opposite of Christ. Boniface is presented as he prepares himself for a public appearance, adorning himself in fine clothes, expensive rings, and elegant robes. When the

Pope's procession meets the humbler procession of Jesus, Fo portrays Boniface's hypocrisy by showing him unrobing and covering himself with mud in feigned humility before Christ.

Up until the meeting with Jesus, Boniface has been satirized for his vanity and arrogance. When altar boys wrinkle his clothes he threatens to hang them by their tongues, a punishment, Fo explains, actually used by Boniface to deal with religious dissidents. Fo uses this graphic image as a recurring bit of black comedy. Each time the altar boys displease him, Boniface mimes hanging them by their tongues. Fo mimes hammering the tongue into the wall, then his hands become the tongue swinging in the wind. Next he transforms himself into a boy as he would appear if his body were hanging suspended from the tongue.

By shifting from the subject to the object of the threat and from the close-up of the tongue to a long shot of the hanging victim, Fo tells the story as if he were a camera shooting the scenes. The sequence is repeated several times throughout the piece from different angles and for shorter durations, as if miniature flashbacks of the original threat were inserted into a corner of the stage. With such montage techniques Fo insures that the audience never gets lost in the characterization of the Pope and is continually reminded of the contextual frame of religious tyranny within which the action takes place.

IMMEDIACY AND AUDIENCE INVOLVEMENT

Fo talks to the public directly through prologs, intentional narrative interruptions, and improvised responses to spontaneous situations that arise onstage. Fo's intimate rapport with large crowds gives his performances an immediacy that elicits the public's active involvement in an ongoing dialog of ideas. Fo challenges the audience with a phrase or gestures, and they respond with laughter or applause. Using his public as a collaborator, Fo structures his monologs with the rhythms of their responses in mind. During his performances the integration of the audience seems unplanned, but when Fo advises other actors of his material in rehearsals, he explicitly directs them to anticipate the public's response at specific moments. Rehearsing monologs with student actors, Fo will play the role of the audience responding to each line, so that the student learns to transform the monolog into a dialog with the public.

The immediacy of the audience is central to Fo's retelling of the miracle when Jesus turns water into wine. Fo initially presents two competing storytellers. One is an angel who tells the official version of the story in a detached style that does not take into account the public's desires. The other storyteller is a drunk who claims to have been present at the miracle and offers an earthy account of the celebration that speaks more directly to the audience's spirit of revelry. The drunk plucks the angel's feathers, chases him away, and proceeds to tell his Dionysian version of the miracle, emphasizing the pleasures of drinking wine with an inebriated ecstasy that serves as a direct call to the senses of his audience. He invites them to feel, smell, and taste the wine with him as he relives the pleasures of Jesus' miracle. In one sequence he drinks wine as if bathing in it, mimes the passage of the red liquid as it seeps through his veins, and expresses the depth of his pleasure with a gigantic burp that sends the aroma of the wine across the countryside. In a cinematic transition the expansive burp opens up the landscape of the action, and Fo presents the trail of the wine's aroma leading to a man on horseback who smells it and shouts out with gratitude, "Jesus sei di / vino" ("Jesus you are divine / of wine"). Fo's vocal and visual shifts have been building up to this climactic shout, which inevitably results in applause from the audience appreciating the pun. The sequence is structured in a way that would render its rhythms incomplete without the culminating punctuation of the audience's gleeful response.

Arguing that drinking wine could never be a sin if Jesus offered it to his mother, the drunk is implicitly urging the public to challenge the angel's pious attitudes and celebrate the liberating effects of wine. To strengthen his argument, the drunk reasons that Adam and Eve would never have been tempted by the snake to eat the apple if there had been wine in the garden for them to drink. The performance is a masterpiece of comic rhetoric designed to persuade the audience to abandon the angel's puritan point of view and accept a more joyous vision of religion. As the story progresses, the drunk's argument becomes funnier and more reasonable at the same time. The public is swayed by his comic logic about Adam in the garden of Eden: if Adam had been like the drunk, the human race would still be living in Paradise. Fo's success in persuading the audience can be measured in their roars of laughter and applause at moments like the horseman's yell.

A TAPESTRY OF POLITICS AND POETRY

Fo weaves the technical elements of his epic clowning into a dense theatrical tapestry in which politics and poetry are inseparable. His comic rhythms grow out of the dialectic between freedom and oppression that is at the core of the stories he tells. Each slapstick crescendo is orchestrated around a liberating triumph over injustice. Generated by the conflict between the powerful and the powerless, the frantic tempo of Fo's farces is an implicit tribute to his characters' abilities to outwit their oppressors and survive.

Fo's montage-like use of shifting perspectives is linked to his political beliefs. Presenting a situation from multiple points of view enables him to emphasize the relationship between individual behavior and its cultural context. The theatrical jump-cuts in Fo's performances suggest a complex interaction between history, economics, religion, morality, and mundane current events. Fo's comedy exists at the overlap between the private and the public domains.

The relationship between Fo and his audiences reveals another aspect of this overlap. The public is included in the performance because Fo believes in their intelligence. He speaks to them with a direct and candid simplicity that transforms spectators into Fo's co-conspirators against injustice.

All of Fo's techniques coalesce in the powerful conclusion to his story of Jesus and the wine. Having just presented Adam's rejection of the Serpent in favor of a glass of wine, the drunk offers a toast to God, the audience, and the earth beneath his feet. Tilting the glass to the public, Fo is graciously thanking them for their involvement. Pouring a few drops on the ground he is paying homage to the earthy impulses that stand in opposition to the repressive censorship of the angel he battled at the beginning of the piece. And raising the glass toward heaven he shifts the focus from the mundane to the spiritual world. This simple, skyward motion is the last gesture of the story, and it is charged with startling eloquence. Having defied the authority of heaven, the buffoon strikes a pose that momentarily transforms him into an angel in spite of himself. The closing sequence epitomizes the spirit of Fo's epic clown in the breadth of its vision, the depth of its feeling, and the generosity with which it embraces the world beyond the stage.

NOTE

[1] This work with Dario Fo was supported by a Sheldon Fellowship from Harvard University.

Mimi D'Aponte (essay date 1989)

SOURCE: "From Italian Roots to American Relevance: The Remarkable Theatre of Dario Fo," in *Modern Drama*, Vol. XXXII, No. 4, December 1989, pp. 532-44.

[*In the essay below, D'Aponte assesses the impact Fo has had on American theater.*]

> Clowns are grotesque blasphemers against all our pieties. That's why we need them. They're our alter egos.
>
> (Dario Fo, Cambridge, May 1987)[1]

Americans writing about theatre have been pronouncing Dario Fo's work extraordinary, whether for performance or political reasons, or for both. "For the past decade," claimed Joel Schechter in 1985, "Dario Fo has been Europe's most popular political satirist."[2] "So many theatres have included Fo in their recent seasons," wrote Ron Jenkins in 1986, "that he has become the most-produced contemporary Italian playwright in the U.S."[3] American producers interested in social satire seem to have become less leery of this zany Italian genius who publicly thanked his "fellow actor," Ronald Reagan, for the marvelous promotion afforded his work when the State Department denied him an American visa for several years.

Dario Fo is the brilliant successor of a comic tradition of mime and improvisation which extends not only back to

*Fo receiving the Nobel Prize from Sweden's King Carl XVI Gustav,
10 December 1997.*

Greek *phlyakes* and Roman *fabulae*, but also includes both medieval *giullari* (to whom he so often refers) and Italian *commedia dell'arte*. He is, in addition, the heir of two twentieth-century Italian geniuses of the comic spirit—Totò and Eduardo. The first connection is evident from the transcription of Fo's remarks filmed to honor Totò (1898-1967) in 1978 and published in English translation last year. He pronounces Totò an "epic actor" (nomenclature he often applies to his own technique)[4]—"he uses all the elements which allow a break with naturalism."[5] Fo also states that Totò is true to the *commedia dell'arte* tradition since, by using body and face in opposition to one another, he creates a true mask (Fo's use of masks and puppets in the 50s and 60s was extensive).[6] Finally, Fo celebrates gleefully Totò's destruction of the fourth wall by citing an example of Totoian conversation with a tardy audience member:

> If someone arrived late when the show had started, Totò interupted everything and said: "So you've come at last? . . . We were really worried . . . Do sit down . . ."[7]

This dialog is identical to one which Fo engaged in with a late-comer to the James Joyce Theater in New York City during a May 1986 performance of his signature piece, **Mistero Buffo.**

> You will find a[n] . . . authentic . . . version of its [commedia dell'arte's] artificial clowning in the Neapolitan comedian Totò. And for another side of the tradition—not famous at all unfortunately—you must go to Eduardo.[8]

The other twentieth-century figure with whom Fo must be compared is Eduardo De Filippo (1900-84). Referred to familiarly by Italians as "Eduardo," and by Eric Bentley as the "Son of Pulcinella," this prolific Neapolitan actor/playwright exemplified a strongly realistic tradition of acting. In 1950 Bentley identified Eduardo as perhaps the finest actor in Italy today "more likely . . . to be the heir of *commedia dell'arte* than any other important performer now living."[9] There was a precision to Eduardo's performances which was uncanny, which left the viewer with the sense of having witnessed the quintessential interpretation of the character in question.[10] This "polish" seems to be what Fo, in speaking to acting students in London, termed *"souplesse."*

> What makes . . . great swimmer[s] is the fact that they have coordination. You're hardly aware of how their bodies move . . . you hardly see them breathe . . . *That* is *souplesse.* It's the same *souplesse*, litheness, that great actors have. They don't show that they are exerting themselves. They make you forget that they are acting.[11]

Fo possesses *"souplesse"* to an astonishing degree and he practises a performance style probably closer to the "Ruzzante" form of *commedia* which he admires than "any other important performer now living."[12] Fo sees himself as the inheritor of the "realistic" acting style of the Italian popular theatre which, he explains, encompasses an epic dimension as well:

> The epic style derives from realism. But it is characterised by the self-aware detachment of the actor; the actor is critical of what he acts. He does not confine himself to conveying information, to telling something, and then letting the audience sort it all out. He seeks to provide the audience with the necessary data for a reading of the piece.[13]

As I hope to demonstrate later in this paper, Fo's performance style also exemplifies Bentley's admiring words about Eduardo: "a series of statements, vocal and corporeal . . . beautiful in their clean economy . . . in [their] relation to each other and to the whole."[14]

Like Eduardo before him, Fo is a highly successful Italian playwright who has created excitement in international theatre circles. Eduardo wrote domestic tragi-comedies produced in translation around the world which, as Bentley put it, were both traditional and original and in which he "put his finger on the black moral spot."[15] Fo's theatre has been defined at various times as agit-prop, throw-away, political, improvisational, a theatre of blasphemy, and popular. His first translator in the United States, Suzanne Cowan, wrote in 1979:

> To give a full account of Dario Fo's theatrical career would really be tantamount to writing a history of postwar Italy, because his work can only be understood as a continuous, uniquely creative response to the major social and political developments of the past thirty years.[16]

Like Eduardo before him, Fo has been greeted with instant popularity in many countries while being given, initially at least, a somewhat cooler reception in the U.S.[17] The failure, for example, of Eduardo's *Saturday, Sunday and Monday* in 1974 Broadway production despite its huge British success in 1973 seems to have been a virtual blueprint for Fo's British-American experience with **Accidental Death of an Anarchist.** This "grotesque" farce about a "tragic farce"[18] achieved tremendous success in London during 1979-81, only to open and close rapidly on Broadway in Fall of 1984.

What seems clear, however, is that Fo's work has created an ongoing interest in American university and repertory theatres which Eduardo's did not. This is due in part to an increased American awareness of international theatre trends fostered by the academy's more frequent conference and exchange programs, and also perhaps by more frequent mass-media culture coverage. Continued American interest in Fo's work springs also from our desire to stay abreast of such trends: Tony Mitchell, in the first English-language book devoted to Fo, states flatly that by 1978, "Fo was already the most widely performed playwright in world theatre."[19] But it is the fact that Fo and Rame have finally been able to practise their crafts of acting and directing in this country that has led to acclaim in the American theatre about this extraordinary team.

Dario Fo's performance of **Mistero Buffo** (**Comic Mystery Play**) and Franca Rame's performance of **Tutta Casa, Letto, e Chiesa** (**It's All Bed, Board and Church**) at the James Joyce Theatre after a tour which played in Boston, New Haven, and Washington, D.C. were remarkably different from usual Off-Broadway fare. Two immediate adjustments of perspective were built into this Obie-award-winning experience. The verbal comedy of these one-person shows, performed on alternate evenings, worked through instant translation (Ron Jenkins as translator for Fo took on the persona of straight-man) and projected overhead sub-titles. Also, the house remained half-lit throughout performance in order to permit interaction with the audience, something accomplished with ease and intimacy despite the "language barrier." Rame's work was a series of monologs treating the "sexual slavery of women" and played "in a style that recalls the sexy, comic intelligence of Mae West."[20] "Dario Fo mesmerizes in **Mistero Buffo**" began *The Boston Globe* review,[21] for each audience was treated to an astounding range of both physical comedy and historical context, which Fo wove anew each evening

as he proceeded deftly through the fresh improvisation of a show encompassing a dozen texts.

> For several of the scenes, Fo employs "grammelot"—a nonsense language he invents phonetically as if it were Northern Italian dialect, English, French, Italian. He becomes transformed, before our eyes and without costume or prop, from a chatty fellow letting us in on historical gossip, into an Italian peasant, a French advisor to the king, an English lawyer of high place, a pope. Each sketch is politically biting, physically hilarious and theatrically successful in its maintenance of character.[22]

In reviewing **Mistero Buffo** for *The New York Times*, Mel Gussow introduced Fo as "an outrageous gadfly" and mentioned Richard Pryor, Father Guido Sarducci and Monty Python by way of comparison. Mr. Gussow concluded with mention of other names:

> With his mobile face and body, he is a cartoon in motion, loping across the stage with the antelopean grace of Jacques Tati, doing a Jackie Gleason away-we-go to demonstrate the Italian perfection of the art of women-watching.[23]

Both sets of references are on target. Fo's performance was unforgettable because it conjured up a complex battery of historical and cultural perspectives, while simultaneously satirizing their contingent political realities. Clad in black work-day jersey and slacks and sharing a bare stage with only his translator, Fo created in the mind's eye of his audience chaotic crowds, lavish costumes, and dramatic conflicts resolved by the machinations of a laughing clown-narrator in favor of those without power.

Fo's formidable powers of persuasion through laughter illuminate his on-stage persona. These same powers are seen from another perspective in his work as teacher and director. Most immediately obvious is the appeal of the comradeship and community which Fo creates about him, beginning with that strong emotional, intellectual, and artistic partnership which he and Franca Rame, his wife, have shared for thirty-four years. This partnership extends not only to their own acting company, currently La Comune of Milan, but also to the manner in which Fo and Rame interact with any company.[24] While Western theatre is by definition an art form organized in hierarchical fashion, Fo's concept of how to work in the theatre appears consistently egalitarian. This philosophy ultimately translates into a specific reality: everything which appears on stage and/or takes place on stage is in some fashion touched by Fo. Whatever the form of this nurturing, its manner is one of co-authorship, of "we" rather than of "I" and "you."

Along with this comradeship comes a powerful charisma which Dario Fo possesses and uses automatically, effortlessly in his quest for the ideal performance of his troupe. He is a director whose every syllable and step on stage are noted by everyone, near and far. Members of the American Repertory Theatre, a young, vital professional company with excellent credentials, spoke glowingly of their learning under Fo's tutelage during rehearsals for **Archangels Don't Play Pinball** in Spring 1987. "Dario exerts an amazing influence—he has a way of working with actors. No one at ART has ever attained this popularity."[25] "I want to get a grant to follow Dario Fo around. This is the guy I've been waiting to learn from all my life."[26] A visiting university director added, "I'm on leave this year. I'd be in Milan if Dario were in Milan. I'm in Cambridge because he's here."[27] Such remarks take on additional weight when one realizes that they represent English-speaking theatre folk describing their Italian-speaking theatre mentor. Dario's ability to communicate goes beyond the limitation of language.

Then there is the power of example. Fo the performer is able to illustrate what Fo the director has to say. Fo and Rame conducted five theatre workshops in London in late spring 1983 the transcripts of which were subsequently published and translated. The student/teacher exchanges during these sessions underscore the credibility in the theatre of a director who practises in his own performances what he preaches to his students. For example:

> QUESTION When you did the three situations exercise earlier, the only way that we spectators could laugh at the comedy of it was because we already understood the situation, because you had explained it to us. But how, then, if you are the actor, creating the situation, how do you express it without using even more obvious methods of expression?

> DARIO FO Theatre has always had *prologues,* even when they are not declared as such. There is an old tradition of theatre in Italy, which had prologues which were really masterpieces. In fact, the rest of the plays has often been lost, and the prologues have remained in their own right. There is, for example, the famous prologue: . . . "Ah, if I could only become invisible." The situation is already presented in it . . . in that one sentence it already gives you the situation. The actor comes on and explains the things he could do if he was invisible. (*He acts out the prologue*)[28]

The enjoyment of watching the persuasive power of Fo's directing and teaching is enhanced by the knowledge that what he offers his actors and students alike is empowerment—empowerment as actors and empowerment as authors. The answer to two questions posed to him demonstrate something of the private Dario Fo's modest character and a sense of the public Fo's ability to teach effortlessly, with *"souplesse."*

> QUESTION What influence do you want your work to have on American theatre?

> DARIO FO I don't know.

> QUESTION What is the connection between political theatre and improvisation?

> DARIO FO The choice of an improvisational form of theatre is already a political one—because improvisational theatre is never finished, never a closed case, always open-ended.

> *Improvisational theatre is open on a space level.* If we are performing in a large theatre, a stadium which seats 5000 in one night and in a factory which accommodates 300 the next, we must improvise, by necessity, and without a dozen rehearsals. Out of necessity we signal to one another and stretch out what we do to fill the stadium or contract it to fit into the factory.

> *Improvisational theatre is open on an emotional level.* Audiences are not the same every evening. Different things have happened to them on a political level. Someone may have been shot, someone may have died; an audience is an emotionally different entity every night. The actor in an improvisational theatre is open to audience mood and builds upon it, using it as a springboard for what he is going to do.

> *Improvisational theatre is open on an intellectual level.* New events happen every day. These events can't be ignored, but must be included, and the old ones, if they are no longer useful, put aside. The *commedia dell'arte* troupes were often the chroniclers of their times, bringing to their often ill-informed audiences up-dates of what was going on in the country of the audience that evening and of what was going on in outlying countries. *Improvisational theatre must be a theatre of ideas, not merely of technique.*[29]

Fo's last statement holds the heart of the matter. It is clear that his concept of theatre is both improvisational and political, and it is also clear that he demands a body of knowledge, a challenge to the intellect, from a theatrical event. So do many theatre artists. What is unique about Fo is that, rather than coveting that creative act known as "playwriting" as is traditional, he asks of his actors that they become his co-writers.[30] "After I leave [the actors] must read newspapers every day and listen to and watch news broadcasts every day, and include pertinent material into the **Archangel** performances."[31] When an actor had suggested that perhaps one person be put in charge of updating the text, this was Fo's reply: "No, no, no one has to be in charge—you all do it! Every actor must practice self-discipline, trying out material and judging its effectiveness carefully, eliminating it if audience reaction is not favorable."[32] It is in this manner that Fo empowers his actors to grow, to stretch, to develop, for he invites them not simply to interpret someone else's ideas, but also to initiate their own.

Which brings us to Dario Fo, playwright, produced in translation in the United States. How, given Fo's convictions concerning improvisation about current political events, does this work? A quick production/publication profile offers several revealing statistics. To date there have been American, English-language productions mounted of six full-length works by Fo (**We Won't Pay! We Won't Pay!, Accidental Death of an Anarchist, Almost By Chance A Woman: Elizabeth, Archangels Don't Play Pinball, About Face** and **A Day Like Any Other**) and two full-length works by Fo and Rame (**Orgasmo Adulto Escapes from the Zoo** and **Open Couple**). Since 1979 there have been at least one, but as many as three American productions of these works annually. Fo's plays have been mounted by regional theatres, touring groups, university theatres, Off-Broadway and Broadway producers. In addition to numerous texts imported from Great Britain, there are currently available American publications of five of the works produced here. Plans are in progress for an American translation of Fo's four-hundred-page theoretical work on theatre, *Manuale minimo dell'autore* (Torino: Einaudi, 1987). Finally, both American journalists and scholars have begun writing about Fo to the extent that their major contribution to an already impressive European bibliography of secondary sources about his work appears imminent.

Each published introduction or preface to a Fo work contains some reference to the need to update or adapt material, while at the same time preserving the playwright's intention. Such directives suggest the problems inherent in revision. "A Note on the Text," which introduces Samuel French's edition of *Accidental Death of an Anarchist,* for example, reads in part:

> For the Arena Stage production and the subsequent Broadway production . . . Nelson [the adaptor] revised the dialogue for the American stage, and added some references to current politics . . . Subsequently, Fo asked for further changes . . . Future productions may require further alteration of political references, unless our President is elected for a life term, and outlives the century.[33]

Ron Jenkin's "Translator's Preface," which introduces *Theater*'s edition of *Elizabeth,* offers both directive and sound explanation:

> For the American version of the play Mr. Fo and I have substituted references to American politics for the original references to Italian politics. This text is presented only as a record of what was prepared for the Yale Repertory Theater production. It should not be performed without prior approval from the translator and playwright. . . . Their [Fo's and Rame's] work cannot be translated without reference to their performance technique, and translations of their work should not be performed without taking their performance style into account. It is delicately balanced between detachment and passion, tragedy and comedy, intimacy and showmanship.[34]

A perusal of American reaction to Fo's work indicates frequent critical reference, both positive and negative, to the current American politics alluded to during the course of a Fo play. Three writers had three different reactions to this question when they reviewed the Broadway production of *Accidental Death* in 1984:

> The play may have deserved to be successful in Italy, where its dealing with an actual case of police defenestration was doubtless audacious and salutary. But it has far less resonance here, and the manner in which Nelson has dragged in American references is obvious and safe.

> Although it's ostensibly an Italian subject, the play has been given emphatic contemporary American application by adaptor Richard Nelson, whose version

includes some hilarious speeches for the masquerading hero about current U.S. politics.

> There are references to the Great Communicator's belief that trees pollute the air and to his habit of sleeping in cabinet meetings . . . Not all of these jokes take wing, but it is somewhat refreshing on Broadway to hear political subjects mentioned at all.[35]

Despite the ongoing need for relevant revision, *We Won't Pay, Accidental Death,* and *About Face* are, thanks to multiple American productions, "here to stay." These three plays appear to have graduated from the stage of "experimental" or "alternative" theatre and, will, I believe, be accepted as an integral part of contemporary international repertory desirable in American theatre schedules. Fo has in essence, during the period 1979-1988, established a base, a modest body of dramatic literature which is recognized by the collective American theatre mind.

This base of three dramatic works realistically represents Fo's social and political concerns while at the same time appropriately casting him as a writer of comedy and satire. In *We Won't Pay,* the richness of which as a drama has been competently described in this journal,[36] the grave social question of economic ineptitude on a national scale is lampooned by the madcap manner in which Mr. everyman worker and Mrs. everywoman wife deal with insufficient salaries and inflationary prices. The hilarity of the piece is caught in the unforgettable image of women leaving the supermarket with goods they have refused to pay for and which they eventually transport as unborn "babies" beneath their coats.

In *Accidental Death of an Anarchist* the frightening specter of institutional "justice" applied to an innocent victim is raised to the high art of grisly grotesque as an actual case becomes the focus of farce. Real-life anarchist Giuseppe Pinelli was arrested in late 1969, erroneously accused of having planted a bomb which killed sixteen people in a Milan bank, and "fell" to his death from a window of the Milan police station. The Fool of Fo's play portrays a mad graduate of many an asylum who arrives to interrogate police hierarchy about this scandal, who stays to re-enact Pinelli's "fall," and who seems to re-appear once again before the horrified police personnel.

In *About Face* the limitations of both management and underdog perspectives on life and love are broadly satirized by a series of fabulous switches of fate. Caricatured Fiat magnate, Gianni Agnelli, becomes, thanks to an auto accident, amnesia, and the wrong plastic surgery, a factory worker in his own plant. He is eventually "exchanged" out of this humdrum existence by both the return of his memory and the co-operation of government officials to whom he writes threatening letters.

In the first two plays the principal key, both to sociopolitical bite and to hilarity, is the mistaken identity of the protagonist. In *Accidental Death* police officials on stage labor under the delusion that a bureau inspector is creating havoc in their midst, while we in the audience know that a mad, self-styled investigator come from a paradise where real justice reigns is loose on the boards. In *About Face* some characters work to improve the health of someone they take for an injured factory worker, while others discover and then protect the Agnelli identity behind the surgically applied incognito. In *We Won't Pay* a series of chaotic misunderstandings pave a double-edged path to social criticism and to side-splitting laughter. In an amazing scene from Act II, the police lieutenant casing the protagonist's flat searches the "pregnant" women he finds there; he is rewarded by imagined blindness when they tell him about a pregnant saint's husband who lost his sight and when, coincidentally, the long-unpaid-for electric lights suddenly dim.

When each play's ruse has been stretched to the most insane absurdity imaginable, Fo snaps us back to epic disengagement, usually through a long-winded speech delivered by a leading character which jars us into remembering a current political problem. In *About Face,* for example, Antonio/Agnelli offers a final diatribe about the power of the state equalling the power of money and caps it with, "So Aldo Moro gets 15 bullets in his gut to protect me."[37] And from the seemingly safe shores of such "reality," we laugh madly at the horrific foibles of human society.

As suggested at the start of this essay, Fo's performance style is reminiscent of Totò and of Eduardo. While the contours of his double life as actor and internationally acclaimed playwright also recall Eduardo's career, Fo's playwriting evokes the works of two other countrymen, one of the Roman era and the other of ours. His consistent reliance upon the dramaturgical misreading of the who and the what harkens back to those comedies of Plautus from whose brilliant feats of mistaken identity and misunderstanding Shakespeare was to borrow liberally. It is also relevant to point out the common fixation about identity which Fo shares with Luigi Pirandello, whose characters' tortured peregrinations lead us finally to learn only that neither we nor they are certain of who they are. When questioned by a Harvard student as to whether Pirandello had influenced him, Fo replied: "Pirandello and I deal with the same themes [illusion and reality] but I'm an optimist."[38]

In considering Fo's impact on theatre in the United States, it seems that two developments are taking place, the direction of which, attributable to a variety of forces, is surely Foian. The first is a new awareness, for us, that the actor need not necessarily put his own ideas aside or neglect to have ideas of his own. During his and Franca's London workshop of May 1983, Fo asserted:

> In my opinion it is more important for actors to learn to invent roles for themselves . . . to learn to be authors . . . *all* actors should do this. In my opinion, the most important criterion for any school of drama is that is should teach its actors to be authors. They must learn how to develop situations.[39]

A *New York Times* issue chosen at random in January 1988 describes the Actors Studio search for a new direction which will include "a mandate to revive the Actors Studio's Playwright-Director's Unit and integrate its work with that of the actors." After more than fifty years of proclaiming the primacy of the actor's individual self-expression, the American citadel of "the method" has come to recognize, for instructional purposes at least, the natural relationship between acting and playwriting. The same issue of the *Times* includes Mel Gussow's enthusiastic review of the American Place Theatre's *Roy Blount's Happy Hour and a Half*: "For 90 minutes we are, figuratively, at a bar with the author and raconteur as he expounds wittily on his shaggy life and his and our hard times."[40]

American actors who author and American authors who act have been aided and abetted by a rich backdrop of vaudeville history and its subsequent chapters in television and radio shows. More recent sources of inspiration have been our own inventive brand of improvisational group theatre (beginning with Chicago's original Second City company in the early sixties and for two decades receiving multiple resurrections around the country) and our new brand of solo, mimetic clowning (the work of the West Coast's "New Vaudevillians" in the eighties). It is fascinating, in this latter connection, to note a clear example of Fo's direct influence. The actor Geoff Hoyle, who played the lead in the 1984 San Francisco Eureka Theatre production of *Accidental Death,* was subsequently invited to play the lead in the 1987 ART production of *Archangels Don't Play Pinball* directed by Fo. During my interviewing in Cambridge, two actors made mention of Fo's considerable influence on Hoyle. Later the same summer, *New York Times* reviewer Jennifer Dunning offered accolades to Hoyle for his part in the "New Vaudevillian" *Serious Fun!* Festival at Lincoln Center.[41]

The second development in contemporary American theatre which reflects a Foian flavor is our renewed awareness of a need for theatre which speaks frequently to social and political concerns. The Eureka Theatre Company mentioned above has produced four of Fo's plays to date and has recently been awarded a substantial federal grant specifically earmarked to develop new American plays dedicated to social concerns.[42] The recent outpouring of powerful political theatre from South Africa, the growing awareness of the impact of the aids epidemic around the world, the fear of nuclear holocaust shared by all nations have brought to the American theatre a new sense of urgency about the subject matter of our plays. Examining our own psyches is no longer enough.[43]

On the broad canvas of world theatre, Dario Fo's mark is visible. He has chosen to place his enormous talents at the service of everyman and everywoman, making it plain that those who have no power are his concern. He supports the have-nots by using the theatre as a forum for paring the powerful down to size. His arms are those available to the economically and politically powerless: physical agility and intellectual wit. In Fo's version of stage reality, presidents and popes are adroitly relieved of prestige and power as ordinary people become aware of their own potential. Fo synthesizes past, present, and future concerns of society as he weds an appreciative sense of tradition with satirical but hilarious situations in which bureaucratic bunglings of immense proportions victimize the common people.

To a student in London who asked him if theatre could change the world, Fo responded: "I believe that neither theatre, nor any form of art, can, in itself, change anything . . . Not even great art."[44] But Dario Fo is a performance artist and a playwright whose comically costumed message, *beware institutional power*, has been heard around the world. Both his comedy and his message are nourishing our theatre today.

NOTES

[1]"Dario Fo: Andiamo a Ridere," *A.R.T. News*, 7, 4 (May 1987), 6.

[2]Joel Schechter, *Durov's Pig* (New York, 1985), p. 142.

[3]Ron Jenkins, "Clowns, Politics and Miracles," *American Theatre*, 3, 3 (1986), 12.

[4]*Dario Fo and Franca Rame: Theatre Workshops at Riverside Studios, London*, (London, 1983), pp. 23-26.

[5]Dario Fo, "Toto: The Violence of the Marionette and the Mask," *Theater*, XVIII, 3 (1987), 8.

[6]A. Richard Sogliuzzo, "Dario Fo: Puppets for Proletarian Revolution," *The Drama Review*, 16, (1972), 75-77.

[7]Fo, *Theater*, 10.

[8]Eric Bentley, *In Search of Theater* (New York, 1953), p. 274.

[9]Bentley, pp. 274-275.

[10]When I observed Eduardo perform in Rome in 1970 and in Naples in 1971, I was particularly impressed with what, at the time, I described as "polish": Mimi D'Aponte, "Encounters with Eduardo De Filippo," *Modern Drama*, 16 (1973), 351.

[11]*Fo and Rame: Workshops*, p. 41.

[12]*Fo and Rame: Workshops*, p. 8.

[13]*Fo and Rame: Workshops*, p. 6. During this session, Fo goes on to explain that Brecht had to invent a mechanical method of detachment, since, as he himself stated, there existed no tradition of popular theatre in German theatre.

[14]Bentley, p. 275.

[15]Bentley, p. 268.

[16]Suzanne Cowan, introduction, *Orgasmo Adulto Escapes from the Zoo*, by Franca Rame & Dario Fo (New York, 1985), p. vii.

[17]Mimi D'Aponte, "Eduardo De Filippo: *Three Plays*," *Italica*, 55(1978), 283.

[18]See Tony Mitchell, *Dario Fo: People's Court Jester* (London, 1984) pp. 59-62.

[19]Mitchell, *Dario Fo*, p. 95.

[20]Ron Jenkins, "Team Playing," *The Boston Globe Magazine*, 27 April 1986, p. 64.

[21]"Dario Fo mesmerizes in 'Misterio Buffo'," *The Boston Globe*, 2 May 1986, p. 44.

[22]Mimi D'Aponte, "Improvisational Notes," *Commonweal*, 113 (1986), 503.

[23]Mel Gussow, "Dario Fo's 'Mistero Buffo,' a One-Man Show," *The New York Times*, 29 May 1986, p. C20.

[24]In Cambridge I observed Fo help move scenery, as well as sing along with his cast for an album recording: I was also regaled with a first-hand account of how, when directing someone at odds with his part, Fo kissed the hand of that overly tense actor to demonstrate the approach he was looking for.

[25]Peter Gerety, Interview at American Repertory Theatre, Cambridge, 27 May 1987.

[26]John Bottoms, Interview at ART, Cambridge, 27 May 1987.

[27]Robert Scanlon, Interview at ART, Cambridge, 27 May 1987.

[28]*Fo and Rame: Workshops*, p. 22.

[29]Dario Fo, Interview in Cambridge, 26 May 1987.

[30]Pirandello was a spokesman for this traditional attitude in Italian theatre. In an essay entitled "Illustratori, attori e traduttori" he declares that illustrators, actors and translators are merely interpreters of the playwright's original creative work.

[31]Fo, Interview.

[32]Fo, Interview. Fo is consistent in his teaching. These remarks reflect the same line of reasoning offered his students in London in 1983 when he said, "The ideal situation would be for the pieces that you have acted out to be written down, transcribed as dialogue, given back to you, and then used as the basis for fresh improvisation. And so on, as a continuing process." *Fo and Rame: Workshops*, p. 34.

[33]Dario Fo, *Accidental Death of an Anarchist*, adapted by Richard Nelson (New York, 1987), p. 6.

[34]Ron Jenkins, "Translator's Preface," *Almost By Chance a Woman: Elizabeth*, by Dario Fo, *Theater*, XVIII, No. 3 (1987), 64-65.

[35]John Simon, *New York*, 26 November 1984, p. 76; *Variety*, 21 November 1984, p. 140; Robert Brustein, "Exploding an Anarchist Play," *The New Republic*, 17 December 1984, p. 26.

[36]Martin W. Walsh, "The Proletarian Carnival of Fo's *Non si paga! Non si paga!*," *Modern Drama*, 28, (1985), 211-222.

[37]See note 13 above; Dario Fo, *About Face*, trans. by Dale McAdoo and Charles Mann, *Theater*, 14, 3 (1983), 40.

[38]"Dario Fo: Andiamo a Ridere," *A.R.T. News*, 7, 4 (1987), 1.

[39]*Fo and Rame: Workshops*, p. 40.

[40]Jeremy Gerard, "Actors Studio, Long in Turmoil, Seeks a New Artistic Director," *The New Times*, 26 January 1988, p. C15; Mel Gussow, "Stage: Roy Blount in Humorists' Series," *The New York Times*, 26 January 1988, p. C17.

[41]Gerety and Bottoms, Interviews; Jennifer Dunning, "Stage: New Vaudevillians at Serious Fun! Festival," *The New York Times*, 4 August 1987, p. C16.

[42]Telephone interview with Richard Seyd, Associate Producing Director for the Eureka Theatre Company, January 1988.

[43]Before going on to the Cambridge walk/interview, I was invited to the Fo-Rame apartment to visit and eat with other guests: a translator/writer from the area, a director from Portland, Maine, and a second director from Sofia, Bulgaria. Throughout the two hours of conversation Franca

continued to work at the large living room table on the sub-titles for an up-coming San Francisco opening of *Open Couple*. Dario came back and forth from the kitchen where he was cooking spaghetti. The scene seems, in retrospect, a marvelous metaphor for the international stature of Dario Fo's popular theatre: New England, New York, Italy, and Bulgaria were sharing an improvised meal in the midst of which work for a play on the West Coast went on.

[44]*Fo and Rame: Workshops*, p. 42.

Stuart Hood (essay date 1992)

SOURCE: An introduction to *Dario Fo Plays: One*, Methuen Drama, 1992, pp. ix-xv.

[*In the essay below, Hood provides a broad survey of Fo's career.*]

Dario Fo represents a tradition in Italian theatre that gave the world comic figures like Pulcinella and Arlecchino. The lineage of his writing and performance can be traced back to the Commedia dell'Arte of the Renaissance which established the cast of cunning servants, swaggering swordsmen, lecherous old men and star-crossed lovers with their masks and conventional costumes that held the stage for more than two hundred years and from which Punch and Judy derive. But further back still he draws on the older tradition of the *giullari*, the wandering performers of the Middle Ages with their tradition of disrespect for the authorities and the church, and on the slapstick of clowns like Zanni, which is the Venetian version of Giovanni and the name from which we get the word 'zany'. These Zannis—peasant clowns from the valley of the Po—developed a tradition of mime and the convention of *grammelot*: a mixture of dialect words and onomatopoeia, a language that was no language and yet one audiences could latch on to and understand and still do. These are kinds of theatre, Fo argues, that in turn have their roots centuries earlier in the Latin farces of Plautus and Terence, which drew on performances with masked actors that were popular and rude—indeed popular because rude and disrespectful. Fo's theatrical mission is therefore one with a trajectory that takes him away from the formal scholarly dramas of the Renaissance courts just as it does from the bourgeois plays of the nineteenth century and the 'well-made' plays of our own time. The art of comic acting, of working with masks, of mime and of *grammelot* he has taken and developed in order to create a modern popular theatre.

Born in 1926 in North Italy, he grew up in a society of lakeside fishermen, smugglers and storytellers; from them, he says, he learned 'the structure of dialect—above all learned the structure of a primordial, integral language'. That structure and that language were to be the basis of one of his theatrical monologues developed at first for radio and later for the theatre, which he reached by way of art school and stage design. In the Fifties—along with his extremely talented wife Franca Rame—he became the equivalent in Italian theatre of a successful West End actor; but the couple abandoned this career to search for

a new audience that was not composed of middle-class playgoers. By the Sixties they had found that audience and were playing to huge crowds in new venues: circus tents, parking lots at factories or the cultural centres of the Italian Communist Party. They and their company became part of the radical political movements of the day. But their connection with the Communist Party was of short duration for the Communists were inflexible in terms of sexual and other politics and unable to understand or approve of that disrespect for established authorities, which large numbers of people—especially the young—felt in those days and to which Fo gave expression.

It is to this period that **Mistero Buffo** (1969) belongs. It is explicitly based on medieval and later texts and the traditions of the *giullari* but in terms of Fo's own development it reflects his subversive reading of Scriptures which is certainly anti-clerical but on another level reflects the view that the Christian tradition is capable of being interpreted in a radical, life-affirming way—the same view as inspired the radical priests working in the *favelas* of South America. Thus his version of *The Marriage at Cana*, as narrated by a drunken guest, is an affirmation of life and the need to enjoy it. What characterises these retellings of Bible stories is the fact that the narrator or chief character in the sketches is frequently a disadvantaged spectator of events—the man who is robbed at the raising of Lazarus or the blind man who, along with his lame mate with his trolley, sees Jesus pass on the way to Calvary and flees from the danger of being 'miracled' by a glance from him. For if they are made whole they will be robbed of their only livelihood. But Fo's anger, which is all the fiercer for being expressed in comic terms, is reserved for the Pope in all his magnificent vestments who spurns Jesus as a poor and worthless creature. It is not surprising therefore that Fo has had problems with the Church and with conventional believers—Franco Zeffirelli, the film director, took exception to the 'satirical reworking of the Gospels' for which the public, he argued, was not ready. Yet in the course of two and a half years, as Fo toured Italy, **Mistero Buffo** attracted a global audience which Fo puts at more than a million spectators—25,000 on one evening alone in Milan and 14,000 in Turin.

Accidental Death of an Anarchist is a political play which is at once a farce and deeply serious. It dates from the Seventies, that murky period in modern Italian history which saw the discontents of young people—schoolchildren, students and workers—take aggressive form in dress and social behaviour. It was also a period of political hysteria in the media and the established political parties—a hysteria which encouraged certain forces on the Right, among the security services and the army, to pursue (with the connivance of the authorities) a 'strategy of tension'. The result was a series of bombings that killed a number of innocent people. One such explosion in a bank in Piazza Fontana, Milan, in December 1969 killed sixteen people and wounded eighty-eight. The authorities and the press laid the blame on 'anarchists', one of whom, Giuseppe Pinelli, 'fell' from a fourth-floor window in the police headquarters where he was being interrogated. Fo wrote his bitterly ironic play about this 'accidental death' as an act of political intervention when a Left-wing paper *Lotta continua* was on trial for accusing the police of murder. When, many years later, there was a proposal to remove the plaque commemorating Pinelli's death, his reaction typically was to go to Milan and restage the piece.

The play is a farce; the main character, who proceeds to investigate the incident and in doing so reveals the idiocy of the lies spun by officialdom, is on the face of it mad, but his madness is like Hamlet's—a weapon that uncovers truths no one dare formulate in the sensible, 'real' world. The power of the play derives from the tension which Fo deliberately sets up between the comedy arising from confusions of identity, always one of the principal elements of farce, and the tragic circumstances surrounding the death of an innocent man. It is one of his most important tenets that laughter opens people's minds and renders them receptive to ideas they might otherwise reject. The dangers of the course he and his wife, Franca Rame, embarked on during this highly volatile political situation are demonstrated by his arrest by the authorities for disrespect to the American president and—a much graver matter—her kidnapping by Fascists for her courageous support of movements on the Left that included women, workers and the parents and relatives of political prisoners. Franca Rame has explained their stance in these terms:

> In order to feel at one with our political commitments it
> was no longer enough to consider ourselves democratic,
> left-wing artists full of sympathy for the working-class
> and the exploited . . . the lesson came to us directly
> from the extraordinary struggles of the working people,
> from the young people's fight against authoritarianism
> and injustice in the schools and from their struggle for a
> new culture and relationship with the exploited classes
> . . . We had to place ourselves entirely at the service of
> the exploited and become their minstrels.

The movement of the Sixties and Seventies developed outside the framework of the established political parties and invented its own methods of struggle. Some of these were a kind of civil disobedience and *autoriduzione*, a tactic by which workers of their own accord limited their working hours and output; the tactic was extended to include the refusal to pay higher prices for pop concerts or cinemas. The slogan *Can't Pay? Won't Pay,* which has found an echo in the anti-poll-tax protests in Britain, was adopted by Fo as the title of one of his successful comedies from this period. But political protest took other forms such as the tactics adopted by the Red Brigades with their policy of armed struggle, kidnapping and political murder—what was described as 'the strategy of annihilation'. The most clamorous example was the capture and killing in 1978 of the Christian Democrat politician and ex-prime minister Aldo Moro. His fate was surrounded by mysteries which have never been resolved. One view is that having been held captive for almost two months—a period during which he appealed to his political allies and the authorities

to come to terms with his captors—he was in the end abandoned by his own Christian Democrat colleagues in order to demonstrate that they were not 'soft on terrorism'.

The hysteria and hypocrisy of the times led Fo to write ***Trumpets and Raspberries,*** a two-act play which is included in this volume as another example of his use of comic invention to make a political intervention. It concerns, again, a confusion of identities: a Fiat shop steward sees what appears to be a terrorist attack on Agnelli, the boss of Fiat; he covers the badly-burned industrialist with his jacket before fleeing from the scene; the disfigured Agnelli is taken to hospital where he is mistakenly identified as the shop steward. He is interrogated by the police, who are convinced that he is a Left-wing terrorist, but they break off their investigations when it becomes clear that their 'terrorist' has such knowledge of dubious goings-on in high places that any further police action would be dangerous.

In the original performance in January 1981, Fo played both the workman and the industrialist, the latter being so swathed in bandages and connected to pulleys that he is little more than a human puppet (a situation that recurs in Fo's work). The mainspring of the comic action derives, in the tradition of classical farce, from confusions and misrecognitions; the cutting-edge, in the original Italian production, was provided by sharp comments on prominent politicians of the day, their hypocrisy and 'the stench of corpses' (to use Fo's words) which accompanied it. The political temperature was raised several degrees when at the end of one performance three women, all relatives of political prisoners, came on stage and read the text of a complaint about conditions in the maximum security gaols where the prisoners were and on whose behalf Franca Rame had sent an appeal to Amnesty International. The ensuing press campaign was astonishing and unrestrained. The row over what was inaccurately described in some papers as a demonstration in favour of the Red Brigades spread to Parliament and the Senate where there were calls for the censorship of parts of the play. Today we read and see it at a different political conjuncture but it stands up as splendid comic writing and a comment on power and its abuse that is still valid.

Fo's work came to be strongly marked by the thinking of the women's movement and by the impetus he received from collaboration with Franca Rame. He was thus inspired to write a number of plays like ***The Open Couple,*** along with monologues for his wife dealing with the position of women in our society. What was remarkable about them was the degree to which the texts evolved in a dialogue with audiences—to the point where it is very difficult to discover what the final text is. The veiw of the text as something open to alteration, without closure, is in a tradition familiar in the popular theatre and to the travelling troupes like the family into which Franca Rame was born; it goes back to the Commedia dell'Arte in which the plot was merely an outline around which the actors improvised and in which they inserted their *lazzi*, their comic routines, and reactions to the audiences of the day.

Fo's skill as a performer lies precisely in his ability to improvise, to spin out a comic moment to its limits in a manner that draws on these traditions. His skill as a writer lies in his prolific ability to write texts for farces, of which two examples have been included here. *The Virtuous Burglar* is based on a classic confusion of identities, on the improbable assembling in one place, one flat, one room, of couples who had rather not be discovered there. Fo has an apparently inexhaustible repertoire of variants on these age-old situations which to this day never fail to work with audiences. Such a piece too is *One Was Nude and One Wore Tails* which exploits the same mechanisms while driving home the old saying about clothes making the man. These are texts which on the page are deceptively simple; they depend for their success on a highly developed style of acting to which speed and agility give an almost balletic quality.

Since the heady days of the Sixties and Seventies Dario Fo has faced the problem that confronts many people on the Left—how to express their feelings about the great social changes in European society, the shifting of the political parameters, the confusions about goals, about ends and means. In one of his latest works *The Pope and the Witch* he takes as his target social attitudes to the drugs problem—in another he deals with the prejudices inherent in certain perceptions of aids, always using to discuss these most controversial topics the skills he has learned from the past, whether as performer, writer or director. It is a measure of his reputation as director that he was invited—the first foreigner to be so honoured—to direct a production of Molière's *Malade Imaginaire* at the Comédie Française.

But Fo is also a controversial figure. Not everybody accepts his interpretation of the medieval texts on which much of his work is founded. There are those who find that he devalues the role of the director in favour of the performer. It is possible for a recent volume on the Italian theatre by an important Italian publisher to contain no reference to his work. There are those who reject his attempt to create a popular culture drawing on old traditions as a counter to the culture of consumerism and the mass media. Not long ago the Italian bishops were outraged by one of his television sketches. There are others who dispute his version of the history of Italian theatre.

What there is no denying is the range and variety of his work. This volume aims to provide a sample drawn from an immense output that goes back more than thirty years and shows no sign of slackening.

Joseph Farrell   (essay date 1998)

SOURCE: "Variations on a Theme: Respecting Dario Fo," in *Modern Drama*, Vol. XLI, No. 1, Spring 1998, pp. 19-29.

[*In this essay, Farrell discusses the difficulties inherent in attempting to translate Fo's works. Fo, he states, "requires more than standard translation techniques. He requires deep understanding tempered by affection. The adapter is a presence in Fo translation because he is needed."*]

A translator is conventionally expected to content himself with a condition of self-effacing invisibility, which surpasses anything even Victorian parents once imposed on their offspring. The good translator should be neither seen nor heard. He should fade into the background, and should expect that if his presence is noted, it is as a prelude to some censure or reproach. A translator will receive attention only when responsible for some gaffe, transgression or solecism which will require discussion and correction at a later date, once the guests have withdrawn.

The way Dario Fo's translators have come to be viewed confirms this rule. Their sin is to have made themselves noticed. Fo, as is endlessly repeated, is the most frequently performed living playwright in the world today, which is another way of saying that he has more translators than any other playwright in the world today. The nature of the performed versions of Fo's work has aroused a high level of controversy, and it appears that there has been greater interest in the process of transposing a Fo text from its original Italian into other languages than has been accorded the same process with any other writer.[1] The nature of the translated text employed for production, principally the perceived confusion of roles between translator and adapter, has puzzled and enraged critics. Fo himself has contributed to the general air of disapproval. As he told an interviewer, in reply to a question about the productions he had seen:

> I have seen few good works. Some were respectable, others appalling, either on account of the actors, the director or the text itself, which had been supposedly corrected but often cheapened.[2]

Fo has himself protested vociferously about specific productions, and specific published versions of his work. Although neither Dario Fo nor Franca Rame speak English, they subject translations identified as suspect to rigid, if idiosyncratic, scrutiny by having the debated translation re-translated into Italian. This process creates difficulties of its own, as the resemblance between an original text and a re-translation is comparable to that between a bullet in the barrel of a gun and a bullet which has ricocheted off a steel plate. A further level of difficulty is added by the nature of Fo's scripts. When they deal with contemporary political topics, as was the case with *Accidental Death of an Anarchist,* they are subject to regular rewrites in the light of changing circumstances and new developments. And in all cases, his plays are subject to reshaping in the light of audience response or of reconsideration by Fo or Rame. On at least one occasion, a translator was censured because his translation was based on a fifth draft, but once re-translated, the comparison was made to the fourth draft. Various cuts and additions which were put down to the translator's intrusive, slapdash or high-handed disregard for the original were actually the result of rewrites undertaken by the author.

Obscenity or vulgarity are especially delicate areas. Personal relations scarcely ever feature in Fo's work. Both Fo and Rame are scrupulous about the language they employ on stage, and in none of Fo's works is there any material which could, in the linguistic register employed, offend the most demanding Calvinist or Carmelite conscience. Even the recent *Zen and the Art of Screwing*[3] conforms to this rule. It was written not by Dario Fo but by his son Jacopo, and Franca Rame performed it because she viewed it as a work which would further the sexual education of the young. On the other hand, in his own play **An Ordinary Day,** Fo features the case of a woman who receives phone calls from other women who believe they are calling some outré analyst. One of the callers is a prostitute who reports that, in an excess of professional *pruderie*, she has bitten off the testicles and related attachment of one of her clients. For the attachment in question, Fo employed the term *coso*, an imprecise, colloquial term which translates as "thingummy." In my translation I set aside such nicety and opted for the candid form "prick." This was re-translated in Milan as *cazzo* and did not pass inspection. It was excised at Franca Rame's insistence with the same ruthlessness the fictional prostitute had demonstrated towards the original offending member.[4]

For different reasons, Fo was irritated with the version of **The Pope and the Witch** that was staged in Britain. The play deals both with the problem of drug taking and with corruption in the Vatican. Fo chose to give the Cardinals who surround the Pope the deliberately flat titles of First Cardinal, Second Cardinal, and so forth. Adapter Andy de la Tour decided that this was unduly colourless and re-christened the Cardinals with the names of the Italian national football team which had received international publicity by winning the World Cup. This attempt to raise the level of whimsy drew, quite reasonably, Fo's ire. In the face of his protests, the publishers made a supposedly comical gesture at appeasement by inserting a correction slip, which they, presumably, believed equal to Fo's own sense of the grotesque. It read: "The characters' names shown in the cast list were subsequently changed, at Dario Fo's request, as follows: Cardinal Vialli is *now* Cardinal Pialli, Cardinal Schillaci is *now* Cardinal Stillaci. . . ."[5]

Fo had requested no such thing, but his objection went deeper than the invention of inappropriate or witless names. It concerned the spirit in which his plays were to be performed; the refusal of directors and actors to grapple with the balance between zany invention and seriousness of social purpose which is of the essence of his theatre; and the consequent impulse to seek facile laughs at every

turn, even when it upset the vision behind the work. His is not mindless, slapstick farce in which any excess can be justified provided it raises one extra laugh. The central problem with translating and staging Fo is to find a means of expressing and conveying the political fire while respecting the framework of farce. Fo has in various occasions defined his own theatre as combining "riso con rabbia" (laughter with anger) and both elements are of importance. The balancing act requires sensitivity, but the failure even to aim for it has meant that there sometimes seems to be an Italian Fo who walks on lines parallel to, but never quite coinciding with, the tracks on which British Fo, German Fo and French Fo walk.

The need to find such a synthesis of the laughter and the anger in the target language will often require a transcending of the limits normally allowed to translation. It is here that one collides with Fo's supposed supporters. No one has been so crass as to propose outright literalism, but the objection to the standard renderings of his work outside Italy takes the form of bewilderment over the (omni)presence of the adapter. One could note, in parenthesis, the curious fact that none of the exponents of translation studies have been able to incorporate the adapter into any theoretical framework. "It hardly seems useful to debate whether or not *adaptation* is still translation," write Basil Hatim and Ian Mason in their useful work on translation.[6] It may not be useful in general, but it is indispensable in the case of Dario Fo.

There can be no dispute over the facts. However they have been presented in programme notes or in published editions, few of the works that have been staged, most especially in English, have been translations. The problem is to establish whether an adaptation is as welcome as a virus infecting a healthy organism, or whether it can function as a tonic restoring a waning life. Some definitions are in order. A translation is a process of reproduction, replication or transference in which the changes are purely linguistic and do not involve wider redirection of the plot or switches of setting, epoch or culture. To be such, a translation must eschew alterations to structure and characterisation, and must respect the more intangible system of values underlying the source text. This does not involve literalism but it does involve a rehabilitation of the much-maligned concept of fidelity, in the sense given to that term by George Steiner in what remains the most profound analysis of the nature and aims of translation:

> The translator, the exegetist, the reader is *faithful* to his text, makes his response responsible, only when he endeavours to restore the balance of forces, of integral presence, which his appropriative comprehension has disrupted. Fidelity is ethical, but also, in the full sense, economic. By virtue of tact, and tact intensified is moral vision, the translator-interpreter creates a condition of significant exchange.[7]

The distorting presence of the translator cannot be avoided, but of itself that does not negate the validity of an aspiration to fidelity founded on an awareness of, and an attempt to maintain or restore, a previously existing balance. The nature of that balance in Fo will be discussed later.

An adaptation, on the other hand, is free of the restraints of fidelity, however it is defined. The adapter may aspire to be a co-creater, and perhaps it is helpful to view his work as the equivalent of the musical variation on a theme rather than as an operation of finding linguistic equivalences. There may be, for instance, parallels between various cults in the society described by Petronius in his *Satyricon* and the "New Age" beliefs held by certain sections of society as the Millennium approaches, but any writer who published a modern *Satyricon* updated to focus on such sects in New York or London would not be considered, and would not consider himself, to be producing a translation, any more than did James Joyce when he wrote *Ulysses*. At times, this process may have gone so far that the adaptation is a new work, in direct conflict with the original. The playwright David Hare expressed his distaste for Arthur Miller's adaptation of Ibsen's *An Enemy of the People* on the grounds that Miller had been so shocked by the anti-democratic stance adopted by the protagonist that he had in consequence arrogated to himself the right to soften that position.[8] Miller could reply that his operation had been transparent.

The suggestion has been made that Fo has suffered from similar distortions without the benefit of transparency. "The problem in Fo's case," writes David L. Hirst, for whom it is indeed a problem, "is that the translations made in Britain have—with one exception—been effected by a combination of translator and adapter."[9] Tony Mitchell similarly entitles his consideration of English language versions "Adapting Fo," and while he and Hirst agree that only one work escapes general censorship, they disagree over which work that is. For Mitchell that play is **We Can't Pay? We Won't Pay!,** a view Hirst dismisses with a polemical spleen others would find appropriate only when describing the activities of neo-fascist pederasts.[10] Hirst puts forward the case in favour of **Accidental Death of an Anarchist,** which he regards as being "a playing script of immense vitality which exploits to the full the potential of both farce and of witty comedy of manners," even if he is compelled to add that "the adaptation is obliged to follow the implications of its inexorable movement away from its source to a radically different target."[11]

In both intellectual and practical terms, the problems are complex. Certain recent critics have gone so far as to view "subversive intent" as a quality to be prized in a translator and to extol translation as "production" rather than "reproduction,"[12] but this is hardly satisfactory. The majority of readers expect to make contact with Dostoevsky and not with his translator when they pick up *Crime and Punishment*. But if fidelity is a goal, fidelity to what? Vladimir Nabokov was forthright. "When the translator sets out to render the 'spirit' and not the mere sense of the text, . . . he begins to traduce his author."[13] Nabokov's views appeared as a foreword to his

translation of Pushkin, but the situation of a playwright is more difficult. Fo himself makes a distinction between "theatre" and "dramatic literature." He consigned Pier Paolo Pasolini to the domain of "dramatic literature" on the grounds that he had no feeling for the rhythms of theatre, no sense of dramatic tension, no understanding of the primacy of the actor, no grasp of the demands of immediate communication with an audience in real time. If all theatrical texts occupy an indeterminate, intermediate space between literature and performance, not all lie on the same meridian between those two poles. Fo's preference is for those plays that incline towards performance and away from literature, as his own do. Put differently, Fo's scripts have much in common with the *canovaccio* of *commedia dell'arte*: they are, of course, more than outline plots intended as a prompt for improvisation, but they are less than the finished, polished scripts produced by such other Nobel Prize-winning dramatists as Bernard Shaw or Eugene O'Neill. The "mere sense" Nabokov referred to could not be, for Fo, something that can find expression solely on the printed page. Their "interpretation" requires a subsequent act of enhancement. Where Shaw insisted that his printed plays be furnished by the full apparatus of stage directions to assist readers who would, he wrote, be always more numerous than spectators, Fo tended towards a view he attributed to Brecht:

> Brecht once said, rightly, of Shakespeare: "A pity it reads so beautifully. It is its only defect, but a great one." And he was right. However paradoxical it may seem, a genuine work of theatre should not at all appear a pleasure when read: its worth should only become apparent on the stage.[14]

The achievement of that pleasure requires the collaboration of those equipped to detect and convey it in its fullness. Neither a translator nor a director can claim to be faithful to Fo if they limit themselves to the beauty of the words on the page. Works so deeply theatrical by nature as are Fo's only reach ripeness when they are "interpreted," or "translated" into production by other hands. Those involved in bringing a play to stage are, as has been often remarked, involved in a work of translation, or adaptation, in the prime sense. Theatre is essentially ensemble creativity, with the writer *primus inter pares*, and perhaps not even *primus*. As was noted by George Steiner, the Italian and French word *interprete* can be used to denote either an actor or an interpreter.[15] The poet or novelist has to contend with no comparable intermediaries. The ensemble creative process, with its concomitant legitimisation of intervention by other minds into the communication between writer and audience, has been a source of some resentment to certain Italian dramatists, even of the highest stature. Leonardo Sciascia wrote three plays and claimed he would have continued writing plays had he not "clashed with the figure of the director."[16] The director was an obstacle.

Even more intriguing is the case of Luigi Pirandello, the last Italian playwright to win the Nobel Prize before Dario Fo. The role of actor as interpreter irked Luigi Pirandello, who always regarded the actor as no more than a cumbersome intrusion in the process of communication between the author and the audience. In his play *Tonight We Improvise*, Pirandello used the character Hinkfuss to satirise the figure of the director who, it must be remembered, was only making his first appearance in Italian theatre around that time. Although Susan Bassnett suggested that the quarrel between Hinkfuss and the actors in that play was an externalisation of a debate inside Pirandello about the potential of theatre,[17] the surface meaning—that Pirandello had no fondness for the craft of either actor or director—is at least equally likely. Pirandello was at best ambiguous about the theatrical revolutions worked by his contemporaries Reinhardt and Piscator. In one of his theoretical essays, "L'azione parlata" [Spoken Action], Pirandello writes in near-mystical terms about a theatre without flesh-and-blood actors where the author's voice would materialise of its own accord.[18] The full scope given to the interventions of the director, designer, scenic artist, lighting designer, actor in the co-operative venture which is theatre was something Pirandello never relished. It diminished the exclusive role of the writer. It is for this reason that Paolo Puppa went so far as to say that "Pirandello did not love the theatre."[19]

Pirandello considered theatre a bastard genre, which dethroned the writer's text. No one could say anything comparable about Dario Fo, who if not a *figlio d'arte* by birth, is the all-round man of theatre, for whom the script occupies no royal position. He belongs to the quintessentially Italian tradition of the actor-author, and part of the reason that the conferring of the Nobel Prize aroused so much controversy in Italy may be that in his own country Fo is considered primarily an actor, whereas abroad he is viewed primarily as an author. In principle he accepts a view which makes the script the written equivalent of a stage prop, to be reworked as needed—or at least when another writer is involved. If it is granted that theatre requires a variety of acts of translation, from a number of sources, there remains the fundamental question of whose act of interpretation can be accorded legitimacy. The dilemma could be clarified, if not resolved, by reference to three very different productions:

(1) In 1994, the celebrated German director Peter Stein produced a Russian-language version of *The Oresteian Trilogy*, which updated the play's great themes of victor's power, victim's impotence, the craving for revenge and the cruel whims of predestination.[20] Stein rejected the original Athenian setting in favour of a brutally modern context recalling the Gulf War which had been fought some months before the first production. Although Stein's Agamemnon returns from the Trojan war bearing the weaponry of his own time, the work was played out against a background of incessant noise from missiles, anti-aircraft guns, rifle and cannon fire. The defeated were simultaneously Iraqis and Trojans.

Some critics slated the production, but none implied that the shift of focus and the directorial transfer from Greece to some indefinite location around Kuwait was other than legitimate. The position of director as interpreter, or translator, is now beyond debate.

(2) In 1981, an English-language version of Fo's own **Accidental Death of an Anarchist** had its premiere at Wyndham's Theatre in London's West End. The company was a left-wing fringe company, Belt and Braces, and although the translation was done by Gillian Hanna, the main influence was that of Gavin Richards, who was adapter, director and lead actor.[21] Fo was present on the opening night and was enraged at what he regarded as a misinterpretation of his work. Several people tried to explain to him the differences between British and Italian traditions of comic writing and performance, attempting to placate him—for he needed placating—by talking of the vibrancy of a music hall tradition which had provided the inspiration of the British production. Was Fo, of all authors, entitled to his annoyance?

(3) In the same year, 1981, the *Teatro stabile* in Turin put on a work by Dario Fo entitled **L'opera dello sghignazzo** (**The Raucous Opera**). In the programme and in the subsequent published version, it was described as being based on "John Gay's *Beggar's Opera*, and on some ideas from my son Jacopo."[22] Acknowledgement was also made of the contribution of poets and rock singers including Allen Ginsberg, Patti Smith, Frank Zappa and Donovan. There was no reference to Bertolt Brecht or to his work, known in English as *The Threepenny Opera*.

In reality, the Berliner Ensemble, who invited Fo to direct a new production of Brecht's *Threepenny Opera*, initiated the project. When they saw what Fo intended doing, and the modification he intended introducing into Brecht's text, they withdrew in horror and refused him permission to make any use of Brechtian material for any production anywhere. Fo professed himself mystified and outraged by this elevation of Brecht's play into an untouchable sacred text. He devised a strategy to circumvent the legal veto imposed by Brecht's heirs. As is well known, Brecht's play was itself a reworking of John Gay's original, but John Gay is dead and gone and has no heirs to threaten recourse to law. When he was invited by the theatre directors in Turin to stage his work there, Dario Fo did what Brecht had done: he went back to Gay's *The Beggar's Opera* and recast it in his own way. Or so he said, and no one could challenge him.

In his introduction to the published version of **L'opera dello sghignazzo,** Fo justified his original script by reference to Brecht's own theories and went on to provide what appears a manifesto for translators, at least translators of Fo.

> From the moment I first received an invitation from the Berliner Ensemble to stage *Threepenny Opera*, it seemed to me essential to set to work on Brecht's text with that open-minded irreverence Brecht had himself recommended. "When you find yourself faced with the task of producing some work by an illustrious

author flee from the terrorism of the classics," he insisted. "If you wish to display the slightest regard for the ideas which classic works contain, treat them without respect." Personally, since Bertolt Brecht has been himself reduced to the status of a classic, I took him at his word and threw myself at him (his text, naturally) feet first, boots on.

(5)

This principle is radical enough in itself, but Fo does not stop there. He goes on to state that some operation of updating is not only desirable but indispensable.

> Another tricky piece of advice from Brecht was his repeated invitation to transfer the script into the space and time of the present, "especially since ours are times of tragic and desperate dejection." [. . .] Certainly Brecht, if he were alive today and had to produce this play, would introduce into the script the tragically urgent problem of drugs, of kidnapping, of the internationalised, industrialised organisation of terrorism, of crime, of the robotic sex market, of widespread, worthless psychoanalysis, the mass media etc, not to mention the question of the somewhat trivial level to which the political world has sunk . . . everywhere.

(5)

There are precedents of the highest order for Fo's notions. Writing of his own theatre, Vladimir Mayakovsky, whose work was well known to Fo, wrote: "In the future, all persons performing, presenting, reading or publishing *Mystery Bouffe* should change the content, making it contemporary, immediate, up-to-the-minute."[23] What Fo preached and practised vis-à-vis Brecht on that occasion became his watchword for his own subsequent forays into the field of directing. When he produced Stravinsky's *Histoire d'un Soldat* for La Scala, Molière's *Le Bourgeois Gentilhomme* for the Comédie Française or Rossini's *Il Barbiere di Siviglia* for the Pesaro Festival, he behaved not as a Stanislavskian servant of author's text, but as an exponent of director's theatre. He reinterpreted freely, introducing mime scenes and regarding Molière and Rossini as examples of late *commedia dell'arte*. When he incorporated the medieval *giullare* sketches into **Mistero buffo,** he gave himself a freedom of manoeuvre that clashes with his view of how his theatre should be regarded.[24]

Of course Fo is a creative genius who operates within a tradition and reshapes the tradition by virtue of his intervention. He plunders the work of his predecessors, as artists have always done. "Immature poets imitate; mature poets steal," was T. S. Eliot's formulation.[25] Manet reshaped, or stole from, Poussin, as did Picasso with Velazquez, Dante with Virgil, Eliot with Dante and Fo with everyone. Nevertheless, as regards the views he has expressed on responsibilities towards authors, it is hard to avoid the conclusion that there is some form of inconsistency involved. As director or interpreter, Fo takes to himself the role of inspired and liberating contributor to the creative process, but wants his own directors and translators to be artisans, to be hewers of his wood and

drawers of his water. It is not just a question of the superior claims of "genius." The paradox is that it is anything but clear that his translators would be doing his theatre justice by assuming the workaday role he confers on them. Fo the actor is the best translator of Fo the author, but in his absence the job has to be done by someone else. Translation of Fo requires audience-centred techniques, which do not necessarily coincide with the author-centred translation he himself prefers. It could be added that translation sets itself varying objectives, as Ben Belitt, the distinguished translator of Pablo Neruda and Jorge Luis Borges, expressed in his own sparkling words:

> We serve a multiple, and not a univocal, function. "We translate to accomplish different ends. For the functions do differ. Some translate in order to exist supinely on the opposite side of the page as a trot to pace subservient readers who cannot or will not construe the language and meanings for themselves. [. . .] Others translate to deepen their own progressive absorption in a sustaining talent: there is a vast body of translation in which the enlightened disclosure of admiration is primary—a kind of substantive embodiment of *praise*. Certainly, the eminent and odd, like Rilke, Pope, Baudelaire, Hölderlin, Marianne Moore, Lowell, have always been allowed their own keyboard and predominant sound."[26]

No doubt Fo, when he turned his attention to Brecht, Ruzzante, Molière or the *giullari*, would merit the classification "eminent," leaving his own translators to content themselves with a categorisation among the merely "odd," but the motivation in both cases is the "disclosure of admiration." If Fo is to make an impact abroad, he requires more than standard translation techniques. He requires deep understanding tempered by affection. The adapter is a presence in Fo translation because he is needed.

To say that some modification or enrichment of the sort which Fo himself routinely brings to his own work by his on-stage presence is not to say that all existing translations or adaptations can be sanctioned. If it is agreed that the adaptation of Fo's **Il ratto della Francesca** into *Abducting Diana* was a work of unredeemed crassness,[27] that the attribution of those moronic names to the Cardinals in **The Pope and the Witch** was a symptom of a profound misunderstanding which was made manifest in the resultant production, it has also to be conceded that the "faithful" translation of **An Ordinary Day** did Fo's theatre no favours. One of the problems with the latter was that it provided no guidance to directors who have now a stereotyped image of Fo and his theatre, and who, being unwilling to respect the darker tone which emerged in that play, insisted on presenting it in the style of the slapstick of his earlier years.

No matter whether the starting point is the farce or the politics, there is the same need with Fo as with other, more obviously "serious" playwrights, to identify the inner vision and to respect that vision as well as the quirks, oddities, idiosyncrasies and comic predilections of the surface. However paradoxical it may appear, this has been best done by such works as the translation-adaptation that is *Accidental Death of an Anarchist,* now become the all-purpose protest play from Tokyo to London. In that work, the cultural references have been altered to allow it to refer to the plight of airport protesters in Japan or spy-scandals in Britain, but this has prevented it suffering the fate of *Uncle Tom's Cabin* or *Gulliver's Travels*, both works that began life as political satires. The international success of that play is a testimony to the theatrical mastery of Fo, to his skill in imagining original theatrical situations and to his expertise in devising structures marrying the extra-theatrical passion to appropriate theatrical techniques, but also to the value of a process which, combining translation and adaptation, conveys all these qualities to other cultures. The result might be, for purists, a variation on a theme, but the music is Fo's.

NOTES

[1]For a discussion of Fo in translation, see Tony Mitchell, *Dario Fo: People's Court Jester* (London, 1984), 94-110; David L. Hirst, *Dario Fo and Franca Rame* (London, 1989), 73-107; Tim Fitzpatrick and Ksenia Sawczak, "Accidental Death of a Translator: The Difficult Case of Dario Fo," in *About Performance* (University of Sydney Working Papers 1, 1995).

[2]Dario Fo, interview in *Sipario*, August-September, 1985, quoted in David Hirst, 73-4, translation mine.

[3]Jacopo Fo, *Zen e l'arte di scopare* (Bussoleno, 1995).

[4]Dario Fo, *Una giornata qualunque* (Milan, 1983): Joseph Farrell, trans. *An Ordinary* Day by Fo and Rame, in *The Open Couple* and *An Ordinary Day* (London, 1990).

[5]Dario Fo, *The Pope and the Witch*, adapted by Andy de la Tour from a translation by Ed Emery (London, 1992).

[6]Basil Hatim and Ian Mason, *Discourse and the Translator* (London and New York, 1990), 18.

[7]George Steiner, *After Babel: Aspects of Language and Translation* (London, 1975), 302.

[8]David Hare, "Pirandello and Brecht," interview by David Johnston in *Stages of Translation*, ed. Johnston (Bath, 1996), 140.

[9]Hirst, 75. See note 1.

[10]Mitchell, 96-8; Hirst, 81-4. See *We Can't Pay? We Won't Pay!*, by Dario Fo, trans. Lino Pertile, adapt. Bill Colvill and Robert Walker (London, 1978). Revised as *Can't Pay? Won't Pay!* (London, 1982).

[11]Hirst, 81, 91; see note 1. *Accidental Death of an Anarchist*, by Dario Fo, trans. Gillian Hanna, adapt. Gavin Richards (London, 1980).

[12]Barbara Folkart, "Modes of Writing: Translation as Replication or Invention," *Romance Languages Annual*, 5 (1994), xvii.

[13]Vladimir Nabokov, translator's foreword to *Eugene Onegin*, by Aleksander Pushkin (New York, 1964), ix.

[14]Dario Fo, *The Tricks of the Trade*, trans. Joseph Farrell, ed. Stuart Hood (London, 1981), 183.

[15]Steiner, 27-8. See note 7.

[16]Leonardo Sciascia and Davide Lojolo, *Conversazione in une stanza chiusa* (Milan, 1981), 66, translation mine.

[17]Susan Bassnett-McGuire, *Luigi Pirandello* (London, 1983), 66.

[18]Luigi Pirandello, "L'azione parlata," in *Saggi, poesie, scritti varii*, vol. VI of *Opere di Luigi Pirandello*, ed. Manlio Lo Vecchio-Musti (Milan, 1981), 66, translation mine.

[19]Paolo Puppa, *Dalle parti di Pirandello* (Rome, 1987), 293, translation mine.

[20]Peter Stein, director, *Orestes*, opened 29 January 1994, Theatre of the Russian Army, Moscow.

[21]See *Accidental Death*, note 11.

[22]Dario Fo, *L'opera dello sghignazzo* (Milan, 1982), 5. Subsequent references appear parenthetically in the text.

[23]Vladimir Mayakovsky, prologue to *Mystery-Bouffe*, trans. Guy Daniels, in *Twentieth-Century Theatre: A Sourcebook*, ed. Richard Drain (London, 1995). 177.

[24]Dario Fo, *Mistero buffo: Giullarata popolare*, ed. Franca Rame (Verona, 1974).

[25]T.S. Eliot, "Philip Massinger," in *Selected Essays, 1917-1932* (New York, 1982), 182.

[26]Ben Bellitt, "Translation as Adam's Dream: A Conversation," interview by Edwin Honig in *Adam's Dream: A Preface to Translation* (New York, 1978), 32.

[27]See Dario Fo, *Il ratto della Francesca* (Milan, 1986) and *Abducting Diana*, trans. Robert Lowe, adapt. Stephen Stenning (London, 1995).

MISTERO BUFFO

Tony Mitchell (essay date 1984)

SOURCE: "*Mistero Buffo*: Popular Culture, The Giullari and the Grotesque," in *Dario Fo: People's Court Jester*, Methuen, 1984, pp. 10-33.

[*Mitchell offers a detailed examination of* Mistero Buffo. *This work, he declares, "and its many offshoots, together with the countless improvised routines and sketches on topical events which Fo frequently makes up on the spot, reveal him as the 'theatrical animal' that he is, and show his unique capacity for turning a one-man show into a piece of epic and total theatre."*]

Italian actor-playwright Dario Fo, who also combines the roles of director, stage designer, song-writer, and political campaigner, has in recent years become the most widely-performed dramatist in the European and world theatre. He has himself performed his solo *pièce celêbre*, *Mistero buffo,* throughout Europe, Eastern Europe, Scandinavia, and in Canada and Peru, and it has become one of the most controversial and popular spectacles of the post-war European theatre. When *Mistero buffo* was presented on Italian television in 1977, after Fo had performed it live more than 1,000 times to audiences in Italy of more than a million and a half, and throughout the world to an estimated 40 million, public outcry from sources as varied as the Vatican (who described it as 'the most

Fo in performance.

blasphemous show in the history of television,')[1] and the Italian Communist Party, was as vociferous as the widespread public acclaim.

What Fo had done, virtually single-handedly, was to distil the popular, comic, irreverent elements of mediaeval mystery plays and religious cycles into a political and cultural onslaught against the repressions of the Catholic Church and the landowning classes throughout history, and express them in the language of the Italian peasantry (and, by extension, every class of oppressed people), fuelled by the epic-didactic concepts of Brecht and Mayakovsky, and the political precepts of Mao Tse-tung and Gramsci.

RECOVERING 'ILLEGETIMATE' FORMS OF THEATRE—THE GIULLARI

The title ***Mistero buffo*** (literally 'comical mystery') is borrowed from *Misteria buff*, an 'epic-satirical representation of our times' written by the Russian poet Mayakovsky in 1918, a hymn to socialist optimism and 'the road to revolution' which was performed under Meyerhold's direction with Mayakovsky playing the role of the Man of the Future. The play deals with seven couples representing the proletariat of different countries who are encouraged by the Man of the Future to steal Jove's thunderbolts for electricity, expel the devils from hell and the angels from heaven (including Rousseau and Tolstoy), and who finally create a promised land full of 'good things' such as machines, cars, trains, technology and food. Mayakovsky has been a constant influence in Fo's plays, one of which, ***The Worker Knows 300 Words, the Boss Knows 1,000—That's Why He's the Boss*** (1969) has the Russian poet as one of the protagonists in a series of stories intended to convey a sense of the urgency of building a working-class culture. However, the origins of Fo's ***Mistero buffo*** reside in the surviving texts and descriptions of the *giullari*, the mediaeval strolling players who performed in the streets and piazzas of Europe:

> *Mistero* (mystery) is the term used since the second and third centuries AD to describe a sacred spectacle or performance. Even today in the Mass we hear the priest announce 'In the first glorious mystery . . . In the second mystery . . .' and so on. So *Mistero* means a sacred performance, and *mistero buffo* means a grotesque spectacle.[2]

In extracting the grotesque elements of the mystery plays, Fo's intention is to bring to the foreground their popular origins, and mock the pomp and postures of the church hierarchy while popularising Christ and biblical legend, which is seen from the mediaeval peasant's point of view.

> The inventors of the *mistero buffo* were the people. From the first centuries after Christ the people entertained themselves—although it was not merely a form of entertainment—by putting on and performing in spectacles of an ironic and grotesque nature. As far as the people were concerned, the theatre, and particularly the theatre of the grotesque, had always been their chief means of expression and communication, as well as putting across ideas by means of provocation and agitation. The theatre was the people's spoken, dramatised newspaper.[3]

At the basis of almost all of Fo's 40 or so plays is the theatrical tradition of the *giullare* (the Italian equivalent of the French *jongleur* and the Spanish *juglare*), the mediaeval strolling player who busked and performed to the peasants of Europe, frequently on the run from persecution from the authorities, censorship, and co-option into the courts, from which arose the 'official' tradition of the commedia dell'arte. Fo's task in ***Mistero buffo*** is the retrieval and recovery of this unofficial, 'illegitimate' theatre contained in the original repertoire of the *giullari* before it was appropriated and transformed by court influence, a process described by one of Fo's foremost Italian commentators, Lanfranco Binni:

The 'epic theatre' of the mediaeval *giullari*, in which the *giullare* became the choral, didactic expression of an entire community and the feelings, hopes and rebellion of exploited people to whom he performed in a piazza, projected their desire for liberation from the religious sphere set up by the authorities. Performances expressed an insistently human passion, with a human, exploited, peasant Christ who refutes the injustices of the hypocritical religion of the rich to such an extent that this 'epic theatre' of the *giullari* was either physically suppressed (by persecuting the *giullari* and cutting off their heads) or neutered and re-translated into an aristocratic vein. Thus the *giullare* who performed in the piazza, sharing a rapport with whoever recognised themselves and their own sufferings in his stories, became the 'court jester' who had the sole task of entertaining courtiers, so that his expressions of anger and hope through physical means and rapport with others was transformed into the recitation of verses of 'quality' whose chief value lay in the weaving of amorous rhymes, or even the dehumanised, objectified description of peasants 'at work', mocked for their 'vulgarity' or transferred into an aristocratic context and given an abstract, 'pastoral' dimension, accompanied by flutes and amorous sighs for gentle nymphs.[4]

A common misconception is that the theatrical traditions of farce and comedy in Fo's theatre stem from the commedia dell'arte, but the *giullari* are essentially pre-commedia, the popular, unofficial mouthpieces of the peasant population, while the performers of the commedia are regarded by Fo as the professional 'court jesters' officially recognised by the ruling classes. Although a number of his routines are culled from the repertoires of *comici dell'arte* like Ruzzante and Zanni who survived the transition from piazza to court, Fo sees these performers as essentially idiosyncratic and rebellious in terms of the canons of the commedia, and peasant rather than court figures. Fo himself in the context of the contemporary Italian theatre experienced the acclaim and stature of a 'bourgeois court jester' when he became a prominent figure in the established, mainstream Italian theatre during the mid-sixties, only to renounce this position of commercial success and seek an alternative, 'fringe' theatre network, performing in factories, piazzas, and *case del popolo* (Communist Party community centres) to a predominantly non-theatre-going audience.

LANGUAGE AS BURLEQSUE—GRAMMELOT

One of the most notable features of ***Mistero buffo*** is its language, which Fo describes as 'fifteenth century Padano', a mixture of the various dialects of the Po valley, Lombardian, Venetian and Piedmontese, which are adapted, sometimes modernised, and frequently parts are completely invented, and even treated as an incomprehensible foreign language which relies on the actor's physical illustration and verbal explanation. Mime, action and gesture assume primary importance, and Fo has continually modified and stylised the language of the plays to such an extent that it functions more as a codified system of sounds similar to 'scat song' in jazz. Particularly when performing outside the Po valley, Fo developed an onomatopoeic language which served to complement his mimic gestures and express the physicality of situations rather than conveying information about the situations, which Fo frequently consigned to an explanatory prologue.

Alongside this emphasis on the physical sound-structure of the Padano dialect, Fo also elaborated a totally invented language called *Grammelot*—a phonic, abstract sound-system in which few recognisable words of any language occur, and which relies on suggestion. In his prologue to *Zanni's Grammelot,* with which he frequently opens performances of *Mistero buffo,* Fo explains the tradition of *Grammelot*:

> *Grammelot* is a form of theatre that was re-invented by the actors of the commedia dell'arte, but it goes back to even before the 1500s. It was developed as an ono-matopoeic theatrical technique to put across concepts by way of sounds which were not established words in the conventional sense. *Grammelot* was invented by the *comici dell'arte* to escape censorship, and when they fled to other countries in the 1500s because of the enormous repression they suffered under the Council of Trent, which effectively denied them the possibility of performing in Italian towns and cities. The majority of them went to France, and we are told that, in order to make themselves understood, they used a form of language similar to French, although only a few words were actually French. Just as there is a foreign language *Grammelot,* so too there is an Italian one, particularly in its dialects. The most famous *Grammelot* was Zanni's. Zanni is the prototype of all the masks of the commedia dell'arte, or at least the father of the most important ones, such as Harlequin. But he's no invented character, he was real. The character of Zanni is directly linked to a category of people, or at least a social class: the peasants of the Po valley and the mountains that extend down to the Po valley.[5]

In fact Fo, reviving the tradition of Zanni, first developed *Grammelot* when he performed *Mistero buffo* in France in 1973, and in the course of performances he has even built up an American *Grammelot* in a piece called *The American Technocrat,* which he has performed at anti-nuclear rallies: a grotesque parody of an American nuclear technician in which he mimes and makes the sounds of aeroplanes and space craft, producing perhaps one recognisable English word in ten (such as 'yeah' or 'OK'—Fo speaks fluent French but virtually no English), but with a deceptively exact inflexion and accent. He also uses this American *Grammelot* in his frequent topical burlesques on American politics, such as his famous impersonation of President Ford tripping while getting out of a helicopter and almost getting killed by the blades, and in one of his asides in the television version of *Mistero buffo,* he relates how *The American Technocrat* caused several Americans to walk out of a Paris performance precisely because they couldn't understand a word of what he was saying, but could detect he was satirising Americans.

Grammelot then, chiefly functions in *Mistero buffo* and some of Fo's other plays, such as the version of Stravinsky's *Soldier's Tale* which he rewrote and directed for La Scala in 1978, where it was used to embody the different dialect the soldier spoke, as a form of burlesque mimicry, and Fo has extended its onomatopoeic potentials to more modern contexts such as the Grandfather's simulated drug hallucinations in *Mother's Marijuana is the Best* (1976) and to a representation of the working of factory machinery and a production line in *Mistero buffo,* in a highly orchestrated gibberish of machine language. Perhaps the most apt description of the language of *Mistero buffo* was given by the critic Renzo Tian: 'Padano, which is reminiscent of Ruzzante but isn't the language of Ruzzante insofar as its concern is to provide an example of an imaginary Esperanto of the poor and disinherited.'[6] In *Knock Knock! Who's There? Police!* (1972), his sequel to *Accidental Death of an Anarchist,* Fo recounts another branch of *Grammelot* which places it in the tradition of Molière, through the mouthpiece of a Superintendent of Police whom Fo performs in the play:

> Scapino, Antonio Scapino, went to France in the 1500s and met Molière . . . and immediately Molière said 'Save me, you must save me, they've censored my latest play *Tartuffe*, and cut the entire ending. You must help me!' 'But I'm a bad actor, and I'm even worse in French.' 'Yes, but you act with gestures, with your face, your hands, you're an extraordinary mime—you come out and act with gestures, and add the odd word or two here and there for effect, or just snort or mutter or talk nonsense, it makes no difference—you put your message across with your hands, with gestures, with pantomime, and they can't censor that.' 'All right then, but who do I have to play, what do I have to say, what's my character?' 'A servant—you can call yourself Scapino, you're a servant in one of the richest households in France, whose eldest son goes into politics, and you teach this youth all the tricks of the trade, the art of hypocrisy, of *tartuffaggine*, the ultimate in Jesuitry . . . OK?' . . . Now for your information this marvellous talk is called *Grammelot*, it's all muttered and spat out in a continuous stream. It doesn't matter if you can't pick up the words, the gestures are what matter.[7]

In this extraordinary set-piece, Fo is using the character of the Police Superintendent to describe *Grammelot* as an example of the speechifying antics of the Italian Christian Democratic Party in the 1970s, which illustrates how Fo continually makes historical leaps to refer to present political reality, a technique which is continually present in *Mistero buffo.* His use of *Grammelot* and the techniques of the *giullari* is educational in serving to stress and illustrate the origins of popular culture, but no mere academic, intellectual exercise, since he continually roots his historical didacticism in contemporary political and social reality to score comic points and make gags at the expense of political authority figures. As the critic Jean Chesneaux has put it:

> Dario Fo is indifferent to both the elitist little world of the professional scholars and to that of theatre professionals. He has moved out of that world to find the workers and the common people. For Dario Fo

history is an active relationship with the past, and a distant epoch like the Middle Ages—as *Mistero buffo* shows—can be just as fertile as a more recent period when it comes to fuelling the active social struggle of the present. What matters is the political quality of this link between the present and the past, not the distance of centuries.[8]

The language used in *Mistero buffo,* in both its inventiveness and its historic complexity, is a major factor in Fo's achievement in bringing to life the origins of an essentially popular, politically aware, peasant theatre, and prove it can be entertaining and enjoyable as well as culturally and politically relevant to popular audiences. In freeing this popular theatrical culture from the academic and bourgeois mystifications it has been subjected to over the centuries, he restores its wit, comedy and enjoyment value by taking imaginative liberties with it while illustrating to his audience a key concept which he extrapolates from Gramsci: 'If you don't know where you come from, you don't know where your potentialities lie.'[9]

ADDRESSING THE AUDIENCE—PROLOGUES, INTERLUDES AND ASIDES

The diverse nature of the material in *Mistero buffo,* the complexity of Fo's verbal acrobatics, his continual paring, modification and stylisation of the texts, and the 'living newspaper' aspect of the spectacle, have obviated often lengthy explanatory prologues to the individual pieces Fo performs. These prologues have become concretised into *discorsi* or *interventi*, direct addresses in which Fo speaks to the audience to explain the situation of a particular piece, using satirical illustrations from topical political events, incorporating impersonations of popes and politicians as well as analyses of current events. These have in turn become an expected part of the performances, set pieces and sketches which exist alongside and complement the *canovacci* (improvisations to a theme) which comprise the source material of *Mistero buffo.* Fo traces these asides to Cherea, a contempoary of Ruzzante's:

> . . . sometimes when he was performing he'd pretend there was a wasp annoying him . . . Eventually the wasp was flying all over the place, off the stage and into the audience even. Cherea would follow it and involve the audience in the grotesque situation. Ruzzante also used direct address with his audiences, not for any aesthetic contrast, but to enable them to participate in the events on stage with a constant awareness of their fiction.[10]

A key concept in Fo's theatrical praxis is his adoption of the concept of 'breaking down the fourth wall', and these moments in which he addresses the audience directly are similar to Brecht's alienation effects, allowing the audience to detach itself from the historical frame of reference of the pieces and make contemporary analogies. Fo's topical sketches, such as Pope John-Paul II skiing, his impersonation of John-Paul I as a grinning simpleton whom he compares to Pinocchio, or Paul VI riding a brakeless bicycle down the hill in Castel Gandolfo, or a skit about *carabinieri* spotting UFOs, become performance

vehicles in themselves, contextualising the religious and spiritual aspects of the biblical plays by producing a modern counterpoint. As a reviewer of a performance in Milan in March 1979 described it:

> The *discorsi*, analyses and polemics have their own separate place in the spectacle, introducing and motivating the individual pieces Fo performs or relates. The structure of *Mistero buffo* takes the form of a text, an explanation, and another text. The fact that the explanations are as entertaining and as well received as the pieces in the play doesn't change the situation. The opposition between language and dialects, between direct dialogue with the audience and fictional story-telling to an ideal audience, between mime and the display of vocal resources, distinguishes perfectly the two areas of the spectacle, which are integrated and complementary, both bringing laughter and applause.[11]

The form of the *discorsi* or asides is modified in the same way as the texts themselves—according to audience response, feedback and discussion. Fo frequently ends performances with what he refers to as the 'Third Act'—debates and discussion with the audience, who express criticisms and suggestions which often help shape the development of the play in terms of political content, style, language and entertainment value.

Fo regards his audiences as an essential element of the process in which he shapes his performances, and their reactions are a strong factor in his elaboration of the frequent improvisations he makes around the texts of *Mistero buffo* as well as in the prologues and *discorsi*. The rhythm of each performance of the play he sees as being the result of a spontaneous but guided (by the performer) collaboration between the comic and a participating audience who it is the comic's job to keep involved and participating by means of a technique he refers to as 'fishing for laughs':

> The comic fishes for laughs by virtually throwing out a comic line, or a hook, into the audience. He indicates where the audience's reaction has to be gathered in and also virtually where the hook is cast, because otherwise the tension built up between stage and audience would die down. Winding in the hook doesn't mean snuffing out the audience reaction, but correcting its flow with a flick of the rod. The comic's ability lies in knowing that if he carries on for a while on the same tack he'll snap the audience's capacity to keep up with his theme. So he breaks into the stage action, using something extraneous (a spectator's funny way of laughing, for example, or imitating the way La Malfa speaks). [Ugo La Malfa: economist and statesman, leader of the Italian Republican Party (PRI) and Minister of Foreign Trade and the Budget until his death in 1979.] Then the comic casts out the hook again, for a bigger laugh (although he can fish for laughs by casting out the hook more than once before provoking one big laugh) . . . One could talk endlessly about techniques of laughter. In Nancy Lecoq gave veritable lessons about techniques of laughter: head laughter, throat laughter, silent laughter, side-splitting laughter, rolling in the aisles . . . I think, however, the audience's real way of laughing

can be divided into just two types: when it is symptomatic of involvement in the play and when it is not. The difference lies between the mechanical reaction of laughing and the relationship through which an audience collaborates in building the play. The first is about the star-satisfaction of the comic who sees the effects of his technique and is pleased with himself, and it is quite different from the comic's reaction to a sort of confrontation which prompts him immediately, on the spot, into developing what he is saying, preferably through improvisation, and the action he is building up on stage with the audience. The comic provokes the audience's laughter with his resources, but audience laughter is a response which itself recharges the comic—it's not just a technique—maybe even feeding the yeast of his stage reactions in the course of a given play, or maybe just adding to the further exercise of his craft . . . All popular theatre requires the audience to be 'inside', and take part in the rhythm of laughter.[12]

THE TEXTS IN PERFORMANCE

Fo has excavated the texts which he uses as a basis for his performance in *Mistero buffo* from a wide variety of Latin, Provençal, Italian, Middle English, and even Yugoslavian, Czech and Polish sources, but the criterion behind his choice and adaptation of the texts is based on a desire to highlight their popular aspect as vehicles of the people's struggle against capitalistic and ecclesiastical oppression. This frequently involves a process of stripping down rather than augmentation, paring away the additions and superimpositions of subsequent adaptors of the original texts (who include even Dante), rescuing the material from the appropriations of 'cultural aristocrats'. In *Rosa fresca aulentissima* (*A Fresh Delicate Rose*) for example, Fo is dealing with a story which is presented in school textbooks as a coy, courtly love story of a boy whose physical lust is checked by the polite blandishments of the girl who is the object of his lust. Fo restores the tale to a brutal example of sexual oppression in which the boy, a rich tax collector, is able to have his way with the girl, and owing to a special wealth protection law, can even charge her with rape, rather than vice-versa.

Mistero buffo has frequently been attacked from academic quarters as well as from Vatican sources. In a book entitled *Giullari e Fo* (1978), Michele Straniero retitles the play 'Mistero Bluff', and sets out to debunk Fo's spurious sense of history, producing a list of historical inaccuracies and anachronisms which occur in *Mistero buffo* (such as, for example, the fact that the term 'mystery' is not found in the Mass but in the Rosary), and accusing Fo of falsifying historical facts and simplifying the popular elements of his source material. Straniero maintains that Fo, in his zeal to reappropriate popular culture from the mystifying hands of bourgeois commentators, ignores or multilates texts which are of bourgeois origin, in what he describes as 'inviting young people to burn books instead of reading and criticising them and discussing the difficulties of cultural mediation, together with the importance of mastering sources like these which the bourgeoisie tends to keep to itself.'[13] Fo regards such

arguments as arid and over-academic, while pointing out that many of the historical inaccuracies that Straniero picks up are deliberately ironic anachronisms: 'Only a person as deficient in irony as Straniero wouldn't notice they were put there deliberately.'[14] In reply to the 'book burning' charge, Fo points to the lengthy bibliography included in the published edition of the play, the fact that some of his material, such as the Apocryphal pieces, are in fact culled from bourgeois sources, the numerous university theses on mediaeval theatre sparked off by *Mistero buffo,* together with the increase of sales of books on the subject.

There is no doubt that Fo's intentions in *Mistero buffo* are didactic and educational, but in performance he stresses the entertainment and amusement to be gained from his mediaeval popular sources, and one is more than willing to forgive him a few ironic anachronisms. Performances of *Mistero buffo* frequently last up to four hours—no two performances are ever the same, and the critic Chiara Valentini has estimated that if all the pieces Fo has performed in *Mistero buffo* were placed end to end, the performance would last an entire day. Fo performs alone on a bare stage, dressed in black sweater and trousers, with no lighting effects and the aid of only a microphone slung round his neck to carry his voice to the outer reaches of the vast halls, sports stadiums, converted cinemas, deconsecrated churches, public squares and open spaces he has performed the play in. He keeps up a constant patter of witty repartee, constantly ad-libbing with the audience, rather like a thinking-man's Lenny Bruce, displaying a staggering physical dexterity, continually changing character, and running through an enormous variety of grotesque, vain, pathetic and comic characterisations of human folly, using his hooded eyes, Chaplinesque mouth, and physical largeness and gaucheness in a mimic style often reminiscent of Jacques Tati. (Fo studied with the French mime Jacques Lecoq in the 1950s, and Lecoq taught him how to use his large frame, long limbs and big feet to advantage, and his lollopping physique together with his vastly expressive face seem capable of evoking any number of physical idiosyncracies.)

Fo establishes an instant rapport with his packed audiences of enthusiastic and predominantly young supporters who often spill onto the stage at the actor's invitation. Using the familiar, informal *tu* form, he ad libs, (in one performance in Vicenza during a thunderstorm he conversed with the thunder, addressing it as the voice of God), and jokes with the spectators. One particularly noteable performance took place in April 1974, in a field opposite the newly occupied Palazzino Liberty, which Fo and his group La Commune had virtually squatted in and adopted as their home theatre. The audience was estimated at about 30,000 and as Fo recalls:

> At least 30 per cent were people from the local area: housewives, old age pensioners, workers, entire families, and hundreds of children, who caused inevitable confusion during the performance, running around, getting lost . . . I had to interrupt the play every ten

minutes to find the mothers of kids who were up on the stage crying desperately.[15]

Typically, Fo used the situation to improvise a discussion about the necessity for more state-run crêches. A sense of solidarity develops between actor and audience, also due to the fact that audiences often have to undergo a police search before entering the theatre because of Fo's status as a politically subversive figure in Italy. *Mistero buffo* is a prime example of 'epic' theatre in the true sense of the word, at once a recreation of popular history and culture and an affirmation of the political potency of this recreation.

THE TV PERFORMANCES

For the television transmission of *Mistero buffo,* which took place in April and May of 1977 (in four parts), and which can be regarded as a definitive version of the play, Fo was filmed in performance on his home base in the Palazzino Liberty, in front of a live audience, with whom he improvised, swapped quips, and went through his array of political caricatures, such as his satirical portrait of the then Italian Prime Minister, Giulio Andreotti. A definitive performance then, in the sense that it was transmitted to an audience of some 5 million, and that Fo has only rarely performed *Mistero buffo* since then, but subject to the spontaneous developments which always take place in a live performance of the play. A live audience has always been an important aspect in Fo's shaping and reworking of the play, both in terms of the method he adopts in trying out his texts as public readings and listening to audience suggestions, and in terms of the adaptations he makes as a result of this audience feedback. As Fo has said,

> *Mistero Buffo* has always relied on improvisation, since the audience is involved in it and doesn't play a passive part, since it imposes its rhythms, and provokes off-the-cuff lines. This type of theatre is recreated from performance to performance, and is always different, and never repetitive.[16]

The television performance is worth describing in some detail, since the highly idiosyncratic and virtually untranslatable language of the play, and the demands it makes on the actor, make it an unrepeatable performance, an 'epic' and 'total' theatre experience which establishes Fo as an actor/dramatist of unique status. *Mistero buffo* is also the lynch-pin of Fo's prodigious output of theatre works, propagating most of the theatrical and political concepts which are embodied in a different dimension in his other plays.

ZANNI'S GRAMMELOT

The piece with which Fo opens *Mistero buffo* is a *lazzo*, or improvised sketch from the commedia dell'arte, as it was performed by one of its greatest exponents. Zanni, Fo explains in his introduction to the piece, represents the plight of the peasants of the Po valley, who were displayed by the 'origins of capitalism' in the Middle Ages, and forced to abandon their land because they couldn't face the competition of imported produce. So Fo as Zanni represents a starving peasant who, in his hunger, imagines

that he is eating himself—which Fo represents in minute gestural detail. He then mimes Zanni's dream, in which he prepares an enormous Pantagruelian feast, stirring an enormous bubbling pot of *polenta*, frying chicken, eggs, cheese and sauce, making the sounds of the boiling pot, the sizzling meat and the rising steam, representing the pans and the cooker with gestures in mid-air, and then abruptly making everything disappear, as Zanni, awakening from his dream, hunts down and captures a fly, dismembers it and eats it with all the relish of someone devouring the feast he has dreamed up previously, distending his stomach grotesquely. The ironic epicureanism of the sketch conveys a desperation and self-parody which combines hunger and anger. Fo's onomatopoeic utterances and mimed gestures are a prime example of what he refers to as a theatre of *gesto mimico* (mimed gesture), which

> originates from an extremely old tradition, but which has been renewed through the generations, and allows past and present to coexist simultaneously, while amplifying the point being made on stage by continually fixing it on the level of technical experience, projected out to the audience without verbal retractions connected with lighting or atmosphere.[17]

Zanni's Grammelot is followed by another *Grammelot*, *The Story of Saint Benedict of Norcia,* about a wall-builder who founded an order of levitating monks who become concerned about their bellies when their cook also starts levitating, which induces the monks to abandon the spiritual sophistication of contemplating their navels in favour of cultivating the land in order to fill their stomachs.

THE MASSACRE OF THE INNOCENTS

In *The Massacre of the Innocents* Fo represents a number of different characters, presenting a mad woman who has substituted a sheep for her dead baby, and who is accosted by a soldier who takes the sheep for a baby. The woman then tells her story to a statue of the Madonna, and the Madonna unsuccessfully attempts to console her. Fo alternates between the mother, the ruthless and merciless soldier, and the Madonna with impressive speed and physical differentiation, while emphasising the peasant environment of deprivation of the distraught mother, who at the end goes off rocking the sheep and singing it a lullaby. Fo avoids sentimentality both through the grotesqueness of the situation he depicts, and the 'chorality' of his performance, in which he is continually swopping characters like a quick-change artist. The unusual pathos and sense of tragedy of this piece is immediately juxtaposed with a comic, grotesque, almost Beckett-like performance, *The Morality of the Blind Man and the Cripple.*

THE MORALITY OF THE BLIND MAN AND THE CRIPPLE

This sketch is attributed to Andrea della Vigna in the fifteenth century, but exists also in French and Belgian versions. A blind man and a cripple join forces, the latter riding on the former's back, and run into Christ on his way to Calvary. They try to flee and hide from Christ, since they don't want to run the risk of being cured of their afflictions by a miracle, which would oblige them to look for work with a master and lead considerably harder lives. In their attempt to avoid Christ's glance, the blind man trips and the pair fall in a heap at the feet of Christ, who heals them and leaves them in disgrace.

Here a grotesque situation of peasant degradation exists alongside a revolutionary message which advocates by implication the overthrow of the *padroni*—the masters and landowners, while also pinpointing the charlatanry of contemporary beggars in a way which echoes Peachum's rabble of false cripples and afflicted in Brecht's *Threepenny Opera*. In the piece Fo 'doubles up' between two very distinct and separate physical types—the blind man who has lost his dog, and the cripple who has lost his cart, presenting them comically, and almost naturalistically, although he frequently speaks the words of one character while physically representing the other, which is an example of his concern with presenting a theatre of situation rather than identifying with the characters he plays. It is characteristic that he does not represent Christ in the piece, but makes him a described objective presence whom his two protagonists are trying to avoid, and thus the focus of the piece is not 'supernatural', concentrating exclusively on the misery and deprivation of their plight.

THE WEDDING FEAST OF CANAAN

Like the previous piece, **The Wedding Feast of Canaan** presents one of Christ's miracles from the people's point of view, playing down the supernatural overtones to stress the joyous, Dionysian, pagan view of the gospels, presenting Christ as a catalyst for festivity and enjoyment and even Bacchanalian excess. The piece begins with an argument over who is going to present the story, between a stiff, refined archangel who wants to present the correct, official and celestial version of the miracle, and an ape-like, drunken, shambling wedding guest who wants to tell the story from a more earthy, boozy and materialist point of view. In this dialectic, the Drunk, a character linked to Fo's line of peasant protagonists like the Blind Man, the Cripple, and Zanni, prevails through brute force and vulgarity and chases the archangel off the stage, after plucking some of the feathers out of his wings. The Drunk then narrates the wedding feast from a fool's point of view, emphasising the pleasure principle, and relishing his description of the epicurean delights of the feast (echoing Zanni's dream about his meal) and expressing the full 'tragedy' of the discovery that the wine has turned into vinegar (and not run out as in the official version, which is changed to the focus of a *contadino*, or peasant farmer). He describes Christ's entrance like that of a magician, and goes into a rapturous, onomatopoeic and alliterative description of the miracle and the resulting wine which he proceeds to get drunk on. Commenting on Christ's insistence that his mother try the wine as well, he reflects that if Adam had had a good glass of wine in his hand when he and Eve were tempted by the serpent and the apple, or if the apple had been made into good cider, the Fall of Man could have been avoided, along with the

necessity to work. This hedonistic and decidedly secular irreverence, which includes the Drunk's vision of heaven as a vat of wine, is free of the socialist condemnation of the excesses of alcohol as an escape from the rigours and constraints of working-class life which one might except. Fo, in the tradition of the Lombardian travelling players, embraces an almost utopian vision of communal festivity in which the joys of food and drink play an important part.

Mistero buffo was shown on Italian television at the same time as Franco Zeffirelli's comparatively pious and reverent film version of the gospels, *Jesus*. Fo and Zeffirelli had a debate about their disagreements over interpreting the gospels, which was set up by the newspaper *La Repubblica*. Zeffirelli maintained that **Mistero buffo** was too 'scurrilous' to be shown to 'unprepared television audiences', and that its 'elitist' political satire would be over the heads of television audiences. It is difficult to see how popular forms and traditions can be regarded as elitist, and Fo defended his position by attacking the lack of a popular viewpoint in Zeffirelli's film:

> Zeffirelli's most serious defect is the fact that he has stifled the festivity, joy and fantasy which exist in all Christian popular tradition and also in the gospels, where there are moments of great festivity and real community. The miracle of the wedding feast of Canaan, for example, the transformation of water into wine. This is one of the greatest passages in the gospels, and it's strange that Zeffirelli censored it. In his *Jesus* there's no miracle of Canaan, and it's a serious omission, because the audience doesn't get the idea that Christ is also the god of joy and spring, the social and religious continuation of Dionysus . . . His film was a ruling class operation, because he has cut out all the popular content of the gospels.[18]

Fo's emphasis on community and festivity is part of a political vision of popular culture in which the spirit of enjoyment and even excess plays an important part. The 'popularity' of **The Wedding Feast of Canaan,** and the fact that it is frequently requested by live audiences, is ample proof of the success and comprehensibility of Fo's cultural operation. 'Popular culture,' he has stated, 'doesn't mean just taking things that are of the people *per se*. It means taking everything that the masters have taken from that culture and turned upside down, and revealing their origins and developments.'[19] **The Wedding Feast of Canaan** is an outstanding example of this operation, while Zeffirelli's film is a perpetration of the 'masters' ' viewpoint of that culture.

THE ORIGIN OF THE GIULLARE

La nascita del giullare (**The Origin of the Giullare**) is a key text of **Mistero buffo,** and derives from a twelth century Sicilian text of Eastern origin. It reveals the peasant origins of the *giullare* and the secular, down to earth, popular nature of their treatment of Christ and supernatural religious events. A serf discovers a mountain and cultivates it with crops until a landowner tries to confiscate the now fertile land, calling on a bishop to lend his support to the appropriation and give it the sanction of the Church. When the peasant still refuses to give up his land, the landowner rapes the peasant's wife in front of his children. The peasant's family deserts him, and he is about to hang himself, having lost his land as well, when a man arrives and asks him for water. The peasant obliges, offering him some food as well. The man then reveals that he is Christ, confirming the peasant's growing suspicions, and promises to perform a miracle which will give the peasant 'a new language' which will 'cut like a knife', deflating and mocking the class of landowners and overlords. Christ makes the peasant a *giullare*, and instructs him to spread the message of his oppression and that of his class throughout the country.

So the mission of the *giullare* is political rather than religious, despite its sacred origins, and his message is the subversive mockery of the ruling class. Fo performs the piece in the first person as the *giullare*, presenting Christ as an ordinary person without supernatural trappings. The *giullare* originates from poverty, degradation and anger, which gives his satire a strong cutting edge. As Fo explains:

> All the forms in which the *giullare* expresses himself are intrinsically satirical, because of the very fact that he . . . originates from the people and takes their anger in order to give it back to them, mediating it with the grotesque, and with rationality, so that the people can become aware of their own condition. When I relate the origin of the *giullare* in *Mistero buffo,* I'm able to tell the story in a convincing way because I believe in it, I believe in the mission which the *giullare* originally chose for himself as the jester of the people. I also believe in it because I've experienced what it means to be the jester of the bourgeoisie. When we put on plays for . . . occupied factories, our greatest joy was being able to follow our comrades' struggles from close at hand, and then to make use of them.[20]

Fo identifies with the *giullare*, and sees his role as the modern equivalent of the mediaeval *giullare* playing to an industrial working-class audience instead of mediaeval peasants. In fact in *The Origin of the Underling,* his companion piece to *The Origin of the Giullare,* Fo makes a historical leap in order to relate the predicament of the mediaeval peasant to that of the modern working class, breaking out of the story to mime a worker on the production line programmed as to when he can go to the toilet so as not to slow down the conveyor belt. This serves to contextualise the predicament of the mediaeval peasant as the original form and the cultural heritage of the modern working class.

THE ORIGIN OF THE UNDERLING

This text is presented in virtually its original form, as used by the *giullare* Matazone da Caligano. It relates the creation of the peasant-serf 'from an ass's fart' after Adam has refused to lend his rib, so the master can have someone to do his unpleasant work for him. The master teaches the serf, under the guise of religious instruction, that his lot is to be a vulgar, repellent creature, who nevertheless has an

eternal soul, through which he can transcend the misery of his fate. Then an angel appears to instruct the landowner how to treat the serf, concluding 'How can this idiotic serf have a soul when he was born from an ass's fart?', thus revealing the overlord's religious blackmail and sowing the seeds for the peasant's revolt and rejection of his lot. Fo sees a strong affinity between the underling and the *giullare* in the fact that both are soulless and see through the overlord's religious duping. The origin of the underling is also the origin of the *giullare*:

> The *giullare* was an underling; he was oppressed—maybe he was even born from an ass like the underling, as the *giullare* Matazone describes the first underling born on this earth. If the *giullare* had a soul, he would feel it like lead, and wouldn't be able to fly because the soul would weigh him down, and he'd say, as Bonvesin de la Riva suggests, 'You should thank God you haven't got a backside, soul, because I'd kick it till it was black and blue.' It's because he was born without a soul that the *giullare* can refuse to accept the blackmail of 'having a good conscience', and prick and gnaw away at the overlord with his satire, and arm the oppressed against him.[21]

THE RESURRECTION OF LAZARUS

The chameleon-like capacity of Fo's mimicry is taxed to the utmost in *The Resurrection of Lazarus,* where he represents an entire crowd of people straining to see Christ's miracle of raising Lazarus from the dead. First he portrays the cemetery guard receiving the first arrivals, and then, through a series of one-line utterances and physical changes, the curious, pushing and voyeuristic crowd gathering and renting chairs for a ring-side view, with brief vignettes of a sardine-seller and even a pickpocket. As Fo states in his spoken introduction to the piece:

> The text of *The Resurrection of Lazarus* is a virtuoso's battle horse because the *giullare* often found himself having to play as many as 15 or 16 characters one after the other, with no way of indicating the changes except with his body—by striking a posture, without even changing his voice. It's the kind of piece which calls on the performer to improvise according to the audience's laughter, cadences, and silences. In practice, it's an improvisation which requires occasional ad-libbing.[22]

The piece is a satire on the 'mystical experience' of a miracle, and Fo's performance emphasises the fairground spectacle aspect of the miracle, which is seen from the peasant spectators' point of view, complete with references to the smell of the decomposing body and the worms inside it, as the cries of the market sellers mix with the sounds of bets being made on the outcome of the miracle, and the final cries of admiration and astonishment are mixed with the shouts of the person whose pocket has been picked, in a truly 'choral' finale. Here the allusiveness of Fo's performance is paramount, as he suggests characters and situations with a few swift gestures and changes of position, which rely on the audience's imagination to fill in the details. Here the audience is virtually presented with a mirror image of itself in terms of assisting at a prestidigious spectacle in which the spectator plays an active role. As Fo has explained:

> I am able to express my personal resources as a comic, because I *believe* in the *giullaresque* function of the comic. The ability of the mediaeval *giullare* to play as many as 15 characters . . . depended on the necessity of doing everything on his own. It wasn't just exhibitionistic wishful thinking. We know that the mediaeval *giullari* performed their plays alone from the stage directions in the texts and their allusions to doubling. Even the most able inventions of the *giullare* required audience participation. The play of allusions and the collaboration of the audience who picked them up, redoubled the poetic and comic charge. So what has been referred to as a 'didactic operation' wasn't really so at all, at least not in the sense that the audience was indoctrinated. Rather their imaginations were stimulated—this was the only way they could reach an awareness of their origins, their past, and their culture.[23]

When Fo and the Associazione Nuova Scena first began working on *Mistero buffo* in 1969, the original intention was to have the plays performed by more than one actor, but this idea was rejected as impracticable after experimentation, as it detracted from the necessary allusiveness of the performance of the *giullare*, and broke the rhythm and flow of the pieces, as well as filling in too much unnecessary detail by introducing minor subsidiary characters who frequently had very little to do and distracted attention from the principal comic's performance. By performing alone, Fo brings a predominantly imaginative element to Brecht's idea of didactic entertainment, which requires not only rational detachment from the audience in *Mistero buffo,* but also an imaginative filling-in and fleshing-out of details and situations rather in the same way as listening to a radio play requires (hence no costumes and no lighting effects), and where there is no space or time for the actor to detach himself from the characters he is playing, who are often only fleeting vignettes in a narrative.

BONIFACE VIII

Fo's allusive mimic capacity also relies on the audience's imagination in *Boniface VIII,* where, as the critic Paolo Puppa has described,

> On a completely bare stage, the audience's imagination is directed towards real objects which are conjured up with a minimum of signs; everything that is named is shown. The pope's charismatic dressing-up is shown in this way, while he recites an ancient extra-liturgical chant, assisted by priests and attendants . . . The aesthetic aspect . . . is exalted in tandem with the political connotations, since the self-investiture lays bare the power which it accumulates by building up its own connotations.[24]

Boniface VIII is introduced by an account of that pope's celebrated Good Friday orgy in 1301, with an array of prostitutes, bishops and cardinals. Candles are extinguished at three metres distance by farts. The piece presents Pope Boniface preparing for a ceremony, singing a hymn, and praying—the prayer becoming a response to an interrogation by Christ, who finally, appearing invisibly, kicks the pope. Fo mimes in detail Boniface's fastidious dressing-up, choosing caps, mirrors, gloves and cloaks, in an illustration of the capacity of fascistic authorities to oscillate between supreme arrogance and potency and abject self-deprecation and servitude. When Boniface is confronted by Christ carrying the cross, played by Fo as a country bumpkin, in the line of the *giullari,* he becomes mincing and masochistic, releasing a monk he has imprisoned and even kissing him for Christ's benefit, although he is unable to disguise his disgust. Fo's Boniface could almost take his place unnoticed in Pasolini's *Salò*; as Puppa points out, Fo's Boniface 'dressing-up' is almost a direct Italian equivalent to Hitler's preparation for public appearances in Brecht's *Arturo Ui*—both lay bare the narcissism which lies behind the temptations of absolute power.

Fo takes a number of historical liberties in *Boniface VIII,* for which he has been severely criticised, but the implied political leap of the imagination in the piece, especially in his anachronistic reference to a peasant communard movement in the same historical period, is executed with such theatrical skill that his detractors are inevitably disarmed. Zeffirelli's comments on the piece are a typical example:

> Satire about the church and the papacy's bad worldly operations is as legitimate as any other form of satire, but it's a different matter when it's extended to the subject of the gospels. I don't think it's right to elaborate the contents of the gospels in a satirical way.[25]

Fo's satirical Christ is unacceptable to Zeffirelli, although he is forced to admit that 'Fo is one of the greatest Italian theatrical phenomena and his performances are always brilliant. I am also aware that the scurrility of his theatre derives from the roots of our theatre, from Plautus and the commedia dell'arte.'[26]—an opinion which leads Fo to discriminate between 'those who become militants of the proletariat, and those who become militants of the Vatican'.[27]

TEXTS FROM THE PASSION

The television version of *Mistero buffo* also included four 'Texts from the Passion': the first of these, *Death and the Madman,* presents a Madman playing a Tarot-like card game while the inn-keeper of the hotel where he is staying announces that thirteen people have come for supper. Meanwhile the Madman wins a large sum of money, and the game culminates in his drawing the card of Death. At this point Death enters in the form of a beautiful virgin, grieved by her task of coming to take Christ away. The Madman proceeds to seduce her and divert her from her duty. The role of the Madman, (*Il Matto*), combines the characters of the *villano* (underling) and the *giullare,* and is a prototype of the protagonist of Fo's later play, *Accidental Death of an Anarchist,* who is also called *Il Matto* (the Maniac) and wreaks similar havoc in a much more modern political context. In *Mistero buffo* he is part fool, part idiot, part pagan and part charlatan, a profane character-actor who is also capable of laudable motives—his attempts to seduce Death are a ploy to warn Christ.

Mary Comes to Know of her Son's Sentence, performed by Franca Rame, relates the attempt by the friends of the Madonna to conceal Christ's crucifixion from his mother, who finds out what is going on only when she sees Veronica with the imprint of Christ's face after the scourging and the crowning of thorns. This piece is a prototype of a series of mother figures whom Franca Rame has performed in Fo's plays since the 1960s, highlights of which were gathered together in a television show, *Parliamo di donne* (*Let's Talk About Women*), which was broadcast by RAI (Radio e Televisione Italiana) as part of the 1977 Fo season. Rame's mother figures . . . have a toughness, political awareness, and sense of sisterhood which sometimes risks sentimentality in their more tragic manifestations—a factor which in Fo and Rame's collaborations after *Mistero buffo* becomes a springboard for parody of the archetypal Italian *mamma*—but here Mary's total acceptance of Mary Magdalene and her determined desire to find out the truth about what is happening to Christ make her a very gutsy figure. The piece ends with Mary's realisation that Christ is about to be crucified, but is cut off as she rushes off in desperation to look for him, and there is no direct presentation of her maternal emotion (unlike Brecht's *Mother Courage,* for example).

In *The Madman beneath the Cross,* the Madman presents the stripping and preparation of Christ for the crucifixion as a theatrical spectacle, while the Roman soldiers bet on the number of hammer blows needed to nail him to the cross. The Madman and the Soldiers then play cards for Christ's clothes in a kind of grotesque 'Strip Jack Naked', and the Madman reveals that he has collected the thirty pieces of silver that Judas has thrown away, and offers them in exchange for Christ's body. When Christ voices his refusal of the Madman's offer, the latter concludes that Christ is mad. At this point the Madman-Samaritan becomes angry and embittered, declaring that the only really appreciable action Christ performed was driving the money-lenders from the temple, through which he is seen to be a representative of the militant proletarian in his ingenuous but well-motivated desire to reroute the course of history and justice.

In the fourth text from the passion, Franca Rame returns to perform *Mary's Passion at the Cross,* in which, rather like Fo's Madman, but in a more distraught fashion, the Madonna tries to bargain with the Roman soldiers to save Christ from being crucified. Graphically envisaging the crucifixion, she offers a silver ring and gold earrings to the soldiers, who claim that they are just doing their job, and that to accept her bribes is more than their job is worth. The Archangel Gabriel appears to attempt to explain to Mary the purpose of her son's death, and it is left ambiguous as to whether the Archangel's appearance

is a 'real' supernatural manifestation or a hallucination of the grief-stricken Madonna. Mary accuses him of not understanding the condition of being a mother, since he was a mere messenger at the Annunciation, and Gabriel apologetically reminds her that her grief, 'your sacrifice and your son's sacrifice will split the heavens, and enable men for the first time to enter into paradise'.[28] Gabriel has the last word, and the implied irony and the avoidance of sentimentality, are immediately apparent.

At the end of the second television transmission of *Mistero buffo* Fo added a *Grammelot* of English origin, dating from the end of the sixteenth century, **The English Lawyer,** the story of a man on trial for raping a girl of the nobility. Like **A Fresh Delicate Rose,** the piece turns the tables on plaintiff and defendant, the English lawyer in a brilliantly histrionic display proving that the girl is to blame for the rape because her physical attributes and provocative appearance induced the 'poor' young man to rape her—an argument which is still frequently used in Italian rape cases in the present day.

MAO TSE-TUNG AND A CHINESE MISTERO BUFFO

Fo's concern with re-representing inherited culture from a popular point of view which clashes with official received ideas of the gospels and the history of the Catholic church is a process he regards as needing constant renewal, and his use of the popular theatrical roots of the Christian tradition is continually aligned with popular working-class culture:

> Unfortunately centuries of history haven't supplanted the necessity of teaching the people to become conscious of their condition. Mao Tse-tung insisted that party intellectuals should make it their concern to retrieve and research popular culture, which has been submerged and camouflaged by priests, aristocrats and the like, and give it back to the people for them to make use of. But as soon as they start making use of it on their own, they tend to gloss it over again, and superimpose all the tricks and forms which are inherent in the fact that the ruling class has always imposed this culture, it becomes necessary to take it back and clean it up again in a continual process which is carried out in collaboration with the people. The problem of the history of the origin of man, his exploitation and the historical development of this, is fundamental to all workers' struggles—this applies to each and any member of the proletariat who is capable of carrying out the revolution which is constantly being talked about.[29]

Fo is not pontificating if one considers the mindlessly grotesque films, television shows and live entertainment which are continually on offer for working-class spectators in Italy, which includes the type of 'popular spectacles' offered by the Italian Communist Party in their summer celebrations, the 'Feste dell'Unita', which frequently cater to the lowest common denominator of popular culture, the variety show.

The success of *Mistero buffo* on Italian television, and the high audience figures, which were helped along by the free 'scandal' publicity afforded by the Vatican's outrage at the play, brought Fo across to the widest possible range of audiences. The television version of *Mistero Buffo* formed part of a 20 hour retrospective of Fo's major plays, and as a result Fo virtually dropped the play from his ample repertoire, performing it mostly abroad, until three years later, in keeping with his belief in the necessity for a constant renewal of his diffusion of popular culture, he returned to the Italian stage (or rather 'fringe' network) with a second edition of *Mistero Buffo,* entitled *La Storia della tigre e altre storie (The Story of the Tigress and Other Stories),* first performed in 1980, in the same theatrical conditions as *Mistero buffo.* Interviewed in Rome during his premiere of the piece in a converted cinema rented by a feminist organisation, *Casa della donna,* Fo commented on the need for the 'community spirit' of performing to live audiences in a politically-charged situation:

> People are tired of solitude, which television only serves to make more acute. And cinema is no substitute for cohesion or collective movement. The theatre, on the other hand, gives people the opportunity of really meeting one another, especially the type of theatre that we and other rank-and-file groups put on, where there's a real sense of involvement and participation. And in recent years the need to get together has increased considerably.[30]

The Story of the Tigress is based on a story which Fo heard in Shanghai in 1975, as related to a Chinese audience of 20,000, by a local country story-teller who performed in a minority dialect, which was translated into Mandarin and then into Italian for Fo, who subsequently took Michelangelo Antonioni to task for his voyeuristic view of China presented in the documentary *Cina-Chung Kuo.* The dialect of the piece reminded him of his own adapted Padano dialect in *Mistero buffo,* and so he set about preparing a Padano version of the story, trying it out in public, reshaping it, and in fact ultimately expanding it from 15 to 45 minutes, sharpening the details, presenting a 'final' version before a script of the piece even existed:

> The audience's participation was a decisive factor. I've had the right sort of support from my audiences in a very precise way, and I've also noticed where there were lapses and slips, and passages which needed cutting and adjusting.[31]

The story concerns a Chinese soldier from Mao's army who is wounded during the war of liberation against Chiang Kai-shek, with gangrene setting in. He tells his comrades to leave him in a cave, where, like Romulus and Remus, he is looked after by a tigress and adopted into her family, teaching them how to cook meat in exchange for learning the laws of survival in the jungle. When his wound finally heals, he persuades the tiger family to accompany him to his home town, and the tigers help the local inhabitants to get rid of the last vestiges of Chiang Kai-shek's army by intimidating them with their roars. After the war is won, the Popular Government takes over the town's administration, and are intimidated

by the tiger family, whom they try to have sent to the zoo, since they maintain that the tigers are a redundant force under the peace-time regime. The villagers are not happy with this proposed solution, and at the end they use the tigers to chase away the new administration. The piece ends with a tedious polemical speech by one of the new administrators, exhorting the people to obey him, a speech which is punctuated by an almighty roar from the family of tigers. In the Chinese context of the fable, as Fo explains in his spoken introduction to the piece, the tiger represents the spirit of self-management, self-determination and endurance, which aligns the story with the context of occupied factories where Fo frequently performs:

> The tiger has a very precise allegorical significance: they say that a woman, or a man, or a people, have the tiger when they are confronted by enormous difficulties, and at the point where most people are inclined to flee, scarper, run away and abandon the struggle, piss off and even reach the point of denigrating themselves and everything generous they've done before, they insist on standing firm and resisting . . . Another clear allegorical meaning the tiger has, which is perhaps fundamental, is this: a person has the tiger when he never delegates anything to anybody, and never tries to get other people to resolve his own problems . . . The person who has 'the tiger' gets directly involved in the situation, participating in it, controlling it, verifying it, and being on the spot and responsible right up to the end.[32]

The reference to striking workers is obvious. Fo's introduction spells out the contemporary political implications of the fable and indicates his continuous involvement in working-class political struggles from the inside, as well as his role as a cultural spokesman for the extra-parliamentary Italian left.

From the performance point of view, *The Story of the Tigress* is a tour de force. Fo plays the soldier with his gangrenous leg, and the tigress, relishing her roars, snarls and growls, which he modulates through a whole range of emotions, even representing the deer she brings back for her cubs, whose childlike playfulness he represents charmingly without ever stooping to the compromise of getting down on all fours. He even represents a bullet coming out of the soldier's gun, and winds up the piece as a pompous party bureaucrat personifying the denial of the spirit of the tigress, which charges the whole piece, in an exhilarating way. One of the most hilarious sequences in the play is when the tigress gives roaring lessons to the soldier's countrymen. As Renzo Tian describes it:

> Dario Fo does all this . . . without using words. At the most there are some fragments of words. He moves a few centimetres and becomes the teacher, then becomes the pupil, strains his vocal chords to an almost frightening extent, saws the air with his long paws, does both the real roars and the apprentice ones, and multiplies his hands, legs and utterances to let us 'see' rather than just hear the roaring class. And he succeeds. He succeeds because he has adopted everything that's been going round the theatre theory scene about gesture, mime, the *giullare,* body language, metaphor and

audience involvement, and he incorporates it all into the sole ingredients of dust and sweat, without mediators, without indirect asides, and without playing his cards close to his chest.[33]

Fo's onomatopoeic language, which here even transcends *Grammelot* in its representation of the world of the tigers, not only manages to translate the context of the Chinese fable into an easily comprehensible contemporary Italian context, but also can be understood by a multinational audience, as the English critic John Francis Lane, reviewing the Rome performance of the play, testifies:

> It is an invented language which he speaks as if he (and we) spoke it naturally. It isn't too difficult to understand, even if the pace at which he rambles on requires a great deal of concentration on the part of listeners of any language background . . . As happened a few weeks ago, when I watched Fo perform for an audience of British theater (sic) people who didn't understand Italian and weren't getting much help from Fo's official translator, he revealed an ability to communicate concepts and images with characters and events and ideas. One man in three hours runs the whole gamut of theatrical experience from primitive self-expression to the latest invention of media sophistication.[34]

Much of the international success of Fo's work is due to the fact that he is an 'animal of the stage', as the Italian expression goes, capable of communicating through sound and gesture in a way which leaves language barriers behind. As Fo himself has said, referring also to Franca Rame's performances and the plays they have collaborated on together:

> We're often asked why our plays are performed so frequently abroad. Part of the answer is this: we talk about real things, which we re-interpret in an ironic and satirical vein. We talk about Italy, but in countries like Germany and France, talking about Italy means talking about their problems.[35]

THE 'OTHER STORIES'

The three other stories in Fo's second edition of *Mistero buffo* are adapted from the Apocryphal gospels, and hence much more similar to the first edition of the play than is *The Story of the Tigress*.

The first of these, *The Child Jesus' First Miracle,* presents Christ as a Palestinian immigrant in Egypt who, out of bbredom and loneliness, starts performing bizarre tricks like projecting lightning from his eyes, working up to his first miracle, which is a political act—he changes the son of the owner of the city into a terracotta pot, because he never allows the other children to play with him and ride his horses. Mary persuades Christ to change the boy back to his original form, since she and Joseph have just found a job and have no wish to be on the run again. Another of Fo's 'Gospels of the Poor', which invariably have a political twist to them, is *The Sacrifice of Isaac,* in which the sacrifice is revealed to have been based on a bet between God and the devil as to the extent of Abraham's love for God. This is revealed to Isaac only after the Angel

has appeared to stop Abraham carrying out the killing. The piece ends with Isaac throwing a stone which lands on his father's head, claiming that it has come from heaven and is for his own good, using the same logic as his father has in preparing him for the sacrifice. The piece illustrates Fo's irreverence for the official gospels, which he uses as a basis for religious satire, and here attacks the traditional notion of patriarchal power invested in the father figure. *Daedalus and Icarus* deals with the same theme of the power fathers exert over their children, dealing with Icarus and Daedalus lost in the labyrinth they have built themselves for Gnossus, and ending with Icarus' tragic fall as he tries to fly. The piece is based on a story by the Greek satirical poet of the second century BC, Luciano di Samosata, whom Fo claims was one of the first ever satirists, and a big influence on Rabelais, whose influence in turn is omnipresent in *Mistero buffo.* Fo uses *Daedalus and Icarus* to stress the importance of the imagination and inventiveness, and to attack resorts to surrogate substitutes for the imagination like drugs, horoscopes and UFOs. In exhorting his audience to seek out more creative activities, Fo himself presents a formidable example.

THE OBSCENE FABLES

Il fabulazzo osceno (*The Obscene Fable*) is the third edition of *Mistero buffo,* based on more secular sources, which Fo first performed in March 1982. It consists of a group of three stories, all tried out and developed by Fo in public with an audience, which deal with popular sexuality and scatology in a way which was usually censored by Mediaeval church and state authorities, but which was preserved through oral tradition. Fo recounts how he was unable to find any academic source material for the stories, and hence has added his own embellishments to the pieces, which convey a popular spirit of bawdry and earthy humour similar to that of Boccaccio, but with more political bite. The *fabulazzo osceno* is a Franco-Provençal story (which Fo plays in roughly the same dialects he uses in *Mistero buffo,* with a bit of Provençal dialect thrown in to tease the audience) of the type known as *Fablieux,* and Fo stresses that they are obscene in the erotic and anti-scandalous sense, as opposed to mere dirty stories. As the American critic Joel Schechter, whose commentary on Fo's performance of the plays in Gubbio I am indebted to, has explained in his excellent article, 'Dario Fo's Obscene Fables':

> Few of the tales that Fo recites can readily be found in books. He discovers them in obscure sources, invents details, and turns them into performance scenarios. In doing this he brings to the public some chapters of Italian history and folklore that went unrecorded because the scholars who preserved past culture favoured the ruling class; it was not in their interest for stories of political and sexual unrest to survive . . . Fo notes that Popes and noblemen in the middle ages were free to write obscene literature, and circulate it among their friends, while stories for the general public survived—if they survived at all—through the oral tradition of minstrelsy in which Fo places himself.[36]

The first piece, *Il Tumulto di Bologna* (*The Bologna Riot*), is 'obscene' in the sense that it deals with excrement, which the local peasants of Bologna in 1334 used as weapons in their revolt against papal legates and the Provençal troops protecting the Pope. Fo mimes with relish the local peasants throwing buckets of shit over the walls of their fortress, and the high-ranking Vatican officials being splattered by it, changing from the role of a detached narrator to those of the gleeful participants in this ultimately successful peasants' revolt, and of the disgruntled and finally banished Vatican troops.

The second piece, *La parpàja tòpola* (*The Butterfly-Mouse*) is a twelfth century sexual fable about a wealthy but simple-minded goatherd who is tricked on his wedding night by his wife, who has been married off to him to avoid scandal arising from the fact that she has been having an affair with the local parish priest. When her new husband finally returns from a put-up wild-goose chase on their wedding night, she, tired from her frolicking with the priest, tells him she has left her sex at her mother's house, and when he insists, she instructs him how to go about getting it. The goatherd goes to his mother-in-law's house, and is given a cardboard box with a cloth and a mouse in it, and told not to open it until he gets back to his wife. But he is impatient, and unwraps the parcel, and the 'sex' ('topola' is a pun on the Italian word for mouse) escapes. At the end of the story the goatherd's wife takes pity on him and tells him the mouse has come home of its own accord, showing him where her vagina is. Fo originally intended this piece to be performed by Franca Rame, but she demurred due to 'certain passages which were so crude in their erotic satire, and so ruthless in their paradoxicality, that they made me feel uneasy. I would have had to do violence to myself to manage to play it: the perennial condition of sexual inhibition of a woman faced with the blackmailing myth of modesty and shame.'[37] The piece is a satire on Victorian-type sexual repression and euphemisms, which frequently amount to the imposition of ignorance, and Fo's performance is in itself a revolt against censorship and sexual oppression.

Fo prefaces his third story in *Il fabulazzo osceno* with an improvised monologue about the P2 scandal in Italy, which he performed on its own in an extended form in Pisa in 1982, after the secret lodge P2 had been exposed and shown to include some of the most prominent Italian politicians, businessmen, industrialists and even entertainers, making it a type of secret Mafia which contained more power and influence than the Italian government. In this *P2 Prologue,* Fo simply talks to his audience, acting out situations and inventing allusions and analogies as he goes along—it is spontaneous theatre. He is particularly scathing about the role of entertainers in the Lodge, and the theatrical overtones of Italian public life:

> P2 is a totally Italian story, with all the drama of espionage, slaughter and crime, but also all the ridiculousness of farce. An example? One of the members of P2 was Claudio Villa, the king of song, who immediately admitted everything, since he's no politician and so has nothing to be ashamed of. Well, Gelli (the head of P2) took Villa into P2 for just one reason: women. The king of song directed a revue company and Gelli invited them all to his house in Arezzo, to have a few dancing girls . . . Don't you find it funny (*buffo*) that a Masonic Lodge doesn't allow women to be members, and yet Gelli used his secret lodge to get some dancing girls? Don't get me wrong, having dancing girls can be a wonderful thing, but can you imagine a country where secret sects are used to get access to women? . . . Compared to these masons, terrorists are mere amateurs. They don't just strike at the heart of the state, they've taken over its eyes, brain, heart, stomach and all the rest.[38]

Fo goes on to describe scenes which recall the orgies of **Boniface VIII,** and uses the political scandal to tease out sexual high-jinks in order to prove his point about the double-standards of sexual repression and the sexual decadence of church and state authorities in whose interest sexual repression operates. Here Fo reveals the real 'living newspaper' aspect of his theatre, in which he is continually editorialising and improvising sketches based on events in the news, which he changes in every performance, providing a live running commentary and dramatisation of political news.

The piece which follows the *P2 Prologue, Lucio e l'asino* (*Lucio and the Donkey*), has sexual overtones similar to those between Bottom and the Queen of the Fairies in *A Midsummer Night's Dream*; a poet suffering from 'phallocratophantasmagoria' tries to perform an Ovidian transformation of himself into an eagle, imitating Jove's famous miracle, in an attempt to increase his sexual prowess. He mixes the wrong potion, however, and ends up as a donkey, who is robbed by brigands and forced to carry the beautiful daughter of a wealthy family. Fo portrays the randy, constantly sexually aroused donkey with vigour and high comedy, using onomatopoeic sounds to parody male sexual ambition in a way which echoes ancient Greek comedies like *Lysistrata*. As a donkey, the poet is constantly kicked in the testicles by all and sundry, but manages to rescue the girl and return her to her parents, who seek to gratify his insatiable sexual appetite with horses. After they discover his ability to write, they sell him to a circus, where he is rented out to an aristocratic lady for sexual purposes, which leads to his employment in the circus in a love-making act with a slave girl. He then discovers the antidote for his metamorphosis and is changed back into a man. He seeks out the lady with whom he made love as a donkey, only to be rejected by her on the grounds that he is no longer an exceptional representative of the Priapic principle, but merely a man like any other. This fable originates in the second century BC, and was written by Luciano di Samosata, a Greek satirical poet who lived in Italy, and whose writings were later an influence on Machiavelli, Rabelais and Voltaire. The 'obscene fables' reveal Fo in a more 'scabrous' vein than *Mistero buffo,* exploring a more Rabelaisian vein of satire than the religious subjects of the earlier texts, while also illustrating how he has ventured into the field of sexual politics, a process which started with his television compilation *Parliamo di donne* in 1976, and which has become a dominant feature in his subsequent collaborations with Franca Rame.

Il fabulazzo osceno concludes with a revised and adapted version of Franca Rame's monologue about the 'suicide' of the German terrorist Ulrike Meinhof, *Io, Ulrike, Grido . . . (I, Ulrike, Cry . . .)*, which was first performed on a stage covered in cellophane in Milan in 1977 to commemorate the first anniversary of Meinhof's death. Here it is presented as an 'obscene tragedy' and used to focus on political torture and the 'obscene' Italian *legge sui penitenti*, a law which offers reduced sentences to terrorists who give information to the state about terrorist activities, (like British supergrasses) which often leads to the conviction of innocent people. The monologue, based on letters and documents by and about Ulrike Meinhof, is a bleak, static and intense depiction of her attempts to stay sane and rational in prison, and overcome the oppressive torture of sterile, white silence by painting the colours of West German consumerist capitalism and speculating about the 'state clean-up' which will harness dissent and stamp out all forms of protest and political opposition in West Germany after the Stammheim deaths. The Fos are careful to point out that they do not agree with the ideology of the Baader-Meinhof group, but use the monologue as a vehicle to condemn the sense of apathy and impotence which has blighted much of the post-1968 revolutionary Left and extra-parliamentary political groups both in Germany and Italy since the late 1970s.

This piece is a rare example in the Fo canon of direct political address in a non-comic form, and illustrates a growing sense of disillusionment with the heady, optimistic and positive form of communal didactic theatre of the early days of *Mistero buffo,* which runs parallel with a more general decline in political protest and Left-wing constructivism in Italy since the late 1970s, a factor I shall return to in the latter part of this book.

Mistero buffo and its many offshoots, together with the countless improvised routines and sketches on topical events which Fo frequently makes up on the spot, reveal him as the 'theatrical animal' that he is, and show his unique capacity for turning a one-man show into a piece of epic and total theatre. His presence as an actor, director and frequently designer, charges his plays with a dynamism both stylistic and political which is often far less apparent in the printed texts of his plays (most of which are in fact only written down after Fo has knocked them into shape through performance, and exist as records of performances rather than constructed literary texts). *Mistero buffo* is an unrepeatable experience tailor-made for and by Fo, which fortunately surmounts language barriers (at least to a certain extent), as a performance by another actor in translation would be virtually inconceivable. This has, however, happened on two occasions in Brussels—first in

November 1972, when Arturo Croso performed *Mistero buffo* in French and Flemish at the TRH and then in February 1983, when Charles Cornette performed selections from *Mistero buffo* under the title *La Jonglerie* at the Atelier rue Ste-Anne.

There have also been at least two attempts to stage *Mistero buffo* in English. Some of the pieces were performed in a puppet show format by Malcolm Knight and his Black Box and Maskot Puppet Theatre in Scotland and at the 1983 Edinburgh Festival, relying on rod and glove puppets to illustrate the gestural range of Fo's monologues in Knight's own translation. In 1984 a young, six-member English and American collective theatre group called the 1982 Theatre Company did an 'ensemble' version of *Mistero buffo,* which included one performance at the Half Moon Theatre in February 1984. The group worked from a very accurate, literal translation of the pieces by Ed Emery, who also translated the Fo Riverside Theatre Workshops and has done a number of other Fo plays in English. The 1982 Theatre Company adapted *The Hymn of the Flagellants, The Slaughter of the Innocents, The Marriage at Canaan, The Morality Play of the Blind Man and the Cripple, The Birth of the Peasant* and *The Birth of the Jongleur* into a condensed, 90 minute production which maintains the spirit of the original from an oblique, contemporary standpoint, with little attempt made at finding an English equivalent of Fo's *Grammelot*. Using a collective style reminiscent of Paul Sills' Story Theatre and the Bread and Puppet Theatre (appropriately, as this latter group was also an influence on Fo's stagecraft), and performing without sets and costumes, the group simplified Fo's texts into a modern English idiom, frequently resorting to corny jokes and slapstick devices in a limited but likeable dramatisation of the monologues. Many of Fo's necessary explanatory and introductory prologues to the pieces were maintained, while an extract from the Wakefield Mystery Cycle's *Shepherd's Play* was interpolated to illustrate similarities between Fo's sources and the English Mediaeval Mystery Play tradition. These similarities involve not only features of dialect, but also the religious mystification of texts by academic commentators, as the group indicated by reading a footnote from the English texts which suggested that the Shepherd's expression of misery at his plight was merely intended to reflect the greater sufferings of Christ. Ensemble 'alienation devices' were incorporated, like performing the *Morality of the Blind Man and the Cripple* with two actresses, and staging the conflict between the Angel and the Drunk in *The Marriage at Canaan* as a battle between two actors trying to upstage each other. By drawing on English theatre traditions such as pantomime and music hall double acts, the group's performance was rooted in a 'popular' format. A modern political parallel illustrating 'state brutality similar to that of the sixteenth century' was made by reciting Franca Rame's account of her improvised *interventi* at the gates of the Fiat factory in Turin in 1980 after the wholesale sackings there. While sacrificing most of the onomatopoeic richness and mimic range of Fo's performance of ***Mistero buffo,*** the 1982 Theatre Company production did demonstrate that by approaching the pieces from a respectful distance, an English equivalent to Fo's 'popular theatre', albeit impoverished, is possible.

NOTES

[1] Dario Fo, *Mistero buffo*, Bertani, Verona, 1977, p. xix.

[2] *Ibid.*, p. 9.

[3] *Ibid.*, p. 9.

[4] Lanfranco Binni, *Dario Fo*, Il Castoro, 1977, p. 52.

[5] *Mistero buffo*, *op. cit.*, pp. 4-5.

[6] In Chiara Valentini, *La storia di Dario Fo*, Feltrinelli, 1977, p. 125.

[7] Dario Fo, *Pum, pum! Chi e? La polizia*, Bertani, Verona, 1974, pp. 234-5.

[8] *Il teatro politico di Dario Fo*, Mazzotta, 1977, p. 6.

[9] *Ibid.*, p. 60.

[10] In Valentini, *op. cit.*, p. 128.

[11] Ugo Volli, in *La Repubblica*, 3 March, 1979.

[12] In Erminia Artese, *Dario Fo parla di Dario Fo*, Lerici, 1977, pp. 53-5.

[13] Michele Straniero, *Giullari e Fo*, Lato Side, 1978.

[14] In *Panorama*, 21 November, 1978.

[15] Artese, *op. cit.*, pp. 84-5.

[16] *Mistero buffo*, p. vii.

[17] Artese, p. 19.

[18] *Mistero buffo*, p. xx.

[19] *Il teatro politico di Dario Fo, op. cit.*, p. 72.

[20] Artese, pp. 51, 68.

[21] *Ibid.*, p. 140.

[22] *Mistero buffo*, p. 100.

[23] Artese, pp. 139-140.

[24] Paolo Puppa, *Il teatro di Dario Fo*, Marsilio, 1978, pp. 113-4.

[25] *Mistero buffo*, p. 215.

[26] *Ibid.*, p. 213.

[27] *Ibid.*, p. 217.

[28] *Ibid.*, p. 184.

[29] *Artese.*, p. 137.

[30] In *Il Messaggero*, March 30, 1980.

[31] Dario Fo, *La storia della tigre*, La Commune, 1980, p. 3.

[32] *Ibid.*, pp. 8-9.

[33] In *Il Messaggero*, March 30, 1980.

[34] In *The International Daily News*, April 1, 1980.

[35] In *Il Messaggero*, March 30, 1980.

[36] *Theater*, Vol. 13, No. 4, Winter 1982, p. 88.

[37] Dario fo, *Il fabulazzo osceno*, La Commune, 1982, p. 1.

[38] In *La Repubblica*, 30 May, 1981.

J. L. Wing (essay date 1993)

SOURCE: "The Iconicity of Absence: Dario Fo and the Radical Invisible," in *Theatre Journal*, Vol. 45, No. 3, October 1993, pp. 303-15.

[In the following essay, Wing contends: "By presenting [in Mistero Buffo*] a kind of fragmented iconicity—fragments of characters, fragments of actions and interactions—Fo has shaped a dramatic montage in which the shifting perspectives force a sense of community. There is no time to identify privately with one character or point of view; the spectator is too busy in every given moment, working on the collective creation of the event."]*

In demonstration of the mysterious power of *absence* as a staging technique, Italian playwright/performer Dario Fo recounts an intriguing tale of a performance at a mental institution for "untreatable cases" in Turn, Italy.[1] Fo was in the midst of a skit involving an archangel and a drunk, in which he, himself, played both characters, a task which compelled him continuously to speak to the empty spot where he had just "placed" his antagonist. At one point, as he was impersonating the drunk who was trying to get a word in edgewise, a patient began berating the (absent) archangel for stifling the drunk's story, screaming," Let him talk, you bastard! Otherwise I'll come up there and give you a kick in the halo!" Somewhat astonished at this response from a spectator he was told hadn't spoken in years, Fo told a group of acting students, "The amazing thing was that she was raging at the character whom I had sketched out in the air; she was pointing at the spot where I had left him." Later other inmates who had been tied to their beds expressed a desire to get up on stage and speak out against oppressive conditions in the hospital. This astonishing response raises questions not only about the nature of "insanity," but also about an art form based fundamentally on presence. How did Fo shape his staging so that absence signified profoundly, so much so that, in this case at least, it induced the mute and powerless to speak? And what are the theoretical implications of this iconic nothingness?

If theatre is an iconically dense representational medium, as many theorists indicate, interpretation of that iconicity has become increasingly open to debate. As a signifier, the icon is a tease: there is simply too much there. Since, as Keir Elam tells us, "the governing principle in iconic signs is similitude,"[2] our tendency as spectators is to naturalize the icon—to assume that it *means* what it *is*. This essentialist temptation is especially apparent when considering the phenomenon of the actor. In a valuable discussion of the slippery relation between the icon and its referent in various theatrical genres, for example, Marvin Carlson contends that "the one element which almost invariably involves iconic identity—is the actor, a human being who represents a human being."[3] Having made this assertion, Carlson hastens to cite the exception of puppetry, much as Elam, wrestling with the same problem ten years earlier, came up with immediate contradictions involving Elizabethan boy actors and Greeks playing gods.[4]

The troubling link between iconicity as "the visual component of meaning"[5] and the physical presence of the actor has proved to be an especially rich source of analysis for feminist theorists, who problematize the social and psychological constructions of the subject in relation to the female body displayed on the stage (or screen).[6] As Laura Mulvey pointed out in her influential essay on film theory in 1975, visibility and pleasure are inextricably linked in the Western configuration of the unconscious.[7] Whether considered from a Freudian or Lacanian perspective, this link is devastating to the female subject, so much so that Mulvey proposes deleting pleasure from the representational configuration altogether.

> It is said that analysing pleasure, or beauty, destroys it. That is the intention of this essay. The satisfaction and reinforcement of the ego that represent the high point of film history hitherto must be attacked; not in favor of a reconstructed new pleasure, which cannot exist in the abstract, or of intellectualized unpleasure, but to make way for a total negation of the ease and plenitude of the narrative fiction film.[8]

Since the pleasure/vision collusion derives from psychological theories which are fundamentally ideological in nature, as Kaja Silverman demonstrates (because they are configured within a culture which already valorizes the male), the most promising approach for a feminist critique of theatrical representation would seem to involve a radical deconstruction of its ideological apparatus. But is this possible without condemning us all to what Mulvey calls "intellectual unpleasure"?

Such a deconstruction is, of course, precisely the project to which Bertolt Brecht addressed himself, when he proposed foregrounding the mechanics of theatrical production in order to break with what he called "culinary theatre," which he equated to an illusionistic meal, easily digested and forgotten. According to Brecht, holistic representation of character or narrative is objectively, *realistically* misguided:

> The continuity of ego is a myth. A man is an atom that perpetually breaks up and forms anew. The bourgeois theatre's performance always aim at smoothing over contradictions. . . . Conditions are reported as if they could not be otherwise. . . . If there is any development it is always steady, never by jerks. . . . None of this is like reality, so a realistic theatre must give it up.[9]

Brecht's solution to bourgeois realism—what might be called his "atomic theory" of representation—features a radical perceptual realignment, which, through various "distancing" techniques, co-opts the spectator as collaborator, rather than passive witness to the performance event.

In Walter Benjamin's terms, the spectator in Brecht's configuration in fact co-produces the event, a concept which has ethical implications:

> *An author who teaches nothing, teaches no one.* What matters, therefore, is the exemplary character of production, which is first able to induce other producers to produce, and second to put an improved apparatus at their disposal. And this apparatus is better the more consumers it is able to turn into producers—that is readers or spectators into collaborators. We already possess such an example. . . . It is Brecht's epic theatre.[10]

According to Roland Barthes, this process implies a disruption of the standard semiotic equation, in which the signifier flows inexorably toward the signified on an ideologically closed circuit:

> Consciousness of the unconsciousness, consciousness that the audience should have of the unconsciousness which prevails on stage: this is the theatre of Brecht. . . . The function of the system here is not to hand on a positive message (it is not a theatre of signifieds), but to make it understood that the world is an object that must be deciphered (it is a theatre of signifiers).[11]

The perceptual "gap" which results from Brecht's denaturalized signification strategy has been appropriated by both film and theatre scholars recently in order to conceptualize an alternative to the ideological entanglements of subjectivity and the gaze. For example, Elin Diamond has shown how the Brechtian "alienation" strategy can be applied to a feminist theatre critique:

> *Verfremdungseffekt* . . . challenges the mimetic property of acting that semioticians call iconicity, the fact that the performer's body conventionally resembles the object (or character) to which it refers . . . by alienating (not simply rejecting) iconicity, by foregrounding the expectation of resemblance, the ideology of gender is exposed and thrown back to the spectator.[12]

In a series of incisive articles, Diamond has applied her observations to show how Caryl Churchill's theatre, in particular, uses a Brechtian approach to challenge ideological presumptions, especially those involving gender construction. Among other considerations, Diamond analyzes how Churchill's dramaturgy makes visible what is normally *in*visible (showing us Val's perceptions as a Ghost in *Fen*, for example) as a means of rupturing a perceptual complacency which equates icon with identity.[13] In this paper, I want to consider how Dario Fo uses the Brechtian formulation to do just the opposite—to make the normally visible *in*visible—in pursuit of a similar goal: to force the spectator into an active and critical collaboration with the representational process in order to challenge "the ideological nature of the seeable."[14]

Fo's manipulation of absence is most apparent in the one-actor skits he regularly performs under the aegis of ***Mistero Buffo*** (the title refers to the medieval mystery plays which are his source material).[15] For Fo, the crucial common factor of all these skits is their historical lineage in the medieval craft of the wandering players, or *guillari*, which he attempts to reconstruct in his performances. This reconstruction centers initially not on visual gaps but on historical gaps in surviving texts, which Fo claims have been sentimentalized and mystified for centuries by academics who were complicitous with power structures which squelched dissent. To recover the original vitality and intent of the medieval pieces, it is necessary to reconstitute the performative elements that linger between the words, the gestural traces that functioned as, "*the* determining part of the representation, precisely to get across to the public those allusions which it was too dangerous to write down in full."[16] Fo contends that to take everything literally is to misrepresent it:

> The text belongs to a precise social class, the one which controls the power. Opposed to it there is another theatric lexicon composed of text, pause rhythm; a lexicon in which many times the word is dependent on a situation.[17]

Fo's insistence on the "theatric lexicon" links up handily with the argument against "privileging the text," flourishing for some time now among Italian semioticians, such as Marco de Marinis and Franco Ruffini who both insist on the importance of evaluating the entire theatrical process rather than focusing on either a text or a definitive production.[18] De Marinis's objection to the idea that a virtual performance is somehow already prefigured within each dramatic text—a necessary condition for the reduction of theatre to a set of codifiable sign systems which can then be definitively analyzed—parallels Fo's notion that the key to a performance lies in the absence between the words. If absence is the uncodifiable, creative core of the performance, then its very unpredictability is potentially threatening to a structure (academic or political) that thrives on codes.

However, Fo's appropriation of absence transcends an opposition to text alone. In the process of attempting to recover the original gestural satire latent in the medieval pieces, to reconstruct absence, he has uncovered a representational strategy which, like Brecht's, fundamentally destabilizes the semiotic foundation of illusionistic representation. Ironically, given Fo's forthright Marxist epistemology, the primary source for his gestural reconstruction is the rich iconography of religious paintings of the period. Fo claims that many of these paintings, which he likens to medieval cartoon strips,[19] represent a synchronomous and multi-faceted narrative, embodying what Fo sees as an optimum epic style which transcends the merely linguistic. "When (medieval) painters tell a story they are outside language," Fo suggests. "They don't show the perspective of only one person. They show diverse points of view . . . the same scene from behind, from the front, from a distance."[20]

Obviously this simultaneous, multiple perspective has ideological implications for theatrical representation. On the

one hand, the sense of multiplicity, of cacophony, of popular culture represented by a performer in the public marketplace recalls Bakhtin's theory of the carnivalesque; both Fo and Bakhtin identify an anarchical exuberance in the type of public performance which "precisely because of its unofficial existence was marked by an exceptional radicalism, freedom and ruthlessness."[21] This theatrical exuberance is anything but benign; indeed, according to Bakhtin, it poses an explicit threat to any power structure which depends on its representation as "eternal, immovable, and absolute."[22]

For Fo, however, the practical challenge which presents itself is precisely one of performance: how does one reconstruct this rich iconography, this popular, pluralistic perspective? A tempting solution would be to attempt a kind of literal mimesis, to reconstitute the original image, using one actor per figure. In the case of the *Mistero Buffo* sketches, however, Fo came to the conclusion that the pieces were clearly intended to be performed by one actor alone. According to Fo:

> The giullari almost always worked on their own; we can see this from the fact that, in the text, things that happen tend to be indicated by the actor splitting himself between (the) parts, and by allusion, so that the full comic and poetic weight of the piece is heightened by the free play of (the spectator's) imagination.[23]

The requisite representational strategy, then, would need to insure that the spectator's imagination is engaged in maximum movement, in order to create the necessarily simultaneous and multiple iconicity. This prescription calls for a kind of "motion picture," and indeed Fo deliberately incorporates cinematic techniques into his performance. A closer look at a few of the *Buffo* pieces will serve to illustrate Fo's approach.

Fo claims that *The Resurrection of Lazarus*, was a *piece de resistance* among medieval *giullari*, requiring an astounding virtuosity, in which one actor would represent some fifteen different characters in succession. "The principle theme of the piece," according to Fo, is "a satirization of everything that passes for the moment of mystery":

> The satire is aimed at the miracle mongers, the magicians, the conjurer's art of the miraculous, which is an underlying feature of many religions, including Catholicism . . . here though, the story of the miracle is told from the standpoint of the people. The scene is set as though it were about to be performed by a great conjurer, a great magician, somebody who is able to do extraordinary and vastly entertaining things.[24]

Clearly the "vastly entertaining conjurer" in question is analogous to Fo, himself, and indeed Fo's strategy depends on a kind of theatrical sleight of hand which needs to be "set up" as meticulously as a magic trick. To emphasize the deliberate derivation from religious icons, and to entice audience collaboration in a "pictorial" reconstruction, Fo always precedes the Mystery sketches with slides.[25] In the case of *Lazarus*, he often shows one of his own drawings, which he claims to have copied from the original sketches for a fresco in a Pisa cemetery. Fo's drawing represents part of a crowd scene, which features one of the figures picking the pocket of another. Although this particular action clearly serves Fo's intention of irreverent demystification, his general configuration of the *Lazarus* is remarkably similar to many versions extant throughout southern Europe and the Near East. According to Emerson Swift, in *The Roman Sources of Christian Art*, the resurrection of Lazarus is one of the most frequently painted scenes in medieval Christian iconography,[26] many versions of which feature the multiple perspective of a crowd of people. The action is invariably more or less centripetally focused—that is, the figures are grouped in semi-circular arrangements around a central axis, that of the "miracle." But perhaps more significant than the striking similarities between all these scenes and Fo's enactment of them, is Fo's one glaring omission: although the paintings invariably feature the figures of Jesus and Lazarus as protagonists of the figural narrative, Fo notably does *not* embody either of these characters; rather, he quite deliberately chooses to restrict his impersonation to the crowd witnessing the event: Jesus and Lazarus may be at the center of the iconic text, the visual narration, but in Fo's demystified version, they are significantly demoted to mere projected absences.

Fo "positions" the fifteen odd characters he chooses to indicate in a semi-circular configuration around an invisible gravesite which he "places" center front. He effects these characters with a kind of staccato, strobe-light effect, introducing them through a precise, swift gestural technique he calls the *invito*, a kind of shorthand acting notation:

> [the *invito* is a] synthesis created by the shortening of the rhythm of images. For the audience, therefore, the transition whereby the character comes onto the stage does not exist; it has been cut out, shortened out. . . . [in this way] the description [of the character is] made by the movement of the actor's body even before he [says] the words describing what [is] happening.[27]

By using this *invito* technique, Fo manages to engage spectatorial collaboration in the creation of a three-dimensional, virtually cinematic "crowd scene" perspective. The mood of the piece, decidedly more carnevalesque than sublime, reflects Fo's contention that the skit is a "satire of everything that contributes the mystical experience"[28] A gatekeeper haggles with the crowd over attendance fees, hawkers sell chairs and refreshments ("Getcha redhots! Hot n'delicious! Bring you right back from the dead!"), latecomers fight with earlybirds for the best seats and old codgers gossip about Jesus's family ("they don't let him go out alone, because he's a little crazy"). When Lazarus's corpse is finally uncovered, reeking and crawling with worms, one entrepreneur takes advantage of the spirited debate over whether Jesus can pull the miracle off by calling for bets. The sketch peaks at the moment of the resurrection, with shouts of celebration, interspersed with the cries of the woman who discovers that her purse has been snatched in the commotion: the final words, ringing out in a kind of staccato opposition are: "Bravo! . . . Ladro (thief) . . . Bravo! . . . Ladro . . . Bravo . . . Ladro!"[29]

In Fo's incredibly complex configuration, then, the very core of the piece, the miracle, is represented by absence—absent protagonists (Jesus and Lazarus), witnessed by a crowd of spectators, which at any given moment exists almost entirely in the imagination of the theatrical spectator, who is thus mirrored, but in a manner which would seem to have escaped at least some of the ideological constraints of a literal mimesis. Meanwhile, the miracle itself, which could be said to represent a liberation from death (significantly linking ancient fertility rituals to the Christian ritual to the theatrical ritual) is undercut by the theft; and it is *precisely* this subversion of the miraculous by the profane which serves as the basis for Fo's own dialogic theatricality. Whether Fo's strategy is ultimately constraining or liberating is a question which is often lost in the dazzling virtuosity of Fo's performance, as he both evokes and exorcises the crowd of characters with such speed and precision that the mind of the spectator is set on a collision course within itself to reconstruct a known event from proffered puzzle pieces that are contradictory, irreverent and finally profanely seductive. French critic Bernard Dort describes the process of piecing together Fo's Lazarus as an adventure in semantics:

> At each moment a double (or triple or quadruple) play of meaning is invested in an image or emotion. . . . By his gestures which remain unfinished—as though suspended between the past and the present—and his words which recall the gestures but which never completely resolve them . . . , Fo addresses nothing but the imagination of the spectator: he literally puts the spectator into movement. He obliges him to adapt himself ceaselessly, to multiply his points of view and perspectives. He forces him into debate.[30]

Fo's dynamic montage is a result of a confluence of carefully constructed framing strategies which are largely borrowed from film techniques, although Fo claims a theatrical lineage for them:

> . . . long before the invention of cinema with all its up-to-date equipment every actor worth his salt managed to compel every spectator with any sensitivity or culture to employ the identical camera, the identical fields and counter-fields of vision, identical universal focus, identical wide-angle lens. . . .[31]

"Compel" would seem to be the operative word here, and indeed Fo's appropriation of filming strategy leads to an interesting dilemma: if, as Laura Mulvey tells us, "cinematic codes create a gaze, a world, and an object, thereby producing an illusion cut to the measure of desire,"[32] then does Fo's utilization of cinematic techniques render him complicitous in the illusion/desire entanglement? Certainly he controls the site of the gaze, but what does it mean when the object "to-be-looked-at," the theatrical icon, is absence, nothingness? To what extent is the *manner* in which he compels focus fundamentally different from that of the filmic "eye"? It is certainly the case that Fo's intervention in the interpretation of his *mise-en-scene*, although intensively manipulative, is nevertheless absolutely dependent on an on-going co-conspiracy with the audience which is absent in the cinematic relationship.

Orchestration of the spectatorial "lens" to which Fo refers requires an acting technique which could be described in semiotic terms as somewhat more indexical than iconic.[33] That is to say that within this configuration, it is the actor's job not to create character or essence, but rather to set up an interpretive code and to act as the mediator of that code for the audience.[34] Again, Fo shapes this role of mediator in cinematic terms, exercising a canny adaptation of the link between ideology and perception

> [which] arises from a particular psychological attitude which on different occasions compels the spectators, almost as though they were using a series of lenses, to frame the images produced by the actors in different ways. The decisive factor is the way the audience is persuaded by the actor to focus on one detail of the action or on the totality of the action, by the use of the lenses unknowingly stored in the individual brain.[35]

This notion of an individual perceptual "lens" links up with De Lauretis's contention that perception is relative to context, a context that must be destabilized in order to break ideology's stranglehold on iconicity;[36] and it is precisely *context*, or conceptual framing, which is the key to Fo's theatrical technique. Fo ensures the perceptual collaboration of his working-class audience by employing a traditional actor's trick he calls the *intervento* to insinuate himself as the crucial intermediary between historical oppression and theatrical liberation. In order to establish this intermediary function, Fo uses the context of medieval fables featuring a *giullare* who is "born without a soul," and can therefore speak out against oppression by refusing to "give into the blackmail of a good conscience."[37] Fo's analogy features himself as the *giullare* while the medieval peasant for whom the *giullare* speaks is clearly Fo's own working-class audience. Within this equation, Fo then manipulates the *intervento*, or disruptive commentary, as a kind of ideological tracking device, to foreground the trans-historical parallels.

An example of this "metatheatrical" manipulation[38] occurs in *La Nascita del Villano* (*The Birth of the Peasant*),[39] a text which Fo incorporates virtually intact from a piece done by the *giullare*, Matazone da Caligano, in the six-teenth century. It features the "miraculous" birth of a peasant from a donkey's fart, followed by the appearance of an angel who stipulates a "dress code" for the peasant, requiring a garment with a convenient slit so he can relieve him without losing time from his work:

> As soon as he's born, in the buff
> Give him an old piece of cloth
> To bag him up with a few stitches
> And make him a good pair of britches
> Pants with a slit—no zipping
> So he doesn't waste any time pissing.[40]

At this point in the presentation, Fo abandons the character of the angel and addresses the audience directly: "You know, this guy seems to have a lot in common with the bosses today!"[41] After telling about a factory in Verona, where the management declared 11:25 a.m. to be the only time for a bathroom break and where the workers when on strike, according to Fo, "[t]o be allowed to pee when they felt the urge,"[42] Fo leads the audience back to a historical perspective by proceeding to impersonate both the landlord and the angel. When the landlord justifies his exploitation by telling the peasant that this is his fate on earth but his immortal soul will transcend terrestial suffering, the angel unwittingly subverts the religious blackmail by blurting out, "How can this stupid serf have a soul when he was blown out by a donkey's fart?"[43]

What the authoritative angel sees as a critical absence, however, Fo identifies as a source of power, forging a bond between the peasant and the *giullare* as blood brothers inn a material struggle; for the immortal soul that they both lack is really nothing more than a kind of spiritual blackmail used to ensure passive behavior on the parts of those who "buy into it." But even more important to the dialectical process than the declarative climax is a catalytic *intervento*, through which Fo has deftly compelled a perceptual link between the medieval peasant and the contemporary factory worker, a configuration which, as one critic notes, is differentiated from a fundamentally static vision ("*Plus ca change . . .*") by the "continuous mobility of the text" which sets itself up as constant interruption, opposition and debate.[44] The complexity of this representational structure undergoes individual permutations in each of Fo's ***Mistero Buffo*** skits.

In ***Le nozze di Cana*** (***The Wedding at Cana***),[45] for exam-ple, the skit which somehow impelled the mute to speak at the Turin mental hospital, Fo creates a direct dialectical opposition between two ideological "matrices," in this case representing divergent interpretations of a biblical story. As in all the medieval pieces, the underlying theme here is the overturning of officially sanctioned, "authorized" versions of gospel stories and church history, to be replaced with a populist notion of religious tradition in which the char-acter Jesus is seen as a working-class hero, described by one observer as "a human, exploited peasant Christ who refutes the injustices of the hypocritical religion of the rich."[46] Again Fo constricts interpretation by constructing a didactic framework for the piece, insuring a perceptual link between Christ and fertility rituals by showing a slide of a *sacre rappresentazione*,[47] depicting a Palm Sunday proces-sion, in which Dionysus, Bacchus and Christ all take part. Using the Brechtian device of eliminating the suspense by telling the fable before enacting it, Fo then explains the significance of the earlier deities to his proposed skit:

> Jesus Christ became Bacchus [who] at a certain point is seen standing on a table, shouting to all the celebrants, "Drink, gentlemen, be merry." Be happy, that's what counts: don't wait for paradise hereafter, paradise is here on earth. [This is] exactly the opposite of the doctrine they teach you from childhood on, when they explain that one must endure, that we are in a vale of tears . . . not everyone can be rich, there are those who

do well and those who do poorly, but everyone will be compensated when we are in heaven . . . be calm, be good, and don't rock the boat . . . Now instead this Jesus Christ of the *giullarta* says, "Rock the boat and be happy!"[48]

In this irreverent configuration, then, Fo represents Christ not only as "just another god," but as an ill-behaved one at that, a rabble rouser, the veritable life of comedy's requisite party. As in the other *giullaresque* sketches, however, the Christ of **The Wedding at Cana** is not directly impersonated by Fo, but is rather a projected absence, an invisible referent of the two oppositional characters alternately "placed" onstage by Fo. Using a technique which Fo calls, *sdoppiamento*, or splitting, Fo sets up a dramatic confrontation between two unlikely antagonists: the first is the archangel, who speaks in the polished Venetian dialect of an aristocrat and affects, as Fo says, "pretty gestures;" he is, of course the *alazon*, or pretender, in the archetypal configuration. Opposing him is a subarticulate, drunken oaf, who speaks in a coarse, peasant dialect peppered with obscenities, and who is barely able to hold himself upright due to his inebriated condition. For the archangel, authority and text are inseparable. As the two struggle for the audience's attention, the archangel repeatedly intones the same litany, as though repetition itself increased credibility:

> (To the drunkard) Be quiet! I must begin because I'm the prologist. (To the audience) Good people, everything that I tell you is true, because it all comes from books and from the Gospels. What comes from them is not fantasy . . .[49]

The drunkard, on the other hand, appeals only to his own experience for veracity:

Me too, what I want to tell you isn't fantasy. I enjoyed a drunkenness so sweet, so beautiful, that I never want to get drunk in this world again, so I won't forget this fantastic drunkenness that is on me now![50]

However "well-spoken" the angel, however, his supposedly divinely sanctioned text is no match for the corporeal subversion of the drunkard. In an apparently benign attempt to cooperate with the edicts of censorship, the drunkard, explores the possibilities of non-verbal communication:

> DRUNKARD: . . . I'll think, think, think, and use my eyes . . . and they'll understand.
>
> ARCHANGEL: No.
>
> D: But I don't make noise with my brain.
>
> A: You're making noise!
>
> D: I'm making noise with my brain? Dammit! I must really be drunk! Holy shit!
>
> A: Don't breathe!
>
> D: What? I can't breathe? Not even with my nose? I'll burst!
>
> A: Burst!

> D: Ah . . . but if I burst, I'll make noise, huh?[51]

Here physical excess and textual purity are in direct conflict and the constant play between the presence and absence of each creates a troubling tableau indeed if Fo's configuration is in any sense "an illusion cut to the measure of desire."[52] According to comic convention, however, the implications are somewhat more direct: forbidden to express himself through his own body, the drunkard proceeds to subvert the physical authority of the angel plucking his feathers, and eventually kicking him offstage. Thus far, the structure of the piece follows the pattern that Ron Jenkins has identified as "a dialectic between freedom and oppression [in which] each slapstick crescendo is orchestrated around a liberating triumph over injustice."[53] Again Fo plays both parts, using the *invito* to defy conventional standards of iconicity: at any given moment, he is a presence addressing an absence, which he has established as a presence in the spectator's imagination. That the "absent" figure is every bit as "real" to the audience as the (temporarily) incarnated one is evidenced by Fo's experience at the mental hospital, which would certainly seem to indicate that his configuration of the absent Other is an empowering strategy for his audience. The voiceless in this case not only identified with the oppressed clown, they were actually enticed by the empty space to join in his revolutionary behavior. On this evidence alone, one might conclude that although Fo's ideological framing devices constrict interpretation somewhat, his use of absence produces a kind of iconic underdetermination, which would seem to invite participation. This is true, not only in the *Cana* dialogue, but also in Fo's staging of the story of the medieval Pope, Boniface.

If the sanctimonious posture of the authoritative archangel is subverted by the finally triumphant voice of the opposing clown in **The Wedding at Cana,** the representational dialectic of **Bonifacio VIII**[54] is somewhat more complex. Iconographically, Fo structures the piece as a processional, although it is important to keep in mind that this configuration is indeed "in mind"—the only figure actually on stage at any given time is Fo himself. Unlike the "heteroglossia"[55] of **Lazarus,** or the dialectical opposition of **The Wedding of Cana, Boniface** is a true monologue—only the protagonist of the piece, the medieval Pope of the title, has a voice. Nevertheless, the silent, subversive forces of a procession of choirboys in the background are no less potently evoked in the minds of the spectators than the irrepressibly voluble drunkard of Cana.

As in the other skits, Fo straddles theatrical "frames," functioning alternatively as the craftsman and the character. As the storyteller with a microphone, he introduces his subject by recounting historical horror tales of Boniface's repressions of both penitential religious orders and the early communards of Lombardy and Piedmont, gleefully punctuating the narration by miming Boniface's grotesque torture techniques, which included nailing dissenters by their tongues to the doors of offended nobility. Then, in a sly shift of historical perspective, Fo assures the audience that the present Pope has nothing whatsoever in common with Boniface, after which he proceeds to tell "Pope stories" which imply just the opposite. Having thus set up a vivid and grotesque analogy between the present Pope and his medieval counterpart, Fo launches into his impersonation of Boniface, who is in the process of getting dressed for an important procession: as he is weighted down by increasingly more opulent garments, Boniface irritably interrupts his liturgical chant to berate his incompetent choirboys, finally threatening one with a tongue hanging. The dialectic in this representation involves an opposition which is set up within the figure of Boniface, himself. Fo foregrounds the Pope and then situates the choirboys behind him, so that Boniface effectively upstages himself each time he turns to admonish them, a configuration which causes him to subvert himself as the voice of authority. In addition, the opulent signs of wealth and power, progressively accumulated upon his body, cause him to be grotesquely weighted down, and finally, literally "tripped up," as one of the choirboys steps on his mantle.

This vision of an arrogant, cruel and grotesquely ornamented Pope is suddenly interrupted when Boniface sees Jesus coming up another street, leading a procession of penitents. When one of his underlings points out that it would be wise to be seen as a humble servant of Christ (in whose name, after all, he supposedly derives his own spiritual authority) Boniface throws off his jewels, smears mud on his face and obsequiously presents himself to Jesus, who doesn't recognize him ("What do you mean, what's the Pope?") After several ludicrous attempts at self-abnegation, the Pope becomes increasingly more impatient ("Pay attention to me, you twit!") Finally he goes to far and is seen to be "flung a long way by a terrible kick in the butt."

Like the clown/drunkard of Cana, "Christ" has presumably been pushed too far. In this case, however, the only visible representation of his revenge, is enacted by the character, Boniface, on himself, as he stumbles grotesquely across the stage, consumed by humiliation and rage. In Fo's brilliant staging configuration, the power that pushes this raging alazon out—the triumphant comic empowerment—emanates from nothing other than absence, an iconicity of nothing. One could argue that Fo has infused this nothing, this absence, with a "Christ" character, but it is clear that whatever is there, it is nowhere if not in the mind of the spectator. If it is a "signifying space," it would seem to signify a force created by the collaborative imagination of performer and audience together, a force which is seen to eject an agent of oppression. Because it is not embodied, this force evades overdetermination. If Fo's use of "iconized absence" is an effective strategy for "denaturaliz[ing] identity," in Kaja Silverman's terms, "by emphasizing at every conceivable juncture its imaginary bases,"[56] then it would certainly seem to be a promising scheme for breaking down an oppressively encoded entanglement of iconicity and ideology in theatrical representation. By emphasizing the mechanics of perception, Fo has transferred the "burden of iconicity . . . from the representation to the viewer's judgement,"

and it would seem that he has considerably empowered the viewer's judgement in the process.[57]

As I have indicated throughout this essay, Fo's theatrical framing devices create a deliberate interpretative constraint, a kind of "forced perspective," which is scarcely free of ideological entanglements. Nevertheless, Fo has succeeded, at the very least, in setting up an extraordinarily dynamic theatrical dialogue. Indeed Fo has said that the purpose of his theatre is to create a debate, that he doesn't want his theatre to "rain down vertically on people's heads."[58] By presenting a kind of fragmented iconicity—fragments of characters, fragments of actions and interactions—Fo has shaped a dramatic montage in which the shifting perspectives force a sense of community. There is no time to identify privately with one character or point of view; the spectator is too busy in every given moment, working on the collective creation of the event, an event which is tossed back and forth through the time and space of the theatrical protoplasm like Brecht's atomic particles of humankind.

NOTES

An earlier version of this paper was presented at the Association for Theatre in Higher Education conference in New York City in August, 1989.

[1]Dario Fo, *The Tricks of the Trade*, trans. Joe Farrell (London: Methuen, 1991), 131.

[2]Keir Elam, *The Semiotics of Theatre and Drama* (London: Methuen, 1980), 21.

[3]Marvin Carlson, *Theatre Semiotics: Signs of Life* (Bloomington: Indiana University Press, 1990), 76.

[4]Elam, *Semiotics*, 23.

[5]Teresa de Lauretis, *Alice Doesn't: Feminism, Semiotics, Cinema* (Bloomington: Indiana University Press, 1984), 45.

[6]For extremely useful overviews of the theoretical implications of female subjectivity in theatrical performance, see: Sue-Ellen Case, *Feminism and Theatre* (New York: Methuen, 1988); Jill Dolan, *The Feminist Spectator as Critic* (Ann Arbor: University of Michigan Press, 1988); and Gale Austin, *Feminist Theories for Dramatic Criticism* (Ann Arbor: University of Michigan Press, 1990).

[7]Laura Mulvey, "Visual Pleasure and Narrative Cinema," *Screen* 16 (Autumn 1975): 6-18. Reprinted in *Issues in Feminist Film Criticism*, ed. Patricia Erens (Bloomington: Indiana University Press, 1990), 28-40.

[8]Ibid., 30.

[9]Bertolt Brecht, *Brecht on Theatre*, trans. John Willet (New York Hill & Wang, 1964), 15, 277.

[10]Walter Benjamin, "The Author as Producer," in *Art After Modernism*, ed. Brian Wallis (Boston: Godine, 1984), 306.

[11]Roland Barthes, "The Tasks of a Brechtian Criticism," trans. Peter W. Mathers, *New Theatre Quarterly* 9 (Spring, 1979): 30.

[12]Elin Diamond, "Brechtian Theory/Feminist Theory: Toward a Gestic Feminist Criticism," *The Drama Review* 32 (Spring 1988): 84.

[13]Elin Diamond, "(In)Visible Bodies in Churchill's Theatre," *Theatre Journal* 40 (May 1988): 188-204. See also the following articles by Elin Diamond: "Closing No Gaps: Aphra Behn, Caryl Churchill, and Empire," in Phyllis R. Randall, ed. *Caryl Churchill: A Casebook* (New York: Garland, 1988), 161-74; "Refusing the Romanticism of Identity: Narrative Interventions in Churchill, Benmussa, Duras," *Theatre Journal* 37 (Oct. 1985): 273-86; and "Mimesis, Mimicry, and the 'True-Real,'" *Modern Drama* 32 (March 1989): 58-72.

[14]Diamond, "(In)Visible Bodies," 191.

[15]Dario Fo, *Mistero Buffo* (Veron: Bertoni, 1974). The title translates as *Comic Mystery*, and refers to a type of travesty of medieval mystery plays. Fo explains the term in his introduction to this edition: "*Mystery* was the word already in use in the first and second century after Jesus Christ to designate a spectacle, a sacred representation . . . thus *Mystery* means, 'sacred representation,' *Mistero Buffo* means, 'grotesque spectacle.'" My translation.

[16]Dario Fo, "Lettura della Disputatio mensium de Bonvesin de la Riva," *Quaderni di Teatro* 3 (1979): 75.

[17]Laura Mulvey, "Visual Pleasure and Narrative Cinema," *Screen* 16 (Autumn 1975): 6-18. Reprinted in *Issues in Feminist Film Criticism*, ed. Patricia Erens (Bloomington: Indiana University Press, 1990), 28-40.

[18]See Marco de Marinis, *Semiotica del Teatro* (Milan: Bompiani, 1982) and Franco Ruffini, "Semiotica del Teatro: recognizione degli stude," *Biblioteca Teatrale* 9 (1974): 34-81.

[19]Fo, *Tricks*, 58.

[20]Ron Jenkins, "Clowns, Politics and Miracles: The Epic Satire of Dario Fo," *American Theatre* 3 (1986): 15.

[21]Mikhail Bakhtin, *Rabelais and His World* (Bloomington: Indiana University Press, 1984), 71.

[22]Ibid., 83.

[23]Dario Fo, *Mistero Buffo*, trans. Ed Emery, ed. Stuart Hood (London: Methuen, 1988), 37.

[24]Ibid., 64.

[25]My description of the staging of the "Lazarus" and "Pope Boniface VIII" pieces is based on my observations of Fo's performance of the skits at the Yale drama school in April, 1984.

[26]Emerson Swift, *The Roman Sources of Christian Art* (Westwood, Conn: Greenwood, 1951), 55.

[27]Dario Fo and Franca Rame, *Theatre Workshops at Riverside Studios*, London (London: Red Notes, 1983), 19.

[28]Tony Mitchell, "Dario Fo's 'Mistero Buffo': Popular Theatre, the Giullare, and the Grotesque," *Theatre Quarterly* 36 (1979): 12.

[29]Fo, *Buffo* (1974): 100-110. Translations are mine, unless otherwise noted.

[30]Bernard Dort, "Dario Fo: Un Acteur Epique," *Travail Theatral* 15 (1974): 116. My translation.

[31]Fo, *Tricks*, 13

[32]Mulvey, "Visual Pleasure," 11.

[33]Elam, *Semiotics*, 26. Elam identifies the indexical function as a "pointing to." His observation that "there are instances where what predominates on stage is a 'pointing to' rather than an imagistic mode of signifying" would seem to apply directly to Fo's technique in the *Buffo* skits.

[34]For a comprehensive discussion on the problems of a fixed "typology of signs" in relation to performance analysis, see Patrice Pavis, *Languages of the Stage: Essays in the Semiology of Theatre* (New York: PAJ, 1982): 14-21.

[35]Fo, *Tricks*, 44.

[36]For example, in discussing Eco's critique of iconic signs, De Lauretis explains: "There is no such thing as an iconic sign; there are only visual texts, whose pertinent units are established, *if at all*, by the context. . . . The key concepts here are context, pertinence, and purposefulness (of the codes)." De Lauretis, *Alice*, 47.

[37]Erminia Artese, *Dario Fo Parla di Dario Fo* (Cosenza: Lerici, 1977), 140. My translation.

[38]Marina Cappa and Roberto Nepoti, *Dario Fo* (Rome: Gremese, 1982), 80.

[39]Fo, *Buffo* (1974), 89-99.

[40]Fo, *Buffo* (1974). All quotations "The Birth of the Peasant," are from this edition and are my translations.

[41]Fo, *Buffo* (1974), 92.

[42]Ibid.

[43]99.

[44]Cappa, Fo, 81.

[45]Fo, *Buffo* (1974), 56-72. Subsequent quotations from "The Wedding at Cana" are from this edition and are my translations.

[46]Lianfranco Binni, *Dario Fo*, Il Castoro 123 (1977): 52.

[47]"Medieval mystery play." For an excellent overview of the *sacre rappresentationi*, see, Cesare Molinari, *Lo Spettacolo drammatico nei momenti della sul storia dalle origini ad oggi* (Milan: Mondadori, 1972), 93-108.

[48]Fo, *Buffo* (1974), 56.

[49]Ibid., 59.

[50]Ibid.

[51]Ibid., 61.

[52]Mulvey, "Visual Pleasure," 11.

[53]Ron Jenkins, "Dario Fo: The Roar of the Clown," *The Drama Review*, 30 (1986): 178.

[54]Fo, *Buffo* (1974): 110-127. Translations mine.

[55]Mikhail Bakhtin, *The Dialogic Imagination: Four Essays*, ed. Michael Holquist, trans. Caryl Emerson and Michael Holquist (Austin: University of Texas Press, 1981). According to Bakhtin, *heteroglossia* connotes, "a multiplicity of social voices and a wide variety of their links and interrelationships" (p. 263), Bakhtin conceptualized *heteroglossia* as a means of indicating "the primacy of context over text" (428).

[56]Kaja Silverman, "Fassbinder and Lacan: A Reconsideration of Gaze, Look and image," *Camera Obscura* 19 (1989): 62.

[57]De Lauretis, *Alice*, 64. In her chapter on "Imaging," De Lauretis draws from theories of visual perception to suggest strategies for, "construct(ing) the terms of another frame of reference, another measure of desire" (68).

[58]Dario Fo, "Some Aspects of Popular Theatre," trans. Tony Mitchell *New Theatre Quarterly* 1 (1985): 136.

ACCIDENTAL DEATH OF AN ANARCHIST

Suzanne Cowan (essay date 1979)

SOURCE: "Dario Fo, Politics and Satire: An Introduction to *Accidental Death of an Anarchist*," in *Theater*, Vol. 10, No. 2, Spring 1979, pp. 7-11.

[*Cowan presents a brief survey of Fo's career and the background of* Accidental Death of an Anarchist, *and offers a concise appreciation of the play itself.*]

I The Author

Dario Fo is one of Italy's most popular and successful playwrights. He is also an actor, director, choreographer, set and costume designer, painter, graphic artist, poet, musician, scholar, cultural organizer and political activist. Such extraordinary versatility approaches the fifteenth and sixteenth century ideal of the cultivated individual; it may not seem surprising that Fo comes from the country which gave birth to the popular concept of the "Renaissance man." However, in the most fundamental respect, his work arises out of the specific conditions of contemporary Italian society, and reflects the profound social, economic and political tensions which have marked that society since the fall of the Fascist regime.

Born in 1926, son of a working-class family from northern Lombardy, Fo inherited from his immediate environment both a strongly democratic, anti-fascist political persuasion, and a love for popular drama in the form of highly imaginative "yarns" invented and spontaneously narrated by local townspeople. As a boy, he showed marked talent for drawing, and was sent to study art at the famed Brera Academy in Milan. However, the atmosphere of turmoil and political ferment which pervaded Italy during the period following Italy's liberation from Fascism and German occupation inspired him to become more directly involved in the collective life of his city. After a few years studying architecture at the University, his growing interest in stage design and decoration, as well as a gift for improvisational comic narration, led him to the theater. Following a debut as bit-performer in some flashy musical variety shows, he wrote and co-directed two very successful satirical revues, performed in an experimental style similar to that of the cabaret theater. These shows, produced in 1953 and 1954, launched Fo both as a writer-director-performer and as a thorn in the side of the ruling conservative establishment. Due to their outspoken jibes against the country's major political and social institutions, they were pounced upon by the press. Right-wing critics subjected them to such a barrage of pressure and government censorship that they were eventually forced to close down.

After a brief stint as film actor and set-designer, Fo returned to the theater with a series of short sketches based on a wide variety of comic techniques, particularly nineteenth century semi-popular melodrama and French farce.

In these dramatic "collages," Fo was assisted by his wife, the gifted actress (now also a producer and director in her own right), Franca Rame. The two formed their own stage company, *La Compagnia Dario Fo-Franca Rame*, in 1959, and for the next nine years enjoyed great popular and commercial success with a series of seven "bourgeois" comedies: so-called because they were performed mainly before middle-class audiences within the regular professional theater circuit. Despite this fact, the plays reflected Fo's continuing research into the roots of popular drama. They also extended his use of grotesque comedy as an instrument of political and social criticism, attacking such formidable institutions as the Italian governmental bureaucracy, armed forces, Catholic church, major corporations, and penal system. The last and most technically ambitious of these comedies, produced in 1967, was a ferocious denunciation of United States imperialism and the war in Vietnam.

During this period, Fo had interrupted his primary theatrical activity twice: the first time in 1962, when he and Franca Rame wrote, directed and starred in Italy's most popular television series (from which they resigned when the state-controlled television network attempted to censor the politically controversial elements of their script), and later in 1966, in order to direct a spectacle of traditional songs, performed by non-professional musicians from rural and working-class backgrounds. However, Fo's definitive break with the commercial theater occurred only in 1968, when the convergence of a number of political struggles—the world-wide protest movement against the Vietnam war, the French students' and workers' uprising, cultural revolution in China, and a wave of labor unrest and social agitation throughout Italy—led him to seek a new way of communicating with a new kind of public. Like thousands of other European artists at that time, he became convinced that it was indispensable to transform the products of his creative labor from market commodities into instruments of social and political change. He therefore determined to "stop playing the jester of the bourgeoisie," and place his skills directly at the service of the Italian working class and revolutionary movement.

The *Compagnia Fo-Rame* was dissolved, and in its place arose *Nuova Scena*, a co-operative theatrical organization allied with the Italian Communist Party. In addition to providing financial backing and publicity, the Party made available to *Nuova Scena* its vast, well-organized cultural and recreational network. This permitted the troupe to perform in numerous locations traditionally ignored by professional touring companies: factories, union halls, workmen's association and local party headquarters, agricultural co-operatives, and so on. In its two years of existence, *Nuova Scena* presented four major plays, all written, directed and principally performed by Dario Fo. The performances were greeted with enthusiastic acclaim by working-class audiences throughout the country. Their unorthodox "third act," consisting of open debate about the issues which had been raised by a play, kept spectators sitting in the improvised performing areas sometimes for hours after the last lines had been recited. Despite their success with the public, however, the plays drew increasing criticism and disapproval from the Communist Party. They took open issue with a number of strategic choices and commitments made by the Party leadership, and, what was even worse, invited the rank-and-file to subject these choices to open debate. This threatened to carry participatory democracy a bit too far for cautious party functionaries, who began threatening to censor the shows and finally went so far as to declare them "off-limits" to local militants. Consequently, in 1970, following extensive self-criticism, debate and internal friction, Fo and Rame (along with several other members of the company) seceded from *Nuova Scena* and founded *Il Collecttivo Teatrale La Comune*: a completely self-supporting theater collective, independent of both "bourgeois" and "revisionist" cultural organizations, and linked to the revolutionary left wing of the working-class movement.

Since the formation of *La Comune*, Fo has written and produced over twenty-five works: plays, "collages" consisting of short monologues and sketches, scenarios, hurriedly constructed shows intended as a response to specific recent political events or local conditions, new folk music shows. He has also composed poems, songs, and satirical articles; performed his plays in several European countries, visited China, appeared again on television (this time without threat of censorship, since restrictions on the public media were largely lifted with the passage of a reform statute in 1976); taught courses on popular theater and poetry; directed an opera at *La Scala*, organized a vast cultural-political network with chapters all over the country; spent time in jail, given hundreds of speeches, and become involved in a myriad of political struggles, ranging from a tug-of-war with the recalcitrant Milan city council over control of a large, neglected building *La Comune* wished to use for its permanent headquarters, to a national campaign in defense of civil rights for both "political" and "common" prisoners.

To give a full account of Dario Fo's theatrical career would really be tantamount to writing a history of postwar Italy, because his work can only be understood as a continuous, uniquely creative response to the major social and political developments of the past thirty years. Since his break with the commercial stage, this relationship might even be described as one of mutual conditioning, since his "theater" (using the term in its broadest sense) has become not only a critique of prevailing society, but an attempt to change it, by contributing—as directly as art can ever allow—to the struggle for socialism.

II BACKGROUND OF THE PLAY

Late in the afternoon of December 12, 1969, a bomb exploded inside the *Banca Nazionale dell'Agricolture* in downtown Milan, killing sixteen people and wounding eighty-eight. The event had enormous political repercussions all over Italy. It touched off an immediate police roundup of left-wing activists and sympathizers; throughout the country, members of "far-left" organizations, and numerous Communist Party militants as well, were arrested and brought to police headquarters for identification. Many were held for days without bail or legal assistance of any kind.

Soon after the terrorist attack, a young Milanese railroad worker named Giuseppe Pinelli, member of a small anarchist group, was summoned to central police headquarters for "questioning." He was kept in prison for three days, during which time he was repeatedly and brutally interrogated by the police. On December 15, during the course of an examination by Inspector Luigi Calabresi and several other officers, he "precipitated" from the fourth-story window of the building. Pinelli's death and was officially declared a suicide, and taken as a confession of guilt. In the meantime, an ill-starred Roman anarchist named Pietro Valpreda, along with two other members of his group, were arrested in a police dragnet and formally indicted for the bombing. They remained in jail for nearly four years before being brought to trial.

During the months which followed Pinelli's death and the arrest of the three anarchists, thousands of political activists were engaged in an intense effort to discover the truth about the crimes. They were operating under the most unfavorable circumstances: the police and law courts had responded to the bombing by launching a fierce campaign of repression and intimidation against the left. Names of some 14,000 workers, students, union organizers and political militants were placed on file with the police; there were hundreds of arrests and searches. The official organs of the mass left-wing parties reflected the distress and bewilderment of their leadership. It was primarily due to the work of the independent left that, in such an atmosphere, the real facts of the case could be brought to light. When they did emerge, they bore scandalous and frightening implications.

Thousands of reports, documents, testimonies and pieces of circumstantial evidence, gathered and painstakingly correlated over many months, led to the inescapable conclusion that the bombings of Piazza Fontana (site of the *Banca dell'Agricolture*) had been planned and executed by members of a neo-Fascist organization. Moreover, these attacks did not constitute an isolated incident. Similar crimes of lesser magnitude had been committed by other right-wing groups, working with the protection and complicity of international fascist and paramilitary organizations, large industrialists, the armed forces, secret service, police, law courts, and sectors of the government itself, supported in part by the American Central Intelligence Agency. What emerged, then, was the picture of a systematic campaign of violence and terror, in which "small" fascists (like the two who were eventually tried and convicted for the bombings, only to be released on a technicality a few years later) figured as little more than errand-boys at the service of much higher authorities. The basic objective of this campaign, commonly known as the "strategy of tension," was to create such an intense climate of fear and mistrust, that the military and right-wing forces would at last be granted authority to exterminate the entire radical opposition and seize control of the organs of state power.

The wave of public protest and anger aroused by Pinelli's death forced the Italian high court to open an investigation into its causes. A good part of the *dossier* on this official "suicide," as well as transcripts of informal statements made by people directly or indirectly involved in the case, were made available to the public through "information leaks" and the work of persistent investigators. As a traditional ally of the police and one of the country's leading reactionary institutions, the court attempted both to suppress information about the case and to obliterate all traces of evidence pointing toward fascist responsibility for the terrorist attacks. Pinelli's widow and mother, supported by a wide range of progressive organizations, repeatedly attempted to prevent the court from burying pertinent information and "whitewashing" the police. In the course of a lengthy series of inquiries and hearings, the "official" version of the event was exposed as a threadbare tissue of contradictions, misstatements and outright lies. Nevertheless, the court at last ruled that there were insufficient grounds for indictment. Presiding judge Vittorio Occorsio ordered the investigation definitively closed. Charges against police chief Marcello Guida, principal investigator Calabresi, and the other officers involved in the case were dropped, and Pinelli's widow was denied legal compensation even for the costs of the trial.

III THE PLAY

Morte accidentale di un anarchico, which Dario Fo called "a grotesque farce about a tragic farce," had its debut in December, 1970, almost exactly one year after the events which inspired it. It is built upon one central dramatic device: the charade—or, to be more precise, an interlocking network of charades. From the play itself, which "pretends" to be a transposition onto Italian soil of an event which actually took place in the United States, to the chameleon-like central character, the Fool, the entire comedy revolves around a series of equivocations and impostures. The most important of these are not discernable within the text of the play itself, because they presuppose a knowledge of the real people after whom the main characters were modelled. In this comedy *à clé*, the Casually Dressed Inspector is Luigi Calabresi, head of the team which conducted Pinelli's interrogation; the Chief is recognizable as Marcello Guida, primary spokesman for the police department and charged with the task of covering up its responsibility for the anarchist's death; and the newspaper woman is a thinly-veiled portrait of Camilla Cederna, a courageous, independent reporter who played a fundamental role in exposing the *pista nera*, or "black path" of evidence leading to fascist responsibility for the Milan bank bombing. Only the protagonist plays himself, and of course this "self" is composed of nothing more than layer upon layer of disguises.

Rather than the *dénouement* typical of classic farce, *Accidental Death of an Anarchist* "resolves" itself in another pretense, a genial trick of mirrors. No sooner does the false

judge meet his fate, in an "accident" almost identical to the one which had killed the hapless anarchist, than the real judge (or is he?) appears on the scene—to begin the play all over again, in a manner of speaking. Thus the layers of illusion and make-believe which were applied, one upon the other, throughout the dramatic action, are now stripped away again; but only to reveal a new charade in place of the original one. The grotesque comedy of false appearances extends even to the formal structure of the plot.

Fo's clever manipulation of the "play-within-a-play" paradigm, and the artifice of a theater piece constructed like a Chinese box, are certainly pleasing to the imagination. However, behind the purely aesthetic appeal of this design lies a clearly political intent. While the show is based entirely upon documentary fact, its outlandish trickery and caricature prevent it from ever falling into flat, naturalistic description of events. It creates a dialectical synthesis of chronicle and fantasy, social criticism and circus tomfoolery. Most important is the analogy constantly suggested between "reality" and "fiction." The Fool's successive disguises are preposterous, but no more so than the all-embracing disguise which dominates the entire play: the legal cover-up of the facts behind Pinelli's death. By maintaining the play's "charade," extending its flamboyant pretense all the way around to the original starting point, Fo creates a continuous process of deception. In this respect, *Accidental Death of an Anarchist* is a faithful reproduction of the real process of deception, the true grotesque comedy, which—like the play itself—does not begin with the death of an anarchist, nor end with a judicial inquiry, but continues to repeat itself over and over again in the form of repression and violence, official lies and conspiracies of power.

Pina Piccolo (essay date 1986)

SOURCE: "Farce as the Mirror of Bourgeois Politics: *Morte Accidentale di un Anarchico,*" in *Forum Italicum,* Vol. 20, No. 2, Fall 1986, pp. 170-81.

[*Piccolo analyzes Fo's use of farce in* Accidental Death of an Anarchist *to achieve "his political goal of demystification of power."*]

> —MATTO . . . Allora, come diceva Totò in una vecchia
> farsa, il questore in questura a quest'ora non c'era . . .

These lines, sardonically delivered by Il Matto in *Morte accidentale di un anarchico* by Dario Fo, offer a microcosm of the comic sources used by the playwright. Whether the play be a "giullare" polyphonic monologue as *Mistero buffo,* or a farce-play, as *Morte accidentale,* diverse forms of the popular comic tradition such as the farce, *varietà, fabulatori* storytelling techniques, *beffe* are combined to produce a theatrical work bent on demystification.

In focusing on Fo's innovative treatment of traditional farce, taking *Morte accidentale* as an example, this article will link the aesthetic choices made by the playwright to his political goal of demystification of power.

As the polyphonic monologue is, for Fo, the best vehicle to express demystification of viewpoint, the farce is the tool that best lends itself to the recreation of contemporary ruling class' politics. Its accelerated rhythms, its inclination towards deception as modus operandi, its freedom of movement unbound by the demands of rigorous logic allow it to mimick the unfolding of today's politics of repression, of bourgeois alliances, of the network of mystification those in power use to maintain legitimacy.

A first analysis of the play reveals its construction as a series of Chinese boxes governed by the dialectic between deception and discovery. Enclosed by this structure, the comic is unleashed in a variety of ways: through the switching of point of view, carnivalesque reversals, parody, breeches of communication due to intersecting levels of deception, one liners based on the awakening of dormant metaphors, gags, and so on. Paradoxically, the farce, a standard-bearer of fictionality in the theater, is entrusted with the task of separating truth from falsehood.

FARCE: MECHANISM AND DEMYSTIFICATION

The connection between farce and politics was pointed out by Karl Marx in *The Eighteenth Brumaire of Louis Bonaparte*: referring to re-occurrences in history, Marx said that when history repeats itself twice, the first time it is as tragedy—the second time as farce. Fo reverses this chronological order to two levels of reality: bourgeois politics heaps tragedy on the oppressed in real life (as in the case of the anarchist Pinelli), but the stage must recreate it as farce in order to demystify power and instill rage leading to political action. In fact, in explaining his grotesque treatment of a tragic event such as Pinelli's death, Fo said:

> abbiamo preferito liberare lo spettatore dal timor panico del Potere, questo 007, questo gigante con i piedi di argilla. . . . Non vogliamo che lo spettatore vada a casa contento perché si è indignato abbastanza e si è liberato e ora è in pace con se stesso. Vogliamo capire con il pubblico cosa c'è sotto quella macchina, perché esiste, se ne abbiamo colpa noi, come si fa a combatterla. Vogliamo smontare a pezzi tutte le macchine del potere: verranno fuori costruzioni grottesche.[1]

Power defined as a machine lends itself easily to representation by farce, a theatrical genre that does not hide its fictionality, with the pretense of bringing a "slice of life," a genre that declares loudly its essence of theatrical machine. Conversely, something that is a construction can be easily dismantled, and thus in farce Fo's enthusiasm for demystification finds an ideal tool.

Studies in the farce by Bentley first, and Jessica Milner-Davis later, have stressed the reliance of the genre on the mechanical, on repetition, on accumulation, on reversal and symmetry. According to Milner-Davis, so predictable is the structure of this art form that a typology of the genre can be easily developed, classifying the products as humiliation farces, deception farces, reversal ones and so on.[2] Bentley points out that the mechanical characteristics of the farce inhibit the function of social criticism: its distorted mirror reflects a world "in the image of the Apes" thus leaving no constructive counter-model.[3] This objection is overruled by Fo, who seeks the constructive moment not in the representation itself but in the debate and action it engenders. For him, the farce, then, can be a weapon of criticism preparing the ground for political action.

Unlike Bentley, Fo maintains that the element of distortion belongs more to reality than to the idiosyncrasies of the genre. In the epoch of the decay of imperialism, history with a capital "H" has lost all pretense of awesome dignity that characterizes tragedy; instead it moves and unfolds with the less-than-dignified, jerky and disjointed tempo of the farce. Unlike the period Marx described, in current times there can be no Napoleons to lend a tragic dimension to bourgeois politics. We are left with the Questore of *Morte accidentale*, the Fanfani of *Il Fanfani rapito* and the Agnelli of *Clacson, trombette e pernacchi*, who lend themselves marvelously to farce.

In addition, the mechanical paradigm that governs the farce can be seen functioning for those who in real life are part of the State machine as well. Individual personality, creativity and loyalty can occasionally create interferences in the smooth functioning of the State, but in the final analysis it is the needs of those who have set up the mechanism that guide or sacrifice the individual bureaucrat or politician. This situation was recreated in a very effective manner in the farce *Clacson, trombette e pernacchi* (1981). In the scene dealing with the Moro kidnapping and the decision of the State to sacrifice a prominent and loyal political figure, Fo highlighted with an "about face" how the situation would have been different had Agnelli (the owner of the State) been kidnapped. In that case, the rigid mechanisms of the State would have become "haywire" and more "flexible" measures adopted.

Thus for Fo the minor, neglected genre of farce becomes the appropriate mirror that reflects, undistorted, the behavior of rulings circles: like them it makes no bones about disguise and trickery, like them it creates and follows mechanisms.

L'ANARCHICO: ACT I

Following Brecht's prescription to sing of dark times when the times are such, in December 1970, Dario Fo staged the premiere of *Morte accidentale di un anarchico*[4] (commonly abbreviated *L'anarchico*). The events that inspired Fo's play, while tragic in their outcome, were no less farcical than farce itself. Almost precisely a year earlier, on December 12, 1969, a young railroad worker, Pino Pinelli, member of an anarchist circle, died by "accidentally" precipitating from the fourth story window of police headquarters in Milan. He had been brought in three days earlier during a nation-wide round up of leftists following an explosion at the Banca Nazionale del-l'Agricoltura in Milan. The bomb had left sixteen dead and eighty-eight wounded. The authorities held the Left responsible for the act. Thus thousands brought in for questioning were denied bail and legal assistance, many were brutally interrogated and detained well beyond the legal limit. Pinelli was among these, but unlike the rest he lost his life in the process. The official police version of the "accident" and the press called it a suicide, a tacit admission of guilt on Pinelli's part. In spite of harsh repression and renewed efforts to cover it up, in a year's time, the Left, and in particular its revolutionary wing, was able to discredit the police version of the an-archist's death. It pointed to the neo-fascists as authors of the bombings and linked all this up to a strategy employed by rightist forces within the government and the army, *la strategia della tensione*.[5] *L'anarchico* does not take the form of a documentary reconstruction of these events. In fact, the plot structure draws heavily from other theatrical precedents, notably Gogol's *The Inspector General*. From that play, Fo takes the situation of concern created in a guilty bureaucracy by the arrival of an inspector, but unlike Gogol, he uses the mechanisms of deceit and discovery for counter-informational purposes. In fact, this time authentic police reports with all their incongruities and gaps serve as a foundation for the movement of the farce. The police characters are modeled after the real police authorities in-volved in the cover-up. The journalist is highly reminiscent of Camilla Cederna, the reporter who investigated the case for *L'Espresso*.

Il Matto, a modern day version of the Fool, who has been certified insane by the proper institutions of the State, is the dynamic force that is unleashed in the play. Like most of Fo's protagonists, Il Matto is a mixture of the Knave and of the Fool, using the qualities of cunning and candor whenever appropriate to the goal of demystification. The continuous switching from one type to the other causes disorientation to those who seek to mystify. Il Matto enjoys unrestrained freedom in organizing situations and *coups de théâtre*, in making and shifting alliances with the other characters, in changing his persona to play various arms of the State.

The play starts off at police headquarters, in the office of Police Inspector Bertozzo, who is interrogating a suspect charged with impersonating a psychiatrist. This first situ-ation is the largest and all encompassing of the Chinese boxes, the one situation that gives rise to the hilarity of the last part of Act II. In relating to Bertozzo details about his histrionism, *i.e.* his mania for impersonating different char-acters, Il Matto resorts to procedures typical of grotesque realism.[6] As in the catalogues and series originating in carnivalesque culture, the highly heterogeneous is found in a contiguous position when Il Matto says he has im-personated a captain of the *bersaglieri*, a naval engineer, a surgeon and a bishop.

However, his greatest dream remains that of playing the judge. A large part of the first scene prepares the ground for the figure of the judge which will have a prominent role throughout the farce. In his description of judges, Il Matto performs one of the first acts of demystification involving switching of point of view. After comparing the deleterious effects of old age on the factory worker, the bank teller, the miner, all of whom are dismissed because of poor health or low productivity, Il Matto describes the judge, the one person on whom age bestows the virtue of Solomonic wisdom:

> Vedi dei vecchietti di cartone tutti impaludati: cordoni, mantellini di ermellino a tubo con le righe d'oro che sembrano tante comparse del Fornaretto di Venezia, traballanti, con delle facce da tappi della val Gardena . . . con due paia d'occhiali legati con le catenelle, che se no li perdono . . . non si ricordano mai dove li hanno appoggiati. Ebbene 'sti personaggi, hanno il potere di distruggere o salvare uno come e quando vogliono. . . .

(144)

Here demystification is accomplished through degradation: the anachronistic vestments, aimed at inspiring awe for the institutions of justice and to indicate their continuity with the past, are degraded to the rank of costumes worn by extras in an amateur production of a minor play, the very physiognomy of wisdom is likened to the face of a lush from an unglorious valley. Old age in its shortcomings is emphasized by the two pairs of spectacles held by chains, but any sweetness possibly evoked by a grandfatherly figure is promptly exorcised by the mention that "these characters" (again the deception of the stage) are in charge of people's lives and deaths.

Again, the judge appears at the closing of the scene, this time in a predominantly mimic dimension. Dismissed by a highly irascible Bertozzo, Il Matto returns to reclaim his papers but finds the office empty. Snooping around he disposes of warrants and complaints, finds the police depositions regarding Pinelli's case and he is about to leave when, with farcical precision, the telephone rings. Il Matto picks it up and spurred by the suggestions of his interlocutor claims to be a certain inspector Anghiari of Rome. He learns from the Sporty Inspector, who is phoning him from the office in which Pinelli was interrogated, that a reviewing judge is being sent by the central government to look into the anarchist's case. Il Matto-Anghiari plays into the fears of the Sporty Inspector by telling him he knows the reviewing judge, an anti-fascist stickler for justice who spent ten years in prison during Mussolini's times. After hanging up, an enthusiastic Matto practices the demeanor appropriate to a "Democratic" judge, one that might instill terror into the hearts of the police.

The second scene opens utilizing intersecting bits of de-ception. While on the phone, Il Matto had been pro-voked by the Sporty Inspector suggesting that both himself (Anghiari) and his colleague Bertozzo could not wait to see the nefarious effects the reviewing judge would have on his career and that of his boss, the Chief of Police who had formerly been a guard in one of Mussolini's jails. The Sporty Inspector avenges himself by giving the candid Bertozzo a black eye and then comes back into his office massaging his fist. A mysterious and severe figure, darkly clad inquires as to the source of the mechanical action—could it be a tic, a sign of hyprocrisy, a hint of insecurity, or feelings of guilt? Annoyed by the intruder's rudeness, the Sporty Inspector bangs his fist on the table, eliciting the following response from Il Matto.

> MATTO: Impulsivo! Ecco la controprova! Dica la verità, non è un tic . . . lei ha dato un pugno a qualcuno non più di un quarto d'ora fa, confessi!

(149)

Mimicking police methods of interrogation and deduction, Il Matto relies on a breech between the levels of deception. He had set up the Sporty Inspector to hit Bertozzo in the preceding round of deception, now on the second round he seeks to impress the inspector as all knowing, taking advantage of the fact that the inspector does not know his identity from round one. Having introduced himself as the reviewing judge, and demanding the full collaboration of the inspector and the chief of police, he seeks to increase the anxiety of the guilty police authorities. Again with the same techniques, Il Matto asks whether the police knew of his arrival. The inspector denies it and Il Matto points to his pulsating vein, a tic which conveniently (in a genre fond of the mechanical) acts as a lie detector and a further threat to the police attempt at cover-up.

This second box of deception is organized mainly around the police versions of Pinelli's death. Il Matto disorients the two policemen pretending alternatively to be interested in unmasking the cover-up or in corroborating their story. Demystification is achieved by different means ranging from carnivalesque reversals to explosions of logic *a la* good soldier Schweick. In the first instance, Il Matto gives the police a taste of their own medicine. According to the first version of the events, the anarchist jumped in a crisis of depression caused by prospects of losing his job and reputation. The police, using one of their usual tricks to extort a confession, had in fact claimed that his comrade and friend from Rome, the anarchist Valpreda, had confessed to planting the bombs and therefore there was no escape for him.

Il Matto, playing the scrupulous judge chord, set up his *beffa* by telling the policemen that the central government had decided to use them as scapegoats to quell a furious public opinion scandalized by the overt miscarriage of justice represented by Pinelli's death. Faced in their turn with the prospect of losing their jobs and reputation, as victims of the *Ragion di Stato* and as interchangeable puppets of a higher mechanism, the two are disconsolate. But as Il Matto proves, it takes more than psychological depression to leap out of a high fourth floor window. In fact as Il Matto forcibly drags them toward the window urging them to throw themselves and pushing them, they have to admit that external force, is necessary in order to make the leap.

The most spectacular of reversals, however, is experienced as the judge now playing on the collaborating chord, pretends to aid the policemen in finding *una versione organica* (a jab at Italian political phraseology), a plausible version of the events. Since according to a second version four hours had elapsed between the police's announcement of Valpreda's confession and the leap, Il Matto fills the four hours with attempts by the police to cheer up Pinelli. Pushing carnivalesque reversal to its limits Il Matto has the police claiming a weak spot for railroad workers who remind them of choochoo trains, a weakness that led them to sing, in a chorus, the hymn of the anarchists in order to help improve Pinelli's mood.

Another method of fighting mystification practiced by Il Matto is that of exploding the logic of those in power. As the policemen justify their serious suspicions about Pinelli's implication in a previous bombing at a railroad station, Il Matto reverses their logic:

> QUESTORE—Però avevamo dei sospetti . . . Dal momento che l'indiziato era l'unico ferroviere anarchico di Milano . . . era facile arguire che fosse lui . . .
>
> MATTO—Certo, certo è lapalissiano direi ovvio. Così, se è indubbio che le bombe in ferrovia le abbia messe un ferroviere, possiamo anche arguire di conseguenza che al palazzo di giustizia di Roma, quelle famose bombe le abbia messe un giudice, che al monumento al milite ignoto le abbia messe il comandante del corpo di guardia e che alla banca dell'agricoltura, la bomba sia stata messa da un banchiere o da un agrario a scelta.

(152-53)

In the introduction to the play Fo wrote that one of his main aims was to demystify the "mediating" image of the State, its appearance of standing above the classes and from that position impartially regulating their demands. Adhering to the Leninist theory of the State as the expression of the irreconcilability of class interests, Fo takes pains throughout the farce to deal with the issue. In this first act, he accomplishes that by making references to the continuity between the fascist state and the current "democratic" one. Of course, the Chief of Police and former fascist guard is the target. Il Matto keeps him in constant suspense by hinting knowledge of his identity. He says that his face looks familiar, perhaps they met at the camp? A highly improbable place for a Chief of Police to have been. Later as he counts the pages of the police deposition after page "ventisette," he meaningfully lets drop not Ventotto but Ventotene (the name of the city where the prison was located). Later yet talking about old-time anarchists, the ones that were "kicked around from land to land" he asks him whether he had any experience with such people. Resorting again to the power of the mechanical, Il Matto concludes one of his sentences with the exhortation *"A noi"* which is promptly repeated as the Fascist slogan by the Chief.

Besides the demystification of the actual events surrounding Pinelli's death, and more generally of the role of the

State, in the first act, demystification of the Stage occurs as well. The contiguity between real life and theater is invoked in the prologue, where Fo states that the events about to be told transpired in the U.S. in the thirties, and had as their victim an anarchist by the name of Salsedo. Of course, the audience should not be surprised if the events recounted bear a certain similarity to the events that took place in Milan because:

> qualora apparissero analogie con fatti e personaggi della cronaca nostrana, questo fenomeno è da imputarsi a quella imponderabile magia costante nel teatro che, in infinite occasioni, ha fatto sì che perfino storie pazzesche completamente inventate, si siano trovate ad essere a loro volta impunemente imitate dalla realtà!

> (141)

This transposition could be interpreted in various ways: as a safeguard against censorship, and/or as a way of pointing out the universality of the role of the State, so that Pinelli's story would not be interpreted just as a Milanese miscarriage of justice.

Later on, throughout the first act, frequent mentions are made of the diaguises of theater, of acting styles (the police version of Pinelli's depression is chastized as being too melodramatic, worthy of actress Franca Bertini). The police depositions are often called stage directions and script by Il Matto, and in reconstructing the events he calls on the policemen to "play the part." Thus the deception of a cover-up is likened to the deception of a stage.

L'ANARCHICO: ACT II

In the second act, after a fairly tranquil beginning that simply continues the judge's and the police's efforts to arrive at a plausible version, major *coups de théâtre* occur, as in fireworks, one after the other.

A certain switch in the rhythm had perhaps been signaled by the preponderance of quick *varietà*; exchanges in dismantling the police version. Again the logic of the cover-up is the target as Il Matto inquires whether the sun set after Midnight, on the night of December 12, the only explanation for an open window in the cold Milanese climate. The remonstrations of the policemen who claim that it was not cold and the window was open on account of the smoke, are met by Il Matto's remarks:

> MATTO—Ah si? Quella sera il servizio metereologico ha dato per l'Italia temperature da far barbellare un orso bianco, e loro non avevano freddo, anzi . . . "primavera!" Ma che cosa avete: un monsone africano personale che passa di qui ogni notte, o è la "corrente del golfo" che vien su per il"tombone di san Marco" e vi passa sotto casa con le fogne?!

> (164)

Images of extreme cold and extreme heat are placed side by side, as are also images of the exotic and of the familiar, in a grotesque procedure aimed at un-masking a blatant lie.

The sequence that relies most heavily on *varietà*; techniques is perhaps the series of exchanges concerning the mysterious anarchist's shoe, that was supposedly left in a guard's hand as he had attempted to stop the anarchist's suicidal leap. Since Pinelli landed with two shoes, Il Matto seeks a number of plausible explanations: (a) the guard, with Speedy Gonzales celerity had reached the falling anarchist and properly put the missing shoe on before he reached ground, (b) Pinelli was a triped, or (c) he was wearing galoshes.

The third box of deceit is set up as an external interference: the *diabolus ex machina* is a journalist arriving to interview the Chief of Police. To spare the policemen the embarassment of admitting they are being investigated by the government, Il Matto promises to change his persona and to aid them in moments of need against the perspicacious press. The alliance of the three against the journalist, however, is problematic for the police because the newly-emerged captain of scientific police, Matto-Banzi-Piccinni, complete with patch over the eye, wooden leg and arm (mementos of the Foreign Legion and of the Green Berets) oscillates between "brilliant" rescue operations and giving too much credit to the radical press version of the events. As the captain plays out the press scenario in which the beaten, unconscious anarchist was leaned out of the window to regain consciousness with the fresh air and was "lost" by careless police, the Chief rebuffs the captain with the question, "Have you taken leave of your senses?" Responding from the first box of deceit and awakening a dormant metaphor, the "Captain" answers, "Yes, sixteen times," which of course the chief does not catch. The mechanical element in the language itself is thus harnessed to lend power to the dialectic between deception and discovery. This type of "interference" occuring between the levels of deception explodes to its full force with the entrance on the scene of Bertozzo, who knows the real captain Banzi-Piccinni and would like to unmask the impostor. The alliance between Il Matto and the two policemen tightens up in this new situation, but for equivocal reasons: the two policemen fear that Bertozzo will reveal the captain's identity to be that of the reviewing judge of box two, whereas Il Matto justly fears that Bertozzo has recognized him as the "certified insane" of box one. A physical dismemberment of the Banzi-Piccinni persona by Bertozzo, who single-handedly tries to carry out a bit of demystification of his own, leads Il Matto to put on yet another disguise: he is now a Bishop, in charge of police security for the Pope. The various disguises offer Il Matto a chance to parody the idiosyncrasies and specialized jargons of each of the arms of the State. Paradoxically the Bishop translates a long Latin quote that chastizes the journalist's efforts at investigative reporting. The passage points out the cathartic effect scandal has on the public, the "democratic" re-assurance it gives that even if things are rotten, people will know about them. Thus demystification has reached a whole gamut of functions: the police, the army, the press, yet it is not ready to stop. After the outrageous utterances of Il Matto-Bishop, alliances start shifting. The three policemen again stand united in their mission of defending the State, as Bertozzo reaffirming the weapon-based power of the police points his gun on all present, demands that the "farce" be stopped, and orders an agent to handcuff everyone to a coat rack. Escalating the discourse of weapons Il Matto claims he has a detonator, demands to be released so he can go to the press, and chains all remaining. Suddenly, the lights go out, and Il Matto is heard screaming as he falls out from the infamous window.

This sets up the situation for box of deception number four as "mystified" policemen, handcuffed to the coat rack, express their regrets for his untimely death and point to their handcuffed condition as proof of innocence. However they end up accidentally revealing their deceit when Bertozzo salutes the departing journalist by easily slipping his right hand out of the handcuff. In a circular fashion the play "ends" with the arrival of a fat and mysterious bearded character, whom the policemen attack believing him to be the resilient Matto, but as the beard and the belly prove to be real they are introduced to the newly arrived reviewing judge.

At this ending one would be tempted to shout the Pirandellian question: Reality or fiction? The frustration may be due to Fo's overindulgence in presenting the contiguity between life and theater. Fo's play on the lines of the demarcation between reality and theater has been carried out well into the second act, especially in an earlier scene in which the chief of police had summoned his infiltrators in the audience. Promptly actors sitting among the spectators had responded, but Il Matto hastened to clarify that those were only actors, but that real police agents were likely to be sitting among the audience keeping a keen eye on "subversive elements" (173-4). Thus the contamination between farce and the politics of reaction reaches its climax in this warning delivered by the Commissario, but in reality issued by Fo, the revolutionary playwright.

Paradoxically, in a farce bent on demystification and on distinguishing the truth from falsehood, the boundaries between the fictionality of theater and the essential nature of bourgeois society become indistinguishable, the farce being chosen as the appropriate mirror reflecting the modes of operation of a decaying class.

The confusion of limits between truth and fiction practiced by Fo respects the grotesque's gusto for a free play of boundaries, and its aversion for exactness and singleness of meaning as pointed out by Bakhtin. Fo's predilection for the multiple, be it the structure of deceit *en abyme*, the polyphonic monologue, or the contamination farce/politics of reaction is a central feature that must be stressed and further investigated if one is to understand Fo's specific contribution to the ongoing debate on political theater.

NOTES

[1] In Erminia Artese, ed. *Dario Fo parla di Dario Fo* (Cosenza: Lerici, 1977), p. 58.

[2] Jessica Milner-Davis, *Farce* (London: Methuen, 1978), pp. 28-60.

[3] Eric Bentley, *The Life of the Drama* (New York: Atheneum, 1962), pp. 248-51.

[4] Dario Fo, *Morte accidentale di un anarchico* in *Compagni senza censura*, vol. 1 (Milan: Mazzotta, 1973), pp. 137-182. All parenthetical quotations are to this edition.

[5] With the investigation of the Pinelli case a whole picture emerged of sponsorship and protection of right wing violence by certain sectors of the government, and even C. I. A. involvement. The goal of the systematic campaign of violence and terror was to destabilize the country by creating a climate of tension and fear (hence the terms *Strategia della tensione*, and *Strage di stato*), that would be blamed on the Left, thus justifying repression against it and an eventual seizure of all organs of State power by the armed forces.

Dozens of books give extensive documentation of this strategy, notably Camilla Caderna, *Pinelli: una finestra sulla strage* (Milan: Feltrinelli, 1971) and Marco Sassano, *La politica della strage* (Florence: La Nuova Italia, 1972).

[6] Mikhail Bakhtin, *Rabelais and his World* (Cambridge: M. I. T. press, 1968), pp. 24-34.

Joylynn Wing (essay date 1990)

SOURCE: "The Performance of Power and the Power of Performance: Rewriting the Police State in Dario Fo's *Accidental Death of an Anarchist*," in *Modern Drama*, Vol. XXXIII, No. 1, March 1990, pp. 139-49.

[*In the following essay, Wing maintains that the form of* Accidental Death of an Anarchist *reinforces its content. The provisional, ever-changing nature of the play, she argues, demonstrates that the "notion of a single, monolithic, political truth is shown to be as corrupt as the notion of a unified, cohesive, theatrical representation."*]

Italian playwright Dario Fo has been exploring the radical relationship between power, violence, and comedy for the past forty years.[1] In a wide variety of plays and performance events which feature theatrical techniques culled from the fertile traditions of his homeland, fo weaves comedy's ancient ploys into a complex production mode featuring a type of grotesque physical paradox which he calls "black mime,"[2] in order to attack a power structure which he sees as immobile and static. In his popular 1970 piece, ***Accidental Death of an Anarchist,*** he appropriates the archetypical comic fool figure, as a "histrio-maniac,"[3] in order to attack the pretensions of the police state and naturalistic theatre simultaneously. In the course of the action, illusionistic theatre is equated with the believable cover-up, and the process of theatre itself becomes the farcial mechanism upon which the unidimensional, solid front of authority is shattered by the provisionality of its own plot line.

Fo wrote *Accidental Death of an Anarchist*[4] in 1970 as a type of informative "teatro a bruciare,"[5] intended to expose an officially sanctioned network of lies and cover-ups surrounding the police murder of a young railroad worker, Giuseppe Pinelli. After a bomb killed sixteen people in Milan in 1969, the police arrested Pinelli, who subsequently died in a fourth-floor "fall" from the window of the police station. In order to cover up responsibility for Pinelli's death and to divert attention from their own failure to investigate the possible perpetrators of the bombing, the police devised a story in which Pinelli supposedly committed suicide in remorse for his guilt over the bombings. Years later the authorities arrested several fascists, including a high official in the Italian secret police, and they were convicted of the bombings. In the meantime, however, official investigations of the event abounded, and the police officer implicated in Pinelli's death by the left wing newspaper, *Lotta Continua*, sued that publication for libel. The resulting enquiries and trials provided Fo with a wealth of topical information ripe for satire. Fo describes his dramatic strategy in this play as "an exercise in counterinformation":

> Using authentic documents—and complete transcripts of the investigations carried out by the various judges as well as police reports—we turned the logic and the truth of the facts on head. But the great and provocative impact of this play was determined by its theatrical form: rooted in tragedy, the play became farce—the farce of power.[6]

If the illusionistic text resembles the human ego in that it "thrives by repressing the process of its own making," as Terry Eagleton points out,[7] then Fo's strategy in *Anarchist* is clearly a direct attack on the quasi-mystical unity of both. Fo crafts his "farce of power" as an assault on holistic illusionism by characterizing the performance text as fundamentally a mode of production which is therefore subject to the active intervention of its audience.[8] In order to provoke the spectator's active collaboration in the theatrical process, Fo employs a variety of oppositional techniques which function to subvert or split audience perception. He then exploits that perceptual disjunction as a Brechtian *Verfremdungseffekt* in which "the habitual mode of representation, where the public is kept at a distance, [is] completely subverted and the spectators completely implicated."[9] Recurring oppositional techniques in Fo's theatrical arsenal include didactic introductions and interventions (*discorsi*), ostensibly spontaneous byplay with the audience (*interventi*), grotesque exaggerations of slapstick conventions (*tormentoni*), blocking patterns in which a background figure (usually the fool) "upstages" a power figure, corporeal distortions (or "disarticulations" of the actor's body), and conscious fragmentation of character and script alike.

In *Accidental Death of an Anarchist,* Fo crafts a sense of audience complicity from his first moments onstage. As in all of his productions, he frames the play with an apparently informal introduction. In fact, the prologue is every bit as orchestrated as the ostensibly more polished formal "script."[10] In this case, Fo contextualizes the play with a prologue about the previous "defenestration" of an American anarchist named Salseda:

> This play tells about a real event that took place in America in 1921. It's only to make the plot more immediate, hence more dramatic, that I transposed all the action to our times. So, it's set, not in New York, but in a nice Italian town somewhere. Let's say, Milan.[11]

This geographic and chronological disjunction serves to distance the event, in a Brechtian sense, by placing the dramatic action within a deliberate historical and ironic perspective. But the arbitrary dislocation of the plot also signals a deliberate construction, requiring a conscious conspiracy on the part of the audience.[12] This technique sets the subsequent unravelling of the authorized police version of the events leading to Pinelli's fatal fall squarely within the framework of fiction: if it is ONLY a story, it is obviously subject to the creative interventions of its author. In the process of enactment, however, it becomes clear that more than one notion of author/authority/authorized has been set in motion. On the one hand the authority of Dario Fo, the author of the play, is challenged by the very characters he has created (for example, at one point the lone female actor exclaims, "Why is there only one woman's part in his blasted play?" [p. 41]). Concomitantly, Fo's ostensible (or ostended, in Umberto Eco's sense)[13] fiction in turn challenges the officially authorized version of Pinelli's fall. Meanwhile, the authority of theatrical representation itself is subverted by a series of disruptive strategies which persistently undermine the integrity of the performance text.

This performance *glissage* is apparent from the moment Fo appears onstage, in the guise of "The Maniac," and an actor playing the police Inspector, Bertozzo, announces:

> I ought to warn you that the author of this sick little play, Dario Fo, has the traditional irrational hatred of the police common to all narrowminded left-wingers and so I shall, no doubt, be the unwilling butt of endless anti-authoritarian jibes.
>
> (p. 1)

In an instantaneous fulfillment of this prediction, Bertozzo's side-kick, the Constable, gets his finger caught in a mousetrap. This moment of slapstick sends several interpretative signals to the audience: it implicates the Maniac as the source (author) of the ensuing comic action and it signals a rupture in the representation, since Bertozzo can comment on the action before it takes place. The implication of actions "authored" in the process of the representation is magnified for an Italian audience, which recognizes the playwright, Dario Fo, in the part of the Maniac. This phenomenon also facilitates a potent political/theatrical dialectic, since the author so obviously performs in the two dimensions simultaneously.

Although some of this dynamic is undoubtedly lost in the translation into other cultures and other productions, the clarity of the Maniac as a theatrical device remains intact. Functioning as the instigator of the comic action, he is easily re ignizable as a stock *eiron* type, manifested variously as u. nety slave" of Roman comedy, the vice character in medieval drama, and the resourceful villain in Shakespeare.[14] Fo quite consciously exploits this historical lineage in order to attack the assumptions of realistic theatre.[15] When Fo's Maniac is arrested for the crime of "impersonation," he pleads insanity, claiming to suffer from "Histrionic mania." Ironically, the role he is accused of impersonating is that of an authority on psychology, blatantly modeled on Sigmund Freud. This characterization sets up a syllogism of comic contradiction: if the Maniac were sane, his impersonation of Freud would be fraud. Since he is not, his Freud is not fradulent. Therefore, a credible Freud depends on insanity.

This sanity/insanity opposition is compounded when considered from a theatrical perspective because realistic representation hinges fundamentally on the notion of the dramatic character as a psychologically integrated entity, a concept developed and promulgated by the work of the influential director and theoretician, Stanislavski, and often linked with Freud's percepts. For Stanislavski, the creation of character is necessarily based on the model of individual consciousness. As Stanislavski's didactic alter-ego, The Director, explains to a pupil in *An Actor Prepares*:

> . . . Always and forever, when you are on the stage, you must play yourself. . . . this is the best and only true material for inner creativeness. Use it, and do not rely on drawing from any other source.[16]

Fo, on the other hand, labels Stanislavski's technique of identifying the actor with the character "the worst type of reactionary, conservative, bourgeois position in history." For Fo, character is clearly pluralistic:

> If . . . I try to create the vision of a community, a chorus, a communion, obviously I'm not going to be too concerned about talking about myself—I'm talking about collective problems. If I seek out collective problems, what I'm saying and the language I use will be different; it'll be forced to be epic . . .[17]

Fo's strategy throughout the play involves a complex series of oppositions which stem from a demolition of character. The Stanislavskian ideal, in which character is seen as an integrated, logically motivated, and psychologically decipherable entity, is the implied counterpoint of a violent theatrical dialectic in which Fo presents character as fragmented, utterly arbitrary, and insanely contradictory. Not only does the lead actor impersonate a series of blatantly improbable characters, seemingly at whim, but it becomes increasingly clear as the play progresses that all the actors are "role-playing," trying on personalities and motivations to fit an improvisatory scenario which the Maniac/author proffers as a logically constructed, well-motivated plot line.

But it is precisely on the issue of "motivation" that Fo's merger/rupture of theatre and politics hinges. In order for the public (audience) to be convinced that the anarchist committed suicide, a believable motivation must be supplied. Moreover, the events leading to his leap must be logically constructed (a well-made plot). It therefore becomes the task of the troupe onstage (led by the Maniac in the guise of an investigating judge) to create a standard realistic representation, featuring a believable plot with which the audience can identify. The opposition/rupture lies in the fact that what they so desperately try to make believable is patently untrue: the anarchist didn't jump—he was pushed. Thus a particular mode of theatrical representation (realistic) becomes inextricably implicated with its counterpart in politics (the believable cover-up).

The central paradox throughout *Anarchist* is that the Maniac manipulates fiction to get at the truth. This manipulation is effected through the theatrical "action" of "rewriting the script."[18] According to the cops' initial story line, the anarchist throws himself out the window in a "raptus" of remorse and guilt. The Maniac-as-judge, however, points out that this version implicates the police, because the victim's suicidal state of mind, or "raptus," too easily can be traced to police intimidation. Paradoxically, in his rejection of the authorized script, the Maniac simply states the truth, which has become an unacceptable fiction in this context:

> You arrest a free citizen, hold him beyond the legal time limit, and then traumatise him by telling him you have absolute proof that he is a bomber which you later state you didn't have at all. . . . We're dealing with a campaign of sustained psychological violence followed by a public exhibition of outrageous and contradictory lies.

(pp. 16-17)

The cops, interpreting this statement as a kind of motivational proofreading, hasten to produce a revised account, featuring a four-hour time lapse between the end of the interrogation and Pinelli's leap. This rewrite is an attempt to eliminate the cops' culpability, on the grounds that however badly the anarchist may have felt at the end of the interrogation he could after all have had a mood change in four hours. The Maniac, however, points out a flaw in the new plot line as well: if the anarchist was no longer upset, why did he jump? His original motivation hinged on "raptus." Without this emotional authenticity on the part of the lead character, the public can hardly be expected to "identify with" the story.

Again fiction and reality intersect at odd angles. In pointing out the flaw in the new plot line, the Maniac suggests lethal consequences for the cops: someone, after all, has to "take the fall" for the failed fiction in the theatrical/political arena. In a parody of the notion of "military honor," the Maniac suggests that the cops jump out the window, as "the only decent thing left." Faced with this "point of ritual death,"[19] the cops respond with a kind of desperate creativity. They beg the Maniac to help them produce a third version, combining the critical mood change after the initial interrogation with a convincing motivation for jumping.

The first requirement is effected primarily through a comic disjunction of language, a technique which Fo has already introduced into the production with his persistent associations of linguistic paradox with the notion of "script." For instance, in the original version of Pinelli's investigation, the police Superintendent's first line to the anarchist is, "It's no use trying to pull the wool over my eyes, sonny." When the Maniac insists that the language be reconstructed in a "documentary" mode, however, the Superintendent eagerly obliges: "Right you filthy pox-ridden pansy you piss me about one more time and I'll . . ." (p. 14). The authorized discourse of the official transcript is thus shown to be an arbitrary construct, in which the truth of the result lies in style rather than substance.

If language is shown to be arbitrary, however, it is also seductively entertaining as one of the primary tools of the theatrical craft. Fo's Maniac convinces the cops that style alone will seduce the public into believing in the anarchist's mood change. In a purported effort to establish the cops as sympathetic characters who are emotionally supportive of their charge and therefore innocent of forcing him into a despair-driven suicide, the Maniac deliberately leads them into a series of verbal contortions which undermine the very goals they are supposedly designed to achieve. His first plot involves a nostalgic reversion to childhood:

> MANIAC Think. Didn't you have a little train set when you were a nipper?
>
> PISSANI Yes.
>
> . . . . .
>
> MANIAC Tell me, did it go "whoo! Whoo!"
>
> PISSANI Yes.
>
> MANIAC Wonderful. How did it go?
>
> PISSANI Whoo! Whoo!
>
> SUPERINTENDENT I had one too.
>
> MANIAC Let's hear it.
>
> SUPERINTENDENT Chchch Whoochch chWhooWhoo!
>
> (p. 21)

The improbable paradox of power figures spouting nonsense is indeed funny, but Fo's subversion transcends the merely comic, for his goal is an attack on the integrity of language itself. By using nonsense to foreground the materiality of the dramatic discourse Fo effectively estranges the signifying process itself, calling attention to the arbitrary nature of the cops' utterances.[20] Having thus established a linguistic equation in which cops' words = zero signification, the Maniac launches his subversive talents against dramatic structure. In a kind of generic two-step, he switches from farce and nursery rhyme to pathos and melodrama, manipulating the performance with all the hype of a Hollywood movie mogul:

> MANIAC Who believes anything you say? No one. Why? Because besides being evident garbage your stories lack the tiniest vestige of humanity. No warmth. No laughter. No pain. No remorse. SING!
>
> (p. 22)

The performative paradox which results from this harangue is a rousing rendition of the anarchist anthem, sung by a chorus line of fascistic Milanese cops. Fully equating "theatrical" with "political" credibility, the cops are convinced that they have at last created a scenario that is emotionally convincing. But the Method requires more than emotional recall. Psychological motivation must, after all, be consistent with character and plot. When they finally realize that their empathetic style has backfired (by making them look ridiculous) the cops place the blame on failed theatre ("We sang. We showed you how warm and human we are"). They beg the Maniac to orchestrate one last attempt at a plausible motivation for the anarchist's fall. When eventually it becomes apparent, however, that their defense rests upon the preposterous premise that the anarchist had three feet, the cops' desperate improvisation degenerates into a grotesque parody of a "falling out among thieves," and the truth is revealed:

> PISSANI I only did it on your orders!
>
> SUPERINTENDENT Me!? Me?! You weren't involved all of a sudden.
>
> CONSTABLE Please! Sir!
>
> SUPERINTENDENT Keep out of it! It's all me now! You didn't enjoy yourself, of course?!
>
> PISSANI I was having a laugh. Yes. You said that, didn't you Constable.
>
> CONSTABLE Yes.
>
> SUPERINTENDENT Some laugh! Ha! Laughing now, aren't we?!
>
> PISSANI I was just scaring him. *You* are the nutter!
>
> SUPERINTENDENT I'm a nutter!?
>
> CONSTABLE Please.
>
> PISSANI Well you bloody pushed him, chum!
>
> (pp. 27-28)

Having manipulated the cops into confessing the truth to his fictional judge, Fo proceeds to push the theatrical/political paradox a step further, into the realm of the grotesque. Late in the play, the cops coax the Maniac to assume yet another character, that of "forensic expert," Captain Piccini, for the purpose of deflecting the questions of an investigative reporter who is about to arrive on the scene. Fo incarnates "Piccini" as a preposterous conglomeration of such blatantly bogus body parts that he is transposed into a virtual marionette. The Piccini "puppet" features a wooden leg, a detachable wooden hand, a crutch, a glass eye (also detachable) and an outrageously fake moustache and wig. As though this physicialization were somehow too subtle, "Piccini" then proceeds to underline his grotesque condition with each phrase and gesture in such a way as to oppose or contradict every dramatic action that could be construed as constitutive of social, political, or psychological stability and order. His hand comes off when he attempts to shake hands. Just as he finishes a particularly lucid account of the anarchist's jump, his eye pops out. Then when one cop winks at another in an attempt to gain his cooperation, Piccini drops his eye in a glass of water and swallows it. Soon after the revelation that paid informers are the "eyes and ears of the state," the Maniac punctuates a comment about the state's gruesome excesses by removing his wooden leg. He rips off his ersatz eyepatch while announcing "Corruption is the rule." As the scene builds, it becomes increasingly evident that the grotesquely corrupted body of the "Maniac" and the body politic are theatrical reflections of each other.

"Piccini's" savage self-demolition is a deliberate implementation on Fo's part of a particular kind of grotesque physical paradox employed in the "black mime" tradition of Lecoq, Moretti, and the late Sicilian comedian, Toto,[21] in which overt physical abuse builds to what Fo calls "a point of paroxysm." In a recent essay on Toto's techniques, Fo articulates a fundamental relationship between power, violence and comedy:

> [The actor] works on the basis of paradox—at the limits of paranoia . . . [in order to attack] whatever is sacred and essential in power, to destroy it at the heart of that pyramid which assures its stability.[22]

This "paroxysm" of violence is realized by combining conventional slapstick routines with the use of a comical prop, a jerry-rigged bomb, which functions both to mirror the original crime and to bring the theatrical/political analogy full circle. The slapstick devolves onto the straight-man cop, Bertozzo, who walks into the Piccini/reporter scenario carrying the bomb. Significantly, Bertozzo's potential danger lies more in his inadequate dramatic imagination than in any actual weapons he may supply. Since he has not been a player within the microcosm of the cops' various provisional *scenarii*, he does not understand that effective improvisation hinges on cooperation and support. Theatrically incompetent, he is unable to participate in presumptions of character and disguise. When he thwarts the proposed scenario by insisting that "Piccini" is not Piccini, he receives the brunt of an increasingly savage barrage of slapstick violence, during which he is kicked, punched, pinched, gagged, and wrestled to the floor. Clearly the intensity of the violence is *outré*, a *tormentone*, a transgression of any rational sense of cause and effect. But Fo creates this grotesque exaggeration deliberately to exploit the theatrical/political analogy; the bomb and the slapstick are reflections of each other.

The real danger for the cops, however, lies in potential accountability, and it therefore resides in the dramatic script rather than in the theatrical gesture; thus it is precisely when the Maniac begins to "drop character" and tell the truth that Bertozzo "recognizes" him as the "impostor":

MANIAC (*to the* Reporter) Are you trying to get us to admit that instead of chasing idiotic anarchists and relying on informers and agents inside the revolutionary left, we should be concentrating our efforts on paramilitary fascist organisations . . . !

. . . . .

SUPERINTENDENT Has he gone mad?

. . . . .

BERTOZZO . . . Mad!!! It's him!!! It's that fucking maniac! It's him!

(p. 37)

Once more, a sanity/insanity opposition aggressively undermines the script. If the official lies of the state (which Bertozzo is, after all, paid to protect) are accepted as "sane," then anyone telling the truth is *ipso facto* insane. Since the Maniac has histrionic powers, in order to defeat him Bertozzo must gain control of the theatrical representation. Admitting "this is the only way I can get you to listen to me," he grabs a gun and forces the others to line up against the proscenium, shouting a warcry against fourth-wall realism ("AGAINST THE FUCKING AUDIENCE!") as he ruptures any pretense of illusionism by demanding that the Maniac reveal his "true identity." Obligingly, the Fo/Maniac then does just that, abandoning the dramatic script for an *intervento* about current political events.

No two versions of ***Accidental Death of an Anarchist*** end exactly in the same way, but all share a provisional *dénouement*. In the Gavin Richards adaptation, reality and theatre become dangerously intertwined as the Maniac slowly divests himself of his layers of disguise while playing a tape of the cops' earlier confession. To underscore the power of this particular script, he tosses the bomb to the reporter, forcing her to make a difficult choice:

MANIAC Here. . . . Have you the stomach for this? There's the keys to the handcuffs. I'm off. You can't chuck the bomb out of the window, it's a public street. So . . . Release them, write your story, but the evidence will die with me and this bunch will undoubtedly be acquitted. Don't release them and you become my accomplice—you join the ranks of the extremists. It's all yours.

(p. 44)

Two endings ensue. In the first, the reporter escapes. An explosion follows. The Maniac lauds the "happy ending" and abruptly exits. In the midst of the audience's applause he then returns to announce the second version, in which the reporter frees the cops and they, in turn, handcuff her to the window frame before they exit, laughing. By refusing to grant a closure to the script, Fo has pinioned it in a state of perpetual rupture. It is not simply a case of an unresolved ending: every layer or theatrical frame of the play is provisional. The micro-play of the comic cops acting out script revisions mirrors the macro-play, ***Accidental Death of an Anarchist,*** with its unresolved *dénouement.*

Ultimately the reflectors are turned toward the audience, for it is the spectator who is finally implicated in the position of author/ity. The notion of a single, monolithic, political truth is shown to be as corrupt as the notion of a unified, cohesive, theatrical representation. The truth, for Fo, is that both history and theatre are collective processes created through rupture, opposition, and the frightening, improvisatory power of choice.

NOTES

An earlier version of this paper was presented at the Semiotic Society of America Conference in Cincinnati in October, 1988.

[1]Fo's first play, *Ma la Tresca ci divide*, was produced in Luino, Italy in 1948. Since then he has written, directed and acted in more than fifty pieces. A chronological description of Fo's work through 1983 can be found in Tony Mitchell's *Dario Fo: People's Court Jester* (London, 1984).

[2]Fo makes a distinction between what he calls the "white mime" of the classical Pierrot tradition, in which performers wear whiteface and affect delicate gestures, and "black mime," which stems from popular performers in the Middle Ages and features the "vulgar" gestures of everyday life.

[3]Fo coins the term, *istrionomania*, from the Latin "histrionem," via the Etruscan term, "ister," which referred to professional players imported into Rome in the fourth century B.C.

[4]Published Italian versions of the play can be found in *Compagni senza censura*, vol. 2 (Milan, 1973), *Le commedie di Dario Fo*, (Torino, 1974) and in a separate edition (Verona, 1972). English adaptions include the Gillian Hanna, Gavin Richards version (London, 1980) and Suzanne Cowan's translation, in *Theater*, 10 (1979), 13-46. The play is subtitled "A Grotesque Farce About a Tragic Farce."

[5]Literally, "theatre to burn." Suzanne Cowan translates this phrase as "throw-away theatre." See "The Throw-away Theatre of Dario Fo," *The Drama Review*, 19 (1975), 103-113.

[6]Dario Fo, *Accidental Death of an Anarchist*, trans. Gavin Richards (London, 1980), p. iii. Unless otherwise noted, subsequent quotations from the play will be taken from this edition and cited in the text by page number.

[7]Terry Eagleton, *Literary Theory: an Introduction* (Minneapolis, 1983), p. 170.

[8]For an analysis of Brecht's theories applied to a Marxist conception of the spectator as producer, see Walter Benjamin, "The Author as Producer," in *Art After Modernism: Rethinking Representation*, ed. Brian Wallis (Boston, 1984), pp. 297-309.

[9]Dario Fo, "Toto: The Violence of the Marionette and the Mask," trans. Stuart Hood, *Theater*, 18 (1987), 10.

[10]For a perceptive analysis of the notion of the privileging of the dramatic text in relation to performance, see Marco De Marinis, *Semiotica del teatro* (Milan, 1982).

[11]Fo, *Morte accidentale di un anarchico* in *Le commedie di Dario Fo*, p. 37. My translation.

[12]For a review of Roland Barthes's seminal articles on the connection between Brechtian theory and a semiotic analysis of performance, see "Barthes on Theatre," trans. Peter W. Mathers, in *Theatre Quarterly*, 9 (1979) 25-30.

[13]See Umberto Eco, "Semiotics of Theatrical Performance," *The Drama Review*, 21 (1977), 107-117.

[14]See Bernard Spivack, *Shakespeare and the Allegory of Evil* (New York, 1958). Spivack argues that certain Shakespearean villains, most notably Iago and Edmund, are direct adaptations of the medieval vice figure.

[15]See Mikhail Bakhtin's *Rabelais and his World*, trans. Helene Iswolsky (Bloomington, 1984), for an analysis of the socially transformative implications of ancient theatrical rituals, such as the Feast of Fools, in which peasants parodied those in power.

[16]Constantin Stanislavski, *An Actor Prepares*, trans. Elizabeth Reynolds Hapgood (New York, 1936), p. 167.

[17]Dario Fo, "Popular Culture," trans. Tony Mitchell, *Theater* 14 (1983), 52.

[18]This tactic effectively undermines what Marco De Marinis calls the "privileged status of the verbal text in the Western theatrical tradition," by forcing the dramatic script into a continuous slippage in which it constantly plays out its own vulnerability. See De Marinis, "Dramaturgy of the Spectator," *The Drama Review*, 31 (1987), 100 - 114.

[19]Northrop Frye, *Anatomy of Criticism* (Princeton, 1957), p. 179. According to Frye, this frequently occurring dramatic device is a reminder of the demonic, dangerous elements that lurk beneath comedy's surface.

[20]For a discussion of the semiotic implications of the use of nonsense in the performance text, see Keir Elam, *The Semiotics of Theatre and Drama* (London, 1980), pp. 17, 19.

[21]Moretti was the famous Arlecchino in Strehler's 1947 production of *Arlecchino servitore di due padroni*, staged at the Piccolo Teatro. Lecoq was Moretti's pupil; Fo, Lecoq's.

[22]Fo, "Toto," p. 7.

FURTHER READING

Gussow, Mel. "Dario Fo's Barbed Wit Is Aimed at Many Targets." *The New York Times* (14 August 1983): 3, 11.
　　Appreciative survey of Fo and his works.

Hirst, David. *Dario Fo and Franca Rame*. Basingstoke, Hampshire: Macmillan, 1989, 218 p.
　　Biographical and critical study of Fo and Rame's career together.

Jenkins, Ron. "Drawing from the Imagination: The Comic Art of Dario Fo." *Aperture* 132 (Summer 1993): 12-19.
　　Offers an appreciation of Fo and a translated excerpt from Fo's *Johan Padan and the Discovery of the Americas.*

———. "The Nobel Jester." *American Theatre* 15, No. 2 (February 1998): 22-4.

Applauds the awarding of the Nobel Prize for literature to Fo, considering it a "courageous and controversial choice."

Mitchell, Tony, comp. *File on Fo*. London: Methuen, 1989, 108 p.

Casebook that provides a descriptive catalogue of Fo's pieces, a chronology, and primary and secondary bibliographies.

Pertile, Lino. "Dario Fo." In *Writers & Society in Contemporary Italy*, pp. 167-90. New York: St. Martin's Press, 1984.

Traces Fo's career and wonders whether "Fo did not, despite himself, pander to the lowest cultural denominator of the farce, the belch and the raspberry, and thus promote, or at least contribute to, the blight of counter-productive vulgarity which is the bane of recent Italian popular culture."

Sogliuzzo, A. Richard. "Dario Fo: Puppets for Proletarian Revolution." *The Drama Review* 16, No. 3 (September 1972): 71-7.

Focuses on Fo's use of puppets in politically satirical pieces.

Tait, Phoebe. "Political Clown." *Drama* 157 (Third Quarter 1985): 28-9.

Profile of Fo. "Fo's extraordinary comic talents," Tait observes, "stem not from a literary basis so much as from an actor's sensitivity and a familiarity with the stage and most importantly an immense respect and appreciation of his audience."

Walsh, Martin W. "The Proletarian Carnival of Fo's *Non si paga! Non si paga!*" *Modern Drama* XXVIII, No. 2 (June 1985): 211-22.

Analysis of *We Won't Pay! We Won't Pay!* that seeks to "examine the particular way it works, establish its integrity *as a play* within the broad tradition of farcical comedy, and . . . demonstrate the continued relevance of traditional, popular forms for the politically committed theatre."

Additional coverage of Fo's life and career is contained in the following sources published by Gale Research: *Contemporary Authors*, Vols. 116, 128; *Contemporary Literary Criticism*, Vol. 32; *Discovering Authors: Modules*, **Dramatists Module;** *Major 20th-Century Writers.*

Maria Irene Fornes
1930-

INTRODUCTION

Fornes is a pioneering avant-garde dramatist who helped create the off-off-Broadway forum during the 1960s. Unlike most of her contemporaries, she has continued working in small, non-commercially oriented theaters for over thirty years. In 1972 she co-founded the New York Theater Strategy—an organization that produced the work of experimental playwrights—and she served in various capacities, from bookkeeper to president, until the company dissolved in 1979. Fornes' works have earned her an unprecedented seven Obie Awards, the highest recognition for off-Broadway productions.

BIOGRAPHICAL INFORMATION

Fornes was born in Havana, Cuba, and attended public schools there. After her father's death in 1945 she immigrated to the United States with her mother and sister; she became a naturalized U.S. citizen six years later. Fornes began a career as a painter and in 1954 went to Europe to study painting. While in Paris, she attended Roger Blin's original production of Samuel Beckett's *Waiting for Godot*, an event that changed her life in the direction of playwriting. Of the production, Fornes has said: "I didn't know a word of French. I had not read the play in English. But what was happening in front of me had a profound impact without even understanding a word. Imagine a writer whose theatricality is so amazing and so important that you could see a play of his, not understand one word, and be shook up. When I left that theater I felt that my life was changed, that I was seeing everything with a different clarity." Fornes began writing plays of her own, and her first to be produced, *The Widow*, was staged in 1961. She has also directed plays, principally her own, and she has said that for her directing is an integral part of the composition process. Besides an unprecedented seven Obie Awards for distinguished playwriting and direction, Fornes has received numerous other awards and scholarships throughout her career, including Yale University fellowships in 1967 and 1968; Rockefeller Foundation grants in 1971 and 1984; an American Academy and Institute of Arts and Letters Award in Literature in 1985; and a Playwrights U.S.A. Award in 1986.

MAJOR WORKS

The surrealistic elements of Beckett's writing have influenced Fornes' plays, which are unconventional in their

structure, dialogue, and staging. Emphasizing neither plot nor character development, the plays are often symbolic rather than realistic and at times contain both brutality and slapstick humor. Fornes is mainly concerned with human relationships, though a social and political consciousness is also evident in many of her plays. In her first important play, *Tango Palace*, Fornes presents ill-fated male lovers who enact such roles as father-son and teacher-pupil. They gradually become engaged in a metaphysical power struggle that ultimately ends in murder. *The Successful Life of 3*, a romantic spoof for which Fornes received her first Obie Award, features characters named He, She, and 3, who meet in a doctor's office and become involved in a love triangle. Their archetypal relationship is delineated through a series of short, unrelated sketches in which the sense of disconnection helps explain the dynamics of their love. Fornes' next Obie Award-winning play, *Promenade*, contains perhaps her strongest social criticism. In this comedy of manners, two guileless, lower-class prisoners, 105 and 106, escape from their jail cell in quest of the evil they know to exist in the world, but which they have never seen. Their flight leads them to direct confrontation with the wealthy for the first time, and 105 and 106 learn that the rich are cruel, while the poor are "rich" in spirit and kindness. However, unable to pinpoint evil because they cannot identify it, the uncorrupted prisoners willingly return to the "freedom" of their cell.

Fefu and Her Friends marks a change for Fornes to a somewhat more conventional approach to drama. With this pivotal work Fornes begins to emphasize realistic, three-dimensional characters rather than symbolic and surreal action. The play revolves around eight female friends who have gathered at a New England country home for a reunion weekend in 1935. Frought with tension and underlying violence, however, the play culminates with the apparent murder of one of the friends. Innovative staging highlights this work, which also won an Obie. Scenes in Act II, for instance, take place in different rooms simultaneously; the audience, split into groups, physically moves from room to room. The play's action, viewed in no particular sequence, stresses the redundant lives of women in a chauvinistic society. Through a blend of quick humor and stream-of-consciousness dialogue, Fornes illuminates the concerns and social ills of the Depression era from a female perspective. *Mud*, also grounded in realism, is set on an Appalachian farm, where Mae, her husband, Lloyd, and Henry, who becomes Mae's lover after Lloyd is accidentally crippled, live in gloom and ignorance. After Mae learns that knowledge and communication are the keys to power, she prepares to leave the stifling farm, but the inarticulate Lloyd kills her.

Fornes treats the themes of sexual politics and the failure of communication in other plays as well. *The Danube* centers on Paul and Eve, whose difficulty communicating is punctuated by the broadcasting of a foreign language instruction tape before each scene. The title character in *Sarita* is an adolescent Cuban girl from the South Bronx who harbors a self-destructive, unrequited love for a young man. Confused by contradicting Cuban and American values and unable to stay away from the boy, Sarita ultimately stabs him to death. *The Conduct of Life*, an Obie Award-winner, focuses on the personal and sexual life of Orlando, a Latin American soldier whose duty is torturing prisoners for his military government. Rather than showing the audience the particulars of Orlando's job, Fornes conveys his heartless temperament by depicting his violent relationship with his wife, whom he harasses and ridicules, and his twelve-year-old female servant, whom he rapes and enslaves. Through the link between Orlando's private and public lives, Fornes comments on the brutality of political oppression. Another Obie Award-winning play, *Abingdon Square*, is set in New York City in 1905 and conveys the sense of stagnation felt by Marion, a fifteen-year-old girl married to a middle-aged man. Marion escapes her confining world through sexual fantasies. When a young man helps her discover her true self, she begins to acknowledge the importance of her own needs and desires.

CRITICAL RECEPTION

Despite her accomplishments, Fornes has not received significant public attention. Her plays are neither widely reviewed nor have they been subject to numerous interpretations, perhaps because critics are unable to categorize Fornes' constantly evolving experimental style. Fellow dramatist Lanford Wilson has commented: "She's one of the very, very, best—it's a shame she's always been performed in such obscurity. Her work has no precedents, it isn't derived from *anything*. She's the most original of us all." The commentary that exists praises Fornes for her subtle social criticism and economy of style. Susan Sontag has asserted: "Fornes has a near faultless ear for the ruses of egotism and cruelty. Unlike most contemporary dramatists, for whom psychological brutality is the principal, inexhaustible subject, Fornes is never in complicity with the brutality she depicts. . . . Fornes's work has always been intelligent, often funny, never vulgar or cynical; both delicate and visceral."

PRINCIPAL WORKS

PLAYS

The Widow 1961
There! You Died 1963; produced as *Tango Palace,* 1964; revised, 1965
The Successful Life of 3: A Skit for Vaudeville 1965
Promenade [music by Al Carmines] 1965; revised 1969
The Office 1966
The Annunciation 1967
A Vietnamese Wedding 1967
Dr. Kheal 1968
Molly's Dream [music by Cosmos Savage] 1968
The Red Burning Light, or Mission XQ3 [music by John Bauman] 1968
Aurora [music by John Fitzgibbon] 1972
The Curse of the Langston House 1972
Cap-a-Pie [music by José Raúl Bernardo] 1975
Washing 1976
Fefu and Her Friends 1977
Lolita in the Garden 1977
In Service 1978
Eyes on the Harem 1979
Evelyn Brown (A Diary) 1980
Blood Wedding [adaptor; from a play by Federico Garcia Lorca] 1980
Life Is Dream [adaptor; from a play by Pedro Calderon de la Barca] 1981
A Visit 1981
The Danube 1982
Mud 1983
Sarita [music by Leon Odenz] 1984
No Time 1984
The Conduct of Life 1985

Cold Air   [adaptor and translator; from a play by Virgilio Piñera]   1985
A Matter of Faith   1986
Lovers and Keepers   [three one-act musicals; music by Tito Puente and Fernando Rivas]   1986
Drowning   [adaptor;   from   a   story   by   Anton Chekhov]   1986
Art   1986
The Mothers   1986; revised as *Nadine,* 1989
Abingdon Square   1987
Uncle Vanya   [adaptor; from a play by Chekhov]   1987
Hunger   1988
*And What of the Night?   [four one-act plays]   1989
Oscar and Bertha   1992
Terra Incognita   [music by Roberto Sierra]   1992
Summer in Gossensass   1995

*The four one-act plays that comprise this work are: *Hunger, Springtime, Lust,* and *Nadine* (formerly *The Mothers*).

AUTHOR COMMENTARY

I Write These Messages That Come (1977)

SOURCE: "I Write These Messages That Come," in *The Drama Review,* Vol. 21, No. 4, December 1977, pp. 25-40

[*In the following, Fornes discusses her writing methods.*]

Thoughts come to my mind at any point, anywhere—I could be on the subway—and if I am alert enough and I have a pencil and paper, I write these *messages* that come. It might be just a thought, like a statement about something, an insight, or it could be a line of dialog. It could be something that someone says in my head.

I have a box filled with these scribbles. Some of them are on paper napkins or the backs of envelopes. These things are often the beginning of a play. Most of the lyrics of the songs that I write are based on these notes—as opposed to a play, which, once it starts, / make. I usually gather a number of those things that have some relation—again, I do not even know why I consider that they are related—and I put them together. I compose something around those messages using a number of lines that have come into my head.

Now sometimes I am trying to get myself organized, and I am sharpening pencils and doing all those things. So I go to that pile of notes—it's a mess because it is scribblings. Sometimes I cannot read what I wrote because often I make notes in dark theatres when I am sitting through a play. (A lot of thoughts come into my mind when I am watching a play, especially a play that I am not at all absorbed by.) I start typing through some of these things and very often I find things I cannot imagine why in the world I thought they were anything special. They are the most mundane thoughts or phrases. Sometimes I think,

"There is some value here that I do not recognize now, but at *some* point I thought, 'this is a message.' It must be that it is, but I have lost the thought." When that happens I often type it out and leave it, even though it is without any faith at all. I leave it because at some point I did have this faith.

The feeling I have about these messages is very different from what I have about what I am writing when it is / writing. I might write something that I like, and it feels good. But the feeling I have about those other things is really as if it is a message that comes in an indivisible unit. I feel if a word is changed, then it is lost. A thought comes—sometimes I do not have a pencil with me—I try to repeat it in my head until I get to a pencil. I know I must remember the exact construction of the sentence. I might be wrong, you see. It could be that it does not matter more or less how it is said. But still I feel that it is a block and that is how it should look, whether it is a page of dialog that comes in the message or three pages or one line.

That dialog then could become a play. When I am to write a work, I never start from a blank page. I only start from one of these things that I do, that I receive. Sometimes I start a play from one line of dialog. It has to be something that has the makings of a play.

The only play that I started from an idea—and it was an idea that was very clear in my head—and that I sat down and wrote was **Tango Palace**. I think it is quite clear that that is how it is written because the play has a very strong, central idea. None of my other plays does. They are not Idea Plays. My plays do not present a thesis, or at least, let us say, they do not present a formulated thesis. One can make a thesis about anything (I could or anyone could formulate one), but I do not present ideas except in **Tango Palace**. I lost interest in that way of working.

The play writes itself. The first draft writes itself anyway. Then I look at it and I find out what is in it. I find out where I have overextended it and what things need to be cut. I see where I have not found the scene. I see what I have to do for the character to exist fully. Then I rewrite. And of course in the rewrite there is a great deal of thought and sober analysis.

One day I was talking to Rochelle Owens, and I was telling her how when I start working on a play the words are just on paper. Perhaps I will see some things or I hear something. I feel the presence of a character or person. But then there is a point when the characters become crystallized. When that happens, I have an image in full color, technicolor. And that *happens*! I do not remember it happening, but I get it like *click*! At some point I see a picture of the set with the characters in it—let us say a picture *related* to the set, not necessarily the exact set.

The colors for me are very, very important. And the colors of the clothes the people wear. When it finally happens, the play exists; it has taken its own life. And then I just listen to it. I move along with it. I let it write itself.

I have reached that point in plays at times. I have put scripts away then and picked them up three years later, and, reading them, suddenly I see that same picture with the same colors. The color never goes away. It could be ten years later. The play exists even if I have not finished writing it. Even if it is only fifteen pages. It is like an embryo that is already alive and it is there waiting.

I am always amazed how an audience knows when a play is finished. That is something that I have always found very beautiful. Sometimes when I go to the theatre when it is not written in the program that there is going to be an intermission, and when it is quite clear that something has ended, people say, "Is it over?" But they say it with surprise. The actors have left the stage, but it does not look over. People know. And then when it is really over, there is that immediate knowledge that it has ended, and people applaud. In that same way, I know when a script has completed itself. I sense the last note of the play.

One play of mine has about three endings. It looks like it has ended, but then there is another ending, and then there is another ending. These are *almost-endings*, and they do not have that total satisfaction of a real ending. It could have been that I could have left it. But probably people would have been asking, "Is it over?" "Oh, it's over."

The characters: they talk. And when it talks, a character starts developing itself. I never try to reproduce a real character. I did, in fact, try to reproduce real people that I knew in one play. **The Office.** I got into trouble because the characters in the situation were from real life, and I changed a lot of things in the play. I felt that I lacked the objectivity to make the play really sharp and for me to be sure exactly what I was doing. Since I started with a reality of what happened, it was the event that was important. And that event would not work for the play.

I know a lot of people write either about a real person or else they put a familiar character into an invented situation. I find that it just confuses me, that I do not see that as useful for me in any way.

In that same conversation with Rochelle Owens, I told her about my colors. She found it very interesting. And I said, "You mean you don't see color when you write? I thought everybody saw color!" But she does not. I asked what happens to her, and she said she hears voices. She hears the sound of what the play is saying. Sometimes she is writing and she knows that a sentence should be bah-bah-bah-bah, but the words do not come immediately. Rather than stopping, she goes on and she leaves that blank space. She goes on because the other words are coming. She knows how it has to sound, and she goes back to it. It comes in exactly that form. That is very different from my own work.

Everything that I have written has had a different start. *Successful Life of 3* started when I heard two men speaking to each other. One of them was an actor I knew.

That conversation was actually in my head. Not that I wanted to write the play for that actor, it is just that he was there and this other guy was there, and he did not have a very definite face. That caught my imagination completely. I wrote the play in two weeks.

At the same time, I was writing **Promenade,** which I wrote as an exercise I gave myself. I wrote down the characters on one set of index cards. On another set of cards, I wrote different places. I shuffled them together. I picked a card that said, "The Aristocrats." And I picked the card that said, "The Prison." So the play started in prison for that reason. But I found it very difficult to write a scene with aristocrats in prison, so the first thing that happened was that they were digging a hole to escape. I wanted to get them out of there.

For some reason it worked for me that the prisoners remained prisoners. And in the next scene, they were at a banquet where there were aristocrats. After that, I found using the cards for the characters was not helping me at all. But I kept using the place cards. That is why the play has six different locations. I would write a scene and when I was finished writing that scene I would turn to the next card. That was the order the scenes came in.

By the way, I find doing exercises very valuable. It is good for me not to do things too deliberately: to have half my mind on something else and *let* something start happening. I am really very analytical. I like analyzing things, but it is better for me not to think very much. Only after I have started creating can I put all my analytical mind into it.

Most of my plays start with a kind of a fantasy game—just to see what happens. *Fefu and Her Friends* started that way. There was this woman I fantasized who was talking to some friends. She took her rifle and shot her husband. Also, there is a Mexican joke where there are two Mexicans speaking at a bullfight. One says to the other, "She is pretty, that one over there." The other one says, "Which one?" So the first one takes his rifle and shoots her. He says, "That one, the one that falls."

So in the first draft of the play, Fefu does just that. She takes her rifle and she shoots her husband. He falls. Then she explains that they heard the Mexican joke and she and her husband play that game. That was just my fantasy: thinking of the joke, how absurd it was. But I do not know what came first, the shooting fantasy or the memory of the joke. (Finally, I left the joke out of the play.)

I started *Fefu and Her Friends* about thirteen years ago. There was just that scene. Then three years later I started again. Then there was a woman in a wheelchair. The play was very different then, but the spirit was actually quite similar. About five years ago, I started really writing, really seeing what had to be done and shaping it. And that was much closer to what it is today. Early this year, I decided I wanted to do that play—finish it and put it on. I just sat down and did it.

A playwright has a different distance from each script. Some are two feet away, and some are two hundred feet away. *Fefu* was not even two inches away. It is right where I am. That is difficult to do when one feels close. A different kind of delicacy enters into the writing. Each day I had to put myself into the mood to write the play. I wrote it in a very short period of time, in a very intense period of writing, where I did nothing but write, write, write. Every day I would start the day by reading my old folder (a different folder from the one where I keep my "messages"), where I have all my sufferings, personal sufferings: the times when I was in love and not, the times I did badly, all those anguishes which were really very profound. There were times that I just had to sit down and write about it because I felt anguish about it. It was not writing for the sake of writing; it was writing for the sake of exorcism. A lot of those things had been in this folder for many years. I had never looked at them. That was where the cockroaches were, so to speak.

I would start the day by reading something from that folder. Actually, there were even a couple times when I used things I found there, but most of it is garbage, really garbage, a collection of dirt: the whining, the complaining. But it would put me into that very, very personal, intimate mood to write.

I never before set up any kind of environment to write a play! This was the first time that I did that because the play was different. I had to reinforce the intimacy of the play.

Then I would put on the records of a Cuban singer, Olga Guillot. She is very passionate and sensuous. She is shameless in her passion. And I wrote the whole play listening to Olga Guillot. (My neighbors must have thought I was out of my mind.) There was one record, *Añorando el Caribe*, that particularly seemed to make my juices run. I just left it on the turntable and let it go on and on and on. The play had nothing to do with Olga Guillot. Her spirit is very different. She is very dramatic. And Fefu is very subtle and very delicate. But her voice kept me oiled.

I started the final writing of *Fefu* in February, 1977. At that time, I had about a third of the play written. It opened May 5, 1977. In those three months, I finished writing, I cast it, and I rehearsed it. I finished the play four days before it opened. I do not mean the very last scene. There were scenes in the middle I had to do. I made no revisions during rehearsals. I have to do some rewriting of the play now. I believe I must approach the rewrite in the same way as before: with the pile of writing and Olga Guillot.

Space affected *Fefu and Her Friends*. In late February, I decided to look for a place to perform the work. I had finished the first scene, and I had loose separate scenes that belonged somewhere in the second part of the play. I did not like the space I found because it had large columns. But then I was taken backstage to the rooms the audience could not see. I saw the dressing room, and I thought, "How nice. This could be a room in Fefu's house." Then I

was taken to the greenroom. I thought that this also could be a room in Fefu's house. Then we went to the business office to discuss terms. That office was the study of Fefu's house. (For the performance we took some of the stuff out, but we used the books, the rugs, everything that was there.) I asked if we could use all of their rooms for the performances, and they agreed.

I had written Julia's speech in the bedroom already. I had intended to put it on stage, and I had not yet arrived at how it would come about. Part of the kitchen scene was written, but I had thought it would be happening in the living room. So I had parts of it already. It was the rooms themselves that modified the scenes which originally I planned to put in the living room.

People asked me, when the play opened, if I had written those scenes to be done in different rooms and then found the space. No. They were written that way because the space was there. I had to figure out the exact coordination for the movements between one scene and the other so the timing would be right. I had rehearsed each scene separately. Now I was going to rehearse them simultaneously. Then I realized that my play, *Aurora,* had exactly the same concept. There was the similarity of two different rooms with simultaneous life. I did not consciously realize until then that it had some connection with *Aurora.*

I mention this because people put so much emphasis on the deliberateness of a work. I am delighted when something is not deliberate. I do not trust deliberateness. When something happens by accident, I trust that the play is making its own point. I feel something is happening that is very profound and very important. People go far in this thing of awareness and deliberateness; they go further and further. They go to see a play and they do not like it. So someone explains it to them, and they like it better. How can they *possibly* understand it better, like it better, or see more of it because someone has explained it?

I am very good at explaining things. And whatever I do not understand, I can even invent. There are people who do beautiful work and do not know why, and they think it is invalid. Those who are not good at explanation are at a disadvantage, but their work is as valid.

I think it is impossible to aim at an audience when writing a play. I never do. I think that is why some commercial productions fail. They are trying to create a product that is going to create a reaction, and they cannot. If they could, every play on Broadway that is done for that purpose would be a great success. They think they know. They try and they fail. I know I do not know, but even if I did, I do not think I would write for the audience.

As a matter of fact, when the audience first comes to one of my plays, my feeling is that they are intruders. Especially when I have directed the play, I feel that I love my play so much, and I enjoy it so and feel so intimate with the actors, that when opening night arrives I ask, "What are all those people doing in my house?" Then it changes, of course, especially if they like it. I might even think I wrote it for them if they like it. I love to have an audience like a play. But during the work period, they are never present. Basically I feel that if I like something, other people will like it, too.

I think there is always a *person* I am writing for. Sometimes it is a specific person that I feel is there with me enjoying it in my mind. In my mind, that person is saying, "Oh, yes, I love it!" Or if it is not a specific person, it is a kind of person. It might be someone who does not really have a face, but it is a friend, someone who likes the same things. If we saw a play, we both would like it or we both would dislike it. So in a way I am writing for an "audience." But it is not for the public, not for the critics, not the business of theatre.

I feel that the state of creativity is a very special state. And most people who write or who want to write are not very aware that it is a state of mind. Most people when they cannot write say, "I can't write. I'm blocking." And then at another point they are writing a lot and they cannot stop; it appears to be a very mysterious thing, writing. Sometimes the Muse is speaking and other times it is not. But I think it is possible to put oneself in the right state of mind in the same manner that some people do meditation. There are techniques to arrive at particular states of consciousness. But we artists do not know the techniques. I do not know, either. I learned to do it with *Fefu and Her Friends* with my notes and record. But who knows? Maybe I could have done the play anyway.

I find that when I am not writing, *starting* to write is not difficult—it is impossible. It is just excruciating. I do not know the reason, for once I get started it is very pleasurable. I can think of nothing more pleasurable than being in the state of creativity. When I am in that state, people call me, say, to go to a party, to do things that are fun, to do the things where usually I would say, "Oh yes! Of course!" And nothing seems as pleasurable as writing.

But then I finish writing, and that state ends. It just seems that I do not want to go back to it. I feel about it the same way I feel about jumping off a bridge. And to keep from writing, I do everything. I sharpen pencils. In the past few days, it has been a constant thing of sitting at a typewriter and saying, "Oh! Let me get my silverware in order!" It seems very important because, when I might need a cup of coffee, the spoons will be all lined up. Incredible. It is incredible. So I go back to the typewriter. I say, "Oh! I need a cup of coffee." And then, "I better go get a pack of cigarettes so I'll have them here." And then there is starching my clothes. That is something I started this summer. It is a very lovely thing. I make my own starch. I have to wash my clothes. I have to let them dry, then starch them. They are hard to iron. I usually do not press my clothes. I just wear them. But now that I am writing, all my jeans are starched and pressed and all my shirts are starched and pressed. Anything is better than writing.

Interview with Fornes (1988)

An interview with Maria Irene Fornes, in *In Their Own Words: Contemporary American Playwrights*, by David Savran, Theatre Communications Group, 1988, pp. 51-69.

[*In the conversation below, Fornes and Savran talk about a number of issues relating to Fornes' dramas, including influences on her work, the content of her plays, and the political role of theater.*]

Born in Havana, Maria Irene Fornes came to New York with her mother in 1945, when she was fifteen years old. She studied painting in night school and with Hans Hoffman in Provincetown before going to Paris to paint for three years, returning to New York in 1957 as a textile designer. Three years later, having read only one play—*Hedda Gabler*—she suddenly got the idea for *Tango Palace.* "I stayed home for nineteen days and only left the house to go buy something to eat," she recalls. "I slept with the typewriter next to me." In the 1960s she was active in the Off-Off Broadway movement and wrote a series of dazzling, inventive fantasies, including *The Successful Life of 3* (1965), an almost comic-strip version of an erotic triangle; *Promenade* (1965, revised and expanded 1969), a vaudevillian celebration of unexpected juxtapositions, with music by Al Carmines; and *Molly's Dream* (1968), about a waitress's wistful fantasies.

In the early seventies she went through a fallow period, which came to an abrupt end in 1977 with the first production of *Fefu and Her Friends,* a play much more somber and emotionally violent than her early works. It was followed by a series of passionate and political works, including *Evelyn Brown* (1980), based on the diary of a servant in turn-of-the-century New Hampshire; *The Danube* (1982), about nuclear war; *Mud* (1983), an examination of a lethal erotic triangle; and *The Conduct of Life* (1985), about women held in thrall to a petty Latin American tyrant, torturer and rapist.

Despite the sharp differences between her early and her later plays, all of Fornes's work can be seen as a relentless search for a new theatrical language to explore what theatre has always been about: the difference between text and subtext, between the mask and the naked face beneath it, between the quotidian and the secret, between love and the fear and violence always threatening its fragile dominion. Fornes's early plays are filled with a slightly melancholic cheer, the result of an interplay between a sequence of fantastic and whimsical interactions and the underlying knowledge of unrequited desire and unfulfilled hopes—or in the words of her Dr. Kheal, "Contradictions compressed so that you don't know where one stops and the other begins." *Promenade,* for example, is peopled by a variety of symbiotic pairs, escaped convicts and a jailer, rich socialites and servants, ladies and gentlemen, a mother and her children. It is a comedy about the failure to make connections, searching for its plot in the same way that the jailer searches for his prisoners or the mother for her lost children. Throughout the play the pairs keep missing each other and although they delight in the unexpected turns, there is an intimation of a darker reality always held at bay. At the end the mother asks the two convicts, "Did you find evil?" And when they tell her "No," she assures them, "Good night, then. Sleep well. You'll find it some other time."

Even in these early works Fornes's revolutionary use of language is evident. From the first, she has honed speech to a simple, concrete and supple essence, whether in dialogue or as here, in the song of the convicts from *Promenade:*

> When I was born I opened my eyes,
> And when I looked around I closed them;
> And when I saw how people get kicked in the head,
> And kicked in the belly, and kicked in the groin,
> I closed them.
> My eyes are closed but I'm carefree.
> Ho ho ho, ho ho ho, I'm carefree.

This is language surprisingly capable of expressing complex shades of emotion and mobilizing a rich and understated irony.

One way of approaching Fornes's recent work is to see a reversal in the relative tonalities of surface and depth, the action now much more ominous, the characters no longer the "cardboard dolls" of *Promenade* but beings who breathe and sweat. The change is heralded in the first scene of *Fefu* when the title character, discussing her husband's belief that women are "loathesome," compares her fascination with it to turning over a stone in damp soil. The exposed part "is smooth and dry and clean." But that underneath "is slimy and filled with fungus and crawling with worms. It is another life that is parallel to the one we manifest." Fefu warns, "If you don't recognize it . . . (*Whispering.*) it eats you." All of Fornes's later plays are explorations of the dark underneath. In *Fefu* Fornes unearths the workings of a furtive misogyny and its destructive power. The seven women who join Fefu at her country house are all, to some degree, victims of the men, with their "natural strength," hovering just offstage. "Women have to find their strength," Fefu explains, "and when they do find it, it comes forth with bitterness and it's erratic." Those among them unable to recognize their internalization of masculine attitudes are destroyed.

The plays since *Fefu,* written in a great diversity of styles, explore the workings of violence—psychological, political and sexual—and the self-destruction toward which it leads, with the aim of teaching, of asking the spectator to understand and to make another choice. *The Danube* was conceived when, by chance, Fornes came across a Hungarian-English language record. "There was such tenderness in those little scenes," she recalls. When asked to write an antinuclear play, Fornes thought of the sadness she felt for "the bygone era of that record, and how sorrowful it would be to lose the simple pleasures of our own." Set on the eve of World War II, the play charts the gradual decay of a civilization along with the emotional

and physical destruction of its well-meaning protagonists. It ends with a "brilliant white flash of light," and then, darkness.

Fornes's plays differ from those of most of her contemporaries in that almost all are set either in a preindustrial society or on the far edge of middle-class culture. They are filled with a deep compassion for the disenfranchised, for whom survival—rather than the typically bourgeois obsession with individual happiness and freedom—is the bottom line. They do not delight, even covertly, in suffering but take a stand unequivocally against dehumanization and violence in its myriad forms. Perhaps it is in this context that her revolutionary use of language is best understood, its simplicity and beauty signaling, in the midst of violence and decay, a verbal utopia in which things are called by their proper names and brutality is so embarrassingly evident that it can no longer hold sway.

OCTOBER 29, 1986—RIVERIA CAFE, SHERIDAN SQUARE, NEW YORK CITY

[David Savran]: *What got you interested in theatre?*

[Maria Irene Fornes]: A play that I wanted to write got me interested in theatre. I was not a playwright. I was not in theatre because at that time theatre was not a very interesting art.

When was that?

1959, '60. At that time the most advanced writers in the American theatre were Tennessee Williams and Arthur Miller. That *was* the American theatre. Important theatre took place on Broadway. The beginning of the avantgarde theatre came from Europe: Samuel Beckett, Eugene Ionesco and Jean Genet. It was as if those European writers were inviting us. But even when these writers became known here, it took a few years before we actually started doing their work.

For years most of my friends were in the arts. They were writers—novelists, poets—or painters. I didn't know anybody in theatre. So I was never at a rehearsal of a play. I never knew an actor who would talk about rehearsals or auditions or anything like that. Very few people I knew went to the theatre. I do remember going to see *A Streetcar Named Desire* because word filtered down that it was interesting. But when I started to write a play, although it did have something to do with some theatre I had seen, it had nothing to do with a general affection for or interest in the theatre.

So you were more attracted to European theatre?

In '55, I think it was, or '54, I saw the original production of *Waiting for Godot* in Paris, directed by Roger Blin. I'd just arrived in Paris and I didn't know a word of French. But I was so profoundly upset by that play—and by upset I mean turned upside down—that I didn't even question the fact that I had not understood a word. I felt that my life had been turned around. I left the theatre and felt that I saw everything so clearly. Maybe it was just a clear night, but it was such a physical experience. I felt that I saw clarity. Maybe that night something in me understood that I was to dedicate my life to the theatre. My feeling was that I understood something about life. If you'd asked me then what it was I'd understood, I couldn't have told you. If I had understood the text it still wouldn't have been clear. Of course, I knew the play had something to do with slavery and freedom.

I was a painter and lived in Paris for several years. I was not interested in writing. I came back to New York in '57 and the next year, I think it was, I saw a production of *Ulysses in Nighttown*, with Zero Mostel, directed by Burgess Meredith. It was performed in a place—on West Houston Street, I think—that was not ordinarily used as a theatre. And that too had a profound effect on me. But still I didn't think I wanted to write a play. I just thought, "How wonderful, what an incredible thing."

Then in 1960, or maybe it was 1959, I had an idea for a play. I was obsessed with it. And I started writing it. Most of the people I knew, especially writers, said, "Theatre's a very difficult medium. You have to learn how to write a play, otherwise it won't be put on." I thought that was very funny because I never thought that I would write a play to put it on. I had to write this play because I had to write this play. It was as personal as that. I never thought of a career or a profession. So I wrote it. And writing it was the most incredible experience. A door was opened which was a door to paradise.

Which play was that?

That was ***Tango Palace.*** I imagine there are few writers who have such a sharp beginning. Usually a person's interest in theatre or literature starts early. Then one day you decide that you'd like to do something. It's very gradual. For me, it was like when you miss a step and fall into a precipice. I didn't even decide that I was going to step into it. And there I was, flying up!

What about other influences? Arthur Miller, Tennessee Williams?

I don't like Arthur Miller at all. I don't like Tennessee Williams' plays very much either, because it seems to me that he celebrates a kind of feminine neurosis, that he sings praise to it. I don't like that. But I don't dislike him the way that I dislike Arthur Miller. I feel love for Tennessee Williams, like someone I knew. In his writing you see the spirit of somebody with delicate feelings who was beat up as a child and lives in a world of pain and tears with a kind of complacency. Maybe complacency is not the right word. Maybe it's masochistic—the feeling that you cannot escape it. So you have a longing for beauty and for romance, you dream that Prince Charming's going to take you away from it all. I don't see the point of that at all. I feel we're fortunate that no matter how terrible things are, we live in a society where we have the freedom to take action, even if some people make this difficult for you, or

if you're disabled from your upbringing. I understand how one can be mangled psychologically, but still your effort should be to find your vitality and move on.

I don't romanticize pain. In my work people are always trying to find a way out, rather than feeling a romantic attachment to their prison. Some people complain that my work doesn't offer the solution. But the reason for that is that I feel that the characters don't have to get out, it's *you* who has to get out. Characters are not real people. If characters were real people, I would have opened the door for them at the top of it—there would be no play. The play is there as a lesson, because I feel that art ultimately is a teacher. You go to a museum to look at a painting and that painting teaches you something. You may not look at a Cezanne and say, "I know now what I have to do." But it gives you something, a charge of some understanding, some knowledge that you have in your heart. And if art doesn't do that, I am not interested in it.

I don't know what my work inspires, because I'm never the spectator. But I'm horrified to think that my work in any way would suggest there is no way out. I've been told by some women, for instance, that by killing Mae in **Mud,** I have robbed them of the possibility of thinking there's a way out. "If she cannot escape," they said, "how can we?" I feel terrible that I have made them lose hope. The work that has most inspired me to action or to freedom is not work that's saying, "Look, I'm going to show you how you too can do it."

Kafka's *The Trial*, like *Waiting for Godot*, gave me the experience of a remarkable energy inside me. Pozzo beats on Lucky and at the end Lucky doesn't get free, but it doesn't matter because I do! I've never been anybody's slave but when I see that I understand something. Josef K. may get guillotined or go to the electric chair but, rather than saying "I'm doomed," I learn from his behavior. I know what my intention is, but I don't know if, after seeing **Mud,** it would be difficult to feel, "I'm getting out." I know that most people don't feel depressed by it.

*So many of your plays have apocalyptic endings, where an amazing thing happens, like the burst of light at the end of **The Danube**. It's as though you're not so much ending a situation as producing a shock wave directed at the spectators, which makes them deal with what they've seen.*

Maybe I have to be a little more careful with that. As I'm writing the play, I suffer with the characters and I share their joys—or else I can't write. I am dealing with them for a long time and then analyzing, breaking the play down, trying to see if it works. I become a technician and start moving things around. It could be that the shock is more violent to the audience than it is to me, because often that violent moment has to do with the violence of ending the work. That's a violence to an author.

Often, when you've become very involved in the life of a character, when you're riveted, and the play ends, you have a feeling of rupture. This world has died. But maybe that feeling of rupture is deeper in me . . . after all, audiences are involved in it for an hour and a half or two hours. But I've been involved for one to three years. I don't know how to end a play unless . . . who's going to kill whom? It could be that it's so violent for me that I transfer it to the stage. But to a member of the audience who doesn't have the same sense of loss when it's over, it's a shock, right? You say it is startling. I experience Mae's death, for instance, as a natural thing. I don't see how they could possibly let her go.

In retrospect it becomes an inevitability. The ending makes me go back to discover why.

I think usually the people who have expressed to me their dismay at Mae's being killed are feminist women who are having a hard time in their life. They hang onto feminism because they feel oppressed and believe it will save them. They see me as a feminist and when they see Mae die, they feel betrayed. I say "they," as if it were a multitude of people. A couple of people have said, "How could you do this to me?"

They expect positive role models. This also comes up in regard to black theatre. Some people are disturbed to see, for example, a black man who is as oppressive as the white man he's fighting against.

I don't believe in role models because I don't believe in that expression. I've never played a role in my life, and role playing to me is the beginning of death. You have to be yourself and you have to find wisdom and enlightenment within yourself. The moment you're playing a role, you're faking it, pretending you're this or that. I know that's not what they mean but the choice of the word is unfortunate.

We have the potential to learn by example or by demonstration. If you're trying to teach people to be careful when they cross the street and not just trust the light, and you show them a film where someone doesn't look and a drunk driver comes by and kills him, you're not saying, "You're going to get killed," You're saying, "Look what happened to this person. You look and don't get killed." That is a classic way of teaching. But maybe that's old-fashioned and I am an old-fashioned person.

How do you begin a play? Plot, characters, a situation?

Usually characters, but not characters that I choose or people I meet and about whom I say, "I'm going to write a play about them." They're characters that come to the page. I was so inspired when I wrote *Tango Palace.* I didn't ask for it, it just came into my mind and possessed me. Considering that it was my first play, it was easy to write. And it received a production at the San Francisco Actor's Workshop, very well directed by Herbert Blau and very well acted by Robert Benson and Dan Sullivan. Then it was published shortly afterwards in a college book of literature, among writers like Aristotle and Shakespeare

and you can imagine . . . When you have a first experience like this, you're always looking to repeat it.

I tried to find ways to be possessed again. I devised writing games—I put descriptions of characters on a number of cards and places on other cards, and shuffled them. I wrote *Promenade* like that. I took one card and it said The Aristocrats and I took another card and it said The Cell. All the locations followed the cards I was getting. And I found that it was possible to be caught up again in a kind of writing where the characters take over and they do what they do and you have nothing to do with it. All you do is write down what's happening. If I don't write that way, the dialogue is very flat and tedious. I have to force the writing out. When the characters take over, it's fluid and fast and interesting. And you are as surprised as when you see something in the theatre and don't know what's going to happen next.

For six years now, I've been teaching playwriting at INTAR. I have an ideal situation there. This year we are meeting every morning at 9:30 for thirteen weeks, which is very intensive. Usually we meet three times a week for six months. First thing, we do half an hour of yoga. Then I give them a writing exercise. I have invented exercises that are very effective and very profound. They take you to the place where creativity is, where personal experience and personal knowledge are used. But it's not *about* your personal experience. Personal experience feeds into that creative place. It's wonderful to see that people can learn how to write.

My writing has been coming from the lab for the last five years. It has changed my style of writing. *Tango Palace* was very passionate. I realized after I wrote it that I didn't know yet how to write painful things without going through agony myself. So I started to write things that were lighter because I just didn't want to suffer. I'm not going to jump into fire so that I can be inscribed in the roster of great writers. But now, through my exercises, I know how to do it. My students know how to do it.

Right now we're in the second week of work. Today we were doing an exercise and one of the writers started sobbing. He was in the lab last year so he knows how to go into that and come out. It's not unusual for me to look over and see someone filled with tears. And you say, "Oh wow, I wish I were there because that must be something good." But he was sobbing and he stopped writing. So I went over behind him and said, "Are you okay?" He said yes. And I said, "Do you need anything?" because I thought maybe he needed comforting. He was okay; he was going through pain, but so what? After a while he went and blew his nose. He looked in the mirror and said he didn't look as pretty when he cried as Natalie Wood so he better stop [laughs]. Pain can be channeled—it's like what actors do. Actors go into the most agonizing thing and they're shaking and you think, "My God, how can they do this every night?" You want to say, "My poor darling. Let me hold you for a while to comfort you." And you go back to the dressing room, and they look like they've just been swimming in the Caribbean. They look radiant, and you're a wreck. So that's how I write [laughs].

It's wonderful to have that every day, with a group of people. We do our yoga quietly. I give them an exercise. We hardly ever talk. We write all morning. The last half-hour, they read. At first, I have a lot to say but I don't criticize the writing. I see if they are trying to write according to some other person's rules. You can tell from the dialogue—if it doesn't have any real life, you know they're following some idea of how people write.

Writing every day is wonderful. You may feel, "I'm not inspired," but maybe after half an hour you begin to be able to write. At home I would say, "Okay, I'll do something and then I'll write." And then I don't write that day. I don't write the next day. After a month of not writing, I don't know how to write. I forget. If you write every day, it's like another kind of existence. There's something in you that changes. You're in a different state.

How long have you been directing your own scripts?

Since 1968 with *Molly's Dream.* That summer there was a workshop for playwrights at Tanglewood in connection with Boston University. They had a company of fine actors. The plays were done in elaborately directed readings, with a lot of people memorizing as much as they could. Robert Lewis was the director of the program, but he wasn't directing any of the plays. I told him I wanted to direct and he said, "No. The directors will direct." I said, "But this is a playwrights' project and, as a playwright, I need to direct this play." He said no. I was annoyed, but I asked Ed Setrakian because I knew him as an actor and liked him and thought, "Why not?"

Then Ed started doing things that I didn't think were right. The play was very simple and he was making it too abstract. So I went to Bobby Lewis and said, "This is not right. He's asking people to do this bizarre behavior. The play's a kind of movie fantasy where people behave normally." So Bobby Lewis said, "You have to ask Ed to do it the way you want. And if you have any problems, I'll talk to him." So Ed did what I asked and then he said to me, "I haven't been able to sleep because of what you're doing to me." And I looked at him and said, "Ed, I'd rather you don't sleep than I don't sleep."

I'd always been so timid. When a director would say "Boo," I would acquiesce. But that situation taught me never again to give in. I didn't want to make Ed not sleep. I wanted to do it myself. If then it doesn't come out right, I did it wrong and nobody else has to suffer. I promised myself that I wasn't going to let anyone else direct my work. And I didn't care if it never got done again.

So I went to New Dramatists—I was a member there—to do *Molly's Dream* again. I wanted to do it with Julie Bovasso. They said, "All right, but we have to get you a director." I said, "No, I want to direct it." They said,

"There's a rule here that playwrights are not to direct." And I started screaming, "I'm directing or I'm quitting. If this is a playwrights' organization, you have to do what is good for the playwrights. What are you going to lose?" So they made an exception for me. I directed Julie Bovasso and it was a bumpy ride. I didn't know her history of quitting and throwing chairs at directors. It worked because I didn't have a director's ego. I just wanted her to do my play. And she was wonderful.

I direct the first production of my plays and often the second. *Sarita*'s going to be done a second time in San Francisco. They wanted me to direct it but I can't. It's too exhausting and I have too much writing to do. I wish I were directing it because I usually make changes in the second production. With the first production, sometimes I haven't finished the play.

So you're active as a writer while you're directing the first production.

Often I'm writing the play. Since *Aurora,* the play after *Molly's Dream,* I have never had a finished play before I started rehearsal. Usually I have a first draft of most of the play. It still needs a lot of rewriting but at least the scenes are there. *Aurora* and *Fefu and Her Friends* were not finished until three days before opening. For *Eyes on the Harem* I had something like three little pages written when we started rehearsal.

During the summer when I work at Padua Hills Playwrights' Workshop in California, we're supposed to write a play for a particular place, a particular grove. For me that's a first draft, or not even a first draft, because usually they want only forty minutes. Then I write more and it becomes a longer play. *The Danube* and *Mud* came from California. *The Mothers* I did last summer at Padua. It may be called something else when it's a big play.

The printed version of *The Conduct of Life* is different from the performance you saw. Orlando's speeches about his sadism were written after the play was first produced.

When I saw the play I really disliked the character, he's such a horrible man. But from reading it, I understood him much better.

The difference is partly in the writing, and partly in the fact that the actor was a young man without much experience. When you work Off-Off Broadway—which means there's no money—there are a number of excellent actresses available. It's much harder to get men. Men don't work for nothing. There are more parts for them, more jobs. If they don't start making money from acting after, say, a couple of years of acting classes and one or two more of auditioning, they quit. Women don't because either they have a husband to support them or they are dedicated to the theatre. They will spend their whole life working a job and acting wherever they can.

Do you read the critics?

I never read a review until people tell me whether it's good or bad. It makes me too nervous. So if people say, "It's excellent," or "It's so-so," or "It's terrible," then I can read it. But I usually read it quickly. Maybe a year or two later, I pick up a review and say, "Oh, I thought this was worse, actually it does say things that are good, that are interesting."

I'm sure critics hate to have a playwright think this, but I find there's very little I learn about my work from reading the reviews. A lot of the critics—not from the *New York Times*, but the *Voice*—are talking to the playwrights, as if we're having a conversation and they're saying, "Look, Irene, it's time you did this." But I don't find that they are usually insightful enough. Maybe I'm being unfair, since I find when I read a review a few months later, it reads differently from the way it first did. Maybe I never find it insightful because I'm so guarded. But I think I'm right to be guarded because there's a difference between having a private conversation and a public one. A negative review is read by everybody. And not only that, but the people who read a negative review—"It was terribly slow"—won't go to see the play. You lose your audience because the critic wanted to have a conversation with you. When you have the power of the media and you tell everybody I'm stupid, that's not a conversation.

But the Village Voice *has been very supportive of your work.*

I owe my life in the theatre to the *Village Voice*. If the *Village Voice* did not exist, I don't know if I would be writing now. Richard Eder was positive about my work when he was with the *Times*. Since he left, about nine years ago, the *Times* never comes and when they do come, it's just hell. Marilyn Stasio has been supportive but she doesn't get much of a chance at the *Post*. They print Clive Barnes and they print reviews that she writes when they feel like it. I complain about the *Voice* because to me they are the only paper. I don't complain about the *Times* critics because to me they don't exist. They don't say anything.

They fulfill a function in the marketplace. Frank Rich doesn't have anything to offer people working in the theatre.

It's just for businessmen. They say to this guy: yes, no or so-so. They should just print that in the newspaper: SO-SO, in large type. I think a journalist, a critic of value, is someone who can teach, who can persuade people to stretch themselves a little bit. I don't mean doing the playwrights a favor or art a favor, I mean helping the audience understand something. Critics are not doing that.

Aunt Dan and Lemon *was one of the very few recent plays for which, I think, Rich did fulfill that role.*

I didn't like the play because I feel it is promoting fascism.

I didn't read the play as promoting fascism but forcing the spectator to confront his own fascist sympathies.

But you know who Wally Shawn is. You know he's not a fascist. How do ordinary people know who he is? It's not that he has to say straight out, "I'm showing you how stupid people are. Listen to how stupid this girl is who's saying it's decent and normal to be fascist." But there is something about where the heart of the author is. When your heart is dubious and perhaps you take a little too much pleasure in sadistic things, it may be confusing.

I don't know anything about Wally Shawn's politics. I know of his father and I saw him in *My Dinner with Andre*, where he was playing a poor writer. Well, he's not poor so I thought, he's playing a part. I don't know whether he's a fascist or so intellectual, so sophisticated, like Andre with his thing about burying himself to experience death. You don't know how far these people can go with, "Let's experience it." Maybe he thinks it's a good idea to go around and kill people. I don't know! I bet you that most people left the theatre saying, "I think Reagan is right. We have to eliminate all the people in Honduras and Nicaragua that are standing in our way."

I saw it as being about Reagan too, but about the incredibly seductive power of his fascism.

But how do you know that Wally Shawn is not pro-Reagan? That girl was a little too convincing for me. When she said, "We're not really compassionate, we are, maybe, a little embarrassed"—something like that—there was something so intelligent about that line. This is too dangerous. If he means to say, "Watch out, look how quickly you can turn," he shouldn't do it so convincingly. Don't hypnotize me into believing that it's right because then, what are you doing? You are creating murderers, the same way they do when they brainwash men who join the marines.

In the theatre I wanted to shout, "No!" I felt outraged. Then I looked around and I became more interested in watching the audience. I don't think people were thinking, "How wrong this girl is." I thought they were thinking, "Is it true, what I'm being told?" You know how many people in that audience actually don't have compassion, but only a little disgust? And you know how many are liberal, just because they think it's right? I felt him convince half that audience. I thought, "The reviewers didn't think that because either they know Wally and they know he has a tender heart or because they think, 'Wally Shawn couldn't be writing this fascistic thing.'" And they all saw it as you feel it was intended. Let's hope most people read the reviews.

When I wrote Orlando's speeches in **Conduct of Life,** I worked very hard to try to imagine the experience of a sadist. I went through hell. It was so difficult. It was so ugly. I have written violent things and they all come out of me . . . easy, natural. I have a monster in me. I have many monsters in me. But that particular one, Orlando, is not in me, I don't understand it. It was a nightmare for me to write those speeches. But I hope that I didn't write them too convincingly. If I did, I would eliminate them from the play. And I feel that Orlando is less dangerous because not many people, especially people who go to the theatre, are going to abuse little girls.

What Wally Shawn is proposing, that they support Reagan, is not as drastic as that. You just go into the voting booth and think, "I want to keep my comfortable life, so I won't tell anybody." That's easy.

In **The Danube** *you use some Hungarian, in the sections of translation. That makes me think of your own position. How is it for you writing in a second language?*

I came here when I was fifteen and that is precisely the time you begin to become your own person, when you are no longer's a child. You begin to go outside your family or school and venture on your own, you start thinking thoughts that you can't share with your family. So when I started thinking independently—or rather, when my thinking connected to society rather than home—it all happened in English. If I want to talk about simple things, I can do it equally well in Spanish or English. When I start talking about thoughts, if I speak Spanish, I have to translate all the time.

For many years I've admired your use of a language that's simple and straightforward, and very poetic.

My vocabulary in English is very limited. When I read a newspaper or magazine article I'm constantly finding words that I don't know. I don't mean technical words. But words I don't use. So I look them up and then I forget what they mean. And it may be that because my knowledge of the language is limited, I always have to be sure of what I'm saying because I have nothing else. I can't say, "I'll put a fancy phrase in here and cover up," because I don't know how to write a fancy phrase. So I have to think, "What does the character want to say? What is the reality of what's happened? What is the need? What is it inside him that can be said to depict him?" I think more of painting, of a character painting a picture, getting a picture clear.

At the same time, it seems your plays are about the impossibility of language to comprehend experience, about the difference between text and subtext. Doctor Kheal says that you can't talk about beauty.

It's become fashionable to say that about language and I'll tell you why I object. Evidently the directors of some productions of **The Danube** believe that I use the language tape to show how we're prisoners of language and how we repeat, as if there were a recording going and we were puppets. Unfortunately, there's also the image of puppets in the play which confirms this for them. Can you imagine? Language is the greatest gift that we have. We've been sitting here talking for two hours. And to think that I would say, "We are imprisoned by language"?! But they have people act like puppets. Don't they understand that this play is about life and the destruction of life? You can't blame language if you don't know how to use language, if

you stop thinking. It's like a computer, you just press a key and you get a whole sentence. That's how so many people use language. It's gotten to the point if you don't use set paragraphs, people don't understand what you're saying.

People often speak about my work as being singular. What's singular is that each person's speech is full of little pieces, how they really think, one word at a time. People are very simple. But they are specific about each little detail. Even if it's just, "Oh, good morning, how are you? How's your daughter?" Maybe I leave out one word that, when I talk, I don't. Words that are useless, like "actually." I take those little words out.

But you were asking me about **Doctor Kheal.** Of course, language is language and life is life. There's no question about it. The number of things you can experience and don't know how to express are infinite. And it is true that sometimes we think we're experiencing only those things we know how to talk about. But that doesn't mean that language is shit. Language is a miraculous thing, probably the greatest gift we have. But it doesn't substitute for life. People who try to use it that way are in trouble. They have to know what experience is. But also they have to try using this incredible tool to clarify what they are experiencing. Because I'm a writer, I know how much work that is. Doctor Kheal has a hard time explaining beauty. So? He explains everything else. It's just that for a moment he would rather experience it. He's saying, "How could one ever come near it? I bow my head in front of it." A way of expressing your awe is to say, "Words fail me." That's language.

How does the American theatre look from your perspective?

You could say that the regional theatre, the Broadway theatre and the Off-Off Broadway theatre are schools of theatre. The theatres are training writers they've never seen, young artists who see whose plays get done all the time and whose plays don't get done at all.

You can go to the school without walls, which is Off-Off Broadway. There's more freedom there. There's more variety. But there, nobody's paid, so you can't demand too much.

I feel that the regional theatres have betrayed the playwrights. Their training has turned too many into documentary writers. Some people are doing actual documentaries, like Emily Mann and Adrian Hall. But that's just journalistic, those pieces are not going to last. That's not theatre literature. It may be serious and subtle work but it's not a play. Plays are written with a bit of that mentality, too. Even if the story is not about a current situation, there's a correlation with something happening right now, like corruption in City Hall.

The regional theatre depends too heavily on subsidies. It's inevitable. I'm not saying that they should do something different. There are less brains on Broadway but more energy. It's a business. I think that the regional theatre is more frightened than the Broadway theatre.

Do you think that's true of the Off-Broadway companies here? Manhattan Theatre Club, Playwrights Horizons, Second Stage?

Those are part of the regional-theatre aesthetic. But I don't go to the theatre enough to be able to say that with great conviction. The timidity comes from being afraid of losing your subscribers. If you lose your subscribers or your single-ticket buyers, you lose part of your funding. Because the more money you make at the box office, the more money you're given. It makes a certain business sense but it has nothing to do with art. And they're afraid, especially when they get into bigger expenses. Part of this has to do with the Equity scales. They have every reason in the world to be afraid. I think that they would put on *anything* that they could get an audience for.

Just recently, I've seen some of the regional theatres opening up to my work. I know my work has changed. It's more accessible, more emotional. There's more of a plot. Maybe they're not changing and I'm changing. I don't know. Maybe they're looking for something and writers who are less conventional will have an opportunity to be done on this large a scale. But it's not all good news because if the audience doesn't like it. . . . Of course any art always depends on sales. Theatre has become an unnatural thing, unlike television or film. So it has to be subsidized.

When I wrote my first play, I was writing because I wanted to write. And I still feel that a little bit. I do it for my own evolution. That doesn't mean I don't want theatres to put on my work, that I don't want audiences to flock to the theatre, that I don't want critics to write fantastic things, that I don't want to get every award there is. If it happens, it's part of my evolution.

Was there a time when you felt you weren't making progress?

After **Promenade** was done at the Promenade Theatre. Actually, I think it had started a little before. Up through **Tango Palace, Successful Life of 3, Dr. Kheal** . . . some of those were humorous but there was more there too. And then I started to repeat. I think in **Aurora** I tried to repeat **Promenade.** It wasn't conscious. And **Molly's Dream,** too, in a way. Those plays were more charming than substantial. They had less muscle. That's why I find my exercises in writing are so important. I think the worst thing for a writer is to write in only one way. It's not from being lazy or clever, you just get into a rut. You don't know you're in a rut. You say, "That's how I write." But if you do those exercises, you write from so many different places and your writing seems so peculiar. Afterwards, you look at it and say, "No, it's not peculiar. It was just peculiar for me. I'd never written from that place before."

Also, the Off-Off Broadway writers started to feel indifference from the people who had been our producers. They started getting excited by directors.

You're talking mid-seventies.

Even earlier, late sixties. The period when the writers were the main energy source in the Off-Off Broadway theatre was only two or three years. I think that '65 was really the beginning of the flowering. I don't know if Sam Shepard, Lanford Wilson, Rosalyn Drexler or Rochelle Owens was writing before that. I started in '65. The first thing that I heard about was Rosalyn Drexler's *Home Movies.* That may have been '64. By '69 already the directors had taken over—Tom O'Horgan, Open Theatre.

Richard Schechner founded the Performance Group in '67.

It's so important to have interest from outside, to have a theatre that wants your work, actors who ask, "Can I be in your play?" And we had Michael Smith in the *Voice.* He was our critic in our paper. You need that. A group of people coming with excitement to the theatre, that's all I need. But I do need that. I cannot write in isolation.

Are there any favorites among your plays?

There are favorites but usually it's the one that I'm working on, the one that I don't really understand yet. Like when you're in love, it means you don't really understand the person. When you understand the person, it's *a* love, rather than *in* love. I think **Fefu** is a very beautiful play. I did it in Minneapolis in May and working with it again, I find it's a very moving play without being sentimental. Men who are more feminine in their nature, more artistic, feel it as deeply as women. There are some men who don't know what's happening. They say, "What? Is there a play there? Is there anybody on the stage?" **Mud** I think is a little jewel.

I'm worried about **The Conduct of Life** because I only did it once. When I do a play once I feel that I don't yet understand it fully. And I worry whether it would work as well if I didn't direct it. I know **Mud** would work. I saw one production of it which wasn't good and yet it worked. But **Conduct of Life** may have a strange soul to it.

How so?

I don't know how it reads. Recently there was a reading of it at Los Angeles Theatre Center. I got a call from the director. He wanted to talk about casting, so I said, "Please, above all, Orlando should look like a very ordinary person, a nice guy. You meet him and he's like someone who works in an office and has a nice job." And he said, "Fine." For Letitia he said he had a very strong woman. Then he asked, "How old is Olimpia?" I said, "Olimpia's a middle-aged woman." He had cast a young girl. I said, "She's a housekeeper, a woman who cleans. She's short and heavy." An attractive girl would throw the balance of the play. I don't even know if the play would work.

He was thinking, too, of women being oppressed. All those women are strong. Nena is a strong woman, a strong child. It's not just women being oppressed. When you have a nut, a crazy person like that, everybody's oppressed. It's the oppression of a sadist. It has nothing to do with women. So a playwright has to be careful. I thought it was so obvious that Olimpia is an illiterate housekeeper that I didn't specify that she's middle-aged, overweight and unattractive. How can you say Olimpia's being oppressed? She runs the house! A servant is a job like any other. You work. When you go to work in an office, are you oppressed? You think that everybody should be a boss?

People like to draw a clear line between victim and victimizer. It's frightening for people to recognize their role in the maintenance of this system.

I don't think Olimpia, Nena and Letitia are maintaining the situation. I remember shortly after the Castro takeover there was a group of Cuban exile artists. They wanted me to go to meetings, to have readings, and they said, "It's not political." So I went. They had readings of poetry and discussions of painting and stuff like that. Then one day they passed an anti-Castro manifesto around that we were supposed to sign. It talked about the Red monster and the language was extreme. I said, "No, I don't want to sign." They were indignant and asked, "Are you in favor of Castro?" I said, "Not really. I'm not in favor of Castro but I'm not against him either. I don't know enough." And they said, "If you're not against him, you're for him." I'm not for him and don't tell me what I am because I know what I am. It's like saying if people don't fight the system, then they are for the system. That's not so. People have to survive. If you don't go out and get a gun and shoot the general, it doesn't mean you're supporting the system.

Letitia is in love with Orlando, but I don't think she's a masochist. She discovers horrible things, that he's in love with a child. She discovers what he is and she shoots him, because she cannot live around him. Before that she has enough information to realize what he is, but she cannot face it. But that doesn't mean that she's supporting the system. There is an oppressor in that play, but it's not Orlando, who is just a peon in the political system. It's the generals.

I don't think everybody there is supporting the system. What are they going to do? Olimpia has a job. She has to survive. You think she's going to say, "You son of a bitch. I'm not going to work in this house anymore. I'm going to go out and starve." We can do that in this country. Here, if Olimpia leaves a job, she's employed the next day somewhere else, because she's a good housekeeper and knows how to cook. But not in other places. So you cannot say, if you don't fight it, you're with it.

It may not be true in Latin America, where survival is the bottom line. But in this country so many people are passively complicit with an oppressive regime. That's a very serious problem.

Are you supporting Reagan because you don't go out and shoot him?

No.

Do you know how many people in other countries think that you are? Because you are going around with your little tape recorder and doing your little interviews instead of fighting.

There are ways of being politically active besides picking up a gun.

Letitia is just an ordinary woman who doesn't know anything. She's just in love with this guy. She's not political. She's not even intelligent. And Olimpia is an imbecile! Do you expect her to be political? And Nena? You expect her to be political? I expect you to be political. I expect me to be. We're supposed to be. It's been going on how many years now?

Six.

It's getting worse and worse. There isn't even a strong opposition as there was in the sixties. I would say that we are parties to this, but not them. We have the knowledge, the intelligence, the perspective. We know what's right and what's wrong.

What does this mean then in terms of bringing about social change, for people who don't have the perspective we have?

They cannot bring about social change. They don't know what's possible.

What can they do?

The only thing they can do is act emotionally. Letitia acts emotionally. She kills Orlando. Not because he has betrayed her, but because he attacks her physically. When he does, she shoots him.

OVERVIEWS AND GENERAL STUDIES

Bonnie Marranca (essay date 1984)

SOURCE: "The Real Life of Maria Irene Fornes," in *Performing Arts Journal*, Vol. VIII, No. 1, 1984, pp. 29-34.

[*In the following essay, Marranca describes the essential characteristics of Fornes' drama, praising the "warm delicacy and grace that distinguish it from most of what is written today."*]

Ever since *Fefu and Her Friends* Maria Irene Fornes has been writing the finest realistic plays in this country. In fact, one could say that *Fefu* and the plays that followed it, such as *The Danube* and now *Mud,* have paved the way for a new language of dramatic realism, and a way of directing it. What Fornes, as writer and director of her work, has done is to strip away the self-conscious objectivity, narrative weight, and behaviorism of the genre to concentrate on the unique subjectivity of characters for whom talking is gestural, a way of being. There is no attempt to tell the whole story of a life, only to distill its essence. Fornes brings a much needed intimacy to drama, and her economy of approach suggests another vision of theatricality, more stylized for its lack of exhibitionism. In this new theatricality, presence, that is, the act of being, is of greatest importance. The theatrical idea of presence is linked to the idea of *social being* expressed by character. The approach is that of a documentary starkness profoundly linked to existential phenomenology.

Fornes's work goes to the core of character. Instead of the usual situation in which a character uses dialogue or action to explain what he or she is doing and why, her characters exist in the world by their very act of trying to understand it. In other words, it is the characters themselves who appear to be thinking, not the author having thought.

Mud, which has as its center the act of a woman coming to thought, clarifies this process. Here is a poor rural trio, Fornes's first lower depths characters, which consists of Mae, Lloyd and Henry, all who lead lives devoid of any sense of play or abandonment; their lives are entirely functional. Each of them exists in varying relations to language—Mae through her desire to read and acquire knowledge realizes that knowledge is the beginning of will and power and personal freedom; Henry, who becomes crippled in an accident during the course of the play, must learn again how to speak; Lloyd, barely past the level of survival beyond base instincts, has no language of communication beyond an informational one. *Mud* is the encounter of the characters in seventeen scenes which are separated by slow blackouts of "eight seconds," the story of struggles for power in which Henry usurps Lloyd's place in Mae's bed, and Lloyd kills Mae when she eventually walks out on Henry and him and their destitute existence. The violence committed in this play is the violence of the inarticulate.

Through the plays of Bond, Kroetz, Fassbinder, Wenzel, Vinaver, to name a few, a new and different realism stripped bare, plays that outline the contemporary vision of tragedy, came into drama in the seventies in Europe. These extreme reworkings of realism prove that the heritage of epic performance opened up by Brechtian dramaturgy, namely, the concept of *gestus*, still is a major source on which to build the new dramatic vocabulary. But this refinement of realism, to the extent that it could be called a movement, never happened here, largely because of the heavy input of psychology and speech in American theatre, the scant interest in stylized gesture and emotion, the lack of attention to the nuances of language as a political condition. (Though one could point to such plays as Tavel's *Boy on the Straight-Back Chair*, Shepard's *Action*, Mamet's *Edmond*, Shank's *Sunset/Sunrise* as steps toward

an American rethinking of realism, they are only isolated phenomena.) What Fornes has done in her approach to realism over the years, and *Mud* is the most austere example of this style to be produced in the theatre on this side of the Atlantic, is to lift the burden of psychology, declamation, morality, and sentimentality from the concept of character. She has freed characters from explaining themselves in a way that attempts to suggest interpretations of their actions, and put them in scenes that create a single emotive moment, as precise in what it does not articulate as in what does get said.

She rejects bourgeois realism's cliches of thought patterns, how its characters project themselves in society; she rejects its melodramatic self-righteousness. Though her work is purposely presented in a flat space that emphasizes its frontality, and the actors speak in a non-inflected manner, it is not the detached cool of hyper- or super- or photo-realism, but more emotive, filled with content. Gestures, emptied of their excesses, are free to be more resonant. *The Danube* resounds with the unspeakable horror of nuclear death precisely because it is not named.

Mud's scenes seem, radically, to be a comment on what does not occur in performance, as if all the action had happened off stage. Her realism subtracts information whereas the conventional kind does little more than add it to a scene. She turns realism upside down by attacking its materialism and in its place emphasizing the interior lives of her characters, not their exterior selves. Hers is not a drama infatuated with things, but the qualities that make a life. Even when Henry buys Mae lipstick and a mirror in which to see herself, the moment is not for her a cosmetic action but a recognition of a self in the act of knowing, an objectification, a critique of the self.

There is no waste in this production. Fornes has always had a common sense approach to drama that situates itself in the utter simplicity of her dialogue. She writes sentences, not paragraphs. Her language is a model of direct address, it has the modesty of a writer for whom English is a learned language. She is unique in the way she writes about sexuality, in a tender way that accents sexual feelings, not sex as an event. It is a bitterly sad moment when Henry, his body twisted, his speech thick with pain, begs Mae to make love to him: "I feel the same desires. I feel the same needs. I have not changed." Emotion is unhidden in her plays. Just as language is not wasted, so the actors don't waste movements. Each scene is a strong pictorial unit. Sometimes a scene is only an image, or a few lines of dialogue. This realism is quotational, theatre in close-up, freeze frame. Theatre made by a miniaturist: in *The Danube* an acted scene is replayed in front of the stage by puppets, creating a fierce honorableness in its comment on human action. It is not imperialistic in its desire to create a world on the stage invested with moral imperatives, it is interested only in tableaux from a few lives in a particular place and time. Each scene presents a glimpse of imagery that is socially meaningful.

The pictorial aspect of this realism signifies an important change in theatrical attitudes towards space. It brings about a reduction of depth and a flattening of the stage picture which allude to a new pictorialism in drama. Whereas traditional realism concerned itself with a confined physicality determined by "setting," the new realism is more open cosmologically, its characters iconic. That is one of the reasons why this emotive, aggressive realism is rooted in expressionist style. (Expressionism keeps realism from becoming melodrama.) It is not coincidental that contemporary painting should also turn to expressionism after a period of super-realism, in order to generate an approach to emotion, narration and content. If styles change according to new perceptions of human form and its socialization, then painting and theatre, arts that must continually revise their opinions of figuration, should follow similar directions in any given period. Today, the exaggerated theatricality in everyday life has brought painting and theatre closer together.

The new realism would be confined by mere setting, which is only informational, it needs to be situated in the wider poetic notion of "space" which has ontological references. In the ecology of theatre, setting is a closed system of motion while space is more aligned to the idea of landscape which influences theatre, not only in writing but in design, as a result of now regarding the stage as "performance space." The very idea of space itself indicates how much the belief that all the world's a stage has been literalized. The concept of theatrical "space" alludes to the global repercussions of human action, if only metaphorically.

In recent years Fornes has become such a self-assured director that the movement in her productions seems nearly effortless, totally inhibiting actorly artificiality. She doesn't force her actors' bodies on us in an attempt for them to dominate space. She leaves spaces on the stage unused. She makes the actors appreciate stillness as a theatrical idea, they are considerate toward other theatrical lives. And Fornes acknowledges the audience by giving them their own space and time in the productions. In *Mud* the short scenes and blackouts emphasize this attitude toward reception. They leave room for the audience to enter for contemplative moments. The authorial voice does not demand power over the theatrical experience. It is not territorial. There is room for subjectivity, as a corrective to evasive objectification, on the part of all those involved in the making and witnessing of the event. *Fefu and Her Friends* is the play that most literally invites the audience into the playing space—there were five of them to be exact—and for this Fornes created a style of acting that seemed, simply, a way of talking, it was so real.

Fornes has found her own stage language, a method of discourse that unites play, actor and space in an organic whole that is always showing how it thinks, even as it allows for fragments of thought, unruly contradictions. One of the characteristics of Fornes's plays is that they offer characters *in the process of thought*. Her characters often question received ideas, conventions, the idea of emotion, even how one engages in thought. "What would be the use of knowing things if they don't serve you, if they don't help you shape your life?" asks Mae, an only partially literate woman who yet is dignified with a mind, however limited in its reach. All thought must be useful to characters and find meaning through life itself, to allow life its fullest expression. *Mud* is imbued with a feminism of the most subtle order, feminism based on the ruling idea that a free woman is one who has autonomy of thought. So, it does not matter to the play that Mae is murdered because the main point has already been made: Mae is free because she can understand the concept of freedom.

On one level, Fornes's plays equate the pleasure of thinking with the measure of being. That so many of her plays, *Dr. Kheal, Tango Palace, Evelyn Brown,* besides those already mentioned here, to one degree or another deal with the acquisition of language, alludes to what must surely be one of her consistent interests: the relationship of language to thought to action. The dramatic language is finely honed to exclude excessive qualifiers, adjectives, clauses. Sentences are simple, they exist to communicate, to question. There is a purity to this language of understatement that does not assume anything, and whose dramatic potential rests in the search for meaning in human endeavor. That is why the human voice, as an embodiment of social values, has so significant a place in this kind of writing.

Fornes's work has a warm delicacy and grace that distinguish it from most of what is written today. Apart from her plays there is little loveliness in the theatre. And yet I must stop to include Joseph Chaikin and Meredith Monk in this special group of artists for they also reflect this "loveliness" of presence. Loveliness?—a humanism that guilelessly breathes great dignity into the human beings they imagine into life, and so propose to reality.

Working for more than twenty years in off-Broadway's unheralded spaces, Fornes is an exemplary artist who through her writing and teaching has created a life in the theatre away from the crass hype that attends so many lesser beings. How has she managed that rare accomplishment in this country's theatre—a career? What is admirable about Fornes is that she is one of the last of the real bohemians among the writers who came to prominence in the sixties. She never changed to fit her style to fashion. She has simply been busy writing, experimenting, thinking. Writers have still to catch up to her. If there were a dozen writers in our theatre with Fornes's wisdom and graciousness it would be enough for a country, and yet even one of her is sometimes all that is needed to feel the worth of the enormous effort it takes to live a life in the American theatre.

Susan Sontag (essay date 1986)

SOURCE: A preface to *Maria Irene Fornes: Plays*, PAJ Publications, 1986, pp. 7-10.

[*In the following essay, Sontag extols Fornes' growth as a dramatist. "The plays," she states, "have always been about wisdom: what it means to be wise. They are getting wiser."*]

Mud, The Danube, The Conduct of Life, Sarita—four plays, recent work by the prolific Maria Irene Fornes, who for many years has been conducting with exemplary tenacity and scrupulousness a unique career in the American theatre.

Born in Havana, Fornes arrived in this country with her family when she was fifteen; in her twenties she spent several years in France (she was painting then), and began writing plays after she returned to New York, when she was around thirty. Although the language in which she became a writer was English, not Spanish—and Fornes's early work is inconceivable without the reinforcement of the lively local New York milieu (particularly the Judson Poets Theatre) in which she surfaced in the early 1960s—she is unmistakably a writer of bicultural inspiration: one very American way of being a writer. Her imagination seems to me to have, among other sources, a profoundly Cuban one. I am reminded of the witty, sensual phantasmagorias of Cuban writers such as Lydia Cabrera, Calvert Casey, Virgilio Piñera.

Of course, writers, these or any other, were not the conscious influences on Fornes or any of the best "downtown" theatre of the 1960s. Art Nouveau and Hollywood Deco had more to do with, say, The Theatre of the Ridiculous, than any plausible literary antecedents (Tzara, Firbank, etc.). This is also true of Fornes, an autodidact whose principal influences were neither theatre nor literature but certain styles of painting and the movies. But unlike similarly influenced New York dramatists, her work did not eventually become parasitic on literature (or opera, or movies). It was never a revolt against theatre, or a theatre recycling fantasies encoded in other genres.

Her two earliest plays prefigure the dual register, one völkisch, the other placeless-international, of all the subsequent work. **The Widow,** a poignant chronicle of a simple life, is set in Cuba, while **Tango Palace,** with its volleys of sophisticated exchanges, takes place in a purely theatrical space: a cave, an altar. Fornes has a complex relation to the strategy of naivete. She is chary of the folkloristic, rightly so. But she is strongly drawn to the pre-literary: to the authority of documents, of found materials such as letters of her great-grandfather's cousin which inspired **The Widow,** the diary of a domestic servant in turn-of-the-century New Hampshire which was transformed into **Evelyn Brown,** Emma's lecture in **Fefu and Her Friends.**

For a while she favored the musical play—in a style reminiscent of the populist parables in musical-*commedia* form preserved in films from the 1930s like René Clair's *A Nous la Liberté.* It was a genre that proclaimed its innocence, and specialized in rueful gaiety. Sharing with the main tradition of modernist drama an aversion to the reductively psychological and to sociological explanations,

Fornes chose a theatre of types (such personages as the defective sage and the woman enslaved by sexual dependence reappear in a number of plays) and a theatre of miracles: the talking mirror in **The Office,** the fatal gun wound at the end of **Fefu and Her Friends.** Lately, Fornes seems to be eschewing this effect: the quotidian as something to be violated—by lyricism, by disaster. Characters can still break into song, as they did in the dazzling bittersweet plays of the mid-1960s, like **Promenade** and **Molly's Dream** and **The Successful Life of 3.** But the plays are less insistently charming. Reality is less capricious. More genuinely lethal—as in **Eyes on the Harem, Sarita.**

Character is revealed through catechism. People requiring or giving instruction is a standard situation in Fornes's plays. The desire to be initiated, to be taught, is depicted as an essential, and essentially pathetic, longing. (Fornes's elaborate sympathy for the labor of thought is the endearing observation of someone who is almost entirely self-taught.) And there are many dispensers of wisdom in Fornes's plays, apart from those—**Tango Palace, Doctor Kheal**—specifically devoted to the comedy and the pathos of instruction. But Fornes is neither literary nor antiliterary. These are not cerebral exercises or puzzles but the real questions, about . . . the conduct of life. There is much wit but no nonsense. No banalitics. And no non sequiturs.

While some plays are set in never-never land, some have local flavors—like the American 1930s of **Fefu and Her Friends.** Evoking a specific setting, especially when it is Hispanic (this being understood as an underprivileged reality), or depicting the lives of the oppressed and humiliated, especially when the subject is that emblem of oppression, the woman servant, such plays as **Evelyn Brown** and **The Conduct of Life** may seem more "realistic"—given the condescending assumptions of the ideology of realism. (Oppressed women, particularly domestic servants and prostitutes, have long been the signature subject of what is sometimes called realism, sometimes naturalism.) But I am not convinced that Fornes's recent work is any less a theatre of fantasy than it was, or more now a species of dramatic realism. Her work is both a theatre about utterance (i.e., a meta-theatre) and a theatre about the disfavored—both Handke *and* Kroetz, as it were.

It was always a theatre of heartbreak. But at the beginning the mood was often throwaway, playful. Now it's darker, more passionate: consider the twenty-year trajectory that goes from **The Successful Life of 3** to **Mud,** about the unsuccessful life of three. She writes increasingly from a woman's point of view. Women are doing women's things—performing unrewarded labor (in **Evelyn Brown**), getting raped (in **The Conduct of Life**)—and also, as in **Fefu and Her Friends,** incarnating the human condition as such. Fornes has a near faultless ear for the ruses of egotism and cruelty. Unlike most contemporary dramatists, for whom psychological brutality is the principal, inexhaustible subject, Fornes is never in complicity with the brutality she depicts. She has an increasingly expressive relation to dread, to grief and to passion—in **Sarita,** for example, which is about sexual passion and the incompatibilities of desire. Dread is not just a subjective state but is attached to history: the psychology of torturers (*The Conduct of Life*), nuclear war (*The Danube*).

Fornes's work has always been intelligent, often funny, never vulgar or cynical; both delicate and visceral. Now it is something more. (The turning point, I think, was the splendid *Fefu and Her Friends*—with its much larger palette of sympathies, for both Julia's incurable despair and Emma's irrepressible jubilation.) The plays have always been about wisdom: what it means to be wise. They are getting wiser.

It is perhaps not appropriate here to do more than allude to her great distinction and subtlety as a director of her own plays, and as an inspiring and original teacher (working mainly with young Hispanic-American playwrights). But it seems impossible not to connect the truthfulness in Fornes's plays, their alertness of depicting, their unfacile compassionateness, with a certain character, a certain virtue. In the words of a Northern Sung landscape painter, Kuo Hsi, if the artist "can develop a natural, sincere, gentle, and honest heart, then he will immediately be able to comprehend the aspect of tears and smiles and of objects, pointed or oblique, bent or inclined, and they will be so clear in his mind that he will be able to put them down spontaneously with his paint brush."

Hers seems to be an admirable temperament, unaffectedly independent, highminded, ardent. And one of the few agreeable spectacles which our culture affords is to watch the steady ripening of this beautiful talent.

Gayle Austin (essay date 1989)

SOURCE: "The Madwoman in the Spotlight: Plays of Maria Irene Fornes," in *Making a Spectacle: Feminist Essays on Contemporary Women's Theatre*, edited by Lynda Hart, The University of Michigan Press, pp. 76-85.

[*In this essay, Austin examines Fornes' "use of the madwoman figure and the image of confinement on stage."*]

The madness of women has been a major concern in the work of feminist theorists such as Sandra M. Gilbert, Susan Gubar, Elaine Showalter, Hélène Cixous, and Catherine Clément. Female madness is also a rather common image in drama and has been used by male playwrights for centuries. As Showalter points out, Ophelia was *the* major image of female madness in Victorian England.[1] The madwoman's use by female playwrights has been far less frequent, however, reflecting their much smaller numbers. But in the last decade, Maria Irene Fornes has used the image to great advantage in three of her plays.

Fornes, a Cuban native who has been writing plays in New York City since the early 1960s, is a major figure in the off-off-Broadway scene and the winner of several Obie awards. Her work is notable for many reasons, one

of which is its portrayal on stage of complex female characters and of the female unconscious. Three of her plays, *Fefu and Her Friends* (1977), *Sarita* (1984), and *The Conduct of Life* (1985), contain madwomen figures who are speaking, acting subjects. Examining these plays through a feminist lens focused on the madwoman figure shows Fornes to be a playwriting exemplar in both form and content.

Sandra M. Gilbert and Susan Gubar's *The Madwoman in the Attic*[2] develops work on a female tradition and traits of women's writing using nineteenth-century fiction and poetry only. In applying to women writers Harold Bloom's theory about the male writer's "anxiety of influence," they find that the woman writer experiences an "anxiety of authorship" or "a radical fear that she cannot create, that because she can never become a 'precursor' the act of writing will isolate or destroy her" (49). She seeks a precursor who "proves by example that a revolt against patriarchal literary authority is possible" (49). Contemporary women writers of fiction and poetry may feel less of this anxiety than women of earlier centuries because they have female precursors, but women playwrights are still in need of more such models than they presently have. Wider dissemination of criticism and production of Fornes's work would be one step in lessening some "anxiety of authorship." But for the nineteenth-century woman writer, this anxiety left a mark on her writing.

Women writers coped by "*revising* male genres, using them to record their own dreams and their own stories *in disguise*." Gilbert and Gubar call these works palimpsestic: "works whose surface designs conceal or obscure deeper, less accessible (and less socially acceptable) levels of meaning" (73). Very often the madwoman appeared in these palimpsestic works, "not merely, as she might be in male literature, an antagonist or foil to the heroine," but as "the *author's* double, an image of her own anxiety and rage" (78). The irony, of course, is that by "creating dark doubles for themselves and their heroines, women writers are both identifying with and revising the self-definitions patriarchal culture has imposed on them" (79).

One of the best examples of the use of the mad double is that of Bertha Mason Rochester in *Jane Eyre* (1847). In their detailed analysis of that novel, Gilbert and Gubar point out the many ways in which Bertha does what Jane wishes she might do, "is the angry aspect of the orphan child, the ferocious secret self Jane has been trying to repress" (360), and "not only acts *for* Jane, she also acts *like* Jane" (361). They conclude that "the literal and symbolic death of Bertha frees her [Jane] from the furies that torment her and makes possible . . . wholeness within herself" (362).

Another device used in these palimpsestic works is that of confinement (and sometimes escape). Very often female characters felt space anxiety in houses or rooms, and sometimes it was the madwoman who was so confined. (Bertha was not only mad but confined to the attic of her husband's house.) One paradigm of such imagery is "The Yellow Wallpaper" (1890) by Charlotte Perkins Gilman, in which a recent mother is confined to a garret room and forbidden to write as treatment for a nervous disorder. The woman worsens and eventually sees, locked behind the wallpaper of the room, a woman whom she helps escape by tearing off much of the wallpaper. Madness and confinement meet again in this story and together tell a powerful tale of female experience. This paradigm, however, is not one confined to the nineteenth century, or to women writers of prose.

Fornes's 1977 play *Fefu and Her Friends*[3] has a cast of eight women, has very little conventional plot, and takes place in five separate audience/stage spaces. The setting is described as follows:

> *New England, Spring 1935*
>
> *Part I. Noon. The living room. The entire audience watches from the auditorium.*
>
> *Part II. Afternoon. The lawn, the study, the bedroom, the kitchen. The audience is divided into four groups. Each group is guided to the spaces. These scenes are performed simultaneously. When the scenes are completed the audience moves to the next space and the scenes are performed again. This is repeated four times until each group has seen all four scenes.*
>
> *Part III. Evening. The living room. The entire audience watches from the auditorium.*
>
> (p. 6)

The house is Fefu's and the other characters are women who gather there to discuss a fundraising program for a vaguely defined cause related to education. The action of the play is the interactions of the women over the course of one afternoon and evening. It demonstrates the synapses between women when they are not with men. As Fefu says early in the play:

> Women are restless with each other. They are like live wires . . . either chattering to keep themselves from making contact, or else, if they don't chatter, they avert their eyes . . . like Orpheus . . . as if a god once said"and if they shall recognize each other, the world will be blown apart." They are always eager for the men to arrive. When they do, they can put themselves at rest, tranquilized and in a mild stupor. With the men they feel safe. The danger is gone. That's the closest they can be to feeling wholesome. Men are the muscle that cover the raw nerve. They are the insulators. The danger is gone, but the price is the mind and the spirit. . . . High price [author's ellipses].
>
> (p. 13)

The play itself proceeds to dramatize a bit of that "danger" that occurs when female raw nerves are not insulated by men.

Part of the play's effect has to do with the close proximity of the audience to the performers in the smaller, enclosed spaces of the scenes in Part II. Audience members on two of the four sides of each room seem to "eavesdrop" on the conversations that take place there, more intimate than in the other two parts. The audience is split up, has to move around physically, must become active in order to see the entire performance. This unusual use of space has been remarked upon in criticism of the play, but has not seemed to have an influence on many other plays. It is one of many ideas this play presents that might profitably be explored by other writers, as well as critics. It is a play that must be experienced to be fully comprehended. Part of its effect comes from confining the audience in the same limited space the characters inhabit. The play also exhibits a feminist use of the madwoman.

The character of Julia enters Part I in a wheelchair and another character describes how Julia fell down at the same moment a hunter shot a deer, and from that moment has not been able to walk. While delirious, Julia said "That she was persecuted.—That they tortured her. . . . That they had tried her and that the shot was her execution. That she recanted because she wanted to live. . . ." (15). Fefu recalls that years ago Julia "was afraid of nothing," and that "she knew so much."

In Part II in the bedroom, as the stage direction says, *"Julia hallucinates. However, her behavior should not be the usual behavior attributed to a mad person"* (23). In her monologue, Julia relates persecution such as that which had been described in Part I. She was beaten, but never stopped smiling. She recites: "I'm not smart. I never was. Neither is Fefu smart. They are after her too. Well she's still walking!" She guards herself from a blow. Later she says, "Why do you have to kill Fefu, for she's only a joker? 'Not kill, cure. Cure her.' Will it hurt? (*She whimpers.*) Oh, dear, dear, my dear, they want your light" (24-25). She then recites a prayer that gives many of the reasons man has considered woman evil. Julia finally says, "They say when I believe the prayer I will forget the judges. And when I forget the judges I will believe the prayer. They say both happen at once. And all women have done it. Why can't I?" (25).

In Part III, after a rehearsal of the fundraising "show," Julia has a long speech in which she says, "Something rescues us from death every moment of our lives," and that she has been rescued by "guardians." However, she is afraid one day they will fail and "I will die . . . for no apparent reason" (35). Later on, Fefu, alone on stage, sees Julia walk, and seconds later she reenters in her wheelchair. Near the end, Fefu and Julia struggle, Fefu telling her to try to walk and to fight. Julia says she is afraid her madness is contagious and tries to keep away from Fefu. Fefu wants to put her own mind to rest and loses courage when Julia looks at her. She finally asks Julia to "Forgive me if you can," and Julia says, "I forgive you" (40). Fefu gets a shotgun used earlier in the play, goes out, a shot is heard, Julia's hand goes to her forehead and as it drops, blood is seen, and Julia's head drops. Fefu enters with a dead rabbit and all the women surround the dead Julia.

This series of scenes, interspersed among others, establishes the "madwoman" Julia as Fefu's double. The play itself, taking place less than ninety years after *Jane Eyre*, has a certain "feel" of the nineteenth century and there are striking similarities between Fefu/Julia and Jane/Bertha. Julia acts out the repressed, angry side of Fefu by struggling with the "guardians," and perhaps her death frees Fefu at the end of the play. But Fornes is a twentieth-century woman and the differences are also striking. The play is as if written by Jane and Bertha, with Rochester pushed offstage, his control lessened by his absence. Julia is not in the attic, but in the spotlight, speaking the truth for herself as subject alternately with speaking the text of male conventional attitudes about women in her "prayer." Fefu and Julia together, overtly bonded and overtly in conflict, make an open statement of women's predicament in the public forum of the theatre.

In the end, Fefu does what Julia cannot—acts. The madwoman is "killed" by her double. This action has many possible interpretations. For Helene Keyssar, ". . . Julia chooses not to fight but to yield. Fefu, however, will not let Julia go. Unable to reinvigorate her friend verbally, Fefu moves to Julia's symbolic terrain and shoots a rabbit." The meaning of this act for Keyssar is that, "Symbolically at least, and on stage where all things are possible, the woman-as-victim must be killed in her own terms in order to ignite the explosion of a community of women."[4] For Beverley Byers Pevitts, "if we recognize ourselves as women, 'the world will be blown apart.' When this does happen, the reflection that was made by others will be destroyed and we will be able to rebuild ourselves in our own image, created by woman." Julia, then, "is the one who is symbolically killed in the end of the play so that the new image of herself can emerge."[5]

In an interview with this writer in April, 1987, Fornes answered questions about the madwomen in her plays:

> Julia is really not mad at all. She's telling the truth. The only madness is, instead of saying her experience was "as if" there was a court that condemned her, she says that they did. I guess that's what makes her mad rather than just a person who is a visionary. The elements of her fantasy are visionary—they are completely within the range of clear thinking. Her fantasies are very organized.

The use of confinement in *Fefu* is also both like and unlike its use in nineteenth-century fiction. On the stage confinement is a visual, visceral reality. In Part II of *Fefu* the audience is confined, along with the actors, in the separate spaces of a woman's house. In the bedroom there is a particular sense of confinement because it is, *"A plain unpainted room. Perhaps a room that was used for storage and was set up as a sleeping place for Julia. There is a mattress on the floor"* (23). In its original production, this was the smallest space in the play and with the same number of audience members in the space as had been in larger spaces, there was a greater sense of confinement associated with Julia than with the other characters. As has

been mentioned, there is a contrasting sense of escape or release for Julia at the end of the play, which is underlined by the audience's memory of her in that cramped bedroom. By making the audience experience crowding, the play shows the metaphor to be "social and actual," as Gilbert and Gubar say of women's use of the image, as opposed to men's "metaphysical and metaphorical" use of it. Julia does not possess the ability to leave the room. This fact is reinforced by the presence of Julia's wheelchair in the small bedroom, helping to further crowd the audience and to visually remind them that Julia possesses no means to leave this confinement.

Two other plays by Fornes, both included in a volume of her plays published in 1986,[6] also make good use of the madwoman figure and the image of confinement on stage. *Sarita* (1984) tells the story of a Hispanic girl of thirteen from the South Bronx, who passionately loves a boy who is habitually unfaithful to her. Over the course of the eight years of the play (1939-47) Sarita is loved by a young soldier, but is drawn back to her obsessive former love until she is driven to kill him and goes mad. The play takes place in twenty short scenes over two acts, with the inclusion of many songs whose lyrics are written by Fornes. While the story itself may seem familiar in outline, it becomes fresh because it is told from the point of view of the young woman involved. Rather than, as in so many plays in the standard canon, seeing how the madwoman affects the lives of those around her, we see how events and emotions make a lovely young woman go mad. Sarita is her own subject, speaking and acting for herself.

Fornes sees Sarita's madness as quite different from Julia's in *Fefu*:

> I think Sarita goes mad because when you are pushed to such a state of emotional upheaval as to murder the person that you loved, I think going mad is normal. If you don't go mad it's a coldness, callous. It's like having a fever. It's normal to have a fever when you have a bug in your system—it's part of the system protecting itself and I think to break down is inevitable.

Fornes's description of Sarita's "fever" echoes in many ways Catherine Clément's discussion of the hysteric in her book written with Hélène Cixous. In southern Italy women dance a tarantella to rid themselves of spider bites, though, as she states, "because tarantulas do not exist in this region, we have to conclude that these are psychical phenomena."[7] The hysteric speaks with her body and performs socially unacceptable acts because she has a "bug" in her system. Sarita also breaks her "fever" in this manner.

The scenes between Sarita and her lover take place in a narrow, box-like kitchen area above and behind the main stage area. The kitchen is the space in which Sarita is confined, waiting for the return of her lover, and suffering the pangs of sexual longing. She does not enter or leave this space in view of the audience, but is simply there when lights come up and go down. Her "social and actual" confinement is keenly portrayed.

The Conduct of Life (1985) also portrays the confinement of a young Hispanic woman, played in the original production by the same actress, Sheila Dabney, who won an Obie award for her performance as the original Sarita. ***Conduct*** concerns a trio of women who are in subservient positions in the house of a Latin American army officer, Orlando. The most confined of the trio is Nena, a young street girl Orlando picked up and brought first to a warehouse, then to his cellar, to sexually abuse and sometimes feed. The other two women are Olimpia, a servant in the house who sometimes works or plays with Nena, and Leticia, Orlando's wife, who thinks she is a mother figure to Orlando. Over the course of nineteen scenes, with no intermission, set in the present but visually presented as anytime from the 1940s onward, the audience sees Orlando brutalize Nena in the name of love and sexuality, and drive his wife to shoot him at the end. Again, Nena is confined in a box-like space above and behind the main stage area, and then is brought down into the cellar area. Again, her confinement is actual and cannot be escaped. But in this play the similarities among Nena, Leticia, and Olimpia present a view of women as subjects under subjugation that echoes Cixous and Clément in their discussion of Freud's patient, Dora.

From the beginning of the play, madness is discussed. In her first speech, to Orlando and his male friend, Alejo, Leticia says she would throw herself in front of a deer to prevent its being killed by "mad hunters," and Orlando responds with, "You don't think that is madness? She's mad. Tell her that—she'll think it's you who's mad." When Orlando leaves, Leticia confesses to Alejo:

> He told me that he didn't love me, and that his sole relationship to me was simply a marital one. What he means is that I am to keep this house, and he is to provide for it. That's what he said. That explains why he treats me the way he treats me. I never understood why he did, but now it's clear. He doesn't love me.
>
> (p. 69)

In the next scene Orlando brings Nena into the warehouse room. The scene is brief—a few words and then:

> (*He grabs her and pushes her against the wall. He pushes his pelvis against her. He moves to the chair dragging her with him. She crawls to the left, pushes the table aside and stands behind it. He walks around the table. She goes under it. He grabs her foot and pulls her out toward the downstage side. He opens his fly and pushes his pelvis against her. Lights fade to black.*)
>
> (p. 70)

In the next scene Olimpia is introduced through a long monologue in which she tells Leticia, in detail, what she does in order to prepare breakfast for the family in the morning. The accumulation of detail is comical, but the link between the two women is established clearly, as both women must "keep this house," while Orlando is oblivious to what either is doing or thinking. The two women bicker over what is to be served for lunch and dinner, Olimpia asserting her will point for point with Leticia. Though Olimpia is the servant, Leticia's only action as the "boss's wife" is to hand money to Olimpia to go shopping at the end of the scene.

Orlando forces sex on Nena two more times, the second time reaching orgasm, and then giving her food and milk. The lines of similarity among the three women become clearer as the scenes progress. When Leticia goes away on a trip, Orlando slips Nena into the house and down to the cellar. Orlando and Alejo talk about a man Orlando interrogated and who is dead. Orlando insists he just stopped him from screaming and then the man died. He does not see himself as being the cause. The connection between political torture and subjugation of women is made by the juxtaposed, rapidly intercut scenes.

Leticia senses there is a woman in the house to whom Orlando is making love, and she feels there is nothing she can do. Orlando tells Nena that "What I do to you is out of love. Out of want. It's not what you think. I wish you didn't have to be hurt" (82). Leticia pleads with Orlando, "Don't make her scream," and Orlando responds, "You're crazy" (82). Then he says, "She's going to be a servant here," and in the next scene Nena is cleaning beans with Olimpia and speaking, for the first time at length, about her grandfather and how Orlando found her and "did things" to her (83-84). Nena sounds like Julia in *Fefu* when she says he beats her "Because I'm dirty," and "The dirt won't go away from inside me" (84). Leticia feels he is becoming more violent because of his job. She does not appear to perceive the fact that his violence at work and home come from a common root. The three women finally sit together at a table as the lights come down on scene seventeen.

In the final scene, Orlando forces Leticia to say she has a lover and to make up details of their meeting. When Orlando physically hurts Leticia, she screams and then, *"She goes to the telephone table, opens the drawer, takes a gun and shoots Orlando. Orlando falls dead. . . . Leticia . . . puts the revolver in Nena's hand and steps away from her."* Leticia asks, "Please . . ." and Nena *"looks at the gun. Then, up. The lights fade"* (88).

The play is over. The doubled madwomen figures have come together, one acting for the other as well as herself, then (possibly) asking help of her double in ending her own torment. The release here is different from that at the end of *Fefu*. The killing of the intolerable lover is more complex than that in *Sarita*. Women are linked by their subjugated roles. The actions of the man make them mad, but they manage both to act and to connect despite their madness and confinement. And the man's self-deception about what he is doing to the women around him is linked to the wider political realm.

When asked to comment on the madwoman in ***Conduct*** compared to ***Sarita,*** Fornes explained:

Certainly, if you think of Leticia after the murder she would probably go through something similar, but I think Leticia would be able to cope a little better. She would have to go through a period of understanding everything. But I thought you meant the person who goes mad in **The Conduct of Life** was Nena. . . . Nena is much more vulnerable; Leticia is a strong person. She's older and more in possession of herself. But Nena is ill, she's been battered, she's abused. I think she's closer to madness than Leticia.

Fornes touches on a central point here; both Leticia and Nena are different aspects of the "madwomen" figure. Nena in her near-mute state when in the presence of a male and Leticia in "speaking" with a gun are similar to Hélène Cixous's description of Freud's patient, Dora: "like all hysterics, deprived of the possibility of saying directly what she perceived . . . still had the strength to make it known." And the role of love in the women characters'"conduct of life" is echoed in Cixous's statement: "The source of Dora's strength is, in spite of everything, her desire."[8]

Clément, in disagreeing with Cixous, finds that the hysteric's eccentricity is tolerated because she is not really threatening to the basic social structure. Fornes makes her hysterics have a clear effect and balances them with a third figure, the "maid." Unlike the "maid" in Freud's writing, Olimpia is not a seductress. She represents housework, the nonsexual side of the wife's duties, while Nena is the merely sexual, though the husband does bring her into the house and make her play the role of a "maid." As Cixous quotes Freud, "'the servant-girl is the boss's wife repressed,' but in Dora's case, Dora is in the place of the boss's wife: the mother is set aside."[9] But in Fornes's case not too far aside, for the mother appears in the form of the wife, Leticia. The play illuminates both Cixous's ideas about the hysteric and Clément's social concerns: "The family does not exist in isolation, rather it truly supports and reflects the class struggle running through it. The servant-girl, the prostitute, the mother, the boss's wife, the woman: that is all an ideological scene."[10]

Taken together, these three plays give a broad picture of the effects of confinement and madness on women in the twentieth century. In both **Fefu** and **Conduct** Fornes shows us a multiple female character, composed of individuals but, as seen on the stage, a whole that is more than its parts. She shows us what Showalter considers "the best hope for the future. . . . In the 1970s, for the first time, women came together," to challenge the dominant ideology and propose their own alternative, including political activism.[11]

By taking an audience *into* the attic the madwoman there can no longer be seen as a mere "metaphorical" disturbance. By letting the madwoman speak for herself, Fornes has performed a radical act. On the stage we *see* her, and other women, escape confinement in various ways. And by placing her women in the spotlight, Fornes helps the audience, as well as future women playwrights, escape restriction by form, society, and themselves.

NOTES

[1]Elaine Showalter, *The Female Malady: Women, Madness, and English Culture, 1830-1980* (New York: Pantheon Books, 1985; reprint ed., New York: Penguin Books, 1987), 10-11.

[2](New Haven: Yale University Press, 1979). Subsequent page numbers in parentheses.

[3]In *Wordplays* (New York: Performing Arts Journal Publications, 1980). Subsequent page numbers in parentheses.

[4]*Feminist Theatre* (New York: Grove Press, 1985), 125.

[5]"Fefu and Her Friends," in *Women in American Theatre: Revised and Expanded Edition*, ed. Chinoy and Jenkins (New York: Theatre Communications Group, 1987), 316.

[6]*Maria Irene Fornes: Plays* (New York: Performing Arts Journal Publications, 1986). Subsequent page numbers in parentheses.

[7]Hélène Cixous and Catherine Clément, *The Newly Born Woman*, trans. Betsy Wing (Minneapolis: University of Minnesota, 1986), 19.

[8]Ibid., 154.

[9]Ibid., 151.

[10]Ibid., 152.

[11]Showalter, 249-50.

W. B. Worthen (essay date 1989)

SOURCE: "*Still Playing Games*: Ideology and Performance in the Theater of Maria Irene Fornes," in *Feminine Focus: The New Women Playwrights*, edited by Enoch Brater, Oxford University Press, 1989, pp. 167-85.

[*In the following essay, Worthen explores "the operation of the mise-en-scène on the process of dramatic action" in Fornes' plays.*]

> Isidore, I beg you.
> Can't you see
> You're breaking my heart?
> 'Cause while I'm so earnest,
> You're still playing games.
>
>   *Tango Palace*

A clown tosses off witty repartee while tossing away the cards on which his lines are written; a love scene is played first by actors and then by puppets they manipulate; the audience sits in a semicircle around a woman desperately negotiating with invisible tormentors: the plays of Maria Irene Fornes precisely address the process of theater, how the authority of the word, the presence of the performer, and the complicity of the silent spectator articulate dramatic play. Throughout her career Fornes has pursued an eclectic, reflexive theatricality. *A Vietnamese Wedding* (1967), for instance, "is not a play" but a kind of theater ceremony: "Rehearsals should serve the sole purpose of getting the readers acquainted with the text and the actions of the piece. The four people conducting the piece are hosts to the members of the audience who will enact the wedding" (p. 8). In **Dr. Kheal** (1968) a manic professor addresses the audience in a form of speech torture; the stage realism of **Molly's Dream** (1968) rapidly modulates into the deliquescent atmosphere of dreams. **The Successful Life of Three** (1965) freezes the behavioral routines of a romantic triangle in a series of static tableaux, interrupting the actors' stage presence in a way that anticipates "deconstructive" theater experiments of the seventies and eighties.[1] And the "Dada zaniness" of **Promenade** (1965; score by Al Carmines)—a musicla parable of two Chaplinesque prisoners who dig their way to freedom—brilliantly counterpoints Brecht, Blitzstein, Bernstein, and Beckett, viewed "through Lewis Carroll's looking-glass."[2]

Despite their variety, Fornes' experiments share a common impulse: to explore the operation of the mise-en-scène on the process of dramatic action. Rather than naturalizing theatrical performance by assimilating the various "enunciators" of the stage—acting, music, set design, audience disposition—to a privileged gestural style encoded in the dramatic text (the strategy of stage realism, for instance), Fornes' plays suspend the identification between the drama and its staging.[3] The rhetoric of Fornes' major plays—**Fefu and Her Friends** (1977), **The Danube** (1983), and **The Conduct of Life** (1985)—is sparked by this ideological dislocation. At first glance, though, to consider Fornes' drama as "ideological" may seem capricious, for Fornes claims that except for **Tango Palace** her plays "are not Idea Plays. My plays do not present a thesis, or at least, let us say, they do not present a formulated thesis" ("I write these messages" [p. 27]). But to constrain theatrical ideology to the "thesis play"—as though ideology were a fixed body of meanings to be "illustrated" or "realized" by an "Idea Play" or an "ideological drama"—is to confine ideology in the theater too narrowly to the plane of the text.[4] For like dramatic action, theatrical action—performance—occupies an ideological field. Performance claims a provisional "identity" between a given actor and dramatic "character," between the geography of the stage and the dramatic "setting," and between the process of acting and the play's dramatic "action."[5] The theater also "identifies" its spectator, casts a form of activity within which subjective significance is created. In and out of the theater, ideologies function neither solely as "bodies of thought that we possess and invest in our actions nor as elaborate texts" but "as *ongoing social processes*" that address us, qualify our actions with meaning, and so continually "constitute and reconstitute who we are" (Therborn, pp. 77-78). Whether the audience is explicitly characterized (as in Osborne's *The Entertainer* or Griffiths' *Comedians*), symbolically represented (as by the spotlight in Beckett's *Play*), or mysteriously concealed by the brilliant veil of the fourth wall, performance refigures "who we are" in the theater. Our attendance is represented in the "imaginary relationship" between "actors," "characters," and "spectators," where ideology is shaped as theatricality (Althusser, p. 153).

Trained as a painter, Fornes is, not surprisingly, attracted to the visual procedures of the mise-en-scène. Her interest in the stage, though, stems from a theatrical rather than an explicitly political experience, Roger Blin's 1954 production of *Waiting for Godot*: "I didn't know a word of French. I had not read the play in English. But what was happening in front of me had a profound impact without even understanding a word. Imagine a writer whose theatricality is so amazing and so important that you could see a play of his, not understand one word, and be shook up" (Cummings, p. 52). The theatricality of *Godot* is deeply impressed on Fornes' pas de deux, **Tango Palace** (1964). Like Beckett, Fornes contests a rhetorical priority of modern realism: that stage production should represent an ideal "drama" and conceal the process of performance as a legitimate object of attention. An "obsession that took the form of a play" (Cummings, p. 51), **Tango Palace** takes place in a stage utopia, decked out with a chair, secretary, mirror, water jug, three teapots, a vase, and a blackboard—theatrical props rather than the signs of a dramatic "setting." The rear wall contains Isidore's "shrine," an illuminated recess holding his special props, as well as Isidore himself: a stout, heavily rouged, high-heeled, androgynous clown. The stage is Isidore's domain: when he gestures, his shrine is lit; at another gesture, chimes sound. To begin the play, Isidore creates his antagonist—Leopold, a handsome, business-suited man delivered to the stage in a canvas bag. Isidore introduces him to the set and its props ("This is my whip. [*Lashing* Leopold] And that is pain" [p. 131]), choreographs his movements, and gradually encourages him to play the series of routines that occupy their evening. Like Isidore's furniture, their mutual performances are classical, "influenced by their significance as distinct types representative of the best tradition, not only in the style and execution but in the choice of subject" (p. 130). Isidore's stage is a palace of art, its history contained in its accumulated junk: "the genuine Persian helmet I wore when I fought at Salamis" (p. 132), a "Queen Anne walnut armchair. Representing the acme of artistic craftsmanship of the Philadelphia school. Circa 1740," a "Louis Quinze secretary" (p. 130), a "rare seventeenth-century needlework carpet," a "Magnificent marked Wedgwood vase," a "Gutenberg Bible" (pp. 136-37). Consigned to the stage, where behavior becomes "acting," where objects become props and history a scenario for role-playing, Isidore and Leopold engage in a fully theatricalized combat, rehearsing a series of contests ordered not by a coherent plot but by the violent, sensual rhythms of the tango.[6]

Although the events of **Tango Palace** often seem spontaneous, they are hardly improvised; the play pays critical attention to the place of the "text" on the stage. The dramatic text is usually traced into the spectacle, represented not as text but as acting, movement, speech, and gesture. The text of **Tango Palace,** though, is assigned a theatrical function, identified as a property of the performance. For Isidore's brilliance is hardly impromptu; his ripostes are scripted, printed on the cards he nonchalantly tosses about the stage.

> These cards contain wisdom. File them away. (*Card*)
> Know where they are. (*Card*) Have them at hand.

(*Card*) Be one upon whom nothing is lost. (*Card*) Memorize them and you'll be where you were. (*Card*) . . . These are not my cards. They are yours. It's you who need learning, not me. I've learned already. (*Card*) I know all my cards by heart. (*Card*) I can recite them in chronological order and I don't leave one word out. (*Card*) What's more I never say a thing which is not an exact quotation from one of my cards. (*Card*) That's why I never hesitate. (*Card*) Why I'm never short of an answer. (*Card*) *Or a question*. (*Card*) Or a remark, if a remark is more appropriate.

(pp. 133-34)

Isidore at once illustrates, parodies, and challenges the absent authority of the text in modern performance: "Study hard, learn your cards, and one day, you too will be able to talk like a parrot" (p. 135). *Tango Palace,* like Beckett's empty stages and Handke's prisons of language, explores the rich tension between the vitality of the performers and the exhausting artifice of their performance, the impoverished dramatic conventions, false furnishings, and parrotlike repetition of words that are the only means of "life" on the stage. Yet Isidore's text also suggests the inadequacy of this dichotomy by demonstrating how the theater insistently textualizes all behavior undertaken within its confines. The more "spontaneously" Leopold struggles to escape Isidore's arty hell, for instance, the more scripted his actions become: "Leopold *executes each of* Isidore's *commands at the same time as it is spoken, but as if* He *were acting spontaneously rather than obeying*":

ISIDORE AND LEOPOLD: Anybody there! Anybody there! (*Card*) Let me out. (*Card*) Open up! (*Card*)

(p. 136)

Even burning Isidore's cards offers no relief, since to be free of the text on the stage is hardly to be free at all. It is simply to be silent, unrealized, dead:

LEOPOLD: I'm going to burn those cards.

ISIDORE: You'll die if you burn them . . . don't take my word for it. Try it.

(LEOPOLD *sets fire to a card.*)

What in the world are you doing? Are you crazy?

(ISIDORE *puts the fire out.*)

Are you out of your mind? You're going to die.

Are you dying?

Do you feel awful?

(ISIDORE *trips* LEOPOLD)

There! You died.

(p. 139)

Tango Palace dramatizes the condition of theater—the dialectical tension between fiction and the flesh—and implies the unstable place of theater in the world that surrounds it, the world that Leopold struggles to rejoin.

The theater can offer only illusion, not the gritty reality, the "dirt" that Leopold wants: "What I want, sir, is to live with that loathsome mess near me, not to flush it away. To live with it for all those who throw perfume on it. To be so dirty for those who want to be so clean" (p. 157). Isidore's "cave," like Plato's, can only provide illusion, yet in *Tango Palace*—as in any theater—artifice is inextricably wrought into the sense of the real. Even Leopold's final execution of Isidore serves only to extend their mutual struggle, for Isidore's impossibly stagey death is followed naturally by his equally stagey resurrection, as he returns dressed like an angel, carrying his stack of cards and beckoning to Leopold; "Leopold *walks through the door slowly, but with determination*. He *is ready for the next stage of their battle*" (p. 162).

Tango Palace provides a vision, an allegory perhaps, of how the stage produces a reality, but produces it as image, performance, theater. Since *Tango Palace,* and especially since *Fefu and Her Friends,* Fornes' plays have become at once more explicitly political in theme, more rigorous in exploring the ideological relation between theatrical and dramatic representation, and more effectively engaged in repudiating the "burden of psychology, declamation, morality, and sentimentality" characteristic of American realism (Marranca, p. 70). Indeed, Fornes' recent work frequently frames "realism" in an alienating, critical mise-en-scène that alters our reading of the performance and of the drama it sustains. *The Danube,* for instance, presents a love story between an American businessman and a Hungarian working girl. This parable of East-West relations develops the tentative romance against a distant background of European conflict and against the immediate physical debilitation of the cast, who seem to suffer from radiation sickness: they develop sores, become crippled, feeble, ragged, and ashen. Although many scenes in *The Danube* are minutely "realistic" in texture, the play's staging intervenes between the spectator and the conventions of realistic performance by interrupting the defining moment of realistic rhetoric: the identification of stage performance with the conventions of social behavior. The play is staged on a platform—not in a stage "room"—held between four posts that serve an openly theatrical function: postcardlike backdrops are inserted between the rear posts, a curtain is suspended from the downstage pair, and between scenes smoke is released from holes in the platform itself. In its proportions the set is reminiscent of a puppet theater, and much of the action seems to imply that the characters are manipulated by an outside agency. And, as in *Tango Palace,* the text of *The Danube* is again objectified, held apart from the actors' charismatic presence. In fact, it was a "found object" that stimulated Fornes' conception of the use of language in the play:

Fornes was walking past a thrift shop on West 4th Street, saw some 78 rpm records in a bin, liked the way they looked even before she knew what they were . . . so she bought one for a dollar. Turns out it was a language record, the simplest sentences, first in Hungarian, then in English. "There was such tenderness in those little scenes," she recalls—introducing people, ordering in restaurants, discussing the weather—"that when the Theater for the New City asked me to do an antinuclear piece, I thought of how sorrowful it would be to lose the simplest pleasures of our own era."

(Wetzsteon, p. 43)

Many scenes of *The Danube* open with a language-lesson tape recording of the opening lines of stage dialogue: we hear the mechanical inflections of the taped English and Hungarian sentences and then the actors onstage perform the same lines in character, naturally.[7] On the one hand, this technique emphasizes the elocutionary dimension of language, how speech is already textualized in the procedures of social action—*"Unit One. Basic sentences. Paul Green meets Mr. Sandor and his daughter Eve"* (p. 44); *"Unit Three. Basic sentences. Paul and Eve go to the restaurant"* (p. 49). Yet although the tape recordings underscore the "text" of social exchange, the actors' delivery—insofar as it is "naturalistic," spoken "with a different sense, a different emphasis" (p. 42)—necessarily skews our attention from the code of social enactment to the "presence" or "personality" it seems to disclose. Onstage, *The Danube* suspends the identification between language and speech. The performance dramatizes the problematic of "social being," the dialectical encounter between the individual subject and the codes of his or her realization, the "intersection of social formations and . . . personal history" (de Lauretis, p. 14). In fact, to speak in an "unscripted" manner is simply to act incomprehensibly, to forego recognition. The characters' infrequent, trancelike monologues are not only spoken out of context, they are apparently unheard by others on the stage.[8] We see the characters physically deteriorate, but they repeatedly deny that their illnesses are out of the ordinary; when they speak textbook patter, they can be realized as "social beings," but when they attempt to speak expressively, they speak to no one, not even to themselves. To be known in *The Danube* is necessarily to "talk like a machine," say only what the "machines" of language and behavior permit one to say (p. 62).

The Danube discovers "the poisons of the nuclear age" in the processes of culture (Rich). The machine of language and the cognate conventions of social life—dating, work, medicine, international relations—represent and so inevitably distort the human life they sustain, the life that visibly decays before our eyes. This is the point of the two brilliant pairs of scenes that conclude the play. In scene 12 Paul's illness finally drives him to the point of leaving Hungary and Eve; the scene is replayed in scene 13, as *"Paul, Eve, and Mr. Sandor operate puppets whose appearance is identical to theirs."* Scenes 14 and 15 reverse this procedure, as scene 14 is played first by puppets and then repeated in scene 15—culminating in Eve's poetic farewell to the Danube and a blinding flash of white light—by the actors. Like the tape recordings, the puppet scenes disrupt the "natural" assimilation of "character" to the actor through the transparent gestural codes of social

behavior. Like the language they speak, the gestures that constitute "character" are shown to be an autonomous text, as effectively—though differently—performed by puppets as by people. The proxemics of performance are shown to occupy the "intersection" between individual subjectivity and the social codes of its representation and recognition. Conventions of politics, codes of conduct, and systems of signification frame the platform of social action in *The Danube*; like invisible hands, they guide the human puppets of the stage.

The formal intricacy of *The Danube* opens a dissonance between speech and language, between the bodies of the performers and the gestures of their enactment, between life and the codes with which we conduct it. This somber play typifies Fornes' current investigation of the languages of the stage, which are given a more explicitly political inflection in *The Conduct of Life.* Set in a Latin American military state, *The Conduct of Life* prismatically reflects the interdependence of politics, power, and gender. The play takes the form of a loose sequence of negotiations between Orlando (a lieutenant in the military) and his wife, Leticia; his commander, Alejo; a domestic servant, Olimpia; and Nena, a girl Orlando keeps in a warehouse and repeatedly rapes. Husband and wife, torturer and victim, man and woman, master and servant: from the opening moments of the play, when we see Orlando doing jumping jacks in the dark and vowing to "achieve maximum power" by being "no longer . . . overwhelmed by sexual passion" (68), the play traces the desire for mastery through a refracting network of relations—work, marriage, career, politics, sex.

Rape is, however, the defining metaphor of social action in the play, and the warehouse scenes between Orlando and Nena emblematize the play's fusion of sexual and political relations. Alejo may be rendered "impotent" by Orlando's vicious torturing of an opponent (p. 75), but torturer and victim are bound in an unbreakable embrace. Indeed, Orlando speaks to Nena much as he does to justify his regime: "What I do to you is out of love. Out of want. It's not what you think. I wish you didn't have to be hurt. I don't do it out of hatred. It is not out of rage. It is love" (p. 82). Orlando's rhetoric is chilling; that this "love" should be reciprocated measures the accuracy of Fornes' penetrating examination of the conduct of social power. Late in the play, Nena recounts her life—sleeping in the streets, living in a box with her grandfather ("It is a big box. It is big enough for two" [p. 83])—and how she came to be abducted by Orlando. She concludes:

> I want to conduct each day of my life in the best possible way. I should value the things I have. And I should value all those who are near me. And I should value the kindness that others bestow upon me. And if someone should treat me unkindly, I should not blind myself with rage, but I should see them and receive them, since maybe they are in worse pain than me.

(pp. 84-85)

Rather than taking a resistant, revolutionary posture, Nena accepts a Christian humility, an attitude that simply enforces her own objectification, her continued abuse. Beaten, raped, owned by Orlando, Nena finally adopts a morality that—grotesquely—completes her subjection to him and to the social order that empowers him. Indeed, when Leticia learns how to conduct her own life—by killing Orlando—she also reveals how inescapably Nena's exploitation lies at the foundation of this world: she hands the smoking revolver to Nena, who takes it with *"terror and numb acceptance"* (p. 88).

Finally, *The Conduct of Life* uses the disposition of the stage to reflect and extend this vision of social corruption. The stage is constructed in a series of horizontal, tiered planes: the forestage area represents the living room; a low (eighteen-inch) platform slightly upstage represents the dining room; this platform steps up (eighteen inches) onto the hallway; the hallway is succeeded by a three-foot drop to the basement, in which are standing two trestle tables; a staircase leads to the platform farthest upstage, the warehouse. The set provides a visual emblem of the hierarchy of power in the play. More significantly, though, the set constructs a powerful habit of vision for the spectators. The living and dining rooms—those areas of public sociability where Olimpia serves coffee, Leticia and Orlando discuss their marriage, Olimpia and Nena gossip while preparing dinner—become transparent to the audience as windows onto the upstage sets and the occluded "setting" they represent: the warehouses and basements where the real life of this society—torture, rape, betrayal—is conducted.

As in *The Danube,* the staging of *The Conduct of Life* dislocates the familiar surfaces of stage realism. On occasion, however, Fornes renders the ideological process of theater visible not simply by disrupting familiar conventions but by dramatizing the audience's implication in the conduct of the spectacle. Indeed, Fornes' most assured play, *Fefu and Her Friends,* explores the ideology of stage gender through a sophisticated use of stage space to construct a "dramatic" relation between stage and audience. The play conceives the gender dynamics implicit in the realistic perspective by disclosing the gendered bias of the spectator's interpretive authority, "his" transcendent position above the women of the stage. The play opens at a country house in 1935. The title character has invited a group of women to her home to rehearse a brief series of skits for a charity benefit to raise money for a newly founded organization. In the first scene the women arrive and are introduced. Many seem to have been college friends, two seem to be lovers, or ex-lovers. Much of the action of the scene centers on Julia, who is confined to a wheelchair as the result of a mysterious hunting accident: although the bullet missed her, she is paralyzed from the waist down. In part 2, Fornes breaks the audience into four groups that tour Fefu's home—garden, study, bedroom, and kitchen: "These scenes are performed simultaneously. When the scenes are completed the audience moves to the next space and the scenes are performed again. This is repeated four times

until each group has seen all four scenes" (p. 6). In part 3 the audience is returned to the auditorium. The women rehearse and decide the order of their program. Fefu goes outside to clean her shotgun, and suddenly a shot rings out; Julia falls dead, though again she does not seem to have been hit.

In the theater, the play examines the theatrical poetics of the feminine not only as "theme" but in the structuring of the spectacle itself, by unseating the spectator of "realism" and dramatizing "his" controlling authority over the construction of stage gender. Early in the play, for instance, Fefu looks offstage and sees her husband approaching: "Fefu *reaches for the gun, aims and shoots. Christina hides behind the couch. She and* Cindy *scream. . . . Fefu smiles proudly. She blows on the mouth of the barrel. She puts down the gun and looks out again"* (p. 9). As Fefu explains once Phillip has regained his feet, "It's a game we play. I shoot and he falls. Whenever he hears the blast he falls. No matter where he is, he falls." Although Phillip is never seen in the play, his attitudes shape Fefu's stage characterization. For as she remarks in her first line in the play, "My husband married me to have a constant reminder of how loathsome women are" (p. 7). The shooting game provides an emblem for the relation between vision and gender in *Fefu,* for whether the shells are "real" or "imaginary" ("I thought the guns were not loaded," remarks Cindy; "I'm never sure," replies Fefu [p. 12]), the exchange of power takes place through the "sighting" of the other.[9]

The authority of the absent male is everywhere evident in *Fefu,* and particularly is imaged in Julia's paralysis. As Cindy suggests when she describes the accident, Julia's malady is a version of Fefu's "game": "I thought the bullet hit her, but it didn't . . . the hunter aimed . . . at the deer. He shot":

> Julia and the deer fell. . . . I screamed for help and the hunter came and examined Julia. He said, "She is not hurt." Julia's forehead was bleeding. He said, "It is a surface wound. I didn't hurt her." I know it wasn't he who hurt her. It was someone else. . . . Apparently there was a spinal nerve injury but the doctors are puzzled because it doesn't seem her spine was hurt when she fell. She hit her head and she suffered a concussion but that would not affect the spinal nerve. So there seems to be no reason for the paralysis. She blanks out and that is caused by the blow on the head. It's a scar in the brain.

(pp. 14-15)

The women of *Fefu and Her Friends* share Julia's invisible "scar," the mark of their paralyzing subjection to a masculine authority that operates on the "imaginary," ideological plane. The hunter is kin to Julia's hallucinatory "voices" in part 2, the "judges" who enforce her psychic dismemberment: "They clubbed me. They broke my head. They broke my will. They broke my hands. They tore my eyes out. They took away my voice." Julia's bodily identification is broken down and reordered according to the "aesthetic" canons prescribed by the male voice ("He said that . . . to see a woman running creates a disparate and incongruous image in the mind. It's antiaesthetic" [pp. 24-25]), the silent voice that characterizes women as "loathsome." This internalized "guardian" rewrites Julia's identity at the interface of the body itself, where the masculine voice materializes itself in the woman's flesh. Other women in the play envy "being like a man. Thinking like a man. Feeling like a man" (p. 13), but as Julia's coerced "prayer" suggests, to be subject to this representation of the feminine is to resign humanity ("The human being is of the masculine gender"), independence ("The mate for man is woman and that is the cross man must bear"), and sexuality ("Woman's spirit is sexual. That is why after coitus they dwell in nefarious feelings" [p. 25]). The subliminal masculine voice inscribes the deepest levels of psychological and physiological identification with the crippling gesture of submission:

(*Her head moves as if slapped.*)

JULIA: Don't hit me. Didn't I just say my prayer?

(*A smaller slap.*)

JULIA: I believe it.

(p. 25)

Fornes suggest that "Julia is the mind of the play," and Julia's scene articulates the shaping vision of *Fefu* as a whole, as well as organizing the dramatic structure of part 2. In the kitchen scene, for instance, Fornes recalls Julia's torture in Paula's description of the anomie she feels when a relationship breaks up ("the break up takes place in parts. The brain, the heart, the body, mutual things, shared things" [p. 27]); the simultaneity of the two scenes is marked when Sue leaves the kitchen with soup for Julia. Sue's departure also coordinates Julia's prayer with the concluding section of the kitchen scene. Julia's submission to the voice in the bedroom is replaced by Paula and Cecilia's suspension of their unspoken love affair: "Now we look at each other like strangers. We are guarded. I speak and you don't understand my words" (p. 28). This dramatic counterpoint invites us to see Paula and Cecilia's relationship, Cindy's violent dream of strangulation (in the study scene), Emma's thinking "about genitals all the time," and Fefu's constant, nightmarish pain (in the lawn scene) as transformations of Julia's more explicit subjection.

The action of *Fefu and Her Friends* takes place under the watchful eyes of Phillip, of the hunter, of Julia's "guardians," a gaze that constructs, enables, and thwarts the women of the stage: "Our sight is a form they take. That is why we take pleasure in seeing things" (p. 35). In the theater, of course, there is another invisible voyeur whose performance is both powerful and "imaginary"—the spectator. *Fefu and Her Friends* extends the function of the spectator beyond the metaphorical register by decentering "his" implicit ordering of the theatricality of the feminine. First performed by the New York Theater Strategy in a

SoHo loft, the play originally invited the spectators to explore the space of Fefu's home. In the American Place Theatre production, the spectators were invited, row by row, to different areas of the theater—a backstage kitchen, an upstairs bedroom, the garden and study sets—before being returned to the auditorium, but not to their original seats.[10] At first glance, Fornes' staging may seem simply a "gimmick," a formalist exercise in "multiple perspective" something like Alan Ayckbourn's *Norman Conquests*.[11] Yet Ayckbourn's trilogy—each play takes a different set of soundings from the events of a single weekend—implies that there could be, in some mammoth play, a single ordering and relation of events, one "drama" expressed by a single plot and visible from a single perspective. In this regard the structure of *The Norman Conquests*, like its philandering hero, Norman, exudes a peculiarly masculine confidence, "The faith the world puts in them and they in turn put in the world," as Christina puts it (p. 13). Despite Fornes' suggestion that "the style of acting should be film acting" ("Interview," p. 110), *Fefu and Her Friends* bears little confidence in the adequacy or authority of the single viewing subject characteristic of both film and fourth-wall realism. In this sense, *Fefu* more closely approximates the decentering disorientation of environmental art than "some adoption by the theater of cinematic flexibility and montage."[12] Different spectators see the drama in a different sequence, and in fact see different plays, as variations invariably enter into the actors' performances. Fornes not only draws the audience into the performance space, she actively challenges and suspends the epistemological structure of realistic vision, predicated as it is on an invisible, singular, motionless, masculine interpreter situated outside the field of dramatic *and* theatrical activity. By reordering our function in the theatrical process, *Fefu* reorders our relation to, and interpretation of, the dramatic process it shapes.[13]

As Cecilia says at the opening of part 3, after we have returned to the auditorium, "we each have our own system of receiving information, placing it, responsibility to it. That system can function with such a bias that it could take any situation and translate it into one formula" (p. 29). In performance, *Fefu and Her Friends* dramatizes and displaces the theatrical "system" that renders "woman" visible: the predication of feminine identity on the sight of the spectator, a "judge." Fornes regards traditional plot conventions as naturalizing a confining set of feminine roles: "In a plot play the woman is either the mother or the sister or the girlfriend or the daughter. The purpose of the character is to serve the plot" ("Interview," p. 106). In this sense Fornes' theatrical strategy may be seen as an attempt to retheorize the interpretive operation of theatrical vision. Fornes replaces the "objective" and objectifying relations of masculine vision with the "fluid boundaries" characteristic of feminist epistemology.[14] As Patrocinio Schweickart argues, summarizing Nancy Chodorow and Carol Gilligan, "men define themselves through individuation and separation from others, while women have more flexible ego boundaries and define and experience themselves in terms of their affiliations and relationships with others" (Schweickart, pp. 54-55). The consequences of this distinction have been widely applied and have become recently influential in studies of reading, studies which provide an interpretive analogy to the action of Fornes' dramaturgy. Schweickart suggests that in a feminist, reader-oriented theory, "the central issue is not of control or partition, but of managing the contradictory implications of the desire for relationship . . . and the desire for intimacy" (p. 55). David Bleich, surveying actual readings provided by his students, suggests that "women *enter* the world of the novel, take it as something 'there' for that purpose; men *see* the novel as a result of someone's action and construe its meaning or logic in those terms" (p. 239).[15] Writing the play, Fornes sought to avoid "writing in a linear manner, moving forward," and instead undertook a series of centrifugal experiments, exploring characterization by writing a series of improvisational, extraneous scenes (Cummings, p. 53). But while Fornes again disowns political or ideological intent ("I don't mean linear in terms of what the feminists claim about the way the male mind works," she goes on to say), her suspension of plot organization for a more atmospheric or "environmental" procedure articulates the gendered coding of theatrical interpretation. Perhaps as a result, the staging of *Fefu* challenges the institutional "objectivity" of theatrical vision. For the play not only realizes Julia's absent voices, it casts us as their speakers, since we enact the role of her unseen, coercive tormentors. The play reshapes our relation to the drama, setting our interpretive activity within a performance structure that subordinates "plot" to "environment" and that refuses our recourse to a single, external point of view.

The "educational dramatics" of *Fefu and Her Friends* not only alert us to the paralyzing effect of a patriarchal ideology on the dramatic characters; they also imply the degree to which this ideology is replicated in the coercive "formula" of realistic sight.[16] As Emma's speech on the "Environment" suggests ("Environment knocks at the gateway of the senses" [p. 31]), the theatrical activity of part 2 reorders the traditional hierarchy of theatrical perception—privileging the drama to its performance—and so suspends the "objective" absence of the masculine eye. *Fefu* criticizes the realistic theater's order of subjection, an order which, like "civilization," is still "A circumscribed order in which the whole has not entered"; even Emma's "environment" is characterized as "him" (p. 32). In *Fefu and Her Friends,* vision is achieved only through a strategy of displacement, by standing outside the theatrical "formula" of realism in order to witness its "bias." The play undertakes to dramatize both the results of that bias—in the various deformations suffered by Julia, Fefu, and their friends—and to enact the "other" formula that has been suppressed, the formula that becomes the audience's mode of vision in the theater. To see *Fefu* is not to imagine an ideal order, a single, causal "plot" constituted specifically by our absence from the performance. For *Fefu and Her Friends* decenters the absent "spectator" as the site of authentic interpretation, replacing "him"

with a self-evidently theatricalized body, an "audience," a community sharing irreconcilable yet interdependent experiences. The perspective offered by the realistic box set appears to construct a community of witnesses, but is in fact grounded in the sight of a single observer; the realistic audience sees with a single eye. *Fefu* challenges the "theory" of realistic theater at its source by dramatizing—and displacing—the covert authority of the constitutive *theoros* of naturalism and the social order it reproduces: the offstage man.[17] In so doing, *Fefu* provides an experience consonant with the play's climactic dramatic event. Much as we are returned to the auditorium in part 3, to assume the role of "spectator" with a fuller sense of the social legitimacy embodied in that perspective, so Fefu finally appropriates the objectifying "bias" of the unseen man in order to defend herself—and free Julia—from its oppressive view. Fefu cleans the play's central "apparatus" and then assumes the hunter's part, the "sight" that subjects the women of the stage:

> (*There is the sound of a shot.* CHRISTINA and CECILIA *run out. Julia puts her hand to her forehead. Her hand goes down slowly. There is blood on her forehead. Her head falls back.* FEFU *enters holding a dead rabbit in her arms. She stands behind* JULIA.
>
> FEFU: I killed it . . . I just shot . . . and killed it . . . Julia.
>
> (p. 41)

Despite the success of *Fefu and Her Friends* and of several later plays—*Evelyn Brown* (1980), *Mud* (1983), *Sarita* (1984)—addressing gender and power issues, Fornes refuses to be identified solely as a "feminist" playwright (Cummings, p. 55). Spanning the range of contemporary theatrical style (experimental theater, realism, "absurd" drama, musical theater, satiric revue), Fornes' drama resists formal or thematic categorization. What pervades her writing is a delicate, sometimes rueful, occasionally explosive irony, a witty moral toughness replacing the "heavy, slow, laborious and pedestrian" didacticism we may expect of "ideological" drama. Brecht was right, of course, to encourage the members of his cast to play against such a sense of political theater: "We must keep the tempo of a run-through and infect it with quiet strength, with our own fun. In the dialogue the exchanges must not be offered reluctantly, as when offering somebody one's last pair of boots, but must be tossed like so many balls" (Brecht, p. 283). Like Brecht's, Fornes' theater generates the "fun," the infectious sophistication of a popular art. Juggling the dialectic between "theater for pleasure" and "theater for instruction," Fornes is still—earnestly, politically, theatrically—"playing games."

NOTES

[1]Fornes describes *The Successful Life of Three* as arising from her association with the Actors Studio: "The first play that I wrote that was influenced by my understanding of Method was *The Successful Life of*

Three. What one character says to another comes completely out of his own impulse and so does the other character's reply. The other character's reply never comes from some sort of premeditation on my part or even the part of the character. The characters have no mind. They are simply doing what Strasberg always called 'moment to moment.'" Insofar as Fornes applies acting exercises to the techniques of dramatic characterization, she seems accurately to have evaluated her relationship to Strasberg: "I was very impressed with Strasberg's work as an actor's technician or a director's technician but I would completely ignore anything he would say about aesthetics" (Cummings, p. 52).

[2]See Barnes; Stephen Holden compares the play to Bernstein's *Candide*, Beckett, and Carroll; and Daphne Kraft describes the play as a hybrid of "Marc Blitzstein's 'The Cradle Will Rock' and Leonard Bernstein's 'Candide.'"

[3]See Pavis, p. 44.

[4]See Bigsby, p. 23, and Terry Eagleton's suggestive account of the relation between text and production in *Criticism and Ideology* (pp. 64-68).

[5]On "identification" and ideology, see Burke, p. 88 and *passim*.

[6]Martin Washburn suggests not only that Fornes has "absorbed the continental traditions" but that "Isidore may actually represent the toils of continental literature which the playwright wants to escape."

[7]It should be noted that some scenes have no taped opening, some have a tape recording of the opening lines only in Hungarian, and some scenes proceed throughout in this manner: English tape, Hungarian tape, actor's delivery.

[8]As, for instance, when a waiter delivers a sudden, trancelike tirade: "We are dark. Americans are bright.—You crave mobility. The car. You move from city to city so as not to grow stale. You don't stay too long in a place. . . . Our grace is weighty. Not yours. You worship the long leg and loose hip joint. How else to jump in and out of cars" (p. 52).

[9]The gun business derives from a joke, as Fornes reports in "Notes on *Fefu*": "There are two Mexicans in sombreros sitting at a bullfight and one says to the other, 'Isn't she beautiful, the one in yellow?' and he points to a woman on the other side of the arena crowded with people. The other one says, 'Which one?' and the first takes his gun and shoots her and says, 'The one that falls.' In the first draft of the play Fefu explains that she started playing this game with her husband as a joke. But in rewriting the play I took out this explanation" (p. 38). It's notable that the gun business dates from Fornes' original work on the play in 1964, as she suggests in "Interview," p. 106.

[10]Although he seems to have disliked leaving his seat, Walter Kerr offers a description of the procedure of the play; see his review of *Fefu and Her Friends*. Kerr's painful recollections of his displacement are recalled several months later, in "New Plays Bring Back Old Songs." See also Pat Lamb ("at stake here is the quality of experience, of life itself"); and the unsigned review of *Fefu and Her Friends* in the *Village Voice*, May 23, 1977 ("this enclosed repetitiveness sums up entire trapped lifetimes").

[11]In Ayckbourn's trilogy the same romantic comedy is replayed three times. In *Table Manners* the audience witnesses a series of misadventures transpiring over a country-house weekend and hears about a variety of offstage events; in *Living Together* these offstage events and others are dramatized while we hear about (and recall) the now-offstage events of the first play; in *Round and Round the Garden* the material from the first two plays is now offstage, and we witness a third series of scenes.

[12]Stanley Kauffman's reading of the play's filmic texture is at once shrewd and, in this sense, misapplied: "I doubt very much that Fornes thought of this four-part walk-around as a gimmick. Probably it signified for her an explanation of simultaneity (since all four scenes are done simultaneously four times for the four groups), a union of play and audience through kinetics, some adoption by the theater of cinematic flexibility and montage. But since the small content in these scenes would in no way be damaged by traditional serial construction, since this insistence on reminding us that people actually have related/unrelated conversations simultaneously in different rooms of the same house is banal, we are left with the *feeling* of gimmick."

[13]As Richard Eder remarked of the bedroom scene, "Julia is lying in bed, and we sit around her. Our presence, like that of the onlookers in Rembrandt's 'Anatomy Lesson,' magnifies the horror of what is going on." See also Feingold.

[14]For this phrase I am indebted to my colleague Joan Lidoff.

[15]In terms of the theatrical structure of *Fefu and Her Friends*, it is also notable that Bleich's male students not only tended to "see" the novel from "outside" its matrix of relationships but tended to privilege the "plot" in their retellings: "The men retold the story as if the purpose was to deliver a clear, simple structure or chain of information: these are the main characters; this is the main action; this is how it turned out. . . . The women presented the narrative as if it were an atmosphere or experience. They generally felt freer to reflect on the story material with adjectival judgments, and even larger sorts of judgments, and they were more ready to draw inferences without strict regard for the literal warrant of the text, but with more regard for the affective sense of human relationships in the story" (p. 256).

[16]Emma's speech on acting is taken from the prologue to Emma Sheridan Fry, *Educational Dramatics*. Elsewhere in the book Fry defines the "dramatic instinct" as the process that relates the subject to its environment: "It rouses us to a recognition of the Outside. It provokes those processes whereby we respond to the attack of the Outside upon us" (p. 6).

[17]As Jane Gallop describes it, "Nothing to see becomes nothing of worth. The metaphysical privileging of sight over other senses, oculocentrism, supports and unifies phallocentric sexual theory (theory—from the Greek *theoria*, from *theoros*, 'spectator,' from *thea*, 'a viewing'). *Speculum* (from *specere*, 'to look at') makes repeated reference to the oculocentrism of theory, of philosophy" (pp. 36-37).

BIBLIOGRAPHY

Althusser, Louis. "Ideology and Ideological State Apparatuses." In *Lenin and Philosophy and Other Essays*, translated by Ben Brewster. London: NLB, 1971.

Ayckbourn, Alan. *The Norman Conquests*. Garden City, N.J.: Doubleday, 1975.

Barnes, Clive. Review of *Promenade*, by Maria Irene Fornes. New York *Times*, June 5, 1969, 56.

Bigsby, C. W. E. "The Language of Crisis in British Theatre: The Drama of Cultural Pathology." In *Contemporary English Drama*, edited by C. W. E. Bigsby, pp. 10-51. New York: Holmes & Meier, 1981.

Bleich, David. "Gender Interests in Reading and Language." In *Gender and Reading*, edited by Elizabeth A. Flynn and Patrocinio P. Schweickart, pp. 234-66. Baltimore: Johns Hopkins University Press, 1986.

Brecht, Bertolt. *Brecht on Theatre*. Edited and translated by John Willett. New York: Hill and Wang, 1964.

Burke, Kenneth. *A Rhetoric of Motives*. Berkeley: University of California Press, 1969.

Chodorow, Nancy. *The Reproduction of Mothering: Psychoanalysis and the Sociology of Gender*. Berkeley: University of California Press, 1978.

Cummings, Scott. "Seeing with Clarity: The Visions of Maria Irene Fornes." *Theater* (Yale) 17, no. 1 (Winter 1985), 51-56.

de Lauretis, Teresa. *Alice Doesn't: Feminism, Semiotics, Cinema.* Bloomington, Ind.: Indiana University Press, 1984.

Eagleton, Terry. *Criticism and Ideology* [1976]. London: Verso, 1978.

Eder, Richard. "Fefu Takes Friends to American Place." New York *Times*, January 14, 1978, 10.

—————. Review of *Fefu and Her Friends*, by Maria Irene Fornes. *Village Voice*, May 23, 1977, 80.

Feingold, Michael. Review of *Fefu and Her Friends*, by Maria Irene Fornes. *Village Voice*, January 23, 1978, 75.

Flynn, Elizabeth A., and Patrocinio P. Schweickart, eds. *Gender and Reading.* Baltimore, Md.: Johns Hopkins University Press, 1986.

Fornes, Maria Irene. *The Conduct of Life. Plays.*

—————. *The Danube.* In *Plays.*

—————. *Dr. Kheal.* In *Promenade and Other Plays.*

—————. *Fefu and Her Friends.* In *Wordplays: An Anthology of New American Drama.* New York: Performing Arts Journal Publications, 1980.

—————. "I Write These Messages That Come." *Drama Review* 21, no. 4 (December 1977), 25-40.

—————. "Interview." *Performing Arts Journal* 2, no. 3 (Winter 1978), 106-11.

—————. *Molly's Dream.* In *Promenade and Other Plays.*

—————. "Notes on Fefu." *SoHo Weekly News*, June 12, 1978, 38.

—————. *Plays.* New York: Performing Arts Journal Publications, 1986.

—————. *Promenade.* In *Promenade and Other Plays.*

—————. *Promenade and Other Plays.* New York: Winter House, 1971.

—————. *The Successful Life of Three.* In *Promenade and Other Plays.*

—————. *Tango Palace.* In *Promenade and Other Plays.*

—————. *A Vietnamese Wedding.* In *Promenade and Other Plays.*

Fry, Emma Sheridan. *Educational Dramatics.* New York: Lloyd Adams Noble, 1917.

Gallop, Jane. "The Father's Seduction." In *The (M)other Tongue: Essays in Feminist Psychoanalytic Interpretation*, edited by Shirley Nelson Garner, Claire Kahane, Madelon Sprengnether. Ithaca, N.Y.: Cornell University Press, 1985.

Gilligan, Carol. *In a Different Voice: Psychological Theory and Women's Development.* Cambridge, Mass.: Harvard University Press, 1982.

Holden, Stephen. Review of *Promenade*, by Maria Irene Fornes. New York *Times*, October 25, 1983, C8.

Kauffman, Stanley. Review of *Fefu and Her Friends*, by Maria Irene Fornes. *New Republic*, February 25, 1978, 38.

Kerr, Walter. Review of *Fefu and Her Friends*, by Maria Irene Fornes. New York *Times*, January 22, 1978, D3.

—————. "New Plays Bring Back Old Songs." New York *Times*, June 13, 1978, C1, C4.

Kraft, Daphne. Review of *Promenade*, by Maria Irene Fornes. Newark *Evening News*, June 5, 1969, 74.

Lamb, Pat. Review of *Fefu and Her Friends*, by Maria Irene Fornes. *Chelsea Clinton News*, January 19, 1978.

Marranca, Bonnie. "The Real Life of Maria Irene Fornes." In *Theatrewritings*. New York: Performing Arts Journal Publications, 1984, pp. 69-73.

Pavis, Patrice. "On Brecht's Notion of *Gestus*." In *Languages of the Stage: Essays in the Semiology of the Theatre.* New York: Performing Arts Journal Publications, 1982, pp. 37-49.

Rich, Frank. Review of *The Danube*, by Maria Irene Fornes. New York *Times*, March 13, 1984, C13.

Schweickart, Patrocinio P. "Reading Ourselves: Toward a Feminist Theory of Reading." In *Gender and Reading*, ed. Elizabeth A. Flynn and Patrocinio P. Schweickart, pp. 31-62. Baltimore, Md.: Johns Hopkins University Press, 1986.

Therborn, Göran. *The Ideology of Power and the Power of Ideology.* London: NLB, 1980.

Washburn, Martin. Review of *Tango Palace*, by Maria Irene Fornes. *Village Voice*, January 25, 1973.

Wetzsteon, Ross. "Irene Fornes: The Elements of Style." *Village Voice*, April 29, 1986, 42-45.

Toby Silverman Zinman (essay date 1990)

SOURCE: "Hen in a Foxhouse: The Absurdist Plays of Maria Irene Fornes," in *Around the Absurd: Essays on Modern and Postmodern Drama*, edited by Enoch Brater and Ruby Cohn, The University of Michigan Press, 1990, pp. 203-20.

[*In this essay, Zinman detects elements of the theater of the absurd in several of Fornes' plays.*]

"Where do female playwrights stand in relation to the tradition of the theater of the absurd?" This question was posed to me by the editors of this volume. Never mind its invitation to tokenism. Never mind its invitation to specious, gender-based generalizations. Better to say something than nothing.

I went back to Martin Esslin's *The Theatre of the Absurd* to find some clues; scanning the index yielded only one female playwright's name: Gertrude Stein, and she is described as a precursor, linked to dadaism and surrealism rather than absurdism, and Esslin points out that the works she describes as "plays" are really "short abstract prose poems in which single sentences or short paragraphs are labelled act I, Act II, and so on. . . . When, towards the end of her life, Gertrude Stein wrote a play with plot and dialogue, *Yes Is for a Very Young Man*, it turned out to be a fascinating but essentially traditional piece of work. . . ."[1] So the question remained.

  reductio ab Absurdo:

The theater of the absurd revolutionized the modern stage in both form and content; that is, absurdist drama is distinguished by its "metaphysical anguish"[2] stemming from our culture's loss of meaning, value, and certitude, as well as by the way such drama communicates this vision through its concrete images, its abandonment of rational discourse, and its insistence on showing rather than saying that life is senseless, thereby revealing a profound mistrust of verbal language. Using these basic ideas, which Esslin provided us all with nearly thirty years ago, it was easy to eliminate many of the most visible women playwrights—Marsha Norman, Beth Henley, Pam Gems, Tina Howe, Wendy Wasserstein, and Nell Dunn, for example—because they are obviously writing varieties of realistic drama. Even when they violate those conventions (as Wasserstein does in Heidi's interior monologues) it is within a realistic framework. Even when they exaggerate the conventions of realism, as Emily Mann does in *Still Life*, it is to press theater more toward the journalistic (this happened; they live in Minnesota; they said these words to me) and further from the imagistic. Even when they depart from realism through song and dance, as Ntozake Shange does in *Colored Girls*, it is discursively. When Shange and Mann recently collaborated on a musical play, *Betsey Brown*, which tries to raise both racial and feminist issues, the results were so blatantly discursive as to seem sophomoric.

It is necessary to acknowledge at this juncture that Americans have never gravitated toward absurdist drama—perhaps because, as Esslin argues,

> the convention of the absurd springs from a feeling of deep disillusion . . . which has been characteristic in countries like France and Britain in the years after the Second World War. . . . [but] The American dream of the good life is still very strong. In the United States the belief in progress that characterized Europe in the nineteenth century has been maintained into the middle of the twentieth. It is only since the events of the 1970's—Watergate and defeat in Vietnam—that this optimism has received some sharp shocks.
>
> (311)

The logic of this reasoning would lead us to believe that women *would* have embraced the theater of the absurd, since they have experienced "deep disillusion," but this is not the case. Thus, it becomes even more interesting to see that although many women writing for the stage use many of the methods of the theater of the absurd, testifying to the power of the inheritance, they do not share its vision.

Many of the overtly political women dramatists, of whom Caryl Churchill and Joan Holden are brilliant examples, could be eliminated from my "answer" to the editors' question by virtue of their commitment to radical social change. This is necessarily an optimistic position, while theater of the absurd assumes the Beckettian premise "Nothing to be done," the line with which *Waiting for Godot* begins. The new feminist theater, too, obviously believes that there is much to be done. The very enunciating of the polemic—despite an absurdist framework or technique—has, surely, at its base, a belief that remediation of societal as well as individual attitudes is feasible.

On the other hand, Adrienne Kennedy, who in some way shares the absurdists' metaphysic of despair, uses methods far closer to expressionism. To see life as symbolic nightmare, heavily invested in and with Christianity as Kennedy does, is, almost certainly, to miss out on the humor. And a strong sense of the ludicrous is essential in—and to—the absurdist playwright.

So it was with a sense of relief that I answered the editors' question with the works of Maria Irene Fornes. To consider Fornes within the absurdist tradition becomes even more interesting when one considers that she is usually regarded as a feminist playwright, despite her rejection of the label. While it is certainly plausible to read her plays as feminist documents, recognizing them as absurdist theater shifts their meanings and effects considerably. Fornes is, to my mind, committed to the theater, not to politics, and she has said, "When we start respecting imagery and sensibility, the gender of the writer will be the last thing we think of."[3]

In *Feminist Theatre*, Helene Keyssar mentions Fornes's administrative work in founding the Women's Theatre Council, which collapsed in 1973 and gave rise to a new group called Theatre Strategy, of which Fornes was president. It is important to note that this group's commitment was not to feminism but "to sending experimental plays across the country."[4] But Keyssar insists that it is in "Fornes's fifteen or more plays that we see the best evidence of the theatrical weapons she deploys in the service of feminism" (122). Gayle Austin comes to a similar conclusion; choosing three of Fornes's plays, *Fefu and Her Friends*, *Sarita*, and *The Conduct of Life*, she declares: "Examining these plays through a feminist lens focused on the madwoman figure shows Fornes to be a playwriting exemplar in both form and content."[5] W. B. Worthen, who discusses Fornes's ongoing theatrical experiment, her "eclectic, reflexive theatricality,"[6] centers his discussion on the sexual politics of the stage-spectator relationship. Although he acknowledges that "Fornes refuses to be identified solely as a 'feminist' playwright" and that her work "resists formal or thematic categorization,"[7] he nevertheless reads *Fefu and Her Friends* in a strong feminist light. The way Fornes's drama changes if one changes the lens or the light is most clearly revealed by reexamining *Fefu*, her best known play.

The action of this play takes place in Fefu's New England house where eight women, many of whom are old friends, have met to plan and rehearse a fundraising program for an educational project. It is a spring day in 1935. This location in time and space creates an immediate disjunction, in that these women seem contemporary—in their verbal as well as their body language—and, given that this is 1935, in that there are no signs of financial hard times in these women's circumstances (cars, jobs, travel, clothes, sense of leisure). It is, nevertheless, croquet, not frisbee, that they go out to the lawn to play, but they may be using flamingos for mallets.

Fornes's characteristic emphasis on the visual rather than the verbal, a crucial absurdist preference, may well stem from the fact that she spoke Spanish before she spoke English (she emigrated from Cuba when she was fifteen) and that she saw the original Roger Blin production of *Waiting for Godot* in Paris when she did not understand any French.

I felt that my life had been turned around. . . . I felt I saw clarity. Maybe that night something in me understood that I was to dedicate my life to the theatre. . . . If you'd asked me then what it was I'd understood, I couldn't have told you. If I had understood the text it still wouldn't have been clear.[8]

And, too, Fornes was a painter (she studied with Hans Hoffman)[9] before she was a playwright. Fornes, who teaches playwriting at INTAR, the Hispanic American Arts Center in New York, uses visualization exercises as her primary pedagogic technique, designed to "get past thinking of writing as 'how to phrase something,'"[10] since her own creative process hinges on the visual:

> But then there is the point when the characters become crystallized. When that happens, I have an image in full color, technicolor. And that *happens*! I do not remember it happening, but I get it like *click*! At some point I see a picture of the set with the characters in it—let us say a picture *related* to the set, not necessarily the exact set.[11]

The most startling "picture of the set with the characters in it" we are given in *Fefu* is an image early in act 1: Fefu picks up a double-barrelled shotgun and shoots her husband, who is offstage, outside on the lawn; he then, we are told, gets up and brushes himself off.

Fornes tells us that the idea for *Fefu* began with the image of a woman shooting her husband, and it took her years to get from that scene to the whole play. She writes:

> Most of my plays start with a kind of a fantasy game—just to see what happens. ***Fefu and Her Friends*** started that way. There was this woman I fantasized who was talking to some friends. She took her rifle and shot her husband. Also there is a Mexican joke where there are two Mexicans speaking at a bullfight. One says to the other, "She is pretty, that one over there." The other one says, "Which one?" So the first one takes his rifle and shoots her. He says, "That one, the one that falls."
>
> So in the first draft of the play, Fefu does just that. She takes her rifle and she shoots her husband. He falls. Then she explains that they heard the Mexican joke and she and her husband play that game. That was just my fantasy: thinking of the joke, how absurd it was.[12]

Although the joke was eliminated from the finished play, the absurdity was not. The game Fefu and Phillip play, which so scandalizes Christina and Cindy, is an absurdist image of their marriage—of, perhaps, marriage itself, of the universal, permanent warfare of male/female relationships. Consider the opening dialogue of the play:

> FEFU: My husband married me to have a constant reminder of how loathsome women are.
>
> CINDY: What?
>
> FEFU: Yup.
>
> CINDY: That's just awful.
>
> FEFU: No it isn't.

> CINDY: It isn't awful?
>
> FEFU: No.
>
> CINDY: I don't think anyone would marry for that reason.
>
> FEFU: He did.
>
> CINDY: Did he say so?
>
> FEFU: He tells me constantly.
>
> CINDY: Oh, dear.
>
> FEFU: I don't mind. I laugh when he tells me.
>
> CINDY: You laugh?
>
> FEFU: I do.
>
> CINDY: How can you?
>
> FEFU: It's funny.—And it's true. That's why I laugh.
>
> CINDY: What is true?
>
> FEFU: That women are loathsome.
>
> CINDY: . . . Fefu!
>
> FEFU: That shocks you.
>
> CINDY: It does. I don't feel loathsome.
>
> FEFU: I don't mean that you are loathsome.
>
> CINDY: You don't mean that I'm loathsome.
>
> FEFU: No . . . It's something to think about. It's a thought.
>
> CINDY: It's a hideous thought. . . .
>
> FEFU: Cindy, I'm not talking about anyone in particular. I'm talking about . . .
>
> CINDY: No one in particular, just women.
>
> FEFU: Yes.
>
> CINDY: In that case I am relieved. I thought you were referring to us. (*They are amused.* FEFU *speaks affectionately.*)
>
> FEFU: You are being stupid.
>
> CINDY: Stupid and loathsome. (*To* Christina.) Have you ever heard anything more . . .[13]

One might write a play about how "loathsome" men find women and about the self-loathing that is both cause and effect of this, and about how women deeply resent loving men, about the terrible interplay of dependence and self-assertion, about the terrible interplay of sexual passion and contempt, but then, one might be Strindberg. To contain all that in one image of Fefu's shooting Phillip with a rifle, into which *he* may have placed real bullets instead of blanks, is to make the stage speak in the powerful shorthand of concrete images. Further, to read the play as a feminist call to arms is to respond as Cindy does—it is to take the cosmic joke personally. Fornes theatrically demonstrates that it is naive and profitless to assume that the complex enmity inherent in such relations is remediable. The Mexican joke is funny and grotesque and horrible all at once, because it is about brutality and self-defeating stupidity, about simultaneous wish fulfillment and wish denial, about the random victim and the victimizer, about the privileging of action over speech and how powerful and dangerous that can be; it is about the Absurd.

All of this is contained in the stage image of Fefu with her shotgun, an image repeated at the close of the play, in the controversial concluding scene wherein Julia, in a wheelchair since her "hunting accident," begins to bleed from the forehead, as though the bullet with which Fefu kills a rabbit has struck her. This scene undoes the tacit realistic explanations of the earlier mysterious story of the deer hunter. Julia, we have been told, fell to the ground in the woods when the hunter shot a deer. There is no medical evidence of harm, yet she can no longer walk. The audience's easy, reassuring diagnosis of psychosomatic paralysis is reinforced, especially since we and Fefu see Julia walking in one scene. Look, the spectator can say, see how the male establishment has victimized her and how she has internalized that victimization. This is to assume realism; that is, such a peculiar event must be accounted for, and psychological exegesis is the one most comfortable to our culture. It is, further, to assume that Julia is a symbolic character whose meaning can be expressed. This is fundamental to the feminist readings of the play; for example, Keyssar sees Julia as the symbol of feminine yielding in the face of the "enormity of the struggle women must undertake," and that "woman-as-victim must be killed . . . in order to ignite the explosion of a community of women."[14]

But the bleeding wound on Julia's forehead after Fefu shoots the rabbit has also been viewed as "miracle" by Susan Sontag,[15] which also suggests the play is realistic and that the only way of explaining such a "violation of the quotidian" is mystically. This, too, I think, mistakes the vision and therefore mistakes the genre. But, if we see the play as absurdist, then the images do not have to be explained; they are theater, not life, and speak with the language of the contemporary stage. Consider, for example, a stratlingly similar image: the bleeding forehead at the conclusion of Sam Shepard's *Red Cross*.

It may be useful to note here that the only play Fornes had read before she started to write plays was *Hedda Gabler*,[16] and one might see Fefu's shotgun as an absurdist transmutation of Hedda's pistol; Fefu is not about to shoot herself to escape male dominance, but she may, in the shooting of the rabbit/Julia at the end, have shot the Hedda principle. This is to suggest not only the feminist act of destroying that female character who symbolizes a yielding to male dominance (or the equally self-destructive suicidal refusal to yield to male dominance), but also the destruction of the Hedda principle in theatrical terms: the rejection of the well-made, realistic play replete with explanations and meaningful actions; the well-furnished house party revisited and revised.

Perhaps the play's most subtle yet radical assault on the realistic is that its characters spring from different modes of theatrical creation: the naturalistic, the symbolic, the histrionic, and the absurdist. This is not merely to say that they exist on different levels of fictive reality—the difference, say, between the actors and the characters in Pirandello's *Six Characters in Search of an Author*. It is also that they belong to different kinds of playwriting, and the play is, formally, built on the collision of these modes.

Julia's long speeches explaining her torment at the hands of her male oppressors—

> I told them the stinking parts of the body are the important ones. . . .
>
> (24)

and

> The human being is of the masculine gender. . . .
>
> (25)

and

> I feel we are constantly threatened by death. . . .
>
> (35)

—are discursive lumps in the texture of the play. It might be useful to note here that in explaining why she dislikes Arthur Miller's and Tennessee William's plays, Fornes said, "I don't romanticize pain. In my work people are always trying to find a way out, rather than feeling a romantic attachment to their prison."[17] They do not, of course, find it; this quest for escape and the defeat of the quest is fundamental to the absurdist vision. By extension of these remarks, one might assume that Julia is a character out of a Miller or a Williams play. Julia defines herself as neurotic, suffering heroine, while Julia as character is defined by Fornes as a manifestation of symbolic realism. Fefu, on the other hand—by far the least verbal character in the play—is an absurdist character; she speaks as well as acts in presentational images.

Thus, it is through an image rather than an argument that Fefu shows Christina that she, too, is "fascinated with revulsion," the image of the smooth, dry stone whose underside is "slimy and filled with fungus and crawling with worms. It is another life that is parallel to the one we manifest" (9). This is more than an appeal to Christina to open her mind to the excitement of grappling with uncomfortable ideas; it is a testimony to theatrical possibilities, an assertion that the stage can show us the life beneath the realistic surface. Fefu's account of the monstrous, mangled cat whom she feeds and fears and who fouls her kitchen is really an image, not a story; like Albee's dog in *Zoo Story*, Fornes's cat is full of unarticulable meaning; it speaks Fefu's "constant pain," which is far less explicable than Julia's.

Like an audience that has come for realism and found absurdity, the guests in Fefu's house find her shocking and puzzling. The refined Christina, who is new to the group, expresses much of the honest, dismayed reaction of audiences to theater of the absurd and to Fefu who is the incarnation of it:

> She confuses me a little. . . . I don't know if she's careful with life. . . . I suppose I don't mean with life but more with convention. I think she is an adventurer in a way. . . . Her mind is adventurous. I don't know if there is dishonesty in that. But in adventure there is taking chances and risks, and then one has to, somehow, have less regard or respect for things as they are. That is, regard for a kind of convention, I suppose. I am probably ultimately a conformist, I think. And I suppose I do hold back for fear of being disrespectful or destroying something—and I admire those who are not. But I also feel they are dangerous to me. I don't think they are dangerous to the world, they are more useful than I am, more important, but I feel some of my life is endangered by their way of thinking.
>
> (22)

This defines the play's mode—or collision of modes, as they are embodied not just in the minds of the characters themselves but in the very way the characters have been conceived.

That the play is about theater rather than politics is most straightforwardly suggested by the plot—the planning of the fundraiser, which is far more a rehearsal than a meeting. The star of the show the next day will be Emma, the most flamboyant character of the group, whose clothing is costume and whose speech, the centerpiece of their meeting, is performed for us rather than just assigned to a position in the program as the others are. Her speech uses a long passage from "The Science of Educational Dramatics," by Emma Sheridan Fry, an early twentieth-century teacher, full of inspirational phrases and the passionate belief that theater can teach—not as a pulpit for a particular ideology, but as a liberating catalyst of the human spirit. The rousing image that concludes Emma's speech enjoins her audience—and, by extension, us—to intrepid action: "Let us, boldly, seizing the star of our intent, lift it as the lantern of our necessity, and let it shine over the darkness of our compliance. Come!" (32). And the image of the "constant stars" of Shakespeare's sonnet 14, which Emma recites in the second act, suggests the same human capacity to convert "truth and beauty" to the storehouse of art, thus forestalling doomsday. The star image is linked to Fefu, for it is she who asks, "Have you been out? The sky is full of stars" (39).

If we read this in pursuit of a feminist interpretation, we see that Fefu sends them all out of doors, into that realm designated by the play as the male domain. Only Julia cannot or will not go, and remains confined indoors, in her wheelchair, in her timidity and terror. Fefu tries to rescue Julia ("Fight, Julia!" [40]) but when Julia retreats into weakness and fear, Fefu must reject her: "You're contagious. . . . I'm going mad too" (40). Politically, Fefu rejects Julia's paralyzing deference, although the

concluding scene, Julia wounded or dead and the women gathered around her, remains ambiguous. Are they lending their support to the murder? Are they appalled? Mystified? Sorry? Glad? The text does not tell us, although there is nothing to suggest that this is a triumphant moment. If anything, there is clearly madness on both "sides." There is no escape in this play; both Julia and Fefu are victims and victimizers; in Fornes's version of the Mexican Joke, it does not matter which end of the rifle you are on.

The image functions as a metadramatic analogy as well. Aesthetically, Fefu's shooting of the rabbit/Julia is Fornes's rejection of the confining conventions of symbolic realism. She sends her friends out into the brilliant night, rejecting "the darkness of our compliance" and accepting the theatrical adventure of the theater of the absurd.

Perhaps even more bizarre than the collision among kinds of characters is that between "educational dramatics" and the theater of the absurd, since many of Fornes's plays are about teaching and learning, and since theater of the absurd is distinguished by its nondidacticism. Like the joyful, histrionic Emma and her namesake, Emma Sheridan Fry, Fornes believes in theater as a liberating force. In an interview she said that

> the play is there as a lesson, because I feel that art ultimately is a teacher. You go to a museum to look at a painting and that painting teaches you something. You may not look at a Cezanne and say, "I know what I have to do." But it gives you something, a charge of some understanding, some knowledge that you have in your heart.[18]

And, although the plays are various in size, shape, and style, one of the patterns that can be traced from the early (*Tango Palace,* 1960) to the recent (*Mud,* 1983) is the repeated use of the teaching/learning pattern; as Susan Sontag points out,

> People requiring or giving instruction is a standard situation in Fornes's plays. . . . (Fornes's elaborate sympathy for the labor of thought is the endearing observation of someone who is almost entirely self-taught.) And there are many dispensers of wisdom in Fornes's plays, apart from those—*Tango Palace, Doctor Kheal*—specifically devoted to the comedy and the pathos of instruction.[19]

Dr. Kheal (1968) is her most obviously absurdist play. Flagrantly indebted to Ionesco's *The Lesson,* it lacks both the intellectuality and the sexual menace of its precursor. But *The Lesson* is an absurdist play about power and language, while *Dr. Kheal* is an absurdist play about absurd theatre itself, a totally self-reflexive piece. In it, the professor, dwarfed by the set composed of blackboard, water glasses, and demonstration charts—Fornes specifies that "he is small, or else the furniture is large"—plays both questioner and respondent, actor and audience, as he attempts to instruct on a range of subjects from poetry to brussels sprouts. The conclusion of Dr. Kheal's lesson is "Man is a rational animal,"[20] while the conclusion of

Dr. Kheal's lesson is to have demonstrated how foolish and pedantic the rational can be. This entire short play becomes a concrete stage image indicting rationality, and thereby also indicting the sort of drama that assumes the viability of the conventional elements of drama—dialogue, action, conflict—all of which are parodied here.

A far more subtle and disturbing treatment of teaching and learning happens in Fornes's first play, *Tango Palace* (1960), a two-hander about Isidore, "an androgynous clown," and Leopold, "an earnest youth." It, too, indicts rationality, although it is harder to tell how. One would do well to be guided by Fornes's preface:

> To say that a work of art is meaningful is to imply that the work is endowed with intelligence. That it is illuminating. But if we must inquire what the meaning of a work of art is, it becomes evident that the work has failed us. . . .
>
> To approach a work of art with the wish to decipher its symbolism, and to extract the author's intentions from it, is to imply that the work can be something other than what it demonstrates, that the work can be treated as a code system which, when deciphered, reveals the true content of the work. A work of art should not be other than what it demonstrates. It should not be an intellectual puzzle. . . . If there is wisdom in the work it will come to us. But if we go after it, we become wary, watchful. We lose our ability to taste.[21]

This is a critical caveat indeed. It also sounds like a substantial manifesto of the theater of the absurd. If we apply it to *Tango Palace,* it provides a gloss on the play. Both Isidore and Leopold are interested in wisdom: Isidore mockingly asserts his possession of it; Leopold urgently wishes to acquire it. Isidore's gaudy appearance (he is stout, with long hair, men's clothes, high heels, lots of makeup, and a corsage) announces, among other things, the refusal to let us know who we are looking at (surely the most basic, instantaneous perception of another person is to identify gender), but lack of clarity is Isidore's stock in trade. In contrast, Leopold, who is born into the play by crawling out of a canvas sack ("Look what the stork has brought me" [13]), is young, handsome, and wearing a business suit; we know exactly who he is. Once again, Fornes builds a play on jarring incongruities rather than old-fashioned conflict.

The vehicle of instruction in *Tango Palace* is a limitless pack of cards, each inscribed with a cliché ("All is fair in love and war") or with a piece of the play's dialogue. The cards seem to be cue cards after the fact, or perhaps they suggest that there is nothing new under the sun, that all dialogue is a rerun, thereby discrediting both written and spoken language. Isidore offers them, pompously, to Leopold: "These cards contain wisdom. File them away. *(card)* [is flipped.] Know where they are *(card)* Have them at hand. *(card)* Be one upon whom nothing is lost. *(card)*" (16). When Leopold mishears or missays a cliché—"All's fair . . ." in the vulgar, common fashion ("Not love *in* war. Love *and* war!"), Isidore smacks

him. Once the communication battle becomes physical, it escalates quickly, and soon both characters have been stabbed, although nothing is permanent here, not even death. Nothing is sacred either, since the religious images and allusions are bandied about lavishly, as Isidore opens his arms wide and is killed with a sword, but it is Leopold who says, solemnly and incorrectly, "It is done." If "cleanliness is close to godliness *(card)*," both "stink." The contest continues in a preposterously clichéd heaven, complete with harps and clouds and angels; Fornes's first play is its own theatricalized manifesto.

The no-exit set, complete with giant padlock on the door, is made far more interesting by Isidore's collection of eighteenth-century furniture (suggesting the museum room in Stanley Kubrick's film 2001), and forms a visual contrast to Isidore's outlandish shrine filled with bullfighting equipment and the beetle masks (debt to Kafka's "Metamorphosis"?). The image of the two men (?) playing (?) at bulls and matadors suggests the grotesque cruelty of the "astounding elegance" of blood sport, which is supposed to yield wisdom and truth. "As I stick each banderilla on your back I'll reveal the answer to a mystery. And then. . . . *(taking the sword)* the moment of truth. . . . As eternal verity is revealed to you, darkness will come upon your eyes . . ." (28). (Debt to Kafka's "The Penal Colony"?)[22]

The nature of this strange play is finally emblematized in itself; Isidore gives Leopold a drawing lesson on the blackboard, teaching him how to draw a "portrait of a mediocre person" by connecting three dots and adding an eye dot and a mouth line to the resulting triangle. But this easy system will not yield a portrait of Leopold, since

> all we can establish is that I am at the top. And way down at the bottom is you. There is no other point. We therefore can't have an angle. We only have a vertical line. The space around us is infinite, enclosed as it may be, because there is not a third person. And if the space around us is infinite, so is, necessarily, the space between us.
>
> (20)

This oxymoronic image of the infinity of enclosed space is, to my mind, the image of the absurdist stage. The lack of a third character, one that might resolve the tension of two points symmetrically suspended, is the hallmark of absurdist drama as it theatricalizes absence and redefines linearity and chronology. That it takes two to tango is precisely the point here.

In another early play, *The Successful Life of Three* (1966), easily recognized as absurdist, the teaching/learning motif reappears to show us that stupidity and ignorance allow for a "successful life"—whereby rivalry, greed, criminality, incompetence, and ineducability allow these two men and one woman to tolerate their existence. Fornes requires in her headnote to the play that each character has one characteristic facial expression—She has a "stupid expression," He "looks disdainful," and Three looks "with intense curiosity"; the note further specifies that these are to be played "very deadpan."[23] The required lack of emotional range clearly rejects the traditional theatrical aesthetic, and creates an absurdist version of Greek masks (absurdist partly because they miss the importance and clarity of comedy and tragedy, and partly because live human faces are being used as masks).

The Successful Life of Three begins with the literalizing of a cliché:

> *Three takes a shoe off and drops it. At the sound of the shoe, He becomes motionless, his arms suspended in the air. Three looks at He, and freezes for a moment.*
>
> THREE: What are you doing?
>
> HE: Waiting.
>
> THREE: What for?
>
> HE: For the other shoe to drop.
>
> THREE: Ah, and I was wondering what you were doing. If I hadn't asked, we would have stayed like that forever. You waiting and me wondering . . . That's the kind of person I am. I ask . . . That's good, you know.
>
> HE: Why?
>
> THREE: *** [Asterisks signify their characteristic expression.]
>
> HE: Why?
>
> THREE: It starts the action.
>
> HE: What action did you start?
>
> THREE: We're talking.
>
> (43-44)

After this metadramatic opening, each of the play's conventional dramatic situations—middle-aged man and young man as rivals for "a sexy young lady," a thief getting caught by the police, the achievement of financial success with an invention—is meaningless, devoid of the emotional component convention demands. The other shoe never drops, as it never does in absurdist drama.

Sontag asks us to "consider the twenty-year trajectory that goes from *The Successful Life of 3* to *Mud,* about the unsuccessful life of three."[24] Although this play, typical of Fornes's recent work, seems far more naturalistic than the earlier plays, both Sontag and Bonnie Marranca[25] have been at pains to define the redefinition of realism these later plays, *Mud* and *The Conduct of Life* (1985), imply. Just as these two plays continue Fornes's career-long discussion—and celebration—of learning and teaching (and, thus, of the viability of received wisdom), so they also continue her interest in the stage as visual field.

Mud pulls against its apparent realism by creating a series of seventeen scenes, each of which ends with a *tableau vivant*, an eight-second freeze "which will create the effect of a still photograph."[26] Thus the play becomes a photograph album, ironically using the art form most easily associated with realism to break the stage realism.

Like *The Successful Life of 3*, this is a play about a love triangle of two men—one older, one younger—and one woman, but here the play ends in the woman's death, as Lloyd, who refuses to let her leave, shoots her with a rifle. This play, like most of Fornes's others (*Tango Palace, Fefu, Conduct of Life, The Danube, Sarita*), ends with a murder. Fornes has said, "I don't know how to end a play unless . . . who's going to kill whom?"[27] This seems to me more a function of an ontology than of politics; the violence is emblematic of a catastrophic vision of human life rather than of tyranny and oppression. The catastrophe at the end of *Mud* is still another reworking of the appalling Mexican joke discussed earlier—the literalizing of the metaphor to create a new image, far more powerful than the easily laughed-off metaphor of the joke.

Mud's capacity to move us deeply lies in Mae's human longings to learn, the value of different kinds of knowledge, and the eloquence of the poetic language that speaks that knowledge. Mae reads from a textbook about starfish—"The starfish is an animal, not a fish. He is called a fish because he lives in the water. The starfish cannot live out of the water . . ." (27)—and this information is transformed into the beauty of her final speech as she lies dying on the kitchen table: "Like the starfish, I live in the dark and my eyes see only a faint light. It is faint and yet it consumes me. I long for it. I thirst for it. I would die for it. Lloyd, I am dying" (40).

It would be easy to read this as a feminist play, but Fornes has specifically rejected her idea of the feminist interpretation:

> I think usually the people who have expressed to me their dismay at Mae's being killed are feminist women who are having a hard time in their life. They hang onto feminism because they feel oppressed and believe it will save them. They see me as a feminist and when they see Mae die, they feel betrayed.[28]

Mud is not immediately recognizable as an absurdist play; nevertheless, it participates in the most basic premises of the theater of the absurd: structurally, it builds on inaction at the conclusion of each scene; theatrically, it conveys, through images rather than explanations, the terrible conflicting human needs inherent in human relationships; linguistically, it demonstrates simultaneously both the inadequacy and the dazzling beauty of words.

Just as *Mud* can be mistaken for a conventionally realistic play or a conventionally feminist play, *The Danube* (1982) is often mistaken for a conventionally absurdist play, along the lines of Ionesco's *The Bald Soprano*, since it depends on foreign language tapes and seems to depict people as puppets. It would be equally easy to read *The Danube* as a feminist work as well, but in fact, although both elements are present, such exclusionary interpretations diminish the play's range and power. Rather than a reductive post-Edenic diatribe, Fornes gives us glimpses into the male-female relation in all its dangerous symbiosis. Similarly, she avoids a prefabricated indictment of the failure of devalued language.

In a statement that seems worthy of an absurdist in the widest and deepest meaning of the term, Fornes has said:

> A way of expressing your awe is to say, "Words fail me." That's language.[29]

NOTES

[1]Martin Esslin, *The Theatre of the Absurd*, 3d ed. (New York: Doubleday, Pelican, 1983), 397.

[2]Ibid., 23.

[3]*Performing Arts Journal*, "Women Playwrights Issue," 7, no. 3 (1983): 91.

[4]Helene Keyssar, *Feminist Theatre* (New York: Grove, 1985), 121.

[5]Gayle Austin, "The Madwoman in the Spotlight: Plays of Maria Irene Fornes," in *Making a Spectacle*, ed. Lynda Hart (Ann Arbor: University of Michigan Press, 1989), 76.

[6]W. B. Worthen, "*Still Playing Games*: Ideology and Performance in the Theater of Maria Irene Fornes," in *Feminine Focus: The New Women Playwrights*, ed. Enoch Brater (New York: Oxford University Press, 1989), 167.

[7]Ibid., 180.

[8]Quoted in David Savran, *In Their Own Words: Contemporary American Playwrights* (New York: Theatre Communications Group, 1988), 54.

[9]Ibid., 51.

[10]Quoted in Neena Beber, "Dramatis Instructus," *American Theatre*, January 1990, 24.

[11]Maria Irene Fornes, "I Write These Messages That Come," *Drama Review* 21, no. 4 (December 1977): 27.

[12]Ibid., 30.

[13]Maria Irene Fornes, *Fefu and Her Friends* (1978), in *Word Plays* (New York: PAJ Publications, 1980, 7-8. All further page references will appear in parentheses in the text.

[14]Keyssar, *Feminist Theatre*, 125.

[15]Susan Sontag, preface to *Maria Irene Fornes Plays* (New York: PAJ Publications, 1986), 8.

[16]Savran, *In Their Own Words*, 51.

[17]Ibid., 55.

[18]Ibid., 56.

[19]Sontag, *Fornes Plays*, 8.

[20]Maria Irene Fornes, *Dr. Kheal*, in *A Century of Plays by American Women*, ed. Rachel France (New York: Richards Rosen Press, 1979), 184. The play's title, although often written *Doctor Kheal*, appears with the abbreviation *Dr.* in this edition, as it does in its more recent publication in the collection titled *Promenade and Other Plays* (New York: PAJ Publications, 1987).

[21]Maria Irene Fornes, *Tango Palace*, in *Playwrights for Tomorrow*, vol. 2, ed. Arthur H. Ballet (Minneapolis: University of Minnesota Press, 1966), 9. All further page references appear in parentheses in the text.

[22]Fornes has said that *The Trial*, like *Godot*, gave her "an experience of incredible energy inside me" (Savran, *In Their Own Words*, 56).

[23]Maria Irene Fornes, *The Successful Life of Three: A Skit for Vaudeville*, in *Playwrights for Tomorrow*, vol. 2, ed. Arthur H. Ballet (Minneapolis: University of Minnesota Press, 1966), 42. All further page references appear in parentheses in the text.

[24]Sontag, *Fornes Plays*, 9. Writing the title as Sontag does, with the figure 3 rather than the word *Three*, eliminates the ambiguity that it may be the character, Three, whose success the play is about. It is worth noting, too, that this play is dedicated to Susan Sontag. The word *Three* is used in the play's first publication in *Playwrights for Tomorrow*.

[25]Bonnie Marranca, "Maria Irene Fornes and the New Realism," *Performing Arts Journal*, no. 22 (1984): 29-33.

[26]Maria Irene Fornes, *Mud*, in *Maria Irene Fornes Plays*, 16. Further page references appear in parentheses in the text.

[27]Savran, *In Their Own Words*, 56-57.

[28]Ibid., 57.

[29]Ibid., 65.

Assunta Bartolomucci Kent (essay date 1996)

SOURCE: "Early Plays, 1963-1968: Production, Experimentation, 'Learning the Ropes,'" in *Maria Irene Fornes and Her Critics*, Greenwood Press, 1996, pp. 89-117.

[*Kent here explores Fornes' early development as a playwright.*]

> I just got this obsessive idea, as if you have a nightmare. . . . Only it was not a nightmare. It was an obsession that took the form of a play and I felt I had to write it.
>
> —Fornes, in Cummings, *Yale Theater*

> Maria Irene Fornes . . . helped clear a way through the claustrophobic landscape of Broadway vapidity and Off-Broadway ponderous symbolism by making theatre that was fresh, adventurous, casual, fantastic, perceptive, and musical.
>
> —Phillip Lopate, *New York Herald*

Until age thirty, Fornes was a student of 'life' and the visual arts. But after writing her first play in 1960, she focused on the crafts of theatre production and soon became an active, eclectic member of the 1960s avant-garde, working with groups ranging from the Method-based Actors' Studio to the wildly experimental Judson Poets.

As a new playwright and avid student of theatrical practice, Fornes experimented with old and new dramatic and performative styles, assimilating elements from such models as Beckett, Ionesco, and Genet to her already-developed aesthetic sensibility. While still learning the ropes, she made significant contributions to teaching and producing as well as to playwriting, winning two Obies as well as numerous fellowships and grants. . . . Although she had only begun writing in 1960, by 1965 she was teaching playwriting at the Teachers and Writers Collaborative in New York and at drama festivals and workshops (Kuhn 158). As soon as she won the right to direct her own new plays, she incorporated directing into her writing process. After opportunities to produce new plays began to dry up in New York in the late '60s, Fornes ran a playwrights' producing organization.

In her early plays (1963-1968), Fornes experimented with form and genre, and playfully parodied popular entertainment and social conventions. Yet she also infused these otherwise rather generalized satires with a surprising dramaturgical 'reality': closely observed and denaturalized representations of small everyday things (objects, dialogue, actions) and straightforward presentations (almost direct transmission) of dreams, desire, and fantasy. Even in these early works, amidst zany situations and campy musical numbers, Fornes threaded uncanny characterizations of the injustices and inanities that we tend to naturalize, rationalize, or turn into innocuous statistics. Fornes would insist that her quirky presentations are not abstractions, but rather theatrical explorations of the "surrealism" of how other people, those "outside our circle of friends," choose (or are forced) to conduct their lives (in Marx 8).

In this chapter I chronicle Fornes' genesis as a playwright and analyze her published plays from the 1960s. I pay special attention to plays such as ***The Successful Life of 3*** and ***Promenade*** which are often omitted from feminist reviews of her work because they contain baffling or possibly sexist images and are difficult to categorize. I hope to shed light on these early plays by re-placing them into the context of Fornes' development as a playwright and of the venues in which they were created and/or produced. Although Fornes functions as a bard/jester throughout her oeuvre by staging contradictions and unsettling assumptions, in these early plays she is clearly working as a jester/satirist, pointing up society's ills and illogic but refraining from overt recommendations. (In her later work, she becomes increasingly the jester/judge, warning her audiences of the interwoven consequences of personal and social relations.)

From 1954-1957, Fornes lived in Europe. Originally intending to paint in an isolated Spanish fishing village, but after less than a week she moved to Paris and from there made short excursions throughout Europe (Harrington 34). Although Fornes continued to work at painting, she recalls:

> my painting had never really reached a personal depth for me. Painting, I always had to force myself to work. I never found that place where you're touching on something vital to your own survival, to your own life.

> (in Cummings 52)

However, while living in Paris, she chanced to see the original 1954 Roger Blin production of *Waiting for Godot*. She found the play to be "the most powerful thing of all—not only in theater but in painting, film, everything!" (in Betsko 155). Even though she "didn't understand enough French to know what was being said, [she] understood the world, the sphere in which it took place. [She] got the rhythm" (Harrington 34). Seeing the Parisian production of *Endgame* confirmed Beckett as a model for her:

> Imagine a writer whose theatricality is so amazing and so important that you could see a play of his, not understand one word, and be shook up. When I left the theater I felt that my life was changed, that I was seeing everything with a different clarity.

> (in Cummings 52)

However, she did not immediately begin writing but worked as a textile designer upon her return to New York in 1957.

In the winter of 1957-1958, she saw an adaptation of James Joyce's *Ulysses in Nighttown* (directed by Burgess Meredith with Zero Mostel),[1] which most impressed her because it was staged in a place on West Houston "not ordinarily used as a theatre" (in Savran 55). To this day, Fornes' playwriting and directing reveal her painterly sensitivity to the deployment of space; she often instructs actors to hit precise blocking marks at key moments (although sometimes such directions also allude to and gently parody familiar movie shots). For example, in ***Night*** she directed an actor to finish his fall on a precise mark so that when his scene partner kneels to comfort him, they will be framed by a romantic "special" (light). But whether film-based or not, Fornes stages every scene with the care of a designer; she attends to the symbolic and psychological effects of positioning, color, and visual weight. Designing images and directing actors as elements of design are as integral to her creative process as scripting dialogue.

The formative play-going experiences mentioned above eased Fornes' transition from painting to writing by showing her the communicative power of visual and environmental aspects in theatre and the immense potential for creating striking effects by experimenting with these elements. Although direct references to her art study occasionally appear in her work, such as the turbulent sky backdrop for ***Nadine*** (1989) inspired by a Hans Hofmann painting, Fornes' artistic background is more consistently evident in memorable theatrical images intended to arrest audience attention, even if they do not fully understand the import or allusions of the accompanying text.

Fornes actually began writing in 1960 with a challenge to then-roommate Susan Sontag, "How silly! If we want to write, why not sit down and write?" And so they did. They continued to write regularly, and for about six months, Fornes and Sontag read and criticized work with a group of friends (Harrington 34). Although influences between lifelong associates are difficult to determine, and in this case we know that Fornes reads very little while Sontag has kept abreast of Fornes' new work, in the 1960s Fornes and Sontag shared an interest in camp, parody, and popular culture.[2]

After struggling as a painter and then trying her hand at short stories, Fornes found in playwriting a suitable outlet for her imagistic, conversational creativity (Harrington 34). Her first finished play, ***The Widow*** (1961), was based on her translation of letters "written to my great-grandfather from a cousin who lived in Spain" (in Betsko 155). And though this play was produced in New York, broadcast in Mexico, and won two writing awards, Fornes was still reworking it in 1966 and did not include it in her first published anthology, *Promenade and Other Plays* (1971).

Fornes made her avant-garde playwriting debut in 1963 with *Tango Palace* (originally *There! You Died*), which premiered at the San Francisco Actor's Workshop under the direction of Herb Blau. She had become pleasurably obsessed with the writing of *Tango Palace:*

> It came out of nowhere—almost like a dream. . . . When the idea came to me I stayed home for 20 days and only left the house to go buy something to eat. . . . I slept with the typewriter next to me.

> (in Harrington 34)

> Writing it was the most incredible experience. A door was opened which was a door to paradise.

> (in Savran 55)

Tango Palace charts the existential struggles between Isidore, an "androgynous" master/teacher, and his/her earnest young captive Leopold, a reluctant student and follower. They engage in a series of nasty Beckettian games during which Leopold is rewarded with blows. Isidore's seductiveness and cruelty, his/her insistence on master/slave narratives, and the highly theatrical use of props and scenarios (such as a tango, a duel, and a bull-fight) are reminiscent of Genet. While the play makes no direct references to feminism, Fornes' exploration of seduction and the entrapment of an unwilling object of desire would interest many feminists. Fornesian hallmarks include an ironic view of interpersonal relations, an interest in language use, and the portrayal of characters who strive (often unsuccessfully) to free themselves from oppressive situations.

Isidore constantly flips cards at the unwilling 'student' that contain the sentences and phrases of their previous dialogue. Isidore insists that if Leopold will only memorize the cards, he will never hesitate nor be short of an answer, a question or "a remark, if a remark is more appropriate" (Tango 134). Through Leopold's refusal to "learn that way," Fornes criticizes rote education. This is also her first play which warns against the deadening effect that a reliance on set phrases and concepts produces in speakers, impeding their ability to express themselves and to connect with others.[3]

In *Tango Palace,* the struggle ceases only when Leopold kills Isidore rather than emulate his teacher's "rottenness," but in the last scene of the play, Isidore reappears as a challenging angel and Leopold, sword in hand, steps forward to resume their battle on the next plane. Despite this circular (or perhaps spiraling) 'conclusion,' Fornes does not expect audiences to be disheartened but rather energized, as she had been by Franz Kafka's *The Trial* and Beckett's *Waiting for Godot.*

> Pozzo beats on Lucky and at the end Lucky doesn't get free, but it doesn't matter because I do! I've never been anybody's slave but when I see that I understand something. Josef K. may get guillotined or go to the electric chair but, rather than saying "I'm doomed," I learn from his behavior.

> (in Savran 56)

Likewise, Fornes hopes that audiences will learn something about themselves and human relations from watching the trials of her combatants. Their battle resumes on the next plane, because Fornes sees life as a series of confrontations which challenge people to make decisions and to keep struggling.

A number of Fornes' plays end with frustrated characters trying to 'shoot' their way out of some sort of emotional and physical entrapment or dilemma.[4] Since Fornes does not advocate violence as a good solution, it may be that she wants to examine the conditions under which low-power 'victims' become capable of striking out in order to free themselves. Perhaps then Leopold must confront Isidore again (though not in the same situation and probably not in a setting so fully controlled by Isidore) in order to struggle towards a better understanding of his entanglement with Isidore (his complicity perhaps) and to find a better solution. In addition, the seeming imbalance between Leopold's entrapment in unfamiliar contexts (which could be read as a judgment that society and social relations cannot be changed) is balanced by Fornes' next play, *The Successful Life of 3,* in which characters are placed in an anarchistic universe in which they are only constrained to the extent that they willingly obey social conventions and the wishes of others.

As *Tango Palace* begins, Isidore's domineering behavior seems extreme, even absurd. But as the play proceeds, Fornes' hunch about "the relationship between a mentor of some sort and a student" (in Betsko 158) evolves into a psychologically realistic critique of the dynamics of master-student relations (especially in the arts) during those years just before widespread student revolt against educational policies. Like a poet-prophet, Fornes often pinpoints such tensions and contradictions before they fully erupt in the society at large. Until recently, she assumed that her (largely "privileged poor" bohemian and liberal middle-class) audiences were with her, or at least not far behind, in their perceptions of social dynamics, an assumption less and less true the farther she has worked from the New York avant-garde. This gap or delay between Fornes' vision and audience perception may be responsible in part for the delay of wider acceptance and understanding of her later plays until several years after they premiere. Her growing recognition of this problem may in part explain the more individualized characters and more explicit rendering of social contexts in her later work.

Tango Palace was a highly successful and personally rewarding premiere. Fornes was pleased with the directing and acting of the San Francisco production, and she received an Office for Advanced Drama Research (OADR) playwriting grant to polish the script for the second volume of Arthur Ballet's anthology, *Playwrights for Tomorrow*. The play also won her a place in the Prentice-Hall literature anthology, *Concepts of Literature* (1966), "among writers like Aristotle and Shakespeare and you can imagine . . . when you have a first experience like this, you're always looking to repeat it" (in Savran 58).

Under the auspices of the OADR, Fornes wrote and directed *The Successful Life of 3: A Skit for Vaudeville* which was presented on a double bill with *Tango Palace* in January 1965 at The Firehouse, an avant-garde venue in Minneapolis. As soon as she returned to New York, the Open Theatre staged *The Successful Life* as part of its 1964-1965 production season at the Sheridan Square Playhouse (*Life* 163). However, Richard Gilman (theatre critic and Open Theatre affiliate) as well as most company members "were unhappy with [Chaikin's] production of the play," which they felt had not done "justice to Miss Fornés' imagination and dramatic powers" (Gilman, in *Promenade and Other Plays* 1). In his restaging, Gilman presented Fornes as "a kind of radical parodist" by foregrounding her "sense of the incongruities and discontinuities of language" (1). Gilman's production, which emphasized Fornes' "fruitfully illogical" depictions of "social inanity" (1), won Fornes an Obie; soon after, the play was produced overseas and published in two anthologies (*Nasso* 244).

Even though the play premiered in Minnesota, New York critic Bonnie Marranca claims that *The Successful Life of 3* "reflects the early Open Theatre approach to drama," because the play's "many changes in character, mood, and situation, and its completely exteriorized (unemotional) and abstract approach to human behavior" were well-suited to the "transformation" techniques then popular at the Open Theatre (Marranca, *Playwrights* 56). However well the play was eventually served by Open Theatre actors, Marranca's implication of one-way influence belies the genesis of the piece and Fornes' relationships with several divergent theatre groups, in particular the Actors' Studio, the Open Theatre, Judson Poets' Theatre, and New Dramatists.

The Actors' Studio, begun in 1949, was a place where actors could hone their skills under the direction of Method director/teachers, such as Elia Kazan, Robert Lewis, and (in the 1960s) Lee Strasberg, all veterans of the Group Theatre (Henderson 274). From 1931 to 1941, Group members sought to emulate the Moscow Art Theatre's naturalistic style of acting by living and working together; their resulting American interpretation of early Stanislavski technique became known as *the Method* (274). As disseminated by the Actors' Studio, the Method style has been characterized as "unconventional, deeply felt, and psychologically detailed," "more impulsive than calculated and more openly emotional than intellectual" (186). Despite the obvious stylistic differences between Fornes' early experimental works and typical Method vehicles by Arthur Miller and Tennessee Williams, Fornes shared with Strasberg a desire to discern and convey psychological truths and to stage behaviors motivated by impulse and emotion rather than by conscious logic and cool rationality.

In the mid-1960s, Fornes observed scenework at the Actors' Studio to familiarize herself with actor/director relationships and the rehearsal process. She also took Method-based classes at Gene Frankel's school: beginning acting, which included sensory exercises, and directing, "which just means you get the experience of not knowing what to say to an actor . . . [which] you might as well go through at school" (52). Although Fornes recognized their aesthetic differences from the outset and would "completely ignore" Strasberg's comments about aesthetics, she was "very impressed with Strasberg's work as an actors' . . . [and] directors' technician" (in Cummings 52). Nonetheless, Fornes' exposure to Method principles changed her writing style:

> My writing became organic. I stopped being so manipulative. In *Tango Palace,* I felt I knew what needed to happen in a scene and that the writing was serving me. You can see the moments when a character is speaking for my benefit rather than from their own need. . . . I [began] applying the Method technique for the actor to my writing and it was bringing something very interesting.
>
> (52)

But it was also while working with new directors at the Actors' Studio that Fornes had her first clashes over the traditional separation between the director's and the playwright's role in producing new plays. Even though she was invited to rehearsal, she was forced to silently note her reactions to the acting and direction and discuss them with the director outside rehearsal (52). Fornes' experience confirmed Lanford Wilson's warning about playwrights' traditionally submissive position in rehearsal. He had explained to her that the playwright is treated "like a girl . . . [who has] to be nice to this guy [the director] who is going to . . . choose the right actors for my play because . . . I am very talented, but I don't really understand anything" (in Betsko 160). Such rude introductions to general theatre practice notwithstanding, Fornes had a more satisfying and fruitful experience with the 'conventional' Actors' Studio than with one of their most notable challengers, the Open Theatre.

In 1963, a group of actors and writers dissatisfied with Method acting, naturalistic plays, and Broadway commercialism formed the Open Theatre (OT) in order to develop a new, more physical or "external" acting style (Poland lxi; Henderson 167). Many members had been students of Nola Chilton, a Method teacher who "had evolved a series of exercises designed to prepare the actor for performing in absurdist dramas where the usual techniques of psychological preparation seemed inappropriate" (Bigsby 98). Joseph Chaikin, a former Chilton student and Living Theatre actor who soon dominated the OT, ran a workshop through which he hoped to "redefine the limits of the stage experience" (Roberts 503-504). He orchestrated physical and vocal exercises and improvisations in discussion with observers, including non-member affiliates such as Gilman, Gordon Rogoff, Paul Goodman, and Susan Sontag (Fornes' former roommate and lifelong colleague) (Malpede 185).

Although Chaikin would have preferred to focus exclusively on non-performative workshops, at the urging of Gilman, the Open Theatre performed short plays and improvs at the end of 1963, and in 1964-1965 mounted a season of "ten plays, from Brecht's *Clown Play* and T. S. Eliot's *Sweeney Agonistes* to works by [Jean Claude] Van Itallie and Maria Irene Fornes" (101). Except for this atypical season, playwrights who joined the Open Theatre were expected, as "integral participants in the group experience," to submit text for improvisation rather than present finished scripts (Poland lxi).

Fornes joined the OT in late 1963. Although she "found their work interesting," she had expected to be "much more active, that Joe would be more interested in [her] ideas . . . [but she soon] realized that they were interested in doing whatever it is they were going to do" (Interview). When she made comments about works in progress "that [she] thought would improve things, they were ignored; so [she] continued to go and just watch and hang around" (Interview). For example,

> Joe and Jean-Claude Van Itallie [the OT's principal playwright and Chaikin's companion] were working on "The Airplane Piece." It was an attack on the 'Powers that Be' . . . in which a plane crashes but the people in 1st class are protected. And I said that the theory may be right in other things but that in those days airplanes usually crashed head first and since 1st class is in the front, it doesn't work for this thing. And he just ignored me. He was not interested in being accurate. How can he be interested in having a symbol that's incorrect! . . . I felt that [at the OT] there was a lot of principle and a lot of political ideas, but they were so fuzzy around the edges. I didn't like that. Of course, I also didn't like the fact I was not treated respectfully.
>
> (Interview)

Given her feelings about the feminization and disempowerment of playwrights, Fornes was not satisfied with Chaikin's general method of using playwrights' work like found text, extracting as little as one sentence or phrase from a scene or play, sometimes only for its aural rhythm, and making it the basis for his guided improvisations. However, she did share Chaikin's belief that good theatre is a "controlled experience, that it must transcend privatism, and that the intuitive must remain subordinated to a central intelligence provided by the writer and the director" (Bigsby 103). But in practice they differed sharply because Chaikin only truly shared the directorial role with Van Itallie, while Fornes was already beginning to make directing part of her playwriting process. Like a number of actors who left the OT to escape Chaikin's "necessary tyranny" (100), Fornes drifted away from the OT and toward the more democratic, chaotic, and for her, "heavenly" Judson Poets' Theatre (Interview).

In relation to *The Successful Life of 3,* Fornes disagreed with both Strasberg's and Chaikin's belief that Method techniques were only suited for 'naturalistic' theatre: "A method actor should be able to work in a play of O'Neill as well as Ionesco as well as Shakespeare. . . . What you need is to be aesthetically aware, and to understand that imagination is a part of natural life" (in Cummings 53). As discussed in Chapter 2, Fornes' belief that imagination along with dreams and visions are "a part of natural life" coincides with the magical-realist worldview. Given this belief and her particular experiences with the Actors' Studio and the Open Theatre, it is less ironic that Fornes describes *The Successful Life of 3* as the first play that "was influenced by my understanding of Method" (52). "What one character says to another comes completely out of his own impulse. . . . The other character's reply never comes from some sort of premeditation on my part or even the part of the character" (52). Fornes adapted Strasberg's "moment-to-moment" work (not anticipating lines and reactions by focusing on the moment rather than the outcome of the scene or story) in order to restrain her analytical urges until after she had gained access to the sort of creative energy that had produced *Tango Palace.*

In *The Successful Life of 3,* 3, an intensely curious and randy middle-aged man, worms his way into a permanent threesome with SHE, a sexy young lady, who handles difficult questions by stopping to "think with a stupid expression" and HE, a handsome and disdainful young man to whom SHE is married for ten of the play's sixteen years (*Life* 165). Serious moral questioning of sexual promiscuity and media stereotypes as well as narrative links between the cartoonlike vignettes are suspended in order to highlight the vagaries of conversational logic, sex and marriage, and masculine rivalry.

Fornes' terse scenes with their rapid shifts in interpersonal dynamics were well-suited to "transformational" acting techniques in which the character, setting, and tone of one scene abruptly transforms into an entirely different emotional and behavioral texture in the next. Yet the characters in *The Successful Life,* however erratic and superficial they seem compared to their naturalistic counterparts, show more continuity and individual development than typical transformational characters and the continuing 'evolution' of two of her three characters provides much of the interest in Fornes' play.

The title of *The Successful Life of 3* points up Fornes' double-edged interest in 3's nonconformist method of succeeding in life. On the one hand, the play celebrates 3's facility for flouting social strictures and making his way in the world as it is; on the other hand, this satire exposes the kind of anarchistic opportunism necessary to survive in a world in which 'free' enterprise, aggressive marketing, and self-promotion carry the day. Most interesting from a feminist point of view, however, are the changes in SHE. For the first half of the play, SHE acquiesces in having sex with 3 whenever he mentions it, raising "too many" children and eternally peeling potatoes as HE's wife; in short, doing 'what women are supposed to do.' Later in the play, SHE leaves both HE and 3 to go to the movies and marries the theatre owner only to return when 3 has made a pile of money. Eventually, she comes 'home' for good, declaring that "I'm too old and tired and I've had too many men. I'm just going to sit here and rest for the rest of my life" (*Life* 196). Even in this early comedy, Fornes draws attention to women's traditionally constrained freedom of choice and creates a character who asserts herself in order to improve her life.

Within this 'playing space,' Fornes manages to broaden a comic type, the 'dumb sexy broad,' by moving SHE through a series of sexual/marital relationships in which (without stretching the intellectual capabilities of the character) SHE learns from her experiences and enters middle age resolutely celibate. Fornes allows SHE to move from the status of object through constrained agency to an equal partnership with the men. With pointed irony, Fornes arranges for this journey from object to agent to be accomplished not by an exceptional woman, but by an ordinary 'dumb broad.'

In addition, Fornes uses the constant switches in character and situation to explore differing (power) relations between women and men. By discarding naturalism's tendency to reproduce accepted stereotypes of gendered roles, transformations opened up a possible space for female characters to act as agents and even to be in situations where they are equal to or more powerful than male characters. This 'creative playing space' (in Ruddick's sense of the term)[5] was more easily opened up in the production as well as the writing because actors and directors (as well as the playwright) were freed from trying to represent round, 'authentic' male and female characters that a naturalistic linear plot would seem to require.

By looking at *The Successful Life* as a series of status games, it becomes apparent that HE, the young attractive white male, has most to lose and that SHE, the acquiescent sex object, has most to gain; from the very beginning 3 establishes himself as an unconventional character who gets what he needs. From the first scene, paunchy, ordinary-looking 3 horns in on HE's privileged access to desirable females. HE marries SHE and becomes a "husband and father" in name only as it is 3 who does "all the screwing and make[s] all the money" (*Life* 183). Notably, it is SHE who is first referred to by a personal name, "Ruth." Only quite late in the play is 3 referred to as Arthur and in both cases, he is being scolded, first for being a thief and then for being mean. HE, the stereotypical leading man and protagonist, never achieves a personal name, and by adhering to the most rigid code of acceptable social behavior for his "role" (chasing desirable women, settling down as a husband and father, reluctantly getting a job), HE loses out. 3 achieves higher status by questioning assumptions, taking risks, and going directly for what he wants. SHE gains highest status in the end by moving from desired object to active seeker of her own enjoyment, and by setting rules and limits on her interactions with others.

Fornes returns to this scenario of a 'dumb woman' living with two equally limited men in her more serious later play, *Mud* (1983), in which categorizations of victim and oppressor, manipulated and manipulator are complicated by changes in the fortunes of the three characters. *The Successful Life* also contains glimpses of interpersonal dynamics and bits of dialogue that reappear as late as 1990 in *Nadine.* Upon re-examining these texts, I believe this foreshadowing signals Fornes' persistent interest in familial, economic, and sexual relations that do not conform to the 'American social norm' of the monogamous heterosexual middle-class couple with two children. In fact, many of Fornes' plays consider the variety of ways in which people form households, make a living, speak to one another, and assimilate elements of popular culture (e.g., movies, social dancing, bullfights, jokes, and fashion shows). In *The Successful Life,* characters, who are themselves living in an implausible filmic world, frequently view and refer to movies and movie characters. They live in a *menage á trois*, work as a store detective, an "Alec Guinness type gangster" (190), or Zorro, and speak in jokes, puns, and *non sequiturs.*

In this two-dimensional comedy, Fornes points out that middle-class people are often most noticeably constrained by their own acceptance of societal mores; or in other words, that people often participate in their own constraint or domination. In *The Successful Life,* no one is forced by violent action or words or by serious legal compulsion to submit to the others' wishes. In fact, the only violent act is committed by 3, a private citizen against a policeman. (Once HE and 3 have given up their rivalry and accepted their triangular relationship with SHE, and the police no longer serve to remove first one and then the other rival for SHE's attention, 3 blithely shoots a policeman whose entrance threatens to disturb their now-comfortable threesome.) Early in the play, SHE consents, albeit without thorough consideration, to perform her 'womanly duties'; her life begins to change only when SHE/Ruth leaves, chooses other partners, refuses menial chores, and sets the conditions under which she will return to a relationship with HE and 3. The men do nothing to force or even dissuade her once she has stated a firm decision. Both 3 and SHE gain status by taking risks and flouting social mores, and though they soon tire of their new ventures, they return with the experiential knowledge to make new decisions.

The show ends with all three characters singing a paean to ignorance: "O let me be wrong, but oh not to know it." It is a very knowing ignorance (and certainly not innocence) that Fornes' characters are promoting. The lyrics might be paraphrased, O let us arrange our affairs in our own unconventional ways without encountering any compelling reasons not to proceed according to our perceived needs at the moment.

Fornes reports that *The Successful Life of 3* started when she heard a conversation in her mind between an actor she knew and another unfamiliar man. "That caught my imagination completely. I wrote the play in two weeks" ("Messages" 29). But such spontaneous inspiration could not always be counted on, and Fornes began seeking ways to be "possessed again" (in Savran 58).

Thus, Fornes' most widely acclaimed play of the 1960s, the campy-satiric musical *Promenade* (1965, music by Al Carmines), resulted from a card game she devised to keep her analytic mind busy and out of the way of her creativity. She inscribed index cards with character types and settings, then shuffled the cards and laid out one card for characters and one for setting. When she dealt "aristocrats" and "prison" and found this pairing incongruous, she knew right away that in the first scene of *Promenade* the prisoners would dig a hole and escape (in Cummings 29). The prisoners' journey to an aristocratic party, the scene of a car accident, a park, a battlefield, and eventually back to jail was dictated by the 'hand' of settings Fornes dealt herself.

This exercise is reminiscent of composer John Cage's and choreographer Merce Cunningham's aleatory techniques. For example, Cunningham would set the direction and sequence of a dance by following the pattern created by throwing Chinese sticks; he and Cage presented concerts in which music and dance that had been created independently of each other were performed at the same time. However, Fornes introduced chance not so much to replace linear narrative with abstract form but rather to make way for irrational, fantastic ideas and images that her conscious mind tended to censor—a goal Fornes shared with San Francisco choreographer Ann Halprin, who sought to imbue modern dance with the "freedom to follow intuition and impulse in improvisation" (Banes 1983, xvii). In the early 1960s, a group of younger choreographers (who formed the Judson Dance Theatre collective) extended Cunningham's and Halprin's experiments by integrating everyday movements, objects, and costumes with play and random activity. They found a congenial (and rent-free) place to rehearse and show their work at Judson Church in Greenwich Village. Fornes shared the Judson dancers' view that traditional "methods, techniques, and definitions that were once avant-garde . . . [are now raw material] to be sampled, borrowed, criticized, subverted" (xv). Therefore, it is not surprising that *Promenade* also found an audience and an enthusiastic production team at the Judson Church.

The young Reverend Al Carmines, resident composer and advocate for the arts, inspired the congregation at Judson to make their Washington Square church a place where artistic experimentation would be unencumbered by "the usual rules of approval and disapproval" (McDonagh 1970, 97). The congregation voted to refrain from censoring artistic work because of language or form; they agreed that all work must "be allowed to grow and flourish in order that any might survive" (97). This ethos also produced a community audience at Judson who took a "passionate, prejudiced, and proud" interest in all the artists who worked at the Church and who were remarkably receptive to "the

bizarre" (97). The cross-fertilization between the various arts housed under one friendly roof resulted in Judson Dance members choreographing movement passages for Judson Poets' Theatre productions, and in Fornes serving as a resident costume designer for Judson from 1965-1971. It was also at Judson that Fornes had enjoyed the sensuous, multi-media Happenings of Jim Dine and Claus Oldenburg (Harrington 34).

Produced in 1965, *Promenade* may well have been "the apotheosis of the Judson style" (Marranca, "Playwrights" 58), with its trenchant wit and obtuse humor, zaniness and high camp characterizations. Artistic director Carmines provided a richly melodious score of thirty-two numbers, ranging from German cabaret and torch songs to parodies of musical comedy and operetta, for Fornes' amusing and sometimes baffling lyrics and rather slight book. Looking at it from the aesthetic side (as Marranca does), Fornes' triumph lies in entertaining her audience with "an insane wonderful story that is even moralistic!" (57).

The story follows prisoners 105 and 106 after they escape from the buffoonish jailer who is too busy exacting sexual payment from female visitors to notice that the inmates are digging out. The escapees attend a high-class party during which the idle rich sing paeans to unrequited love and infidelity, and the ladies jump out of their dresses in imitation of Miss Cake, the full-bodied consort of the boorish Mayor/Warden. When the insouciant Servant is caught mocking these inane pastimes, Mr. S puts her in 'her place':

> It's sad your career depends on our whim.
> On with your work, my dear, or you'll get thin.
> You see, even if you're here, and we're also here,
> You are not near, isn't that clear?
>
> (*Promenade* 211)

Before leaving the party, 105, 106, and the Servant steal all the valuables from the drowsing overfed aristocrats.

When the trio comes upon a man injured by a hit-and-run driver, Fornes gives us a commedia-style lazzo in which the prisoners put their numbered jackets frontwards and backwards on the injured man. When the stupid jailer 'finds' his suspect(s) and carts the injured man off to jail in their stead, they sing the song "Clothes Make the Man," comically inverting the usual snobby implications of the adage. Next, 105 and 106 encounter their Mother who has been looking for her infants for years and who does not recognize them as adults. They respond by singing:

> It's to age that we owe what we are.
> In fact, we're grateful for the passing of time.
>
> (234)

Phyllis Mael is partially right that in *Promenade* "social criticism is evident but attenuated by the absurdity of its presentation" (190). Nevertheless, Fornes' facility for imaging social ironies is already evident in these early plays. In the battlefield scene, badly injured working-class soldiers discuss how they were conscripted into serving as cannon fodder. Despite falling bombs, the rich continue their moveable feast among the carnage. After the Mayor has called the wounded men to attention for review by their 'betters,' the party-goers callously unwind the soldiers' bandages and proceed to use both gauze and soldiers in an oblivious Maypole dance, while the Mother tries unsuccessfully to stop them. After the rich wander off leaving the waging of the (Vietnam?) war to the lower classes, the Mother and the Servant cradle the wounded men in a double piéta.

Having exposed the rich and powerful as social parasites, Fornes turns our attention to how the oppressed survive in an unfair world. The newly healed soldiers persuade the other workers to take advantage of the aristocrats' free wine and entertainment. The Mother, who "has been sad ever since [she] pitied a despicable man," displays an ambivalent reaction: she distances herself from the destitute man, thanking God that she "is better than he is," but also acknowledges that "there are many poor people in the world, whether you like or not" and wishes that she could go to a place "where a human being is not a strange thing" (265). The Servant goes off to think about what she has learned, having nearly succumbed to the seductions of material possessions, which she had originally donned in order to demonstrate that "riches make you dumb" (238-240). 105 and 106 come to the most poignant and frightening conclusion:

> When I was born I opened my eyes,
> And when I looked around I closed them;
> And when I saw how people get kicked in the head,
> And kicked in the belly, and kicked in the groin,
> I closed them. I closed them.
> My eyes are closed but I'm carefree.
>
> (254)

I disagree with Bonnie Marranca's opinion that the prisoners, 105 and 106, are "total innocents . . . [who] turn their backs on the rich and their riches, and the cruelties of life" and who find "'freedom' in their cells" and in their "'rich' inner lives" (*Playwrights* 56). On the contrary, Fornes offers for consideration the prospect of prisoners 'choosing' willful ignorance to avoid witnessing the domination and abuse of the poor. In these examples, Fornes demonstrates how peers influence one another to conform to their class positions by accepting the 'generosity' of the rich, by setting themselves above and apart from their 'less fortunate' neighbors, by aping the wealthy, or by closing their eyes and "being carefree." In other words, Fornes exposes some of the workings of *habitus* in maintaining and reproducing class divisions.[6]

But since Fornes' audiences are not comprised primarily of either the wealthy or the working poor, most of the lyrics, in the prisoner's song for example, are aimed at "privileged-poor" bohemians and the middle-classes who (collectively) have the resources and knowledge to change social relations. When the prisoners sing "A poor man doesn't know where his pain comes from. . . . A poor man's life is sour and he doesn't know who made it so" (253), Fornes is asking the audience to open their eyes and to recognize structural social inequalities and the pain and waste they cause. She appeals to her audience to side with the poor against the "madmen" who "feel sure" only about "stupid things . . . money, power, adulation":

> I know what madness is
> It's not knowing how another man feels
> A madman has never been
> In another man's shoes
>
> Madness is lack of compassion
>
> (254).

Here Fornes targets the consciences of her particular audience—people willing to pay to watch her aesthetically challenging and politically complicated works. In answer to David Savran's suggestion that the 'victims' in her play, *The Conduct of Life* are complicit in their own oppression, Fornes responded that it is not the responsibility of the most oppressed to bring about social change but of those like herself, her audiences, and the interviewer, who "have the knowledge, the intelligence, the perspective . . . [to] know what's right and what's wrong . . . [and] what's possible" (in Savran 69). Although I believe that Fornes is reacting against middle-class complacency and the convenient notion that fundamental social change can come only from the most oppressed classes, at times her statements seem to betray little faith in the knowledge and capabilities of oppressed people. Such ambiguity also appears in the lyric "A poor man doesn't know where his pain comes from" but as we will see throughout her oeuvre, Fornes' depiction of the strength and striving of extremely limited characters seems to undercut these hints of condescension. Although delivered in an easy-to-swallow, if zany, cabaret-style vehicle, the social and political issues introduced in *Promenade* will be revisited in harsher, darker, and subtler form throughout Fornes' works into the 1990s.

Promenade returns in the end to its predominantly light and ironic tone with a full cast lullaby, "All Is Well in the City":

> All is well in the city,
> People do what they want.
> They can go to the park.
> They can sleep all they want.
> And for those who have no cake,
> There is plenty of bread.
>
> (266)

Here, Fornes pokes fun at the anaesthetizing closure of musical comedies while at the same time exposing for consideration a singularly American version of the palliative ascribed to Marie Antoinette, who faced much more strenuous unrest than most people could discern in the United States when **Promenade** premiered in 1965.

In this piece, Fornes walks the line between mere entertainment, avant-garde obscurity, and didacticism, and does so with bardic aplomb. Readily apparent is her tribute to and subversion of movies and popular entertainment from the 1920s and '30s: the vaudeville turns, the lazzi of mistaken identities, the torch songs about cruel-hearted lovers and unfulfilled desires. Her sympathy for those who must serve the boorish wealthy and who are disciplined by their henchmen is easily accessible and perhaps made a bit too palatable by bright music and comic approach. And like the Servant, who finds herself dangerously attracted to the wealth she would eschew, Fornes risks reinvoking the gender and class stereotypes of the popular forms she satirizes. When I first saw the illustration of a buxom nude woman jumping out of a cake which graces the soundtrack record jacket and listened to the song, "Four Naked Ladies," I was dismayed (as I imagine other feminists might be). However, on closer examination, I found Miss Cake to be an intriguing character, part rebel and part accomplice to the smarmy Mayor. In her quirky song of seduction, Miss Cake dares the men to love a full-figured mature woman:

> Let the fruit ripen on the tree
> For if not, the meat will harden.
> I'm the peach of the west.
> Chicken is he who does not love me . . .
>
> For there's more to the cake than the icing.
> A morsel I'm not, I'm a feast.

> (217)

I also realized that the women who wished "to be naked too" were the female version of the discredited aristocrats and that, just in case the audience missed Fornes' critique, the Servant refers to their ridiculous behavior in her subsequent mockery of the rich. Thus, even in these early '60s plays, Fornes boldly staged sexuality and questioned conventional sexual relations while protecting her actors from gratuitous physical display. Miss Cake appears in an ample leotard and tights decorated with feathered fringe while the "naked ladies" remove only their dresses and remain in outlandishly decorated teddies, stockings, shoes, and hats.

Critics have noted that the Mother's song questions the conventional nature of Truth (e.g., Mael 189):

> I have to live with my own truth.
> I have to live with it.
> You live with your own truth.
> I cannot live with it.
> I have to live with my own truth whether
>   you like it or not.
>
> I know everything. Half of it I really know.
> The rest I make up. The rest I make up.

> Some things I'm sure of, of other things I'm too
>   sure, and of others I'm not sure at all.

> (265)

But the critics do not connect the Mother's (and Fornes') understanding—that each person must make up from moment to moment a provisional version of truth and reality—with Fornes' call for people to take action, to grow and to improve their lives no matter what their material circumstances. Although Fornes does not believe that the purpose of her plays is to persuade people to take a particular course of action, her plays exhibit low-power characters' (failed or successful) attempts to create tactical spaces for change and resistance. These "demonstrations," coupled with Fornes' satirical dislodging of unconsciously held assumptions about social relations, present the possibility that elements of her plays may function as (Peircian) signs and thus affect the "experience" and "habits," or dispositions, of the audience.

Throughout the remainder of the '60s, Fornes continued to write light, often comedic social commentaries while experimenting with varying presentational modes: ritual, music hall, lecture, and film as well as vaudeville and musical theatre styles. In 1966, Jerome Robbins (co-director of the New York City Ballet, Broadway choreographer, and sometime Judson patron) backed a Broadway production of Fornes' **The Office,** which previewed but never opened.[7] Fornes believes that she "got into trouble" with this play because she tried to transport characters from real life into an invented situation, a method of writing that she found more confusing than useful ("Messages" 28).

In **Dr. Kheal** (1967), a popular and much performed comic-didactic 'lecture,' Fornes combined the idiosyncratic wit and wordplay of **Promenade** with the paradoxes and teacher-student dynamics of **Tango Palace**. Professor Kheal, whose name synthesizes 'kill' and 'heal,' teaches that in reality such seeming opposites actually coexist:

> Don't you know that you can take a yes and a no and push them together, squeeze them together, compress them so they are one? That in fact that is what reality is? Opposites, contradictions, compressed so that you don't know where one stops and the other begins?

> (*Dr. Kheal* 72)

However, Kheal's ambiguous reality is tempered by *balance*, "a state of equilibrium between opposing forces," and by *will*:

> Does the thing happen, or does one do it? . . . Through will. . . . Can I make my own life. Construct my own life? . . . Of course not, you fool. Of course you can.

> (64)

Kheal concludes this discussion with a paradox: "Either you do it, or else it does itself. Life, that is. What other way is there? None" (65).

By presenting free will and determination as binary opposites, and having her provocateur handle the resulting
tension by first maintaining that you *both* can and cannot
construct your own life and then later insisting that *either*
you do life or life does itself, Fornes wished to question
audience members' understanding of individual agency in
relation to the power of social forces. It is worth remembering that during a time when many artists and young
people were holding 'the Establishment' responsible for
both interpersonal and international ills, Fornes held that
(middle-class) individuals were in great measure responsible for their own happiness within given circumstances
(Harrington 34). By taking this jestic position within a
"revolutionary" movement (Shepard 32), Fornes seemed to
be pointing toward a clear-eyed and unromanticized conception of the shifting and contingent power of individuals
to construct a life within networks of social power. *Dr.
Kheal* introduces this and other germinal ideas that will recur throughout Fornes' later plays, darker works in which
she continues to investigate subjects-in-practice, constantly
evolving subjects interacting with provisionally stable institutions as well as with other subjects-in-practice.[8]

Despite her aversion to overtly political groups and "didactic" drama, Fornes contributed two plays to the Vietnam
War protests: *Vietnamese Wedding* (1967), a participatory theatre-style event for adults in which the audience
was encouraged to humanize the 'enemy' by enacting a
Vietnamese version of a familiar ritual (. . .); and the disjointed collaboration, *Red Burning Light* (1968, music by
John Bauman).[9] This piece combined the 1960s penchant
for staging raunchy behavior (scratching, belching, hump-
ing, sticking out tongues, exposing breasts) with music
hall routines, including slapstick comedy, exotic dances,
ballads, chorus lines, and lots of 'sexy' jokes, in an unfocused attempt to poke fun at U.S. chauvinism, imperialism,
and militarism. In a generous *Village Voice* review of the
LaMama production, Robert Pasolli describes *The Red
Burning Light of the American Way of Life* (*RBL*) as
a burlesque "ramble through some military and political
adventures" (59). For Pasolli, the play was less about
politics per se than eroticism and carnality (a frequent
Fornes topic) (59). He praises the piece for subtly making
the "point" that "American imperialism is an incidental
form of run-away and largely impotent sexuality, [that]
the proverbial red light burns at the heart of our national
experience" (59). But Pasolli also remarks the "mockingly
bad dirty jokes" and the "parody of Madame Butterfly in
a bumps and grinds [*sic*] dance" without connecting them
to any specific social commentary or to the Vietnam-era
military frame of the story. Near the end of the review,
he dedicates two column inches to the performance of a
"perfect dumb stripper," praising especially the actress's
"young and attractive body, which most strippers lack"
(59). This sexist and objectifying perspective was typical
for 1969, and perhaps encouraged by Fornes' presentation of stereotypical characters such as "the sexy young
lady" and "a bosomy lady general" (*RBL* 21). However,
Pasolli's superficial reading falls disappointingly short of

his trenchant explications of Fornes' other early works; but
since Fornes radically revised the script before publication,
I cannot fairly judge either the effectiveness of the actual
performance or Pasolli's response to it.

Although the erotic dances were cut in the published
version, sexual talk and raunchy behavior still dominate
the text. This otherwise insignificant romp merits attention,
however, for the surprising degree to which Fornes infuses
biting, if inchoate, critiques of the unfounded sense of
supremacy that underlies the sexual double-standard as well
as U.S. assaults on 'native' populations through preaching
and tourism as well as military campaigns. Fornesian
ideas and images that will reappear in more polished
form abound: remote bombings produce "small amounts of
smoke in various places" onstage (as in *The Danube*) (*RBL*
55); the dangerous misuse of language such as parroting
political double-speak, euphemisms, and even song lyrics;
and the frivolity and inattention of relatively well-off
characters in contrast to the hard-earned knowledge and
striving of the oppressed. In the published version, two
particularly chilling instances stand out: a young soldier's
naive ballad about the "strange" transformation of the
tropical jungle into a "flat, gray, brittle and dry" land
where "breathing is rather hard," and the U.S. military's
oblivious repetition of Kooly-Kooly's song:

> I coom flom li del
> To tell woo woo yell pay
> Yool skin ill be toln flom yool boly
> And yul ees ill be peerce and fol flum
> Deil sodet.
>
> And yul lims ill be pooty of blud and bown
> As main wer.
> Ha ha ha. Ha ha ha. Ha ha ha.
> Yool ill pay, if not heel in lel.
>
> (*RBL* 50)
>
> I come from the dead
> To tell you you will pay.
> Your skin will be torn from your body,
> And your eyes will be peirced,
> And fall from their sockets.
>
> And your limbs will be putty of blood and bone.
> As mine were.
> Ha ha ha. Ha ha ha. Ha ha ha.
> You will pay, if not here, in hell.
>
> (52)

As in much of Fornes' work, these songs warn oppressors
and their compliant or complicit followers that they are
not immune from the adverse effects of their destructive,
thoughtless, and chauvinist beliefs and behaviors. Even in
this flawed experimental work, Fornes manages to stir up
the ambivalence and ambiguities that blur the necessarily

contextual boundaries between sexy and sexist, civilization and barbarism, liberation and re-inscription.

In *Molly's Dream* (1968, music by Cosmos Savage), a lonely barmaid falls asleep while reading a romantic Western. She dreams of encounters between herself and Jim, a man draped with previous female admirers, and between John (Wayne) and Shirley Temple-like Alberta. Unwilling to become part of Jim's harem, even though "it felt right to be near him," Molly adopts a jaded, wiser, and unhurtable Marlene Dietrich persona (*Molly* 93). After watching the other characters try on a series of rigidly gendered movie roles—dispassionate macho man, well-hung (with holsters) gunslinger, Dracula, Superman, baby doll, and perfect bride and groom—Molly drops the Dietrich and explains to Jim that "in order to become what we are, we have to go through many stages" (123).

In *Molly's Dream,* Fornes manages to share her fascination with romance and at the same time critique role-playing and the movie images that shape and limit expressions of desire. She parodies naturalized representations of masculine rivalry and sex appeal and of females as victims, children, or concubines. Fornes usefully complicates Molly's reaction to reading a love story: rather than simply providing emotional escape from loneliness and boredom, the story provokes Molly's psychic journey from sexual attraction, through heartbreak and feigned indifference, to acknowledgment and restraint of this particular desire since its satisfaction would cost her autonomy and individuality. Perhaps Fornes was ahead of her time in exploring the complexities of how women identify with film, theatre, and fiction (key issues for feminist critics of the late 1980s), for the play was deemed too "romantic" by some feminist standards in 1968.[10]

Fornes explained this potential contradiction to interviewer Scott Cummings in the context of some (radical) feminists' rejection of (heterosexual) romance.

> I remember having what became almost an argument with a friend of mine who is very political . . . about *Molly's Dream.* She said it was romantic and meant it as a criticism and I said, "Yes, isn't it?" and meant it as a high compliment. I remember we were in a bar, we were drinking beer, and I said, "Have you ever been with a person when just being with them makes you see everything in a different light. A glass of beer has an amber, a yellow that you've never seen before and it seems to shine in a manner that is—" and she said, "Yes!" and I said, "That is romantic! That is romance!" and she said, "Well, in that case. . . ." I said, "It *is* more beautiful. It isn't that you want it to be more beautiful or that you are lying to yourself. It *is*. Your senses are sharpened."
>
> (in Cummings 55)

In response to Cummings' comment that "there is a power in that feeling that can make a character do things that are not in his or her own best interest," Fornes replied,

"Romance is romance. It's like intelligence. Now you can say that some people are so intelligent that sometimes they become too mental and brainy and it leads to their destruction" (55). In these comments, Fornes defends her attempt to separate for herself and for her audience general concepts from how they function in particular contexts. As Helene Keyssar pointed out, in *Molly's Dream* Fornes both celebrates Molly's enlivened senses and sensibilities and critiques cinematic depictions of romantic relationships as seen through Molly's eyes, that is, from a particular female character's perspective.

From an historical perspective, one can see that *Molly's Dream* combines Fornes' early parodic style with harbingers of the more serious treatment of gender and other inegalitarian social relations in her later plays. For example, the zany filmic context of *The Successful Life of 3* with its broadly satiric swipes at two-dimensional B-movie characters is toned down in *Molly*; the fictional roles are separated from the protagonist's 'real life,' held up for scrutiny, and criticized for their negative influence on gender relations. Molly's self-discoveries are clearer and deeper than the muted changes in consciousness exhibited by SHE, but less profound than the painful and poignant insights grasped by female characters in *Fefu* and *Mud*. Molly was also the first published Fornes play since *The Widow* (1961) to center on a female protagonist; in all her later plays, the central protagonist(s) would be female (and sometimes also male) characters.

Feminist critics in the early 1980s who liked the play tended either to simplify Fornes' exploration of gender roles (Keyssar 122) or to assume that because Molly is still dreaming when Jim comes back that she has missed her chance for true love (Mael 190). They fail to note, however, that Jim returns draped with luggage *"which resembles in color the Hanging Women's costumes"* (*Molly* 124). No Prince Charming, Jim hesitates in the doorway, laden with baggage from old relationships, while Molly tries on and then discards conventional (and ultimately unsatisfactory) subject positions in her dreams. More interesting from a theoretical point of view is Fornes' placement of Molly in a dream state or, to use Lisa Ruddick's term, a liminal or "transitional" space (Ruddick 3-4), a time and place reserved for the playful experimentation necessary to develop a strong and evolving sense of self, a space usually denied women by their gendered roles as sex objects and caregivers.[11] Turning her magical-realist respect for psychic events to feminist account, Fornes arranges for Molly to raise her (feminist) consciousness by making use of the relative freedom of a subconscious dream state.

Like her protagonists, Fornes used the experimental venues of the 1960s as a "creative play space" in which to experiment with a range of production (and producing) styles, and to learn the crafts of theatre by practicing them. Although *Molly's Dream* (in 1968) was her last published play until 1977, Fornes continued to work in the theatre, as a director and producer as well as playwright.

PLAYWRIGHT/DIRECTOR

When *Molly's Dream* was first produced "in an elaborately directed reading" for a Tanglewood writing workshop, Fornes had wanted to direct her own project. She reluctantly acquiesced when Robert Lewis (workshop leader and prestigious Broadway director) insisted that only "directors will direct" (in Savran 59). Fornes chose Ed Setrakian as her director because she knew and liked him as an actor; but when he began "making [the play] too abstract . . . [and] asking people to do this bizarre behavior," she complained to Lewis. Rather than being allowed to take over the direction, Fornes was forced to ask the director to do what she wanted.

> So Ed did what I asked and then he said to me, "I haven't been able to sleep because of what you're doing to me." . . . And I said, "Ed, I'd rather you don't sleep than I don't sleep." . . . But that situation taught me never again to give in. I didn't want to make Ed not sleep. I wanted to do it myself. If then it doesn't come out right, I did it wrong and nobody else has to suffer. I promised myself that I wasn't going to let anyone else direct my work. And I didn't care if it never got done again.
>
> (59-60)

Later in 1968, when New Dramatists offered Fornes a second production of *Molly's Dream,* she threatened to quit the playwrights' organization if they would not support her need as a playwright to direct her own work. They made an exception and from that production on, Fornes has directed the first and, whenever possible, the second and third productions of her new scripts.

In retrospect, Fornes recalls

> I never saw any difference between writing and directing. . . . Of course, they are different things, but they are sequentially and directly connected. So that to me rehearsing was just the next step [in writing a play]. To continue working on it was natural.
>
> (in Cummings 52)

However, for a playwright to direct her own plays or for a woman to direct at all is still not considered "natural" in professional theatre. In addition to crossing the gender-marked division between 'feminine' playwriting and 'masculine' directing, Fornes also challenged producers' 'traditional wisdom' that women directors could not command sufficient respect from and control over (predominantly male) casts and crew. Thus Fornes tends to select artistic collaborators who already believe in her work (such as Anne Militello, who has lit more than ten Fornes productions). In such a positive atmosphere, Fornes claims that she often wields "a power that is almost hypnotic" (160). During my observation of her directing at Trinity Rep in 1989-1990, Fornes commanded the respect due a seasoned director as well as the rapt attention due an indisputable authority on the enigmatic sensibility of her plays.

Since making it a practice to direct her own new plays, Fornes claims that she has never finished a script prior to rehearsal. (She began rehearsals for *Eyes on the Harem* [1978], which garnered an Obie for direction, with only three pages of finished dialogue [in Savran, 60]). She uses the rehearsal time to try out preliminary or even "extra" scenes with actors as part of the writing/editing process. Fornes' technique of seeing characters and hearing dialogue in action before a script is finalized contributes to the imagistic theatricality of her scripts. Directing also allows her to strengthen a play's structure so that it can withstand the multiple interpretations of directors, actors, designers, and audiences in subsequent productions (in Betsko 158). In addition to these aesthetic reasons, Fornes' insistence on directing was also the move of a woman writer taking over the next step in the production of meaning, as well as the means of production.

PLAYWRIGHT/PRODUCER

By the end of the 1960s, the wide-open experimental theatre environment began to change. Fornes notes, "by '68 already the directors [e.g., Chaikin, Richard Schechner, and Tom O'Horgan] had taken over. Most of the playwrights who were active in the early years of the off-off-Broadway movement became sort of outcasts" (in Cummings 53). Women playwrights, in particular, found that they were required to make "horrible compromises to get produced" or that in the hands of some directors their plays were transformed into "vehicle[s] for feminine violation" (Megan Terry; Rosalyn Drexler, in Gussow 44). In 1972, Fornes joined with other avant-garde women playwrights (Terry, Drexler, Julie Bovasso, Adrienne Kennedy, and Rochelle Owens) to form the Women's Theater Council (WTC), a cooperative theatre to produce women's work. Fornes explained in an New York Times article about the establishment of the WTC that "Men are writing out of their dreams. Ours are feminine dreams. Now we can say yes, we are women" (in Gussow 44).

But no one would fund the Women's Theater Council because they "had no track record" (Terry, in Betsko 385), even though all six women had been produced and reviewed throughout the 1960s and five had won Obies for playwriting. Undaunted, they joined forces with a number of male playwrights, including Ed Bullins and Sam Shepard (Keyssar 21), and formed the New York Theater Strategy (1972-1979), which Fornes ran (almost single-handedly) for five of its six years. Theater Strategy shared the virtues and vices of 1960s off-off-Broadway venues which allowed playwrights to set their own pace, to test ideas without inordinate worries about pleasing the audience, and "to be involved with [their own] work—and that of others twenty-four hours a day" (Paul Foster, in Bigsby 26). At the time, running Theater Strategy "twenty-four hours a day" suited Fornes' idiosyncratic, do-it-yourself methods and gave her an opportunity to learn every aspect of avant-garde theatre on the job and to work on numerous productions of new plays. Not until 1977 after directing and producing her own new play *Fefu and Her Friends,* did she hire managerial help and begin her current prolific period of writing.

CHANGING WRITING STYLE

The years 1969-1977 were a relatively fallow period for Fornes as a playwright. Although the heavy production schedule at the New York Theater Strategy pre-empted full-time writing, Fornes also felt that with *Aurora* (unpublished, produced 1973), and even with *Molly's Dream,* that she had begun to repeat herself, and so during the early 1970s, she worked to change her writing style, the hardest and "most important thing for a writer to do" (in Cummings 54).

Writing *Tango Palace* had been an exhilarating but "very passionate" experience, a spontaneous burst of creativity that 'took possession' of Fornes (in Savran 59). This spontaneity produced a surprisingly good first play but provided Fornes with no techniques for writing "painful things without going through the agony [her]self" or for accessing her creativity at will (in Savran 59). This explains the rather abrupt change in tone from *Tango*'s dark psychological probing to the lighter satire of her other early plays, "I started to write things that were lighter because I just didn't want to suffer" (59). Throughout the 1960s, she experimented with games and exercises in order "to find ways to be possessed again" (58). Sometimes she "found that it was possible to be caught up in a kind of writing where the characters take over, [where] it's fluid and fast and interesting" (in Savran 58); but at other times, she procrastinated, re-arranging her silverware, starching her jeans, doing anything to avoid writing (Fornes, "Messages" 40).

While managing Theater Strategy and helping other playwrights, casts, and directors solve creative problems, Fornes continued to lead writing workshops for which she devised yoga- and visualization-based warm-ups and adapted Method and improvisational acting techniques for use in writing plays. During this time, she came to believe that playwrights, like actors, could "gain an enormous depth by going to the past, to the future, to other times that are between [those] scenes" actually included in the final script (in Cummings 53-54). In her own work, Fornes uses the "extra" scenes produced through this research method to enrich her characters' often brief appearances onstage and to 'instantly' revise scripts in rehearsal. (During rehearsal for *Night,* I noted that Fornes was able to add, cut, or rearrange speeches and scenes during the actors' rest breaks.)

These techniques, in conjunction with staging preliminary (written) text as part of the writing process (which allows experimentation with the visual, aural, and relational dimensions that actors provide), enable Fornes to identify areas to be clarified and/or text to be pared away. Watching the script in performance greatly facilitates Fornes' aim to circumvent easy catharsis or closure and allows her to delete lines and actions that undercut her vision of the contradictory, ambiguous nature of human realities. From

these writing experiments in the 1960s and '70s, Fornes developed a two-phase writing process: an initial 'additive' stage which invites creativity and admits irrational ideas and images, followed by a 'subtractive' phase during which she analyzes and edits (both on paper and on stage) selections from a rich repository of relevant material. *Fefu and Her Friends* (1977) was the first product of her changing writing/directing process.

By the time Fornes returned to full-time authorship with *Fefu* (1977), she had experimented with many forms and styles in a variety of '60s venues and gained valuable production experience while managing the New York Theater Strategy. As a 'convert' to theatre at age thirty, Fornes set out to learn all the crafts of her new field, meanwhile producing significant experimental works. Beginning with *Fefu,* Fornes shifted from free-wheeling satires of character types and forms of entertainment, to studies of rounder characters in more particularized, real world contexts. Yet, as we will see, she retained her fascination with the irrational and the unconscious elements of human experience, elements to which she maintained access through her increasingly controllable creative process.

NOTES

[1]*Ulysses in Nighttown*, dramatized and adapted by Marjorie Barkenton under supervision of Padraic Colum (New York: Random House, 1958).

[2]Fornes says of her early relationship with Sontag:

> We exchanged ideas compulsively. I wasn't a reader, and culture isn't something about which you can say, okay, I'm going to get some now. So I couldn't go to her, she had to come to me. We were always talking.
>
> (in Harrington 34)

[3]In *Promenade*, a maidservant mocks the inanity and disconnection of aristocratic chatter, and more trenchantly, in *Night*, mentally unbalanced but oddly perspicacious Helena asserts that when people use "false words which have nothing behind them . . . they feel a little cheated later, debilitated. If you use words without meaning, you feel debilitated" (*Night*, "Lust" 13).

[4]In addition to *Tango Palace*, Fefu in *Fefu and Her Friends*, Leticia in *The Conduct of Life*, Lloyd in *Mud*, Joseph in *Night*, and half-seriously 3 in *The Successful Life*; also, Sarita in *Sarita* and Nadine in *Night* attack their oppressors with a knife.

[5]See Ruddick section of Chapter 2 for a discussion of the importance of creative play in self-development.

[6]For my discussion of Bourdieu's definition of *habitus* and related concepts, see Chapter 1.

[7]The manuscript is unavailable since Fornes never finished the script to her satisfaction.

[8]For a discussion of 'subjects-in-practice,' see the Gardiner section of Chapter 1.

[9]The original production of *The Red Burning Light Or: Mission XQ3*, was directed by Fredric de Boer and choreographed by James Barbosa for the Open Theatre's 1968 European tour. By the second production (at LaMama E.T.C. in New York), the show had gained three more

director/choreographers including Fornes and Judson colleague Remy Charlip and a second composer, Richard Peaslee.

[10]A noteworthy exception is Phyllis Mael's 1981 explication of *Molly's Dream* which anticipates poststructuralist theories about the workings of cinema by remarking Fornes' exploration of cinema's (and theatre's) influence on people's dreams and fantasies.

[11]For an introductory discussion of "transitional space" and "self-creating play," see the Ruddick section of Chapter 2.

BIBLIOGRAPHY

Banes, Sally. *Democracy's Body: The Judson Dance Theatre 1962-64.* Ann Arbor, MI: U of Michigan P, 1983.

Betsko, Kathleen, and Rachel Koenig. *Interviews with Contemporary Women Playwrights.* New York: Beech Tree, 1987.

Bigsby, C. W. E. *A Critical Introduction to Twentieth-Century American Drama.* Vol. 3: *Beyond Broadway.* Cambridge: Cambridge UP, 1985.

Cummings, Scott. "Seeing with Clarity: The Visions of Maria Irene Fornes." *Yale Theatre* 17 (Winter 1985): 51-56.

Fornes, Maria Irene. *Abingdon Square.* In *American Theatre,* February 1988: 1-10 (pull-out section).

————. *And What of the Night?* Unpublished manuscript from Trinity Repertory Company production, January 5, 1990, Providence, RI. (Includes four parts: *Nadine, Springtime, Lust,* and *Hunger.*)

————. *The Conduct of Life.* Fornes, *Maria Irene Fornes: Plays* 65-88.

————. "Creative Danger." *American Theatre,* September 1985: 12-13.

————. *The Danube.* Fornes, *Maria Irene Fornes: Plays* 41-64.

————. *Dr. Kheal.* Fornes, *Promenade and Other Plays* 59-74.

————. *Fefu and Her Friends.* New York: PAJ, 1978.

————. *Fefu and Her Friends.* Directed by Carolyn Connelly, Arts Alliance, Northwestern U, Evanston, IL, November 1989.

————. *Fefu and Her Friends.* Directed by Sally Harrison-Pepper, Miami U, Oxford, OH, February 1994.

————. "I Write These Messages That Come." Transcribed and ed. Robb Creese. *The Drama Review* 21.4 (1977): 26-40.

————. "In response to the New York Times Magazine article: 'Women Playwrights: New Voices in the Theatre' by Mel Gussow on the occasion of Norman's ''Night, Mother.''" Ed. Gail Austin. *Performing Arts Journal* no. 21 (1983): 90.

————. Langston Lecture. Department of Theatre, U of Texas at Austin. March 12, 1992.

————. *Maria Irene Fornes: Plays.* New York: PAJ, 1986.

————. *Molly's Dream.* Fornes, *Promenade and Other Plays.* 75-126.

————. *Mud.* Fornes, *Maria Irene Fornes: Plays.* 13-40.

————. *Promenade.* Fornes, *Promenade and Other Plays* 201-72.

————. *Promenade and Other Plays.* New York: Winter House, 1971.

————. *Promenade.* Audio recording. Lyrics by Al Carmines. Directed by Lawrence Kornfeld. RCA Victor, Stereo-LSO, 1161, 1969.

————. *Promenade.* Archival video recording of Stadium II production. Dir. Beth Kattelman. Ohio State University, November 13, 1990.

————. *Red Burning Light Or: Mission XQ3.* Fornes, *Promenade and Other Plays* 19-58.

————. *Sarita.* Music by Leon Odenz. Fornes, *Maria Irene Fornes: Plays* 89-145.

————. *Sarita.* Program notes. By Rick Foster, dramaturg. Dir. Stanley E. Williams. Lorraine Hansberry Theatre, Potrero Neighborhood House, San Francisco, January 16, 1987.

————. *The Successful Life of 3.* Fornes, *Promenade and Other Plays* 163-200.

————. *Tango Palace.* Fornes, *Promenade and Other Plays* 127-62.

————. Telephone interview with Assunta Kent. January 23, 1993.

————. *Vietnamese Wedding.* Fornes, *Promenade and Other Plays* 5-18.

————. *What of the Night? Women on the Verge: Seven Avant Garde Plays.* Ed. Rosette C. Lamont. New York: Applause, 1993. 157-236.

Gussow, Mel. "New Group to Offer Plays by Women." *New York Times,* February 22, 1971: 44.

Harrington, Stephanie. "Irene Fornes, Playwright: Alice and the Red Queen." *Village Voice,* XI.27 (April 21, 1966): 1, 33-34.

Henderson, Mary C. *Theatre in America: 200 Years of Plays, Players, and Production.* New York: Abrams, 1986.

Keyssar, Helene. *Feminist Theatre: An Introduction to Plays of Contemporary British and American Women.* New York: Grove, 1985.

————. "Drama and the Dialogic Imagination: *The Heidi Chronicles* and *Fefu and Her Friends.*" *Modern Drama* 34 (1991): 87-106.

Kuhn, John G. "Fornes, Maria Irene." *Contemporary Dramatists.* 158-60.

Mael, Phyllis. "Fornes, Maria Irene" in *Dictionary of Literary Biography* 7. Ed. John MacNichols. Detroit: Gale Research, 1981. Pt. 1: 188-91.

Malpede, Karen. *Three Works by the Open Theatre.* New York: Drama Book Specialists, 1974.

Marranca, Bonnie, and Dasgupta, Gautam. *American Playwrights, A Critical Survey.* New York: Drama Book Specialists, 1981. 53-63.

Marx, Bill. "Mother Avant-Garde: The Courage of Maria Irene Fornes." *The Newspaper.* Section Two (Arts & Entertainment). Providence, RI: January 11, 1990. 1, 8.

McDonagh, Don. *The Rise and Fall and Rise of Modern Dance.* New York: Dutton, 1970.

Nasso, Christine, ed. "Fornes, Maria Irene." *Contemporary Authors.* Detroit: Gale Research P, n.d. Vols. 25-28, 1st ed.: 243-245.

Pasolli, Robert. "You Take a Yes & a No." *Village Voice,* April 17, 1969: 44.

Poland, Albert, and Bruce Mailman, eds. *The Off Off Broadway Book: The Plays, People, Theatre.* New York: Bobbs-Merrill, 1972.

Roberts, Vera Mowry. *On Stage: A History of Theatre.* New York: Harper & Row, 1974.

Ruddick, Lisa. "Can Psychoanalysis Make Room for the 'Spirit'?" Panel on "The Self After Postmodernism." MLA Convention. San Francisco, December 30, 1991.

Savran, David. "Maria Irene Fornes." *In Their Own Words: Contemporary American Playwrights.* New York: Theatre Communications Group, 1988. 51-69.

Shepard, Richard. "Lyrics Preceded a Hit Musical's Music." *New York Times,* June 6, 1969. 32.

Diane Lynn Moroff (essay date 1996)

SOURCE: "Palimpsests," in *Fornes: Theater in the Present Tense*, The University of Michigan Press, 1996, pp. 117-30.

[*In the essay below, Moroff investigates "the theatrical palimpsest in Fornes's theater, the simultaneous literary and visual texts that are theater."*]

The theater dramatizes, makes perceptible, literary themes; concepts are made visual; they exist—as they do in life—in both language and the image. We do not only hear about abuse, for example, we can see it; we see Orlando's molestation of Nena. There is no opportunity in the theater for the spectator to forget context either for thought or for action; we cannot forget that Shakespeare's Othello is a Moor surrounded by Caucasians or that Hamlet is forced to see Claudius actually sit on his father's throne. Like the self more generally, the theatrical character is defined by context, by whom as well as what it comes up against. Chekhov made certain to keep the spectators' gaze on the cherry orchard, whose branches brush the stage space, in order to give us more insight into the characters' contentions with the past. The orchard is an image of that past, and, as the characters enact their conflicts in the very context of what has compelled those conflicts, their struggles become more than abstraction.

In this chapter I explore the theatrical palimpsest in Fornes's theater, the simultaneous literary and visual texts that *are* theater. Fornes has with increasing care highlighted the palimpsestic nature of the theater, particularly to illuminate the functioning and intersection of her characters' labors for power and the realization of their desires.

Her characters are frequently sexual, always sensual and emotional, always physical. For thirty years Fornes has complemented each of her character's intelligence with his or her sensuality. That meaning invoked by what characters say to one another is mediated by what the spectator sees the characters do to one another as they act out their sensuality. Her characterizations become more unstable and more authentic simultaneously; through the imaging of characters' desires, we see how the self can be simultaneously powerful and powerless, how desire can be simultaneously punishing and enabling.

Typical of Fornes's dichotomies, desire makes her characters impervious and vulnerable simultaneously. It is both selfish and necessary, punishing and rewarding to the self and to the other, central to the complex and ambiguous tasks of attaining subjectivity and objectivity. Desire formulates the subject and necessarily engenders an object, but its obscuring of boundaries threatens the integrity of both the lover and the beloved in Fornes's plays, even while it contributes to their sense of completion.

Within individual plays and within her oeuvre, a haunting lyricism results from the patterns that emerge when characters act out their desires in struggles for power over themselves and one another. The history of Fornes's theater has been, in fact, a history of representing that desire and its complicated web of simultaneous targets and aspirations: the achievement of a self, the procuring of a lover, the forging of a satisfactory role within a community—each of which act violently disrupts the self and the other.

Fornes has been consistently devoted to relationships as the most productive narrative context for the representation of what it is to be human. She has been consistently devoted, too, to the body as the site of that drama, which lends a particularly sensual quality to her stages, obscuring a line between mere physicality and sexuality. In the tradition of sensual writers like Anaïs Nin, Fornes uses physicality to explore some of the less tangible, more elusive connections between people. She often substitutes exposition and psychology with the equally telling image. As Ross Wetzsteon suggests, "Fornes's heart doesn't seem to be in psychologizing, she seems to use it only to *depsychologize* the scene, she's much more comfortable explaining to the actress how she wants her to sit down—that's the kind of grounding she focuses on" ["Irene Fornes: The Elements of Style," *Village Voice* 31, No. 17 (19 April 1986): 42-5]. The subtleties of characters' relationships are often defined by physical gestures, ranging from pouring bourbon and bringing soup in *Fefu* to the exhibitionist masturbation in *Mud* to explicit sexual foreplay in *Sarita*. Characters are always undergoing a process of definition through their physical interactions with others. Whether explicitly sexual or not, these interactions are profoundly intimate and symbolic of desire.

Fornes's characters have internalized the theater, watching themselves and one another as if they were watching performances. Their sensuality, in turn, takes on highly theatrical attributes; sensuality is projected outward into the image of the character: the spectator *sees* that sensuality in order to comprehend characters' words and actions. In this chapter I read moments of simultaneous texts—the narrative and the image—in the four plays discussed in the preceding chapters [*Fefu and Her Friends, Mud, Sarita,* and *The Conduct of Life*], as well as in *Abingdon Square* (1987) and in *What of the Night?* (1993), in order to explore character often as the result of the convergence of the literary and imagistic texts of desire and power.

* * *

Within the theatrical world of *Fefu and Her Friends* the relationships that matter most are the relationships the spectator sees. The visual text subsumes the supposed social and cultural text of "a man's world." The omission of men from *Fefu,* particularly when considered in light of Fornes's thematic and formal scope over thirty or so years, may be directly responsible for any empowerment of its women. The women are allowed to recreate their relationships—for that matter, they are allowed to have relationships—without the mediation of a *Conduct of Life*'s Orlando, for example. The palimpsest of the women's interactive presences over their tortured narratives of oppression, fear, and anger offers the women redemption. The space for desire ultimately unmediated by men often allows for that desire's productivity.

In *Fefu* characters are largely defined by their desires, and whatever *images* of desire—sexual or otherwise—Fornes provides are between women. Men are referred to, particularly Fefu's husband, Phillip, but they remain beyond the audience's field of vision. Therefore, though heterosexual desire makes it into the dramatic text, it does not make it into the theatrical text. Even when the topics of the women's conversations cover characters, real or imaginary, outside of their theatrical event, their concerns are with themselves and one another above all else. Their desires, as imaged in this theatrical event, are for the comfort and support of the women with whom they share this space. And those desires are responded to.

Fefu's other desire, ostensibly for her husband, is both punishing and enabling. She experiences her desire for Phillip as ultimately damaging to her autonomy. But that desire is finally proxy for a desire for her own self's health. In the play's last act Fefu tells Julia that Phillip has left her:

> His body is here but the rest is gone. . . . I torment him and I torment myself. I need him, Julia. . . . I need his touch. . . . I need the person he is. I can't give him up. *(She looks into Julia's eyes.)* I look into your eyes and I know what you see. It's death. Fight!

> (139-40)

The irony of "His body is here"—when his body is not here—foregrounds the productive possibilities of even unmet desire in Fefu's experience. Fefu imagines that Julia sees her need for Phillip as a kind of "death" to herself, but, to the contrary, she implies, it saves her. It is not Phillip who can save her but the desire for Phillip; "his body is gone," but Fefu does not finally need his body on this stage in order to experience her own desire—which is a way of avoiding the death that has been the consequence of Julia's eradication of her own capacity to desire.

In *Mud, Abingdon Square,* and *Sarita* Fornes concerns herself with the components of a woman's desire—how desire is constructed as both self-nurturing and as defense against persecution. Fornes increasingly explores women's characters in her later work: *The Successful Life of 3*'s lackadaisical She makes way for *Mud*'s rebellious Mae; the romantic Molly of *Molly's Dream* makes way for the sexually and emotionally complex heroine of *Sarita.* Acting out desire becomes largely responsible for the producing of a woman's role, sometimes against societal expectations.

Mud depicts Mae's thwarted desires for a realized self in the image of the voyeuristic sex imposed upon her by Henry and Lloyd. At separate moments in the drama both Lloyd and Henry masturbate in front of Mae. Though both insist that they do so in efforts to compel Mae to make love to them—that is, in an inverted process of lovemaking or seduction—both are in fact putting on performances that Mae is compelled to watch. Their masturbations are meant to master Mae by forcing her into the position of voyeur, unwittingly and unwillingly included in their sexual acts; she is necessary for the masturbator's climax. While Mae's verbal exchanges with Henry and Lloyd *say* that all of their behavior results from the frustrations of poverty, ignorance, inability to communicate, and unfulfilled needs—or even from Mae's manipulations as she aggressively seeks power—the theatrical image of the men's masturbations demonstrates that the men prevent the possibility for Mae of productive "intercourse."

Lloyd and Henry's supposed desire for Mae is punishing for all the characters in the constrained dramatic world of *Mud.* Unexamined and fettered, that desire is never realized as a desire for their own autonomy; repressed, it then violently reemerges as a coveting of Mae, which, in an effort to prevent her from leaving the stage, compels Lloyd to kill her, leaving him and Henry bereft. Mae's desire is subject to these same constraints; her repressed desires reemerge purely selfishly as a desire to improve herself but with no awareness of the need to alter context to do so. For Mae, however, her desire is enabling as well: she becomes a poet and achieves self-love, even if only at the moment of her death—though the visual palimpsest offers no cause for celebration. Her dead and bloody body eclipses anything that has been productive about her desire.

Marion of *Abingdon Square* resembles Mae, though in a completely different world, a world of wealth and privilege, a genuinely beautiful world not of a dark kitchen embedded in mud but of space and light, of French doors and gardens. Her dramatic life begins as pure romance, her much older husband-to-be, Justin, singing Handel to her, her husband's son Michael her dancing partner and friend. But Marion, like Mae, feels crippled by her ignorance. Her education was interrupted by the death of her parents, and she feels she does not "yet comprehend a great many things" (6). That assessment is followed by a scene in which she and her cousin Mary muse upon the sexual lives of others and are then consumed with guilt. Marion seeks to use her self-education as punishment for that guilt; she studies Dante's "Purgatorio" by standing painfully in her overheated attic, "on her toes with her arms outstretched, looking upward" (11). Her self-education is excruciating. She explains to her great-aunt Millie, who finds her in this posture:

> I feel sometimes that I am drowning in vagueness—that I have no character. . . . I do this to strengthen my mind and my body. I am trying to conquer this vagueness I have inside of me. This lack of character. . . . This weakness.

> (13)

Marion constructs her own palimpset; she essays to offer up an image of herself as strong in contrast to her profound experience of weakness.

Eventually, Marion extends her search for self-definition into a blatant using of men. When her books and religion do not work, Marion becomes a writer of sorts, keeping a daily "diary," which is really a fictional revisioning of her life. She writes in a lover, a mysterious man with the first initial *F*, who does in fact enter her life through the streets of New York's West Village and eventually through her husband's French doors. But even then he is not the lover she initially takes. Marion protects herself from an actual lover by taking instead the house painter (their one sexual encounter leads to the conception of her child). Terror of her own sexual desire and the subsequent indication of a powerful and dangerous self to Marion necessitate the continuation of the self-denying pattern begun with marrying a much older man, to whom Marion feels indebted but not in love. In time, something like courage, but more like need, compels her to live her devised fiction. Frank becomes her lover, and she even relocates herself into another space, into an apartment for "privacy" on Abingdon Square.

Despite Marion's increasing aggression, these are futile steps to alter a resolute context, which is that of a young, orphaned woman, insufficiently educated, fettered by marriage, controlled by the men who benignly enough are the masters of that context. Marion finally becomes motivated by what is figured as sexual desire above all else, eventually depicted as destructive. Inevitably, it destroys her marriage to Justin and hence terminates her companionship with Michael, who insists he must remain faithful to his father. Frank acts the typically elusive lover, who insists they must be careful and so distances himself from her. Marion had hoped through her fiction to become alive, to live her own life, but she experiences the consequences of that vitality as threatening even to that unrealized self: "When I sinned against life because I was dead I was not punished," she insists. "Now that life has entered me I am destroyed and I destroy everything around me" (34).

Fulfilling the prophecy of the larger script in which she acts—that is, the script that defines her as a young wife, inherently and futilely rebellious—Marion becomes a menacing sexual animal, at least according to Justin. After their separation he tells Michael:

> Last week I followed her to a dance parlor. . . .
> Marion's behavior is irrational. She's not sane. . . .
> I followed her in and I took a table by the window.
> A man wearing a soldier's uniform greeted her. They
> started dancing. And moved to a dark corner. She knew
> I was there looking at her and that's why she did what
> she did. They kissed and caressed lewdly. I've never
> seen such behavior in public.
>
> (35)

Marion accepts Justin's definition of her. She describes to Mary her instinct to murder Justin by shooting him, which would give her "a great satisfaction. A satisfaction equal to flushing a toilet. . . . I am crude. I know I'm crude. I know I'm uncivilized" (36). Though Marion is essentially

humbled and prostrate at Justin's bedside as he is likely to die from a stroke, the drama holds her responsible for his death: her lifelong repression engendered a violence that fell over into all of their lives (Justin's stroke was the consequence of a scene in which the two stood facing each other with guns). With great and sad irony, Marion becomes the abuser as the consequence of the abuse of a world that gave her no room for self-definition; she is an agent only when acting *against* others, imaged via her instigated sexual encounters, each of which tell the story of a woman reduced to a kind of physical hysteria in efforts to achieve a self.

The eponymous protagonist of **Sarita** is one of the only female characters Fornes's audience actually sees making love. But when Sarita makes love—either physically with Julio or verbally with Mark—she is not giving love or sex as much as taking her own satisfaction. Sarita is empowered by her impulses toward self-fulfillment. While Fornes celebrates Sarita's sexuality, particularly by contrasting her with her mother, Fela, who has effectively been deadened by her passionless life, she also suggests that Sarita's desire is what causes her tragedy. Sarita is so consumed with desire for Julio that she has sex with him repeatedly at the cost of both her self-esteem and her marriage with Mark. Ironically, it is Julio who clarifies Sarita's conduct; he eventually asks her for money, confirming that he has been playing her prostitute.

Although Sarita never comes to the realization, Fornes illustrates that Sarita's desire for Julio has been misdirected from the start. Sarita's real desire, projected onto Julio and contextualized by an affair, has been for her own self. As discussed in chapter 4, Fornes spends considerable time imaging Sarita in the act of making love. Those images, when viewed through the lens of Fornes's appreciation of Sarita's sexuality, suggest that her lovemaking in this sense has been masturbatory in the most productive of ways: she has been trying to care for herself. And to a degree she succeeds, in that she survives this drama and that she is eventually responsible for liberating both herself and Julio from their roles. Though the process involves her murdering Julio, and hence Sarita's loss of the apparent object of her desire, Fornes hints that Sarita may be on the brink of understanding her desire's misdirection. That even after her various crimes—abandonment of her child, adultery, murder—Mark is at her side at the play's end, providing an audience for her confessions, offers Sarita the opportunity and the context in which she may learn to restructure her desire.

The palimpsests within **The Conduct of Life** are largely formulated by the shifting relationships between Orlando and Nena; his active sexual abuse of her confirms his power over her, but her goodness, her endurance, and her sturdy position over his dead body at the play's end dramatically overturn that narrative.

While Orlando sexualizes every encounter, even comparing the torture of political prisoners to horses mating, the women in the drama undo that imagery. Virtually anti-climactically, Nena's progress is from sexual victim to innocent child, brought up from the torture chamber in the cellar to the safety of the kitchen, where she shells peas with Olimpia. A drama that focuses on the reverberations of political violence characterized by rape and mutilation of genitalia concludes in a space in which circumspect if aggressive women control the stage.

In **Conduct,** as in **Fefu,** Fornes returns to the redemptive possibilities of the relationships between women. Orlando's links with each of the female characters in the play become the models for links between the female characters. The women repeat certain of Orlando's behavior: Leticia sometimes abuses her power over Olimpia; Olimpia mimics Orlando's violent language; Leticia chooses to emulate her husband's denial of his abuse of Nena. But, while all of Orlando's abuses can be characterized as sexual abuses in that they are experienced by his victims as suppression of their human desires, none of the women can indulge in such objectification. Even Leticia, who has jealous cause, can never objectify Nena, as Orlando does everyone who crosses his path, from the political prisoners he tortures to his wife to his abducted child-mistress.

As Nena's literal master, Orlando's abuse of Nena is far more profound than Lloyd and Henry's abuse of Mae in **Mud.** Orlando repeatedly masturbates *against* Nena:

> Look this way [Orlando says to Nena]. I'm going to do something to you. . . . Don't move away. *(As he slides his hand along her side.)* I just want to put my hand here like this. . . . This is all I'm going to do to you. . . . (He pushes against her and reaches an orgasm.)
>
> (76)

Orlando rapes Nena, makes her his voyeur, his audience, all for the specific sake of overpowering her. Ironically, however, Orlando's corruption of desire obliterates his own self in addition to threatening Nena's. His efforts in the play's final scene to force Leticia into the role of corrupt desirer (he tries to force a "confession" from her concerning a nonexisting lover) results in his erasure from this drama. The sheer violence of his desire can only be destructive.

The brutality of his mastery of Nena prevents any physical escape for her; ominously, her only option is to close off feeling, to lose that part of herself. But, rather than allow that complete repression of herself, Nena desperately pursues her own aptitude for kindness, and she succeeds: "If someone should treat me unkindly, I should not blind myself with rage, but I should see them and receive them, since maybe they are in worse pain than me" (85). Nena transforms her role as Orlando's voyeur into a productive role; she rejects her status as his victim and, in fact, in that manner overpowers him, even while she is physically defeated by him throughout the drama.

Nena's capacity is explicitly dependent on her particular grasp of her role as voyeur, her awareness of the transcendent and complex palimpsests. She understands Orlando's desire for an audience to his sexual behavior because all of her life she has been searching for "anyone watching over me" (84). While Orlando steals his audience—imprisoning his victims, demanding the attention of his spectators—Nena receives her as a gift. Even Nena's monologue explicitly acknowledges the need for an audience, her dependence on her spectators' presence. She tells her story precisely because she believes Olimpia is watching over her, and she concludes her horrible litany of Orlando's abuses with the gift of example: "I should value the things I have. And I should value all those who are near me" (85). In her way Nena is Fornes's most pathetic victim to date—by far the most abused and least able to protect herself from that abuse—and yet Nena is also Fornes's greatest heroine. Utterly ensnared in a dangerous drama, and in Orlando's violent theatricality, Nena still rejects that role. Nena's image moves from a sexualized object to a spiritual, inviolable agent of good, representing Fornes's theme of the possibility for moral perpetuation by example. By becoming the most powerful figure—the one holding the gun—on **Conduct**'s stage, Nena illustrates the transformation of her own palimpsest.

Fornes's most recent published play, **What of the Night?** returns to nearly pure absurdist theater, with particular emphasis on the image as context for the violence of sexuality. The play consists of four plays in turn, **Nadine, Springtime, Lust,** and **Hunger** (some of which have been published and performed independently).[1] While characters may be traced through each play, the context (time and place) differs so completely from play to play that until **Hunger** only characters' names are recognizable. An overall system is suggested by the inclusion of a few familiar elements but undermined by the complete novelty of each new play. That chaotic order is largely what the play is about: it describes the patterns of abuse from adult to child, the consequences of abuse of power, and the explosive fragmentation of the self in a violent world. Each play has at its center a sexually explicit encounter; each encounter is also brief and virtually superimposed on the narrative.

The title character of **Nadine** is an impoverished mother in the Southwest, 1938, a prostitute whose son, Charlie, makes some money for the family by stealing for Pete, who is forty years old, "stupid and mean" (159). Pete is abusive to Charlie; he hits and cheats him and speaks vulgarly to his girlfriend, Birdie. Nadine, in an effort to force Pete to give Charlie more of what he is due, offers Pete sex:

> *Nadine walks behind Pete. She puts her hand inside his jacket and squeezes his breast. He grabs her arm to remove it but begins to shake. His eyes roll. She lowers her hand to his crotch. He quivers. He pants and grunts. His eyes roll.*

Nadine insists, "You got to pay," while Pete *"whimpers and stamps his feet. He growls and drools"* (166). Nadine's seduction resembles abuse; the image of their "successful" sexual encounter (Pete reaches orgasm and gives Nadine three dollars for Charlie, one "on her cleavage" [167]) conveys the violence of these characters' desperation. While **Nadine** ends with the smallest hint of hope when Birdie chooses to leave this stage behind and, in turn, thwarts Pete's efforts to rape her, the image of the only adults on the stage, parental figures of sorts, engaging in something like a mutual rape, suggests that the likelihood of the children escaping unscathed is slight at best.

In **Springtime** even the silhouette of the abusive figure destroys the lives of two lovers. The play centers a male character, whom the audience meets only once, in the midst of a romance between Rainbow and Greta. Midway through the play, and after much talking about him, Ray's brief presence in the women's bedroom is shocking. His intrusion into what is otherwise the women's space destroys the sanctity of that space.

Ray casts a menacing shadow over the women's love affair, imparting danger at his first mention. Rainbow, to earn money for Greta's medicine, has apparently been coerced by Ray into something resembling prostitution: "I had to agree," Rainbow tells Greta, "to do something for him. . . . Meet someone" (84). But Ray's villainy in these women's eyes does not last the course of the drama; either naively or wishfully, the women see his influence over them as redemptive. Though Greta battles both jealousy about Rainbow's relationship with Ray and fear for what Ray does to Rainbow, she also attributes to him the role of a savior. She believes Ray has saved Rainbow from a life of crime, has made her "impeccable" when once she was "peccable" (86). And Rainbow insists that Ray has been a friend to her, that she "understands" him, that "he's not what he appears to be" (85).

From the audience's perspective both Greta and Rainbow are being generous, even ingenuous. The facts appear to be that Ray is Rainbow's pimp and that he hires her out for pornographic photography. He not only takes advantage of Rainbow's need but, eventually, of Greta's need as well. The audience learns that Greta too has been having sex with Ray (or "something," which is all the information Fornes offers), possibly in an effort to free Rainbow from him.

Greta's and Rainbow's romance is never private; it is never only their own but always the man's too. Fornes may be suggesting that a romance between two women can never be their own because the cultural context for romance is heterosexual. Or Fornes may be suggesting that romance in general can never belong solely to its participants, that expectations of the form control the lovers' behavior. Ray controls the progress of Greta and Rainbow's relationship, preventing either of them from ever being truly honest and from giving what they want to give to each other. When Greta discovers Rainbow's photographs, Rainbow says: "I don't mind. It's for you" (87). In order to be able to give her love to Greta, and to take care of her, Rainbow must pass through the conduit of male sexual desire; in order for Greta to save Rainbow's dignity, she too must pass through that conduit. When their relationship ends, the audience is to understand that Rainbow leaves Greta because their relationship does not satisfy her criteria: "For me," she says, "to love is adoring. And to be loved is to be adored" (88). But the audience has no evidence that Greta has not fulfilled her part in Rainbow's formula. The evidence we do have is that Ray has come between them, prevented the women's desire. His sexual role has determined the fate of Greta's and Rainbow's narrative.

Lust opens with Ray, "passionate and driven," and Joseph, "a self-contained businessman," discussing a boy's welfare, Ray urging Joseph to fund the boy's education. While the dialogue runs its formal course ("I'm asking the foundation to help him financially"; "How can I help?" "With a scholarship and additional funds for medical expenses"),

> *Ray speaks, Joseph sits next to him. He reaches for [a] blanket and covers their middle. He puts his arm around Ray's waist and twists him around so Ray's back is to him. He pulls Ray's pants down and begins to move his pelvis against him.*
>
> (194)

The visual text of their sexual encounter, which both men admit feels "quite natural" to them, overwrites the literary text. The men's sexual relationship and its power dynamics serve as context for the rest of the relationships in the play.

Helena, Joseph's daughter, enters immediately after the men have zipped up their pants. She is hysterical and needy, almost a parody of what a woman would be in Joseph and Ray's world, and Joseph arranges for Ray to marry her, clearly in order to watch over this ailing woman. The play focuses largely therein on Ray and Helena's inability to communicate and Ray's rise to power over Joseph. A series of Ray's dreams dominate the tableaux, including one in which Ray masturbates against his own image in the mirror while a woman yells angrily at him from another room, and another in which he demands, "Measure my cock" (206), to another unknown woman. Helena ends the play walking her father around the stage until "he becomes more and more debilitated [and] he falls to the ground inert and naked but for his shorts"; she concludes that, though her father knew that if he had a son he could have been "like you [Ray], distasteful in every way . . . he said that he still wished I had been a boy" (218). None of the relationships in this play exist independently of the primary relationship described by the image of the sexual exchange between Joseph and Ray.

A number of characters return for the final play, **Hunger**, compelling the spectator to seek out connections between the other plays, as a rhyme returns the reader to the word it echoes. **Hunger** is an emotionally tender narrative, marked by significantly less violence in the moment but also by the vexing depiction of the characters who have been permanently marred by the violence of the other vignettes from **What of the Night?** Charlie is now damaged, "a portly old man," "pensive," with "a scar on his forehead" (219). He does not recognize Birdie, his childhood girlfriend, but is drawn to her nonetheless. The sexual encounter in **Hunger** is tentative and tender. Charlie admires Birdie, now seventy-four. He takes her hand, she touches the side of his face, and he puts his arm around her waist and draws her to him: "I would like to know what it feels like to put my body against yours. I knew you'd feel fresh. Like water. Like I've had you in my arms" (225), he says. Though Birdie stops the embrace there, the tenderness of their union—this moment of articulated and imaged desire—pervades the rest of the drama, which offers the portrait of Ray reduced, like King Lear, to homelessness, rage, and fear. The play's final image is the foursome of Birdie, Charlie, Ray, and Ray's companion, Reba; Charlie wraps a blanket around Birdie's shoulder, Reba offers Birdie some sherry to help her ease her way into their world, and Ray, who had harmed Birdie back in **Lust,** "stretches his arm to her," sobbing (235).

An angel enters the abandoned warehouse that houses, and apparently will house forever, these sufferers. The angel too is impaired, "one of his wings is broken and hangs behind him" (219), and he walks, "shuffling his feet with short wide steps" (234). His gracelessness is accentuated by what he has brought to feed the characters; he spills his box full of animal entrails on the floor, and, like animals in turn, the four elderly characters kneel down to eat. Birdie, not yet inured to these victuals, gags and faints. Reba remarks:

> She's not used to this.—*[To the Angel.]* Next time would you bring her something she can eat? Something she likes. *[To Birdie.]* What would you like? . . . Bring her some bread and coffee and some juice and cream. . . . She should have some vegetables, carrot sticks! . . . And also a little red wine. . . . Or sherry's better, I think. . . . Would you like a little liqueur?

(235)

Reba is the one character in the final play of **What of the Night?** new to the drama. Her role is defined entirely as caretaker, first of Ray then of Birdie. She has a strength and endurance possible only by having not lived through the first three plays, by coming to life at the moment of her dramatic presence as a nurturer. But, kind as she is, she cannot conceal from the spectator that desire has been reduced to the simple if sensual need for food, as Reba articulates it and as the characters' postures, bent over that food, illustrate.

The repression of characters' desire in **What of the Night?** recalls the repression of **Conduct**'s Nena. Orlando's abuse of Nena in the basement restrains her growth; she remains a child, experiencing desire as a child will for little more than the company and safety available in the kitchen. In Nena, Fornes re-presents all of her victims: victims to others' abuse of power, victims to structures others have created as well as those to which the individual has contributed, to politics and to art. And, in Nena, Fornes

re-presents the vulnerability inherent to our theatrical lives. But, in her, Fornes also offers the power of a particular kind of spirit, naive maybe but optimistic enough, young enough, to be entrusted with even the most dangerous of our props and roles—the gun Leticia hands her, the story she asks her to tell.

* * *

The goal for perhaps all of Fornes's characters—from the somewhat two-dimensional characters of **Tango Palace** or **The Successful Life of 3** to the complex victimized victimizers of **The Conduct of Life** or **Mud**—is a health that can be characterized sexually, intellectually, and spiritually. To inhabit healthily the theatrical self can mean access to one's sexuality. Many of Fornes's characters seek specifically a sexual contentedness: Leopold, Dr. Kheal, She, Molly, Sarita, Fefu—there is at least one in virtually every play. The process toward that sexual contentedness is self-theatricalization, literally role-playing, performing, soliloquizing, displaying: theatrical seductions of other characters and members of the audience. In turn, a healthy sexuality—self love, in the final account—enables characters to find good roles to play, to rearrange their stages, to rewrite their dramas. Often these moments are the implied moments just beyond the play's end. This could be Nena's fate, Fefu's, Sarita's. And the spectator's.

As may well be said for all theater, the spectator is the final player in Fornes's theater. Sometimes the character of the audience is explicitly acknowledged by Fornes, but, even when that character is less explicit, the audience's role in the creation of the drama is manifest. Spectators play voyeurs in Fornes's drama; their roles as witnesses make them responsible for the turn of events.

The increasingly violent subtexts of Fornes's plays reflect not only the reality of our increasingly violent world but also the more subtle violence to the human spirit that this physical violence does. The transformation of Fornes's characters' sexuality, from She and 3's playfulness, for example, to Orlando's perversities, describes a sensual deadening. In her more recent work many of Fornes's characters die at their drama's end, presumably because by that point in their dramatic and theatrical narratives their bodies are only shells. Fornes's dramas increasingly link sex to violence, not in order to moralize but, rather, to re-present, with impact, the extent of human powers. Fornes's images of the potential violence of role-playing do not strike me as cynical. To the contrary, they are her version of the honest truth meant to spur her audience to action.

Fornes has exceptional respect for, and hence exceptionally high expectations of, her audience; she expects our relationships with her characters to be as honest as are her relationships with them. She expects us to learn from their mistakes. We are to take the theatrical presences of Fornes's characters literally, to locate ourselves within the theatrical presents of her dramas, and then to embrace her theatrical images as wonderfully, or dangerously, real.

NOTE

[1]An earlier version of *Nadine* was first performed as *The Mothers* at the Padua Hills Festival, Los Angeles, 31 July 1986. *Hunger* was first produced by Engarde Arts, New York City, 1 March 1988. *Springtime* and *Lust* and the four plays as a unit were first performed by the Milwaukee Repertory Theater as *And What of the Night?* 4 March 1989 (*Women on the Verge* 1993, 158).

FEFU AND HER FRIENDS

Beverly Byers Pevitts (essay date 1981)

SOURCE: "*Fefu and Her Friends*," in *Women in American Theatre: Careers, Images, Movements*, edited by Helen Krich Chinoy and Linda Walsh Jenkins, Crown Publishers, 1981, pp. 316-20.

[*In the following, which was first published in 1981, Pevitts reads* Fefu and Her Friends *as a feminist play.*]

Maria Irene Fornes explores basic feminist issues in her play, *Fefu and Her Friends.* Although set in 1935, the play explores lives of contemporary women. The sensibility, the subject matter, the "universal" female characters, and the very structure of the play are clearly feminist. The eight women's lives viewed in *Fefu* are seen, especially in the second part of the play, as being repetitive and capable of being viewed in any random sequence; yet even as women we do not respond negatively to this suggestion. In the very repetition of the four scenes that are played simultaneously we view intimately women's need for women. Although the title character says women need men because we cannot feel safe with each other, the other characters prove her wrong as they interact.

In *Fefu and Her Friends* Fornes defines what can happen when women recognize their own worth, and each other: "And if they shall recognize each other, the world will be blown apart." The play is a delicate piece on the surface and resilient underneath. It is fluid, structured like music, a "fugue," says the playwright. The play takes place in an affluent New England home in 1935. Eight female characters are introduced: they discuss woman's loathsomeness, settle relationships among themselves, rehearse speeches, and recount visions. Fornes's nonstereotypical characters speak as selves, not in roles of mother, daughter, bitch, witch, or virgin. She breathes into her characters humor and intelligence. The loving of one's self and the despising of one's self are both examined as well as woman's inclination *not* to trust other women. Fornes calls the play totally female, "it's so profoundly us."

Women find themselves in a familiar world in this play in which characters and character relationships mean more than plot, and structure is more important than character. The audience viewing the play is brought into the play as they are moved from room to room of the house. The opening and closing scenes are played in the living room of Fefu's home, but the four scenes played within this framework, Part Two, are played simultaneously in four different rooms. The cyclical four scenes reveal the characters tenderly interacting, bound up in each other's lives. By moving to the characters' spaces, the audience knows the reason(s) all eight of these women are getting together. One discovers intimately with the performers "how woman feels about being a woman."

Fornes builds the play like an architect, with a sense of progress and a sense of performance:

> A playwright has to have a very abstract mind and has to see a play like an architect. One has to see the whole building and also structure and foundations and how these things are made and see it so it doesn't fall apart. . . . The novel is more delicate, the construction of a play is "tougher."

Fefu is cinematic, in both structure and acting style. The framework of Part One and Part Three contains all of the characters. The four scenes with simultaneous life, Part Two, that nest between the two framework parts, contain within each scene only two or three characters interacting. These "substance scenes" present not plot but character development and relationships. The play incorporates stop action, jump cuts, and replay as the audience moves from room to room to room to see each of the four scenes in Part Two. As one flows from space to space, and as each scene is repeated four times, the rooms have simultaneous life. The scenes and the parts of the play are interrelated by accretion of the whole. The through line of action, the passage of time, is merely the sequence of events. The women arrive, they greet each other in Part One. They separate, they read, they share, they rest, they discuss, they play croquet in the second part. Part One is morning, Part Two is afternoon, and Part Three is early evening and contains the climactic event scene.

There are five different environments. Experiencing the play, kinesthetically moving from room to room, becomes more important than following a story. In a proscenium setting the audience has a fixed perspective. In *Fefu* the audience moves about the rooms of the house. The movement is special because the audience is enclosed with the performers within the four walls. The audience is on only two sides of the rooms in the four simultaneous scenes in Part Two, and when the audience looks at the performers they do not see other audience members behind the players. It is, as Fornes expressed it, rather like being a witness. The audience is experientially involved in the play, not following a linear story. Instead, they overhear conversations, witness a series of encounters.

Scenes are intricately interwoven. Cindy and Christina are in the study through which Sue passes on her way with the soup to Julia's bedroom where Julia lies in bed hallucinating. Paula and Cecilia revive and resolve an old relationship in the kitchen while Fefu and Emma play croquet on the lawn. The linkage of the four scenes is both linear and vertical. A rhythm of involvement and disengagement works through all six scenes of the play. Fefu, like Sue, weaves through two other areas of the four playing areas during the four simultaneous scenes. These two characters link the scenes through all of Part Two. Fefu moves through the study/living room to the kitchen for lemonade and back out to the lawn. The fourth (last) time she takes other characters with her while Paula moves to the study/living room to play the piano.

In the third part of the play, the audience comes together again as a whole after having viewed the four separate groups while each of the scenes played four times. "If the timing is not impeccable there will be no scene," says Fornes. If someone other than Fornes were to direct the play, she thinks it would be very difficult to do unless it were thought of as music. She also comments,

> Style is different in the first and third scenes from the style in the center of the play. These scenes are more theatrical in style and take on a larger life. The shape that a play of mine takes has to do with my own need for a certain creative output.

Fornes says that with plot we are concerned with the mechanics of how we manage in the world, so play without plot deals with the mechanics of the mind, some kind of spiritual survival, a process of thought. The temporal awareness of the characters is related to the segmentation of the play's structure. The audience is pulled into this play that is as fluid and free as water. They are captured in its depth perceptually and physically by moving to the characters' spaces as well as by perceiving them visually and aurally.

The central scene of the play is Julia's hallucinating scene in bed in Part Two. It is a moving scene in which the character speaks clearly thoughts many women know.

> The human being is of the masculine gender. The human being is a boy as a child and grown up he is a man. Everything on earth is for the human being, which is man. . . . Woman is not a human being. She is: 1—A mystery. 2—Another species. 3—As yet undefined. 4—Unpredictable; therefore wicked and gentle and evil and good which is evil.—If a man commits an evil act, he must be pitied. The evil comes from outside him, through him and into the act. Woman generated the evil herself.—God gave man no other mate but woman . . .—Man is spiritually sexual, he therefore can enjoy sexuality. His sexuality is physical which means his spirit is pure. Women's spirit is sexual . . . Their sexual feelings remain with them till they die. And they take those feelings with them to the afterlife where they corrupt the heavens, and they are sent to hell where through suffering they may shed those feelings and return to earth as man.

Julia's thesis in *Fefu* is "the mind like the body is made to suffer to such a degree as to become crippled."

In the opening scene of *Fefu,* the title character points out that "women are loathsome." She gives the proof by reasoning the rational male way, by comparing woman to a rock that on the exterior "is smooth and dry and clean" and is on the internal, interior, underneath side "slimy, filled with fungus and crawling with worms." This represents, she says, "another life that is parallel to the one we manifest." She continues, "If you don't recognize it . . . it eats you." The exterior appearance of woman and the interior appearance of woman can be readily compared to the image woman has been made into—the commercial view of the world (provided by men) into which women re-create their own images already created for them. The two sides of the rock represent how women feel about the image that has been created of them. And if we (women) do not realize it and recognize it, the underneath side does rot with the fungus and worms found there. If we do recognize this image, as Fefu later tells us, if we recognize ourselves as women, "the world will be blown apart." When this does happen, the reflection that was made by others will be destroyed and we will be able to rebuild ourselves in our own image, created by woman. The character Julia, trapped and oppressed, who at one point of her life was "afraid of nothing," and "knew so much" that the others wondered how one so young could know so much, is the character who is symbolically killed in the end of the play so that the new image of herself can emerge.

For many women becoming a feminist has caused a personal transformation. *Fefu* and some of the other contemporary plays by women concern themselves with the expression of this transformation, the transformation of the personal into mythos. Playwright Tina Howe suggests:

> If a woman really explored the areas that make her unique as a woman, was radical in her femininity, the commercial theatre would be terrified. For a woman to deal artistically with her womanhood is a dangerous territory and hard to write. I keep a distance from the more radical feelings I have as a woman, partly from the fear I have of being stoned to death and partly because those feelings are very personal. I'm not so sure I could handle them, but I think it's high time someone did.

Plays by women playwrights are coming to have a feminist consciousness. Whether the writers actively intend their work to reveal this or not, the experience of coming to know the truth about one's self and one's society is revealed in plays by women. Maria Irene Fornes says that *Fefu and Her Friends* is a feminist play.

> The play is about women. It's a play that deals with each one of these women with enormous tenderness and affection. I have not deliberately attempted to see these women "as women have rarely been seen before." I show the women as I see them and if it is different from the way they've been seen before, it's because that's how I see them. The play is not fighting anything, not negating anything. My intention has not been to confront anything. I felt as I wrote the play that I was surrounded by friends. I felt very happy to have such good and interesting friends.

Fornes says her plays are not "idea plays," neither do they, as the playwright says, "present a formulated thesis." This play with no walls takes on the fragility of fine, thin, hand-blown crystal. Fornes says that in the process of auditioning extremely talented people she came to view the play as if it had glass walls and that she felt some of these people would break the walls. When she views plays far away from herself, she says the characters become two dimensional, that they are like drawings rather than like flesh and blood. In a realistic play one can feel the characters "breathe"; in a more abstract play it is the play that breathes, not the characters. In *Fefu and Her Friends* the characters "breathe"; it is an extraordinary play because it explores some of the very basic fears and issues of feminist sensibilities and yet it is a personal feminist statement. Maria Irene Fornes's play is as fluid as water, as fragile as breakable glass, and as durable as the metaphoric rock.

Penny Farfan (essay date 1997)

SOURCE: "Feminism, Metatheatricality, and *Mise-en-scène* in Maria Irene Fornes's *Fefu and Her Friends*," in Modern Drama, Vol. XL, No. 4, Winter 1997, pp. 442-53.

[*In the following essay, Farfan maintains that, for Fornes, there exists an "organic relationship" between the writing and the directing of her plays.*]

The first time that Maria Irene Fornes attended a rehearsal of one of her plays, she was amazed to be informed by the director that she should not communicate her ideas about staging directly to the actors but should instead make written notes that they would discuss together over coffee after rehearsal. This exclusion of the playwright from the rehearsal process seemed to Fornes "like the most absurd thing in the world."[1] As she later commented,

It's as if you have a child, your own baby, and you take the baby to school and the baby is crying and the teacher says, "Please I'll take care of it. Make a note: at the end of the day you and I can talk about it." You'd think 'This woman is crazy. I'm not going to leave my kid here with this insane person.'[2]

Since her initial theatrical experience, Fornes has directed many of the first productions of her own work, having resolved that if she did not direct, the "work would not be done" at all.[3] She has "never [seen] any difference between writing and directing"[4] and for this reason she rarely goes into rehearsal with a completed script in hand.[5]

The organic relationship between dramaturgy and *mise-en-scène* in Fornes's work is perhaps nowhere more evident than in her 1977 play *Fefu and Her Friends,* in the middle section of which the audience is divided into quarters, taken out of the main auditorium, and rotated through four intimate playing areas representing rooms in Fefu's house, where the actresses simultaneously repeat interlocking yet distinct scenes four times, once for each section of the

audience. Fornes arrived at this unique staging by chance while she was looking for a space in which to present her as-yet-unfinished play:

I did not like the space I found because it had large columns. But then I was taken backstage to the rooms the audience could not see. I saw the dressing room, and I thought, "How nice. This could be a room in Fefu's house." Then I was taken to the greenroom. I thought that this also could be a room in Fefu's house. Then we went to the business office to discuss terms. That office was the study of Fefu's house . . . I asked if we could use all of their rooms for the performances, and they agreed.

I had written Julia's speech in the bedroom already. I had intended to put it on stage and I had not yet arrived at how it would come about. Part of the kitchen scene was written, but I had thought it would be happening in the living room. So I had parts of it already. It was the rooms themselves that modified the scenes which originally I planned to put in the living room.

People asked me, when the play opened, if I had written those scenes to be done in different rooms and then found the space. No. They were written that way because the space was there.[6]

Yet while Fornes attributes the staging of *Fefu and Her Friends* to chance, she has also stated, "When something happens by accident, I trust that the play is making its own point. I feel something is happening that is very profound and very important."[7] Indeed, as I will argue here, in reconfiguring the conventional performer-spectator relationship, Fornes's *mise-en-scène* in *Fefu and Her Friends* realizes in theatrical terms an alternative model for interaction with the universe external to the self such as that proposed by the metatheatrical actress/educator-character Emma as a means of transforming Fefu's pain. In this respect, *Fefu and Her Friends* posits postmodern feminist theatre practice as a constructive response to the psychic dilemmas of the play's female characters. As Emma says, "Life is theatre. Theatre is life. If we're showing what life is, can be, we must do theatre."[8]

Set in New England in 1935, *Fefu and Her Friends* involves eight women who seem to share a common educational background and who gather at Fefu's house to prepare for what seems to be a fundraising project relating to education. One of these women, Julia, suffers from a mysterious and apparently psychosomatic illness that became evident a year earlier when she collapsed after a hunter shot a deer. She has not walked since and still occasionally blanks out. Alone in her bedroom in Part Two, Julia undergoes a long hallucination punctuated by threats and blows from invisible "judges" who seem to epitomize patriarchal authority (33-6). During the course of her hallucination, she reveals that the onset of her illness was a punishment for having got "too smart" and that the conditions of her survival were to become crippled and to remain silent about what she knows. Even now, however, though she attempts to appease the judges by reciting a creed of the central tenets of patriarchal ideology, Julia remains covertly but essentially defiant and unindoctrinated, challenging conventional wisdom relating to women and attempting to get the judges off the trail of her friend Fefu, who is also considered to be "too smart" (34). Thus, in the 1930s context in which the play is set, Julia's physical symptoms both express and suppress her resistance to women's subordination within patriarchal society, as did those of the "smart" female hysterics treated by Sigmund Freud, Josef Breuer, and others around the turn of the century.[9]

Described by Fornes as "the mind of the play—the seer, the visionary,"[10] Julia herself implies that her insights into the patriarchal construction of female inferiority are repressed common knowledge when she states at the end of her Part Two monologue, "They say when I believe the prayer I will forget the judges. And when I forget the judges I will believe the prayer. They say both happen at once. *And all women have done it.* Why can't I?" (35, emphasis added). Julia's connection to the other characters in the play is borne out by the simultaneous staging of Part Two, when, at the same time that she is in the bedroom reciting the patriarchal creed under threat of violence from invisible tormentors, Paula is in the kitchen describing the pain of breaking up with her lover Cecilia, Cindy is in the study recounting a nightmare about an abusive male doctor, and Emma and Fefu are on the lawn discussing Emma's obsession with genitals and Fefu's "constant pain" (29). Fornes's sense of the appropriateness of a certain amount of sound-spill between the various playing areas in Part Two suggests that Julia's forbidden knowledge functions as the intermittently or partially audible subtext underlying all the characters' interactions, which have been described by W.B. Worthen as "transformations of Julia's more explicit subjection."[11]

The connection between Julia and the other characters is confirmed in Part Three of *Fefu and Her Friends* when the women reminisce about their college days in terms that resonate with and confirm the reality of her hallucinations: female intelligence is associated in these recollections with madness, while college professors and doctors are represented as actual versions of Julia's hallucinated judges and are referred to similarly, by means of the pronoun "they" (55-66). Elaine Showalter has written that "hysteria and feminism . . . exist on a kind of continuum" and that "[i]f we see the hysterical woman as one end of the spectrum of a female avant-garde struggling to redefine women's place in the social order, then we can also see feminism as the other end of the spectrum, the alternative to hysterical silence, and the determination to speak and act for women in the public world."[12] The common educational background of the women in *Fefu and Her Friends* signifies their shared experience of the pressure to become indoctrinated into the system of beliefs outlined in Julia's prayer. At the same time, the reunion of these women on the basis of their ongoing commitment to education may suggest a fundamental concern on Fornes's part with representing characters engaged in the project of researching alternative modes of response to the knowledge

articulated by the hysteric Julia as "the mind of the play." In this sense, the term *Lehrstück* or "learning play" that Bonnie Marranca has used to describe Fornes's 1987 work *Abingdon Square* is applicable to *Fefu and Her Friends* as well.[13]

Julia aligns herself explicitly with Fefu, implying that she also is too smart and is therefore in similar danger of punishment by the judges; and indeed, of all the characters in the play, Fefu is most directly involved in the struggle that has left Julia crippled. Fefu is married to a man she claims to need and desire, but who has told her that he "[married her] to have a constant reminder of how loathsome women are" and who engages her in a terrible "game" whereby he falls to the ground after she shoots at him with a rifle that has thus far been loaded with blanks but that he has threatened one day to load with a real bullet (7, 11-13). Fefu's interest in the male-associated activities of shooting and plumbing and her assertions that she "like[s] men better than women" and that she "like[s] being . . . thinking . . . [f]eeling like a man" (15) indicate that her strategy for coping with the pain of her marriage is male-identification, but this mode of response is problematized by the presence of female friends who cause her to confront the patriarchal construction of female inferiority. In the opening scene, for example, Cindy forces Fefu to acknowledge a discrepancy between what her husband Phillip says about women being "loathsome" and what she herself knows of women based on her own personal experience (7-9). This invalidation of her posture of male-identification makes being around women a dangerous situation for Fefu. As she states in Part One,

> Women are restless with each other. They are like live wires . . . either chattering to keep themselves from making contact, or else, if they don't chatter, they avert their eyes . . . like Orpheus . . . as if a god once said"and if they shall recognize each other, the world will be blown apart." They are always eager for the men to arrive. When they do, they can put themselves at rest, tranquilized and in a mild stupor. With the men they feel safe. The danger is gone. That's the closest they can be to feeling wholesome. Men are muscle that cover the raw nerve. They are the insulators. The danger is gone, but the price is the mind and the spirit . . . High price.—I've never understood it. Why?—What is feared?—Hmmm. Well . . .—Do you know? Perhaps the heavens would fall.
>
> (15)

The devastating recognition scene that this speech anticipates occurs near the end of the play when, in a moment that may support Julia's assertion that "[h]allucinations are real" (44), Fefu "sees" Julia walking and understands that her illness is a psychosomatic response to an insight that she will not or cannot communicate except through the hysterical paralysis of her body (55). Unaccepting of what she perceives as Julia's passive and voluntary submission, Fefu tries to force her to her feet to fight and then takes action herself, exiting to the lawn with the now-loaded rifle. Like the hunter who shot a deer and mysteriously injured Julia, Fefu now shoots a rabbit and Julia once more suffers the wound, which this time may be fatal (59-61).

Beverley Byers Pevitts has argued that the death of Julia signifies the symbolic killing off of woman as created by the dominant culture in order to enable the emergence of a new self-determined female identity,[14] yet Fornes's assertion that her characters should not be seen as symbolic or representative figures makes Pevitts's positive interpretation of the ambiguous ending of *Fefu and Her Friends* problematic.[15] With regard to this question of the play's ending, Fornes's starting premises for her work on *Fefu* may perhaps be instructive. By her own account, she began writing the play with two "fantasy" images in mind. The first image was of a "woman . . . who was talking to some friends [and then] took her rifle and shot her husband"; the second was a joke involving "two Mexicans speaking at a bullfight. One says to the other, 'She is pretty, that one over there.' The other one says, 'Which one?' So the first one takes his rifle and shoots her. He says, 'That one, the one that falls.'"[16] In the completed play, Fornes has brought these two starting premises together so that, however indirectly, Fefu shoots Julia rather than her husband Phillip and, in doing so, takes the place of the men in the "joke" who objectify women to the point of annihilation. Notably, in Part One of the play, Julia remarks of Fefu's use of the gun, "She's hurting herself" (22); inasmuch as taking up the gun is a male-associated strategy of domination, Julia's observation is correct.[17] In this *Lehrstück*, then, Fefu's male-identification is ultimately as self-destructive and ineffectual a strategy of resistance to women's subordination within patriarchal culture as Julia's hysteria.

After Fefu and Julia, the actress-educator character Emma may be of greatest significance in the play, her metatheatrical status serving to call attention to the transformative potential of performance that Fornes herself explores through her *mise-en-scène*. Emma's somewhat comical admission to Fefu that she "think[s] about genitals all the time" and that she is amazed that "people act as if they don't have genitals" (27) may signify an intuitive awareness on her part of the operation of a sex/gender system that naturalizes culturally constructed gender norms by obscuring their superimposition on sexed bodies, yet her involvement in the struggle that is at the heart of the play is less explicit and direct than that of either of the two main characters. Subsequent to their discussion of genitals, Fefu confides to Emma that she is living in a frightening state of "constant pain" that is "not physical" and is "not sorrow" (29) but that is threatening to overwhelm her. She associates this pain with a black stray cat that has been "coming to [her] kitchen":

> He's awfully mangled and big. He is missing an eye and his skin is diseased. At first I was repelled by him, but then, I thought, this is a monster that has been sent to me and I must feed him. And I fed him. One day he came and shat all over my kitchen. Foul diarrhoea. He still comes and I still feed him.—I am afraid of him.
>
> (29)

Left alone on stage, Emma responds to this story by *"improvis[ing] an effigy of Fefu"* and reciting before it Shakespeare's Sonnet 14:

> Not from the stars do I my judgment pluck.
> And yet methinks I have astronomy;
> But not to tell of good or evil luck,
> Of plagues, of dearths, or seasons' quality;
> Nor can I fortune to brief minutes tell,
> Pointing to each his thunder, rain, and wind,
> Or say with princes if it shall go well
> By oft predict that I in heaven find.
> But from thine eyes my knowledge I derive
> And, constant stars, in them I read such art
> As truth and beauty shall together thrive
> If from thyself to store thou wouldst convert:
> Or else of thee this I prognosticate,
> Thy end is truth's and beauty's doom and date.
>
> (29)

Through this brief performance, Emma attempts to counteract Fefu's superstitiously passive submission to the black cat as an ominous manifestation of some negative external force that has control over her fortunes, reciting Shakespeare's words to assert Fefu's own power to transform the world outside herself actively by using her inner resources to reproduce in it her own version of reality. Emma thus introduces performance as a potentially constructive mode of response to the forces that oppress Fefu and that she accepts as her lot in her own form of paralysis; for as Assunta Kent has pointed out, Fefu's unwillingness "to risk losing all the old familiar constraints and habits"—her dependence on a husband who finds her and all women "loathsome"—is ultimately as crippling as Julia's hysteria, "[reducing Fefu's] potentially revolutionary ideas to shocking comments" and "[making] a game of her hostility toward her distant husband."[18]

Emma's views on the transformative potential of performance are clarified through her dramatization in Part Three of an extraordinary and mystical passage from a 1917 book by Emma Sheridan Fry entitled *Educational Dramatics* (*Fefu,* n 46). In this passage, Fry argues that instead of shutting ourselves off from the vast realm of experience that the forces of "[e]nvironment" represent as they seek entry into our beings, we should embrace these forces, confident in the knowledge "that 'all' is ours, and that whatever anyone has ever known, or may ever have or know, we will call and claim." According to Fry, we are "[a] creation of God's consciousness coming now slowly and painfully into recognition of ourselves," and "[c]ivilization" is as yet "[a] circumscribed order in which the whole has not entered." In meeting Environment as "our true mate that clamors for our reunion,"

[we] will seize all, learn all, know all here, that we may fare further on the great quest! The task of Now is only a step toward the task of the Whole! Let us then seek the laws governing real life forces, that coming into their own, they may create, develop and reconstruct. Let us awaken life dormant! Let us, boldly, seizing the star of our intent, lift it as the lantern of our necessity, and let it shine over the darkness of our compliance.

(47-8)

Notably, the first name of Fornes's actress-character echoes that of the author of this passage, yet her last name is given as Blake so that she cannot be interpreted as a fictionalized version of Fry (46). Through her performance of Fry's text, then, Emma exemplifies the active response to the environment that Fry proposes, taking the text into herself yet at the same time transforming it so that its call for a subject who will break out of a socially conditioned and compliant relation to a male-personified environment in order to come to a new state of consciousness resonates with the feminist thematics that underlie Fornes's play, where the two main characters are in different ways paralyzed by internalized oppression.[19]

The performance model that Emma advocates and enacts through her representation of Fry's text is analogous to Fornes's *mise-en-scène*, and this analogy in turn casts the *mise-en-scène* in implicitly feminist terms. Feminist performance theorists such as Jill Dolan and Elin Diamond have drawn on the work of film theorist Laura Mulvey to argue that women traditionally have been positioned as objects of the male gaze in theatrical representation.[20] However, while Fornes's image of the man at the bullfight who identifies the woman he desires by gunning her down suggests a fundamental resistance to this objectifying male gaze, W.B. Worthen's reading of *Fefu and Her Friends* as a critique of "the gender dynamics implicit in the realistic perspective" in which Fornes "unseat[s] the spectator of 'realism'" in order to "dramatiz[e] 'his' controlling authority over the construction of stage gender" is more problematic.[21] More specifically, Worthen's argument relies on the notion that "[t]he action of [the play] takes place under the watchful eyes of Phillip, of the hunter, of Julia's 'guardians,'" as well as of the spectator, who, as yet "another invisible voyeur," is aligned with Julia's "unseen, coercive tormentors."[22] In endowing non-characters with offstage dramatic presence in order to consider how Fornes *de*constructs the role of the spectator in realism, Worthen shifts his focus away from the characters onstage and, in doing so, neglects to take fully into account how Emma's metatheatrical discourse advocating an active new relation to the environment applies to Fornes's *re*construction of the spectator that she brings into the world of the play.[23]

Fornes has stated of *Fefu and Her Friends* that she "expected that the audience would feel as if they are really visiting people in their house,"[24] but the "nice middle-class girls from Connecticut"[25] who in this sense play hostess to the audience defy conventional representations of femininity by setting the terms of their guests' entertainment.

Thus, the simultaneous staging and sound spill in Part Two provide spectators with a theatrical experience that corresponds with the characters' own experience of the intrusion into consciousness of critical feminist insights. Moreover, spectators drawn deliberately into the world of the play are cast less as Julia's judges, as Worthen has argued, than as her confidants, the community she feels she needs to join with her in hallucinating if she is to avoid "perishing" (44). Cecilia says at the beginning of Part Three of *Fefu,* "We cannot survive in a vacuum. We must be part of a community, perhaps 10, 100, 1000"; notably, it is Fefu's refusal to enter into Julia's hallucinatory world to see what it is she sees that causes her to fire her fatal shot and thereby to replicate the man in the joke that was the starting premise for the play. Working against objectification through her reconfiguration of the actor/spectator relationship and her manipulation of aesthetic distance, Fornes fosters community by facilitating identification. At the same time, however, she insists on the need to recognize difference within community by representing multiple and simultaneous perspectives on—and/or versions of—the action in Part Two. As Cecilia concludes, "the concern of the educator [is] to teach how to be sensitive to the differences in ourselves as well as outside ourselves, not to supervise the memorization of facts. [. . .] Otherwise the unusual in us will perish. As we grow we feel we are strange and fear any thought that is not shared with everyone" (44).

Fornes's *mise-en-scène* literalizes philosopher María Lugones's metaphor of "'world'-travelling" as the process by which identification—and therefore identity—is constituted. "[T]he failure to identify" is, for Lugones, "the failure to see oneself in [others] who are quite different from oneself."[26] Describing her own experience of alienation from her mother, Lugones recalls the necessity of ceasing to see "through arrogant eyes":

> Loving my mother also required that I see with her eyes, that I go into my mother's world, that I see both of us as we are constructed in her world, that I witness her own sense of herself from within her world. Only through this travelling to her "world" could I identify with her because only then could I cease to ignore her and to be excluded and separate from her. Only then could I see her as a subject even if one subjected and only then could I see how meaning could arise fully between us.[27]

As Lugones concludes, "travelling to someone's 'world' is a way of identifying with them . . . because by travelling to their 'world' we can understand *what it is to be them and what it is to be ourselves in their eyes.* Only when we have travelled to each other's 'worlds' are we fully subjects to each other."[28] The identification process that Lugones is concerned with "is of great interest" to Fornes as well; as she has rather amusingly stated,

> it is through identification that we learn to become whole human beings. . . .
>
> [If] we do not allow our imagination to receive the experiences of others because they are of a different

gender, we will shrivel and decay, and our spirit will become a dry prune and we will become ill and die and we will not go to heaven because in heaven they do not allow dry prunes.[29]

Elin Diamond has pointed out that the process of identification that is constitutive of identity implies at the same time transformation of the self by the other and is thus radically destabilizing, so that "[t]he humanist notion of identity as a model that the self enacts over time—that is unique, unified, coherent, and consistent—is belied precisely by the temporality, the specific historicity of the identification process."[30] In the production of *Fefu* at the American Place Theatre in 1978, after moving audience members into the world of the characters in Part Two, Fornes returned them to seats other than those that they had occupied at the start of the play,[31] a literal shifting suggestive of the transformative potential that Diamond maintains is inherent in the act of identification that Lugones calls "world-travelling."

I have argued that the metatheatrical dimensions of *Fefu and Her Friends* implicate Fornes's *mise-en-scène* as a constructive response to the feminist problematics that generate the play's action.[32] Fornes's own account of the reception of the 1978 production indicates the tenacity of conventional identification patterns, however, and raises questions about the effectiveness of *Fefu and Her Friends* as feminist theatre. As Fornes recalls, "a lot of the men" who stayed on for post-show discussions at the American Place Theatre

> wanted to know where the men in the play were; they wanted to know whether the women were married. They insisted on relating to the men in this play, which had no male characters. If the name of a man was mentioned that was the person they wanted to identify with. There was a man who thought the play was about Phillip (he is the husband of the central character and he never appears on stage nor is he very much talked about).[33]

There is a utopian quality to the metatheatrical character Emma's envisioning of the total integration of subject and environment in a less "circumscribed" civilization of the future, and the failure of identification evident in Fornes's account of the early reception of *Fefu and Her Friends* suggests that, like the feminist critical writing that Tania Modleski has described, the play that was first staged in 1977 and that is now a foundational text in feminist theatre was "simultaneously performative and utopian, pointing toward the freer world it [was] in the process of inaugurating."[34] I will close, then, by reiterating Emma's statement on the potential of theatre to effect social transformation: "Life is theatre. Theatre is life. If we're showing what life is, *can be*, we must do theatre" (22, emphasis added).

NOTES

[1]Maria Irene Fornes, "Seeing with Clarity: The Visions of Maria Irene Fornes," interview by Scott Cummings, *Theater* (Yale), 17:1 (1985), 52.

[2]Ibid.

[3]Maria Irene Fornes, interview, in *Interviews with Contemporary Women Playwrights*, by Kathleen Betsko and Rachel Koenig (New York, 1987), 159.

[4]Fornes, "Seeing with Clarity," 52. See note 1.

[5]Maria Irene Fornes, interview, *In Their Own Words: Contemporary American Playwrights*, by David Savran (New York, 1988), 60. Fornes states in this interview that she finished writing *Fefu and Her Friends* only three days before the show opened (60).

[6]María Irene Fornés, "'I write these messages that come,'" *The Drama Review* 21:4 (1977), 35-7. [Following her first published anthology Fornes has dropped the use of accents in the name.]

[7]Ibid., 37-8.

[8]Maria Irene Fornes, *Fefu and Her Friends* (New York, 1978), 22. Subsequent references appear parenthetically in the text.

[9]Elaine Showalter has noted that many turn-of-the-century female psychiatric patients were better educated and more intellectual than was customary for women of their day and that their unconventionality in this respect was perceived by male doctors to be related to their disorders. *The Female Malady: Women, Madness, and English Culture, 1830-1980* (New York, 1985), 145-64.

[10]Maria Irene Fornes, interview by Bonnie Marranca, *Performing Arts Journal* 2:3 (1978), 107.

[11]Maria Irene Fornes, interview by Allen Frame, *Bomb: A Tri Quarterly on Art, Fiction, Theatre and Film*, 10 (Fall 1984), 28; W.B. Worthen, "Still Playing Games: Ideology and Performance in the Theater of Maria Irene Fornes," in *Feminine Focus: The New Women Playwrights*, ed. Enoch Brater (New York, 1989), 177.

[12]Showalter, 161. See note 9.

[13]Bonnie Marranca, "The State of Grace: Maria Irene Fornes at Sixty-Two," *Performing Arts Journal*, 14:2 (1992), 25.

[14]Beverley Byers Pevitts, *"Fefu and Her Friends,"* *Women in American Theatre: Careers, Images, Movements: An Illustrated Anthology and Sourcebook*, ed. Helen Krich Chinoy and Linda Walsh Jenkins (New York, 1981), 318-19.

[15]See Fornes, interview by Marranca, 106. See note 10. For a similar critique of Pevitts's interpretation, see Assunta Bartolomucci Kent, *Maria Irene Fornes and Her Critics* (Westport, CT, 1996) 126-66. My analysis of *Fefu* shares several points of convergence with Kent's but differs in its emphasis on metatheatricality and *mise-en-scène*.

[16]Fornes, "'I write these messages,'" 30. See note 5. In a panel discussion published as "Women in the Theatre" in *Centerpoint: A Journal of Interdisciplinary Studies* 3:3-4 (1980), Fornes further stated, "I started [*Fefu and Her Friends*] because I had six dresses that I bought in a thrift shop, 1930s dresses, chiffon, lovely. I wanted to write a play about women so I could use these dresses. But the dresses were never used for this production; they were used for another one. So, the play started as one about women" (36).

[17]On this point of the gun, it may be worth noting that, according to David Savran, the only play that Fornes had read up to the time she wrote her first play *Tango Palace* was Ibsen's *Hedda Gabler*. See Savran, introduction to Fornes, interview, *In Their Own Words*, 51. See note 5. The title character commits suicide with the gun she has inherited from her father General Gabler. Hedda's death is the result of two contradictory aspects of a patriarchal legacy that has unsuited her for conventional feminine roles but has at the same time left her unable to envision for herself a viable alternative.

[18]Kent, 131. See note 15.

[19]While my analysis focuses on Julia, Fefu, and Emma, the metaphor of paralysis may also be extended to the other characters in the play. Worthen 176, see note 11; Kent 144, see note 15; and Deborah R. Geis, "Wordscapes of the Body: Performative Language as *Gestus* in Maria Irene Fornes's Plays," *Theatre Journal*, 42:3 (1990), 297.

[20]Laura Mulvey, "Visual Pleasure and Narrative Cinema," *Art after Modernism: Rethinking Representation*, ed. Brian Wallis (New York, 1984) 361-73; Jill Dolan, *The Feminist Spectator as Critic* (Ann Arbor, 1988) and "Desire Cloaked in a Trenchcoat," *Presence and Desire: Essays on Gender, Sexuality, Performance* (Ann Arbor, 1993) 121-34; and Elin Diamond, "Brechtian Theory/Feminist Theory: Toward a Gestic Feminist Criticism," *TDR*, 32:1 (1988), 83, 89.

[21]Worthen, 175. See note 11.

[22]Worthen, 177, 179. See note 11.

[23]For a related critique of Worthen's analysis, see Kent 134-36. See note 15.

[24]Fornes, interview by Marranca, 108. See note 10.

[25]Fornes, interview, in *Contemporary Women Playwrights*. See note 3.

[26]María Lugones, "Playfulness, 'World'-Travelling, and Loving Perception," *Making Face, Making Soul: Haciendo Caras: Creative and Critical Perspectives by Women of Color*, ed. Gloria Anzaldúa (San Francisco, 1990), 393.

[27]Ibid., 394.

[28]Ibid., 401.

[29]Maria Irene Fornes, "The 'Woman' Playwright Issue," ed. Gayle Austin, *Performing Arts Journal* 7:3 (1983), 90.

[30]Elin Diamond, "The Violence of 'We': Politicizing Identification," *Critical Theory and Performance*, ed. Janelle G. Reinelt and Joseph R. Roach (Ann Arbor, 1992), 396.

[31]See Walter Kerr, "Two Plays Swamped by Metaphors," review of *Fefu and Her Friends* at the American Place, *New York Times* (22 January 1978), D3.

[32]My argument is perhaps further substantiated by the fact that, according to Assunta Kent, the characters and "interpersonal dynamics" depicted in *Fefu* were "based in part" on Fornes's observations of the "short-lived" Women's Theater Council, which she co-founded with avant-garde women theatre artists Megan Terry, Rosalyn Drexler, Rochelle Owens, Julie Bovasso, and Adrienne Kennedy (121, 114, 211). See note 15.

[33]Fornes, "'Woman' Playwright Issue," 90-1. See note 29.

[34]Tania Modleski, *Feminism Without Women: Culture and Criticism in a "Postfeminist" Age* (New York, 1991), 48.

FURTHER READING

Betsko, Kathleen, and Rachel Koenig. "Maria Irene Fornes." In *Interviews with Contemporary Women Playwrights*, pp. 154-67. New York: Beech Tree Books, 1987.
    Conversation in which Fornes talks about her methods of constructing and directing her plays, the "female aesthetic" in drama, and other topics.

Chaudhuri, Una. "Maria Irene Fornes." In *Speaking on Stage: Interviews with Contemporary American Playwrights*, ed. Philip C. Kolin and Colby H. Kullman, pp. 98-114. Tuscaloosa: University of Alabama Press, 1996.
    Interview in which Fornes discusses her dramaturgy and the reception and interpretation of her works.

Gargano, Cara. "The Starfish and the Strange Attractor: Myth, Science, and Theatre as Laboratory in Maria Irene Fornes' *Mud*." *New Theatre Quarterly* XIII, No. 51 (August 1997): 214-20.
    Argues that in *Mud* Fornes "uses the theatrical space as her laboratory—a place to explore the interface between our society's construction of the world and our evolving artistic and scientific vision."

Geis, Deborah R. "Wordscapes of the Body: Performative Language as *Gestus* in Maria Irene Fornes's Plays." *Theatre Journal* 42, No. 3 (October 1990): 291-307.
    Analyzes Fornes' plays from the perspective of the "fragmentation" of signification between "the languages of the body . . . and the spoken language of the character."

Keyssar, Helene. "Drama and the Dialogic Imagination: *The Heidi Chronicles* and *Fefu and Her Friends*." *Modern Drama* XXXIV, No. 1 (March 1991): 88-106.
    Investigates the collision of voices or points of view in *Fefu and Her Friends*. "The World that Fornes has created in *Fefu*," Keyssar argues, "is one in which not only Julia and Fefu herself but each of the women struggles with her own voice and brings into the conversation the diverse historical elements of her own linguistic consciousness."

Koppen, Randi. "Formalism and the Return to the Body: Stein's and Fornes's Aesthetic of Significant Form." *New Literary History* 28, No. 4 (Autumn 1997): 791-809.
    Contends that in Fornes' work, as in Gertrude Stein's, "it is precisely the attention to and foregrounding of form which suspends one kind of viewing (abstracting, masterful) and institutes another, one which is intimate, attentive, and meditative."

Marranca, Bonnie. "The State of Grace: Maria Irene Fornes at Sixty-Two." *Performing Arts Journal* XIV, No. 2 (May 1992): 24-31.
    Appreciation of Fornes that considers her an "unabashed moralist" and *Abingdon Square* "a counter-reformation for our ideological age in which responsibility for one's actions is regarded as a hindrance to personal fulfillment."

O'Malley, Laura Donnels. "Pressing Clothes / Snapping Beans / Reading Books: Maria Irene Fornes's Women's Work." *Studies in American Drama, 1945-Present* 4 (1989): 103-17.

Explores the concept of "women's work" through "an analysis of ritual action" in several of Fornes' plays and the playwright's "own perspective on ritual."

Wolf, Stacy. "Re/presenting Gender, Re/presenting Violence: Feminism, Form and the Plays of Maria Irene Fornes." *Theatre Studies* 37 (1992): 17-31.

Argues that "in *Fefu and Her Friends* and *The Conduct of Life*, Fornes' formal devices . . . allow spectators to perceive the manner in which acts of violence position each character a perpetrator or victim, as empowered or disempowered, and to see how each character's relationship to violence signifies his or her power in terms of gender."

Additional coverage of Fornes' life and career is contained in the following sources published by Gale Research: *Contemporary Authors, Revised Edition*, Vols. 25-28; *Contemporary Authors New Revision Series*, Vol. 28; *Contemporary Literary Criticism*, Vols. 39, 61; *Dictionary of Literary Biography*, Vol. 7; *Hispanic Writers*; *Major 20th-Century Writers*.

Susan Glaspell
1876-1948

INTRODUCTION

Glaspell is known as an important figure in the development of modern American drama and as a cofounder of the influential Provincetown Players theater group. In many of her plays Glaspell used experimental techniques to convey her socialist and feminist ideals, portraying female characters—some of whom never appear onstage—who challenge the restrictions and stereotypes imposed on them by society.

BIOGRAPHICAL INFORMATION

Glaspell was born in Davenport, Iowa. She graduated from Drake University in Des Moines in 1899 and accepted a position as a reporter at the *Des Moines News* the same year. After she published several short stories in such magazines as *Harper's Monthly* and the *American Magazine*, Glaspell left journalism to concentrate on publishing novels and short fiction. In 1913, Glaspell married George Cram Cook, a noted socialist. Dissatisfied with American popular theater, the couple moved to Provincetown, Massachusetts, and cofounded, with a group of writers, artists, and intellectuals, the Provincetown Players. Inspired by the independent theater movement in Europe, which had presented the works of Henrik Ibsen, Emile Zola, August Strindberg, and Maurice Maeterlinck, among others, the Provincetown Players were dedicated to developing an American theater movement alternative to the commercial theater of Broadway. The Provincetown "little theater" group included such writers as Djuna Barnes, Edna Ferber, Neith Boyce, Edna St. Vincent Millay, Paul Green, and Eugene O'Neill, most of whom wrote, directed, and acted for the group. The Provincetown Players began to disband with the personal successes of some of the members, including Glaspell. After the failure of his own work outside the company and what he considered the defection of other members, Glaspell's husband also resigned from the group. Glaspell and her husband moved to Greece and resided there until Cook's death in 1924. The following year, Glaspell married Norman Matson. In 1931, she received a Pulitzer Prize for *Alison's House*, the last of her plays to be produced. She served as midwestern director of the Federal Theater Project for a brief period before returning to Provincetown to write novels. Glaspell died of pneumonia in 1948.

MAJOR WORKS

While Glaspell achieved some success with her novels—most notably her last two, *Ambrose Holt and Family* and *Judd Rankin's Daughter*—she is best remembered as one of the first American experimental playwrights. For one of her first plays, *Trifles*, Glaspell turned for inspiration to a murder case she had covered as a reporter. Glaspell's lead characters, Mrs. Hale and Mrs. Peters, accompany the sheriff and two other men to the isolated farmhouse of Minnie Wright—who dominates the play, yet never appears onstage—to collect some clothes for her while the men search for evidence to use in her trial for the murder of her husband. Surveying Minnie Wright's kitchen, the women piece together a motive from such evidence as untidy stitching on a quilt Minnie was constructing and a strangled canary in her sewing basket. The three male characters search the rest of the house fruitlessly, leaving the women to their "trifles." In her starkly realistic rendering of the characters and incidents, Glaspell disputed the notion that women's concerns and activities within the home are trivial, and exposed the harsh life frontierswomen endured in a male-dominated social and legal system. In *Bernice*, Glaspell again used the technique of keeping offstage the character who motivates the action of the play, which takes place following the death of the title character. Glaspell focuses on Bernice's friends and relatives, who attempt to understand her life and death, but can only articulate their thoughts in abstract, usually meaningless words and phrases. *The Verge*, which is generally acknowledged to be Glaspell's most ambitious work, is presented from the point of view of Claire Archer, a botanist who develops new species of plants. Claire rejects traditional gender and social roles and, with the exception of her friend Tom, is misunderstood by everyone because of her desire to transcend the limits of human reality. The play ends with Claire on the brink of madness, having failed to create a new form of life, speaking in a cryptic mix of poetry and prose.

CRITICAL RECEPTION

After receiving critical acclaim during her lifetime, Glaspell fell into obscurity after her death and has only lately been rediscovered due to an increase in feminist scholarship. Because of the experimental nature of many of her plays, she is considered with Eugene O'Neill to be a founder of modern American drama. Her one-act play *Trifles* and the short story into which she adapted it, "A Jury of Her Peers," are widely anthologized as exemplars of their respective forms. Additionally, critics note Glaspell's contribution to the canon of midwestern American literature, citing her use of frontier landscapes and elements of her Iowa upbringing in her work. While some commentators initially regarded her plays as overly intellectual and inaccessible to the average audience, she is now generally considered to be one of the most important figures in modern American drama and twentieth-century feminist literature.

PRINCIPAL WORKS

PLAYS

Suppressed Desires [with George Cram Cook] 1915
Trifles 1916
Close the Book 1917
The Outside 1917
The People 1917
Tickless Time [with Cook] 1918
Woman's Honor 1918
Bernice 1919
Inheritors 1921
The Verge 1921
Chains of Dew 1922
The Comic Artist [with Norman Matson] 1928
Alison's House 1930

OTHER MAJOR WORKS

The Glory of the Conquered (novel) 1909
The Visioning (novel) 1911
Lifted Masks (short stories) 1912
Fidelity (novel) 1915
The Road to the Temple (biography) 1926
"A Jury of Her Peers" (short story) 1927
Brook Evans (novel) 1928
Fugitive's Return (novel) 1929
Ambrose Holt and Family (novel) 1931
Cherished and Shared of Old (juvenilia) 1940
The Morning Is Near Us (novel) 1940
Norma Ashe (novel) 1942
Judd Rankin's Daughter (novel) 1945

OVERVIEWS AND GENERAL STUDIES

Arthur E. Waterman (essay date 1966)

SOURCE: "Dramatic Achievement," in *Susan Glaspell*, Twayne Publishers, 1966, pp. 66-91.

[*In the essay below, Waterman surveys Glaspell's major plays and assesses her significance as a playwright.*]

If the Provincetown's chief contribution to American drama was its dedication to the American playwright, Susan Glaspell proved the merit of that faith. Since most historians of American theater equate the Provincetown with the accomplishment of O'Neill, they overlook that theater's devotion to the new dramatist and misconstrue both its purpose and final triumph. When he met the Players, O'Neill was already a confirmed playwright, who would have reached greatness without them. It was great luck that brought the Provincetown and O'Neill together; both profited enormously from the relationship. O'Neill found a stage where he could experiment and develop; the Players found a potentially major dramatist whose work would time and again save their sagging treasury. Although the Players knew they had assured success with O'Neill, to their credit they never sacrificed their policy of opening the playhouse to any American writer in order to make money or fame from one of his plays. Instead, they sent his more popular dramas uptown, so they could produce other less successful works. There is no evidence to support the claim that O'Neill deliberately used the group to foster his own career, nor is there any support for the idea that the Provincetown changed its essential aim to exploit O'Neill's talent. They met at a crucial time in each other's career: the playhouse needed playwrights, and the playwright needed a playhouse.

After the original organization was broken up by Cook's departure for Greece in 1922, O'Neill, Kenneth Macgowan, and Robert Edmond Jones took over the playhouse and formed a new Provincetown. Its purpose, however, was quite different from the first theater; it was now a commercial enterprise, existing to produce O'Neill's plays and other works, not necessarily original nor American, in competition with the uptown theaters. Perhaps the best explanation of the relationship between O'Neill and the Provincetown was given by O'Neill. "I owe a tremendous lot to the Players," he said, "they encouraged me to write, and produced all my early and many of my later plays. But I can't honestly say I would not have gone on writing plays if it hadn't been for them. I had already gone too far ever to quit."[1]

Unlike O'Neill, Susan Glaspell was not a practicing playwright when she began to write plays for the Playwright's Theatre. She tells us she had never "studied" playwriting—meaning, I suppose, that she had not consciously analyzed the techniques and the traditions for the drama as she had for fiction. She picked up her own dramatic practices from the plays she saw being done around her and gradually worked out her own method by writing one-acts for the Provincetown.

She had no dramatic training and no continuous influence in the theater other than the Provincetown. Her development as a playwright is almost completely within the scope of that theater. Whatever she accomplished in drama, therefore, is largely due to the influence of the Provincetown; thus, her final stature as a dramatist is a convenient measure of its importance.

I ONE-ACT PLAYS

From early in 1915 to late 1918 the Provincetown produced seven one-acts written by Susan Glaspell. The first was *Suppressed Desires* (1915), a collaboration between the Cooks. It is an amusing skit which satirizes the Villagers' sudden, often misguided enthusiasm for Freudian theories. Henrietta Brewster, who has "taken up" psychoanalysis, gratuitously interprets the dreams of Stephen, her husband, and of Mabel, her sister. According to Henrietta, Stephen's dream of a melting wall shows his desire to escape from his job as an architect; and Mabel's dream that she is a hen being ordered to "Step, Hen" proves that she loves a man named Eggleston. To save their "living Libidos," Mabel and Stephen visit a psychoanalyst. His interpretation of their dreams varies considerably from Henrietta's version, for he says that Stephen's dream means that he wants to escape from his marriage; and Mabel's dream is an unconscious desire for her brother-in-law: she wants "Step-hen" and she longs to replace "Hen-rietta." Faced with a husband about to desert her and with a sister who dreams of taking him away, Henrietta renounces Freud; she has decided that it is better to keep desires suppressed.

Like several plays done in the early years by the Provincetown, *Suppressed Desires* pokes fun at an aspect of Village life. Cook's *Change Your Style* spoofed Provincetown art schools; Neith Boyce's *Constancy* mocked the proponents of free love. Unlike these other satires, *Suppressed Desires* has become a classic of its kind: "Now it has been given

by every little theater, and almost every Methodist church; golf clubs in Honolulu, colleges in Constantinople; in Paris and China and every rural route in America."[2]

The play's continuing popularity stems from the very funny lines, the simple staging, and its ease of casting and presentation: all of which make it ideal for amateur theaters. In addition, the topical nature of psychoanalysis has persisted throughout the twentieth century. Freud is still a mystery to the average man and his theories are liable to broad and frequently comic misinterpretations, so the satire has not lost its appeal. Other plays on the subject, such as Alice Gerstenberg's *Overtones* (also produced in 1915), have remained popular but not so consistently and universally in demand as *Suppressed Desires.*

The Wharf Theater was started primarily because the Cooks could not get *Suppressed Desires* put on by any established playhouse. Once they had begun their own theater, they had to have more plays to keep it going. This became Miss Glaspell's chief function in the Cook household: At her husband's insistence she wrote plays while she sat, she tells us, in the old wharf until the scenes began to shape themselves in her mind.

As we might expect, her first play written without the help of Cook, *Trifles* (1916), was closer to her fiction than any of her later plays; indeed, the play was turned with minor changes into the short story *"Jury of Her Peers." Trifles* was adapted perfectly to the bare wooden Wharf Theater, where its simple plot line and immediate appeal were most effective. *Trifles* is different from her other one-acts in that it is neither satiric nor overtly idealistic. With its precise realism, exact details, accurate dialogue, and conscious awareness of certain Midwestern ingredients, it is local color on stage. We expect men like John Wright to live on the prairie, women like Minnie Foster to marry him; and the sudden violence after twenty years of repression seems inevitable in that bleak Iowan homestead. An English reviewer, S. K. Ratcliffe, who saw one of the repeat performances in New York, recognized the Midwestern qualities of the play more clearly than the American reviewers, who accepted them without comment: "As played by the New York company *Trifles* proves itself an undeniable little masterpiece; but it is so purely American that I doubt whether the two women could be played by English actresses with equal effect."[3]

Trifles is far and away Miss Glaspell's most popular play; indeed, it is one of the most popular one-act plays ever written in America. Like *"Jury of Her Peers,"* the play has been frequently anthologized and used as an example of structure and craftsmanship in texts on dramatic technique.

In the one-acts she wrote during the next two seasons, Susan Glaspell imitated the plays she saw other playwrights doing, but she occasionally added her own characteristic idealism. She satirized both conventional behavior and Village nonconformity in *Woman's Honor* (1918). In it, a young man, who nobly refuses to name the woman who could provide his alibi in a murder case, is beseiged by a whole line of women, such as The Shielded One, who are anxious to sacrifice their honor to his welfare. Both his false idealism and the ladies' contempt for their reputations receive the barbs of Miss Glaspell's wit. In the end, the suspect is ready to plead guilty rather than face any more women prating about their honor. This kind of play is quite easy to write and produce, so it is not surprising that the early bills of the Provincetown and the Washington Square Players contain many of these satiric sketches. Nor is it surprising that Susan Glaspell would write several of these clever one-acts in her early attempts at playwriting.

Close the Book (1917) laughs at the *poseur* who insists on unconventionality and at the snobbish small-town matron who hides her family's black sheep within a closed book on genealogy. The humor comes when Jhansi, who believes she is a gypsy, defends her ancestry to her fiancé's family—"I am a descendent of people who never taught anybody anything!" (*Plays*, 68)—and the respectable family's attempt to disguise its humble origins. Jhansi turns out to be a milkman's daughter, so the family must pity her for being as good as they are. The play succeeds because of the dialogue, especially Jhansi's lines, which make the most of the comic turnabout. Here is Jhansi when she discovers her mundane origins:

> So *this* is what I was brought here for, is it? To have my character torn down—to ruin my reputation and threaten my integrity by seeking to muzzle me with a leg at Bull Run and set me down in the Baptist Sunday-School in a milkwagon! I see the purpose of it all. I understand the hostile motive behind all this—but I tell you it's a *lie*. Something here [*Hand on heart*] tells me I am not respectable!
>
> (*Plays*, 84).

Miss Glaspell not only satirized the fads of Village life but also tried to speak for the idealism that was behind the Villagers' revolt against propriety. Plays like O'Neill's *Fog* and Louise Bryant's *The Game* contain abstract characters who express vague idealistic sentiments, and Miss Glaspell's ***The People*** (1917) follows these plays in the way it states abstract notions. Her play deals with the struggle for survival of a radical newspaper devoted to the social revolution. The editors are ready to stop publication until the people speak through the voices of a boy from Georgia, a fisherman from New England, and a woman from Idaho. Each tells what the paper means to him as each tries to articulate an idealistic faith: "It was wonderful to ride across this country and see all the people. . . . I had thoughts not like any thoughts I'd ever had before—your words like a spring breaking through the dry country of my mind. I thought of how you call your paper 'A Journal of the Social Revolution,' and I said to myself—This is the Social Revolution! Knowing that your tombstone doesn't matter! *Seeing*—that's the Social Revolution" (*Plays*, 57). Moved by such sentiments, the editors decide to keep the paper going.

The weakness in the play is that nothing happens; there is no action. The high-sounding speeches are too vague; for, as Isaac Goldberg said, ". . . the characters merge into caricature, and the spectator listens to the preachment of some beautiful thoughts that live as words, as ideas, but surely not as drama."[4] In trying to give dramatic expression to her ideals, Miss Glaspell was faced with the same difficulty she had in her novels, and as yet she had not discovered a solution.

The Outside (1917) is a more interesting attempt to make drama from idealism—to put into direct dramatic terms her concern with that vague something she calls "the meaning of life." The setting of the play is the lifesaving station on the edge of Provincetown, once the scene of many dramatic fights with death. It is now inhabited by Mrs. Patrick and her taciturn servant Allie Mayo: two women who have chosen this isolated place to escape from being involved in life. As the play opens, a lifesaving crew takes over the living room in a vain attempt to save a drowned sailor. Mrs. Patrick resents this intrusion on her privacy: she sees it as a way of making her feel some emotion over the dead seaman. Allie is moved to cry out against Mrs. Patrick's desire to wall herself in. Like her mistress, Allie has sealed herself off from the world, refusing to talk. But now she must speak: "That boy in there—his face—uncovered something—[*Her open hand on her chest. But she waits, as if she cannot go on; when she speaks it is in a labored way—slow monotonous, as if snowed in by silent years.*] For twenty years, I did what you are doing. And I can tell you—it's not the way" (*Plays*, 109).

Searching for some symbol of her personal feelings, Allie, who compares the search for life with the land's fight against the ever-encroaching sea, calls the treeline at the edge of the sand the Outside, where the fight for survival goes on and where, significantly, life wins. She warns Mrs. Patrick not to bury her life: "I know where you're going! . . . What you'll try to do. Over there. [*Pointing to the line of woods.*] Bury it. The life in you. Bury it—watching the sand bury the woods. But I'll tell you something! *They* fight too. The woods! They fight for life the way the Captain fought for life in there!" (*Plays*, 111). In spite of herself, Mrs. Patrick is moved; and, as the curtain falls, she feels the pull of the life-force, and recognizes that she cannot bury herself from life.

Although the play begins with the excitement of the rescue, little happens from then on. The broken speech of Allie—played in the original production by Susan Glaspell—states the meaning of the play. But Allie cannot show us the full life; she can only cry out against an empty one. The play is a considerable improvement over ***The People,*** but it is still vague; it still lacks some kind of action that could project the ideas. Miss Glaspell can talk about life—although Allie's lines are spoken "in a labored way," indicating how difficult it was to put into words, let alone deeds, the abstract message—but Miss Glaspell cannot show us the life she admires. Even Ludwig Lewisohn, who was always highly impressed by her plays, said of ***The Outside,*** "her attempt to lend a stunted utterance to her silenced creatures makes for a hopeless obscurity."[5]

Tickless Time (1918), another collaboration between the Cooke, successfully merges the idealism and satire found in many of the early plays done by the Provincetown but without the confusing awkwardness this combination often resulted in. In the play, Ian Joyce makes a sundial which he says is "a symbol of man's whole search for truth—the discovery and correction of error—the mind compelled to conform step by step to astronomical facts—to truth" (*Plays*, 277). In his passion for absolute truth, he buries all their clocks; they will live above the erroneous tick. The cook races vainly between the kitchen and the sundial—dinner loses to a shadow. When Ian has to correct for the sun's variations, his wife realizes that they have not found perfection and digs up the clocks. Throughout the play, the clocks are exhumed and reburied several times as time itself becomes a relative absolute. Finally, they decide to keep both sundial and clocks: they will serve truth while they live by error.

The play is very funny; it is as witty in its way as *Suppressed Desires,* which indicates that Cook had a decided flair for light comedy. It was based on his attempt to establish his own "relation to truth beyond our world" by building just such a sundial. *Tickless Time* recognizes the idealism that was fundamental in the lives of the Players, but it also laughs at their sometimes extreme and bizarre expressions of that faith. Set in a comic framework, this idealism is less ponderous; but, like the sundial, it is still there at the close of the play and still valid.

We might say that in these one-acts Miss Glaspell had not yet found her dramatic voice. Two are collaborations, one is close to the short story, the others try various techniques and attitudes ranging from witty satire to hesitant idealism. She had little difficulty writing satiric sketches, but she had yet to find the techniques that would permit her to say something serious in dramatic form, with dramatic focus. Her idealistic plays stumble into vagueness, and her comedies skim the surface of life. Moreover, these one-acts follow quite consistently the same kinds of plays other playwrights and little theaters were doing. They show, therefore, how dependent she was on her contemporaries; and they also indicate that Miss Glaspell was still looking for a dramatic tradition she could use. Writing these short plays and also absorbing stagecraft by acting in and directing her own plays and those by others, she was learning to be a playwright in the best way possible. When the Provincetown Players moved to its new theater in 1918 and to a satisfactory stage with, by then, an experienced company, she was ready to move with them: she was ready to write full-length plays.

II BERNICE

In its insistence on producing only original plays by native playwrights, the Provincetown was attempting to establish a theater which would reflect the modern American scene. There was, however, no accepted dramatic tradition for this unique aim. Broadway, caught in the web of Romantic melodrama, offered little help. The new American playwright had for his models the European playwrights who had developed symbolic Expressionism into a useful technique, plus the native tradition which was slowly reaching toward Realism in theme and characterization. Trained in the local-color tradition in fiction, Miss Glaspell had little trouble using realistic techniques on stage. *Trifles* shows how easily and how well she could create a slice of life. But when she tried to go beyond realism, as in the groping dialogue of *The People* and *The Outside,* she could not find the dramatic means to render her ideas: She had not yet successfully created an American vision for an American audience. This skill had to be developed by trial and error, by constant experimentation in a theater like the Provincetown where she could gradually weld Realism and Expressionism into a new and personal dramatic form.

The Provincetown produced many types of plays, from the starkly realistic *Cocaine*, by Pendleton King, to the highly symbolic *The Spring*, by George Cram Cook. Some of its most satisfying moments came from an unusual play presented in exceptional terms, as in *Aria Da Capo*, by Edna St. Vincent Millay. The basic direction the theater took, however, was determined by the plays of the two leading playwrights, Eugene O'Neill and Susan Glaspell, in whose works American Realism and European Expressionism merged. O'Neill, who was never exclusively a Provincetown playwright and who grappled with the problem of technique all his life, swung from the realism of *Anna Christie* to the symbolism of *The Emperor Jones*, eventually outgrowing the limited abilities of the Players. And in her own way, Susan Glaspell also faced the need to experiment, to adapt different techniques to different themes; but, unlike O'Neill, she confined her themes to the contemporary American scene and remained with the Provincetown from its beginning to its end.

In her first full-length play, *Bernice* (1919), she uses a technique that she had tried earlier in *Trifles* and was to use later in *Alison's House*: She translates an idealistic theme into action and dialogue through a heroine who never appears on stage. Bernice is dead when the curtain rises; but she influences the actions of all the characters who gather at her home. The crucial question of the play, the dramatic tension, comes from a conflict over the meaning of her death.

Bernice's philandering husband, Craig, and her best friend, Margaret, react very differently when they hear that Bernice was a suicide. Craig interprets her death as proof of her love for him and of her grief at his infidelity. Margaret is at first skeptical because she cannot believe anyone so full of beauty and tenderness would kill herself. Then the maid confides to her that Bernice died of natural causes, but, knowing her death was near, she asked that Craig be told she took her own life. This revelation shocks Margaret, for it seems to indicate that Bernice chose this unusual way to punish her unfaithful husband. Unwilling to accept Bernice's apparent cruelty, Margaret searches for another explanation and finds it in Craig's subsequent behavior.

Thinking his wife died for his sake, Craig finds a new purpose in his life. When Margaret suggests that his behavior need not be different simply because of Bernice's death, he replies, "*Need* not? You think I want the old thing back? Pretending. Fumbling. Always trying to seem something—to feel myself something. No . . . even more than it makes me want to die it makes me want to—Oh, Margaret, if I could have Bernice now—*knowing*. And yet—I never had her until now. This—has given Bernice to me" (*Plays*, 226). Realizing that Craig has now dedicated his life to being worthy of Bernice's sacrifice, Margaret sees the meaning of her strange last wish: it was a selfless gift, "a gift to the spirit. A gift sent back through the dark" (*Plays*, 229).

The burden of the play lies in the dialogue. There is so little action on stage that it is a drama of discovery through words. The essential action in the play, Bernice's death, has occurred before the play begins; what is left is the discovery of the meaning of her death and her last request. The limited action suited the small Provincetown stage perfectly and the emphasis on the rendition of the lines, rather than upon any complex stage business, suited the method-acting prevalent at that amateur theater. *Bernice,* a "mood" play of quiet yet deep emotion, appealed to those wanting a drama of ideas that ignores the superficial movements of everyday living in order to concentrate on the meaning of life. Ludwig Lewisohn pointed out the special appeal of the play: "beneath the surface is the intense struggle of rending forces. Bernice is dead, but a drama sets in that grows from her last words to her old servant and it is a drama that moves and stirs and transforms."[6]

As in *The Outside,* Miss Glaspell attempted in *Bernice* to express the significance of an intense life; and, as in the one-act play, Miss Glaspell eschews overt action for quiet mood. She suggests in this play and in others like it, especially *Alison's House,* that deeply felt beliefs are best expressed in an indirect way through a gradual revelation with ever-increasing feeling: through words not deeds, thoughts not acts, impressions not factual details. This concept was contrary to Broadway's insistence that a stage-story be all action and all surface. Heywood Broun praised Susan Glaspell in 1916 for showing other playwrights how to handle this most difficult manner of telling a story on stage: "Playwrights of our day, and of a good many previous days, for that matter, have gone ahead in the belief that an off-stage story is a poor story."[7] *Bernice* goes too far perhaps from concrete reality. It needs something—some crisis, or motive for action—to give an outward framework to the more important inner conflicts. It does show, however, that Miss Glaspell's apprenticeship was over; she could write full-length plays.

III INHERITORS

Inheritors (1921) is almost as idealistic as *Bernice,* but presents its theme in more active and realistic terms. In a strict sense it is a war play, for it is concerned with the war's effect on a Midwestern college. In its broadest

extension, the play dramatizes the decline of faith in the twentieth century and defines the effects on contemporary life. It is Susan Glaspell's most serious play about the American Dream: about its origins in the pioneers' vision of an agrarian utopia; its promise of freedom and hope for the oppressed; and its lessening before the newer forces of prejudice and blind "Americanism," especially in the Midwest where it had once beckoned so brightly.

The play opens in 1879 when Silas Morton announces that he will donate land to establish a state university. He is supported by Felix Fejevary, a refugee from Hungarian tyranny, who wants to repay America for giving him freedom. Silas hopes that his gift will make up for his feelings of guilt over taking the land from the Indians in the first place. Each man sees the college as a means of repaying his debt to the country, and each idealistically hopes that the future can bring recompense for the past.

Act Two brings us to 1919, the fortieth anniversary of Morton College. Fejevary's son, president of the board of trustees, wants a state grant for the school; but he must convince Senator Lewis that the college is not a hotbed of radicalism. The radicals on campus consist of one professor who defended conscientious objectors during the war; a few Hindu students; and Madeline Morton, granddaughter of Silas. She defends the Hindus against the "gang tactics" of the American students who are led, ironically, by Fejevary's son; and she defies any authority that interferes with her freedom. Each main character represents a different approach to the problem of maintaining the college's independent and idealistic traditions amid the fears of an uncertain present. Professor Holden pleads with Madeline to forsake her defense of the minority. Since he has compromised his beliefs to keep his job, he tries to influence her by making her see the price she will have to pay: "I can't see you leave that main body without telling you all it is you are leaving. It's not a clean-cut case—the side of the world or the side of the angels. I hate to see you lose—the fullness of life" (143). Her father, Ira, also tries to persuade her not to become involved in other peoples' difficulties. Like the Ira in the short story **"Pollen,"** he is a misanthrope, who has lost his son in the war, his wife from diphtheria; he is, therefore, afraid of the challenge of modern life.

But Madeline cannot detach herself from suffering humanity. She finds strength in her grandfather's vision of the future and in the natural justice of the wind's spreading pollen from one cornfield to another. She says, "The world is all a moving field. [*Her hands move, voice too is as of a moving field.*] Nothing is to itself. If America thinks so—America is like father. I don't feel alone any more. The wind has come through—wind rich from lives now gone. Grandfather Fejevary, gift from a field far off. Silas Morton. No, not alone any more. And afraid? I'm not even afraid of being absurd!" (153).

The three acts of the play cover three generations, which divide it roughly into past, present, and future. The first act establishes the dream, the vision of the future that will bring about the hopes of the Midwestern pioneer and the grateful immigrant. The second act places Morton College in the present day to show reaction to the effects of the war. Senator Lewis personifies everything wrong that came out of the war. He is one-hundred percent American: almost ludicrous in his jingoism and quite dangerous in his narrow-mindedness. Fejevary is caught in his practical desire to have the means serve the end, as he tries to discover some middle ground between conservatism and liberalism. The third act carries us ahead to several possible solutions to the dangers of Act Two. Ira has become an isolationist who is politically and morally cut off from the problems of man; he has gone the way Senator Lewis will go if pushed far enough. Fejevary's son insists on an absolute conformity that would exclude any dissent. Madeline represents the impractical vision of her ancestors: freedom and brotherhood at any price, the dream of possibility based on her heritage and her reaching into the future.

Significantly, *Inheritors* raises questions it does not answer. Although Madeline is the heroine with right on her side, she is warned again and again of the serious consequences of her intransigence. As we know today, any solution will inevitably be ambiguous; there is a dramatic splendor in holding fast to one's principles, but it is a lonely splendor which can be singularly ineffective in the complex world. Miss Glaspell hints at the ambiguity of Madeline's position, but her play, unlike a novel, does not allow for complicated political and moral solutions. *Inheritors* is almost too full as it is; for, without a strong actress playing Madeline, it is in danger of becoming sidetracked by the problems of Professor Holden and the tragedy of Ira. With a good actress in the lead—Ann Harding in the Provincetown production, Eva Le Gallienne in the Civic Repertory production in 1927—the play can be a compelling, disturbing dramatic experience.

"But that a dramatist of ideas has taken her place in the theater, of that there can be no doubt—and this through the agency of a little, rather dingy, but proudly insurgent theatre."[8] This review of *Inheritors* by J. Ranken Towse touched on two of its noteworthy qualities: it illustrates the Provincetown's faith in the American playwright and in the American heritage; and it is a serious play of ideas. Treating an important issue of its time (and our own), the play calls for a rededication to the virtues of the past—without denial of the dangers of commitment. It avoids any complex symbolism of the kind that had made Cook's *The Spring*, which treated the same theme, confused and turgid. Susan Glaspell meets her ideas head on. In *Inheritors* she is not depicting a vague concern with the meaning of life, as she was in *Bernice,* but an immediate problem. Her technique, therefore, is more direct, her structure clearer. She dramatizes the theme through characters who are almost extreme representatives of several positions, and whose clash leaves no doubt as to the nature of the problem. Once more Miss Glaspell's intimate knowledge of the Midwest gives her art a detailed

accuracy that makes her play credible and purposeful. She knew the Midwestern college so well that she recognized it as the ideal setting for a conflict between modern conformity and the older frontier tradition of integrity and independence. In its setting, its characters, its dramatic conflict, *Inheritors* is at once satiric and idealistic—as realistic as *Trifles* and as provocative as any play of ideas.

Although not all the critics liked the play—Alexander Woollcott felt it was "painfully dull, pulseless and desultory"[9]—they could not ignore it. Ludwig Lewisohn, one of the most enthusiastic reviewers, recognized the importance of its theme to a postwar audience:

> It is the first play of the American theatre in which a strong intellect and a ripe artistic nature have grasped and set forth in human terms the central tradition and most burning problem of our national life, quite justly and scrupulously, equally without acrimony and compromise.
>
> No competent critic, whatever his attitude to the play's tendency, will be able to deny the power and brilliancy of Miss Glaspell's characterization. . . . She has recorded the tragic disintegration of American idealism.
>
> The memorable dramatic occasion of the year is on MacDougal Street where Susan Glaspell has added to the wealth of both her country and her art.[10]

Ten years later Lewisohn looked back on *Inheritors* and re-emphasized its significance: "*Inheritors*, moreover, was more than a stirring play; it was in its day and date, a deed of national import. While Broadway blazed and buzzed, both history and literature were being made on MacDougal Street."[11]

IV THE VERGE

The critics could not mistake *The Verge* (1921) for a typical murder mystery as they had *Bernice,* for they knew by the end of the first act they were watching a play unique in American drama. They were seeing Miss Glaspell's most extreme rendition of the individual's reaction against convention to seek her own meaning from life. It is as if Miss Glaspell were testing her own ideas by magnifying them in order to examine the delicate balance that must be maintained between freedom and conformity. Claire Archer, the most radical woman ever presented on the American stage, is quite different from the ordinary woman. As a result, she shocked some viewers, bewildered others, and delighted feminists who saw her as the personification of their desire for an independent life. Miss Glaspell makes clear, however, her own reservations about such ultimate independence.

As a wife and mother Claire is expected to assume the responsibilities of her station in society. But she refuses. She hates her ancestors, is unfaithful to her husband, rejects her daughter; and she refuses to be gracious, hospitable, or feminine. Declining to be "locked in" by convention, she compares her instinct for revolt with the plants she grows;

Plants do it. The big leap—it's called. Explode their species—because something in them knows they've gone as far as they can go. Something in them knows they're shut in to just that. So—go mad—that life may not be prisoned. Break themselves up—into crazy things—into lesser things, and from the pieces—may come one sliver of life with vitality to find the future. How beautiful. How brave (34).

The play develops through a series of rising climaxes which end each act and which carry Claire closer to the "big leap." She says she is trying to break through to "otherness," and to do so she leaves her husband, rejects her lover, and destroys her latest plant mutant because it would not meet the challenge of new life but retreated to its original form. Claire will not compromise; the plant must go ahead or die. Throughout the second act she desperately looks for someone to join her on "the verge." As she moves from passion to hysteria, she attacks the ordinary people around her, saying, "I'm tired of what you do—you and all of you. Life—experience—values— calm—sensitive words which raise their heads as indications. And you *pull them up*—to decorate your stagnant little minds—" (69). By Act Three Claire knows she will have to go ahead alone. Her new plant, "The Breath of Life," has made the breakthrough, and Claire intends to follow it. When her lover tries to stop her, she insanely chokes him to death as her passion breaks the bounds of reason. The curtain falls on her singing madly; she feels that she has crossed over literally to God.

We must realize that Claire has gone too far. Like many of Susan Glaspell's heroines she seeks some form of expression for the complete life. She can mouth sentiments Miss Glaspell must have felt herself, but Claire's final actions indicate that the playwright was making her an extreme case for dramatic purposes and was acknowledging the limitations that have to be placed on aspiration, the boundaries beyond which no one may go.

The Provincetown's production of *The Verge,* with Margaret Wycherly playing Claire, was apparently confusing. Stark Young, who recognized the attempt to do something new, felt the acting hurt the play. Woollcott objected to the vague language and didn't like Claire as a character. Percy Hammond, who liked both play and performers, wrote; "The play is good, but not great. Yet, it must be added, most of our American dramatists would be proud of such a default of greatness; indeed, only two or three of them could so fail."[12]

This mixed reception from viewers and critics alike stems partly from the ambiguous nature of Claire's personality. She goes mad before our eyes, she commits a number of reprehensible crimes, yet she is treated sympathetically. Claire carries the play; she is at once its heroine and its villain. Unlike most plays, certainly most Broadway shows, *The Verge* views life through the eyes of a true rebel—a mad visionary whose perspective may shock us but whose insights also force us to review our own mundane limitations and to find some logic in her passionate out-burst

against "stagnant little minds." Given what Miss Glaspell wanted to do—present the extreme feminist—there was no better, no more dramatic way to present her than through Claire's own forceful personality, ambiguous though it may be.

The dramatic problem in the play was how to give adequate expression, both verbal and symbolic, to Claire's desires. In earlier attempts to dramatize this yearning for life—in *The Outside,* for example—Miss Glaspell relied on a choked, stammering dialogue, full of words like "otherness" and "outness." Although there is some of this labored speech in *The Verge,* she adds several new techniques to convey her theme of extreme behavior. The plants and the new DeVries mutation theory give a scientific and psychological basis to Claire's actions. In her several attempts to articulate her position, Claire breaks into poetry which reads like an odd mixture of George Cram Cook and Emily Dickinson:

> I have the faith that can be bad as well as good.
> And you know why I have the faith?
>   Because sometimes—
> from my lowest moments—beauty has opened as the
> sea. From a cave I saw immensity.
> My love, you're going away—
> Let me tell you how it is with me;
> I want to touch you—somehow touch you once before
> I die—Let me tell you how it is with me.
> I do not want to work,
> I want to be;
> Do not want to make a rose or make a poem—
> Want to lie upon the earth and know.
>
>   (82)

No wonder the critics were in disagreement over the quality of the acting. Such lines, shifting from prose to poetry, must have been extremely hard to say; but, read well, they could be quite moving.

The most interesting device in the play is the use in the manner of some European playwrights of an Expressionistic setting which is distorted and unrealistic in order to suggest the twisted reachings of Claire and her plants: The set *"is a tower which is thought to be round but does not complete the circle. The back is curved, then jagged lines break from that, and the front is a queer bulging window—in a curve that leans. The whole structure is as if given a twist by some terrific force—like something wrung"* (58). Better than any other device, the setting suggests the Surrealistic—that is, other-worldliness—of Claire's search and actions; and the set makes more acceptable the madness at the end of the play. We are in an absurd world in *The Verge,* a twisted, straining place, where things and people stretch out but do not quite reach some impossible, non-human perfection. The dome, which eased the staging considerably, provided for many unique lighting effects. Clearly Miss Glaspell knew her craft by now, knew what she could achieve on that tiny stage in the way of lighting and setting.[13] Even Alexander Woollcott, who never liked any of Susan Glaspell's plays, said that *The Verge* "is beautifully mounted, a little art and a little skill creating a more satisfying suggestion of earth and air and sky than can be managed with immense expenditure by the allegedly wiser producers of Broadway."[14]

The Verge is one of the first plays in the American theater to employ Freudian symbolism in its setting: it weaves the design of the set into the meaning of the play, and it forsakes realism in character, dialogue, and staging to achieve Expressionistic effects. It is Susan Glaspell's most experimental play, both in technique and theme; and, although there were widely divergent views about its success, it was at least an innovation in the dramatic art of its day.

V CHAINS OF DEW

I have not been able to discover a copy of the last Glaspell play produced by the Players, *Chains of Dew* (1922). Fortunately, Heywood Broun summarized the plot in his review:

> *Chains of Dew* is about a poet. Among his little group of radical friends in New York the opinion prevails that Seymour Standish would unquestionably be a great poet if only he could be freed from the environment of his home. They feel that his limitations are a dull wife, a devoted mother and a position of prominence in a respectable little town in the middle west.
>
> And so, when he goes back to his chains, his friends follow him. One of them is a young woman agitating for birth control. She thinks that she can compel Standish to take a position which will force him to break with his wife and his home and find freedom which they believe to be essential to his best work. Much to the surprise of the conspirators, they find his wife sympathetic and enthusiastic about their beliefs. She is eager to defy the smug community in which she lives. It is Standish who is revealed as a prig.
>
> Eventually the poet's mother reveals the truth about her son, which is that he is addicted to the secret vice of sacrifice. The animating force behind his poetry has been his feeling of martyrdom. He enjoys thinking that his wife is a sweet dunderhead who is holding him back. Her display of intelligence and initiative devastates his whole scheme of life.
>
> And so his wife makes a great sacrifice. She abandons all effort to be a person and becomes once more merely a wife and mother, in order to provide the proper atmosphere of oppression which her husband needs in order to write poetry.[15]

Broun liked the play but objected to the poor performance it was given at the Provincetown. Since this was the last play to be done by the Players and since Miss Glaspell was in Greece when it was produced, it is no wonder that the performance was ragged. *Chains of Dew*, however, does continue the Midwestern concerns of her plays and becomes the basis for the plot of her later novel *Ambrose Holt and Family* (1931) in which Blossom Holt sacrifices her own desires for the sake of her poetic husband. With a

few conspicuous exceptions, notably *The Verge,* her plays are Midwestern in setting and attitude. The Midwestern wife in this play is superior to her phony husband and his Eastern friends: not only is she morally superior but she also has a sense of identity, of independence, which they lack. *Inheritors* criticized certain aspects of American society and found a moral corrective in the Midwestern legacy; and later, when she had to choose a setting for *Alison's House,* Miss Glaspell placed the play in Iowa along the Mississippi. This consistent Midwesternism in her art caused one critic (Woollcott) to say she was old-fashioned; another, to speak favorably of her distinctive American traits (Lewisohn); and still another, to claim she oversteps national boundaries (Goldberg). Although Miss Glaspell was primarily an experimental playwright, she never completely shook off the literary traditions of her fiction. In this respect she plainly illustrates that peculiar mixture in the Provincetown of old-fashioned idealism and modern experimentation.

In the announcement "To Our Playwrights" the Provincetown Players said, "We have given two playwrights to America, Eugene O'Neill and Susan Glaspell."[16] There can be no question that Susan Glaspell's plays were a major factor in the success of the Playwright's Theatre. After *Bernice* no drama critic could overlook her plays, and every New York newspaper carried reviews of her last three plays. Only in a playhouse like the Provincetown could American Realism and European Expressionism unite to begin a new movement in American drama. Only in an experimental theater could Miss Glaspell find the means and the opportunity to develop her dramatic talent by freely experimenting with themes and techniques as she worked out her dramatic method. In return she wrote eleven plays exclusively for that theater and served it in countless other ways: for eight years she devoted her time, energy, money, and creative capacity to it. When she left it, its experimental period was over but its legend was assured.

Before the Provincetown, plays of ideas came mainly from foreign writers like Shaw and from a few scattered attempts by native dramatists. Miss Glaspell hit home because her plays were distinctly American, distinctly contemporary. Thus *Inheritors,* although it might have been acceptable to Broadway for its well made form, would have been rejected because of its painful conclusions; and *The Verge,* with its highly experimental form and radical views, could have appeared in no other theater than the Provincetown.

VI THE COMIC ARTIST

After Cook's death in 1924, Miss Glaspell traveled in Europe where she met Norman Matson, whom she married in 1925. In 1927 she published *The Road to the Temple,* which she said she wrote "to make Jig [Cook] realized by more people." Writing his biography led her apparently to a consideration of the relationship between the artist's life and society, for her last two plays are concerned with the conflict between the private life of an artist and the public's right to his art. This theme is especially true of *Alison's House* and is one of the major problems in *The Comic*

Artist (1928), a collaboration between Miss Glaspell and Norman Matson.

The "comic artist" is Karl Rolfe, a successful cartoonist, whose creation, "Mugs," symbolizes man's pathetic and comic striving for heroism. In spite of his good intentions, Mugs always falls short of his aspirations, with tragicomic results. Karl would like to be a serious artist, but he limits himself to cartooning in order to make money. His wife sees Mugs as a source of income; therefore, she nags Karl into minimizing his talent. Karl's brother, on the other hand, wants him to develop his artistic gift and tries to mediate some balance between Karl's personal life and his artistic possibilities. The result is tragedy. In a foolish, heroic, Mugs-like gesture, Karl dies trying to save his wife, whom he mistakenly thought was drowning. Thus the spirit of Mugs permeates the play. Although everyone acts with the best of intentions, nothing ends satisfactorily. The play suggests that, when people bungle in the life of an artist, they bring misery, regardless of their motives.

Performed first in London in 1928 and then in the West-port Playhouse in 1931, *The Comic Artist* did not reach Broadway until 1933. It was not a success. The reviewer for *Newsweek* said it contained "strained literary writing made up principally of forced situations developed in tedious scenes."[1] The play is strained, and it is more literary than dramatic. It contains an unhappy combination of serious ideas that Miss Glaspell wrote into it and frivolous comedy that, I suspect, Norman Matson was responsible for. There is an annoying inconsistency in the play, both in method and theme, as its two authors work at cross purposes. At one place a woman speaks lines that sound like other Glaspell heroines: "And there in the garden, all of a sudden—as some people are eager to know who will win a football game or who killed Dr. Hall, I was eager to know what life means!" (40). This speech runs counter to a lot of trivial stage business designed to give movement and light farce to the play. The dramatic effect, that mood of quiet tension so characteristic in Miss Glaspell's plays, is ruined by a shifting tone and by awkward comic devices.

VII ALISON'S HOUSE

Alison's House (1930) is as controlled in its tone and as consistent in its movement as *The Comic Artist* is not. Inspired by reading Genevieve Taggard's *The Life and Mind of Emily Dickinson* and still intrigued by the dramatic potential of a play treating the conflict between the artist and the world—and perhaps sensing that *The Comic Artist* had failed to do dramatic justice to this theme—Miss Glaspell wrote her version of Emily Dickinson's "quarrel with the world." Because she was not permitted to use Miss Dickinson's name nor any of her poetry, Susan Glaspell named her heroine Alison, set the play in the Midwest, and used Emerson's poems. Nevertheless, Alison Stanhope is a thinly disguised Emily Dickinson.

What Miss Glaspell did to solve the difficult problem of conveying Emily Dickinson on stage was to continue her technique of keeping the central character off-stage. Alison has been dead for eighteen years when the play begins; we know her through her influence on the different members of the Stanhope family. On the last day of the nineteenth century the family is preparing to move from its house. We begin on a note of resignation: the century, the house, and the eldest member of the family—all are passing away.

This melancholy mood is disrupted by a reporter who has come to write a story about Alison before her effects are moved. Because there has been a persistent rumor that Alison was in love with a married man, the Stanhopes resent the public's curiosity about her life. Each member of the family reacts differently to the reporter's intrusion: Ted wants to exploit her reputation for his own profit, Alison's brother is resigned to the fact that she belongs to the world, Louise fears a scandal may emerge, and Agatha zealously guards Alison's property by refusing to let anyone enter her room and by even trying to burn Alison's unpublished work. Agatha cries, "I say she does not belong to the world! I say she belongs to us. And I'll keep her from the world—I'll keep the world from getting her—if it kills me—and kills you all!" (25). When Agatha dies in Act Two, the strongest defender of Alison's privacy is gone. Her unpublished poems are passed on to Elsa, the person most like Alison. The poems tell the "story she never told. She has written it, as it was never written before. The love that never died—loneliness that never died—anguish and beauty of her love!" (139).

So the problem of what to do with the unpublished material is made more dramatic by the revelation that it tells of a love affair which will reflect on the Stanhope name. Alison's father wants to burn the poems, but Elsa (to the accompaniment of New Year's bells) convinces him that the poems belong to the future: "She loved to make her little gifts. If she can make one more, from her century to yours, then she isn't gone. Anything else is—too lonely" (154). As the new century dawns, as a new life begins for the family, the quiet mood of resignation that began the play has now shifted to a new note of rebirth; and the play ends.

Once again, and for the last time, Susan Glaspell found the right dramatic situation to render her implicit faith in the human condition. There is just enough tension in the conflict among the members of the family to create dramatic excitement. The climaxes in each act, especially Agatha's death in Act Two, continue the tension into the next act, so that the dramatic line, the rising tautness of the play, is sustained from first to last, unbroken by any false notes. This single, finely balanced key is supported by the unities of setting and time—the play takes place within one house during one day. *Alison's House* demonstrates conclusively that Susan Glaspell's most effective and most characteristic dramatic technique was her centering a play around an off-stage character: Minnie Wright, Bernice, Alison. Somehow this generates a peculiar tension, like a hushed whisper that grows stronger as the play progresses. She can keep us believing in the idealistic nature of her heroine because the heroine remains abstract. Never seeing her, we accept her as a vision, an abstraction, which we might not do if she were to materialize in some particular action. Alison is a spirit, an ideal who represents the love that finally causes the regeneration at the end of the play. She is an unseen force who symbolizes the hope the play evokes.

For these reasons—the overt conflict, the unities, the unbroken dramatic line, and the effect of Alison—this play is one of Miss Glaspell's finest. The quiet but unmistakable turn in Act Three to a new note of hope is most impressive, as the unobtrusive symbols of time—a new day, a new year, a new century—tell us a new spirit has risen. The old concerns passed with Agatha's death. Now Alison can be received as a poet, and her personal life will be overshadowed by her artistry.

A great deal of the power of this play depends on the ability of the actors to hold the suspense through the shift in tone without breaking down into sentimentality. With Eva Le Gallienne playing Elsa, the Civic Repertory Theatre's production was so successful that *Alison's House* won the 1931 Pulitzer Prize in drama.[18] In no other play was Miss Glaspell in such perfect control of her characters, her dialogue, her symbols, and her ability to create a sustained mood. *Alison's House* has remained a popular play among amateur theaters and is generally recognized as one of the highlights of the American theater in the 1930's. It was, therefore, a fitting close to her dramatic career.

VIII IMPORTANCE AS A PLAYWRIGHT

The publication of Miss Glaspell's plays in 1920 and of her separate plays in 1921 and 1922 offered the critics a chance to review her dramatic work. Both Ludwig Lewisohn and Isaac Goldberg discussed the importance her plays had in the new drama beginning to appear in America. Lewisohn saw clearly the particular American qualities of her vision:

> Behind Miss Glaspell's hardihood of thought hover the fear and self torment of the Puritan. She is a modern radical and a New England schoolteacher; she is a woman of intrepid thought and also the cramped and aproned wife on some Iowa farm. She is a composite, and that composite is intensely American. She is never quite spontaneous and unconscious and free, never the unquestioning servant of her art. She broods and tortures herself and weighs the issues of expression.
>
> Her comedy . . . is never hearty. It is not the comedy of character but of ideas. . . .[19]

Goldberg, who touched on the effect her writing plays of ideas had on her dramatic language, compared her art in this respect to O'Neill's:

> Glaspell's intensity of thought . . . induces a straining toward wit, an eminently intellectual process; her humor . . . presupposes persons of sophistication. As O'Neill inclines toward the masterful man, so she leans toward the rebellious woman. Where the author of *The Hairy Ape* spurts out words like the gushing of a geyser, Glaspell is reticent, laconic. . . .

> Now, Miss Glaspell is indeed very sensitive in the way she feels feeling, and by that very token is she the woman of thought. . . .[20]

What these critics are in effect saying is that, while Miss Glaspell is of major importance as a dramatist of ideas, she paid a price for this achievement. She had to foresake a lyrical drama for an intellectual one. Consequently, there are few moving speeches in her plays; she hesitates with words, groping for the language her characters need to express their ideas. This results in that brooding quality Lewisohn speaks of: a unique mood which comes partly from the sparseness of speech, partly from the limited stage action, and partly from the particular techniques she used to help the words convey her ideas. She employed expressionism in *The Verge,* created an off-stage heroine in *Bernice* and *Alison's House,* and treated realistically a specific issue in *Inheritors.* As Goldberg says, her feeling supports her thought; her ideas emerge not so much from the lines spoken, but from the atmosphere engendered by the situation and the techniques.

Miss Glaspell's work at the Provincetown was a major reason for the appearance of new realistic plays on Broadway about 1920. Zona Gale's *Miss Lulu Bett,* which won the Pulitzer Prize in 1921, was a study of a repressed Midwestern woman—one not unlike Minnie Wright in *Trifles.* Rachel Crothers, who was writing plays at this time which treated the position of the modern woman, reached some of the conclusions found in *The Verge,* Other plays, such as Elmer Rice's *The Adding Machine* (1923) and John Howard Lawson's *Processional* (1925), used Expressionism as a means to convey ideas in drama. It would be inaccurate, however, to say that these plays were directly influenced by Miss Glaspell's plays—or that, without her and the Provincetown, there would have been no modern American drama. But it is safe to say that her work paved the way and that the Provincetown created a climate where original plays by American playwrights were acceptable to the Broadway producers and to the theater public. The sudden outbreak of new realistic plays in the 1920's was no accident. Miss Glaspell's plays of ideas, which experimented with various techniques in order to create an intellectual drama, and the Playwright's Theatre's conspicuous achievement were important aspects in the rise of modern American drama.

Although Miss Glaspell was not the first American dramatist to treat life realistically on stage, she was one of the first to gain a measure of success, both critical and popular, without catering to the demands of the uptown producers. Her plays were amazingly modern for their time. She wrote on the new woman in all her weakness and glory; she treated psychoanalysis when it was still very new in this country. She depicted in varying form the little magazine, the Bohemian, the war's effect on the sensitive minority, and the difficulty of individualism in the modern world. She brought to the American stage a procession of memorable women, from the repressed midwestern farm-wife to the most radical feminist. Furthermore, she created this panorama of the new age without losing her ability to evoke the more traditional aspects of our culture, especially those of the Midwest.

So her plays have these unique qualities: an interplay among the intellectual, experimental, and traditional elements in our society; an attitude of strong idealism controlled by her probing intellect; a coexistence of the most modern themes and characters with the traditional beliefs of the older generations; and, in her major plays, a successful integration of these diverse qualities into a harmonious, dramatic unity. This surely is an achievement. In her accomplishment she justified the Provincetown's faith in the American playwright.

Although Susan Glaspell published no plays after **Alison's House,** she retained an interest in the theater throughout her life.[21] She regularly attended the productions of various groups who put on plays in Provincetown. She was director of the Midwest Play Bureau for the Federal Theatre for over a year, and she stimulated the writing of plays about the Midwest. Thus she was an observer and patron of the drama after her active participation in the theater had ended.

NOTES

[1]Quoted in Barrett H. Clark, *Eugene O'Neill: the Man and His Plays* (New York, 1929), p. 43.

[2]*Road to Temple*, p. 250.

[3]S. K. Ratcliffe, "An American Dramatist—and Some Players," *New Statesman and Nation*, XVII (July 9, 1921), 386. It is worth noting that this review published in England shows how far the story of the Provincetown had traveled by 1921.

[4]Isaac Goldberg, *The Drama of Transition* (Cincinnati, 1922), p. 475.

[5]Ludwig Lewisohn, *The Drama and the Stage* (New York, 1922), p. 103.

[6]Ludwig Lewisohn, *Expression in America* (New York, 1932), p. 394.

[7]Heywood Broun, "The Drama," New York *Herald Tribune*, November 14, 1916, p. 7. Broun, who was one of the earliest admirers of Miss Glaspell's plays, was reviewing *Trifles*; his remarks can apply, however, to several of her plays.

[8]J. Ranken Towse, "The Play," New York *Evening Post*, March 23, 1921, p. 9.

[9]Alexander Woollcott, "Second Thoughts on First Nights," New York *Times*, March 27, 1921, section 7, p. 1.

[10]Ludwig Lewisohn, *Nation*, CXII (April 6, 1921), 515. Much of this review is reprinted in Lewisohn's *Expression in America*, p. 395.

[11]*Expression in America*, p. 395.

[12]Percy Hammond, New York *Herald Tribune*, November 16, 1921, p. 10.

[13]For a photograph of the set for *The Verge*, see *Theatre Arts*, VI (January, 1922), 12, or *The Provincetown*, p. 81.

[14]Alexander Woollcott, New York *Times*, November 15, p. 23.

[15]Heywood Broun, New York *World*, April 29, 1922, p. 11.

[16]*The Provincetown*, p. 92.

[17]*Newsweek*, I (April 29, 1933), 26.

[18]Most critics were surprised that *Alison's House* was awarded the Pulitzer Prize. They thought that either Philip Barry's *Tomorrow and Tomorrow*, or Lynn Rigg's *Green Grow the Lilacs* would have been a better choice. For a summary of the critical reception accorded *Alison's House*, see *The Best Plays of 1930-1931*, ed. Burns Mantle (New York, 1932), pp. vii, 222ff.

[19]Ludwig Lewisohn, *Nation*, CXI (November 3, 1920), 509-10.

[20]*Drama of Transition*, pp. 472-73.

[21]Miss Glaspell wrote another play, *The Big Bozo*, based on Harl Cook's escapades on a motorcycle, but it has never been produced.

Christine Dymkowski (essay date 1988)

SOURCE: "On the Edge: The Plays of Susan Glaspell," in *Modern Drama*, Vol. XXXI, No. 1, March 1988, pp. 91-105.

[*In the following essay, Dymkowski investigates the "preoccupation with the limits of experience" displayed in Glaspell's plays.*]

Until recently, Susan Glaspell has been little more than "a footnote in the history of drama," remembered chiefly for her association with Eugene O'Neill and the Provincetown Players; her contemporary reputation as one of the two most accomplished playwrights of twentieth-century America may come as a legitimate surprise even to serious students of dramatic history.[1] Her plays have rarely been performed by professional companies and, apart from the often-anthologized **Trifles,** have been unavailable in print;[2] such marginalization of Glaspell's work is the most obvious way in which her drama can be said to be "on the edge." Its own preoccupation with the limits of experience is another.

Central to Glaspell's plays is a concern with fulfilling life's potential, going beyond the confines of convention, safety, and ease to new and uncharted possibilities, both social and personal. This need to take life to its limits and push beyond them implies a paradoxical view of life's margins as central to human experience—as the cutting edge that marks the difference between mere existence and real living. This edge is imbued with both possibility and danger, the one concomitant with the other; Glaspell makes this clear not only in the plays but in her account of her response to the Provincetown dunes:

> I have a picture of Jig [her husband] at the edge of
> the dunes, standing against the woods, that line he and
> I loved where the woods send out the life that can
> meet the sand, and the sand in turn tries to cover the
> woods—a fighting-line, the front line.[3]

It is, in the widest sense, the front line between life and death.

This focal point is at once evident in the titles of some of Glaspell's plays: **The Outside** and **The Verge** speak for themselves, while *Trifles* ironically alludes to the discrepancy between the vitality of women's experience and the male view of it as petty. Indeed, inherent in almost all of Glaspell's work is a consciousness that identifies women as outside the mainstream of life and thus capable of shaping it anew.

The paradoxically central nature of the edge informs Glaspell's theatrical methods and themes. Her first play, *Trifles* (1916),[4] illustrates its use in several ways, the irony of the title already having been noted. The plot revolves around the visit to a farmhouse by County Attorney Henderson and Sheriff Peters to investigate the murder of John Wright; they are accompanied by the farmer who discovered the murder and, almost incidentally, by the farmer's and sheriff's wives. The men's assumption is that Minnie Wright, already in custody for the crime, has killed her husband, and they are there to search the house for clues to a motive. The audience undoubtedly sees them as protagonists at the start of the play.

The stage directions immediately call attention to the women's marginality: the men, *"much bundled up"* against the freezing cold, *"go at once to the stove"* in the Wrights' kitchen, while the women who follow them in do so *"slowly, and stand close together near the door"* (p. 36). The separateness of the female and male worlds is thus immediately established visually and then reinforced by the dialogue:

> MRS. PETERS (*to the other woman*) Oh, her fruit; it did freeze. (*to the* Lawyer) She worried about that when it turned so cold. . . .
>
> SHERIFF Well, can you beat the women [*sic*]! Held for murder and worryin' about her preserves.
>
> COUNTY ATTORNEY I guess before we're through she may have something more serious than preserves to worry about.
>
> HALE Well, women are used to worrying over trifles.
>
> (*The two women move a little closer together.*)
>
> (p. 38)

Not surprisingly, the women are relegated to the kitchen, while the men's attention turns to the rest of the house, particularly the bedroom where the crime was committed: "You're convinced that there was nothing important here—nothing that would point to any motive," Henderson asks Peters, and is assured that there is "Nothing here but kitchen things" (p. 38). However, while the men view the kitchen as marginal to their purpose, the drama stays centered there where the women are: contrary to expectation, it becomes the central focus of the play.

Ironically, it is the kitchen that holds the clues to the desperation and loneliness of Minnie's life and yields the women the answers for which the men search in vain; moreover, the understanding that they do reach goes beyond the mere solving of the crime to a redefinition of what the crime was. Mrs. Hale blames herself for a failure of imagination: "Oh, I *wish* I'd come over here once in a while! That was a crime! That was a crime! Who's going to punish that? . . . I might have known she needed help! I know how things can be—for women. I tell you, it's queer, Mrs. Peters. We live close together and we live far apart. We all go through the same things—it's all just a different kind of the same thing" (p. 44). The empathy both women feel for Minnie leads them to suppress the evidence they have found, patiently enduring the men's condescension instead of competing with them on their own ground. Conventional moral values are overturned, just as the expected form of the murder mystery is ignored: the play differentiates between justice and law and shows that the traditional "solution" is no such thing.

Just as Glaspell sets the play in the seemingly marginal kitchen, she makes the absent Minnie Wright its focus, a tactic she was to use again in *Bernice* and *Alison's House;* although noted by critics,[5] this use of an absent central character has not received much comment. It is yet another way in which Glaspell makes central the apparently marginal—indeed, in stage terms, the non-existent. It is a point I will return to in discussing the later plays.

Woman's Honor (1918),[6] like *Trifles,* is concerned with the gulf between female and male experience, centering on the ways men define and limit the world in which both sexes live and the ways in which women challenge those definitions and limitations. At its start, it appears to focus on Gordon Wallace, a man accused of murder who refuses to give an alibi because his "silence shields a woman's honor" (p. 121); without his knowledge, his lawyer Foster has leaked the fact to the press in the hope that "Wives—including . . . jurors' wives—will cry, 'Don't let that chivalrous young man die!' Women just love to have their honor shielded" (pp. 123-24).

Foster is quickly proved wrong as a succession of women enter the sheriff's conference room, all ready to provide Wallace with the alibi he so desperately needs, despite the loss of "honor" this will entail. Unlike the men, none of the women have names but are described somewhat expressionistically in the stage directions as the Shielded One, Motherly One, Scornful One, Silly One, Mercenary One, and Cheated One. As these seemingly anonymous figures discuss their motives and attitudes towards "woman's honor," they acquire far more reality than the men, who become ciphers pushed from center stage.[7] What has seemed the play's central human situation—a young man "ready to die to shield a woman's honor" (p. 124)—becomes totally unimportant, indeed farcical, as the action progresses. The women have gathered not so much to save Gordon Wallace as to destroy an empty idea.

The reasons behind the women's action are as varied as their names and, except for the Silly One who finds Wallace's attitude "noble beyond words," belie male attitudes towards them; however, the behavior of the Silly One undermines her position—she is a *"fussily dressed hysterical woman [who] throws her arms around the* Lawyer's *neck,"* exclaiming "I cannot let you die for me!" (pp. 135, 131). The only other dubious motive comes from the Mercenary One, who makes it quite clear she has financial reasons for her presence; it eventually emerges that the women have been talking at cross-purposes, and she has come to apply for a stenographer's job.

The discussion among the rest of the women identifies "woman's honor" as a male concept, beneficial only to men; the Scornful One indicates its hypocrisy on several levels:

> So you were thinking of dying for a woman's honor. (*He says nothing.*) Now do you think that's a very nice way to treat the lady? (*He turns away petulantly.*) Seems to me you should think of *her* feelings. Have you a right to ruin her life? . . . A life that somebody has died for is practically a ruined life. For how are you going to think of it as anything but—a life that somebody has died for? . . . Did it ever strike you as funny that woman's honor is only about one thing, and that man's honor is about everything but that thing? . . . Now woman's honor means woman's virtue. But this lady for whom you propose to die has no virtue. . . . You aren't dying to keep her virtuous. I fancy few lives have been laid upon that altar. But you're dying to keep us from knowing what she is. Dear me, it seems rather sad.

> (pp. 133-35)

The Motherly One agrees that the notion is an empty one not worth dying for, but wonders if it should perhaps "be kept us, as . . . it gives men such noble feelings." The Scornful One replies: "That man—the one [who seduced me] when I was seventeen—he's that sort. He would be of course. Why this instant his eyes would become 'pools of feeling' if any one were to talk about saving a woman's honor" (p. 139).

Eventually the discussion focuses on which of the women should stay to provide the alibi. It is agreed that the Motherly One has "too many other things to do" and that the Scornful One is not appropriate because "Woman's honor never hurt" her (p. 150); since the Silly One subscribes to male ideals, the choice is between the Shielded and Cheated Ones.[8] The decision involves choosing between personal and political objectives: the Cheated One insists on providing the alibi as a means of self-determination and personal fulfillment ("It's the first thing I ever wanted to do that I've done," p. 154), while the Shielded One wishes to claim she spent the night with Wallace as a means of freeing "all [women] smothered under men's lofty sentiments towards them" (p. 146). A vagueness about the way in which the Shielded One will liberate all others of her type weakens the play somewhat: the women are inconsistently treated as types or as individuals according to thematic needs. Nevertheless, the women aim at a resolution that will involve both the Shielded and the Cheated Ones, thus encompassing both personal and general salvation.[9] Although we do not hear what this solution might be, it is clear that it is reached: "Here! Yes! On the night

of October 25—(*Their heads together in low-voiced conference with* Lawyer . . .)" (p. 155). At this point, however, the prisoner, who is now both marginal and powerless, attempts to regain control; he "*slips around the* Cheated One . . . *and makes for the door. It opens in his face, and the doorway is blocked by a large and determined woman.* Prisoner *staggers back to* Lawyer's *arms*" and says, "*Oh, hell. I'll plead guilty*" (pp. 155-56), as the play ends.

The comedy of the conclusion entails one of Glaspell's serious concerns; her preoccupation with "the battle between the life force and the death force" has already been admirably discussed elsewhere.[10] Wallace's life-denying attitude, however, gains added meaning when placed within the context of being on the edge. The imbalance of power between the sexes acts as an advantage to women, a disadvantage to men, when they reach the "front line" of struggle and change. It is precisely *because* "men . . . determine the world in which . . . women are . . . required to live" that women may have a perspective on it of which men are incapable;[11] they have always been on the outside looking in. Their position on the edge gives them an alternative power—the power to move beyond what is, just as the women in *Trifles* and *Woman's Honor* move beyond male definitions of crime and justice and honor. Men placed on the edge, however, are excluded from a power to which they subscribe—Wallace, put in this position, cannot reshape his world from a new perspective; he can only affirm the old one. He prefers to die rather than redefine his notion of woman's honor. The perspective of gender can go some way to explain the inherent optimism of Glaspell's plays, even though they center on women who have died or go mad or face long spells in prison, as well as the unwitting pessimism and defeatism of so much of O'Neill's work.[12]

By recreating the Provincetown coastline that Glaspell describes in *The Road to the Temple,* the setting of *The Outside* (1917) embodies the life/death struggle inherent in the edge:

> . . . *through [an] open door are seen the sand dunes, and beyond them the woods. At one point the line where woods and dunes meet stands out clearly and there are indicated the rude things, vines, bushes, which form the outer uneven rim of the woods—the only things that grow in the sand. At another point a sand-hill is menacing the woods. . . . The dunes are hills and strange forms of sand on which, in places, grows the stiff beach grass—struggle; dogged growing against odds. At right . . . is a drift of sand and the top of buried beach grass is seen on this.*

> (p. 48)

The set's significance is not left to the audience's inference but is underlined by the dialogue: Allie Mayo, embracing "The edge of life," speaks *tenderly* of the "Strange little things that reach out farthest," while Mrs. Patrick gloats that they "will be buried soonest"; Allie recognizes that they will nevertheless "hold the sand for things behind them" and so contribute to life (pp. 54, 53). Mrs. Patrick, who throughout the play has denied life and struggle, finally starts to *"feel . . . her way into the wonder of life,"* understanding what it is to "Meet . . . the Outside" (p. 55).

Both women had originally retreated from life as a result of losing their husbands, and in dramatizing their re-embracing of it, the play affirms women's autonomy. The relationship between women and men in the play is, however, more complex than this statement suggests, and, not surprisingly, the perspective of gender also informs critical interpretation of it: Bigsby regards the male life-savers, who at the beginning of the play struggle unsuccessfully to revive a drowned man, as catalysts of the change ("paradoxically, [with Allie they] succeed in their efforts 'to put life in the dead,'" 1987, p. 13), while Ben-Zvi sees Glaspell's focus "on the failure of men to accomplish what women can do. . . . [The men's] physical activity has proven a failure. The passive, mute Allie, however, is victorious in her own personal resuscitation of Mrs. Patrick" (1982, pp. 25-26). While a persuasive interpretation of the play can encompass both viewpoints, Glaspell's focus is unquestionably on the women and on the triumph of Allie's vision, which goes beyond the men's mere recognition of the life/death struggle to an understanding of the way in which that struggle itself shapes life.

While the line between woods and dunes in **The Outside** locates its focus in a symbolic struggle between life and death, the edge in **Bernice** (1919),[13] Glaspell's first full-length play, is the interaction between literal life and death. The play focuses on the recently-deceased title character, whose body lies in a room just off-stage. Despite her physical absence from the action, the play creates and reinforces Bernice's presence in several ways. First, the setting is *"The living-room of Bernice's house in the country,"* and it is clear that Glaspell expected the stage set to create a powerful sense of her character: *"You feel yourself in the house of a woman you would like to know . . ."* (p. 159); furthermore, the house's evocation of its dead owner begins the action of the play:

> FATHER Bernice made this house. (*Looking around.*) Everything is Bernice. (*A pause.*) Change something, Abbie! (*With growing excitement.*) Put something in a different place. [He moves some of the furnishings.] (*. . . helplessly.*) Well, I don't know. You can't get Bernice out of this room.
>
> (p. 160)

In addition, the other characters all focus on their relationships to Bernice, and indeed, relate to each other *through* that relationship. Their focus on the dead woman is theatrically realized by their constant approaches to the closed door behind which her body lies, the door itself acting as this play's concrete symbol of the edge. In fact, these approaches dramatize the continuing development of their relationship to her—for example, Bernice's faithless husband cannot bring himself to enter the room when he first arrives at the house, but eventually finds a solace there unavailable from any of his fellow-mourners. Through the

characters' discussions and the action on stage, Glaspell makes her dead hero the vital mover of the drama.

That drama focuses, as implied, on the way the other characters—father, friend, husband, sister-in-law, and maid/companion—understand Bernice, and on the way that understanding shapes and transforms their lives.[14] Craig, horrified to learn from Abbie, the maid, that Bernice killed herself, blames his infidelities for her action and berates himself for underestimating her passion for him: Margaret, her friend, cannot believe that Bernice took her own life, and when she forces the truth from Abbie—that Bernice, ill on her deathbed, made her promise to deceive Craig—she is devastated by the thought that Bernice's "life was *hate*" (p. 206). By the end of the play, Margaret understands that the deception was Bernice's final gift to Craig, one that breaks the mould of his life up till then and so gives him the opportunity to reach beyond his limits.

As always, this need to "break through" the "bounded circle" of life is Glaspell's central concern (p. 202), and again, it is the character on the edge who is most successful in doing so; the dead Bernice has far more effect on the other characters than anyone else in the play. However, this influence is not simply due to the way death can alter relationships; despite Bernice's isolated country life, Margaret, who has devoted herself to active work for political and social causes, can say:

> I do things that to me seem important, and yet I just do *them*—I don't get to the thing I'm doing them for—to life itself. I don't simply and profoundly get to *life*. Bernice did.
>
> (p. 200)

The audience need not take Margaret's assessment on trust, but recognition of Bernice's achievement does depend on an understanding of power, an understanding determined in the play by gender. Craig's unfaithfulness to Bernice arose from his failure to dominate her, to "have" her completely (see pp. 174, 186); as Margaret explains, he "turned to women whom [he] could have" and "'had' all of them simply because there was less to have" (p. 197). He could not appreciate Bernice because he had not "the power to reshape" her, and as Margaret astutely remarks, he wanted "no baffling sense of something beyond" him (pp. 174, 197). Thus, Glaspell depicts male occupation of the central position in a woman's life as limiting for both, keeping them within the "bounded circle" of life. This is not "the power to reshape" that Craig thinks it is, but merely the power to circumscribe.

By using her death to convince Craig that he had the power over her he yearned for, Bernice, from her remote position, exercises a liberating power of her own. Craig now rejects his old life as "make-believe": "Pretending. Fumbling. Always trying to seem something—to feel myself something" (p. 226). Bernice's father recognizes that her spirit was generous enough to give as much as possible, but that paradoxically its very greatness meant she could not give "all she was" (p. 223). Even more paradoxically, the play shows how that magnanimity could clothe itself as something venal, and in so doing, manage "to give—what couldn't be given" (p. 226). Glaspell makes clear that Bernice's power over Craig is not one imposed on him, like man's power over woman, but one which allows him free scope. As Bernice's father remarks, "she wanted me to do what—came naturally to me. . . . She was never trying to make us some—outside thing" (p. 194).[15]

Inheritors (1921), Glaspell's next play, emphasizes that growth into new ways of being *is* organic rather than imposed: just as the pollen from Ira's corn blows across neighboring fields, making other corn richer (see p. 155), so humankind develops from a desire to extend oneself; in discussing the evolution of the hand, for example, one character explains that "from aspiration has come doing, and doing has shaped the thing with which to do" (p. 116). True life is process, not product: "we aren't *finished* yet" (p. 117). Thus, the edge in this play is "the impulse to do what had never been done" (p. 116), which develops human potential. Importantly, this potential is both individual and social; the two are inextricable in this play.

The structure of *Inheritors* allows Glaspell to explore the development from impulse to achievement. Act I takes place in 1879, when the pioneer Silas Morton and his Hungarian refugee friend Felix Fejevary discuss Silas's intention to found a college for the girls and boys of the cornfields; the next three acts, set in 1920, show what has happened to the ideals of forty years before. Right from the beginning of the play, Glaspell takes every opportunity to highlight ironically the betrayal of earlier ideals through present self-interest. The action is set on the fourth of July, 1879—Independence Day, but the celebrations mentioned commemorate the Civil War of a decade earlier. Grandmother Morton, the first settler in the area with her husband and son Silas, "never went to bed without leaving something on the stove for the new ones that might be coming" (p. 107), but now balks at Silas's plan to give away some of their vast land holdings to start a college. The portrait of Lincoln which hangs in the Morton farmhouse during Act I is ironically recalled by the audience in the next act when his inaugural address, affirming the right to revolution, is subverted by a state senator and a bigoted student (pp. 123-24); the latter, the grandson of the "revolutionist" Fejevary, is hounding Indian students who call for an end to British imperialism in their country. He can say without any conscious irony: "This foreign element gets my goat" (p. 122). The dangers of moving from the edge to the center are made very apparent.

It is entirely appropriate and theatrically effective that the portrait of Silas Morton hanging in the college library should overhear the giddiness and snobbery of students in whom he had hoped to nurture sensitivity and love of learning: they dissolve into hysterical giggles because another student is "trying to run a farm and go to college at the same time" (p. 125). It also overhears the discussion between Fejevary's son, now president of the Board of Trustees, and State Senator Lewis about the "radical" views of Professor Holden, who has championed the cause of his former student Fred Jordan, a conscientious objector still held in solitary confinement two years after the war's end (see pp. 119-20, 136); so that the college can receive money from the state, Fejevary agrees to silence the professor. As he later explains to Holden, "we [the college] have to enlarge before we can grow. . . . Yes, it is ironic, but that's the way of it" (p. 131).

Everything in the play goes to show that that is *not* "the way of it"; while Holden is eventually compromised by the need to pay his wife's medical bills, Madeline Fejevary Morton, granddaughter of the pioneer and the revolutionary, is able to "go . . . against the spirit of this country" (p. 140), standing up for the rights of the persecuted Indian students and refusing to use her privileged position as a way of escaping the consequences of her assault on the police. In discussing her decision with Holden, Madeline articulates the dangers and potential of being on the edge: "I'd like to have been a pioneer! Some ways they had it fierce, but think of the fun they had! A whole big land to open up! A big new life to begin! . . . Why did so much get shut out? Just a little way back—anything might have been. What happened?" Holden answers that "It got—set too soon," and Madeline concludes that prosperity was the cause: "That seems to set things—set them in fear." She understands the importance of "Moving" and regrets that "We seem here, now, in America, to have forgotten we're moving. Think it's just *us*—just now" (p. 151). The town itself epitomizes her analysis: once a settlement at the very edges of civilization, nurturing people of vision and courage and generosity,[16] it is now a city in the heart of the nation, full of unthinking conformists. Its college students are happy to act as strike-breakers, and the only courage that is recognized is in fact a fear of being different: those who went to war "had the whole spirit of [their] age with [them]" (p. 134), unlike the truly courageous Fred Jordan.

In the last three acts of the play, those characters with the greatest integrity are the most marginal ones. Seen by society as both extremists and outsiders, in stage terms Fred Jordan and the Indian students do not exist: they never appear. However, near the beginning of the last act, Glaspell provides this stage direction, which occupies several minutes of performance time:

> *Rises, goes to* [the] *corner closet. . . . She gets a yard stick, looks in a box and finds a piece of chalk. On the floor she marks off* Fred Jordan's *cell.* [It is "two and a half feet at one end, three feet at the other, and six feet long."] *Slowly, at the end left unchalked, as for a door, she goes in. Her hand goes up as against a wall; looks at her other hand, sees it is out too far, brings it in, giving herself the width of the cell. Walks its length, halts, looks up.*

(pp. 143-44)

In this way, Glaspell makes the absent Fred Jordan the center of our attention, without having him appear on stage. The audience is forced to imagine the experience of this political prisoner through Madeline's imagining of it; indeed, because the focus is on Madeline's *attempt* to experience Fred Jordan's confinement, the audience's mental and emotional engagement is greater than it would have been if Jordan were actually shown on stage in his cell.

Madeline, as hero, is of course central in terms of plot and stage presence, but she chooses to marginalize herself in the society which the play depicts. When Holden tries to dissuade her from "do[ing] a thing that [will put her] apart," fearing she will thereby lose the "fullness of life," Madeline pinpoints the self-interest that leads him to this view: "You don't think that—having to stay within—or deciding to, rather, makes you think these things of the—blight of being without?" She dismisses his argument, neatly summarizing Glaspell's own view: "I don't see it—this fullness of life business. . . . I think that in buying it you're losing it" (p. 152).

While *Inheritors* deals with the social and political signifi-cance of being on the edge, *The Verge* (1921) is concerned solely with the individual. Its hero, Claire, experiments with plants, hoping to shock them "out of what they were—into something they were not." Her goal is to break "the old pattern," a prison that substitutes form for life. For Claire, the edge is a jumping-off-point for "otherness," for liberation from old and dead ways of being: "anything may be—if only you know how to reach it" (pp. 76-77, 86). Her experiments have led to two potentially new plants: the Edge Vine, which eventually runs "back to what it broke out of," and Breath of Life, "alive in its otherness" (p. 62).[17]

Claire's attempt to create new plant forms is, of course, analogous to human potential: "We need not be held in forms moulded for us. There is outness—and otherness." The way to such creation is through destruction of the old order: "If it were all in pieces, we'd be . . . shocked to aliveness. . . . Smash it" (p. 64). Claire's understanding informs her otherwise incomprehensibly urgent plea to her conventional husband to "Please—please try [your egg] without salt" (p. 62) and validates a response to her daughter which others condemn as unnatural: Elizabeth, in her own words, studies "the things one studies" and does "the things one does" and "Of course . . . is glad one is an American" (p. 74); it is not surprising that Claire is repulsed by the idea that such a daughter "ever moved [her] belly and sucked [her] breast" (p. 78).

Although another critic has found Claire's name ironic,[18] her vision is essentially the same as Madeline Morton's, and as clear. Indeed, her clarity seems to be underlined by the amorphousness of the names of the men who sur-round her—Tom, Dick, and Harry, respectively her friend, lover, and husband. However, Tom's surname, Edgewor-thy, distinguishes him some-what from the others; it links him with the idea of the edge and, more particularly, with Claire's Edge Vine, which had the chance to be other, but

"Didn't carry life with it from the life it left" (p. 77). Tom shares Claire's aspirations and values, but to a limited extent: whereas she is terrified that she will "die on the edge," without achieving "otherness" (pp. 86, 78), he is content with merely being "outside life" (p. 72). When Claire suggests to him that their friendship and shared sympathy should lead to a fulfilling sexual relationship, one that may help to achieve the otherness she desires (p. 89), Tom refuses on the grounds that it would instead be a going-back. His concern for her, however, is suspect: while in sympathy with Claire's aims and ideas, he has also shown himself afraid of them. Tom realizes that the "door [to otherness is] on the far side of destruction" (p. 71), but he cannot face the risks, even vicariously. He warns Harry not to try to stop Claire's botanical experiments: "If she can do it with plants, perhaps she won't have to do it with herself" (p. 71). Again, Glaspell shows woman as the risk-taker and seer.

Tom's position as an avoider is not redeemed by his ultimate desire for sexual union with Claire. Instead of meeting her on the basis she had earlier proposed, he claims her according to the old pattern of female and male relationships: "I'm here to hold you from where I know you cannot go" (p. 99). Claire, who like Breath of Life wants to create herself anew, recognizes that Tom "fill[s] the place—should be a gate" and strangles him, ultimately achieving her freedom in madness.[19]

That Claire's madness *is* liberating in the way she desires is determined by her own attitude to madness and sanity. She repeatedly refers to the latter as a prison: "sanity. . . . [is] made a virtue—to lock one in. . . . Things that [grow] take a sporting chance—go mad—that sanity mayn't lock them in— . . . from life—that waits" (p. 65; see also pp. 70, 78, 82, 89). She has always supposed that "If one ever does get out . . . it is—quite unexpectedly, and perhaps—a bit terribly" (p. 63). In this way, Claire's madness at the end of the play is a personal triumph, but one to be understood symbolically rather than realistically.[20]

Glaspell's choice of settings gives her further opportunity to emphasize her theme. Acts I and III take place in Claire's greenhouse laboratory, Act II in her private tower. Both places are extremities of the house she lives in, and yet all the action of the play occurs there. Moreover, these edges force awareness of their centrality—all the characters are drawn into them, *must* enter them, in order to engage with Claire. Indeed, the comedy of the first act revolves around the retreat of Tom, Dick, and Harry to the greenhouse in order to eat breakfast comfortably; Claire has diverted to it all heat from the house so that the plants' temperature may be consistently maintained in the freezing weather.

Glaspell's decision to depict Claire's tower complete on stage actively involves the audience in the tension between the edge and the center; her stage directions at the begin-ning of Act II explain that the tower's "*back is curved, then jagged lines break from that, and the front is a queer bulging window. . . ."* Claire *is seen through the huge ominous window as if shut into the tower* (p. 78). It is most unusual for a playwright to separate characters from the audience with an actual physical barrier rather than a merely imagined fourth wall; seen through and enclosed by the glass, Claire is both the focus of the audience's attention and an outsider in its world. The tower, at once isolating Claire and making her its center,[21] resembles Breath of Life, an "outer shell" with "something alive" and glowing within it (p. 96; s.d., p. 92); we hardly need Tom's reference to the plant as a "womb [Claire] breathes to life" (p. 97) to recognize the metaphor's aptness both for Claire's experiment and Glaspell's stage-picture. By identifying Claire in her tower with an embryo in the womb, Glaspell underlines several ideas: the organic nature of growth and development, the naturalness of the violence of creation, and the uniquely female capacity to give birth to new life; it is not only Tom's personal failings which prevent his journeying as far as Claire.

The Verge, which itself moves across different dramatic genres, is in many ways Glaspell's most complete expression of the complexities of being on the edge, and forms a fitting conclusion to this discussion.[22] Throughout her career as a playwright, Glaspell was preoccupied with the central importance of people and ideas outside the mainstream of life, and the sterility of the status quo. Her consistent point-of-view, however, did not lead to a depressing staleness but to wide experimentation with different dramatic genres and theatrical devices which would embody her ideas. Her present appeal should in fact be wide: her relative critical neglect offers scholars and theatre historians varied research opportunities; her perspective on women and her creation of a variety of strong female protagonists should attract feminist critics, actors, and audiences; her insistence on the dangers of complacency should find a ready response in those who despair of the social and political myopia not just of Reagan's America but also of most other western democracies.

Glaspell clearly deserves a more central place in the history of twentieth-century American drama than she has so far been given. That she has not is in large part due to her sex. To those who will retort that Glaspell gave up the theatre, writing only one play between the end of her association with the Provincetown Players in 1922 and her death in 1948, while O'Neill went on from strength to strength, the answer is simply that gender contributed to those developments as well.[23] Theatre, like the critical scholarship that determines "major figures," is still male-dominated, its edges inhabited by women. It is time those edges were seen as the challenging and important areas Glaspell recognized them to be.

NOTES

[1]Quotation from Introduction, *Plays by Susan Glaspell*, ed. C.W.E. Bigsby (Cambridge, 1987), p. 30 [hereafter referred to as Bigsby, 1987]. For recent reappraisals of Glaspell, see also Gerhard Bach, *Susan Glaspell und die Provincetown Players: Die Anfänge des modernen amerikanischen Dramas und Theaters* (Frankfurt, 1979) and Bigsby, *A Critical Introduction to Twentieth Century American Drama: Vol. 1 1900-1940* (Cambridge, 1982), pp. 25-35 [hereafter referred to as Bigsby, 1982]. An example of Glaspell's contemporary reputation can be found in James Agate's review of *Inheritors* for the *Sunday Times*: "I am inclined to think it ranks with *The Master Builder*," quoted on flyleaf, Susan Glaspell, *The Road to the Temple* (London, 1926).

[2]Bigsby's recent collection of Glaspell's plays contains only *Trifles*, pp. 35-45; *The Outside*, pp. 47-55; *The Verge*, pp. 57-101; and *Inheritors*, pp. 103-57; future references to these plays will be to this edition.

[3]*Road to the Temple*, p. 221.

[4]Glaspell had a year earlier co-authored a play, *Suppressed Desires*, with Jig Cook.

[5]E.g., Bigsby, 1982, pp. 25-26; Sharon Friedman, "Feminism as Theme in Twentieth-Century American Women's Drama," *American Studies*, 25 (1984), 75.

[6]Susan Glaspell, *Woman's Honour*, in *Plays* (Boston, 1920), pp. 119-56. All further references to this play appear in the text.

[7]The lawyer is off stage for a good part of the play, and stage directions indicate Wallace looking *"like one at bay"* (p. 129), giving *"the impression of being crowded into a corner"* (p. 138), and finally attempting to escape (p. 156).

[8]At this point the lawyer returns, and as she does in *Trifles*, Glaspell takes the opportunity to underscore female solidarity and male incomprehension of it:

> LAWYER Ladies—ladies—quarreling? I'm sorry to find you in this mood. I had hoped while you were here together you might—arrive at some understanding. . . . Now why must women always dislike each other?
>
> MOTHERLY ONE (*In her motherly way.*) If I were you I'd try not to talk much.
>
> LAWYER Why not?
>
> SCORNFUL ONE She has a kind heart. Now I—I'd let you talk.
>
> LAWYER Sometimes it seems quite as well not to try to follow women.
>
> SCORNFUL ONE Sometimes even better.
>
> (pp. 151-52)

[9]The Scornful One makes this clear in suggesting that they "save *both* of them through Gordon Wallace," p. 155.

[10]See Bigsby, 1987, pp. 12 ff.

[11]Bigsby, 1987, p. 12, makes this comment without seeing its implications; he continues: "But, *remarkably it seems*, [women] retain a grasp on moral realities. . . ." (my italics).

[12]Cf. Bigsby, 1982, p. 44: "More often than not, [O'Neill's] plays are not about a glorious struggle against fate, an heroic pursuit of the unobtainable. They are concerned with the desperate illusions which are the acknowledgement of defeat." Similarly, in comparing the two playwrights, Linda Ben-Zvi comments that "O'Neill [is] committed to a tragic world where human suffering leads to awareness, perhaps, but not to victory; Glaspell, to a more optimistic, meliorative world" ("Susan Glaspell and Eugene O'Neill: The Imagery of Gender," *The Eugene O'Neill Newsletter*, 10 (1986), 27). I was able to obtain only a photocopy of Ben-Zvi's article, together with her previous one, "Susan Glaspell and Eugene O'Neill," *The Eugene O'Neill Newsletter*, 6 (1982), 21-29, after I had finished writing my own; although her emphases are different, many of her ideas anticipate and complement mine.

[13]*Bernice: A Play in Three Acts*, in *Plays* (Boston, 1920), pp. 157-230. All further references to this play appear in the text.

[14]The responses range from her sister in law's total incomprehension to her friend's eventual complete understanding.

[15]The discrepancy in Glaspell's judgement of the likely effects on "A life that somebody has died for" (*Woman's Honor*, p. 134) is more apparent than real, if one considers gender. Margaret expects Craig to be destroyed by the belief that Bernice has killed herself for him: "I . . . can't *stand* it to see anyone go down under a thing he shouldn't have to bear" (pp. 215-216); she shares the view of the Shielded One in *Woman's Honor* that such knowledge will ruin a life. This is the female perspective, one very different from that of the male in his dominant position. Ironically, Craig's transcendence of his limitations would not be possible without those limitations being present in the first place: his very self-centeredness and self-importance (which Glaspell presents not just as personal but as generic failings) allow him to accept Bernice's sacrifice as proof of his value and then to act from that validated sense of self. Glaspell implies that a woman in a similar situation would not think herself worth such a sacrifice.

[16]Glaspell's concern in this play with the betrayal of American Indians might seem to belie my point. However, she makes clear that the relationship between the earliest settlers and the Indians was not exploitative, but one of mutual respect (see p. 105). It was "after other white folks" came that trouble began—in other words, once this edge was subsumed into the normal.

[17]Glaspell is also aware of the trap of creation; Claire, in speaking of Breath of Life and its achieving otherness, says, "Out? / You have been brought in" (p. 96). The battle at the edges of life is a constant one: stasis is defeat.

[18]Bigsby, 1982, p. 30.

[19]It is worth pointing out that Tom has told Harry he would "go so far as to stop [his] existence" if it would help Claire; Claire herself calls her murder of Tom her "gift" to him. (She echoes Margaret in *Bernice*, p. 229: Bernice's lie to Craig was "a gift to the spirit.") Considering these points together with Tom's identification with the Edge Vine, the action should perhaps also be understood as a way of keeping Tom true to the best in himself. Cf. Claire's explanation of her earlier action: "I should destroy the Edge Vine. It isn't—over the edge. It's running, back to—'all the girls' [a reference to Elizabeth's conformity]," p. 77.

[20]The way in which the play's own changing form mirrors its content has already been pointed out by Bigsby, 1982, p. 29.

[21]While it is true that the other characters are also seen through this window, the tower is Claire's and very much identified with her.

[22]It is worth noting that *Alison's House* (1930), Glaspell's last play, concerns itself with the same ideas and uses many of the same tactics as her earlier works (New York, 1930). Focusing on the way old-fashioned, conventional morality hinders self-fulfillment, the play is appropriately set on December 31, 1899—the edge between one century and another—and ends at midnight, with "distant bells ring[ing] in the century" and new values (pp. 154-55). The battle between the old and the new in the Stanhope family takes place through the agency of their aunt/sister Alison, a famous poet, who has been dead for eighteen years and in whose house the action is set. The resolution of Act III occurs in Alison's bedroom, and Glaspell conjures up a sense of her presence and influence in ways similar to those used in *Bernice*.

[23]Glaspell's last play for the Provincetown Players was *Chains of Dew* (1922), which was never published. Besides *Alison's House* (1930), she also wrote *The Comic Artist* (1928) with Norman Matson. It is significant that Glaspell's productive years coincided with her involvement in an amateur group which, besides supporting new writers, was equally open to women as to men.

Linda Ben-Zvi (essay date 1989)

SOURCE: "Susan Glaspell's Contributions to Contemporary Women Playwrights," in *Feminine Focus: The New Women Playwrights*, edited by Enoch Brater, Oxford University Press, 1989, pp. 147-66.

[*Ben-Zvi assesses the ways that Glaspell's work paved the way for modern feminist writers, arguing that while Glaspell's "particular experiments may at first glance seem removed from those of women writing in modern and postmodern modes of the sixties, seventies, and eighties . . . they are in fact part of the same ongoing search for dramatic means to depict female experience."*]

The name Susan Glaspell is followed in her biographical sketches by some of the most illustrious credentials in all of American theater history: cofounder of the Provincetown Players, the seminal American theater company; prodigious playwright, who contributed eleven plays to the Provincetown theater in its seven years of existence, surpassed only by Eugene O'Neill, who wrote fourteen under the aegis of the group;[1] talented actress, praised by the visiting French director Jacques Copeau for her moving depiction of character;[2] director of her own plays, including *The Verge,* one of the first expressionist dramas seen on the American stage; winner of the Pulitzer Prize for drama in 1931 for her play *Alison's House,* only the second woman to be so honored; head of the Midwest bureau of the Federal Theatre Project in Chicago in the thirties, credited with reviewing over six hundred plays and instrumental in the production of several important works by black playwrights; significant influence on others, particularly Eugene O'Neill, who she brought to the Provincetown theater in the summer of 1916 and with whom she continued to have a close personal and professional relationship until her departure for Greece with her husband in 1923, thus ending the original Provincetown experiment.[3]

Few have been so successful in so many areas of theater, yet, ironically, few have so completely disappeared from the dramatic canon as Susan Glaspell. Critics in her own period such as Heywood Broun, Ludwig Lewisohn, Isaac Goldberg, and Barrett Clark praised her and O'Neill for creating an indigenous American dramatic idiom, experimenting with new forms and new subject matter, and leading the way for those who followed.[4] Yet while O'Neill's reputation grew over the years, Glaspell was virtually ignored by subsequent critics.[5] In the forty years following her death, only one book devoted to her dramas and novels and only one biographical essay on her life appeared.[6] And with the exception of her first one-act play, *Suppressed Desires,* which has remained a standard work for amateur theater companies, her other writings—six one-act and six full-length plays and eleven novels—were allowed to go out of print.[7]

Interest in Glaspell and her work began to resurface only in the last ten years, when research devoted to women writers uncovered her masterpiece **Trifles**, and the play, along with the short story version, **"A Jury of Her Peers,"** began to appear in anthologies of women's writing, particularly Mary Anne Ferguson's popular *Images of Women in Literature* and Judith Barlow's drama collection *Plays by American Women: The Early Years.*

While feminist criticism has brought Glaspell's name back from the dead and uncanonized, it has not yet produced studies of Glaspell's contributions to dramatic writing. Most discussions of her plays concentrate on them as documents of female exploitation and survival.[8] Certainly, they are important because they are among the first modern writings to focus exclusively on female personae, but they go even further. They offer a new structure, a new dramatic language appropriate to their angle of vision, and a new depiction of character which accommodates the experience of the central figure they delineate, a woman seeking her way in a hostile and often unfamiliar world.

Glaspell's relevance to women playwrights is particularly important because she illustrates in the body of her works the kinds of questions they must face, questions of form determined by the sensibility that the plays embody. Glaspell was among the first writers to realize that it was not enough to present women at the center of the stage. If there were to be a radical break with plays of the past, women would have to exist in a world tailored to their persons and speak a language not borrowed from men. She shared this awareness with her contemporary Virginia Woolf, who, in a 1920 essay, described the problems of female representation on the stage:

> It is true that women afford ground for much speculation and are frequently represented; but it is becoming daily more evident that lady Macbeth, Cordelia, Clarissa, Dora, Diana, Helen, and the rest are by no means what they pretend to be. Some are plainly men in disguise; others represent what men would like to be, or are conscious of not being; or again they embody the dissatisfaction and despair which afflict most people when they reflect upon the sorry condition of the human race.
>
> (p. 65)

Glaspell's women *are* what they seem to be: tentative and often halting, trying to find themselves and their voices. Her explorations on the stage are similar to those described by the critic Susan Rubin Suleiman in her 1986 essay entitled "(Re)Writing the Body: The Politics and Poetics of Female Eroticism":

> Women, who for centuries had been the *objects* of male theorizing, male desires, male fears and male representations, had to discover and reappropriate themselves as *subjects*. . . . The call went out to invent both a new poetics and a new politics, based on women's reclaiming what had always been theirs but had been usurped

from them; control over their bodies and a voice with which to speak about it.

(p. 65)

Glaspell, seventy years earlier, was aware of both responsibilities. She offered a form, a poetics, and a politics which Suleiman and others writing today describe as vital to female-centered art. Glaspell saw that if the world portrayed is the world of women—if the locus of perception is female—then her plays would have to strive for a shape which reinforces this new vantage point and a language which articulates it. And while her particular experiments may at first glance seem removed from those of women writing in modern and postmodern modes of the sixties, seventies, and eighties—who employ transformations, nonrepresentational situations and characters, fragmented temporal and spatial distinctions—they are in fact part of the same ongoing search for dramatic means to depict female experience. A study of Glaspell's works thus provides illustrations of how women can function as protagonists and how structures, language, and subject matter can act as extensions of such women-centered drama.

PIONEER ROOTS

When Susan Glaspell first came to New York with her husband George Cram Cook in April 1913, she was disturbed by the theater she saw. In *The Road to the Temple,* her biography of Cook, she writes, "Plays, like magazine stories, were patterned. They might be pretty good within themselves, seldom did they open out to—where it surprised or thrilled your spirit to follow. They did not ask much of you, those plays." Like O'Neill and the other contributors to the Provincetown Players, she was conscious of the limitations of traditional dramatic form. The Dublin-based Abbey Theatre had toured America in 1911 and had shown the possibilities of dramas not limited to narrowly defined shapes. Yet Glaspell's desire to smash existing structures stems from more than the contemporary abhorrence of limitation, permeating the society in which she moved: Greenwich Village in the first decades of the century. To understand Glaspell's work with form and language, it is necessary to understand something of her biography. Her wish to see plays which "open out" and require the audience "to follow" springs most directly from her pioneer roots.

Susan Glaspell was born in Davenport, Iowa, in 1876,[9] a grandchild of one of the early settlers of the territory. When asked to compile notes for a biographical sketch, she wrote, "Though my home has for some years been in the East, almost everything I write has its roots in the middle west; I suppose because my own are there."[10] In an essay for *Twentieth Century Authors* she repeats this idea: "I have never lost the feeling that is my part of the country" (pp. 541-42).

The impetus for pioneers such as her ancestors, that thing that made them leave comfortable homes for unknown places, continually puzzled Glaspell and became the central motif in all her writing. In *The Road to the Temple* she asks, "What makes a man who has an orchard or a mill in Massachusetts or New York where there is room enough for him . . . get into a covered wagon and go to Indians, rattlesnakes, to the back-breaking work of turning wilderness into productive land.""They go to loneliness and the fears born in loneliness," she says of these pioneers. Young enough herself to remember her grandmother's stories, Glaspell also recognized the difficulty facing the following generations. How do those who come after retain the pioneering spirit? In *Inheritors,* her historical drama, the protagonist Madeline Morton says to her college professor Dr. Holden, "Just a little way back—anything might have been. What happened?" He answers (speaking with difficulty), "It got—set too soon." Unlike O'Neill, who attributed America's failure to an inability of the country to "set down roots," Glaspell saw roots as dangers, marks of fixity and stagnation, usually leading to stultifying institutions against which her characters struggle, much as their pioneering forebears did, in order to move into a new sphere, if not of place then of spirit.

While Glaspell indicates that both men and women need constantly to question institutions and to change them and themselves if both become too rigid—a situation she describes in *Inheritors*—it is to her women characters that she usually attributes this desire for change. It is they who seem to suffer most from the fixity of society. Glaspell continually sunders the stereotype of women desiring stability and the comfort of place. Her works stand in juxtaposition to arguments such as the one set forth in Leslie Fiedler's *Love and Death in the American Novel,* where women are depicted as perpetuators of the status quo, those agents of society against whom male characters battle by going down the Mississippi, into the wilderness, on the road. Invariably in the world Glaspell describes, it is the women, not the men, who want to "lit out," for fixity impinges more directly on them than on the men.[11] As figures of power—American versions of Ibsen's "pillars of society"—the male characters in Glaspell's works have most to lose by change, they hew most closely to routine, and allow virtually no freedom to the women with whom they live. Glaspell's women, for the most part, are required to uphold traditional patterns and remain in place—both physically and mentally.

Mrs. Peters in *Trifles* is typical of such personae. She is described as "married to the law," and expected as such to mouth the ideas of her husband, the sheriff, to trace his conservative path, reflecting his opinions and his decisions. Mr. Peters and the men in the play are untouched and unchanged by the events they witness at the scene of a murder; they are "the law," and the law, Glaspell indicates, is a fixed thing incapable of dealing with either nuances of a case or variations of human behavior. Mrs. Peters, however, assimilates the evidence she stumbles across; she "opens out" into new areas of self-awareness. It is her emancipation which becomes the central theme of the play, overshadowing the murder investigation, the ostensible subject of *Trifles.*

In *The Verge,* Glaspell's expressionist masterpiece, her protagonist Claire Archer experiments with plants in an attempt to move vicariously in new directions that have not been attempted before. Her "Edge Vine" timidly clings to the familiar patterns of the species, and she destroys it. It is to the plant she calls "Breath of Life" that she next turns, hoping that in its courageous "thrusting forward into new forms" it will enter worlds which she too wishes to know. When asked why she breeds new plant forms that do not seem "better" than the familiar varieties, she attempts to explain: "These plants (*beginning flounderingly.*)—perhaps they are less beautiful—less sound—than the plants from which they diverged. But they have found—otherness. (*Laughs a little shrilly.*) If you know what I mean?" When her husband tries to stop her words as he has tried to stop her experiments, she continues excitedly, "No; I'm going on. They have been shocked out of what they were—into something they were not; they've broken from the forms in which they found themselves." In Claire's own life, "form" takes the familiar configurations: wife, mother, friend, lover. She too would move outward, but she is kept back by a circle of men appropriately called Tom, Dick, Harry—friend, lover, husband—and by her sister and child. "Out there—lies all that's not been touched—lies life that waits. Back here—the old pattern, done again, again and again. So long done it doesn't even know itself for a pattern," Claire says to those who thwart her in her desires.

In *Inheritors,* again woman is shown as pioneer, this time not seeking emancipation from conventional gender roles or attempting exploration into unknown areas, but seeking the reinstatement of democratic values which have been subverted in succeeding generations. Madeline Morton, the protagonist, refuses to believe that the practices of America in 1920, with its Red-baiting, condemnation and imprisonment of conscientious objectors, and limitations on freedom of speech, are correct. An "inheritor" of the pioneering spirit of her grandfather, she alone questions the values of the "100 percent Americans" whose jingoism reflects the period in which the play is set and in which it was written.

PIONEER FORM

The image of pioneering is a recurrent one in all of Glaspell's plays; it shapes all her writing. Yet what makes her significant as a model for modern women playwrights is less the paradigm itself than the fact that Glaspell creates a form which reinforces it. Like modern playwrights such as Beckett and Pinter, she recognizes that it is not enough to have subject matter discuss new ideas; a playwright must also offer a dramatic form appropriate to the ideas expressed. The impossibility of logic and linearity cannot be adequately shown in a conventional three-act play which abides by the laws of time and place; so, too, the desire of women characters to break the rules of their societies cannot be depicted in plays which follow conventional rules. The form of a Glaspell work becomes an extension of the theme: each play attempts to break with the formulaic conventions of dramaturgy so pervasive during her period and to offer possible new structures to shape the explorations of her female personae.

Nothing in a Glaspell play is linear. Plots do not have clearly defined beginnings, middles, and ends; they self-consciously move out from some familiar pattern, calling attention as they go to the fact that the expected convention will be violated, the anticipated order will be sundered. If the play seems to be a traditional detective story, as in *Trifles,* the emissaries of the law—the men—will not be the focus of attention. The center of interest, instead, will be the women, those peripheral, shadowy figures in the play who have come on the scene to accompany their husbands and each other.

The notion of linearity in Glaspell's plays is always connected with suppression and with social institutions which have become rigid and confining. For example, the men in *Trifles* walk and talk in straight lines, crisscrossing the scene of the murder as they crisscross the facts of the murder case. When Mr. Hale, a witness to the murder scene, relates his story, he is chided by the district attorney to recount just the facts. "Well Mr. Hale, tell just what happened when you came here yesterday morning." Whenever Mr. Hale veers in the slightest way from the straight narrative line, the county attorney returns him to the narrow parameters of the discourse. "Let's talk about that later, Mr. Hale. I do want to talk about that, but tell now just what happened when you got to the house." In his insistence on the limitations of discourse, the attorney makes clear that he is able to proceed only in prescribed ways. It is significant that Mr. Hale is not part of the legal system; he seems less confined by the narrowness of the lawmen and more in spirit with the freer, unstructured methods of the women, one of whom is his wife. Yet because of his sex, Mr. Hale is afforded the privileges of the men. He is not confined to the kitchen, but follows the attorney and the sheriff around the house seeking clues which will help convict Mrs. Wright, the woman accused of strangling her husband.[12]

Unlike the men, Mrs. Hale and Mrs. Peters show flexibility in their actions and their words. They are limited by the patriarchal power structure clearly working within the scene Glaspell describes, but they are free in the limited confines of the kitchen where the play takes place. One of Glaspell's radical departures is to place the action in the kitchen, one of the few plays of the period to follow *Miss Julie* in doing so. But unlike in Strindberg's play, there are no men in this female province to control the action. Here the women freely retrace the steps of Mrs. Wright.[13] Slowly, almost without volition, they piece together the motive for murder, quilting a pattern of awareness as they randomly move across the stage and speak about the events of the case.

The central image Glaspell chooses for this play is quilting, and, like quilters, her female characters carefully sew together disconnected pieces, making new patterns out of old materials, intuitively sifting through the details

around them without any preconceived pattern limiting their actions. It is they who solve the case, not the lawmen who are committed to set ways of investigation.

The dichotomy Glaspell presents is between male fixity—the fixity of a society gone rigid—and female exploration at the outskirts of that society in the world of women, among "trifles." She underlines this dichotomy by offering a form which has the same randomness and openness as the quilting process itself, in apposition to the constrained, formalized actions of her male characters.

Even more innovative is Glaspell's manipulation of point of view. What she is able to do in this play and in her other works is to force the audience to share the world of her women, to become fellow travelers with her pioneering protagonists. While the men in *Trifles* are almost immediately shunted offstage and only appear as they traverse the playing area of the kitchen, the women remain stationary. It is with them that the audience—men and women—remain, not privy to the conversations of the men, not afforded their mobility. The audience is therefore forced to see the world through the eyes of Mrs. Hale and Mrs. Peters. As a bond is gradually forged between the women and the absent one for whom they act as surrogates and judges, a bond is gradually created between the women and the audience who has gained some insights into their female world and has—at least for the duration of the play—seen as they see. When, at the end of the work, Mrs. Hale places the box containing the strangled bird into her pocketbook in order to destroy the incriminating evidence which provides the only motive for murder, the audience generally applauds her gesture and by so doing becomes itself an accessory to the act.[14]

By placing women at the center of the drama and the audience captive in the kitchen with them, Glaspell does more than merely upend the conventional detective format or offer an unusual locale for a play—at least in 1917. She actually overturns the very hierarchical values of the society she depicts. The men in the play chide "the ladies" for being concerned with the "trifles" of the farm kitchen: the unbaked bread, dirty towel rack, and sewing left undone. Yet Glaspell indicates during the course of the play that such "trifles" can reveal truths, that the concerns of women may have as much significance as the "facts" of men.

She overturns both conventional dramatic form and conventional gender demarcations and values in her other plays as well. In *The Outside* men again play the seemingly active agents. They are lifesavers who attempt to resuscitate a drowning victim. And again—as in *Trifles*—men are unsuccessful; their attempts to save life fail. But as they go through the motions of resuscitation, two women—a maid and her employer—watch silently and themselves perform another kind of "lifesaving." As in *Trifles,* once more Glaspell depicts the inarticulate power of women to understand the shared experiences of other women, unstructured by language but nevertheless communicated through mutually shared pain. Using single words, pauses, and broken sentences, the maid, Allie Mayo, reaches out to the other woman, Mrs Patrick, drawing her back to the life she has rejected. Little outward action occurs, but once more Glaspell indicates that events of great moment may take place in near-silence among those not accustomed to heroic deeds; individuals may be saved by a few well-chosen words, by a gesture, by "trifles," as well as by physical valor.

In *The Verge* Glaspell's protagonist is less fortunate than the two women in *Trifles* and *The Outside;* she is afforded no victory in her quest for freedom. Unable to move "outside," like the plant she has cultivated, Claire Archer reverts to one of the two traditional ends for women who would break with societal restrictions. She lapses into madness, a variation on the suicide that so often is the end of pioneering women, at least in literature in the early part of twentieth century. Glaspell's great accompishment in this play is to provide a perfect dramatic structure to shape her hero's efforts. Antedating O'Neill's *Hairy Ape* by several months, she creates one of the first expressionist settings in American theater.[15] The play has an odd, open-ended shape to it, depicted visually on the stage by the two playing areas: the narrow, low greenhouse in which Claire works and the tower—*"a tower which is thought to be round but does not complete the circle,"* the stage directions say. Claire calls it her "thwarted tower." Both areas are lit in special ways. In act 1, patterns are superimposed on the greenhouse *"as if—as Plato would have it—the patterns inherent in abstract nature and behind all life had come out."* Periodically, light from a trapdoor illuminates the laboratory. The interior of the tower in act 2 is dark and brooding, lit by an old-fashioned watchman's lantern whose "innumerable pricks and slits in the metal create a marvelous pattern on the curved wall—like some masonry that hasn't been."

The form of the play is also experimental. Beginning like a conventional comedy of the twenties—weekend guests discomforted because the heat in the house has been diverted to the plants in the greenhouse—the play moves in act 2 to a psychological investigation of Claire that stands in odd juxtaposition to the levity and ambiance of act 1. Yet this discontinuity between acts seems to be Glaspell's way of once more having form reinforce theme. Repeatedly in act 1 Claire is chided by the men around her to be "cheerful," "witty," "fun." Enforced gaiety is what Claire wishes to escape as much as she wishes to escape the restrictive roles of traditional womanhood. By contrasting the style and mood of the laboratory scene with the introspective world of the tower, Glaspell indicates the forces working on her protagonist. Only in her tower home is Claire relatively free to pursue a course not dictated by others. However, there are still stairs which lead up to her haven, more often trod than the parallel stairs which lead from her laboratory down to a temporary, subterranean refuge. She may escape down the latter, but she cannot avoid the intrusions of those who will ascend the former.

In act 3, again in Claire's laboratory, as she waits for the unveiling of her new plant form, the tensions between the two styles of the preceding acts and the two venues explode in violence. Using the same ending that O'Neill will employ in *The Hairy Ape*—the hug of death—Glaspell has her protagonist strangle Tom, the man who presents the greatest obstacle to her freedom. She then concludes her play with Claire lapsing into insanity, what appears to be the only refuge from the world depicted in the play. Conflating the initial comedy of manners and the psychological investigation, Glaspell creates a play which fits no simple category, a fitting structure for a protagonist who wishes to escape easy classification.

PIONEER LANGUAGE

Glaspell's plays foreground women and provide open, unrestricted, asymmetrical dramatic structures in which women operate. The same can be said for the language characters use. Repeatedly, Glaspell connects language to action. Since her women are exploring new areas of their lives, they find traditional language unsuited to their needs. They may be women unused to speech or women all too aware that the words they speak do not express their thoughts. In either case the results are the same. Her characters are virtually inarticulate, or are rendered so because of the situations in which they find themselves. The most common punctuation mark she uses is the dash. It is used when the character is unsure of the direction in which she is going, as yet unprepared to articulate consciously a new awareness or unwilling to put into words feelings and wishes which may collapse under the weight of words.

One of Glaspell's most important contributions to drama is to place these inarticulate characters in the center of her works, to allow them to struggle to say what they are not sure they even know. While O'Neill's personae usually end statements with exclamation points, Glaspell has the courage to allow her women to trail off their words in pauses, devices against the tyranny of language. And while those inarticulates O'Neill does present are unable to speak because of the limits of their class or education, Glaspell's women, despite their class, share the limitations of their gender and find speech difficult. It fails to describe the new areas into which they are attempting to move and is often perceived as the language of male experience.

In many ways Glaspell's recognition of the inherent connection between female independence and language makes her a forerunner of contemporary feminist critics who see language at the heart of any possible realignment of the sexes. While Glaspell did not write essays about the subject, her plays speak to the same concerns that occupy feminist critics such as Julia Kristeva, Hélène Cixous, and Luce Irigaray.[16] And while Glaspell's struggles to create a female language do not go as far as those espousing *écriture féminine* would probably accept, they are predicated on some of the same beliefs: that women's subjugation in society is connected to the subjugation imposed by language.

Prefiguring psychoanalytic critics such as Irigaray, Glaspell actually offers on the stage the absent woman—woman as void—against whom male characters react, upon whom they impose a shape—much as Woolf described—making of the absent woman a kind of palimpsest upon which to inscribe their own identities, desires, and language. Bernice in the play of that name, Alison in *Alison's House,* and Mrs. Wright in *Trifles* are all hovering presences who never appear. Since they are not physically present, their voices are co-opted by males who speak for them. This dramatic depiction of woman as void is one of Glaspell's most innovative and modern techniques, employed by contemporary women playwrights as well as by feminist critics.

One of the most direct examples of male usurpation of female speech appears in *Trifles,* which begins with Mr. Hale acting as the spokesperson for the absent Mrs. Wright. Her words come through his mouth. The women present say nothing as the voice of man speaks the words of woman. Only when the women are alone does sound come, and it is—and remains—a halting sound. Yet as the awereness of their shared subjugation develops, the women begin to seek a verbal form for this knowledge. Appropriately, it is a language of stops and starts, with lacunae—dashes—covering the truths they still cannot admit or are unused to framing in words. What the audience sees and hears are people learning to speak, constructing a medium of expression as they go. The way is not easy, and the language they frame is awkward. But it is clearly their language, no longer the words of others which they have been taught to speak.

One of the most effective moments in the play, a point of anagnorisis, is when Mrs. Peters recalls the time when she too felt powerless, like Mrs. Wright, and she too had murder in her heart: "When I was a girl—my kitten—there was a boy took a hatchet, and before my eyes—and before I could get there—if they hadn't held me back I would have—hurt him." Unwilling or unable to say more, Mrs. Peters talks in half sentences, covering her growing awareness in pauses more telling than the words she actually employs. The sentence becomes a verbal concomitant to the patchwork investigation the two women have conducted in the kitchen.

In another section of *Trifles,* Glaspell points directly to the connections between quilting and growing awareness, doing so through seemingly flat, banal phrases. Three times during the course of the play, the women discuss the stitches Mrs. Wright has used for her work. The first time the men overhear them and laugh when Mrs. Hale asks, "I wonder if she was goin' to quilt it or just knot it." Several minutes later the question turns to a qualified statement when Mrs. Peters says, "We think she was going to—knot it." The last words of the play, after the women have hidden the evidence and silently rebelled against their husbands, are Mrs. Hale's: "We call it knot it." From interrogative to qualified statement to assertion—the sentences mark the changes in the women, changes the men overlook because they do not hear the import of the words the women use.

To the men, the words refer to "trifles"; the language is foreign, the shape of the sentences irrelevant. That seems to be Glaspell's point. The women speak in a different voice, to use Carol Gilligan's apt phrase. There is the voice of law and fact and the voice of connection and caring.[17] The two voices do not hear each other. What is important, however, is that the audience, who has begun to decipher the words of women, can understand the import of the lines as the men with whom these women live cannot. The audience has begun to listen to, if not to speak in, "a different voice."

Glaspell employs other alterations of language in *The Verge.* In that play Claire Archer suffers from too many words, other people's words. When she desires to express her own ideas, she finds herself unable to do so because the words she must use are already misshapen by the uses others make of them. "I'm tired of what you do," Claire tells her fatuous sister,

> you and all of you. Life—experience—values—calm—sensitive words which raise their heads as indications. And you *pull them up*—to decorate your stagnant little minds—and think that makes you—And because you have pulled that word from the life that grew it you won't let one who's honest, and aware, and troubled, try to reach through to—what she doesn't know is there.

Unsure of what she seeks, Claire realizes the dilemma she faces: the language which is her only means of investigation is the language of those she would leave behind. It is against the fixed forms of the society which Claire inveighs, just as it is against the imposition of an alien language which she struggles.

To compound the problem, Claire also recognizes that when trying to give voice to ideas which are still inchoate, she forces upon them a pattern that limits the exploration itself. "Stop doing that!" she demands of language, "—words going into patterns; They do it sometimes when I let come what's there. Thoughts take pattern—then the pattern is the thing." Here Glaspell refers not to the limits women experience speaking the language of men but to the limits of language itself.

PIONEER SUBJECT MATTER

Claire Archer is one of the first female characters in drama whose main concern is to create a new language and whose failure illustrates the difficulties in doing so. Sixty years later, in his play *Not I,* Samuel Beckett would place a gaping mouth eight feet above the stage and reenact a similar struggle for articulation of self—and a similar failure. By making language the primary focus of the struggle for selfhood, Glaspell is radically expanding the possibilities of thematic material for theater and the uses of stage language.

Further, Glaspell was one of the first women playwrights to present female personae engaged in violent acts: killing a husband offstage in *Trifles,* strangling a lover onstage in *The Verge.* Glaspell's choice of subject matter in both plays may not seem shocking or innovative in the contemporary period, where a playwright depicts a woman taking the grotesque shape of a circus freak and having her genitals excised (Joan Shenkar's *Signs of Life*); or examines lesbianism, homosexuality, and masturbation as liberating alternatives to, or perhaps direct results of, colonial values and mores (Caryl Churchill's *Cloud Nine*); or describes the ritual slaughter of a random male (Maureen Duffy's *Rites*); or depicts lady mud wrestlers performing in a bar in New Jersey (Rosalyn Drexler's *Delicate Feelings*); or makes Joan of Arc and Susan B. Anthony fellow travelers (Lavonne Mueller's *Little Victories*). Yet, in her own period, Glaspell's material was culled from events and subjects considered sacrosanct, controversial, and—in the case of *Inheritors*—subversive. Her first play was *Suppressed Desires,* written in collaboration with her husband, George Cram Cook. It parodied a movement which her own circle of friends in Greenwich Village took most seriously: psychoanalysis. "You could not go out to buy a bun without hearing of someone's complex," Glaspell wrote about her first days in New York in 1913. Blind adherence to analysis becomes the comic subject of the play, subtitled *A Freudian Comedy*. It was one of the first plays written in America to employ, albeit sarcastically, the new theories Freud introduced to the country only a few years before in his Clark University lectures.[18]

Glaspell consistently wrote about controversial topics throughout her career, sometimes treating them to ridicule, sometimes offering them a platform for development. For example, her last play for the Provincetown theater, *Chains of Dew* (1922), has as its protagonist a young woman named Nora (the name probably borrowed from Ibsen) whose mission is to spread news about contraception and who in the process radicalizes the women with whom she comes into contact in the play and, by extension, those in the audience.

Glaspell's most challenging use of subject matter, however, comes in the play *Inheritors*. In order to appreciate the risks taken in this work, it is necessary to have some idea of the climate in which the play was written in 1920. In 1917, as a result of Woodrow Wilson's declaration of war—an act Glaspell and her friends vigorously opposed—Congress passed the Selective Service Act, which required general conscription for eligible males, exempting only those who on narrowly specified grounds opposed all wars. Others resisting the draft for moral or political reasons were tried as deserters, and when convicted often faced brutal treatment. Along with conscription, Congress also enacted laws intended to quell dissent about the war. The Espionage Act, on pain of a ten-thousand-dollar fine and twenty years in jail, made it illegal to refuse duty or impede recruitment in the military. The appended Sedition Act went further and prohibited uttering, printing, or writing any disloyal, profane, or scurrilous language about the form of government in the United States. Various alien laws made it a crime, punishable by deportation, to speak out against America or any of its allies.[19]

During the postwar period the theater was generally silent about such abuses in society. Burns Mantle's *Best Plays of 1920-21* lists such hits as *Good Times* and *Irene*. Glaspell's *Inheritors* was the exception to this escapist fare. It directly condemns the treatment of conscientious objectors after the war, the deportation of aliens and strikebreakers, and the abridgment of personal freedom of speech. The play also makes direct references to the excessive patriotism which persisted after the end of the war. "That's the worst of a war—you have to go on hearing about it for so long," and "Seems nothing draws men together like killing other men," and "The war was a godsend to people who were in danger of getting on to themselves" were lines still liable to bring Glaspell—like her protagonist—a possible fine and jail sentence under the espionage and sedition laws. Glaspell's friends Big Bill Haywood, head of the Wobblies, Emma Goldman, and Jack Reed had already experienced the effects of the repression. Yet Glaspell went ahead with her play, which was well received and may have had some part in reversing the climate of the period. It is interesting to note that as a mark of the universality of the issues Glaspell raises, the Hedgerow Theatre of Moylan, Pennsylvania, headed by Jasper Deeter, an original member of the Provincetown Players, performed the play every year from 1923 to 1954, except during the war.[20] When the play was revived by the Mirror Repertory Company in New York in 1983, the critics all mentioned one point: the picture of the past which it offers is as valid in the eighties as it was for Glaspell's audience in 1921.

Glaspell's focus on contemporary issues—either to mock them or to promulgate them—follows a tradition among women playwrights which goes back as far as Mercy Otis Warren and forward to Megan Terry and Maria Irene Fornes. Yet when Terry wrote *Viet Rock* in the sixties and Fornes wrote *The Danube* and *The Conduct of Life* in the eighties, they risked far less censure or danger than Glaspell faced in her own stand against a repressive society.

As important as her political positions were in keeping alive the tradition of outspoken women playwrights, Glaspell is probably most important to women writers as an example of someone who dared to give dramatic shape to the struggles of women. The two women in *Trifles* can be prototypes of Everywoman; Claire Archer can be a fictional surrogate for feminist ideologues who are presently engaged in altering language to fit their own needs and possibilities. Certainly, Glaspell is not the only woman playwright who provides a her/story from which others may draw sustenance. Those writers represented in Barlow's collection—Mowatt, Crothers, Gale, and Treadwell—as well as innovators such as Gerstenberg and those many, until recently anonymous black women playwrights of the twenties and thirties, offer a body of works that open up the range of experimentation for the present group of women playwrights.[21]

I would argue that having read the work of Glaspell and other women writing at the beginning of the century, one has a better idea of the ongoing movement which is American women's drama. There is the shadow of Glaspell and the others behind such experiments as the Women's Project of the American Place Theatre, which one of its participants described as giving to women "a place to raise their voices without apology" (p. 13). While Helene Keyssar in *Feminist Theatre* is correct in saying that it was only in the late sixties that playwrights "*in significant numbers* became self-consciously concerned about the presence—or absence—of women as women on stage" (p. 1, my italics), there were women much earlier in the century, and before, who shared these concerns and wrote plays which led the way. Susan Glaspell was one of the most important of these pioneering playwrights. Although she has been ignored by those who shape the canon, she should not be ignored by those who are attempting to reconstitute it.

NOTES

[1]Over the seven-year period in which the original theater company functioned, there were one hundred original American plays produced by fifty playwrights, thirty-three of them women. See Helen Deutsch and Stella Hanau, *The Provincetown: A Story of the Theatre*, and Robert Karoly Sarlos, *Jig Cook and the Provincetown Players: Theatre in Ferment*.

[2]Sarlos reports that Copeau was "'touched to the depth of his soul' by Susan Glaspell's acting in her own play, *The People*. Copeau confessed that 'the simplicity of her presence' made him understand as no previous experience has 'the importance of relinquishing current theatre techniques, even at the price of a prolonged period of groping'" (p. 73).

[3]See Linda Ben-Zvi, "Susan Glaspell and Eugene O'Neill," *Eugene O'Neill Newsletter 9: Special Issue on O'Neill and Women* (Fall, 1982), 15-24; and Linda Ben-Zvi, "Susan Glaspell, Eugene O'Neill, and the Imagery of Gender," *Eugene O'Neill Newsletter* 11 (Spring 1986), 22-27.

[4]See Isaac Goldberg, *The Drama of Transition* (pp. 472-81); Ludwig Lewisohn, *Drama and Stage* (pp. 102-10) and *Expressionism in America* (393-98). For an annotated bibliography of the critical responses to Glaspell's plays and those of other Provincetown members, see Gerhard Bach, *Susan Glaspell und die Provincetown Players*.

[5]Among contemporary critics only C. W. E. Bigsby discusses Glaspell as an equal to O'Neill and as a writer whose works deserve serious attention. See C. W. E. Bigsby, *A Critical Introduction to Twentieth-Century American Drama*, vol. 1, *1900-1940* (pp. 25-35). Bigsby has also recently edited a collection of Glaspell's plays (*Trifles, The Outside, The Verge,* and *Inheritors*).

[6]See Arthur Waterman, *Susan Glaspell*, and Marcia Noe, *Susan Glaspell: Voice from the Heartland*.

[7]Glaspell's one-act plays are *Suppressed Desires* (written with George Cram Cook), *Trifles, The People, Close the Book, The Outside, Woman's Honor,* and *Tickless Time* (written with Cook). Her full-length plays include *Bernice, Inheritors, The Verge,* and *Chains of Dew* (all written for the Provincetown Players); *The Comic Artist* (written with Norman Matson in 1928); and *Alison's House* (written in 1931 and awarded the Pulitzer Prize in that year). Thanks to Bigsby's collection, Glaspell's major plays are once more available.

[8]See Annette Kolodny, "A Map for Rereading: Gender and the Interpretation of Literary Texts," in *The New Feminist Criticism; Essays on Women, Literature, and Theory* (pp. 46-62).

[9]Although Glaspell listed her birth year as 1882 in biographical articles, she was actually born July 1, 1876. The Scott County Registrar's office lists no birth certificate for Glaspell, but the Iowa census of 1880 notes a four-year-old Susie Glaspell, a five-year-old Charles, and a one-year-old Frank, children of Elmer and Alice (Keating) Glaspell residing at 502 Cedar Street, Davenport, Iowa. Also, a diary of Glaspell's aunt on file at the Berg Collection of the New York Public Library, which houses both Glaspell's and Cook's papers, indicates that on the alleged date of her birth in 1882, the entire Glaspell family, including Susie, came to visit. Finally, Drake University, where Glaspell received a Ph.D. degree, lists her age at the time of her admission in 1897 as 21.

[10]This description is found in Glaspell's papers in the Berg Collection.

[11]It is interesting to note that while O'Neill gives lip service to freedom—"and at last be free, on the open sea, with the trade wind in our hair" (from his first poem)—a close study of his works indicates that he places his characters in closed spaces and has them yearn for fixity and home. For example, on the fictional steamer *Glencairn* the playing areas are closed, cramped quarters, with small, crowded bunks and foreshortened spaces. In *Bound East for Cardiff* and *In the Zone*, action is confined to the forecastle. While *The Moon of the Caribees* is set on deck—one of the few sea plays that is—only a small strip of it is seen, and the action always seems to move below, out of sight. The best example of the freedom of sea life metamorphosing into the fixity of home is found in *The Hairy Ape*, where Yank, while ridiculing the idea of home, shows how he has made a new home of his furnace world. He spends most of the play attempting to regain this home after he is ousted from it. Progressively in O'Neill's later works, his male characters seek surrogate homes and indicate that freedom, for them, is not as important as the security of home. A comparison of the plays of O'Neill and Glaspell indicates how the traditional stereotypes of male freedom and female domesticity are destroyed. See Linda Ben-Zvi, "Freedom and Fixity in the Late Plays of Eugene O'Neill," *Modern Drama 31: Special Centenary Issue on O'Neill* (May 1988), 16-27.

[12]To get a strong sense of the physical linearity that exists in the work, see the film version by the director Sally Hackel, entitled *A Jury of Her Peers*.

[13]It is possible to see *Trifles* as an answer to *Miss Julie*, a play Glaspell would have known. There are several parallels that indicate she may have had the play in mind when she wrote her own "woman's version." In both plays the female character has a pet bird that is killed by a man. In *Miss Julie* Jean kills Julie's bird before sending Julie off to her own death. In *Trifles* the woman takes revenge for the destruction of her pet and for her own death of the spirit by killing her husband by slow strangulation, the appropriate act to fit his crime.

[14]When I was organizing a special session on Glaspell for the Modern Language Association, I received a letter from a professor at an eastern law school telling me that he taught *Trifles* to new first-year law students because of the audience's pardoning of an illegal act.

[15]See Linda Ben-Zvi, "Susan Glaspell and Eugene O'Neill," and "Eugene O'Neill and the Imagery of Gender," in *The Eugene O'Neill Newsletter*. In both articles I agree that Glaspell's *Verge* is an important influence on O'Neill's *Hairy Ape*. At the time he was composing his play, O'Neill was meeting his neighbor Glaspell every afternoon after working on his manuscript, his wife Agnes reports. As an indication of how completely O'Neill critics ignore Glaspell and her influence on O'Neill, it is interesting to note that not one has ever mentioned the striking similarities between the two plays and the fact that O'Neill was in such close association with her during its composition. They prefer to cite such speculative

sources as the film *The Cabinet of Dr. Caligari* and the play *From Morn to Midnight*, works O'Neill knew less well than he knew *The Verge*.

[16]For a sampling of French feminist criticism, see Elaine Marks and Isabelle de Courtivrons, eds., *New French Feminisms: An Anthology*. For a sample of American feminist criticism, see Elaine Showalter, ed., *The New Feminist Criticism: Essays on Women, Literature, and Theory*.

[17]Carol Gilligan, *In a Different Voice*. Gilligan's discussion of the differences between male and female language and approaches to problem solving is directly connected to *Trifles*, which clearly reinforces Gilligan's observations.

[18]For a discussion of Glaspell's use of Freudianism on the stage, see W. David Sievers, *Freud on Broadway*.

[19]To get an idea of the climate in America after the First World War, see Frederick C. Giffin, *Six Who Protested*; Burl Noggle, *Into the Twenties*; Zachariah Chafee, *Freedom of Speech*; and H. C. Peterson and Gilbert C. Fite, eds., *Opponents of War: 1917-1918*. In the last book the authors list a celebrated case of a conscientious objector named Fred Robinson who was mistreated long after the war. Glaspell's character Fred Jordan may have been based on Robinson.

[20]Former actors associated with the Hedgerow Theatre gave a reading of *Inheritors* at the Modern Language Association meeting in Los Angeles in 1982. Organized by Gail Cohen, the production included Hedgerow alumni Henry Jones and the late Richard Basehart.

[21]In the past few years, several books devoted to black women playwrights have appeared. In 1988 Beacon Press brought out the plays of Marita Bonner, edited by Joyce Flynn and Bonner's daughter, and New American Library published an anthology of black woman playwrights entitled *Nine Plays by Black Women*, edited and with an introduction by Margaret B. Wilkerson.

BIBLIOGRAPHY

Bach, Gerhard. *Susan Glaspell und die Provincetown Players: Die Anfänge des modernen amerikanischen Dramas und Theaters*. Frankfurt-am-Main: Lang, 1979.

Ben-Zvi, Linda. "Susan Glaspell and Eugene O'Neill." *Eugene O'Neill Newsletter 9: Special Issue on O'Neill and Women* (Fall 1982), 15-24.

————. "Susan Glaspell, Eugene O'Neill, and the Imagery of Gender." *Eugene O'Neill Newsletter* 11 (Spring 1986), 22-27.

————. "Freedom and Fixity in the Late Plays of Eugene O'Neill." *Modern Drama* 31: *Special Centenary Issue on O'Neill* (May 1988), 16-27.

Bigsby, C. W. E. *A Critical Introduction to Twentieth-Century American Drama*. Vol. 1, *1900-1940*. Cambridge: Cambridge University Press, 1982.

————, ed. *Plays by Susan Glaspell*. Cambridge: Cambridge University Press, 1987.

Chaffee, Zacariah. *Freedom of Speech*. New York: Harcourt Brace, 1921.

Deutsch, Helen, and Stella Hanau. *The Provincetown: A Story of the Theatre*. New York: Russell and Russell, 1931.

Fiedler, Leslie. *Love and Death in the American Novel*. Rev. ed. New York: Stein and Day, 1966.

Giffin, Frederick C. *Six Who Protested: Radical Opposition to the First World War*. Port Washington, N.Y.: Kinnekat Press, 1977.

Gilligan, Carol. *In a Different Voice*. Cambridge, Mass.: Harvard University Press, 1982.

Glaspell, Susan. *Inheritors*. Boston: Small, Maynard, 1924.

————. *The Outside* in *Plays*. Boston: Small, Maynard, 1920.

————. *The Road to the Temple*. New York. Frederick Stokes, 1927. Rev. 1941.

————. *Suppressed Desires* (with George Cram Cook) in *Plays*.

————. *Trifles* in *Plays*.

Goldberg, Isaac. *The Drama of Transition*. Cincinnati: Stuart Kidd, 1922.

Keyssar, Helene. *Feminist Theatre*. New York: Grove Press, 1985.

Kolodny, Annette. "A Map for Rereading: Gender and the Interpretation of Literary Texts." In *The New Feminist Criticism*, edited by Elaine Showalter, pp. 46-62. New York: Pantheon, 1985.

Kunitz, Stanley J., and Howard Haycraft, eds. *Twentieth Century Authors*. New York: H. W. Wilson, 1942.

Lewisohn, Ludwig. *Drama and the Stage*. New York: Harcourt, 1922.

————. *Expressionism in America*. New York: Harpers, 1932.

Marks, Elaine, and Isabelle de Courtivrons, eds. *New French Feminisms: An Anthology*. Amherst, Mass.: University of Massachusetts Press, 1980.

Miles, Julia, ed. *The Women's Project*. New York: Performing Arts Journal Publications and the American Place Theatre, 1980.

Noe, Marcia. *Susan Glaspell: Voice from the Heartland*. Macomb, Ill.: Western Illinois Monograph Series, no. 1, 1983.

Noggle, Burl. *Into the Twenties*. Urbana, Ill.: University of Illinois Press, 1974.

Peterson, H. C., and Gilbert C. Fite, eds. *Opponents of War: 1917-1918*. Madison, Wisc.: University of Wisconsin Press, 1957.

Sarlos, Robert Karoly. *Jig Cook and the Provincetown Players: Theatre in Ferment*. Amherst, Mass.: University of Massachusetts Press, 1982.

Showalter, Elaine, ed. *The New Feminist Criticism*. New York: Pantheon, 1985.

Sievers, W. David. *Freud on Broadway*. New York: Hermitage House, 1955.

Suleiman, Susan Rubin, ed. *The Female Body in Western Culture*. Cambridge, Mass.: Harvard University Press, 1986.

Waterman, Arthur. *Susan Glaspell*. New York: Twayne, 1966.

Woolf, Virginia. *Women and Writing*. Edited by Michele Barrett. New York: Harcourt Brace, 1979.

Veronica Makowsky (essay date 1993)

SOURCE: "Passive Resistance to Active Rebellion: From *Trifles* to *The Verge*" and "Ghostly Revenants and Symbolic Sons: Fugitives Return," in *Susan Glaspell's Century of American Women: A Critical Interpretation of Her Work*, Oxford University Press, 1993, pp. 59-82, 101-16.

[*The following excerpts provide a broad overview of Glaspell's development as a playwright.*]

Glaspell did not publish a novel between *Fidelity* in 1915 and *Brook Evans* in 1928, the years of her involvement with the Provincetown Players, her sojourn in Greece with Cook, and her period of mourning for his death. She is, of course, best known for the plays she wrote during that period, particularly the widely anthologized *Trifles* (1916), and many critics consider the plays her major works because they are an exciting, innovative contribution to American drama. In terms of her fiction, though, the plays are not a startling flowering or reversal, but can be seen as the thematic and symbolic bridge between Glaspell's early and late novels.[1] In keeping with this thematic continuum, this chapter will examine the plays that focus on women, particularly the theme of maternity, for in these plays motherhood becomes disassociated from sweetness and light and increasingly linked to entrapment and oppression.[2] In contrast to the self-sacrificial struggles of Ernestine Hubers in *The Glory of the Conquered* (1909) or the long self-immolation of Ruth Holland in *Fidelity,* Glaspell creates dramatic heroines who begin to realize that in living for others they are destroying themselves. As Adrienne Rich states in her book on motherhood, "Oppression is not the mother of virtue; oppression can warp, undermine, turn us into haters of ourselves."[3]

Glaspell's fiction has been considered much more conventional than her plays, but the difference is one of degree; it is not a *volte face*. Although the heroines of her plays are more visibly, vocally, and sometimes violently, rebellious than those of her novels, her fictional heroines are hardly models of decorum. In *The Glory of the Conquered,* Ernestine Hubers manages to pursue her career as an artist and learn the methods of scientific research despite sexism on all sides; in *The Visioning,* Katie Jones leaves the safety and comfort of the military brass for the uncertainties of life with a socialist organizer and artist; although *Fidelity*'s Ruth Holland lives with a married man for years, she leaves him to pursue her own interests when he is free to marry but she no longer loves him.

Similarly, in formal terms, Glaspell's plays have been found more innovative than her fiction. For instance, the distinguished Eugene O'Neill and Glaspell scholar Linda Ben-Zvi states:

> Nothing in a Glaspell play is linear. Plots do not have clearly defined beginnings, middles, and ends; they self-consciously move out from some familiar pattern, calling attention as they go to the fact that the expected convention will be violated, the anticipated order will be sundered.[4]

Ben-Zvi is undoubtedly correct, but I see this difference as less a rebellion against the conventional well-made play and more of a continuation of some of the techniques of Glaspell's novels, which often begin *in medias res*, do not follow a conventional courtship to marriage pattern, and often end with the question of the heroine's future left open. Glaspell's dramatic use of understated gestures and comments also derives from her apprentice fiction; as early as 1904, her fictive heroine Christine Holt observes:

> At crucial times people acted just as they did in the commonplace hours—really they acted more so. And that would be a good feature to bring out in the play.

The tragedy of the play must be very quiet, very conventional, and commonplace.[5]

The relative lack of action and plethora of ideas and meditative speeches in Glaspell's plays also arises from her work as a writer of women's fiction; in the restricted sphere of the domestic, a woman's life is mainly interior, inside her own mind as well as inside her home.

Glaspell's plays may not be formally or thematically antithetical to her fiction, but the difference in the degree of rebellion is significant. The rebellions of her fictional women are private while those of her dramatic heroines sometimes lead them to the public sphere of demonstrations, courts, and prison; these heroines do include two murderesses, a number of confessed adulteresses, and a police-basher. Their actions demand that the patriarchal world consider their feelings and situations as something more than domestic "trifles."

The increased degree of rebelliousness in Glaspell's plays has a number of causes, personal, generic, and cultural. First, in biographical terms, Glaspell was married to a believer and practitioner of free love whom she loved; she did not want to live without him, but his numerous affairs made him hard to live with, and her anger finds an outlet in these plays, sometimes quite specifically against Cook and sometimes against patriarchal men in general.[6] Secondly, her situation with the Provincetown Players as playwright, actress, and co-founder gave Glaspell an artistic freedom and control quite unusual for a woman. In *Feminist Theories for Dramatic Criticism*, Gayle Austin points out:

> The writing of plays requires mastering to some degree a male-dominated, public production machinery, something that relatively few women have been able to do over the long history of the form, and consequently there is not as large a body of extant plays by women as there is of novels.[7]

The liberating effect of Glaspell's transition to a different genre was augmented by her sense of a new audience: she was no longer trying to appeal to conventional middle-class female readers of fiction, but to the avant-grade of Greenwich Village and Provincetown, including her fellow members of the feminist Heterodoxy Club.

Glaspell's first solo dramatic effort is the justly celebrated one-act play *Trifles* (1916). Mrs. Peters and Mrs. Hale accompany some male authorities to the remote farmhouse of Minnie and John Wright where they are supposed to collect some personal belongings for the imprisoned Minnie while the men try to establish a motive for Minnie's alleged strangling of her husband. As numerous critics have demonstrated, the men stomp about loudly and authoritatively but cannot find the clues because they are unable to read quiet, domestic "trifles."[8] In contrast, Mrs. Peters and Mrs. Hale realize that the disordered kitchen, ragged sewing, and strangled canary indicate that the isolated Minnie would accept no further abuse from her cold, stingy husband and revenged the death of her pet and friend by killing John the same way.[9] The women display female solidarity by concealing the dead bird, and their conclusions, from the men.

The sympathy of Mrs. Hale and Mrs. Peters arises not only from sisterly solidarity but from the two women's self-identification as mothers, in contrast to the childless Minnie. Love, particularly maternal love, is associated with sound and its absence with silence. Mrs. Hale wonders "how it would seem never to have had any children around," and Mrs. Peters can tell her: "I know what stillness is. When we homesteaded in Dakota, and my first baby died. . . ."[10] They realize that the pet was a kind of child-substitute for the solitary Minnie; the canary's voice was to displace the silence of a coldly authoritarian husband and replace the sounds of the unborn children. Mrs. Hale notes, "If there'd been years and years of nothing, then a bird to sing to you, it would be awful—still, after the bird was still" (26). Mrs. Peters even remembers a similar loss and response: "When I was a girl—my kitten—there was a boy took a hatchet, and before my eyes—and before I could get there—If they hadn't held me back I would have—hurt him" (25).

Their maternal feelings not only help Mrs. Hale and Mrs. Peters understand the importance of the canary to Minnie, but also help them direct their solicitude toward Mrs. Wright herself through the memory of Minnie as a vulnerable, pretty young girl who loved singing in the choir. Mrs. Hale makes the identification clear when she states that Minnie "was kind of like a bird herself—real sweet and pretty, but kind of timid and—fluttery. How—she—did—change" (22). Mrs. Hale finally places the blame for that change on John Wright: "She used to sing. He killed that, too" (25). Through the traditional literary metaphor of the bird's song as the voice of the soul, the women acknowledge that John Wright not only killed Minnie's canary, but her very spirit.

Adrienne Rich justly observes that "powerless women have always used mothering as a channel—narrow but deep—for their own human will to power."[11] Similarly, Glaspell is not idealizing motherhood or maternal feelings here but demonstrating that these rural women have no outlets for expression aside from domesticity focusing on children, though Minnie Wright lacks even that. After noting John Wright's nullity as a husband, Sharon P. Friedman states, "If a husband and children are the determinants of most women's lives, then Minnie has nothing; she is nothing."[12] Glaspell's early fiction repeatedly identifies artistic creativity with motherhood, but Minnie Wright is not allowed that outlet either, through an unfinished quilt or vicariously through the voice of the canary. In a sense, as Annette Kolodny has written, Glaspell is also exploring the plight of the woman writer; her "trifles" are as unnoticed and unappreciated by her culture as are Minnie's domestic artifacts by the investigating men.[13]

Glaspell demonstrates that maternal feelings are a double-edged sword in that they make Mrs. Hale and Mrs. Peters sympathize with Minnie's childlessness and want to protect her as if she were a child, but their maternal devotion also prevents them from helping Minnie until it is too late.[14] Mrs. Hale, played by Glaspell in the original production, declares, "I know how things can be—for women. We live close together and we live far apart. We all go through the same things—it's all just a different kind of the same thing" (27). She realizes that her narrow focus on her own domicile and children have kept her from nurturing Minnie, and cries, "Oh, I *wish* I'd come over here once in a while! That was a crime! That was a crime! Who's going to punish that?" (27). Not the men certainly, who want the women locked into separate domestic spheres and would like them to accept the blame, which really belongs to men. When she makes this comment Mrs. Hale is empathetic, but masochistic; not until she conceals the evidence with Mrs. Peters at the end of the play does she silently place the guilt where it really belongs.

If one regards Mrs. Hale and Mrs. Peters as the heroines of *Trifles,* their rebellion must be characterized not as active insurrection but as passive resistance, which is all these women can realistically achieve under the circumstances. If Minnie Wright is the central figure of *Trifles,* the play may seem different since she does murder her oppressor, but the glimpses we get of her after the killing, through Mr. Hale's spoken memories, indicate the ineffectual nature of her act. She has moved herself from her rocking chair in the center of the kitchen to a "small chair in the corner" (8), as if she is acknowledging her marginalized and outlaw status. She keeps rocking as if she knows that she must comfort herself the way a mother would a child. Most tellingly, she is largely silent, except to laugh when Mr. Hale mentions that he came to see if John Wright wanted a telephone and to tell him "I sleep sound" (7) as her excuse for not hearing the killing. Both these sounds are in effect silences that point to her past and future silencing: John had cut her off from the sounds of human voices, and her sleep in the grave will be sound and silent if she is convicted of murder. Even a rebellious woman like Minnie knows that men may be laughable in their blindness but that they still have overwhelming power. Women like Mrs. Hale and Mrs. Peters are limited to the divisive expression of biological maternity as a diversion from more culturally powerful creativity.

Glaspell's next play, *The People* (1917), does not ostensibly concern the position of women, but the character played by Glaspell in the original production, the Woman from Idaho, is a spokesperson for the playwright, and her catalytic role indirectly comments on the place of women in society.[15] A periodical based on *The Masses, The People: A Journal of the Social Revolution*, is about to fold because of insufficient funds and the competing idiosyncrasies of the staff. The real problem, though, is that the staff, most importantly the Editor, have lost faith in the people and become deracinated intellectuals.[16] They are recalled to their faith by three representatives of the people who appear in the office: the Boy from Georgia, who has left his date and a dance; the Man from the Cape, who has left his oyster bed; and the Woman from Idaho, who has left the tombstone she earned for herself as a form of security.

The Woman from Idaho in many ways seems a continuation of *Fidelity*'s Ruth Holland who left the hinterlands for exciting new cultural movements in New York City. The Woman describes her vision from the train: she saw a plain with horses and cows the way Ruth had perceived her western valley with sheep, a place of confinement, conformity, silence, and death. It is also a landscape that Minnie Wright would easily recognize.

> A plain, dark trees off at the edge, against the trees a little house and a big barn. A flat piece of land fenced in. Stubble, furrows. Horses waiting to get in at the barn; cows standing around a pump. A tile yard, a water tank, one straight street of a little town. The country so still it seems dead. The trees like—hopes that have been given up. The grave yards—on hills—they come so fast. I noticed them first because of my tombstone, but I got to thinking about the people—the people who spent their whole lives right near the places where they are now. There's something in the thought of them—like the cows standing around the pump. So still, so patient, it—kind of hurts. And their pleasures:—a flat field fenced in.[17]

Only the words of the Editor of *The People* had managed to bestir her from this landscape of pure physicality ending in death.

By the end of the play, however, the Woman from Idaho has herself become so articulate that she inspires the Editor and his staff to continue to publish their journal; in other words, she seems like an embodiment of the traditional woman as the muse of an artistic man, but Glaspell manages to evade this trap: although the Woman from Idaho is meant to be a representative of the silent masses, she is actually much more eloquent than the intellectuals at the office, as her speech describing the rural deathscape indicates. In the context of the play, her change is caused because the words of the Editor fertilized her so that she brought forth inspirational speech: "When my work was done that night, I read your wonderful words. They're like a spring—if you've lived in a dry country, you'll know what I mean" (54). Like a pregnant woman, she is an icon of the past, the present, and the future, and her speech, like that of a child, spurs its father, the Editor, to work for the future in the endless evolutionary progress that is Glaspell's vision of maternal creativity for men and women. Only the Woman from Idaho realizes that the social revolution is not a product, but a process: "*Seeing*—that's the Social Revolution" (57), Glaspell's Greenwich-Village version of *The Visioning.*

In *The People,* Glaspell presents men and women alternately inspiring one another in an endless creative process, but in *The Outside* (1917) she initially depicts women without men, and they seem as sterile as the landscape that surrounds them. Mrs. Patrick has left her husband over some unspecified betrayal and is living in bitterness in an

appropriately abandoned lifesaving station on Cape Cod with her silent servant Allie Mayo who lost her husband to the sea twenty years earlier.[18] The women's willed wasteland is invaded and revivified by two male life-savers who bring in a drowned man. Despite Mrs. Patrick's seemingly callous attempts to drive them out, they attempt to resuscitate him. Their efforts are unsuccessful, but the example of their fervor and persistence seems to bring Allie Mayo back to life, as the words of The Editor had revived The Woman from Idaho. Allie Mayo was played by Glaspell in the original production, and like Mrs. Hale and the Woman from Idaho, is her spokesperson. She tells Mrs. Patrick, "For twenty years, I did what you are doing. And I can tell you—it's not the way."[19]

The women's situation is examined through the title image, "the outside." They live outside the town where the last vegetation meets the sand "on the outside shore of Cape Cod" (99). The life-savers see the vegetation as valiant, as courageous as their own efforts to save the drowning man, but like that effort, they believe it is opposed by Mrs. Patrick. Bradford declares, "I believe she *likes* to see the sand slippin' down on the woods. Pleases her to see somethin' gettin' buried, I guess" (105). The vegetation is ugly, stunted by its struggle against wind and sand, but Allie Mayo tells Mrs. Patrick that it should be valued because "strange little things that reach out farthest" are the necessary beginnings of life "and hold the sand for things behind them. They save a wood that guards a town" (112) where "children live" (113).

As Linda Ben-Zvi has observed, "The image of pioneering is a recurrent one in all of Glaspell's plays; it shapes all her writing."[20] Pioneering is also closely associated with motherhood for Glaspell, as in the image of the vegetation on the outside sheltering the children within. Mrs. Patrick seems to realize this in her last speech of the play, "Meeting the Outside!", which she "cannot say . . . mockingly . . . ; in saying it, something of what it means has broken through, rises. Herself lost, feeling her way into the wonder of life" (117). The last line of the play, one which surely only the most gifted of actresses could convey, is the bracketed stage direction, "It grows in her as slowly (Curtain)" (117). The line is incomplete, but one possible conclusion is that "it grows in her as slowly as a child," that "wonder of life." To pioneer for humanity is a form of motherhood because it also prepares the way for the future, and in *The Outside* Glaspell depicts two women who may become such pioneers, though they are not biological mothers.

Glaspell's next play, *Woman's Honor* (1918), is her finest comedy because the humor and the message are mutually supportive, not detractive. In a sense, Glaspell's earlier plays had also addressed the question of a woman's honor. Is it more honorable to murder your husband than endure his abuse? Is women's honor better served by concealing a crime than revealing it to a male-dominated judiciary that cannot fathom its motive? Is honor maintained by the respectability of earning your own tombstone or by continuing to grow and live in raffish Greenwich Village? Do women without men, women on the outside, have any honor or importance at all? In *Woman's Honor* Glaspell hilariously explores competing definitions of that term while exploding the double standard.

Gordon Wallace, a prisoner, faces a death sentence because he refuses to provide an alibi for the night of October twenty-fifth; he declares himself "ready to die to shield a woman's honor."[21] In a conference room at the sheriff's house, his lawyer Mr. Foster tells him that he had determined to save him from his "romantic course" (122) by publishing the story in the newspaper so that "wives—including, I hope, jurors' wives—will cry, 'Don't let that chivalrous young man die!'" (123). Six women appear in the room, five of them ready to sacrifice their honor by claiming that they were with Wallace on the night in question. They are identified by their particular feminine roles, not individual names, as if to emphasize the ways the concept of woman's honor warps the lives of all sorts of women. Three embody positive cultural myths, such as the Virgin Madonna, and three epitomize the negative ones, such as witch-bitch.

The Silly One is the virgin, a foolish one at that, since she wants to give up her honor for the romantic notion of saving a knight, the equally silly Gordon Wallace. Her inability to perceive reality is demonstrated when she at first embraces Mr. Foster, mistaking him for Wallace. She speaks in romantic cliches, such as "Love is so beautiful. So ennobling!" (132) and "Love conquereth all things" (135). By the end of the play, through her exposure to the other women, she has shifted her allegiance further from romantic claptrap and closer to feminist solidarity when she tells the Shielded One, "I will give my life for yours, my sister!" (148). Her consciousness may have changed its focus, but not necessarily been raised, since her last line in the play is "Love is so beautiful!" (155).

The Shielded One is maiden as prospective wife, a wealthy young woman whose honor will be preserved so that she will best exhibit the status of her husband. Her discomfort with her role as icon and commodity is displayed by her willingness to surrender her "honor," and by the questions she raises: "What *is* woman's honor?" (144); "Aren't we more than things to be noble about?" (145); and "Is it true that women will not help one another? That they are hard and self-seeking?" (151). As the latter question indicates, she wants sisterly solidarity, not the divisive competition over men that she views as a form of prostitution: "I speak for all the women of my . . .—under-world, all those others smothered under men's lofty sentiments toward them! I wish I could paint for you the horrors of the shielded life. [*Says 'shielded' as if it were 'shameful'.*]" (146). The parody of a fate worse than death continues as she declares of the shielded life, "I'd rather die than go back to it!" (147).

The Motherly One represents the Madonna, a woman beyond sexuality who consequently has no "honor" worth

saving in a culture that values women as commodities for their appearance and ability to give sexual pleasure. She is a nurse who sees sacrificing her "honor" as an extension of her roles as mother and professional. She regards men as spoiled children who treat the concept of woman's honor like a toy. "I should really hate to take it from them entirely" (145), she indulgently observes, but she recognizes that the toy can be dangerous unless she places it under her maternal purview: "It would be just like a lot of men to fuss around about a woman's honor and really let it hurt somebody" (136). By the end of the play, the Motherly One becomes more interested in nurturing her fellow women than in preserving the inane Wallace; she tries to provide them with opportunities for speech and mediates their competing claims.

The Mercenary One is the ostensibly negative counterpart of the Silly One since she also does not understand what is happening, but for quite different reasons. She has come to the prison to apply for a stenographer's job. She needs to make a living and has no time for abstractions such as woman's honor. The other women mistakenly believe that she has arrived to sell Wallace her reputation so that he can save his life; they accuse her of being "hard" and lacking "woman's self-respect" (142). Glaspell is quite clearly indicating that the shelter and trap of woman's honor is restricted to a materially privileged group of women who are too caste-ridden to empathize with a woman who must work outside her home.

In effect, the women have accused the Mercenary One of a kind of prostitution, but, unlike the Shielded One, they do not recognize the kind of prostitution to which women subject themselves in the name of love. The Scornful One, however, does perceive it, as her name indicates. She was outside the privileged class of women whose honor is shielded so that one man alone may own it. To the assembled women, she describes the hypocrite who took her honor when she was seventeen: "Why, this instant his eyes would become 'pools of feeling' if any one were to talk about saving a woman's honor" (139). She is the most realistic of the women, the one who can truly understand that the concept of woman's honor is a way to limit and dehumanize women: "Woman's honor is only about one thing, and . . . man's honor is about everything but that thing" (134). Without the privilege, or burden, of a woman's honor, she is free to be the best person she can: "You see honor camouflages so many things—stupidity, selfishness—greed, lust, avarice, gluttony. So without it you're almost forced to be a decent sort—and that's sometimes wearing" (139).

The Scornful One's derision is directed not only at hypocritical men, but at her fellow women who have not been compelled to develop her kind of strength, particularly the "coward" (137) who was really with Wallace on October twenty-fifth but will not appear to save him. Although the Scornful One had initially wanted to destroy the concept of woman's honor through her parodic sacrifice, by the play's end she wants all the women to work together to preserve the young and salvageable, "to save *both* of them [the Shielded One and the Silly One] through Gordon Wallace" (155); in other words, she wants to make women the subjects here and a man their object or tool.

The sixth woman who appears is the Cheated One, played by Glaspell in the original production. She has lived the respectable monogamous life of the Motherly One, but there is no indication in the text that she has been relieved of her role as sex object through having children. She tells the other women,

> I've been cheated. Cheated out of my chance to have a man I wanted by a man who would have what he wanted. Then he saved my woman's honor. Married me and cheated me out of my life. I'm just something to be cheated. That's the way I think of myself. Until this morning. Until I read about Gordon Wallace. Then I saw a way to get away from myself. It's the first thing I ever wanted to do that I've done. You'll not cheat me out of this. Don't you try!
>
> (154)

The rape of her body followed by the matrimonial rape of her spirit has made her as suspicious of her fellow women as she is of men. She is so embittered that even her way of getting away from herself is actually an affirmation of that self: "The only unfortunate woman I'll think about is myself" (154). At the end of the play, she is still unable to join the huddle of women, but she does hover about the edge if only "not to be cheated of what is being said" (156). Through the Cheated One, Glaspell is demonstrating that a woman's martyrdom for honor does not make her a saint, but quite the contrary: the repeated denial of a woman's identity and volition can make her a monster of selfishness as she desperately tries to compensate herself for what has been wrested from her.

Gordon Wallace claims to esteem women so highly that he would die for their honor, but his misogynistic use of chivalry is unmasked at the conclusion of the play. He is so horrified by the sight of the united women that when a seventh woman appears, "large and determined" (156), he declares, "Oh, *hell. I'll plead guilty*" (156), and the curtain descends. Christine Dymkowski notes, "Men placed on the edge . . . are excluded from a power to which they subscribe—Wallace, put in this position, cannot reshape his world from a new perspective; he can only affirm the old one."[22] Or, as Sharon P. Friedman puts it, "He would rather die than relinquish his control of the situation."[23] Gordon Wallace may also be unwittingly speaking the truth because he and his fellow subscribers to the concept of woman's honor are guilty of the dishonoring of woman's autonomy.

In a sense, *Bernice* (1919), Glaspell's first three-act play, is another version of *Woman's Honor,* with Bernice as an unselfish version of the Cheated One; her philandering husband, the shallow writer Craig Norris, as a more sophisticated Gordon Wallace; and the other women characters representing alternate women's roles. As Act One begins,

Bernice has died, and her father and devoted servant Abbie await the return of Craig, his conventional sister Laura Kirby, and Bernice's closest friend, social activist Margaret Pierce. Upon their arrival, the examination of Bernice's life and motives begins, obtusely by the men and perceptively by most of the women, much as in the case of *Trifles'* Minnie Wright. Abbie later informs Craig that Bernice committed suicide, and Craig then takes "credit" by telling Margaret, "You think I didn't matter. But Bernice *killed* herself because she loved me so!"[24]

In Act Two, Margaret learns from Abbie that Bernice died of natural causes; she did not kill herself but requested that Abbie tell Craig that she did. Margaret interprets this as a vengeful attempt to devastate unfaithful Craig with guilt, an act that indicates that Bernice's "life was *hate*" (206). So disillusioned is Margaret that she refuses to enter the bedroom where Bernice lies. In Act Three, Margaret sees that Bernice's gesture has indeed improved Craig since he renounces his world of "make-believe" (226) and insists on rearranging the room as Bernice always kept it. Margaret realizes that Bernice's true motive was to remove Craig's insecurity by giving him a sense of how valued he was, so the play ends with Bernice remaining the paragon that almost everyone considers her.

"Saint" *Bernice* is a curiously defensive play, as if Glaspell protests too much the transcendent goodness of her heroine. Although she seems to present Bernice as a martyr and saint, the cost of her canonization seems too high: in a brief reference at the beginning of Act Two, Abbie says that Bernice died of stomach ulcers (180); she may well have been killed by repressed anger, the good girl's disease. The play's uncomfortable sense of conflicting messages may emanate from Glaspell's own confusions, as Marcia Noe speculates:

> *Bernice* may be more easily understood if viewed in the context of Susan Glaspell's life with Jig Cook, who, like Craig Norris, was unfaithful to his wife and, much of the time, unsuccessful as a writer. Could *Bernice* have grown from a fantasy of Susan's in which she killed herself to punish Jig for his infidelity, all the while rationalizing that the act would bring him to his senses and shock him into living up to his potential as a writer?[25]

Noe's explanation seems plausible since Bernice does seem to be indulging in the behavior of a petulant child who threatens, "You'll be sorry when I run away." Glaspell may also be attempting to reassure herself about her childless state in that Bernice has also suffered a stillbirth, as well as about her choice of a career as an artist rather than a social reformer. She may be asking woman's traditional guilty question: Have I done enough for others or have I actually devoted too much attention to myself? Glaspell presents her defense of Bernice, and herself, through the contrasting lives of the other women characters as well as through their refracted composite portrait of Bernice.

Through the character of Laura, Glaspell defends Bernice against her failure to become a conventional wife and mother. Laura is the only character in the play who does not revere Bernice; instead she blames her for not having "the power to hold Craig" (186) from straying and for failing to "value Craig's work" (188). Laura is the kind of woman who wants other women to be as miserable as she is in order to validate her suffering. Despite her limited perspective, she has a moment of insight when she is attempting to help organize Bernice's funeral and comments, "Really I do like control" (209). Her drive for autonomy must find its channel, limited though it is.

Clearly, Bernice should not have joined Laura in deformed domesticity, but Margaret's career presents a more problematic alternative. Like many of Glaspell's Greenwich Village friends, Margaret is a social reformer; she currently works in Chicago, "trying to get out of prison all those people who are imprisoned for ideas" (187). However commendable Margaret's goals, she is shown to have made the poorer choice because, as she tells Craig, "We give ourselves in fighting for a thing that seems important and in that fight we get out of the flow of life. We had meant it to deepen the flow—but we get caught" (198). Since Bernice's dying word was Margaret's name, she clearly means to get Margaret back into that flow by causing her to perceive and appreciate what the play presents as a totally unselfish act, her last message to Craig. Margaret is like a disciple who has her faith tested in order to prove herself a worthy successor to the apotheosized Bernice, and Margaret's final words show that she has succeeded: "Oh, in all the world—since life first *moved*—has there been any beauty like the beauty of perceiving love? . . . No, not for words" (230).

The emotional core of the play, though, resides in Bernice's attempt to defend herself against the charge of thwarting Craig's potential by failing to surrender her very soul to him. Craig regards marriage as a power struggle from which the man should emerge the victorious master of his slave-object-wife; he comments that Bernice had "a life in her deeper than anything that could be done to her. . . . I never *had* Bernice" (173). He childishly justifies his affairs as attempts to gain her exclusive attention: "A man's feeling is different. He has to feel that he moves—completely moves—yes, could destroy—not that he would, but has the power to reshape the—" (174). Margaret perceptively tells him, "Those love affairs of yours—they're like your false writing—to keep yourself from knowing that you haven't power" (2000). Craig is supposedly redeemed when Bernice lets him believe he had enough power to make her take the role of abandoned wife and kill herself in jealousy and grief. The play suggests that Bernice has proven herself a "true woman" in rescuing Craig, but the rescue is based on a lie, as if men cannot bear too much reality.

Glaspell not only defends Bernice against putative lapses as conventional woman and social reformer, but asserts her virtues as a mother, though without biological children, and as an artist, despite her lack of a tangible medium. Bernice mothers everyone: as we have seen, from the grave she nurtures Craig and Margaret; when alive, she cared for her childish and withdrawn father and guided and inspired her servant Abbie, played by Glaspell in the original production. Abbie seems to glory in her self-abdication, like a child who wants to please and emulate what she perceives as the perfect mother or master: "It was the *main* thing in my life—doing what she wanted" (164). In some ways, the unsatisfactorily ethereal Bernice and dog-like Abbie become more palatable if one regards them as complements who together form a whole. Bernice thinks and inspires while Abbie acts and confronts the consequences. Glaspell, however, seems unable to create such a complete woman in this play unless it is Margaret, who at the final curtain has learned from Bernice and Abbie to rekindle the vision that will make her activism meaningful.

A more positive way to view Bernice may be as a sort of Henry Jamesian artist-in-life, like Milly Theale in *The Wings of the Dove* or Maggie Verver in *The Golden Bowl*, who uses life as a medium to create beauty and wholeness, often at significant cost to herself. As Sharon P. Friedman aptly observes, "Bernice has imagined and executed the scenario from which the drama emerges."[26] C.W.E. Bigsby sees this staging as a form of female empowerment, "one in which the determining voice and actions are those of women who deliberately create the dramas within which men are obliged to act."[27] Bernice has not produced biological children or artistic artifacts, but her legacy to the future, through Craig the artist and Margaret the reformer, will help promote human evolution, the process that Glaspell considered of paramount importance, much as do Mrs. Patrick and Allie Mayo in *The Outside* and the Woman from Idaho in *The People*. That may be Glaspell's ostensible or intended theme, but her subtext works against it since, to return to the Jamesian analogy, like Milly Theale, Bernice is dead and, like Maggie Verver, the valorization of her marriage is based on unacknowledged deceit.

Glaspell's last major Provincetown plays, *Inheritors* (1921) and *The Verge* (1921), continue to explore the nonbiologically maternal roles of social reformer and artist while examining the influence of biological mothers, for good or ill, upon their daughters. The cultivation of new types of plants is the central metaphor in both plays, suggesting that the development of the species, or offspring, may come only at great cost to the gardener, already a mutant-mother herself.

In *The Road to the Temple,* Glaspell comments that "new country is a good place to look at society. When you see grandfather, father and son you see human society, with personal quality, luck and changing conditions making destiny." Glaspell returns to the Midwest in *Inheritors* for the purpose of examining two "species" over time, the Fejevary and Morton families, but with just as much emphasis on the maternal as the paternal line.[28] In Act One, on the Fourth of July, 1879, Silas Morton decides to promote intellectual independence by donating a beautiful and valuable hill on his farm for the site of a new college, despite the objections of his mother and the cash of a land-developer. One of his motives was his own regret over his lack of education, a deficiency he realized from the society of his cultivated best friend, the aristocratic Hungarian immigrant Felix Fejevary, a liberty-loving revolutionary forced to flee his native land.

Act Two takes place in 1920, as if Glaspell intends it for a warning to chauvinistic postwar America. Felix Fejevary II, son of the immigrant, is now president of Morton College, and he is discovered in the college library reassuring an influential state senator that such subversive elements as Professor Holden will be silenced so that the senate will appropriate large sums for the college. He is distracted from his machinations by the sound of a fracas outside. Fejevary's son Horace, a jingoistic student, has tried to silence two student demonstrators from India. When the police saw trouble beginning, they grabbed the darker-skinned students somewhat roughly. Horace's cousin and fellow student Madeleine, granddaughter of Silas Morton and the first Felix Fejevary, rushed impulsively to the Indians' aid and hit the policeman with her tennis racket.

Acts Three and Four concern Madeleine's gradual realization that her spontaneous blow for freedom is really her true inheritance from the past and her wisest course for the future. In Act Three, President Fejevary is again busily selling out freedom of speech in the ironic setting of the library as he threatens to dismiss Professor Holden unless he stops protesting the mistreatment of Fred Jordan, a former student who is imprisoned for his unpopular conscientious objection to the recent war. Fejevary's threat is particularly nasty since Holden is the sole support of an invalid wife. Fejevary is once more interrupted in his sleazy activities by Madeleine, this time as she defends her action because the Indian students are "people from the other side of the world who came here believing in us, drawn from the far side of the world by things we say about ourselves."[29] She hears a new uproar involving the Indian students and rushes out to rejoin the fray as the act's curtain descends.

In Act Four, a week after her arrest, Madeleine holds to her resolve to go to prison, like Fred Jordan, rather than deny her beliefs, despite the pleas of her father Ira, her Aunt Isabel, the vanquished Professor Holden, and the possible love interest of Emil Johnson. Madeleine's move from the tennis court to the police court may seem rather abrupt. Why isn't Madeleine more like her fellow students and foils, Doris and Fussie, whose idea of a good time is making fun of a farm boy by pretending to be infatuated with him? Glaspell has, however, carefully prepared us for Madeleine's difference by her portraits of Madeleine's female ancestors and their foils, suggesting that women of every generation have the potential to be pioneers and further humanity's development, though in quite different ways.

Silas Morton's mother, called Grandmother in Act One, is a literal pioneer. Interestingly, no mention is made of Silas'

deceased wife, rebellious Madeleine's actual grandmother, as if to give schematic emphasis to the first generation of pioneers. Grandmother fought the Indians singlehandedly when she was attacked, once throwing one into her cellar and standing on the door, but she also could befriend them, trading cookies for fish, because she understands their motivation: "We roiled them up considerable. They was mostly friendly when let be. Didn't want to give up their land—but I've noticed something of the same nature in white folks" (104). Grandmother also identifies with another marginalized group, her fellow women. She tells the first Felix Fejevary that when she left the house, she would always leave some food for the settlers stopping for a respite before proceeding further west. Her longing for sisterly companionship is manifest as she tells him,

> There was a woman I always wanted to know. She made a kind of bread I never had before—and left a-plenty for our supper when we got back with the ducks and berries. And she left the kitchen handier than it had ever been. I often wondered about her—where she came from, and where she went (107).

This memory is another version of *Trifles* in that one woman speculates about another through examining her housekeeping, but in this instance to be inspired by her strength, not chastened by her destruction.

Despite her empathy as a young woman, in her senescence Grandmother tries to prevent Silas from deeding the hill to the college, exclaiming, "I worked for that hill! And I tell you to leave it to your own children!" (115). Her foil is the cultured Old Mrs. Fejevary who "did have an awful ladylike way of feeding the chickens" (106). Through Grandmother, Glaspell is indicating that the very virtues that promote pioneering, courageous visioning, and industry are so strenuous that they can only be sustained for a limited duration without intellectual and cultural resources like those of Old Mrs. Fejevary; the solitary and untutored pioneer soon slips back into the narrow nurturing of her own family, rather than the human family.

The next generation also contains two contrasting women. Madeleine's Aunt Isabel, wife of the second Felix, is a woman who is very warm and caring toward her family and her own kind but is unable to empathize with those who are different. In a statement typical of the era's xenophobia, she tells her niece, "These are days when we have to stand together—all of us who are the same kind of people must stand together because the thing that makes us the same kind of people is threatened" (147).

Fortunately, Madeleine has a more generous female role model, her deceased mother, Madeleine Fejevary Morton, sister of President Fejevary. Young Madeleine initially knows very little of her mother since her widowed father Ira finds the subject so painful. On the day of her twenty-first birthday, the day she must turn herself into the judge, Madeleine makes some fudge in an attempt to celebrate her birthday by herself since she is alienated from her family. She later tells her Aunt Isabel,

And then that didn't seem to—make a birthday, so I happened to see this [a Hungarian dish], way up on a top shelf, and I remembered that it was my mother's. It was nice to get it down and use it—almost as if mother was giving me a birthday present (147).

Madeleine does receive a present from her mother through the unlikely mediation of her father Ira, a fanatical developer of a new breed of corn, who, in Grandmother and Isabel's way, refuses to share it with other farmers. As he tries to prevent Madeleine from choosing prison, Ira tells her how her mother died.

Then *she* came—that ignorant Swede, Emil Johnson's mother—running through the cornfield like a crazy woman—"Miss Morton! Miss Morton! Come help me! My children are choking!" Diphtheria they had—the whole of 'em—but out of this house she ran—my Madeleine, leaving you—her own baby—running as fast as she could through the cornfield after that ignorant woman. . . . That was the last I saw of her. She choked to death in that Swede's house. They lived (154).

Madeleine proves herself her mother's daughter when she decides to hurt her family for their and America's ultimate good by standing up for her principles, no matter what the cost.

Like the corn that Ira Morton grows, Madeleine combines the best of her different strains, the Mortons' hard work and neighborliness and the Fejevarys' cultural breadth and rebelliousness. She could also be regarded as a kind of mutant, and in the human world, such pioneers can be rejected and destroyed for their difference, no matter what benefits humanity may ultimately reap from them.

Madeleine may gain strength from challenging the system, but she could be willfully choosing her self-destruction in an oppressive world, as does Claire Archer in *The Verge.* Early in the play, Claire's husband Harry humorously comments upon Claire's blunt language: "This is what came of the men who made the laws that made New England, that here is the flower of those gentleman of culture."[30] Harry will learn, however, that this is no beneficent plant like Ira's corn, but a monstrous mutant formed by the pressures of patriarchal strictures on a venturesome and creative woman.[31]

Claire, like Ira Morton, expresses her autonomy and creativity through her plants, and, also like Ira, is jealous of her private space, the greenhouse that she considers her room of her own; she even tells her husband, "I'll not have you in my place!" (61). She describes one of her experiments, the Breath of Life plant, to her lover Dick:

I want to give fragrance to Breath of Life—the flower I have created that is outside where flowers have been. What has gone out should bring fragrance from what it has left. But no definite fragrance, no limiting enclosing thing. I call the fragrance I am trying to create Reminiscence. Reminiscent of the rose, the violet, arbutus—but a new thing—itself. Breath of Life may

be lonely out in what hasn't been. Perhaps someday I can give it reminiscence (63-64).

As her close friend Tom, an explorer, perceives, "If she can do it with plants, perhaps she won't have to do it with herself" (71). Unfortunately, as in the case of Mrs. Patrick and Allie Mayo in *The Outside,* watching plants, whether they are scrubby beach bushes or Breath of Life, will not suffice, for Claire wants to be a woman on "the outside" or "the verge."[32]

Mrs. Patrick is perceived as monstrous by the lifesavers for her bitter reclusiveness and at least initially by the audience for her attempt to bar the drowning man from her house. Glaspell presents Claire Archer as similarly armored in her own problems. Even at the beginning of the play, she does not care about the comfort or feelings of others. On a frigid, snowy day, she has all the house's heat directed to the greenhouse to preserve her plants and then objects when her husband and guests wish to breakfast there, a gesture that at first seems a comic eccentricity but by the play's end can be seen as part of Claire's willed withdrawal from others.

Glaspell is not unproblematically presenting Claire as a monster of egotism since the men who surround her, the representative Tom, Dick, and Harry, do not seem worthy of much serious attention. Her husband Harry just wants a wife who will be the life of the party so he tries to fit her horticultural experiments into a suitably feminine paradigm: "That's an awfully nice thing for a woman to do—raise flowers" (65). Her lover Dick just wants his ego boosted by a beautiful woman who belongs to another man; he dismisses her experiments as "merely the excess of a particularly rich temperament" (65). The man who does understand her experiments, the ironically named explorer Tom Edgeworthy, is unwilling to risk the challenge of an experimental relationship with Claire; he is about to run away on his next journey to avoid exploring his own or Claire's inner space. When he offers to keep Claire "safe" (99), she is momentarily lured, but then shoots him because, as she says, "I'd rather be the steam rising from the manure than be a thing called beautiful!" (99).

Glaspell not only presents a heroine who rejects her assigned role as man's plaything, but challenges an even more basic cultural assumption, the unwavering, self-sacrificial devotion of a mother for her child. In an ironic reversal of the usual intergenerational scene, Claire rejects Elizabeth, her daughter from a previous marriage, because she is *not* a rebel. The now-adult Elizabeth recalls an "idol" given to her mother by Tom: "I dressed the idol up in my doll's clothes. They fitted perfectly—the idol was just the size of my doll Ailine. But mother didn't like the idol that way, and tore the clothes getting them off" (73). Claire is authoritarian in her denial of Elizabeth's play, conventional though the child's game may be. She does not explain her reasons to Elizabeth, but remains inarticulately violent and destructive, caring more about her own sense of appropriateness than about her daughter's treasured doll-clothes.

This remembered scene aptly foreshadows Claire's total rejection of the grown Elizabeth, who, unsurprisingly, received the remainder of her upbringing from Claire's traditional sister Adelaide. When Elizabeth arrives after a year's absence and tries to "embrace" her mother, Claire defensively holds a box that she is carrying in front of her and says, "Careful, Elizabeth. We mustn't upset the lice" (74), though she apparently considers it acceptable to upset her own daughter. Claire compares her other great experiment, the Edge Vine, to Elizabeth, telling her, "I should destroy the Edge Vine. It isn't—over the edge. It's running, back to—'all the girls'" (77). At the end of the scene, she does try to uproot the Edge Vine, exclaiming, "Why did I make you? To get past you!" (78). She strikes Elizabeth with the vine and declares, "To think that object ever moved my belly and sucked my breast" (78).

This scene is shocking today, but in 1921 it must have been even more so to the recent heirs of Victorian mother-worship for whom Adelaide appears to speak when she upbraids her sister Claire, "A mother who does not love her own child! You are an unnatural woman" (85). Again, though, Glaspell complicates her portrait of Claire as a monster, a Medea, when Claire later tells Tom about her son by Harry who died when he was a small child.

> I was up with Harry—flying—high. It was about four months before David was born—the doctor was furious—pregnant women are supposed to keep to earth. We were going fast—I *was* flying—I had left the earth. And then—within me, movement, for the first time—stirred to life far in air—movement within. The man unborn, he too, would fly. And so—I always loved him. He was movement—and wonder. In his short life were many flights. I never told anyone about the last one. His little bed was by the window—he wasn't four years old. It was night, but him not asleep. He saw the morning star—you know—the morning star. Brighter—stranger—reminiscent—and a promise. He pointed "—Mother," he asked me, "what is there—beyond the stars?" A baby, a sick baby—the morning star. Next night—the finger that pointed was—(*suddenly bites her own finger*) But, yes, I am glad. He would have tried to move and too much would hold him. Wonder would die—and he'd laugh at soaring (87).

Claire expected David to "soar" for her since he was a male and "pregnant women are supposed to keep to earth."[33] In *Of Woman Born*, Adrienne Rich describes a similar expectation.

> I wanted to give birth, at twenty-five, to my unborn self, the self that our father-centered family had suppressed in me, someone independent, actively willing, original—those possibilities I had felt in myself in flashes as a young student and writer, and from which, during pregnancy, I was to close myself off. If I wanted to give birth to myself as a male, it was because males seemed to inherit those qualities by right of gender.[34]

Unlike Claire, though, Rich went on to raise three sons, participate in the feminist movement of the 1960s, and do her own soaring herself as expressed in her great poetry.

Some forty years earlier, Claire sees her own option for vicarious accomplishment closed by her son's premature death, and even wonders if such a repressive society would allow male self-expression since "too much would hold him." Claire tries to express herself through her plants, fails, and ends the play as a mad murderess, singing "Nearer My God to Thee." When we seek an explanation for Claire's debacle, her lack of a feminist sisterhood is a necessary but not sufficient cause. Linda Ben-Zvi provides the essential difference between Claire and Rich, and Claire and Glaspell, when she writes,

> Since [Glaspell's] women are exploring new areas of their lives, they find traditional language unsuited to their needs. They may be women unused to speech or women all too aware that the words they speak do not express their thoughts. In either case, the results are the same. Her characters are virtually inarticulate, or are rendered so because of the situations in which they find themselves. The most common punctuation mark she uses is the dash. It is used when the character is unsure of the direction in which she is going, as yet unprepared to articulate consciously a new awareness or unwilling to put into words feelings and wishes which may collapse under the weight of words.[35]

Because they cannot speak, many of them act self-destructively: Minnie Wright, Mrs. Patrick, Allie Mayo, Bernice Norris, Madeleine Fejevary, and Claire Archer.

Almost all of Glaspell's heroines are, in one sense or another, childless: Minnie, the Woman from Idaho, Mrs. Patrick, Allie Mayo, the Scorned One, the Cheated One, Bernice, Madeleine, and Claire. They are also artists without viable mediums of expression. Minnie Wright expects her canary to sing for her; The Woman from Idaho wants to inspire the Editor to write for her; the six women in ***Woman's Honor*** can only protest their situations, in effect save their own lives, through saving the life of a foolish male-chauvinist; Mrs. Patrick and Allie Mayo see the stunted vegetation on the outside of Cape Cod as their living symbol; Bernice uses her death to make changes she could not achieve by living; Madeleine Morton expresses her sense of injustice by hitting a policeman and will presumably be imprisoned; and Claire Archer, thwarted by patriarchy, the death of her son, and the failure of her daughter and her plants, projects her own rage one step further by shooting a man and imprisoning herself in her own madness.

None of these heroines seem to have Glaspell's own outlet for her creative, maternal passions, her artistry with words and structure. This may be depressing, but it is realistic, for how many women, or, for that matter, men, are so gifted? The hope lies in Glaspell's speech, her maternal legacy to that better future in which she so fervently believed. The agonized voices, and silences, of her women on the edge, are, as Allie Mayo hesitantly declaims in her last speech of the play, the "stunted straggly line that meets the Outside face to face—and fights for what itself can never be. Lonely line. Brave growing" (116).

. . . . .

In her play ***Alison's House,*** Glaspell presents a ghostly revenant whose piquant personality and famous poems haunt her family and admirers eighteen years after her death. Alison Stanhope is based on Emily Dickinson, but the poet's family would not allow Glaspell to use the Dickinson name or quote from her poems.[36] Even so, Alison is characterized by many of the traits we readily associate with Dickinson: a white dress (124); sherry-colored eyes (147); a love of Emerson's poetry (97); a non-literary sister as devoted watchdog; and a rebellion against the conception of God as a stern and unloving patriarch (103).[37] Through the play, Glaspell evaluates the consequences of one aspect of Dickinson's life, her unconsummated love for a married man, here rendered as Alison Stanhope's renunciation of a married Harvard professor in answer to the pleas of her scandal-fearing brother (140-41).

A cheerful and uplifting reading of the play would stress that by renouncing an earthly lover and biological children, Alison could become the perfect mother through nurturing her symbolic children, nephew Eben and niece Elsa, and through her poems that sustain other women, her spiritual daughters. Unlike an often harassed biological mother, Aunt Alison has the time and energy to manifest "playfulness" (92) toward Eben and Elsa by presenting them with charmingly quaint gifts like "pebbles from the river" (36). Since she is not required to raise them and be their daily disciplinarian, she can side with them against authority. When they disobey, she says, "Alison knows" and "Alison won't tell" (36). Her use of the third-person sounds at once childlike and godlike, as does her more consolatory, "Come to Alison. . . . Alison will make it right" (113). Eben even trusts her enough to show her his youthful attempts at poetry. In other words, Alison seems like the perfect mother, sufficiently powerful to assist, but still enough of a child to understand.

In accordance with such an optimistic reading of the play, to the women of the future Alison's nurturing legacy is her recently discovered love poetry. These verses express for other women what they are incapable of articulating for themselves. In the catharsis that Alison provides for them, they can find succor and solace. As Ann, a young woman newly in love, declares, "Alison said it—for women" (150), and so once again Alison proves herself the ideal mother-figure.

The play, however, is much more ambiguous than this emphasis on Glaspell's typical themes indicates.[38] The first, and, until Alison, the only woman artist-protagonist in Glaspell's plays and novels, is Ernestine Hubers of her first novel, ***The Glory of the Conquered*** (1909). Ernestine did manage to have it all, albeit sequentially, as she achieved artistic mastery despite and because of submerging her career in that of her husband. Sandra M. Gilbert and Susan Gubar find this absence of women artist-figures typical of women writers of Glaspell's era: they face their fears of a woman's life without art "by imagining characters who are unable to achieve the aesthetic release their authors themselves attain by the very creation of these figures."[39] When Glaspell creates her second major artist, twenty years after the first, she returns to the late nineteenth-century notion that a woman can either be an artist or a mate, not both.

Glaspell, however, is presenting a devastating critique of these rigidly defined, mutually exclusive roles for women. Alison's legacy, the life and art of renunciation, is not an unmixed blessing. Her sister Agatha is so obsessively jealous a caretaker that she will not even reveal what kind of pen Alison used (27). Agatha is another example of Glaspell's strong sense of the evils of living vicariously; had Alison run away with her lover, Agatha might have been compelled to live her own life. Another victim is Alison's brother Stanhope who remained in an unhappy marriage, despite his love for another woman, out of a foolish consistency; he chooses to suffer as he compelled Alison to do.

The younger generation also has lost at least as much as they have gained from Alison's legacy. Her nephew Eben, following the renunciatory pattern set by his aunt, is trapped in a marriage to Laura, a woman as rigidly conventional as the Laura of ***Bernice,*** and so he is unable to write poetry (74). (One might also speculate that he suffers from the anxiety of influence in regard to his famous aunt.) Alison's niece Elsa follows the example of Alison's spirit, not her actions, by living with a married man, but, like ***Fidelity***'s Ruth Holland, finds that sin can be as mundane as virtue, remarking that "Love doesn't have to clothe itself" (115). Alison's much younger nephew Ted, born after her death, sees her legacy as ripe for exploitation: he anticipates great profits from the publication of her love poetry, and, more immediately, to gain better grades on his English themes by telling his professor private details about Alison. Alison's biological descendants are unhappy whether they renounce love for duty like Agatha, Stanhope, and Eben, endure scandal for love like Elsa, or are oblivious to everything but gain like Ted.

Because Alison's descendants are not artists, they are unable to transcend the banalities of their chosen lives. She does, however, have a spiritual heir, another of Glaspell's symbolic sons, the aspiring poet Richard Knowles, who is sent to the Stanhope mansion by his newspaper to cover its sale and the dispersal of the family and Alison's personal effects. There he meets and falls in love with Stanhope's secretary Ann, who loves poetry but cannot write it, and tells Knowles, "I wish I could. . . . That's why I'm so grateful to Alison" (6). Knowles has been walking by the river, as was Alison's custom, and proposes that Ann join him. He tells her that as he walked, it was as if [Alison's] thoughts were there. They must have been hers—for they were better than mine. And it seemed to me if you would walk there with me—you and I together—well, that she wouldn't be gone.

(96)

Knowles, the symbolic son, can have it all, the poetic legacy of his ghostly mother Alison and the quotidian love of his earthly muse Ann.

Alison's House is an appropriate conclusion for Glaspell's works of the 1920s, for the play's action occurs during the dismantling of Alison's house, as if to suggest that her experience as woman and artist, however painful and limited, can find no place in the modern world. The new house of art will actually be the old dwelling, slightly remodeled, that we readily recognize as the traditional prerogative of the male artist with his ever-subservient female muse. The only gleam of light in these works of the late twenties is that in Richard Knowles, Evans Leonard, and John Knight, Glaspell seems to be anticipating a new, more sensitive, more androgynous kind of man. Sadly, she is bidding farewell to her hopes for her symbolic daughters since they seem bound to the eternal wheel of following or reacting against the warped and warping legacies of their ghostly mothers.

NOTES

[1] I am providing the dates of the first production of each of Glaspell's plays, not their dates of publication.

[2] I am not discussing Glaspell's collaborations with George Cram Cook, *Suppressed Desires* (1915) and *Tickless Time* (1918), or her collaboration with Norman Matson, *The Comic Artist* (1928), because of the difficulties of thematic attribution, nor do I examine the one-act farce *Close the Book* (1917) because it is so light and is not particularly relevant to an examination of women's roles. As part of my discussion of the revenge of the dutiful daughters in Chapter 7, I mention *Chains of Dew* (1922) when I discuss the novel into which Glaspell converted it, *Ambrose Holt and Family* (1931). *Alison's House* (1930) is treated in Chapter 6 with the other "ghostly" women of that period of Glaspell's writing.

[3] Adrienne Rich, *Of Woman Born: Motherhood as Experience and Institution* (New York: Norton, 1986, 1976), xxxv.

[4] Linda Ben-Zvi, "Susan Glaspell's Contributions to Contemporary Women Playwrights" in *Feminine Focus: The New Women Playwrights*, Enoch Brater, ed. (New York: Oxford U P, 1989), 152.

[5] Susan Glaspell, "Contrary to Precedent," *Booklovers* (January-June 1904): 236.

[6] Marcia Noe, "Susan Glaspell: A Critical Biography" (University of Iowa, Ph.D., 1976), Ann Arbor: University Microfilms International, 1981, 94. Robert K. Sarlos cites Ida Rauh, Edna St. Vincent Millay, Louise Bryant, and Eunice Tietjens as some of Cook's putative lovers and the sources of Glaspell's jealousy during the Provincetown days; "Jig Cook and Susan Glaspell: Rule Makers and Rule Breakers" in *1915, the Cultural Moment: The New Politics, the New Woman, the New Psychology, the New Art and the New Theatre in America*, Adele Heller and Lois Rudnick, ed. (New Brunswick, NJ: Rutgers U P, 1991), 258 n9. Ellen Kay Trimberger points out that free love worked more to the advantage of already culturally privileged Greenwich Village males and against women who preferred

monogamy; "The New Woman and the New Sexuality: Conflict and Contradiction in the Writings and Lives of Mabel Dodge and Neith Boyce" in *1915, the Cultural Moment*, 105, 108.

[7] Gayle Austin, *Feminist Theories for Dramatic Criticism* (Ann Arbor: U of Michigan P, 1990), 2.

[8] The articles I found particularly helpful are: Karen Alkalay-Gut, "Jury of her Peers: The Importance of Trifles," *Studies in Short Fiction*, 21 (1984): 1-9; C.W.E. Bigsby, "Introduction" to *Plays* by Susan Glaspell (Cambridge: Cambridge U P, 1987), 9-12; Judith Fetterley, "Reading about Reading: 'A Jury of Her Peers,' 'The Murders in the Rue Morgue,' and 'The Yellow Wallpaper,'" in *Gender and Reading: Essays on Readers, Texts, and Contexts*, ed. Elizabeth A. Flynn and Patrocino P. Schweickart (Baltimore: Johns Hopkins U P, 1986): 147-64; Sharon P. Friedman, "Feminist Concerns in the Works of Four Twentieth-Century American Women Dramatists: Susan Glaspell, Rachel Crothers, Lillian Hellman, and Lorraine Hansberry" (New York University, Ph.D., 1977), Ann Arbor: University Microfilms International, 1977, 111-28; Annette Kolodny, "A Map for Rereading: Or, Gender and the Interpretation of Literary Texts," *New Literary History*, 11 (1980): 451-67; and Beverly A. Smith, "Women's Work—*Trifles*?: The Skill and Insights of Playwright Susan Glaspell," *International Journal of Women's Studies*, 5 (1982): 172-84. Glaspell later turned *Trifles* into a short story, "A Jury of Her Peers," *Everyweek* (March 5, 1917).

[9] Beverly A. Smith argues that Minnie Wright may have been physically as well as emotionally battered. "Women's Work—*Trifles*?: The Skill and Insights of Playwright Susan Glaspell," *International Journal of Women's Studies*, 5 (1982): 172-84.

[10] Susan Glaspell, *Trifles* in *Plays* (Boston: Small, Maynard, 1920), 25, 26. Subsequent references to this play will be indicated within the text.

[11] Rich, 38.

[12] Sharon P. Friedman, "Feminist Concerns in the Works of Four Twentieth-Century American Woman Dramatists: Susan Glaspell, Rachel Crothers, Lillian Hellman, and Lorraine Hansberry" (New York University, Ph.D., 1977), Ann Arbor: University Microfilms International, 1977, 124.

[13] Annette Kolodny, "A Map for Rereading: Or, Gender and the Interpretation of Literary Texts," *New Literary History*, 11 (1980): 463.

[14] C.W.E. Bigsby calls Mrs. Hale and Mrs. Peters' earlier neglect of Minnie Wright "a failure of sisterly solidarity." "Introduction" to *Plays* by Susan Glaspell (Cambridge: Cambridge U P, 1987), 11. The women's behavior is also an example of what Sara Ruddick finds one of the dangers of motherhood in a patriarchal, competitive society, that "a parent may feel compelled to preserve her *own* children, whatever befalls other children," or, in the case of *Trifles*, other women; "Maternal Thinking" in *Mothering: Essays in Feminist Theory*, Joyce Trebilcot, ed. (Totowa, NJ: Rowman and Allanheld, 1983, 1984), 217. Two more examples of exclusive mothering are Grandmother and Isabel Fejevary in Glaspell's *Inheritors*.

[15] My supposition that Glaspell played roles that were particularly significant to her is supported by the impression of the French director Jacques Copeau who saw her in *The People*:

I observed on the stage a young woman of modest appearance, with a sensitive face, a tender and veiled voice. She was absolutely lacking in technique. She did not have the slightest notion of it. . . . And only at the end of her speech, she reached out her two arms simply, and she became suddenly silent, looking out straight ahead as if she was continuing to live her thoughts in the silence. Well, that gesture was admirable, and there was in that look a human emotion that brought tears to my eyes. I had a real woman before me, and the tears which she made me shed were not those involuntary tears brought on sometimes by the nervous excitement of the theater. They were real tears, natural tears, natural, human as she was.

Quoted in Noe, 103.

[16]For the history and ideology of *The Masses*, see Eugene E. Leach, "The Radicals of *The Masses*" in *1915, the Cultural Moment*, 27-47.

[17]Susan Glaspell, *The People* in *Plays* (Boston: Small, Maynard, 1920), 57. Subsequent references to this play will be indicated within the text.

[18]The life-saving station was modeled upon the one in which Eugene O'Neill lived.

[19]Susan Glaspell, *The Outside* in *Plays* (Boston: Small, Maynard, 1920), 109. Subsequent references to this play will be indicated within the text.

[20]Ben-Zvi, 152.

[21]*Woman's Honor* in *Plays* by Susan Glaspell (Boston: Small, Maynard, 1920), 124. Subsequent references to this play will be indicated within the text.

[22]Christine Dymkowski, "On the Edge: the Plays of Susan Glaspell," *Modern Drama*, 31 (1988), 95.

[23]Friedman, 148.

[24]*Bernice* in *Plays* by Susan Glaspell (Boston: Small, Maynard, 1920), 176. Subsequent references to this play will be indicated within the text.

[25]Noe, 108.

[26]Friedman, 161. She also comments that "Glaspell, in this play, is clearly glorifying the power of insight and imagination over whatever necessary gains are made through political and social struggle" (161).

[27]Bigsby, 16.

[28]*The Road to the Temple* (New York: Frederick A. Stokes, 1927, 1941), 12. A genealogy in Glaspell's papers in the New York Public Library's Berg Collection indicates that the Mortons are partially modelled on Glaspell's own ancestors. In *The Road to the Temple*, Glaspell mentions the founding member of the Cook family in Iowa, Ira, and his friendship with the Morton family (7). *The Road to the Temple* also provides another possible inspiration for *Inheritors*: Glaspell states that Cook wrote as story in which the "swing of the pendulum moves this family back and forth between idealism and materialism" (93-94) over the generations. The prototype of *Inheritors'* Grandmother appeared in Glaspell's one-act comedy *Close the Book* (produced in 1917; *Plays* [Boston: Small, Maynard, 1920], 63-96).

[29]*Inheritors* in *Plays* by Susan Glaspell, C.W.E. Bigsby, ed. (Cambridge: Cambridge U P, 1987), 139. Subsequent references to this play will be indicated within the text.

[30]*The Verge* in *Plays* by Susan Glaspell, C.W.E. Bigsby, ed. (Cambridge: Cambridge U P, 1987), 64. Subsequent references to this play will be indicated within the text.

[31]J. Ellen Gainor also notes the identification of Claire with plants. "A Stage of Her Own: Susan Glaspell's *The Verge* and Women's Dramaturgy," *Journal of American Drama and Theatre*, 1 (1989): 84.

[32]See Dymkowski, 95-96; 100-102.

[33]Gainor presents a similar interpretation of Claire's relationship to her son by citing French feminist criticism: 91-92.

[34]Rich, 193.

[35]Ben-Zvi, 156.

[36]For more on the Dickinson-Stanhope parallels, see Waterman, 86-87; Marcia Noe, "A Critical Biography of Susan Glaspell" (University of Iowa, Ph.D., 1976), Ann Arbor: University Microfilms International,

1981, 175; and Gerhard Bach, *Susan Glaspell und die Provincetown Players* (Frankfurt: Peter D. Lang, 1979), 188-89. I like to think that Glaspell would have quoted Dickinson's "'Houses'—so the Wise Men tell me—" if she had had the permission of the Dickinson estate since the poem concerns the unfulfilled promises of the house of the patriarchy: Number 127 in *The Complete Poems of Emily Dickinson*, Thomas H. Johnson, ed. (Boston: Little, Brown, 1960), 59.

[37]*Alison's House* (New York: Samuel French, 1930). Subsequent references to this play will also be indicated within the text.

[38]Critics generally dislike *Alison's House* because it is a "well-made play" and so a retreat from Glaspell's experimental Provincetown plays; for an excellent assessment along these lines, see C.W.E. Bigsby's "Introduction" to *Plays* by Susan Glaspell (Cambridge: Cambridge U P, 1987), 26-29. Cynthia Sutherland argues that the play is a thematic retreat in that it "safely distanced controversial feminist issues by presenting women tethered by Edwardian proprieties rather than more immediately recognizable topical restraints"; "American Women Playwrights as Mediators of the 'Woman Problem,'" *Modern Drama*, 21 (1978): 330. I am taking Sutherland's argument a step further to assert that *Alison's House* represents a surrender, not just a retreat, in the context of Glaspell's other works of the late 1920s.

[39]Sandra M. Gilbert and Susan Gubar, *No Man's Land: The Place of the Woman Writer in the Twentieth Century*. Volume I: *The War of the Words* (New Haven: Yale U P, 1988), 182.

Yvonne Shafer (essay date 1995)

SOURCE: "Susan Glaspell (1876-1948)," in *American Women Playwrights, 1900-1950*, Peter Lang, 1995, pp. 36-57.

[*Shafer offers a concise literary biography of Glaspell and an appraisal of her work.*]

Susan Glaspell (1876-1948) was one of the most talented and original women playwrights writing in the first half of the century. Her name is closely associated with the famous Provincetown Players which she and her husband George Cram Cook founded. Most of her plays were forgotten from the thirties to the eighties in the United States although her one-act *Trifles* was frequently anthologized and performed. In recent years Glaspell has attracted the attention of scholars and some of her plays have been revived. During her lifetime she wrote thirteen plays, fourteen novels, and over fifty short stories, essays, and articles. In 1931 she became the second woman playwright to receive the Pulitzer Prize. After receiving this award for *Alison's House* she wrote no plays which were produced, and this mysterious withdrawal from a successful theatrical career has perplexed historians and critics. An examination of Glaspell's life and career provides a tenable explanation for her withdrawal from playwriting, and also reveals the extent to which she was influenced by German Expressionism but remained the quintessential American in her philosophical and social outlooks.

Glaspell was born in Iowa in "the heartland of America" on July 1 during the centennial of the founding of the United States. American history and democratic ideals are an important part of her writing. She was one of the few women attending Drake University in the late nineteenth century. There she published stories, acted as literary editor of the college newspaper, and won prizes in oratorical competitions which frequently had set topics dealing with the nature of Americanism. After finishing her education, Glaspell worked for two years as a reporter for the *Daily News* in Des Moines. By 1889, only two years out of college, she was earning her living by writing short stories.

Living in her hometown, Davenport, she was involved in radical groups which believed in the New Thought and opposed conservative, small-town politics and social outlooks. Far from being oppressed by a melancholy *fin de siècle* feeling, Americans were imbued with a feeling of growth, the sense that progress was inevitable, and that a new century with great possibilities was around the corner. Although, as one writer puts it, Glaspell was "raised in the 19th century tradition that idealized patriotism, piety, and competition, progress, and respectability" (Noe 66), she was, in fact, quite a rebel who shocked her friends and family by carrying on a romance with George Cram Cook, a married man with a divorce in his past. With Cook she shared the many interests which were reflected in her novel *The Visioning* (1911). These included biological and social Darwinism, divorce laws, trade unions, prison reform, socialism, pacifism, and feminism. These interests inform her plays and give a depth and richness to the characters.

Glaspell's upbringing in the Midwest gave her a great admiration for the strong pioneers who created the cities by the rivers where she was raised, and she emulated them in breaking new ground in her playwriting and fighting for what she believed was *truly* American. According to Lawrence Langner, she was a "delicate woman with sad eyes and a sweet smile who seemed fragile as old lace, until you talked to her and glimpsed the steel underneath" (*The Magic Curtain* 70). A final element in what might be described as progressive Americanism was the strong belief in democracy she shared with Cook, whom she married in 1913. So strong was this belief that she and Cook ultimately went to Greece to find the source of democracy and there Cook died.

Shortly after Cook and she were married they went to Provincetown, Massachusetts. There they associated with bohemians, writers, artists, and radicals such as John Reed. They established the Provincetown Players in 1915 and worked with Robert Edmond Jones and others who were excited by experimental theatre and by German Expressionist plays in particular. Jones was an important influence on Glaspell, for he spent the time before World War I in Germany and brought back sketches of scenery and descriptions of plays. He contributed greatly to the enthusiasm for the New Stagecraft in America. Glaspell had traveled in Europe while Cook was getting his second divorce and had seen European productions. One of the central artistic impulses which permeated the productions of the Provincetown Players was that of Expressionism,

most clearly seen in the plays of Susan Glaspell and Eugene O'Neill, the two outstanding playwrights produced by the group. In her use of Expressionism Glaspell was far ahead of most American playwrights, and it is only through a realization of the significance of Expressionism in her plays that they can be fully understood.

Expressionism developed as a formal movement in Germany after World War I, but the techniques utilized in Expressionism appeared earlier in such plays as Strindberg's *Ghost Sonata* and *A Dream Play*. Seeking a new, deeper realism, the Expressionists wrote plays (often called monodramas) in which everything was viewed through the perspective of the protagonist. Since the protagonist was usually suffering from the indifference or brutality of society, the settings mirrored her/his angst, and were sharply angled and distorted. Shafts of light and an intense use of chiaroscuro were typical. Characters were purposefully presented as types, not individuals, and were given names such as The Boss, The Wife, or The Poet. The language involved sharp staccato exchanges and telegraphic monologues. Glaspell often used Expressionistic techniques and was one of the first playwrights in America to do so. She began before the general awareness of Expressionism was developed through the showing of the film *The Cabinet of Dr. Caligari* in 1921, the Theatre Guild presentation of Kaiser's *From Morn to Midnight* in 1922, and the performance of O'Neill's Expressionist plays, such as *The Hairy Ape* (1922).

In 1914 Glaspell wrote a one-act play called **Suppressed Desires** with Cook, but had no intention of becoming a playwright. She was enjoying a lucrative career writing short stories and novels. However, Cook wanted a play to complete a bill with O'Neill's *Bound East for Cardiff.* When she responded that she had never written a play alone, he answered, "There is a theatre there waiting—go look at it!" (**The Road to the Temple** 130). The result was her highly acclaimed play, **Trifles.** Not enough attention has been paid to this imperative expressed by Cook: there was always "a theatre there waiting" for both Glaspell and O'Neill. Plays were both welcomed and needed, and experimental approaches were encouraged by the Provincetown Players in marked contrast to the American commercial theatres. The idealism, the yearning for excellence, and the belief in the possibility of great American art was expressed in many statements put forth by Cook and others.

As Cook left Provincetown to go to New York to find a theatre for the group, he shouted to Glaspell from the train, "WRITE . . . ANOTHER . . . PLAY!" (**The Road to the Temple** 250). Between 1915 and 1922 she wrote eleven plays, worked on the productions, and acted in most of them. One can fairly say that because of the Provincetown Players she gave herself entirely to the creation of American plays influenced by German methods of writing and staging. When the Provincetown Players seemed to move in a more commercial direction and there was dissension among the members, Cook and Glaspell left for Greece and she turned away from the theatre.

Suppressed Desires, the first of the Provincetown plays can seem merely a frivolous satire on Freudianism in America, but is, in fact, a carefully crafted comedy which has held the stage for over seventy-five years. As Sievers has noted, it "is an ingenious and delightful satire on the effects of amateur psychoanalysis in the hands of a giddy faddist" (*Freud on Broadway* 53). It still delights an audience and does not seem dated although it was very much a response to the intense interest in Freud when it was written. Glaspell once exclaimed, "You could not buy a bun without hearing of someone's complex" (qtd. in Sievers 53). The source of the comedy is Henrietta's obsession with psychoanalysis and her adulation of Dr. Russell. When her sister Mabel comes to visit, she describes a dream of being a wet hen who is commanded to "Step hen! Step hen!" Henrietta interprets Mabel's dream as an aversion to her husband and a suppressed desire for a writer. Throughout the action she urges both Mabel and her own husband Stephen to go to Dr. Russell with their dreams, pointing out the dangers of suppressing desires.

However, the tables are turned when to Henrietta's dismay Dr. Russell informs Mabel that she indeed has a suppressed desire, but it is for Stephen (Step hen). The final blow comes when Stephen goes to the psychoanalyst and returns with the information that he has a suppressed desire to leave Henrietta. She is shocked into a repudiation of the doctor and psychoanalysis and it seems that her marriage will take a more reasonable course. As for Mabel's suppressed desire, Stephen tells her, "You just keep right on suppressing it" (341). The amusing characterizations, the witty satire, and the clever dialogue combine to make this play a most effective comedy which maintains its appeal despite the passage of time. In contrast to many of her later plays, it is essentially realistic.

Trifles was first performed in Provincetown in 1916. Since that time it has become famous as is the short story based on it called *"A Jury of Her Peers"*. The situation in the play was suggested to Glaspell by a murder case she covered when writing for the newspaper in Des Moines. The basic situation is that a man has been found strangled in his bed and his wife, Mrs. Wright, claims not to know who killed him. The play begins as the County Attorney and the Sheriff have come to investigate the murder and find the motive. With them are the Sheriff's wife, Mrs. Peters, and the wife of the neighbor who discovered the murder, Mrs. Hale. Although the men mock them for their attention to small domestic details ("just like women!"), the two wives piece together a picture of the painful, lonely life Mrs. Wright has led, and what probably caused her to murder her husband. A major fact is the discovery of a murdered song bird—the only element of pleasure in the household. They also feel very guilty because they did not try to help Mrs. Wright with their friendship. Mrs. Hale cries, "Oh, I *wish* I'd come over here once in a while! That was a crime! That was a crime! Who's going to punish that?" (701). In the end the men, in their attention to "important" matters, have missed the explanation of the crime, and the women, bonded by their sympathy

and understanding, do not reveal it. As Ozieblo observed, "Although Glaspell never again used female bonding as the main theme of a play, it surfaces in *Bernice* and is significant in the later *Alison's House*" (74).

The play is of note for its effective mood, realistic dialogue, and dramatic impact. Despite the absence of overt dramatic conflict, the play does not seem static and there is suspense in the action. It is notable in Glaspell's career as it is the first of several plays in which the central figure in the story does not appear in the play. By the end of the play Mrs. Wright's character is as vivid and detailed as if she had been in the play, but all of the material is presented through skillful exposition. Her husband's character is also developed in this manner. This technique was later used by Glaspell in *Bernice* and *Alison's House*. As Sharon Mazer has recently commented, the unusual construction of the play may not be noticed today:

> Its radicalism may be as easy to miss for the modern audience as the details of Minnie Foster's story are for its male "audience." But by leaving the primary female character off-stage and then reconstructing her through the eyes of the women on the stage, Glaspell effectively and theatrically exposes the construction of "woman" and the way women are perceived, and provides a vivid opportunity to begin to see the way these women do.
>
> (Mazer 88)

The influence of Strindberg is seen in this play and in other works produced by the Provincetown Players—O'Neill was particularly impressed by his plays. Like *Miss Julie*, the action of this one-act play is set in a kitchen and domestic details are important in the setting and the action. Also the servant Jean kills Miss Julie's finch which causes her to reveal her intense hatred for him. Glaspell makes the murdered song bird an element which leads to Mrs. Wright's murder of her husband.

Trifles has received praise from critics throughout the years, especially for the structure. Writing in 1916, Heywood Broun said, "The play is a striking illustration of the effect which may be produced by a most uncommon method. It shows that indirection need not be denied to the playwright if only he is clever enough to handle this most difficult manner of telling a story for the stage" ("Best Bill Seen at the Comedy" 7).

Writing in 1962, Donald Fitzjohn also praised the playwright's technique:

> [*Trifles*] is not simply a play of detection, in which the two women discover the missing motive for a murder and decide to suppress the evidence. That is the plot on the surface level only. Fundamentally it is a play about compassion; although this is never mentioned specifically. In fact, one of the most interesting things about *Trifles* is the use made of implicit rather than explicit dialogue. By this means a vivid picture is created for the audience of the lives of two people who never appear.
>
> (*English One-Act Plays of Today*, viii-ix.)

After its initial performance in Provincetown the play was produced in New York. Its success led to productions throughout the United States and in other countries. In 1928 a Scottish group won the first prize in the Little Theatre Tournament with the play.

The People was written in 1917 and produced by the Players at Macdougal Street with Glaspell in the major role of The Woman From Idaho. (She was considered one of the best actresses in the group.) The setting and the subject matter are typical of Expressionism. The play takes place in a newspaper office of a liberal newspaper, *The People*. At a time of financial crisis the progressive editor (appropriately played by Cook) is about to give in to various pressures and close the paper. As if called up by his mind, abstract characters arrive from the entire United States—one country, despite its regionalism—and prevail upon him to continue to inspire Americans everywhere. Reluctant to listen to their pleas (i.e. the pleas of his own enlightened consciousness), he is nonetheless moved to continue his work by The Woman. She is a character who has come in response to an idealistic editorial written by the Editor. Her speech, written long before *Our Town*, presents a message similar to that in Wilder's play, emphasizing the importance of seizing and experiencing life and the beauty of nature:

> We are living now. We shall not be living long. No one can tell us we shall live again. This is our little while. This is our chance. And we take it like a child who comes from a dark room to which he must return—comes for one sunny afternoon to a lovely hillside, and finding a hole, crawls in there till after the sun is set. I want that child to know the sun is shining upon flowers in the grass. I want him to know it before he has to go back to the room that is dark. I wish I had pipes to call him to the hilltop of beautiful distances. I myself could see further if he were seeing at all. Perhaps I can call you; you who have dreamed and dreaming know, and knowing care. Move! Move from the things that hold you. If you move, others will move. Come! Now. Before the sun goes down.
>
> (10)

This and her other long speeches are typical of the nonrealistic monologues found in Expressionistic plays by Walter Hasenclever, Georg Kaiser, and other German playwrights. When properly read, they do not sound like realistic dialogue, but have a stylized, staccato rhythm.

Unfortunately this play has been viewed as an unsuccessful attempt at social realism. Even Rachel France, while generally appreciative of the experimental approaches used by Glaspell, wrote, "*The People* is one of Glaspell's more obviously flawed efforts. Aside from its static quality, the play never settles on any one form, be it burlesque or straight satire. And the cast, made up mostly of cartoon characters, are all too often given to lofty, serious pronouncements" ("Susan Glaspell" 218).

Although *The People* is a minor work, it represents an effective theatrical challenge to realistic playwriting and

is still moving when produced. In the early part of the play there is an amusing use of satire with such characters as Earnest Approach, Light Touch, and The Anarchist. So little attention was paid to the non-realistic approach in this and other Glaspell plays that a few years later when Thornton Wilder began writing such plays as *The Long Christmas Dinner* and *Pullman Car Hiawatha* many critics treated them as entirely new and original—and many theatre historians still do.

Close the Book (1917) is a mildly amusing satire which is chiefly of interest now because of its setting in an Iowa University town and the characterization of the central character, Jhansi. In both of these elements it prefigures the later and more important Glaspell play *Inheritors*. The play presents the results of a conflict between a rebellious young woman student, an important family in the community, and the administration of the university. Jhansi revels in her position as an outsider, an adopted gypsy child with outlaws for ancestors, as much as she scorns the proper family ancestors whose pictures adorn the walls of her fiancé's home. When documents are produced to prove she is really quite respectable, she is furious: "So this is what I was brought here for, is it? To have my character torn down—to ruin my reputation and threaten my integrity by seeking to muzzle me with a leg at Bull Run and set me down in the Baptist Sunday School in a milk wagon! I see the purpose of it all. I understand the hostile motive behind all this—but I tell you it's a *lie*. Something here (hand on heart) tells me I am not respectable!" (58)

When she is forced to admit to her heritage, she and her fiancé start digging through the records to find out disreputable things about their ancestors. Finally the grandmother suggests that they all "close the book." The point of view seems to be that we should be proud of our ancestors, but not deny their humanity by elevating them to sainthood. As Ozieblo observed, "As a result of her first-hand experience, Glaspell was never tempted to sentimentalize pioneer life" (68). Glaspell, of course, was proud of the pioneers who established the towns and universities in the midwest. Some of the material for the play may have been suggested by her experiences at Drake University and the University of Iowa where Cook was a professor. As Bartholow V. Crawford commented, "The work of Susan Glaspell reveals considerable variety in form, setting, and style; but there is also a degree of continuity and coherence in ideals and point of view. . . . The Middle Western scene was for her not something to be lived down or forgotten, but one of her richest resources" (518).

Arthur Hornblow fairly described the effect of the play in his review for *Theatre* Magazine, noting that it was "far fetched and futile, a sad falling-off from either *Trifles* or *Suppressed Desires*." He concluded, "The skit started off well and the character of Jhansi . . . was a well-drawn character, but long before its close the story faded into nothing but talk" (356).

The Outside (1917) is a far more impressive play whose power has not been diminished by the passage of time. In addition to its own merits, it is interesting as a study for the later play *The Verge*. The setting provides immediate interest in the play. Glaspell's description is typical of her interest in the visual aspects of a play which contribute to its theatricality and symbolic qualities. Her detailed description takes up nearly a page of the script. The setting is an old life-saving station, now bleak and cheerless, with a barn type door at the back which opens to reveal the sand dunes: "At another point a sand-hill is menacing the woods . . . through the open door the sea is also seen" and outside the door the stiff beach grasses "struggle; dogged growing against odds" (69).

As the play begins two men are seen attempting to resuscitate a drowned man. The highly symbolic play is developed with a number of paradoxes. For example, this place devoted to saving lives is now housing a dead man and is the home for two women dead in life. Outside, the sand dunes continually kill the trees and plants, yet they are covered with new plants. This play is a good example of Glaspell's belief in social and biological Darwinism.

The apparent conflict in the play is between the captain who wants to keep trying to bring the dead man to life and Mrs. Patrick who insists she must have her home to herself. Beyond that, however, is the deeper conflict between Mrs. Patrick and nature: she wants to deny life and growth because she has been deserted by her husband. She has spent the winter in the station with only a servant, Allie Mayo, a Provincetowner hired particularly because she rarely speaks.

However, the attempt to restore life to the sailor has moved Allie. She starts to come back to life herself—come in from the outside—and to convince Mrs. Patrick to do so. Although the play is not Expressionistic in style, this character who has been silent for so long finds difficulty in speaking and utilizes a telegraphic style of speaking typical of Expressionism. As she tries to convince Mrs. Patrick she says, "I know where you're going! . . . What you'll try to do. Over there. (Pointing to the line of woods.) Bury it. The life in you. Bury it—watching the sand bury the woods. But I'll tell you something! They fight too. The woods! They fight for life the way that Captain fought for life in there! (Pointing to the closed door.)" (76)

Ultimately, her stilted eloquence and nature, itself, convince Mrs. Patrick against her will to come in from the outside. Death leaves the house as the drowned sailor is carried away. Mrs. Patrick tries to mock the others, but as Allie has said, life grows over buried life and the "Spring will return when she is ready to know it is Spring. Life and the outside must meet" (79). Mrs. Patrick's final line indicates the struggle she is undergoing and what the result will be: "(bitter, exultant) Savers of life! (To Allie Mayo) You savers of life! "Meeting the Outside"! Meeting—(But she cannot say it mockingly again; in saying it, something of what it means has broken through, rises. Herself lost, feeling her way into the wonder of life.) Meeting the Outside! (It grows in her slowly.)" (80).

Not surprisingly this mood piece with little action received a mixed critical response. Glaspell's usual supporter, Ludwig Lewisohn commented, "Her attempt to lend a stunted utterance to her silenced creatures makes for a hopeless obscurity" ("The Drama and the Stage: 'The Outside'" 103). Maurice Maeterlinck received much the same criticism for his Symbolist plays such as *Pélleas and Mélisande* and *The Intruder*. In recent years Pinter's plays baffled the public and critics when first performed. Glaspell, like these two playwrights created a mood of mystery and explored human relationships utilizing silence, pauses, mystery, and indirection. Glaspell's use of setting, language and characterization contribute to a moving and theatrically effective play which might be even more poignant on the stage now than when it was written. It should be noted that the idea for the setting was suggested by the life-saving station (remodeled by Mabel Dodge) where O'Neill and his wife entertained their friends, and where, one stormy day, Susan Glaspell and Jig Cook listened to O'Neill reading *The Emperor Jones*.

Another one-act play in the Expressionistic mode is the comedy *Woman's Honor* (1918). Whereas in many of her plays prison reform and feminism are treated as central, serious concerns, here Glaspell touches lightly on the subjects. The play is a comical treatment of a standard subject: an innocent man is awaiting trial for murder because if he revealed his alibi he would destroy a woman's honor. When his lawyer makes this public, abstract personifications of Woman come forth offering their help: The Motherly One (who enters knitting), The Scornful One, The Silly One, and others all offer to give up their honor and say he spent the night of the murder with them. The characters are essentially products of the vision of women held by The Prisoner and, by extension, men in general. Each woman exists only as a type, perceived, and to a degree created by men.

Glaspell used a great deal of humor in this play. German Expressionism was generally very serious, but in Glaspell's plays and later American Expressionist plays such as Elmer Rice's *The Adding Machine* (1923) and Kaufman and Connelly's *Beggar on Horseback* (1924) there is a strong emphasis on comedy. An example of a comic scene in *Woman's Honor* is the arrival of The Mercenary One. She appears to be a prostitute which causes the women to reveal their scorn for her. The scene concludes:

> SCORNFUL ONE—Woman's honor doesn't play much part in your young life, does it? Or woman's self-respect, either.
>
> MERCENARY ONE—(Rising) Say, you think you can sit there and insult me? I don't know what you are, but I'll have you know I'm an honest working girl! I heard they were going to take on another stenographer down here, but I don't like the *atmosphere* of this place. (She leaves.)

SILLY ONE—(*Settling herself with relief.*) It was a mis-understanding. Ah, life is paved with misunderstanding.

(141-143)

The women have committed the same "crime" as The Prisoner in prejudging the woman and interpreting her responses in a preconceived fashion. The Prisoner is forced to listen to the stereotyped speeches from the women because he has perceived women as types, rather than respecting them as individuals. As the play rises to a climax, the women voice their objections to the roles in which The Prisoner, The Lawyer, and other men have cast them. In desperation, The Prisoner rejects all their offers of aid and cries in frustration, "Oh, hell, I'll plead guilty" (156). (This line, of course, relates to more than the false accusation of murder.)

In this play the abstract characters of Expressionist drama help to make the point that men's perceptions of women marginalize them and prevent them from perceiving reality through their own eyes. The play is at once a comic presentation of the feminist viewpoint and a light parody of the many realistic plays in which a woman sacrifices her honor to save a man.

As in *Trifles* and *The People,* in *Woman's Honor* Glaspell played an important role, The Cheated One. Since she directed *The People* and acted in both plays, the necessary Expressionistic style was created by her, so there was no possibility the audience would perceive the plays as realism. Again, from the point of view of realism, the play is not successful. France dismisses it by saying that it was less experimental than *The Outside,* and that Glaspell "turned to a device already overworked at the Provincetown Players—characters with abstract names" ("Susan Glaspell" 219).

Glaspell again collaborated with Cook on *Tickless Time* (1916). It is typical of a number of early Provincetown plays which related to the types of people in the group and their interests, and which are set in homes in Provincetown or apartments in Greenwich Village. As in *Suppressed Desires,* the play satirizes an obsession of one character which threatens to ruin the household of an otherwise happily married couple. Ian Joyce has worked for weeks to create an accurate sun-dial. Carried away by the idea that a sun-dial relates to truth and nature, Ian convinces his wife Eloise that they should bury all their clocks and live by the sun-dial.

Having set up a funny situation, the playwrights then initiated a series of misadventures resulting from it. Funny pieces of business, such as the cook dashing in and out of the garden trying to time the browning of onions and the cooking of beef, and the sounds of the alarm clock and the cuckoo from their graves at the foot of the sundial enliven the action. A funny visual effect is created, too, with her return after Ian has buried the sundial: "Annie and Ian appear and march across from gate to house, Annie triumphantly bearing her alarm clock, Ian—a captive at her chariot wheels—following with suitcase, shawl-strap and long strings of bags around his wrist. A moment later Ian comes out of the house, looks at each dug-up thing and stands by the grave of the sun-dial. His idealistic concept of time has been undercut by the pragmatism of the cook, who has the last word, calling in a flat voice from the house, 'It's dinner time!'" (150-151).

The play was another effective comic collaboration between Glaspell and Cook. It may have been self-satire in part, with Ian representing Cook going off on a half-cocked idea and Glaspell supporting him. While it does not have the depth of her works written alone, it was a pleasing satire which would still be effective on-stage today. First performed in 1918, it was revived in 1921. When O'Neill's *The Emperor Jones* was moved to Broadway and then taken on tour, it replaced Lawrence Langner's *Matinata.* (Either of the plays must have seemed a rather odd curtain raiser for O'Neill's powerful play.) Following the American tour the play was part of the bill in London and a subsequent revival in New York.

Glaspell's first full-length play was produced in 1919. *Bernice* is a realistic three-act play unusual in that the figure of Bernice never appears. The play is really a type of mystery play in which the several characters search for the explanation of Bernice's death. Visitors to the house, Margaret and sister-in-law, converse at length about the baffling circumstances of Bernice's death. The servant, Abbie, falsely tells Bernice's husband Craig that she committed suicide because she loved him too much to bear his infidelities.

Glaspell's examination of the character of Bernice gives an interest to the play and also provides a comment on the expectations regarding the conduct of a wife in this period. The sister-in-law (as in the later play *Alison's House*) speaks for the standard conservative viewpoint of society. She condones her brother's affairs because she thinks Bernice was too independent to be a good wife. Craig shares this view, saying, "Margaret, I wish I could tell you about me and Bernice. I loved her. She loved me. But there was something in her that had almost nothing to do with our love. . . . Well, that isn't right, Margaret. You want to feel that you have the woman you love. Yes—completely. Yes, every bit of her!" (58). In the concluding scenes Margaret decides to let Craig believe that he really did have all of Bernice. She sees that Bernice, in her great compassion and understanding, gave him in death what she was incapable of giving him in life. Glaspell created the image of a woman too intelligent and independent to act only as the pillar of support for a weak husband.

The play was not a major success and was not revived, but it reveals Glaspell's growing ability to move beyond the one-act form. Some critics described it as simple and cleverly constructed. The reviewer for the *Nation,* while praising the play as a whole, noted some of its problems: "*Bernice* is not for the commercial stage. It is too subtle, too slow, too real. The characters actually talk, they do not speak for the benefit of the audience. They grope for the solution of their problems with a reality that is actually painful. And their problems are not the problems of the stage but of souls today, the souls of young people seeking reality, and the souls of old people escaping it" ("Bernice" 702-703).

Two years later, Glaspell produced a full-length play which had considerable success and demonstrated her capabilities as a playwright much more clearly than in **Bernice.** Although **Inheritors** was produced in 1921, and is very much rooted in the society of that time, the themes in it seem very contemporary. In the play Glaspell presented her concerns about the nature of American society, academic freedom, the effects of war on society, the treatment of Indians by the pioneers, and twentieth century antipathy toward foreigners in America. The style of the play is realistic, but the three-act structure has an interesting element. The first act takes place on the Fourth of July in 1879 and concludes with the decision to found a college, and the second and third acts are set in the college in 1920. The effect of the structure is to emphasize that American society faces the same problems and concerns despite the passage of time. Again, Glaspell's Darwinism is in evidence: Silas, a rich farmer, wants to found a college in order to help all the children, not just his own, and to improve America. He says with asperity to the people who oppose him, "Why the buffalo here before us was more than we if we do nothing but prosper. God damn us if we sit here rich and fat and forget man's in the makin'" (42).

In the first act there is an emphasis on war, with concern expressed by Silas's mother that men never tire of talking about war, "Seems like nothing draws men together like killing other men" (p. 8). Various points of view about America are expressed through the arguments about what Silas should do with his land. At the end of the act, he gives the deed of land to Fejevary, a revolutionary nobleman who fled from Hungary to make a new start in America. Fejevary will organize the college to pay his debt to his new homeland.

In the second act the conflict concerns the question of free speech and the right to protest. Glaspell was reacting to the recent oppression related to the World War I. She was appalled by the 1917 and 1918 Espionage and Sedition Acts. Hundreds of IWW members and 95 leaders of the radical organization were found guilty on charges of draft evasion and conspiracy to cripple the war effort by fomenting strikes. They were given long jail sentences and heavy fines.

Glaspell's central figure, Madeline is the granddaughter of Fejevary, and shares his idealism. Another idealistic character is Professor Holden, who has been criticized by a state senator for defending conscientious objectors. The senator has come to celebrate the fortieth anniversary of the founding of the college, but the day is marred by student protests led by a Hindu. In the course of these,

Madeline assaults a police officer and she and the Hindu are put in jail. The complexity of society is mirrored by the complexity of the characters. Madeline seems at once admirable and painfully naive. One character talks about how as a foreigner his father was welcomed to America and in the next breath says the Hindus should be deported. The question of freedom of speech is emphasized because the college wants money from the state to expand, but the money will not be forthcoming if professors speak their minds. The senator expresses his view very clearly, "Oh—a scholar. We can get scholars enough. What we want is Americans" (48).

The third act is one of decisions. Professor Holden decides he must keep his mouth shut because of his sick wife. Madeline has become less naive and realizes the future that awaits her if she stands up for her beliefs. She has been warned, "Do you know that in America today there are women in our prisons for saying no more than you've said here to me!" (113). In a dramatic scene, she chalks out on the floor the small space of a prison cell. Nevertheless, she refuses to compromise, and at the end of the act puts on her hat and coat and walks out facing a future in prison.

The role of Madeline was a major opportunity for Ann Harding and was a turning point in her career. Glaspell understudied her and was praised highly by William Archer who saw her perform the role. The critics praised the acting, particularly that of Harding, but generally did not praise the play as a whole. Terms such as preachy, dull, turgid, and wordy were used by many critics. O. W. Firkins was one of the enthusiastic critics, and praised the themes and technique: "Dramatic movement may not assimilate the propaganda, but is continually active around and beneath it; the dialogue is hardly describable by any tamer adjective than brilliant, the play of intelligence is keen and varied, and the work while anything but impartial, is at least entitled to the solid praise of generous and thoughtful partiality" (344-345).

Eva Le Gallienne admired the play and decided to revive it at the Civic Repertory Theatre in 1927. Brooks Atkinson wrote that the play was verbose, but "Miss Glaspell's pure understanding of the American pioneer tradition remains as a quality rare in the theatre" ("Pioneer Traditions" 1). Writing in *Vogue*, David Carb expressed the view that the play had not dated:

> The assertion that it concerns mainly the injustices and fetishes in the wake of the World War I requires explanation—they cause the explosion, but the explosives are conditions which are as true today as they were seven years ago and seven decades ago and seven decades before that. The arrogance of wealth, intolerance, the smudging of a fine idea by the soiled hands of politics and finance, education having to lower its banner before economic necessity, the bold dream of one generation made ugly and perverse by the compromise of the next—all of those conditions remain.

(138)

Although *Inheritors* is overwritten, it is a dramatic and courageous piece of work which remains of interest today. It is less exciting than some of her other plays in part because of its three-act, realistic structure. There was talk of a New York revival in 1967 when it would have been very topical, but it failed to materialize. Unfortunately, it was given a weak revival in 1984 with Geraldine Page, surrounded by lesser actors, playing a very small role. The play suffered because of the production (Lipsius 10). Given the contemporary quality of the themes and the characterization it is likely that a carefully pruned script might succeed today in a university theatre.

In 1921 Glaspell wrote *The Verge,* one of the most daring and demanding American plays written in this decade. Here her Darwinian beliefs and her idealism come together in a serious, innovative play which puzzled many critics who could only perceive in it a realistic depiction of a neurotic feminist. The settings for the play by Cleon Throckmorton emphasized the non-realistic, Expressionistic style: the first is a strange greenhouse in which the architecture and the exotic, strangely hybridized plants express Claire's visions and aspirations:

> The Curtain lifts on a place that is dark, save for a shaft of light from below which comes up through an open trap door in the floor. This slants up and strikes the long leaves and huge brilliant blossom of a strange plant whose twisted stem projects from right front. Nothing is seen except this plant and its shadow. A violent wind is heard. A moment later a buzzer. It buzzes once long and three short. Silence. Again the buzzer. Then from below—his shadow blocking the light, comes Anthony, a rugged man past middle life;—he emerges from the stairway into the darkness of the room. Is dimly seen taking up a phone.

(58)

The second setting is a tower in which Claire works. This is her private place and can only be reached by a difficult climb up a spiral staircase. She seeks relief in this bizarre room from the world which is stifling her. It is, "A tower which is thought to be round but does not complete the circle. The back is curved, then jagged lines break from that, and the front is a queer bulging window—in a curve that leans. The whole structure is as if given a twist by some mysterious force—like something wrung" (78).

Claire, who breeds new species of plants (including the Edge Vine), wants to become something more than people have been, to think things never thought before, to dare things women have never dared. She is caught in the social situation of the America Glaspell rejected: rigid, static, intolerant, uncreative, and provincial. Claire represents the American woman who has the potential for something great. But the constraints of a patriarchal society have warped and perverted her so she can no longer interact with people. She has rejected her family (including her daughter whom she regards as an unsatisfactory experiment), she rejects her first and second husbands, and a lover. In the final scene (which, like most of the action, would be quite

ridiculous if played as realism) she strangles the man she loves because she realizes that to accept his love would be to stop, to find a wall instead of a gate. She says, "I'm fighting for my chance. I don't know—which chance" (98). As the play ends, she has stepped into the madness which she rightly perceives as the only way she can move beyond the life—and the men—she scorns. Had it not been for the Provincetown Players it is highly unlikely that Glaspell would have written this play or that it would have been produced: the theatre was there waiting.

The Verge proved puzzling and irritating to many critics in 1921. However, there were a few critics who wrote appreciative notices. Ludwig Lewisohn wrote, "Susan Glaspell has a touch of that vision without which we perish" ("The Verge" 709). Kenneth Macgowan tried to find things to praise, but had to conclude that, "The play is clogged, not only with a figure that affrights so many, but with abstruse phrases and very lengthy talk" ("Seen on the Stage" 49). A typical review was written by Robert A. Parker, who characterized Claire as "the type of erotic, neurotic, ill-tempered, and platitudinous hussy who dramatizes herself into a "superwoman" and even 'puts it over' on her gentlemen friends. . . . If she [Glaspell], like the feminine majority of her audiences, accepts this fraudulent female as an authentic "superwoman", we can only express our opinion that Claire is not convincing" (296).

Many years after the play opened, O'Neill biographer Louis Schaeffer dismissed it as one of Glaspell's lesser efforts (325). It is not hard to see why critics found the play difficult (although apparently there was a sympathetic audience). The opening dialogue sets the expectation of a witty comedy which is not fulfilled, the dialogue shifts from prose to poetry in several scenes, and the setting is peculiar to those accustomed to realism. Finally, Claire's character is hard to accept. (Several critics noted that Margaret Wycherly gave a beautiful performance in a difficult role.) She tries to strike her daughter with the thorny Edge Vine, she makes incredible demands on people, and she tells her sister she is "a liar and thief and whore with words!" (82). In 1921 the general public was not prepared for Glaspell's searing, passionate, non-realistic exploration of the position of women in society. Stephen Rathbun predicted the play would find acceptance in the future, saying, "Mayhap a century or two from today . . . *The Verge* will be as much of a stage classic as *Hamlet* is today. Perhaps in those future years thought will count more than plot and the exploration of the soul will be more important to theatregoers than action on a mundane plane" (4). There have been some revivals in recent years and contemporary appreciation of the play may lead to others. Sievers said the play "is one of the truly remarkable pieces of psychological literature of our times. The author draws a terrifyingly real portrait of manic-depressive psychosis. . . . *The Verge* is possibly the most original and probing play that had been written in America by 1921" (70-71). In an extended analysis of the play Ozieblo wrote that at the end, "Claire, a female Faust, now is her own God and cannot be reached by societal structures and compunctions;

she has broken out and is free existentially, alone in the transcendental beyond. Like the protagonist of *Inheritors,* Claire rejects the laws of the patriarchal world, but unlike her she refuses to deal with them on their own terms" (71).

With the play *The Comic Artist* (1928) Glaspell again collaborated with a man, this time Norman Matson, whom she had met after Jig Cook's death in Greece. The play has something of the style of S.N. Behrman's high comedy critiques of American society without his wit, unfortunately. It was performed in London in 1928, then at the Westport Playhouse in 1931, and finally on Broadway in 1933. The play ran for only 21 performances despite the presence of the talented Blanche Yurka in the leading role of Eleanor. The conclusion of the play differs from the published version (1927), which may indicate a compromise in an attempt to please the public with a happy ending.

The plot of the play is fairly simple: into the seaside home of a happily married painter comes a cynical woman of the world, her daughter who is beautiful but materialistic and selfish, and the idealistic cartoonist who is married to her and is the brother of the painter. Through the action and exposition it is revealed that the mother was attracted to the painter in Paris, but that he fell in love with her beautiful daughter Nina instead. He subsequently left Nina, so she married his brother Karl, as second-best. The key figure in the play, however, is Eleanor, a compassionate, nurturing woman, slightly older than her painter husband, Stephen. Throughout the play she supports her husband and Karl, even when the passion between Stephen and Nina again ignites. In the published ending, Karl is frightened into believing Nina has thrown herself in the ocean, and in trying to save her is killed. However, in the Broadway version nobody dies and Karl takes Luella and Nina back to New York, leaving Eleanor and Steven alone trying to rebuild their lives (Papke 81).

The play may be read as an allegory about a Paradise based on old, earthy, honest American values which is invaded by a serpent in the form of Luella, the worldly-wise American who has raised her daughter, the temptress Eve figure, to emulate her Parisian life of luxury and decadence. Although the play is not successfully or convincingly constructed, it has interest because there are some elements in it which relate to Glaspell's life and her outlook. The character of Stephen seems to have been modeled on her exuberant, Dionysian, would-be artist, Jig Cook. Cook mixed the powerful wine punches for the Provincetown Players' parties and Stephen pours the wine he makes from beach plums; Cook wanted to be a playwright, but he was a weak writer next to Glaspell and O'Neill, Stephen wants to be a modern Da Vinci, but concludes he is a mediocre painter; Cook and Stephen share a tendency to philosophize about the meaning of life. Perhaps most importantly from Glaspell's point of view, Cook was strongly attracted to women as is her character Stephen. The setting for the play is an old home redolent of American values, like many of the homes in Provincetown.

It is not surprising that the play was a failure. It was a weak collaboration to begin with, the altered ending seemed contrived, and the play was presented in New York when Glaspell's reputation was at a low ebb. As Papke commented, "This last major production on the American stage of a Glaspell work, then her collaboration with Matson, that fact elided by most critics who treated the play as if Glaspell must bear all responsibility for it alone, did not serve to shore up her reputation as a dramatist or stand as a strong finale to her experimentation with that art form" (84).

The reason for the decline in Glaspell's reputation was her play *Alison's House,* which was written after *The Comic Artist,* but produced before it in 1931. This play was the most controversial that Glaspell wrote because it won the Pulitzer Prize for 1930-31. It is ironic that this honor brought the critics down on Glaspell and on the Pulitzer Prize Committee.

The play was inspired in part by Glaspell's interest in the life of Emily Dickinson. The play is about a character similar to Dickinson. As in some of Glaspell's earlier plays, the "central" character is not in the play. The play opens eighteen years after the poetess Alison Stanhope has died. Her house is being cleared and sold by her relatives. The crass new owners plan to modernize and set up an inn for tourists. As in *Inheritors,* the play involves a struggle between the values of two different generations. But in this case, the sympathy is with the younger people who are more honest and more devoted to Alison's memory. The play has a realistic three-act structure, and shows the influence of Chekhov's *The Cherry Orchard.* There is very little story line and the characters discuss their differing viewpoints at length. In the first act it is established that Alison loved a married man, but renounced her love and shut herself up in the house to write poetry. In contrast, her niece, Elsa, did not renounce her love for a married man, but ran off with him. The family is surprised when she appears late in the first act. Stanhope's unpleasant daughter-in-law, Louise, represents the conservative, narrow-minded American values Glaspell rejected throughout her writing career. She refuses to stay in the house if Elsa does.

In the course of the three acts, Elsa's Aunt Agatha attempts to burn down the house in order to destroy Alison's unpublished poems, then changes her mind and gives them to Elsa just before she dies. The last act is taken up with the discovery that the poems reveal Alison's love for the married man, her loneliness, and the depth of the love affair. Arguments are presented for and against destroying the poems, and the play concludes with the decision to publish the poems.

One of the obvious differences between this play and *The Cherry Orchard* is that Chekhov peopled his play with many fascinating characters but Glaspell's seem rather familiar types. Elsa is the most interesting character and she is only in the first and second acts briefly. She dominates the last act and then the interest rises because the spirit of Dickinson/Alison is present. Richard Lockridge wrote, "In the struggle between centuries, between ideals, Miss Glaspell has found the material for at least one act of clear and moving drama. For that act alone *Alison's House* is infinitely worthwhile" (32). In fact, Glaspell might have been able to create a very successful one-act play on this subject. Another problem with the play is the scandal of divorce and the disgrace of unmarried people living together. This element was very quick to date in a period of changing social values. Of course these subjects were close to Glaspell's heart: she had fallen in love with a married man who divorced his wife to marry her and at the time she wrote the play she was living with Norman Matson and was not married to him.

The unusual element in the play for many critics was the absent heroine. Most critics felt Glaspell was unsuccessful in creating the presence and vitality of the Dickinson figure. Mark Van Doren reflected the majority opinion, writing, "Miss Glaspell has written before, and written better, about the influence of a dead woman upon her family and friends. It is an interesting theme, if a somewhat artificial one, and much might be done with it. But very little has been done in the present instance, and the little that has been done is offensively false" (590-591). Those critics who did not see the play at the Civic Repertory Theatre and went to see it uptown (after the award) were generally baffled about why it had won over such plays as *Once in a Lifetime* and *Elizabeth the Queen*. Their negative reviews, which panned Glaspell, her play, and the prize committee, killed ticket sales and the play closed after two weeks.

Contemporary critics could not understand how the play won the Pulitzer Prize, and this has continued to puzzle some people. There were several factors which contributed to the committee decision. The first is in the nature of the award (which has since been changed). The award was for the play which would best represent the high values of American life. Despite its faults, *Alison's House* fulfilled that quality admirably. As a Los Angeles reviewer wrote when Le Gallienne presented it on tour, "[It is] a drama of an intense realism, a realism which somehow exudes the spirit of a real American, an America which still bears herself with dignity and reverence" (Blon, n.p.) Another factor was the outstanding performance given by Eva Le Gallienne as Elsa. Yet another factor was the wish to encourage intellectual drama of the type presented by Le Gallienne at the Civic Repertory at low prices. Defending the decision in 1944, committee member Walter Prichard Eaton wrote of the choice between a Theatre Guild production and "Miss Le Gallienne's struggling Civic Repertory Company." He concluded that he had no apologies as *Alison's House* was a good play, and that seeing it again in 1941, "it was still a moving and provocative play which deserved a recognition Broadway refused" (qtd. in Toohey, 93). The play was selected by Burns Mantle as one of the ten best of the year. Ultimately the quality of the play was summed up by the title of John Mason Brown's review: "*Alison's House*. Some Fine Moments, But a Disappointing Play by Miss Glaspell" (12).

Glaspell was naturally disappointed in the critical and popular response. She returned to her career as a novelist. She wrote only one more play, *The Big Bozo,* and it was never produced. Her last involvement in theatre was as head of the Mid-west Federal Theatre Project in the late thirties. Her play *Inheritors* was produced by the Federal Theatre Project in Jacksonville, Florida.

When Susan Glaspell died in 1948 her theatrical activities were largely forgotten. She was a talented actress, an outstanding playwright, and an idealistic intellectual who made many contributions to the American theatre. She wrote theatrically effective roles which provided opportunities for many fine actresses including Ann Harding, Blanche Yurka, Eva Le Gallienne, and herself. She was inspired to work in the theatre through connection with three idealistic theatrical organizations: the Provincetown Players, the Civic Repertory Theatre, and the Federal Theatre Project. Unlike most playwrights, she had no wish for Broadway success and did not seek financial success in Hollywood. Many of her plays have held the stage and others should be produced. Glaspell was technically proficient and highly imaginative. Some of her longer plays were criticized for verbosity, but a good director could easily cut them for production. When her plays appeared in a new edition in 1988, critic Michael Goldman called her "the only playwright of her generation worthy of comparison with O'Neill" (n. p.). He called his review "The Dangerous Edge of Things" and that was where Susan Glaspell worked. Because of the experimental approach taken by the theatres with which she worked she was free from commercial pressures and able to apply various techniques to subjects which reflected her idealism and her belief in the potential greatness of America. Edythe M. McGovern recently summed up Glaspell's career by saying,

> Because her work in the theater was of necessity much more experimental than her work in other genres, Glaspell's main significance stems from her Province-town connection, not only as a playwright, but, more importantly, as an innovator instrumental in changing the course of American drama forever. The most striking hallmark of her best writing is her consistent emphasis on the need for human beings to fulfill their highest potential by utilizing what is desirable from the past and applying it with faith and courage to the future.

> (146)

BIBLIOGRAPHY

BOOKS

Bigsby, C.W.E., ed. *Plays by Susan Glaspell*. Cambridge: Cambridge Univ. Press, 1987.

Cerf, Bennett and Van H. Cartmell, eds. *Thirty Famous One-Act Plays*. New York: Random House, 1949.

Clements, C.C., ed. *Sea Plays*. Boston: Small, Maynard, 1925.

Fitzjohn, Donald, ed. *English One-Act Plays of Today*. London: Oxford University Press, 1962.

France, Rachel, ed. *A Century of Plays by American Women*. New York: Richards Rosen Press, 1979.

Gassner, John. *Twenty-Five Best Plays of the Modern American Theatre: Early Series*. New York: Crown, 1949.

Glaspell, Susan. *Alison's House*. New York: French, 1930.

————. *Bernice*. London: Benn, 1924.

————. *Inheritors*. Boston: Small, Maynard, 1921.

————. *The Outside*. In: Clements, C.C., ed., *Sea Plays*.

————. *The People and Close the Book*. New York: Frank Shay, 1918.

————. *Plays*. New York: Dodd, Mead, and Co., 1931.

————. *The Road to the Temple*. New York: Stokes, 1927.

————. *Trifles*. In: Gassner, *Twenty-Five Best*.

————. *The Verge*. In: Bigsby, *Plays*.

————. and George Cram Cook. *Suppressed Desires*. In Cerf, *Thirty Best*.

————. and Norman Matson. *The Comic Artist*. London: Benn, 1927.

Langner, Lawrence. *The Magic Curtain*. New York: Dutton, 1951.

Lewishohn, Ludwig. *Drama and the Stage*. New York: Harcourt, 1922.

Mainiero, Lina, ed. *American Women Writers*. New York: Ungar, 1979.

Makowsky, Veronica. *Susan Glaspell's Century of American Women*. New York: Oxford University Press, 1993.

Mazer, Sharon. "Instructor's Manual," *The Anthology of Drama*. New York: Harcourt, Brace Janovich, 1993.

Papke, Mary E. *Susan Glaspell: A Research and Production Sourcebook*. Westport: Greenwood Press, 1993.

Robinson, Alice M., Vera Mowry Roberts, and Milly S. Barranger, eds. *Notable Women in the American Theatre*. New York: Greenwood Press, 1989.

Schlueter, June, ed. *Modern American Drama: The Female Canon*. New Jersey: Associated Univ. Presses, 1990.

Sheaffer, Louis. *O'Neill: Son and Artist*. Boston: Little, Brown and Company, 1973.

Sievers, W. David. *Freud on Broadway*. New York: Hermitage House, 1955.

Toohey, John L. *A History of the Pulitzer Prize Plays*. New York: The Citadel Press 1967.

ARTICLES

Ben-Zvi, Linda. "Susan Glaspell." Robinson, *Notable Women* 341-346.

Crawford, Bartholomew W. "Susan Glaspell." *The Palimpsest* (December 1930): 517-521.

France, Rachel. "Susan Glaspell." *Dictionary of Literary Biography*. 7: 215-223.

Goldman, Michael. "The Dangerous Edge of Things" *New York Times Literary Supplement* 5 Dec. 1988: 139.

McGovern, Edythe M. "Susan Glaspell." Mainiero, *American Women Writers* 144-46.

Noe, Marcia. "Susan Glaspell." *Dictionary of Literary Biography* 9: 66-71.

Ozieblo, Barbara. "Rebellion and Rejection: The Plays of Susan Glaspell." Schlueter, *Modern American Drama* 66-75.

Shafer, Yronne. "Susan Glaspell: German Influence, American Playwright." *Zeitschrift für Änglistik und Amerikanistik* (December 1988): 333-38.

REVIEWS

Atkinson, J. Brooks. "Pioneer Traditions: Miss Glaspell's Intelligent Portrayal of a Vital Period in American History—The New Playwrights." *New York Times* (20 March 1927): sec 8, p. 1.

Blon, Katherine T. von. "*Alison's House* Presented." *Los Angeles Times* (22 February 1933).

Broun, Heywood. "Best Bill Seen at the Comedy." *New York Tribune* (14 Nov. 1916): 7

Brown, John Mason. "The Play: *Alison's House*, Some Fine Moments, but a Disappointing Play by Miss Glaspell, Inspired by Emily Dickinson's Life." *New York Evening Post* (2 December 1930): 12.

Carb, David. "Seen on the Stage—*Inheritors*." *Vogue* (1 May 1927): 138.

Firkins, O. W. "Drama: *Inheritors* at Provincetown and *Nice People* on Broadway." *The Weekly Review* (13 April 1921): 344-346.

Hornblow, Arthur. "Little Simplicity." *Theatre* Dec. 1918: 347.

————. "Some Time." *Theatre*: Dec. 1918: 346.

Lewishohn, Ludwig. "Drama: *The Verge*." *Nation* (14 December 1921): 708-709.

Lockridge, Richard. "Play of a Poet: *Alison's House*, An Awkward, Poignant Play, Offered at Civic Repertory. *New York Sun* (2 December 1930): 32.

Macgowan, Kenneth. "Seen on the Stage—*Inheritors*." *Vogue* (15 May 1921).

Review of *Bernice*. *Nation* (3 May 1919): 702-703.

Parker, Robert A. "Drama—Plays Domestic and Imported." *Independent* (17 December 1921): 296.

Rathbun, Stephen. Review of *The Verge*. *The Sun* (19 November 1921): 4.

Van Doren, Mark. "Drama: The Pulitzer Prize Play." *Nation* (27 May 1931): 590-591.

TRIFLES

Beverly A. Smith (essay date 1982)

SOURCE: "Women's Work—*Trifles*? The Skill and Insights of Playwright Susan Glaspell," in *International Journal of Women's Studies*, Vol. 5, No. 2, March/April 1982, pp. 172-84.

[*In the following, Smith examines Glaspell's presentation of women in* Trifles *and she analyzes the play as "a possible fictional representation of a [spouse] battering."*]

INTRODUCTION

SHERIFF *(rises)*: Well, can you beat the woman! Held for murder and worrin' about her preserves.

COUNTY ATTORNEY *(getting down from chair)*: I guess before we're through she may have something more serious to worry about.

HALE: Well, women are used to worrying about trifles. *(The two women move a little closer together.)*[1]

Susan Glaspell

The same aspects of life which the male characters in *Trifles* see as ordinary and insignificant are in truth vital parts of the female experience shared by the female characters onstage and off. Playwright Susan Glaspell's ironic use of the word "trifles" is an early key indication of her skills as an artist and as a social observer. It is doubly, and sadly, ironic that her skill and her subject matter have been underestimated or acknowledged in a simplistic manner.

Since its first appearance in 1916, *Trifles* has become one of the most frequently anthologized American dramas, used both as a model of the one-act form and more recently as an example of women's literature. However, critical discussions of the play have been sketchy at best and reflective of the male/female divisions in the play. In his monograph study of Glaspell as a novelist and dramatist, Arthur Waterman acknowledges the fame of *Trifles* as deserved, "an example of structure and craftsmanship."[2] He is correct in that *Trifles* is a taut, compact drama concerning the visit of five persons, three men and two women, to a farmhouse where Minnie Wright probably strangled her husband John while he slept. Although the on-stage characters reveal much about themselves, Sheriff Peters, County Attorney Henderson, Hale, the Wrights' neighbor who found the body, Mrs. Peters, and Mrs. Hale reveal even more about the lives and personalities of Minnie and John, whom the audience never sees. Waterman does not examine in detail the structure, symbolism, and insights which he praises, but instead he consigns the play to the category of "local color on stage," "with its precise realism, exact details, accurate dialogue, and conscious awareness of certain Midwestern ingredients."[3] The drama inherent in the commission and investigation of a murder is well-known. Glaspell does more than place that drama in a Midwestern setting. For this play subtly explores such human experiences as disintegration of a marriage, bitter loss of innocence, psychological and physical spouse abuse, assault, breakdown of human communication, stress born of frustration and few alternatives, and bonding of individuals with shared experiences.

Feminist critics have praised Glaspell's recognition of female bonding, once stereotypically the reserve of males, the gender that waged war and played team sports. Harriet Kriegel notes that "the women in *Trifles* demonstrate their sympathy with and understanding of another woman's plight when they are confronted with her violent retaliation against her husband's domination and brutality."[4] In focusing on the insights of Glaspell the feminist, it is too easy to overlook the skills of Glaspell the playwright. Kriegel does not examine the development of the bonding or the integral part that process has in sustaining the drama's suspense. Cynthia Sutherland argues that Minnie Wright, as symbolized by her caged, then strangled pet canary, is a "stifled wife" who has "enacted her desperate retaliation" for having had to abandon a career.[5] There is virtually no evidence that Minnie aspired to a singing career, other than her years in the church choir before her marriage. On such meagre support, to ascribe such career aspirations to a woman of World War I rural America is anachronistic. Minnie's aspirations for humane companionship and communication were in some respects more modest than career aspirations, but nonetheless more vital to her existence as a functioning, rational human being.

Although previous critics have been insightful and essentially correct in their comments on *Trifles,* the play's dramatic technique and observations on human behavior merit more detailed examination. At the outset of such an examination, it is essential to point out that there are alternative explanations for the characters' conduct and multiple meanings to the literary devices, both qualities being the marks of a fine literary work which demands something of its performers and its audience or readers. This paper first explores the play's structure and symbolism and then the play's social insights, although these two aspects are too well integrated to be dealt with in complete separation.

THE ARTISTRY OF SUSAN GLASPELL

Glaspell provides an extensive description for a deceptively simple set. The audience sees only one room of John and Minnie Wright's farmhouse, the kitchen, which in farm communities traditionally has been the center of family life and the woman's domain. This kitchen saw the extinction of a family's life, and investigators invade Minnie's kitchen, much as they invade her life. The bedroom, where John was strangled with a rope while sleeping, and the parlor are off-stage. A bedroom may conceal many of the secrets of a marriage, none more serious than the murder of a spouse. The two informal investigators, Mrs. Hale and Mrs. Peters, who remain in the kitchen, learn more of this bedroom's secrets than do the formal investigators who visit the actual murder scene. Searching for requested clothing, the women do enter the parlor, a room in other homes set aside for visitors and special family occasions, of which Minnie enjoyed very few. When Minnie's parlor finally receives visitors, she is not there and the family occasion is not one to celebrate.

The kitchen has several examples of incompleted chores and limited spending on household goods. Bread left rising, unwashed pans under the sink, a dirty towel hanging on a rack, a table half-wiped are all signs of interrupted or unfinished work, but the time of and the reasons for those interruptions are open to speculation. Such untidiness could have resulted from Minnie's poor housekeeping, which by extension included the murder of the head of the household. Were tasks customarily left undone, or did their incompletion mean a shock or emergency had taken place?

An uncurtained window links a desolate interior with the harsh weather outside. Were the Wrights too poor or John too miserly to buy curtain material? Were they so secluded physically, and in other ways, that they did not need curtains? Or was Minnie so disheartened that she did not bother to make and hang curtains or to replace faded wallpaper? Did she neglect her duties, whiling away lazy days in her unpainted rocking chair, or did she use the sedative of its steady movements to soothe the distress of her faded life?

The five characters who enter this scene are the young County Attorney Henderson, Sheriff and Mrs. Peters, and Mr. and Mrs. Hale, the Wrights' closest neighbors and long-term residents of the area. At first the men dominate the action and dialogue while the women stand by, shaking with cold and fear. The initial description of Minnie comes from these men, who arrive already convinced of her guilt and lacking only a final piece of evidence to complete the case against her. But it is the women who remain on stage for virtually the entire act, evolve a more complete description of Minnie, and eventually take decisive action, on much the same basis as had Minnie. The women form, in the words which Glaspell used for a later story based on *Trifles,* "a jury of her peers."[6] In a sense, the women are also defense counsel, convincing both themselves and the audience of the soundness of their judgment. The men act as clerk of courts, announcing "the indictment," and, similarly preview their upcoming functions as prosecutor, head law enforcement officer, and chief prosecution witness.

Hale had come to the Wrights to ask whether they wanted to join him on a party-line telephone. Coming on Minnie alone and rocking in her chair, he found it difficult to communicate face-to-face. She "looked queer," "kind of done up," "as if she didn't know what she was going to do next," and she laughed strangely, but was not excited, when she announced her husband was upstairs dead "of a rope around his neck." Sitting quietly pleating her apron, Minnie claimed not to know the murderer of her husband despite the fact she had lain next to John on the bed. Minnie's reactions, the circumstances of John's death, and the lack of other suspects, as the childless Wrights lived alone, leave only the discovery of something "that would point to any motive." But, as the Sheriff says, there is "nothing here but kitchen things," trifles "women are used to worrying over." Performing in some respects as a Greek chorus, the men believe themselves to be the voice of the community's conscience. Each of the four times they come on-stage, they reiterate two themes, Minnie's guilt and the inconsequential nature of kitchen things, the women's domain and the equal of their scanty intelligence. Unlike the Greek chorus, however, they lack prophetic insights and perfect hindsight.

They certainly lack a knowledge of the irony inherent in their own remarks; the objects and intellects which they discount have the true worth, a value recognized by the women and Susan Glaspell. Some ordinary objects, a jar of cherry preserves, a log-cabin patterned quilt, and a bird and its cheap cage, provide clues to Minnie's past, the women's sympathetic understanding, and Glaspell's symbolism. Searching the kitchen, Henderson puts his hand onto the shelf where Minnie keeps her home canning. With no one there to keep up the house's fires, the cold had frozen and burst the glass jars. Disdainful of Minnie's housekeeping, Henderson withdraws his hand and washes at the sink. Like Pilate, he leaves judgment to others, but unlike the Biblical figure, Henderson does so unknowingly.

Left alone Mrs. Hale and Mrs. Peters honor Minnie's request to check her cherry preserves, and they find only one jar remaining intact. Knowing the effort needed to put up preserves, the women recognize Minnie's loss. The previous hot summer she had spent days of backbreaking labor picking, cleaning, and cooking over a coal stove to provide a vital part of the family's diet until the next growing season. Canning was also a source of pride, the mark of her ability to carry out her prescribed domestic role. Other women won blue ribbons at county fairs for their canning; Minnie's jars stayed on the shelf until used.

Minnie herself stayed on the shelf, alone and unbefriended on the farm, until the coldness of her marriage, her life in general, broke her apart. Her secrets kept under pressure burst from their fragile containers and created, as one character says about her preserves, "a nice mess." The single intact jar symbolizes the one remaining secret, the motive to complete the prosecutor's case. Almost by reflex, Mrs. Hale claims this jar. Near the play's close, both women decide to use the jar as a deception, so as to spare Minnie the knowledge of her loss. More importantly, they spare her another loss, that of her freedom or her life, for they conceal evidence of a motive, the final incident that prompted Minnie to kill. They lie to and for Minnie to protect her—to clean up her mess.

Accidently Mrs. Peters discovers Minnie's handsewn quilt blocks, sections of a log cabin pattern. The bright pieces are some of the few colorful things in the dreary kitchen. Utilitarian bed covers, quilts also express their makers' creativity and skill. Minnie's quilt was destined to warm the Wrights' bed, but it would never have dissipated that other, greater coldness between the two. Almost certainly, Minnie saved scraps of old dresses, flour sacks, and worn-out shirts, bits of a family's history, and mixed those with new bright material. Similarly, the other women link scraps of Minnie's past together to tell her story. Like the quilt, this story puts pieces in a different order and may have additional elements.

A broken cage and a strangled bird are the last of Minnie's possessions the women find. A symbol of her restricted life, the bird cage is not the "gilded cage" of song and folklore. It is a cheap cage to match her own poverty, the result of fate or John's stinginess. The circumstances of her life have been more restrictive than real bars. Virtually held in solitary confinement, she has been shut off from childhood friends and neighbors, with only the taciturn John to share the isolation which he probably created. Did the pet canary's singing break the silence and brighten her days? Was the canary, silent or tuneful, an all too painful reminder of an irrevocable youth of white dresses and church choirs and of a bleak future sliding into old age? A more detailed discussion of her bird and Minnie herself appears in the next section on the bonding of Mrs. Peters and Mrs. Hale to one another and to the absent Minnie. But with just these examples, the jar of preserves, the log cabin quilt, and the caged bird, Glaspell's mastery of symbolism is evident. A major question remains. What insights into human behavior does Glaspell make while effectively using carefully honed literary devices and structure?

THE BONDING OF WOMEN

Susan Glaspell, as critics have noted, depicts female bonding, the sympathetic cooperation of women with past experiences, current dissatisfactions, and future hopes in common. Stereotypically women have been held to be so devious and jealous as to be incapable of complex, lasting bonds with other women, rivals in a desperate search for male shelter. Supposedly in return for such protection, women submerge their identities and sacrifice their independence to their husbands, whose dominance has been buttressed by the legal system and social pressures. Cut off from outside support, including other women, wives then cheerfully absorb themselves in the trivial, mundane tasks of housekeeping and childcare. The dichotomous stereotype is that women are by nature crafty, devious men-haters who plot revenge for years, behind a façade of respectability and domesticity. In truth, married, home-oriented women have always been capable of and engaged in independent action and deep relationships with other women.[7] Just as some women can be intelligent, forceful, dedicated, and kind, others can be stupid, submissive, vain, and cruel. And women can have diametrically opposed characteristics at different times in their lives and in changing situations. To argue otherwise is to deny an essential part of their humanity.

Why do Mrs. Hale and Mrs. Peters deceive their husbands, whom they have previously obeyed, and jointly conceal damaging evidence against Minnie Wright? Why did Minnie kill her husband with whom she had lived in apparent harmony for decades? Mrs. Hale and Mrs. Peters are physically dissimilar characters, according to Glaspell's directions. Mrs. Peters "is a slight, wiry woman, a thin, nervous face." Mrs. Hale "is large and would ordinarily be called more comfortable looking." From their entrance, the women stand apart from the men, clustered at the stove. The men talk with a rough familiarity born of working together and knowing one another. The women seem less acquainted and never call each other by their first names. But at the men's first disparaging remarks about Minnie's housekeeping and women "worrying over trifles," the

women move closer together. Finding the sticky shelf of preserves, a dirty hand-towel, and unwashed pans, County Attorney Henderson asks the women to agree that Minnie was "not much of a housekeeper." Mrs. Hale, the more forceful of the two, defends Minnie and herself: "there's a great deal of work to be done on a farm." Men, whose "hands aren't always as clean as they might be," help dirty the towels; men share blame for what goes wrong in a home. If Minnie did not have "the homemaking instinct," Mrs. Hale does not know "as Wright had, either" or that "a place'd be any cheerfuller for John Wright's being in it." Having told the women to "keep an eye out for anything that might be of use to us," the men go to investigate the bedroom and leave the women alone to collect a change of clothing for Minnie. The women find more than clothing.

As the men's footsteps, and influence, echo over their heads, the women speak back and forth to each other for the first time. Against Mrs. Hale's complaint that she would "hate to have men coming into my kitchen, snooping around and criticizing," Mrs. Peters defends the men as doing "no more than their duty." Restless to do something, Mrs. Hale rearranges the unwashed pans Henderson kicked out of place, pulls at the dirty towel, and picks up, then drops Minnie's bread dough. Unable to do anything about these, she cleans the unbroken jar, whose significance has already been discussed, sighs, and moves to sit down in the rocking chair, where her husband had found a dazed Minnie the previous morning. Her touch starts the empty chair rocking. The chair evokes Minnie's presence for both women, and, perhaps to dissipate that image, they return to their assigned job. The sole time they leave the kitchen, they come on additional evidence of Minnie's dismal life, her clothing. A long-time community resident, Mrs. Hale remembers Minnie, as Minnie Foster, "one of the town girls singing in the choir," who "used to wear pretty clothes and be lively." Mrs. Hale blames John, not Minnie's disinterest, for the shabby clothing: "Wright was close," miserly with money, words, and feelings. Mrs. Peters, who had never known the youthful Minnie, remembers a request for an apron, something "to make her feel more natural," and, as the women may well think, something to hide her other clothing.

The women do bring something that they have been thinking out into the open. Mrs. Hale, again taking the lead, asks her companion, "Do you think she did it?" Sympathetic from the outset, Mrs. Hale does not think she did. Expressing uncertainty, Mrs. Peters remains disturbed by the manner of John's death: "It must have been done awful crafty and still . . . a funny way to kill a man, rigging it all up like that." After all, "the law is the law." From her law officer husband, Mrs. Peters has learned that "Mr. Henderson is awful sarcastic in speech and he'll make fun of her sayin' she didn't wake up."

While they examine the quilt blocks, the women themselves feel the edge of male sarcasm. Their innocent question—"wonder if she was goin' to quilt or just knot it?"—is laughed at by the men intent on another knot Minnie tied.

But the women feel the laughter is directed at their own lives, spent dealing with domestic tasks. It is all the more galling that the laughter comes from the men for whom they have done these tasks. Mrs. Hale says, "I don't see as it's anything to laugh about." Mrs. Peters who *"looks abashed"* at the laughter too, still makes apologies: "Of course they've got awful important things on their minds."

Until this point the play's structure and actions hold to a pattern: the men's derisive, preoccupied comments aimed at the absent Minnie and the two women; some sympathy, but little action from Mrs. Hale, Minnie's neighbor who has known Minnie since childhood; the muted concern with Minnie and defense of the men by Mrs. Peters who only has talked with Minnie under detention. Now, when the women look again at the quilt pattern, the pattern of Minnie's life, there is a change. Too many male jibes and too many examples of Minnie's deprivations have accumulated. Mrs. Hale looks at a quilt block:

> Here, this is the one she was working on, and look at the sewing! All the rest of it has been so nice and even. And look at this! It's all over the place! Why, it looks as if she didn't know what she was about!

The women's eyes meet and glance at the door to check on the men's return. Suddenly Mrs. Hale pulls out the awry stitches, her acknowledged reason being, "Bad sewing always made me fidgety." Mrs. Peters, faced with evidence of Minnie's anger or sudden emotion, rationalizes: "I sometimes sew awful queer when I'm just tired." Previously not bothering to finish wiping the table, Mrs. Hale takes decisive action to help Minnie. And Mrs. Peters no longer makes excuses solely for men.

When Mrs. Peters discovers a broken bird cage, the pace quickens, with each woman supplying clues to the importance of this item; Mrs. Hale remembers a salesman who came through a year before selling canaries. And Mrs. Peters knows the broken cage was not created by a hungry cat. Minnie had told the Sheriff's wife that she feared cats. The bird cage triggers a series of remembrances from Mrs. Hale. As a young girl Minnie "was kind of like a bird herself—real sweet and pretty, but kind of timid and—fluttery. How—she—did—change." Mrs. Hale holds two persons responsible for that change, John Wright and herself. John did not drink and "kept his word as well as most" and "paid his debts." "But he was a hard man," "like a raw wind that gets to the bone." Mrs. Hale blames herself for not having visited her childhood friend, even though the farm "weren't cheerful" and is "a lonesome place and always was." Disturbed by her own guilt, she returns to commonplace things, a gathering of sewing items so that Minnie will be less lonely in jail. Instead of her scissors, the two women find something that cuts more deeply.

In a pretty box is a canary with a broken neck. Mrs. Peters says, "Somebody—wrung—its—neck," the same four-word cadence Mrs. Hale had used to describe Minnie. The implication is clear. At this dramatic point, the men return, not having dropped their worn jibe about "quilt or knot." Henderson sees the dead canary, but not its significance. More importantly *both* women lie so that he will ignore the bird. Henderson's mistake is to ignore the women as well.

Left alone the women talk *"in the manner of feeling their way over strange ground, as if afraid of what they are saying, but as if they cannot help saying it."* Afraid that she herself might have killed on impulse, yet driven to confess, Mrs. Peters relates that as a girl she had seen a boy hack to death her kitten. "If they hadn't held me back I would have—(*catches herself, looks upstairs where steps are heard, falters weakly*)—hurt him." She also knows "what stillness is," having homesteaded in Dakota and lost a child. Minnie did not have a child, only the bird. Mrs. Peters still insists that the "law has got to punish crime." Mrs. Hale blames herself: "Oh, I *wish* I'd come here once in a while!" At this point they agree to lie to Minnie about her preserves to protect her. For the same reason, but with more serious consequences, the two lie to the men when they return the final time.

The men make another joke, this instance at Mrs. Peters' expense. The Sheriff's wife rejects the idea that she is married to the law, "Not—just that way." Minnie had reached the limit of her endurance when John killed the bird. Mrs. Peters reaches her limit with that derisive analogy. She, not Mrs. Hale, is the first to hide the bird with the purpose of carrying it away. When she cannot get it into her bag, she goes to pieces, and Mrs. Hale takes over. Mrs. Hale, who has been sympathetic to Minnie Wright from the outset, has the last word. To the prosecutor's facetious, repetitive question about the quilt, she replies with her hand holding the concealed bird, "We call it—knot it, Mr. Henderson." The bond among the women is the essential knot.

MINNIE FOSTER WRIGHT—A BATTERED WIFE STRIKES BACK?

Although Mrs. Hale and Mrs. Peters would not have used the term, they believe Minnie has been psychologically battered by a cold, close husband, her childlessness, the demanding work of farm life, and the isolation of her home. Under multiple pressures, she cracked. What she endured for years was burdensome, but the killing of her pet was one weight too many. It should be noted that Mrs. Hale and Mrs. Peters are never certain that John strangled the bird or that Minnie killed John. The women harbor an element of doubt, even if only to assuage one aspect of their own guilt. The women leave many of their conclusions unspoken, allowing each other and the audience to make judgments. It is possible that they left one conclusion even more veiled than others, namely the possibility that John physically battered Minnie. No one saw Minnie with a black eye; no one reported female screams coming from the Wright household. However, no one saw Minnie regularly or lived nearby. Minnie does fit, at least in some respects, the psychological/social pattern of the battered wife. And the marriage bears some of the characteristics common to a battering relationship.

The number and quality of studies on battered women have drastically increased in the past five years.[8] The problem, however, has haunted marriages and female/male relationships for centuries. There have been a few recent historical studies on battering. Those studies argue that the reasons for and patterns of this violence resemble those found in present-day studies. Therefore, it seems legitimate to use both historical and modern examinations to explore this early 20th century play as a possible fictional representation of a battering.

Elizabeth Pleck notes that: "Despite the legal sanctions for police arrest of abusive husbands and the belief of many Americans that wifebeating was illegitimate, American legal justice in the Victorian age was mostly ineffectual." To procure a divorce, "relatively rare" and "highly stigmatized," a wife had to prove cruelty and "also had to show that she had not provoked him or continued with him thereafter."[9] Sometimes when courts did not provide protection through criminal or divorce action, members of the women's families and communities stepped in. These vigilantes meted out informal, often physical, punishment to those who went beyond disciplinary chastisement of their wives.[10] Nancy Tomes speaks of a similar rough justice in the working-class districts of 19th century London, where "neighbors tried to prevent or moderate a wife beating by a combination of surveillance and reproach." Alcohol and poverty increased the "tensions centered around questions of privilege and allocation of resources." Tomes believes that the recorded decline of violence originated with "a rising standard of living that made the male's position within the family easier to maintain" or that meant larger, single-family homes where "violence may have become more private."[11] The decline may have been real, or the "dark figure" of unreported crime may have grown with the social changes.

Isolation was certainly a characteristic of Minnie and John's life. First, there was the physical isolation of the farm, "down in a hollow and you don't see the road." Isolation on a poor farm in the grasp of a severe winter produced stress, a factor in starting and continuing abuse in a relationship. Another type of isolation could have been self-imposed. "Battered women tend to isolate themselves so that friends and family do not find out how bad their life really is."[12] Shabby clothing may not have been the only reason Minnie left the church choir and stayed out of the Ladies' Aid, when the companionship of other women, ladies' aid, might have eased her loneliness. For John, the party-line telephone was more than an unnecessary expense; it was a threat to the "growing sense of exclusivity and possession."[13] Minnie was his alone.

What brought Minnie and John together originally? Bruce Rounsaville reports that battered women are frequently "under some sort of pressure to become involved with a man at the time of meeting the partner. . . ."[14] The social, financial, and psychological pressures on women, especially in pre-World War II rural society, to marry have been long acknowledged. "The message they received was that in order to be successful and popular with the boys, it was necessary to give their power away." And men, consciously or unconsciously, used violence to enforce this patriarchal society.[15] The women most vulnerable to battering report "a benign, paternalistic, 'dresden-doll' kind of upbringing."[16] Mrs. Hale remembers Minnie Foster as "real sweet and pretty, but kind of timid and fluttery," who "wore a white dress with blue ribbons and stood up there in the choir and sang." Dresden-dolls are breakable.

There are several types of persons found to be parts of battering relationships. "A particularly volatile combination seems to be a jealous, possessive man with paranoid tendencies and a counter-dependent, indomitable, passive-aggressive woman."[17] Apparently Minnie had spent 30 years being the dutiful spouse in the demanding role of a farmer's wife before she struck back. John, as Hale relates, rejected the telephone "saying folks talked too much anyway, and all he asked was peace and quiet. . . ." Did people talk too much about him? Was John jealous of the canary salesman who visited the lonely Minnie and left behind a noisy reminder of himself?

Minnie would not have been unique in staying in such a marriage, because battered women report feeling helpless, powerless even when alternatives do exist.[18] And alternatives were fewer for Minnie, living when battered women's shelters had not been developed, divorce was difficult and disapproved of, and career opportunities were severely restricted.

Abused women have struck back, sometimes with provocations similar to John's strangling of the bird. Some criminologists argue that persons, for various reasons, precipitate or bring on their victimization. Studies of victim precipitation show that males are "considerably more likely to precipitate homicide than females."[19] John's actions fit one of the types of precipitation, a victim "seeking to punish or create a position in which control can be exerted over the person to be precipitated."[20] Also, in some respects, Minnie fits the profile of the female homicide offender. In contrast to male homicide offenders, women much more often kill spouses and lovers, "interacting victims" who "contributed to a great extent to their own fate by their lifestyle; by their behavior towards the doer; and by creating permanent conflict situations. . . ."[21] Elizabeth Suval and Robert Brisson could be describing Minnie when outlining the model of the female homicide offender:

> . . . she has experienced considerable socio-economic deprivation. . . . She is likely to have had a rural background and relatively strong family life, . . . She may have learned strong affectional needs and formulated high expectations of interpersonal relationships but they have not been realized. When conflicts developed, perhaps she lacked the ability to recognize and select less disasterous ways of solving her problems.[22]

Nor is Minnie's method of killing unique. On the surface, it would be easy to relegate her to that group of evil, sly women who stealthily poison, stab, or otherwise eliminate their mates—the black widow spider personified. From Cesare Lombroso through Otto Pollak to this day, criminologists have all too readily labeled "the female deadlier than the male," virtually because of her gender. Gabriella Rasko has taken another, somewhat different view. Most often women do kill latent or predisposed victims, the sick, the old, their children, and sleeping spouses. Ordinarily these persons would be stronger than their killers, and they are the persons women have been traditionally involved with. "Thus, the 'choice' of a 'perfidious,' indirect, concealed or open way of attack is not a question of 'masculine' or 'feminine' psychology, but of a situational-technical nature, determined by the available means and by the given balance of forces in the situation."[23]

Would Minnie Foster Wright have been convicted of murder? Would her conviction have been assured had the prosecutor found the bird and guessed its importance? A recent series of spousal murders has led to a number of law journal articles which explore the question of the battered woman who kills her partner. More than 60 years separate Minnie's fictional case from these real cases. The legal definitions of murder, manslaughter, and self-defense have evolved in that time, but many points discussed today are present in Minnie Wright's case. She could have entered an insanity plea. She was so dazed when found by Hale that she may not have known the nature and quality of her act. But it is difficult to know how such a plea would fare today, much less in the formative period of psychiatry.[24]

Could she have entered a plea of self-defense? While arguing that a husband has no legal right to beat his wife, many courts in early 20th century America would have agreed with a present-day criticism of the self defense plea:

> To establish a 'battered wife' defense comparable to self-defense, as some would propose, would be to exempt a class of citizens from the penalties imposed by law for homicide. This would not only validate a kind of vigilante justice the law is supposed to preclude. . . .[25]

Others disagree. They point to the "retreat rule" of self-defense and manslaughter cases, which says that a defendant "must have personal knowledge and assurance of his ability to retreat in safety, regardless of what a reasonable man might have believed." A defendant, in other words, cannot plea self-defense if she/he could have left the place of confrontation. However, women remain in battering relationships because they believe, rightly or wrongly, that there are no alternatives, no places to run to or to hide in. Battered women are subject to repeated beatings and mental abuse, cumulative terror in the home, a place from which the courts have held that defendants do not have to retreat. Also, "to reduce murder to manslaughter (or self-defense) the battered wife defendant must be able to show that she was so overcome by passion that she was unable to cool down in the interval of time between the provocation and the homicide."[26] The incompleted tasks in Minnie's kitchen argue that she acted very soon after the provocation, John's strangling of the bird. Moreover, for

a reduction of the charges, the court must hold that "under similar circumstances, a reasonable person would have been similarly provoked and that, consequently her arousal and her deed are, if not justifiable, then understandable."[27]

What constitutes a "reasonable man" in such cases? With women excluded from many states' juries, would men in Minnie's society have understood her situation? Hale shows some sympathy with her, but he is dominated by the other, more closed-minded men. In Minnie's case, by the play's end, the more important jury has already sat and rendered a verdict. The women, "representatives of the accused's community,"[28] decided that Minnie should not be found guilty and, as a result, suppress evidence. The crime that will haunt them is not the suppression of evidence, but their part in the suppression of Minnie: "That was a crime! Who's going to punish that?" Late, but not too late for Minnie and for themselves, they discover:

> . . . how things can be—for women. I tell you it's queer, Mrs. Peters. We live close together and we live far apart. We all go through the same things—it's all just a different kind of the same thing.

NOTES

[1] Susan Glaspell, *Plays* (Boston: Small, Maynard and Co., 1920), p. 10.

[2] Arthur Waterman, *Susan Glaspell* (New York: Twayne Publishers, 1966), p. 69.

[3] Ibid.

[4] Harriet Kriegel, "Introduction," *Women in Drama* (New York: New American Library, 1975), p. xxxiii.

[5] Cynthia Sutherland, "American Women Playwrights as Mediators of the 'Woman Problem,'" *Modern Drama*, 21 (1978), 323.

[6] Susan Glaspell, *A Jury of Her Peers* (London, Benn, 1927).

[7] Carroll Smith-Rosenberg, "The Female World of Love and Ritual: Relations between Women in Nineteenth-Century America," *Signs*, 1 (1975), 1-29. For summary of recent studies on social bonds, see: Scott Henderson, "A Development in Social Psychiatry: The Systematic Study of Social Bonds," *Journal of Nervous and Mental Disease*, 168, 2 (1980), 63-69. Social bonds seem to be especially important for middle-aged women: Joan F. Robertson, "Women in Midlife: Crises, Reverberations, and Support Networks," *Family Coordinator*, 27 (1978), 375-82. Robertson argues that social bonds, much more than menopause, determine the stability of middle-aged women.

There have been, of course, other literary examples of social bonding among women. Two interesting examples, short stories, preceded *Trifles*: Mary Wilkins Freeman's "The Revolt of Mother" (1890) and Hamlin Garland's "A Day's Pleasure" (1891). From other women and for or with their children, the leading female characters find the strength to face or overcome their problems in rural environments.

[8] For some basic studies of the problem, see: Terry Davidson, *Conjugal Crime: Understanding and Changing the Wife-Beating Pattern* (New York: Hawthorn Books, 1978); Richard J. Gelles, *The Violent Wives* (San Francisco: Glide Publications, 1976); Maria Roy, ed., *Battered Women: A Psychosociological Study of Domestic Violence* (New York: Van Nostrand Reinhold, 1977); Suzanne K. Steinmetz and Murray A. Strauss, eds., *Violence in the Family* (New York: Dodd, Mead, and Co., 1974); Lenore E. Walker, *The Battered Woman* (New York: Harper and Row, 1979);

William Goode, "Force and Violence in the Family," *Journal of Marriage and the Family*, 33 (1971), 624-36; Linda S. Labell, "Wife Abuse: A Sociological Study of Battered Women and Their Mates," *Victimology*, 4 (1979), 258-67; Suzanne K. Steinmetz, "Wife-Beating: A Critique and Reformulation of Existing Theory," *Bulletin of the American Academy of Psychiatry and the Law*, 6 (1978), 322-34; and Suzanne K. Steinmetz, "Violence Between Family Members: A Review of Recent Literature," *Marriage and the Family Review*, 1 (1978), 3-16.

[9] Elizabeth Pleck, "Wife Beating in Nineteenth-Century America," *Victimology*, 4 (1979), 64; see also: Susan Brownmiller, *Against Our Will: Men, Women, and Rape* (New York: Simon and Schuster, 1975).

[10] Pleck, "Wife Beating," pp. 67-72.

[11] Nancy Tomes, "A 'Torrent of Abuse': Crimes of Violence Between Working Class Men and Women in London, 1840-1875," *Journal of Social History*, 11 (1978), 335, 334, 341.

[12] Lenore E. Walker, "Battered Women and Learned Helplessness," *Victimology*, 2 (1977-78), 530.

[13] R. Emerson Dobash and Russell P. Dobash, "Wives: The 'Appropriate' Victims of Marital Violence," *Victimology*, 2 (1977-78), 438.

[14] Bruce J. Rounsaville, "Theories in Marital Violence: Evidence from a Study of Battered Women," *Victimology*, 3 (1978), 25.

[15] Walker, "Battered Women," p. 529; Dobash and Dobash, "Wives," p. 343.

[16] Walker, "Battered Women," p. 529.

[17] Rounsaville, "Theories," p. 22.

[18] Walker, "Battered Women," pp. 525-34; and Rounsaville, "Theories," p. 18.

[19] Lynn Curtis, "Victim Precipitation and Violent Crime," *Social Problems*, 21 (1974), 597.

[20] James J. Gobert, "Victim Precipitation," *Columbia Law Review*, 77 (1977), 515; and LeRoy G. Schultz, "The Victim-Offender Relationship," *Crime and Delinquency*, 14 (1968), 134-41.

[21] Gabrielle Rasko, "The Victim of the Female Killer," *Victimology*, 1 (1976), 397. For other studies, see: Marvin Wolfgang, *Patterns in Criminal Homicide* (New York: John Wiley & Sons, 1966); Ellen Rosenblatt and Cyril Greenland, "Female Crimes of Violence," *Canadian Journal of Criminology and Corrections*, 16 (1974), 173-180; Stephen Norland and Neal Shover, "Gender Role and Female Criminality: Some Critical Comments," *Criminology*, 15 (1977), 87-104; David A. Ward, Maurice Jackson and Renee E. Ward, "Crimes of Violence by Women," in *Crimes of Violence*, ed. Donald Mulvihill et. al. (Washington, D.C.: U.S. Government Printing Office, 1969), pp. 843-909. See also: Mary S. Hartman, *Victorian Murderesses* (New York: Schocken Books, 1976).

[22] Elizabeth M. Suval and Robert C. Brisson, "Neither Beauty nor Beast: Female Criminal Homicide Offenders," *International Journal of Criminology and Penology*, 2 (1974), 33-34.

[23] Rasko, "Victim," p. 398.

[24] Jacques M. Quen, "Anglo-American Criminal Insanity in Historical Perspective," *Journal of the History of the Behavioral Sciences*, 10 (1974), 313-23; and Charles E. Rosenberg, *The Trial of the Assassin Guiteau: Psychiatry and Law in the Gilded Age* (Chicago: Univ. of Chicago Press, 1968).

[25] Marilyn Hall Mitchell, "Does Wife Abuse Justify Homicide?" *Wayne Law Review*, 24 (1978), 1731. See also: A.D. Eisenberg and E.J. Seymour, "The Self-Defense Plea and Battered Women," *Trial*, 14, 7 (1978), 34-42.

[26] Nancy Fiora-Gormally, "Battered Wives Who Kill: Double Standard Out of Court, Single Standard In?" *Law and Human Behavior*, 2 (1978), 138-39, 137.

[27] Ibid., p. 137.

[28] S. Baseden Vandenbraak, "Limits on the Use of Defensive Force to Prevent Intramarital Assaults," *Rutgers Camden Law Journal*, 10 (1979), 659. See also: Lewis La Rue, "A Jury of One's Peers," *Washington and Lee Law Review*, 33 (1976), 841-76.

Linda Ben-Zvi (essay date 1992)

SOURCE: "'Murder, She Wrote': The Genesis of Susan Glaspell's *Trifles*," in *Theatre Journal*, Vol. 44, No. 2, May 1992, pp. 141-62.

[*In the essay below, Ben-Zvi investigates a murder trial that Glaspell covered as a reporter as a likely basis for* Trifles.]

In the preface to her book *Women Who Kill*, Ann Jones explains that her massive study of women murderers began with a quip. After working through a reading list which included *The Awakening*, *The House of Mirth*, and *The Bell Jar*, a student asked her: "Isn't there anything a woman can do but kill herself?" Jones responded, "She can always kill somebody else."[1]

Women killing somebody else, especially when that somebody is male, has fascinated criminologists, lawyers, psychologists, and writers. Fascinated and frightened them. Fear is the subtext of Jones's book: "the fears of men who, even as they shape society, are desperately afraid of women, and so have fashioned a world in which women come and go only in certain rooms; and . . . the fears of those women who, finding the rooms too narrow and the door still locked, lie in wait or set the place afire."[2] Or kill.

Women who kill evoke fear because they challenge societal constructs of femininity—passivity, restraint, and nurture; thus the rush to isolate and label the female offender, to cauterize the act. Her behavior *must* be aberrant, or crazed, if it is to be explicable. And explicable it must be; her crime cannot be seen as societally-driven if the cultural stereotypes are to remain unchallenged.[3]

Theatre loves a good murder story: violence, passion, and purpose. The stuff of tragedy is the stuff of the whodunit; *Oedipus* is, among other things, the Ur-detective story. Therefore, it is not surprising that contemporary dramatists should turn to murder—to murder by women—as sources for plays. And, following the thesis of Jones's book, it is also not surprising that the most powerful of the dramas, those that are more than exempla, docudramas, or hysterogenic flights, should be written by women who share with Jones an awareness that often the murderer, like the feminist, in her own way "tests society's established boundaries."[4]

Three plays of this century, based on murder cases and written by American women are Sophie Treadwell's *Machinal*, Wendy Kesselman's *My Sister in This House*, and Susan Glaspell's *Trifles*. All do more than rework a tale of murder; they reveal in the telling the lineaments of the society that spawned the crime. *Machinal*, written in 1928 and successfully revived in New York in 1990, is loosely based on one of the most sensational murder cases of the 1920s: Ruth Snyder and Judd Gray's killing of Snyder's husband. Diverting attention from that other case of 1927—Sacco and Vanzetti—articles blazed, "If Ruth Snyder is a woman then, by God! you must find some other name for my mother, wife or sister."[5] Treadwell turns this tabloid hysteria on its head. Her Ruth is neither aberrant nor insane; she is ordinary, unexceptional, exactly someone's mother, wife, or sister, worn down by the societal machine of the title.

More disturbing because less easily domesticated is the equally famous 1933 murder case, from Le Mans, France, in which two maids, the sisters Christine and Lea Papin, bludgeoned, stabbed, and mutilated the bodies of their employer and her daughter: Mme. and Mlle. Lancelin. The crime was directed against women; however, the two plays that have sprung from the murder—Jean Genet's *The Maids* and Kesselman's *My Sister in This House*—focus on repressed sexuality and its relation to power, victimization, and enforced gender roles, Kesselman's version moving beyond the acts of horror to implicate "the rage of all women condensed to the point of explosion."[6]

While Treadwell and Kesselman reconstitute celebrated murder cases and alter the historicity to shape their readings of female experience, Glaspell's *Trifles* takes its leave from a previously unknown source; therefore, it has been impossible until now to determine what contextual material Glaspell employs and how she reworks it in order to create her one-act masterpiece and its fictional offshoot, **"A Jury of her Peers."**[7]

In *The Road to the Temple*, her biography of her husband George Cram Cook, Glaspell offers a brief comment on the genesis of the play, and on the conditions under which it was written. In the summer of 1916, she, Cook, and other transplanted Greenwich Village writers, artists, and political activists were summering in Provincetown, Massachusetts, and, for the second season, were amusing themselves by staging their own plays on a fishing wharf, converted at night to a makeshift theatre. At the end of July, Glaspell had brought Eugene O'Neill to the group, and they had staged his play, *Bound East for Cardiff*. Now they needed a play for their third bill. As Glaspell tells the story, Cook urged her to supply one:

> I protested. I did not know how to write a play. I had never "studied it."
>
> "Nonsense," said Jig. "You've got a stage, haven't you?"
>
> So I went out on the wharf, sat alone on one of our wooden benches without a back, and looked a long time

at that bare little stage. After a time the stage became a kitchen—a kitchen there all by itself. . . . Then the door at the back opened, and people all bundled up came in—two or three men, I wasn't sure which, but sure enough about the two women, who hung back, reluctant to enter that kitchen.[8]

Whenever she became stuck at a certain point in the writing, Glaspell would walk across the narrow street that separated the wharf from her home, and sit once more in the theatre until she could visualize the scene; after structuring it on paper she would test it in the actual space where it would be played. And so *Trifles* was written under conditions many playwrights would envy.[9]

As for its genesis, she claimed it was based on an actual murder case: "When I was a newspaper reporter out in Iowa, I was sent down-state to do a murder trial, and I never forgot going into the kitchen of a woman locked up in town." In numerous interviews throughout her life, she offered variations on this memory; but she never provided the name of the murderer or the details of the trial.[10]

In the process of completing research for a biography of Susan Glaspell, I discovered the historical source upon which *Trifles* and **"Jury"** are based: the murder of a sixty-year-old farmer named John Hossack on December 2, 1900, in Indianola, Iowa. Glaspell covered the case and the subsequent trial when she was a reporter for the *Des Moines Daily News*, a position she began full-time the day after she graduated from Drake University in June 1900, a twenty-four-year-old woman with a Ph.B. in philosophy and several years of newspaper work in Davenport and Des Moines behind her.[11] Although her general beat was the Iowa statehouse, and she would later say that the experiences there provided her with sufficient material to quit her job a year later and turn to fiction, it was the Hossack murder case that was the central story of her brief journalistic career.

Although not as sensational as the Snyder or as horrific as the Papin case, the Hossack killing also focuses on a woman accused of murder. The investigation and subsequent trial offer one more example of what Jones so graphically details in her book: the process by which juridical attitudes toward, and prosecution of, women are shaped by societal concepts of female behavior, the same concepts that may have motivated the act of murder. However, the position of the author in relation to the material differs among the plays. While Treadwell probably attended the Snyder trial, she was not an active participant in the situations she recasts. Glaspell was. And while Kesselman could make a thorough, dispassionate investigation of the commentary and reactions that surrounded the history of the Papin case, Glaspell was actually a primary contributor to the shaping of public opinion about the woman being tried. The news accounts Glaspell filed, therefore, offer more than an important contextual basis for approaching the fictional texts. They also provide important biographical information about the author and her own personal and artistic evolution, and document the cultural shifts which took place between 1900 when the murder took place and 1916 when Glaspell wrote her play.

II

The case at first glance seemed simple. Some time after midnight on December 2, 1900, John Hossack, a well-to-do farmer, was struck twice on the head with an axe, while he slept in bed. Margaret Hossack, his wife of thirty-three years—who was sleeping beside him—reported that a strange sound, "like two pieces of wood striking," wakened her; she jumped out of bed, went into the adjoining sitting room, saw a light shining on a wall, and heard the door to the front porch slowly closing. Only then did she hear her husband's groans. Assembling the five of her nine children who still lived at home, she lit a lamp, reentered the bedroom, and discovered Hossack bleeding profusely, the walls and bedsheets spattered, brain matter oozing from a five inch gash, his head crushed. One of his sons claimed that the mortally injured man was still able to speak. When he said to his father, "Well, pa, you are badly hurt," Hossack replied, "No, I'm not hurt, but I'm not feeling well."[12]

It was assumed that prowlers must have committed the crime; but when a search of the farmhouse failed to reveal any missing items, a coroner's inquest was called. Its findings were inconclusive. However, after discovering the presumed murder weapon smeared with blood under the family corn crib, and listening to reports and innuendos from neighbors, who hinted at a history of marital and family trouble, the Sheriff arrested Mrs. Hossack, "as a matter of precaution" (5 December) while the funeral was still in progress or, as Glaspell would more vividly report, "just as the sexton was throwing the last clods on the grave of her murdered husband" (14 January).

There was really nothing unique about such a murder in the Iowa of 1900 which if no more violent than it is today was certainly no less so. Sandwiched between ubiquitous advertisements for "Female Nerve Cures" and romantic accounts of the courtships of Vanderbilts and Rockefellers are a whole range of lurid tales that would keep a contemporary tabloid busy—and happy: reports of a woman being set on fire, a farm hand murdering another man with a neck yoke, a young man attempting to kill his parents, and a garden-variety assortment of rural knifings, insanity, and violence.[13] What makes the Hossack case stand out are the extended length of the coverage and the vivid style of the reporter. Her paper seems to have charged Glaspell with two tasks: rousing the readership and insuring that the story stay on the first page. She accomplishes both.

Employing the techniques of Gonzo journalism sixty years before Hunter Thompson, Glaspell filed twenty-six stories on the Hossack case, from the fifteen-line item on page three, dated December 3, 1900 that summarily described the event of the murder, to the page one, full-column story on 11 April 1901 that reported the jury's decision at the

trial. Most are indistinguishable from her own unsigned "Newsgirl" features running in the paper at the time. They make ready use of hyperbole, invention, and supposition, all filtered through one of Glaspell's common devices in her column: a lively, often opinionated persona. Whether labeled "your correspondent," "a representative from the *News*," or "a member of the press," she is a constructed presence who invites the reader to share some privileged information, intriguing rumor, and running assessment of the case and of the guilt or innocence of the accused.

In her first extended coverage of the crime, under the headline, "Coroner's Jury Returns its Verdict this Morning—Mrs. Hossack Thought to be Crazy," Glaspell announces the imminent arrest of the woman, a fact "secretly revealed to your correspondent." She also provides the first of many rumors that become increasingly prominent in her coverage, although never attributed to specific sources: "Friends of Mrs. Hossack are beginning to suggest that she is insane, and that she has been in this condition for a year and a half, under the constant surveillance of members of the family," and "the members of the Hossack family were not on pleasant relations with each other," information which comes as "a complete surprise, as Hossack was not supposed to have an enemy in the world." She concludes by citing the most damaging evidence used against the accused woman throughout her trial: Mrs. Hossack's claim that she lay asleep beside her husband and was not awakened while the murder was taking place (5 December).

Glaspell continues to mix fact, rumor, and commentary, with a superfluity of rousing language and imagery, opening her next report with the reminder that Mrs. Hossack has been arrested for the death of her husband, "on charge of having beaten out his brains with an axe," that the accused woman has employed the legal services of Mr. Henderson and State Senator Berry, that when arrested she showed no emotion and absolutely declined to make any statement concerning her guilt or innocence, and that while her family supported her "the public sentiment is overwhelming against her." How she gleaned this information or arrived at these conclusions, Glaspell does not say. She does, however, provide her first description of the accused woman: "Though past 50 years of age, she is tall and powerful and looks like she would be dangerous if aroused to a point of hatred." She again repeats the rumors of domestic tensions, and quotes a neighbor, named Haines—a witness at the inquest—who implies that Mrs. Hossack had years before asked him to get her husband "out of the way" (6 December).

"Public sentiment is still very much against the prisoner," the 8 December news story begins, reiterating the claim that Mrs. Hossack wanted "to get rid of her husband" and adding that she was willing to pay liberally for the services of anyone undertaking the task—a story "the public generally accepts" and will, therefore, "sympathize with the county attorney in his efforts to convict the woman." In an added development, Glaspell reports that Mrs. Hossack had left home a year before but had been persuaded to return "with the idea of securing a division of the property, but this division had never been made." Although the sheriff had refused all requests to see photographs of the murdered man, Glaspell announces, "a representative of the *News* was accorded this privilege though it must be confessed there is little satisfaction in it" (8 December).

Waiving a preliminary hearing, Mrs. Hossack's attorneys decided to take the case directly to the grand jury which bound her over for trial in April. In the interim the defendant requested and was given bail. The story Glaspell filed immediately prior to the release contains a new element. The reporter, who only days before had described Mrs. Hassock as cold, calm, and menacing, now described her as "worn and emaciated" as she was led from her cell, with "red and swollen eyelids indicating that she had been weeping" (11 December). Since Mrs. Hossack was immediately released after this date and remained in her home until the trial, it is likely that what caused Glaspell to alter her description was her own visit to the Hossack farm, the event she uses as the basis for *Trifles.* From this point on in her reporting, Glaspell's references to the accused woman become more benign, the "powerful" murderer becoming with each story older, frailer, and more maternal.[14]

Glaspell was probably at the farmhouse gathering material for the front page, double-column feature that appeared on 12 December, the most extensive coverage of the pre-trial events. It began with the headline, "Mrs Hossack may yet be proven innocent," followed by the subheadings, "Tide of sentiment turns slightly in her favor—Notified today that she will soon be released—First photographs bearing on the tragedy." The photographs turn out to be three simple pencil drawings: Mrs. Hossack, sitting in a rocking chair, her head bent down, her eyes closed; her dead husband with the two gashes to his head; and the axe, complete with four dots of blood. Captions indicate that the first is "sketched from life," the second "from flashlight photograph of the dead man" that "others tried to obtain access to . . . but failed." In more detail, Glaspell describes her revisionary image of Mrs. Hossack: "the aged prisoner . . . looked up into the officer's face, smiled and remarked that she would be glad to get home again with her children but did not manifest any great degree of joy at the news." Bail, the reader is told, will not be excessive because the accused "is an aged woman and one who would not try in any manner to escape."

As much as she may have altered her own perceptions of Mrs. Hossack and may have tried to influence her readers, Glaspell still had the job of keeping them interested in the case. Borrowing devices from popular detective fiction of the time,[15] she dangles tantalizing questions: the test on the murder weapon may now be known, but the readers will have to wait until the trial to learn the results; the same for the blood stains on Mrs. Hossack's clothing. Glaspell does hint that the results substantiate the claim that the blood on the axe comes from slaughtered fowl, and continues, "if that is true one of the strongest links in the chain of circumstantial evidence is broken. If the blood is human, it will look bad for the accused." If still not intrigued, the reader is given a gruesome detail—a "substance resembling brains" has also been found on the axe—and a rumor that the defense will enter a plea of insanity if their efforts on behalf of their client fail. She must be crazy or innocent "the best people of Indianola" surmise, since visits to the home in the past few months did not indicate problems, but only a wife attentive to her husband's needs, seeing "that he lacked for nothing." Of Mrs. Hossack's character, these unnamed sources reveal, "She is said to be a woman who is quick tempered, high strung, like all Scotch women, but of a deeply religious turn of mind" (12 December).

In the months before the trial, Glaspell filed only three small articles about the case, each one using the opportunity of a new piece of news to summarize the details of the murder, the grisly events becoming more grisly with the retelling. On 23 March she reports that new evidence has emerged "and that in all probability it would result in Mrs. Hossack's acquittal at an early date." She does not say what the evidence is but she offers an important turn in the case. Mr. Haines, the primary source of information about trouble in the Hossack home and the party to whom, it is believed, Mrs. Hossack turned to get rid of her husband, "had gone insane brooding over the tragedy, and was yesterday sentenced to the insane asylum."

Although there had been talk of moving the venue of the trial because of the strong feelings against Margaret Hossack and the fear that an impartial jury could not be found (14 January), the trial finally began in the Polk County Courthouse on 1 April 1901 and was held every day except Sundays for the next ten days. Glaspell had apparently been successful in stirring public interest because she reports that on the first day over 1,200 people attended, far more than the tiny rural court could accommodate and that on the day the jury returned its verdict more than 2,000 were present. Noting the composition of the observers, she says that the "conspicuous feature so far is the large attendance of women in court. Over half of the spectators present today belong to the gentler sex. The bright array of Easter hats lent a novelty to the scene, giving it much the appearance of some social function" (2 April).[16]

The seventy-eight witnesses, fifty-three for the prosecution and twenty-five for the defense, focused on seven specific questions during the trial: (1) Would it have been possible, as his son testified, for John Hossack, who had sustained two traumatic blows—one made with the axe head, the second with the blunt handle—to talk and call for his wife and children; (2) Was the blood found on the axe and the hairs later discovered nearby human, or were they, as claimed by the family, the residue of the turkey killed two days earlier for Thanksgiving; (3) How had the axe, which the youngest son said he placed inside the corn crib after killing the turkey, come to be found under it, in its usual place; (4) Had the axe and Mrs. Hossack's night clothes been washed to remove incriminating stains of blood; (5) Was the dog, who always barked when strangers appeared, drugged on the night of the crime, as family members testified; (6) Had earlier domestic troubles in the Hossack house been resolved and all dissension ceased for over a year before the murder, as the family stated; and (7) Would it have been possible for an intruder or intruders to enter the house through the bedroom window, stand at the foot of the bed and reach up to strike the fatal blows without rousing the woman who slept by her husband's side? An eighth question—what prompted Mrs. Hossack to leave home and wish her husband "out of the way"—only entered the testimony twice. One neighbor, the wife of Mr. Haines, stated that she and her husband had come to aid Mrs. Hossack, who thought her husband would kill the family (3 April). Another neighbor testified that he had to act as protector when Mrs. Hossack returned to her home "in case her husband again maltreated her as she had reason for believing" (2 April).

Glaspell's reports do not suggest that the prosecution or the defense pursued the possibility of violence in the home, and she does not broach the subject herself. Instead her stories of the trial tend to be summaries of testimony by experts and lay people who describe the structure of the brain, the disposition of the body in the bed, and the configuration of the blood spots on the walls. She does pause to describe the shock caused when the Hossack bed was brought into the courtroom complete with bloodstained bedding, and when two vials of hairs were displayed: one found near the axe, the other obtained by exhuming John Hossack.

Interspersed between these accounts are her descriptions of the accused and of those attending the trial. During day one, for example, Glaspell describes Mrs. Hossack's reaction to the recital of counts against her: "Her eyes frequently filled with tears and her frame shook with emotion" (2 April). On the next day, when the murder scene was again invoked, she notes that Mrs. Hossack, who occupied a seat by the Sheriff's wife, surrounded by three of the Hossack daughters and all but one of the sons, broke down and wept bitterly: "Grief was not confined to her alone, it spread until the weeping group embraced the family and the sympathetic wife of Sheriff Hodson who frequently applied her handkerchief to her eyes" (3 April).

Since there were no witnesses to the crime, the prosecution's case was based entirely on circumstantial evidence, and Glaspell often stops in her narration of the testimony to weigh the success of the unsubstantiated arguments, and to prod her readers to keep following the case. After one lengthy argument about how well Mrs. Hossack was able to wield an axe, Glaspell comments: "It must be admitted, however, that the prosecution has not thus far furnished any direct evidence and it is extremely doubtful if the chain of circumstantial evidence thus far offered will be sufficient to eliminate all doubt of the defendant's guilt from the minds of the jurors . . . on the other hand it is claimed by the prosecution attorney that the best evidence is yet to come" (4 April). When Mrs. Hossack took the stand in her own defense and repeated the story she had held since

the inquest, describing how she and her husband had spent a typical evening together the night of the crime—"He sat in the kitchen reading . . . later played with his whip . . . [while] I was patching and darning"—Glaspell observes, "When she left the stand, there seemed to be the impression on the audience that she had told the truth" (8 April). Earlier questions of Mrs. Hossack's sanity apparently were dispelled by her composed appearance in court.

Like the novelist she would soon become, Glaspell saves her most impassioned descriptions for the climax of the trial: the summations by the lawyers. Of State Senator Berry, the defense counsel, she writes:

> It is said to be the master effort of his life . . . at times the jury without exception was moved to tears. Strong men who had not shed a tear in years sat in their seats mopping their eyes and compressing their lips in a vain effort to suppress the emotion caused by the Senator's eloquent pleas.
>
> [9 April]

This lachrymose display, she says, even extended to the prosecution attorneys who were "seen to turn their heads fearful lest the anguish of the family would unman them and the jury would have an impression which they could not afterward remove." The spectators were also moved. When the court was adjourned at noon, she writes, "fully two thousand people went out in the sunshine, their faces stained by the tears which had coursed down their cheeks."

Aside from tears, Berry's chief strategy was to charge that Mr. Haines, "the insane man," was the real murderer. When he had been asked by the Hossack children to come to the house on the night of the murder, he had refused, saying that there were tramps about. It was he who had first implicated Mrs. Hossack by suggesting that she had wanted her husband dead and had sought his aid. And it was Mrs. Haines who had provided some of the most damning evidence about dissension in the Hossack home.

As successful as Berry may have been in concluding for the defense, Glaspell warns her readers that "it is certain that when attorney McNeal closes the argument for the prosecution the effect of Senator Berry's eloquence will have been lost and the verdict, if any at all is reached, can hardly be acquittal" (9 April). Why, she does not say.

On the last day of the trial, County Attorney Clammer and Mr. McNeal summarized for the prosecution; and, as Glaspell predicted, McNeal was able to rouse the audience with his indictment—"She did it, gentlemen, and I ask you to return her in kind . . . she has forfeited her right to live and she should be as John Hossack, who lies rotting beneath the ground." He too had his own bombshell: Margaret Hossack had been pregnant and given birth to a child before their marriage. This, McNeal claimed, was the dark secret often referred to in the trial, the story Hossack said he would take to his grave, and the reason for the unhappiness in the Hossack home. Just how a pregnancy thirty-three years earlier could have been the sole cause of trouble in the marriage and how it proved Mrs. Hossack's guilt in the murder of her husband was not clear; but, as Glaspell reports, it provided the jury with the impression that she was a woman who could not be trusted. It was with this revelation that the trial ended (10 April).

The case went to the jury on 10 April, the judge presenting the following charge:

> when evidence consists of a chain of well authenticated circumstances, it is often more convincing and satisfactory and gives a stronger ground of assurance of the defendant's guilt than the direct testimony of witnesses unconfirmed by circumstances.

[11 April]

In less than twenty-four hours the jury returned its verdict. Margaret Hossack was found guilty as charged and was sentenced to life imprisonment at hard labor. Glaspell reported the outcome, but made no comment on the finding.

It was the last story she filed in the case; it was also the last story she filed as a reporter for the *Des Moines Daily News*. Immediately after the trial, she resigned and returned home to Davenport to begin writing fiction, and by the summer of 1901 she had moved to Chicago and enrolled in the graduate English program at the University of Chicago. Therefore, she may never have learned the final disposition of the Hossack case, for the story was not yet over. In April 1901 lawyers Henderson and Berry lost an appeal with a lower court, but in April 1902 the Supreme Court of the State of Iowa agreed to hear the case. Citing several instances where the trial judge had ruled incorrectly on the evidence, the higher court overturned the original conviction and requested a new trial.[17] A second trial took place in Madison County, in February 1903. This time the jury, after twenty-seven hours of deliberation, was unable to reach a verdict: nine voted for conviction and three for acquittal.[18] In papers filed in April 1903, the prosecutor stated that since no further information had surfaced, it would be a waste of taxpayers' money to ask a third jury to hear the case.[19] Mrs. Hossack, then near sixty and in failing health, was ordered released, and was allowed to return to her home, her guilt or innocence still in question.

Eight years earlier, a court in Fall River, Massachusetts had freed Lizzie Borden because they could not imagine that a refined, New England "Maiden" who wore demure silk, carried flowers, and wept copiously in court could wield the axe that slew her family. So strong were the prevailing views about femininity, that even the prosecuting attorney found it hard "to *conceive*" of the guilt of "one of that sex that all high-minded men revere, that all generous men love, that all wise men acknowledge their indebtedness to."[20]

What is striking in the Hossack case is how ready the community was to assume the guilt of "one of that sex." Unlike Lizzie, who quickly read the signs of the time and played the part that was demanded of her—she learned to cry in court—Margaret Hossack, for all her

tears and Glaspell's mid-course correction and subsequent, embellished descriptions of "the frail mother of nine," did not win over the jury. The jury may not have been convinced that she was guilty of murder, but she certainly was guilty of questionable female behavior. She had left her husband, discussed her marital troubles with neighbors, and—most damaging—had been pregnant before marriage. To have found such a woman innocent or to have explored the question of justifiable homicide would have been unthinkable in the Iowa court of 1901. Such a direction in the trial would have necessitated an investigation of the family, the power wielded by the husband, his physical abuse over a long period, and the circumscribed lives of the wife and children; both the prosecution and, tellingly, the defense seemed loath to pursue such investigations. Instead, as Glaspell's accounts indicate, their cases were each discourses in evasion, argued on small, tangential points, few of which addressed the central issue of motive. Even the Supreme Court ruling, which acknowledged John Hossack's repeated beatings of his wife—with his hands and with a stove lid—couched its findings:

> The family life of the Hossacks had not been pleasant perhaps [sic] the husband was most to blame. He seems to have been somewhat narrow minded and quite stern in his determination to control all family matters.[21]

However, absent from the seven points on which the Supreme Court reversed the lower court decision was abuse. In fact the court argued that prior relations in the family should not have been introduced in the original trial since harmony had been established for over a year. Domestic life, thus, remained untarnished.

Why such juridical sidestepping? Because John Hossack was a pillar of the society, he had been nominated "for some of the highest offices in Warren County" (12 December), and "the twelve good men" Glaspell describes sitting in judgment of Mrs. Hossack were all men who knew him well and who had a vested interest in protecting his name if they could no longer protect his person. The women attending the trial in their Easter finery—perhaps even the sympathetic Sheriff's wife—might have been able to offer a different reading of the case, but they were not accorded the opportunity in the court or in the newspaper accounts Glaspell filed. Sixteen years later, in her play Glaspell offers them the opportunity to be heard.

III

Trifles begins at home. A murder has been committed, a man strangled while he slept; his wife—who claimed to be sleeping beside him at the time—has been accused of the crime and taken to jail to await trial. Those prosecuting the case, County Attorney Henderson and Sheriff Peters, have returned to the scene to search for clues that will provide "a motive; something to show anger, or—sudden feeling," and explain "the funny way" the man was murdered, "rigging it all up like that."[22] Accompanying them are Mr. Hale, who found the body; Mrs. Peters, the Sheriff's wife, charged with bringing the accused woman some of her things; and

Mrs. Hale, who keeps her company in the kitchen below while the men move around the upstairs bedroom and perimeter of the farmhouse searching for clues.

In the absence of the wife, the women, like quilters, patch together the scenario of her life and her guilt. As they imagine her, Minnie Foster is a lonely, childless woman, married to a taciturn husband, isolated from neighbors because of the rigors of farm life. When they discover a bird cage with its door ripped off and a canary with its neck wrung, they have no trouble making the connection. The husband has killed the bird, the wife's only comfort, as he has killed the bird-like spirit of the woman. The motive and method of murder become clear to them as the signs of sudden anger they infer from the half-wiped kitchen table, and Minnie's erratic quilt stitching. Based on such circumstantial evidence, the women try the case, find the accused guilty, but dismiss the charge, recognizing the exigencies that led her to the act. In the process of judging, they become compeers: Mrs. Peters recognizes her own disenfranchisement under the law and her own potential for violence, and Mrs. Hale recognizes her failure to sustain her neighbor and thus her culpability in driving the desperate woman to kill.

This brief summary indicates how few specific details remain in Glaspell's revisioning of the Hossack case. There is mention of "that man who went crazy" (4), but he is not named or connected to the events.[23] Of the names of the participants, only Henderson is used, assigned to the country attorney rather than the defense lawyer. Margaret Hossack has been renamed Minnie Foster Wright, the pun on the surname marking her lack of "rights," and implying her "right" to free herself against the societally sanctioned "right" of her husband to control the family, a right implicit in the Hossack case.[24]

Glaspell's most striking alterations are her excision of Minnie and the change of venue. The accused woman has been taken away to jail before *Trifles* begins, her place signified by the empty rocking chair that remains in her kitchen. By not bringing Minnie physically on to the stage, the playwright focuses on issues that move beyond the guilt or innocence of one person. Since the audience never actually sees Minnie, it is not swayed by her person, but by her condition, a condition shared by other women who can be imagined in the empty subject position. And by situating her play in the kitchen, not at the court, in the private space where Minnie lived rather than the public space where she will be tried, Glaspell offers the audience a composite picture of the life of Minnie Wright, Margaret Hossack, and the countless women whose experiences were not represented in court because their lives were not deemed relevant to the adjudication of their cases. Most important, by shifting venue, Glaspell brings the central questions never asked in the original Hossack case into focus: the motives for murder, what goes on in the home, and why women kill.

Motives are writ large in *Trifles.* The mise-en-scène suggests the harshness of Minnie's life. The house is isolated, "down in a hollow and you don't see the road" (21)—dark, foreboding, a rural, gothic scene. The interior of the kitchen replicates this barrenness and the commensurate disjunctions in the family, as the woman experienced them. Things are broken, cold, imprisoning; they are also violent. "Preserves" explode from lack of heat, a punning reminder of the causal relationship between isolation and violence. The mutilated cage and bird signify Wright's brutal nature and the physical abuse his wife has borne. Employing expressionistic techniques, Glaspell externalizes Minnie's desperation and the conditions that caused it.[25] She also finds the dramatic correlative for revenge. Rather than use an axe, this abused wife strangles her husband: a punishment to fit his crime. So powerfully does Glaspell marshall the evidence of Minnie's strangled life, that the jury on the stage and the jury who observe them from the audience presume the wife's "right" to take violent action in the face of the violence done to her. They see what might cause women to kill.

When Glaspell turns to the characters in her play, she again reworks the figures from the Hossack case, offering a revisionary reading of their roles in the original trial. The lawmen in *Trifles* bear traces of the original investigators: the County Attorney and the Sheriff. Mr. Hale, however, is Glaspell's invention, a composite of the Indianola farmers who testified at the Hossack trial, his name possibly derived from Mr. Haines. By introducing a man not directly charged with prosecution of the case, Glaspell is able to show patriarchal power and privilege, the united front that judged Margaret Hossack. She also illustrates the process through which an individual joins the ranks. In **"A Jury of her Peers,"** she goes to great lengths to indicate Mr. Hale's awkwardness at the beginning of the story, as he relates the details of the case, and how easily he is intimidated by the County Attorney. However, when he is allowed—by virtue of his gender—to go upstairs with the men of law, it is Hale, not they, who directly taunts the women: "But would the women know a clue if they did come upon it."[26] Glaspell ironically describes Hale as speaking "with good natured superiority" when he declares, "women are used to worrying over trifles" (44). Gender transcends class here, as it did in the original trial, where the farmers, jurors, and lawyers had a common connection: they were male and as such they were in control of the court and the direction of the testimony.

However, Glaspell also indicates that the privileged club does have a pecking order. Mr. Hale is recently admitted—or more likely, only temporarily admitted—and, therefore, more likely to chide those below him in order to gain favor with those above. A similar desire to ingratiate themselves with the law and to establish a camaraderie that temporarily suspended class was clearly apparent among the farmers of Indianola, eager to play a part in convicting Mrs. Hossack, some so ready that their zeal in intruding themselves into the investigation was cited in the Supreme Court reversal.

Constructing her category of men across class lines, establishing their connectedness based on legal empowerment and rights, Glaspell summarily dismisses them to roam about on the periphery of the tale, their presence theatrically marked by shuffling sounds above the heads of the women, and occasional appearances as they scurry out to the barn. With her deft parody, Glaspell undercuts the authority the men wielded in the original case, and throws into question their sanctioned preserve of power. They physically crisscross the stage as they verbally crisscross the details of the crime, both actions leading nowhere, staged to show ineffectuality and incompetence.

In her version of the Hossack case, the women, also drawn across class lines, occupy the men's place, standing in stage center and functioning as the composite shaping consciousness that structures the play.[27] Glaspell carefully chooses the two women who will usurp legal agency. Mrs. Peters is the wife of the Sheriff, patterned after Sheriff Hodson's wife, whose acts of kindness to Margaret Hossack seem to have stayed in Glaspell's memory. At first, Mrs. Peters parrots the masculinist view and voice of her husband, defending the search of the home as the men's "duty." However, she gradually comes to recognize that marital designation—wife of the Sheriff—offers her no more freedom than it does Minnie; in fact, it completely effaces her as an individual. Glaspell illustrates this condition by having the women identified only by their surnames, while, at the same time, they seek to particularize Minnie, referring to her by both her first and her maiden name.[28]

To the men, however, Minnie is John Wright's wife, just as Mrs. Peters is the Sheriff's wife: "married to the law" (*Trifles*, 29), "one of us" ("Jury," 37), she "doesn't need supervising" (*Trifles*, 29). Even Mrs. Hale at the beginning of **"Jury"** assumes that Mrs. Peters will be an extension of her husband and will share his views of murder. However, as Mrs. Peters slowly ferrets out the facts of Minnie's life—the childlessness, the isolation—and conflates the experience with her own early married days, she begins to identify with Minnie. It is when she comes upon the bird cage and the dead canary that she makes the most important connection: an understanding of female helplessness in front of male brutality: "When I was a girl—my kitten—there was a boy took a hatchet, and before my eyes—and before I could get there—[covers her face an instant] If they hadn't held me back I would have—[Catches herself, looks upstairs where steps are heard, falters weakly]—hurt him" (*Trifles*, 25).

It is significant that Glaspell attributes to Mrs. Peters, the Sheriff's wife, the memory of a murder with an axe, the murder weapon in the Hossack case, and offers as sign of brutality the dismemberment of an animal, a trace, perhaps, of the turkey in the original case. In the reversal of roles that Glaspell stages—in having Mrs. Peters act in lieu of her husband, dispensing her verdict based on her reading of the case and the motives for murder—she destroys the notion that a woman is her husband. She also stages what a woman may become when given legal power: a subject

acting under her own volition, her decisions not necessarily coinciding with her husband's or with the male hegemony. She becomes self-deputized.

If Mrs. Peters is taken from life, so too is Mrs. Hale, a possible surrogate for the young reporter Susan Glaspell.[29] Just as Mrs. Peters recognizes her own potential for murder in the face of powerlessness, and this recognition motivates her to act and to seize the juridical position, so Mrs. Hale comes to her own awareness in the course of the play. What she discovers in the kitchen of the Wright home is her own complicity in Minnie's situation, because of her withheld aid. "We live close together and we live far apart. We all go through the same things—it's just a different kind of the same thing," she says, summarizing her insight about "how it is for women" (27). In light of the Hossack case and Glaspell's role in sensationalizing the proceedings and in shaping public opinion, the lines appear to be confessional; so to her question, "Who's going to punish that?" (27), Mrs. Hale's words seem to indicate Glaspell's awareness in 1916 of her omissions and commissions in 1901: her failure to act in Margaret Hossack's behalf, and her failure to recognize the implications of the trial for her own life.

Given this awareness, it may seem strange that when Glaspell has the opportunity to retry Margaret Hossack and change the outcome of the case, she does not acquit the woman, or, as KayAnn Short argues, give her "her day in court" to prove her innocence.[30] Instead she has Mrs. Peters and Mrs. Hale assume Minnie's guilt and—as in the original trial—base their findings on circumstantial evidence instead of incontrovertible proof. However, when approaching *Trifles* in relation to the Hossack case, it becomes clear that acquittal is not Glaspell's intention, not why she wrote the play. Whether Margaret Hossack or Minnie Wright committed murder is moot; what is incontrovertible is the brutality of their lives, the lack of options they had to redress grievances or to escape abusive husbands, and the complete disregard of their plight by the courts and by society. Instead of arguing their innocence, Glaspell concretizes the conditions under which these women live and the circumstances that might cause them to kill. She thus presents the subtext that was excised from the original trial and that undergirds so many of the cases cited in Ann Jones's study: men's fears of women who might kill, and women's fears of the murder they might be forced to commit. In so doing, she stages one of the first modern arguments for justifiable homicide.[31] By having Mrs. Peters and Mrs. Hale unequivocally assume Minnie's guilt and also assume justification for her part, Glaspell presents her audience/jury with a defense that forces it to confront the central issues of female powerlessness and disenfranchisement and the need for laws to address such issues.[32]

However, Glaspell does not actually present the victimization of women or the violent acts such treatment may engender; instead she stages the potential for female action and the usurpation of power.[33] By having the women assume the central positions and conduct the investigation and the trial, she actualizes an empowerment that suggests that there are options short of murder that can be imagined for women. Mrs. Peters and Mrs. Hale may seem to conduct their trial sub rosa, because they do not actively confront the men; but in Mrs. Hale's final words, "We call it—knot it, Mr. Henderson" (30), ostensibly referring to a form of quilting but clearly addressed to the actions the women have taken, they become both actors and namers. Even if the men do not understand the pun—either through ignorance or, as Judith Fetterley suggests, through self-preservation—the audience certainly does.[34] It recognizes that the women have achieved an important political victory: they have wrested control of language, a first step in political ascendancy; and they have wrested control of the case and of the stage. Not waiting to be given the vote or the right to serve on juries, Glaspell's women have taken the right for themselves. Her audience in 1916 would get the point. It would have understood that Glaspell is deconstructing the very assumption of the law's incontrovertibility, its absolutist position.[35] Mrs. Peters and Mrs. Hale, by suturing into their deliberations their own experiences and fears—just as the men in the Hossack case had done—illustrate the subjective nature of the reading of evidence, and, by implication, of all essentialist readings.

In 1916 it would have been clearer than it often is to contemporary audiences that Glaspell is more concerned with legal and social empowerment than with replacing one hierarchy with another; that women's surreptitious action may comment less on women's natures than on the political systems that breed such behavior; that women do not speak "in a different voice," but speak in a manner deriving from their different position under the law, that is, from their common erasure. Glaspell's depiction of the conditions of her women is close to what Catherine MacKinnon describes in *Feminism Unmodified*: women's actions—their voices—deriving not from some innate nature but from the ways they have been forced to speak and to act. MacKinnon suggests that if legal and social changes could occur, it would then be time to decide how a woman "talks."[36] When women are powerless, she argues, they "don't just speak differently. A lot, [they] don't speak." Speech is "not differently articulated, it is silenced."[37] In *Trifles* Glaspell, like MacKinnon, posits gender as a production of the inequality of power under law, "a social status based on who is permitted to do what to whom."[38]

IV

That Susan Glaspell was able to reshape the events of the Hossack case in order to focus on contemporary issues in 1916 can be attributed to at least two causes. The first is biographical. Glaspell herself had changed in the sixteen years that separated the trial from the composition of the play. When she covered the Hossack case, she was twenty-four, right out of college; when she wrote *Trifles,* she had just turned forty, and had already published three well-received novels, thirty-one short stories, and a collection of short fiction, all focusing on the lives of women. She had also spent a year in Paris, and had lived in Chicago, Greenwich Village, and Provincetown, before her marriage at the age of thirty-seven to fellow Davenport native George Cram Cook.[39]

It is a mistake to claim that Glaspell was a slumbering midwestern woman until Cook brought her to life and political awareness when they married. Before her marriage, and even before her coverage of the Hossack case, she was already something of an iconoclast, aware of the imposition of cultural restriction on women, at least as they had an impact on her own life and the lives of the women she observed as Susie Glaspell, the eighteen-year-old Society Editor of a local Davenport newspaper. However, her nascent feminism was based on the class structure of the city. She was poor in a town that valued wealth; she worked in a society where women were expected to find others to work for them.

What she seems to have experienced for the first time in her coverage of the Hossack case was a legal rather than social powerlessness that cut across class lines: the testimony of Mrs. Hossack, the ladies in their Easter finery attending the trial, and even the Sheriff's wife were equally silenced. While Glaspell may have felt sympathy, if not empathy, for Mrs. Hossack when she entered her kitchen in 1901, and while she may have been aware of the skewed nature of the trial, she was not able to translate this experience or insight into her writing, certainly not into her newspaper reports. As Ann Jones shows in her description of the coverage of a variety of murder trials of women during the period, the news accounts offer what the society will bear. The possibility of exploring the implications of the Hossack trial in terms of gender roles or of pursuing the question of justifiable homicide would have been unthinkable in Iowa in 1901, even if Glaspell had consciously been moved to do so.

In 1916, it was not. If Glaspell had changed, so had society. Although the general public might still resist such positions, the people for whom Glaspell fashioned her theatre, if not her fiction, would certainly see the Hossack trial in light of their own agitation for the nineteenth amendment, women's rights, socialism, and the dismantling of absolutist thought in all areas.[40]

At the time she wrote *Trifles,* Glaspell was living in a community passionately concerned with socialism and feminism; she herself was a founding member of Heterodoxy, the New York-based group of women whose numbers included activists Maria Jenny Howe, Crystal Eastman, Elizabeth Irwin, Mary Heaton Vorse, and—for a time—Charlotte Perkins Gilman.[41] The audience for the Provincetown Players was already a body of the committed, who in 1916 agitated for suffrage and for social reform that would redress class distinctions in America, and who for the most part were opposed to Wilson and the war. Unlike many suffragists, their arguments were usually posited on a materialist rather than an essentialist reading of gender, concerned either with class struggles of which gender limitations were part or with enlightenment ideals of individualism applicable to both women and men. They did not romanticize femininity; most debunked the "cult of the home." Their major concern was in insuring "that women shall have the same right as man to be different, to be individuals not merely a social unit," and that this individualism would manifest itself in legal and social freedom.[42] It was for this audience and at this time that Glaspell returned to the Hossack case.

Trifles, therefore, is grounded in a double-focused historical context: the Iowa of 1901 and the Provincetown of 1916, the two periods leaving traces and providing many of the tensions and fissures that produce the contemporary feel of Glaspell's best works. Thus posited, her writing acts as a palimpsest for the shifting roles of women in the early twentieth century, and for her own shifting attitudes toward the possibilities for women and for herself. It is either a testament to the skill with which Glaspell constructed *Trifles* and *"A Jury of her Peers,"* or proof of how little women's lives have changed since 1916 that contemporary feminist critics still use the play and story as palimpsests for their own readings of contemporary feminist issues, readings that still point to some of the dilemmas which faced Glaspell and her personae in 1901 and in 1916: how to free women from the stereotypical roles into which they have been cast, how to articulate their lives and their rights without reinscribing them in the very roles against which they inveigh, how to represent female power not victimization, in short how to represent Margaret Hossack. However, in reading the works through a contemporary grid, critics should be careful of turning them into contemporary tracts, assuming that just because Glaspell offers a picture of two women who bond she is arguing for a higher moral ground for women, romanticizing femininity and home, arguing sexual difference, or the categorization of women under a fixed moral genus.[43] Given her own interests and concerns at the time, and her own relation to the Hossack case, it is more likely that her play and story are illustrating the need to provide both male and female voices in court—and in art—if human experience is not to be forever subsumed under the male pronoun and if women's voices are to be heard not as difference but as equally registered.

NOTES

[1]Ann Jones, *Women Who Kill* (New York: Holt, Rinehart and Winston, 1980), xv.

[2]Ibid., xvi.

[3]At the turn of the century, the father of modern criminology, Cesare Lombroso, offered a checklist of physical qualities that would identify women who might kill: they "approximate more to males . . . than to normal women, especially in the superciliary arches in the seam of sutures, in the lower jaw-bones, and in peculiarities of the occipital region" (Jones, *Women Who Kill*, 6).

[4]Jones, *Women Who Kill*, 13.

[5]Ibid., 257.

[6]As qtd. in Lynda Hart, "They Don't Even Look Like Maids Anymore: Wendy Kesselman's *My Sister in This House*," in *Making a Spectacle*, ed. Lynda Hart (Ann Arbor: University of Michigan Press, 1989), 145.

[7]Unless otherwise specified, when I mention *Trifles*, I am also assuming "A Jury of her Peers."

[8]Susan Glaspell, *The Road to the Temple* (New York: Frederick Stokes, 1927), 255-56. Glaspell's comments in *The Road to the Temple* are often misleading. The book is hagiography, and just as she constructed other scenes to make them more dramatic—and to dramatize the role of Cook—she may be doing so here. That she should want to portray his role in her shift to drama as that of a mentor encouraging his tutor is, however, revealing. It may be attributed to Cook's recent death in Greece, her return alone to Provincetown, and her immediate love affair with Norman Matson. See Kathleen Carroll, "Centering Women Onstage: Susan Glaspell's Dialogic Strategy of Resistance," Diss. University of Maryland, 1990; and Ann Larabee, "Death in Delphi: Susan Glaspell and the Companionate Marriage," *Mid-Western Review* (1987): 93-106 for other explanations. Glaspell offers variations on this scene in notes for the book. In one version, she writes, "I began writing plays because my hisband [sic] George Cram Cook made me [crossed out and replaced with "forced me to"]. 'I have announced a play of yours for the next bill,' he told me, soon after we started the Provincetown Players. I didn't want my marriage to break up so I wrote 'Trifles . . .'" (Notes from Berg Collection, New York Public Library).

[9]Judith Barlow, in an unpublished essay entitled "Susan's Sisters: The 'Other' Women Writers of the Provincetown Players," suggests that Glaspell may have also been influenced by her friend Neith Boyce's play *White Nights*, a work produced by the group the year before, that has as its theme a troubled marriage and a wife who wishes independence. See Barlow, *Susan Glaspell: A Collection of Critical Essays*, ed. Linda Ben-Zvi (unpublished). *White Nights*, first published in 1928, is reprinted in Rachel France, ed., *A Century of Plays by American Women* (New York: Richards Rosen, 1979).

[10]Glaspell, *The Road to the Temple*, 256.

[11]Glaspell first started writing for newspapers after she graduated from high school in Davenport, Iowa, in 1894. She covered local news and social events for the *Trident*, the *Davenport Morning Republican*, and the *Weekly Observer*, which listed her as Society editor, under the name Susie Glaspell.

[12]Susan Glaspell, "The Hossack Case," *Des Moines Daily News*, 4 December 1900. Glaspell reported the story from 2 December 1900 to 13 April 1901; references to Glaspell's *Des Moines Daily News* stories will appear in the text.

[13]Glaspell may have covered the story about murder by a neck yoke, or at least read of it, because she appropriates the method for use in *Trifles*.

[14]It is possible that Glaspell was actually accompanied to the Hossack house by the Sheriff and the County Attorney, who made several trips there during this period to gain evidence. One of the points cited by the Supreme Court of Iowa in its opinion on the trial was the possible impropriety of having the same County Attorney who would conduct the trial gather the evidence. There is no indication, however, that the Sheriff's wife also traveled to the Hossack farm, although the possibility exists that she did.

[15]See Jones, *Women Who Kill*, 111-16.

[16]The Hossack case was not unique in the number of women in attendance. Jones offers examples of irate ministers commenting on the large number of women who attended celebrated murder trials around the same period. In one case, a minister comments that, "It is a strange thing that women, under no compulsion whatever, are found in large numbers in every notorious trial everywhere, and the dirtier the trial the more women

usually will be found in attendance" (*Women Who Kill*, 139). He does not conjecture about this phenomenon.

[17]See State vs. Hossack, Supreme Court of Iowa, 9 April 1902, *Northwestern Reporter*: 1077-81. There were seven procedural points upon which the Supreme Court of Iowa based its reversal, the most significant of which were the following: that the hairs found under the corn crib were not proven to be from the murder weapon and had been taken by the County Attorney and given to the Sheriff and could not, therefore, be introduced as evidence; that the dissension in the Hossack house had abated at least a year prior to the murder, and could not, therefore, be introduced in the case.

[18]See Polk County Transcripts of Court Records, Case #805, 2 April 1901-3 March 1903.

[19]Warren County Court Records, Hossack Trial, April 1903. I thank the Warren and Polk County Court Recorders' Offices for their help in securing these files.

[20]Jones, *Women Who Kill*, 231.

[21]*Northwest Reporter*, 9 April 1902.

[22]Susan Glaspell, *Trifles*, in *Plays* (Boston: Small, Maynard, and Co., 1920), 15. All further page references appear in the text.

[23]See Elaine Hedges, "Small Things Reconsidered: Susan Glaspell's 'A Jury of her Peers,'" in *Women Studies* 12 (1986), 89-110. Rpt. in *Susan Glaspell: A Collection of Critical Essays*, ed. Linda Ben-Zvi. Hedges discusses insanity in rural American life and also the practice of women on the plains having canaries to provide them company.

[24]For other associations connected with the name, see Karen Alkalay-Gut, "Murder and Marriage: another Look at *Trifles*," in *Susan Glaspell: A Collection of Critical Essays*, ed. Linda Ben-Zvi.

[25]Glaspell often employed expressionistic techniques in her plays. See Yvonne Shafer, "Susan Glaspell and American Expressionism," in *Susan Glaspell: A Collection of Critical Essays*, ed. Linda Ben-Zvi. Shafer discusses expressionism in the one-act plays *The People* and *Woman's Honor*, and in the full-length play *The Verge*. Also see Linda Ben-Zvi, "Susan Glaspell and Eugene O'Neill," *The Eugene O'Neill Newsletter* 6 (1982): 22-29, and Linda Ben-Zvi, "Susan Glaspell, Eugene O'Neill, and the Imagery of Gender," *Eugene O'Neill Newsletter* 10 (1986): 22-28 for further discussions of expressionism in Glaspell's plays.

[26]Susan Glaspell, "A Jury of her Peers," in *Everyman*, 5 March 1917, 42. All further page references appear in the text.

[27]Mrs. Peters and Mrs. Hale are of different classes, a fact visually captured by the filmmaker Sally Heckel, in her version of "A Jury of her Peers" (Texture Films). Mrs. Hale wears a plain, cloth coat and head scarf; Mrs. Peters has a fur tippet and large, feathered hat. Their language also bears signs of their classes—a technique Glaspell often repeats. In *Trifles*, Mrs. Hale makes grammatical errors, has unfinished sentences, drops letters. Mrs. Peters speaks in a grammatically correct manner befitting the Sheriff's wife. For example, Mrs. Hale's, "I wonder if she was goin' to quilt it or just knot it?" becomes Mrs. Peters's, "We think she was going to—knot it," the omitted *g* being Glaspell's way of marking different education and position. What joins the women is the men's categorization of them, predicated on gender, erasing difference, dismissing individuality.

[28]At the time Glaspell was writing the play, the question of women taking their husband's names was a political issue. One of Glaspell's friends, Ruth Hale, launched a movement called the Lucy Stone League which supported married women who chose to keep their maiden names. See Judith Schwarz, *Radical Feminists of Heterodoxy: Greenwich Village 1912-1940* (Lebanon, NH: New Victorian Publishers, 1982), 14, 58, 83. Also see Liza Maeve Nelligan, "'The Haunting Beauty of the Life We've

Left': A Contextual Reading of Susan Glaspell's *Trifles* and *The Verge*," in *Susan Glaspell: A Collection of Critical Essays*, ed. Linda Ben-Zvi. Glaspell, like her fellow writers Neith Boyce, Mary Heaton Vorse, and others never assumed her husband's name.

[29]When the Provincetown Players staged the play, Glaspell chose to play Mrs. Hale and had her husband, George Cram Cook, play Hale.

[30]Kay Ann Short, "A Different Kind of the Same Thing: The Erasure of Difference in 'A Jury of her Peers,'" *Susan Glaspell: A Collection of Critical Essays*, ed. Linda Ben-Zvi.

[31]One could argue that the precedent for staging a case of justifiable homicide for women was established in *The Oresteia*, where the motives leading to Clytemnestra's murder of Agamemnon are delineated, or would be if one affixed to the work the murder of Iphigenia, as Ariane Mnouchkine recently has done in a production of Aeschylus' trilogy at the Théâtre du Soleil that is prefaced by Euripides' *Iphigenia in Aulis* (see *New York Times*, 27 March 1991: B-3, for a description of this performance). For a discussion of contemporary wife battering cases and the plea of justifiable homicide, see Jones, *Women Who Kill*, Chapter 6.

[32]In most of Glaspell's plays, there is a political component that is directly connected to particular events of her period, which would be immediately evident to her audience, but which is often lost in contemporary discussions of her works. In *Suppressed Desires*, for instance, she takes on a noted anti-feminist of the period, one Professor Sedwick, who had said, "All women were hens" (reported in the *New York Times*, 18 February 1914). In the play, Glaspell and Cook play on the name Step-hen, parodying both Freudianism and Cook's childhood pronunciation of the word (*Road*, 25). However, they also are answering Sedwick, a reference her audience would immediately have understood. Even more overtly, *Inheritors* challenges contemporary issues such as the Alien and Sedition laws, and the Red Scare, and *Chains of Dew* argues for birth control. For the relation between events of her period and Glaspell's plays, see Barbara Ozieblo, "Suppression and Society," in *Susan Glaspell: A Collection of Critical Essays*, ed. Linda Ben-Zvi, and J. Ellen Gainor, "*Chains of Dew* and the Drama of Birth Control," in *Susan Glaspell: A Collection of Critical Essays*, ed. Linda Ben-Zvi.

[33]See Judith Butler, "Performing Acts and Gender Constitution: An Essay in Phenomenology and Feminist Theory," in *Performing Feminisms: Feminist Critical Theory and Theatre*, ed. Sue-Ellen Case (Baltimore: Johns Hopkins University Press, 1990), 270-82, on the problems of staging victimization and thus representing the very condition the writer may wish to dismantle.

[34]See Judith Fetterley, "Reading about Reading: 'A Jury of Her Peers,' 'The Murder in the Rue Morgue,' and 'The Yellow Wallpaper,'" in *Gender and Reading: Essays on Readers, Texts, and Contexts*, eds. Elizabeth A. Flynn and Patrocinio P. Schweickart (Baltimore: Johns Hopkins University Press, 1986).

[35]Questions concerning the binding nature of law were hotly debated in 1916—a time of war and protest against that war—in issues of *The Masses* and other periodicals with which Glaspell was connected.

[36]Catherine MacKinnon, *Feminism Unmodified: Discourses on Life and Law* (Cambridge: Harvard University Press, 1987). While acknowledging the work of such writers as Carol Gilligan, MacKinnon argues that Gilligan "achieves for moral reasoning what the special protection rule achieves in law: the affirmative rather than the negative valuation of that which has accurately distinguished women from men, by making it seem as though those attributes, with their consequences, really are somehow ours, rather than what male supremacy has attributed to us for its own use. For women to affirm difference, when difference means dominance, as it does with gender, means to affirm the qualities and characteristics of powerlessness" (38-39). What is relevant about MacKinnon's argument in relation to *Trifles* and "Jury" is her emphasis on law and

enfranchisement. Reading Glaspell through MacKinnon allows the critic to move beyond the questions of "different voice" that were the critical bulwarks of the first moment of Glaspell criticism. For example, see Linda Ben-Zvi, "Susan Glaspell and Eugene O'Neill," "Susan Glaspell, Eugene O'Neill, and the Imagery of Gender," and "Susan Glaspell's Contributions to Contemporary Women Playwrights," *Feminine Focus: The New Women Playwrights*, ed. Enoch Brater (New York: Oxford University Press, 1988), 147-66; Karen Stein, "The Women's World of Glaspell's *Trifles*," *Women in American Theatre*, eds. Helen Krinch Chinoy and Linda Walsh Jenkins (New York: Theatre Communications Group, 1987), 253-56; Karen AlkalayGut, "'A Jury of her Peers': The Importance of Trifles," *Studies in Short Fiction* 21 (1984): 3-11; and Karen Malpede, "Introduction," *Women in Theatre* (New York: Limelight, 1983). See also the more recent materialist readings: Judith Stephens, "Gender Ideology and Dramatic Convention in Progressive Era Plays, 1890-1920," in *Performing Feminisms: Feminist Critical Theory and Theatre*, ed. SueEllen Case (Baltimore: Johns Hopkins University Press, 1990), 283-93; Kay Ann Short, "A Different Kind of the Same Thing: The Erasure of Difference in 'A Jury of Her Peers,'" in *Susan Glaspell: A Collection of Critical Essays*; Liza Maeve Nelligan, "The Haunting Beauty from the Life We've Left: A Contextual Reading of Susan Glaspell's *Trifles* and *The Verge*," in *Susan Glaspell: A Collection of Critical Essays,*; Kathleen Carroll, "Centering Women Onstage: Susan Glaspell's Dialogic Strategy of Resistance," Diss., University of Maryland, 1990; and Linda Williams, "'A Jury of her Peers': Marlene Gorris's 'A Question of Silence,'" *Postmodernism and Its Discontents: Theories and Practices*, ed. E. Ann Kaplan (London: Verso, 1988), 107-15. However, it should be noted that as much as MacKinnon's ideas, as used here, may provide one way of approaching *Trifles*, it is hard to imagine that Glaspell would have supported MacKinnon's stance on censorship as a way of alleviating pornography. Repeatedly in her writing, Glaspell objected to any form of censorship, for any reason. She was involved in several anti-censorship cases, one involving the attempted banning of a book by the Davenport Public Library in 1910, and in later controversies surrounding celebrated censorship cases.

[37]MacKinnon, *Feminism Unmodified*, 39.

[38]Ibid., 8.

[39]Glaspell's marriage parallels almost exactly the paradigm Caroline Heilbrun presents in *Writing A Woman's Life* (New York: W. W. Norton, 1988), a marriage near middle age that is scandal-ridden and that both forces the woman out of society and allows her a freedom such societal marginalization provides.

[40]It is important to note that *Trifles* and "A Jury of her Peers" were written for different audiences. The fiction, appearing in the popular magazine, *Everyweek*, 5 March 1917, stresses identification between the reader and Mrs. Hale, a familiar farm housewife, and leads to a reading that seems to romanticize housework and traditional feminine roles far more than *Trifles* does. For example, in the story version, Glaspell has Mrs. Hale say, "The Law is the law and a bad stove is a bad stove. How'd you like to cook on this?," an image and a question with which her readers could identify, just as they could identify with Mrs. Hale's sudden call from her own kitchen to travel to the kitchen of Minnie Wright. One of the anomalies in the criticism of the two works is the failure of most critics to note that there are two versions of the same basic story and to take into consideration the differences in accordance with the nature of the audience and the differences implicit in the genre. Two of the most influential essays on these works use "Jury" and make no reference to the more subtle and radical *Trifles*. See Annettee Kolodny, "A Map for Re-Reading: Or Gender and the Interpretation of Literary Texts," in *The New Feminist Criticism*, ed. Elaine Showalter (New York: Pantheon, 1985), 93-106, and Judith Fetterley, "Reading about Reading: 'A Jury of her Peers,' 'The Murder in the Rue Morgue,' and 'The Yellow Wallpaper.'" When Linda Williams compares the Dutch film "A Question of Silence" to Glaspell's work, she also uses "Jury" not *Trifles*. See Williams, "'A Jury of her Peers.'"

[41]See Judith Schwarz's description of Heterodoxy in *Radical Feminists of Heterodoxy*, in which she lists Glaspell as a founding member; also see Nancy Cott, *The Grounding of Modern Feminism* (New Haven: Yale University Press, 1987), for a detailed study of the feminist movement in New York in the years 1910-1920; and June Sochen, *The New Woman in Greenwich Village, 1910-1920* (New York: Quadrangle, 1972), for a description of the period and of Glaspell's relation to feminists in Greenwich Village. In her *Women and American Socialism, 1870-1902* (Champaign: University of Illinois Press, 1981), Mari Jo Buhle discusses how Glaspell "created female characters as working-class women with capacities to feel intensely, to understand injustice rather than internalizing oppression, and when conditions allowed to strike back at their oppressors" (203).

[42]These quotations are taken from the *New York Times* (18 February 1914) report concerning a meeting organized by Heterodoxy president Marie Jenny Howe at Cooper Union, billed as "the first feminist meeting ever convened." At the time Glaspell was in Davenport, after suffering a miscarriage, but many of her friends were there, and she would most likely have been in the audience, if not on the dias. For other references to articles on feminism written between 1913-1916, see Cott, *The Grounding of Modern Feminism*. I thank Liza Maeve Nelligan for calling my attention to the Rally, and for sharing her research on heterodoxy and the feminist movements of the period with me.

[43]Five years later Glaspell would write *The Verge*, her most powerful and most feminist play. Her persona, Claire Archer, would demand a life not circumscribed by the traditional roles assigned to women-mother, caregiver, hostess-and would stand in juxtaposition to her daughter and her sister, who represent conventional women whose gender does not provide them with an insight into Claire's life or her aspiration. In *The Verge* Glaspell also pursues feminism as a "transvaluation of values" on a Nietzschean model. See Cott, *The Grounding of Modern Feminism*, 296, in relation to Dora Marsden and a similar position. Also see Nelligan, "The Haunting Beauty of the Life We've Left," and Carroll "Centering Women Onstage."

Judith Kay Russell (essay date 1997)

SOURCE: "Glaspell's *Trifles*", in *The Explicator*, Vol. 55, No. 2, Winter 1997, pp. 88-90.

[*In this essay, Russell argues that the three women depicted in* Trifles *bear "strong resemblance" to the three Fates of Greek mythology.*]

On the surface, Susan Glaspell's one-act play **Trifles** focuses on the death of an oppressive husband at the hands of his emotionally abused wife in an isolated and remote farm in the midwest. Beneath the surface, the collective behaviors of Mrs. Hale, Mrs. Peters, and Mrs. Wright in Glaspell's play bear strong resemblance to those of the Fates (Clotho the Spinner, Lachesis the Disposer of Lots, and Atropos the Cutter of the Thread) in Greek mythology. Although Glaspell brings new vigor to the myth, the attention given to Mrs. Hale's resewing the quilt, the change in Mrs. Peters's perspective on law and justice, and the rope placed by Mrs. Wright around her husband's neck are nonetheless grounded in the story of the Three Sisters who control the fate of men.

Mrs. Hale embodies the qualities of Clotho the Spinner, the sister who spins the thread of life. Mrs. Hale subtly suggests that Mrs. Wright is not the sole agent in the death of Mr. Wright. On the surface, Mrs. Hale's ungrammatical reference to that event, "when they was slipping the rope under his neck" (79), can be attributed to improper subject and verb agreement, which is not uncommon in certain regional dialects. However, the use of the plural pronoun and singular verb subtly suggests the involvement of more than one in a single outcome, and it foreshadows the conspiracy of the three women and their efforts to control the outcome or the fate of all characters. Furthermore, the information concerning the domestic life of the Wrights is supplied, or spun, mainly by Mrs. Hale; she describes Mr. Wright as "a hard man," and, with her recollections of the young Minnie Foster (now Mrs. Wright) as "kind of like a bird" (82), she establishes the connection of Mr. Wright's involvement in the physical death of the canary and spiritual death of his wife. The condescending manner in which the men joke about the women's concern regarding Mrs. Wright's intention "to quilt or just knot" the quilt evokes a defensive remark from Mrs. Hale in which she hints that it is unwise to tempt fate; she asserts, "I don't see as it's anything to laugh about" (79-80). Finally, by "just pulling out a stitch or two that's not sewed very good" and replacing it with her own stitching (80), Mrs. Hale symbolically claims her position as the person who spins the thread of life.

The second member of the Three Sisters, Lachesis the Disposer of Lots, is personified by Mrs. Peters. The viability of the thread spun by Mrs. Hale depends on the actions and reactions of Mrs. Peters. To claim her position as the member of the Fates responsible for assigning destiny, she must abandon objectivity and move toward subjectivity. Her objectivity is exemplified by her assertion that "the law is the law" and her view on physical evidence as she informs Mrs. Hale, "I don't think we ought to touch things" (79-80). The sight of the dead canary and the recognition that "somebody—wrung—its—neck" marks Mrs. Peters's initiation into subjectivity and the sisterhood (83). The discovery of the dead bird awakens Mrs. Peters's suppressed childhood memories of rage toward the "boy [who] took a hatchet" and brutally killed her kitten (83). In her mind, the kitten, Mrs. Wright, and the bird become enmeshed. Mrs. Peters realizes that the dead bird will be used to stereotype Mrs. Wright as a madwoman who overreacts to "trifles." At this point, Mrs. Peters emerges from the shadow of her role as the sheriff's wife and becomes "married to the law" (85). Her new concept of law subjectively favors justice over procedure. She claims her position as the sister who dispenses the lots in life when she moves to hide the bird and thus denies the men "something to make a story about" (85).

Mrs. Wright represents Atropos the Cutter of the Thread. Symbolically, Mrs. Wright is first linked to Atropos in Mr. Hale's description of her "rockin' back and forth" (73), a motion similar to that made by cutting with scissors. The connection to Atropos is further established when Mrs.

Peters discovers the dead bird in Mrs. Wright's sewing box and exclaims, "Why, this isn't her scissors" (83). Ironically, the dead canary takes the place of the scissors: The death of the bird is directly tied to the fate of Mr. Wright. In addition, Mrs. Wright assumes mythical status through her spiritual presence and physical absence from the stage. Mr. Hale relates that in his questioning of Mrs. Wright, she admits that her husband "died of a rope round his neck," but she doesn't know how it happened because she "didn't wake up"; she is a sound sleeper (74-75). Mrs. Wright denies personal involvement in the death of her husband, yet she acknowledges that he died while she slept beside him in the bed. Mrs. Wright says, "I was on the inside" (75). Although she may be referring to her routine "inside" position of sleep behind her husband in the bed placed along the wall, Mrs. Wright's statement suggests a movement from the outside (her individual consciousness) to the inside (the collective consciousness of the Fates). Her involvement with the rope of death is the equivalent of severing the thread of life. She did not spin the thread, nor did she assign the lot; she merely contributed a part to the whole, and that collective whole becomes greater than the sum of its parts. For this reason, Mrs. Wright is correct in denying individual knowledge or responsibility in the death of her husband.

In *Trifles,* Mrs. Hale weaves the story or describes the circumstances, Mrs. Peters weighs the evidence and determines the direction of justice, and Mrs. Wright carries out the verdict; although the procedure is somewhat reversed, the mythic ritual is performed nevertheless. Susan Glaspell's use of the Fates, or the Three Sisters, does not weaken her dramatization of women who are oppressed by men. Although some believe that the power of the Three Sisters rivals that of Zeus, Glaspell reminds her audience that, regardless of myth or twentieth-century law, it still takes three women to equal one man. That is the inequality on which she focuses.

WORK CITED

Glaspell, Susan. "Trifles." *Plays By American Women: 1900-1930.* Ed. Judith E. Barlow. New York: Applause Theater Book, 1994. 70-86.

FURTHER READING

Bach, Gerhard. "Susan Glaspell (1876-1948): A Bibliography of Dramatic Criticism." *The Great Lakes Review* 3, No. 2 (Winter 1977): 1-34.
    Annotated bibliography of secondary sources on Glaspell's plays.

———. "Susan Glaspell—Provincetown Playwright." *The Great Lakes Review* 4, No. 2 (Winter 1978): 31-43.
    Traces the influence of the Provincetown Players on Glaspell's development as a writer.

Bigsby, C. W. E. Introduction to *Plays by Susan Glaspell*, pp. 1-31. Cambridge: Cambridge University Press, 1987.
 Presents a history of Glaspell's life and her involvement with the Provincetown Players, as well overviews of *Trifles, The Outside, The Verge*, and *Inheritors*.

Noe, Marcia. *Susan Glaspell: Voice from the Heartland*. Macomb: Western Illinois University, 1983, 97 p.
 Biographical and critical study of the author.

Papke, Mary E. *Susan Glaspell: A Research and Production Sourcebook*. Westport, Conn.: Greenwood Press, 1993, 299 p.
 Contains a complete bibliography of Glaspell's works, plot summaries, production histories, summaries of reviews, and an annotated bibliography of secondary sources.

Waterman, Arthur E. "Susan Glaspell and the Provincetown." *Modern Drama* VII, No. 2 (September 1964): 174-84.
 Declares that Glaspell's "major contribution to American drama lies in the fact that she was a dramatist of ideas. Before the Provincetown, plays of ideas came mainly from foreign writers. . . . Glaspell hit home because her plays were distinctly American, distinctly contemporary."

————. "Susan Glaspell (1882?-1948)." *American Literary Realism* 4, No. 2 (Spring 1971): 183-91.
 Bibliographic essay on Glaspell, including a reception study, a primary bibliography, and a selected bibliography of critical works.

————. "Susan Glaspell's *The Verge*: An Experiment in Feminism." *The Great Lakes Review* 6, No. 1 (Summer 1979): 17-23.
 Views *The Verge* as "a play reaching beyond its obvious feminist emphasis to the larger question of how a society can best direct the energies of its more gifted eccentrics to constructive ends."

Additional coverage of Glaspell's life and career is contained in the following sources published by Gale Research: *Contemporary Authors*, Vols. 110, 154; *Dictionary of Literary Biography*, Vols. 7, 9, 78; *Twentieth Century Literary Criticism*, Vol. 55; *Yesterday's Authors of Books for Children*, Vol. 2.

Tony Kushner
1956-

INTRODUCTION

Kushner is best known for his award-winning *Angels in America* (1991 and 1992), which is unprecedented in its extensive treatment of homosexual themes and its use of gay characters to examine such traditional issues as culture, politics, and history. Focused on the 1980s, *Angels in America* examines American society during the Reagan/Bush years with a strong emphasis on the implications and consequences of AIDS. Kushner's themes encompass the gay experience from repression and hypocrisy through denial and self-loathing to the ultimate goals of self-acceptance and self-love.

BIOGRAPHICAL INFORMATION

Kushner was born in New York City in 1956 and was raised in Lake Charles, Louisiana. His parents were classical musicians, and his mother's performances as an actor influenced the young Kushner toward a career in theater. Though aware of his sexual preference from an early age, Kushner attempted to overcome his homosexuality through psychotherapy. He eventually came to terms with his sexual orientation and opened his writing to homosexual themes. He worked as an assistant director at the St. Louis Repertory Theatre after receiving his M.F.A. in directing from New York University in 1984. He returned to New York in 1987 and produced several of his early works, including *Stella* and *Hydriotaphia*. In 1993 the first part of *Angels in America, Millennium Approaches*, was produced on Broadway to universal acclaim. *Millennium Approaches* won the Pulitzer Prize for drama, the Antoinette Perry (Tony) Award for Best Play, and the New York Drama Critics Award for best play. Kushner won another Tony for best play in 1994 for the second part of *Angels in America, Perestroika*.

MAJOR WORKS

Kushner's early work did not focus strictly on gay themes. The best-known of his first efforts, *A Bright Room Called Day*, for example, examines the responses of a group of friends in pre-World War II Germany to Hitler and Nazism. Kushner then proceeds to make comparisons between the Third Reich and the administrations of United States presidents Reagan and Bush. Kushner's other early works include *Hydriotaphia*, which, inspired by seventeenth-century essayist Sir Thomas Browne, was written in a style

reminiscent of classical and traditional poetry; *The Illusion*, adapted from Pierre Corneille's *L'illusion comique*; and *Widows*, a collaboration with Ariel Dorfman based on that writer's work of the same name. Of course, his most enduring work thus far has been *Angels in America*.

Millennium Approaches comprises the first half of Kushner's two-part drama. Although it features over thirty characters—including the oldest living Bolshevik, the ghost of Ethel Rosenberg, a black drag queen, and an elderly rabbi played by a young Gentile woman—*Millennium Approaches* has five main protagonists: Roy Cohn, the infamous, real-life prosecutor and the former henchman of Senator Joseph McCarthy; Prior Walter, a young man who has been diagnosed with AIDS; Louis Ironson, a Jewish homosexual who is Prior's lover; Joe Pitt, an ambitious, bisexual Mormon who works for Cohn; and Harper Pitt, Joe's wife. Concerned with the characters' relationships with one another as well as the interconnections within America's pluralistic society, the play contains numerous subplots that chronicle the characters' reactions to AIDS, the breakdown of their relationships, and the subsequent formation of new bonds. One storyline, for example, re-volves around Cohn's relentless and absurd pursuit of political power in the Reagan era. The personification of evil and self-interest in the play, Cohn attempts to place Joe Pitt as his man inside the Justice Department. Upon learning that he has contracted AIDS, Cohn denies his own homosexuality and continues with his machinations; defin-ing homosexuals as people who lack political power, he argues that because he has power he is not gay, he is simply a heterosexual who has sex with men. Another plot revolves around the grief that Prior and Harper experi-ence when their respective mates, Louis and Joe, desert them. As Louis and Joe become more involved with one another, both Prior and Harper experience loneliness and various hallucinatory visions: Prior sees himself dancing with Louis while Harper fantasizes about being in Antarc-tica. At the conclusion of *Millennium Approaches*, an angel appears to Prior and pronounces him a prophet. In *Pere-stroika*, the second half of *Angels in America*, the partners learn to accept the losses and changes that occurred in the first half of the play and to transform them into positive experiences, while Cohn, who refuses to learn, dies of AIDS. Prior proclaims his own unique gospel and in the final scene directly addresses the audience, extending the play's message to the entire human community.

CRITICAL RECEPTION

Critical reaction to *Angels in America* has been over-whelmingly favorable. Commentators laud it as the prover-bial great American play, claiming it addresses such topics as the value and inevitability of change, the nature of self-interest and community, and the major political issues of the 1980s: gay rights, the end of the Cold War, the place of religion in modern society, and the ideological struggle between conservatism and liberalism. Critics have also praised Kushner for avoiding the sentimentality that characterizes most dramas that deal with AIDS. Frank Rich, writing about *Millennium Approaches*, has declared the play "a true American work in its insistence on embracing all possibilities in art and life."

PRINCIPAL WORKS

PLAYS

A Bright Room Called Day   1985
Yes, Yes, No, No   1985
Hydriotaphia, or, The Death of Dr. Browne   1987
Stella   [adaptor; from the drama by Johann Wolfgang von Goethe]   1987
The Illusion   [adaptor; from the drama *L'illusion comique* by Pierre Corneille]   1988; revised 1990
Widows   [adaptor with Ariel Dorfman; from a book by Dorfman]   1991
Millennium Approaches   1991
Perestroika   1992

Slavs! (Thinking About the Longstanding Problems of Virtue and Happiness)   1995
A Dybbuk   1997
The Good Person of Sezuan   [adaptor; from the play *Der gute Mensch von Setzuan* by Bertolt Brecht]   1998
†*Death and Taxes: Hydriotaphia and Other Plays*   1999

OTHER MAJOR WORKS

Thinking about the Longstanding Problems of Virtue and Happiness: Essays, a Play, Two Poems, and a Prayer   (miscellany)   1995
Tony Kushner in Conversation   (interviews; edited by Robert Vorlicky)   1997

*These works comprise parts one and two of the two-part drama entitled *Angels in America: A Gay Fantasia on National Themes*.

†This volume includes the plays *Hydriotaphia*; *Reverse Transcription*; *Terminating, or, Sonnet LXXV, or, Lass meine*; *Schmerzen nicht verloren sein, or, Ambivalence*; *East Coast Ode to Howard Jarvis*; and *David Schine in Hell*

AUTHOR COMMENTARY

Interview with Kushner   (1994)

"Tony Kushner Considers the Longstanding Problems of Virtue and Happiness: An Interview by David Savran," in *American Theater*, Vol. 11, No. 6, October 1994, pp. 20-7, 100-04.

[*In the following, Kushner discusses the influences on his work and his development as a writer.*]

When Bill Kushner diligently guided his 14-year-old son Tony through Wagner's 20-hour *Ring* cycle, he little sus-pected his prodigious offspring would end up some two decades later writing *the* theatrical epic of the 1990s.

Angels in America, with its ground-breaking Broadway run scheduled to continue through January '95, has now begun a national tour in Chicago, while theatres around the world scramble to mount their own productions of the most widely acclaimed new American play in mem-ory. From San Francisco's American Conservatory Theater to Houston's Alley Theatre, from the Intiman Theatre Company in Seattle to the Alliance Theatre Company in Atlanta, Kushner's seven-hour, two-part play will be the centerpiece of the 1994-95 season. At the same time, audi-ences in 17 foreign countries (including France, Germany, Japan, Iceland and Brazil) will see home-grown produc-tions of *Angels* over the next year.

From its inception—commissioned by San Francisco's Eureka Theatre Company, it was mounted in workshop and full productions at the Eureka, Los Angeles's Mark Taper Forum and London's Royal National Theatre prior to its April 1993 opening on Broadway—*Angels in America: A Gay Fantasia on National Themes* has altered the face and scale of the American theatre. Having amassed the

Pulitzer Prize for Drama, two best-play Tonys and a spate of other prestigious awards, it has proven, against all odds, that a play can tackle the most controversial and difficult subjects—politics, sex, disease, death and religion—and still find a large and diverse audience. This achievement is even more remarkable when one considers that all five of its leading male characters are gay. Bringing together Jews and Mormons, African- and European-Americans, neo-conservatives and leftists, closeted gay men and exemplars of America's new "queer politics," *Angels* attempts nothing less than the creation of a cosmic-scale history of America in the age of Reagan and the age of AIDS.

Tony Kushner, a self-described "red-diaper baby," was raised in Lake Charles, La., the son of professional musicians. The Kushners' rambling house on the edge of a swamp teemed with pets and resounded with music. Young Tony developed an appreciation of opera and the Wagnerian scale of events from his father Bill (*Moby Dick* remains the playwright's favorite novel), while from his mother Sylvia's involvement in amateur theatrics he learned to appreciate the emotional power of theatre. (He still vividly remembers her performance as Linda Loman in *Death of a Salesman*—and the tremendous identification he felt with her.) But at age six, when he developed a crush on Jerry, his Hebrew school teacher, Tony knew he was not like other boys. Growing up, as he puts it, "very, very closeted," he was intrigued by the sense of disguise theatre could offer. But because he had decided "at a very early age" that he would *become* heterosexual, he avoided the theatre in town, where he knew he would find other gay men.

In the mid-1970s, Kushner moved to New York to attend Columbia University, where he studied medieval art, literature and philosophy and read the works of Karl Marx for the first time. Still fascinated with theatre, he explored the mind-bending experimental work of directors like Richard Foreman, Elizabeth LeCompte, JoAnne Akalaitis and Charles Ludlam; immersed himself in classical and modernist theatre traditions; and got involved in radical student politics. It was not until after he graduated from Columbia, however, that he began to "come out"—and much like Joe Pitt in *Millennium Approaches,* he called his mother from a pay phone in the East Village to tell her he was gay.

Angels in America pays energetic tribute to these diverse experiences and inspirations. Drawing on Brecht's political theatre, on the innovations of the theatrical avant-garde and on the solidly American narrative tradition of Eugene O'Neill and Tennessee Williams, Kushner invents a kind of camp epic theatre—or in his phrase, a Theatre of the Fabulous. Spanning the earth and reaching into the heavens, interweaving multiple plots, mixing metaphysics and drag, fictional and historical characters, revengeful ghosts and Reagan's smarmy henchmen, *Angels* demonstrates that reality and fantasy are far more difficult to distinguish, on stage and in the world, than one might think. It also reasserts, as political activists have insisted since the 1960s,

that the personal is indeed the political: Exploring the sometimes tortuous connections between personal identity (sexual, racial, religious or gender) and political position, it dramatizes the seeming impossibility of maintaining one's private good in a world scourged by public greed, disease and hatred.

Yet *Angels in America* is by no means a play about defeat. On the contrary, it consistently attests to the possibility not only of progress but also of radical—almost unimaginable—transfiguration. Its title and preoccupation with the utopian potential inscribed in even the most appalling moments of history are derived from an extraordinary mediator—the German-Jewish Marxist philosopher Walter Benjamin. In Benjamin's attempt to sketch out a theory of history in "These on the Philosophy of History," written in 1940 as he was attempting to flee the Nazis, this most melancholy of Marxists uses Paul Klee's painting, "Angelus Novus," to envision an allegory of progress in which the angel of history, his wings outspread, is poised between past and future. Caught between the history of the world, which keeps piling wreckage at his feet, and a storm blowing from Paradise, the angel "would like to stay, awaken the dead, and make whole what has been smashed." But the storm "has got caught in his wings" and propels him blindly and irresistibly into an unknown future.

For Kushner, the angel of history serves as a constant reminder both of catastrophe AIDS, racism, misogyny and homophobia, to name only the most obvious) and of the perpetual possibility of change—the expectation that, as Benjamin puts it, the tragic continuum of history will be blasted open. And the concept of utopia to which the angel is linked ensures that the vehicle of enlightenment and hope in *Angels*—the prophet who announces the new age—will be the character who must endure the most pain: Prior Walter, a man born too soon and too late, suffering from AIDS and the desertion of his lover. Moreover, in Kushner's reinterpretation of American history, his utopia is inextricably linked both to the extraordinary idealism that has long driven American politics and to the ever-deepening structural inequalities that continue to betray and mock that idealism.

It is hardly coincidental that *Angels in America* should capture the imagination of theatregoers at this decisive moment in history, at the end of the Cold War, as the United States is attempting to renegotiate its role as the number-one player in the imperialist sweepstakes. More brazenly than any other recent play, *Angels*—not unlike Wagner's *Ring*—takes on questions of national mission and identity. It also attempts to interrogate the various mythologies—from Mormonism to multiculturalism to neoconservatism—that have been fashioned to consolidate an American identity.

At the same time, the play is intent on emphasizing the crucial importance of the sexual and racial margins in defining this elusive identity. In this sense, it seems linked to the strategies of a new activist movement, Queer Nation, whose founding in 1990 only narrowly postdates the writing of the play. This offshoot of the AIDS activist group ACT UP agitates for a broader and more radical social and cultural agenda. Like Queer Nation, *Angels in America* aims to subvert the distinction between the personal and the political, to refuse to be closeted, to undermine the category of the "normal," and to question the fixedness and stability of every sexual identity. Reimagining America, giving it a camp inflection, *Angels* announces: "We're here. We're queer. We're fabulous. Get used to it!"

I interviewed Tony Kushner on a cold Sunday afternoon in January in his apartment on New York's Upper West Side.

[David Savran]: *How did your early ideas about theatre change?*

[Tony Kushner]: As a freshman at Columbia, I read Ernest Fisher's *The Necessity of Art* and was very upset and freaked out by it. The notion of the social responsibility of artists was very exciting and upsetting for me.

Why upsetting?

I arrived from Louisiana with fairly standard liberal politics. I was ardently Zionist and, where I grew up, the enemy was still classic American anti-Semitism. It was a big shock to discover all these people on the left at Columbia who were critical of Israel. My father is very intelligent in politics but very much a child of the Khrushchev era, the great disillusionment with Stalinism. I guess I just believed that Marxism was essentially totalitarianism and I could hear in Fisher a notion of responsibility that is antithetical to the individualist ideology that I hadn't yet started to question.

One of the things that changed my understanding of theatre was reading Brecht. I saw Richard Foreman's *Threepenny Opera* at Lincoln Center in 1976 and thought it was the most exciting theatre I'd ever seen. It seemed to me to combine the extraordinary visual sense that I had seen downtown with a narrative theatre tradition that I felt more comfortable with. There was also the amazing experience of the performance. When Brecht is done well, it is both a sensual delight and extremely unpleasant, and Foreman got that as almost nothing I've ever seen. It was excoriating and you left singing the songs. So I read the "Short Organum" and *Mother Courage*—which I still think is the greatest play ever written—and began to get a sense of a politically engaged theatre.

It was in Brecht that I think I understood Marx for the first time. I understood materialism, the idea of the impact of the means of production, which in Brecht is an issue of theatrical production. I started to understand the way that labor is disappeared into the commodity form, the black magic of capitalism: the real forces operating in the world, the forces of the economy and commodity production underneath the apparent order of things.

Because of Brecht I started to think of a career in the theatre. It seemed the kind of thing one could do and still retain some dignity as a person engaged in society. I didn't think that you could just be a theatre artist. That's when I first read Benjamin's *Understanding Brecht* and decided I wanted to do theatre. Before that I was going to become a medieval studies professor.

Why?

I loved the Middle Ages and I think there's something very appealing about its art, literature and architecture, but I was slowly getting convinced that it had no relevance to anything.

What about the Middle Ages? The connection between art and religion?

I have a fantastical, spiritual side. And when I got to Columbia, I was very impressionable. In the first class I took, a course in expository writing, we did *Beowulf*. I found the magic and the darkness of it very appealing and I was very, very moved—as I still am—by being able to read something 900 years old, or 2,000 years old in the case of the Greeks, and to realize that it isn't in any way primitive. You also realize—although I don't believe in universal human truths—that there are certain human concerns that go as far back as Euripides or Aeschylus.

And of course medieval art and culture predates the development of bourgeois individualism, which you go to great pains to critique.

It's extraordinary to see that great richness can come from societies that aren't individuated in that way. The anonymity of the art is terrifying to a modern person. It's not until very late, really until the beginning of the Renaissance, that you start to have artists identifying themselves. You realize these human beings had a profoundly different sense of the social.

At the same time, I started to get very exciting about Shakespeare and Ben Jonson. I directed Jonson's *Bartholomew Fair* as my first production at Columbia, and it was horrible.

It's a very difficult play.

I didn't start easy—36 parts. I couldn't even find 36 actors. One of them didn't speak English and we had to teach him syllabically. You can't understand most of it anyway, because of the references to things that have long since disappeared, but I had fun doing it and decided at that point—although I'd tried writing a couple of things—that I would become a director because I didn't think that I'd ever write anything of significance. I was also attempting to follow in the footsteps of people I really admired like Foreman, Akalaitis and Liz LeCompte. I thought the best thing to do was to write the text as a director, so I spent two years answering switchboards at a hotel and two years teaching at a school for gifted children in Louisiana. I directed several things there to get over my fear of directing—*The Tempest, Midsummer Night's Dream*—and I did my first take at *The Badan-Baden Play for Learning*, which I'm beginning to think is, next to *Mother Courage*, the best thing Brecht ever wrote. Then I applied to NYU graduate school in directing because I wanted to work with Carl Weber because he had worked with Brecht—and he looked like Brecht. At my second attempt (George Wolfe and I just discovered that we were rejected by him in the same year), I got in.

Your own work, with its multiple plot lines, has some resemblance to Bartholomew Fair, but it is also engaged in the American narrative tradition. What impact have Miller, Williams and O'Neill had on your writing?

Miller, none. I do actually admire *Death of a Salesman*. I can see how, in its time, it had an immense impact. And it's still hard to watch without sobbing at the end. But some of it is a cheat. It's melodramatic and it has that awful, '50s kind of Herman Wouk-ish sexual morality, the supposed tragedy of the little man and all that—but it's incredibly pathetic, or bathetic.

I sneered at O'Neill for a long time, but I'm beginning to realize that two or three of his plays—not just *Long Day's Journey into Night*—are amazing. I've always loved Williams. The first time I read *Streetcar*, I was annihilated. I read as much Williams as I could get my hands on until the late plays started getting embarrassingly bad. I've always thought *Orpheus Descending* is a fascinating play, much more fascinating than the Broadway production directed by that Tory Peter Hall, which I thought was just awful. I'm really influenced by Williams, but I'm awestruck by O'Neill. I don't feel that he's much of an influence because he's from a very different tradition with a very different sensibility.

I think John Guare is a very important writer. *Landscape of the Body*, the Lydie Breeze plays, *House of Blue Leaves* are amazing. Like Williams, Guare has figured out a way for Americans to do a kind of stage poetry. He's discovered a lyrical voice that doesn't sound horrendously twee and forced and phony. There are astonishingly beautiful things scattered throughout his work.

*As I was watching **Perestroika**—the opening tableau, the spectacle, the angel—I also thought about Robert Wilson.*

Hollow grandiosity [*laughs*]. I saw *Einstein on the Beach* at the Met in '76 and was maddened and deeply impressed by it. I'm very ambivalent about Wilson. The best I've ever seen him do—the piece I loved the most—was *Hamletmachine*. Watching *Hamletmachine*, I felt: This is such tough theatre, this is hard work. I was always afraid of making the audience work. But I was horrified by what I saw of *The CIVIL WarS*. It really seemed like Nuremberg time—done for Reagan's Hitler Olympics. What he does to history—this notion of Ulysses S. Grant and Clytemnestra and owls and Kachina dancers—excuse me, but what is this? What's going on here?

So you see a complete dehistoricization?

Absolutely. And to what end? These figures are not neutral, they're not decorative. You do see ghosts of ideas floating through, but it feels profoundly aestheticist in the worst, creepiest way, something with fascist potential. Also, the loudest voice is the voice of capital: This cost so much money, and you've spent so much money to see it. There's a really unholy synthesis happening of what is supposed to be resistant, critical and marginal, marrying big money and big corporate support. Wilson is an amazing artist, but a disturbing one.

Maria Irene Fornes is also very, very important to me. I saw her really experimental stuff like *The Diary of Evelyn Brown*, based on these endless, tedious lists of what a pioneer woman who lived on the plains did during the day—and Fornes just staged them. It was monumentally boring and extraordinary. Every once in a while, this pioneer woman would do a little clog dance. You saw the great tediousness of women's work, and yet it was, at the same time, exalted, thrilling and mesmerizing. Then Fornes moved into plays like *Conduct of Life* and *Mud*. I think she's a great writer and director, and the extent to which she's not appreciated here or in England is an incredible crime and an act of racism. And she's the only master playwright who's actually trained another generation—so many wonderful writers like José Rivera, and Migdalia Cruz and Eduardo Machado.

And then there's Caryl Churchill, who is like . . . God—the greatest living English-language playwright and, in my opinion, the most important English-language playwright since Williams. There's nothing like *Fen* or *Top Girls*. She came to see *Angels* at the National Theatre in London, and I felt hideously embarrassed. Suddenly the play sounded like a huge Caryl Churchill ripoff. One of the things that I'm happy about with **Perestroika** is that it's a bigger and messier work—I found a voice, and it doesn't sound as much influenced by Churchill as **Millennium**.

The important thing about the British socialist writers, even the ones I find irritating, is that their style comes out of the Berliner Ensemble touring through Britain—they have a strong Marxist tradition they're not at war with, and they've found a way (Bond, of course, did it first) to write Marxist, socialist theatre that has a connection with English-language antecedents. So it was very important for me to read Brenton, Churchill, Hare and Edgar. During the late '70s, when there was nothing coming out of this country, they seemed to be writing all the good plays.

*As the subtitle of **Angels** makes plain, this play recognizes that gay men have been at the center of certain crucial themes and identities in our national life. How do you see **Angels** in relation to the development of queer politics?*

I'm in my late thirties now and of the generation that made ACT UP and then Queer Nation—a generation stuck between the people who created the '60s and their children. I see traces of the Stonewall generation, of Larry Kramer and even, to a certain extent, Harvey Fierstein—but also the generation of [filmmaker] Greg Araki and [actor] David Drake, that Queer Nation, Boy Bar kind of thing. I feel that I'm part of a group of theatre people that includes Holly Hughes, David Greenspan, Paula Vogel . . . As I've said in other interviews, I think of it as a change from the Theatre of the Ridiculous to the Theatre of the Fabulous.

The Queer Nation chant—"We're here. We're queer. We're fabulous. Get used to it!"—uses *fabulous* in two senses. First, there's *fabulous* as opposed to *ridiculous*. In *The Beautiful Room Is Empty*, Edmund White writes about the Stonewall rebellion being a "ridiculous" thing for the people who were involved: It was a political gesture, what Wayne Koestenbaum calls "retaliatory self-invention," a gesture of definance. That's the essence of the ridiculous. And the drag gesture is still not completely capable of taking itself seriously. I don't want to talk in a judgmental way, but there's still a certain weight of self-loathing, I think, that's caught up in it. You couldn't say that Charles Ludlam was self-loathing. But there is a sense in which masochism (I'm sounding like Louis [the character in *Angels*] now) and flashes of intense misogyny—when another victim of oppression is sneered at and despised because of her weakness—come from the fact that one hates one's own weakness. There's a certain embracing of weakness and powerlessness in the Ridiculous.

John Waters, too, is a good example of that.

Yes. And there's also an incompatibility with direct political discourse. How can you be that kind of queer and talk politics? Of course, what AIDS forced on the community was the absolute necessity of doing just that—of not becoming a drab old lefty, or old new lefty, but maintaining a queer identity and still being able to talk seriously about treatment protocols and oppression.

So there's *fabulous* in the sense of an evolutionary advance over the notion of being ridiculous, and *fabulous* also in the sense of being fabled, having a history. What's very important is that we now have a consciousness about where we come from in a way that John Vaccaro and Charles Ludlam, when they were making pre-Stonewall theatre, didn't have. Think back to [avant-garde performer and filmmaker] Jack Smith, that whole tradition of which he was the most gorgeous and accomplished incarnation. Ludlam died before ACT UP started. Had he lived, there's no question but that he would have had no problem with it. I knew nothing about his theoretical writings when he was alive, I just knew he was the funniest man I'd ever seen. But he was working through a very strong politics and theory of the theatre, and I'm sure the times would have made many amazing changes in his art.

So I feel we're another step along the road now. It's incumbent upon us to examine history and be aware of history, of where we've come from and what has given us the freedom to talk the way we do now. We're the generation that grew up when homophobia wasn't axiomatic and universal, and when the closet wasn't nailed shut and had to be kicked open.

*The progress narrative you're constructing here makes me think that **Perestroika**'s idea of history is not only rooted in dialectical materialism but also in your belief in the possibility of progress and enlightenment.*

As Walter Benjamin wrote, you have to be constantly looking back at the rubble of history. The most dangerous thing is to become set upon some notion of the future that isn't rooted in the bleakest, most terrifying idea of what's piled up behind you.

When I started coming out of the closet in the early '80s, and was going to the Coalition for Lesbian and Gay Rights meetings, they were so bourgeois and completely devoid of any kind of Left political critique. There was no sense of community with any other oppressed groups, just "let's get the gay rights bill passed in New York and have brunches and go to the gym." It was astonishing to discover that only 10 years before there had been the Gay Activist's Alliance and the Lavender Left and hippie gay people, and I thought, "What happened? Where did they go?" Of course, they went with the '60s. But ACT UP changed all that. Now it's hard for people to remember that there was a time before ACT UP, and that it burst violently and rapidly on the scene.

*It seems to me that this development of queer politics has in part prepared for the success of **Angels in America**.*

Absolutely. It kicked down the last door. The notion of acting up, much more than outing, is what really blew out liberal gay politics. I mean, you depend upon the work that's done by the slightly assimilationist but hard-working, libertarian, civil rights groups, like the NAACP, but then at some point you need the Panthers. You need a group that says, "Enough of this shit. This is going too slow. And if we don't see some big changes now, we're going to cause trouble. We really are here. Get used to it." Up until that point, the American majority—if there is such a thing—fantasizes that the noise will just go away, that it's a trend, a swing of the pendulum. The way *Angels in America* talks, and its complete lack of apology for that kind of fagginess, is something that would not have made sense before.

Unlike Torch Song Trilogy, *in which Arnold just wants to be normal,* **Angels in America**, *along with queer theory and politics, calls into question the category of the normal.*

Right. Creating the fiction of the white, normal, straight, male center has been the defining project of American history. I'm working on a play about slavery and reading 18th-century texts, and it has been the central pre-occupation in American politics for the entire time during which this land has been trying to make itself into a country. The founding fathers weren't getting up and arguing about making homosexuality legal, but it's been an ongoing issue. And in this century, it's been an obsession during various times of crisis. It always seems to me that in the concerns of any group called a minority and called oppressed can be found the biggest problems and the central identity issues that the country is facing. Because of Brecht, and from reading the history of the collapse of the Weimar Republic when I was writing **A Bright Room Called Day,** I realized that the key is the solidarity of the oppressed for the oppressed—being able to see the connecting lines. This is one of the things that AIDS has done, because it's made disenfranchisement incredibly clear across color lines and gender lines.

I keep thinking of that line from Walter Benjamin's: "Where we perceive a chain of events, [the angel] sees one single catastrophe which keeps piling wreckage upon wreckage and hurls it in front of his feet." The scene in **Perestroika** *really took my breath away, seeing the wreckage behind the scrim.*

And there's a whole scene that we didn't perform because it just didn't play: These very Benjaminian, Rilkean angels are listening on an ancient radio to the first report of the disaster at Chernobyl. Benjamin's sense of utopianism is also so profoundly apocalyptic: a teleology, but not a guarantee, or a guarantee that Utopia will be as fraught and as infected with history. It's not pie in the sky at all.

I think that is also a very American trope. In *The American Religion,* Harold Bloom keeps referring to this country as the evening land, where the promise of Utopia is so impossibly remote that it brings one almost to grieving and despair. Seeing what heaven looks like from the depths of hell. It's the most excruciating pain, and even as one is murdering and rampaging and slashing and burning to achieve Utopia, one is aware that the possibility of attaining Utopia is being irreparably damaged. People in this country knew somewhere what they were doing, but as we moved into this century, we began to develop a mechanism for repressing that knowledge. There's a sense of progress, but at tremendous cost.

It's Prior who carries the burden of that in **Angels.** *Embedded even in his name is the sense that he's out of step with time, both too soon and belated, connected to the past and future, to ancestors and what's to come.*

He's also connected to Walter Benjamin. I've written about my friend Kimberly [Flynn], who is a profound influence on me. The line that Benjamin wrote that's most important to her—and is so true—is, "Even the dead will not be safe if the enemy wins." She said jokingly that at times she felt such an extraordinary kinship with him that she thought she was Walter Benjamin reincarnated. And so at one point in the conversation, when I was coming up with names for my characters, I said, "I had to look up something in Benjamin—not you, but the prior Walter." That's where the name came from. I had been looking for one of those WASP names that nobody gets called anymore.

Despite all these utopian longings, at the center of both **Bright Room** *and* **Angels** *are characters, Agnes and Louis,*

who are, in one way or another, liberals. In both plays you've well-intentioned liberals whose actions are at an extraordinary remove from their intentions. Why?

I've never thought of Louis and Agnes as a pair, but they really are. I think they're very American. American radicalism has always been anarchic as opposed to socialist. The socialist tradition in this country is so despised and has been blamed so much on immigrants. It's been constructed as a Jewish, alien thing, which is not the way socialism is perceived anywhere else in the world, where there is a native sense of *communitas* that we don't share. What we have is a native tradition of anarchism, and that's a fraught, problematic tradition. Ronald Reagan is as much its true heir as Abbie Hoffman. Abbie Hoffman was an anarcho-communist and Ronald Reagan is an ego-anarchist, but they're both anarchists.

The strain in the American character I feel the most affection for and that has the most potential for growth is American liberalism, which is incredibly short of what it needs to be, incredibly limited and exclusionary—and predicated on all sorts of racist, sexist, homophobic and classist prerogatives. And yet, as Louis asks, why has democracy succeeded in America? I really believe that there is the potential for radical democracy in this country, one of the few places on earth where I see it as a strong possibility. There is an American tradition of liberalism, of a kind of social justice, fair play and tolerance—and each of these things can certainly be played upon in the most horrid ways. (Reagan kept the most hair-raising anarchist aspects of his agenda hidden, and presented himself as a good old-fashioned liberal who kept invoking FDR.) It may just be sentimentalism on my part because I am the child of liberal-pinko parents, but I do believe in it—as much as I often find it despicable. It's sort of like the Democratic National Convention every four years: It's horrendous, and you can feel it sucking all the energy from progressive movements in this country, with everybody pinning their hopes on this sleazy bunch of guys. But you do have Jesse Jackson getting up and calling the Virgin Mary a single mother; on an emotional level, and I hope also on a more practical level, these are the people in whom to have hope.

None of the characters in **Angels**, *though, is involved with mass-movement politics.*

That's because the play is set—and I think this is very important—at a time when there's no such thing in the United States for generally progressive people. For someone like Belize, there isn't anything: The Rainbow Coalition has started to waffle and fall apart. And there is nothing in the gay community—there's the Gay Pride parade, and Gay Men's Health Crisis getting humiliated at the City Council in Newark every year—1984-85 was a horrible, horrible time. It really seemed as if the maniacs had won for good.

What Martin says in **Millennium** now seems like a joke that we can all snigger at, but at the time, I just wrote what I thought was most accurate. The Republicans had lost the Senate, but would eventually get that back because the South would go Republican. There would never be a Democratic President again, because Mondale was the best answer we could make to Ronald Reagan, the most popular President we've ever had. So none of these people had anything they could hook into, which is the history of the Left. When the moment comes, when the break happens and history can be made, do we step in and make it or do we flub and fail? As much as I am horrified by what Clinton does—and we could have had someone better—we didn't completely blow it this time.

I'm interested in father-son relationships in the play—the way that Roy Cohn is set up as the masochistic son of a sadistic father, Joseph McCarthy, and how he, in turn, is a sadistic father to Joe. Isn't a sadomasochistic dynamic really crucial for mapping so many of the relationships in the play? Both Louis and Harper seem amazingly masochistic, in very different ways.

I want to explore S&M more because feel that it's an enormously pervasive dynamic, that it's inextricably wound up with issues of patriarchy, and that there are ways in which it plays through every aspect of life. I think it's something that needs to be understood, thought about and spoken about more openly.

We subjects of capitalist societies have to talk about the ways in which we are constructed to eroticize and cathect pain, as well as the way pain is transformed into pleasure, and self-destruction into self-creation. What price must we finally pay for that? Until now, there's been a kind of dumb liberation politics—all forms of sexual practice are off-limits for analysis, and S&M is fine, we just leave it in the bedroom. But of course it's not just the kind of S&M that's acted out that needs to concern us. I think that sexuality should still be subject to analysis, including the question of why we're gay instead of straight, which I think has nothing to do with the hypothalmus or interstitial brain cells, but has to do with trauma.

But isn't all sexuality rooted in trauma?

We're just good Freudians. Yes, it's all trauma and loss, and the question is, are there specific forms of trauma? I believe that there is an etiology of sexuality that's traceable if anybody wants to spend the money on an analyst. Oedipus is still legitimate grounds for exploration and inquiry. And I think that the notion of the cultural formation of personalities is of tremendous importance. Roy's generation of gay men, for example, had that kind of deeply patriarchal, gender-enforced notion of the seduction of youth—the ephebe and the elder man. That comes down from the Greeks, homosexuality being a form of tutelage, of transmission, of dominance and submission. It felt to me that that would absolutely be part of Roy's repressed, ardent desire for Joe. Then what you see replicated in the blessing scene is a form of love which has to flow through inherited structures of hierarchical power.

These are some of the oldest questions with which we've been torturing ourselves: What is the relationship between

sexuality and power? Is sexuality merely an expression of power? Is there even such a thing as a "sexuality"? If we buy into the notion of the construction of these forms of behavior, and the construction of personalities that engage in these behaviors, do we believe in the *de*construction of these forms? What is that deconstruction? There's the issue of reforming the personality to become a socialist subject: By what process, other than submission, does the individual ego become part of a collective? Is there a process other than revolution, other than bloodshed, agony and pain—which is fundamentally masochistic—by which we can transform ourselves? That's a big question, and it turns you toward things like Zen.

That's the question of the play: What is there beyond pain? Is Utopia even imaginable?

If our lives are in fact shaped by trauma and loss—and as I get older it seems to me that life is very, very profoundly shaped by loss and death—how do you address that? How does one progress in the face of that? That's the question that the AIDS epidemic has asked. There is no place more optimistic than America, in the most awful way (like "Up with People!"). These questions make so many people queasy, and become the subject of so much sarcasm, but identity is shaped, even racial identity. If there weren't bigots, there wouldn't be a politics of race. There has to be a politics of difference that speaks to the presence of enormous oppression and violence and terror. The more we know about history, the more we realize—and this is an important thing about sadomasochism—that it never ends. You can see in our present moment a thousand future Sarajevos. You know that when you're 90, if you live so long, they'll still be fighting. Even after the Holocaust, the monsters are still among us. And can you forgive? That's why I ask this question of forgiveness, because its possibility, like that of Utopia, is undertheorized and underexpressed.

Relating to the question of forgiveness, why do you use Mormons in the play, along with Jews? The angels are so clearly Old Testament angels, angels of the vengeful God. How does that tie in with the Mormon religion?

There are interesting similarities between Mormonism and Judaism. They both have a very elusive notion of damnation. It's always been unclear to me, as a Jew, what happens if you don't do good things. Presumably you don't go to Paradise. There *is* a Hell, but, even among the Orthodox, there isn't an enormous body of literature about it—it's not like Catholicism. Mormonism has a Hell but it also has three or four layers of Heaven.

Also, like Judaism, Mormonism is a diasporic religion, and it is of the book. It draws its strength very much from a literal, physical volume, which isn't sacred like the Torah—but it's all about the discovery of a book. Neither religion is about redemption based on being sorry for what you've done and asking for forgiveness. The hallmark of Mormonism is, "By deeds ye shall be known." Ethics are defined by action, and that is also true in Judaism. Your intentions make very little difference to God. What counts is what you do and whether you're righteous in your life. That appeals to me. It also feels very American.

I started the play with an image of an angel crashing through a bedroom ceiling, and I knew that this play would have a connection to American themes. The title came from that, and I think the title, as much as anything else, suggested Mormonism because the prototypical American angel is the angel Moroni. It's of this continent, the place in Mormon mythology that Jesus visited after he was crucified. It's a great story—not the Book of Mormon, which, as Mark Twain said, is chloroform in print, but the story of Joseph Smith's life and the trek, the gathering of Zion. The idea of inventing a complete cosmology out of a personal vision is something I can't imagine a European doing. I guess Swedenborg and Blake sort of did that, but it didn't become a theocratic empire. And unlike Swedenborg's vision (which is rather elegant and beautiful) and Blake's (which is extraordinarily beautiful but mostly incomprehensible), it's so dumb. It's naive and disingenuous. It's like Grandma Moses, the celestial and the terrestrial heavens with all this masonry incorporated into it. It's American gothic.

I wanted Mormons in this play. I find their immense industry, diligence and faith moving. The symbol of Utah and of the Mormon kingdom of God is a beehive, which is, in its own way, a socialist, communist image. There were in fact a lot of experiments in Utah of communally owned property, which is what Joseph Smith originally dictated, with wealth held in common, and experiments with controlled economies. Their social experiments were independent of, but similar to, European socialist, communal notions of the 19th century.

Now, they're right-wing and horrible. But the Mormons I've met, I've actually liked. There's something dear and nice about them. When I was working on Joe, I wanted to write a conservative man that I actually liked. I didn't finally succeed [*laughs*], although I feel that he gets somewhere and will ultimately be redeemable, in *Angels,* part three.

You're working with Robert Altman now to turn **Angels** *into a movie.*

Yes, I'm writing the screenplay. *Nashville* had a profound impact on me, with its extraordinary interweaving of stories. I wanted somebody I respected and whom I knew would make the film version very unlike the stage play. I'm completely confident of that [*laughs*]—Altman allows a certain kind of messiness to be a part of his aesthetic, which appeals to me a lot, and I'm sure he's the only person in Hollywood who would have said immediately, as he did, that we have to do two films.

I hope I can get him to deal with the difficult question of gay sexuality. He hasn't always been great about that, but I can't believe that he'd want to do this without being aware

that there are going to be men naked in bed together, or in the park. This can't be another one of those films with two men lying in bed with the bedsheet pulled up against their pecs. I think it will be very important, given the way that Altman improvises, that he has some gay actors in the cast. I don't want to see a lot of straight people trying to figure out what it's like.

You're working on another play?

I haven't completely committed myself to what the next big one is going to be, but I have two that are cooking: One is about Vermeer—it's sort of a history of capitalism; the other is a play about a slave named Henry Box Brown who mailed himself out of slavery in a box to Philadelphia. Then I discovered by a fluke that Henry Box Brown wound up in England and toured English textile towns trying to get them to boycott Southern cotton before the Civil War. When I was working on **Millennium** at the National, I went to one of the towns, and I've just unearthed a whole treasure chest of amazing characters from the Industrial Revolution. George Wolfe is going to direct it both here and at the National, probably with white British actors and African-American actors.

So you remain committed to writing history plays.

There's a kind of safety in writing a history play—you can make up everything. It insulates you to a certain extent from the assault of everyday life. But I've also decided to write more **Angels in America** plays, and those may be the only ones in which I deal with contemporary reality.

When I was writing **Perestroika** this summer, I got very, very angry at the characters. At first, I thought it was because I was sick of them, but now I've come to realize that I hated the idea of not being able to work on them anymore. I want to know what happens to them. I already have most of the plot of part three in my head. It won't be continuous, but I could have a cycle of nine or ten plays by the time I'm done. The characters will get older as I get older. I'll be bringing in new ones and letting characters like Roy go. I'm excited about that. I think it's harder to write that kind of play than a history play.

Although I think of **Angels in America** *as a history play.*

In a sense, it is—although when I started writing it, it wasn't. It receded into the past. As it gets older, it will become increasingly about a period of history. There is a danger for me of writing too much out of books, because I'm sort of socially awkward and not much of an adventurer. I don't want to write only about the past. Brecht never wrote anything about his contemporaries, did he?

Arturo Ui.

Except it's set in Chicago and they're speaking in a very different way.

What about the learning plays?

But again, they're drowned in pseudo-Confucian poetry and set in China and other places.

But in all of his work he was historicizing his particular moment.

Exactly. That's all you can ever do.

Notes about Political Theater (1997)

SOURCE: "Notes about Political Theater," in *The Kenyon Review*, new series Vol. XIX, Nos. 3/4, Summer/Fall 1997, pp. 19-34.

[*In the essay below, Kushner argues the need for a committed political theater in America.*]

In his essay on Theodore Dreiser, E. L. Doctorow quotes Dreiser's critical description of himself as a young man: "Chronically nebulous, doubting, uncertain, I stared and stared at everything, only wondering, not solving." This is, Doctorow comments, "a perfect description of the state of readiness in a novelist."

And, I might add, in playwrights, perhaps even more so. The art of playwriting is not fundamentally a narrative art like novel writing; it is dialogic, it proceeds from contradiction, not cause and effect; not "this happens and then this and then this," but more "This happened. Oh yeah? Who says so?"

It is a cruel thing to ask playwrights to present themselves directly to audiences or readers, stripped of many layers of protection, production, interpretation with which we habitually accoutre ourselves. All of which is to say that I hope the following, which is an attempt to define what I mean when I say that I consider myself a writer of political theater, isn't too noodleheaded. Noodleheadedness is an important thing for playwrights to cultivate in themselves, but it is not in any other circumstance necessarily a social grace.

I do theater because my mother did it. Sylvia Deutscher Kushner was a professional musician by training, a bassoonist, and one of the first American women to hold a principal chair in a major orchestra (the New York City Opera orchestra at the age of eighteen); and she was an amateur actress of considerable emotional depth and power, a real tragedienne. Most of her theatrical performances were given between my fifth and ninth years, during which period she was the leading lady of the Lake Charles, Louisiana Little Theater. I remember the particularly intense experience of watching her—as Linda Loman, as Anne Frank's mother, as Betty the Loon (in *The Effect of Gamma Rays on Man-in-the-Moon Marigolds*). She was elegant onstage, and beautiful. She screamed and slapped people, she defied Nazis, she tormented an older woman who reminded me of my grandmother. She was thrilling; she had power; she made people weep. I experienced total identification. A theater queen was born.

The first time I saw her act she was in a melodrama called *A Far Country*; she played a woman, loosely based on Anna O., afflicted with hysterical paralysis, who was being treated by Sigmund Freud. I was four years old. My mother was carried onstage in each scene by a tall man. I dreamed about being paralyzed and being carried like that, by a tall man, onstage, before an applauding audience. Months after the play closed my mother took a lengthy trip to New York City, and I woke up paralyzed the morning after her departure. I couldn't move for two days, and then I was fine. My pediatrician conjectured that my condition probably resulted from some sort of allergic reaction to farmyard animals I'd encountered on a nursery school outing the previous day, but was he Sigmund Freud? What did *he* know? I still don't know if my problem was the result of psyche or soma or, more likely, some combination of the two. I choose to think of it as an early calling to that arena of hysterical and historical conversion, the stage. I remember wondering during those two days of immobility if the Far Country referred to in the play's title was New York.

It seems to me best to begin by confessing to the originary impulse behind my choosing to do theater, specifically political theater, the definition of which is a large part of what I'll be addressing, rather than occupy myself in some other, possibly more useful, certainly more stable and less crazy-making, profession. Beginnings are important. I wish I could lay claim to a missionary urge, a grand calling or revolutionary pragmatism: I will be an artist because through art I can best change the world, but the truth is that I drifted into theater like a potential addict drifts into an opium den, predestined from an early age, borne aloft on the crosscurrents of Oedipus and Narcissus.

All psychology has its origins in the public sphere; the world outside is experienced, introjected, becomes the stuff of which we are made, our private selves, and is then reinserted into the public sphere as we interact with the world around us. Public, private, public: my mother onstage; me in my dreams, onstage; me as a grown-up theater artist, returning the world ingested to the real world, whatever that may be (don't ask me, I work in theater). There is a ceaseless motion between these domains; boundaries blur. The public is the private, or, as feminism puts it, the personal is political.

The genesis of my politics is no loftier, no less mundane nor more free of family drama than the genesis of my theatrics. I have a healthy appetite for politics, for history, for political theory. I inherited this from my parents, New York-New Deal liberals transplanted to the Deep South, who in turn inherited it from their parents—all of us indebted to the insatiable curiosity, skepticism, pessimistic optimism, ethical engagement, and ardent pursuit of the millennium that is, for me, the most valuable heritage of nearly two thousand years of Diasporan Judaic culture. And I learned politics through numerous episodes in my youth of mild anti-Semitism and not-so-mild homophobia. The rest is just generalizing from a few deeply etched particulars, returning anger absorbed to the world that generated it in the first place; again, public becomes private becomes public. People who work in the theater, which is never pure, should be comfortable with this dialectical impurity, this seesaw mixing-up of spheres, this paradox. And it is a paradox: the personal is the political, and yet it is important, somehow, to maintain a distinction between the two. Which is to say that the personal and the political are the same, and aren't.

In a lot of theater in this country, the personal is what you make art out of and the political is what you try to avoid discussing at parties; or maybe an occasional current event worms its way into the theater you do, which is fine. Politics in moderation spices up the proceedings, adds a contemporary punch to that tired second act in which Joe Sr. and Joe Jr. have it out in the kitchen following a late-night drinking spree, as long as the *real* issues are adhered to: Joe Jr.'s rotten childhood, caused by Joe Sr.'s rotten childhood. The personal is personal, the political is personal, and the problems of Joe, father and son, must ultimately be ascribed to that old villain, human nature, the precise character of which is inferred but never too closely examined, understood by all to be ambivalent, competitive, lonely, sinful, incurious, and anti-intellectual. There is a great dread of inflicting the political upon the psychological, true locus of the aesthetic event, a question, as E. H. Carr says, of the class-based division between science and the humanities, of *tone*: politics is too noisy, too bristling with elbows and arguments, too impolite. The mildly depressed effect of most American psychotherapeutic discussion is more comfortable for those who go to the hushed Palace of Art to be comfortable. Those problems are generally deemed most interesting which are unsolvable, which no political theory or belief in human agency can address, which lie *beyond* politics, beyond history, in the realm of destiny, tragedy, and myth.

The notion that everything flows from a single source (human nature, destiny, you name it) is fundamentally undialectical. The insistence on the primacy of a kind of simplistic, essentialist psychology—of the personal as ultimate pre-condition for all human activity—is, as everyone from Marx to Brecht to Roland Barthes tells us, a pronouncement from the heart of the great historical project of capitalist myth-making: the transformation of that which is social, cultural, and political, and hence changeable, into nature, which is immutable and eternal. In art as in life the predominant aesthetic of theater as it is practiced in this country is still something called Naturalism, which originally purported to show human beings living life in real conditions of existence, and which is now a weary and worn-out system of conventions and received notions about the great themes of life that shows a tenacity and survivorship second only to capitalism itself. It can be seen in its most naked form on television now, and in film; in the theater we've learned to trick Naturalism up in formalistically experimental clothing, but we still traffic mainly in visions of ultimate futility presented, all such fanciness aside, as unmediated tellings of the truth of the world.

Everything is personal; everything is political. We are trained to see the personal, the psychological (although our psychological understanding is usually pretty unsophisticated). We are less able to see the political; in life, as in art, much energy is devoted toward blurring the political meaning of events, or even that events *have* a political meaning. Hence, the recent news that in Harlem three black children died after a thirty-story fall when their apartment in a public housing high-rise caught fire was everywhere described as a "tragedy." "Tragic," like "natural," is one of those rhetorical dead ends that stops the mind from reaching to the full awfulness and criminality of an event. The correct response to tragedy is tears, not rage. Tragedy offers catharsis, and transcendence; its spectators are ennobled by having witnessed it. Its victims, of course, are dead, but *tragically* dead, which is somehow more elegant than plain old dead. It has that classical ring. The presence of a malign kind of human agency is elided, uncomfortable questions not asked: what sorts of indifference to the lives of what sorts of people produces thirty-story buildings that have no adequate routes of escape, and why is it almost always black kids or Latino or Chicano kids, and children of the poor, falling down elevator shafts, out of unprotected windows, getting hit by stray bullets? Do stories such as these speak about the cruelty of life or about the cruelty of poverty and racism?

Without losing sight of the personal, I would argue that everything is rife with political meaning, is political, that all theater is political: when theater artists assiduously avoid politics, we deny the existence of the political and are making a political statement, committing a political act. Omission, as the saying goes, is commission. The act of wishing away the world of political struggle is a deeply reactionary gesture. Brecht says it: We live in a time when "to talk of trees / is almost a crime / because it implies silence about so many atrocities."

If all theater is political, then is there an animal called *political theater*, distinct from other kinds of theater? If all life is political, then politics ceases to exist as a meaningful category; swallowed up by its own universality, it disappears. Since it's true that everything is political (though not exclusively so) it becomes meaningless to talk about political and nonpolitical theater, and more useful to speak of a theater that presents the world as it is, an interwoven web of the public and the private; and theater that distorts by eliminating one entire facet of human experience, or of theater of the left and theater of the right, or theater that negates the status quo and theater that supports it, theater of the oppressed and for the oppressed, or theater of and for the oppressors.

It is incredibly hard to use, unembarrassedly, words like *oppressed* and *oppressors*, even in an essay, and even more so onstage. We feel that the rhetoric of politics is somehow enlarded with failure, tainted with betrayal and a partisan-driven simplicity; we feel we've heard it before, which is interesting, considering how thoroughly purged of such talk our drama actually is.

A great deal of the theater done in this country is two things: bad (by which I mean unimaginative, boring, unsatisfying, simplistic, and ugly) and reactionary (by which I mean racist, sexist, imperialist, homophobic, and so on). The commercial theater is now largely the property of Andrew Lloyd Weber, *The Phantom* and *Cats* and *Les Mis*, and in the most tasty recent development, the Walt Disney Corporation, which is buying and refurbishing an old Times Square porno palace, chasing out the real rats, and providing the Corporate Mouse with a permanent theatrical residence for the performing of god-knows-what kind of simulacra drama. The commercial theater is really interesting only for the squalor and kitsch of its increasingly creepy spectacle. It must be visited as one visits a mental patient who is growing daily more noisily psychotic and whose prognosis, sadly, is far from good.

The "serious" theater, mostly the not-for-profit regional theater, is better, but still riven with problems. It is racist, mostly by virtue of its completely excluding minorities, frequently by condescension and occasionally by direct assault. It is unrelentingly, untiringly misogynist, hatred of women remains the mainstay of its diet, a song it never tires of singing. It is imperialist. Last season I saw, back to back, two plays the titles of which, in the name of discretion and self-preservation I will not divulge, each making use of the same identical strategy: white, wealthy people from America discovering themselves through an encounter with a third-world culture, in which the real story is the uses to which the lives and usually the sufferings of nonpersons (mostly nonwhite persons) can be put in the ongoing moral and spiritual development of *people like us*. It's the Oliver Stone theme, it's what E. M. Forster eighty years ago was smart enough at least partially to avoid doing, reproducing in fiction an act of unregenerate colonialism; we seem in the years intervening to have misplaced his sensitivity. In general, plays about other countries are really excuses for setting "American" problems in exotic locales; and the issue of what happens when writers attempt representations of other peoples, a very complex issue indeed, is usually angrily and summarily dismissed. "I am an artist. I'll write about anything I want." Misguided libertarianism overrides, in a gesture fraught with the arrogance of power—overrides the demands of the liberation struggles of foreigners, of indigenous groups of disenfranchised people.

We have done better with male homosexuals in recent years; my career attests to that. It shouldn't be ignored that the attention focused on homophobia after generations of silence and worse has been greeted simultaneously with querulous inquiries as to why there needs to be *so much* homo drama. And lesbians are virtually as invisible on mainstages in this time of "tolerance" as they have ever been.

Our forays into theater that addresses political or historical issues are generally misguided and embarrassing. We write history plays which, because they are written for audiences that know no history, in a theater that has been stripped of its pedagogic capabilities, are ludicrously oversimplified and hence denuded of meaning except for easily graspable platitudes about love (history as soap opera) or liberty (history as the endless rehashing of high-school civics). We live in terror of seeming partisan; we playwrights too often adopt a stance of cynical sophistication that delights in revealing the essential corruption or essential stupidity or essential decency of both over- and underdog. This easy relativism makes political analysis impossible, but at least we don't "insult" our subscribers by preaching or seeming didactic. We are in the lamentable position of having to eschew most political issues because we simply have no vocabulary with which to discuss them. Our aesthetic codes preclude complex political discourse far more effectively than any government censor could hope to accomplish. Theater people are guiltily aware of the need for theater to have a social, if not political, impact; we always talk about doing work that matters, that "means something." We proceed from this nondescript "something" to an avoidance of the very resources and tools which would enable us to create work that fits that description. I'm reminded of that exercise-freak character Lily Tomlin does. She says, plaintively, "I always said I *am* somebody, I *am* somebody; I guess I shoulda been more specific."

The principal antagonists and agents of our drama are individuals, usually white men, or families, usually white families. The individual is important to us; he gives us something to "care" about. We are apparently incapable of caring about issues, or ideas, or communities, or at least we believe ourselves to be; if *we* personally are capable of such empathic leaps, we assume it is our audience that is unable and must be served up a regular menu of individuals and their individual problems. The family is regularly hauled into service as the contemporary stand-in for fate: that which must be struggled against and, inevitably, succumbed to. Both phenomena, the individual and the family, are given validation by being treated as facts and forces of nature. The travails of both reduce, on some level, to issues of boundary, territory, and turf, which is to say real estate, which is to say private property ownership, which is to say capitalism, but the theater chooses to leave it all at the level of individualized turf battles and tribal warfare, concealing what is historically determined and politically charged behind the mask of instinct and "natural" desire.

(To digress to the cinematic, to Spielberg's *Schindler's List*, the crown jewel in the oeuvre of history's most financially successful, and maybe least ambivalent and hence most aesthetically successful reactionary artist: In this immensely popular film it is not the agonies of multitudes who arouse empathy in the largely unexplored heart of the film's protagonist, but rather a little girl [a decidedly goyische looking little girl] in a colorized red dress. There are no ethical systems invoked, as if the manifest insufficiency of these is enough to explain their absence, merely a tug of the heartstrings produced by an endangered cherub. The drama is the drama of the dependence of ineffectual multitudes on the exceptional man, who, for motives Spielberg never attempts to guess at, is a deliverer, all his operatic protestations at the film's conclusion notwithstanding. And the film's final image, predictably, is that of Liam Neeson, who plays Schindler, standing alone, placing a rose at the grave of the real Schindler—Schindler admiring himself, his godlike abilities, an image of complete narcissism and self-promotion which is the film's, and its director's, truest passion.)

I worry that I'm misrepresenting myself, the affable fellow I mostly am (though I have a friend who goes to the theater with me and has nicknamed me the "Bilious Faggot"). All this carping and complaining, it's as if some secret critic within was being born. I think it's come forth to fill a vacuum; namely, my inability to articulate a theory of the theater. In the absence of such a scheme, my most useful instrument for self-definition, and hence some explanation of what I try to do when I make theater, is to describe as thoroughly as possible the kind of theater I don't like. I would venture to say that there's more bad theater produced, percentage-wise, than bad film or bad novels or bad paintings or bad poetry (well, maybe there's more bad poetry). And bad theater is, for me at least, maybe the worst aesthetic experience imaginable. Because it is, in addition to offensive and boring and all the other things other instances of bad art can be, excruciatingly embarrassing.

The embarrassment factor is critical to the theatrical event. It's what gives every moment on stage part of its unique power. What we refer to when we speak sentimentally about the "power of the live event" is merely the frisson, becoming rarer in this age of electronic simulation, of being proximate to something that can end up soaring or falling flat on its ass. Both the sublime and the ridiculous being embodied in the same being produces a kind of tension that engages us equally as decent people, as masochists and as sadists. The human drama of salvation and damnation is always present on stage when the live actor can at any moment slip or redeem himself. This makes the theater more interesting than commodity-form art, and more scary. An actor lacks the warrantied dependability of a Lexus or a Sony digitalized minidiscman; but those things can only work perfectly or be replaced, whereas even a bad actor can have a brilliant moment.

It's hard to talk politically about the theater, a world that's many things but has always been tainted, tawdry, and superfluous. It's very important not to devalue the tainted, the tawdry, and the superfluous and indeed, the essential tackiness and falseness of the theater is its greatest aesthetic asset and political strength. Nevertheless, attempts to combine overt political intent with dramatic event have produced, throughout history, more embarrassing failures than glowing successes. Even the greatest successes have been regarded with a certain justifiable suspicion: Why, if you really want to be engaged politically, don't you actually *do* something instead of spending a colossal amount of time imitating the things other people do?

Peter Schumann of Bread and Puppet Theater (one of the political theater's more notable successes) acknowledged this in a wonderful program note many years ago when he wrote about the inescapable guilt of artists "fooling around in a world of trouble."

I am a professional playwright. I betray my bourgeois origins and aspirations by the pride I take in declaring: I get paid money to do art. Money bestows validity. It holds out an enticing possibility—that I may be able (be allowed) to live in comfort doing what I love to do, that I will be spared the painful dichotomy of work-for-money versus work-for-love. Millions of people all over the world work out their lives at jobs that offer them no pleasure, or almost none. There *are* prices too high to pay for the great good fortune of earning a living as an artist, but the high price is frequently hidden. The bill is delivered later. We can find ourselves much deeper in debt than we'd imagined.

It is in the crush of the marketplace, that it is useful to disentangle the personal and the political, to restore for a moment their separate distinctions. The personal is private; there is a membrane, however permeable it may be, that divides inside from outside. The private is a preserve, a place of resistance—of the erotic, the human, against a world grown increasingly pornographic, toxic, violent, and technologically nonhuman. The political, in one sense, is a realm of conscious intent to enter the world of struggle, change, activism, revolution, and growth, even in the face of the fearfulness, the caution and conservatism of the past-haunted interior. In times of struggle and oppression the names with which we identify become very important. If we are in opposition to the established order, it's strategically necessary and personally fortifying to call oneself an oppositionist, or something less clunky if it's available. Assimilation is dangerous if we attempt to blend in with an order that's out to destroy us. Identifying oneself as a pariah, as Other, if that's what we are, is an important political act. We take the right and privilege of definition away from the oppressor, we assume the power of naming ourselves. This is a lesson every gay man and lesbian learns: the closet doesn't protect us, it only shames and enervates. Strength rests in open declaration.

So I call myself a political theater artist, even though it's sometimes embarrassing to say it, even though my on-again, off-again activism makes me feel a bit fraudulent in calling myself a political anything. It feels much like coming out of the closet felt, only a bit lonelier. In making the claim, at least, I put myself on the line, publicly, and this helps to keep me from slipping in the face of temptation. I am a political theater artist of the left; this means I can't direct plays I find reactionary, even if that means giving up paying work. It means I can't applaud work that seems to me offensive to a group of people fighting for their own liberation. If I am a political theater artist of the left, I am committed to do work that participates as fully as possible in the struggles of the oppressed for power, in the desperate need for economic democracy, for socialism, for feminism, for environmentalism, for an end to bigotry of all kinds, for the building of a better world. Because the world can be much better than it is.

I have no idea how to do political theater—well, that's disingenuous, I have a few ideas, but certainly no solution and no system. I know that most overtly political theater today is guided more by good intention than by good politics, solid thinking, imagination, or talent. And there are theaters that produce work of sometimes questionable political intent whose brilliance at formalist experimentation makes an evening with them more exhilarating, disturbing, and even liberating than anything else being produced (the Wooster Group or Richard Foreman, for example). Or realism, for that matter, can't be discounted. Mamet's *Glengarry Glenn Ross* is a recent instance of brilliant, political drama, a fresh and vicious and rigorous assault on the high human cost of life in the free market. Mamet's career is as interesting to me as the career of any playwright; he's so great, troubling, ideologically slippery. After *Glengarry* he writes *Oleanna*, which is endlessly smart and fascinating and ultimately, infuriatingly false; and then *Cryptogram*, which I regard as one of the masterpieces of our dramatic literature. Don't be doctrinaire or *too* partisan; in other words, the theater is as confusing and as surprising as life.

I decided in college that playwriting was a dignified and worthy occupation only after reading Brecht, and I wanted to be a playwright like Brecht, who, while writing plays, articulated a theory of the theater for which those plays were intended. Few other playwrights have attempted this, and none with anything approaching the impact and importance of Brecht's writings, extending in influence from the theater into every medium and into political theory proper. Brecht did not invent his theater out of the whole cloth; nor, in fact, is it accurate to describe the various attempts Brecht made at writing for and about a new kind of theatrical experience as cohering, finally, into a single solution. Brecht joined himself to the most exciting, daring, politically attractive theater of his time, and then figured out the terms of the praxis, the synthesis of idea and practice, that created it. He began to describe a theater aesthetic that married the illusion/reality paradigm at the heart of all Western theater since the Italian Renaissance and Shakespeare to its counterpart in Marx. The distinction Marx makes between the *real* and the *social*, between the world of illusion created by relationships between producers of commodities, and some unknowable *real* of which the *social* is an imaginary reflection, between the real labor which creates goods in a commodity-producing system, and the form of the commodity into which the traces of labor, of human relationship has disappeared. Theater, like dialectical materialist analysis, examines the magic of perception and the political, ideological employment to which the magic is put.

Marxism is very important, very useful; it's hard to understand the political economy without it. We don't need orthodox Marxists, but we do need Marx, his theories of alienation, commodity fetishism, dialectical materialism, and his understanding of the formative role played by economics and the forces and the relations of production. Without Marx, and without the body of socialist theory and history to which he remains the most significant contributor, critiquing capitalism is like trying to learn how to speak without anyone to teach us. The mysteries of the present crisis will not yield themselves up to good, old-fashioned common sense; the reason we live under a capitalist system is *not* because people are greedy and weak (although people *are* greedy and weak); there are tools available for understanding, but we are afraid of them. Every nation on earth, from Europe to Asia to Central and South America to Africa, reads and discusses Marxist, socialist, and communist political theory and critical thought—except America. Marx, and the whole intellectual history of radicalism, revolution, socialism, and communism that's been buried with him (much of it American intellectual history) must be unearthed, reexplored, and come to terms with. This is not a task or privilege for scholars and academics alone; artists also need to dig in.

It's very difficult to convince people of this now. The collapse of the Soviet bloc was widely heralded as relieving us of the obligation to understand socialist theory, along with the many other blessings it has brought us—the civil war in Bosnia, the gulf war, and Zhirinovsky. It's a great thing that the Soviet bloc fell apart, it was long overdue; in part because it now frees us to examine socialism untrammeled by the need to defend its ongoing failure in Russia, a defense which ought never to have been undertaken.

Political problems are complex and can be understood only through research. History must be explored, particularly the history of the great periods of transition: the sixteenth century in France and England; the seventeenth century in Holland, when capitalism came into its own; the great age of industry and imperialism from 1860-1914; the crisis of the modernist period from 1918-1945; the sixties. Revolutions are undertheorized and approached with insufficient appreciation of the complexity and the impenetrability of great uprisings, such as the French, the Russian, and the Los Angeles.

Americans sufer from collective amnesia; our own past is lost to us. Theater has always had a vital relationship to history; the examination and, yes, the *teaching* of history has got to be accounted a function of any political theater.

At the turn of the century, the lecture hall was a kind of popular theater, regularly attended by huge audiences of every class who must have believed that oratory and rhetoric were legitimate forms of entertainment, and, even more important, so was pedagogy. There was nothing mutually exclusive about being instructed and having a good time. Important political movements, grassroots populism and anarchism, for example, were chiefly disseminated and promulgated in lecture halls. There has been a falling off; all that is left of the Theater of Ideas is scientology, and

Americans reject the pedagogical function of theater. If it wants to teach something, it had better make sure that it never gets caught in the act. Our aversion to education in the theater is hardly surprising, considering how boring, unsensual, and worthless most American education is. People become allergic to the learning process. Theater people share this allergy with their audiences.

People who make political theater are told that they're preaching only to the converted. The converted need preaching to as much as the unconverted, and will usually prove far more responsive and interested in change. The preaching-to-the-converted line is invoked to deplore the ostensible uselessness and solipsism of political art, which will frequently draw its audience from the left rather than the right. It's a line predicated on an entirely false notion of how the struggle works and who is doing the struggling. Good political theater asks complicated questions; it explores; it doesn't offer simple dogma. Those who are involved in the struggle to change the world need art that assists in examining the issues at hand, which are usually incredibly complex. A good preacher is essential to any faith, and all the more essential to a nonhierarchical, pluralistic faith. The converted have a lot to think about.

It is immensely difficult, if not impossible, to write a play intended to enter into public discourse that is free of any reference to current event, to news. It's hard to understand why anyone would want to. There's an old fantasy that if one writes a play void of any reference to the world in which we live, void of all reference to political parties, to popular culture, to money and to global conflict, one will be producing something more able to gliding through this present distasteful moment and up into that hyperborean realm toward which, we are told, all artists aspire: eternity, universality, immortality—the canon. Nothing seems plainer to me than that the work that has attained such status was not designed to do so, but rather came out of the *urgent now*; that any such universality as a work may claim must proceed from its particulars to the general, and that art that strives for universality winds up being generic, and dull; and also, finally, that eternity is a very long time, and immortality almost certainly an impossibility.

Artists use their private, unconscious lives as fodder for artistic creation. Problems arise when our unconscious isn't politically correct, and whose is? This is a real dilemma, but I believe that people shouldn't feel safe in putting unmediated fantasy onstage. Unmediated fantasy, granted, has a kind of nightmarish magnetism, but it's probably less magnetic to others than it is to you. Take cold showers, read a few books, and remember that in the real world people who act out their private fantasies are frequently called insane.

Theater, including political theater, without private fantasy doesn't exist, and it would be absolutely no fun to watch if it did. The membrane separating the political and the personal is permeable, as I've said, and the greatest critical thinkers invariably resort to a prose bordering on poetry in trying to untangle the knotty problems of existence. We can't make good politics without access to our souls. Clarity helps; we will have more luck in the struggle between what we would like to be and what we are if we don't lose sight of what we are.

Theater that isn't entertaining isn't worth doing. Theater that's explicitly political has to be *very* entertaining and *very* well done or it will be *very* easily dismissed. If we do political theater, theater that will be perceived as political, that addresses political issues or addresses issues politically, we are starting out with one big strike against us. We will have to be better than most, not just as good as. When people see a family psychodrama that doesn't work, they say "This play didn't work." When they see a play about unionism in the 1980s that doesn't work, they will say "I hate political theater." We can't afford to be mediocre.

The theater of images probably isn't enough. I can't see how it's possible to do political theater that's as subtle and complex as it needs to be without words. People's aural attention span is, at this point in history, terminally brief. I don't know what to do about that, but I know it's a *big* problem, and not one that should be solved by avoidance, by serving up pictures without words, or with the barest minimum possible. Images are important, but words are at the barricades. Images are ambiguous, offer shelter from certain meaning. Words will pin us down, positionally. Structuralist and post-structuralist theories about the flow and unfixity of meaning are useful, certainly, and are all too infrequently examined by theater practitioners, but even given a field of uncertainty surrounding every word we utter, words limit the possible number of meanings to a few generally agreed upon and hence are irreplaceable if we actually want to say something.

Theater frequently winds up being about theater as much as it's about anything else. Theater about theater has political value. The way in which we, as artists, impact upon and change our profession and our art is important, though not really as important as stopping the bombing in Sarajevo or getting affordable health care. Or getting Newt Gingrich out of Congress. Or Trent Lott. Or Jesse Helms. Or practically *every* Republican politician. But I digress. There is a line past which activism is demanded rather than acting. But if acting is what you do well, then you should do it, and try to make it as valuable, which is to say as socially and politically informed, as possible. Anyone in the theater who cares about the world will spend his or her life on the horns of this predicament. Brecht confessed to Walter Benjamin that, if asked by a heavenly tribunal whether he cared more about the world or the theater, he'd probably have to say the theater. The story makes sense; he wouldn't have been as great as he was if he'd answered otherwise. Being an artist takes up a lot of time and energy. The processes of art are slow, and not particularly in sync with the faster-pulsing processes of the real world. But the demands of art can easily become excuses for inaction.

When the time comes to march, I hope I'll fall in step, even if I'm in tech with first preview only two days away. I worry about a life spent imagining life, about the necessary removal from life that art entails. Sometimes I feel Plato was right to banish poets from the Republic: artists spend their lives weaving truth into artifice; even the greatest have only succeeded in making great artifice, and although there's something glorious about that, art's an activity that can, when viewed in the proper lighting, look a bit sleazy.

* * *

Queernation, a group born out of ACT UP and the AIDS militant movement, but directed primarily at issues of lesbian and gay enfranchisement and power, used to have a slogan: "We're here, we're queer, we're fabulous, get used to it." "Fabulous" became a popular word in the queer community. It was never *un*popular, but for a while it became a battle cry. "FABULOUS!" It was part of a new queer politics, carnival and camp, aggressively fruity, celebratory, and tough as a street-wise drag queen. "Fabulous" was roughly the gay equivalent of that undefinable, ineffable thing young black people used to identify as soul, and perhaps now identify as "badness"—which Jews identify as *menschlichkeit*. If you possess it, you don't need to ask what it is; when you attempt to delineate it, you move away from it. "Fabulousness" is one of those words which provide a measure of the degree to which a person or event manifests a particular oppressed culture's most distinctive, invigorating feature.

What are the salient features of fabulousness? Irony. Tragic history. Defiance. Gender-fuck. Glitter. Drama. It is not butch. It is not hot—the cathexis surrounding fabulousness is not necessarily erotic. Fabulous is not delimited by age or beauty. Style has a dialectical relationship to physical reality. The body is the Real. Style is Theater. The raw materials are reworked into illusion. For style to be truly fabulous, one must completely triumph over tragedy, age, physical insufficiencies, and just as important, one's audiences must be made aware of the degree of transcendence, of triumph: must see both the triumph and that over which the triumph has been made. In this the magic of the fabulous is precisely the magic of the theater. The wires show. The illusion is always incomplete, inadequate; the work behind the magic is meant to be appreciated.

I'm gay and identify myself most strongly within the homosexual community and as a gay theater artist. I see the work I do as part of a movement of people who are similarly identified, and who, I have begun to suspect, are making the next chapter in the history of American gay theater, which has at times been intimately linked to American theater period, and has become increasingly distinct. Our antecedent is Charles Ludlam, who died of AIDS in the early '80s, and who was, in addition to being the funniest man who ever lived and a brilliant consumer and regurgitator of theatrical style and legend, the founder and chief arbitrator of the Theater of the Ridiculous.

The Ridiculous as a category is brilliantly defined by Ludlam in his manifesto: the Theater of the Ridiculous, Scourge of Human Folly, with such maxims as "You are a living mockery of your own ideals: either that, or your ideals are too low." The Ridiculous, with its roots stretching back into the 1950s, became the first openly gay aesthetic. For me its defining moment was not a theatrical one but rather the political act that began the modern gay liberation movement, the Stonewall Riots, which took place on the night of Judy Garland's funeral in 1969, and which was begun in a spirit of both rage and parody, as drag queens, consciously and with considerable irony, hurled bricks and abuse at cops in imitation, even parodic imitation, of the Black Panthers, chanting "Gay is good!" as the queer version of "Black is beautiful!" At the threshold of community, of liberation, at the threshold of transforming closet drama from tragedy into comedy (a step beyond Genet because it's funnier) homosexuals learned the essential strategy of divesting ourselves of furtiveness. We have dragged—and I do mean dragged—the trappings of the underworld, the demimonde onto the avenues in broad daylight, and yet we aren't yet capable of seeing ourselves as subjects. We are ridiculous; we are the mirror of the larger ridiculousness that is the world; and yet we are ridiculous, not yet able to take ourselves quite seriously enough. Certain locutions are forbidden the Ridiculous because they collapse the distance irony provides between pain and its articulate expression, a distance which can be safely collapsed only after coming into real power, when hopes, even remote hopes of redress are at hand.

The tensions between the comic and the serious: taking ourselves too seriously, we cease to be gay. Becoming subjects cannot mean becoming unfabulous; becoming people must mean becoming gay people, not straightmen. Becoming humorless, we lose connection to the most vital parts of our culture (my fear, for instance, that this piece is too dour and sour and will fail to get me a date). The Fabulous incorporates the ridiculous. It is the next step, not a rejection. It is a necessary corrective to the dead earnestness of the butch, corporate, gay Republican assimilationist camp, if you pardon the expression. The Fabulous is the assertively Camp camp, the rapturous embrace of difference, the discovering of self not in that which has rejected you but in that which makes you unlike, and disliked, and Other.

The Fabulous is the recovery of the power of the Bakhtinian, the magic of the grotesque, the carnivalesque: politics as carnival, as Halloween, as theater. We can see this in the amphibious nature of the gay pride parade, simultaneously angry demonstration, identity assertion, and Mardi Gras. In part fabulousness is a bestowing of power by merely believing in it; if I dress like a nun I become invested. And this is true. I would rather be blessed by Sister Dementia Praecox than by Cardinal O'Connor. Art is like this. There's nothing there, but that nothing has power; it grows to something of great constancy, but howsoever strange and admirable.

If we are moving from a Theater of the Ridiculous to a Theater of the Fabulous, I would guess that this development also has something to do with telling stories, of having arrived as a community with a history—of both oppression and liberation. We are now fabulous in part because we are fabulists, fabled, organized, and powerful enough to have the luxury to begin to examine the past and interpret it. And to pass it along to our descendants, openly. For homosexuals to work to create a history is for us to say that there will be those who come after—to say to the straight world, some of your children will be queer.

And the Fabulous is interested in exploring magic, the spirit, the soul, which the iron irony of the Ridiculous could do only in sidelong glances. In part this magic has the same pedigree as Shakespeare's, as Brecht's, as Marx's, in the uneasy relationship between the real and the imaginary, in which human activity plays a mediational role between the material and the ideal. Marx writes: "We ground consciousness in life activity, in social being," all too familiar an idea to closet cases and proud drag queens alike. Marx also writes: "In direct contrast to German philosophy, which descends from heaven to earth, here we ascend from earth to heaven." Which is *divine*, which is what queers have been exclaiming, performing, enunciating in a thousand thrilling, discomforting, fabulous ways since oppression and resistance created us. And I suspect, for identity-based politics and a politics of sexuality and gender, as well as for all progressive politics of the left, the millennium is at hand and the time has come to reconsider the rationalist basis of our political theories, not to leap dumbly into some ersatz New Age, but to begin to explore the role of faith, prayer, and soul in a politics that is concerned, as ours must be, with irreparable loss, with community and with the sacrifices community entails, and with the most difficult and necessary thing of all, hope.

Great, bewildering changes are afoot. This is a period of transition; it makes contradictory sense or none at all sometimes. In 1992 the country decided to try to address the consequences of a thirteen-years-and-longer betrayal of everything fundamentally decent and hope-providing in American history and American constitutional democracy. The forty percent of our population that is reliably progressive, civic-minded, farsighted and fair, having had enough of the Reagan counterrevolution, elected an administration mandated to push forward a program that could, with luck, get us back at least to where we'd arrived by the 1960s—and then maybe go further. AIDS, breast cancer, the increasingly toxic environment and the failing national health had awakened an appetite for federal intervention in our outrageous health-care problems; and one had hoped this might in turn remind the nation of the usefulness of federally funded social programs, against poverty, for education, for creating work and rebuilding the crumbling infrastructure, and the crumbling economy.

But today there is everywhere a recrudescence of Reaganism in its '90s version, Forrest Gumpism, aka "It hurts to think"—of which the 104th Congress was a particularly nightmarish incarnation. The 105th Congress promises nothing in the way of improvement. The right is in trouble, but it will also certainly continue to be trouble, always dependably its meanest and most perverse when it feels itself losing its grip on power. And it has already gained so much ground. Enfranchisement and pluralism and multiculturalism are derided as "quota-mongering," the growing pains of democracy are successfully deplored and derided by the right as the birth of a culture of victimology and complaint. The shelves of our bookstores are groaning under the weight of the thousand-and-one newly published defenses mounted on behalf of the canon, for the purpose, ultimately, of perpetuating exclusion and marginalization, and all at a time when urban city schools are war zones, with fifty kids to a class, offering no art instruction or science labs or individualized attention; at a time when there is nearly no affordable quality public higher education, and the lives of our citizens are sacrificed to a new passion for balanced budgets and an old passion for slashing the taxes of the rich.

We have entered into an age the politics of which I like to call neo-barbaric, in that the previously unassailable fundamentals of civilization, of community, are under attack, and logic, causality, even coherent narrative are gone. Every dreary speech of the last presidential campaign, every inarticulate senator and representative we tune in on declaiming on C-SPAN; every line of clotted, pinched prose in the Savonarola-screeds penned by justices like Rehnquist and Scalia, serve to degrade an already dangerously degraded level of public discourse and literacy; the Big Lie is back too—a surefire warning sign of fascism. The third wave of the revolution that was the backlash against the sea changes of the sixties has arrived in Washington; the *freikorps* commandos of Iran-Contra/Reaganism are now firmly in control of Congress. Today it seems to me that if the angel of the apocalypse has in fact appeared, in time for the millennium, it isn't shaped like a pillar or wheel of fire or a multi-winged trumpeting seraph; its form is the balanced budget. The world ending these days is figured in the appalling spectacle of the world's people believing that all the money in the planet has vanished somehow, the world's peoples preparing accordingly, not for a grand opera of dark flood waters inundating and miracle cities shining atop clouded hills, of clashing armies of angels and demons, but rather for an endless winter dwindling, which no one believes any of us will ultimately survive; scarcity, not deluge and catastrophe, is the apocalypse. If paradise arrives it will be pricey, impermanent, and exclusively for the wealthy (and probably located on one of those Microsoft islands near Seattle). The *Dies Irae* is looming as the fate of the poor, the marginal, the immigrant, the refugee, the disenfranchised, the vulnerable. We are in terrible trouble. We must watch out.

It seems to me that the usual assumptions and expectations may be less reliable than they have been in the past, and this is exciting and scary. I believe that the secrets of theater—that a life lived at play is preferable to a life lived in drudgery; that things are not always what they seem to be; that the unpredictability and vibrancy of actual human presence contains an inimitable power and a subversive potential; that there is an impurity, a fluidity at the core of existence—these secrets speak to the liberationist, revolutionary agenda of our day. I continue to believe in the usefulness, and effectiveness, of this increasingly marginalized profession and art. But I believe that for theater, as for anything in life, its hope for survival rests in its ability to take a reading of the times, and change.

MILLENNIUM APPROACHES

PERFORMANCE REVIEWS

Frank Rich (review date 5 May 1993)

SOURCE: "Embracing All Possibilities in Art and Life," in *The New York Times*, 5 May 1993, pp. C 15-16.

[*In the following review of the New York production of* Millennium Approaches, *Rich declares the play "a true American work in its insistence on embracing all possibilities in art and life."*]

"History is about to crack open," says Ethel Rosenberg, back from the dead, as she confronts a cadaverous Roy Cohn, soon to die of AIDS, in his East Side town house. "Something's going to give," says a Brooklyn housewife so addicted to Valium she thinks she is in Antarctica. The year is 1985. It is 15 years until the next millennium. And a young man drenched in death fevers in his Greenwich Village bedroom hears a persistent throbbing, a thunderous heartbeat, as if the heavens were about to give birth to a miracle so that he might be born again.

This is the astonishing theatrical landscape, intimate and epic, of Tony Kushner's *Angels in America,* which made its much-awaited Broadway debut at the Walter Kerr Theater last night. This play has already been talked about so much that you may feel you have already seen it, but believe me, you haven't, even if you actually have. The new New York production is the third I've seen of *Millennium Approaches,* as the first, self-contained, three-and-a-half-hour part of *Angels in America* is titled. (Part 2, *Perestroika,* is to join it in repertory in the fall.) As directed with crystalline lucidity by George C. Wolfe and ignited by blood-churning performances by Ron Leibman and Stephen Spinella, this staging only adds to the impression that Mr. Kushner has written the most thrilling American play in years.

Angels in America is a work that never loses its wicked sense of humor or its wrenching grasp on such timeless dramatic matters as life, death and faith even as it ranges through territory as far-flung as the complex, plague-ridden nation Mr. Kushner wishes both to survey and to address.

Subtitled "A Gay Fantasia on National Themes," the play is a political call to arms for the age of AIDS, but it is no polemic. Mr. Kushner's convictions about power and justice are matched by his conviction that the stage, and perhaps the stage alone, is a space large enough to accommodate everything from precise realism to surrealistic hallucination, from black comedy to religious revelation. In *Angels in America,* a true American work in its insistence on embracing all possibilities in art and life, he makes the spectacular case that they can all be brought into fusion in one play.

At center stage, *Angels* is a domestic drama, telling the story of two very different but equally troubled young New York couples, one gay and one nominally heterosexual, who intersect by chance. But the story of these characters soon proves inseparable from the way Mr. Kushner tells it. His play opens with a funeral led by an Orthodox rabbi and reaches its culmination with what might be considered a Second Coming. In between, it travels to Salt Lake City in search of latter-day saints and spirals into dreams and dreams-within-dreams where the languages spoken belong to the minority American cultures of drag and jazz. Hovering above it all is not only an Angel (Ellen McLaughlin) but also an Antichrist, Mr. Leibman's Roy Cohn, an unreconstructed right-wing warrior who believes that "life is full of horror" from which no one can escape.

While Cohn is a villain, a hypocritical closet case and a corrupt paragon of both red-baiting and Reagan-era greed, his dark view of life is not immediately dismissed by Mr. Kushner. The America of *Angels in America* is riddled with cruelty. When a young WASP esthete named Prior Walter (Mr. Spinella) reveals his first lesions of Kaposi's sarcoma to his lover of four years, a Jewish clerical worker named Louis Ironson (Joe Mantello), he finds himself deserted in a matter of weeks. Harper Pitt (Marcia Gay Harden), pill-popping housewife and devout Mormon, has recurrent nightmares that a man with a knife is out to kill her; she also has real reason to fear that the man is her husband, Joe (David Marshall Grant), an ambitious young lawyer with a dark secret and aspirations to rise high in Ed Meese's Justice Department.

But even as Mr. Kushner portrays an America of lies and cowardice to match Cohn's cynical view, he envisions another America of truth and beauty, the paradise imagined by both his Jewish and Mormon characters' ancestors as they made their crossing to the new land. *Angels in America* not only charts the split of its two central couples but it also implicitly sets its two gay men with AIDS against each other in a battle over their visions of the future. While the fatalistic, self-loathing Cohn ridicules gay men as political weaklings with "zero clout" doomed to defeat, the younger, equally ill Prior sees the reverse. "I am a gay man, and I am used to pressure," he says from his sick bed. "I am tough and strong." Possessed by scriptural visions he describes as "very Steven Spielberg" even when in abject pain, Prior is Mr. Kushner's prophet of hope in the midst of apocalypse.

Though Cohn and Prior never have a scene together, they are the larger-than-life poles between which all of *Angels in America* swings. And they could not be more magnetically portrayed than they are in this production. Mr. Leibman, red-faced and cackling, is a demon of Shakespearean grandeur, an alternately hilarious and terrifying mixture of chutzpah and megalomania, misguided brilliance and relentless cunning. He turns the mere act of punching telephone buttons into a grotesque manipulation of the levers of power, and he barks out the most outrageous pronouncements ("I brought out something tender in him," he says of Joe McCarthy) with a shamelessness worthy of history's most indelible monsters.

Mr. Spinella is a boyish actor so emaciated that when he removes his clothes for a medical examination, some in the audience gasp. But he fluently conveys buoyant idealism and pungent drag-queen wit as well as the piercing, open-mouthed cries of fear and rage that arrive with the graphically dramatized collapse of his health. Mr. Spinella is also blessed with a superb acting partner in Mr. Mantello, who as his callow lover is a combustible amalgam of puppyish Jewish guilt and self-serving intellectual piety.

The entire cast, which includes Kathleen Chalfant and Jeffrey Wright in a variety of crisply observed comic cameos, is first rate. Ms. Harden's shattered, sleepwalking housewife is pure pathos, a figure of slurred thought, voice and emotions, while Mr. Grant fully conveys the internal warfare of her husband, torn between Mormon rectitude and uncontrollable sexual heat. When Mr. Wolfe gets both of the play's couples on stage simultaneously to enact their parallel, overlapping domestic crackups, *Angels in America* becomes a wounding fugue of misunderstanding and recrimination committed in the name of love.

But *Angels in America* is an ideal assignment for Mr. Wolfe because of its leaps beyond the bedroom into the fabulous realms of myth and American archetypes, which have preoccupied this director and playwright in such works as *The Colored Museum* and *Spunk*. Working again with Robin Wagner, the designer who was an essential collaborator on *Jelly's Last Jam*, Mr. Wolfe makes the action fly through the delicate, stylized heaven that serves as the evening's loose scenic environment, yet he also manages to make some of the loopier scenes, notably those involving a real-estate agent in Salt Lake City and a homeless woman in the South Bronx, sharper and far more pertinent than they have seemed before.

What has really affected *Angels in America* during the months of its odyssey to New York, however, is not so much its change of directors as Washington's change of Administrations. When first seen a year or so ago, the play seemed defined by its anger at the reigning political establishment, which tended to reward the Roy Cohns and ignore the Prior Walters. Mr. Kushner has not revised the text since—a crony of Cohn's still boasts of a Republican lock on the White House until the year 2000—but the shift in Washington has had the subliminal effect of making *Angels in America* seem more focused on what happens next than on the past.

This is why any debate about what this play means or does not mean for Broadway seems, in the face of the work itself, completely beside the point. *Angels in America* speaks so powerfully because something far larger and more urgent than the future of the theater is at stake. It really is history that Mr. Kushner intends to crack open. He sends his haunting messenger, a spindly, abandoned gay man with a heroic spirit and a ravaged body, deep into the audience's heart to ask just who we are and just what, as the plague continues and the millennium approaches, we intend this country to become.

Linda Winer (review date 5 May 1993)

SOURCE: "Pulitzer-Winning 'Angels' Emerges from the Wings," in *New York Newsday*, 5 May 1993.

[*In this review, Winer asserts that* Angels in America *is "a fierce and wonderful play— uncompromising and compassionate, unflinchingly partisan and intensely well-informed, as intimate and entertaining as it is monumental and spiritual."*]

The Angel has landed, at long last. In the final moment of *Angels in America,* she and her big fluffy wings came crashing through the ceiling into the bedroom of a dying man with AIDS. "Greetings, prophet!" she proclaimed to the shocked, emaciated figure on the bed. "The great work begins!"

Actually, it had begun three-and-a-half hours earlier.

Tony Kushner's Pulitzer Prize-winning gay epic, which opened at the Walter Kerr Theater last night after probably the longest foreplay in Broadway history, is a fierce and wonderful play—uncompromising and compassionate, unflinchingly partisan and intensely well-informed, as intimate and entertaining as it is monumental and spiritual.

But first, a correction: It's important to note that this is only *half* a fierce and wonderful play. The second half, subtitled *Perestroika,* is being reworked and won't open until the fall, when the two massive chunks will be available in repertory to tear us apart and, we hope, put us back together. This first part, *Millennium Approaches,* is engrossing and devastating by itself, but leaves basic relationships unresolved, motives undefined, questions tantalizingly unanswered.

Thus, in addition to all the other new and dangerous provocations this fearless work brings to safe old Broadway, we now have a cliffhanger that will leave us dangling for months. With a lesser work, nobody would remember. With this one, we cannot forget.

As careful readers may have guessed by now, ***Angels in America, A Gay Fantasia on National Themes: Millennium Approaches*** has not been crushed by the hype and acclaim that tailed it from London to the Los Angeles production at the Mark Taper Forum last November. It is a pleasure to report that those two words—eagerly anticipated—which had begun to seem permanently grafted on a title that didn't need any extra weight, did not oversell it.

It's also a relief to see that director George C. Wolfe, hired after the Taper opening to fix the Oskar Eustis production that many of us didn't think was broken, got it right. Ron Leibman's justly acclaimed Roy Cohn is still staggering proof of the seductive appeal of nonstop evil. Stephen Spinella and Joe Mantello still take your breath away as Prior Walter, the flamboyant AIDS-racked WASP, and Louis, the liberal angst-racked Jewish lover who abandons him.

Wolfe has made three cast changes—one even exchange (Jeffrey Wright as the gay nurse / former drag queen Belize) and two improvements (Marcia Gay Harden and David Marshall Grant as the troubled young Mormon couple). Wolfe reblocked the 30-odd scenes to fit the sleek new Robin Wagner scenery, fine-tuned the already harrowing performances for a bit more warmth and away from some of the easier laughs. He also left enough of the L.A. production alone that the omission of any mention of Eustis in the credits seems impolite, if not unjust.

And justice is very much on Kushner's mind, both as indictment of the Republican years and atonement for our moral unraveling before the apocalypse. Set in 1985, smack into Reagan / Bush and 15 years before the Big 2000, "Angels" uses gay life and AIDS as the eye of a storm that has all the raw destruction and promise of an end-of-the-century myth.

Kushner uses a huge canvas, but a very delicate brush. This is a play of big ideas—politics, religion, love, responsibility and the struggle between staying put and our need to move, preferably forward. Kushner likes to drop everyday people into hallucinations, fever dreams, and stage magic that looks home-made and awesome at the same time. Kushner likes to name names—Joe McCarthy, the Reagan kids, Jeane Kirkpatrick—and he likes characters who have opinions on everything, from American racism to the hole in the ozone, from Ed Meese to medieval history.

And, yet, this heretofore almost unknown playwright is such a delightful, luscious, funny writer that, for all the political rage and the scathing unsanitized horror, the hours zip by with the breezy enjoyment of a great page-turner or a popcorn movie.

Eight actors play 20 characters, who, despite the scope of the discourse, never come together in groups larger than duets or the occasional trio. Every so often, two different couples play out their scenes as if in split-screen cinema, and sometimes one character's drug trip intersects with someone else's dementia.

We start with a solo in the Bronx, an old rabbi delivering a eulogy over the casket of an old immigrant he didn't know, musing on the ancient culture she brought on her back, about the "great voyage" we cross every day because of her and her dying breed, in the "melting pot where nothing melted." It's a beautiful, sardonic monologue, which sets the stage for the broad vision, the sense of loss and the sense of humor to follow.

From there, we meet the rest—friends, lovers, but mostly unlike types whose lives overlap in surprising but eerily logical ways. There is Harper, the depressed agoraphobic Mormon wife with a Valium addiction, and Joe, her straight-arrow Republican lawyer husband, trying to deny his homosexuality.

There's Louis, an over-educated word processer at Joe's circuit court, who worries some of Kushner's most passionate and hilarious moral dilemmas into the ground, but cannot endure the "vomit and sores and disease" that challenge our American belief in the constant historical progress toward happiness. Faced with Prior's purple spots and diarrhea, Louis bolts.

And then there is Cohn, the omnivorous right-wing power-broker and closet gay, trying to recruit young idealistic Joe to fix the disbarment case against him—and denying he has AIDS because "homosexuals are people with zero clout." Leibman, in the bravura role of his career, starts out in a cadenza, working the phones in multiple conversations, and, just when you think Leibman is so over-the-top he'll turn into Jerry Lewis, he finds even darker corners.

As for the other actors peopling this vast universe, Grant has just the right combination of boyishness and rigidity as the struggling Joe, Harden does wonders with the clingy, mad-housewife role that seemed impossibly irritating in L.A., though even Harden can't make those imaginary trips with Mr. Lies, her fantasy travel agent, work. Kathleen Chalfant is so perfect as Joe's Mormon mother and as the ghost of Ethel Rosenberg that we forgive her weak rabbi and physician, and Wright is a lovely combination of endearing and no-nonsense as Belize.

Spinella is unforgettable as the ravaged but still ironic Prior, so long-boned and thin we feel we could fold him up and slide him under the door. Mantello gets the best speeches and has to do the most hateful things, all with lovable charm. Ellen McLaughlin's angel is suitably angelic in one of Toni-Leslie James' graceful costumes, and Wagner's sets, with its computerized moving panels, keeps things simple without shortchanging the special effects.

There were some boos at the end of the preview I attended, and we can only guess why. Maybe the mainstream Broadway audience was shocked, maybe somebody was related to Jeane Kirkpatrick, maybe somebody yearned for Cohn's deferred dream of a Republican presidency and Supreme Court forever. Or, maybe, someone just didn't want to have to wait until fall to find out how this important story ends. This, we understand.

John Simon (review date 17 May 1993)

SOURCE: "Of Wings and Webs," in *New York* Magazine, Vol. 26, No. 20, 17 May 1993, pp. 102-03.

[*Although he admires* Millennium Approaches, *Simon finds the work truncated and incomplete without its second half,* Perestroika.]

How nice it would be to have stumbled upon *Angels in America* on some far-off stage in London or Los Angeles, unencumbered by the hurrahing heralds of "Genius!" or the demurring trumpeters of "Trumpery!" One could then have mused, "Who would have imagined that Tony Kushner, the author of the grandiosely vacuous *A Bright Room Called Day,* would make such progress? At least now he is writing from the inside out rather than, wrongly, the reverse." But before we elevate *Angels in America* to the rank of masterpiece, we must ponder both its surtitle and its subtitle.

The surtitle, *A Gay Fantasia on National Themes*, should remind us that this effort to be national or ecumenical is, after all, a minority report. Not so much a minority of one, which the true artist always rightly is, as a minority of one percent (if we espouse the latest official figure) or 5 to 10 (the proposed counterfigures for homosexuals in America), which is both too much and too little. It is dangerous for the playwright to speak chiefly and tendentiously for such a social minority. And the subtitle, *Millennium Approaches,* literally a reference to the year 2000, should alert us to the second half of *Angels,* entitled *Perestroika,* still only approaching, as it is being revised by the author for an autumn opening. When we have both parts in tandem or in repertory, we shall be better able to determine whether the American theater has achieved a milestone, an artistic millennium, or just another, longer and more pretentious, *Jeffrey.*

Angels, Part One, is an attempt to encapsulate the Reagan-Bush era in the story of two families or quasi-families. One is the Mormon and seemingly heterosexual couple, Joe and Harper Pitt—joined later by Joe's mother, Hannah—who come east from Utah, to play out a kind of return of the pioneers to New York and Washington. The other is the more complicated ménage of Louis Ironson and Prior Walter, a homosexual couple, in which Prior falls prey to AIDS, and Louis to cowardice. Louis, a clerical worker, drifts, like Joe, into the orbit of Roy Cohn, the play's devil figure (although Mr. Lies, the spirit of drugs and thus a fake travel agent, is another, lesser, one). Cohn aspires to crooked control of New York, Washington, and the country by creating a fake family of filial acolytes, who are to be his spies and agents in the centers of power. He is, moreover, so evil as to deny his homosexuality and AIDS.

To complement the eastward journey of the Mormons (significantly known as Latter-day Saints), there are two westward journeys: that of Louis's ancestors, the European

Jews, one of whose last true representatives, a grandmother, is eulogized at start of play as (significantly for Kushner's thirst for ecumenism) the Last of the Mohicans. And that of Prior's Anglo ancestors, ghosts who go west to haunt their scion, although his business is really with the future, with the angel of death and the afterlife—perhaps even God, the good father, unlike Roy, the bad one.

But it is too early to talk extensively and conclusively about a play that, however long, is only half a play. To be sure, it is also unfair to open such a half-play without its second part, especially when one hears from the West what a mess *Perestroika* was there. So, are the Salt Lake City real-estate agent and the Bronx bag woman, who now seem obtrusive danglers, essential to the grand plan? Are Harare's Valium-induced gibberings about Antarctica and the ozone layer germane to what follows? Are those biblical references—Lazarus resurrected, Jacob and the angel—to become properly integrated symbols? And, apropos integration, will the black homosexual Belize and his argument with the Jewish Louis give rise to a reconciliation of blacks and Jews? Will, as the title *Perestroika* implies, Europe join America in the action? Will the fact that some male roles are played by a woman assume valid meaning? Tune in next fall.

George C. Wolfe has directed with almost too much inventiveness, while Robin Wagner's scenery and Jules Fisher's lighting perform what they are supposed to—miracles. Only the costumes and music fall rather short. Ron Leibman is more Roy Cohn that Cohn himself ever was, even though many of his lines are (unacknowledgedly) taken directly from Cohn's dicta. Joe Mantello is properly slippery as Louis—all honor to Kushner for not making his alter ego more appealing. As Prior, the excellent Stephen Spinella is spindliness incarnate (or disincarnate), the most frighteningly real onstage AIDS patient; I hope this good actor doesn't starve himself for his craft. Good, too, are David Marshall Grant as a saint uneasily heading for the gay life, and Jeffrey Wright as a philosophical black drag queen.

Marcia Gay Harden's Harper is a lot less moving than she might be; Ellen McLaughlin and Kathleen Chalfant truly manage only one role each, though the variety demanded from them may be excessive. The two most important things about *Angels in America* are both good news and bad. The good is that, for all its three and a half hours, the play doesn't ever bore you; the bad is that it is unfinished, and that it is hard to see how Kushner—or anyone—could pull such far-flung ambitions, such heterogeneous though homosexual strands together into one tightly knit, ravelproof whole.

Robert Brustein (review date 24 May 1993)

SOURCE: "Angles in America," in *The New Republic*, Vol. 208, No. 21, 24 May 1993, pp. 29-31.

[*In the review below, Brustein, despite some reservations, judges* Angels in America *"the authoritative achievement of a radical dramatic artist with a fresh, clear voice."*]

Tony Kushner's **Angels in America**—or rather the first of its two parts, **Millennium Approaches**—may very well be the most highly publicized play in American theater history. It is certainly one of the most peripatetic. Originally planned for a 1989 opening at San Francisco's Eureka Theater, then performed in full workshop at the Mark Taper in Los Angeles, later produced by the Eureka Theater in 1990, still later by the Royal National Theatre in London in early 1992, then staged along with its second part by the Mark Taper in Los Angeles in late 1992, and now mounted on Broadway after bypassing one of its scheduled sponsors (the New York Public Theater), **Angels in America** has received unanimous praise at every step in its journey.

Meanwhile its author, and latterly its Broadway director, George C. Wolfe, have been inspiring feature stories in countless newspapers and magazines. Awarded a Pulitzer Prize before it even opened in New York, the play will doubtless win multiple Tonys, the Critics Circle Prize, next year's Outer Circle Award and any other honors still being stamped by theatrical trophy factories. A hungry media machine collaborating with a desperate industry has turned the second dramatic effort of a relatively young playwright into that illusory American artifact, The Great American Play.

In short, **Angels in America** is being regarded less as a work of the imagination than as a repository of high cultural hopes and great economic expectations. And burdened with such heavy baggage, it virtually invites close scrutiny at the customs desk, which is to say, a classic critical debunking. This will surely come, but don't expect it from me. I have a few reservations about the script and more about the New York production. But for all the hype and ballyhoo, and granted that one is judging an unfinished work, I would rather join in welcoming the authoritative achievement of a radical dramatic artist with a fresh, clear voice.

Indeed, the real question is how such a dark and vaguely subversive play could win such wide critical acceptance. (Wide audience acceptance is not quite as likely.) Compare how long it took Mamet to find success on Broadway, and consider how many gifted writers such as Sam Shepard, David Rabe, Maria Irene Fornes, Christopher Durang, Wallace Shawn and Craig Lucas, among others, have still not achieved majority status.

As noted, Kushner's new play satisfies special extra-dramatic needs. More intrinsic appeals are suggested in the subtitle, "A Gay Fantasia on National Themes." **Angels in America** is, first and foremost, a work about the gay community in the Age of AIDS—an urgent and timely subject fashionable enough off-Broadway, now ripe for the mainstream. It is also a "national" (that is, political) play in the way it links the macho sexual attitudes of redneck homophobes in the '80s with those of red-baiting bullies

in the '50s. It is a "fantasia" not only in its hallucinated, dreamlike style but in the size and scope of its ambitions. (O'Neill, among others, has accustomed us to associate greatness with epic length and formal experimentation.) And it is a very personal play that distributes blame and responsibility as generously among its sympathetic gay characters as among its villains.

In short, despite its subject matter, **Angels in America** is not just another contestant in the Theater of Guilt sweepstakes. Compare it with any recent entry on the same subject and you will see how skillfully Kushner navigates between, say, the shrill accusations of Larry Kramer's *The Destiny of Me* and the soggy affirmations of William Finn's *Falsettos*. It is Kushner's balanced historical sense that helps him avoid both self-righteousness and sentimentality. His balanced style helps as well—angry but forgiving, tough-minded but warmhearted, ironic but passionate, mischievous and fantastical. Kushner is that rare American thing, an artist-intellectual, not only witty himself but the gauge by which we judge the witlessness of others. His very literate play once again makes American drama readable literature.

Kushner takes his title from one of his more memorable lines, "There are no angels in America, no spiritual past, no racial past." But if our country offers few figures of saintly virtue to satisfy our hopes for history, the author provides plenty of hallucinations, dreams, apparitions, ancestral ghosts. There is even a mute tutelary deity, garbed like a figure in a grammar-school pageant, who comes crashing through the ceiling at the conclusion of the play, to the sound of beating wings. (Sam Shepard's unfinished *War in Heaven* is about another angel who crashes onto an American landscape.)

While they are no angels, most of Kushner's characters have their positive side. What he wishes to celebrate is the joy and courage with which they explore their sexuality in a dangerous world. His main subject is how people display, discover and affirm the fact that they are gay. (Only one of his major characters isn't homosexual and she's having a nervous breakdown.) But despite Kushner's sense that America is essentially a queer nation in every sense of the phrase, his dramatis personae are a fairly representative grouping of contemporary American types: Joseph Pitt, a Mormon lawyer; Harper, his Valium-addicted wife; Louis Ironson, a Jewish computer technician; Prior Walter, his Brahmin lover now dying of AIDS; Belize, a former transvestite now turned male nurse—and Roy Cohn.

The presence of this malignant conservative icon heightens the political dimension of the play. As Joe McCarthy's former henchman, Cohn proudly assumes credit for the execution of Ethel Rosenberg (a phantom who appears near the end). But although he identifies homosexuality with subversion, he suffers from Karposi's sarcoma himself. Cohn stubbornly refuses to admit he is gay ("Roy Cohn is not a homosexual. Roy Cohn is a heterosexual man . . . who fucks around with guys"), mainly because gays have no political power. But it is another sign of Kushner's achievement that he is almost able to make this monster appealing (the warm-hearted, totally confused Joe Pitt even expresses love for him). Roy Cohn is a classical dramatic villain who remains the play's most fascinating figure, a feat worthy of Racine, who, tradition tells us, wrote his *Phédre* in order to prove he could make an audience sympathize with a criminal character.

Alternating between intellectual debates and feverish dreams, *Angels in America* lacks an animating event or action, which is a major structural flaw in such a long (three-and-a-half-hour) work. The compensation is a gallery of wonderful characters, thirty in all, played by eight actors. The pivotal figures are Cohn and Prior, two men dying of AIDS, with two other men, the married Mormon Joseph Pitt, discovering his own sexuality, and Louis, discovering his own cowardice, revolving around these contrasting poles in various attitudes of guilt and sympathy. Louis abandons Prior when his disease reaches an advanced stage, though he seeks a pickup in Central Park in punitive disregard for his own physical health. And it is Louis, deploring the marginality of gays, who reflects on the difficulty of love in a country on the edge of a serious nervous breakdown. ("In the new century, I think we will all be insane.")

This ominous premonition regarding the new century, the expectation of divine retribution, sends shivers through this play. The sense of fatality is Greek but the prediction belongs to Ibsen, who believed that "all mankind is on the wrong track" and that the ghosts of the past and the future would retaliate for all our failed ideas and broken promises. As the ghost of Ethel Rosenberg says to the dying Cohn, "History is about to break wide open. Millennium approaches." *Angels in America* foreshadows these future schisms in the form of radical and sexual strife, the failures of liberalism, the absence of a genuine indigenous culture—and at the same time, curiously, manages to offer a trace of redemption. One redemptive feature, certainly, is a strong-voiced, clear-eyed dramatic artist capable of encapsulating our national nightmares into universal art.

The good news is the play. The not so good news is the New York production. In his notes, Kushner wrote that "the play benefits from a pared-down style of presentation, with minimal scenery," though he wanted the magical effects to be "amazing." But at $65 for an orchestra ticket, it was inevitable that the physical production would be lavish. Robin Wagner's setting is made up of cold blue marbelized panels that seem appropriate only when one of the characters lands up in Antarctica. Usually the design chills an otherwise warm-blooded work. More disconcerting is the designer's literalism in displaying a New York skyline outside Roy Cohn's window and the canyons of Utah for a brief (cut-table) scene about a character moving from Salt Lake City, even glaciers and ice flows in a South Pole fantasy. And far from being amazing, the special effects could use advice from Industrial Light and Magic.

I saw the production some days before its postponed opening, and it has undoubtedly improved, but I wasn't certain that George C. Wolfe, though extraordinarily gifted as a showman, possessed the temperament to realize such a subtle play. The evening contained a few touching scenes (particularly Louis dancing with the stricken Prior at the end), but the staging often seemed more appropriate to musical comedy than to serious drama. (Two scenes played simultaneously among four characters reminded me of the Jets and Sharks chorus in *West Side Story*.)

And must of the acting lacked depth. Admittedly, the gay characters are highly theatrical (they make continuous references to Broadway shows), but if they don't possess a solid core of truthfulness, then it is hard to identify their humanity. I much admired Joe Mantello as the suffering ironist Louis Ironson, Stephen Spinella as the cadaverous Prior Walter and Ellen McLaughlin in a number of doubled roles, all from the original California cast. But many of the major characters are either too bland or too heightened to be believable. Suspended between show business and domestic business, the production lacks command, which is a shame because this is a play that requires a director as authoritative, and actors as intelligent, as the author.

As for Ron Leibman's Roy Cohn, it is clearly over the top. Leibman, who has the mouth and teeth of a barracuda and a nasalized vocal instrument that sounds like Jerry Lewis blowing a klaxon, plays the part as a Dickensian monster, shouting, screaming, barking, stabbing his finger and slapping his thighs. He's so apoplectic you fear for his health, but he carries you along by the sheer force of his personality. I couldn't help admiring his outrageous audacity, and I also liked the Restoration fop he played in one of Prior's hallucinations. (Leibman would be terrific as the brutal Manly in Wycherly's *Plain-dealer*.)

For me the central concern is not the quality of this production (there will be many more in the future), but rather how its talented author will cope with all our deadly critical embraces and still continue his creative development. To be frank, the signs thus far are not exactly promising. The moment commercial interest surfaced for *Angels in America,* there were enough personal betrayals, expedient decisions, fractured loyalties and postponed promises to confirm the playwright's conviction that there are no angels in America—only angles. The Broadway producers, risking millions on a problematic venture, are of course expected to protect their investments. But very few of the creative people involved acted with much honor in this undertaking, not the director who broke his commitment to another theater in order to take the assignment, nor the author who agreed to drop his original designer, members of the original cast and the original director (also his close friend) after *The New York Times* signaled some displeasure with the L.A. production. The decision to bypass the Public Theater may even have hastened JoAnne Akalaitis's departure.

Perhaps to compensate for all the shattered friendships and broken agreements, Kushner has insisted that Wednesday matinee tickets be sold at cheap prices (thus passing the moral debt to his producers in the form of reduced revenue). But one suspects that for all his professed loyalty to non-profit theaters and "downtown audiences," he is rationalizing for the sake of a Broadway splash. We have had enough theater history (notably, Tennessee Williams's career after *Cat on a Hot Tin Roof*, when he reluctantly allowed Kazan to soften the ending) to tell us that personal deception is not compatible with artistic development. Still, I have enough faith in Kushner's intelligence and self-knowledge (after all, he created Louis Ironson) to believe he won't deceive himself long, and may even turn this experience to creative advantage. The great theatrical subject, which O'Neill pursued all his life and only captured when he created James Tyrone, is how the bitch goddess success blights the life of the American artist. Who is presently learning more about this theme—and is more qualified to write about it—than the author of *Angels in America*?

John Lahr (review date 31 May 1993)

SOURCE: "Angels on Broadway," in *The New Yorker*, Vol. LXIX, No. 15, 31 May 1993, p. 137.

[*In the review below, Lahr argues that* Millennium Approaches, *"which is gay in subject matter and theme, is about America, about justice, about decency, and about heart."*]

"And how else should an angel land on earth but with the utmost difficulty?" Tony Kushner wrote to the cast of *Angels in America,* his saga about gay life and the politics of sexuality, when its two parts made their American première at the Mark Taper Forum, in Los Angeles, last fall. "If we are to be visited by angels we will have to call them down with sweat and strain." All the sweat and strain in transferring this ambitious epic to Broadway are now over, and its first part, *Millennium Approaches,* under the expert stewardship of the director George C. Wolfe, has landed in fine fettle at the Walter Kerr Theatre. The New York version has benefitted and borrowed from its two previous award-winning productions, at the Royal National Theatre, in London (the Evening Standard Award), and at the Taper (the Pulitzer Prize). The script is leaner, the acting dynamics are more defined, the cast is more uniformly up to the performing mark. On balance, despite casting quibbles and a reductive set, the production comes closest so far to the pulse and the depth of Kushner's gorgeous work.

The power of *Angels in America* is in the combination of Kushner's wise heart and shrewd narrative. Here, teeming with good talk and good humor, is that almost forgotten ingredient of contemporary American theatre—good story. Instead of doing "political theater," Kushner does theatre

politically. Taking its epigraph from the Stanley Kunitz poem "The Testing-Tree"—

In a murderous time
the heart breaks and breaks
and lives by breaking—

Angels in America is essentially about betrayal and how the heart learns or doesn't learn to live with loss. Louis, unable to deal with illness, abandons his lover, Prior, who has AIDS; Joe, an ambitious bisexual Mormon Republican legal clerk, abandons his dippy pill-popping wife, Harper; and the rapacious Roy Cohn abandons everybody. Within these crude parameters, Kushner has made something magical and mysterious which honors the gay community by telling a story that sets its concerns in the larger historical context of American political life. The vehicle for this thematic crossover is the hectoring, unscrupulous right-wing lawyer Roy Cohn. ("Roy Cohn is a heterosexual man, Henry, who fucks around with guys," he tells the doctor who has made the diagnosis of AIDS.) As written, Cohn is one of the great evil characters of modern American drama. In him Kushner personifies the barbarity of individualism during the Reagan years, and also the deep strain of pessimism that goes with the territory. "Love; that's a trap. Responsibility; that's a trap, too," Cohn tells Joe, whom he sees as a potential "Royboy" to pull strings for him in the Justice Department. "Like is full of horror; nobody escapes, nobody; save yourself." In transferring his incandescent performance as Cohn from California to New York, Ron Leibman has become almost Jacobean in the snarling, vigorous excess of his performance. It's a choice that is lapped up by the audience but is lamentable for the play. *Perestroika,* the second part of the saga, which centers largely on Cohn's story, is scheduled to join *Millennium Approaches* in October. By then, with any luck, both the story line and Leibman's emotional progression will have found their proper equipoise.

Otherwise, Wolfe's production is elegant and understated. Wolfe, who believes that the greatest show on earth is the sight of human beings exhibiting their feelings, has downplayed the fantastical and concentrated his considerable theatrical imagination on making every emotional moment clear and compelling. (On the two nights I visited the play, the audience rose en masse at the finale to give it a standing ovation.) Wolfe's greatest contribution to the evening is the unshowy but fine filigree work on the performances of Stephen Spinella, as the dying Prior, and Joe Mantello, as the anguished and droll Louis—performances that have grown stronger, clearer, and more subtle in the move to Broadway. Wolfe has also added David Marshall Grant as Joe, Marcia Gay Harden as Harper, and Jeffrey Wright as the retired drag queen Belize, all of whom bring a rich felt life to paradoxical personalities and keep the moral stakes of the drama high. Wolfe, who takes over as producer at the Public Theatre after this production, sees Kushner's play as a kind of watershed. "If we wanted to know what America was becoming, we used to look at the center—that which was constituted as normal, American,

Protestant, and white," he told me. "Now, if we want to know where America is and where it's going, we need to look at the fringe. The fringe is now the center. This play, which is gay in subject matter and theme, is about America, about justice, about decency, and about heart. A friend of mine has a good line—'If they're running you out of town, get in front and pretend it's a parade.' Well, now the people who were being run out of town are saying, 'We're the parade. And we're not going anywhere. So deal.'" But neither Wolfe nor Kushner practices the polemic he preaches. Instead of imposing personality on ideas, the production lets ideas emerge through Kushner's careful observation of personality.

At the beginning of **Angels in America,** a rabbi speaks over the coffin of one Sarah Ironson, who came from the shtetl to the Bronx. "You can never make that crossing that she made," he says to us. "For such Great Voyages in this world do not any more exist." But they do. Kushner has made one, and through the blessings of his great gifts of humor and empathy so do we. He brings us news of that most beautiful, divided, and unexplored country—the human heart.

PERESTOIKA

PERFORMANCE REVIEWS

Frank Rich (review date 24 November 1993)

SOURCE: "Following and Angel for a Healing Vision of Heaven on Earth," in *The New York Times*, 24 November 1993, pp. C 11, 20.

[*In this assessment of* Perestroika, *Rich considers the play "a true millennial work of art, uplifting, hugely comic and pantheistically religious in a very American style."*]

If you end the first half of an epic play with an angel crashing through a Manhattan ceiling to visit a young man ravaged by AIDS, what do you do for an encore?

If you are Tony Kushner, the author of **Angels in America,** you follow the angel up into the stratosphere, then come back home with a healing vision of heaven on Earth. **Perestroika,** the much awaited Part 2 of Mr. Kushner's "Gay Fantasia on National Themes," is not only a stunning resolution of the rending human drama of Part 1, **Millennium Approaches,** but also a true millennial work of art, uplifting, hugely comic and pantheistically religious in a very American style.

Set at once in New York City in the real plague year of 1986 and on a timeless, celestial threshold of revelation, it has the audacity to ask big questions in its opening moments: "Are we doomed? Will the past release us? Can we change? In time?" And then, even more dazzlingly, come the answers delivered in three and a half hours

of spellbinding theater embracing such diverse and compelling native legends as the Army-McCarthy hearings, the Mormon iconography of Joseph Smith and the MGM film version of *The Wizard of Oz.*

The opening questions are asked by a character who never reappears: a blind Russian man who is the world's oldest living Bloshevik. *Perestroika* is aptly titled not because it has much to do with the former Soviet Union but because it burrows into that historical moment of change when all the old orders, from Communism to Reaganism, are splintering, and no one knows what apocalypse or paradise the next millennium might bring. "How are we to proceed without theory?" asks the cross, aged Bolshevik. Not the least of Mr. Kushner's many achievements is his refusal to adhere to any theatrical or political theory. *Angels in America* expands in complexity as it moves forward, unwilling to replace gods that failed with new ones any more than it follows any textbook rules of drama.

Even so, Mr. Kushner does not neglect the intimate tales of the characters who captured the audience's imagination in Part 1. The show at the Walter Kerr Theater, where both parts will now play in repertory, is still driven by two antithetical AIDS patients, the 31-year-old free spirit Prior Walter (Stephen Spinella) and the closeted old right-wing cynic Roy Cohn (Ron Leibman). Louis Ironson (Joe Mantello), the leftist Jewish lover who deserted Prior, begins an affair with the Republican, Mormon lawyer Joe Pitt (David Marshall Grant) early in Part 2, even as Joe's wife, Harper (Marcia Gay Harden), continues to drift in a Valium-induced fantasy of Antarctica. Belize (Jeffrey Wright), the black former drag queen, turns up as Cohn's sassy hospital nurse while Joe's mother (Kathleen Chalfant), who has left Salt Lake City and now works at the Mormons' Visitor Center in New York, becomes an equally unlikely solace to Prior.

The collisions of these people are often more comic than you might expect. In classical terms, *Perestroika* is a comedy, for it brings all its characters' conflicts into more or less peaceful resolution, with much laughter along the way. When Louis and Joe go to bed, for instance, their irreconcilable political differences turn their coupling into a riotous ideological fistfight—"a sex scene in an Ayn Rand novel," in Louis's aghast summation—even though the utter selfishness of both men, guiltless conservative and guilty liberal alike, binds them closer than their knee-jerk party lines admit. When Ethel Rosenberg (Ms. Chalfant) returns from the grave to exchange wisecracks with Cohn and then say the kaddish for him, Mr. Kushner rebalances the scales of justice and revives the gallows humor of Lenny Bruce even as he blankets the scene with the reconciliatory poetic cadences of the prayer. How much more cosmically comic can you get?

Still more so, as it happens. The crux of *Perestroika* is the tying up of the greatest dangling thread from Part 1: that final-curtain arrival of the Angel who anoints Prior a prophet. As played by Ellen McLaughlin with down-to-earth puckishness, the Angel proves something of a comedian in Part 2. Up to a point. She is also, as Prior comes to realize, an angel of stasis and death. Pursuing a fever dream as vivid as the one that propelled Judy Garland to Munchkinland, Prior climbs to a heaven resembling the earthquake-shattered San Francisco of 1906. Given a red epistolary book and robe, if not red slippers, he encounters a conclave of angels on his way to deciding just what kind of prophet he will be when he returns to a home that God seems to have abandoned.

Prior's searching pilgrimage is echoed throughout *Perestroika* by the Mormon, Jewish and black characters and implicitly by their pioneer, immigrant and enslaved ancestors. As Prior journeys to heaven, so the Mormon mannequins in a wagon-train diorama come magically to life, Belize is possessed by the ghosts of Abolitionist days while Louis must wrestle with his discarded Jewishness. Only Cohn stays adamantly put, canonizing himself as "the heartbeat of modern conservatism" even as he consigns Henry Kissinger and George Schulz to history's dustbin along with the more expected names on his enemies' list.

It takes an artist of Mr. Kushner's talent and empathic powers to elevate Cohn, a mere scoundrel in real life, into a villain of such wit and cunning that he becomes mesmerizing theatrical company. Mr. Leibman, his face ashen, his eyes rimmed in red, his stooped posture wrapped in a demonic green robe, plays him with savage grandeur in *Perestroika,* as a sweaty pulp of rage and hatred and blasted nerves. A whirligig of malevolence, he barks "Find the vein, you moron!" to Belize one moment, then blackmails Iran-contra conspirators for a supply of AZT the next. As always, his telephone serves as an extra appendage—his last word in *Angels in America,* like his first, is "Hold!"—but now the cord is entwined with the many tubes of his illness. This does not stop Mr. Leibman, in an absolutely terrifying scene, from ripping loose of his IV, his poisoned blood spurting everywhere to make one last hypocritical plea that Joe, his gay protégé, return to his heterosexual marriage.

This patient from hell notwithstanding, George C. Wolfe, the director, and Robin Wagner, the designer, have slightly lowered the temperature of *Angels* for its second half, as befits a text in which hallucinations overwhelm any quarrelsome domestic or political reality. Much of the action takes place in a cool, dark limbo that, as lighted by Jules Fisher and flecked with jazz by the composer Anthony Davis, both captures the literal setting (largely New York City during a spring rain) and conveys the pregnant end-of-millennium mood. The roles that grow markedly in Part 2—Mr. Wright's agent provocateur of a nurse, Ms. Chalfant's no-nonsense yet strangely comforting matriarch and especially Mr. Grant's Joe—are beautifully rendered. Like the impressive Mr. Mantello, Mr. Grant has an unusual knack for finding humor and shading in a character whose self-righteousness is matched only by his callousness to a partner in desperate need.

Yet the heart of the play is Prior Walter, as acted by the extraordinary Mr. Spinella. "I'm not a prophet," he protests early in Part 2. "I'm a sick, lonely man." Deserted by his lover, thin to the point of emaciation, covered with the lesions of Kaposi's sarcoma, Prior is the one who must bear the weight of the future on his slender shoulders. While Mr. Spinella looks like God's avenger in the quasi-clerical black cape and hood he wears for much of the evening, his performance is the opposite of Mr. Leibman's Cohn. He is beyond anger.

"The worst thing about being sick in America is you are booted out of the parade," Cohn says. Prior, who has an "addiction to being alive" refuses to be booted. He wants to "live past hope," he tells the angel of death. "I want more life." Appropriately, *Angels in America* is one play of the AIDS era that does not end at a memorial service but with the characters gathered in expectation on a brilliant day, before Bethesda Fountain in Central Park. The year of this epilogue is 1990, and though Prior is now leaning on a cane like the Bolshevik of the prologue and is nearly as blind, Mr. Spinella radiates joy. "This disease will be the end of many of us, but not nearly all," he says. "The world only spins forward."

People no longer build cathedrals as they did a thousand years ago, to greet the next millennium, but *Angels in America* both spins forward and spirals upward in its own way, for its own time. If anything, Prior's description of statuary angels like the one in the fountain honoring the Civil War dead could stand for Mr. Kushner's fabulous play: "They commemorate death, but they suggest a world without dying."

"Bye now!" cries a smiling Mr. Spinella as this great epic draws to a close, raising his long arm and throwing it back in an ecstatic wave. His indelible gesture feels less like a goodbye than a benediction, less like a final curtain than a kiss that blesses everyone in the theater with the promise of more life.

Linda Winer (review date 24 November 1993)

SOURCE: "'Angels' II: Still Playful, and Still Profound," in *New York Newsday,* 24 November 1993.

[*In this review, Winer regards* Perestroika *as "playful and profound, extravagantly theatrical and deeply spiritual, witty and compassionate, furious and incredibly smart," but concedes that it has some significant flaws.*]

When last we saw our friends from *Angels in America*—and they do feel like intimate friends by now—a big fluffy angel had crashed through the bedroom ceiling of the man dying of AIDS. "Greetings, Prophet!" she declared to the horrified, wasted figure on the bed. "The great work begins!"

Lest anyone fear that Tony Kushner has lost his sense of proportion in the six months since the first half of his monumentally celebrated epic opened to distracting approval on Broadway, you should know right off what the suffering man says back to the angel. *"SHOO!"* is what he says, flinging his long skinny fingers at her fearsome winged holiness. He says, adorably, "Shoo!"

So Part II, *Perestroika,* finally opened at the Walter Kerr last night after the longest cliffhanger in Broadway history, not to mention an autumn of unfortunately public previews, cancellations and false starts that made Kushner's legions of admirers seriously nervous. Like the Pulitzer Prize-winning first half, *Millennium Approaches,* this one runs 3 1/2 hours, and we're delighted to report that, again, it breezes by like no time at all.

Like the first part, it is playful and profound, extravagantly theatrical and deeply spiritual, witty and compassionate, furious and incredibly smart. It's impossible to imagine anyone captivated by the beginning not wanting—more, *needing*—to go back for the end.

And, yet, it is equally likely that most will not find it as satisfying. Kushner has been trying to get *Perestroika* right since 1990 and, though the version directed by George C. Wolfe is far less confused than the one at the Mark Taper Forum in Los Angeles last November, it does have some pretty major clunkers.

Kushner has given himself the largest possible task—reorganizing the philosophical design of the world in the chaos brought by Reagan-era amorality, the death of Soviet communism, AIDS, and, perhaps, the incipient apocalypse. So he gets opaque or pedestrian when he stretches farthest into the theoretical. We forgive him for not being able to solve the problems of the earth and heaven in a play, or even two plays. We're also crazy about him for trying.

This is not to say we're not still let down by the ending, which, after hours of staggeringly clear-eyed insight and cosmic promise, ties a pretty bow around it all in an epilogue more worthy of Tiny Tim at Christmas than Kushner at the end of the world. But it's a tribute to Kushner, Wolfe and their wonderful actors that any end would leave us missing the prospect of these people and their stories in our lives again.

Kushner begins exactly where he left off, with the angel in Prior Walter's room. But, first, we're somewhere in the former Soviet Union with the oldest living Bolshevik, named Prelapsarianov, as in Eden before Eve's lapse. Unlike the old rabbi who began *Millennium* by mourning the immigrants brave enough to come to an unknown land, this old man is warning against change—against rejecting the ideals of communism—without having a replacement theory. He evokes the evening's first of many images of social structure as skin, declaring, "If you don't have any skin, we cannot, we must not, move ahead."

Moving ahead, moving at all, is on Kushner's mind in *Angels,* though he doesn't come out with it much until *Perestroika*—which, you may remember, means rebuilding—and it may not be all that clear by the end. The addled angel herself (played with beautiful aerial somersaults and a demented little cough by Ellen McLaughlin) is saddled with the Big Speeches about movement and stasis, and they are fairly impenetrable.

She has come to Prior Walter (the magnificent Stephen Spinella) to urge mankind to stop moving, to turn back, "to let deep roots grow." It seems God has fallen in love with his human creation and abandoned the angels. Meanwhile, Louis (played with ever-more angst-ridden desperation by the irresistible Joe Mantello) has abandoned his sick lover Prior, and Joe, the closeted-gay Mormon Republican lawyer (David Marshall Grant, on the exquisite line between hypocrite and victim), has left his depressed, Valium-hallucinating wife Harper (Marcia Gay Harden, even more impressive than before as a woman who could be really annoying).

Roy Cohn (Ron Leibman, ever-deepening his portrait of the seduction of evil) is dying of AIDS. Although we miss the scene from the L. A. production in which he returns for the lawsuit between God and the angels, his death inspires Kushner to one of the most haunting among the many haunting scenes—Ethel Rosenberg channeling the Kaddish through Louis as he steals Roy's AZT. Kathleen Chalfant is sterling as Ethel, and actually perfect as Joe's Mormon mother, who, because Kushner understands the power of the connections between unlike forces, befriends Prior. Jeffrey Wright, too, has gotten even better as Belize, the black gay nurse. Kushner and Wolfe have deepened the racial conflicts and made Belize a constant source of wisdom.

Designer Robin Wagner has managed to keep the dozens of scenes flowing, with special effects that are spectacular, yet with a sweetly homemade look, especially a Mormon diorama that comes hilariously to life. Kushner is still naming names, including Ed Koch and Ollie North, with quotes from Dorothy of Oz, Blanche of *Streetcar*, Joseph Welch of the McCarthy hearings. Although. some of the messages could be reduced to billboard slogans here—"we're all connected," "choose life"—Kushner wants us to know that people don't just die from AIDS, they also live with it.

Although the first part of *Angels* can stand alone as a formidable piece of theater, the second is definitely dependent on the other. Ideally, one should not wait too long after *Millennium* before seeing what happens to the characters in *Perestroika*. In a perfect world, the whole thing would have been ready to stage at the same time and theatergoers would not have had to keep the flame burning so long themselves.

Of course, Kushner is not writing about a perfect world. If he were, we would not need him so very much.

John Simon (review date 6 December 1993)

SOURCE: "Angelic Geometry," in *New York* Magazine, Vol. 26, No. 48, 6 December 1993, p. 130.

[*In the following evaluation of* Perestroika, *Simon notes that the play "aspires to epic status and, with its free-ranging action and propulsive energy, does approach it," but ultimately, he argues, it "goes nowhere."*]

After an intermission of six months, and with more delays than a NASA launching, Part Two of *Angels in America, Perestroika,* has finally opened. Tony Kushner might have continued fiddling with it even longer, except that Frank Rich, an *Angels* enthusiast, is quitting his post as chief drama critic of the *Times,* and his successor is said to be an only lukewarm *Angelist:* hence the need to catch Rich before he leaves. Actually, and not altogether surprisingly, the best assessments of *Angels in America* so far have come not from us drama critics but from outsiders: Andrew Sullivan, the homosexual editor of *The New Republic,* in his column of June 21, 1993; and the psychiatrist Yale Kramer, in a penetrating analysis in last July's issue of *The American Spectator.* More about them later.

Continuing where Part One, *Millennium Approaches,* left off, *Perestroika* supplies the same virtues and vices. Kushner is a funny fellow, and there is both nicely elaborated humor and rapid-fire wit throughout much of the three-and-a-half-hour span. When Hannah Pitt, the Mormon mother, her burlap hair in a shopworn bun, confronts her son's lover's lighter-than-air ex-lover, Prior Walter, who has just corroborated his homosexuality, she leaps to the enthymeme "Are you a hair-dresser?" "Well," he answers, "it would be your lucky day if I was." Later, when Prior finds being a prophet onerous, he asks Hannah, who knows her Bible, what God does with prophets who refuse their vision. She replies, "He feeds them to whales." But, of course, the jokes get nastier, as when the clue in a guessing game, "New York's No. 1 closeted queen," elicits the response "Koch" and huge audience laughter.

Further, Kushner handily sustains interest not only with his dialogue but also with artful construction, as he shifts among his three main stories: the affair of the AIDS-crossed lovers, Prior and Louis Ironson (the author's alter ego); the latent-homosexuality-and-rampant-dementia-crossed Mormon spouses, Joe and Harper Pitt (note the wife's masculine-sounding name); and the dying Roy Cohn and his circle. That circle includes Joe, chief clerk to a high-ranking judge and Louis's current lover; Belize, Roy's black male nurse and verbal sparring partner, who was Louis's lover before Prior; and the ghost of Ethel Rosenberg. If all this sounds a bit contrived, well, it is. Yet even as the overlapping or simultaneous scenes can add zest, they can also spread confusion; moreover, they unduly protect the author from committing himself to any one of his characters.

The play aspires to epic status and, with its free-ranging action and propulsive energy, does approach it. Yet epic has to sweep across a more representative canvas. Here the straight characters are few, and either mad or marginal. And whereas the author of this "Gay Fantasia on National Themes" has the right to his limitations, he must also bear their consequences, all the more so since even his homosexual figures are confined to certain types while excluding others.

Lastly, Kushner has written good parts for the actors, indeed challenging multiple roles for most of his cast of eight. (Sometimes, when he arbitrarily casts women as men, he overdoes it.) With snazzy direction from George C. Wolfe, Kathleen Chalfant, David Marshall Grant, Marcia Gay Harden, Ron Leibman, Joe Mantello, Ellen McLaughlin, Stephen Spinella and Jeffrey Wright perform impressively, supported by the witty sets of Robin Wagner, cheeky costumes of Toni-Leslie James, and well-nigh gestic lighting of Jules Fisher. Only Anthony Davis's music misses.

But the fact remains that *Angels in America*—and especially Part Two, from which we expect a resolution—goes nowhere. Great drama need not provide answers (and seldom does), so long as it raises the right questions; *Angels,* for all its attitudinizing, may not raise any. On the most mundane level, it dodges the issue of AIDS; though Prior is dying of it for seven hours, the final tableau implies full remission or, at any rate, denies us the dramatically necessary impact of his death. On the most metaphysical level, Prior is proclaimed a prophet by the visiting angel and even mounts to Heaven where a conclave of angels, in a particularly ill-written scene, grants him return to Earth. Why?

Kushner doesn't tell and, as usual, hedges his bets. In this June-moony Heaven (the act is titled "Heaven, I'm in Heaven"), Prior meets Harper, who is there for no better reason than that she has experienced a long-delayed orgasm. Kushner wants to have things both ways: either to play it safe, or so as not to have to know what he is talking about.

In the aforementioned essay, Yale Kramer showed, in great and compelling detail, that Kushner is pleading not just for homosexuality but also and especially for transgression, a life-style of flouted complaisance and flaunted socially unacceptable excess. And Andrew Sullivan argued that "gay life—and gay death—surely awaits something grander and subtler than this," for "the script itself never ascended . . . above a West Village version of Neil Simon." To which I would add that even the play's central concept of the homosexual hero as prophet and consort of angels was long ago anticipated by Rimbaud, who pronounced himself angel and seer. And I mistrust any writer who (in a Sunday piece in the *Times*) commits the pleonasm "from whence." Granted, this was acceptable in Shakespeare's day, but we've come a long way since then—grammatically up, and dramatically down.

John Lahr (review date 13 December 1993)

SOURCE: "Earth Angels," in *The New Yorker*, Vol. LXIX, No. 42, 13 December 1993, pp. 129-33.

[*In this assessment, Lahr declares* Perestroika *"a masterpiece."*]

Tony Kushner wrote **Perestroika,** the second part of **Angels in America,** in what he describes as "an incredible eight days I spent at the Russian River, in Northern California, in April of 1991, ten months after my mother died." The play was a tape-measure job—three hundred pages, five acts—that would take six hours to perform. After finishing the epilogue, Kushner threw his belongings in his car and set off down through the Napa Valley toward San Francisco. Almost immediately, life began to imitate the play's marvels and resonances. "When I got in the car, this magical thing happened," Kushner told me the day before he jetted off to watch the London production of his superbly expanded and polished final product (it had been reworked in collaboration with its director, George C. Wolfe, and the New York cast of **Millennium Approaches**), at the Royal National Theatre, and five days before the same version opened on Broadway. "I turned on the radio, and the first thing that came on was 'American Pie.' I started to lose that station, so I switched to the next station. It was Simon and Garfunkel, singing 'America.' Then a group called, I think, the Black Crowes, singing the song 'She Talks to Angels.' Then I switched to a classical-music station that was playing Mozart's bassoon concerto, which was one of my mother's practice pieces. That was amazing. Really amazing." When Kushner got to San Francisco, he installed himself and his humongous manuscript in a café on Market Street and called his friends. "For the entire evening, people came by," he said. "It was a huge party. I ran up this immense bill on bottles of champagne. It was worth it. I really didn't know if, especially after my mother died, I'd ever finish the play, which bracketed my mother's death, and contains it—a form of mourning and a form of not letting go."

Perestroika—the word is the Russian for "rebuilding"—dramatizes the work of mourning: the struggle to embrace both loss and change. The play is immense in its wisdom of the heart; every line sings with hurt and humor. Although Kushner has cut the playing time and the number of pages by half, the five-act structure remains intact, parceled neatly around two intermissions, and is crucial to Kushner's vision of the play's metaphor. "**Perestroika** doesn't have that classical cadence, that one-two-three punch—a beginning, a kickup, and a bang," he says. "**Perestroika** doesn't rise and fall in the same way. It's iambic pentameter: 'this and then this and then this and then this and then this.' It's epic. You experience each act very much as an installment of a journey, and you feel, I hope, that at the end you've arrived at a huge place. It's very tricky. For me, the bulk of it—the epic nature of it—becomes part of what it's about: this incredible struggle I feel people have to wage in order to be able to change themselves."

At the end of **Millennium Approaches,** all the characters have come to grief and to stalemate. The Mormon wife, Harper, has lost her bisexual lawyer husband, Joe Pitt. Hannah Pitt, Joe's mother, has sold her house in Salt Lake City to move to New York. The defiantly macho Roy Cohn has contracted AIDS. Prior Walter, also suffering from AIDS, has been abandoned first by his lover, Louis, and then, apparently, by his senses, as an angel crashes through the ceiling of his apartment at the finale to announce that Prior is a prophet and she is the messenger. But of what? In **Perestroika,** the angel turns out to be an angel of stasis, part of the forces of entropy creating the climate of collapse which Prior has either to join or to reject. She carries a red-and-gold "Tome of Immobility, of respite, of cessation." Suspended above Prior and somersaulting occasionally to make a point, the angel (the strong-jawed, fierce-eyed Ellen McLaughlin) is the voice of retreat in the face of overwhelming loss. "Forsake the Open Road," she tells him, sounding like a retrograde Walt Whitman. To Kushner, who is staunchly agnostic, the angel "embodies the longing for a cosmic regression which is so profound that it becomes deeply reactionary and destructive." For the new production, Kushner has cut a lot of the cosmic flimflammery from the début version of **Perestroika** (which was at the Mark Taper Forum, in Los Angeles), and, by showing Prior to be as puzzled as the audience by the angelic visitation, has made it more dramatic. Prior wants to know if the angel is there to damn or save him. "In the Judeo-Christian tradition, the Day of Wrath is both the day of wrath and the coming of the Kingdom of God," Kushner says. "The honey of Heaven may or may not come. You don't get the answer. You get an absolute maybe." Is Prior a prophet? Or is the visitation a dream? In his quandary, Prior (played, by Stephen Spinella, with a poignant and ever-increasing comic command) bolts from the angel. "He is running, he thinks, in defiance of the angel's command to 'be still,'" Kushner wrote in his notes to the director of the English production, Declan Donnellan, "and of course in the process is running himself to death." Prior and all the characters in **Perestroika** teeter on this delicate, terrifying balance between resignation and action. Choice is made harder because the characters have been abandoned both by God and by ideology. A note of historical confusion is sounded in the prologue by the oldest living Bolshevik, Aleksii Antedilluvianovich Prelapsarianov, who in the play's first beats raises the question of change. "The Great Question before us is: Can we Change? In Time? And we all desire that Change will come," he says. His old eyes hidden behind sunglasses, Aleksii goes on to scold the audience about "this Sour Little Age," and warns: "If the snake sheds his skin before a new skin is ready, naked he will be in the world, prey to the forces of chaos. . . . Have you, my little serpents, a new skin?"

At the beginning of **Perestroika,** the skins of all the characters are by no means thick. They evade the excruciating pain of loss by an obsession with fantasy or with flesh. Harper is distracted by grief. "I'm stuck," she says. "My heart's an anchor." ("What I love in the character," Kushner wrote in his notes to the director, "is that she is both very brave and amazingly inventive in her avoidance, she creates spectacular routes of escape and then unravels them because she knows they're untrue.") Marcia Gay Harden gives Harper's poetry and pottiness fine definition as she acts out her anguish by chewing down a tree at the Botanic Garden arboretum and, later, spending hours at the Mormon diorama at the Visitors' Center in New York, looking at "The Great Trek," because the main figure reminds her of Joe. "When they push the buttons he'll start to talk," she tells Prior, who is there to learn more about angels. "You can't believe a word he says but the sound of him is reassuring. It's an *incredible* resemblance." Cohn, now pasty and shrunken as he lies in a hospital bed, still wields his furious power as a bulwark against change. He dies, significantly, echoing the words with which he's introduced in *Millennium Approaches.* "A nice big box of drugs for Uncle Roy!" he shouts on the phone, blackmailing someone into getting him some AZT. "Or there'll be seven different kinds of hell to pay!" In a perfectly modulated and unforgettable performance, Ron Leibman, with his tongue darting out and with bloodshot eyes shrinking to beads of hate in his gnarled face, turns the bedridden Cohn into a kind of iguana of invective. The hectoring generates a self-hypnotic sense of power, which cuts Cohn off from his loss. "Tough little muscle," he says of his heart. "Never bleeds."

Prior, on the other hand, is full of raw, contradictory feelings, still imagining Louis's return and confessing to feeling "lascivious sad." Louis, for his part, is just plain lascivious. He assuages his guilt by submerging himself in appetite. "What he wants from Joe is the sort of impossible, cost-free salvation Joe seems to offer," Kushner writes. "To get this, Louis has to submit to Joe—politically, sexually, psychologically." As Louis, Joe Mantello has continued to extend the subtlety of his marvelous characterization, and superbly savors the self-loathing in Louis's sexual narcotics. Louis forces himself to connect with Joe Pitt, his ideological opposite, as a kind of penance. "The nose tells the body—the heart, the mind, the fingers, the cock—what it wants," he says, licking Joe's cheeks in one of the most extraordinary seduction scenes I've ever seen, "and then the tongue explores, finding out what's edible, what isn't, what's most mineral, food for the blood, food for the bones, and therefore most delectable." Louis puts his hand down the front of Joe's pants, pulls it out, and smells and then tastes his fingers. "Chlorine. Copper. Earth," he says, and makes his move. Joe falls in love with Louis. This is one of Kushner's major discoveries in the rewrite, and allows him to extend their relationship beyond political squabbling to the play's more central issue: Where do love and justice meet? "I mean you say law isn't Justice and Justice isn't morals," Louis says in the middle of one of their bouts of lovemaking, "but really, who if not the Right is putting the Prude back in Jurisprudence?" David

Marshall Grant makes Joe at once sweetly expansive in love and obtusely closed down in life. When, late in the play, Louis and Joe square off against each other over Joe's ghostwriting of reactionary legal decisions, Joe continues to bleat, "It's law, not justice, it's power, not the merits of its exercise, it's not an expression of the ideal, it's . . ." And there's an ugly fight, in which Louis gets bloodied. "It's literally having blood on his hands that makes Joe get it," Kushner wrote in his notes.

The black nurse, Belize, is the character who mediates between the living and the dead, and between Louis and Prior. As Belize, Jeffrey Wright comes into his own in *Perestroika,* stamping the character with a distinctive, camp combination of fury and fun. When Cohn boasts, "Pain's . . . nothing, pain's life," Belize counters, "Sing it, baby." Belize is the play's moral bellwether. He tips off Louis to Joe's ghostwriting and to his relationship to Cohn, and it's also Belize who recognizes in Cohn not just the "polestar of human evil," as Louis calls him, but a fallen gay brother. "A queen can forgive her vanquished foe," Belize says. "It isn't easy. . . . Forgiveness. Which is maybe where love and justice finally meet." He engineers an epiphany of love and justice by getting Louis to say Kaddish over Cohn's dead body while he steals Cohn's AZT to prolong Prior's life. In this exquisite scene, Kushner manages to act out both anger and atonement by having Louis and the ghost of Ethel Rosenberg finish the prayer, saying in counterpoint, "You sonofabitch."

For most of the characters, the play's arc leads to an acceptance of loss and to a new kind of strength in solitude. "Sometimes, maybe lost is best," Harper tells Joe, who returns on the rebound from Louis. "Get lost, Joe. Go exploring." She hands him her Valium stash and exits from their symbiotic relationship into a hard-won, clear-eyed independence. In an airplane on the way to San Francisco, she thinks of the hole in the ozone layer and has a vision of dead souls floating up "like skydivers in reverse, limbs all akimbo, wheeling and spinning." The departed clasp hands and form a web that repairs the hole. "Nothing's lost forever," she says in one of Kushner's most gorgeous speeches. "In this world, there is a kind of painful progress. Longing for what we've left behind, and dreaming ahead."

Prior, too, has fought his way to a spiritual place. He climbs a neon ladder to Heaven and confronts a congress of angels, the Council of Continental Principalities. "We live past hope. If I can find hope anywhere, that's it, that's the best I can do," he tells them, finally rejecting the "Tome of Immobility" and able to receive the gift of the dead, which is a renewed sense of life. "I want more life," he says. Prior becomes strong enough to accept his isolation and his death. "This is my life, from now on, Louis. I'm not getting 'better,' "he says. Louis declares his love for Prior and asks to come back, but Prior, while acknowledging love, also acknowledges that some hurts are irreparable. "You can't come back," he finally tells Louis. "Not ever. I'm sorry. But you can't." Mourning has led him to a new way of being. "To face loss. With grace. Is key, I think, but it's impossible," he says.

There's comparable gallantry in the passionate restraint of George C. Wolfe's production. Wolfe inherited *Millennium Approaches* when the script was frozen, after its successful London and Mark Taper productions, but here, in reimagining *Perestroika* for Broadway, he has been free to impose his swift, unfettered intelligence on the material. As a result, the play is tighter, sharper, more scenically and emotionally streamlined than *Millennium Approaches.* Robin Wagner's set is simpler and more effective; and Jules Fisher, the maestro of the lighting board, shapes an array of subtle and suggestive moods.

Just before the Epilogue, Hannah Pitt (the formidable Kathleen Chalfant), whose rigidity has lost her the allegiance of her homosexual son but who learns tolerance through her friendship with Prior, takes leave of him in the hospital, promising to come again. "Please do," Prior says, invoking Tennessee Williams: "I have always depended on the kindness of strangers." Hannah, who has no self-pity and doesn't seem to know the famous line, rounds on Prior, saying, "Well, that's a stupid thing to do." It's a big laugh, but it's also telling. Not since Williams has a play-wright announced his poetic vision with such authority on the Broadway stage. Kushner is the heir apparent to Williams' romantic theatrical heritage: he, too, has tricks in his pocket and things up his sleeve, and he gives the audience "truth in the pleasant disguise of illusion." And, also like Williams, Kushner has forged an original, impressionistic theatrical vocabulary to show us the heart of a new age.

At the finale, which jumps forward four years, to 1990, with Prior still alive and chatting happily with his "family"—Louis, Belize, Hannah—beneath the angel at the Bethesda Fountain in Central Park, Kushner takes another leaf from Williams' book. He lets Prior stop-start the vivacious chat the way Tom Wingfield does in *The Glass Menagerie.* "The world only spins forward. We will be citizens. The time has come," Prior says to us, turning upstage and then, almost as an afterthought, turning back to deliver the ineffably moving envoi. "Bye now," he says. "You are fabulous creatures. And I bless you: *More Life. The Great Work Begins.*" And on that note of blessing—at once elegiac and adamant—the characters take leave of us. But, long after the ovation is over, we retain their sense of life and struggle and miracle. In the strict sense of the word, we *are* all fabulous—"the subjects of whom stories are told." And Kushner, in his big-hearted and almost reckless bravery, has told a great story. There will be those who will regret the subject matter, or the length, or the cosmic folderol. But the carping hardly matters. *Perestroika* is a masterpiece.

Robert Brustein (review date 27 December 1993)

SOURCE: "The Great Work Falters," in *The New Republic*, Vol. 209, No. 26, 27 December 1993, pp. 25-8.

[*Here, Brustein states that* Perestroika *"features the wittiest writing, and brightest sensibility, of any play in memory. But it not only has little in the way of structure, it also lacks the important dramatic component of a central action, or animating event, to push it forward. Most serious, it fails to prove its thematic premise, that an insistently homosexual perspective can be the basis for a universal worldview."*]

At the conclusion of *Millennium Approaches,* the first part of Tony Kushner's *Angels in America,* an angel crashes through the ceiling of Prior Walter's bedroom and announces: "The Great Work Begins." At the start of Part II, titled *Perestroika,* a doddering Bolshevik complains that humankind cannot function without the equivalent of Marxist theory. *Perestroika* makes a heroic, if partly ironic, effort to furnish that alternative theory through the conception of a totally sexualized universe. But despite its admirable ambitions and for all its extraordinary qualities, *Perestroika* seems more a repetition than a culmination of the Great Work promised by the initial design.

Like *Millennium Approaches, Perestroika* is alive with fierce intelligence and sharp scenes. It contains the same engrossing conflicts and engaging central characters. A kind of extraterrestrial soap opera (akin to "Twin Peaks"), it continues to mix reality and dreams—personal relationships and supernatural shenanigans—in a dazzling display of style. It features the wittiest writing, and brightest sensibility, of any play in memory. But it not only has little in the way of structure, it also lacks the important dramatic component of a central action, or animating event, to push it forward. Most serious, it fails to prove its thematic premise, that an insistently homosexual perspective can be the basis for a universal worldview.

Even more than *Millennium Approaches, Perestroika* looks at politics and metaphysics almost entirely through the prism of sex and interpersonal transactions. The ailing Prior Walter ejaculates when the Angel first descends, and experiences erection whenever she reappears. While she chants *"Ectasis in Excelsis,"* he humps a sacred text (the stage direction reads: "If they had cigarettes, they'd smoke them now"). He learns that "Heaven is a city much like San Francisco," where many of the angels are gay or lesbians, engaging in perpetual copulation and producing a Protomatter (called "Angelic Spooj") that glues the universe together. Even Hannah, the stern mother of the gay Mormon, Joe Pitt, gets turned on to the point of orgasm by the lesbian angel. Similarly, Conservative Joe and Liberal Louis discuss their political differences while making out in Jacob Riis Park ("The more appalling I find your opinions the more I want to hump you," Louis admits), and Roy Cohn's reactionary politics are almost entirely explained by his being a closet queen.

Then there is the specter of AIDS, which surrounds this play like an evil miasma, with its attendant horrors of emergency rooms and I.V.s, diseased tissues, lesions, sarcomas, pneumonia and blindness. Though Prior is still alive at the end of the play, he and Cohn are dying of the disease throughout the long evening, inspiring Kushner to write at least four death scenes and two resurrections. (Cohn's dying is presided over by his archnemesis, Ethel Rosenberg, who later prompts Louis in his recitation of the kaddish over Cohn's body.) Kushner comes perilously close to suggesting that this plague is heaven-sent—not, as the fundamentalists would have it, as a punishment for sin, but as a sign of God's abandonment of humans around the time of the 1906 San Francisco earthquake (in heaven, Prior enjoins the angels to take this deadbeat Dad to court for desertion). Prior's refusal to despair, or to let us avert our face from this ghastly specter, are the qualities that anoint him as the Prophet of *Angels in America.*

In the conclusion, he, Louis and Belize are sitting near the Bethesda Fountain in Central Park, presided over by a stone statue of another Angel. The Bethesda Angel is associated with healing properties, and when the millennium comes, all who are afflicted will be enabled to bathe in her fountain. After Prior and Louis argue over Gorbachev and perestroika, and Louis and Belize dispute the rights of Palestinians, Prior reflects on the scourge that is killing him, and his comments are worth quoting: "This disease will be the end of many of us, but not nearly all, and the dead will be commemorated and will struggle on with the living, and we are not going away. We won't die secret deaths any more. The world only spins forward. We will be citizens. The time will come."

It is a moving statement on behalf of all who suffer the torments of this deadly affliction, and, for once, Kushner's mordant jests in the face of the horror modulate into pure feeling. But the swelling inspirational tone of his coda takes a sharp turn toward bathos with Prior's concluding lines, delivered directly to the audience: "Bye now. You are fabulous creatures, each and every one. And I bless you. *More life*. The Great Work Begins." The "Bye now" is unfortunate enough. But unless Kushner is assuming that everybody in the theater is HIV-positive, there is more than a trace of audience-stroking in these curtain lines. To be blessed as "fabulous creatures" after watching three and a half hours of painful death scenes, sexual betrayals, corrupt politics and cynical metaphysics in a "terminally crazy and mean America" suggests that sentimentality is the down side of Kushner's rhetoric, just as high camping is the flip side of his wit. For every surprising conjunction of clauses or skillful interlapping of scenes, there is a vaudeville skit or a gay wise-crack to trigger the laugh machine. (Kushner has a particular weakness for gags about hairdressers and Fauberge cologne better left to the Theater of the Ridiculous.) Those frequent lapses prevent *Angels in America* from fulfilling its extraordinary potential, as does our growing realization that the play's length is less a sign of richness than of the author's

incapacity to edit out repetitions or focus on an integrated action.

For the subject of AIDS does not readily accommodate itself to any single worldview. It is an appalling disease that has claimed many of our close friends in the arts, but it will not lend itself to metaphor any more than cancer or tuberculosis does, and it does not reduce itself to moral outrage any more than bubonic plague or syphilis does. "I am dying. Why doesn't somebody help us?" asked the *Times*'s Jeffrey Schmalz before he succumbed to AIDS himself. Who but an absent God can answer his heartbreaking question? Until a cure is found, the disease is real to us helpless humans less as a moral or political issue than as a particularly miserable and recalcitrant biological fact. Among the many AIDS plays, only Paul Rudnick's whimsical *Jeffrey* seems to recognize the practicalities of the problem, since it concerns a gay man who doesn't spend his time assigning blame but rather determines (though he fails) to stay celibate to save his life.

Kushner indicts his straight characters less for remaining indifferent to AIDS than for failing (*pace* Roy Cohn) to acknowledge their own homosexuality. And he condemns the gay world not for spreading the disease so much as for failing (*pace* Louis Ironson) to remain loyal to the friends who contract it. Personal loyalty and mutual support remain the highest values this author can imagine. Yet a pervasive sense of victimization wraps around his play like a shroud. The bleeding finger writes, and having writ, fails to move on.

My main criticism of George C. Wolfe's direction of *Millennium Approaches* is that it applies Broadway accessories to a serious play. Oddly, these values seem entirely appropriate to the more commercially inclined *Perestroika.* Robin Wagner's scene design is now considerably more modest, and therefore considerably more effective, than his sets for Part I, consisting of simple furniture strategies rather than large location pieces. And the extravagant acting fits better inside a play with large theatrical gestures. I found Ron Leibman's shrieking and kvetching Roy Cohn just as impressive in Part II of *Angels in America,* though he is still on the outlandish side of reality. His mercurial shifts in tone and volume, his incredible rattling pace, mark him as the only actor alive who can interrupt himself. Stephen Spinella's feverish, spasmodic, emaciated Prior Walter is still enormously affecting, and David Marshall Grant's Joe Pitt remains a model of tortured propriety. Ellen McLaughlin is compelling both as a butch nurse and as the gyrating calisthenic Angel, Jeffrey Wright is a marvelously bitchy Belize and Kathleen Chalfant is dignified in a variety of older male and female roles. Only Marcia Gay Harden's Harper Pitt remains embedded in sitcom, though Joe Mantello's Louis Ironson, vocally whiny and physically itchy, began to pall on me a little this time, too. But then the actor is charged with playing so many sex scenes in front of an audience that he's probably a little strung out.

Scene from the 1993 production of Millenium Approaches. *Stephen Spinella as Prior Walter and Ellen McLaughlin as the Angel.*

ANGELS IN AMERICA

CRITICAL COMMENTARY

Gordon Rogoff (essay date 1993)

SOURCE: "Angels in America, Devils in the Wings," in *Theater*, Vol. 24, No. 2, 1993, pp. 21-9.

[*In the essay below, Rogoff sardonically traces the evolution of* Angels in America, *maintaining that the changes made in the course of its various stagings lessened the work.*]

As one who lives a life rather than a "lifestyle," I'm not sure what a gay play, let alone a gay fantasia, might be. But there they fly, those miniprovocations and tiny half-thoughts, now glued permanently to whatever may be dredged from the experience of seeing George C. Wolfe's musical-comedy version of Tony Kushner's **Angels in America: Millennium Approaches,** subtitled "A Gay Fantasia on National Themes." Well, if not exactly a musical-comedy, a play now underscored with so much musical blather instructing us what to feel or think, that it might just as well go all the way. A few years ago at the Public Theatre, Wolfe made a lovely, sensual Caribbean mess out of Brecht's *The Caucasian Chalk Circle*, a scattershot entertainment that never enlightened but was intoxicating fun to watch until the awful Azdak came on, proceeding to be weighty and witless. At the time, it looked like Wolfe's bad luck with a not-so-good actor. With *Angels* in mind, however, it looks like Wolfe's revenge on complication and intelligence.

Poor T. K., caught now in the national theme he's too astute to suffer gladly—the success that dislodges good work from its resolute rage so that a huge public might see it as a user-friendly temper tantrum. It's tiring to repeat Steven Marcus's captivating phrase from years ago—"In America, nothing fails like success"—but from one era to another, it's likely to rear itself again as the most succinct, if not the best, explanation. *Angels* is inescapably the newest case-in-point, moving from the usual 15 minutes of famous workshops and readings where, if history is witness, it might have quickly reached the usual oblivion, to a groundswell of attention that followed hard upon Declan Donnellan's production last year at Britain's National Theatre. Suddenly it became flavor-of-the-year, just in time to attract the attention of all those producers—off-Broadway, regional, and Broadway—who had let it slip away while mounting their clone-seasons: *Oleanna Glen-Seagull Meets the Baltimore Waltzing at Lughnasa*. At last, went the newly coined, quickly conventional wisdom, a serious play both funny and—oh those words tripping off the press releases again—relevant, meaningful, haunting, about-something, desperately moving, movingly filled with meaning about the most desperate tragedy of our times short of Bosnia and Somalia, of course.

Not to be outdone by flacks, the dutiful army of reviewers has checked in by now with their own hyperbolic yelps, led by Warwick the Kingmaker, Frank Rich of the *New York Times*, forsaking his available dash and gift for the fluent, colorful line in favor of hard sell—"the most thrilling American play in years." And what a relief that must be for the 13 Broadway producers, already high on what one of them, shouting to the rehearsing company, referred to as "our Pulitzer Prize." (The exact quote: "We did it! We won the Pulitzer!") Maybe Kushner feels a flashing moment of pain at his evident loss of ownership, but why should any American playwright begrudge his own hard-won 15 minutes on the yellow-brick road to movie contracts and half-ownership of Chemical Bank? Somebody has to be one of the Chosen, every few years at least, though it can't be easy to recall the last 20 years of Tennessee Williams, banished from Broadway and hounded as a failure, the curse of Marcus striking again.

The worst of it for Kushner is that he surely doesn't need Warwick to tell him he's good, though with the system what it is, he's not likely to be king without an official crowner. So once Rich's review was dispatched from London, the rest fell into place like all those dominoes that used to strike terror into the American imperium,

still another reminder that, in late-century America, battles are often won while wars are always lost. To be fair, Kushner's options were not enviable, however well he might reason from the evidence of his own play, in which similar tensions between heroism and sell-out loom over every decisive encounter. As James Joyce put it, surely not imagining American theater's distorting mirror, yet nonetheless aware of any artist's essential loneliness, "The artist, like the God of creation, remains within or behind or beyond or above his handiwork, invisible, refined out of existence, indifferent, paring his fingernails."

Gnawing is more like it for the American playwright, likely to lose something along the way, whether remaining semivisible or dubiously indifferent. In New York, at least, he has to know that Broadway has no recent record of playing host to delicately poised new work, having long ago arranged matters so that 2,000 years of dramatic literature would intrude only on those rare occasions when subsidized imports (the Royal Shakespeare's *All's Well that Ends Well*) or a movie star's periodic need to confirm his out-of-practice pedigree (Dustin Hoffman's Shylock) would act as what merchants used to call "loss-leaders," profitless merchandise meant to lure customers back for more conventional goods. Otherwise, only partisans lifting themselves on billowing clouds of denial can have missed the plainly visible signs: producers now are faceless conglomerates, leveraging the various sell-outs over which they preside in order to meet their not-so-original perception that the public can be seduced for an instant from the tube only by offering what the tube does all the time, usually more efficiently. And what an irony lies there for collectors, the moguls battering the public into submission by claiming they know what is wanted while viewers sink deeper into sofas, meekly letting the laugh-track inform them that they're happy.

Enter George C. Wolfe, Warwick's truly Chosen one, hired by the New York Shakespeare Festival to direct that *Chalk Circle* extravaganza, ready in the wings, as it finally turned out, to replace JoAnne Akalaitis at the NYSF after Warwick's ceaseless shrieks for her head, just as he was miraculously in place when all previous directors of *Angels*—Donnellan, David Esbjornsen, and Oskar Eustis—were out-of-the-picture for one reason or another. Now, let's try fairness again, and concede that some of those reasons could be sound, especially for Kushner. Unlike me, he might not have been mightily impressed by Donnellan's London production, clearly conceived for the small, black-box Cottlesloe Theatre, furniture rolled on and off by actors to the bare stage backed by the largest American flag ever seen, through which the Angel crashed in *Millennium*'s final moment. (Still another one for irony collectors: the Broadway flying machine, no doubt a technological improvement over the *Peter Pan* machines that used to work well enough, was evidently so far ahead of the mere mortals charged to run it that the opening had to be delayed for a week.) Esbjornsen, who had directed a San Francisco workshop production, was never really a New York contender, and despite John Lahr's insistence in the *New Yorker* that Eustis, in Los Angeles, had directed a better production than Donnellan's, the pressure was already on for Kushner to scrap both designer and director for the Broadway sweepstakes, thus inadvertently declaring that New York can have only one Warwick, and it ain't going to be Lahr, no matter how hard the new *New Yorker* tries to move to the head of the chattering class.

Oh dear, what a thickening of plots, enough to nourish entire armies of conspiracy theorists. But wouldn't it be better to try fairness yet again? Somebody may have reminded Kushner of how Frank Rich hollered Hallelujah when Caryl Churchill's *Serious Money* played in London and opened later at the Public, leading Joseph Papp to move it to Broadway in the reasonable expectation that Warwick would come through again. Unaccountably, it was not to be: Turnabout in reviewing is never fair play, but the *Times* enjoys immunity, so if Warwick entertains a second thought, who can ask for anything more? You win some, you lose some, thus runs the world away, as the man said while not killing the Kingmaking King in Elsinore.

So what's a playwright to do?

Let's track this rueful morality play more carefully, at last. In April 1993, Kushner permitted his friend, Michael Mayer, to direct third-year students from the Graduate Acting Program of NYU, in *Perestroika,* Part II of *Angels.* In "A Letter from the Playwright," published in the program, he tells us that he had hoped originally to use the NYU production "to try out rewrites" for the projected Broadway production in October. Before playing in the November 1992 Mark Taper Forum production, *Perestroika* had been a five-act play, "twice its current length." With admirable candor, however, Kushner reports that rewriting time eluded him as the Broadway production of *Millennium* became more consuming than he could have guessed. "I've been crazed with anxiety and distracted to the point of madness," he writes, "and so we've decided to go with the L.A. version intact, warts and all."

No need to search for subtext here: Kushner lost months of rewriting time not only by submitting to interviews coast-to-coast, but by giving himself over to the full play of hysteria common to all Broadway productions, 13 instant experts fussily protecting their investors' cash flow while still another director—Wolfe—plots new blocking for many of the same actors who had evidently negotiated their roles with some effectiveness for Eustis in November. Meanwhile, Robin Wagner was rigging swiveling panels, automated platforms sliding on with set-piece furnishings, sometimes decorated with pastel backdrops and huge wafts of smoke; add to this that humongous musical score, including a snatch of Montserrat Caballe's *Norma* for anyone in need of a familiar reference point, such as a Terrence McNally play, and it's easy to see why Kushner might be crazed. Just as well, too, since Mayer's diamond-clear production may be the last time he'll have a chance to recall the virtues in plain speaking: just as Donnellan

honored Kushner with bull's-eye simplicity in London's *Millennium,* so did Mayer in NYU's *Perestroika.* No longer within, behind, beyond, or above his handiwork, Kushner was deeply immersed in the handiwork—and mischief—of all the others. One mercy for him, anyway, is that neither Wolfe nor the producers pressed him the way Elia Kazan once pressed Tennessee Williams to put Big Daddy into the third act of *Cat on a Hot Tin Roof.* Appearances notwithstanding, Broadway no longer demands wholesale textual changes, or so it seems from this example; instead, these co-conspirators merely rearrange tonalities, emphasis, balances, and meaning: loudness and sentimentality are in, politics and sex are out.

Now: My own subtext should be clear enough. Try as I'd like to keep up the fairness game, I'm not positioned to offer anything but comparisons, some of them invidious, which can hardly come as a surprise. If I had to guess, I'd say that if a review of Bach's *A minor Mass* in 1749 declared that it was "the most thrilling German Mass in years," I might have turned from devout Lutheran to confirmed doubter. Luckily for Saxons at the time, and surely for the diligent, unexpectant Kapellmeister himself, it was only when the *Credo* was performed in 1786 that some loopy Hamburg critic fell from his pew to write that it "was one of the most excellent pieces of music ever heard," high praise, indeed, and not a moment too soon. Hyperbole on behalf of Bach was no more common than performances almost a century later, and then the first shout came from the Zürich music publisher, Hans Georg Nägeli, "that for such things we have indeed a small public." Not for want of trying: Nägeli was surely right and sober in 1818 when he called the *B minor Mass* "the greatest musical work of art of all times and nations," though I hate to think of how this claim might have affected Beethoven and Schubert, then pursuing their trade without prizes, without much praise—and not many performances for that matter.

It was my good fortune, then, to come upon *Millennium* in the spirit of a passerby slipping into a Leipzig church long before Nägeli had launched his lavender prose. More to the point, I saw it during a long London weekend featuring Paul Scofield's baleful, basset-hound Shotover and Vanessa Redgrave's delirious, flying-saucer Hesione in Shaw's certifiably masterful *Heartbreak House.* I was entitled to guess that, whatever the obvious merits of Jonson's *The Alchemist,* Pinter's *The Caretaker,* or Kushner's *Millennium Approaches,* no performance could match Trevor Nunn's production in the full grip and majesty of Shaw's appalled vision of the modern world's final blast. Nor—or so I allowed myself to think—would anyone dare to try.

But you know the rest: I had not reckoned with young Kushner, wrestling, like the aging Shaw, with his own version of apocalypse, undaunted by both history and the history of playwriting, so intensely involved in contrapuntal narrative and what, at first glance, appears to be a sweeping command of Swiftian irony joined to an unyielding Jacobean anguish. As much as anything, I added

Angels to my short list out of curiosity about an American play gaining its early renown in London, much like *The Zoo Story* in Berlin more than 30 years ago. Furthermore, as a card-carrying sceptic when American vowels trip not-so-lightly off British tongues, I was entertaining the complacent notion that the actors would be resorting to broad rasps masquerading as A-mur-kin speech.

By the fourth scene of *Millennium,* in which Louis Ironson and his lover Prior Walter chat about the funeral of Louis's grandmother and their missing cat, both discussions emerging quickly as metaphor rather than small talk, it was clear that Kushner's gifts are at once novelistic and theatrical: not for him the niggling domestic quarrel or joking insult; instead, he races over a psycho-political landscape with the laser beam that has already eluded Bill Clinton, juggling a half-dozen tales daringly into an epic horror story about gays, Jews, Mormons, right-wing power-nuts, endemic American racism, abandoned women, fiction truer than fact meeting documentary fact (Roy Cohn) overwhelmed by lies and self-deception—all of them converging on the most abandoned adoration of theater doing what it does like no other written form, density shining out from translucent vision.

The British actors, too, were another surprise, Henry Goodman's Roy Cohn having transformed Whitechapel into Flatbush, the others mostly in charge of an unself-conscious, never-illustrated idiom, Salt Lake or New York, that was usually graceful, proportioned, and never arch or outlandish. Best of all was Marcus D'Amico's Louis, the young Jew (at last!) as hunk, light-years from Woody-Dustin nerdhood, the best and the brightest without a doubt, but no more in sight of leadership or sainthood than any other hero *manqué*. D'Amico is noble in carriage and demeanor while retaining the fragrant intensity of the self-appointed victim looking eagerly over his shoulder for his next ravisher. Louis can't bear responsibility for another's pain, yet D'Amico gives him the intelligent presence of Hamlet, the lightning wit of Mercutio, and the spluttering fury of Hotspur. With D'Amico, that peculiar achievement of actors at their best begins to take over, lifting the play from our customary expectations about sympathy into a realm where reality can have full sway: Louis is a god who behaves like a shit.

It was in New York, however, that I began to understand the full measure of D'Amico's—yes, and Donnellan's—success with Kushner's precarious balancing act. For one thing, George C. Wolfe turns every scene into a chorus line of quips and demonstrations. Ron Leibman's Roy Cohn is encouraged to take toothsome bites out of the moving scenery, literally hijacking attention from the central miseries in the American century in order to make claims on a raucous display of sympathy for the biggest shit of them all. Here, indeed, is the rasp and unfocused energy I feared from the British, not just a matter of caricatured accent or cartoon violence, but an unmannerly display of antic disposition gone haywire, selfish, and stupid. Worse, it's highway robbery of Louis's centrality—Louis,

the other Jew, the one who doesn't give a damn about clout or power, the talented, princely intelligence whose unspoken text is that he could be the lawyer that Cohn has become, but some miserable doubt survives that prevents him from pursuing ambition of any kind. Instead, he works as a word processor in the court system, nowhere to go but down into the interior of his constantly examined life. Broadway's Joe Mantello makes an honorable accounting of Louis, the embittered clerk, but he's not part of a production that seeks any further news from the text. On the contrary, his is a dutiful, on-the-line version of Louis being merely disloyal, unfaithful, a cowardly kitten rather than a lion in heat.

But, as I've come to realize after NYU's *Perestroika,* Louis's mysterious reticence, his incapacity to seize feeling from reason, his refusal to dwell in the house of his instinctive wisdom, is Kushner's stalwart unhappiness, too. The play's ambitious reach is the mirror image of Louis's retreats. Like so many in the audience of *Millennium,* whether in England or America, I had every reason to guess that the Angel's arrival before Prior's sickbed was the signal of his imminent departure, death at last having dominion over the simplest and saddest of characters. "The Great Work begins," she declares, only to reveal in the next play that it's beginning more for Prior than the others. To my astonishment, then, *Angels* may be an AIDS play after all, with Wolfe heading for the slobbering jugular because he knows that current events are better box-office than Louis's cosmic battles and failures, most especially current events that dwell on effect instead of cause.

The kicker here is that if Kushner wished merely to be current, he would have had to be more inclusive, offering a rainbow coalition of super-shifts and sappy saints—more WASPs, surely more fundamentalists, one real Lesbian at least, a Native American to go with the Eskimo who passes through the Mormon wife's fantasy, and no doubt some country-western twangers, Hispanics, CEOs, students, seniors, and maybe even a token president or Supreme Court justice or car salesman, real estate agent, talk-show host, or perhaps David Schine, the forgotten man in the real Roy Cohn saga. That Kushner is selective is a sign of a practical dramatist, not given to pageant playwriting, wholly committed to the power of image, metaphor, and resonance. Then, too, if he had wanted to write an exclusively gay or AIDS play, his models could run the gamut from those early Gore Vidal and James Baldwin novels in which the horrified gay man was on a long suicide trajectory, to *Boys in the Band*'s self-laceration, *As Is*'s romantic grief, or *The Normal Heart*'s rage against gay trimmers and closeted politicians—in short, a play identifying itself with pioneer clichés and journalistic agitation.

Millennium, however, is its own model, even if *Perestroika*—and Wolfe—are jerking it back to more familiar territory. Kushner, if I may try my own shortcut, is stalking big game in country already charted by those distinctly un-American types, Genet and Foucault, acknowledging the extravagant sexiness of the hunt, the famished need to fill oneself up with defiance and experiment. True, Louis is only a beginner, not likely to get more than a "C" in Foucault 101, but he's on the edge of always testing the unthinkable, which, like it or not, is how gays can make meaning out of a universe that forbids choice. In Central Park, he finds momentary adventure with a leather-clone who can't take him home because he lives with his parents. Kushner pushes swiftly past this irresistibly funny reversal into the briefest erotic encounter. (Stage direction: "They begin to fuck.") Louis has sought both sex and humiliation, even surrendering to the possibility that the rubber has broken. But the ultimate disgrace comes after the man pulls out, Louis getting slapped for sending his "best to Mom and Dad."

"It was a joke," he says, left only with hapless truth and forlorn grace. Kushner's mastery here is complete; time could scarcely be more compressed, tension more breathless, danger more severely linked to sex itself as the most contingent symbol available. Even more, perhaps, this is Kushner's encounter with every kind of limit, even including what can be shown and dramatized, not least to an audience of straight men, especially, unwilling to look at men holding hands in public. If this is a dare, however, it's not one that escapes Wolfe's soft touch: where Donnellan gave the fuck its own expansive time in what amounted to an act of unforgiving presence, Wolfe throws a literal spotlight over Louis's agonized face as he jolts up from the first thrust. Louis admits he can't relax; Wolfe is admitting he has to relax all those tight-asses out there so ready to be disgusted by what they're unwilling to know. This is a spotlight on gay clichés disrupting a play fighting to be gay in ways undreamt in old theologies, gay or straight.

The signals are, however, that Kushner's most challenging dangerous instincts are losing the fight. What we know now is that Louis, like the rest of us, had greatly exaggerated Prior's death. Kushner eventually lets the ghost of Ethel Rosenberg say *Kaddish* with Louis over Roy Cohn's corpse, but the joke is on both of them because Cohn, too, refuses to die, at least for a moment. As in *Millennium,* the other stories keep colliding with one another: Roy Cohn's protégé Joe, the Mormon abandoner of his wife, has become Louis's lover and a literal gay-basher, his mother abandons Salt Lake City, soon finding orgasmic ecstasy with the Angel, and Louis (well, the actor playing Louis) turns into his dead grandmother playing cards in a heaven that sounds like the old Grand Concourse. And, if you're still following me and can credit what I'm recounting, the suffering survivors end up on a Central Park bench proclaiming that Hope, if not the thing with feathers, is at least a glimmering on the otherwise bloodied horizon. In short, Kushner, for all his prodigal anger, enjoys seven hours of first-rate story-telling that fizzles into a short commercial message telling couch potatoes what they always clamor to know.

Have I reason to be disappointed? You bet I have. Not merely because Kushner is a dramatic poet settling for

less, but because he hasn't given Louis the full sway of his own tragical-comical-historical imagination. Instead, he punishes him with a more punishing affair while rewarding Cohn with a sardonic last laugh (very funny, indeed, and Kushner should have stopped right there) followed by the dignified death no AIDS victim ever enjoys. But if it's only natural to be enthralled, as Milton was, by the powerful lure of an omnivorous devil, it's not necessarily the only goal for an energetic playwright, especially one who has found a protagonist capable—as D'Amico revealed—of living in the full, consequential glare of his own lighthouse intelligence.

Suddenly, it looks as if Louis, on a course with destiny, has been thwarted by his playwright into a course with triviality. Think of what would have happened if Peer Gynt had been shoved into his own play's side shows, the onion never peeled and his fate allied to Oswald's in *Ghosts*, leading everybody to conclude that the play is really about a disease that dares—or dares not—speak its name. This transparent absurdity is surely no more Kushner's subject than syphilis was Ibsen's. Yet, with Wolfe ferreting out the side-shows—and who can wholly blame him for leaping at the bait?—Kushner's dark rendezvous with stratospheric gods slips into footlight follies.

You'd be right to surmise by now that I've begun to jam all these experiences into one giant Kushnerian stew pot, mixing up Donnellan's seasonings with Wolfe's heavy dousings of sugar and honey, unable to rescue the true wonders of *Millennium* from the still-rewritable detours in *Perestroika*. It's Louis, of course, with his dynamo mouth and tortured sin-tax, who keeps insisting on his right to a play of his own. The life at stake here is the retreating conscience of the nation, not only a gay man claiming space while rightly screaming from the rooftops that it's about time, but a life grappling with loss even before it happens, unable to cruise neatly and completely past the murmuring adjudicators within his heart. God spare him from the slaphappy claims of those, including myself, who love him too uncritically and more than he can ever know.

Ross Posnock (essay date 1994)

SOURCE: "Roy Cohn in America," in *Raritan*, Vol. 13, No. 3, Winter 1994, pp. 64-76.

[*In this essay, Posnock compares the historical Roy Cohn to Kushner's depiction of him in* Angels in America.]

"I'm immortal Ethel," the dying Roy Cohn tells the visiting specter of Ethel Rosenberg in his final words in Tony Kushner's *Angels In America: Millenium Approaches.* "I have forced my way into history. I ain't never gonna die." The prospect of cheating death might have struck Cohn in real life as the ultimate coup in the art of the deal. So what if bodily extinction is the price, Cohn might have reasoned; that's what entering history costs these days. Legendary at working all the angles, Cohn possessed an insatiable appetite for the pleasures and perils of wheedling, welshing, cajoling, extorting. His was a life of sheer performativity, free of legal or moral qualms. Laws existed to transgress, boundaries to violate; even dining with others became the occasion for going too far. As a startled Winston Churchill and many lesser luminaries discovered, Cohn would soon be using his fingers to eat off one's plate without ceremony or shame. As in most matters, he was indulged, a response that began with his worshipful mother. Her son from the start was a fluent liar and hypocrite (the zealous guardian against the red menace successfully pulled every string to avoid the draft) who never apologized and never explained. *Defiance* was the apt name of his ninety-nine-foot yacht, which Cohn was rumored to have scuttled for the insurance money. He prided himself on not being nice; "fuck nice," Kushner's Cohn snarls, and it could serve as an epitaph.

Cohn was a monstrous brat whose pugnacity was as histrionic as everything else about him; all this makes him a natural for theatrical representation. And, lucky as always, Cohn has found, in Kushner and the actor Ron Leibman, two sympathetic interpreters. (At this writing, **Perestroika,** part 2 of **Angels,** has yet to open in New York, and my discussion is confined to part 1.) "This Roy is a work of dramatic fiction," Kushner says in a note to the play; yet his fiction derives its pungency from being steeped in the details of Cohn's biography. Kushner's Cohn is a satanic figure so seductive that he threatens to explode the play's central Christian conceit of millenarian redemption. Kushner both honors and attempts to contain Cohn's disarming power. He contains it most obviously by reducing the play to a struggle between demon and angel. But before discussing **Angels** in more detail I want to describe Cohn as he has otherwise become known to us, and then set him in a larger cultural context, one that can illuminate a subject that also concerns Kushner—the status of postmodern heroism.

As more than one of his friends remarked, from an early age Cohn set his own rules. Power brokering was his consuming passion, and young Roy was precocious in leveraging his father's stature as a Bronx judge: at age thirteen he was gossip columnist for the Bronx *Home-News*; by sixteen he had fixed his first parking ticket as a favor for one of his teachers at Horace Mann; at twenty he graduated from Columbia's law school; and at twenty-three he was Assistant United States Attorney for the trial of the Rosenbergs. Here the allergy to constraint that would mark his career fully emerged, as he sought, in secret illegal communications to Judge Kaufman, death for the Rosenbergs. Soon Joe McCarthy was proudly calling him "my strong right arm." Cohn rose to national renown as the Senator's vicious boy-henchman, expert in publicly humiliating and smearing alleged communists and homosexuals (nearly all of them Jewish), and threatening to "wreck the army" when they balked at his incessant demands that his handsome and wealthy friend G. David Schine be given an easy ride. It is still startling to recall how much of the Army-McCarthy hearings revolved

around Cohn's "power whim," in the words of one fellow lawyer, his determination to bend the United States Army to his will.

Cohn's reputation, if not his boss's, survived the televised ordeal, and before too long he was thriving as the ultimate inside operator, an immensely successful Park Avenue "legal executioner" on behalf of New York City's political, social, and criminal elite. Always contemptuous of the genteel legal establishment, "owning" more judges than anyone, he relished his outlaw status. He did business with Democrats and Republicans alike, since, as he liked to say, not party but power is what counts. The parties that counted were often those he gave; recently come to light is a private one he hosted at the Plaza Hotel in 1958 for his mentor Edgar Hoover, who appeared, it is alleged, as "Mary," elegant in a fluffy black dress.

That Cohn, this American Torquemada, was himself a Jew and a homosexual (he always called them "fags") as well as a self-described "momma's boy" who lived forty of his fifty-nine years with his mother, tempts one to regard him not only as not nice but pathologically conflicted and self-loathing. His life seems a virtual hothouse of fifties neuroses, with momism and the closet under particular cultivation. Yet it would be misleading to confine Cohn to the Eisenhower era. He was never one to let history pass him by. By the time of his death in 1986, the suffocating fifties were just a memory, mom was gone, and while he never came out of the closet, his homosexual practices had long been conspicuous to those in the know. His mother's death in 1967 had left Cohn free unabashedly to enjoy his increasingly lavish sexual tastes, which included maintaining a stable of beautiful young men (always introduced as Roy's "nephews") and making frequent forays into the orgiastic nightlife of Studio 54, where his annual birthday bashes were held. For years Cohn had been the most famous New York homosexual not in show business. Yet even as he was dying of AIDS, and even though he had been outed by an enemy in the early eighties, he fiercely denied his sexual preference on "Sixty Minutes."

Just this sketch of his career suggests that Cohn provides the psychocultural critic a remarkable window to observe the sort of intricate psychic mirroring and exchanges between subversive and countersubversive that Michael Rogin has found in his important studies of American political demonology in the cold war. But the case of Roy Cohn is especially fascinating at least in part because it disarms or renders irrelevant psychoanalytic explanations as well as conventional moral judgments; they become something like the intellectual equivalent of the handwringing of a feckless liberalism—well meaning but beside the point. The effort to psychologize or moralize Cohn looks under or above him, thereby missing a fabled weapon of his own power—the gaze. Cohn's gaze emanated from a remarkable face: even in snapshots his intimidating and compelling physical ugliness assaults the eye. Photographed with a Donald Trump, a George Steinbrenner, a Barbara

Walters (his perennial beard), Cohn's priapic head, thick scarred nose, hooded reptilian eyes and deadly frozen stare are baleful. "I early learned," Murray Kempton has said, "that Roy had no interior to speak of." Armed with a photographic memory, he was known to speak in court for hours without stopping, without notes and seemingly without breathing. A "depth" reading fails to enter Cohn's uncanny aura that projected both menace and charm but also a sense of belonging to a race other than the strictly human.

In retrospect, his species seems that of pop American *Übermensch*, a lineage of amoral, lethal prodigies that begins in the twenties with Leopold and Loeb, who were devout readers of Nietzsche and, as is likely, *Crime and Punishment*. Unlike these two real life Raskolnikovs, contemporary supermen have a passion for executing not the perfect murder but the hostile takeover, and reaping tens of millions from insider trading. The Milkens and Boeskys and their progeny were, in the mid-eighties, the "masters of the Universe" in Tom Wolfe's phrase, and the "big swinging dicks" made famous in *Liar's Poker*. While he may share their indifference to limits and their love of putting in the fix, Cohn is without the asceticism that conditions the eighties money culture of excess in which a regime of the hundred-hour work week forced a Milken to gobble lunch at his desk.

Cohn may be closer to that "most revolutionary—and deeply serious—of post-war Nietzscheans," Michel Foucault, or, rather, the Foucault whom James Miller depicts in his much discussed recent biography. Miller presents this central hero of contemporary sensibility in his last decade of life as a quester in search of "limit experience," that boundary where death and pleasure bleed into each other. Foucault's search took him to San Francisco's leather underground where, enraptured, he experimented in consensual S/M. While admittedly an odd couple, Cohn and Foucault share more than death from AIDS. Their common ground could be described as a hedonistic antihumanism, if we accept Foucault's definition of humanism as "everything in Western civilization that restricts the desire for power." In passing beyond restriction, both enjoyed male orgies of "bodies and pleasures."

Foucault's passion for living dangerously prompts Miller to ask what it might mean to live a life beyond good and evil. In a wholly different key, Cohn's life poses similar questions and answers. Living "beyond" entails, among other things, acts of self-making constrained neither by the imperative to tell the truth nor by the inside/outside dichotomy that structures liberal individualism. The exemplary individual, Miller quotes Foucault, "is not the man who goes off to discover himself, his secrets, his hidden self; he is the man who tries to invent himself." Indifferent to the American therapeutic ethos, with its mantras of "personal growth" and "finding oneself," Cohn made the will to power the keystone of his self-creation. And as adamantly as any postmodernist, he insisted that the personal and political are one. Politics, the game of power,

"the game of being alive," as Kushner's Cohn says, defined his sexuality as surely as it defined every other aspect of his life.

In America "there's only the political and the decoys and the ploys to maneuver around the inescapable battle of politics," says the Jewish intellectual Louis Ironson in Kushner's play. Louis goes on to explain that "there are no gods here, no ghosts and spirits in America, there are no angels in America, no spiritual past, no racial past." This list of absences echoes Henry James's famous lament in 1879 about the thinness of American culture, and also Tocqueville's thesis (*Democracy In America* is explicitly referred to). More important, it provides Kushner with an intellectual context for suggesting how individualism so easily blossoms into demonic luxuriance amid the great vacant secular spaces of America, land of Amnesia. Thus Cohn, a man without interior, is also a representative American in the weightless age of Reagan. As unbounded as America, Cohn contrasts with the burdened Louis, still feeling ancestral ties to the old world, though in the very process of burying those ties. Early on he attends his grandmother's funeral, fears he has abandoned her, and seeks solace from the rabbi who, in the play's opening scene, has conducted the service. Made uneasy by Louis's urgent need to confess, the rabbi tells him "better you should find a priest. . . . Catholics believe in forgiveness. Jews believe in guilt," a distinction that will prove pivotal at the angelic denouement.

Ironson and Cohn never meet in part 1. But as the two dominant Jews in the play, a comparison is inevitable. Cohn's emotional antithesis, Ironson (the name suggesting his weighty concerns, which are leavened by his caustic wit) is consumed by introspection and abstraction, with questions of moral justice, guilt, and self-condemnation as he contemplates leaving his lover dying of AIDS. Louis's self-loathing serves to set off in bold relief what may be the most scandalous thing about Cohn's scandalous life—his unembarrassed pleasure in the sheer wielding of clout, in being Roy Cohn. A warrior joy is at the center of both Kushner's dramatic fiction of Cohn and of Ron Leibman's exultant, volcanic portrayal.

"I wish I was an octopus, a fucking octopus. Eight loving arms and all those suckers." These are Cohn's opening lines, spoken at his desk while working with delight an immense array of flashing phones, improvising with a half dozen different callers just the right mix of obscenity, charm, viciousness, apology, and deal making, all the while sharing bites of a sandwich with his young protégé, a Mormon lawyer named Joe Pitt, who patiently waits for his undivided attention. The scene stages and is about virtuoso performance, as Cohn's octopus-wish concisely frames what the rest of the scene enacts—his delirious, near-animal excess, greed, orality, and invasiveness. "God bless chaos," he mutters at one point.

Captivating from the start, Kushner's Cohn hopes to inspire Joe Pitt, "my pretty young punk friend" as he calls him, to be a "Royboy" and act as his "eyes" in the Justice Department where disbarment proceedings against Cohn are beginning. On the verge of acknowledging his desires for men and leaving his wife, Joe draws out Roy's paternal side. As if declaring his own version of the Greek ideal of *philia* (friendship), Cohn says: "the most precious asset in life, I think, is the ability to be a good son. . . . I've had many fathers, I owe my life to them, powerful, powerful men. Walter Winchell, Edgar Hoover, Joe McCarthy most of all. . . . I brought out something tender in him. He would have died for me. And me for him." Roy's tone darkens as he concludes with a paean to the chill rigor of the *Übermensch* ethos: "Like a father to a son I tell you this: Life is full of horror; nobody escapes, nobody; save yourself. . . . Don't be afraid; people are so afraid; don't be afraid to live in the raw wind, naked, alone. . . . Learn at least this: What you are capable of. Let nothing stand in your way."

Both satanic tempter—"Transgress a little Joseph. There are so many laws; find one you can break"—and Nietzschean overreacher—"Make the law, or [be] subject to it. Choose"—Cohn casts a seductive spell on Joe and the audience. And, clearly, on Kushner himself. After all, how does Roy Cohn, one of the most despised figures in gay political culture, whose lifelong gay-hating and sexual denials earned the words "Coward. Bully. Victim." on the AIDS quilt, manage to emerge, swaggering, at the center of one of the first works of gay theater to succeed with a mainstream Broadway audience?

Kushner's audacity in giving Cohn center stage deserves the praise it has received. Yet the meaning of Cohn's presence in the larger thematics of *Angels* raises the issue of the play's coherence. The muddle of the work derives from the fact that Kushner's ultimate ambitions are at cross purposes: he aims somehow to assimilate the Nietzschean figure of Cohn to the play's explicitly redemptive and Christian project. In his final scene, Cohn receives a visit from a heavenly emissary—Ethel Rosenberg—whose execution, he earlier told Joe, was his "greatest accomplishment." When a defiant Roy declares that he has "forced" his way into history, Ethel one-ups him by announcing: "History is about to crack wide open. Millenium approaches." Since she is on the side of the Angels, Ethel's prediction of history's imminent end is soon ratified by Kushner: amidst the heavy beating of wings, falling plaster, and white light, the play concludes with the descent of an angel to the bedside of the AIDS-stricken hero. "The great work begins: The Messenger has arrived," the Angel intones; surely the second coming is at hand. The play's hunger for a salvation of soulless America seems satisfied: there *are* Angels in America after all!

Has Roy Cohn, then, been brought to such intense dramatic life only for the purpose of receiving absolution? This seems to have been Kushner's stated intention. In an interview he has declared his need to "forgive" this man whom he hated. "Forgiveness may be the hardest political question people face. If there isn't something called

forgiveness, if there isn't a statute of limitations on crime . . . there will never be peace and progress. But forgiveness, if it means anything, has to be incredibly hard to come by. . . . Forgiveness can never be unambivalent. But how else do we set ourselves free from the nightmare of history?" Yet Cohn in life, and certainly on stage, never sought forgiveness. No Nietzschean does, since forgiveness is too close to pity, the emotion of *ressentiment*. Forgiveness likely seemed to Cohn as meaningless as believing one can escape the nightmare of politics and history. What is more, Cohn makes clear in *Angels in America* that history and politics are not things from which one can choose to be free. For Kushner's Cohn, politics are bodily, inseparable from breathing, a conception that literalizes and thus tropes upon some of the most prestigious Left shibboleths of the day.

Given the disparity between Kushner's intentions and what the play achieves, it is hard to resist the Blakean conclusion that he is of the devil's party without knowing it. The play, in short, is sharply at odds with itself. Blake meant to praise Milton, and to suggest art's openness to moral complication, its willingness to explore, indeed embrace, the corrupt, even as it wreaks havoc on one's cherished beliefs. In creating his Cohn, Kushner, perhaps unknowingly, affirms such openness. Cohn/Leibman commandeers the play, inspiring its most powerful writing and dwarfing the absorbing but largely familiar domestic subplots unfolding around him. Nothing, not even the arrival of an angel, is strong enough to topple him. Unwittingly on the side of Satan, Kushner's undeniable achievement is his nonredemptive portrayal of Cohn, a characterization whose telos is not to forgive but to witness unflinchingly Cohn's self-affirming moral indifference. To appreciate Cohn's will to power requires first elaborating the ramifications of the play's dominant metaphor of the end of history.

The literal and figurative deus ex machina that concludes part 1 of *Angels* expresses a fantasy of ending history that seems more escapist than sublime. Earlier the play had indirectly invoked another context for history's end, namely Hegel's. Louis Ironson alludes to his "neo-Hegelian positivist sense of constant historical progress toward happiness or perfection or something" as he explains to the rabbi why he is having trouble accepting his lover's illness. Maybe a person imbued with this Hegelian sense of progress, Louis avers, finds it hard to "incorporate sickness into his sense of how things are supposed to go. Maybe . . . he isn't so good with death." Louis's remarks, never clarified or enlarged upon, recall the argument of Hegel's most influential modern interpreter, Alexandre Kojève, who said that history has ended with the achievement of a "universal homogenous state"—liberal democracy—where master/slave rivalries are at last reconciled by the advent of universal recognition of equality. Thus every man is "completely satisfied," free of the threat of war, free to enjoy prosperity and animal-like contentment.

Kojève's Hegelian thesis has recently been injected into the zeitgeist. Francis Fukuyama's best-selling *The End of*

History and the Last Man recontextualizes and reinterprets Kojève to explain the sudden collapse of communism and the end of the cold war. Yet Fukuyama is indebted to Nietzsche (by way of Leo Strauss) rather than to Hegel or Kojève for his particular emphasis—that the end of history is a decidedly mixed blessing, for "we risk becoming secure and self-absorbed last men, devoid of . . . striving for higher goals in our pursuit of private comforts.""Last men" is Nietzsche's scornful phrase for those who emerge at the end of history and thrive amid the spiritual hollowness of technocratic modernity. The appearance of the last men announces the triumph of the slave morality bred by liberal democracy, which produces selfish citizens absorbed in feathering their own nests. Acknowledging neither masters nor gods, last men seek only comfortable self-preservation as their bulwark against their greatest fear, which is mortality. So Louis is quite right: believers in the Hegelian sense of progress aren't "so good with death." In the Age of Reagan, implies Kushner, all of us are last men, for, as Louis puts it, "we all know" what it is like to be "Reagan's kids," to be part of a family that isn't "really a family . . . there aren't any connections there, no love," and children and parents "don't even speak to each other except through their agents."

The last man, in Nietzsche's view, is at one extreme, and the Superman is at the other. The pivot of their differences is recognition, which Kojève defines as the desire to control the desire of other men. "To be really, truly man, and to know that he is such," a human being needs to impose himself "on the other as the supreme value," says Kojève, an action that "necessarily takes the form of a fight," a battle to the death "for pure prestige carried on for the sake of recognition." To Hegel, the demand for equal recognition, driven forward by the reality of slavery, constitutes the motor both of the human psyche and of history. Yet the universalized recognition that makes possible both democracy and the last man is precisely what the Superman deems undiscriminating, hence worthless, what only a slave could desire. This is Nietzsche's aristocratic revision of Hegel's more democratic historicism. The only valuable recognition, says Nietzsche, is the desire to be recognized as better than others. While all vital democratic societies nurture the desire for recognition of equality, the quest for superiority must also be kept alive as the animating force of all creativity and genuine freedom. In contemporary multicultural, relativist America, where the prestige of victimhood is high, the drive to superiority, as Fukuyama points out, is stigmatized and thus is sublimated into such domains as entrepreneurship, foreign policy (short decisive wars in distant countries), and sports.

In some humans the craving for superiority is less sublimated, the battles for prestige and recognition less mediated. Those too obviously hungry we call vulgar. But Roy Cohn's vulgarity may be unmatched. So inflamed was his desire to be recognized that it burned through layers of civilizing insulation, exposing to view the raw literalness, the naked avidity, of his need. Nietzsche's *Übermensch*, who is indifferent to others as he creates his own values,

might in fact scorn Cohn as being enslaved to recognition. For each time he picked up the phone he was testing the reach of his clout; every time he floated a deal, sought a favor, bought a judge, the outcome of the battle for pure prestige was on the line. Enslaved or not, however, those who refuse to sublimate their passions often startle and compel us by awakening our repressed envy.

Casting off the mediations that condition the rest of us, Cohn's relation to the political was so visceral that it obliterated any outside from which it might be judged. Kushner acutely grasps this and in a remarkable speech has Cohn reveal his embodied politics. When Joe Pitt calls Roy "unethical," Cohn replies:

> What the fuck do you think this is, Sunday School? . . . This is gastric juices churning, this is enzymes and acids, this is intestinal is what this is, bowel movement and blood-red meat—this stinks, this is *politics*, Joe, the game of being alive. And you think you're . . . What? Above that? Above alive is what? Dead! In the clouds. You're on earth, goddammit! Plant a foot, stay a while.

A body politic indeed; for Cohn, politics is the condition of being alive and thus not something about which one can have a judgment. Thus Joe's verdict of "unethical," however justified, is uttered from an illusory perch outside life and shrivels in the void of Cohn's moral nihilism. A similar fate awaits Kushner's attempted forgiveness of Cohn.

What makes the fusion of body and politics in Kushner's Cohn particularly unsettling is that it eerily echoes that liberating slogan: the personal is the political, a phrase meant to dissolve the allegedly pernicious bourgeois separation of private from public. That Cohn's embodied politics in the play also collapses both realms into each other cautions against assuming that the imperative of our current critical age—death to all binary oppositions—is inevitably the first signpost on the road to social justice.

In merging the personal and political, the homophobic Cohn, as Kushner presents him, empties the category of homosexuality of positive content. This is dramatized in an already well-known scene in *Angels*. As his doctor tells him he has AIDS, Cohn taunts him, daring him to say "Roy Marcus Cohn you are a homosexual" on pain of having him [Cohn] destroy his career. Roy rejects the label *homosexual* to describe himself not out of shame, since he is incapable of feeling that, but because "what a label refers to . . . [is] clout. Not who I fuck or who fucks me, but who will pick up the phone when I call, who owes me favors." Homosexuals, Cohn goes on to say, "are not men who sleep with other men. . . . Homosexuals are men who know nobody and who nobody knows. Who have zero clout. . . . Roy Cohn is not a homosexual. Roy Cohn is a heterosexual man . . . who fucks around with guys."

This self-invention is Kushner's Cohn at his most Nietzschean, as he transvalues sexuality by equating it with power rather than with identity. Cohn's views were formed in the closeted America of the fifties, the advent of his power brokering. Existing sub rosa, homosexuality was beneath the political, bereft of public life, adrift in a dead zone of "zero clout." And to men like Cohn or his mentor Hoover, for whom politics was not simply a domain of existence but instead the very "game of being alive," the notion of homosexuality as an identity was tantamount to a condition of living death—the absence of power and of self-mastery. Its political label—as un-American—was the sum of its negativity.

Kushner's Cohn forces us to be skeptical about assuming that a hidden reality of agonizing sexual self-hatred rages inside him. Such an assumption is derived from the modern therapeutic regime that constructs sexuality itself as a constitutive truth of identity. In short, Kushner's Cohn asks us to entertain the possibility that Cohn was neither out nor closeted. Rather, Cohn (and Hoover) found the negation called homosexuality irrelevant to himself and regarded his preference for men as the Greeks did—as a matter of taste, not something expressing his "very nature, the truth of his desire, or the natural legitimacy of his predilection." The words are Foucault's to describe our modern notion of sexuality, which sharply differs from male sexuality in ancient Greek "experience, forms of valuation, and systems of categorization." Perhaps we are closer to Rome since, like us, Rome came after, inflating self-regard to imperial dimensions of arrogance and becoming a decadent imitation of the Greek ideal of boy love. At one birthday bash Studio 54 served as Roy's Rome, where his Greek taste was both made explicit and parodied: his toga-clad "nephews," reports Sidney Zion, crowned their "Uncle" with golden laurel leaves, singing "Happy Birthday" to a Roy "looking every bit the modern Emperor Hadrian."

Emperor Cohn, like Kushner's Cohn, tells us something about the character of postmodern heroism. Here, again, a comparison with Foucault suggests itself. Yoking them together reminds us that embarrassing, even grotesque excess is less an impediment to than the condition of both men's attainment of a certain bizarre grandeur. Their *Übermensch* status is laced with comic incongruities: Cohn the icy "legal executioner" and sissy momma's boy; Foucault, the brooding philosopher of power and wide-eyed tourist on Folsom Street as if enacting a leather-jacketed update of *The Blue Angel*. This all-too-human parodic Nietzscheanism reflects a logic implicit in Foucault's insistence that his S/M experiments were not to be understood as repeating those of de Sade, his great predecessor in sexual anarchy. De Sade had valorized genital sex, whereas Foucault's "limit experience" sought what he called a "nondisciplinary eroticism" that invented "new possibilities of pleasure with strange parts" of the body. The nondisciplinary severs bodily from sexual pleasure, a "desexualization of pleasure" that Foucault jocularly summed up with the mock slogan "erections are out!"

This last phrase, a new take on the more familiar "small is beautiful," encapsulates the "second time as farce" quality that may be the signature of the postmodern. The heroic bid to topple Western sexuality from its dual identity as both genitally organized and the deepest truth of subjectivity ends as the quest for impotence. Granted, Foucault's is an *achieved* impotence attainable only to the sexual outlaw of "limit experience," one who risks going "Beyond Sex," as he puts it. But granting this does not deny that under such conditions the heroic uneasily contains its own incipient demolition, as Superman threatens to collapse into "last man."

Postmodern heroism's pervasive irony often is intended to function preemptively, as a healthy purgative, washing away any totalizing impulses that might cross the precarious boundary between the superhuman and the inhuman. As Nietzsche before him, Foucault discovered, in Miller's words, how "ruthless and unrelenting" must be the effort to "identify and uproot the inhuman—and to identify and tear out the fascism in us all." The project may be impossibly self-defeating—its very rigor reinforces the condition meant to be extirpated. But Foucault thought that the struggle against the attractions of totalitarian power—sexual and political—was important. As a lifelong addict of brutal power, Roy Cohn likely underwent no such ascetic struggle, endured no such tension. To have revealed the scandal of Cohn's unrepentant pleasure in power is Kushner's signal achievement, one that survives his proferring of forgiveness.

David Savran   (essay date 1995)

SOURCE: "Ambivalence, Utopia, and a Queer Sort of Materialism: How *Angels in America* Reconstructs the Nation," in *Theatre Journal*, Vol. 47, No. 2, May 1995, pp. 207-27.

[*In the essay below, Savran attempts to answer the question of why "a play featuring five gay male characters [is] being universalized as a 'turning point' in the American theatre, and minoritized as the preeminent gay male artifact of the 1990s."*]

Critics, pundits, and producers have placed Tony Kushner's ***Angels in America: A Gay Fantasia on National Themes*** in the unenviable position of having to rescue the American theatre. The latter, by all accounts, is in a sorry state. It has attempted to maintain its elite cultural status despite the fact that the differences between "high" and "low" have become precarious. On Broadway, increasingly expensive productions survive more and more by mimicking mass culture, either in the form of mind-numbing spectacles featuring singing cats, falling chandeliers, and dancing dinnerware or plays, like *The Heidi Chronicles* or *Prelude to a Kiss*, whose style and themes aspire to "quality" television. In regional theatres, meanwhile, subscriptions continue to decline, and with them the adventurousness of artistic directors. Given this dismal situation, ***Angels in America*** has almost singlehandedly resuscitated a category of play that has become almost extinct: the serious Broadway drama that is neither a British import nor a revival.

Not within memory has a new American play been canonized by the press as rapidly as *Angels in America*.[1] Indeed, critics have been stumbling over each other in an adulatory stupor. John Lahr hails *Perestroika* as a "masterpiece" and notes that "[n]ot since Williams has a playwright announced his poetic vision with such authority on the Broadway stage."[2] Jack Kroll judges both parts "the broadest, deepest, most searching American play of our time," while Robert Brustein deems *Millennium Approaches* "the authoritative achievement of a radical dramatic artist with a fresh, clear voice."[3] In the gay press, meanwhile, the play is viewed as testifying to the fact that "Broadway now leads the way in the industry with its unapologetic portrayals of gay characters."[4] For both Frank Rich and John Clum, *Angels* is far more than just a successful play; it is the marker of a decisive historical shift in American theatre. According to Rich, the play's success is in part the result of its ability to conduct "a searching and radical rethinking of the whole esthetic of American political drama."[5] For Clum, the play's appearance on Broadway "marks a turning point in the history of gay drama, the history of American drama, and of American literary culture."[6] In its reception, *Angels*—so deeply preoccupied with teleological process—is itself positioned as both the culmination of history and as that which rewrites the past.

Despite the enormity of the claims cited above, I am less interested in disputing them than in trying to understand why they are being made—and why *now*. Why is a play featuring five gay male characters being universalized as a "turning point" in the American theatre, and minoritized as the preeminent gay male artifact of the 1990s? Why is it both popular and "radical?" What is the linkage between the two primary sources for the play's theory of history and utopia—Walter Benjamin and Mormonism? And what does this linkage suggest about the constitution of the nation? Finally, why has queer drama become *the* theatrical sensation of the 1990s? I hope it's not too perverse of me to attempt to answer these questions by focusing less on the construction of queer subjectivities per se than on the field of cultural production in which *Angels in America* is situated. After all, how else would one practice a queer materialism?

THE ANGEL OF HISTORY

The opposite of nearly everything you say about *Angels in America* will also hold true: *Angels* valorizes identity politics; it offers an anti-foundationalist critique of identity politics. *Angels* mounts an attack against ideologies of individualism; it problematizes the idea of community. *Angels* submits liberalism to a trenchant examination; it finally opts for yet another version of American liberal pluralism. *Angels* launches a critique of the very mechanisms that produce pathologized and acquiescent female bodies; it represents yet another pathologization and silencing of women. A conscientious reader or spectator might well rebuke the play, as Belize does Louis: "you're ambivalent about everything."[7] And so it is. The play's ambivalence, however, is not simply the result of Kushner hedging his bets on the most controversial issues. Rather, it functions, I believe—quite independently of the intent of its author—as the play's political unconscious, playing itself out on many different levels: formal, ideological, characterological, and rhetorical. (Frank Rich refers to this as Kushner's "refusal to adhere to any theatrical or political theory."[8]) Yet the fact that ambivalence—or undecidability—is the watchword of this text (which is, after all, *two* plays) does not mean that all the questions it raises remain unresolved. On the contrary, I will argue that the play's undecidability is, in fact, always already resolved because the questions that appear to be ambivalent in fact already have been decided consciously or unconsciously by the text itself. Moreover, the relentless operation of normalizing reading practices works to reinforce these decisions. If I am correct, the play turns out (*pace* Frank Rich) to adhere all too well to a particular political theory.

Formally, *Angels* is a promiscuously complicated play that is very difficult to categorize generically. Clum's characterization of it as being "like a Shakespearean romance" is doubtlessly motivated by the play's rambling and episodic form, its interweaving of multiple plotlines, its mixture of realism and fantasy, its invocation of various theological and mythological narratives, as well as by its success in evoking those characteristics that are usually associated with both comedy and tragedy.[9] Moreover, *Perestroika*'s luminous finale is remarkably suggestive of the beatific scenes that end Shakespeare's romances. There is no question, moreover, but that the play deliberately evokes the long history of Western dramatic literature and positions itself as heir to the traditions of Sophocles, Shakespeare, Brecht, and others. Consider, for example, its use of the blindness/insight opposition and the way that Prior Walter is carefully constructed (like the blind Prelapsarianov) as a kind of Teiresias, "going blind, as prophets do."[10] This binarism, the paradigmatic emblem of the tragic subject (and mark of Teiresias, Oedipus, and Gloucester) deftly links cause and effect—because one is blind to truth, one loses one's sight—and is used to claim Prior's priority, his epistemologically privileged position in the text. Or consider the parallels often drawn in the press between Kushner's Roy Cohn and Shakespeare's Richard III.[11] Or Kushner's use of a fate motif, reminiscent of *Macbeth*, whereby Prior insists that Louis not return until the seemingly impossible comes to pass, until he sees Louis "black and blue" (2:89). Or Kushner's rewriting of those momentous moral and political debates that riddle not just classical tragedy (*Antigone, Richard II*) but also the work of Brecht and his (mainly British) successors (Howard Brenton, David Hare, Caryl Churchill). Or the focus on the presence/absence of God that one finds not just in early modern tragedy but also in so-called Absurdism (Beckett, Ionesco, Stoppard). Moreover, these characteristics tend to be balanced, on the one hand, by the play's insistent tendency to ironize and, on the other, by the familiar ingredients of romantic comedies (ill-matched paramours, repentant lovers, characters suddenly finding themselves in unfamiliar places, plus a lot of good jokes). Despite the ironic/comic tone, however, none of the interlaced couples survives the onslaught of chaos, disease, and revelation. Prior and Louis, Louis and Joe, Joe and Harper have all parted by the end of the play and the romantic dyad (as primary social unit) is replaced in the final scene of **Perestroika** by a utopian concept of (erotic) affiliation and a new definition of family.

Angels in America's title, its idea of utopia, and its model for a particular kind of ambivalence are derived in part from Benjamin's extraordinary meditation, "Theses on the Philosophy of History," written shortly before his death in 1940. Composed during the first months of World War II, with fascism on its march across Europe, the darkness (and simultaneous luminosity) of Benjamin's "Theses" attest not only to the seeming invincibility of Hitler, but also to the impossible position of the European left, "[s]tranded," as Terry Eagleton notes, "between social democracy and Stalinism."[12] In this essay, Benjamin sketches a discontinuous theory of history in which "the services of theology" are enlisted in the aid of reconceiving "historical materialism."[13] Opposing the universalizing strategies of bourgeois historicism with historical materialism's project of brushing "history against the grain" (257), he attempts a radical revision of Marxist historiography. Suturing the Jewish notion of Messianic time (in which all history is given meaning retrospectively by the sudden and unexpected coming of the Messiah) to the Marxist concept of revolution, Benjamin reimagines proletariat revolution not as the culmination of a conflict between classes, or between traditional institutions and new forms of production, but as a "blast[ing] open" of "the continuum of history" (262). Unlike traditional Marxist (or idealist) historiographers, he rejects the idea of the present as a moment of "transition" and instead conceives it as *Jetztzeit*: "time filled by the presence of the now" (261), a moment in which "time stands still and has come to a stop" (262). Facing *Jetztseit*, and opposing all forms of gradualism, Benjamin's historical materialist is given the task not of imagining and inciting progressive change (or a movement toward socialism), but of "blast[ing] a specific era out of the homogeneous course of history" (263).

The centerpiece of Benjamin's essay is his explication of a painting by Paul Klee, which becomes a parable of history, of the time of the Now, in the face of catastrophe (which for him means all of human history):

> A Klee painting named "Angelus Novus" shows an angel looking as though he is about to move away from something he is fixedly contemplating. His eyes are staring, his mouth is open, his wings are spread. This is how one pictures the angel of history. His face is turned toward the past. Where we perceive a chain of events, he sees one single catastrophe which keeps piling wreckage upon wreckage and hurls it in front of his feet. The angel would like to stay, awaken the dead, and make whole what has been smashed. But a storm is blowing from Paradise; it has got caught in his wings with such violence that the angel can no longer close them. This storm irresistibly propels him into the future to which his back is turned, while the pile of debris

before him grows skyward. This storm is what we call progress.

[257-58]

In Benjamin's allegory, with its irresolvable play of contradictions, the doggedly well-intentioned angel of history embodies both the inconceivability of progress and the excruciating condition of the Now. Poised (not unlike Benjamin himself in Europe in 1940) between the past, which is to say "catastrophe," and an unknown and terrifying future, he is less a heavenly actor than a passive observer, "fixedly contemplating" that disaster which is the history of the world. His "Paradise," meanwhile, is not the site of a benign utopianism but a "storm" whose "violence" gets caught under his wings and propels him helplessly into an inconceivable future that stymies his gaze.

Benjamin's allegory of history is, in many respects, the primary generative fiction for **Angels in America.** Not only is its Angel clearly derived from Benjamin's text (although with gender reassignment surgery along the way—Kushner's Angel is "Hermaphroditically Equipped"), but so is its vision of Heaven, which has *"a deserted, derelict feel to it,"* with *"rubble . . . strewn everywhere"* (2:48; 121). And the play's conceptualizations of the past, of catastrophe, and of utopia are clearly inflected by Benjamin's "Theses," as is its linkage between historical materialism and theology. Moreover, rather than attempt to suppress the contradictions that inform Benjamin's materialist theology, Kushner expands them. As a result, the ideas of history, progress, and paradise that **Angels in America** invokes are irreducibly contradictory (often without appearing to be so). Just as Benjamin's notion of revolution is related dialectically to catastrophe, so are **Angels**'s concepts of deliverance and adjection, ecstasy and pain, utopia and dystopia, necessarily linked. Kushner's Angel (and her/his heaven) serve as a constant reminder both of catastrophe (AIDS, racism, homophobia, and the pathologization of queer and female bodies, to name only the play's most obvious examples) and of the perpetual possibility of millennium's approach, or in the words of Ethel Rosenberg (unmistakably echoing Benjamin), that "[h]istory is about to crack wide open" (1:112). And the concept of utopia/dystopia to which s/he is linked guarantees that the vehicle of hope and redemption in **Angels**—the prophet who foresees a new age—will be the character who must endure the most agony: Prior Walter, suffering from AIDS and Louis's desertion.

Within the economy of utopia/dystopia that **Angels** installs, the greatest promise of the millennium is the possibility of life freed from the shackles of hatred, oppression, and disease. It is hardly surprising, therefore, that Roy Cohn is constructed as the embodiment and guarantor of dystopia. Not only is he the paradigm of bourgeois individualism—and Reaganism—at its most murderous, hypocritical, and malignant, but he is the one with the most terrifying vision of the "universe," which he apprehends "as a kind of sandstorm in outer space with winds of mega-hurricane velocity, but instead of grains of sand it's shards and splinters of glass" (1:13). It is, however, a sign of the play's obsessively dialectical structure that Roy's vision of what sounds like hell should provide an uncanny echo of Benjamin's "storm blowing from Paradise." Yet even this dialectic, much like the play's ambivalences, is deceptive insofar as its habit of turning one pole of a binarism relentlessly into its opposite (rather than into a synthesis) describes a false dialectic. Prior, on the other hand, refusing the role of victim, becomes the sign of the unimaginable, of "[t]he Great Work" (2:148). Yet, as with Roy, so Prior's privileged position is a figure of contradiction, coupling not just blindness with prophecy, but also history with an impossible future, an ancient lineage (embodies by Prior 1 and Prior 2) with the millennium yet to come, and AIDS with a "most inner part, entirely free of disease" (1:34). Moreover, Prior's very name designates his temporal dislocation, the fact that he is at once too soon and belated, both that which anticipates and that which provides an epilogue (to the Walter family, if nothing else, since he seems to mark the end of the line). Prior Walter also serves as the queer commemoration of the Walter that came before—Walter Benjamin—whose revolutionary principles he both embodies and displaces insofar as he marks both the presence and absence of Walter Benjamin in this text.[14]

Throughout *Angels in America,* the utopia/dystopia coupling (wherein disaster becomes simultaneously the marker for and incitement to think Paradise) plays itself out through a host of binary oppositions: heaven/hell, forgiveness/retribution, communitarianism/individualism, spirit/flesh, pleasure/pain, beauty/decay, future/past, homosexuality/heterosexuality, rationalism/indeterminacy, migration/staying put, progress/stasis, life/death. Each of these functions not just as a set of conceptual poles in relation to which characters and themes are worked out and interpreted, but also as an *oxymoron,* a figure of undecidability whose contradictory being becomes an incitement to think the impossible—revolution. For it is precisely the conjunction of opposites that allows what Benjamin calls "the flow of thoughts" to be given a "shock" and so turned into "the sign of a Messianic cessation of happening" (262-63). The oxymoron, in other words, becomes the privileged figure by which the unimaginable allows itself to be imagined.

In Kushner's reading of Benjamin, the hermaphroditic Angel becomes the most crucial site for the elaboration of contradiction. Because her/his body is the one on which an impossible—and utopian—sexual conjunction is played out, s/he decisively undermines the distinction between the heterosexual and the homosexual. With her/his "eight vaginas" and "Bouquet of Phalli" (2:48), s/he represents an absolute otherness, the impossible Other that fulfills the longing for both the maternal and paternal (or in Lacanian terms, both demand and the Law). On the one hand, as the maternal "Other," s/he is constituted by "[d]emand . . . as already possessing the 'privilege' of satisfying needs, that is to say, the power of depriving them of that alone by which they are satisfied."[15] On the other hand, "[a]s the law

of symbolic functioning," s/he simultaneously represents the "Other embodied in the figure of the symbolic father," "not a person but a place, the locus of law, language and the symbolic."[16] The impossible conjunction of the maternal and the paternal, s/he provides Prior with sexual pleasure of celestial quality—and gives a new meaning to safe sex. At the same time, s/he also fills and completes subjectivity, being the embodiment of and receptacle for Prior's "Released Female Essence" (2:48).

Although all of these characteristics suggest that the Angel is constructed as an extratemporal being, untouched by the ravages of passing time, s/he comes (quite literally for Prior) already culturally mediated. When s/he first appears at the end of **Millennium,** he exclaims, "*Very* Steven Spielberg" (1:118). Although his campy ejaculation is clearly calculated as a laugh line, defusing and undercutting (with typical postmodern cynicism) the deadly earnestness of the scene, it also betrays the fact that this miraculous apparition is in part the product of a culture industry and that any reading of her/him will be mediated by the success of Steven Spielberg and his ilk (in films like *Close Encounters of the Third Kind* and *E.T.*) in producing a particular vision of the miraculous—with lots of bright white light and music by John Williams. To that extent, the appearance of the Angel signals the degree to which utopia—and revolution!—have now become the product of commodity culture. Unlike earlier periods, when utopia tended to be imagined in terms of production (rather than consumption) and was sited in a preceding phase of capitalism (for example, in a preindustrial or agrarian society), late capitalism envisions utopia through the lens of the commodity and—not unlike Walter Benjamin at his most populist—projects it into a future and an elsewhere lit by that *"unearthly white light"* (1:118) which represents, among other things, the illimitable allure of the commodity form.[17]

Although the construction of the Angel represses her/his historicity, the heaven s/he calls home is explicitly the product (and victim) of temporality. Heaven is a simulacrum of San Francisco on 18 April 1906, the day of the Great Earthquake. For it is on this day that God "[a]bandoned" his angels and their heaven *"[a]nd did not return"* (2:51). Heaven thus appears frozen in time, *"deserted and derelict,"* with *"rubble strewn everywhere"* (2:121). The Council Room in Heaven, meanwhile, *"dimly lit by candles and a single great bulb"* (which periodically fails) is a monument to the past, specifically to the New Science of the seventeenth century and the Englightenment project to which it is inextricably linked. The table in the Council Room is *"covered with antique and broken astronomical, astrological, mathematical and nautical objects of measurement and calculation. . . ."* At its center sits a *"bulky radio, a 1940s model in very poor repair"* (2:128) on which the Angels are listening to the first reports of the Chernobyl disaster. Conflating different moments of the past and distinct (Western) histories, Heaven is a kind of museum, not the insignia of the Now, but of *before,* of an antique past, of the obsolete. Its decrepitude is also symptomatic of the Angels' fear that God will never return. More nightmare than utopia, marooned in history, Heaven commemorates disaster, despair, and stasis.

Because of its embeddedness in the past, the geography of Heaven is a key to the complex notion of temporality that governs *Angels in America.* Although the scheme does not become clear until *Perestroika,* there are two opposing concepts of time and history running through the play. First, there is the time of the Angels (and of Heaven), the time of dystopian "STASIS" (2:54) as decreed by the absence of a God who, Prior insists, "isn't coming back" (2:133). According to the Angel, this temporal paralysis is the direct result of the hyperactivity of human beings: *"YOU HAVE DRIVEN HIM AWAY!,"* the Angel enjoins Prior, "YOU MUST STOP MOVING!" (2:52), in the hope that immobility will once again prompt the return of God and the forward movement of time. Yet this concept of time as stasis is also linked to decay. In the Angel's threnody that ends the Council scene, s/he envisions the dissolution of "the Great Design, / The spiraling apart of the Work of Eternity" (2:134). Directly opposed to this concept is human temporality, of which Prior, in contradistinction to the Angel, becomes the spokesperson. This time—which is also apparently the time of God—is the temporality connected with Enlightenment epistemologies; it is the time of "Progress," "Science," and "Forward Motion" (2:132; 50). It is the time of "Change" (2:13) so fervently desired by Comrade Prelapsarianov and the "neo-Hegelian positivist sense of constant historical progress towards happiness or perfection" so precious to Louis (1:25). It is the promise fulfilled at the end of *Perestroika* when Louis, apprehending "the end of the Cold War," announces, "[t]he whole world is changing!" (2:145). Most important, the time of "progress, migration, motion" and "modernity" is also, in Prior's formulation, the time of "desire," because it is this last all-too-human characteristic that produces modernity (2:132). Without desire (for change, utopia, the Other), there could be no history.

Despite the fact that this binary opposition generates so much of the play's ideological framework, and that its two poles are at times indistinguishable, it seems to me that this is one question on which *Angels in America* is not ambivalent at all. Unlike the Benjamin of the "Theses on the Philosophy of History," for whom any concept of progress seems quite inconceivable, Kushner is devoted to rescuing Enlightenment epistemologies at a time when they are, to say the least, extremely unfashionable. On the one hand, *Angels in America* counters attacks from the pundits of the right, wallowing in their post-Cold War triumphalism, for whom socialism, or "the coordination of men's activities through central direction," is the road to "serfdom."[18] For these neoconservatives, "[w]e already live in the millennial new age," we already stand at "the end of history" and, as a result, in Francis Fukuyama's words, "we cannot picture to ourselves a world that is *essentially* different from the present one, and at the same time better."[19] Obsessed with "free markets and private

property," and trying desperately to maintain the imperialist status quo, they can only imagine progress as regression.[20] On the other hand, *Angels* also challenges the orthodoxies of those poststructuralists on the left by whom the Marxian concept of history is often dismissed as hopelessly idealist, as "a contemptible attempt" to construct" grand narratives" and "totalizing (totalitarian?) knowledges."[21] In the face of these profound cynicisms, *Angels* unabashedly champions rationalism and progress. In the last words of *Perestroika*'s last act, Harper suggests that "[i]n this world, there is a kind of painful progress. Longing for what we've left behind, and dreaming ahead" (2:144). The last words of the epilogue, meanwhile, are given to Prior who envisions a future in which "[w]e" (presumably gay men, lesbians, and persons with AIDS) "will be citizens." *"More Life"* (2:148), he demands.

Kushner's differences with Benjamin—and the poststructuralists—over the possibility of progress and his championing of modernity (and the desire that produces it) suggest that the string of binary oppositions that are foundational to the play are perhaps less undecidable than I originally suggested. Meaning is produced, in part, because these oppositions are constructed as interlocking homologies, each an analogy for all the others. And despite the fact that each term of each opposition is strictly dependent on the other and, indeed, is produced by its other, these relations are by no means symmetrical. Binary oppositions are always hierarchical—especially when the fact of hierarchy is repressed. *Angels* is carefully constructed so that communitarianism, rationalism, progress, and so forth, will be read as being preferable to their alternatives: individualism, indeterminacy, stasis, and so forth ("the playwright has been able to find hope in his chronicle of the poisonous 1980s"[22]). So at least as far as this string of interlocked binary oppositions is concerned, ambivalence turns out to be not especially ambivalent after all.

At the same time, what is one to make of other binarisms—most notably, the opposition between masculine and feminine—toward which the play seems to cultivate a certain studied ambivalence? On the one hand, it is clear that Kushner is making some effort to counter the long history of the marginalization and silencing of women in American culture generally and in American theatre, in particular. Harper's hallucinations are crucial to the play's articulation of its central themes, including questions of exile and of the utopia/dystopia binarism. They also give her a privileged relationship to Prior, in whose fantasies she sometimes partakes and with whom she visits Heaven. Her unequivocal rejection of Joe and expropriation of his credit card at the end of the play, moreover, signal her repossession of her life and her progress from imaginary to real travel. Hannah, meanwhile, is constructed as an extremely independent and strong-willed woman who becomes part of the new extended family that is consolidated at the end of the play. Most intriguingly, the play's deliberate foregrounding of the silencing of the Mormon Mother and Daughter in the diorama is symptomatic of Kushner's desire to let women speak. On the other hand, *Angels* seems to replicate many of the structures that historically have produced female subjectivity as Other. Harper may be crucial to the play's structure but she is still pathologized, like so many of her antecedents on the American stage (from Mary Tyrone to Blanche DuBois to Honey in *Who's Afraid of Virginia Woolf?*). With her hallucinations and "emotional problems" (1:27), she functions as a scapegoat for Joe, the displacement of his sexual problems. Moreover, her false confession that she's "going to have a baby" (1:41) not only reinforces the link in the play between femininity and maternity but also literally hystericizes her. And Hannah, despite her strength, is defined almost entirely by her relationship to her real son and to Prior, her surrogate son. Like Belize, she is given the role of caretaker.

Most important, the celestial "sexual politics" (2:49) of the play guarantees that the feminine remains Other. After his visitation by the Angel, Prior explains that "God . . . is a man. Well, not a man, he's a flaming Hebrew letter, but a male flaming Hebrew letter" (2:49). In comparison with this masculinized, Old Testament-style, "flaming"(!) patriarch, the Angels are decidedly hermaphroditic. Nonetheless, the play's stage directions use the feminine pronoun when designating the Angel and s/he has been played by a woman in all of the play's various American premières. As a result of this clearly delineated gendered difference, femininity is associated (in Heaven at least) with "STASIS" and collapse, while a divine masculinity is coded as being simultaneously deterministic and absent. In the play's pseudo-Platonic—and heterosexualized—metaphysics, the "orgasm" of the Angels produces (a feminized) "protomatter, which fuels the [masculinized] Engine of Creation" (2:49).

Moreover, the play's use of doubling reinforces this sense of the centrality of masculinity. Unlike Caryl Churchill's *Cloud 9* (surely the locus classicus of genderfuck), *Angels* uses cross-gender casting only for minor characters. And the crossing of gender works in one direction only. The actresses playing Hannah, Harper, and the Angel take on a number of male heterosexual characters while the male actors double only in masculine roles. As a result, it seems to me that *Angels,* unlike the work of Churchill, does not denaturalize gender. Rather, masculinity—which, intriguingly, is always already queered in this text—is produced as a remarkably stable, if contradictory, essence that others can mime but which only a real (i.e., biological) male can embody. Thus, yet another ambivalence turns out to be always already decided.

THE AMERICAN RELIGION

The nation that *Angels in America* fantasizes has its roots in the early nineteenth century, the period during which the United States became constituted, to borrow Benedict Anderson's celebrated formulation, as "an imagined political community, . . . imagined as both inherently limited and sovereign."[23] For not until the 1830s and 1840s, with the success of Jacksonian democracy and the development of the ideology of Manifest Destiny, did a sense of an imagined community of Americans begin to solidify, due to a

number of factors: the consolidation of industrialization in the Northeast; the proliferation of large newspapers and state banks; and a transportation revolution that linked the urban centers with both agricultural producers and markets abroad.[24]

It is far more than coincidence that the birth of the modern idea of America coincided with what is often called the Second Great Awakening (the First had culminated in the Revolutionary War). During these years, as Klaus Hansen relates, "the old paternalistic reform impulse directed toward social control yielded to a romantic reform movement impelled by millennialism, immediatism, and individualism." This movement, in turn, "made possible the creation of the modern American capitalist empire with its fundamental belief in religious, political, and economic pluralism."[25] For those made uneasy (for a variety of reasons) by the new Jacksonian individualism, this pluralism authorized the emergence of alternative social and religious sects, both millennialist evangelical revivals and new communities like the Shakers, the Oneida Perfectionists, and, most prominently and successfully, the Mormons.[26] As Hansen emphasizes, "Mormonism was not merely one more variant of American Protestant pluralism but an articulate and sophisticated counterideology that attempted to establish a 'new heaven and a new earth. . . .'" Moreover, "both in its origins and doctrines," Mormonism "insisted on the peculiarly American nature of its fundamental values" and on the identity of America as the promised land.[27]

Given the number and prominence of Mormon characters in the play, it should come as little surprise that Mormonism, at least as it was originally articulated in the 1820s and 1830s, maintains a very close relationship to the epistemology of *Angels in America.* Many of the explicitly hieratic qualities of the play—the notion of prophecy, the sacred book, as well as the Angel her/himself—owe as much to Mormonism as to Walter Benjamin. Even more important, the play's conceptualization of history, its millennialism, and its idea of America bring it startlingly close to the tenets of early Mormonism. Indeed, it is impossible to understand the concept of the nation with which *Angels* is obsessed (and even the idea of queering the nation!) without understanding the constitution of early Mormonism. Providing Calvinism with its most radical challenge during the National Period, it was deeply utopian in its thrust (and it remains so today). Indeed, its concept of time is identical to the temporality for which *Angels in America* polemicizes. Like *Angels,* Mormonism understands time as evolution and progress (in that sense, it is more closely linked to Enlightenment epistemologies than Romantic ones) and holds out the possibility of unlimited human growth: "As man is God once was: as God is man may become."[28] Part of a tremendous resurgence of interest in the millennium between 1828 and 1832, Mormonism went far beyond the ideology of progress implicit in Jacksonian democracy (just as *Angels*'s millennialism goes far beyond most contemporary ideologies of progress).[29] Understood historically, this utopianism was in part the result of the relatively marginal economic status of Joseph Smith and his followers, subsistence farmers and struggling petits bourgeois. Tending "to be'agin the government,'" these early Mormons were a persecuted minority and, in their westward journey to Zion, became the subjects of widespread violence, beginning in 1832 when Smith was tarred and feathered in Ohio.[30] Much like twentieth-century lesbians and gay men—although most contemporary Mormons would be appalled by the comparison—Mormons were, throughout the 1830s and 1840s, attacked by mobs, arrested on false charges, imprisoned, and murdered. In 1838, the Governor of Missouri decreed that they must be "exterminated" or expelled from the state. In 1844, Smith and his brother were assassinated by an angry mob.[31]

The violent antipathy towards early Mormonism was in part the result of the fact that it presented a significant challenge to the principles of individualist social and economic organization. From the beginning, Mormonism was communitarian in nature and proposed a kind of ecclesiastical socialism in which "those entering the order were asked to 'consecrate' their property and belongings to the church. . . ." To each male would then be returned enough to sustain him and his family, while the remainder would be apportioned to "'every man who has need. . . .'" As Hansen emphasizes, this organization represents a repudiation of the principles of laissez-faire and an attempt "to restore a more traditional society in which the economy was regulated in behalf of the larger interests of the group. . . ."[32] This nostalgia for an earlier period of capitalism (the agrarianism of the early colonies) is echoed by Mormonism's conceptualization of the continent as the promised land. Believing the Garden of Eden to have been sited in America and assigning all antediluvian history to the western hemisphere, early Mormonism believed that the term "'New World' was in fact a misnomer because America was really the cradle of man and civilization."[33] So the privileged character of the nation is linked to its sacred past and—as with Benjamin—history is tied to theology. At the same time, this essentially theological conceptualization of the nation bears witness to the "strong affinity," noted by Anderson, between "the nationalist imagining" and "religious imaginings."[34] As Timothy Brennan explains it, "nationalism largely extend[s] and modernize[s] (although [does] not replace) 'religious imaginings,' taking on religion's concern with death, continuity, and the desire for origins."[35] Like religion, the nation authorizes a reconfiguration of time and mortality, a "secular transformation of fatality into continuity, contingency into meaning."[36] Mormonism's spiritual geography was perfectly suited to this process, constructing America as both origin and meaning of history. Moreover, as Hans Kohn has pointed out, modern nationalism has expropriated three crucial concepts from those same Old Testament mythologies that provide the basis for Mormonism: "the idea of a chosen people, the emphasis on a common stock of memory of the past and of hopes for the future, and finally national messianism."[37]

This conceptualization of America as the site of a blessed past and a millennial future represents—simultaneously—the fulfillment of early nineteenth-century ideas of the nation and a repudiation of the ideologies of individualism and acquisitiveness that underwrite the Jacksonian marketplace. Yet, as Sacvan Bercovitch points out, this contradiction was at the heart of the nationalist project. As the economy was being transformed "from agrarian to industrial capitalism," the primary "source of dissent was an indigenous residual culture," which, like Mormonism, was "variously identified with agrarianism, libertarian thought, and the tradition of civic humanism." These ideologies, "by conserving the myths of a bygone age" and dreaming "of human wholeness and social regeneration," then produced "the notion of an ideal America with a politically transformative potential." Like the writers of the American Renaissance, Mormonism "adopted the culture's *controlling* metaphor—'America' as synonym for human possibility," and then turned it against the dominant class. Both producing and fulfilling the nationalist dream, it "portray[ed] the American ideology, as all ideology yearns to be portrayed, in the transcendent colors of utopia."[38] A form of dissent that ultimately (and contradictorily) reinforced hegemonic values, Mormonism reconceived America as the promised land, the land of an already achieved utopia, and simultaneously as the land of promise, the site of the millennium yet to come.

I recapitulate the early history of Mormonism because I believe it is crucial for understanding how ***Angels in America*** has been culturally positioned. It seems to me that the play replicates both the situation and project of early Mormonism with an uncanny accuracy and thereby documents the continued validity of both a particular regressive fantasy of America and a particular understanding of oppositional cultural practices. Like the projects of Joseph Smith and his followers, ***Angels*** has, from the beginning, on the levels of authorial intention and reception, been constructed as an oppositional, and even "radical" work. Structurally and ideologically, the play challenges the conventions of American realism and the tenets of Reaganism. Indeed, it offers by far the most explicit and trenchant critique of neoconservatism to have been produced on Broadway. It also provides the most thoroughgoing—and unambivalent—deconstruction in memory of a binarism absolutely crucial to liberalism, the opposition between public and private. ***Angels*** demonstrates conclusively not only the constructedness of the difference between the political and the sexual, but also the murderous power of this distinction. Yet, at the same time, *not despite but because of these endeavors*, the play has been accommodated with stunning ease to the hegemonic ideology not just of the theatre-going public, but of the democratic majority—an ideology that has become the *new* American religion—liberal pluralism.[39]

The old-style American liberalisms, variously associated (reading from left to right) with trade unionism, reformism, and competitive individualism, tend to value freedom above all other qualities (the root word for liberalism is, after all, the Latin *liber*, meaning "free"). Taking the "free" individual subject as the fundamental social unit, liberalism has long been associated with the principle of laissez-faire and the "free" market, and is reformist rather than revolutionary in its politics. At the same time, however, because liberalism, particularly in its American versions, has always paid at least lip service to equality, certain irreducible contradictions have been bred in what did, after all, emerge during the seventeenth century as the ideological complement to (and justification for) mercantile capitalism. Historically, American liberalism has permitted dissent and fostered tolerance—within certain limits—and guaranteed that all men in principle are created equal (women were long excluded from the compact, as well as African American slaves). In fact, given the structure of American capitalism, the incommensurability of its commitment both to freedom and equality has proven a disabling contradiction, one that liberalism has tried continually, and with little success, to negotiate. Like the bourgeois subject that is its production and raison d'être, liberalism is hopelessly schizoid.

The new liberalism that has been consolidated in the United States since the decline of the New Left in the mid-1970s (but whose antecedents date back to the first stirrings of the nation) marks the adaptation of traditional liberalism to a post-welfare state economy. Pursuing a policy of regressive taxation, its major constituent is the corporate sector—all others it labels "special interest groups" (despite certain superficial changes, there is no fundamental difference between the economic and foreign policies of Reagan/Bush and Clinton). In spite of its corporatism, however, and its efficiency in redistributing the wealth upward, liberalism speaks the language of tolerance. Unable to support substantive changes in economic policy that might in fact produce a more equitable and less segregated society, it instead promotes a *rhetoric* of pluralism and moderation. Reformist in method, it endeavors to fine tune the status quo while at the same time acknowledging (and even celebrating) the diversity of American culture. For the liberal pluralist, America is less a melting pot than a smorgasbord. He or she takes pride in the ability to *consume* cultural difference—now understood as a commodity, a source of boundless pleasure, an expression of an exoticized Other. And yet, for him or her, access to and participation in so-called minority cultures is entirely consumerist. Like the new, passive racist characterized by Hazel Carby, the liberal pluralist uses "texts"—whether literary, musical, theatrical or cinematic—as "a way of gaining knowledge of the 'other,' a knowledge that appears to replace the desire to challenge existing frameworks of segregation."[40]

Liberal pluralism thus does far more than tolerate dissent. It actively enlists its aid in reaffirming a fundamentally conservative hegemony. In doing so, it reconsolidates a fantasy of America that dates back to the early nineteenth century. Liberal pluralism demonstrates the dogged persistence of a *consensus politic that masquerades as dissensus*. It proves once again, in Bercovitch's words, that

[t]he American way is to turn potential conflict into a quarrel about fusion or fragmentation. It is a fixed match, a debate with a foregone conclusion: you must have your fusion and feed on fragmentation too. And the formula for doing so has become virtually a cultural reflex: you just alternate between harmony-in-diversity and diversity-in-harmony. It amounts to a hermeneutics of laissez-faire: all problems are obviated by the continual flow of the one into the many, and the many into the one.[41]

According to Bercovitch, a kind of dissensus (of which liberal pluralism is the contemporary avatar) has been the hallmark of the very idea of America—and American literature—from the very beginning. In this most American of ideologies, an almost incomparably wide range of opinions, beliefs, and cultural positions are finally absorbed into a fantasy of a utopian nation in which anything and everything is possible, in which the millennium is simultaneously at hand and indefinitely deferred. Moreover, the nation is imagined as the geographical representation of that utopia which is both everywhere and nowhere. For as Lauren Berlant explains, "the contradiction between the 'nowhere' of utopia and the 'everywhere' of the nation [is] dissolved by the American recasting of the 'political' into the terms of providential ideality, 'one nation under God.'"[42] Under the sign of the "one," all contradictions are subsumed, all races and religions united, all politics theologized.

DISSENSUS AND THE FIELD OF CULTURAL PRODUCTION

It is my contention that *Angels*'s mobilization of a consensual politic (masquerading as *dis*sensual) is precisely the source not only of the play's ambivalence, but also of its ability to be instantly recognized as part of the canon of American literature. Regardless of Kushner's intentions, *Angels* sets forth a project wherein the theological is constructed as a transcendent category into which politics and history finally disappear. For all its commitment to a historical materialist method, for all its attention to political struggle and the dynamics of oppression, *Angels* finally sets forth a liberal pluralist vision of America in which all, not in spite but because of their diversity, will be welcomed into the new Jerusalem (to this extent, it differs sharply from the more exclusionist character of early Mormonism and other, more recent millennialisms). Like other apocalyptic discourses, from Joseph Smith to Jerry Falwell, the millennialism of *Angels* reassures an "audience that knows it has lost control over events" not by enabling it to "regain . . . control," but by letting it know "that history *is* nevertheless controlled by an underlying order and that it has a purpose that is nearing fulfillment." It thereby demonstrates that "*personal* pain," whether Prior's, or that of the reader or spectator, "is subsumed within the pattern of history."[43] Like Joseph Smith, Tony Kushner has resuscitated a vision of America as both promised land and land of infinite promise. Simultaneously, he has inspired virtually every theatre critic in the U.S. to a host of salvational fantasies about theatre, art, and politics. And he has done all this at a crucial juncture in history, at the end of the

Cold War, as the geopolitical order of forty-five years has collapsed.

Despite the success of the 1991 Gulf War in signaling international "terrorism" as the successor to the Soviet empire and justification for the expansion of the national security state, the idea of the nation remains, I believe, in crisis (it seems to me that "terrorism," being less of a threat to individualism than communism, does not harness paranoia quite as effectively as the idea of an evil empire). If nothing else, *Angels in America* attests both to the continuing anxiety over national definition and mission and to the importance of an ideological means of assuaging that anxiety. In *Angels,* a series of political dialectics (which are, yet again, false dialectics) remains the primary means for producing this ideological fix, for producing dissensus, a sense of alternation between "harmony-in-diversity and diversity-in-harmony." The play is filled with political disputation—all of it between men since women, unless in drag, are excluded from the political realm. Most is centered around Louis, the unmistakably ambivalent, ironic Jew, who invariably sets the level of discussion and determines the tenor of the argument. If with Belize he takes a comparatively rightist (and racist) stance, with Joe he takes an explicitly leftist (and antihomophobic) one. And while the play unquestionably problematizes his several positions, he ends up, with all his contradictions, becoming by default the spokesperson for liberal pluralism, with all *its* contradictions. Belize, intriguingly, functions unlike the white gay men as an ideological point of reference, a kind of "moral bellwether," in the words of one critic.[44] Because his is the one point of view that is never submitted to a critique, he becomes, as David Román points out, "the political and ethical center of the plays." The purveyor of truth, "he carries the burden of race" and so seems to issue from what is unmistakably a "white imaginary" ("[t]his fetishization," Román notes, "of lesbian and gay people of color as a type of political catalyst is ubiquitous among the left").[45] He is also cast in the role of caretaker, a position long reserved for African Americans in "the white imaginary." Even Belize's name commemorates not the Name of the Father, but his status as a *"former drag queen"* (1:3), giving him an identity that is both performative and exoticized. He is the play's guarantee of diversity.

The pivotal scene for the enunciation of Louis's politics, meanwhile, is his long discussion with Belize in *Millennium* which begins with his question, "Why has democracy succeeded in America?" (1:89), a question whose assumption is belied by the unparalleled political and economic power of American corporatism to buy elections and from which Louis, as is his wont, almost immediately backs down. (His rhetorical strategy throughout this scene is to stake out a position from which he immediately draws a guilty retreat, thereby making Belize look like the aggressor.) Invoking "radical democracy" and "freedom" in one breath, and crying "[f]uck assimilation" (1:89-90) in the next, he careens wildly between a liberal discourse of rights and a rhetoric of identity politics. Alternating

between universalizing and minoritizing concepts of the subject, he manages at once to dismiss a politics of race (and insult Belize) and to assert its irreducibility. Yet the gist of Louis's argument (if constant vacillation could be said to have a gist) is his disquisition about the nation:

> this reaching out for a spiritual past in a country where no indigenous spirits exist—only the Indians, I mean Native American spirits and we killed them off so now, there are no gods here, no ghosts and spirits in America, there are no angels in America, no spiritual past, no racial past, there's only the political.

[1:92]

For Louis, America hardly exists as a community (whether real or imagined). Rather, for this confused liberal, America is defined entirely by its relationship to the "political." With characteristic irony, Kushner chooses to present this crucial idea (which does, after all, echo the play's title) in the negative, in the form of a statement which the rest of the play aggressively refutes. For if nothing else, *Angels in America*—like *The Book of Mormon*—demonstrates that there are angels in America, that America is in essence a utopian and theological construction, a nation with a divine mission. Politics is by no means banished insofar as it provides a crucial way in which the nation is imagined. But it is subordinated to utopian fantasies of harmony in diversity, of one nation under a derelict God.

Moreover, this scene between Louis and Belize reproduces millennialism in miniature, in its very structure, in the pattern whereby the political is finally subsumed by utopian fantasies. After the spirited argument between Louis and Belize (if one can call a discussion in which one person refuses to stake out a coherent position an argument), their conflict is suddenly overrun by an outbreak of lyricism, by the intrusion, after so much talk about culture, of what passes for the natural world:

> BELIZE: All day today it's felt like Thanksgiving. Soon, this . . . ruination will be blanketed white. You can smell it—can you smell it?
>
> LOUIS: Smell what?
>
> BELIZE: Softness, compliance, forgiveness, grace.

[1:100]

Argumentation gives way not to a resolution (nothing has been settled) but to the ostensible forces of nature: snow and smell. According to Belize, snow (an insignia of coldness and purity in the play) is linked to "[s]oftness, compliance, forgiveness, grace," in short, to the theological virtues. Like the ending of *Perestroika,* in which another dispute between Louis and Belize fades out behind Prior's benediction, this scene enacts a movement of transcendence whereby the political is not so much resolved as left trailing in the dust. In the American way, contradiction is less disentangled than immobilized. History gives way to a concept of cosmic evolution that is far closer to Joseph Smith than to Walter Benjamin.

In the person of Louis (who is, after all, constructed as the most empathic character in the play), with his unshakable faith in liberalism and the possibility of "radical democracy," *Angels in America* assures the (liberal) theatre-going public that a kind of liberal pluralism remains the best hope for change.[46] Revolution, in the Marxist sense, is rendered virtually unthinkable, oxymoronic. Amidst all the political disputation, there is no talk of social class. Oppression is understood not in relation to economics but to differences of race, gender and sexual orientation. In short: *an identity politic comes to substitute for Marxist analysis*. There is no clear sense that the political and social problems with which the characters wrestle might be connected to a particular economic system (comrade Prelapsarianov is, after all, a comic figure). And despite Kushner's avowed commitment to socialism, an alternative to capitalism, except in the form of an indefinitely deferred utopia, remains absent from the play's dialectic.[47] Revolution, even in Benjamin's sense of the term, is evacuated of its political content, functioning less as a Marxist hermeneutic tool than a *trope*, a figure of speech (the oxymoron) that marks the place later to be occupied by a (liberal pluralist?) utopia. *Angels* thus falls into line behind the utopianisms of Joseph Smith and the American Renaissance and becomes less a subversion of hegemonic culture than its reaffirmation. As Berlant observes, "the temporal and spatial ambiguity of 'utopia' has the effect of obscuring the implications of political activity and power relations in American civil life."[48] Like "our classic texts" (as characterized by Bercovitch), ***Angels*** has a way of conceptualizing utopia so that it may be adopted by "the dominant culture . . . for its purposes." "So molded, ritualized, and controlled," Bercovitch notes (and, I would like to add, stripped of its impulse for radical economic change), "utopianism has served . . . to diffuse or deflect dissent, or actually to transmute it into a vehicle of socialization."[49]

The ambivalences that are so deeply inscribed in ***Angels in America,*** its conflicted relationship to various utopianisms, to the concept of America, to Marxism, Mormonism, and liberalism, function, I believe, to accommodate the play to what I see as a fundamentally conservative and paradigmatically American politic—dissensus, the "hermeneutics of laissez-faire." Yet it seems to me that the play's ambivalence (its way of being, in Eve Sedgwick's memorable phrase, "kinda subversive, kinda hegemonic"[50]) is finally, less a question of authorial intention than of the peculiar cultural and economic position of this play (and its writer) in relation to the theatre, theatre artists, and the theatre-going public in the United States. On the one hand, the Broadway and regional theatres remain in a uniquely marginal position in comparison with Hollywood. The subscribers to regional theatres continue to dwindle while more than half of Theatre Communications Group's sample theatres in their annual survey "played to smaller audiences in 1993 than they did five years ago." Moreover, in a move that bodes particularly ill for the future of new plays, "workshops, staged readings and other developmental activities decreased drastically over the five years studied."[51]

On the other hand, serious Broadway drama does not have the same cultural capital as other forms of literature. Enmortgaged to a slew of others who must realize the playwright's text, it has long been regarded as a bastard art. Meanwhile, the relatively small public that today attends professional theatre in America is overwhelmingly middle-class and overwhelmingly liberal in its attitudes. Indeed, theatre audiences are in large part distinguished from the audiences for film and television on account of their tolerance for works that are more challenging both formally and thematically than the vast majority of major studio releases or prime-time miniseries.

Because of its marginal position, both economically and culturally, theatre is a privileged portion of what Pierre Bourdieu designates as the literary and artistic field. As he explains, this field is contained within a larger field of economic and political power, while, at the same time, "possessing a relative autonomy with respect to it. . . ." It is this *relative autonomy* that gives the literary and artistic field—and theatre in particular—both its high level of symbolic forms of capital and its low level of economic capital. In other words, despite its artistic cachet, it "occupies a *dominated position*" with respect to the field of economic and political power as whole.[52] And the individual cultural producer (or theatre artist), insofar as he or she is a part of the bourgeoisie, represents a "dominated fraction of the dominant class."[53] The cultural producer is thus placed in an irreducibly contradictory position—and this has become particularly clear since the decline of patronage in the eighteenth century and the increasing dependence of the artist on the vicissitudes of the marketplace. On the one hand, he or she is licensed to challenge hegemonic values insofar as it is a particularly effective way of accruing cultural capital. On the other hand, the more effective his or her challenge, the less economic capital he or she is likely to amass. Because of theatre's marginality in American culture, it seems to be held hostage to this double bind in a particularly unnerving way: the very disposition of the field guarantees that Broadway and regional theatres (unlike mass culture) are constantly in the process of having to negotiate this impossible position.

What is perhaps most remarkable about ***Angels in America*** is that it has managed, against all odds, to amass significant levels of both cultural and economic capital. And while it by no means resolves the contradictions that are constitutive of theatre's cultural positioning, its production history has become a measure of the seemingly impossible juncture of these two forms of success. Just as the play's structure copes with argumentation by transcending it, so does the play as cultural phenomenon seemingly transcend the opposition between economic and cultural capital, between the hegemonic and the counterhegemonic. Moreover, it does so, I am arguing, by its skill in both reactivating a sense (derived from the early nineteenth century) of America as the utopian nation and mobilizing the principle of ambivalence—or more exactly, dissensus—to produce a vision of a once and future pluralist culture. And although the text's contradictory positioning is to a large extent defined by the marginal cultural position of Broadway, it is also related specifically to Tony Kushner's own class position. Like Joseph Smith, Kushner represents a dominated—and dissident—fraction of the dominant class. As a white gay men, he is able to amass considerable economic and cultural capital despite the fact that the class of which he is a part remains relatively disempowered politically (according to a 1993 survey, the average household income for gay men is 40% higher than that of the average American household).[54] As an avowed leftist and intellectual, he is committed (as *Angels* demonstrates) to mounting a critique of hegemonic ideology. Yet as a member of the bourgeoisie and as the recipient of two Tony awards, he is also committed—if only unconsciously—to the continuation of the system that has granted him no small measure of success.

A QUEER SORT OF NATION

Although I am tempted to see the celebrity of *Angels in America* as yet another measure of the power of liberal pluralism to neutralize oppositional practices, the play's success also suggests a willingness to recognize the contributions of gay men to American culture and to American literature, in particular. For as Eve Sedgwick and others have argued, both the American canon and the very principle of canonicity are centrally concerned with questions of male (homo)sexual definition and desire.[55] Thus, the issues of homoeroticism, of the anxiety generated by the instability of the homosocial/homosexual boundary, of coding, of secrecy and disclosure, and of the problems around securing a sexual identity, remain pivotal for so many of the writers who hold pride of place in the American canon, from Thoreau, Melville, Whitman, and James to Hart Crane, Tennessee Williams, and James Baldwin—in that sense, the American canon is always already queered. At the same time, however, unlike so much of the canon, and in particular, the canon of American drama, *Angels in America* foregrounds explicitly gay men. No more need the reader eager to queer the text read subversively between the lines, or transpose genders, as is so often done to the work of Williams, Inge, Albee, and others. Since the 1988 controversies over NEA funding for exhibitions of Mapplethorpe and Serrano and the subsequent attempt by the Endowment to revoke grants to the so-called NEA four (three of whom are queer), theatre, as a liberal form, has been distinguished from mass culture in large part by virtue of its queer content. In the 1990s, a play without a same-sex kiss may be entertainment, but it can hardly be considered a work of art. It appears that the representation of (usually male) homosexual desire has become the privileged emblem of that endangered species, the serious Broadway drama. But I wonder finally how subversive this queering of Broadway is when women, in this play at least, remain firmly in the background. What is one to make of the remarkable ease with which *Angels in America* has been accommodated to that lineage of American drama (and literature) that focuses on masculine experience and agency and produces women as the premise for history,

as the ground on which it is constructed? Are not women sacrificed—yet again—to the male citizenry of a (queer) nation?

If Kushner, following Benjamin's prompting (and echoing his masculinism), attempts to "brush history against the grain" (257), he does so by demonstrating the crucial importance of (closeted) gay men in twentieth-century American politics—including, most prominently, Roy Cohn and two of his surrogate fathers, J. Edgar Hoover and Joseph McCarthy. By so highlighting the (homo)eroticization of patriarchy, the play demonstrates the always already queer status of American politics, and most provocatively, of those generals of the Cold War (and American imperialism) who were most assiduous in their denunciation of political and sexual dissidence. Moreover, unlike the work of most of Kushner's predecessors on the American stage, *Angels* does not pathologize gay men. Or more exactly, gay men as a class are not pathologized. Rather, they are revealed to be pathologized circumstantially: first, by their construction (through a singularly horrific stroke of ill luck) as one of the "risk groups" for HIV; and second, by the fact that some remain closeted and repressed (Joe's ulcer is unmistakably the price of disavowal). So, it turns out, it is not homosexuality that is pathological, but its *denial*. Flagrantly uncloseted, the play provides a devastating critique of the closeted gay man in two medicalized bodies: Roy Cohn and Joe Pitt.

If *Angels in America* queers historical materialism (at least as Benjamin understands it), it does so by exposing the process by which the political (which ostensibly drives history) intersects with the personal and sexual (which ostensibly are no more than footnotes to history). Reagan's presidency and the neoconservative hegemony of the 1980s provide not just the background to the play's exploration of ostensibly personal (i.e., sexual, marital, medical) problems, but the very ground on which desire is produced. For despite the trenchancy of its critique of neoconservativism, *Angels* also demonstrates the peculiar sexiness of Reagan's vision of America. Through Louis, it demonstrates the allure of a particular brand of machismo embodied by Joe Pitt: "The more appalling I find your politics the more I want to hump you" (2:36). And if the Angel is indeed "a cosmic reactionary" (2:55), it is in part because her/his position represents an analogue to the same utopian promises and hopes that Reagan so brilliantly and deceptively exploited. Moreover, in this history play, questions of male homosexual identity and desire are carefully juxtaposed against questions of equal protection for lesbians and gay men and debates about their military service. Louis attacks Joe for his participation in "an important bit of legal fag-bashing," a case that upholds the U.S. government's policy that it's not "unconstitutional to discriminate against homosexuals" (2:110). And while the case that Louis cites may be fictional, the continuing refusal of the courts in the wake of *Bowers v. Hardwick* to consider lesbians and gay men a suspect class, and thus eligible for protection under the provisions of the Fourteenth Amendment, is anything but.[56] Unilaterally constructing gay men as a suspect class (with sexual identity substituting for economic positionality), *Angels* realizes Benjamin's suggestion that it is not "man or men but the struggling, oppressed class itself [that] is the depository of historical knowledge" (260). More decisively than any other recent cultural text, *Angels* queers the America of Joseph Smith—and Ronald Reagan—by placing this oppressed class at the very center of American history, by showing it to be not just the depository of a special kind of knowledge, but by recognizing the central role that it has had in the construction of a national subject, polity, literature, and theatre. On this issue, the play is not ambivalent at all.

NOTES

My thanks to Rhett Landrum, Loren Noveck, John Rouse, and Ronn Smith for their invaluable contributions to this essay.

[1]Joseph Roach has suggested to me that the closest analogue to *Angels* on the American stage is, in fact, *Uncle Tom's Cabin*, with its tremendous popularity before the Civil War, its epic length, and its skill in addressing the most controversial issues of the time in deeply equivocal ways.

[2]John Lahr, "The Theatre: Earth Angels," *The New Yorker*, 13 December 1993, 133.

[3]Jack Kroll, "Heaven and Earth on Broadway," *Newsweek*, 6 December 1993, 83; Robert Brustein, "Robert Brustein on Theatre: *Angels in America,*" *The New Republic*, 24 May 1993, 29.

[4]John E. Harris, "Miracle on 48th Street," *Christopher Street*, March 1994, 6.

[5]Frank Rich, "Critic's Notebook: The Reaganite Ethos, With Roy Cohn As a Dark Metaphor," *New York Times*, 5 March 1992, C15.

[6]John Clum, *Acting Gay: Male Homosexuality in Modern Drama* (New York: Columbia University Press, 1994), 324.

[7]Tony Kushner, *Angels in America: A Gay Fantasia on National Themes. Part One: Millennium Approaches* (New York: Theatre Communications Group, 1993), 95. All further references will be noted in the text.

[8]Frank Rich, "Following an Angel For a Healing Vision of Heaven and Earth," *New York Times*, 24 November 1993, C11.

[9]Clum, 314.

[10]Tony Kushner, *Angels in America: A Gay Fantasia on National Themes. Part Two: Perestroika* (New York: Theatre Communications Group, 1994), 56. All further references will be noted in the text.

[11]See, for example, Andrea Stevens, "Finding a Devil Within to Portray Roy Cohn," *New York Times*, 18 April 1993, section 2, 1-28.

[12]Terry Eagleton, *Walter Benjamin, or Towards a Revolutionary Criticism* (London: Verso, 1981), 177.

[13]Walter Benjamin, "Theses on the Philosophy of History," in *Illuminations*, ed. Hannah Arendt, trans. Harry Zohn (New York: Schocken Books, 1969), 253. All further references will be noted in the text.

[14]Tony Kushner explains: "I've written about my friend Kimberly [Flynn] who is a profound influence on me. And she and I were talking about this utopian thing that we share—she's the person who introduced me to that side of Walter Benjamin. . . . She said jokingly that at times she felt such an extraordinary kinship with him that she thought she was Walter Benjamin reincarnated. And so at one point in the conversation, when I was coming up with names for my characters, I said, 'I had to

look up something in Benjamin—not you, but the prior Walter.' That's where the name came from. I had been looking for one of those WASP names that nobody gets called anymore." David Savran, "The Theatre of the Fabulous: An Interview with Tony Kushner," in *Speaking on Stage: Interviews with Contemporary American Playwrights*, ed. Philip C. Kolin and Colby H. Kullman (Tuscaloosa: University of Alabama Press), forthcoming.

[15]Lacan, "The Signification of the Phallus," in *Ecrits: A Selection*, trans. Alan Sheridan (New York: Norton, 1977), 286.

[16]Elizabeth A. Grosz, *Jacques Lacan: A Feminist Introduction* (London: Routledge, 1990), 74, 67.

[17]Benjamin maintained a far less condemnatory attitude toward the increasing technologization of culture than many other Western Marxists. In "The Work of Art in the Age of Mechanical Reproduction," for example, he writes of his qualified approval of the destruction of the aura associated with modern technologies. He explains that because "mechanical reproduction emancipates the work of art from its parasitical dependence on ritual, . . . the total function of art" can "be based on another practice—politics," which for him is clearly preferable. Benjamin, "The Work of Art in the Age of Mechanical Reproduction," *Illuminations*, 224.

[18]Although one could cite a myriad of sources, this quotation is extracted from Milton Friedman, "Once Again: Why Socialism Won't Work," *New York Times*, 13 August 1994, 21.

[19]Krishan Kumar, "The End of Socialism? The End of Utopia? The End of History?," in *Utopias and the Millennium*, ed. Krishan Kumar and Stephen Bann (London: Reaktion Books, 1993), 61; Francis Fukuyama, *The End of History and the Last Man*, quoted in Kumar, 78.

[20]Friedman, 21.

[21]Aijaz Ahmad, *In Theory: Classes, Nations, Literatures* (London: Verso, 1992), 69. Ahmad is summarizing this position as part of his critique of poststructuralism.

[22]David Richards, "'Angels' Finds a Poignant Note of Hope," *New York Times*, 28 November 1993, II, 1.

[23]Benedict Anderson, *Imagined Communities: Reflections on the Origin and Spread of Nationalism* (London: Verso, 1991), 6.

[24]See Lawrence Kohl, *The Politics of Individualism: Parties and the American Character in the Jacksonian Era* (New York: Oxford University Press, 1989).

[25]Klaus J. Hansen, *Mormonism and the American Experience* (Chicago: University of Chicago Press, 1981), 49-50.

[26]See Ernest R. Sandeen, *The Roots of Fundamentalism: British and American Millenarianism 1800-1930* (Chicago: University of Chicago Press, 1970), 42-58.

[27]Hansen, 52.

[28]Joseph Smith, quoted in Hansen, 72.

[29]See Richard L. Bushman, *Joseph Smith and the Beginnings of Mormonism* (Urbana: University of Illinois Press, 1984), 170.

[30]Hansen, 119.

[31]For a catalogue of this violence, see Jan Shipps, *Mormonism: The Story of a New Religious Tradition* (Urbana: University of Illinois Press, 1985), 155-61.

[32]Hansen, 124-26.

[33]Hansen, 27, 66.

[34]Anderson, 10-11.

[35]Timothy Brennan, "The National Longing for Form," in *Nation and Narration*, ed. Homi K. Bhabha (London: Routledge, 1990), 50.

[36]Anderson, 10-11.

[37]Hans Kohn, *Nationalism: Its Meaning and History* (Princeton: Van Nostrand, 1965), 11.

[38]Sacvan Bercovitch, "The Problem of Ideology in American Literary History," *Critical Inquiry* 12 (1986): 642-43; 645.

[39]Despite the 1994 Republican House and Senate victories (in which the Republicans received the vote of only 20% of the electorate) and the grandstanding of Newt Gingrich, the country remains far less conservative on many social issues than the Republicans would like Americans to believe. See Thomas Ferguson, "G.O.P. $$$ Talked; Did Voters Listen?," *The Nation*, 26 December 1994, 792-98.

[40]Hazel Carby, "The Multicultural Wars," in *Black Popular Culture*, a project by Michele Wallace, ed. Gina Dent (Seattle: Bay Press, 1992), 197.

[41]Bercovitch, 649.

[42]Lauren Berlant, *The Anatomy of National Fantasy: Hawthorne, Utopia, and Everyday Life* (Chicago: University of Chicago Press, 1991), 31.

[43]Barry Brummett, *Contemporary Apocalyptic Rhetoric* (New York: Praeger, 1991), 37-38.

[44]Lahr, "The Theatre: Earth Angels," 132.

[45]David Román, "November 1, 1992: AIDS / *Angels in America*," from *Acts of Intervention: Gay Men, U.S. Performance, AIDS* (Bloomington: Indiana University Press, forthcoming).

[46]This is corroborated by Kushner's own statements: "The strain in the American character that I feel the most affection for and that I feel has the most potential for growth is American liberalism, which is incredibly short of what it needs to be and incredibly limited and exclusionary and predicated on all sorts of racist, sexist, homophobic and classist prerogatives. And yet, as Louis asks, why has democracy succeeded in America? And why does it have this potential, as I believe it does? I really believe that there is the potential for radical democracy in this country, one of the few places on earth where I see it as a strong possibility. It doesn't seem to be happening in Russia. There is a tradition of liberalism, of a kind of social justice, fair play and tolerance—and each of these things is problematic and can certainly be played upon in the most horried ways. Reagan kept the most hair-raising anarchist aspects of his agenda hidden and presented himself as a good old-fashioned liberal who kept invoking FDR. It may just be sentimentalism on my part because I am the child of liberal-pinko parents, but I do believe in it—as much as I often find it despicable. It's sort of like the Democratic National Convention every four years: it's horrendous and you can feel it sucking all the energy from progressive movements in this country, with everybody pinning their hopes on this sleazy bunch of guys. But you do have Jesse Jackson getting up and calling the Virgin Mary a single mother, and on an emotional level, and I hope also on a more practical level, I do believe that these are the people in whom to have hope." Savran, 24-25.

[47]See Tony Kushner, "A Socialism of the Skin," *The Nation*, 4 July 1994, 9-14.

[48]Berlant, 32.

[49]Bercovitch, 644.

[50]Sedgwick used this phrase during the question period that followed a lecture at Brown University, 1 October 1992.

[51]Barbara Janowitz, "Theatre Facts 93," insert in *American Theatre*, April 1994, 4-5.

[52]Pierre Bourdieu, "The Field of Cultural Production, or: The Economic World Reversed," in Bourdieu, *The Field of Cultural Production: Essays on Art and Literature*, ed. Randal Johnson (New York: Columbia University Press, 1993), 37-38.

[53]Randal Johnson, Ed. Introd., Bourdieu, 15.

[54]*Gay & Lesbian Stats: A Pocket Guide of Facts and Figures*, ed. Bennett L. Singer and David Deschamps (New York: The New Press, 1994), 32.

[55]See Eve Kosofsky Sedgwick, *Epistemology of the Closet* (Berkeley: University of California Press, 1990), 48-59.

[56]It is not the subjects who comprise a bona fide suspect class (like African Americans) that are suspect, but rather the forces of oppression that produce the class. For an analysis of the legal issues around equal protection, see Janet Halley, "The Politics of the Closet: Towards Equal Protection for Gay, Lesbian, and Bisexual Identity," *UCLA Law Review* (June 1989): 915-76.

Charles McNulty (essay date 1996)

SOURCE: "*Angels in America*: Tony Kushner's Theses on the Philosophy of History," in *Modern Drama*, Vol. XXXIX, No. 1, Spring 1996, pp. 84-96.

[*In the following, McNulty analyzes* Angels in America *in terms of Walter Benjamin's theories of history, finding that* Perestroika *abandons Benjamin's view of history as continuous catastrophe for an unwarranted view of history as a record of progress.*]

AIDS plays have come to be thought of as a phenomenon of the 1980s, as Happenings were of the 1960s. Though the epidemic still rages, the bravely furious genre that began with William Hoffman's *As Is* and Larry Kramer's *The Normal Heart* has for the most part receded into the paragraphs of theater history textbooks. Nicholas de Jongh identifies the central mission of these plays as the fight against "an orthodoxy that regards AIDS as a mere local difficulty, principally affecting a reviled minority."[1] It is not entirely surprising, then, that the category has been said to have drawn to a close. The disease, after all, has been acknowledged, albeit belatedly, to be a widespread calamity; only the morally deaf, dumb, and blind have resisted this assessment, and they most certainly remain beyond the pale of agitprop, no matter how artfully conceived. To make things official, an obituary of the genre appeared in *American Theatre* in October of 1989:

> Recently, AIDS has fallen off as a central subject for new drama. It's no wonder. When, for instance, spectacle and public ritual are so movingly combined in the image and action of the Names Project Quilt, conventional theater seems redundant—at best a pale imitation of the formal, mass expressions that help give shape to real grief and anger. Time and again the spirited protestors of ACT UP have demonstrated that the theater of AIDS is in the streets.[2]

The cult of Tony Kushner's ***Angels in America,*** by far the most celebrated play of the 1990s, would appear, however, to have rendered all this premature. Subtitled *A*

Gay Fantasia on National Themes, Kushner's two-part epic features a deserted gay man with full-blown AIDS battling both heaven and earth. But *Angels* represents not so much a revival of the category as a radical rethinking of its boundaries. For the playwright, the question is no longer what is the place of AIDS in history, but what of history itself can be learned through the experience of gay men and AIDS.

Kushner's angels were inspired not from any Biblical ecstasy but from the great twentieth-century German-Jewish critic Walter Benjamin's "Theses on the Philosophy of History."[3] Benjamin, writing in the spring of 1940 in France only a few months before he was to kill himself trying to escape the German occupation, borrows Paul Klee's 1920 painting *Angelus Novus* to convey his rigorously anti-Hegelian understanding of the movement of history:

> This is how one pictures the angel of history. His face is turned toward the past. Where we perceive a chain of events, he sees one single catastrophe which keeps piling wreckage upon wreckage and hurls it in front of his feet. The angel would like to stay, awaken the dead, and make whole what has been smashed. But a storm is blowing from Paradise; it has got caught in his wings with such violence that the angel can no longer close them. This storm irresistibly propels him into the future to which his back is turned, while the pile of debris before him grows skyward. This storm is what we call progress.[4]

The movement of history is conceived not in terms of a dialectical narrative intent on progress, but as a steadfast path of destruction. All, however, is not lost. For Benjamin, the present represents a crisis point in which there is the opportunity to take cognizance of the homogeneous course of history, and thereby shift a specific era out of it.[5] For Kushner, a gay activist and dramatist enthralled by Benjamin's brooding analysis of history, the present crisis couldn't be more clear. Surveying five years of the first decade of the AIDS epidemic, the playwright casts a backward glance on America's domestic strife, and with it something unexpected flickers into view—the revolutionary chance to blast open the oppressive continuum of history and steer clear into the next millennium.

To realize this Benjamin-inspired vision, Kushner follows the lives of two couples and one political racketeer from the annals of the American closet—all in the throes of traumatic change. Louis, unable to deal with the fact his lover Prior has AIDS, abandons him; Joe, an ambitious Mormon lawyer, wants to abandon the homosexual part of himself, but ends, instead, abandoning his valium-popping wife Harper; and last, but not least, Roy Cohn, sick with AIDS, abandons nothing because he holds onto nothing. In an age in which shirkers of responsibility are encouraged to unite, Louis, the obstructed New York Jewish intellectual, and Joe, the shellacked all-American Mormon protégé of Cohn, spend a month together in bed, while their partners are forced to find ways of coping alone.

"Children of the new morning, criminal minds. Selfish and greedy and loveless and blind. Reagan's children," is how Louis characterizes Joe and himself, in this most troubling trouble-free time. "You're scared. So am I. Everybody is in the land of the free. God help us all,"[6] he says to Joe, sincerely, though at the same time still groping for a way to move beyond guilt and self-consciousness into the intoxicating pleasures of sexual betrayal.

Kushner provides a quintessential American framework for the current historical dilemma in the play's opening scene, which features Rabbi Isidor Chemelwitz's eulogy for Louis's grandmother. Not knowing the departed too well, the Rabbi speaks of her as "not a person but a whole kind of person, the ones who crossed the ocean, who brought with us to America the villages of Russia and Lithuania—and how we struggled, and how we fought, for the family, for the Jewish home, so that you would not grow up *here*, in this strange place, in the melting pot where nothing melted" (1:10). Referring to the mourners as descendants, Rabbi Chemelwitz admits that great voyages from the old worlds are no longer possible, "[b]ut every day of your lives the miles that voyage between that place and this one you cross. Every day. You understand me? In you that journey is. [. . .] She was the last of the Mohicans, this one was. Pretty soon . . . all the old will be dead" (1:10-11). For Kushner, the past's intersection with the present is inevitable, a fact of living; what disturbs him is the increasing failure of Americans to recognize this, the willful amnesia that threatens to blank out the nation's memory as it moves into the next millennium.

This fugitive wish to escape the clutches of the past is concentrated most intensely in Louis, who is faced with the heavy burden of having to care for his sick lover. An underemployed, hyper-rationalizing word processing clerk in the court system, he is unable to come to terms with his current life crisis. In a conversation with his Rabbi, he tries to explain why a person might be justified in abandoning a loved one at a time of great need:

> Maybe because this person's sense of the world, that it will change for the better with struggle, maybe a person who has this neo-Hegelian positivist sense of constant historical progress towards happiness or perfection or something, who feels very powerful because he feels connected to these forces, moving uphill all the time . . . maybe that person can't, um, incorporate sickness into his sense of how things are supposed to go. Maybe vomit . . . and sores and disease . . . really frighten him, maybe . . . he isn't so good with death.

> (1:25)

Louis is determined to "maybe" himself out of his unfortunate present reality—and he's not beyond invoking the heaviest of nineteenth-century intellectual heavyweights to help him out. This peculiar trait is only magnified after he eventually leaves Prior for Joe. One of the more incendiary moments occurs at a coffee shop with Prior's ex-lover and closest friend, Belize. Wishing to ask about Prior's condition, Louis lauches instead into a de Tocqueville-esque diatribe. "[T]here are no gods here, no ghosts and spirits in America, there are no angels in America, no spiritual past, no racial past, there's only the political, and the decoys and the ploys to maneuver around the inescapable battle of politics" (1:92), he explains breathlessly over coffee to Belize, who appears unimpressed by all the academic fireworks. In fact, Belize makes clear that he can see right through Louis's highbrow subterfuge. "[A]re you deliberately transforming yourself into an arrogant, sexual-political Stalinist-slash-racist flag-waving thug for my benefit" (1:94), he asks, knowing all too well from his experience as a gay African American drag queen that history is not simply some dry-as-dust abstraction, but an approximation of the way individuals lead both their public and private lives.

Though Kushner is critical of Louis, he in no way diminishes the gravity of what this character is forced to deal with. Louis has, after all, good reason for wanting to flee. When he confronts his lover on the floor of their bedroom, burning with fever and excreting blood, the full horror of this disease is conveyed in all its mercilessness and squalor. "Oh help. Oh help. Oh God oh God oh God help me I can't I can't I can't" (1:48), he says to himself, mantra-like, over his fainted lover—and who could be so heartless to argue with him? Louis's moral dilemma is compelling precisely because what he has to deal with is so overwhelming. Still, the playwright makes clear that all the talk of justice and politics will not free us from those terrifying yet fundamental responsibilities that accompany human sickness and death. All the Reaganite preaching of a survival-of-the-fittest creed will not exempt us from our most basic obligations to each other. Belize knows this, and he brings the discussion back to the matter at hand, Louis's desertion of his lover at a moment of profound need. "I've thought about it for a very long time, and I still don't understand what love is," he says before leaving Louis alone outside the coffee shop. "Justice is simple. Democracy is simple. Those things are unambivalent. But love is very hard. And it goes bad for you if you violate the hard law of love" (1:100).

Though stalwartly behind Belize's felt wisdom, Kushner observes an analogy between the ambivalence of love and the working out of democracy and justice, the bedroom and the courtroom not being as far apart as most would assume. Louis and Joe's ravenous infidelity, for example, is seen to be in keeping with the general dog-eat-dog direction of the country. During the warm-up to their affair, Joe tells Louis of a dream he had in which the whole Hall of Justice had gone out of business: "I just wondered what a thing it would be . . . if overnight everything you owe anything to, justice, or love, had really gone away. Free" (1:72). Louis, whose motto has become "Land of the free. Home of the brave. Call me irresponsible" (1:72), has found the perfect soulless mate for a self-forgetting fling. "Want some company?" he asks. "For whatever?" (1:73). Later, in Part Two of *Angels,* when the two men get involved, they help each other get over the guilt of leaving their former lovers behind. First Joe:

> What you did when you walked out on him was hard to do. The world may not understand it or approve it but it was *your* choice, what *you* needed, not some fantasy Louis but *you.* You did what you needed to do. And I consider you very brave.

And then, somewhat more reluctantly, Louis:

> You seem to be able to live with what you've done, leaving your wife, you're not all torn up and guilty, you've . . . blossomed, but you're not a terrible person, you're a decent, caring man. And I don't know how that's possible, but looking at you it seems to be. You do seem free.[7]

Joe, giving a new American spin to the phrase the "banality of evil," admits to being happy and sleeping peacefully. And so all would seem to be well in the couple's new-founded East Village love nest, except that Louis has bad dreams.

"In America, there's a great attempt to divest private life from political meaning," Kushner has said on the subject of his play's vision. "We have to recognize that our lives are fraught with politics. The oppression and suppression of homosexuality is part of a larger agenda."[8] In fact, nearly everything under the sun, from valium addiction to VD, is considered part of a larger agenda. For Kushner, politics is an intricate spiderweb of power relations. His most singular gift as a dramatist is in depicting this skein, in making visible the normally invisible cords that tether personal conscience to public policy. The playwright does this not by ideological pronouncement, but by tracking the moral and spiritual upheavals of his characters' lives. AIDS is the central fact of *Angels,* but it is one that implicates other facts, equally catastrophic. Racism, sexism, homophobia, moral erosion, and drug addiction come with the Kushnerian territory, and, as in life, characters are often forced to grapple with several of these at the same time.

Kushner uses split scenes to make more explicit the contrapuntal relationship between these seemingly disconnected narrative worlds. Roy's meeting with Joe, to discuss the junior attorney's future as a "Roy-Boy" in Washington, occurs alongside the scene in which Louis is sodomized in the Central Park Rambles by a leather-clad mama's boy. Louis's mini-symposium at the coffee shop is simultaneous with Prior's medical checkup at an outpatient clinic. Dreams, ghosts, and a flock of dithering, hermaphroditic angels are also used to break through the play's realistic structure, to conjoin seemingly disparate characters, and to reveal the poetic resonances and interconnectedness of everyday life. In a mutual dream, Harper, tranquilized and depressed, travels to Prior's boundoir, where she finds him applying the last touches of his Norma Desmond makeup. In a febrile state known portentously as the "[t]hreshold of revelation" (1:33), the two are endowed with clairvoyant insight, and it is here that Harper learns for sure that her husband is a "homo," and Prior understands that his illness hasn't touched his "most inner part," his heart (1:33-34). Even in his characters' most private, most alone moments, the "myth of the Individual," as Kushner calls it, is shot through with company.[9]

Nowhere is this merging of social realms more spectacularly revelatory, however, than in the presentation of Cohn. Though much is based on the historical record, Kushner publishes a disclaimer:

> Roy M. Cohn, the character, is based on the late Roy M. Cohn (1927-1986), who was all too real; for the most part the acts attributed to the character Roy [. . .] are to be found in the historical record. But this Roy is a work of dramatic fiction; his words are my invention, and liberties have been taken.

> (1:5)

Cohn, however, would have nothing to complain about: Kushner does the relentless overreacher proud. All Nietzschean grit and striving, Kushner's Cohn is forever trying to position himself beyond good and evil. "Transgress a little, Joseph," he tells his Mormon acolyte. "There are so many laws; find one you can break" (1:110). Power alone concerns him. Politics, the game of power, "the game of being alive," defines every atom of his being—even his sexuality, which refuses to be roped into traditional categories. Identity and other regulatory fictions are decidedly for other people, not for Cohn, who informs his doctor that labels like homosexuality

> tell you one thing and one thing only: where does an individual so identified fit in the food chain, in the pecking order? Not ideology, or sexual taste, but something much simpler: clout. Not who I fuck or who fucks me, but who will pick up the phone when I call, who owes me favours. This is what a label refers to.

> (1:45)

Cohn's own claim to transcendental fame is that he can get Nancy Reagan on the phone whenever he wants to. How different this is from Prior's relationship to his own sexuality; on his sickbed, he steels himself with the words: "I am a gay man and I am used to pressure, to trouble, I am tough and strong" (1:117).

But it is Louis, as Ross Posnock has noted, who is Cohn's true emotional antithesis.[10] Though the two share no scenes together, their approaches to the world represent the thematic struggle at the center of Kushner's play. Yes, Louis transforms himself into a Cohn wannabe, but in the end he proves too conscience-ridden to truly want to succeed. Early on, when he asks his Rabbi what the Holy Writ says about someone who abandons a loved one at a time of great need, it is clear that he will have trouble following Cohn's personal dictum: "Let nothing stand in your way" (1:58). "You want to confess, better you should find a priest," his Rabbi tells him. On being reminded that this isn't exactly religiously appropriate, his Rabbi adds, "Worse luck for you, bubbulah. Catholics believe in forgiveness. Jews belief in Guilt" (1:25). Louis is a would-be Machiavel hampered by the misgivings of his own inner-rabbi. "It's no fun picking on you Louis,"

Belize tell him; "you're so guilty, it's like throwing darts at a glob of jello, there's no satisfying hits, just quivering, the darts just blop in and vanish" (1:93). An exemplary neurotic, Louis internalizes the play's central conflict: the debt owed to the past vs. the desire for carte blanche in the future. Or as Louis himself puts it, "Nowadays. No connections. No responsibilities. All of us . . . falling through the cracks that separate what we owe to ourselves and . . . and what we owe to love" (1:71).

AIDS brings this dilemma to a rapid and painful reckoning. Grief has come into people's lives earlier in the late 1980s, occurring where it normally would have been postponed. Kushner believes this sad fact may very well force Americans to confront the consequences of their blind individualism. The trauma of AIDS holds for him the greatest potential source of social change. Early death, governmental back-turning, and whole populations of enraged mourning have created what Kushner would call a state of emergency. The conditions, in other words, are ripe for revolution. Communal consciousness, provoked by loss, has translated into militancy and activism. What's more, Kushner has convinced himself of Benjamin's prerequisite for radical change—the belief that "*even the dead will not be safe from the enemy if he wins*."[11] Haunting ***Angels in America*** is the restive ghost of Ethel Rosenberg, the woman Cohn famously prosecuted and had ruthlessly sentenced to death. "History is about to crack wide open" (1:112), she cries out with a vengeful laugh at her ailing enemy, who taunts her with the idea of his immortality. Indeed, "Millennium Approaches" has become the dead's battle-cry as well as that of the living.

To make clear that the forces of light are rallying against the forces of darkness, Kushner entitles the last act of ***Millennium Approaches*** "Not-Yet-Conscious, Forward Dawning." Even level-headed Belize shares this fervent sense that revolutionary change is coming. Outside the coffee shop, he assures Louis that "[s]oon, this . . . ruination will be blanketed white. You can smell it—can you smell it? [. . .] Softness, compliance, forgiveness, grace" (1:100). It is on this hopeful note that the playwright ends the first part of his epic saga. An angel, crashing through Prior's bedroom ceiling, announces:

> Greetings, Prophet;
> The Great Work begins:
> The Messenger has arrived.

> (1:119)

The Great Work, however, begins with a nay-sayer. Aleksii Antedilluvianovich Prelapsarianov, the world's oldest living Bolshevik, begins ***Part Two: Perestroika*** declaring:

> The Great Question before us is: Are we doomed? The Great Question before us is: Will the Past release us? The Great Question before us is: Can we change? In Time?

> And we all desire that Change will come.

> (*Little pause*)

(*With sudden, violent passion*) And *Theory*? How are we to proceed without *Theory*? What System of Thought have these Reformers to present to this mad swirling planetary disorganization, to the Inevident Welter of fact, event, phenomenon, calamity?

(2:13-14)

Kushner himself doesn't have a theory to offer before the lights come up on Prior cowering in bed with an Angel hovering over him. What the playwright has instead is an insight into the workings of history. "As Walter Benjamin wrote," the playwright reminds, "you have to be constantly looking back at the rubble of history. The most dangerous thing is to become set upon some notion of the future that isn't rooted in the bleakest, most terrifying idea of what's piled up behind you."[12] Kushner understands that the future needs to have its roots in the tragedies and calamities of the past in order for history not to repeat itself. The playwright's very difficult assignment, then, in *Perestroika* is to somehow move the narrative along into the future, while keeping history ever in sight; he must, in other words, find the dramatic equivalent of Klee's *Angelus Novus*, and bring us either to the threshold of a fresh catastrophe or to a utopia that throws into relief the suffering of the past.

Surprisingly, and in most un-Benjaminian fashion, Kushner rushes headlong into a fairy tale of progress. Torn between the reality of protracted calamity and the blind hope of a kinder, gentler millennium, the playwright opts for the latter, hands down. Kushner says of himself that he "would rather be spared and feel safer encircled protectively by a measure of obliviousness."[13] To that end, Prior not only survives his medical emergencies, but the playwright has him traipsing up a celestial scaffolding to heaven. Louis and Joe's torrid affair ends when Louis finds out the identity of Joe's boss. Calling Cohn "the most evil, twisted, vicious bastard ever to snort coke at Studio 54," Louis explodes at his month-long bedfellow, "He's got AIDS! Did you even *know* that? Stupid closeted bigots, you probably never figured out that each other was . . ." (2:111). After Joe punches him in the nose, Louis goes back to Prior, who lovingly tells him it's too late to return. Cohn, at long last, kicks the bucket, only to have Louis and Belize (with help from the ghost of Rosenberg) say Kaddish over him. "Louis, I'd even pray for you," Belize admits, before explaining the reason for his unusual benevolence:

> He was a terrible person. He died a hard death. So maybe. . . . A queen can forgive her vanquished foe. It isn't easy, it doesn't count if it's easy, it's the hardest thing. Forgiveness. Which is maybe where love and justice finally meet. Peace, at last. Isn't that what the Kaddish asks for?

(2:124)

Though the two men end up ransacking the undearly departed's stockpile of AZT, it is Cohn who has the last laugh. In a fleeting moment of monstrous irony, Kushner grants Cohn his dream of immortality by letting him serve as God's defense attorney. Harper, tired of traveling through her own drug-and-loneliness-induced Antarctica, demands Joe's charge card and leaves for the airport to catch a night flight to San Francisco. "Nothing's lost forever," she says before making her final exit. "In this world, there is a kind of painful progress. Longing for what we've left behind, and dreaming ahead" (2:144).

The action concludes in a final pastoral scene in Central Park, in which Prior, Louis, Belize, and (somewhat implausibly) Hannah, Joe's Mormon mother and Prior's newest friend and sometimes caretaker, bask in the sun of a cold winter's day. "The Berlin Wall has fallen," Louis announces. "The Ceausescus are out. He's building democratic socialism. The New Internationalism. Gorbachev is the greatest political thinker since Lenin" (2:145). (Thus the title *Perestroika*.) The soothing story of the healing angel Bethesda is told, after which Prior sends us all contentedly home:

> This disease will be the end of many of us, but not nearly all, and the dead will be commemorated and will struggle on with the living and we are not going away. We won't die secret deaths anymore. The world only spins forward. We will be citizens.
>
> The time has come.
>
> Bye now.
>
> You are fabulous creatures, each and every one.
>
> And I bless you: *More Life*.
>
> The Great Work Begins.

(2:148)

We won't die secret deaths anymore? The world only spins forward? Such uncritical faith in Progress would have been anathema to Benjamin, and to the Kushner of the first part, who so cogently applies the German's uncompromising historical materialism to America's current fin-de-siècle strife. The playwright has quite emphatically turned his attention away from the past and present turmoil, to a future that seems garishly optimistic in contrast. What happened?

There is a definite movement in *Perestroika* away from historical analysis towards a poetics of apocalypse. The pressure of reality seems to have induced an evangelical fervor in Kushner, in which social and political reality has become subordinate to religious fantasy. "The end of the world is at hand," Harper declares, while standing barefoot in the rain on the Brooklyn Heights Promenade. "Nothing like storm clouds over Manhattan to get you in the mood for Judgment Day" (2:101), she adds to the timely accompaniment of a peal of thunder. If that is not enough to convince us, Kushner whisks us around the heavens to hear the angels sing:

> We are failing, failing,
> The earth and the Angels.
> Look up, look up,

269

It is Not-to-Be Time.
Oh who asks of the Orders Blessing
With Apocalypse Descending?

(2:135)

As Frank Kermode points out in *The Sense of an Ending: Studies in the Theory of Fiction*, "[I]t seems to be a condition attaching to the exercise of thinking about the future that one should assume one's own time to stand in an extraordinary relation to it. . . . We think of our crisis as pre-eminent, more worrying, more interesting than other crises."[14] This is, of course, in large part a way to distract from the urgency of the present. Cultural anxiety is often transmuted into the myth of apocalypse; society, too, has its defense mechanisms for dealing with uncomfortable reality. On this point Savran agrees: "Regardless of Kushner's intentions, *Angels* sets forth a project wherein the theological is constructed as a transcendent category into which politics and history finally disappear."[15]

Ironically, though the play is set in a tragic time (a "murderous time" implies the Stanley Kunitz epigraph to **Millennium Approaches**), Kushner steers clear of tragic death, preferring instead to finish on a Broadway upnote. What makes this ending particularly hard to accept is that the playwright hasn't provided any convincing evidence to suggest that the state of emergency has let up in the least. Instead, he focuses on the gains in Prior's inner struggle, his will to live and general spiritual outlook. "Bless me anyway," Prior asks the angels before returning to a more earthbound reality. "I want more life. I can't help myself. I do. I've lived through such terrible times, and there are people who live through much much worse, but. . . . You see them living anyway. [. . .] If I can find hope anywhere, that's it, that's the best I can do" (2:135-36). New Age self-healing now takes precedence over politics, the spirit of individualism infects AIDS, and anger becomes merely an afterthought directed at God. "And if He returns, take Him to court," Prior says in a huff before leaving the cloudy heavens behind. "He walked out on us. He ought to pay" (2:136).

The situation parallels almost exactly the course of public response to AIDS in America. In the second decade of the epidemic little has changed, except for the fact that there is a diminishing sense of crisis. Activism has lulled, militancy has subsided into earnest concern, while conservatism, fundamentalism, and Jesse Helms-style homophobia are on the rise. AIDS, though still deadly, has been symbolically tamed. "Nothing has made gay men more visible than AIDS," Leo Bersani observes in *Homos*.[16] "But we may wonder if AIDS, in addition to transforming gay men into infinitely fascinating taboos, has made it *less dangerous* to look."[17] Troubled by the enormous success of **Angels,** Bersani argues that it is yet another sign of "how ready and anxious America is to see and hear about gays—provided we reassure America how familiar, how morally sincere, and particularly in the case of Kushner's work, how innocuously full of significance we can be."[18]

Bersani offers these comments as part of a larger critique on the Queer movement's spirited, if often hollow, rhetoric of community building, which has come in response to AIDS, and which he views as dangerously assimilationist. Sharing Louis's belief in "the prospect of some sort of radical democracy spreading outward and growing up" (1:80), Kushner insists on the possibility of this kind of Queer (i.e., communal) redemption. Indeed, the playwright has said (with no trace of self-irony) that he finds *Benjamin's* sense of utopianism to be in the end profoundly apocalyptic.[19] Savran explains that, "[u]nlike the Benjamin of the 'Theses on the Philosophy of History,' for whom any concept of progress seems quite inconceivable, Kushner is devoted to rescuing Enlightenment epistemologies."[20] That is to say, "*Angels* unabashedly champions rationalism and progress."[21]

Benjamin's vision, however, seems ultimately far less bleak than either Kushner's or Savran's wishful idealism. Bertolt Brecht's remark on "Theses on the Philosophy of History" seems peculiarly apt: "[I]n short the little treatise is clear and presents complex issues simply (despite its metaphors and its judaisms) and it is frightening to think how few people there are who are prepared even to misunderstand such a piece."[22] Progress was for Benjamin a debased term primarily because it had become a dogmatic expectation, one that left the door open to very real destruction:

> One reason why Fascism has a chance is that in the name of progress its opponents treat it is as a historical norm. The current amazement that the things we are experiencing are "still" possible in the twentieth century is *not* philosophical. This amazement is not the beginning of knowledge—unless it is the knowledge that the view of history which gives rise to it is untenable.[23]

Kushner's brand of progress, in fact, seems dangerously close to that uncritical optimism on which Social Democraatic theory, the antagonist of Benjamin's entire vision, relies:

> Progress as pictured in the minds of Social Democrats was, first of all, the progress of mankind itself (and not just advances in men's ability and knowledge). Secondly, it was something boundless, in keeping with the infinite perfectibility of mankind. Thirdly, progress was regarded as irresistible, something that automatically pursued a straight or spiral course.[24]

For Benjamin, history is essentially the history of trauma. It is the sequence of violent breaks and sudden or catastrophic events that cannot be fully perceived as they occur, and which have an uncanny (in the rich Freudian sense of the word) tendency to repeat themselves. His essay is above all an inducement to consciousness, a clarion call to the mind to wake from its slumber and apprehend this persistent cycle of oppression and the mountain-high human wreckage left in its wake. Benjamin doesn't so much believe, as Savran suggests, that the present is doomed by the past, as that paradoxically in order for a society to free itself to move in a more utopian direction, the fundamental inescapability of the aggrieved past must be vigilantly acknowledged.

In her essay "Unclaimed Experience: Trauma and the Possibility of History," Cathy Caruth makes the crucial point that "the traumatic nature of history means that events are only historical to the extent that they implicate others . . . that history is precisely the way we are implicated in each other's traumas."[25] This insight provides a way to understand not only the sweeping synthesis of Kushner's political vision in *Part One*, but also what may have gone awry in *Part Two*. From the vantage point of the traumatic experience of gay men and AIDS, Kushner taps into a much larger pool of American trauma, from the McCarthy witch hunt and Ethel Rosenberg to Reagan and neoconservatism. That Kushner is able to reveal from such an unabashedly gay, indeed flaming, position these indissoluble political bonds may be surprising to those who cannot conceive of sharing anything in common with men who imitate Tallulah Bankhead. But through the intimate concerns of Prior and Louis's relationship, Kushner opens up historical vistas onto generations of America's oppressed. The question is: were the almost unbearable scenes of Prior's illness, the pain of his and Harper's abandonment, and the punishing hypocrisy of Roy Cohn and his kind so overwhelming, so prolific of suffering, that they forced the playwright to seek the cover of angels?

By the end of *Perestroika,* Kushner stops asking those pinnacle questions of our time, in order to dispense "answers" and bromides—Belize's forgiveness of a rotten corpse; Harper's comforting "[n]othing's lost forever"; Louis's paean to Gorbachev and the fall of the Iron Curtain. By the final scene, Prior learns that "[t]o face loss. With Grace. Is Key . . ." (2:122). This is no doubt sound knowledge. But to be truly convincing it must be passed through, dramatized, not eclipsed by celestial shenanigans peppered with *Wizard of Oz* insight. Surrounded by loved ones, Prior sends us off with hearty best wishes. AIDS has become an "issue" and all but vanished from sight. After convincing us brutally, graphically, of the centrality of AIDS in our history, and of the necessity of keeping the traumatic past ever in sight, the playwright abandons the house of his uncommon wisdom. *Millennium Approaches* may be the most persuasive and expansive AIDS play to date, but, as the silent backtracking of *Perestroika* suggests, the genre needs continuous reinforcing.

NOTES

[1]Nicholas de Jongh, *Not in Front of the Audience: Homosexuality on Stage* (London, 1992), 179.

[2]Alisa Solomon, "AIDS Crusaders Act Up a Storm," *American Theatre* (Oct. 1989), 39.

[3]David Savran, "Tony Kushner Considers the Longstanding Problems of Virtue and Happiness," *American Theatre* (Oct. 1994), 22-23.

[4]Walter Benjamin, "Theses on the Philosophy of History," in *Illuminations*, ed. Hannah Arendt, trans. Harry Zohn (New York, 1968), 257-58.

[5]Benjamin, 265.

[6]Tony Kushner, *Angels in America; A Gay Fantasia on National Themes. Part One: Millennium Approaches* (New York, 1993), 74. Subsequent references will be included in the text, preceded by the numeral 1.

[7]Tony Kushner, *Angels in America: A Gay Fantasia on National Themes. Part Two: Perestroika* (New York, 1994), 38. Subsequent page references will be included in the text, preceded by the numeral 2.

[8]John Lahr, "Beyond Nelly," *New Yorker* (23 Nov. 194), 127.

[9]Kushner, "Afterword," *Perestroika*, 150.

[10]Ross Posnock, "Roy Cohn in America," *Raritan*, 13:3 (Winter 1994); 69.

[11]Benjamin, 257.

[12]Savran, "Tony Kushner," 25.

[13]Kushner, "Afterword," 155.

[14]Frank Kermode, *The Sense of an Ending: Studies in the Theory of Fiction* (London, 1966), 94.

[15]David Savran, "Ambivalence, Utopia, and a Queer Sort of Materialism: How *Angels in America* Reconstructs the Nation," *Theatre Journal*, 47:2 (1995), 221.

[16]Leo Bersani, *Homos* (Cambridge, MA, 1995), 19.

[17]Ibid., 21.

[18]Ibid., 69.

[19]Savran, "Tony Kushner," 26.

[20]Savran, "Ambivalence," 214.

[21]Ibid., 214.

[22]Bertolt Brecht, *Journals 1934-1955*, trans. Hugh Rorrison (London, 1993), 159.

[23]Benjamin, 259.

[24]Ibid., 262.

[25]Cathy Caruth, "Unclaimed Experience: Trauma and the Possibility of History," *Yale French Studies*, 79 (1991), 192.

Carla J. McDonough   (essay date 1997)

SOURCE: "Other Voices, Other Men: Reinventing Masculinity," in *Staging Masculinity: Male Identity in Contemporary American Drama*, McFarland & Company, 1997, pp. 161-69.

[*In the excerpt below, McDonough investigates Kushner's examination of male identity in* Angels in America, *arguing that the play critiques "social assumptions regarding the efficacy of traditional masculinity."*]

Although most of the male characters discussed in this study have put their faith in a set idea of masculinity and manhood, most also suffer confusion and doubt because they feel unable to achieve or maintain that ideal manhood. Mamet's businessmen, Shepard's would-be cowboys, Rabe's soldiers and single men, and Wilson's family men, while sharing some common beliefs about American masculinity, all structure their ideas of manhood by privileging different qualities and structures of that masculinity. In short, although they tend to assume one definition, when set side by side their multiple stories provide multiple perspectives on masculinity. Even within a perspective, such as Shelly Levene's or Levee's, the possibility of other perspectives—of other performances—arises, although these characters try to suppress or discount those options. The predicament of these characters regarding manhood seems to be that in collapsing possibilities in order to solidify their identities, they actually cut off their ability to maintain any identity. Rather than an inherent, unchanging essence, masculinity seems to be, in fact, a construct that needs the mutability these men fear.

Regarding the idea of mutability, it seems pertinent to return to some of the critical concepts raised in the opening chapter, particularly to the ideas posed by James Clifford. Clifford explores both the mutability of human cultures and the impulse to ignore this mutability in favor of accepting culture as monolithic. He argues, however, that the world of the twentieth century has basically made the idea of monolithic culture obsolete: "Twentieth-century identities no longer presuppose continuous cultures or traditions. Everywhere individuals and groups improvise local performances from (re)collected pasts, drawing on foreign media, symbols, and languages" (14). Clifford's analysis of ways for viewing culture, intended to address issues pertinent to anthropologists and ethnographers, offers a useful perspective from which to view the predicament of masculinity in contemporary American drama. Based upon the plays discussed in previous chapters, male characters are all too often lost in a nostalgia for a set version of American manhood that they usually locate in the country's frontier past, but this past is itself merely another construct, a narrative structured a certain way by writing over actual flaws and discrepancies or, as Victor Seidler puts it, by making the differences among actual men "invisible." Joe Dubbert further argues that the idea of a moment in the past in which American manhood was secure is itself a myth that generations of Americans as far back as the 1840s held about a *previous* time. In contrast to this mythologized previous time, the tendency seems to have been to view the *current* moment as one of crisis. This tendency is voiced by both Mamet's and Edmond's belief that the world is "falling apart," and by Austin of Shepard's *True West* when he comments that "nothing is real here." These men, real and imagined, long for a time and place in the tradition of American manhood when the world was whole and "men were men." Although this tradition is largely mythical, to throw out traditions and pasts completely is hardly a solution, as Wilson's Levee and Boy Willie both learn. Instead of embracing or denying *a* history, perhaps the solution is to entertain multiple versions of that history, to accept the "making of masculinities," as Harry Brod entitles his volume of essays on the new men's studies. In short, the solution is to reinvent masculinity. Why does this solution elude the men of these plays, even when confronted in no uncertain terms by the failure of their

monolithic concepts? Clifford comments, "It is easier to register the loss of traditional orders of difference than to perceive the emergence of new ones" (15). Perhaps that is the next task in examining the issue of masculinity in contemporary American drama—not to record old versions of masculinity but to recognize and validate new versions.

Although the plays already treated offer characters trapped in intractable images that betray them, what of explorations of new images of manliness, of manhood? Are alternate viewpoints out there? What about male playwrights who acknowledge this question of male identity and its problems, or who indicate awareness of the centrality of this gender bias? The changes in gender attitudes, the questions raised by feminism, men's studies, and gay studies regarding gender, find their place in more recent work for the stage. Some of the best examples are provided by minority playwrights, those stereotypically outside of the mainstream idea of traditional American masculinity—playwrights who typically get "qualified" with adjectives that supposedly limit their universality. The Chinese-American David Henry Hwang and the gay playwright Tony Kushner offer recent notable examples of powerful drama that explore the problems and entrapments of traditional American concepts of masculinity, and that provocatively critique it. Their plays do not always escape the stereotypes they seek to deconstruct, but their examination is much more consciously disruptive of the traditional portrait of masculinity than are the plays already treated in this study. Although they do not "solve" the gender question for men, they do engage in what Judith Butler calls "gender trouble." By troubling the still waters of the "accepted" version of gender identification, the "accepted" reflection is disrupted, returning a much more distorted image of gender than is usually recognized and leading ultimately to questioning of that image. Instead of writing over the issues that the dominant voice would like to make invisible, these playwrights tend to acknowledge and foreground gender issues for their men. . . .

While Hwang's play [*M. Butterfly*] is enacted on the sweeping canvas of East-West relations, albeit with a distinctly American voice that Hwang insisted upon, Tony Kushner's epic *Angels in America* takes on a wide-angle portrait of America, the first half of which offers us some relevant issues regarding how America's self-image is implicated in issues of gender.

Kushner's part 1 of *Angels in America, Millennium Approaches* (1990), provides a portrait of a decaying American culture. The heart of this decay is located in the tyranny of heterosexuality and competitive masculinity. These two issues are carried chiefly by the stories of Roy Cohn, "a successful New York lawyer and unofficial power broker" (3), and his employee/apprentice Joe Pitt. Like *M. Butterfly*, Kushner's play highlights the gender games being played, and nowhere is the game better mastered than by Roy Cohn. In treating the ideological climate of America at the end of this century, Kushner chooses as his representative of the cutthroat materialism of the 1980s a gay politician who vehemently denies his homosexuality and disparages homosexuals in general for being weak and ineffectual, even as he affirms that he sleeps with men. Roy Cohn's self-image and his value system is rooted upon one principal: power, or what he calls "clout." He associates power with the defining quality of the heterosexual male. Thus his reasoning: because he is powerful, he is not a homosexual but a heterosexual male who happens to sleep with men. Perhaps no other passage in drama, fiction, or poetry so clearly establishes the issues at stake in male fear of homosexuality than does Cohn's rationalization of his orientation. The assumptions and stereotypes regarding male heterosexuality that lead to prejudice and oppression are summed up in Cohn's assertion that the successful American man is supposed to be tough, powerful, dominant, competitive, ruthless, violent, and that these qualities are possible only when associated with heterosexual behavior. Cohn is subsequently a contradiction in terms in being a powerful, ruthless, and competitive man who is also homosexual. He can resolve the contradiction only by denying it because it is impossible for him, in his limited imagination, to combine his definitions of self in any way that falls outside of traditional definitions of "acceptable," heterosexual masculinity.

The issue of acceptable masculinity haunts Joe Pitt as well. His confusion regarding his own identity stems from repressed homosexuality, but his sexuality is intricately entangled with his ideas of appropriate behavior as taught him by his religion (Mormonism) and by his position (a lawyer) within the world of corporate America. Joe's innocence of the system that Roy rules serves to highlight the corruption of that system. Faced with the corruption of this all-American way, Joe finds himself unable to support or to deny such a system. Instead, he offers a rationalization that covers over Roy's belligerent and abusive behavior. When asked by Roy to go to Washington to oversee his political dealings there, Joe refuses, saying:

> There's so much that I want, to be . . . what you see in me, I want to be a participant in the world, in your world, Roy, I want to be capable of that, I've tried, really I have but . . . I can't do this. Not because I do not believe in you, but because I believe in you so much, in what you stand for, at heart, the order, the decency. I would give anything to protect you, but. . . . There are laws I can't break. It's too ingrained. It's not me [107].

Joe indicates that he sees Roy's ways as being decent, but also that they are illegal (indecent). He cannot reconcile this problem, so he decides to quit working for Cohn, even as he indicates his respect and admiration for Cohn.

Roy's response to Joe's desire to equate decency with Roy's methods is to lay out the ultimate incompatibility between decency and the American method of obtaining and maintaining power. He asks Joe, "You want to be Nice, or you want to be Effective? Make the law, or subject to it. Choose" (108). Unlike the hero of the Hollywood western, whom Robert Ray describes as not having to choose between contrasting ideologies, *this* hero is forced to choose between two possibilities. Joe is confronted with the fact that good or decent behavior and powerful or effective behavior are not compatible in Cohn's (America's dominant) ideology. Roy stands for America's history of doing wrong for the supposed sake of right, whether that be blacklisting communists, beating and arresting civil rights demonstrators, bombing civilians in Vietnam, selling arms in return for hostages, or ignoring the "homosexual" disease AIDS. And ultimately Roy sees this belligerent, violent, "illegal" behavior as a mark of his masculinity, his manhood. The fact that Roy has AIDS, then, calls into question his power on many levels. By weakening him physically, it prevents him from being "tough." By associating him with the homosexuality he wishes to deny, it connects him with people perceives to be weaklings.

In contrast to the weakling that Roy assumes every homosexual to be, Kushner offers his audience several gay men whose behavior is as varied as is their situation. Joe, a repressed homosexual, has married a woman whose addiction to valium is exacerbated by knowing that her husband does not really feel for her as a husband should. Joe has wanted to do right, but in following prescribed behavior laid down for him by religious and corporate philosophies, he has brought unhappiness upon himself and his wife. In comparison to the troubled heterosexual marriage of Joe and Harper, Kushner offers the troubled relationship between Louis and Prior, who is dying of AIDS. This relationship offers the audience a portrait in cowardice and courage. Louis's understandable fear of death does not excuse his abandoning his lover, something which Louis is aware of, even as he defends his behavior to their mutual friend Belize. While Louis spends the course of the play trying to escape his responsibilities, both Prior and Joe come to a greater understanding of who they really are and of their own strengths and weaknesses. Prior's hallucinations/visitations particularize his bout with AIDS, moving him away from being a generic "victim." As Prior encounters his ancestry, as he finds out more about his family past, Joe comes to terms with his present family by at last coming out to his mother. Although each of these men's stories is intricately connected to their sexuality in one way or another, their battles are over issues of identity and responsibility that go beyond sex.

Given the range of attitudes and philosophies among these men, it is interesting to note that a recurring critical comment by reviewers of this play is that Kushner's choice of characters to represent America is not appropriately representational because he focuses on gay men. Although some reviewers of this play, such as Clive Barnes and Frank Rich, were comfortable with accepting the themes presented as being "universal," others were uncomfortable with this "gay" portrait of America (Barnes, "Angelically" 210; Rich "Embracing" 15-16). For example, John Simon called this play a "minority report" ("Of Wings" 102). Edwin Wilson commented that *Angels* "presents the closed universe of a homosexual world" (9). In championing the play, John Lahr still commented that it offers a view from the margins, although that view is relevant to understanding the center of the country (137). And Howard Kissel sums up the play as being "about being gay in America" ("Falling" 216). While all of these comments are valid in that the play does treat the lives of gay men and their conflict with the straight culture, the fact that the reviewers assume that homosexuality is a limiting quality to these characters' ability to be representative Americans is quite relevant to the argument at hand. After all, these men are not the established "norm" of heterosexual masculinity, and the critical reluctance to see these non-heterosexual men as the "real" story of American further emphasizes the way that heterosexual masculinity is accepted unquestionably as the universal. Consider, in comparison, that Mamet's heterosexual businessmen in *Glengarry Glen Ross* encountered no such critical reservations for speaking about American business and culture as they encounter some of the same conflicts regarding work and male identity that Kushner's characters face. Of further interest is the fact that although reviewers repeatedly commented on the lack of a heterosexual perspective, none noted that the play offers very little in the way of women's lives and experiences. These critics are not bothered by the masculine bias, but by the issue of homosexuality. The assumption underlying the critique of gay men as representative Americans is that they do not fit into the already accepted representative of American culture whom we have seen in the plays by the previous playwrights. This representative, universal person is male, but he is not gay, Jewish, Mormon, or black as are the main characters in Kushner's play.

Although they treat characters and issues that would seem to be out of the mainstream of appropriate subject matter for drama, these two plays by Hwang and Kushner have been given the stamp of mainstream approval by being awarded two of its most prestigious awards: The New York Drama Critics' Circle Award and the Pulitzer Prize. Both plays met with wide commercial success as well, and have been restaged often in theaters across the country. Do these awards and commercial acceptance indicate a willingness to examine gender issues as now being obviously relevant to America's staging of itself, or do they reflect a desire to make safe these plays by defusing their radicalness? But ultimately, how radical are these two "gender-bending" plays? For all the spectacular staging and plotting, both plays still treat the question of male identity—of what it means to be a real man, although from refreshingly different angles than we have seen in the works of the previous playwrights discussed. In this way, both of these plays fall in line with the critically accepted bias that manhood—its norms and limitations—is the central, universal issue within American drama. These two plays, however, are much less sympathetic to the traditional portrait of the "real" man than are the nostalgic portraits we have witnessed in previous chapters. Indeed, even as they reinforce the idea that to understand American culture is to understand its men (which is, at best, a partial truth), they also critique social assumptions regarding the efficacy of traditional masculinity.

Hwang and Kushner, though, do less for ensconcing the male bias than does the critical reception afforded these two pieces. At the same time that their treatment of male identity calls into question the validity of the traditional concept of manliness, criticism of these two plays tends to overlook the "man question" that they raise in favor of treating the woman question, the race question, or the gay question. Viewers trained to see gender issues as irrelevant to the "norm" of heterosexual man find themselves unable to see any aberrations with that figure. The "aberrations" of woman, of non-white, of homosexual have been made to replace the question raised about white, heterosexual masculinity. Until we can begin to question the norm, how do we hope to address the man question? If Gallimard, Cohn, Troy Maxson, Phil, Teach, and Jake are to be accepted as the "all-American" voice of experience, what kind of gender problems are we writing into our society as normal, acceptable, unquestionable?

Such a question reveals to us a hauntingly pervasive problem within our culture—how "normal" masculinity is often the cause of gender problems that are being displaced upon other genders and upon other issues. In placing such a premium upon a rigidly defined concept of masculinity, and resisting any alterations or evolution of that concept even in the face of its failure to meet contemporary needs, the male characters we have encountered have locked themselves into an image that is fracturing both themselves and their worlds. Audiences and critics alike, in agreeing to "overlook" traditional masculinity and, more importantly, its problems, have helped to ensure the entrapping ideology that locks these men into such (self-)destructive stories. However, perhaps by finally naming the man question, we can at last begin to answer it.

BIBLIOGRAPHY

Barnes, Clive. "Angelically Gay about Our Decay." *New York Post* 5 May 1993. Reprinted in *New York Theatre Critics' Reviews* 53 (1993): 210.

Brod, Harry, ed. *The Making of Masculinities: The New Men's Studies.* Boston: Allen and Unwin, 1987.

Butler, Judith. *Gender Trouble: Feminism and the Subversion of Identity.* New York: Routledge, 1990.

Clifford, James. *The Predicament of Culture: Twentieth-Century Ethnography, Literature, and Art.* Cambridge: Harvard UP, 1988.

Dubbert, Joe. *A Man's Place.* Englewood Cliffs: Prentice Hall, 1979.

Hwang, David Henry. *M. Butterfly.* New York: Plume, 1988.

Kissel, Howard. "Falling Angels: Gay Epic Fails to Take Wing." *New York Daily News* 5 May 1993. Reprinted in *New York Theatre Critics' Reviews* 53 (1993): 216.

Kushner, Tony. *Angels in America, Part One: Millennium Approaches.* New York: Theatre Communications Group, 1993.

Lahr, John. "Angels on Broadway." *The New Yorker* 31 May 1993: 137.

Ray, Robert. *A Certain Tendency of the Hollywood Cinema, 1930-1980.* Princeton: Princeton UP, 1985.

Rich, Frank. "Embracing All Possibilities in Art and Life." *New York Times* 5 May 1993: sec. C, 15-16.

Seidler, Victor J. *Rediscovering Masculinity: Reason, Language and Sexuality*. New York and London: Routledge, 1989.

Simon, John. "Of Wings and Webs." *New York* 17 May 1993: 102-103.

Wilson, Edwin. "Tony Kushner's Gay Fantasia Arrives on Broadway." *Wall Street Journal* 6 May 1993: sec. A, 9.

Jonathan Freedman (essay date 1998)

SOURCE: "Angels, Monsters, and Jews: Intersections of Queer and Jewish Identity in Kushner's *Angels in America*," in *PMLA*, Vol. 113, No. 1, January 1998, pp. 90-102.

[*In this essay, Freedman analyzes* Angels in America *as "the most powerful recent attempt to interrogate the complex interrelation between inscriptions of Jewish and sexual otherness."*]

> *The foreignness of Jews is a kind of difference* unlike others. *They are "those people" whom no label fits, whether assigned by the Gaze, the Concept or the State. . . . [F]or Jewishness, the type is the exception and its absence the rule; in fact you can rarely pick out a Jew at first glance. It's an insubstantial difference that resists definition as much as it frustrates the eye: are they a people? a religion? a nation? All these categories apply, but none is adequate in itself.*
>
> Alain Finkielkraut (164)

The french jewish critic Alain Finkielkraut neatly encapsulates the conundrum that Jews have long posed to the imagination of the West. Jews are doubtless different—but somehow differently different, in ways that differ markedly over time. To sample just a few of the major Western understandings of the Jew is to see how diverse and contradictory models of Jewish identity have been. Installed since biblical times in a position of national marginality, constructed by medieval theologians as outsiders to revealed truth, persecuted in the early modern period as usurers or pawnbrokers (from whom governments did not hesitate to borrow), defined by eighteenth-century philosophers as members of a debased tribe in need of cultural improvement, and viewed by nineteenth-century ethnologists as an irrevocably inferior race whose members should be deported, sequestered, or ultimately exterminated, Jews have historically been defined as many contradictory things (Arendt; Langmuir; Poliakov; Rose). And as a new generation of critics has powerfully argued, this multiply constructed figure has an additional property. Although essential to the many different categories by which human difference has been constructed, the Jew challenges the coherence of these classifications (Cheyette; see also Boyarin and Boyarin). If Jews are a race, why do they look so different from one another? If they constitute a religion, how are they to enter the secular nation-state? And if a nation is defined by shared language and culture, how can these

people who speak numerous languages and who cleave stubbornly to a culture of their own belong?

Nowhere have both these properties of the Jew—giving a shape to otherness and calling such constructions into question—been more evident than in images of sexual transgression, especially in the later nineteenth century, when entirely new classifications of sexual deviance were elaborated: the degenerate, the pervert, the homosexual. For as Sander Gilman and others have argued, these powerful but unstable models of deviance were built on that shifting figure of all-purpose alterity the Jew—often, to add to the irony, by assimilating Jewish intellectuals like Max Nordau, Cesare Lombroso, and Freud (Gilman, *Case* and *Jew's Body*; Pick; Harrowitz). The figure of the monstrous Jewish pervert became a staple of anti-Semitic propaganda first in Europe, then in the United States in the late nineteenth century, but the link between the Jew and the sexual other had been forged in the imaginative literature of Europe and England long before—for instance, in medieval mystery plays, which emphasized the Jew's sexual ravenousness and extrahuman powers. Shakespeare's Shylock is a figure metonymically connected with that other merchant of Venice Antonio, whose homoeroticism echoes and is echoed by the Jew's supposed appetite for unnatural reproduction in the form of usury. (According to the medieval philosopher Nicole d'Oresme, for example, "[i]t is monstrous and unnatural that an unfruitful thing should bear, that a thing specifically sterile, such as money, should bear fruit and multiply of itself" [Shell 51].) And Dickens's Fagin is simultaneously a classic Jewish monster with supernatural powers (Fagin does not leave footprints on marshy ground) and one of the first and most fearsome representatives of the child molester, that new figure of sexual pathology in the late nineteenth century. In a more positive vein, Proust's *A la recherche du temps perdu* can be read as a lengthy attempt to play images of the "race maudite" 'damned race,' the Sodomites, against an equally othered race, the Jews (520). The Jewish other and the sexual other were thus frequently placed in vibrant contiguity in the literary traditions of the West well before sexologists or psychologists or race theorists codified that relation.

And yet the overlapping and mutually constitutive discourses on the Jew and the sexually perverse generate questions about each other that disrupt established categories. Shylock's rapacious Jewishness and Antonio's noble homoeroticism measure each other in a way that undermines any simple characterization of Jewish vice or Christian virtue. And in contrast to Dickens's use of anti-Jewish sentiment to enhance the evil of a perverse villain, the dazzling interplay of images of sexual deviance and Jewish otherness in Proust works to undo any stable code of identity, whether rooted in the faubourg Saint-Germain or the rue du Temple.

This categorizing tradition and its destabilizing work superintend my inquiry into the most powerful recent attempt to interrogate the complex interrelation between inscriptions of Jewish and sexual otherness: Tony Kushner's "gay fantasia on national themes," *Angels in America.* Kushner's two-part epic-comic-tragic-fantastic drama has since its first performances in 1991 and 1993 been received with equal doses of critical praise and audience enthusiasm. *Angels* restored to American theater an ambition it has not enjoyed since the days of Eugene O'Neill or Arthur Miller, even though Kushner's syncretism extends the theatrical medium in ways unimagined by his predecessors, conjoining recent American political history, gay male identity politics, Brechtian alienation devices, Mormon myth-making, Broadway schtick, and cabalistic lore. Along with many other projects, the play undertakes an extensive mapping of the place where figurations of the Jew meet figurations of the sexual other, the deviant, the queer.[1] No other text since *Sodome et Gomorrhe* in *A la recherche* has given such sustained and sympathetic attention to both sides of this complex and long-standing conjuncture. But the disappointment of the play, its flawed conclusion, follows ineluctably from Kushner's need to collapse this parallel and to affirm a vision neither queer nor Jewish. For Kushner desires a dramatic form and an understanding of transcendence that allow a space for queer citizenship in a culture obsessed with the mythography of rebirth and the inevitability of miracle. Much is imaginatively and culturally gained thereby, but it is my doleful task here to suggest that much is lost as well and that what is lost is almost exclusively on the Jewish side of the equation. The play collapses into a traditional assimilationist answer to the questions of Jewish identity it has bravely raised: the price of achieving political efficacy in a Christian-centered culture turns out to be the abandonment of Jewish difference to affirm other forms of difference. In conclusion, I compare Kushner's vision of utopian identity with Walter Benjamin's in "Theses on the Philosophy of History," one of Kushner's inspirations. For in the very text Kushner invokes stands a version of the utopian project that eliminates this kind of Hobson's choice in favor of a politics inspired by but not limited to the definitionless difference culturally inscribed in the figure of the Jew.

The unstable and shifting equation between the sexual transgressive and the Jew is established in *Millennium Approaches,* the first part of *Angels in America.* The play begins with Rabbi Isidor Chemelwitz's eulogizing Louis Ironson's grandmother Sophie in front of Louis and his lover, Prior; one scene later, Prior reveals that he has a Kaposi's sarcoma lesion, "the wine-dark kiss of the angel of death," and proclaims, "I'm going to die" (*Millennium* 21). The fate of Sophie Ironson in America—that "melting pot where nothing melted"—chimes with and ironically foreshadows Prior's, and it is a reminder that his death is too early and starkly inevitable. And the words that Rabbi Chemelwitz speaks of Sophie resonate directly in Prior's experience: "You can never make that crossing that she made, for such Great Voyages in this world do not any more exist. But every day of your lives the miles that voyage between that place and this one you cross. Every day. You understand me? In you that journey is." Although the syntax is stage Yiddish, the language is rich

with implication for the two gay men: the archetype for the transformation of identity, which is the mark of queer experience and survival in the play, is the wandering, rootless, shape-shifting Jew who never finds a home. "You do not live in America," claims the Rabbi. "Your clay is the clay of some Litvak shtetl, your air the air of the steppes" (10). The fate of the Jew, like that of the queer, is to be eternally other even in the utopian land that proclaims itself a haven for all aliens. At the end of the play, Prior proclaims, "We will be citizens," underlining his own alienness even in the quest to overcome it (*Perestroika* 148).

Although Kushner emphasizes the contiguity between the Jew and the queer, he does not insist on positing their common alterity. Instead, he uses each as a metonym for the other, creating an interplay of similarity and difference that conspicuously resists reduction into identity. Early in *Millennium Approaches,* for example, Mormon Joe's homoerotic desire is articulated by his dream of Jacob wrestling with a "golden-hair[ed]" angel, an image both of male-male desire and of the struggle between prophetic vocation and queer identity that resonates throughout the play. The dream vision insists on multiplicity and struggle, even in its articulation of a sexually charged oneness—not only in the homoerotically inflected wrestling match between Jacob (soon to be Israel) and an Aryanized angel but also within Joe, whose identifications are multiple. "I'm . . . It's me. In that struggle," Joe tells his wife, Harper, suggesting that he can be or wants to be both a new Jacob wrestling with the angel for prophetic power and an angel yearning to press his body against a Jewish man's (49).

In yet another important instance of the queer-Jew conjunction, Louis Ironson becomes aware of himself as a Jew only after he encounters anti-Semitism from a Jamaican-born black man in a London gay bar; he says, "I feel like Sid the Yid, you know I mean like Woody Allen in *Annie Hall* with the payess and the gabardine coat" (91). His Jewishness is spotlighted for him—and for the audience—when it comes into contact with the politics of otherness in the gay community. Kushner does not specify which kind of alterity might be more privileged, preferring instead to ironize all possible forms of difference through Louis's experience of their clashing interplay.

Although the richness of this interplay is a tribute to Kushner's skill as a dramatist and cultural critic, that process has a darker, more complex side as well. For at the imaginative center of the play stands its most daring and conflicted representation of the queer-Jew interrelation: Roy Cohn, Kushner's at once most historically specific and most stylized character. The real Roy Cohn was of course a perennially controversial figure in American politics, from his days as chief aide to Joseph McCarthy to his career as a politically connected power broker with ties to right-wing politicians, the mob, and the Catholic Church (see Von Hoffman). He was also a spectacularly self-denying gay man, simultaneously the object of homophobic innuendo by his political opponents and, as one of the first public victims of the AIDS virus, an object lesson to the gay male community of the perils of internalized self-hatred (Cadden). An anonymously contributed panel in the Names Project AIDS memorial quilt expresses this conflation of qualities; it reads, "Roy Cohn. Bully. Coward. Victim." Kushner cites this panel as the source of his interest in Cohn: "I was fascinated [by the panel]. . . . People didn't hate McCarthy so much—they thought he was a scoundrel who didn't believe in anything. But there was a venal little monster by his side, a Jew and a queer, and this was the real object of detestation" (Lubrow 60). And throughout the play, Kushner not only notices but also exploits the process by which Cohn was constructed in the culturally sedimented image of the monstrous Jewish pervert—a "venal little monster . . . a Jew and a queer."

Well before Cohn's opponents invoked the stereotype of the venal little monster, the monstrous Jewish pervert had assumed a specifically American embodiment. For between 1880 and 1920—a time of extensive eastern European immigration, economic upheaval, and class warfare—anti-Semitism entered the American political arena on a massive scale. After the financier Joseph Seligman was barred from hotels in Saratoga, many other Jews were excluded from resorts and vacation hotels; Ivy League universities began establishing quotas for Jewish students; and the eugenicist Anti-Immigration League, which worked to establish the quota-setting Immigration Restriction Act of 1924, grouped Jews with other southern and eastern Europeans (as well as Asians and other "undesirables"). In addition, a flood of books, broadsides, and periodical articles in the mainstream and the more popular (if not populist) press rechanneled the anti-Semitic calumny that permeated Europe—many of the anti-Semitic French journalist Edouard Drumont's most extreme animadversions, for example, were directly reprinted in the anti-Semitic tract *The American Jew* (1888); later, the *Protocols of the Elders of Zion* (c. 1905), a notorious forgery by the Russian secret police, was circulated in the 1920s by no less a figure than Henry Ford. These texts put into American circulation the familiar figure of the Jewish pervert.

These slurs sutured the Jew both to sociopolitical power and to nonprocreative sexual practices. It was as if the perverse political power of the Jew could be expressed only by that figure's indulgence in deviant forms of sexuality. Thus *The American Jew* follows claims about the Jews' financial power with assertions that Jews imported sexual perversion into an otherwise pristine America: "Those certain hideous and abhorrent forms of vice, which have their origin in countries of the East, and which have in recent years sprung into existence in this country, have been taught to the abandoned creatures who practice them, and fostered, elaborated, and encouraged, by the lecherous Jew!" (Selzer 49). The speech of Jews is said to be as disgusting as their behavior:

> The average Jew is disgustingly bawdy in his talk, and interlards his conversation with filthy expressions and obscene words. On the verandas of summer resorts, in

hotel corridors, in the lobbies of theaters, on steamboats, on railway cars, and in public places in general, the Jew indulges in this repulsive peculiarity, to the great annoyance and disgust of respectable Christian women and decency-loving Gentile men. This was one of the habits that made him so objectionable at summer resorts, and has led to his practical exclusion at every first-class summer hotel in the land.

(50)

This image of the licentious or lascivious Jew was rapidly inscribed in narratives of female exploitation, either as an instigator of white slavery or as an exploiter of female workers. A 1909 article in *McClure's* claimed that a cadre of mysterious Jews controlled the prostitution industry in New York—largely by selling their own daughters—and that "one half of all the women . . . in the business . . . started their career in New York" prostitution (Turner 58). *The American Jew* extended the concern to gentiles: "In many of the factories operated by Jews throughout the country, the life of an honest girl therein employed is made simply a hell, by reason of the Jews' predominant lechery" (Selzer 53). These fears exploded when Leo Frank, a Jewish factory owner falsely accused of raping a young female worker, was lynched by an Atlanta mob in 1915—an event that is generally considered the worst anti-Semitic incident in United States history and that was made possible by the network of associations I have cited above. At his trial, Frank was constructed as sexually perverse: a known sodomite in Georgia, a state whose antisodomy laws have remained notorious, Frank favored oral intercourse, his chief accuser testified. This testimony was relevant because the victim, Mary Phagan, died with her hymen intact. Frank was cast by his chief public antagonist, the populist politician Tom Watson, in the image of the gentile-mad Jewish pervert: "[a] typical young libertine Jew . . . dreaded and detested by the city authorities of the North [for] utter contempt of law and a ravenous appetite for . . . the girls of the uncircumcised" (Frey and Thomson-Frey 126; see also Dinnerstein 180). It was on these multiple grounds—as capitalist, despoiler of young gentile women, pervert, and Jew—that Frank was lynched.[2]

Hyperphallic but abjuring the proper exercise of the phallus, politically and economically empowered but turning to the seduction of innocent American virgins, the Jewish male thus enters the American populist imaginary as a peculiar amalgam of sexual and political power, perverting gentile bodies and the body politic with a single gesture. For example, in *McClure's* Turner argued that Jewish control of the prostitution industry was the basis for "a system of political procurers" that buttressed Tammany Hall and thereby polluted the national political process (60). This image is imported into *Angels* through Roy Cohn, one conduit for populist paranoia in the 1950s. "[H]e's like the polestar of human evil, he's like the worst human who ever lived, he isn't *human* even . . . ," Louis cries out when he hears of Cohn's death (*Perestroika* 95). Although usually attentive to the signs of anti-Semitism, Louis participates in the suturing of Cohn and anti-Semitic images of Jewish monstrosity. Kushner's iconography here is quite precise. "Playing the phone" with what the stage directions call "sensual abandon," Cohn cries, "I wish I was an octopus, a fucking octopus. Eight loving arms and all those suckers" (*Millennium* 11). Through the magic of theatrical transformation, he metamorphoses into that very inhuman figure. Fixing cases, buying Broadway seats, cheating clients, Cohn seems to extend his tentacles everywhere.

Indeed, Kushner's Cohn corresponds with uncanny accuracy to one of the most powerful images of anti-Semitic propaganda, which I label, with a nod to Sander Gilman's anatomization of the Jew's body, the Jew's tentacles. In anti-Semitic discourse of the later nineteenth and early twentieth centuries, the Jew's monstrosity is performed by the transformation of the hand—the emblem of warmth, love, and pleasure—into bat wings, vampire talons, spider legs, or octopus tentacles. For example, a late-nineteenth-century illustrated anatomy of the Jew includes not just standard anti-Semitic attributes—"restless suspicious eyes," "curved nose and nostrils," "ill-shapen ears of great size like those of a bat"—but also "long clammy fingers" that reach out to clutch or caress (Selzer, following 108). In much classic anti-Semitic propaganda, these corpse-like fingers extend in a monstrous way that connotes social or sexual power. "The Jew's soft hands and curved fingers grasp only the values that others have produced," claims *The American Jew* (Selzer 99), and according to T.T. Timayenis's *The Original Mr. Jacobs* (1888), "the soft hand almost melting with the hypocrisy of the traitor" is a sign of "physical degradation," which "closely follows upon moral degradation. This is strongly remarked among Jews who, of all the races of men, are the most depraved" (21). Among visual representations that use this trope is Gustave Doré's famous caricature of Mayer Rothschild, *Dieu Protège Israel*, which represents the banker holding the globe and defiling it with his long, batlike talons. In George Du Maurier's *Trilby* (1894), the hypnotizing musician Svengali is represented as a spider filling Trilby's dreams with images of monstrous pestiferousness. Illustrated covers of the *Protocols of the Elders of Zion* depict a brutish Jew pawing a bleeding, violated globe or a spider covering the world with its all-encompassing legs.

Kushner's trope of the octopus functions with particular brilliance in this context: it conjoins an image of the Jew as hyperphallic monster with one that stresses the perverse dimensions of that figure. Indeed, it is the second image that constitutes Kushner's most original addition to the tradition. An octopus, like a spider, has "eight loving arms," but it also has "all those suckers": the multiplication of phalli suggested by the arms is reoriented by the trope of the suckers, which unites implications of cheating, vampirism, and fellatio in a vivid image of monstrosity that is both recognizably Jewish and demonstrably queer.[3] The figure of Cohn thus represents an audacious attempt to think through to the center of anti-Semitic imagery, to the cultural queering of the Jew, and finally to the representation of the Jew as at once monstrous, empowered, and perverse—an image Kushner then installs at the center of the play's most malignant icon of queer-Jewish identity.

Kushner invokes this anti-Semitic iconography throughout the play with amazing accuracy. Cohn is foul-mouthed:

ROY. Christ!

JOE. *Roy.*

ROY (Into receiver). Hold. (Button; to Joe) *What*?

JOE. Could you please not take the Lord's name in vain?

(Pause.)

I'm sorry. But please. At least while I'm . . .

ROY (Laughs, then). Right. Sorry. Fuck.

(*Millennium* 14; ellipsis in orig.)

Cohn seduces an innocent gentile, Joe Pitt, whom he tempts first into big-city life and then into homosexual practices and a homosexual identity (to Cohn's hypocritical chagrin). Cohn embodies stereotypical Jewish lasciviousness and greed by hogging a cache of AZT—one he procures, as anti-Semites might imagine, thanks to his possession of secrets about affairs of state. But the idea of the sexually transgressive is never far from the malign Jew, and when anti-Semitic language surfaces in the play, it is sutured to the notion of queerness. For example, when Belize confronts Cohn about this selfish appropriation of a drug that can help prolong, if not save, Prior's life, Cohn refuses to share, then launches racist epithets at Belize. Belize responds with a string of his own imprecations: "shit-for-brains, filthy-mouthed selfish motherfucking cowardly cocksucking cloven-hoofed pig" (*Perestroika* 61). At once homophobic and anti-Semitic, Belize's curse points to self-hatred among both Jews and queers in a society suspicious of its manifold others. But to call Cohn a "cloven-hoofed pig" is to curse him for being both Jewish and nonkosher: cloven-hoofed animals are kosher; pigs are not. The curse thus echoes the common anti-Semitic habit of conflating Jews with that which they abjure, but it also ironically suggests that Cohn has taken as his totem animal the octopus, a beast as forbidden to observant Jews as the pig. The octopus-loving Cohn proudly casts himself the same way that Belize casts him, as forbidden, taboo, *treyf* in a self-negation that contravenes both his sexual and his religious identity.[4]

This construction of Cohn confronts the most regressive element of the right with a reminder that one of its cynosures was also one of its biggest bogeymen, the perverse Jewish power broker. It also outs Cohn in terms that he would have resented. But Kushner evinces a profound fascination with this character, one that lends **Angels** a remarkable inner tension. For while Kushner keeps killing Cohn off, Cohn keeps rising from the dead, like a zombie or golem. Cohn's death dominates **Perestroika,** all the more so because it seems to occur three or four times. The first instance is the memorable scene in which Cohn fakes his death in front of the ghost of Ethel Rosenberg. By tricking the ghost, Cohn achieves a Nietzschean triumph over the dead even though he cannot beat death. Cohn dics a fcw moments later, and the play even manages to have him properly mourned. Discovering Cohn's body while sneaking in to steal his AZT, Belize urges Louis to remember his grade-school Hebrew and say kaddish, the Jewish prayer for the dead. The ghost of Ethel Rosenberg, hovering by the bedside, prompts Louis when he forgets, then comically has him add a curse:

> LOUIS. Oseh sholom bimromov, hu ya-aseh sholom olenu v'al col Yisroel . . .
>
> ETHEL. V'imru omain.
>
> LOUIS. V'imru omain.
>
> ETHEL. You sonofabitch.
>
> LOUIS. You sonofabitch.
>
> *(Perestroika* 126; ellipsis in orig.)

Blessed and cursed, mourned and mastered, Cohn returns again as a ghost that haunts Joe Pitt. He kisses Joe on the mouth in a moment of overt sexuality that pays tribute to Joe's nervously asserted "outness": "Show me a little of what you've learned, baby Joe. Out in the world." Then Cohn announces his departure to the afterlife with a Shakespearean flourish: "I gotta shuffle off this mortal coil. I hope they have something for me to do in the great Hereafter, I get bored easily" (127). Even after this final appearance, Cohn is brought back yet again when Prior, retreating from heaven, sees Cohn agreeing to take on God as his client. And Cohn is in a sense killed again by the excision of this scene from the Broadway and national touring productions of the play.[5]

These remarkable cursings and blessings, ritualized slayings and compulsive revivals turn Cohn into a great vaudevillian in the twilight of his career making one farewell appearance after another before being dragged offstage in mid-shtick. But they also endeavor to bring Cohn's uncanny power under authorial control. As with that other stage Jew Shylock, the energies gathered in Cohn exceed his author's attempts to order and organize them. The persistence of these efforts to kill Cohn, mourn him, revive him, then kill him again attests to the power he continues to exert over his author. It is also a sign of Kushner's need to master Cohn and all that Cohn allegorically incarnates: homophobia, the most invidious forms of right-wing populism, and McCarthyism. Indeed, the symmetry of the two plots of the play suggests that Cohn functions as the objective correlative of the AIDS virus: he infects Mormon Joe with his political vision just as the virus infects Prior.[6] But Cohn's persistence in the face of multiple deaths suggests that he enacts another allegory as well: that of Jewish power. The fantasy culturally inscribed in the supposed monstrosity of the Jew, after all, is that these persistently marginalized members of a Christian-centered culture possess the greatest amount of what Cohn calls "clout" (*Millennium* 45), a secret power all the

more insidious because it is hidden, one that has persisted over the passage of centuries despite all efforts to eradicate it. This phantasmic image of the Jew with power both attracts and repels Kushner, as his representation of Cohn reveals.

In *Angels,* the emblem of ambivalence about Jewishness is Louis, another queer Jew. But Louis is also a neurotic nebbish. Cohn energizes this ambivalent image by refusing to be a nebbish and by arrogantly asserting the voracious, phallic power ascribed to the Jew under the sign of monstrosity. Cohn's willingness to embody this image, to be the Jew with tentacles, palpably attracts Kushner and also leads to Kushner's equally powerful need to master Cohn dramaturgically—to mourn or to kill him. For to affirm the play's ideological commitment to the full assimilation of queer citizens into an ideal body politic, Kushner must eliminate Cohn and all the phallic aggression he represents. At the end of the play, there is room for angels and angelic queers in a utopian America, but there is no place for monsters.

Cohn's ejection from the play, then, is not to be read as a function of some putative self-hatred[7] but an inevitable aspect of Kushner's social and political program. I am deeply sympathetic to Kushner's politics, but their inscription in *Angels* has disturbing dramatic and ideological consequences. As *Perestroika* lurches toward its climax (like Cohn, it seems to end several times), a Christian thematic surfaces that stresses grace and rebirth. And along with this thematic comes a classic form of emplotment—Shakespearean comedy—that affirms regeneration through the creation of a new, redeemed community. Both these forms have notorious difficulties in reckoning with the figure of the Jew.

Like *Twelfth Night*—or, more relevantly, *The Merchant of Venice*—Kushner's play ends with the evocation of a community as a newly formed, extended, inclusive family, albeit a family with a difference. Composed of various forms of otherness, this family is a redeemed version of the community of others that Louis seeks in the gay bar in London: a Mormon with recently discovered lesbian tendencies, a Jew, and a black male drag queen, all presided over by a WASP man living heroically with AIDS. But given the play's preoccupation with the queer-Jew equation, it is disturbing that Louis, the Jewish member of this queer family, should be represented as querulous and ineffectual. The queer Jew enters the postnuclear family, that is to say, not only as a cultural stereotype (albeit one depicted with some affection) but as a particularly disempowered one. More troubling still is the absence of Cohn and anyone associated with him from this community—for Joe Pitt, too, is banished from the final scenes. Shylock, at least, gets to leave the stage under his own power; no such agency, not even negative agency, is granted to either Cohn or his surrogate son. This elision pushes the play into a more explicitly Christian narrative: it emphasizes the near-miraculous rebirth of Prior after his fever-induced dream vision, for he lives on thanks to the AZT stolen from

Cohn's deathbed by Belize and Louis. Cohn dies, it seems, so that Prior might live to preside over the new queer postnuclear family, at least for the space of the theatrical enactment.

The turn to Christian thematics suggested by the privileging of the Prior plot is confirmed by the imagery and action of the play's final section. At Central Park's Bethesda Fountain, Prior has Louis begin the story of the biblical pool of Bethesda and directs Hannah and Belize to complete it. This moment is undeniably moving, but when considered under the sign of Jewishness it remains deeply problematic. Prior asks Louis to perform an act at once typical and typological, to submerge his own Jewish voice in a chorus of Christian ones. The story of Bethesda that Louis tells has distinctly anti-Jewish overtones in the Book of John, where it precedes Christ's healing of a lame man (Prior walks with a cane as a result of his disease). The miracle increases the persecutorial furor of the Jews, already aroused by Christ's performing such miracles as bringing back the dead (Belize mentions Lazarus earlier in the play). But Christ announces that he is the fulfillment of the Old Testament prophecy to the Jews: "Had ye believed Moses, ye would have believed me, for he wrote of me" (5.46). Needless to say, Christ's words fall on deaf ears. These implications were, I suspect, absent from Kushner's consciousness as he wrote; however, they animate the cultural text to which he is clearly referring, and at this point in the play, that passage is writing him. Louis performs the act that, in the biblical passage Kushner alludes to, Jews exist to accomplish: announcing the new Christian dispensation, then getting out of the way.

The Bethesda angel that hovers over the play's conclusion seems to derive more from Marianne Williamson than from Walter Benjamin, and I want in conclusion to suggest why. This turn to the Christian grows out of the play's most powerful and moving political aspirations. The particular success of *Angels,* after all, is to speak at once to multiple audiences—gay and straight; highbrow and middlebrow; socialist, Democratic, and even Republican—and to argue to those audiences for a mode of civic identity that includes rather than excludes, that creates rather than denies community. To David Savran, this enterprise is problematic, for it recapitulates the liberal pluralist ideology that Kushner has explicitly disavowed.[8] Yet as Savran grudgingly admits, the play's breadth of appeal and generosity of address is the source of its efficacy in a public sphere dominated for several decades by conservative ideologies that articulate the utopian longings historically central to the construction of a distinctive American identity:

> What is most remarkable about the play is that it has managed, against all odds, to amass significant levels of both cultural and economical capital. . . . It does so . . . by its skill both in reactivating a sense (derived from the early nineteenth century) of America as the utopian nation and mobilizing the principle of ambivalence—or,

more exactly, dissensus—to produce a vision of a once and future pluralist culture.

(225)

The evocation of the queer family at the end of *Angels* is a perfect example of this utopian vision of union by dissensus and of the political ends to which Kushner attempts to turn this vision. He offers the image of redeemed community in the guise of a utopian Americanness in which the nation is reconstituted in the image of a postnuclear family made up of quarreling outsiders—in Savran's terms, the very embodiment of union by dissensus. That Kushner is echoing a problematic nationalist discourse is ultimately less important than his appropriation of it for a frankly queer political project—and of the family-as-nation metaphor for a nonprocreative notion of both family and nation that includes all forms of family in a new national narrative. When Prior, the reluctant prophet, having wrestled with his own angels, announces his apocalyptic revelation, he intends to include all the members of the audience in this new union, which is more perfect because it is still divided:

> The world only spins forward. We will be citizens. The time has come.
>
> Bye now.
>
> You are fabulous creatures, each and every one.
>
> And I bless you: *More Life.*
>
> The Great Work Begins.

(Perestroika 148)

Prior predicts that "we"—the members of the queer family—"will be citizens," but to achieve this status, "each and every one" must devise a new form of citizenship and work to construct a redeemed America that can gather gay and straight, black and white, Mormon, Christian, and Jew into a collective identity precisely through the act of quarreling over that identity.

But herein lies the problem with Kushner's achievement, at least when considered from a point of view that stresses the different difference that is Jewish difference. To affirm this project, Kushner must speak in the idiom of mainstream culture while criticizing that culture: he must evoke a utopian ideal of America that exerts political and imaginative power in the social arena but that is substantially less than ideal. As Sacvan Bercovitch has suggested, this American ideal of utopia presents the nation as a perfected version of its flawed predecessors just as in the versions of Protestant theology adopted by American Puritans the Christological narrative serves as a fulfillment of its Jewish antecedents.[9] Ironically, this utopian understanding of America has served for many Jewish intellectuals—including Kushner (and perhaps Bercovitch as well)—as a vector of assimilation into a national drama that had excluded them. "It was impressed upon us," writes Kushner of his childhood, "as we sang America the Beautiful at the Seder's conclusion, that the dream of millennia was due to find its ultimate realization not in Jerusalem but in this country" (*Thinking* 5). But according to Bercovitch, the deployment of a typological schema in the construction of an American national utopia ultimately swallows up the narrative of Jewish history that serves as its antecedent and gloss. Jewish difference becomes not only one part of an ethnic panoply—of a vision of union by ethnic dissensus—but also the shadowy type whose truth is named America (Bercovitch 73-81). In such a schema, the narrative of the biblical Hebrews and even that of the Jewish people may be privileged, but by the very conditions of that privilege, their difference—that which marks them as Jews—is extinguished.

To be sure, Kushner invokes the rhetoric of an American utopia not to elide Jewish difference but to intervene on behalf of a queer politics in a cultural debate over the national destiny: to queer the Puritan, as it were. However, the narrative schema he deploys situates his endeavor on a firmly Christian terrain in an overtly typological way. This effect becomes clearest in the play's final foray into the typological imaginary, the concluding speech of Prior. Prior the arch-WASP reverses Louis's anticipation of the Christian dispensation and speaks a Jewish blessing, marked as such by Kushner in his commentary on the play: "More Life."[10] But the reversal cannot be complete; although the Protestant imaginary can contain Jewishness under the logic of typology, Jewishness is granted no such power vis-à-vis the Christian. Prior's articulation of a Jewish blessing thus continues and indeed confirms the absorption of Jewish type into Christian fulfillment instead of breaking or reversing that pattern. It is troubling that a play beginning with a rabbi's voice extolling "the melting pot that does not melt" ends with the subordination of the Jew to Christian emplotment. But Kushner is determined to find a place for angels in America—somehow.

Is there a way of conceptualizing the utopia *Angels* evokes that would not amalgamate otherness into a culturally palatable unity? Benjamin, one of Kushner's major sources for the play, thought so, and his writings suggest a different model for the consolations *Angels* offers. As I have suggested, Benjamin is everywhere in Kushner's play, from its imagery of apocalypse to its angelic iconography. But Benjamin's presence is felt most powerfully in the final scene. When Prior cries, "The world only spins forward" (a false claim, since the world, which spins on its axis, could be said in that sense to be moving nowhere), his speech alludes to the moment in the "Theses on the Philosophy of History" when Benjamin defines his own utopian vision through the image of a Klee drawing, the *Angelus Novus*:

> His face is turned towards the past. Where we perceive a chain of events, he sees only one single catastrophe which keeps piling wreckage upon wreckage and hurls it in front of his feet. The angel would like to stay, awaken the dead, and make whole what has been smashed. But a storm is blowing from Paradise; it has got caught in his wings with such violence that the angel can no longer close them. This storm irresistibly propels him into the future to which his back is turned,

while the pile of debris before him grows skyward. This storm is what we call progress.

(257-58)

Kushner invokes Benjamin but ignores the complexity of his argument. With its audacious conflation of the angelic and the monstrous, Klee's image serves as a reminder that the difference between angel and monster is often just a matter of perspective. This is the chastening recognition that Kushner's utopianism conspicuously lacks, especially when compared with Benjamin's muted (in Benjamin's word, "weak" [254]) messianism. That the angel is propelled forward by the wind from paradise is less important than the text's clear distinction between the beholder of the angel and the vision the angel experiences. The same nonidentity exists within the collective subject who is the implicit addressee of Benjamin's text. This storm may be what "we" call progress—but Benjamin leaves thoroughly and disturbingly open-ended the questions of who that "we" is and what the relation is between what "we" see and what "we" want to see.

In the space created by that opening lies a less amalgamative, more open-ended model of collective identity that creates a place for divergent understandings of history, progress, paradise, and utopia—even of America.[11] That space provides an escape from the impulse to amalgamate—to assimilate?—the various sorts of otherness that Kushner's utopian project ultimately embodies, despite his juggling of multiple models of alterity until the last act of the play. The beauty and brilliance of *Angels* is that the play points beyond itself—and so imposes hard questions about the nature of identities, Jewish and queer alike, that a less insistent, more troubled vision of utopia would leave in its wake.

NOTES

In writing and revising this essay, I have profited from the advice and counsel of Sara Blair, Philip Blumberg, Daniel Boyarin, Jonathan Boyarin, Bryan Cheyette, Daniel Itzkovitz, Anita Norich, Joseph Roach, and David Scobey. After I had written the piece, I read an excellent essay on the same topic by Alisa Solomon that reaches precisely opposite conclusions.

[1] In this essay I distinguish *sexually perverse, deviant,* and *other* from *queer.* The first three terms are labels imposed on those whose sexual practices are considered outside the norm; the last is used by those who are so labeled to define themselves in a way that contests such categorization (see Warner and Berlant xxvi).

[2] Itzkovitz (esp. 178-79) suggested the relevance of Frank to my argument.

[3] Fellatio and Jewishness are explicitly linked elsewhere in the play; Harper attempts to win Joe back to her bed by telling him that "Mormons can give blowjobs." She learns how to do so not in her temple, however, but from "a little old Jewish lady with a German accent" on the radio (*Millennium* 27).

[4] The real Cohn seems to have felt no need to apologize for or conceal his Jewishness even though he worked for most of his adult life on the fringes of the American right most closely affiliated with anti-Semitism. That Cohn does not represent simple Jewish self-hatred makes the network

of ironies radiating from the cloven-hoofed pig and octopus images an even more powerful expression of Kushner's imaginative conflicts and investments.

[5]The scene appeared in the 1988 production at the Mark Taper Theater, which Kushner considers definitive. But its excision in middlebrow venues like Broadway suggests an act of cultural omission that is consistent with Kushner's political project.

[6]It was Kushner's explicit intention to draw this parallel, according to Oskar Eustis, who commissioned *Angels*, served as a sounding board during its composition, and directed the definitive production.

[7]Kushner is not a self-denying or self-hating Jew, despite his investment in Louis, who he claims dictated the text of *Angels* to him when he was blocked in the early stages of composition (Lecture). Kushner is involved in projects that affirm a cultural Jewishness: he has worked on an adaptation of the Yiddish play *The Dybbuk* and is currently planning a version of *The Golem* as part of a trilogy on the intertwining of race and power in the modern world.

[8]For Kushner's repudiation of liberalism, see *Perestroika* 158.

[9]It can be argued that there are ample doctrinal continuity and shared eschatology in the Christian and Jewish traditions. But as Langmuir observes, typological thinking in the Middle Ages made a primary theological point of the historical insufficiency of the Jews. This view persists in American versions of covenant theology, as Bercovitch shows, and in eighteenth- and nineteenth-century Enlightenment philosophy, as Rose argues. More to the point, Kushner alludes to a biblical passage suggesting the historical supersession of the Jewish people by Christian revelation. According to Ruether, such biblical passages make anti-Judaism (and hence, later in time, fully racialized anti-Semitism) a vital part of the Christian tradition rather than a blot on an otherwise sympathetic vision.

[10]Here is Kushner's account of the origin of the blessing: "The play is indebted, too, to writers I've never met. It's ironical that Harold Bloom . . . provided me with a translation of the Hebrew word for 'blessing'—'more life'—which subsequently became key to the heart of *Perestroika*. Harold Bloom is also the author of *The Anxiety of Influence*, his oedipalization of the history of Western literature, which when I first encountered it years ago made me so anxious my analyst suggested I put it away. Recently, I had the chance to meet Professor Bloom, and, guilty over my appropriation of 'more life,' I fled from the encounter as one of Freud's *Totem and Taboo* tribesmen might flee from a meeting with that primal father, the one with the big knife" (*Thinking* 39). Kushner's ambivalence here is palpable (and reminiscent of Louis). He strikes the culturally mediated stance of the ambivalent Jew in the very act of suggesting how culturally mediated his knowledge of Jewishness is. The same admixture of acknowledgment and disavowal is activated by another powerful Jewish father figure, Roy Cohn.

[11]At the end of *The Anatomy of National Fantasy*, Berlant points to the dangers of this kind of amalgamative thinking: "[I]n the United States, power is erotically attached to America. The national frame is abstract, like a man, or a Statue of Liberty. Since that sentence is false—for a man and a statue are only abstract if you repress their conditions of production—the subject who wants to avoid the melancholy insanity of the self-abstraction that is citizenship . . . must develop tactics for refocusing the articulation, now four hundred years old, between the United States and America, the nation and utopia. She must look, perhaps to her other identities, for new sources of political confederation" (286).

BIBLIOGRAPHY

Arendt, Hannah. *The Origins of Totalitarianism*. 1948. New York: Harcourt, 1951.

Benjamin, Walter. "Theses on the Philosophy of History." *Illuminations*. Trans. Harry Zohn. New York: Schocken, 1969. 253-64.

Bercovitch, Sacvan. *The American Jeremiad*. Madison: U of Wisconsin P, 1978.

Berlant, Lauren. *The Anatomy of National Fantasy: Hawthorne, Utopia, and Everyday Life*. Chicago: U of Chicago P, 1991.

Boyarin, Jonathan, and Daniel Boyarin, eds. *Jews and Other Differences: The New Jewish Cultural Studies*. Minneapolis: U of Minnesota P, 1997.

Cadden, Michael. "Strange Angel: The Pinklisting of Roy Cohn." *Secret Agents: The Rosenberg Case, McCarthyism, and Fifties America*. Ed. Marjorie Garber and Rebecca Walkowitz. New York: Routledge, 1995. 93-105.

Cheyette, Bryan. *Constructions of the Jew in English Literature and Society: Racial Representations, 1875-1945*. Cambridge: Cambridge UP, 1993.

Dinnerstein, Leonard. *The Leo Frank Case*. New York: Columbia UP, 1968.

Eustis, Oskar. Personal interview. 8 Aug. 1996.

Finkielkraut, Alain. *The Imaginary Jew*. Trans. David Suchoff. Lincoln: U of Nebraska P, 1994.

Frey, Robert Seitz, and Nancy Thomson-Frey. *The Silent and the Damned: The Murder of Mary Phagan and the Lynching of Leo Frank*. Lantham: Madison, 1987.

Gilman, Sander. *The Case of Sigmund Freud: Medicine and Identity at the Fin de Siecle*. Baltimore: Johns Hopkins UP, 1993.

———. *The Jew's Body*. New York: Routledge, 1991.

Harrowitz, Nancy. *Antisemitism, Misogyny, and the Logic of Cultural Difference: Cesare Lombroso and Matilde Serao*. Lincoln: U of Nebraska P, 1994.

Itzkovitz, Daniel. "Secret Temples." Boyarin and Boyarin 176-202.

Kushner, Tony. *Angels in America: Millennium Approaches*. New York: Theater Communications, 1993.

———. *Angels in America: Perestroika*. New York: Theater Communications, 1993.

———. Lecture. Bread Loaf School of English. Middlebury. 7 Aug. 1996.

———. *Thinking about the Longstanding Problems of Virtue and Happiness: Essays, a Play, Two Poems, and a Prayer*. New York: Theater Communications, 1995.

Langmuir, Gavin. *Toward a Definition of Antisemitism*. Berkeley: U of California P, 1990.

Lubow, Arthur. "Tony Kushner's Paradise Lost." *New Yorker* 30 Nov. 1992: 59-64.

Pick, Daniel. *Faces of Degeneration: A European Disorder, circa 1848-1918*. Cambridge: Cambridge UP, 1989.

Poliakov, Leon. *Histoire de l'antisemitisme*. 4 vols. Paris: Calmann-Lévy, 1955-71.

Proust, Marcel. *Sodome et Gomorrhe*. Ed. Antoine Compagnon. Paris: Gallimard, 1989.

Rose, Paul. *Revolutionary Anti-Semitism in Germany from Kant to Wagner*. Princeton: Princeton UP, 1990.

Ruether, Rosemary. *Faith and Fratricide: The Theological Roots of Anti-Semitism*. New York: Seabury, 1974.

Savran, David. "Ambivalence, Utopia, and a Queer Sort of Materialism: How *Angels in America* Reconstructs the Nation." *Theater Journal* 47 (1995): 207-27.

Selzer, Michael. *Kike!* New York: World, 1972.

Shell, Marc. *Money, Language, and Thought: Literary and Philosophic Economies from the Medieval to the Modern Era.* Berkeley: U of California P, 1982.

Solomon, Alisa. "Wrestling with *Angels*: A Jewish Fantasia." *Approaching the Millennium: Essays on* Angels in America. Ed. Deborah Geis and Steven Kruger. Ann Arbor: U of Michigan P, 1997. 118-33.

Timayenis, T. T. *The Original Mr. Jacobs.* New York: Minerva, 1888.

Turner, George Kibbe. "The Daughters of the Poor." *McClure's* Nov. 1909: 45-61.

Von Hoffman, Nicholas. *Citizen Cohn.* New York: Doubleday, 1988.

Warner, Michael, and Lauren Berlant. Introduction. *Fear of a Queer Planet: Queer Politics and Social Theory.* Ed. Warner and Berlant. Minneapolis: U of Minnesota P, 1993. vii-xxxi.

FURTHER READING

Brask, Per, ed. *Essays on Kushner's Angels.* Winnipeg: Blizzard Publications, 1995, 154 p.
> Contains two essays on *Angels in America* translated from Danish and German.

Geis, Deobrah R. and Steven F. Kruger, eds. *Approaching the Millennium: Essays on Angels in America.* Ann Arbor: University of Michigan Press, 1997, 306 p.
> Contains essays dealing with the play from a variety of perspectives, including history, politics, and performance.

Hornby, Richard. "Dramatizing AIDS." *The Hudson Review* XLVI, No. 1 (Spring 1993): 189-94.
> Review of *Angels in America* that praises Kushner for avoiding sentimentality in the depiction of AIDS.

Shewy, Don. "Tony Kushner's Sexy Ethics." *The Village Voice* XXXVIII, No. 116 (20 April 1993): 29-32, 36.
> Discusses the commotion surrounding the Broadway production of *Angels in America* and includes an interview with Kushner.

Steyn, Mark. "Communism Is Dead; Long Live the King!" *The New Criterion* 13, No. 6 (February 1995): 49-53.
> Negative assessment of *Angels in America* that finds the play overblown and Kushner a "preposterously well-meaning moralizing sentimentalist."

Weber, Bruce. "Angels' Angels." *The New York Times Magazine* CXLII, No. 49,312 (25 April 1993): 27-31, 48-58.
> Surveys the various productions of *Angels in America* as it made its way to Broadway.

Edmond Rostand
1868-1918

INTRODUCTION

Significant for his revival of Romantic verse drama at a time when Naturalism and Symbolism dominated the French stage, Rostand combined an excellent sense of theatrical effect with a keen wit. His optimistic idealism found its best expression in the comedy *Cyrano de Bergerac*, which has achieved a lasting international reputation.

BIOGRAPHICAL INFORMATION

Born in Marseilles, Rostand was the son of a prominent journalist and economist. After attending local schools, he studied literature, history, and philosophy at the College Stanislas in Paris. He began writing for the marionette theater and had poems and essays published in the literary review *Mireille* at the age of sixteen. Although Rostand later studied law, he never practiced, choosing instead to concentrate on a career as an author. His first drama, *Le Gant rouge*, was produced in 1888 with little success, and his first volume of poetry, *Les Musardises*, received scant critical attention when it was published in 1890. Rostand achieved widespread popularity and critical regard in 1894 with his next play, *Les Romanesques* (*The Romancers*), which was produced at the Comedie Française, and solidified his reputation the following year with *La Princesse lointaine* (*The Faraway Princess*), which he wrote for the actress Sarah Bernhardt. Thereafter, Bernhardt became the principal interpreter of his works, appearing in leading roles in several of his plays. The actor Constant-Benoit Coquelin requested Rostand to write a play that would showcase his versatile skills as an actor, and Rostand complied by creating in 1897 what would become his most popular work, *Cyrano de Bergerac*. Two years later, ill health forced Rostand to retire to his country estate, and in 1901 he was elected to the Academie Francaise, the youngest member ever inducted. He continued to write plays and poetry when his health permitted, leaving his final play, *La Dernière nuit de Don Juan* (*The Last Night of Don Juan*), unfinished at the time of his death in 1918.

MAJOR WORKS

Rostand's poetry has been largely disregarded by critics, and he is remembered primarily as a dramatist. In his early play, *The Romancers*, Rostand rejected the sordid realism of the Naturalist plays then popular, creating a lighthearted satire about two young lovers in search of romance and adventure who discover that romantic love

can exist without the excitement of danger or obstacles to overcome. Rostand further developed the theme of courtly love in *The Faraway Princess*, which relates the story of the troubadour Joffroy Rudel, Prince of Blaye, whose love for the Countess of Tripoli, whom he has never seen, inspires him to travel to see her before he dies. In this play Rostand introduced the theme of tenacious adherence to unattainable ideals that became characteristic of his works.

Cyrano de Bergerac is considered Rostand's dramatic masterpiece, successfully combining humor, romance, and heroic action in expert verse. Based on the life of the seventeenth-century soldier and author Savinien de Cyrano de Bergerac, the play recounts the hero's faithfulness to his ideals despite his recognition that he will never be rewarded for them. For example, he upholds his artistic principles by refusing to bowdlerize his plays in order to have them performed or to cater to a patron in order to live comfortably. Adhering to his principles of friendship, he refuses to compete with his friend Christian for the attention of Roxane, the woman they both love, and refrains from destroying Roxane's false image of Christian when he dies, even though it means foregoing his own chance to achieve happiness with her.

The polish of *Cyrano de Bergerac* aroused expectations which were largely disappointed by the last two plays Rostand completed. *L'Aiglon* (*The Eaglet*), which describes the life of the Duke of Reichstadt, son of Napoleon I, has been criticized for its simplistic and predictable construction. *The Eaglet* enjoyed considerable success in France, but it has never had the international appeal of *Cyrano de Bergerac*. The allegorical verse drama *Chantecler*, in which a barnyard cock upholds his faith in the importance of his role in the world, has received varied critical evaluations. While some commentators find the play too lengthy, obscure, and contrived, others praise it as Rostand's most ambitious and profound work, particularly those critics who view it as a poem to be read rather than performed on stage.

CRITICAL RECEPTION

When Rostand's plays first appeared, some critics believed that they would inspire a return to verse drama and Romanticism. However, his dramas merely stood in contrast to the Naturalist and Symbolist literary movements of his time, rather than causing them to be supplanted. Recent evaluations of Rostand's work have praised his skillful verse and consummate theatricality, but find that his plays lack the thematic complexity and depth necessary to be considered great. Nevertheless, his dramas, particularly *Cyrano de Bergerac*, have maintained their popularity and continue to be performed to enthusiastic reviews.

PRINCIPAL WORKS

PLAYS

Le Gant rouge 1888
Les Romanesques [*The Romancers*] 1894
La Princess lointaine [*The Faraway Princess*] 1895
Cyrano de Bergerac 1897
La Samaritaine [*The Woman of Samaria*] 1897
L'Aiglon [*The Eaglet*] 1900
Chantecler [*Chanticleer*] 1910
*La Dernière nuit de Don Juan [*The Last Night of Don Juan*] 1922

OTHER MAJOR WORKS

Les Musardises (poetry) 1890
Le Cantique de l'aile (poetry) 1910
Le Vol de la Marseillaise (poetry) 1919

**This unfinished work was published posthumously.

OVERVIEWS AND GENERAL STUDIES

Martin Lamm (essay date 1952)

SOURCE: "The First Symbolists," in *Modern Drama*, translated by Karin Elliott, Basil Blackwell, 1952, pp. 152-78.

[*In the following essay, Lamm appraises Rostand's major plays.*]

While Maeterlinck and Claudel had difficulty in gaining stage success with their plays another writer of the same school, but of incomparably lower calibre, Edmond Rostand, succeeded in winning the heart of the great public. *Cyrano de Bergerac* was the theatrical triumph of the century, quantitatively perhaps the greatest that the history of the theatre has ever known. For some years the young author was universally acclaimed as the king of modern drama. This enthusiasm, however, began to wane even during his lifetime, and in histories of literature Rostand is now dismissed with a lack of appreciation which is as unjustified as the earlier excessive praise.

Rostand was an exact contemporary of Claudel but he came from the south, like his master Victor Hugo, and like Daudet and his Tartarin. The passionate troubadour and the boastful Gascon are the two standard types from the South of France. Rostand achieved the feat of combining them in Cyrano, a character with the bravado of a Gascon and the heart of a troubadour.

Before Rostand achieved this tremendous success he had spent his apprentice years in the Symbolist school as a writer of lyric poetry, and later of plays which did not meet with much appreciation and did not deserve to do so.

Rostand's first play, *Les Romanesques* (*The Romancers,* 1894), was an attempt to dramatize the world of Watteau. There was in his nature an element of affectation, and it was precisely in periods characterized by affectation that he found his themes, the period of the troubadour for *La Princesse lointaine,* (*The Faraway Princess*), the period of supreme affectation in which Cyrano is set, and the age of Rococo for *The Romancers.*

The plot of this play, in which two fathers pretend to be enemies in order to tempt their children to fall in love with each other, has also been used in a comedy by Otto Ludwig. It is not certain whether Rostand knew this work, but there is a similar situation in Musset's *A quoi rêvent les jeunes filles* (*What do young girls dream of?*).

It is of Musset and Marivaux that the play reminds us, though it lacks their psychological subtlety. The meaning is not that the young people will be cured of their romantic fancies when they have discovered how they have been puppets in their fathers' hands. The epilogue explains that they have only been deceived about the outer and unimportant appearance of things; in their hearts they have known the truth.

In his next play, **The Faraway Princess,** Rostand throws himself headlong into the most ethereal of romances. The real hero of the play, who does not appear very often on the stage, is the troubadour, Rudel. In character and style he is the perfect expression of the courtly, platonic affections of the Middle Ages. He is a character who has been treated by all the world's romantic writers, Heine, Browning, Swinburne and Carducci.

Like *Pelléas and Mélisande* the story is a variation on the Tristan theme. Rudel is at death's door, but before he dies he wishes to see Princess Mélissinde, for whom he has conceived a lofty passion through the songs of wandering minstrels. When at last he reaches Tripolis he is too weak to go ashore, and sends his friend Bertrand in his place. When the Princess catches sight of Bertrand she takes him for Rudel, and when he reads out the love poem that Rudel composed for the distant Princess she falls in love with him.

Meanwhile Rudel is still alive, though his last hour is near. During his final struggle with death the Princess and Bertrand come aboard, but the chaplain forbids Bertrand to cloud his friend's last hours by telling him of his intended deception. In a scene that is reminiscent of the end of *Hernani*, Rudel dies with his lips pressed against those of the Princess.

The plot anticipates that of **Cyrano.** Roxane is in love with the handsome face of Christian, but at the same time, and without realizing it, she loves the noble soul of Cyrano, for it was he who under the cloak of darkness made a declaration of love in Christian's name and wrote his letters for him.

Rostand's idealism is not profound, but it is genuine. The superficiality of his characterization is plainly apparent here, as well as his liking for startling stage effects. The plot is unnecessarily complicated, and the dialogue tediously wordy.

None of Rostand's early plays was particularly successful, least of all **La Samaritaine (The Woman of Samaria),** with its New Testament subject and the figure of Christ as an actor in the play.

Cyrano de Bergerac made him world-famous at once, and the morning after the première on 28th December, 1897, the French critics were prophesying that this date would mark a new epoch in drama as clearly as *Le Cid* and *Hernani* had done. This exaggeration was disproved by events. **Cyrano** did not turn out to be the beginning of a revolution, not even in France. The play is a vigorous and faithful revival of the great heroic drama of the French classical and romantic periods; it is in no sense a new creation.

Subject to these reservations, however, it cannot be denied that **Cyrano** exercised an influence on modern drama. Its remarkable success was convincing proof that the day of historical drama was not yet past, as critics tended to assert. The increase in the popularity of historical plays in all countries around the turn of the century is not unrelated to **Cyrano de Bergerac,** and it was never really dropped from the repertory lists of French theatres. Even in Sweden it is constantly revived, and always with success. It is unjust, too, to complain of the public's bad taste. The play is remarkable neither for its merits nor its faults. It has no unusual artistic merit, nor does it make greater concessions to the public's liking for stage effects than plays usually do.

Cyrano's struggle against a cruel fate, his ability to stand fast by his ideals in the face of opposition and defeat, his determination to put a brave face on humiliation and poverty, and finally, when all else fails, to go down with a brave gesture—all this is not something particularly French or 18th century; it is universal in its appeal. This play resembles too painstaking a copy of an old master, a typical, average piece of Dutch painting, with a few bold strokes of the brush added by Franz Hals.

Cyrano de Bergerac was a lucky shot. Rostand had found a period which perfectly matched his temperament. The early 17th century was an age of affectation, of idealism and sensibility, of gallant and elaborately turned phrases. When Rostand endowed Cyrano with his own exalted passions and his too brilliant vocabulary he gave the play its natural period flavour.

The beginning of the 17th century was also an age of military bravado, of the *Fronde* and *The Three Musketeers*. When Rostand makes D'Artagnan wish Cyrano luck and shake his hand, he clearly indicates that we are in a period where no act is too heroic to be believed. Cyrano is allowed to vanquish a hundred men and to tell the tale with his characteristic gallows humour. His long nose prevents his being taken really seriously by the audience, even when he is carrying out deeds of incredible heroism or showing a superhuman capacity for selfless resignation and exalted idealism. He has a half-mocking, half-tragic way of looking at himself, but Rostand does not allow us to witness any real soul-searching in him, and he does not even give us the impression that such a thing has ever happened.

Cyrano quickly selects the attitude which he feels honour compels him to adopt, and then abides by it stubbornly to the end. He is perfectly aware that such quixotic behaviour will not earn him esteem, but he is incapable of acting otherwise. The moral rectitude of the hero, which has been emphasized by modern dramatists from Schiller to Ibsen, practically reached its climax with Cyrano, the poet and long-nosed braggart. The effect was smaller and less convincing in him than in many of his predecessors, because he is so completely lacking in any sense of doubt. Cyrano belonged to an age when men acted more from impulse than reflection. He was created by an author who was in complete sympathy with him. This is why Rostand was able to work on audiences to whom the heroes of Kleist, Hebbel and Ibsen, with all their introspection, will always remain incomprehensible.

Nearest to Cyrano probably come Victor Hugo's heroes, for they are based on a similar antithesis. Just as Hernani and Ruy Blas bear noble souls under their robber cloaks or servants' uniforms, so Cyrano's sensitive and poetic soul contrasts with his robust exterior and his extravagant boastfulness. The two sides of his character drive him from one deed to another, each more heroic, more wildly idealistic than the last. He resembles Hugo's heroes in their unceasing desire to excel themselves. The knowledge that Roxane loves the stupid Christian causes him to do something more positive than merely to renounce his claims nobly; he wants Roxane to have Christian and to owe her happiness to him. To do this he determines that Roxane must not realize the extent of Christian's stupidity, so he composes letters for Christian, and takes his place in the dark to make that grand avowal of love which she has demanded. These tactics make it even more certain that he will lose Roxane, but they also give him the bitter-sweet satisfaction of knowing that it is really his soul, as expressed in letters and declarations of passion, that Roxane loves. Cyrano abides by his intention even when, sorely wounded, he visits Roxane in the final act. When he reads Christian's last letter, which he himself has written, his voice betrays his feelings. But when Roxane asks him if he loved her he steadfastly denies it, whispering at the end, "No, no, my love, I did not love you." Two lives have been destroyed for a dream; in the hour of Cyrano's death they both realize this. But Cyrano also knows that this struggle for a dream has been worth while just because it was a struggle, just because more than any other struggle it has demanded courage and sacrifice. In Rudel's song in **The Faraway Princess** Rostand praised that same love, noble because of its hopelessness, "plus noble d'être vaine."

Apart from Cyrano the characters in the play are insignificant. Fair without and hollow within, Christian is the antithesis of Cyrano, in the Victor Hugo style. Roxane says in the final act of the play that she has only loved one person but has lost him twice, a thought which Hugo might have expressed in the same way. Rostand and he both revel in grand period pictures which still retain a festive quality.

Our own generation does not, however, find the play as poetic as did the audiences which filled the Théâtre Porte Saint Martin for six hundred performances, or the reading public which bought more than a million copies. What remains most firmly in the memory is probably the final act, with its autumn mood of falling leaves; the sonorous Gascon song is an imitation of a poem which was wrongly ascribed to the real Cyrano.

The play is like a rich brocade which on close examination is found to contain crudities of colour and gems which are not real, but this is less disturbing because it contains an undertone of burlesque. Less easy to forgive are the hackneyed situations of the Scribe type which occasionally occur in it.

In **L'Aiglon** (**The Eaglet**), which Rostand wrote three years later, we get an impression of the actor anxious to gain the applause of his audience. Here we have a loud-voiced patriotism, sentimental and full of speeches but lacking the ability to laugh at oneself that is to be found in Cyrano.

The play was written for Sarah Bernhardt, then no longer young, and was one of the attractions of the Paris Exhibition of 1900. To read it now is like being confronted in some out-of-the-way place by a vast and pretentious exhibition building, hastily constructed of shoddy material. It may be splendidly painted and equipped to please the eye during the short summer months, but seems frighteningly empty and dismal if put to longer use.

Why Rostand really failed was because he selected a profoundly tragic subject. Napoleon's unfortunate son, Frans of Reichstadt, assumed a burden that was too heavy for him when he tried to win again for France the glory that had been Napoleon's. Rostand did the same when he chose a theme that was too great for his poetic talent. One might almost believe that he realized this better than his critics when one reads his last play, **Chantecler,** where he writes with charming irony of the henhouse and its chief singer, the cock, who believes that his throat can rival that of the nightingale.

The Emperor's son, obsessed by Napoleon's dream, but lacking the power to realize it—this was the essence of the plot, but Rostand could not bring it out without resorting to theatrical devices.

Napoleon himself could not be brought on to the stage, so instead Rostand, in an unlucky moment, introduced a veteran of the Old Guard whose name was Flambeau, and who was a sort of travelling museum of Napoleon's relics. From various corners and pockets of his clothes he produces a snuff-box, a pipe and a glass, all bearing Napoleon's picture or his monogram. The tragic death of the Duke on the stage is also embellished with Napoleonic souvenirs. The cradle which the City of Paris presented at his birth is carried in, and the Grand Cross of the Legion of Honour is hung over his night-shirt. There is a statue of Napoleon in the room, and he hums the tunes of his father's day while he is receiving the sacrament.

The Eaglet is set in Scribe's period; a performance of a Scribe play is announced at a fancy-dress ball at Schönbrunn. This may explain the deliberate Scribe touches in the play, the manoeuvres and counter-manoeuvres and the endless disguises. Flambeau says somewhere that he is never satisfied simply with providing the basic needs, but has a crazy passion to 'faire du luxe.' It is this southern French characteristic which has got the better of Rostand in **The Eaglet.**

Although the faint protests against **The Eaglet** were drowned in shouts of approval, Rostand seems to have realized the validity of the criticisms. He wanted to be a poet, not just a stage technician. After *The Eaglet,* to the surprise of the public and the critics, he retired to the country, taking his family with him, and settled for ten years in a quiet corner of the Pyrenees. Rumours were rife about the great stories that he was going to dramatize, such as Faust and Don Quixote, and there was much disappointment when it was learned that he was actually writing a play about hens in a farmyard, with a cock as the hero. The idea came quite soon after *The Eaglet,* but Rostand had trouble in expressing it. In any case, he was ill at the time and was not confident about his subject. The play was not completed until 1909.

A work which had met so many obstacles and taken so long to write was awaited by public and critics alike with understandable suspicion, and the première did not dispel all doubts. Maeterlinck and his *The Blue Bird* were to triumph three years later, and *Chantecler* did not meet with the recognition it merited. In it Rostand took his revenge for *The Eaglet.* He spent ten years of his life on a play which he must have known the ordinary public would never approve, for *Chantecler* is more of a literary drama and actually a more original piece of work than *Cyrano.*

In most European countries there is a legend to the effect that a cock believes that he causes the sun to rise because he predicts it with his crowing. This notion is elaborated by Rostand in the style of a fable. Chantecler, the name of the cock in *Roman du Renard*, is convinced that without him all would be darkness and nature sunk in eternal sleep. The jeers of envious rivals cannot shake his faith. A golden hen pheasant lures him into the forest away from all his hens, but she cannot accomplish alone her wish to make him forget his mission. She therefore summons to her aid the songster of the night, the nightingale, and at his first note Chantecler feels himself finally defeated. It is the same for him as for all who hear the song of the nightingale; they believe that they are only listening for a minute, but when the singing is ended they find they have been listening all night. The sun has risen, but Chantecler has not summoned it with his crowing. Chantecler suddenly sees that he has lost his throne. When the dog from the farmyard comes to greet him and tell him that everyone wants him back to bring up the sun, he answers in a moment of gloom, "Now they have the faith which I have lost." But his depression only lasts a moment and then he lets fly a full-throated crow. When the pheasant asks in surprise why he has done this he replies that it is his calling. The sun may have risen without his help, but it remains for him to awaken all to life, to open all eyes. "Who sees that his dream has died must die at once, or else rise up in greater strength."

This simple story has sometimes been taken to be an allegory on the fate of mankind, or in praise of the value of daily toil, or as an exhortation to all men to do their duty without too great illusions about its importance. This is a fairly widely held point of view, but we grasp the purport of the play better if we consider what the poet's function is. He cannot give life to nature, but he can open men's eyes to it, and he is most faithful to his calling when he regards himself as a worker among fellow-workers. "If I sing clearly and truthfully, and if every farm has a cock who sings in his place, then there will be no more night," says Chantecler.

Rostand explained that the cock expressed his own dreams, and indeed embodied something of himself. During this ten-year period while he was working on the play he had come to realize that his merits were overrated both by himself and by others. Both in the troubadour of Rudel and in Cyrano he had shown something of himself. Cyrano's self-sacrificing idealism becomes little less than a desperate gamble, a desire to make all the noblest and most extravagant gestures himself. Chantecler is less brilliant and more natural. He is the hero of domestic virtues, the citizen and father of the family, the faithful guardian. But as with all his fellow-countrymen, there is a touch of romance in his blood, and he believes that really he is something quite different. Rostand has brought out the sunny and frankly naive qualities of this Tartarin of a cock in a very human way. He is 'un brave meridional' like Tartarin, who finds it hard to see reality except through the veil of romance. Daudet blames this trait of the southern French on the burning sunshine which seems to shroud everything in a haze. So it is with Chantecler. His imagination is always a stage ahead of reality, and his sensitive soul is often wounded.

In his posthumous play, *La dernière nuit de Don Juan (Don Juan's Last Night)*, Rostand writes a sequel to the Don Juan legend which leaves that most famous of all heroes morally naked. The play was not published until 1921, and it consists of a prologue and two acts which were already complete when the first world war broke out. The best scene is the one where Don Juan, released from hell, is confronted by shades of the thousand and three women whom he has seduced. He has to remember their names, but is always guessing wrong, and the shades mock him as they turn away. Finally they say that he has never known them, never possessed them—it is they who have possessed him, just to pass the time away. Romeo and Tristan are the two real lovers who have left behind something of themselves in those they loved. Don Juan is a mere intruder who has struck down those who are already wounded. He appears to have possessed all women, but in fact has possessed none. There is one single shade whom he has occasionally met but who is not on this list of conquests, the white one, the Ideal. At last the unhappy Don Juan begins to long for hell, but the cruel Devil tells him that a hell of a special sort is reserved for him. He is not destined for eternal fire but eternal theatre; he is to be one of the puppets in the Devil's collection. The play is slightly influenced by the Button-moulder episode in *Peer Gynt*, but the thought is typical of Rostand, namely that only love that is unselfish and idealistic is real.

Joseph Chiari (essay date 1958)

SOURCE: "Edmond Rostand," in *The Contemporary French Theatre: The Flight from Naturalism*, Rockliff, 1958, pp. 32-46.

[*In the essay below, Chiari examines the elements of Romanticism in Rostand's plays.*]

Edmond Rostand is not a major writer, yet somehow he is an important one. His importance lies in the fact that he is not only a kind of reaction to symbolist poetry, but a combination of the two strains—idealism and realism—which at the end of the nineteenth century were contending for pre-eminence, and also the representative of a great tradition in French poetry, the tradition of rhetorical poetry. Rostand's romanticism is counteracted by his rationalism and trust in reality, and these two contending tendencies assume, in turn, the mastery of his creative mind, or blend harmoniously in order to produce his best writings.

Rhetoric, which is found in the best poets, from Shakespeare to Racine, has now become a term of disparagement, yet there is good and bad rhetoric. The aim of rhetoric being to persuade, it may take the form of a conscious effort combining words and gestures in order to create an emotive state which will win over the reader or listener, or it may be a logical, cogent display of reasoning which cannot fail to carry conviction. It is an attempt to convey to the listener or reader a definite experience by means of overwhelming or triumphing over his judgment. Therefore the experience of the listener or reader will not be creative, but will be imposed upon him by the poet; that experience will gain only a temporary acceptance, for as it has not been truly lived and re-created by the listener or reader, it will not become part of his experience; it will not be true knowledge—which is what real poetry should be—it will remain an inferior kind of poetry. The poetry will not rise from the event or the thing described in its simplicity, or complexity, but will be given life with an aim in view, and both its morality and beauty will tend to be explicit and not implicit, as they should be. Poetry in tragedy arises from profound emotions probed to their depths in attempts to lay bare the very sources of being. Poetry in comedy arises from intellectual dispersions or unsuspected associations; the mind, instead of being governed by an overwhelming passion, bubbles freely in irrepressible exuberance according to the theme and subject chosen. That kind of poetry does not imply any revelatory quality of the words, but it does imply the existence of a rhythmical pattern, a musicality of the lines, and also the use of figures of speech which appeal as much to the senses as to the intellect, the whole thing being not a compulsory surge from the whole being of the poet, but rather an "intellectual" creation resulting from the intellect working on emotions as well as on strictly intellectual materials.

It seems to me that the test of whether rhetoric is good or bad lies in its power of conviction. If the author forgets himself, and uses his characters, or one of his characters, in order to expound his own ideas, or if he allows the characters to speak beyond the stage to the audience, then we have bad rhetoric. If a character dramatizes himself unconsciously, or if his words and gestures do not match the emotions or feelings which he is seeking to convey, then we also have bad rhetoric, for the words are no longer there in order to express a given situation, but because the author, carried away by his verbal skill, cannot resist a display of his virtuosity. But if the intellectual excitement, the passionate vehemence or persuasive strength of speech is perfectly in character and situation, whether it be Henry V on the eve of Agincourt or Horace's and Curiace's passionate debate before they engage in single combat, we have excellent rhetoric, or, to be precise, excellent dramatic speech. Good rhetoric is essentially reason at white heat, set upon a goal and wilfully using all the means of impassioned speech and power of emotive suggestion in order to reach it. The words, like waves, roll, pervade and overwhelm the listener until he lies temporarily exhausted or dazed under the impact of this mighty, dissolving stream. Rostand's rhetoric is above all the rhetoric of a burlesque poet, a poet who is making fun of others, as well as of himself. Although he is much less brilliant than either of them, his is the rhetoric of Pope or of Byron, the Byron of *Don Juan*, for instance, who laughs at himself first so that others may not do it. Rostand's Percynet, for instance, sees himself as Romeo, Tristram and all the great lovers of legend and history, but he says that with a smile, and therefore his utterances have a truly dramatic value for they fulfil their purpose. Only when he talks for one moment seriously, too seriously, of his love without any self-consciousness (as in the "stances") does he fall into sentimentality.

Rostand's passions are thoroughly intellectual. They come not from the heart but from the head; they are not forces which can wrench the human soul as storms can wrench minds or trees, they are thought out, although at times mentally felt and expounded with great skill. We have here a kind of rhetoric of passions reminiscent of that of Corneille and sometimes very successful, for like Corneille—though not to the same degree—Rostand was a master of words. But he did not write, he never wrote with his whole being; he wrote from a divided or rather complex, non-integrated personality. If he shared in the romanticism of his time, his Attic salt, his Mediterranean scepticism prevented him from taking himself too seriously and from striking humourless poses. He has his limitations, and they are very great, for he did not have the supreme quality of the poet, imagination, which can make great poetry; but he had equilibrium, and a sound grasp of realities. When that equilibrium is broken, when the balance leans towards the tragic, as in *La Princesse lointaine* or in *La Samaritaine,* Rostand is at his worst, for he is not a tragic poet; but when, as in *Cyrano,* he can temper the most serious situation with self-criticism and laughter—which forestalls laughter at himself—he is at his best, and he achieves a kind of elevation quasi-unique in his genre in France and very reminiscent of Byron.

La Samaritaine, for instance, illustrates the weak aspects of Rostand's romanticism unmitigated by the realism and the sense of humour which generally redeem it. The theme is the triumph of ideal love over physical love. The more one advances through the play, the more one wonders with anguish and increasing disquiet what Jesus had to do in the apotheosis of this new Magdalen—Sarah Bernhardt. The part is all to obviously written for the great actress, who is given as many opportunities as Rostand could provide to display the irresistible charms of her feminine personality, and they are such that even Jesus who is far more man than God, is very nearly carried away by "la forme divine de son bras nu". Indeed, who could resist her, when with her fair locks rippling down her white shoulders she seeks to rouse the mob in the public square or to lead them out of the town, along the dusty roads towards Jacob's Well where Jesus sits? What a tableau, as Rostand calls it! Jesus speaks like Rostand himself; Rostand the inflated, self-conscious poet who could not only always produce a rhyme when needed, but also a triple and quadruple rhyme when those who required them were the ghosts of great prophets who had behind them centuries of vaticination.

Rostand certainly did not seem to understand anything about religion, or he would not have produced that cardboard mock pageantry which might perhaps grace a village fête in Provence and bring sentimental tears to the eyes of old matrons watching the scene, but which has no deep echoes. Jesus cannot be a dramatic character, even in order to partner Sarah Bernhardt. How can he choose, act, hesitate, suffer, since he knows all, suffers all and transcends time and space? To make of him the protagonist of a drama is to reduce him to the husk of what he is, and to show the shallowness of one's sensitiveness. The only drama the greatest drama of all, is the Passion of Christ. We cannot alter the story or the fable, as we may choose to call it, without shattering the whole framework of human sensitiveness. If Jesus moves on earth and utters human words, they must be movements and words which everybody knows, and which have by now become the very texture of the Christian soul. He may be made to behave and to speak in the manner and with the words of Rostand, D. H. Lawrence[1] or any other poet, but then it is no longer Jesus; he becomes a being whom pagans or Martians could perhaps understand, but Christians certainly cannot do so. This is not a point of historical truth; poets can, to a certain extent, alter history and give us poetic truth, but Christ is not *history* but *reality*, permanent and eternal reality, beyond the historical. The greatest poets, Dante or Milton, who have sought to convey to man the idea of the Divine, have understood that; for although Milton makes God and Christ speak, they do so at least in an epic, and not in a drama. A drama, if it deals with the life of Christ, can only take the form of mystery plays which give us as faithful a vision as possible of the life of our Lord as we know it from the Bible.

Pace to *La Samaritaine* and let us pass, with *Cyrano de Bergerac,* to a genre in which Rostand can truly be himself, and in which he has reached his plenitude as a poet-dramatist.

Rostand combines some of the technical skill of Scribe with some of the exuberance of language of Victor Hugo. Besides that, he is both a realist and an idealist. His idealism is akin to that of Victor Hugo; like him, he believes in violent contrasts and in the supremacy of the spiritual over the physical. Cyrano has echoes, sometimes conscious echoes, of Marion Delorme and Ruy Blas—the earthworm in love with a star. Like Victor Hugo, Rostand can unfold brilliant metaphors and coin striking antitheses, and even his most lyrical outbursts, such as Cyrano's words to Roxane in Act III, have that kind of rhetorical brilliance and verbal lusciousness which we find in Victor Hugo. There is no doubt that with regard to rhetoric and themes, Rostand is the most Hugoesque of contemporary French poets. One cannot talk of his imagination; as I have already suggested, I do not think he had much, and whatever he had (and this is where he parts company from Victor Hugo), he certainly did not place a great deal of trust in it. He was too sceptical, too reality-bound, and, in contrast with Victor Hugo, he did not picture himself as the visionary, inspired seer who can descry unknown lands and point the road to his fellow-beings.

Rostand has a definite gift of visual imagery, of which we find many good examples in *Cyrano,* but as soon as he leaves reality he throws himself into a fantastic world in which he obviously does not believe. He has fancy, the kind of power which drags him in any direction but which is incapable of unifying various aspects of things and emotions into a living whole, and he has at times a power of dramatic expression which in its simplicity produces emotional tension and can rise to poetry. The end of the scene between Roxane and Cyrano is an example in which great tension between two characters can lift simple words to poetry. That scene is dramatic and very moving too, for here we see how Cyrano's hopes are drowned in the distractions of Roxane, who is completely carried away by her love for another. Rostand, or Cyrano, could dream beautiful dreams, but these dreams were countered by the wit of a man who knew their defects, and who knew that life could not always be a dream. The whole of Rostand's dramatic creation tends to prove that he believed in the supremacy of the ideal over the spiritual; indeed, in the end Rudel and Cyrano, the poets, the idealists, are those whose love triumphs; but that triumph never takes place in the world here and now, in the world of realities. When these heroes fall in the arms of their beloved, it is always too late, death is already upon them.

Protected by night Cyrano could, through the magic of his words, win Roxane's love, but he knew all too well that the whole thing would not stand the test of light and reason; he knew that Ideal is one thing and Reality another. Rostand did not believe, as Hugo did, in imagination, and his wit springs from that loss of belief. Hugo believed in his visions, in his apocalyptic dreams; Rostand also could dream, but he knew that dreams could not be realized, and he resolved the contrasts between dreams and reality into mockery, as when Cyrano, in Act I scene V, confesses his love for Roxane to his friend Le Bret:

> CYRANO: . . . Avec mon pauvre grand diable
>   de nez je hume
> L'avril,—je suis des yeux, sous un rayon d'argent,
> Au bras d'un cavalier, quelque femme, en songeant
> Que pour marcher, à petits pas, dans de la lune,
> Aussi moi j'aimerais au bras en avoir une,
> Je m'exalte, j'oublie . . . et j'aperçois soudain
> L'ombre de mon profil sur le mur du jardin.
>
> LE BRET (*ému*): Mon ami! . . .
>
> CYRANO: Mon ami, j'ai de
>   mauvaises heures!
> De me sentir si laid, parfois, tout seul . . .
>
> LE BRET (*vivement, lui prenant la main*): Tu pleures?
>
> CYRANO: Ah! non, cela, jamais! Non, ce serait trop laid,
> Si le long de ce nez une larme coulait!
> Je ne laisserai pas, tant que j'en serai maître,
> La divine beauté des larmes se commettre
> Avec tant de laideur grossière!
>
>   (pp. 46-7)

This is extremely moving, it is dramatic and it is poetry. The whole scene, which oscillates between the sentimental dream and the dramatic self-mockery of the main character, is wholly integrated and shows the progressive creation of Cyrano's character.

That power to see himself as he really is, and to laugh instead of crying over what is unchangeable, gives the character a new dimension and increases his dramatic range; it is, if one wishes to call it so, a kind of sense of humour, a quality which is wholly absent from the great romantics like Wordsworth, Shelley or Victor Hugo, who generally wrote on one single plane, but which in this country appears very often in the poetry of the Scots, Burns, Byron and in our time MacDiarmid. The quality of self-critical humour and of laughing at the Devil and even at death itself, is one of the main traits of Scottish poetry. The poetry of the great romantics, with their faith in imagination, their kind of mystical attitude towards the creative act, or the high seriousness of Arnold who could see in poetry a substitute for religion—or, for that matter, German subjectivity from Goethe to Wagner—has no parallel whatever in Scottish poetry. The Scots seem to share with the French a great reverence for the intellect. Rostand, in that respect, is very French indeed; he refuses to confuse reality and visions, he rarely takes himself too seriously, and when he does it is fatal to his art. Strangely enough, another mediterranean, a greater poet than Rostand, yet a man who, like him, believed both in poetry and in reason—Valéry—concluded his artistic life with *Mon Faust*, a dramatic poem in which even

Mephistopheles is derided and made a victim of the author's irrepressible scepticism. Cyrano believes in love but, man of the world as he is, distrusts feelings and fears that other men may laugh at him, so he forestalls them by laughing first. The important thing is that, however shallow Rostand's philosophy may be, he looks at experience not from one single vantage-point, as the great romantics generally did, but from various directions. He may lack depth, but he has complexity and range; he does not attempt to reach for a transcendental order, he deals with reality as he sees it, and Nature, when he describes it, has none of the immanence conferred upon it by Wordsworth or Victor Hugo.

As a play, *Cyrano* has many flaws. When at the end of the balcony scene, for instance, Christian reaps the fruit of Cyrano's rhetoric of love, we cannot help having a certain feeling of revulsion, and we are made aware of the fact that Rostand's great dramatic skill can at times fail him. The death of Christian, which is not quite convincing, nevertheless increases the sympathy of the audience towards him. The last scene of Act I is sheer fantasy, but it does fit with the character of that strange man who is Cyrano. On the contrary, the arrival of Roxane on the battlefield in Act IV, scene iv, and above all the repast which follows, transform the atmosphere of tension into one of tragi-comedy and burlesque. It is a flight into absolute fancy, the characters become unreal and the interest flags. We find ourselves right in the thick of melodrama; the battle is completely artificial, and Rostand can display such a lack of sensitiveness as to make *en joue* rhyme with *je sens sa joue*. In spite of the fact that Cyrano's character is well drawn, the other characters are rather shallow. They are strongly reminiscent of Corneille's heroes in the fact that they are all, in various degrees, good; none of them is evil. The play has no metaphysical depth; life is shallow, language is without profound roots, yet it is nevertheless the language of a poet. Even De Guiche, who at the beginning of the play seems to be the bad one, in the end becomes the good Duc de Gramont who has seen the light and can express himself in poetry:

> Voyez-vous, lorsqu'on a trop réussi sa vie,
> On sent,—n'ayant rien fait, mon Dieu, de vraiment mal!
> Mille petits dégoûts de soi, dont le total
> Ne fait pas un remords, mais une gêne obscure;
> Et les manteaux de duc trainent dans leur fourrure,
> Pendant que des grandeurs on monte les degrés,
> Un bruit d'illusions sèches et de regrets,
> Comme, quand vous montez lentement vers ces portes,
> Votre robe de deuil traine des feuilles mortes.
>
>   (p. 197)

In spite of certain weaknesses, *Cyrano* is Rostand's major dramatic and poetic achievement. Rostand has often enough been dismissed as a mere writer of verse, or a kind of rhetorical poet who was not in fact a poet. Such opinions seem to me to imply a very narrow view of poetry. Granted, Rostand's poetry is different in quality and in degree from that of Shakespeare or Coleridge, or from that of Racine or Baudelaire; still, there are surely various kinds of poetry which can range from that of Shakespeare to that of Rostand.

Cyrano is a heroic comedy in verse, and therefore we cannot expect to find in it the kind of revelatory poetry which we find in *Othello, King Lear* or *Phèdre*. The aims of the poet are here very limited, but they are clear; he does not attempt to confront us with unsolved mysteries, but with the everyday dualism of human nature within definitely human situations.

The dramatic action of *Cyrano* is on the whole sustained, and there are scenes of true dramatic and poetic beauty—the marvellous tirade of Cyrano on noses, for instance, and the reply to the Vicomte which is a brilliantly developed metaphor, are dramatic and produce, through the self-irony of the main character, a heightening of sensibility to which one could hardly refuse the name of poetry. In the same way, the other beautiful speech of Cyrano in the eighth scene of the second act is good wit-poetry; there are plenty of apt images, there is movement, there is rhythm, and it is dramatic; it gives us a full description of Cyrano's character—Cyrano who, once more, abruptly shatters his apparent boastfulness with the confession of his utter dejection. Only a poet, however minor he may be, could fuse such contrasting emotions into the unity which we find in many scenes of *Cyrano*. The scene which follows is not poetry, but it is a good drama, and it adds to the mounting tension. True, the balcony scene, which is Rostand's lyrical flight, does not rise to the heart-rending lyricism of *Romeo and Juliet*, or the poignancy of some of Shakespeare's sonnets, but it is a very dramatic scene, which trembles on the verge of sentimentalism but which nevertheless avoids it and conveys in a poetic way the pathos of Cyrano's situation; the audience is bound to share in that pathos, for it knows that what he says comes from the depths of his heart, and it cannot but feel sympathy for a man who makes use of the sincerity of his passion in order to win a heart which he knows will not belong to him. It is indeed a very "poetical" situation, extremely delicate to handle without raising unwanted smiles or laughter, but it seems to me that by now the complex nature of Cyrano's character is so well accepted and his sincerity, which makes him forget that he is playing a part, seems so genuine, as to make the scene dramatic.

Rostand shows us that the greatest dangers which beset the poet are perhaps the discrepancies which might arise between his aims and the means which he uses to reach them. If, like Maeterlinck, he thinks he can reach poetry by using poetic themes and conventions, he will soon realize that the result will be neither dramatic nor poetic, for the two in that case should go together; but if, on the contrary, like Rostand, he attunes his poetic lyre to the situations he has chosen to describe, to the characters he has chosen to present, then he may, without flights to the summits which the former tried to reach, avoid the marshy ground where Maeterlinck got lost, and walk along a moderately high ground to the accompaniment of a music which, if it does not ravish us, never completely bores us, and which will save his name from oblivion. In his way, Rostand is a poet. He succeeds where Maeterlinck failed, and *Cyrano* is a work which has both an intrinsic and an historical importance. Aesthetically it is successful drama, historically, it is the meeting-point of a long tradition in French literature and the reconciliation of many contrasting traits, amongst the most important, the ideal and the rational; it has echoes of Victor Hugo, Banville, Scarron and others also, and it points the way to Valéry's more elaborate scepticism.

Cyrano marks the apex of Rostand's dramatic career. With *L'Aiglon* and *Chantecler* we have again a break in the equilibrium which produced Rostand's best drama, and consequently we have partial failures. The critics who try to gloss over these dramatic failures by describing them as poems are, to my mind, mistaken. There are true poets like Swinburne, for instance, or W. B. Yeats, who could fail in their attempts to produce good drama because they were first and foremost poets and perhaps not primarily dramatists. *Atalanta in Calydon* may not be a good play, but it certainly contains good poetry. But Rostand was not a poet of Swinburne's or of Yeats' magnitude; he was a versatile, masterly versifier, he had the gift of words, he could juggle with them to the point of inebriation, and also to lapses of appalling bad taste, and he only was a poet when he was a successful dramatist. He could sometimes write good descriptive poetry, and his images often have a Hugoesque splendour, but they are generally clear, visual images, free from psychological complexities or metaphysical symbolism tending towards apocalyptism as is the case with Claudel, for instance, who, like Rostand, resembles Victor Hugo but in a different way. Rostand obviously is, and could only be, a minor poet; in him there is no depth, no power of vision, no confrontation between being and non-being, between time and eternity, none of that awareness which can illumine a man's soul when confronting his finitude and his fate with the infinity of the universe, and which can give rise to moving, heart-rending songs which enable him to transcend time and his earthly plight. Rostand is the kind of poet who, deprived of the lyrical gift to sing himself out of time, can only make poetry out of the characters which compose his drama; and when he fails to be dramatic, he also fails to be a poet. His limited realistic vision, his intellect, which in order to avoid any possible suggestion of presenting Rostand as a thinker should really be described as good common sense, confine him to a kind of poetry which is more often verse than poetry, and which never goes beyond drama.

The critics who try to console themselves by saying that in *L'Aiglon* and in *Chantecler* Rostand's lyrical poetry redeems the lack of dramatic tension, the practical failure in drama, confuse the shadow for the substance. The so-called symbolism of *Chantecler* is so obvious that it does not deserve that name, and it does not require any explanation. Any normal twelve-year-old child would grasp it at once without having to ask his father any awkward questions;

in fact, its obviousness rejoins in its results the very transparent camouflages put on by Maeterlinck's characters. At any moment we expect Chantecler to say: "Well, of course you know who I am, don't you?" just as we are surprised not to hear at certain moments the famous Blue Birds saying these same words. These animals have nothing animal about them; they talk and behave as Rostand and his friends probably did, and we feel that somewhere, some time in Rostand's life, there must have been some hen-pheasant who tried to lure him away from the Dawn, some denigrating blackbird-like colleague, and some high-falutin' lady whose "at homes" were the meeting-place of all the blue-stockings and the wigged hollow-heads of Paris. If, because Rostand obviously speaks through those various characters and borrows more often than not Chantecler's voice, we call that lyricism, we are singularly mistaken. Some speeches certainly sound personal, at times to the point of incongruity, as when Chantecler-Rostand talks of Chénier's death; but lyricism is something more than personal expression of feelings, as Lamartine and Rostand ought to have known. It all depends on the feelings; those expressed here are pretty common alloys, and would require a great deal more refining before they could reach the state of the pure metal. There is in the play a certain amount of wit verse, the kind of wit which brings together things far apart, or suddenly reduces the distances which separate things similar; part of scene iv in the first act is a case in point. There is also some kind of poetry, mostly verbal—the hymn of Chantecler to the sun, and his confidences to the hen-pheasant—interspersed with very bad lapses; and there are throughout the play unbearable puns, unbelievable samples of lack of taste, and a kind of verbal headiness which sprawls endlessly across numerous scenes. It is, all told, a very elaborate, over-elaborate fantasy, which is ingenious, and in parts entertaining as a review, but which will grow older and older, and will not improve with age.

L'Aiglon is on a higher level than *Chantecler.* It is, after *Cyrano,* the most accomplished drama of Rostand. Here he has once more moved away from that mixture of realism and idealism, sentiment and irony, bravado and heroism, which characterizes *Cyrano,* and we are once more faced with a very romantic theme, that of the hero condemned to failure. The action is therefore static; the main character, although he has impulses and velleities of movement, remains motionless. The words are like the sails of a wind-mill gyrating without anything to grind; they strike the air, and nothing but the air, producing a powerful impression of fruitless effort. The result is bombastic, swollen language, gongorism, and long scenes placed where they are for no other purpose than to enable the poet to indulge in a certain form of rhetoric.

The hero is a cardboard hero, an opera prince without any life of his own. He seems to be a combination of certain very feminine aspects of Rostand's character, crystallized in a form which would suit Sarah Bernhardt's acting. The truth is that, although Rostand may be able to conceive a verbal exteriorization of tragedy, and may have the gift of passionate rhetoric which can produce at times epic poetry, he cannot be a tragic poet. He can obviously write mock-heroic verse, as in *Cyrano,* and also heroic verse, as in *L'Aiglon.* The entrance of Flambeau in the ninth scene of the second Act is a good sample of heroic poetry containing striking images:

> Nous qui pour arracher ainsi que des carottes
> Nos jambes à la boue énorme des chemins,
> Devions les empoigner quelquefois à deux mains.

> (p. 92)

Flambeau is the best-drawn character of the play, and it is in him that we find that mixture of heroic grandeur and irony which was greatly responsible for Cyrano's attractiveness. He has bad lapses—at the end, for instance, when he dies saying "Je me suis fait une légion d'honneur"—but on the whole he is moving, convincing, and his language sometimes bears the imprint of epic poetry. There are other samples of epic poetry: the beginning of the tenth scene in Act I, for instance, contains good epic poetry. Indeed, the thing to remember about *L'Aiglon* is that it is only a partial failure, for in spite of lengthy, lifeless scenes, in spite of appalling samples of bad taste and most common puns, such as: "vous ragusassiez!", *L'Aiglon* is at times dramatic and contains a certain kind of poetry. The duke is weak, sentimental, as when he offers to decorate Flambeau, pompous, petulant and childish, as when he wilfully alienates himself from his grandfather's good-will, or merely shilly-shallying, as when he should be strong and escape in order to reach the throne; all these traits show that this sickly and nervous young man was not fit to reign. Like Hamlet[2] whose presence seems to have been haunting Rostand at that time, the young duke is incapable of action. He is ever hampered by what looks like very futile reasons. He nurses Hamletian feelings about his mother's unfaithfulness to the great man, his father. Just as the ghost plays an important part in *Hamlet*, in *L'Aiglon,* Napoleon's great shade dominates the play and overwhelms the weak, golden-haired young man who is torn between his urge to fulfil his father's wish and the anxiety of feeling unequal to this great task. Yet he could at times redeem himself, with the self-irony of "les soldats de plomb de Napoléon II", and Rostand could every now and then knit his speech with splendid Hugoesque images, as when, in Act I, scene viii, the doctor, talking about butterflies in an album, asks the young duke what he is looking at, and the duke replies with the very apt and dramatic words: "L'épingle qui le tue"; or later, in scene xiii, in spite of the weak rhymes:

> Mais haussez au soleil la page diaphane;
> Le mot 'Napoléon' est dans le filigrane!

Or in the middle of the rather sentimental speech of the duke to Flambeau, in the otherwise good scene ix of Act II, when he says:

> Je dois, malgré tant d'ombre et tant de lendemains,
> Avoir au bout des doigts un peu d'étoile encore . . .

There are many examples of such verbal felicity, which, when they fit with the character, are good rhetoric. Even more, the end of scene iv in Act II contains good descriptive, direct poetry; the tension caused by the feelings involved is strong, the images used extremely apt, and the result is quite moving poetry.

NOTES

[1]Jesus, in D. H. Lawrence's story, *The Man Who Died*, suffers the same entirely subjective interpretation.

[2]Hamlet is not incapable of action because he is a weak character or lacks physical courage, it is only because he has too much purity of mind and wants first to discover the truth which underlies his "world out of joint".

Alba della Fazia Amoia (essay date 1978)

SOURCE: "The Masterpieces," in *Edmond Rostand*, Twayne Publishers, 1978, pp. 60-91.

[*Amoia regards* Cyrano de Bergerac *and* The Eaglet *as Rostand's finest works.*]

The two plays that may be characterized as Rostand's most developed and mature works—***Cyrano of Bergerac*** and ***The Eaglet***—were produced in 1897 and 1900, respectively. The former is the glorious burst of the summer of Rostand's life. The latter was written at the beginning of a painful period of illness, destined to become the author's melancholy autumn.

I CYRANO OF BERGERAC: A DREAM IN ACTION

In about three and a half centuries of modern theatrical history, there have been recorded in France only two other triumphs comparable to that of Rostand's ***Cyrano of Bergerac:*** the first was Corneille's *Le Cid*, produced in 1637 during the time of Richelieu; the other, *Le Mariage de Figaro* by Beaumarchais, presented in 1784 in the dawn of the French Revolution.

Cyrano of Bergerac was first produced on December 28, 1897, at the Porte Saint-Martin Theater. Exactly one hour after the curtain had fallen, practically the entire audience was still in the theater applauding. The most curious historic aspect accompanying the play's production was the pessimism that had marked the preparations and rehearsals. Even though the name of Edmond Rostand was well known in turn-of-the-century Paris, the idea of an heroic-comic drama in rhymed alexandrine verse, built on an historic background in the Romantic manner of sixty years earlier, constituted an anachronism. The Parisian public was sophisticated and demanding, but at the same time seemed to be avid for nothing but Imperial plays and easy *pochades* (light comedies).

The Fleury brothers, who were the directors of the Porte Saint-Martin Theater, after having accepted ***Cyrano of Bergerac*** for production, regretted it almost immediately afterward. They were pessimistic about its success and felt that if the play ran for a dozen performances, it would be a stroke of luck. In the face of such a negative attitude, it was decided to hold production expenses down to a minimum. Rostand found himself in the predicament of having to pay for the actors' seventeenth-century costumes—in the amount of one hundred thousand francs—out of his own pocket. As for the stage sets, they were so meager that during the dress rehearsal Rostand broke down and was on the verge of assaulting the stage designer. Notwithstanding the famous Constant Coquelin's zeal for the part of the protagonist which was his, pessimism prevailed throughout the theater. One of the members of the company asked Coquelin what his predictions were regarding the play's success; he answered in a single word, shaking his head negatively: "Dark." Instead, that night of December was to mark the beginning of a glorious career on stages throughout the world for the swashbuckling swordsman-poet, Cyrano of Bergerac. Capricious and unpredictable in its reactions, the Parisian theatrical public had nonetheless been able to discern accents of an authentic poetry behind the verbal virtuosity and the visual artifices of the play.

The story of Cyrano is well known in its broad lines. As told by Edmond Rostand, it reveals an ingenuousness and, in many verses, a quixoticism recalling the author's Spanish ancestry. Cyrano is an unvanquished swordsman and an affected, versatile poet, possessed of an enormous, grotesque nose which "arrives so long ahead of him" that it prevents him from giving free rein to his true nature, that of an incurable sentimentalist. He is secretly enamored of his beautiful cousin, Roxane, who in turn loves the young soldier, Christian de Neuvillette, an attractive man but completely devoid of poetry and wit. Roxane, fearful that the gentle Christian, who has just joined the corps of Gascon cadets, will suffer in the hands of his rough and rude fellow soldiers, entrusts him to her cousin, Cyrano. The latter takes his assignment so seriously and conscientiously that he even composes for Christian highly perfected love letters for his beautiful lady. In fact (in one of the most famous scenes of the play), taking advantage of the darkness, he boldly and passionately declares his love to Roxane, who is on the balcony of her home. Cyrano then altruistically withdraws to allow Christian to receive Roxane's kiss. In the meantime, however, the Count de Guiche, commander of the cadets, has also fallen in love with the beautiful Roxane. Unable to stop the marriage of the enamored young couple, he takes his vengeance by sending Christian and Cyrano to besiege the town of Arras. During the siege, Cyrano's passionate correspondence grows more voluminous, and his letters begin to produce a profound change in Roxane, rendering her love deeper and more spiritual. Now she loves Christian no longer for his external beauty but for his soul—that is, she loves Cyrano. Suddenly and unexpectedly, she appears at the Arras military camp, but on that very day, Christian, who now understands that Roxane has unknowingly fallen in love with Cyrano, has decided to tell her the truth about the correspondence. Realizing he is loved for someone else's spirit and intelligence, he voluntarily seeks his death; he is wounded in battle and dies.[1] Cyrano, out of respect for his friend, keeps the secret for fifteen years. On the verge of death resulting from a long illness caused by a falling beam striking his head, Cyrano, in delirium, confesses his long, immutable and unrequited love to the anguished Roxane. Dying, he lifts his sword high, and his last noble, proud words are: "Stainless, unbent, I have kept . . . / . . . My plume! *mon panache*"[2]

Such is the story that, bursting forth in sonorous verses and in a kaleidoscope of glistening images, has been holding audiences enthralled for almost eighty years. The student who recently declared that, in this age of cosmetic surgery, Cyrano of Bergerac is no longer plausible nor relevant, has, of course, missed the whole point of the play. It is not Cyrano's nose that prevents Roxane from loving him; it is rather the fact that he is not Christian. Even if Cyrano had been endowed with a beautiful nose, Roxane would still not love her cousin. The existence of the handsome Christian, speaking and writing with beauty borrowed from Cyrano's soul, is the image that holds Roxane enthralled, and her "pink lip will inevitably tend toward his blond moustache."[3] Roxane does not find Cyrano ugly, but a normal-nosed Cyrano would not satisfy her esthetically either.

And yet the nose is what has immortalized Rostand's character. Famous actors—Constant Coquelin, Ralph Richardson, José Ferrer, Gino Cervi, Jean Piat, Christopher Plummer—their faces disfigured by an enormous false nose, have been acclaimed and will be remembered for their interpretations of Cyrano of Bergerac. In North America, the character was made familiar through the adaptations and stagings of Walter Hampden and Anthony Burgess. Such an abundance and variety of interpretations of the character of Cyrano suggest that part of this study should concern itself with the figure of the real Cyrano, since Rostand's point of departure for the play was the character of an authentic personage who lived in Paris in the seventeenth century during the time of Richelieu and Mazarin.

Before focusing on the real Cyrano, however, it may be of interest to note that as a young boarder at school, Edmond Rostand, already distinguished among his companions for his talent in composition, had offered to write love letters and poems for a friend of his, who copied them over and sent them to his young girlfriend. This personal recollection somehow imposes itself on the chronicles that have created the immortal trio of Cyrano, Christian, and Roxane. Moreover, Rostand's wife, in her book about her husband, relates an anecdote that sheds light on how the first idea came to the dramatist for the writing of *Cyrano of Bergerac*. Rosemonde states that Edmond was spending a summer in the town of Luchon, a resort in the Haute-Garonne, where he happened to meet, beside a fountain, a young man who obviously had been grievously disappointed in love and was nursing his sorrow. Edmond drew out the boy's story, then spoke to him at length,

consolingly and paternally. For several days, Amédée returned to the fountain to listen to Edmond's "teachings," after which he disappeared. Rostand was quite triumphant when, some time later, he met the young lady involved and she said to him in a burst of passion: "You know, my little Amédée, whom I had judged to be so mediocre, is marvelous: he's a scholar, a thinker, a poet . . .". Amédée was, of course, none of these things; he was just a pale reflection of her ideal, but the idea for *Cyrano* was born.[4]

When Rostand submitted his manuscript of *Cyrano of Bergerac* for publication, he inscribed on the first page:

> It is to the soul of CYRANO that I wished to dedicate this poem. But since it has entered into you, COQUELIN, it is to you that I dedicate it.[5]

Coquelin, as has been noted already, was the first actor to portray the role of the poetic swordsman with the long nose. In the light of Rostand's dedication, it is reasonable to ask how much of the soul of the real Cyrano passed on to the stage, and how much from the stage into the legend; or, better yet, to ask why Rostand's imagination was so fired by the figure of a Gascon cadet who died at the age of thirty-six in the most melancholy obscurity.

The first encounter with the real, historic Cyrano is slightly disappointing: the Gascon cadet was, in fact, not a Gascon, even though he served in the company which subsequently became legendary. Savinien de Cyrano (the name given to our hero at the baptismal font) was born in Paris, of Parisian parents, on March 6, 1619, in one of the oldest and most populous neighborhoods of the capital—Les Halles. The family was rather well off, and enjoyed the prestige of a modest title of nobility. His father's name was Abel de Cyrano; the noble particule, de Bergerac, appeared later, following the acquisition of a castle on the outskirts of Paris. There were, in reality, two castles. The first, Mauvières, still exists today, although much transformed by restorations over the last century. The second castle has disappeared; not even its ruins remain. It is known, however, to have been called Bergerac, and was located near the village of the same name (now called Sous-Forêt) in the Chevreuse valley. According to established usage of the time among noble families, Abel's first child, Denyse, was authorized to use the name Cyrano de Mauvières; the second, Savinien, future swordsman and poet, Cyrano de Bergerac. It was probably the suffix -ac that misled Rostand and prompted him to make his hero a Gascon gentleman. Names of families and villages ending in -ac are, in fact, typical of Gascony. It is possible, too, that the original owners of the castle and fief were Gascons.

In accordance with the practices of the time; male offspring were sent to board with churchmen, and female offspring to convents. Savinien was no exception. His early education at Mauvières was entrusted to a country priest, who also had charge of Cyrano's future friend and apologist, the pious Henry Le Bret. At the age of twelve, after five years of what the great Italian dramatist, Count Vittorio Alfieri, a century later, would have defined as "ineducation," Cyrano left the boarding school. He had won a scholarship for the Collège de Beauvais in Paris, where he remained for six years and learned to detest tradition, cultural Aristotelianism, and the constituted authorities which were the mainstays of seventeenth-century society.

At this point in his life appeared the beautiful lady who was destined to become the inspiration for Roxane. In Rostand's play, her name is Madeleine Robin, and she is in love with the handsome Christian de Neuvillette. The real Cyrano de Bergerac did indeed have a cousin with a not dissimilar name: Madeleine Robineau, bourgeoise by birth, but married to a nobleman, the Baron de Neuvillette. Through her marriage in 1635 she had become a member of Parisian high society and stood out conspicuously among the most highly considered ladies. It was she who took charge of Cyrano's social education. It is not known whether the Baroness de Neuvillette was really a *précieuse* like Rostand's Roxane, but it is known that she had two great passions—good food and dancing—and that, like Roxane, she was noted for her "peach complexion." It was in her company that Cyrano learned the usages of high society and the good manners which he sorely lacked. Whether he was enamored of Madeleine is not known. It is certain, however, that he was profoundly influenced by her and found her fascinating.

The relationship, however, was not destined to last long: Cyrano's father, tired of financing his son's follies, decided to pull tight the purse strings, whereupon Cyrano decided to enlist as a cadet with the Noble Guards of the Gascon Captain, Carbon de Casteljaloux, to whom he had been introduced by his ever faithful friend, Le Bret. Cyrano was wounded in battle at Mouzon in 1639; the following year he left the Cadets and became part of the regiment of the Counts, participating in the siege of Arras—a boring affair, as all sieges are. Cyrano and his companions spent their time smoking and playing cards, just as in the opening scene of the fourth act of Rostand's play. The wife of the newlywed young Count of Canvoye was very much in love with her husband, and a graphomaniac besides—she sent him as many as three letters a day. The Count, who was not very gifted as a writer, in order to hide his embarrassment, turned for help on more than one occasion to Cyrano, who supplied him with love poems to send to his beloved wife. It is probably this historic fact that furnished Rostand with the idea for the famous letter substitution by Cyrano for the handsome but almost illiterate Christian.

The boredom of the siege was broken by an enemy attack. Cyrano, in the front line, was stabbed in the throat by an enemy saber. When he regained consciousness in a rudimentary camp infirmary, he learned that among those who had fallen in battle was the Baron de Neuvillette, Madeleine's husband. The death of Christian at Arras is not, therefore, a literary invention, nor is the widow's withdrawal to a convent. When, in fact, Cyrano left the military service and returned home to convalesce in Paris, he learned that Madeleine was spending her life in prayer

and penitence. He had the opportunity of seeing her in the Convent of the Holy Cross on the day that his sister, Catherine, took the veil. He scarcely recognized Madeleine: her mourning gown was of the poorest sort, her face was devastated by tears and fasting; and the former "peach complexion" was hidden under long gray hair that Madeleine no longer attempted to disguise by artificial coloring. In the face of this manifestation of profound humility, Cyrano experienced a sort of reverse exhibitionism; he fled from the convent, horrified, and vowed never to return.

The ex-Cadet of Gascony now lived as he could, in the intellectual circles of Paris, where he underwent the influence of the famous mathematician and materialist philosopher, Gassendi. Refusing all protectors, he preferred to gain his own reputation for libertine ideas and extravagance. He wrote two fantasies in prose, *Le Voyage dans la lune* and *L'Histoire des Etats de l'Empire du Soleil*, letters, maxims, and even a study of physics. Author also of a comedy (*Le Pédant joué*) and a tragedy (*La Mort d'Agrippine*) that he was unsuccessful in having presented, Cyrano finally was constrained to turn to a protector—Louis, Duke of Arpajon, Marquis of Séverac and Count of Rodez. Notwithstanding the Duke's protection, the presentation of his tragedy was a failure. The audience rioted on the first night because of an innocent line which Cyrano's enemies chose to interpret as a sacrilege. Presentations of the play were suspended and, as a result, requests for the text at the Charles de Sercy publishing house reached an all-time high. The Duke began to regret the protection he had accorded, and Cyrano, too, felt the weight of the attachment. A fortuitous accident—or a plot—hastened their separation: a beam fell from the roof of the ducal residence and struck the poet on the head; he was to remain for a year on the threshold of death. And this is the ambush that is freely evoked by Rostand in the fifth act of his play.

The good Le Bret undertook to have his injured friend transported to the home of a certain Tanneguy for treatment. Madeleine visited him there twice, but her words of comfort apparently must not have been much appreciated, since the dying Cyrano sent word to his cousin, Pierre de Cyrano, who lived in Lannois, begging him to come to fetch him and promising that he would not disturb him for too long—just a few days. Pierre answered the call of distress, arriving at Tanneguy's home on July 25th; Cyrano, wavering, rose from bed, got dressed, went downstairs, and was assisted into the waiting carriage. On July 28, 1655, just a few days later, he was, in fact, dead, in accordance with his promise to his cousin. Cyrano de Bergerac's was a first-class mind whose brilliant fantasies, ingenious scientific hypotheses, and bold religious and political views were prematurely interrupted. Rostand, by reviving him in his celebrated play, contributed much to his fame. Rostand's hero, however, is very different from the real Cyrano, even though many biographical elements in the play are exact and though there are significant similarities between the two figures.

Rostand merely develops the figure of the noble idealist who fights against the reality of ordinary life. His Cyrano, however, never admits to such a reality but creates his own world. In such a personal cosmos, the objective observer might judge him to be the loser, but Cyrano gains for himself his most precious ideal—*panache*. Cyrano's world comprises two existences: the life of each day and the life of love. He cherishes the highest concepts of life and duty; in them are contained the plot of the play and the story of his soul. Rostand dedicated the work to the *soul* of Cyrano. The play is an heroic comedy, which is very close to tragedy. As in a Molière play, not only is the sacrifice of a noble soul seen, but also the struggle of an heroic soul against all the evils of society and even against that love of idealism that can be harmful because of its own strength. From this point of view, Rostand's Cyrano surpasses the real one; love works miracles. It is this love that carries Roxane's soul to a higher level. Cyrano's idealism causes those who approach him to become idealistic, too. But the real tragedy lies in the fact that this idealistic love, which renders Roxane faithful to the memory of Christian, is the source of all of Cyrano's heroism and all his hatred for convention. In the end, it is also the cause of his death. What Cyrano loves so passionately is not Roxane—who, in truth, does not at all deserve his love, at least in the beginning of the play. He loves Love itself. He loves the fantasy that he has invented and which has become his ideal, personified by Roxane. The interest of the play, therefore, lies in the soul of Cyrano. To seize the essence of this great soul and to appreciate the true heroism of the comedy, an analysis of the internal and external figure of Rostand's creation is necessary.

Cyrano may be considered first as an able and clever man with a temperament that, once aroused, can manifest itself sweetly and paternally—but only in intimacy or in a deeply sincere relationship. Usually he is extremely violent. The most important external aspect of his character is the cult of the gesture, of which there are two kinds. First, there is the splendid gesture, the theatrical gesture, the execution of a duel while composing an improvised ballad, or marching at the head of a motley procession to fight single-handed against one hundred men. These are bravuras inspired by Cyrano's grotesque external appearance, but he executes them because he is full of life, energy and goodness—and is timid inside. He is a poet and a creator, but he senses his own ugliness and has lost his love for his own life. This explains the splendor of his verses. At this point, it is almost imperative to quote in their entirety Cyrano's memorable variations on the theme of his big nose:

> Aggressive: "Sir, if I had such a nose,
> I'd cut it off, so much 'twould cut me up."
> Friendly: "It oft must plunge, sir, in your cup;—
> Best make a goblet of a special shape."
> Descriptive: "'Tis a rock,—a cliff,—a cape.
> A cape, quotha? Surely a promontory."
> Curious: "What is that thing,—let's have the story,—
> A tool box, or, perhaps, a writing case?"
> Gracious: "You must love birds to have a place

> Paternally prepared,—I call it sweet,—
> To make a safe perch for their tiny feet."
> Truculent: "Sir, be careful when you smoke,
> Lest you make trouble for all honest folk,—
> Lest neighbors run and cry, 'A chimney fire!'"
> Careful: "Pray hold your head a little higher,
> Else such a weight will surely make you fall."
> Solicitous: "Sir, take a parasol,
> Lest its bright hue be faded by the sun."
> Pedantic: "Aristophanes knew one,—
> Hippocampelephantecamelos
> Was made to carry, certes, such a nose."
> Lightly: "Why, friend, a most commodious rack
> To hang one's hat,—where space will never lack."
> Emphatic: "Fierce Euroclydon, behold,
> Needs all his power to give that nose a cold."
> Dramatic: "'Tis the Red Sea when it bleeds."
> Admiring: "'Tis the sign the chemist needs."
> Lyric: "A conche and you a triton, say?"
> Simple: "A monument. When's visiting day?"
> Respectful: "Come, the landed gentry greet.
> Here's one who has a gable on the street."
> Rustic: "Why look-a-here. A nose? I tell 'un
> 'Tis a prize turnip,—or a stunted melon."
> Soldierly: "Charge, heavy artillery."
> Practical: "Put it in the lottery.
> Assuredly 'twould be, sir, the Grand Prize."
> Or, last, like Pyramus, with streaming eyes:
> "No wonder that nose blushes;—wicked traitor
> Who mars his master, shaming his Creator."
> Here are a few things, sir, you might have said,
> Had you or wit or learning. But instead,
> You wretched fop who trifle with your betters,
> You have no spark of wit; and as for letters,
> You have just four, to write you down a fool.
> Had you one grain, from nature or from school,
> Before these galleries you might have played
> With some such fancies as myself displayed;—
> —But not the fourth part of them all have spoke,
> Nay, nor the half of one,—for I may joke,
> Jest, as my mood or mockery may nerve me,—
> But as I serve myself let no man serve me.[6]

The lines are a fine example of humor and verbal bravura, and yet they convey perfectly Cyrano's self-mockery and inner suffering.

In addition to the splendid gestures, there are Cyrano's heroic gestures, which render his soul so noble and great: the letters he writes for Roxane on behalf of Christian; the balcony scene, in which he directs the unfolding of the lovers' exchange all for his friend's benefit. These magnanimous gestures are so much more beautiful than the others because they are completely gratuitous. They are born of Cyrano's own personal pride and of his heroism. Perhaps the best example, however, of the heroic gesture is the scene that so poignantly combines the comic and the tragic: the scene in which Cyrano detains the Count de Guiche from entering Roxane's home, where her marriage ceremony to Christian is being performed—a ceremony that Cyrano wishes desperately would not take place and yet which he desires fervently for his beloved Roxane's happiness. Pretending to fall heavily, as if from a great height, and lying motionless as if stunned by his fall from the moon, Cyrano intercepts the Count's approach and holds him enthralled for the time necessary for Roxane and Christian to plight their troth. Rostand has cleverly captured the flavor of the real Cyrano's *Le Voyage dans la lune* and *L'Histoire des Etats de l'Empire du Soleil* in the scene, which is worth quoting in part:

> I'm dizzy . . . giddy . . . for like a bomb
> I hurtled from the moon.
>
> . . . . .
>
> Not metaphorically but with force.
> Centuries agone . . . or else, a minute, . . .
> How long I fell, I know not. I was in it . . .
> That saffron ball up yonder in the sky!
>
> . . . . .
>
> Keep nothing from me. On what earthly site
> Have I descended like an aerolite?
>
> . . . . .
>
> I came,—your pardon,—through a waterspout,
> Cloudburst, that left its spray. I have journeyed, sir.
> My eyes are full of stardust. Ha, . . . this spur
> Caught in a comet's tail. This golden tinge.
> Here, on my doublet, is a meteor's fringe.
>
> . . . . .
>
> See, there, on my calf,—mark of a tooth?
> The Great Bear hit me. As I dodged, forsooth
> I missed the Trident but I fell ker-plunk!
> Into the Balances. See, they are sunk!
> They mark my weight. Look how the record lingers.
> If you should tweak my nose between your fingers,
> 'Twould prove a fount of milk . . .
> From the Milky Way.
> Would you believe, Sirius,—I saw this sight,—
> Puts on a cloudy nightcap every night?
> The Little Bear can't bite;—he tries to nip.
> I broke a string in Lyra by a slip.
> I mean to write my travels in a book.
> These stars entangled in my mantle,—look,—
> When I've recorded all my diverse risks,
> These captured stars shall serve as asterisks.
>
> . . . . .
>
> By six sure methods I can rise like vapor.
> I could stand naked like a waxen taper,
> Caparisoned with crystal phials clear,
> Unstopbled, filled with summer's earliest tear,—

> My body to the sunlight I'd expose,
> And it were lifted as the dew arose.
>
> GUICHE: Ho! That makes one way.
>
> CYRANO: And again, I might
> Draw winds into a vacuum,—keep it tight,—
> Rarify them, by glowing mirrors, pressed
> Isosahedron-wise within a chest.
>
> GUICHE: Two!
>
> CYRANO: Then, both mechanic and inventor, I
> Make a steel grasshopper and let it fly
> By swift explosions, till it fire me far
> To the blue pastures of the farthest star.
>
> GUICHE: Three!
>
> CYRANO: Or, since smoke rises in its natural state,
> I'd catch a globeful, equal to my weight.
>
> GUICHE: Four!
>
> CYRANO: Luna loves, what time her bow is narrow,
> To suck beef-marrow, so I'd smear with marrow.
>
> GUICHE: Five!
>
> CYRANO: On an iron disc I'd stand with care,
> And toss a lodestone lightly in the air.
> That is a good way. When the iron flew,
> Drawn by the magnet, as we nearer drew,
> I'd catch the magnet,—toss it up! You see,
> One might keep climbing through eternity.
>
> GUICHE: Six! And all excellent. Now, tell me, pray,
> Which method did you choose?
>
> CYRANO: A seventh way!
>
> GUICHE: Indeed! And what?
>
> CYRANO: Give up! You'd never guess!
>
> GUICHE: Stark mad, but most ingenious none the less.
>
> CYRANO: . . . It is the ocean!
> When the moon moved the yearning tide to motion
> I lay out on the sands, wave-wet, and so
> My head was moved, and lifted . . . lifted slow,—
> Hair holds the water, sir,—and *very* slowly,
> I rose, just like an angel, stiff and holy.
> Effortless, splendid, high above all men
> I rose . . . I rose . . . I felt a shock. . . .

GUICHE: And then? . . .

CYRANO: . . . The time is up, Sir, and I set you free.
The wedding's over.[7]

In the heroic gesture may be seen the tragedy of the man of genius: Cyrano is a poet, a philosopher, an indomitable fencer and an idealist; but he is not successful *because* he is heroic, *because* he is idealistic, and *because* he fears ridicule. His philosophy, as he explains it to Le Bret, is: ". . . Let what will befall / Always I will be admirable, in all."[8] The genuine Cyrano is the Cyrano of the *panache*. He desires to be "admirable in all"—and only for his own satisfaction. This is the explanation of his profound sincerity. Even though he may reiterate many times that it is beauty which he loves, Cyrano loves sincerity and courage above all. He loves Christian mainly because he has made his promise to Roxane to protect him, but also because Christian is courageous. He loves Le Bret because he is sincere. He loves the cadets because they personify courage. He loves the pastry cook, Ragueneau, because he is a poet and writes sonnets on the paper bags in which he wraps his tarts and pies. Cyrano's attitude toward women is the same: he shows esteem for a woman of the lowest social rank and treats her as a princess because she is kind and generous, but he has no sympathy for Ragueneau's wife because she is harsh and insensitive to his poetry and treats her husband badly.

With regard to Roxane, Cyrano has a completely different outlook. At the beginning, his passion is a kind of poetic veneration for her beauty; in her presence he remains wide-eyed and timid. When he learns that it is not himself but rather Christian who is loved by Roxane, his passion increases to the point of becoming poetry for the sake of love. Passion renders Cyrano heroic because it infuses into his noble heart the fire and warmth of his altruistic philosophy:

> . . . Self drops out of sight.
> For thy least good I would give all my own;—
> Aye, though thou knewst it not. . . .[9]

Cyrano loves love more than he loves Roxane, but for him love is Roxane herself. His love is that of a man who has never known a woman intimately. He admits that he has never known "feminine sweetness."

At times, Cyrano is melancholy, but only toward the end of his life, as, for example, when Le Bret notices that he seems to be suffering. Cyrano starts, and cries out that he will never show others his suffering. All must appear heroic. During Roxane's last visit, looking at the falling leaves, he exclaims: "How well they fall!"[10], and later he speaks of "the fullness of Fate's mockery."[11] Cyrano is a man, a hero, from the beginning of the play to the end. He is Gascon only in appearance; within, he is a southerner, litigious, passionate, and a lover of theatrical poses. His is the temperament of Don Quixote.

As for Roxane, she is affected, very light, with little spiritual depth. She is romantic, but without the youthful simplicity of Sylvette in **Romantics**. Her beauty is legendary, like the far-off princess Melissinde's, and her lace handkerchief inspires the starving garrison at the siege of Arras just as the vision of the princess far away encouraged the feverish sailors to continue rowing. Roxane further resembles Melissinde in that neither would ever consider committing a great crime of love. Roxane seeks only an excessively refined sort of love. Little by little, however, the influence of Cyrano's idealism has an impact on her concept of life's values, giving rise to a deep spiritual evolution within her. Ultimately, she is able to say to Christian: "At last I love thee for thy soul alone!"[12] After Christian's death, she is faced with the cruel reality that there is nothing left in life for her, but she maintains an admirable calm. Subsequently, when she learns of Cyrano's love and exclaims: "I loved but once, and twice I lose my love!"[13], although the concept is affected, the cry comes from a heart genuinely in despair, and Roxane is tragically moving. In sum, the figure of the heroine represents a force in Cyrano's life; she is love personified. Just as Bertrand, in **The Princess Far Away,** is not easily defined or explained with respect to Melissinde, so the figure of Roxane is not easily juxtaposed with respect to Cyrano.

Turning to the secondary characters as conceived by Rostand, Christian de Neuvillette may be defined as a provincial youth, a bit out of style, who does not dare to speak to Roxane because he knows he lacks wit. He is very handsome and certainly is courageous because he dares to do something that no other brave soldier would even consider: tease Cyrano about his nose! But he is a simple soldier. He becomes impatient in the role of the affected lover, yet when Cyrano leaves him to his own devices, he is unable to do more than stammer some banalities. In the end, he allows himself to be killed in the siege in order to leave an open, free path for his friend. Christian is genuinely sincere—and therefore is beloved by Cyrano—but his role is reduced to being handsome and consequently being nothing but an obstacle in Cyrano's love life. In this respect, he is the counterpart of Bertrand in **The Princess Far Away.**

Le Bret plays the role of the confidant. Embodying a spirit of good sense, he is a kind of Sancho Panza at the side of Don Quixote. Through the intimate conversations between Le Bret and Cyrano, the latter's character is developed and his ideas and ideals are revealed.

The last of the secondary characters is the Count de Guiche, a true cavalier in Louis XII style, typifying the role of the mundane in comedy. He lacks ideals, except for a sort of personal concept of *noblesse oblige*, but his courage in battle inspires admiration. The only effect that Cyrano's idealism produces in him is to render him a bit dreamy at the end of the play, when he pronounces Cyrano's eulogy. His dreaminess, however, is not an early manifestation of the purification of a soul, but rather the expression of a weak and egotistic character that feels some remorse:

> Envious . . . Yes!
> Sometimes, when one has made life's success,
> One feels,—not finding, God knows, much amiss,—
> A thousand small distastes, whose sum is this;
> Not quite remorse, but an obscure disorder.[14]

Groups and crowds of personages are part of the play, and indeed Rostand shows extraordinary skill in harmonizing large numbers of onlookers with the action of the main characters. The dramatic duel scene and the exit procession are the most striking in *Cyrano de Bergerac*; the pastry cook surrounded by poets and cadets creates an additional unforgettable scene; and, finally, the group scene in the convent garden, under falling leaves, forms a scene of peace and tranquil joy mixed with a nuance of fatality.

Undoubtedly there are some defects in Rostand's masterpiece: too much refinement, too many theatrical gestures. Cyrano is perhaps too much the incarnation of the Romantic hero, with his contrasting physical ugliness and moral beauty. The poetry of the play is pure and lyric, however, because it is sincere. Rostand, the excessively refined stylist, is comfortable in his own preciosity. Rostand, the singer of heroic zeal, is comfortable in his Cyrano. The work, therefore, vibrates with preciosity, heroism, and poetic idealism. Moreover, as Patricia Williams maintains, the play is a strictly classical work in that it is faithful to the Aristotelian precepts, one of which is that a tragedy must be plausible. She affirms that Cyrano "is completely credible, and his actions are completely motivated by his convictions. He is true to life."[15]

The best excuse for Rostand's rhetoric and the best compliment to his dramatic sense are offered, however, by T. S. Eliot, who writes:

> His rhetoric, at least, suited him at all times so well, and so much better than it suited a much greater poet, Baudelaire, who is at times as rhetorical as Rostand. . . . Is not Cyrano exactly in th[e] position of contemplating himself as a romantic, a dramatic figure? This dramatic sense on the part of the characters themselves is rare in modern drama. . . . Rostand had—whether he had anything else or not—this dramatic sense, and it is what gives life to Cyrano. It is a sense which is almost a sense of humour (for when any one is conscious of himself as acting, something like a sense of humour is present). It gives Rostand's characters—Cyrano at least—a gusto which is uncommon on the modern stage. . . . [I]n the particular case of Cyrano on Noses, the character, the situation, the occasion were perfectly suited and combined. The tirade generated by this combination is not only genuinely and highly dramatic: it is possibly poetry also.[16]

Rostand's *Cyrano of Bergerac* will continue to have meaning throughout the ages, will continue to move audiences everywhere, and probably will remain identified with the name of Edmond Rostand long after his other works have sunk into complete oblivion.

II THE EAGLET: THE LYRICISM OF A "POOR CHILD"

Youth frequently inspired Rostand in his choice of heroes and heroines. In *The Eaglet,* it is not the joyful, amorous youth of *Romantics* that is seen, but rather the immaturity and fragility of a young boy, Franz. Known both as the Duke of Reichstadt and the King of Rome, Franz was the son of Napoleon I and Maria Luisa (the daughter of the Archduke Francis I of Austria and Napoleon's second wife). He lived from 1811 to 1832. His claim to the paternal throne of France as Napoleon II (after Napoleon's first abdication in 1814) was at first nominal; a year later, instead, the title was formally established. In his declaration of June 22, 1815, dictated to his brother, Luciano, Napoleon spoke the following words: "My life is finished and I proclaim my son, under the name of Napoleon II, Emperor of the French." The words were repeated aloud by the Emperor himself before the nation's House of Representatives, which recognized the sovereignty of Napoleon II. Even before Waterloo, the divisive maneuver had been suggested by Joseph Fouché, Minister of Police under the Empire (who betrayed Napoleon after the Hundred Days and kept his ministry under the Restoration). Fouché's intention was probably to split the loyalties of the allies between father and son. By bestowing his crown on his son, Franz (who had been living for a year in Austria with his grandfather), Napoleon made some concession to the scruples of Francis I, one of the signers of the declaration of Vienna against the "usurper Bonaparte." The gesture helped to extract his son somewhat from the close custody of Metternich; Austria did not, however, release its grasp on the "Eaglet," fearing in him the bellicose blood of his father. At first it was decided that he would become "Prince of Parma," with hereditary rights (entrusted to his mother, Maria Luisa) to the Duchy of Parma, Piacenza and Guastalla. Then, instead, the title of the Duke of Reichstadt was bestowed on him, with compensation for the loss of effective sovereignty over any territory in the form of lands and rents.

After Waterloo, Fouché passed definitively to the side of the Bourbons, and it was principally due to his pressure that the June 22, 1815 proclamation became, for all practical purposes, a dead letter.

Adolph Hitler, during the course of his exercise of power, made one sentimental gesture toward the French: immediately after his lightning victory over France in July 1940, he ordered that the remains of the King of Rome be removed from the Capucin crypt (Kapuzinerkirche) in Vienna, where they had been reposing for over a century among the tombs of the Hapsburgs. Where the Eaglet's body was once entombed now lies his mother, who died in 1867. Hitler gave the order for Franz' remains to be solemnly transported to Paris—to the Invalides—for interment with those of the Emperor Napoleon exactly one hundred years after the return to Paris of Bonaparte's ashes. He intended this spectacular form of "restitution" to be not so much an act of posthumous justice as a move to attract the sympathy of the French, who have always been sensitive to the memory of Napoleon. The voyage of the remains of the Eaglet took place, however, among general indifference and aloofness, in a Europe racked by war.

A few months later, however, references to the King of Rome began to increase because a nobleman of Trento, Baron de Moll, in going through his family archives, discovered an important document: the diary of one of his ancestors, Captain Giancarlo de Moll, who had lived in the military "household" of the Duke of Reichstadt and had kept watch over him during the long illness that ended in his premature death. The diary was published; it is a cut and dried document with no embellishment yet extraordinarily interesting. It constitutes the most significant testimony that has been preserved in connection with the death of the King of Rome. Precisely because of the lack of sympathy on the part of de Moll, who did not expect his words to be published, and because of the cold detachment of his tone and the indifference with which he speaks of the progress of the illness that was slowly taking Franz to his death, the reconstruction of a fairly accurate portrait of the Duke of Reichstadt is possible. Napoleon II is stripped of his Romantic veils, but he is infinitely more human and more pathetic than the "Prisoner Eaglet" of the Bonaparte tradition. Even now, more than a quarter of a century after the publication of the de Moll diary, the legends of the "Austrian feathers" of Carducci's ode, and of the tempestuous loves that seem to have led Napoleon's son to an early death, are difficult to surrender to reality. The pale, sickly youth, dead at the age of twenty, without having brought salvation to France, remains a tenacious image. Today, his mortuary mask is exposed in the room of Schoenbrunn Palace which had twice been occupied by Napoleon I. Overlooking the vast and impressive gardens of the palace, the room contains, besides the mask, only a stuffed bird—symbol of the Eaglet and, as the Viennese guide today will announce nostalgically, Franz only friend.

The correspondence between Franz and his mother, Maria Luisa of Austria, was continuous and affectionate. They wrote to each other indiscriminately in the two languages in which they were both fluent—French and German. (Franz also spoke Italian rather well—a language that was coming more and more into favor at the Court of Vienna despite the origins of the "usurper Bonaparte.") Some of the boy's letters to his mother are extremely bellicose and justify the phrase pronounced by the old Prince of Ligne who, meeting him as a child of four, found him already to have "military eyes." In fact, the nineteen-year-old Duke wrote to his mother on March 25, 1830:

[P]erhaps I shall be able to participate [in the maneuvers] next year at the head of my battalion. What a great day that will be! All my desires end there, because to push them as far as the joy of a war would be excessive audacity, especially during these times. . . . In truth, I have the sad foreboding that I shall die without having received the baptism of fire. I have already made my decision in case of this terrible eventuality. I shall put into my will that my bier should be brought into the first battle that should occur, so that my soul will

have the consolation, wherever it may be, of hearing whistling around its bones the bullets it has so often desired. . . .[17]

The passage is puerile, and typical of a child who enjoys war-play in the shadow of Napoleon. But in these few lines there is an obscurely prophetic tone. Like a shiver, the presentiment of a precocious death runs through them.

One of Franz's more noteworthy qualities was his independence of judgment. He did not repudiate any aspect of his father's moral heritage despite his Austrian indoctrination. One of his dearest friends, Anton Prokesch-Orten, found him one day absorbed in the reading of the *Memorial of Saint Helena*, which contains Napoleon's testament. The Eaglet read out loud to Anton the fourth paragraph, in which Napoleon exhorts his far-off son never to forget that he was born a French prince. "That," he added," is the rule of conduct of my entire life."

At first glance, Franz, Duke of Reichstadt, looked like a true Hapsburg, with the characteristic protruding upper lip, blond hair and blue eyes. Contrary to most observers, however, Marshal Auguste Viesse de Marmont, the Duke of Ragusa whom the Bonapartists referred to as the "traitor of Essonnes" because he negotiated secretly with the Allies to force Napoleon's abdication, discerned a physical resemblance between Franz and his father. The Eaglet's facial structure, his gestures, and a certain way of inclining his head to one side, were clearly inherited from Bonaparte. None of Napoleon's Corsican ruggedness, however, had passed to his son. That young figure, so full of charm and attractiveness, was, unfortunately, of an alarming fragility. Although there were already some worries about his health in 1826, when the boy was fifteen years old, fears abated after his summer vacation in Austria.

They reappeared, however, five years later, and much more intensely. It was then that gossip began about the young Duke's "excesses" which would inevitably undermine his health. In the liberal circles of Europe, specific accusations were leveled against Metternich and the Austrian court for actually encouraging these excesses in the cynical hope of getting rid of "the Son of the Man." Names were mentioned; the most persistent were those of the dancer Fanny Elssler and the Countess Nadine Károlyi, née Kaunitz. These ladies were, however, merely the objects of a schoolboy's infatuations. Only one woman seems to have inspired a deep sentiment in Franz: Princess Sofia of Bavaria, wife of the Archduke Francis Charles, a maternal uncle of the Duke. Sofia was that "aunt with cousin's eyes," of whom Rostand speaks in such fine imagery. Some historians do not hesitate to attribute to Franz the paternity of Sofia's two sons, Francis Joseph and Maximilian, born a few days before the Eaglet's death. The Court of Vienna had recourse to Sofia so that etiquette should be preserved until the end, and this historic fact is freely evoked by Rostand in his play. The sick Duke not only had to receive the last sacraments of the Church, but he had to receive them in public, in the presence of the Court and the blood Princes. Sofia, eight months pregnant, found a plausible motive for the ceremony, without alarming the dying Franz. Proposing to confess and take holy communion in order to invoke the benediction of God on her childbirth, she urged Franz to do likewise.

Only a few intimates were present in the room, but outside a small crowd hedged around in silence. At a certain moment, during the receiving of the sacraments, the doors opened soundlessly and then closed again. Etiquette was saved. The end came shortly after. Franz's last words, in German, were addressed to his mother: "Ich gehe unter, Mutter, Mutter!" ("Mother, Mother, I am going under!").[18]

Such, then, is the real story of Franz, Duke of Reichstadt and King of Rome. Possibly Rostand used it as the basis for his second masterpiece because in Franz's biography he found inspiration for the negative counterpart of the swashbuckling hero. After the success of *Cyrano of Bergerac,* Rostand felt he had to create something even better, which would have to take the form of a reverse image, since no figure could possibly outdo Cyrano. An ascending creative parabola will be observed in his successive works, reaching its symbolic and lyric apex with *Chanticleer.*

While he was still working on *Cyrano of Bergerac, Le Roi de Rome* by a certain von der Pforten was being performed at the Royal Theater in Berlin. Moreover, the figure of the Eaglet—France's Hamlet—had occupied a place in Rostand's heart for a long time. As a boy, he slept in a bed over which hung a portrait of the Duke of Reichstadt:

> This portrait, he said, had become a sort of friend to me. I saw it from my bed, in the morning, on opening my eyes. It was he who presided over my studies, when I was working alone at my little table. He was present at my first readings, my first dreams, and at my first emotions.[19]

Rostand felt a premonition of his own future in the destiny of the young Duke. The child was enchained by the past triumph of his father and lived in unceasing anguish. Rostand, after *Cyrano of Bergerac,* would never succeed in freeing himself from the anguish of creativity except by creating a new masterpiece.

There were other reasons for the choice of the story of the Duke of Reichstadt. In the dedicatory note of his collection of poems, *Les Musardises,* Rostand declared his love for all those who are mocked, scorned, and disinherited, and for all those who, desiring to do well, in the end achieve nothing. In Rostand's eyes, the Duke of Reichstadt was one who had been mocked and scorned; Fate had decreed that he should accomplish nothing. Ten years after *Cyrano of Bergerac,* then, *The Eaglet* appeared, dedicated to the "two Maurices" in these words:

> Great God! Here is no cause
> Defended or reviled.
> I only bid you pause
> To pity a poor child.[20]

An historic drama in six acts, the play may be considered a masterpiece of lyricism rather than a masterpiece of drama. It is difficult to say whether it is a psychological drama or a kind of dramatized epic poem. Love is relegated to a secondary level, yet the work breathes a certain sentimentality because Rostand simply wanted to bring "the story of a poor child" to the stage. While the plot of *Cyrano of Bergerac* is based on two big lies, heroic and full of verve, *The Eaglet* is not very heroic. It is the tragedy of an unfulfilled dream, and nothing else. Cyrano lived his life scornful of the circumstances surrounding him. He created his personal reality and came very close to triumph even when he failed. The Eaglet hardly lived. He merely created his dream. His desire was to cultivate a legend (like Melissinde in *The Princess Far Away*), but the circumstances of life did not allow his dream to be realized. The illusion did not serve the cause of action. The Eaglet stalls. His hesitation is fatal. In the first of the two sonnets entitled "In the Crypt of the Capucins, at Vienna," found at the end of the play, Rostand declares:

> In vain the scribbler searches what to write.
>   The Poet knows. Historians repeat.
>   My verse may perish, but Time cannot cheat
> Wagram of that pale from against the light.
>
> . . .'Tis not Legend always that deceives.
> A dream is truer far than yellowed leaves.
> Sleep. You were Youth. You were Napoleon's son.[21]

As for the dramatic construction of *The Eaglet,* like *The Woman of Samaria,* its acts are really tableaus, and each is evocative of the eagle symbol. The entire work may be considered as a sequence of events rather than the evolution of a character. The principal setting is nineteenth-century Austria in the Palace of Schoenburnn, at the Court of the Archduke, Francis I. The first act, or prologue, entitled "Fledgling Wings," is set in Maria Luisa's villa in Baden, near Vienna, where everything French is interdicted. A conversation between Metternich and Frederick of Gentz reveals Fouché's intentions of proclaiming the Duke of Reichstadt Napoleon the Second. Metternich is unperturbed by the report, confident that Maria Luisa will prevent the infiltration of the news and the hatching of any plots that might upset her ingenuous tranquillity. At most she has smuggled in a French tailor and a modiste for herself and her son. Against a backdrop of music, entertainment, and festivities are heard conversations with political undertones. A loud cry of "Long live Napoleon!" brings panic to the villa, which is quickly controlled by Metternich. The friends of the Duke of Reichstadt beg him to return to France as Emperor of the French, but he does not feel up to the task and asks for "three hundred sleepless nights" in order to prepare himself. The Duke's tutors arrive on the scene for the daily Austrian history lesson, which Franz boldly and deftly turns into an apotheosis of his father to the consternation and mystification of his teachers, who have censored all of their pupil's reading matter. Maria Luisa appears on the scene; Franz, in a fit of rebellion, rejects his mother's heritage and claims the blood of only a Corsican lieutenant in his veins. But he immediately becomes tender once again and hurries his superbly clad mother off to the dance, begging her to forget and forgive his frenzy and delirium. Frederick of Gentz leads a closely veiled woman into the Duke's chamber: it is the dancer, Fanny Elssler, who, in Franz's arms, recites memorized details of the Imperial Guard's heroic acts, for she is the source of the imprisoned Eaglet's knowledge of Napoleonic history.

In the second act—"Fluttering Wings"—a year has elapsed. The Duke has established his work room in the palace chamber used by Napoleon the First when—twice—he occupied Schoenbrunn. Franz's close friend, the Chevalier of Prokesch-Osten, has been brought to the palace, thanks to the influence of the Archduchess, Franz's aunt. The Duke laments that his partisans have forgotten him, but Prokesch encourages him to make preparations for his return to France. Marshal Marmont, Napoleon's faithful soldier, Seraphin Flambeau, and the Countess Camerata, Franz's cousin, are all plotting together for Napoleon II's triumphal re-entry into Paris.

The third act is entitled "Spreading Wings;" in it, hopes are raised that the Duke of Reichstadt will find the strength to flee Austria. The Emperor Franz is giving audiences to the citizens attired in their Bohemian, Tyrolean, and other national costumes, waiting to present their petitions before the throne. A shepherd enveloped in a great mantle presents his paper to the Emperor:

> A shepherd of Tyrol,
> Orphaned, despoiled and driven from his home
> By ancient enemies, desires to come
> Back to its woods, its skies . . .
> And to his father's land.

The Chamberlain asks the name of the shepherd, who stands erect and shouts: "The Duke of Reichstadt, and his land is France!"[22] His grandfather rebukes him, but then the two begin to reminisce about times past and their deep love for each other. Franz begs his grandfather to give in to his whims once more and allow him to go to Paris, so that he will be able to claim: "This is my grandson, Emperor of France!" The Emperor agrees, and they joyfully embrace, but Metternich appears to thwart their dream. Grandfather and grandson separate like children caught in mischief. The Emperor informs Metternich that he wishes Franz to reign; Metternich accepts on the condition that liberty be muzzled in France and that Napoleon II reign as an Austrian puppet. The Emperor Franz and Metternich fall into agreement, whereupon the Duke of Reichstadt recoils from them in horror. That evening, he sets the signal for the plotters: one of his father's little black hats, placed on the half-open map of Europe. Flambeau stands guard at the Duke's door. Metternich enters, does not see Flambeau in the shadows, and begins to address the hat in a tirade that gives way to an outburst of pure malevolence against Napoleon.

Flambeau steps into the moonlight and stands motionless in the classic pose of a grenadier. Metternich recoils and rubs his eyes, thinking he is having an hallucination. Flambeau pretends that the year is 1809 and the French are quartered in Schoenbrunn; Metternich puts his finger into the flame of one of the candles to test whether he is dreaming. Flambeau plays his part superbly, but when the Duke's chamber door opens and Flambeau proclaims in a sonorous voice: "Emperor Napoleon!" there is seen on the threshold the trembling form of a poor child in a white nightgown, slender and coughing—and Metternich recovers his composure. The Austrian Chancellor flings insults at Franz—"you have the little hat, but not the head"—and succeeds in convincing him of his inherent weakness. Cruelly evoking his ill-fated forebears, Metternich breaks Franz's pride and determination, and at the end of the act, the Duke falls to the ground, a lamentable white heap whose little strength has failed him.

In the fourth act—"Bruised Wings"—the curtain rises on a masquerade ball in the Park of Schoenbrunn. From behind their dominoes, Metternich and Sedlinsky, the prefect of police, discuss the plot which they expect the conspirators to execute during the evening. Metternich has no fear, because he is certain that Franz will remain in hiding and avoid the ball because his pride has been hurt. The Duke does, however, appear at the ball with his friend, Prokesch, but clearly trailing bruised wings. He agonizes over the fact that all his race has had its vein of madness and that he is foredoomed to shadows and despair. Accidentally observing an intimacy between his mother and the Count of Bombelles, Franz is suddenly filled with an upsurge of filial love for Napoleon. He seizes the Count by the throat and flings him to the ground. The gesture saves him from despondency and allows him to face Metternich once again with pride and insolence. Plans are laid for his escape to the Field of Wagram and his subsequent triumphal entry into Paris.

The fifth act—"Broken Wings"—opens with Franz's exultant words: his soul has become vast, he anxiously awaits the sight of his throne, and he already relishes his power. The conspirators gather around him; the Eaglet's foot is in the stirrup ready for the flight. At this moment, however, he is warned that the life of his cousin, the Countess Camerata, who has been posing as the Duke because of their close resemblance, is imperilled. The Duke insists on going to her aid—and his hesitation loses the conspirators' cause. Flambeau stabs himself and lies dying on the Field of Wagram "among the slain, / First for the father,—this time for the Son."[23] The Duke urgently and vividly re-creates Napoleon's battle in order to bring back a cherished and glorious past. Flambeau's last moments are peaceful, for his death comes in the midst of an illusion of victory. The Duke, himself transported by the fantasy he created for Flambeau, is finally brought back to reality by the approach of his Austrian regiment. Like an automaton, he leads the soldiers, giving his orders in the voice of an Austrian officer.

The sixth act (epilogue), entitled "Folded Wings," is set at Schoenbrunn in the Duke's bedchamber. In the feverish disorder of the sick room stands out a small bronze statue of Napoleon the First. The Archduchess, with forced gaiety, visits the horribly wasted Duke who, the Doctor informs her, "takes his milk well." The compliment offends the dying Franz, who "had burned for endless fame, / To shine with warriors, heroes of that ilk," and is "praised for the way in which one takes one's milk!"[24] The Archduchess succeeds in persuading Franz to observe court custom by attending Mass together and taking the sacrament. The Imperial Family looks on unobserved during the elevation of the host, and in the moment of profound emotion and perfect silence, even Metternich is touched by the nobility of the dying Eaglet. In a low, deep whisper, Metternich says: ". . . Oh he was a gallant prince! / . . . Not only to the Lamb of God I kneel."[25] When Franz becomes aware of the room full of people observing him, with calm and supreme majesty he bids his "Austrian family" to leave him, quoting to them the words from the *Memorial of Saint Helena*:

"My son is born a French prince. Let him be
A French prince unto death." Be it known
That I obey. Farewell.[26]

The great vermilion cradle of the King of Rome is brought into the chamber and placed beside the bed of the Duke, who puts his hand between the cradle and the bed, uttering the deeply moving lines:

My life lies in that space.
. . . And Fate has shed
In that dark, narrow space that holds my story,
No single ray of all that blaze of glory![27]

Franz requests that French folk songs be sung to him and that the story of the proclamation of the King of Rome be read to him as he dies. The Duke's head falls forward; his last two words are: "Mama!" and "Napoleon."

In a drama of this type, interest centers on the possible actions to be carried out and on the sequence of events—not on the character of the Duke nor on that of Metternich, which are pre-established from the outset. The figure of Seraphin Flambeau is a memorable one, but his principal *raison d'être* is just to keep the play moving. He is a zealous, active soldier, whose energy is lacking in the Duke's own temperament. Franz finds inspiration in Flambeau and thereby nourishes his own hallucinations. *The Eaglet* is the narrative of a young man locked in struggle with his dreams of grandeur and with his sick body and vacillating temperament, in a hostile, foreign environment which is tragically indifferent to his struggle. Austrian indifference during his lifetime was matched by French indifference to the return of his remains in 1940. The Duke of Reichstadt never made his mark in the world; shadows and obscurity were his destiny, as he himself was able to predict.

Franz, Duke of Reichstadt, is a new Hamlet, but without the philosophy—the philosophy of gloom—of his predecessor.

He is possessed of a double heritage: in his veins runs the blood of Bonaparte and the blood of old Austria. He is a Bonaparte with blond hair: "I've something blonde within that frightens me."[28] He has the nervous, sickly temperament of his mother. He is "too princely;" he never smiles; he is "blonde like Saint George;" "he seems not to be alive." On his own confessions, he is nothing but "a remembrance within a phantom." He is a Romantic hero, like Chatterton, and the weak side of his nature is revealed in a hundred ways. He is as excitable as a child when, for example, he finds the set of painted wooden soldiers; his Tyrol shepherd disguise, donned in order to request help from his grandfather, is nothing but a childish game. He seems to be playing a puerile role even on his deathbed, when he allows his imagination to depict his own funeral ceremony. This weak, Romantic hero, however, erupts with energy in a sort of burst of wrath (for example, when he declares himself to be a "living Wagram"), but these flings are of short duration and produce no concrete results. The most dramatic of them is the one in which he throws himself in fury against the Count of Bombelles, who has lightly kissed the shoulder of his mother. Franz recoils, astonished by his own act, and passes his hand over his brow, saying: "It was not I who laid that braggart low. / The Corsican leapt out and dealt the blow!"[29] Ultimately, Franz realizes that his zeal takes shape only in his dreams; it fades whenever he attempts to put it into action. His dreams are grandiose and heroic, but his own soul inspires loss of faith in himself, and he lives with an inferiority complex. The Duke of Reichstadt created by Rostand has no heroic qualities and he knows that posterity will create a distorted image of him:

When History tells the story of my life,
No one will see my dreams, fierce, stormy, wild, . . .
They will see a go-cart, and a solemn child,
A child not even crying for the moon,
Holding the globe—but as a toy balloon![30]

In *The Woman of Samaria,* Jesus was passionate and at the same time his life, his goodness, his perfection, and all his divinity permitted him to produce miracles. In *The Princess Far Away,* Joffroy Rudel and Bertrand were courageous, and they were also poets. Cyrano was a swordsman, a poet, and stronger than those who envied him. The Duke, however, is nothing but the son of Napoleon. He is a dying soul possessed of a grandiose dream, a figure whose action is entirely inner, whereas the actions of those who have created their own life make themselves felt beyond their inner life. The action of the drama does not develop as an outgrowth of the Duke's behavior; he acts only when everything has been prepared for him by others. Once, in the middle of the drama, he thinks he has the power to act, but in desperation renounces his grandiose dreams to become nothing but a Don Juan. He discovers that he can have power over women only. The psychological study of the Eaglet is excellent, but the manner of presentation spoils the effect and produces an atmosphere of melodrama. Eloquent flings are followed by hesitation and inactivity; a lively hope is followed by a premature death. The Eaglet could not take flight toward France, the country of his Ideal. He dies, and nothing remains of his effort. Doubtless, the figure of the Duke was symbolic of the wave of feeling that swept Europe around 1830. It was an era of sentiment rather than of reason, of dream rather than of action, of timid veneration rather than of heroic admiration, of tragedy rather than of triumph. For this reason, it is difficult to distinguish clearly between the historic Duke and the legendary one. The deeply Romantic poets of the period saw in him the worthy son of Napoleon, whose energy and strong will clashed against the walls of his prison. They made of him a legendary martyr, a symbol of their own feeling of limitation in the face of hard reality. In this climate, the historian's objectivity was lost.

The two characters who arouse the most interest through their often melodramatic actions are Prince Metternich and Seraphin Flambeau. Metternich maintains close surveillance over the Duke, who is *"not-a-prisoner-but"* just let him try "[t]o speak behind closed doors with no one near, / That mushroom there would sprout a listening ear."[31] At night, Metternich penetrates into every corner of the castle, letting himself into every room with his pass-key; he is the spy who spies on the spies. From time to time, he demonstrates the quasi-diabolic skill of the old diplomat. To emphasize his non-heroic aspect, Rostand has created two scenes in the third act that deserve mention: one is the scene in which Metternich pronounces his long tirade over Napoleon's little hat. As he speaks, his hatred for Napoleon's greatness and virtue mount to the point where he loses his usual self-possession and takes the apparition of the grenadier (Flambeau in soldier's costume) for reality, believing he has gone back twenty years in time. The other scene is the one in which he attempts to break the pride of "this terrible child." All his capacity for cruelty and evil is revealed. Metternich is cold, diabolically clever, deprived of any dream or illusion. He is the personification of harsh, earthly logic, and he thereby constitutes the main obstacle in the path of the chimerical Duke.

Seraphin Flambeau, defender of the oppressed, as excessively and outrageously faithful to the son of Napoleon as he had been to the father, is perhaps the most captivating of the secondary characters in the play. It is he who exhorts the Duke to return to France, where youth will rally to him singing Béranger's songs. Admirably courageous, a conspirator in love with liberty and with his country, Flambeau has suffered privation and anguish in his desire for glory and for service to the "little corporal." Full of heroism, condemned to death a thousand times in contempt of court, he has the great defect of "always doing a little more than is necessary." He echoes Cyrano of Bergerac, fighting with a rose in his ear. Certainly, Flambeau is more brusque and less poetic than Cyrano, and he is not a hero who lives in and shapes the present in the mold he desires. Flambeau lives in the glorious past of great victories and tragic sufferings. The spirit of Cyrano is most visible in the scene at the door of the Duke's chamber: donned in his old grenadier's uniform, he forgets that it is not Napoleon the great who is sleeping on the other side of the closed door,

until he is taken by surprise by Metternich. Flambeau's lyricism is real, however, while that of Cyrano is slightly willfully excessive. Cyrano, in other words, consciously seeks the *recherché*, whereas Flambeau does not.

The strong contrast between the spirit of Flambeau and that of the Duke appears clearly in the sublime and unforgettable scene on the battlefield of Wagram. After the failure of the conspiracy, Flambeau lies dying, a victim of his own hand, while the Duke urgently tries to recall the past by relating the progress of Napoleon's battle:

> THE DUKE: We are at Wagram. Just before you fell
> Davoust's division crumpled Neusiedel.
> The Emperor with field glasses watches all
> You got a bayonet thrust. I saw you fall
> And bore you to this slope. . . .
>
> FLAMBEAU: (*struggling*): I am choking! Water! . . .
> Can . . . you . . . see
> The . . . Emperor?
>
> THE DUKE: He moves his hand.
>
> FLAMBEAU: (*closing his eyes, peacefully*): A victory![32]

The Duke's auto-suggestion is a really poetic creation. He produces an illusion in which Flambeau can die with confidence. This is the grand finale to the inglorious catastrophe of the Eaglet and to the illusory life of Franz who, later, on his own deathbed, creates a moving and admirable scene, playing games on the threshold of death in a style worthy of Cyrano's *panache*.

As with all of Rostand's plays, the reader is left with a feeling of insufficient psychological development of the characters. The author's genius reveals itself rather in the memorable pictures that capture a state of being or a particular gesture. Rostand is, above all, a love poet; in **The Eaglet,** he was constrained to put love on a secondary level. Even though love is always very close to an inner, sentimental dream, Rostand nevertheless uses it to accentuate the weakness and uselessness in the character of the Duke. The Eaglet is loved by the devoted Thérèse of Lorget; by his mother, Maria Luisa (who does not understand her son's anguish and who instead amuses herself by listening to light chit-chat at the palace balls); by the carefree dancer, Fanny Elssler; he is loved, indeed, by all women, except the Countess Camerata, an exceptional figure who assumes the proportions of a Cornelian heroine. About her, the Tailor says:

> She who delights to seem untamed and wild,
> Unarmoured Amazon whose proud young face
> Is living seal of her exalted race;
> Fences; breaks thoroughbreds; dares anything.[33]

The Countess Camerata attempts to incite the Eaglet to action. The moment he vacillates, she cries out:

> . . . Be gone! Ah me,
> Sir, if your Father were but here to see
> This sickly lad who wavers, doubts and frets
> How you would make him shrug his epaulettes![34]

In conclusion, I would say that Rostand's **The Eaglet** is a defective masterpiece. There are too many elements of preciosity in it, too many details and excessive refinements that are not essential: the dominoes at the ball, Legions of Honor, overabundant verses on Napoleon's tricolor and star, etc. There are too many disguises: Flambeau is disguised as an Austrian spy or as Neptune; the Eaglet as a Tyrolean shepherd in order to hand his petition to the Austrian Emperor; the Countess as the Duke, etc. There are too many Romantic antitheses in the pale, sickly child who makes his appearance on the scene at the height of the dramatic moment when Metternich expects Napoleon to emerge from the bedchamber. There are too many superfluous literary allusions, weighed down with alliterations, as, for example:

> Each breeze brings in a branch; with every breath
> —Oh miracle to madden a Macbeth!—
> Not only does the forest march to me,
> It swiftly dances in its ecstasy!
> Borne on this sweet wind, lo, the forest flies![35]

On the other hand, and despite certain passages in which the dialogue is too concise, **The Eaglet** contains the great qualities of Rostand's art: lyricism and sincerity. It is a new lyricism, neither affected nor Romantic, but rather sentimental—as it should be in a Court whose atmosphere of music, color, languor and love, so well rendered by Rostand, serves to obfuscate any heroic idealism and zeal. Nevertheless, even if it is sometimes over-sentimental, the feeling of sincerity that prevades such lyricism is inescapable.

The Eaglet has great dreams, noble sentiments, lofty aspirations, and dares to defy the Austrian eagle with grandiose concepts:

> O eagle black,
> Two-headed bird with cruel, weary sight,
> O Austrian eagle, world-worn bird of night,
> An Eagle of the day swept through your path,
> And,—fluttering wildly in your fear and wrath,—
> Not daring to believe, bird black and old,
> You see one eaglet sprouting wings of gold![36]

In the end, however, when everything slides away before his eyes that are closing in death, he returns to the earthy solidity of the old French popular songs. There is no progression of interest in the play, as has already been stated, but Rostand's intention must not be lost sight of: he wished to paint the portrait of a poor child who wanted to outdo himself, a wistful child who would have liked to make history but lived with his face pressed against the glass of the palace of Schoenbrunn. The inner energy of Napoleon's son flowed forth in a personal lyricism. His aspirations were grandiose and sentimental but completely sincere and colored by that fervor of youth that made the heart of every Frenchman palpitate. All of France became mother to that poor child, the Duke of Reichstadt.

NOTES

[1] An interesting case of identification and empathy with the wounded Christian of Neuvillette is analyzed in C. G. Jung, *Symbols of Transformation. An Analysis of the Prelude to a Case of Schizophrenia* (New York, 1956), pp. 34 ff., which includes Jung's interpretation of the character of Cyrano. At the moment when Christian is killed and Sarah Bernhardt throws herself upon him to stanch the bleeding of his wound, Jung's patient felt a real, piercing pain in her own breast, just where Christian was supposed to have received the blow. But the tragic intermezzo with Christian is played against a background of far wider significance, namely Cyrano's unrequited love for Roxane. According to Jung, the identification with Christian is probably only a cover.

[2] *Plays of Edmond Rostand*, translated by Henderson D. Norman (New York, 1921), *Cyrano of Bergerac*, V, 6, p. 360.

[3] Elly Katz, *L'Esprit français dans le théâtre d'Edmond Rostand* (Toulouse, 1934), p. 59.

[4] Rosemonde Gérard, *Edmond Rostand* (Paris, 1935), pp. 10-12.

[5] Norman, *op. cit.*, *Cyrano of Bergerac*, p. 209.

[6] *Ibid.*, I, 4, pp. 233-35.

[7] *Ibid.*, III, 11, pp. 303, 304, 305, 306-07.

[8] *Ibid.*, I, 5, p. 241.

[9] *Ibid.*, III, 6, p. 295.

[10] *Ibid.*, V, 5, p. 352.

[11] *Ibid.*, V, 6, p. 357.

[12] *Ibid.*, IV, 8, p. 334.

[13] *Ibid.*, V, 6, p. 358.

[14] *Ibid.*, V, 2, p. 347.

[15] Patricia Williams, "Some Classical Aspects of *Cyrano de Bergerac*," XIX Century French Studies, I, 2 (Winter 1973), 116.

[16] T. S. Eliot, *Selected Essays 1917 - 1932* (New York, 1932), pp. 25, 28, 29.

[17] Maria Luisa Rizzatti, "L'Aiglon: mito e verità," *Storia Illustrata*, XII, 123 (Feb. 3, 1968), 99.

[18] *Ibid.*, 96 - 106.

[19] Emile Ripert, *Edmond Rostand* (Paris, 1968), p. 115.

[20] Norman, *op. cit.*, dedication preceding *The Eaglet*.

[21] Norman, *op. cit.*, p. 204.

[22] *Ibid.*, *The Eaglet*, III, 1, p. 89.

[23] *Ibid.*, V, 5, p. 180.

[24] *Ibid.*, VI, 1, p. 191.

[25] *Ibid.*, VI, 2, p. 194.

[26] *Ibid.*, VI, 3, p. 196.

[27] *Ibid.*, VI, 3, p. 198.

[28] *Ibid.*, I, 13, p. 45.

Charles Wyndham as Cyrano and Mary Moore as Roxanne, in a 1900 English production of Cyrano de Bergerac.

[29]*Ibid.*, IV, 7, p. 137.

[30]*Ibid.*, VI, 3, p. 197.

[31]*Ibid.*, II, 2, p. 55.

[32]*Ibid.*, V, 5, pp. 181 - 82.

[33]*Ibid.*, I, 9, p. 32.

[34]*Ibid.*, V, 3, p. 175.

[35]*Ibid.*, I, 13, p. 45.

[36]*Ibid.*, III, 3, p. 97.

CYRANO DE BERGERAC

T. S. Eliot (essay date 1920)

SOURCE: "'Rhetoric' and Poetic Drama," in *The Sacred Wood: Essays on Poetry and Criticism*, Methuen & Co., 1920, pp. 78-85.

[*In the following essay, Eliot declares that "in the particular case of Cyrano on Noses, the character, the situation, the occasion were perfectly suited and combined. The tirade generated by this combination is not only genuinely and highly dramatic: it is possibly poetry also."*]

The death of Rostand is the disappearance of the poet whom, more than any other in France, we treated as the exponent of "rhetoric," thinking of rhetoric as something recently out of fashion. And as we find ourselves looking back rather tenderly upon the author of **Cyrano** we wonder what this vice or quality is that is associated as plainly with Rostand's merits as with his defects. His rhetoric, at least, suited him at times so well, and so much better than it suited a much greater poet, Baudelaire, who is at times as rhetorical as Rostand. And we begin to suspect that the word is merely a vague term of abuse for any style that is bad, that is so evidently bad or second-rate that we do not recognize the necessity for greater precision in the phrases we apply to it.

Our own Elizabethan and Jacobean poetry—in so nice a problem it is much safer to stick to one's own language—is repeatedly called "rhetorical." It had this and that notable quality, but, when we wish to admit that it had defects, it is rhetorical. It had serious defects, even gross faults, but we cannot be considered to have erased them from our language when we are so unclear in our perception of what they are. The fact is that both Elizabethan prose and Elizabethan poetry are written in a variety of styles with a variety of vices. Is the style of Lyly, is Euphuism, rhetorical? In contrast to the elder style of Ascham and Elyot which it assaults, it is a clear, flowing, orderly and relatively pure style, with a systematic if monotonous formula of antitheses and similes. Is the style of Nashe? A tumid, flatulent, vigorous style very different from Lyly's. Or it is perhaps the strained and the mixed figures of speech in which Shakespeare indulged himself. Or it is perhaps the careful declamation of Jonson. The word simply cannot be used as synonymous with bad writing. The meanings which it has been obliged to shoulder have been mostly opprobrious; but if a precise meaning can be found for it this meaning may occasionally represent a virtue. It is one of those words which it is the business of criticism to dissect and reassemble. Let us avoid the assumption that rhetoric is a vice of manner, and endeavour to find a rhetoric of substance also, which is right because it issues from what it has to express.

At the present time there is a manifest preference for the "conversational" in poetry—the style of "direct speech," opposed to the "oratorical" and the rhetorical; but if rhetoric is any convention of writing inappropriately applied, this conversational style can and does become a rhetoric—or what is supposed to be a conversational style, for it is often as remote from polite discourse as well could be. Much of the second and third rate in American *vers libre* is of this sort; and much of the second and third rate in English Wordsworthianism. There is in fact no conversational or other form which can be applied indiscriminately; if a writer wishes to give the effect of speech he must positively give the effect of himself talking in his own person or in one of his rôles; and if we are to express ourselves, our variety of thoughts and feelings, on a variety of subjects with inevitable rightness, we must adapt our manner to the moment with infinite variations. Examination of the development of Elizabethan drama shows this progress in adaptation, a development from monotony to variety, a progressive refinement in the perception of the variations of feeling, and a progressive elaboration of the means of expressing these variations. This drama is admitted to have grown away from the rhetorical expression, the bombast speeches, of Kyd and Marlowe to the subtle and dispersed utterance of Shakespeare and Webster. But this apparent abandonment or outgrowth of rhetoric is two things: it is partly an improvement in language and it is partly progressive variation in feeling. There is, of course, a long distance separating the furibund fluency of old Hieronimo and the broken words of Lear. There is also a difference between the famous

Oh eyes no eyes, but fountains full of tears!
Oh life no life, but lively form of death!

and the superb "additions to Hieronimo."[1]

We think of Shakespeare perhaps as the dramatist who concentrates everything into a sentence, "Pray you undo this button," or "Honest honest Iago"; we forget that there is a rhetoric proper to Shakespeare at his best period which is quite free from the genuine Shakespearean vices either of the early period or the late. These passages are comparable to the best bombast of Kyd or Marlowe, with a greater command of language and a greater control of the emotion. *The Spanish Tragedy* is bombastic when it descends to language which was only the trick of its age; *Tamburlaine* is bombastic because it is monotonous, inflexible to the alterations of emotion. The really fine rhetoric of Shakespeare occurs in situations where a character in the play *sees himself* in a dramatic light:

> OTHELLO. And say, besides,—that in Aleppo once . . .

> CORIOLANUS. If you have writ your annals
> true, 'tis there,
> That like an eagle in a dovecote, I
> Fluttered your Volscians in Corioli.
> Alone I did it. Boy!

> TIMON. Come not to me again; but say to Athens,
> Timon hath made his everlasting mansion
> Upon the beachèd verge of the salt flood . . .

It occurs also once in *Antony and Cleopatra*, when Enobarbus is inspired to see Cleopatra in this dramatic light:

> The barge she sat in . . .

Shakespeare made fun of Marston, and Jonson made fun of Kyd. But in Marston's play the words were expressive of nothing; and Jonson was criticizing the feeble and conceited language, not the emotion, not the "oratory." Jonson is as oratorical himself, and the moments when his oratory succeeds are, I believe, the moments that conform to our formula. Notably the speech of Sylla's ghost in the induction to *Catiline*, and the speech of Envy at the beginning of *The Poetaster*. These two figures are contemplating their own dramatic importance, and quite properly. But in the Senate speeches in *Catiline*, how tedious, how dusty! Here we are spectators not of a play of characters, but of a play of forensic, exactly as if we had been forced to attend the sitting itself. A speech in a play should never appear to be intended to move us as it might conceivably move other characters in the play, for it is essential that we should preserve our position of spectators, and observe always from the outside though with complete understanding. The scene in *Julius Cæsar* is right because the object of our attention is not the speech of Antony (*Bedeutung*) but the effect of his speech upon the mob, and Antony's intention, his preparation and consciousness of the effect. And in the rhetorical speeches from Shakespeare which have been cited, we have this necessary advantage of a new clue to the character, in noting the angle from which he views himself. But when a character *in* a play makes a direct appeal to us, we are either the victims of our own sentiment, or we are in the presence of a vicious rhetoric.

These references ought to supply some evidence of the propriety of Cyrano on Noses. Is not Cyrano exactly in this position of contemplating himself as a romantic, a dramatic figure? This dramatic sense on the part of the characters themselves is rare in modern drama. In sentimental drama it appears in a degraded form, when we are evidently intended to accept the character's sentimental interpretation of himself. In plays of realism we often find parts which are never allowed to be consciously dramatic, for fear, perhaps, of their appearing less real. But in actual life, in many of those situations in actual life which we enjoy consciously and keenly, we are at times aware of ourselves in this way, and these moments are of very great usefulness to dramatic verse. A very small part of acting is that which takes place on the stage! Rostand had—whether he had anything else or not—this dramatic sense, and it is what gives life to Cyrano. It is a sense which is almost a sense of humour (for when anyone is conscious of himself as acting, something like a sense of humour is present). It gives Rostand's characters—Cyrano at least—a gusto which is uncommon on the modern stage. No doubt Rostand's people play up to this too steadily. We recognize that in the love scenes of Cyrano in the garden, for in *Romeo and Juliet* the profounder dramatist shows his lovers melting into incoherent unconsciousness of their isolated selves, shows the human soul in the process of forgetting itself. Rostand could not do that; but in the particular case of Cyrano on Noses, the character, the situation, the occasion were perfectly suited and combined. The tirade generated by this combination is not only genuinely and highly dramatic: it is possibly poetry also. If a writer is incapable of composing such a scene as this, so much the worse for his poetic drama.

Cyrano satisfies, as far as scenes like this can satisfy, the requirements of poetic drama. It must take genuine and substantial human emotions, such emotions as observation can confirm, typical emotions, and give them artistic form; the degree of abstraction is a question for the method of each author. In Shakespeare the form is determined in the unity of the whole, as well as single scenes; it is something to attain this unity, as Rostand does, in scenes if not the whole play. Not only as a dramatist, but as a poet, he is superior to Maeterlinck, whose drama, in failing to be dramatic, fails also to be poetic. Maeterlinck has a literary perception of the dramatic and a literary perception of the poetic, and he joins the two; the two are not, as sometimes they are in the work of Rostand, fused. His characters take no conscious delight in their rôle—they are sentimental. With Rostand the centre of gravity is in the expression of the emotion, not as with Maeterlinck in the emotion which cannot be expressed. Some writers appear to believe that emotions gain in intensity through being inarticulate. Perhaps the emotions are not significant enough to endure full daylight.

In any case, we may take our choice: we may apply the term "rhetoric" to the type of dramatic speech which I have instanced, and then we must admit that it covers good as well as bad. Or we may choose to except this type of speech from rhetoric. In that case we must say that rhetoric is any adornment or inflation of speech which is *not done for a particular effect* but for a general impressiveness. And in this case, too, we cannot allow the term to cover all bad writing.

NOTE

[1]Of the authorship it can only be said that the lines are by some admirer of Marlowe. This might well be Jonson.

Clarence D. Brenner   (essay date 1949)

SOURCE: "Rostand's *Cyrano de Bergerac: An Interpretation*," in *Studies in Philology*, Vol. XLVI, No. 4, October 1949, pp. 603-11.

[*In this essay, Brenner examines Cyrano's similarities to traditional French Romantic heroes.*]

Edmond Rostand is said to have become interested in Cyrano de Bergerac in the days of his youth because Cyrano represented a type, *le raté*, which had a great appeal for him.[1] When years later he wanted to compose a play for his friend Coquelin, the life of Cyrano readily suggested itself to him as a subject ideally suited to the talents of that famous actor. The principal traits of character of the hero of his play, as well as most of his accomplishments and exploits, Rostand took from the life of the real Cyrano. He elaborated each of these traits in varying degree by bringing his magnificent imagination to bear on them, and he gave particular emphasis to several which embodied his own ideals. Indeed it is probably true that fundamentally the Cyrano of the play represents to a considerable extent the author himself, the author as he would have liked to be,[2] a fact which must account in part for the remarkable vitality of this dramatic hero. But, in our opinion at least, there is another interesting aspect to this hero: as Rostand gave thought to the portrayal of this character he became aware of the similarity of some of the experiences and some of the traits of his Cyrano with those of certain well-known Romantic heroes of French literature. This gave him the happy idea of associating these heroes with his. He accomplishes this evocation in various ways, as we shall see, and for a very good reason he makes it quite patent. Critics of Rostand, upon seeing or reading his play, have been reminded of one or more of the French Romantic heroes whom I shall presently designate. In no case, so far as I can determine, have they taken the trouble really to verify the validity of their impressions. This attitude is characteristic of nearly all the published criticism of Rostand: it has been to a large degree impressionistic.[3]

It is my purpose to attempt to demonstrate how Rostand evokes through his Cyrano certain French Romantic heroes of the past, and then to indicate another, but closely related, method that he uses to link his play, and perhaps himself, with the works of the great Romantic writers of his country.

Who then are the Romantic heroes that Rostand would have us associate with Cyrano? If we take them more or less chronologically, the first to present himself is Figaro. Be it said at once that the echo of Figaro in Cyrano is less apparent than that of the other heroes we shall mention. But it is there and can be detected by those who know both these characters well. Parallels between the two can be easily drawn. Like Cyrano, Figaro has the wonderful self-confidence, the ready wit, and the resourcefulness which enable him to recover his composure quickly in the presence of adversity and to be "partout supérieur aux événements."[4] His description of himself as an "orateur selon le danger, poète par délassement, musicien par occasion,"[5] would fit Cyrano too. These are obvious similarities. There is no point in attaching more importance to them than that. Where one, if he has a good ear and a good memory, hears echoes of Figaro is in the manner in which Cyrano expresses himself at times.[6] When he allows himself to become sentimental for a moment, as in the speech beginning

> Regarde-moi, mon cher, et dis quelle espérance
> Pourrait bien me laisser cette protubérance!
>
> (Act I, sc. 5)

we can detect something of Figaro expressing himself in similar vein in his well-known soliloquy. In certain scenes that present a battle of wits, such as the one with De Guiche in the Second Act, we can hear Figaro far away sparring with the Count, as in the scene containing the tirade on *god-dam*.[7] One could cite Cyrano's "non merci" speech with the same intent.[8] Figaro is certainly one of the ancestors of Rostand's Cyrano; they belong to the same family of heroes, of this fact there can be do doubt.

We next consider one of the characters created by Victor Hugo, namely Don César de Bazan of *Ruy Blas*. Several critics have stated that Cyrano has reminded them of Don César, but they have not told us why. Since Hugo more than anyone else is Rostand's model for the form and substance of his comedies, it is not surprising to find Don César, more than any other character the model for Cyrano,[9] especially the Don César of the famous Fourth Act. A careful reading of *Ruy Blas* will reveal that Don César has a great deal in common with Cyrano.

We find he is a poet:

> "Je marchais en faisant des vers sous les arcades"
>
> (I, 2)

and

> "Quoi. l'on vous traite ainsi, beautés à l'œil mutin,
> A qui je dis le soir mes sonnets du matin."

He is a brave and reckless swordsman, he loves duels:

> "Mon épée est à vous, je deviens votre esclave,
> Et, si cela vous plaît, j'irai croiser le fer
> Avec don Spavento, capitan de l'enfer."
>
> (I, 2)

and

> "Quand je tiens un bon duel, je ne le lâche pas!"
>
> (IV, 5)

He is gallant:

> "Œil pour œil, dent pour dent, c'est bien!
>   hommes contre hommes!
> Mais doucement détruire une femme! et creuser
> Sous ses pieds une trappe! et contre elle abuser,
> Qui sait? de son humeur peut-être hasardeuse!
>
> . . . . .
>
> J'aimerais mieux, plutôt, qu'être à ce point infâme,
> Vil, odieux, pervers, misérable et flétri,
> Qu'un chien rongeât mon crâne au pied du pilori."
>
> (I, 2)

He is generous:

> "Rien n'est plus gracieux et plus divertissant
> Que des écus à soi qu'on met en équilibre.
> Frère, voici ta part."
>
> (I, 3)

It is the Don César of Act IV who offers the most striking parallel to Cyrano. There can be little doubt that when Rostand wrote the scene[10] in which Cyrano pretends to fall from the moon he had before his mind this act of *Ruy Blas* in which Don César tumbles down the chimney. Note that the latter states, "J'habite dans la lune," and that Cyrano explains, "Je tombe de la lune." When Don César endeavors to conceal his identity from Don Guritan he employs the same elaborate and absurd hocus pocus that Cyrano uses to throw dust in the eyes of De Guiche:

> "Je ne suis plus vivant, je n'ai plus rien d'humain,
> Je suis un être absurde, un mort qui se réveille.
> Un bœuf, un hidalgo de la Castille-Vieille.
> On m'a volé ma plume, et j'ai perdu mes gants.
> J'arrive des pays les plus extravagants."
>
> (IV, 5)

Since the real Cyrano was the author of a *Voyage dans la lune*, it was a clever idea to have him pretend to be an inhabitant of that astral body,—and it is quite possible that Victor Hugo gave Rostand that idea.

There is one more French hero whom Rostand appears to wish us definitely to associate with Cyrano, namely, D'Artagnan of Dumas' *Trois Mousquetaires*. D'Artagnan too was a Gascon and Rostand makes him a member of the same regiment as Cyrano. As a swordsman and duellist he is without a peer in modern French literature prior to Rostand's hero. So it is a neat turn to have him identified as one of those who come forward and congratulate Cyrano after the latter's feat of coordinating perfectly the composition of a ballad and what we might call the "composition" of a duel.

Rostand was a friend and admirer of Théodore de Banville. Among Banville's heroes who have something in common with Cyrano we can think of Riquet à la Houppe who has a deformed body and a beautiful soul. A much closer resemblance is offered by Gringoire who is a poet, a *farceur*, is proud and independent even in the face of poverty, and has a tender and sympathetic side. We can see no evidence. however, of any effort on the part of Rostand to recall these characters of Banville's in a specific manner.

It requires no great effort to find other heroes in the world's literature who resemble Cyrano in type. One of these, for example, is Don Quixote. He has easily come to the mind of a number of critics and he is even mentioned in the play, but we can see in this latter fact nothing more than a reference that is quite appropriate to the occasion. In our opinion Rostand from his own soul breathed life into the skeleton of the original Cyrano and at the same time took occasion to make it evident that *his* Cyrano had something in common with certain French Romantic heroes. The resulting character not only incorporates Rostand's ideals,[11] but he would seem to represent at the same time the ideal French Romantic hero, the last in line and the greatest of a family of such heroes. This second fact, we believe, has been generally overlooked.

Besides employing the character of Cyrano for the purpose, Rostand has taken the occasion in this play to pay his respects to his great French Romantic predecessors in another way. He has directly borrowed from them certain episodes or ideas. This he does openly so that "he who runs may read."

Taking our sources again in more or less chronological order, we find Beaumarchais once more heading the list. The episode in Act III, sc. 1, where Cyrano is obliged to have the theorbo players follow at his heels for a whole day as a result of losing a bet is almost certainly a reminiscence of the scene in Act III, sc. 22, of the *Mariage de Figaro* where Count Almaviva obliges Bazile to follow Grippe-Soleil about and sing to him to the accompaniment of his guitar.

As might be expected, it is Hugo who contributes more references of this type than any other Romantic author. Leon Herrmann would have us believe that *Marion de Lorme* is one of the principal models for Rostand's play.[12] He makes much of the fact that the action of both plays takes place in Paris at almost exactly the same time in the seventeenth century and that Richelieu, though of some

importance in both plots, is never seen upon the stage. There is no evidence, however, that these similarities are more than coincidental. There is one obvious borrowing from *Marion de Lorme* which others before Herrmann had noted. It is Cyrano's gazette in the last act.[13] This gazette is imitated from the scene in Hugo's play[14] where the Comte de Gassé, who arrives from Blois to join his regiment, is made by his comrades to relate the latest news from Paris.

Though Rostand is influenced by Hugo's dramaturgy and by his comic dialogue,[15] no one play of Hugo's serves him exclusively as a model. He owes more to *Ruy Blas*, however, than to any other play. We have already shown that there is undoubtedly something of the character of Don César in the character of Cyrano. Without wishing to overstress the subtle problem of influences, we should like to point out certain interesting parallels between these two plays. Compare with Cyrano's dramatic first entrance in Act I the manner in which Ruy Blas enters the meeting of the king's private council and remains unobserved until he reveals his presence to the surprised courtiers at the psychological moment.[16] On another occasion Ruy Blas brings the queen a message from the king. Then he faints from loss of blood from a concealed wound. The identical handwriting on the message dictated by the king and on the letter the queen has received reveal Ruy Blas as the queen's unknown lover.[17] All this is very similar to the scene in the final act in which Roxane becomes aware of Cyrano's love. There are certain general similarities offered by the scenes between Don César and a duenna and between Cyrano and Roxane's duenna.[18] In both cases the duenna arranges a rendez-vous. Finally it is barely possible that Rostand got his idea for Cyrano's *panache* from this play of Hugo's. For Hugo has the grandees of Spain wear a white plume in their hats as a symbol of their noble rank and of their pride in that rank. Ruy Blas, in the First Act (sc. 3), tells Don César that he would gladly sell his soul to be one of the young grandees he sees about, "la plume au feutre et l'orgueil sur le front!". A few minutes later he has his wish when Don Salluste, having just transformed him into the false Don César, claps such a hat on his head upon the approach of the queen to indicate that that he too is not to be distinguished from the other grandees present. Furthermore, Ruy Blas, at the height of his power and glory, enters the meeting of the king's private council "la plume blanche au chapeau."[19]

We have already indicated how Rostand associates certain attributes of Cyrano with those of D'Artagnan of *Les Trois Mousquetaires*. In addition, Christian's arrival to join the Cadets de Gascogne reminds us of young D'Artagnan's early experiences in the Guards.[20] The siege of Arras recalls vaguely the siege of La Rochelle, as Dumas portrays it. It has been said that Cyrano's action in tying Roxane's handkerchief to a lance so that it may serve as a flag is based on the episode in which D'Artagnan and his friends use a napkin for a similar purpose during the occupation of the Bastion Saint-Gervais.[21] Interesting though they are, it is impossible to make out a case of influence in either of the two parallels just cited.

Among the heroes of Alfred de Musset's plays there are none that approach the Cyrano type sufficiently to warrant any obvious association of them with the Cyrano of the play. However. Rostand at least pays passing homage to Musset in the First Act (sc. 3) where the pages, by means of a hook and a cord, snatch the wig off a "bourgeois" among the spectators assembling for the show in the Hôtel de Bourgogne. This idea is very probably taken from the scene in *Fantasio*[22] where a page tells Elsbeth how someone by the same means removed the wig of the Prince of Mantua.

Théophile Gautier devotes one of the chapters of *Les Grotesques* to a very entertaining sketch of the real Cyrano de Bergerac. There can be almost no doubt that in the two scenes in which Cyrano's nose figures prominently[23] Rostand is consciously imitating the imagination and the picturesque vocabulary that Gautier employs in describing that famous appendage. Indeed it is very possible that Gautier suggested not only the scene in which Cyrano describes his nose, but also the later one in which Christian twits him about it. We do not know the extent of the "researches" made by Rostand preparatory to writing his play, but we may at least make the passing observation that he could have found in Gautier's biographical sketch just about all the basic facts upon which his imagination built up the figure of Cyrano.

It is possible that we have not quite exhausted the list of borrowings from French Romantic literature to be found in **Cyrano de Bergerac,** but we have listed a sufficient number to make our point. The Romantic Period was one of the epochs that most fascinated Rostand. Obviously he had a first-hand acquaintance with the works of his Romantic predecessors. Whether he depended upon an unusually good memory or whether he had recently refreshed his knowledge is of no consequence. The fact to be noted is that his borrowings from these predecessors are so numerous and so widely distributed that they cannot have been made unconsciously. One must conclude that Rostand employed them knowingly and openly as a method of rendering homage to his illustrious literary forbears and as one way of linking his work directly with theirs and of placing his play in a direct line of descent, in a relationship also exhibited by his hero. Let us not forget at the same time that Rostand produced a very original play.

NOTES

[1]Cp. Rosemond Gérard, *Edmond Rostand* (Paris, 1935), p. 8.

[2]"C'est avec la cire de son âme qu'il avait modelé celle de Cyrano. Ces fiertés excessives qui ne veulent rien devoir aux plus proches amis, ces générosités extrêmes qui ne se vengent des ennemis qu'en les écrasant de bienfaits, tout cela était passé tout naturellement du poète dans le héros." *Ibid.*, p. 36.

[3]The most ambitious attempt at an objective consideration of Rostand, that of M. J. Premsela (*Edmond Rostand*, Amsterdam, 1933), reveals the author of the study to be temperamentally and culturally inadequate to

do justice to his subject. Much of the impressionistic criticism is likewise vitiated for the first of these reasons.

[4]*Barbier de Séville*, Act II, sc. 3.

[5]*Mariage de Figaro*, Act V, sc. 3.

[6]An echo of this sort can be heard, for example, in the famous soliloquy in Hugo's *Hernani* (Act IV, sc. 2).

[7]*Mariage de Figaro*, Act III, sc. 5.

[8]Act II, sc. 8.

[9]Of course the contrast between physical deformity and a beautiful soul can also be found in such well-known characters of Hugo as Triboulet and Quasimodo.

[10]Act III, sc. 9.

[11]Pierre Aspesteguy reports that his friend Rostand once said to him: "Je n'exalte en Cyrano que le monde des grandes vertus, la magnanimité, la grandeur d'âme dans le dévouement telle qu'elle doit être; je veux défendre les droits de l'esprit contre les privilèges: naissance, fortune, relations, et particulièrement les atouts de la beauté uniquement physique." *La Vie profonde d'Edmond Rostand* (Paris, 1929), p. 147.

[12]"Marion de Lorme et Cyrano de Bergerac," in *Neophilologus*, X, 2 (January, 1925), pp. 91-95.

[13]Act V, sc. 5.

[14]Act II, sc. 1.

[15]Much of what Don César says in Act IV of *Ruy Blas*, for example, could just as well come from the lips of Cyrano.

[16]Cp. especially the stage direction at the end of Scene 1, Act III. At the end of Act II, scene 2, of *Hernani*, Hugo introduces his hero in a sudden and dramatic manner that parallels Cyrano's entrance even more closely.

[17]Act III, sc. 3.

[18]*Ruy Blas*, Act IV, sc. 4, and *Cyrano de Bergerac*, Act I, sc. 6. Dame Bérarde, the duenna in *Le Roi S'Amuse*, might also enter into this parallelism.

[19]Stage direction at end of Scene 1, Act III.

[20]Cp. *Les Trois Mousquetaires*, Ch. V.

[21]Act IV, sc. 10. *Les Trois Mousquetaires*, Ch. XVI. Cp. H. Platow, *Die Personen von Rostands "Cyrano de Bergerac" in der Geschichte und in der Dichtung*, Erlangen, 1902, p. 67.

[22]The nose has figured quite extensively in literature. Rostand may also have had in mind here the description of the uses of the nose in one of Erasmus's *Colloquia Familiaris* entitled *De Captandis Sacerdotis*. The parallelism is rather close. English sources must be discounted. Cp. Coleman O. Parsons. "Remarks on English Nose Literature," in *Notes and Queries*, 165, 2-4 (1933).

[23]Note, for example, the following passage from Gautier's text: "Si quelqu'un avait le malheur de le regarder et montrait quelque étonnement de voir un nez pareil, vite il lui fallait aller sur le pré.—Et comme les duels de ce temps-là ne finissaient pas par des déjeuners et que Cyrano était un habile spadassin, on courait risque de recevoir quelque bon coup d'épée au ventre et le ramporter son pourpoint percé de plus de boutonnières qu'il n'en avait auparavant, ce qui fit qu'au bout de peu de temps tout le monde trouva la forme du nez de Cyrano excessivement convenable et que tout au plus quelque provincial non encore usagé s'avisait d'y trouver le mot à rire. Il n'est pas besoin d'ajouter que quelque bonne botte poussée à fond apprenait bientôt à vivre au plaisant si elle ne le tuait pas." *Les Grotesques*, nouv. éd., Paris, 1856, p. 183.

Louis Untermeyer (essay date 1954)

SOURCE: "A Foreword," in *Cyrano de Bergerac: A Heroic Comedy in 5 Acts by Edmond Rostand*, translated by Louis Untermeyer, The Heritage Press, 1954, pp. ix-xvii.

[*In the following essay, Untermeyer discusses the genesis, development, and reception of* Cyrano de Bergerac.]

A real flesh-and-blood Cyrano won audiences long before Rostand rhymed him into dramatic immortality. The progenitor of the play's swaggering but self-sacrificing hero, the walking gargoyle, Savinien Cyrano de Bergerac, was born near Paris in 1619. He loved his family's Gascon background, and he hated the routine education to which he was subjected. Even as a youth his spirit was both creative and critical. The principal at the College of Beauvais was the target of his young but already dangerous scorn and, later, was caricatured in a comedy, *Le Pédant Joué,* "The Teacher Tricked." Nevertheless, it was at school that Cyrano formed his closest friendship, a companionship with Henri Le Bret, who became his lifelong mentor and, after Cyrano's death, his editor and biographer.

Once out of school and on the loose in Paris, Cyrano spent his time like any well-to-do seventeenth century blade. He roistered and duelled—anyone who looked twice at his gargantuan nose was likely to be challenged to mortal combat—grew contentious, and quarreled with his father and all his friends except Le Bret. When he got into serious trouble he joined the audacious Cadets, or Guardsmen, of Carbon de Castel-Jaloux, fought violently in Flanders, and, at twenty-one, was seriously wounded during the siege of Arras.

Shortly after 1640 he gave up soldiering and turned to literature. In an effort to curb his irascible temper he studied and even practiced philosophy. He became a playwright, and succeeded in serious drama as well as farce; the much applauded *Death of Agrippina* is said to have been his favorite. His speculative fantasy, *A History of the Republic of the Sun*, was a forerunner of the prophecies of Jules Verne and the science-fiction of our own day, and it is said that Swift got the idea for *Gulliver's Travels* from Bergerac's *A Voyage to the Moon*. (Both are available in translation.)

Death came to Cyrano in life as in the play. As he was returning home one evening, a heavy piece of wood fell from a window and struck him down; it was never discovered whether the blow was designed or an accident. However, differing from his finale in the play, Cyrano did not succumb immediately, but lived in great suffering for a year. He was just thirty-six when he died in 1655.

2

Two and a half centuries after his birth, Cyrano de Bergerac—somewhat idealized but still independent and even more pugnacious and paradoxical—began a new life. His resuscitator was, like himself, a French poet and playwright: Edmond Rostand, not yet turned thirty. Rostand had been a devoted reader of Bergerac and, when he determined to bring Cyrano to the stage, he found that the seventeenth century playwright had made his task fairly easy for him. Rostand took many of the incidents of Cyrano's life and historical references and embodied them in his play; the opening scene immediately projects the mood of an archaic, intriguing, rowdy Paris, diverted by rival coteries and excited by blustering gallantries. Many of Cyrano's actual associates were revived, or revised, and became Rostand's *dramatis personae*: his friend and editor Henri Le Bret; Lignière, a popular versifier and writer of sardonic epigrams; the doughty Carbon de Castel-Jaloux; the fat and affected actor, Montfleury, ridiculed by Molière; two other well-known actors, Bellerose and Jodelet; two of Cyrano's admirers, Cuigy and Brissaille; the suave Antoine, Count de Guiche, who married Richelieu's niece; and Christian (originally Christophe) de Champagne, Baron of Neuvillette, who (as in the play) died at the siege of Arras. History says nothing about Cyrano and Christian-Christopher being friends. Nor is it a fact that Cyrano was in love with his cousin, the intellectual little snob, Madeleine Robineau, the Roxane of Rostand's drama. The prototypes were there, but they needed the magic touch of Rostand's imagination to place them in dramatic relation to each other. Moreover, it needed the poet to communicate, as Rostand declared when he was elected to the French Academy at the age of thirty-four, "ecstasy by means of lyric poetry . . . the morality of beauty."

Cyrano de Bergerac was by no means Rostand's first play. Born in Marseilles in 1868, a product of the land of the troubadours, of Provençal song and dance, Edmond Rostand was fortunate. His family was wealthy; his father was a versifier, essayist, and translator of Catullus. The boy's natural inclination to literature was encouraged from the start. He won prizes at college and, as soon as he received his bachelor's degree, a sinecure was found for him in a bank. But none of the Rostands took the position seriously and soon Edmond devoted himself wholly to writing. At twenty-two he married a young actress-poet and published his first book. It was a volume of verse, **Les Musardises,** and, though it was wholly without originality, it contained a few suggestions of the facility which was to become its author's chief characteristic. At twenty-four a farce in one act, **The Two Pierrots,** was presented at the Comédie Française; it was a variation on the "Laugh, clown, laugh" theme and remained in the repertoire as a curtain-raiser. Two years later Rostand had his first triumph: a satirical fantasy, **The Romancers,** which was a financial as well as an artistic success and won him a prize of 5,000 francs. At twenty-seven, with Sarah Bernhardt in mind, he wrote **The Faraway Princess.** This was another fantasy, based on the legend of the Provençal poet, Jaufré Rudel, who had fallen in love with the Countess of Tripoli, whom he had never seen, and who traveled overseas to Syria to die in her arms. Bernhardt produced the play in her own theatre and was glamorous in the title role.

Browning had woven his own variations around the story in his "Rudel to the Lady of Tripoli"—it was the kind of rhapsodic, moon-mad play that every poet dreams of writing, and it turned Rostand from light satire to a consideration of serious subjects.

Meanwhile, the Dreyfus affair was rocking France, and Rostand did not remain aloof from the controversy. He sided staunchly with Zola, Proust, Anatole France, and others in defense of the victimized Jewish captain. Yet in the midst of the national upheaval, he managed to complete two plays. The first, produced in Holy Week in 1897, was *The Woman of Samaria,* a modern miracle play founded on the Gospel story of Jesus according to St. John. The second was *Cyrano de Bergerac.*

Cyrano was the high point of Rostand's career. Three more plays were still to come, three increasingly ambitious dramas of decreasing merit. The first was *L'Aiglon* (*The Eaglet*) produced in 1900, a dramatized study of Napoleon's unhappy and consumptive young son. Not a completely convincing play, it had moments of true vision and deep pathos; the role of the tragic boy was acted in France by Sarah Bernhardt, in America even more touchingly by the frail Maude Adams. Rostand devoted the next ten years to *Chantecler,* his most experimental and, in some ways, his most searching work. The scene is a barnyard; the actors are the farmside's birds and beasts; the overlord is the strutting cock who believes that his crowing brings up the sun. When it reached Broadway, the title role was played incongruously but charmingly by Maude Adams. Rostand took the fabled world of La Fontaine and the beast-epics of the Middle Ages and gave them the individualized vitality that Chaucer brought to Pertelote and Chauntecleer in "The Nonne Preestes Tale." Overshadowed by *Cyrano,* the play was belittled, and its failure so disheartened Rostand that he retired to his country place in the Pyrenees. His sense of frustration was already indicated in the very character of his defeated heroes: *Cyrano,* whose eloquence is futile and whose nobility serves only to win his beloved for another man; *L'Aiglon,* the sickly Duke of Reichstadt, Napoleon's son, who knows he can never achieve the heaven-storming strength of the Eagle; *Chantecler,* who is forced to learn that his cock-crow does not compel the sun to rise. Another play, *The Last Night of Don Juan,* produced four years after Rostand's death, again revealed beneath the flourishes and gay arabesques the author's unfulfilled dreams and hopeless disillusions. An unfinished drama on the Faust theme was never published. Rostand died December 2, 1918.

3

The first performance of *Cyrano de Bergerac* was literally an historic occasion. The premiere, December 28, 1897, had been awaited with public curiosity and private apprehension. On the opening night Rostand was overcome with nervousness and overwhelmed with surprise. A half-hour before the curtain rose he apologized to the company for having involved them in what was sure to be a disastrous failure; two hours after the curtain had been rung down, the audience was still in the theatre, still applauding, still calling for the author, still crying out names and repeating lines in unprecedented excitement. The great French actor, Constant Coquelin, to whom the play was dedicated and who created the title-role, gives a picture of the scene: "The first night was eagerly awaited by the critics, the literary, and the artistic worlds. The audience that night was undoubtedly the cream of our Parisian public. When the curtain rose on the first act there was not a seat vacant in the theatre. The emotion of a great event was floating in the air. Never, never have I lived through such a night. Victor Hugo's greatest triumph, the first night of *Hernani,* was the only theatrical event that can compare with it, and that was injured by the enmity of a clique who persistently hissed through the performance. There is but one phrase to express the enthusiasm at our first performance—'a house in delirium' alone gives any idea of what took place. As the curtains fell on each succeeding act the entire audience would rise to its feet, shouting and cheering for ten minutes at a time. The coulisse and the dressing-rooms were packed by the critics and the author's friends, beside themselves with delight. I was trembling so that I could hardly get from one costume into another, and had to refuse my door to every one. Amid all this confusion Rostand alone seemed unconscious of his victory."

Thereafter, *Cyrano* became a permanent part of the international theatre. It was translated into every European language and several Oriental tongues, including Japanese. In the excellent German version by the eminent author, Ludwig Fulda, the play was performed again and again. Its peculiar combination of classic manner and baroque style, of beauty and bombast, was a challenge to all translators. There have been at least half a dozen notable English versions. Within a year of its first French presentation four English texts were published: a readable if not too accurate version by two Englishwomen, Gladys Thomas and Mary F. Guillemard; a fairly idiomatic version by Gertrude Hall; a discreet prose rendering by Helen B. Dole, who felt that the ballade and other "arias" were untranslatable and printed them in French, "in their native melody and rhythm"; and a workmanlike approximation by Howard Thayer Kingsbury. It was Kingsbury's version that was presented to a New York audience on October 3, 1898 (less than a year after the Paris opening) with Richard Mansfield in the title role and Margaret Anglin playing the part of Roxane. On the same night another version of Rostand's drama was produced in Philadelphia by Augustin Daly with Charles Richman as Cyrano and Ada Rehan as Roxane.

The play continued to be so successful that it was almost immediately retailored. It became a comic opera which opened in New York on September 18, 1899. "Based" on Edmond Rostand's play, it had a book by Stuart Reed, lyrics by Harry B. Smith, and music by Victor Herbert. The title role was played by the favorite comic of the day, Francis Wilson.

On November 1, 1923, a new English version of what, by that time, was known as "the Rostand classic" featured Walter Hampden in a spirited verse adaptation by Brian Hooker. An operatic arrangement with music by Walter Damrosch was staged in 1930. The text was by the music critic, W. J. Henderson, but the opera failed to win a place either in critical esteem or in the music-lover's heart.

The Hooker version was revived on October 8, 1946, with incidental music by the novelist-musician, Paul Bowles. The revival was staged by José Ferrer, who also acted the title part. Four years later Ferrer appeared in a brilliantly conceived film version, retaining a great part of the original play in Hooker's adaptation.

Two recent versions attempted to capture the swift-running rhymes of the original. The first, highly stylized and desperately spirited, was by the late English poet, Humbert Wolfe. This rendering was made for a film version that was to be produced in England starring Charles Laughton, but was abandoned. The other and more literal rhymed translation was published in Los Angeles in 1947. This was a collaboration, the joint product of Clifford Hershey Bissell, Ph. D., and William Van Wyck, Litt. D., a serious if not always successful effort.

4

It is a platitude to say that the transferring of a poetic work from one language to another involves many difficulties and results in many losses, but that platitude must be repeated. The fusing of separate phrases and stray ideas into a new thing complete in itself—the magic metamorphosis which is poetry—is untranslatable. The translator can expect nothing more than a fair approximation, a paraphrase, which will not sacrifice too much of the meaning at the expense of the music or, contrariwise, give up too much of the music to preserve the meaning. All he can hope for is a good compromise which will keep the rhythm pulsing, the action moving, and the spirit soaring.

The question of rhyme demands separate consideration. In a play of any length, and particularly in a serious play, rhyme is a hazard. This is not true in France, where identities of sound, assonances, and echoes are used freely; in Rostand's language rhyme presents no problems to the Gallic ear. But the English actor—as well as the English audience—is accustomed either to a dramatic prose or variations of the resonant, rolling, and generally unrhymed blank verse perfected by the great Elizabethans. It is this variably sonorous but never cloying speech which has been maintained from the time of Marlowe and Shakespeare to T. S. Eliot and Christopher Fry. On our stage, and especially the modern stage, a long play in rhymed verse sounds both artful and artificial. Worse, it is difficult to follow. The listener grows intent upon the technical device; he waits for the rhymed word which is to cap its predecessor at the end of every line. In his attention to the sound he loses the sense.

Thus, in a completely rhymed translation of *Cyrano,* the too nimble pairing of sounds, the continual matching of similar syllables, the very insistence of the rhymes, is a danger which is also a disservice to the original. For, despite the label, *Cyrano* is a comedy only in a very special sense. It certainly is not a comic comedy—there are countless witticisms, plays on words, puns, and occasional grotesque episodes; but there is nothing essentially humorous in the action. The plight of an ugly man in love with a beautiful woman, an intellectual who woos his beloved for a stupid but handsome man, and loses her himself—this is the substance of a partly ironic, partly pathetic, and finally tragic drama. This is precisely the kind of play which Rostand wrote. The mood throughout is romantic; the language is rich; the tone is alternately sentimental and noble. In short, if it is a comedy at all, it justifies the subtitle which Rostand gave his play: A Comedy-Heroic.

The subtitle is the core of the drama. For "Cyrano" is heroic in the literal as well as the theatrical sense. Here, on one level, is a swashbuckler whose life is a perpetual physical and verbal challenge; a purple patchwork of dazzling swordplay accompanied by the most extravagant rhetoric. And here, on another level, is a man doomed by his own arrogant brilliance. What seems to be romanticism run riot is checked by a grim and even devastating irony. Cyrano's defiant posturing, his grandiose gestures and oratorical fanfares, turn out to be fragments of a career in ruins—a half-braggart, half-hopeless structure of defense, a triumph of despair. Like that other anachronistic grotesque, Don Quixote, Cyrano can face himself only in the cracked mirror of illusion.

In an atmosphere of such contradictory luxuriance, the present translator has attempted to steer a middle course between the Scylla of plain prose and the Charybdis of highly colored couplets. He recognizes that Rostand used a language which is so flexible, so melodious and delicately archaic, that even the most opulent prose fails to suggest the musical character of the work. Therefore, since poetry in one language can be suggested only by poetry in another, blank verse has been chosen as the logical medium—a blank verse which is chiefly colloquial rather than classical, avoiding inversions, straightforward in idiom and modern in tone. However, the famous duelling ballade and other set pieces call for a much more formal treatment. Such lyrical moments are so surcharged with high spirits and exuberance that they inevitably rise, or erupt, into rhyme. Here, as in the body of the blank verse, the translator has tried to strike a balance between the literal meaning of the original text and Rostand's wit, fluency, and flickering eloquence.

Cyrano de Bergerac is little more than half a century old—not a long time in the life of a classic. It continues to be so great a challenge to the interpreter that, within fifty years, no less than ten English translators have offered their renderings, each one vying with his predecessor in a fresh effort to bring the spirit of the original to the printed page. This version is one more evidence of the play's continuing

Scene from an 1898 French production of Cyrano de Bergerac.

appeal. Next to writing his own poetry, there is no greater pleasure for a poet than putting into his own tongue the essence of another poet. It is a dangerous delight, and the present paraphraser hopes he has not too much adulterated Rostand's sparkling words and potent music.

Patricia Elliott Williams (essay date 1973)

SOURCE: "Some Classical Aspects of *Cyrano de Bergerac*," in *Nineteenth-Century French Studies*, Vol. I, No. 2, February 1973, pp. 112-24.

[*In the essay below, Williams interprets* Cyrano de Bergerac *in terms of the Aristotelian definition of tragedy.*]

Edmond Rostand's undisputed chef d'oeuvre, *Cyrano de Bergerac,* is usually and justifiably termed a neo-romantic play, a return to the dauntless, poetic and somewhat bombastic vein of Hugo's *Hernani* and its contemporaries. Traits of the French romantic writers of the 1820's, who rejected the merits of their predecessors, the French classicists, indeed are reflected in *Cyrano.* Yet a careful study of Rostand's dramaturgy reveals that certain classical premises, some of which were stressed by Aristotle, are applicable to *Cyrano de Bergerac.*

Admittedly Aristotle's precepts were established for the appreciation of classical Greek tragedy rather than nineteenth-century French drama; yet the general concepts and standards which he enunciated have continued to guide dramatists as well as critics up to and including modern times. Though some modern scholars such as John Crowe Ransom deny the validity of Aristotle's criteria for evaluating modern literature,[1] Aristotle, as Francis Fergusson points out, "made the most ambitious effort to describe the nature of dramatic art,[2] . . . and the principles of his investigation are still the best we have. . . ."[3] Whether Rostand deliberately adhered to the Aristotelian precepts is a moot point, and not the major question here, for we are simply subjecting *Cyrano de Bergerac* to an Aristotelian analysis.

Aristotle explains tragedy as

> an imitation of an action that is serious, complete, and of a certain magnitude in language embellished with each kind of artistic ornament, the several kinds being found in separate parts of the play; in the form of action, not of narrative; through pity and fear effecting the proper purgation of these emotions.[4]

"Mimesis (imitation), as Aristotle uses the term," explains Dr. Gusta B. Nance, "seems to be an interpretation of life by a creative artist in which interpretation the artist gives a conception of nature (human and physical), representing the probable and necessary, thus giving the universal, the essence of things and men"[5] Rostand interpreted human nature in a man whose excessive sensitivity to an imperfection prevents his obtaining his most cherished goal. He created the confident and proud Cyrano, without peer in bravura, cleverness, wit or poetry: a composite of the ideal French hero. In an era when French morale was at a record low, Rostand painted a hero successful in the respects the nation had stumbled: victorious in battle, positive and confident in action, just in dealing with rivals, generous in spirit, crowned with the *panache* perhaps considered by the French as their exclusive characteristic. Rostand showed the nobility of human nature through his hero, yet kept the action firmly within the realm of probability. Through the particular problem of Cyrano's excessively long nose, Rostand demonstrated universal human nature which permits a relatively inconsequential imperfection to prevent ultimate achievement.

Tragedy is a serious action, that is, opposed to comedy in that comedy "is an artistic imitation of men of an inferior moral bent; faulty, however, not in any or every way, but only in so far as their shortcomings are ludicrous."[6] Samuel Butcher describes tragedy as a picture of human destiny in all its significance.[7] This is not to say that tragedy does not have humorous aspects; consider Cyrano's *tirade du nez*, the opening scene in Act II in Ragueneau's pastry shop, the incident of Cyrano's pretending to have fallen from the moon in order to detain De Guiche. These humorous incidents do not exaggerate a fault or weakness; they do not detract from the total effect of human destiny and its significance.

A complete action, as Aristotle explains, has a beginning, middle, and end. Cyrano, in love with Roxane and exhilarated by their rendez-vous, begins the tragic action by agreeing to help Roxane win the handsome Christian de Neuvillette. The middle is his pursuit of this determined course and his suffering because of his inability to reveal directly his passion to Roxane. The tragic hero experience a reversal of his situation at Christian's death, apparently freeing him to win Roxane for himself. Yet he realizes that through the poetic love letters he has created the image of Christian that Roxane loves. To destroy it would not only dishonor the dead but also would assure Roxane's contempt for him. Clearly the situation is of his own making and he alone is responsible. He must uphold the image of the poetic Christian, even in his dying moments saying, "Non, non, mon cher amour, je ne vous aimais pas."[8]

Rostand ensures his play is of the Aristotelian "certain magnitude" by the stature of Cyrano, the nobility of his actions and of his soul. Cyrano, faced with the moral dilemma of whether to seek his own pleasure or to help Roxane and Christian achieve their happiness, meets it with admirable strength. His *forte* is his intellect ever present and more than sufficient to disguise his true feelings, to advance Christian's courtship with poetic affirmations, to succeed in winning Roxane, to detract De Guiche from interrupting the marriage ceremony, to inspire his fellow soldiers in battle, to fight injustice and mediocrity, and to confront death defiantly.

Morally, Cyrano is neither all good nor all bad, but has strong leanings toward goodness. His misfortune is not the result of his own wickedness, but of his profound value conflict with results in his decision to yield his own interest in Roxane to Christian. This fatal decision is provoked by his deeper than average bent of feeling. With his tragic hero who has aspirations, conflicts, and inhibitions common to everyone, Rostand produces an Aristotelian catharsis by evoking pity for a man who suffers more than he deserves. Fear also is evoked because it is so easy to identify with this man's universal traits.

Aristotle continues: "every tragedy must have six elements according to which the quality of the tragedy is determined: (1) plot, (2) character indicants, (3) thought, (4) spectacle, (5) diction, and (6) music."[9]

The prerequisite which Aristotle considers most important is the plot. He states, "The most important of these is the arrangement of the incidents of the plot, for tragedy is not the portrayal of men (as such), but of action, of life. . . ." (*P*, p. 14). A scrutiny of **Cyrano** shows that Rostand carefully arranged the structure of the plot according to story and form, and constructed it soundly with generally good dramatic techniques. The arrangement of incidents in the plot shows artistically logical developments, prepares the audience for what is coming next, and the action rises consistently to the climax. An initial crisis occurs approximately two-thirds of the way to the climax: to sustain interest, Rostand offers a new setting, a different

and somewhat unrelated activity to provoke curiosity, after which he approaches the climax. Thus, the initial crisis, Roxane's and Christian's marriage in Act III, is followed in the fourth act by the scene change to the battlefield. There the action, after the intense emotion of the third act, shows the calm despair of the weary, hungry soldiers. Suddenly the beautiful and gay Roxane arrives like an angel to bring food and good cheer. Curiously the audience watches as Cyrano reveals to Christian his past letterwriting. The audience's interest grows with Cyrano's preliminary effort to tell Roxane of his love, when the climax, Christian's death, occurs. It seems that the careful structure of the beginning, middle, and end plus the undeniably logical arrangement of events contribute to the successful performance of the play. Rostand's very close attention to the arrangement of incidents of the action leads us to assume that he considered plot a vitally important element.

In presenting criteria for characters, Aristotle lists four necessary qualities: the character should be good, fitting, and exhibit likeness and consistency (*P*, p. 29). He says, "A character will be good if the choice made evident is a good one," (*P*, p. 29) and he explains fitting in these terms: "There is such a thing as manly character, but is not fitting for a woman to be manly or clever" (*P*, p. 29). Preston H. Epps, in his translation the *Poetic of Aristotle*, notes that by likeness Aristotle "seems to mean: likeness in character to the traditional character portrayed" (*P*, p. 29). S. H. Butcher, in *Aristotle's Theory of Poetry and Fine Art*, simply translates this third quality as "true to life."[10] To elucidate consistency, Aristotle avers that "even if the person portrayed in the imitation is inconsistent and has been given this type of character, he must be consistently inconsistent" (*P*, p. 29). He further stipulates that "it is also necessary in character portrayal, just as it was in arranging the incidents, to aim always at what is necessary or what is probable in such a way that when a certain type of person says or does a certain type of thing he does so either from necessity or probability" (*P*, p. 30).

Consider the hero: Cyrano is probably the best developed character in all of Rostand's plays. Each act reveals a new dimension of his personality: in Act I he is bold, courageous, and arrogant in the face of superficiality; Act II shows him in love, in firm control of his emotions when his love is not returned, and generous to protect and to tolerate jibes from his rivals; in Act III his poetic, lyric, and imaginative facets are revealed; Act IV discloses his scorn for cowardice, the lengths to which love has carried him, his joy at the promise of Roxane's recognition, and his despair at the death of Christian; Act V maintains his sense of humor, his devotion to and love for Roxane, and his courage in death. He is completely credible, and his actions are completely motivated by his convictions. In this respect, he is true to life. He is also a type character, the universal hero. He is portrayed consistently as a hero with a physical grotesqueness which prevents him from allowing his passion to develop without constraint. Cyrano is good in the Aristotelian concept, in that his choice to defer to Christian for Roxane's attentions is noble.

Cyrano far outshadows his handsome rival Christian de Neuvillette, a static character, seen consistently from only one point of view. Like Cyrano he is, for the most part, credible, true to life, and sufficiently motivated. He, too, is a type character—a man whose primary asset is his handsomeness—and is manifested throughout the play as the handsome, beloved man in antithesis to the grotesque, unloved Cyrano. His decision to insist that Cyrano tell Roxane of his love for her meets Aristotle's criterion of goodness in character.

Roxane, the heroine of the play, is painted as a beautiful *précieuse*. Rostand's critics usually do not credit her with much depth, yet she possesses the ingenuity common to any woman in love. She is a developing character within a limited scope, credible, and logical in motivation. She is a type character consistently portrayed as an ideal woman.

Although plot is perhaps the most important aspect in Rostand's plays, characterization is also of great significance, for without skillful character creation, the plot's impact would be diminished. The characters who perform the action are credible and consistent because they are well developed. Their attributes accurately reflect the qualities of the persons they are supposed to represent, and the characters are fitting because they have the requisite traits necessary to create the personage properly. Their motives for action are well-founded and clearly expressed.

Aristotle's third constituent element for tragedy is thought. He explains thought as it relates to drama in this manner:

> tragedy is an imitation of an action being carried out by certain individuals who must be certain kinds of persons in character and in thinking—the two criteria by which we determine the quality of an action; for character and one's thinking are two natural causes of action, and it is because of these that all men fail or succeed (*P*, p. 12).

Preston H. Epps, translator of the *Poetics*, comments on the difficulty of assessing precisely what was meant by the Greek word *dianoia*, which he translates as thought. He enumerates the five meanings of the word given in the new Lidell and Scott Greek lexicon as follows: "(1) 'thought, *i.e.*, intention, purpose'; (2) 'process of thinking'; (3) 'thinking faculty, understanding'; (4) 'thought expressed, meaning of a word or passage'; and (5) 'intellectual capacity revealed in speech or action by characters in the drama'" (*P*, p. 12). From his study of the *Poetics* and the context in which the word *thought* is explained, Epps concludes that Aristotle seems to have "had in mind in his use of this word: (1) intellectual deliberative capacity; (2) the process of thinking; and (3) the thoughts one gives assent to and acts upon" (*P*, p. 12). He emphasizes that these are the various meanings of the word that Aristotle seems to have intended and admits that they are not entirely satisfactory.

Without Epps' explanation, Aristotle's further definition of thought would not be completely clear. Aristotle says:

> The third part is the thinking ability of the characters which is the ability to (think out and) say (1) what is possible (within the limits of the situation) and (2) what is fitting—a function which is the same as that of language when used in statesmanship and in oratory. . . .

> Thought manifests itself in what the characters say as they prove or disprove something or make evident something universal (*P*, p. 15).

Consequently, a study of thought necessitates an examination of dialogue both in terms if its technical aspects and its cognitive elements. The technical components of the language will be examined later. The initial consideration of thought will deal with evidence of the rational process in the three leading characters.

Cyrano's ability to perceive the crux of a situation and to give the precise response is evident in Act I in his verbal devastation of Montfleury, in the variety and aptness of all examples in the *tirade du nez*, culminating in the *tour de force* of wit in the impromptu ballade and duel with Le Vicomte de Valvert. This facility of wit is also evidenced in Act III when Cyrano wins Roxane's kiss for Christian and detains the Duc de Guiche during the marriage of Roxane and Christian. Cyrano's reasoning power, however, breaks down in the central theme of the play, his unrequited love for Roxane. Emotions emerge dominant over rational thought. Rather than impassionately constructing a rational plan to achieve his goal—the love of Roxane—he hopelessly accepts her schoolgirlish infatuation with a handsome face, and attributes his failure as rejection because of the physical imperfection of an excessively long nose. Even when his better judgment seems to be emerging in Act IV with his confession to Christian that he has sent daily letters to Roxane, Cyrano is plunged back into the emotional realm by Christian's untimely death. His reason accurately instructs him that this particular moment is inopportune to declare his love. Now it is obvious that Cyrano has strong romantic traits. He is superior, self-conscious, imaginative, a man of active hypersensibility fated by his unfortunate physical appearance.[11] Aristotle would not have the character to collapse at the first sign of challenge (Roxane's apparent rejection of Cyrano) but instead would advocate the character think through all aspects of the situation. Cyrano's proven wit, perception, and persuasiveness are evidence of a potential rational being. The error in or lack of judgment, however, results in the romantic Cyrano, romantic hero of 1898 and all ensuing romantics.

The secondary characters, Roxane and Christian, are not developed enough to display any reasoning ability. They simply react to their emotions.

The element of diction, which takes the form of dialogue in drama, is defined in the *Poetics* as an "expression (of thought) by means of language" (*P*, p. 15).

Cyrano de Bergerac is an extravaganza of dramatic activity. The first act is sheer spectacle of movement, and the episodes quickly succeed each other. Yet the kaleidoscopic events are achieved with grace and a surprising economy of dialogue. On occasion, however, Rostand halts the action completely with soliloquies which demonstrate both the versatility of the character's personality and the talent of the actor. While the extensive length of the play, the multiplicity of episodes, and the soliloquies indicate extravagance in dialogue, the precise words chosen to illustrate the events and moods provide a balancing economy.

When considering the appropriateness of language in revealing character, we recognize that all the characters, even the soldiers, are refined persons. As such, they speak correctly. As a result, the play is only partially realistic in regard to manner of speech. Rostand, however, does make the content of the dialogue conform reasonably to realism. Christian frankly admits he can hold his own in jesting but has little talent for the refined manner of speech necessary to converse with ladies. Roxane's dialogue supports the *précieuse* personality that Rostand has drawn for her. Since Cyrano is the most highly developed character in the play, it is interesting to note how fully his dialogue reveals his personality. His audacious courage is displayed when he challenges anyone who objects to his banishing Montefleury from the stage. The famous *tirade du nez* soliloquy indicates his humor, wit and adjustment to his appearance. The *non merci!* speech reveals his pride and independence. Cyrano's secret dream, his love for Roxane, and the madness he feels in being denied this dream disclose his sensitivity. The hero's poetic skill is exhibited when he impersonates Christian beneath Roxane's balcony. His inventive mind comes to the fore in the scene in which he detains De Guiche while Roxane and Christian are married. Just before dying, Cyrano evaluates his life in his self-composed epitaph:

> Philosophe, physicien,
> Rimeur, bretteur, musicien,
> Et voyageur aerien,
> Grand riposteur du tac au tac,
> Amant aussi—pas pour son bien!—
> Ci-git Hercule-Savinien
> De Cyrano de Bergerac
> Qui fut tout, et qui ne fut rien. . . .[12]

The pace of dialogue is energetic and vivid. While Rostand generally uses the alexandrine couplet, there are several notable exceptions: such as the *ballade* composed during the duel, the epitaph, and Ragueneau's recipe for *tartelettes amandines*. Rostand employs his typical technique of dividing the alexandrine line among several speakers in order to sustain moments of deep emotional feeling. Thus the long play moves at a pace calculated to maintain the spectator's interest.

In the diction (used in the sense of choice of words) of Cyrano, Rostand employs a number of somewhat uncommon words such as *colichemardes, délabyrinthez, escogriffes, estafilade, icosaedre, naisigère, pentacrostiche, pharaminieux, tryanneau*. Moreover, he appears to have invented at least two words: *Hippocampelephantocamelos* and *Regromontanus*. The use of these pedantic and amusing words appropriately serves to support the *précieux* quality of the play. It seems therefore apparent that the language in *Cyrano de Bergerac* effectively sustains dramatic tension, reveals characters and themes.

Regarding his fifth criterion, Aristotle says, "of the remaining elements (*i.e.*, music and spectacle), music has the greatest enriching power" (*P*, p. 15). In *Cyrano*, it has different purposes for each instance in which it is used. In Act I, music accompanies the abortive performance of Clorise and serves to establish the probability of the play within a play, and to separate its action from that of the actual drama. Music in this instance seems quite natural and is readily accepted by the audience. Musicians in Act III, however, are used as dramatic devices. Before the balcony scene, Cyrano assigns each page to a lookout post to warn him by playing an air on the lute if anyone approaches; thus, he is not taken by surprise at the entrance of the capucin or of De Guiche.

The drums, bugles, and fifes are natural accompaniments of seventeenth century warfare; therefore, their use in Act IV is to be expected. Rostand, however, further employs the music of the fifer, who plays old familiar tunes to relieve the men's minds of the miseries of war. This scene also contributes to the effectiveness of Roxane's arrival at camp. The men are saddened by memories of home and family and are quiet, sentimental, and somewhat huddled together. Thus Roxane does not enter a camp of bitterly complaining, miserable, perhaps even argumentative men, but of men receptive to the gentleness, kindness, and beauty she brings.

Rostand uses organ music near the end of Act V to call the nuns to evensong. The music also intimates that Cyrano is dying and sweetens his last moments with thoughts of life transcending earth.

The music in *Cyrano de Bergerac* has dual purposes: that of an obvious literary device and a subtle evocation of emotional responses.

Aristotle's enthusiasm for music does not extend to spectacle. He says that "spectacle, while quite appealing, is the most inartistic and has the least affinity with poetry, for the essential power of tragedy does not depend upon the presentation and the actors. Moreover, for achieving the effects of spectacle, the art of the mechanic of stage properties is more competent than the art of poetry" (*P*, p. 15). The element of spectacle in the sense of *décor* and of *coups de théâtre*, however, has long enchanced drama.

Visual effects increase the richness of *Cyrano de Bergerac.* Each of the five acts takes place in a different setting, which Rostand precisely describes in the stage directions. His artistic and decorative talents are particularly apparent in the detailed directions given for Ragueneau's pastry shop. His purpose in providing for the elaborate settings is to establish mood and atmosphere.

The *coups de théâtre* in this play contribute to the total spectacle. The first four scenes of the first act are
spectacular representations of seventeenth-century life, involving numerous characters with appropriate costumes
and behavior. Rostand heightens the total effect with the
activities of the cut-purses, the pages snatching wigs, Roxane's appearance, Montfleury's performance, and Cyrano's
ensuing termination of the performance. Cyrano's duel
while composing a poem constitutes the high point of the
spectacle. Likewise, the first four scenes of Act II are
spectacular with the numerous bakers and poets. Rostand
enhances these scenes with their activities and with Ragueneau's poetic efforts and frustrations. He deviates from
the crowd spectacle in Act III and uses instead individuals
for *coups de théâtre*. This is illustrated in the balcony
scene when Cyrano assumes Christian's place, and Christian subsequently ascends to Roxane's presence. Roxane's
persuasion of the capucin to marry her to Christian as well
as Cyrano's claim to have fallen from the moon are also
dramatic *coups de théâtre* which enter the realm of the
spectacular.

Perhaps the most spectacular scene in the play is Roxane's arrival at the battlefield in Act IV. The misery of
the soldiers contrasts with the sumptuousness of the coach.
Moreover, horses on stage were then always the ultimate in
theatrical spectacle. Rostand concludes **Cyrano de Bergerac** with the greatest of theatrical devices, the death of
the hero. Thus the *coups de théâtre* in **Cyrano de Bergerac**
vary from the crowd to the individual, from the comic to
the tragic, and from duels and horses to death on stage.

In concluding this consideration of **Cyrano de Bergerac**
in terms of Aristotle's definition of tragedy and six basic
elements for drama, it is again acknowledged that leading drama analysts past and present classify the play as
neo-romantic, completely out of step with its time, yet
unmistakably a box-office success. It is not at all difficult
to apply romantic traits to the play; however, Rostand's
genius lies not only in creating a romantic hero, but also
in the classically structured framework within which he
places the hero.

The tragedy in **Cyrano** is not his death but the irony of
his life—that Roxane's actual love was not the defunct
Christian but the vibrant Cyrano. By revealing the hero
in the "moments of highest mental agitation and deepest
anguish,"[13] Rostand shows the stature of the personality in
the struggle. He has creatively interpreted human destiny in
fundamental, timeless, and universal aspects evoking pity
and fear as described above not only emotionally but also
intellectually.

Aristotle's criteria for drama are clearly applicable insofar
as plot, character, diction, music, and spectacle are concerned. It is the deviation in thought, the character's ability
to reason through a situation rather than yield to an emotional conclusion, which is the springboard for the romantic
tone. Without the careful classical structure in the image
of tragedy on which are superimposed the constituents of

romanticism, the excellent dramaturgy, and superb poetry,
Rostand's romantic hero might never have gotten to the
stage to captivate the hearts of universal romantics.

NOTES

[1]Henry Popkin, "The Drama," in Lewis Leary (ed.), *Contemporary Literature Scholarship. A Critical Review* (New York: Appleton-Century-Crofts,
Inc., 1958), pp. 292-298.

[2]Francis Fergusson, *The Idea of a Theater* (Garden City, N. Y.: Doubleday
and Company, Inc., 1955), p. 242.

[3]Fergusson, p. 248.

[4]S. H. Butcher (trans.), *Aristotle's Poetics* (New York: Hill and Wang,
1961), p. 61.

[5]Gusta B. Nance, Professor Emeritus of Comparative Literature, Southern
Methodist University and Professor of English, Dallas Baptist College,
unpublished lecture.

[6]Lane Cooper, *Aristotle on the Art of Poetry* (Revised edition; Ithaca:
Cornell University Press, 1947), pp. 13-14.

[7]S. H. Butcher, *Aristotle's Theory of Poetry and Fine Art* (Fourth edition;
New York: Dover Publications, 1951), p. 241.

[8]Edmond Rostand, *Cyrano de Bergerac* (Paris: Librairie Charpentier et
Fasquelle, 1930), Act V, scene 5.

[9]Preston H. Epps (trans.), *The Poetics of Aristotle* (Chapel Hill: The
University of North Carolina Press, 1942), p. 13. Hereinafter cited as

[10]S. H. Butcher, *Aristotle's Poetics*, p. 81.

[11]These characteristics of a romantic hero are those discussed by George
Ross Ridge in *The Hero in French Romantic Literature* (Athens: University of Georgia Press, 1959).

[12]Edmond Rostand, *Cyrano de Bergerac*, Act V, scene 6.

[13]Gusta B. Nance, unpublished lecture.

Edward Freeman (essay date 1995)

SOURCE: "*Cyrano de Bergerac*: Mythopoeia Triumphant,"
in *Cyrano de Bergerac*, University of Glasgow French and
German Publications, 1995, pp. 21-47.

[*In the following essay, Freeman considers* Cyrano de
Bergerac *"the perfect vehicle for one of the most comprehensive, polyvalent pieces of myth-making in nineteenth-century French literature."*]

The rapturous reception that was granted to **Cyrano de
Bergerac** by its first-night audience can be accounted for
by the enormity of the conception of the play. In his three
previous full-length plays, Rostand had cast around, with
only moderate success . . . , to develop a style and find a
subject that suited him. Now, in moving from Jesus Christ
[in **La Samaritaine**] to the infinitely less austere figure of
Cyrano de Bergerac, whose *Entretiens pointus* have been
called by Jacques Prévot 'une mise en question ludique
du langage conventionnel', Rostand can give full rein to
his inclination to be linguistically audacious, to create

for himself scenic and verbal challenges of a complexity unprecedented in French theatre history. The result is a vast work four hours long in most performances—that is the perfect vehicle for one of the most comprehensive, polyvalent pieces of myth-making in nineteenth-century French literature. Few plays in any nation's caltural history have ever arrived so opportunely to fill a vacuum:

> Depuis trente ans, le théâtre cherchait une formule de renouvellent, et les tentatives qu'il faisait en tous sens n'aboutissaient qu'à nous mettre à l'école de l'étranger et à étouffer l'esprit national dans l'obscurité ou dans une sorte de neurasthénie brutale. Tout d'un coup, sonna le verbe clair de Cyrano; l'enthousiasme fut indescriptible, exorbitant, excessif; il manifestait la joie de la foule qui exultait parce qu'elle avait retrouvé l'esprit français.

(Calvet, p. 173)

The century that began with Chateaubriand, Hugo and Gautier—and not forgetting Emmanuel Las Cases, biographer of Napoléon I—was both more grandiose and more narcissistic in its myth-making than any other in French history. Rostand ended the century in the same vein. The 'French spirit' that Rostand's audiences were believed by Calvet to have rediscovered in **Cyrano de Bergerac** had, at its core, that amalgam of 1830s' Romantic idealism and Cornelian *générosité*; associated with the age of Louis XIII which Hugo and his contemporaries had tried to capture in some of their works. The central fibre of this core was honorable and if need be, and it usually was, self-sacrificial conduct in the pursuit of love. It had not been greatly in evidence in the French theatre of the 1890s.

LOVE

The same would appear to be true of the real world inhabited by the historical Savinien de Cyrano de Bergerac and his libertine friends Dassoucy and Chapelle. Contemporary accounts suggest that the young Cyrano mixed in a circle of debauchees who spent a lot of time and money (although not much of the latter in Cyrano's case) in drinking and gambling. There are hints that Cyrano may have had a homosexual character—the 'dangereux penchant' hinted at by Le Bret, who elsewhere writes of Cyrano's 'si grande retenue envers le beau Sexe, qu'on peut dire qu'il n'est jamais sorty du respect que le nôtre lui doit'.

Three hundred years later, Jeanne Goldin puts it less coyly: 'Tout ce qui est lié à la physiologie et aux fonctions purement féminines provoque, chez Cyrano, un dégoût qui intéresserait les psychiatres, et il ira jusqu'à expliquer les cas de possession par 'quelques suffocations de matrice' (Goldin, p. 40). Jacques Prévot has very similar doubts about Cyrano's intimate relationships with women, basing them on a detailed analysis of the coded allusions to 'desire' in his *Lettres amoureuses* (*Cyrano de Bergerac poete et dramaturge*, pp. 45-50). In fact Prévot concludes that Dassoucy's *Aventures burlesques* clearly point to Cyrano's homosexual character. At any rate the great restraint towards the fair sex attributed to Cyrano by Le Bret cannot

have been total, for at one stage he had to have long and expensive treatment for syphilis. The illness may even have hastened the end of his short life; this is as plausible a cause as the head injury caused by a falling plank, which occurred fourteen months before his death.

The historical Cyrano, who might thus in his psychosexual nature and general life style have had a certain amount in common two centuries later with a number of Rostand's *fin-de-siècle* predecessors and contemporaries, is totally transformed by the dramatist into something quite different: a sighing gallant, adoring his cousin Magdeleine Robin, by her *précieux* name 'Roxane', from afar. The sublime love that has taken possession of him is destined to be unrequited, or so he believes, because of his misfortune in being endowed with a grotesque nose, 'ce nez qui d'un quart d'heure en tous lieux me précède' (I.v, l. 494). Hugo's Ruy Blas, similarly in thrall to the Queen of Spain, had merely to progress from the state of lackey to prime minister to win her love; Cyrano, for want of the modern science of rhinoplasty, has no such hope. By an inversion that could not have been more typical of Hugo, Roxane loves Christian, who is the antithesis of Cyrano in being sublimely handsome but (of course) grotesquely inept, inarticulate, tongue-tied. He is incapable of pursuing his own courtship of Roxane without the (of course) sublimely altruistic prompting, literally, of Cyrano. We have come a long way from the quarrel between the historic Cyrano and Dassoucy (and the flight of the latter to Italy) over the bedding of a *spitted* 'chapon', i.e. castrato (Prévot, *loc. cit.*, pp 48-9).

Cyrano's heroic sacrifice in furthering Christian's cause is the central theme of the play, and dominates it from start to finish. Rostand exploits a gamut of human situations, escalating in both pathos and dramatic ingenuity, in presenting *générosité*; as the outstanding feature of Cyrano's character. Cyrano writes love letters for his 'rival' and prompts him in the balcony scene (III.vii) with such refined language that he can be quite sure that Roxane is falling in love with *his* words rather than the body and person of Christian. The next logical phase is the definitive sacrifice of his hopes in enabling Christian and Roxane to marry by delaying de Guiche, who has his own plans for Roxane, for a crucial quarter of an hour (III.xiv). By the time this has been achieved, at the end of Act Three, over 1,700 alexandrines have been delivered, almost as many as in a seventeenth-century classical play, and we have witnessed a considerable amount of complex stage action. This is enough material for a similar comedy of amorous quiproquo by Molière, Marivaux or the Beaumarchais of *Le Barbier de Séville* (perhaps *Le Mariage de Figaro* is the only precedent of similar substance to **Cyrano de Bergerac**).

But to suppose that the play could ever have ended at this point, in a kind of platonic coitus interruptus (in the way that *Le Mariage* might arguably have ended after Act Four) is to fail to do justice to the fertility of Rostand's imagination in exploring and exhausting all the psychological possibilities of the love theme. Cyrano dominates the play, but that is not to say that the other characters are pale ciphers. Both Christian and Roxane still have their greatest dramatic moments ahead of them. In Act IV, which is based on the historical siege of Arras in 1640, Rostand invents for Christian an appalling realization: that Cyrano, the writer of countless love letters, ostensibly on his behalf, loves Roxane. And what goes with this is the sudden and shocking awareness that Roxane in turn loves the writer of the letters.

When she asserts that she would even love him if he were ugly, he is hit by a terrible truth: he has enjoyed a love that should have been Cyrano's. The devastation is all the more total for resulting from Roxane's innocent 'Je t'aimerais encore! / Si toute ta beauté tout d'un coup s'envolait . . .' (IV.viii, ll. 2146-7). Never was a fervent declaration of love more deadly. Only Racine could manufacture a scene of tragic irony of such power; certainly there is none such in Hugo (we spot all his shocks looming up well in advance: does anyone watching *Le Roi s'amuse*, soon to be Verdi's *Rigoletto*, not know whose body is in the sack?). Christian is destroyed; throwing himself into the battle with an ardour that is nothing less than suicidal, he is mortally wounded (IV.x). It remains for Cyrano to commit one more sublime gesture: he prevents Christian from dying in a state of despair by pretending that he has told the truth to Roxane and she still loves him nevertheless.

As if that is not enough, there remains a whole act for Rostand to squeeze the last drops of pathos out of the sublimated love of Cyrano for Roxane. For fourteen years Christian's devoted widow has been allowed to persist in the illusion that her vast stock of love letters were all written by Christian. The scene (V.v) in which, once again, a terrible truth pierces an innocent consciousness is another fine example of Rostand's feeling for dramatic moment. And yet again, too, credit must be given to Rostand for the skill with which he breathes fresh life into existing dramatic devices. One of the hoariest, and dullest, of them is the last-act reading out aloud of a letter that makes all clear. And it is not not unknown for this to coincide with the falling of dusk. It settles, with the final curtain, on a momentous day, an expiring life, a doomed social class, an era that can never come again. But now Rostand conjoins and exploits both clichés with an ingenuity for which critics have not given him sufficient credit.

As darkness falls, Roxane accedes to the dying Cyrano's request to be allowed to see Christian's last letter, ostensibly for the first time. When he 'reads' the letter aloud, we are prepared, I think, for her surprise at hearing 'une voix [. . .] que je n'entends pas pour la première fois'. But the moment when the truth *dawns* upon Roxane in the dusk—when she suddenly 'sees' in the darkness that Cyrano cannot possibly be reading the letter—is a remarkable exploitation of the distinctive properties of theatre. Theories of *spécificité*, could do far worse than start here.

If Cyrano is able to recite the letter in the darkness there can only be one reason: he knows it by heart. For Roxane, a series of conclusions logically follows: he knows it because he wrote it (and all the other letters); he wrote them because he loved her (and still does). When Le Bret and Ragueneau burst in, he is prevented from answering the question she can not repress: 'Alors pourquoi laisser ce sublime silence se briser aujourd'hui?' One of the earliest English editors of the play is in one sense right: 'he betrays a secret that he ought to have carried with him to the grave, for the sake of a dead man's memory' (Ashton edition, p. vii). And for the sake of the widow's peace of mind thereafter: Cyrano is fallible as well as mortal. Having only a few moments to live, he cannot find it within him to die without letting Roxane know the truth. As his life ebbs away, he devises the last of the many scenarios he has acted out during the course of the play. As Lauxerois puts it in his edition (p. 205): 'cette lecture [est] l'unique solution entre la parole et le silence'. It is an inspired piece of invention on the part of Rostand to have it divulged in this way, and within a few minutes of stage time at the first performance in 1897, the first of the forty curtain calls was ringing out.

Great and heroic love cannot be repressed. Fourteen years of sublime and stoic silence are enough for anyone: that was what four hundred successive French audiences were evidently happy to hear in 1897-1898. This picture of sublime love and sublimated sexuality made a considerable change from what was normally on offer to Parisian theatregoers in the 1890s. Most of them might have been quite content to ogle the bed-hopping *cocottes* of Feydeau's *L'Hôtel du Libre-échange* (1894) and *La Dame de chez Maxim's* (1891) or enjoy the socially smarter and less sexually manic titillation of *Amoureuse* by Georges de Porto-Riche (1891) and *Les Amants* by Maurice Donnay (1895). Certain dramatists, such as Curel and Brieux, were capable of treating sexual themes and their socio-moral ramifications in a serious and responsible way. In the more audacious plays of the era, which reflected the influence of the newly imported work of the foreign masters, even sexual promiscuity, nymphomania and syphilis were no longer the taboo subjects that they had been twenty years previously. Even when discussion was not explicit, it needed little imagination to tune in to the vibrations coursing through the eponymous heroine of Strindberg's *Miss Julie* or to realize what Oswald was dying of in Ibsen's *Ghosts*.

This was strong meat, but for a while there was stronger on offer. In 1891 the Théâtre Réaliste presented *Prostituée, La Gueuse, La Crapule, La Morte violée* and *L'Avortement* before the author-actor, one Chirac, was eventually put behind bars (see Henderson, pp. 81-2). From this Naturalist perspective, although admittedly it is a caricatural extreme, we are in a better position to appreciate the extensive mythopoeic process at work in **Cyrano de Bergerac** in so far as it embraces not just the hero but Roxane, Christian and even the cadets de Gascogne.

The *précieuse* Roxane has been transformed in Act Five into an ethereally devout and chaste widow, eternally impossible for Cyrano to love except via his after ego, the *personne interposée* of Christian. She could not be further removed from the 'belles aventurières espagnoles et italiennes, voluptueuses et fières créatures, aimant d'un égal amour l'or, le sang et les parfums,' etc, conjured up from the fertile recesses of his own imagination by Gautier (*Les Grotesques*, p. 235) to be the female attractions for the youthful Cyrano 'qui voit Paris pour la première fois'. She and her friends, *marquis* and *précieuses* alike, are a far cry again from the *lurons* who were the real Cyrano's social and sexual familiars.

The mythopoeic process requires that the rest of the play too be bathed in an atmosphere of chivalric fantasy. De Guiche, before redeeming himself as a courageous military commander in Act Four, shapes up to behave like a sinister Buckingham in Dumas's *Trois Mousquetaires* or similar figures in Hugo's plays who do in fact seduce, abduct, rape and kill women. Yet the menace inherent in his unchecked personal authority comes to nothing: the decorum of the sexual climate in **Cyrano de Bergerac** belongs to a far more ideal world than that of French Romantic literature generally. The assimilation of the play to the theatre of Victor Hugo is made often enough, but it is perhaps too facile in at least that one respect. Love in **Cyrano de Bergerac** is essentialized and platonized in a way that points both to Rostand's adolescent study of d'Urfé and to contemporary *fin-de-siècle* influences that were in fact to stay with him for the rest of his career.

To take another example, and one to which we shall return in discussing the war theme, the camp of the cadets de Gascogne at the siege of Arras, so far from evoking the atmosphere of brutality that abounded in the Thirty Years' War, recalls nothing so much as a soldiers' chorus in light opera. It is a company of well-scrubbed and sentimental young men, all identical carbon copies, and emitting not a note of that sexual menace implicit in the designation 'soudards et reîtres' (thugs, brutes) with which Christian tries to warn off Roxane. The Spanish enemy is every bit as decent, indeed, as Latins, perhaps even more so. This is how Roxane breached the enemy lines:

> J'ai simplement passé dans mon carrosse, au trot.
> Si quelque hidalgo montrait sa mine altière,
> Je mettais mon plus beau sourire à la portière,
> Et ces messieurs étant, n'en déplaise aux Français,
> Les plus galantes gens du monde, je passais!

(IV.v, ll. 1952-6)

For the jaded Parisian palate of the late 1890s, then, a significant part of the appeal of **Cyrano de Bergerac** was that it celebrated a code of romantic love and chivalry associated with another age. Superficially at least, a reading of Dumas *père* had already implanted this escapist, heroic ethic in the mythic imagination of the audiences at the Théâtre de la Porte-Saint-Martin. In Venus they had 'retrouvé l'esprit français'; but what of Mars?

ARMS AND THE MAN

Rostand's mythopoeic powers were put to the test far less with Cyrano's martial exploits than with his venereal activities. 'Le démon de la bravoure' is how Le Bret described him in the posthumous biography of 1657 (namely the preface to the *États et empires de la Lune*, the edition republished by the Bibliophile Jacob in 1858 and used by Rostand). The phrase had been picked up and embellished by Gautier in 1844. Cyrano's prowess as a soldier and swordsman, which is so central a part of the heroic national myth of 1897, is based on four details culled from Le Bret. In 1639 Cyrano fought at the siege of Mouzon and was wounded by a musket ball. He then fought at the siege of Arras in 1640 and received a sword wound in the neck. He rapidly achieved notoriety in the duelling culture of his fellows, the Gascon company of Carbon de Castel-Jaloux, and served as a second 'plus de cent fois'. Le Bret would have us believe he also took on a *hundred* opponents (a favourite hyperbole, obviously) in a sword fight at the Porte de Nesle and left two for dead, seven seriously injured, and, we must suppose, ninety-one very shaken. This account is supplied in minimal form by Le Bret, and with little comment.

Gautier adds not very much more, restricting himself to the ironic observation, a propos of the fact that Cyrano's military career was all over by the time he was twenty, 'c'est commencer de bonne heure, et bien des braves militaires servent toute leur vie sans avoir cette bonne fortune d'être aussi honorablement blessés' (*Les Grotesques*, p. 244). He also embroiders colourfully on the theme of the Porte de Nesle incident. The implausible 100-1 odds were already in Le Bret, but the fight now becomes 'cette bataille digne du cid Campéador'. Of the curious statement by Le Bret that although Cyrano was a second in one hundred duels, he never fought in one on his own account, Gautier repeats not a word. He had in fact many pages earlier filled out his virtuoso opening introduction to the essay, three pages on the subject of the nose, by stating that Cyrano would fight a duel with anyone visibly startled by the sight of the exorbitant organ. Gautier's Cyrano is in fact the one to be inherited by Rostand fifty years later: the impetuous *bretteur* who will unsheath at the drop of a hat, a glove, a misplaced reflection.

The main dynamic of Act One is the establishing of Cyrano's character as an eccentric Renaissance intellectual, famous not least for his swordsmanship. In advance of his appearance on stage, his acquaintances describe him in a series of superlatives and absolutes as 'cet homme [. . .] des moins ordinaires' (l. 99), 'le plus exquis des êtres sublunaires' (l. 100), 'Rimeur','Bretteur', 'Physicien','Musicien' (l. 101). But they observe above all that'c'est un garçon versé dans les colichemardes' (l. 95), 'le plus fol spadassin' (l. 107), and that 'il [. . .] pourfend quiconque le remarque' (l. 119). In fact the historical figure that Rostand has chosen to enhance in this way was at this stage of his life, in 1640, an almost totally unknown young man of nineteen or twenty, enjoying a brief interlude between his two short and somewhat unglorious military campaigns. His years as a student of Gassendi lie ahead of him. He will become a literary *touche-à-tout* and a general intellectual dabbler, but never an eminent scientist or musician.

A far greater portion of the imagery in this sequence (contained mostly in the pastrycook Ragueneau's speech) relates to his physical appearance. At first with his 'feutre à panache triple', pourpoint à six basques', 'cape', etc., he resembles nothing so much as a stereotypical, *image d'Épinal* musketeer from the time of Louis XIII to be found in many a Romantic novel or play of the 1820s and 1830s, not just those of Dumas *père*. And to the continuing superlatives, 'plus fier que tous les Artabans', etc, is added a curious kind of conglomerate lexical hyperbole in that the weapon that he itches to unsheath is now a 'colichemarde', now 'l'estoc', now 'son glaive'. Later in the Act it is 'une épée' and 'un espadon'. But then an even more distinctive Rostandian note of fantasy takes over, a comic extravaganza of similarly disparate cultural allusions: 'Monsieur Philippe de Champaigne', 'feu Jacques Callot', 'Artabans', 'l'alme Mère Gigogne', 'Pulcinella, des ciseaux de la Parque'. And what is now indelibly imprinted on the spectator / reader's retina is the physical profile of Cyrano with his nose ('ce nez-là' rhyming with 'Pulcinella'!) and his plumed headgear, as a strutting *coq gaulois*. His sword causes his cloak at the back to lift up 'comme une queue insolente de coq' and is the most striking feature of a sketch done by the author himself. Thus does Rostand establish an image of Cyrano as fiery, fearless and French, in fact 'doublement Français, puisqu'il est gascon'.[1]

The rest of the act is a demonstration of Cyrano's fiery temperament. He banishes Champfleury from the stage after only three lines of his performance of Baro's *Clorise*, and in a packed audience containing not a few people of influence and high office (Richelieu!), not one is man enough at first to defy him. He then humiliates the marquis de Valvert; the act closes with him going off to defend the poet Lignière against the hundred men who wait in ambush for him. Thus far Rostand's Cyrano, as an obstreperous, sword-happy 'Gascon' is not so very different from the countless *fier-à-bras, rodomonts, fanfarons, artabans, matamores* that strut and swagger through European literature from the late Middle Ages onwards, continuing a tradition dating back in fact to the *miles glorious* of Plautus. In that respect Cyrano as a *commedia* type would already have been embedded in the cultural consciousness of Rostand's spectators in 1897 (although presumably rather more of them would have met him in Gautier's *Le Capitaine Fracasse* and Dumas *père*—Rostand has Cyrano congratulated by d'Artagnan, no less—than in Ariosto and La Calprenède).

An aggressive hero of such proportions made a change from the etiolated protagonists of symbolist and decadent literature of the 1890s. Yet it is not what critics are thinking of when they point to the *esprit cocardier* that was stimulated by the play, and which gave such a boost

to French patriotism and military pride at a very sensitive time. To understand why the play had this impact, it is not to the *commedia* braggart, taking on a hundred opponents, that we must look, but to the somewhat different Cyrano of Act Four and his fellow professional soldiers at the siege of Arras. This act occupies a climactic position in the play's structure, and Rostand's mythopoeic enhancement of the role of Cyrano, and through him of the military glory of France, is worth some attention.

It is known that Rostand studied Achmet d'Héricourt's *Les Sièges d'Arras* (1845) and the *Mémoires of the Maréchal de Gramont* (1826) to understand the military operations involved. This is not a lot of preparatory reading, and the latter work is in any case that of a very interested party, the much-promoted Comte de Guiche. That may be of no account, since Rostand is a dramatist not a historian. The fact remains that it is not easy to refute the claim that via this very substantial element of ***Cyrano de Bergerac,*** placed at a strategic point in a play that elsewhere lays great store by feats of arms and military swagger, Rostand has constructed an apologia for war and a paean to French bravura and genius—panache—in the conduct of it.

The historical truth is somewhat different. French military involvement in the Thirty Years' War was low-key, thanks almost entirely to the European-wide political skills of Richelieu. This was how it had to be: in the 1630s, France had not been a major European fighting force for a long time. The country's military capability trailed behind that of the Imperial Habsburgs and even the Swedes and the Dutch as regards arms, equipment, drills, discipline and logistical organization. As a historian has put it, 'Richelieu had a low opinion of the fighting spirit of the French, urged Feuquières to recruit in Germany, and he tried, like Henri IV, to entice the peasants of the Val Telline to serve in the French army' (Treasure, p. 193). Thus the great military battles of the Thirty Years' War, the White Mountain, Lützen, Breitenfeld, the first battle of Nördlingen, and the carnage that accompanied them and notorious atrocities like the sack of Magdeburg in 1631, were experienced mainly by others.

France's political and territorial gains at the end of the Thirty Years' War in 1648, on the other hand, were significant, and were obtained by clever diplomacy and proxy warfare. Such victories as were won by French feats of arms were relatively minor ones like Rocroi and Arras. Full-scale pitched battles against the Spanish, such as Rocroi in 1635, were rare; the siege of Arras in 1640 usually merits only the merest of mentions in histories of the Thirty Years' War.

And what of Gascon involvement in all of this? A statistical analysis by Robert Chaboche of the regional origins of French troops shows that Gascon troop numbers, although slightly higher than those from other provinces of the south, were nothing like those of provinces close to the action such as Île-de-France, Picardy, Champagne and Normandy (Chaboche, pp. 10-24). The Gascons were probably outnumbered by Irish, Germans and Swiss. The overall picture, although unavailable to Rostand before the findings of modern historians, is somewhat different from the one we are presented with in *Cyrano de Bergerac.* As Treasure again puts it:

> An English mercenary, already eleven years a campaigner in the Thirty Years' War, remarked on the difference between the French army at the start of its first season of war, the cavalry crested with feathers and resplendent in scarlet and silver lace, and the ragged deserters who stole away, officers as well as men, before the end.

(p. 192)

But history is one thing, creative literature and theatre roughly based on it are quite another. 'Turoldus' does not appear to have been inhibited by the unavailability of Basque and Arab archives from composing the *Chanson de Roland.* By the end of the 1640s, as Turenne gained in experience, France was emerging as a major military power and gradually breaking the stranglehold of the Habsburgs. Rostand, in *Cyrano de Bergerac,* thus unearthed and held up for admiration what with a little stretch of the imagination could be regarded as a glorious precedent, a balm for the French inferiority complex of the 1890s vis-à-vis Germany. To that part of the nation still suffering psychologically from the lingering wound of Sedan, one of the greatest humiliations in all military history; still feeling the phantom twitches of the severed limbs that were Alsace and Lorraine; increasingly fearful of suspected German machinations; and resignedly voting vast budgetary sums to the arms race of the 1890s, *Cyrano de Bergerac* was a prodigious morale-booster. Marshal Bazaine had surrendered in Metz in 1870 with an army of 170,000 well-equipped men; General Boulanger had shown not much more stomach for a political fight in 1889 and had run away to his mistress in Brussels. But Rostand's commander de Guiche, once he has been provoked into redeeming himself by Cyrano's mention of Henri IV, foregoes his right to retire from the most dangerous zone of action, stays to lead and fight, and saves the day . . . and the lady. Why then, two hundred and fifty years later, should not France again emerge from under the shadow of a powerful neighbour possessing an awesome military machine? And might not war lead to enduring peace? Did France have cause to fear Spain ever again after the end of the Thirty Years' War? It it could happen to the Habsburgs, it could happen to the the Hohenzollerns.

So we see then in *Cyrano de Bergerac* an epic, heroic comedy that plays up military ardour, glory, unfailing courage. These are symbolised by the *panache* associated with the name of Henri IV, whose legendary cry 'Ralliez-vous à mon panache blanc!' would have been lodged in the imagination of every bourgeois patriot in the nineteenth century. Unlike de Guiche at Bapaume, Henri IV would not have abandoned his commander's sash to get out of a tight corner. 'Mais on n'abdique pas l'honneur d'être une cible' (IV.iv, 1. 1862) mocks Cyrano, who—in yet one

more preposterous *coup de théâtre* in a play that groans beneath their weight—has braved a hail of grapeshot to retrieve the sash. Against superior numbers and superior arms, French courage in its supercharged Gascon form is a priceless asset. *In extremis*, it may be the only one. No commentator appears to have noticed the significance of Cyrano's contemptuous, and for once laconic, dismissal of his master's cunning plan to break the siege by espionage and subterfuge. De Guiche's complacent lines, as he makes contact with a Spaniard who is in his pay, are of great interest against the background of the ongoing Dreyfus case and what it revealed about mutual suspicion, espionage and manipulation by Germany and France:

> C'est un faux espion espagnol. Il nous rend
> De grands services. Les renseignements qu'il porte
> Aux ennemis sont ceux que je lui donne, en sorte
> Que l'on peut influer sur leurs décisions.

(IV.iv, ll. 1876-9)

'C'est un gredin' is Cyrano's opinion of the enemy soldier whose venality is the opportunity for the French to save their skins. It is not the Gascon way. Nor, by implication, should it be the French way. The professional soldier Hulot has a similar view of such methods in Balzac's ambivalent novel about war and social disorder *Les Chouans*, yet another Romantic novel that Rostand would have known well from his *lycée* days.

As much as he reinforces an aristocratic ethic of military honour and courage, and pushes back on to his horse, so to speak, an aristocrat who momentarily forget himself, Rostand plays down, indeed totally omits, the real horrors of the Thirty Years' War, the suffering of the common people, famine, riots, insurrections, devastation and religious fanaticism. Callot is mentioned in the second scene of the play, but it is the Callot of the picturesque *Caprices* (for the purpose of contextualizing Cyrano's grotesque appearance—and his name makes an excellent *rime riche* with 'falot'!) not the same Callot whose *Miseries of War* is one of the most poignant records of that tragic era.

The miseries—if that is a strong enough word in respect of a novel in which the large-scale experience of mangled limbs, gangrene, excruciating pain is described in stark and insistent detail—had been a notable feature of Zola's novel about the Franco-Prussian War, *La Débâcle.* It was published in 1892, some twenty-two years after the event, yet only five years before the first performance of *Cyrano de Bergerac.* We surely cannot doubt that Rostand was familiar with it, yet in as much as *any* literary inspiration lay behind Act Four, it is as if he had read nothing since *Les Trois Mousquetaires.*

In a chapter contributed to a thematic work of war history, Adrienne Hytier notes that in these years 'le nombre de candidatures à Saint-Cyr double', and that *revanchards* like Déroulède and Maurras fuelled the fires of nationalism.[2] About the same time, an antimilitarist, pacifist current—smaller and doubtless socially courageous—began to flow. Writers and journalists such as Abel Hermant, Henri Fèvre, Lucien Descaves and Georges Darien began to pull liberals and left-wing Republicans towards the position adopted by Jean Jaurès in the years immediately preceding the First World War. Rostand had to live with a dilemma. *Cyrano de Bergerac* could easily be recuperated by nationalists as late as thirty years after the Franco-Prussian War, and it continued to be popular in the run-up to the First World War, in which, if he had been physically fit, Rostand would willingly have been a combatant. Over seventeen thousand copies of the play were sold in 1917 alone; a derived version by Jean Suberville, *Cyrano de Bergerac aux tranchées*, was published in 1918 with a preface by Rostand. Yet he was far from being the natural ally of the ultra-conservatives who formed their ranks during the precise period of twenty years separating the beginning of the Dreyfus affair and the outbreak of the First World War. It is interesting to note that a copy of Zola's *Paris* was personally dedicated by him to the playwright when it was published in March 1898. The Rostand who was courageous enough to lend his name to the cause of Dreyfus, in defiance of the pro-military elements and interested parties that might naturally derive satisfaction from, and exploit, the patriotism of *Cyrano de Bergerac,* was the late Romantic who had transformed a pre-Classical *miles gloriosus* into a thoroughly nineteenth-century Idealist and Poet. If the play is an apologia for war, it is for war to be fought honorably and in a spirit of idealism, and for its apologists to be the first into the trenches. Rostand may have been naïve, but he was never a rogue.

THE POET

LE VICOMTE: *méprisant* Poète . . . !

CYRANO: Oui, monsieur, poète!

(Liv, l. 394)

Rostand's Cyrano the lover-warrior is also an intellectual, a creator, a poet. Rostand is known to have read most of his seventeenth-century model's work that would have been available for consultation in the 1890s. He also documented himself about the cultural climate of the pre-classical period before Cyrano's death in 1655; he was no stranger to it in any case since his prize-winning essay on d'Urfé and Zola. The *Dictionnaire des Précieuses* by Somaize (1660), Chappuzeau's *Théâtre français* (1674) and the *Dictionnaire critique de biographie et d'histoire* by Auguste Jal (1872) were among a number of scholarly sources called upon. The zeal with which he created an accurate cultural background to the action of Act One has in fact been mildly criticized by Truchet for its naïveté and didacticism. The latter is no doubt right when he situates the reception of *Cyrano de Bergerac* from a sociological point of view in the educational context of the Third Republic. A section of the audience at the Théâtre de la Porte-Saint-Martin was a popular one. To understand its response, Truchet suggests:

Il faut se reporter aux temps héroïques des débuts de l'enseignement primaire obligatoire. Régnait alors, dans le sillage des instituteurs, un touchant appétit de savoir, une foi quelque peu naïve en l'acquisition des connaissances par toutes sortes de moyens, parmi lesquels le théâtre; on allait voir, certes, *Cyrano* pour le plaisir, mais on y allait aussi pour s'instruire. D'où parfois, de la part de l'auteur, un didactisme un peu lourd, qui se manifeste particulièrement vers le début de la pièce, pour reconstituer une atmosphère, enseigner des noms (Philippe de Champaigne, Callot, Rotrou par exemple, ou Montfleury, Jodelet, Bellerose), donner des informations sur des hommes célèbres; ainsi ce vers: "Tiens! Monsieur de Corneille est arrivé de Rouen!" (I, ii).

(Truchet edition, pp. 34-5)

Also among the early audiences was one Émile Magne, a young man of twenty very conscious of having far more than a primary education, and eager to demonstrate it. Within months of the first night of the play, his *Les Erreurs de documentation de 'Cyrano de Bergerac'* (*La Revue de France*, 1898) lavishes sarcasm on Rostand: 'Entrer un instant à l'Arsenal, compulser quelques livres traitant du XVIIe siècle n'eut [*sic*] point constitué un acte d'extrême virilité. Mais Monsieur Rostand est un des admirateurs de celui qui établit le fameux principe du moindre effort et sa comédie s'en ressent' (Magne, p. xii). In the end Truchet's aesthetic objections, his reproaches about the clumsy expository style, are more pertinent than Magne's forensic indignation about Rostand's anachronisms. Magne was scandalised that Rostand believed Baro's *Clorise* was first performed in 1640 (instead of 1631), that Richelieu could have attended a performance of such a mediocre play, that there could ever have been illegal duelling in his presence, etc. Rostand coped serenely with Magne's vituperation and informed him that there were more anachronisms and 'errors' in the play that had not yet been spotted—a teasing provocation to more erudition on Magne's part. The latter's diatribe has most aptly been described by Brun as 'un pavé énorme pour écraser un brillant papillon' (Brun, p. 7): unlike the *pavé de l'ours* in La Fontaine's fable (and Feydeau's curtain-raiser), this brickbat is certainly not hurled well-meaningly.

Appropriately, *Le Pédant joué*, Cyrano's only comedy, is the subject of a more arcane *clin d'œil* by Rostand to the erudite. In the final act, as Cyrano is dying, Ragueneau expresses his disgust that Molière's *Les Fourberies de Scapin* (not in fact performed until 1671!) has apparently plagiarized Cyrano's comic line, put into the mouth of the pedant Granger: 'Que Diable aller faire dans la Galère d'un Turc?' The literary allusion is this time handled more subtly by Rostand than those of Act One. It is once again an example of what Truchet calls 'les charmes de la pièce pour les spectateurs qui avaient fait des études.' The author flatters his audience by allowing it the satisfaction of supplying the full title of the play referred to as *Scapin* and of completing Molière's famous line 'Que diable allait-il faire [. . .] dans cette galère?'. The culmination of the intertextual tease for an educated audience participating in a theatrical crossword puzzle is that Rostand does not tell them what play of Cyrano's the line and scene are taken from.

However, the whole incident is of thematic importance. In his dying moments Cyrano is essentialized as generous. 'Chut! Chut! Il a bien fait!' is his comment on Molière's plagiarism, which any of Rostand's audience who had read *Les Grotesques* would have seen described by Gautier as 'le plus effronté plagiat qu'il se puisse voir'. Ragueneau reports that the scene provoked much laughter. Molière enjoyed a success that with a little more effort and luck on Cyrano's part could have been Cyrano's—and perhaps with a little more probity on Molière's part should have been. Cyrano regrets his lack of success as a writer: 'Oui, ma vie / Ce fut d'être celui qui souffle,—et qu'on oublie!', but is not bitter: 'C'est justice, et j'approuve au seuil de mon tombeau.' The very next line, with its binary rhythm and personal absolutes, encapsulates the nineteenth-century conception of the lover-poet's condition: 'Molière a du génie et Christian était beau'. Cyrano has been graced by neither genius nor beauty, but he has clung proudly to his independence. This interpretation of Cyrano de Bergerac as a Romantic, a dramatic poet who suffers and dies for his principles and for his misfortunes, a noble idealist in a grubby world of hard-headed opportunists, concludes the play and is our abiding vision of Rostand's hero as an incarnation of 'l'esprit français'.

Gautier's vehement denunciation of Molière's plagiarism—if indeed it was one—for being one of the most shameless thefts in cultural history is an appropriate reminder that the Romantic thesis underlying *Les Grotesques* is fundamental to Rostand's conception of Cyrano *qua* poet. Not just of Cyrano, but of his fellow-poets Lignières and Ragueneau and the cohort of 'poètes affamés' of the first two acts of the play, the second of which is actually given the title 'La Rôtisserie des Poètes'. Rostand's Lignière is based in name at least on the real François Payot de Lignières (1628-1704) whom Le Bret counted among Cyrano's friends. He incarnates various features of the Romantic tradition of the poet inherited from Rutebeuf and Villon that Gautier and his fellow anti-Classicists would have admired: poor, a lover of the *dive bouteille*, disapproved of by Boileau, a scourge of the high and mighty—and a potential victim as a consequence ('Une chanson qu'il fit blessa quelqu'un de grand' I.iii, l. 157). 'Poète!' is the anathema, sufficient as an absolute, thrown at Cyrano by the Vicomte, a representative of the same class that organized the hundred against one ambush of Lignières. With the difference that he is a teetotaller, a detail retained from Le Bret, according to whom Cyrano considered drink to be as lethal as arsenic, but given minimal treatment in the play, Rostand's subversive hero is a kindred spirit to Lignière(s) in making enemies among the influential, with in his case fatal consequences.

For the Romantics, poetry should be what it allegedly once was, a joyous, creative activity, rooted in the life of the common people, before it was appropriated and emasculated by courtiers and academicians in the middle of the seventeenth century. Before then, they imagined, poetry could be loved and created by peasants . . . and pastrycooks. Once again an important character of the play, Ragueneau, is based on a historical figure. Cyprien Ragueneau was a pastrycook obsessed with poetry—'portant comme un autre Atlas tout le faix de l'Etat poétique' (Dassoucy, *Aventures burlesques*,)—who finished his days, as in the play, as mediocre an actor as a poet. It is against this background that Rostand's Cyrano must be seen. His opinion of Roxane's *précieux* friends could not be more forthright: 'des singes' (III.iii, l. 1297). He is far more at home wherever poetry is spontaneous, improvised for the pleasure of a popular audience—if necessary, while fighting a duel. In Cyrano's case the result is a far better formal ballad than Ragueneau's recipe in verse for *tartelettes amandines*. Although Rostand omits to exploit a detail to be found in Le Bret—'Je le vis un jour dans un corps de garde travailler à une élégie avec aussi peu de distraction que s'il eût été dans un cabinet fort éloigné du bruit'—clearly, poetic creation in **Cyrano de Bergerac** is part of everyday life, anything but a salon activity.

The five-act structure chosen by Rostand elides the whole period from 1640 to 1655, in which Cyrano's literary career was concentrated. Yet it cannot be said that the final vision of Cyrano as a *poète maudit*, the last in a line from Baudelaire to Rimbaud, Verlaine and Laforgue, is inconsistent with the Cyrano of 1640 as portrayed in the earlier acts. In Act Five, de Guiche, now promoted from the *comte* who fought at Arras to the rank of *duc-maréchal*, regrets that at the pinnacle of his career he feels 'mille petits dégoûts de soi'. Cyrano, however, while suffering from 'l'abandon, la misère . . . la solitude, la famine', can take comfort from having always been independent. 'Ne le plaignez pas trop', urges de Guiche, 'il a vécu sans pactes, / Libre dans sa pensée autant que dans ses actes' (V.ii, ll. 2307-2308).

Fourteen years earlier de Guiche had offered his personal patronage to Cyrano (II.vii), only to have it indignantly rejected when the latter heard that the price of having his tragedy *La Mort d'Agrippine* championed might be that Richelieu, de Guiche's uncle, would suggest a few improvements to the versification: 'Impossible, Monsieur; mon sang se coagule / En pensant qu'on y peut changer une virgule' (II.vii, ll. 931-2). When taken to task by Le Bret, Cyrano launches into the powerful 'Non, merci' tirade (II.viii) against being in the pay of a patron, surrendering one's freedom of thought or suffering any violation of the sacrosanct integrity of the artist's personal expression.

The scene is yet another curious amalgam, typical of the patchwork pastiche style of the play. Cyrano's courageous if arrogant declaration of material and intellectual independence at all costs recalls similar sentiments in key works of the Romantic period, most notably Vigny's *Chatterton*. But a few lines later Rostand pulls a different coloured patch of material out of the scrap box, sews it on the

the garment, and the tone changes. The proud poet-martyr modulates into a bile-spitting misanthropist who, artistic integrity suddenly forgotten, *wants* to be hated: '[Je] m'écrie avec joie: un ennemi de plus!' (II.viii, l. 1022). Cyrano-Alceste—'Déplaire est mon plaisir. J'aime qu'on me haïsse' (l. 1024)—lambasts the eminently reasonable and long-suffering Le Bret / Philinte for his geniality and social skills. This venomous tribute to 'la Haine' (l. 1035) has the merit of historical plausibility, if no other, in that the theme is nearly contemporary with *Le Misanthrope*. And even without going so far as to follow Madeleine Alcover in challenging Cyrano's authorship of the *Mazarinades* (*Cyrano relu et corrigé*;), it is clear that elsewhere the historical Cyrano could be acerbic and vindictive, in his *Lettres satiriques*, for example, at the expense of Scarron and Montfleury. Yet seen in the context of Cyrano's profile as a poet, this *ex nihilo* surge of misanthropy is profoundly unconvincing. The objection must be made that this twenty-line pose fits ill with the nature of Cyrano in the rest of the play. It is difficult to imagine *this* Cyrano, any more than Molière's Alceste, being tolerated for long in a barrackroom full of fun-loving, Gascon musketeers to whom *galéjade* and badinage are second nature.

It is as if the above scene has been pasted in at a late stage of the writing, the better to prepare Le Bret's final portrait of Cyrano in Act V:

> Ses épîtres lui font des ennemis nouveaux!
> Il attaque les faux nobles, les faux dévots,
> Les faux braves, les plagiaires,—tout le monde!

(V.ii,ll. 2293-5)

The anaphoric *faux* is followed up in Cyrano's last delirious speech by a visual rhetoric, for the eye of the reader, in the exclamatioin marks and initial capitals that put one in mind of nothing in nineteenth century poetry so much as Vigny's *Les Destinées*: 'le Mensonge [. . .'] les Compromis, les Préjugés [. . . ,] la Sottise'—these are 'tous [s]es vieux ennemis'. It is meant to be an apocalyptic assortment of vices that Cyrano has spent his life combating, only to be defeated. Yet is there not something bland and unspecific about these demons? Via the rhetoric of the repeated *faux*, the capitalization of the abstract nouns, the hyperbolic *tout le monde*, Rostand would appear to be straining stylistically—for want of a convincing ideological substance—to enhance the mythic stature of a hallowed Romantic hero, the poet-martyr, who had been around for a very iong time by 1897, and about whom he had nothing new to say.

It is a difficult task, yet for achieving by style what can not be achieved by substance Rostand is equalled only by Hugo in nineteenth-century theatre. After four hours of stage time and over two thousand alexandrines he still has a range of literary and scenic tricks to deploy: the dusk, the falling leaves and the autumnal chill; the convent bells and procession of nuns in the background; the pathos worthy of Pixérécourt: 'Ma mère / Ne m'a pas trouvé beau. Je n'ai pas eu de sœur' (the latter historical inaccuracy would

bring the tally to over fifty if Magne were still counting); delirious visions of happier times; Quixotic hallucinations; the grandiose, Pascalian infinities of the last line of the epitaph he has composed for himself, 'Cyrano de Bergerac / Qui fut tout et qui ne fut rien' (V.vi, ll. 2539-40); the *faux-sublime* of possibly the most famous line in the play, 'Non, non, c'est bien plus beau lorsque c'est inutile!' (l. 2557); the gallows humour à la Villon of the play on words: 'je crois qu'elle [la mort] regarde . . . / Qu'elle ose regarder mon nez, cette Camarde' (ll. 2553-4); the death of the hero, sword in hand, like Bayard and Roland at the foot of a tree; like them, he is a Christian knight, 'chez Dieu' (that has been hinted at throughout this act); the dying Beast kissed by Beauty in the last line of the play (a profane form of extreme unction); and finally a slow fade on the aristocratic emblem of the ethos of the whole play, one of the most famous curtain-lines in French theatre:'Mon panache'. Two other emblems, the laurel and the rose, he has yielded up; but, like Henri IV, he is inseparable in death from the legend of his panache. No 1830s' Romantic poet, champion of liberty and martyr to truth, ever had a death scene quite like this.

. . . . .

But what of the Savinien de Cyrano de Bergerac who inspired hostile cabals of *real* 'dévots', whose *La Mort d'Agrippine* was a source of scandal because of the implicit atheism of Sejanus's lines:

> Étais-je malheureux lorsque je n'étais pas?
> Une heure après la mort, notre âme évanouie
> Sera ce qu'elle était une heure avant la vie.

(V.vi)

and who, in the same play, punning on the words *hostie* and latin *hostia* (victim), exposed himself to charges of blasphemy? The Cyrano de Bergerac who would have liked to see Cardinal Mazarin *flambé*; who published a satirical letter 'Contre un Jé . . . [Jésuite] assassin et médisant', and whose *États et empires de la Lune* was purged of potentially dangerous impieties when it was published by the well-meaning Le Bret and de Sercy in 1657? What of Cyrano de Bergerac *libertin*, in short?

The answer is, not much. It is true that Rostand has made a conspicuous and dramatically effective call on the last-named text. In Act Three, scene 13, de Guiche has to be prevented for just a quarter of an hour from reaching Roxane's house. Rostand has Cyrano pretend to fall back to earth after his journey to the moon, and succeed in distracting Guiche by describing the methods he used for his journey (a virtuoso passage for once poorly exploited in the [Jean-Paul] Rappeneau film). Rostand succinctly recycles five to be found in *Les États et empires de la Lune* and one from *Le Soleil*, and invents one of his own for good measure. The scene is an imaginative piece of comic writing worthy of Molière and Beaumarchais. But that is the limit of Rostand's appropriation of this major Cyrano text. When read in conjunction with its companion volume,

Les États et empires du Soleil, under the convenience title *L'Autre Monde*, it is regarded as an early work of comic philosophical fiction on the path that leads to Fontenele, Swift and Voltaire. Rostand of course, like everyone else before 1910, had access only to the 1862 Paul Lacroix edition of the text, expurgated by the timorous Le Bret in 1657. At various points Lacroix indicates in footnotes that 'il y a ici une lacune; mais nous croyons reconnaître que Cyrano avait mis Adam et le Paradis Terrestre dans la lune' (p. 129) and 'on peut supposer que Cyrano racontait comment il avait cueilli un fruit sur l'arbre de la Science' (p. 132). Even allowing for the incompleteness of the edition available to Rostand, the author has responded only in a limited way to the stimulus of what it was nevertheless still known to contain. As Pierre Brun puts it, in the first scholarly study of Cyrano's work, in 1893: 'il y a dans son roman des questions audacieuses et ardues, sinon résolues, du moins posées' (p. 247). Rostand has steered a careful course wide of Savinien de Cyrano the freethinker and of the whole area of religious controversy associated with him in the seventeenth century.

The first two lines of the epitaph composed by Rostand's Cyrano for himself are 'Philosophe, physicien / Rimeur, bretteur, musicien' (V.vi, ll. 2533-4). Neither here or anywhere else in the play is the world *libertin* found. Although Rostand subscribes to the legend that the log that fell on Cyrano's head was aimed, he omits that part of the legend that would have it that the aiming was done by, or at the instigation of, Jesuits. In Rostand's version, de Guiche has heard a rumour that Cyrano could soon have an accident, but it is implicit that the organisers of it are secular. Religious fanaticism and intolerance—the real demons that could have fatal consequences for a *libertin* in the seventeenth century—are significant by their absence from the phantoms hallucinated by Cyrano in his delirium. Furthermore a part of the legend about Cyrano's death that Rostand does accept, as unprovable as the imputation of Jesuit involvement, is that he died *chrétiennement*. It is true that he has Cyrano believe his place in 'paradise'—alongside Socrates and Galileo—will be 'dans la lune opaline', but that is the merest salute to the tradition of Cyrano the freethinker. Rather more does it accord with the image of Cyrano the dying clown, a *pierrot* even more appropriately *lunaire* than any other at the end of the nineteenth century.

The fact remains that despite this Rostandian quirk and the absence of formal last rites, Cyrano has asked Sœur Marthe to pray for his soul and made his intentions clear. The convent of the Dames de la Croix and its good-hearted nuns could hardly have been depicted more reverentialy. Jacques Prévot has argued that *'L'Autre Monde* est un poème' and that 'Cyrano est notre premier poète scientifique en prose' (*Cyrano de Bergerac romancier*, p. 130), That is surely true, and it must be concluded that his poet, the courageous explorer of alternative secular universes, whose place in the intellectual history of the seventeenth century was being established about the time Rostand was writing,

is separated, if not in light years, at least by a considerable distance from the 'vieil ami qui vient pour être drôle'.

THE NOSE AND THE MAN

'Rostand ne semble rien devoir aux *Grotesques* de Gautier, si ce n'est peut-être l'idée d'attacher au nez de son héros l'importance que l'on sait.' (Truchet, p. 36). Although we would not agree that Rostand's conception of Cyrano and of the poetic calling genèrally owes almost nothing to Gautier, the second half of this quotation certainly rings true. As already seen, the historical Cyrano's nose was the cause for mirth for at least two seventeenth century commentators, Dassoucy and Ménage, despite which he had enough aplomb to incorporate a substantial comic passage on the merits of big noses into the *États et empires de la Lune*. Not only did every self-respecting inhabitant of the moon use his nose as a sundial but he was prepared to castrate every male child born with a small nose. What was a *barbarie* to the traveller was a practice reflecting thirty centuries of accumulated wisdom for the lunarians:

> Nous le faisons après avoir observé depuis trente siècles qu'un grand nez est, à la porte de chez nous, une enseigne qui dit: Céans loge un homme spirituel, prudent, courtois, affable, généreux et libéral; et qu'un petit est le bouchon des vices opposés; c'est pourquoi des camus on bâtit les Eunuques, par ce que la république aime mieux n'avoir point d'enfants d'eux que d'en avoir de semblables à eux.

(*Œuvres complètes*, p. 416).

This is clearly the passage that Rostand, prompted by Gautier's gloss in *Les Grotesques*, used as his source for Cyrano's apostrophe to the bumbling 'Fâcheux':

> Vil camus, sot camard, tête plate, apprenez
> Que je m'enorgueillis d'un pareil appendice,
> Attendu qu'un grand nez est proprement l'indice
> D'un homme affable, bon, courtois, spirituel,
> Libéral, courageux, tel que je suis . . .

(I.iv, ll. 290-94)

Another clear, if shorter echo of an original Cyrano text is heard in the next scene, when Cyrano laments to Le Bret that because of 'ce nez qui d'un quart d'heure en tous lieux me précède', he is doomed to remain unloved, 'même par une laide'. This is obviously inspired by Genevote's description to his face of Granger's appearance in *Le Pédant joué*. Amid an epic catalogue of ugly features, the nose stands out: 'son nez mérite bien une égratignure particulière. Cet authentique nez arrive partout un quart d'heure devant son Maître; Dix savetiers de raisonnable rondeur vont travailler dessous à couvert de la pluie' (*Œuvres complètes*, p. 202). Cyrano was thus ambiguous on the subject of noses: allegedly irascible as regards his own (chalking up ten deaths in duels, according to the *Menagiana*), yet capable on at least two occasions in his work of exploiting the comic potential of a prime specimen. It so happens that in presenting it, in *La Lune*, as an indicator of all the moral virtues, and its opposite as a sign of viciousness or of extreme dullness at the least, Cyrano the seventeenth-century humanist was continuing a long tradition of ancient and Renaissance 'nose literature' (to use Coleman Parsons's phrase—p. 235), much of which he may have been familiar with. A late sixteenth-century text referred to briefly in this Parsons nose survey is a treatise by the Italian surgeon Gaspare Tagliacozzi, *De Curtorum Chirurgia*. With woodcut illustrations demonstrating his techniques, Tagliacozzi claimed to to be able to graft on noses from the skin of the upper arm for the benefit of gentlemen who had lost their noses as a result of what was euphemistically known as 'duelling' (he had worked in Naples). Yet there appears to have been no call for the resourceful rhinoplast's services from the *over*-endowed. The work may have been known to our humanist *touche-à-tout*, providing ammunition, as it conceivably could, to one with a sufficient degree of wit and malevolence, for a belief in the viciousness of the nasally challenged.

Although he has felicitously recycled what might just be perceived as a nose complex in Cyrano, Rostand can have known little of the long humanist tradition that lay behind it. Nor, to move on to a human science that was more his own contemporary, could he have foreseen that modern anthropologists would point to non-European traditions which throw interesting light on his particular handling of the theme:

> Le nez, comme l'œil, est un symbole de clairvoyance, de perspicacité, de discernement, mais plus *intuitif que raisonné*.
>
> Pour les Bambaras, le nez est, avec la jambe, le sexe et la langue, un des quatre ouvriers de la société. Organe de flair, qui décèle les sympathies et les antipathies, il oriente les désirs et les paroles, guide la marche de la jambe, et complète en somme l'action des trois autres ouvriers responsables du bon ou du mauvais fonctionnement de la collectivité.
>
> Au Japon, les orgueilleux et les vantards passent pour avoir de longs nez . . .[3]

Intuitive, hypersensitive, articulate, boastful, Rostand's Cyrano is all of these, in so far as such characteristics are believed to be enjoyed by the nasally conspicuous, the *nasigères*, as they were known in the author's Marseille schooldays. Even, too, as an expert swordsman, nimble on his legs—'le nez [. . .] guide la marche de la jambe.' But for the Bambaras of West Africa, for whom the leg complements the nose and the tongue in the passage quoted above, there is a fourth vital appendage for harmonious living, the sexual organ. Is Rostand's hero conspicuous in this respect?

In the section on Love, we have already noted that Rostand's treatment of the theme throughout the play is chaste, idealized, chivalric. For all we know, Christiane, Roxane and Cyrano all die virgins. The ribald, even salacious, tone to be detected in some of the original

Savinien de Cyrano's writing is absent from the play. Rostand is similarly austere as regards any inspiration he can have drawn from *Les Grotesques*; Gautier's essay begins with a sly but clear allusion to the folk belief that a long nose is a sign of a long penis: 'beaucoup de physiologistes femelles tirent aussi de la dimension de cette honnête partie du visage un augure on ne peut plus avantageux' (*Les Grotesques*, p. 231). Among modern critics, Citti and Besnier draw attention to the potential as a phallic symbol of a nose as grotesquely long as Cyrano's in the play, yet are hard pressed to account for Rostand's diffidence in the matter. In Besnier's words, 'Qui aura deviné que [le nez] était (redoublé, en outre, d'une prompte épée) phallique? Rostand dit bien des choses en somme de ce nez, mais pas celle-là: preuve, si l'on veut, que c'est la seule qui compte' (Besnier edition, p. 20). It is well said: Rostand is surprisingly coy. *Par pudeur*, the author who ten years earlier preferred d'Urfé to Zola is choosing to ignore at least two allusions that must have been quite clear to him: one blatant, in a French *grivois* tradition, Gautier's titillating reference to the 'physiologistes femelles'; one less so, if more interestingly Freudian *avant la lettre*, the lunarians' choice of castration as a fate for all infant males unfortunate enough to be born with small noses.

Although the play is replete with verbal audacities, the only one of them that is sexually allusive concerns Cyrano's sword, not his nose: 'La pudeur vous défend de voir ma lame nue?' (Liv, 1. 227). Yet the significance of his nose for a consideration of his maleness, his virility, his *virtù*, is inescapable. Rostand's Cyrano, possessor of an enormous nose, is aggressive in his relations with other assertive or prominent males. He fences verbally or literally with the Fâcheux, Valvert, Montfleury, de Guiche, the Gascons. He flaunts and flashes his sword, his tongue . . . his nose.

To Lignière and Ragueneau, however, males who are victims, he is compassionate and protective. The only woman to whom he is assertive is the latter's flirtatious wife, Lise, (she leads Ragueneau . . . by the nose, as it were). With all other women, the *distributrice*, Roxane, the nuns, he is shy, inhibited, tearful, ashamed of his nose. His sword stays sheathed. And not just his sword: he would appear to share with Christian the implausible record of being the only French soldier in the Thirty Years' War to die a virgin. The man who will take on a hundred men at one time *with his sword* nearly faints and has to be held up by Le Bret when he is faced with the prospect of meeting Roxane face to face. It is only via the *personne interposée* of Christian that he can court her, and when the latter is dead the play is four-fifths over. Is it not tempting to see the fourteen-year-long relationship he then lives with Roxane—an *unnecessarily* platonic relationship—as proof that it is a sublimated homosexual love for Christian that he is mourning? Cyrano's exorbitant nose, then, is a kind of *commedia* mask, an ostensible symbol of virility, yet which by virtue of its very enormity prevents, and above all *protects*, the *vir* from having to do what a *vir* has to do.

NOTES

[1]Émile Magne, *Le Cyrano de l'Histoire*, p. 5.

[2]'Ambiguïté et contradictions (XIXe siècle)', in *La Guerre* (Paris: Bordas, 'Les Thèmes Littéraires', 1975), pp. 117-34 [pp. 123-4].

[3]'Le Nez', in J. Chevalier and A. Gheerbrant, *Dictionnaire des symboles* (Paris: Laffont, 1982), p. 666. Italics supplied.

Unless otherwise indicated, French texts are published in Paris. Textual citations give author's name, then page number.

BIBLIOGRAPHY

I Annotated editions

Ashton, Harry *Cyrano de Bergerac*. Oxford: Basil Blackwell, 1942.

Aziza, Claude *Cyrano de Bergerac*. Presses Pocket, coll. 'Lire et Voir les Classiques', 1989.

Besnier, Patrick *Cyrano de Bergerac*. Gallimard, 'Folio', 1983.

Bird, Edward A. *Cyrano de Bergerac*. Toronto: Methuen, 1968.

Citti, Pierre *Cyrano de Bergerac*. Livre de Poche, 1990.

Lauxerois, Pierre *Cyrano de Bergerac*. Bordas, 1988.

Pavis, Patrice *Cyrano de Bergerac*. (with preface by P. Barillet). Livre de Poche, 1983.

———. *Cyrano de Bergerac*. Larousse, 1991.

Spens, Willy de *Cyrano de Bergerac*. Garnier-Flammarion, 1989.

Truchet, Jacques *Cyrano de Bergerac*. (Éditions de L'Imprimerie nationale, 1983.

Woollen, Geoff *Cyrano de Bergerac*. Bristol: Bristol Classical Press, 1994.

II English Translations

Burgess, Anthony *Cyrano de Bergerac*. London: Hutchinson, 1985.

Hooker, Brian *Cyrano de Bergerac*. New York: Henry Holt, 1923.

Morgan, Edwin *Cyrano de Bergerac*. Manchester: Carcanet Press, 1992.

Norman, Henderson *Plays of Edmond Rostand*. New York: Macmillan, 1921.

III Books and articles on Rostand and his theatre

Amoia, Alba della F. *Edmond Rostand*. Boston: Twayne, (World's Authors Series, no. 420), 1978.

Boillot, Félix 'La Construction de la phrase dans *Cyrano de Bergerac*', *Le Français moderne*, VII (1939), 301-316.

Calvet, Jean *Les Types universels dans la littérature française*. Lanore, 1963, 2 vols. ('Cyrano', vol. I, pp. 173-90).

Gérard, Rosemonde *Edmond Rostand*. Charpentier et Fasquelle, 1935.

Grieve, J.W. *L'Œuvre dramatique d'Edmond Rostand*. Les Œuvres représentatives, 1931.

Haugmard, Louis *Edmond Rostand*. Sansot, 1910.

Howarth, W.D. *Sublime and Grotesque: A Study of French Romantic Drama*. London: Harrap, 1975.

Magne, Émile *Les Erreurs de documentation de "Cyrano de Bergerac."* La Revue de France, 1898.

Rictus, Jehan *Un "bluff" littéraire, le cas Edmond Rostand*. P. Sevin et E. Rey, 1903.

Ripert, Émile *Edmond Rostand, sa vie et son œuvre*. Hachette, 1968.

Vernois, Paul 'Architecture et écriture théâtrales dans *Cyrano de Bergerac*', *Travaux de linguistique et de littérature de l'Université de Strasbourg*, IV, 2 (1966), 111-38.

Williams, Patricia 'Some Classical Aspects of *Cyrano de Bergerac*', *Nineteenth-Century French Studies*, I, 2 (1973), 112-24.

IV Cyrano de Bergerac and his times

Alcover, Madeleine *La Pensée philosophique et scientifique de Cyrano de Bergerac*. Geneva: Droz, 1970.

———. *Cyrano relu et corrigé*. Geneva: Droz, 1990.

Brun, Pierre *Savinien de Cyrano Bergerac, sa vie et ses œuvres, d'après des documents inédits*. Armand Colin, 1893.

———. *Savinien de Cyrano Bergerac, gentilhomme parisien: l'histoire et la légende de Lebret à M. Rostand*. Daragon, 1909.

Cyrano de Bergerac *Histoire comique des états et empires de la lune et du soleil*, ed. P.L. Jacob [i.e. Paul Lacroix, 'Le Bibliophile Jacob'], Delahays, 1858; republished by Galic, 1962). Contains Henry Labret's biographical preface of 1656.

———. *Œuvres complètes*, ed. Jacques Prévot. Belin, 1977.

Gautier, Théophile *Les Grotesques*, ed. Cecilia Rizza. Fasano/Paris: Schena/Nizet, 1985.

Goldin, Jeanne *Cyrano de Bergerac et l'art de la pointe*. Presses de l'Université de Montréal, 1973.

Harth, Erica *Cyrano de Bergerac and the Polemics of Modernity*. Columbia University Press., 1970. Jal, Auguste *Dictionnaire critique de biographie et d'histoire*. Plon, 1872.

Knight, Joseph 'The Real Cyrano de Bergerac', *The Fortnightly Review*, LXX (1898), 207-15.

Lachèvre, Frédéric *Les Œuvres libertines de Cyrano de Bergerac*. Paris, 1920; Geneva: Slatkine Reprints, 1968.

Mason, Haydn *Cyrano de Bergerac: 'L'Autre Monde'*. London: Grant and Cutler, 1984.

Mongrédien, Georges *Cyrano de Bergerac*. Berger-Levrault, 1964.

Parsons, Coleman O. 'The Nose of Cyrano de Bergerac', *The Romanic Review*, 25 (1934), 225-35.

Prévot, Jacques *Cyrano de Bergerac romancier*. Belin, 1977.

———. *Cyrano de Bergerac poète et dramaturge*. Belin, 1978.

Scruggs, C.E. *Charles Dassoucy: Adventures in the Age of Louis XIV*. Lanham, Md., University Press of America, 1984.

Spink, John *French Free-Thought from Gassendi to Voltaire*. London: Athlone Press, 1960.

V Background and thematic studies

Chaboche, Robert 'Les Soldats français de la guerre de trente ans, une tentative d'approche' *La Revue d'histoire moderne et contemporaine*, XX (1973), 10-24.

Hemmings, F.W.J. *The Theatre Industry in Nineteenth-Century France*. Cambridge University Press, 1993.

Henderson, John A. *The First Avant-Garde (1887-1894): Sources of the Modern French Theatre*. London: Harrap, 1971.

Parker, Geoffrey (ed.) *The Thirty Years' War*. London & New York: Routledge, 1984.

Reader, Keith 'Le Phénomène Cyrano: Perceptions of French Cinema in Britain', *Franco-British Studies*, XV (1993), 3-9.

Shattuck, Roger *The Banquet Years: The Arts in France, 1885-1918*. London: Faber and Faber, 1955).

Treasure, G.R.R. *Seventeenth-Century France*. London: Murray, 2nd. ed., 1981.

FURTHER READING

Bentley, Eric. "*Cyrano de Bergerac*, 1897." In *The Play: A Critical Anthology*, pp. 10-147. New York: Prentice-Hall, 1951.

> Presents a brief introduction, the Humbert Wolf translation of the *Cyrano de Bergerac*, and an afterword covering a number of issues, including the plot, characters, themes, and dialogue of the play.

Burgess, Anthony. Preface to *Cyrano de Bergerac* by Edmond Rostand, translated and adapted by Anthony Burgess, pp. v-xiv. New York: Alfred A. Knopf, 1971.

Discussion of the task of translating *Cyrano de Bergerac* that touches on issues of Rostand's style and versification.

Butler, Mildred Allen. "The Historical Cyrano de Bergerac as a Basis for Rostand's Play." *Educational Theatre Journal* VI, No. 3 (October 1954): 231-40.

> Compares Rostand's character with the historical figure and attempts to account for the playwright's deviations from fact in his play.

Cohen, Helen Louise. Introduction to *Cyrano de Bergerac*. In *Milestones of the Drama*, pp. 347-56. New York: Harcourt, Brace and Company, 1940.

> Includes an account of Rostand's dramatic career, background on the historical Cyrano de Bergerac, and a bibliography of secondary sources.

Kilker, J. A. "Cyrano without Rostand: An Appraisal." *The Canadian Modern Language Review* XXI, No. 3 (Spring 1965): 21-5.

> Examines the work of the real Cyrano de Bergerac, himself the author of two plays.

Additional coverage of Rostand's life and career is contained in the following sources published by Gale Research: *Contemporary Authors*, **Vols. 104, 126;** *Discovering Authors*; *Discovering Authors, British Edition*; *Discovering Authors, Canadian Edition*; *Discovering Authors: Modules*, **Dramatists and Most-Studied Authors Modules;** *Major 20th-Century Writers*; *Twentieth-Century Literary Criticism*, **Vols. 6, 37.**

Victor Séjour
1817-1874

INTRODUCTION

Séjour was a pioneering African American playwright who achieved notable success in the nineteenth-century Parisian theater.

BIOGRAPHICAL INFORMATION

Séjour was born Juan Victor Séjour Marcou et Ferrand in New Orleans. His father was Juan Francois Louis Séjour Marcou, who operated a cleaning establishment, and his mother was d'Eloisa Phillippe Ferrand. Séjour's parents held education in high esteem, and they sent their son to the Saint-Barbe Academy, where he proved himself a gifted student. When he was seventeen, Séjour wrote a poem celebrating the anniversary of La Société des Artisans, an association of free black mechanics to which he belonged. Les Artisans greeted the poem with enthusiasm. In 1836, when he was nineteen, his parents sent him to Paris to further his education. In Paris he met Cyrille Bisette, who edited the abolitionist journal *La Revue des Colonies* and who published Séjour's short story "Le Mulâtre" in his magazine in 1837. In 1841 Séjour published *Le Retour de Napoléon*, an heroic ode honoring the French emperor. Séjour's interest in heroic themes and his enthusiasm for Napoleon continued throughout his life. The success of this poem gained him entrance to Parisian literary circles, where he met Alexandre Dumas, *père*, and Émile Augier. Séjour's dramatic career began in 1844 when his five-act play *Diégarias* was performed at the Théâtre-Français. Throughout the 1850s and into the 1860s Séjour was one of the most popular playwrights of the Parisian stage. His plays of the period were warmly received, as audiences enjoyed the grandiose prose, sumptuous costumes, and spectacular settings. In 1860 he was made a member of the French Légion d'Honneur. By 1865, however, public tastes had shifted and Séjour's popularity had begun to wane; by the early 1870s he was destitute and ill. He died from tuberculosis in 1874.

MAJOR WORKS

During his career Séjour had more than twenty plays staged. Among his recurring dramatic themes are family relationships, nationalism, religion, and social justice. His plays reflect the influence of William Shakespeare, as well as his knowledge of other English Renaissance playwrights, such as Ben Jonson, and of French writers, including Victor Hugo, who was clearly a model for Séjour.

Diégarias, a verse drama in five acts, shows affinities to both Shakespeare's *Merchant of Venice* and *The Jew of Malta* by the Elizabethan dramatist Christopher Marlowe. As did Shakespeare, Séjour produced a play about the English King Richard III. And the verse drama *La Chute de Séjan* is possibly an adaptation of Jonson's *Sejanus*. Séjour's use of the monologue in his plays and the high-flown rhetoric of his characters have been compared to similar devices employed by Hugo. His dramas often depict great emotional extremes, focusing on passionate love, hate, jealousy, revenge, and intrigue.

CRITICAL RECEPTION

Séjour's plays were greatly admired and popular in the Paris of his day. Their passionate intensity and complexity were highly praised. But as literary tastes changed, such attributes were disparaged as overblown and convoluted. Today few critics place Séjour among the top ranks of nineteenth-century playwrights; most do, however, commend his achievement in providing thrilling and engaging melodramas to appreciative audiences, and for attaining remarkable success in an arena typically closed to African Americans. Placing him in the context of nineteenth-century Louisiana, T. A. Daley has declared simply: "New Orleans produced no finer poet, no better dramatist . . . than Victor Séjour."

PRINCIPAL WORKS

PLAYS

Diégarias 1844
La Chute de Séjan [*The Fall of Sejanus*] 1844
Richard III 1852
Les Noces vénitiennes [*Venetian Weddings*] 1855
L'Argent du diable [*The Devil's Money*] [with Adolphe Jaime, *fils*] 1856
Le Fils de la nuit [*The Son of the Night*] 1856
André Girard 1858
Le Martyre du coeur [*The Martyrdom of the Heart*] 1858
Le Paletot brun [*The Brown Overcoat*] 1858
Les Grands Vassaux [*The Chief Vassals*] 1859
Les Aventuriers [*The Adventurers*] 1860
Compère Guillery [*Comrade Guillery*] 1860
Les Massacres de la Syrie [*The Syrian Massacres*] 1860
La Tirense de cartes [*The Fortune Teller*] [with Jean-François Mocquard] 1860

Les Mystères du Temple [*The Mysteries of the Temple*] 1862

Les Volontaires de 1814 [*The Volunteers of 1814*] 1862

Les Fils de Charles-Quint [*The Sons of Charles the Fifth*] 1864

Les Marquis Caporal [*The Marquis Corporal*] 1864

Les Enfants de la louve [*Children of the She-Wolf*] [with Théodore Barrière] 1865

La Madone des roses [*The Madonna of the Roses*] [with Barrière] 1868

OTHER MAJOR WORK

Le Retour de Napoléon [*The Return of Napoleon*] (poem) 1841

OVERVIEWS AND GENERAL STUDIES

Charles Barthelemy Roussève (essay date 1937)

SOURCE: "Negro Literature in Ante Bellum Louisiana: Victor Séjour," in *The Negro in Louisiana: Aspects of His History and His Literature*, The Xavier University Press, 1937, pp. 82-90.

[*In the following excerpt, Roussève provides an introduction to Séjour's life and works.*]

If Camille Thierry was the greatest Negro non-dramatic poet in Louisiana before the Civil War, Victor Séjour, the dramatist, considering his works from the point of view of their volume and quality, and the popularity which came to them during his lifetime, was the greatest Louisiana-born Negro poet of his age. Like Thierry, he is represented in *Les Cenelles*.

The story of his rise to glory reads like a romantic novel. The son of Juan François Louis Victor Séjour, native of Santo Domingo, and Éloise Phillippe, of New Orleans, he was born probably in New Orleans June 2, 1817, according to his baptismal record at Saint Louis Cathedral. Some believe, however, that he was born as early as 1809; and the *Dictionnaire Larousse du XXe Siècle* states that his birth occurred in Paris in 1821. While his full name was Juan Victor Séjour Marcou et Ferrand, he chose to be called Victor Séjour. His father operated a prosperous cleaning and dyeing establishment at "25, rue de Chartres," in New Orleans. Séjour studied, as has been mentioned earlier, under Michel Séligny.

Victor Séjour became a member of "Les Artisans," an organization of free colored mechanics incorporated in 1834[1] and still in existence. When he was seventeen years old, Séjour, on the anniversary of the founding of the society, wrote a poem which much impressed the members. In 1836, convinced of his literary talent, his parents sent him to Paris to complete his education and to remove him

from the wretched conditions to which his people were then a prey.

After his graduation he wrote in 1841 an ode, **"Le Retour de Napoléon,"** the quality of which was sufficient to admit him into the literary circles of Paris. There he met Alexandre Dumas and Émile Augier. *Diégarias,* his first drama, was staged at the Théâtre-Français July 23, 1844. His **Chute de Séjan** was also presented there in 1849. Following the production of these heroic dramas in verse, he gravitated toward melodrama. Twenty-one of his works in this style were played in the theatres of Paris. They immediately proved immensely popular, for the Paris theatre-goers came in droves to their premières. Victor Séjour had "arrived."

Really devoted to his mother, when word reached him that she was in need he sailed to New Orleans to her rescue, and thence he returned to Paris.

For an extended period Victor Séjour was the idol of the Parisian theatres. Among his friends was Louis Napoleon, who made him his private secretary. Eventually tastes changed, however; and both his popularity and his purse suffered. Poor and ill, he evinced difficulty in finding directors to present his **Cromwell** and **Le Vampire, Grand Drame Fantastique.** At last, before his **Vampire** could be staged at La Gaieté, Séjour died in a hospital, a victim of galloping tuberculosis, on September 21, 1874. Kind and lovable, he was mourned by many. He is buried at Père La Chaise.

Tall, handsome, and distinguished, with sparkling brown eyes, and with a complexion too dark and lips too large for him to be taken for a Caucasian, Séjour was an impressive figure at Paris in the heyday of his glory. An admirer of Shakespeare and Hugo, he was conversant with the literature of the drama, and he knew all the secrets of the psychology of stagecraft. Kind and generous toward his actors, he earned their love, admiration, and esteem. He continually sought to improve his works, often presenting revised passages on slips of paper to players on their way to the stage.

In the catalogue of his works are dramas in prose and in verse. Among his pieces in prose are **Richard III, Les Noces Vénitiennes, André Gérard,** and **Le Martyr du Coeur,** all of which are in five acts. **Le Fils de la Nuit** and the comedy **L'Argent du Diable** are in three acts. **Le Paletot Brun** is a comedy in one act. Included among his dramas in verse are **La Chute de Séjan** and **Diégarias,** both of which are in five acts. His **Cromwell** and **Le Vampire** were never published. Séjour wrote only one play with an American setting—**Les Volontiers de 1814,** a drama in five acts and fourteen tableaux, dated 1862 and featuring the Louisiana volunteers against the British at the Battle of New Orleans.[2]

Diégarias, the five-act drama in verse with which Séjour started his career as playwright, has its setting in Castile. Its principal characters are Diégarias, a Jew who kept secret, even from his daughter Inès (the only female character), his name and creed; Don Juan de Tello, husband of Inès; Henry IV, king of Castile; and Abdul-Bekri, Moorish spy. The quality of Séjour's style at this early period and the nature of the title-character of the play are revealed in the following passage, spoken by Diègarias to Inès:

> Ta mère . . . ? Elle me dit un mot,
> Et mon coeur étonné se rendit aussitôt.—
> "Fuyons!"—Ma haine avait fait place à ma tendresse.
> Heureux et confians [*sic*] nous partîmes—La Grèce
> Nous reçut.—Lǵ mon sort s'adoucit, je devin
> Riche et puissant. Je fus honoré; mais en vain,
> Le repos me fuyait! mon injure passée,
> Comme un crime, un remords, pesait sur ma pensée.
> Bianca mourut, laissant, dans ses derniers adieux,
> Le désir d'être transportée un jour dans ces lieux.—
> Ce désir fut ma loi.—Je partis.—Par prudence,
> Je pris un autre nom, je cachai ma croyance,
> Si bien qu'après vingt ans . . . vingt ans d'exil enfin,
> Nul ne revit en moi Jacob-Eliacin.—
> . . . .[3]

Victor Séjour's **Richard III** was presented for the first time at the Théâtre de la Porte Saint-Martin on September 29, 1852. The work is respectfully dedicated to the dramatist's father, to whose rectitude and loftiness of spirit Séjour attributed whatever success had crowned his art. In the play, whose background is the War of the Roses, the corpse-strewn career of Richard III unrolls itself to its wretched close. In a gripping scene Richard, asking in marriage the hand of his niece Elizabeth, daughter of the queen dowager, and sister of the murdered children of Edward, is answered thus by the angry princess:

> Ah! gardez votre trône!—Votre trône? Quelle est la femme qui voudrait s'y asseoir? Votre trône?—Non, ce n'est pas une compagne que tu peux avoir, c'est une accomplice; ce n'est pas un coeur candide et pur, c'est une furie qui puisse dormir en paix sous ton toit, dans l'enivrement de tes cruautés! . . .
>
> Oui, tu t'es fait du meurtre une distraction! Oui, tu as tué mes deux frères, Edouard et Richard. Oui, tu as tué mon oncle Rivers, tué mon oncle Clarence, ton frère. Tu t'es fait un marchepied de cadavres pour escalader ce trône que tu viens m'offrir, à moi dont le coeur est morcelé par tes crimes. Oh! l'insensé tyran! la vapeur du sang t'a enivré! Je suis heureux de pouvoir te le dire en face: je ne te hais pas, je te méprise; je ne te hais pas, je te brave; je ne te hais pas, je te chasse![4]

Just before the fall of the curtain in the last scene, as Richard, dead, is ordered placed into the sepulchre in which he had meant, had his plans succeeded, to seal the remains of Elizabeth, the happy people, rid of the ruthless tyrant, cry out hosannas to Elizabeth and her victorious lover Richmond:

> Vive Richmond! vive Elizabeth![5]

Les Noces Vénitiennes, first staged March 8, 1855, is a tale of hate, jealousy, revenge, intrigue, assassination, and heroism, into which is woven, like a golden thread, a beautiful story of love and devotion. The scene is principally in Venice, toward 1553. The principal characters are Orséolo, chief of the Council of Ten; his daughter Albone; and her beloved, Galiéno, a Venetian general. The mortal hatred, centuries old, between the families of Orséolo and Galiéno forms the source of the plot. Some insight into the nature of the play and its characters may be gained from the reading of a few passages. Raspo, a spy, speaks thus, soon after the curtain rises:

> Où est-elle, la différence, entre un homme brusquement assassiné et un homme mort douloureusement dans son lit?[6]

A few lines later Raspo says tersely, "Langue légère, tête de trop."[7] In the act following, Albone, the noble seventeen-year-old beauty, now a captive, declares, "La mort n'est rien, la honte seul est à craindre. . . ."[8] Orséolo, in the fourth act, speaks in this wise to Galiéno: "Dieu a mis les morts entre nous."[9] In the last scene Orséolo dies showering maledictions upon Galiéno, who after many adventures is at last happily united with the beautiful Albone.

While Victor Séjour achieved fame as the author of numerous plays, it must not be forgot that his initial work in Paris was the heroic poem, **"Le Retour de Napoléon."** Probably because it was his only production of sufficient brevity, this ode is the only piece by which he is represented in *Les Cenelles.* . . . The poem illustrates the extent to which the sympathies and interests of Séjour, as well as those of other free people of color in ante bellum Louisiana, were associated with France.

NOTES

[1]According to the present secretary, some of its ante bellum members were white men.

[2]Desdunes, *op. cit.*, pages 38-43; Fortier, *op. cit.*, page 43; Tinker, *op. cit.*, pages 427-31; Gillard, John T., *The Catholic Church and the American Negro*, page 18; and *Dictionnaire Larousse du XXe Siècle*.

[3]*Op. cit.*, Act I, Scene vii, page 9. Prose translation: Thy mother? She told me a word, and my astonished heart immediately understood. "Let us flee!" My hate had given way to tenderness. Happy and confident, we departed. Greece received us. There my fate became less harsh, I became rich and powerful. I was honored; but in vain, rest forsook me! my past suffering, like a crime, a remorse, weighed upon my mind. Bianca died, expressing, in her last farewell, a wish to be brought one day to this land. That wish became my law. I departed. Through caution I took another name, I hid my creed, so well that after twenty years—twenty years of exile, after all—none saw in me Jacob-Eliacin. . . .

[4]*Op. cit.*, Act II, Scene ix, pages 36-37. Translation:

Ah! keep thou thy throne! Thy throne? Where is the woman who would sit thereon? Thy throne? No, 'tis no companion that thou canst have, 'tis an accomplice; 'tis not a heart sincere and pure, 'tis but a fury who could slumber in peace under thy roof, in the frenzy of thy cruelties! . . .

Yes, thou hast made of murder a pastime! Yes, thou didst kill my two brothers, Edward and Richard. Yes, thou didst kill my uncle Rivers, didst kill my uncle Clarence, thy brother. Thou didst make for thyself a footstool of corpses with which to climb to that throne which thou comest to offer to me, to me whose heart has been torn by thy crimes. Oh! the brutish tyrant! the smell of blood has made thee drunk! I am happy to be able to tell it to thy face: I do not hate thee, I scorn thee; I do not hate thee, I defy thee; I do not hate thee, I drive thee hence!

[5]*Ibid.*, Act V, Scene v, page 101.

[6]*Op. cit.*, Act I, Scene i, page 2. Translation: Where is the difference between a man brusquely assassinated and a man painfully dying in his bed?

[7]*Ibid.*, Act I, Scene ii, page 2. Translation: Light tongue, superfluous head.

[8]*Ibid.*, Act II, Scene vii, page 10. Translation: Death is nothing, shame alone is to be feared. . . .

[9]*Ibid.*, Act IV, Scene vii, page 24. Translation: God has placed the dead between us.

A. E. Perkins (essay date 1942)

SOURCE: "Victor Séjour and His Times," in *The Negro History Bulletin*, Vol. V, No 7, April 1942, pp. 163-66.

[*In the essay below, Perkins gives a brief literary biography of Séjour.*]

VICTOR SÉJOUR, GENIUS OF DRAMA

Victor Séjour, the most versatile writer and brilliant dramatist among that unusual group of free colored Creoles who lived in Louisiana, along the Gulf Coast and Atlantic Seaboard, was born in New Orleans, June 2, 1817, illegitimate son of Eloisa Philippe Ferrand, and Juan Francisco Louis, Victor Séjour Marcos, a native of San Marcos (San Dominque).[1] There is a lack of accord as to the date of his birth, varying from 1809 to 1821, but the record in St. Louis Cathedral establishes the correct date of his birth as that above. This *liaison* was legitimized by marriage on January 13, 1825.[2] The child preferred to call himself "Victor Séjour," and by that name he was baptized and known. He was baptized in the St. Louis Cathedral as shown in the register of baptisms for *les hommes de couleur*.[3] His father also abbreviated his own name to François Marcou.[4] He ran a prosperous dyeing establishment at 25 *rue de Chartres*, then the main artery of trade in New Orleans.[5]

Victor received his early education under Michel Seligny at *Saint-Barbe Academy*. Seligny himself had received his education in Paris, says Nathalie Populus Mello, herself a brilliant pupil of Seligny.[6]

The people of color had many wealthy persons among them, and this group formed an organization known as the *Société d'Economic*, founded by Creole artisans.[7] Upon the anniversary of his graduation, at the age of seventeen, he wrote a poem complimentary to these artisans. It made such a profound impression that a subscription was immediately raised to send Victor to Paris to be educated.[8] Incidentally,

this also shows the prosperous condition of some of these free people of color. His parents terminated his studies in Paris in 1836, for reasons of economy.[9] He rested after leaving college for a brief while; then in 1841, he made his literary debut through a heroic poem appearing in *Les Cenelles*,[10] **"Le Retour de Napoléon."** This poem opened the doors of the literary circles of Paris to him, where he met Alexandre Dumas and Emile Augier.[11] It was perhaps his relation to these two famous characters that bent him towards a theatrical career.

Le Théâtre-Français in 1844, enjoyed his *première* adventure in **Diégarias**.[12] While it was pompous and sophomoric, it well disclosed the versatility, wide range of imagination and dramatic powers of the author and actor. Diégariau is a Jew who keeps the secret of his racial identity even from his daughter Inès and Don Juan de Tello, her husband; Henry IV, King of Spain; and Abdul-Bekri, the Moorish spy. After twenty years he confesses himself to Inès. An extract of the translation of his confession follows.

> *Ta mère. . . . Elle me dit un mot. . . .*
> *Fuyons!—Ma haine arait fait place à ma tendresse*
> *Heureux et confiants nous partîmes—La Grece*
> *Nous recut. . . . Je devins*
> *Riche et puissant. Je fus honoré; mais en vain,*
> *. . . Mon in jure passée.*
> *Comme un crime, un remords, pesait sur ma pensée.*
> *Bianca mourut, laissant, dans ses derniers adieux,*
> *Le désir d'être transportée un jour dans ces lieux.*
> *Ce désir fut ma loi. . . .*
> *. . . Après vingt ans . . . d'exil enfin,*
> *Nul ne revit en moi Jacob-Eliacin.*[13]

Séjour's star was rising. "Paris theatre-goers came in droves" to witness his plays. The height of his popularity may be imagined, as well as his ability and culture appreciated, when it is noted that he became in the hey-day of his career private secretary to Louis Napoléon.[14]

Séjour reached the height of his career about 1853, perhaps, when he was thirty-six years old, and in a prose drama of five acts. All Paris turned out to witness his *premières*.[15] A description of the night in the *Porte de Saint-Martin Théâtre* of his first play of **Richard III** may serve to give a faint picture of this quandroon dramatist at the pinnacle. The theater is brilliantly lighted. His voice is clear and vibrant, his movements, precise and elegant, his interpretation and imitation are superb. As the curtain ascends for him a man of olive complexion bows with kingly mien. He commands. His voice rings out over the large audience and the house cheers and cheers. Victor Séjour has "arrived." Describing him a bit more minutely: His brown eyes have the fire and the reflection analogous to the panther on the chase. He is tall, broad-shouldered, and walks with self-assurance. He is descending *le foyer via l'escalier*. He carries a coat on his right arm, and upon close approach to him he resembles *un Français du Midi*. He has heavy lips and is of the exotic type.[16] A woman exclaims from the crowd audibly: *C'est lui! C'est l'auteur,*

Victor Séjour! (It is he! It is the author, Victor Séjour.)[17] Séjour is at the pinnacle. His star swings to its zenith.

HIS MOTHER IN NEED

One might wonder why these free people of color so much sought and loved France. France was free. America was slave. And while the status of free people of color was in Louisiana more nearly, that of the whites, especially the mulatto race, than it was that of the slave, it was not yet without restraint, and at times these peoples, many of them well educated. refined, wealthy, and of the best blood of France, felt painful humiliation at mistreatment. That accounts for much of the desire for many of them to make Paris their home, not less than its classic atmosphere.

A call from his mother, who evidently had lost her husband by death, brought Séjour hastily to her, for she was in great need.[18] But he found his birthplace now unbearable. Whether this state of his mind had been effected by the large freedom and opportunity that Paris had given him or by an actual changed social condition in New Orleans, is not definite. But it was probably both, for it was about this time that Governor Robert Wickliffe had recommended to the Legisature of Louisiana that "Public policy dictates that immediate steps be taken at this time to remove all free Negroes now in the State when such removal can be effected without violation of law. Their example and association have a most pernicious effect upon our slave population."[19]

Phelps says, "A class of quadroons grew up with alarming rapidity, and by a process of natural selection which may be easily inferred, developed just those characteristics which made them dangerous. Many of these quadroons, endowed with superior mental qualities, and ambitions impossible to the pure Negro, won their freedom, and demanded a place in the civilization of the whites."[20]

Séjour did not therefore tarry long in the city of his birth. But while in New Orleans, says Nathalie Populus Mello, he formed a *liaison* with an octoroon who accompanied him upon his return voyage to Paris. From this *liaison* a son was born.[21]

Such unions were not unusual at the time. It was taken by the society as an incident. It was the result of a social condition arising out of slavery. The large number of mixed bloods in Louisiana, and generally upon the Gulf and Atlantic coasts at the time, testifies to the general acceptance of this social condition as a matter of course.

Lyle Saxon says, "Now it must not be assumed that these women were prostitutes—they were not. They were reared in chastity, and they were as well educated as the times would permit. These were for the greater part the illegitimate daughters of white men and their quadroon mistresses. . . . Their chastity was their chief stock in trade, in addition to their beauty. Their mothers watched them as hawks watch chickens, accompanied them to the balls where white men were admitted and did not relinquish their chaperouage until the daughter had found a suitable 'protector.' . . . Sometimes these *liaisons* lasted for years, occasionally for life."[22]

In 1849, Séjour enacted his **La Chute de Sejan,** which seemed to be an adaptation of a play of Ben Johnson by the same name.[23] In all he wrote for various Parisian theatres twenty-four plays,[24] two of which were composed in collaboration with Théodore Barrière, one with Brésil and one with Jamie (fils). In 1856 he played **Fils de la Nuit,** and yet large audiences were flocking to hear him.[25] Both a student and an admirer of Shakespeare and Victor Hugo, he probably knew the latter, as they were both noted dramatists. He understood the psychology of an audience. Desdunes says, "Séjour played the stage with the skill of a master."[26]

HIS STAR BEGINS TO WANE

It was in 1874 that Séjour made a contract with *La Gaiété*; to play **Cromwell** and **Le Vampire,** both fantastic dramas.[27] But Séjour is now fifty-seven. The years are beginning to tell their tale. His revenues have stopped. *Il est maintenant malade et pauvre. (He is now sick and poor.)* On September 21, 1874, he fell to galloping consumption. The curtain coming down upon him swiftly, his tragic passing might well remind one of some of his major dramas.

His old friend, Pergallo, does not, however, forsake him in his last darkest hour. He will take care of the funeral. He conducts the sad and poorly attended cortege to Père-Lachaise. The simple casket is ready to be lowered into the tomb. Here we might wonder where were the crowds that followed him to the theaters and lionized him in the hey-day of his brief, passing glory.[28]

A man dressed in a blouse suit followed the cortege weeping inconsolably. Unauthorized he took hold of the cord.[29]

> *Permettez-moi, s'il vous plait; je suis le manouevre au théâtre.*
>
> *Cette raison u'est pas suffisante.*
>
> *Je le sais, mais je vous prie. Il m'aimait. C'est moi qui tirais toujours la corde du bateau dans le Fils de la Nuit.*

Pergallo yielded to Jean the cord.

There are probably two major reasons for Séjour's relative obscurity in American literature and dramatics. First, Séjour's mother tongue was French, and second, Negroes are not readily admitted into the circle *literati*. It would hardly be contended that Dunbar, Du Bois, William Stanley Braithwaite, James Weldon Johnson, Brawley, Locke, Kelly Miller, and Carter G. Woodson, all admittedly writers of great creative ability, experienced no greater difficulty in entering the circles *literati* than Ralph Waldo Emerson or Joel Chandler Harris experienced. Every one of them met unusual difficulty. Dunbar, because of his inimitable genius of humor and pathos, and Du Bois because of his rich, rare gift in literary expression as well as his unbending philosophy of that higher law of human equality, literally unbarred doors of color locked against them.

Séjour suffered in American even more than these suffered, for regarding Negroes in terms of letters in 1850 was unthinkable in all but Latin America. In the South it was a crime. *Victor Séjour, comme tant d' autres, était obligé de s'éloigner du pays qùi l'avait vu naître.*[30]

Prejudice was sharper against men of color than against women of color in New Orleans, that is, especially when men assumed the intellectual role. The titles *pétite mademoisélle, mademoisélle* and *madame* were terms commonly employed in New Orleans when addressing females of color of marked respectability. In the enumeration of free colored people in Woodson's *Free Negro Heads of Families, 1830*, polite reference frequently occurs, as *Miss* Meleric Borel, *Mme.* Jeanette Alexis, *Mlle.* Htte. Bumchartrean, *Mme.* Theophile, *Ld.* (Lady) Gabrielle, *Widow* T. Daubreuille, *et cetera.*[31] The term *F.L.C.*, Free Lady of Color, was used at times. Without doubt, people of color, men and women, free and slave, were treated better in New Orleans than in any other slave community.[32]

Séjour, however, and many other men of his social level, suffered, and as a result found residence in Paris rather than in New Orleans.[33]

He wrote poetry, drama and prose copiously.[34] No account of his death is found in New Orleans newspapers. The *Tribune*, owned by the Roudenez brothers, San Domingan mulattoes, suspended operation in 1867. But Paris newspapers took account of his death. Announcements of it occurred in *Le Soleil*, September 23, 1874; in *Le Figaro*, September 24-25, 1874; and in *Le Gaulois*, September 22, 1874.[35]

Paul de Saint-Victor gives an analysis of **Les Mysterès du Temple** in the *Renaissance Louisianaise* extolling it, September 24, 1862.[36]

In his compelling personal magnetism over his audiences, in his rare gift of penetration, interpretation, richness of vocabulary and vocal expression he had few equals.

His last days were sad. In his taking leave of the stage there was tragedy,—tragedy such as he himself had so inimitably enacted "before all Paris" as it turned out to see and hear him play.[37]

When he fell before the "fatal malady,"[38] his popuarity had already begun to wane. Tastes were changing.[39] A less serious age was coming on that demanded something light. Yet Séjour, the "unfathered quadroon," born in a slave society that hindered the expression of his genius, had through sheer audacity and courage ventured beyond its pale in quest of freedom and fame and had achieved them,—achieved them at fearful cost and sacrifice.

His was the glory of the setting sun in mystic eclipse, a brilliant and melancholy star moving across the heavens and illuminating its own pathway, and sinking with mournful *éclat* into the darkness below. It is for gratitude and pride to reclaim him and award to him the crown of dramatic excellence that he so grandly sought and achieved.

NOTES

[1]Edward L. Tinker, *Les Écrits de Langue Française en Louisiane au XIXᵉ Siècle*, p. 428.

[2]*Ibid.*

[3]*Register of Baptisms*, St. Louis Cathedral, Vol. XV, p. 174. B. *No. de l'acte*, 871.

[4]Edward L. Tinker, *Les Écrits de Langue Française en Louisiane au XIXᵉ Siècle*, p. 428.

[5]*Ibid.*

[6]*Ibid.*

[7]*Ibid.*

[8]*Ibid.*

[9]*Ibid.*

[10]*Les Cenelles* pp. 55-59.

[11]Edward L. Tinker, *Les Écrits de Langue Française en Louisiane au XIXᵉ Siècle*, p. 428.

[12]Charles B. Rousséve, *The Negro in Louisiana*, pp. 84-85.

[13]Charles B. Rousséve, *The Negro in Louisiana*, pp. 84-85. Translation: "Thy mother . . . ? She spoke a word to me. 'Let us flee!' My hate yielded to tenderness, Happy and confident we departed. . . . Greece received us . . . I became rich and powerful. I was honored, but in vain. My past, suffering, like a crime, a remorse, weighed upon my mind. Bianca (his wife) died, expressing, in her last farewell, a desire to be brought to this land. That wish became my law. After twenty years of exile, after all—none saw in me Jacob-Eliacin."

[14]*Ibid.*, p. 83.

[15]Edward L. Tinker, *Les Écrits de Langue Française en Louisiane au XIXᵉ Siècle*, p. 429.

[16]*Ibid.*, p. 428.

[17]*Ibid.*, p. 429.

[18]Edward L. Tinker, *Les Écrits de Langue Française en Louisiane au XIXᵉ Siècle*, p. 429.

[19]A. E. Perkins, *Who's Who in Colored Louisiana*, p. 32.

[20]*Ibid.*, p. 33.

[21]Edward L. Tinker, *Les Écrits de Langue Française en Louisiane au XIXᵉ Siècle*, p. 429.

[22]Lyle Saxon, *Fabulous New Orleans*, p. 181.

[23]Edward L. Tinker, *Les Écrits de Langue Française en Louisiane au XIXᵉ Siècle*, p. 428.

[24]*Ibid.*

[25]Edward L. Tinker, *Les Écrits de Langue Française en Louisiane au XIXᵉ Siècle*, p. 429.

[26]R. L. Desdunes, *Nos Hommes et Notre Histoire*, p. 39.

[27]Edward L. Tinker, *Les Écrits de Langue Française en Louisiane au XIXe Siècle*, p. 429.

[28]*Ibid.*

[29]*Ibid.*

[30]R. L. Desdunes, *Nos Hommes et Notre Histoire*, pp. 38-39. Note: Free translation n. 47: Victor Séjour, as others, was obliged to leave his native land in order to escape its prejudices.

[31]Carter G. Woodson, *Free Negro Heads of Families*, p. 31 ff.

[32]R. L. Desdunes, *Nos Hommes et Notre Histoire*, p. 39.

[33]*Ibid.*

[34]Edward L. Tinker, *Les Écrits de Langue Française en Louisiane au XIXe Siècle*, p. 430.

[35]*Ibid.*

[36]*Ibid.*

[37]*Ibid.*

[38]*Ibid.-Ante*, p. 8.

[39]*Ibid.*

James V. Hatch and Ted Shine (essay date 1974)

SOURCE: An introduction to *The Brown Overcoat* by Victor Séjour, in *Black Theatre USA: Plays by African Americans, 1847 to Today*, revised and expanded edition, edited by James V. Hatch and Ted Shine, The Free Press, 1996, pp. 25-6.

[*In the following essay, first published in 1974, Hatch and Shine stress the historical importance of Séjour's works.*]

Born in New Orleans on June 2, 1817, of a Creole quadroon mother and a free Black man from Santo Domingo, Juan Victor Séjour Marcon et Ferrand demonstrated a talent for writing poetry early on, at Saint Barbe Academy. At age seventeen, to complete his education, Victor was sent to Paris to remove him from the humiliation imposed upon men of color, even freed men. For the remaining thirty-eight years of his adult life, Séjour acted in plays and wrote dramas for the Parisian theatre. "Tall, handsome and distinguished, with sparkling brown eyes and a complexion too dark and lips too large for him to be mistaken for Caucasian, Séjour was an impressive figure in Paris in the heyday of his glory."[1] Within two years, he had published a novella, **"Le Mulatre" ("The Mulatto")**, but it was his long poem about the return of Emperor Napoleon's body to Paris, *Le Retour de Napoléon*, published in 1824, that brought the young man his fame.

Popular with important literary figures of the day—among them Alexander Dumas père, and the playwright Emile Augier—Séjour began his theatre career in 1844 with a verse drama, **Diégarias**, at the Théâtre Français. Over the following years he wrote twenty other produced plays, many of them full-length romantic historical dramas in the manner of Victor Hugo, whom he admired. In his plays

Séjour "dwells on love of parents and their children, and on the beauty of romantic and marital love. Amid his successes, he dutifully and devotedly brought his parents to Paris, where they lived out their last years. In spite of his plays' high appreciation for marriage and their attractive portrayal of fidelity, Séjour fathered three sons of three mothers out of wedlock."[2]

The reports that Séjour wrote one play with Blacks as characters, **Le Volunteers of 1814**, are false. The play does not concern itself with the siege of New Orleans, but with Napoleon in Europe. He did, however, write a play in 1858, **Le Martyre du Coeur (The Martyrdom of the Heart)**, with one Black character, a Jamaican. It was reported he wrote a five-act drama entitled **L'Esclave (The Slave)**, but the script has never been found.

Séjour penned **The Brown Overcoat** the same year that William Wells Brown published *The Escape* (1858), and it was produced the following year. It is a typical artificial comedy in what was then the degenerated tradition of Molière and Beaumarchais. The dialogue is sometimes witty, often relying on puns that cannot be duplicated in translation. The play has nothing to do with race and little to do with the world.[3]

Yet the play is significant in a collection of this kind, for it was written by a Black American playwright who led a successful nonracial artist's life. Unlike [Ira] Aldridge, he seems to have left the "problem" of racism behind. He integrated into French society and was honored with the title Chevalier and made a member of the Légion d'Honneur. On September 10, 1874, he fulfilled the nineteenth-century's image of the artist by dying in a charity hospital of tuberculosis.

Few of Séjour's plays have been produced, although *The Brown Overcoat*, translated by Townsend Brewster, was produced Off-Broadway on December 6, 1972. The centenary of his death was commemorated with a Séjour production at Loyola University in New Orleans, and at Southern University his likeness appears in a mural of "great Negroes of Louisiana." Along with Ira Aldridge, Séjour pioneered the tradition that if an African American artist could achieve in Europe, that artist might then find some respect at home. Paris in particular became the mecca for many, including Josephine Baker, Chester Hines, Richard Wright, and James Baldwin.

NOTES

[1]Charles Rousseve, *The Negro in Louisiana* (New Orleans: Xavier Press, 1937.)

[2]Charles Edwards O'Neill, *Directary of American Negro Biography* (New York: W. W. Norton, 1982.)

[3]In this European tradition, Paul Laurence Dunbar also wrote one play entitled *Robert Herrick* (c. 1899). The comedy, written in the style of Sheridan and using the poet Robert Herrick as its hero, remains unproduced and unpublished.

Charles Edwards O'Neill (essay date 1978)

SOURCE: "theatrical Censorship in France, 1844-1875: The Experience of Victor Séjour," in *Harvard Library Bulletin*, Vol. XXVI, No. 4, October 1978, pp. 417-41.

[In the excerpt below, O'Neill traces Séjour's experiences with the French censors]

A free man of color born in New Orleans in 1817, Victor Séjour enjoyed a fascinating thirty-year career as a playwright in Paris. With *Diégarias,* staged by the national Théâtre Français in 1844, he made his début. More than twenty of his plays followed on the stages of Paris, including *La Chute de Séjan* (1848), which ran for three and one half months, and *Le Fils de la Nuit* (1856), dedicated to his friend Alexandre Dumas the Elder, which was the most successful of all. His *Cromwell* was played in 1875, seven months after the playwright's death in September 1874.

His life and work link Haiti, whence his father came; Louisiana, his own birthplace; and France, his cultural home. The biography and the literary status of Séjour must be the subject of a book rather than an article. For the moment be it sufficient to say that, although Victor Séjour was not a Victor Hugo or an Alexandre Dumas, he was more than a common playmaker. He was in the second echelon, but he was not just "second rate." Without him one cannot tell the literary history of Second Empire theatre. And without him we cannot complete the history of Louisiana or of Blacks in the United States.

However, within the limits of this article we will focus on only one dimension of that literary history and on only one aspect of Séjour's career, namely his experience in dealing with government censors. Séjour's experience will cast light upon the Second Empire's view of the stage; in particular we will see the government's intense concern over *precisely* what was said on the stage. We will also come to sense the caution and foresight a playwright probably kept in mind as he wrote—or revised what he had written. That there was cooperative dialogue between author and censor also appears; and, strangely, it is thanks to the censorship bureau that we have today the scripts of two Séjour plays which have until now been presumed lost.

SÉJOUR AND THE CENSORS

Censorship by government-appointed readers was a normal part of theatre life in France under Louis-Philippe; it had been restored in 1835 after his regime had for a brief time experimented with removal of controls. The Republic of 1848 promptly abolished censorship of plays. However, the law of 30 July 1850 restored the earlier policy. Before a play could be staged, approval had to be obtained from the Minister of the Interior for Paris productions, from the prefects for those in the departments.[1] In 1853 and 1854 the responsibilities for administration of the national theatres as well as for censorship of Paris theatres were shifted from the Minister of the Interior to the Minister of State of the Household of the Emperor.[2]

The Minister's work was divided between [I] a five-member consultative Examining Commission, whose mission was to examine the manuscripts, confer with directors and authors, and censor the plays, and [2] two-member inspection teams, responsible for executing the decisions of the Examining Commission, seeing the production in rehearsal, and overseeing performances.[3]

Thus, prior to the Second Empire, controls had been removed in 1791, in 1830, and in 1848. Each time the system was reinstalled. General opinion agreed that absolute liberty on the stage was a risk "to the moral, religious and political life of a country."[4]

After the Second Empire fell, the Government of National Defense suspended censorship in September 1870. The "exceptional regime" restored controls in March 1871, and the Third Republic continued them for the rest of the century. The National Assembly in June 1874 provided for inspection of theatres under the Ministry of Public Instruction, Cults, and Fine Arts. The new Republic's administration expected the theatre to be a wholesome school "which would not corrupt . . . [but] would give France the moral greatness becoming to a democracy." The Third Republic intended to grant liberty compatible with public peace, but show severity toward immoral plays.[5]

In the run-of-the-mill operation of censorship, two copies of each play were to be presented to the Ministry of the Interior at least fifteen days before the intended first performance. The Examining Commission would report their conclusions to higher administrators who could bring them to the attention of the Minister himself. At times these conclusions were not followed "either because the [Ministry] did not share the view [of the Commission], or because particular motives or political reasons led [the Ministry] to show itself more indulgent." During the process, "the Commission would receive authors and directors so as to reach an understanding with them on changes it judged useful."[6]

Séjour was thus engaged in dialogue with Commission and Ministry for almost thirty years. Their concerns were expressed in office correspondence which makes it easy for us to follow the relations of Séjour and the censors. The Commission's files of submitted scripts have preserved for us two Séjour plays that were never printed and were presumed lost.

It was to the July Monarchy's censors that Séjour submitted *Diégarias,* his first play. It was approved—with some minor modifications made on the script.[7] Similarly, only a few changes were required in his next few plays or, indeed, none at all, as in the case of *L'Argent du Diable.*[8]

André Gérard, however, was the object of close scrutiny. Its views on the suffering of an injured or disabled worker were allowed to pass, but the rascally Truphème could not be presented as a veteran who had received a decoration![9]

When Séjour brought *Le Martyre du Cœur* to the theatre manager and the Censorship Bureau, it was entitled *Pierre Labo[u]rie.* The scenario, with a workingman devoted to the daughter of a nobleman whom his father had served as valet, would seem to be innocent, sentimental, even sweet. But in 1858, the scars of revolution and class strife were too fresh; certain elements of the original play might prick them raw.

Thus the scheming antagonist, who is out to snare Clarisse, and who, in opposing Pierre, shows only vice in comparison with the worker's virtue, must not be a duke. So "Le Duc" of the original becomes "Lerdac" of the approved play. The transformation is effected by lines written in for Placide, when Lerdac says that he "represents" the now-off-stage Duc de Valmartin. Placide upbraids the schemer for lifting himself up on an honorable name "like a dwarf on stilts. You are a merchant's son, a commoner, and a bit of a usurer besides."[10]

The censor explained his requirements and his reasons: "Following my observations, a number of radical modifications have been carried out on the work. It seemed indispensable to me that the two personages set in opposition be placed on a level less unequal. On one side Pierre Laborie, instead of being of a line of valets, had as father a manager. He is no longer a laborer but an engraving artist." The erstwhile Duke would now be a dishonest agent of the Duke; that is why Le Duc became Lerdac.

This modification, the censor judged, would remove the obnoxious element that was found in the original, and that it was the particular mission of the Censorship Bureau to eliminate. The original version would prolong and aggravate that social antagonism which the government was persistently trying to remove from the national scene. With these changes effected, the Bureau approved the play in time for its opening in mid-March of 1858.[11]

When Séjour and co-author Jean-François Mocquard readied *La Tireuse de Cartes* for production, the Examining Commission was concerned: A dying Jewish infant is baptized by a Christian maid, unexpectedly recovers, and is hidden and raised as a Christian; the Jewish mother, acting as a fortune-teller, seeks relentlessly until she finds the child, who had been adopted into a noble family. The Examining Commission's role was to foresee trouble-causing elements, and here was a play wrought in the heat of controversy. However, Mocquard was of the Emperor's staff. What was the Commission to do? It seems that the play was given exceptional treatment, for, strangely, although a text of every other Séjour play of the Second Empire can be found in the censorship files, *La Tireuse* is not there.

It was, of course, submitted, and a first report was made in late November of 1859. The Examining Commission found that the play "raise[d] a pre-judgment question which [they did] not think they were qualified to resolve. It is a question whether, on the one hand, one wishes to permit the theatre to become henceforth an arena open to religious antagonism, even when that antagonism is not produced except for purely dramatic interest, and whether, on the other hand, in the present political situation on the international and religious scene, it is proper to stage a subject evidently inspired by a recent event, whose repercussions are at the present moment being felt anew."[12] (The recent event was the Edgardo Mortara case.)

Invited by the Minister "to effect modifications . . . of a nature to diminish the dangers and obstacles," the Examining Commission went to work, but they did not expect "to arrive at a completely satisfactory result." They toned down elements that "highlighted religious antagonism." They eliminated lines that seemed blasphemous. They removed a parish priest, and omitted mention of his church and sermon; in the kidnapping there would not even be a superior of a monastery, because he too would be a priest. "We did accept a *superioress*, because she does not have the sacred character [of ordination]; besides she does not appear, but is spoken of only in the exposition of the action."

"As much as possible," the censors explained, "we tried to concentrate the dominant interest of the play on the tenderness, the rivalry of the two mothers."[13] The Minister responsible gave his approval for performance because he "saw nothing in it that could prevent it" from being played. Outside observers, however, seeing the reflection on Pius IX, were surprised, because a play that could have given offense to the Austrian Emperor was blocked at about the same time.[14]

Following the Paris run, *La Tireuse* went out *en province*, where it became a cause of concern to the departmental prefects. In February 1860 the Prefect of the Upper-Garonne Department declined to approve the play in Toulouse; yet he consulted Paris lest he be too severe. His reasoning was that, during the international controversy over the Question of Rome, Toulouse was quiet; no discontent or hostility toward the Emperor or his policy was being manifested by clergy or laity. There was, of course, watchful waiting. The Prefect wanted to keep the quiet tone, wanted to avoid the stirring of recrimination. "I need not add," he wrote to the Minister, "that I intend in no way to fault the work itself and that I am concerned exclusively with the significance that would be given it here."[15] Since the play had not been announced, it was not exactly "cancelled." The Prefect was willing to approve the performance if Paris said to go ahead.[16]

Paris would not take the responsibility. The play had been staged in Paris because, it was judged, no trouble would follow. "If you think it would be otherwise in Toulouse," the Minister responded to the Prefect, "it is for you by the terms of the law itself to make a decision in that regard."[17]

From Grenoble, later that month, the Prefect of the Isère Department also tried to shift the burden to Paris. He too was told to make his decision in the light of local circumstances which he alone could judge.[18]

A different play, also entitled *La Tireuse de Cartes*, a vaudeville work with words by Letellier and music by Abadie, was entered on the government's "List of forbidden plays" as early as 30 December 1853, years before the Mortara affair and the Séjour play.[19] In departmental prefectures these homonyms could easily have been confused.

With minor touches to various lines *Les Aventuriers* (1860) and *Les Massacres de la Syrie* (1860) sailed through censorship. However, in 1861 Séjour's *Les Volontaires de 1814* first went before the censors, carrying the title of *L'Invasion*. In this drama Napoleon I is defeated by the Allies, who march on Paris. The script was rejected outright by the Examining Commission; the head of the Bureau des Théâtres (Cabanis) agreed with the examiners, and the Minister (Waleski) endorsed the rejection.

The trio of examiners was clear and firm: "We cannot propose the authorization of the play entitled *The Invasion,* which with unsettling realism recalls one of the most disastrous periods of our contemporary history. Despite the brilliant comeback which France has made, despite the glorious place which Emperor Napoleon III has reconquered for her among the nations, the deeply painful and humiliating portrayal of the calamities which partisan spirit blames on the First Empire, and presents as the cause of its fall, cannot be laid before the eyes of the public."[20]

The ensemble, rather than particular passages, created the problem. Yet some details were pinpointed. For example, the censors regretted that in one scene "a workingman attributes to the Emperor all the ills that weigh on France, for in going to Moscow, he showed the enemy the path to Paris."[21]

Much reworking was done on this play. Its title was changed from *The Invasion* to *The Volunteers of 1814.* A key aim in the revision was to eliminate scenes and lines that could trigger an anti-regime outburst of scoffing laughter or of insulting catcalls. Finally, the *Volunteers* were allowed to march on stage in April 1862.

Six years later a revival of the play in Laval prompted the Prefect of the Department of the Mayenne to consult Paris. He was advised to assess the circumstances and do as he judged best.[22] This was getting close to the year when another invasion of northeastern France would bring down another Napoleon.

In 1876 the Theatre of Roubaix wanted to stage *Les Volontaires.* The Prefect of the Department of the North consulted Paris, which this time did make the decision—in the negative. The Minister of the Interior asked the Minister of Public Instruction what was the status of Séjour's play. The latter responded that the portrayal on stage of the Emperor Napoleon I, the Emperors of the coalition, and the invasion "would without any doubt produce scandals which the most elementary prudence commands us to avoid."[23] The national wound that was sore and painful in 1861 was—after Sedan—raw and gory in 1876.

The apparently innocent *Les Mystères du Temple* (1862) called forth "numerous observations" from the censors in line with the policy of preserving social harmony. "The author yielded to these observations, and effected the changes which seemed [to the censors] necessary." The play was approved.[24]

Although the censorship office was satisfied with changes of some individual lines in *Les Fils de Charles-Quint* (1864) and the *Le Marquis Caporal* (1864), one republican reviewer would have made the author revise the whole role of Gourdier, the corrupt civil administrator of the revolution.

Séjour's *Les Enfants de la Louve* (1865), set in fifteenth-century England's War of the Roses, awakened "certain scruples" in the Examining Commission, but, nonetheless, won their approval. (One of the examiners was Victor Hallays, who would later write a history of censorship in France.) Two points worried them. "We asked ourselves," they reported, "first, whether in this struggle of exiled princes claiming the throne, some ill-intentioned minds would not be on the lookout for allusions." (Then those minds could lead cheers or jeers in the theatre.) "We asked ourselves, secondly, whether this portrait of a debauched and bloodthirsty king stayed within the bounds of what is admissible in the theatre without becoming a danger for the respect due to the very principle of sovereignty."

But further reflection and a few changes sufficed to clear the play, which seemed "too clearly set in time and place to allow the audience to see anything other than the play itself": England, York, Lancaster, the barbarous fifteenth-century manners, and so on. Besides, it was noted, Séjour's *Richard III,* "raising analogous questions, had been performed some years previously without difficulty."[25]

Séjour's late-career plays, *La Madone des Roses* and *Henri de Lorraine,* passed censorship easily—with the usual touching up of individual lines. His posthumous *Cromwell*'s story is a drama all in itself.

Séjour died at a moment when France was wavering between monarchy and republic. He left behind him the manuscript of a play on Oliver Cromwell, Lord Protector of England, a personage whom Séjour's mentor Victor Hugo had also dramatized. Cromwellian Puritans had beheaded Charles I, and changed England from monarchy to a sort of republic. This was an explosive theme to stage in Paris in the period of doubt that followed the Second Empire, the Franco-Prussian War, and the Commune!

It was the actor, Paul-Félix-Joseph Taillade, who brought Séjour's last opus to the stage. Recalling how the playwright had yearned to have it played, Taillade spoke for the script with the management of the Théâtre du Châtelet.[26]

Maurice Drack (*nom-de-plume* of August-Alfred Poitevin) readied the manuscript for the Châtelet.[27] Opening night was postponed when the Châtelet called in Marc Fournier, the old pro from the Porte-Saint-Martin, to perk up the stage effects—as in the old days of Séjourism. *Cromwell* opened on 24 April 1875.

Later writers have claimed that the play was never staged! Some wondered whether we would ever know the contents of the drama. Thanks to the government censorship bureau's preservation of scripts, we can read Séjour's *Cromwell* in two versions, one an earlier draft of the other. It would be rash to affirm that government censorship rather than artistic judgment is responsible for all the structural changes in the play. But problems aplenty were posed for censors who were expected so to filter a play that it would cause no outcry in the theatre.

Cromwell, in the impassioned rhetoric of a Séjourian protagonist, would hardly have soft lines on royalists! Yet, given the tensions of Paris in the spring of 1875, Séjour's Cromwell had to mind his manners even in outbursts.

In one speech the Protector is in a rage over royalist attempts to assassinate him—"these royalist vampires who have sucked and gone mad with the rich blood of England." Given the royalist-versus-republican tensions, the censors contested the line. Drack proposed to drop "bloodsucking" and to say "these royalist wretches." The censors held their ground; even the word *royalist* had to go.

Onstage that first night Taillade was carried away with his dramatic fervor, and let fly with the suppressed phrase—milder, doubtless, than old Cromwell in reality spoke, but too explosive for Paris in April 1875. "Those royalist wretches!" Republicans in the audience cheered. Royalists whistled—the French version of booing. Uproar! For five or ten minutes bedlam drowned out actors.

In this city still under martial law (*état de siège*) the reaction of the public authorities was immediate. The Governor of Paris, General Louis Paul de Ladmirault, notified the management: "Given the disorder of which the Châtelet was the scene in the course of the performance of 24 April we decree that the performance of *Cromwell* is forbidden."[28]

The press accepted in general the role of censorship in the theatre, but felt that the financial loss suffered by the 800 persons who lived off the Châtelet's revenues was too heavy a penalty for the deed of one actor. Conservative Jules Clarétie expressed confidence that the order would soon be revoked.

In the interim perceptive observers pointed out the ambivalence of the play. The restoration of the Stuarts was foreshadowed. Thus Séjour's *Cromwell* was neither republican nor royalist: it was historical. The audience—or rather a fraction of the audience—had over-reacted. Then others had reacted to the reaction.[29]

Taillade publicly apologized. "I regret a slip which has had such fatal consequences for a director with whom I am on contract, for the authors whose friend I am, for the players whose comrade I am. I am not at all ashamed to admit I made a mistake in altering a text, of which the actor, whatever may be his personal ideas, should remain the faithful interpreter. The only excuse I can offer the public, my sovereign judge, is that, in a stirring situation, I lost my head, and let myself be carried away by an unfortunate accident of improvisation."[30]

Taillade's *amende honorable*, the management's repentant apologies, the cast's willingness to review the entire play carefully in the presence of the censors—all persuaded the Governor of Paris to rescind his order. *Cromwell* reopened on 4 May. With the excitement already gone, with the play censored beyond the normal range, the public did not turn out in numbers sufficient to make up the box-office losses.

Clément Caraguel judged that *Cromwell* was "one of the best dramas staged on the boulevards for two or three years, and it can play for a long time without the public peace being troubled."[31] Peace was troubled no more, but the play lasted only through 24 May.[32]

"Poor Victor Séjour!" Sarcey exclaimed, "Assuredly he did not suspect five or six years ago when he was working on this drama (interrupted by death), that there would be found in it mischievous allusions to a situation that did not yet exist."[33] . . .

This examination of Séjour's experience with the censors has given us insight into the mind of the Second Empire. We see particularly how nervous or sensitive Napoleon III and his government felt *vis-à-vis* the stage. We are surprised to see the official attention to detail, to certain words, to what seem minutiae. Must not this very sensitivity in itself have given heightened political significance to stage dialogue?

Yet Victor Séjour was not a threat to the regime. A man attuned to the cry for justice, Séjour was not in favor of violent revolution but rather of orderly evolution in a social climate of stability and harmony. Since he was generally in favor of Bonapartism, and what Bonapartism said it favored, we can be satisfied that his experience with censors was rather typical, or at least that his work received no harsher treatment than that of others.

NOTES

[1]Albéric Cahuet, *La Liberté du Théâtre en France et à l'Etranger* (Paris: Dujarric, 1902), pp. 215-216; Circulaire Ministérielle, 3 août 1850, in *La Censure Dramatique* ["Administration Théâtrale" at head of title] (Paris: Sagnier, 1873), pp. 82-84.

[2]Cahuet (note 1 above), pp. 218-219.

[3]Victor Hallays-Dabot, *Histoire de la Censure Théâtrale en France* (Paris: Dentu, 1862), pp. 331-332; Cahuet (note 1 above), p. 219; Circulaire aux Directeurs des Théâtres de Paris, 3 août 1850, in *La Censure Dramatique* (note 1 above), pp. 85-87.

[4]Hallays-Dabot (note 3 above), pp. 332-333.

[5]Cahuet (note 1 above), pp. 244-246.

[6]Victor Hallays-Dabot, *La Censure Dramatique et le Théâtre, Histoire des Vingt Dernières Années (1850-1870)* (Paris: Dentu, 1871), p. 6.

[7]Paris, Archives Nationales, Série F21, Numéro 966, 22 juin 1844. These documents are cited hereinafter as AN—thus, AN, F21, 966.

[8]AN, F18, 899, *Richard III*, 3 août 1852; AN, F18, 798, *L'Argent du Diable*, 8 mars 1854; AN, F21, 975, *Noces Vénitiennes*, 6 mars 1855; *Fils de la Nuit*, 8 juillet 1856.

[9]AN, F18, 713, *André Gérard*, décision signifiée 21 avril 1857.

[10]AN, F18, 953, *Martyre du Cœur*, Act I, scene 7.

[11]AN, F21, 974, *Pierre Laborie*.

[12]AN, F21, 975, Commission d'Examen, 25 nov. 1859.

[13]*Idem.*

[14]AN, F21, 996, Ministre d'État de la Maison de l'Empereur to Préfet du Département de l'Isère, 23 mai 1860.

[15]AN, F21, 996, 6 fév. 1860.

[16]*Idem.*

[17]*Idem.*

[18]AN, F21, 996, Préfet to Ministre, 24 fév. 1860; Ministre to Préfet, 23 mai 1860.

[19]AN', F21, 996, *Liste des pièces interdites*, dated Paris, 30 déc. 1853; 7 déc, 1857; 1 mai 1863; 28 déc. 1866.

[20]AN, F21, 975, report on *L'Invasion*, 5 sept. 1861; Cabanis to Waleski, 6 sept. 1861. Undated marginal notation of Ministre.

[21]AN, F21, 975, report of 5 sept. 1861.

[22]AN, F21, 996, Préfet to Ministre, 26 mai 1868; Ministre to Préfct, 29 mai 1868.

[23]AN, F21, 997, 27 oct. 1876; 3 nov. 1876.

[24]AN, F21, 974, report, 12 août 1862.

[25]AN, F21, 977, report, *Les Enfants de la Louve*, 12 avril 1865.

[26]*Figaro*, 25 avril 1875.

[27]*Ibid.*; also Edouard Noël and Edmond Stoulig, *Annales du Théâtre et de la Musique*, 1875 (Paris, 1876), p. 356.

[28]*Journal des Débats*, 27 avril 1875.

[29]*Figaro*, 25 and 26 avril 1875; *Le Temps*, 27 avril and 3, 10, and 17 mai 1875; *Journal des Débats*, 27 avril 1875; *Gazette de France*, 5 mai 1875; *La Presse*, 27 and 28 avril 1875; Noël and Stoulig, *Annales* (note 27 above), pp. 353-357.

[30]*Figaro*, 30 avril 1875, p. 3 (letter to editor).

[31]*Journal des Débats*, 10 mai 1875.

[32]*Figaro*, 24-25 mai 1875.

[33]*Le Temps*, 10 mai 1875, feuilleton.

J. John Perret (essay date 1983)

SOURCE: "Victor Séjour, Black French Playwright from Louisiana," in *The French Review*, Vol. LVII, No. 2, December 1983, pp. 187-93.

[*In the following essay, Perret reviews the French critical reception of Séjour's plays.*]

Victor Séjour (1817-1874), *homme de couleur libre* born in New Orleans, had two plays performed at the Comédie Française and a score at other Parisian theaters. No indication of the author's racial heritage is found in them, and religion is used to plead for tolerance. His first play at the Comédie Française was ***Diégarias*** (1844), which reads like a Hugolian version of *La Juive*. ***La Chute de Séjan*** (1849), his second play, was his last in verse and the last on this stage. Using a *sujet d'actualité*, the massacre of Maronite Christians in Syria in 1860, he showed the results of Moslem fanaticism in ***Les Massacres de la Syrie*** (1860). These same plays also show his three principal weaknesses: (1) out-of-date Romanticism bordering on melodrama, (2) indiscriminate borrowing from classical and contemporary authors, (3) adulation of Napoleon III.

Little is known of Séjour's life. His father, Jean François Louis Victor Séjour Marcou, always called himself Louis Séjour, was a native of St. Marc, Haiti, and an octoroon like Dumas *fils*. With the aid of newspapers we can place him in New Orleans at least as early as 1811. By 1816 he was promoting quadroon balls in the notorious Washington Ballroom at the St. Philip Street Theater in the heart of the French Quarter. Later he became a dry goods merchant with a store on the corner of St. Philip and Bourbon streets and eventually engaged successfully in real estate transactions. In the early 1850s he joined his son in Paris where he died in 1864 according to reports in the New Orleans press.

According to baptismal records of the St. Louis Cathedral, Jean Victor, natural son of M. Jean François Louis Victor Séjour Marcou and Mlle Eloïse Philippe Ferrand of New Orleans, was born 2 June 1817. (The date on his tombstone in Père-Lachaise is incorrect.) Marriage records show his parents married on 13 January 1825, thus legitimizing Victor and his elder brother Louis. His education remains a mystery. There were schools for the children of "free men of color" at the time, but the one he allegedly attended did not exist until the 1840s, at least a decade after his arrival in France in 1830. There, he presumably followed the traditional paths of aspiring writers, except that he would not have had to contend with poverty; his father, to whom he was very devoted, was alive and prosperous. The return of Napoleon's remains in 1841 inspired him to publish a long poem entitled ***Le Retour de Napoléon*** (Paris: Dauvain et Fontaine, 1841) in which the Emperor incarnated France: "Non, non, ce n'est pas moi que l'indigne Angleterre, / Comme un lion captif, retient sur cette terre / Noble France, c'est toi."

In ***Diégarias*** (Paris: César Bajat, 1844), which had its premiere on 23 July 1844 at the Comédie Francaise, we find the devices, good and bad, which Séjour will employ throughout his career: (1) melodramatic characterization, (2) excesses in language, (3) a proclivity for having parents directly or indirectly cause the death of the progeny,

(4) antithesis of the Hugolian variety, (5) use of the union-in-death theme.

Considering his acknowledged masters, one could hardly expect otherwise. In the dedication of ***André Gérard*** (Paris: Michel Lévy Frères, 1857), a melodrama exploited by the flamboyant Frederick Lemaître, he began by eschewing *l'art pour l'art* and putting himself unequivocally on the side of Dumas *fils* and Augier: "Personne plus que moi ne se préoccupe du but et de la moralité du théâtre." He concluded by naming his masters:

> L'art est une succession de sommets. Je me contente d'être placé au degré le plus bas, pourvu que je puisse contempler, sur les hauteurs, mes deux maîtres Shakespeare et Victor Hugo, ces sources de grandeur et vérité. J'aime les torrents, même dans leurs plus bruyantes horreurs; je hais les filets d'eau, même dans leurs fantaisies et leurs grâces.

It is obviously the Hugo of *Hernani* that impressed him. Add Schiller, the elder Dumas, Byron, and one or two others, and one has a good idea of his fundamentally Romantic orientation, an orientation that never changed to accommodate itself to contemporary schools and taste.

Critical reception reflected the times; ***Diégarias*** coming fifteen months after the premiere of *Les Burgraves* was warmly received, as the theater-going public did not realize that the Romantic theater's day had passed. Théophile Gautier, still unabashedly Romantic, offered an encomium. Critics in the 1850s and 1860s tended to be more reserved, tempering praise with counsel. Unfortunately, Adolphe Brisson, Francisque Sarcey's son-in-law, included no entry earlier than 1867 when he condensed the latter's *feuilletons* into eight volumes.[1] The critic was then dealing with an author past his prime and he had few words of praise. The asperity of the tone increased with the years until after Séjour's death the mere mention of his name had an almost paroxysmal effect on the critic. Had Sarcey mentioned him more frequently, he might have conferred a kind of immortality on him as the quintessential bad playwright.

Séjour's first play epitomizes his conception of the theater. Jacob Eliacin, a fifteenth-century Spanish Jew compelled to leave Spain because he courted and married a Christian, fled to Greece where he amassed a fortune as a merchant. After an absence of fifteen years he emerges as Diégarias, the trusted minister of Henry IV of Castille, the object of his subjects' hatred and plotting. Diégarias' main concern, however, is for his daughter Inès, who has been seduced by Don Juan de Tello, a conspirator. Inès loves him and believes naïvely that a sham ceremony had joined them in marriage. At this point, a more classically inclined author would have opted for the Cornelian situation, the affair of state, or for the Racinian one, the mismatched couple of whom only one is in love. Simplicity of plot and economy of action being foreign to our author, he combined both elements with a Scribian use of *péripéties*. The visual

takes precedence over the psychological, as it always will in Séjour's theater.

The resolution of these parallel crises affords the author free dramaturgic rein. A Moor whom Diégarias had treated harshly in Greece informs Don Juan de Tello of Diégarias' background. In a *coup de théâtre*, the seducer bares the secret before the court and saves himself from a forced marriage. Disgraced, stripped of title and rank, Diégarias seems to be at the nadir of his fortune. Yet, he holds the trump card—money. The king and the conspirators will both approach him for support to pay their mercenaries. From the king he demands the head of Don Juan as the price of a loan. Helping the conspirators overturn the throne will rectify the wrongs he suffered because of his religion. As he relishes the thought of this dual vengeance, he takes an oath that is derived from *Othello* (Act III, Scene iii):

> Devant toi, nuit lugubre, et toi, pâle clarté,
> Et vous, astres roulans dans votre immensité,
> Je vous prends à témoin—dussé-je sur ma tête
> Voir tomber en éclats la foudre et la tempête.
>
> (Act IV, Scene vi)

The king keeps his word, and Don Juan is executed. Inès becomes the first of Séjour's lovers to seek reunion in death. As her father savors his first revenge, she swallows poison and serenely awaits death: "J'irai le retrouver dans le sépulchre avare . . . / Le poison réunit quand l'échafaud sépare" (Act V, Scene vii).

Diégarias then tells the assembled nobles the king has traded the life of one of them for gold. He, a Jew, has toppled the throne. He becomes a sort of malevolent Ruy Blas, complete with antithesis, as he taunts the king: "Résignetoi, car ton heure est sonnée, / Le nain s'est fait géant et tient ta destinée" (Act V, Scene viii). The tocsin signaling the revolt is heard. Diégarias' triumph seems complete until he notices his daughter in her death throes. The curtain falls as he sobs: "J'ai voulu me venger . . . j'ai tué mon enfant."

In a review dated 29 July 1844 in *Histoire de l'art dramatique en France depuis vingt-cinq ans* (Paris: Edition Hetzel, 6 vols, 1859) Gautier waxed enthusiastic: "Ce drame est l'œuvre d'un débutant, et il a réussi . . . le public a reçu la pièce du jeune auteur avec un sentiment de bienveillance que nour voudrions lui voir plus souvent pour les essais et les débuts littéraires" (III, 236). Neither the Romantic tendencies nor the patent borrowings from Hugo were seen as faults by Gautier. On the contrary, he saw them as signs of strength:

> Son drame révèle des tendances et des études romantiques; ce sera, pour beaucoup de gens, une occasion de blâme et de reproche; quant à nous qui nous faisons honneur d'appartenir comme disciple à cette école que d'autres ont rendue illustre, nous féliciterons M. Victor Séjour d'avoir imité franchement le plus grand poète

de ce temps-ci. C'est déjà une preuve de talent que de
savoir choisir un bon maître.

                                                    (III, 237)

After praising this "drame habilement charpenté," Gautier
added: "Le style, qui pourrait être plus correct et plus
poétique, a une qualité très importante au théâtre: il est clair
et net, disant ce qu'il veut dire sans trop de concessions à
la rime et à l'hémistiche" (III, 238).

Writing eighteen years after the play's premiere, L. Félix
Savard found it "tout rouge de meurtres," *boursoufflé*,
and completely lacking in verisimilitude: "Ce Juif devenu
ministre, ce roi Henri IV de Castille n'avaient rien de bien
humain. . . ." He pilloried the style by citing this fragment
"Chaque rayon de flamme / Devrait prendre une voix
pour parler à ton âme" and asking rhetorically: "Avez-vous
jamais entendu *parler des flammes*?"[2]

La Chute de Séjan (Paris: Michel Lévy Frères, 1849),
whose premiere at the Comédie Française was on 21 August 1849, shows even more flagrant borrowing. Sejanus,
the Roman emperor, is the first of Séjour's characters to
use the monologue à la Don Carlos in *Hernani*. In addition, his impending doom is predicted in a style that barely
paraphrases Ruggieri's warning to Saint-Mégrin in *Henry
III et sa cour* (Act IV, Scene iii). How closely Séjour
followed his master can be seen by comparing Hernani's
offer to Don Ruy Gomez to one made in *La Chute de
Séjan:*

> Quand tu voudras, seigneur, quel que soit
>   le lieu, l'heure,
> S'il te passe à l'esprit qu'il est temps que je meure,
> Viens, sonne de ce cor, et ne prends d'autres soins.
> Tout sera fait.
>
>   *Hernani* (Acte III, Scene vii)

Séjour even starts with the same rhyme words:

> Ce serment fait; dès lors, tu peux indiquer l'heure,
> Choisir le lieu, l'instant, où tu veux que je meure,
> Soit-il ici, soit ailleurs, fût-ce en un lieu sacré,
> J'en atteste à mon tour les dieux, j'obéirai.
>
>   (Act III, Scene ix)

Before turning to *Les Massacres de la Syrie* (Paris: Barbré,
1860) a final word on sources. Séjour did a *Richard
III* (1852). *Les Noces vénitiennes* (1855) is admittedly
a sequel to Delavigne's *Marino Faliero*, but it opens
with a hall of portraits scene straight from *Hernani*. *Les
Fils de Charles Quint* (1864) owes more than a little to
Schiller's *Don Carlos*. I have seen references to an *Henri
de Lorraine* (1870), but I have not been able to locate a
copy of it. One could assume that it is derived from *Henry
III et sa cour.*

Even with a scant pair of racial allusions, *Les Massacres
de la Syrie* has more than any other of his plays. While
ostensibly the dramatization of an historical event, the play
could be described as a protracted metonymy; Napoleon
III is France and vice versa. In spite of this, the elements
for a good play were not lacking: the dual tensions of the
politico-religious conflict and the love of a Moslem girl
for a giaour.

Ben-Yacoub, leader of the fanatical Drusian sect, plans a
massacre of the Maronite Christians led by Georges de
Moréac. The Druse loves Gulnare, a Moslem foundling
raised by the Moréac family.[3] She, however, loves Georges
de Moréac. Ben-Yacoub's hatred of the giaours is thus
twofold. The historical Ab-el-Kader (1807-1883), former
enemy of the French, has become a staunch ally and
appears in *deus ex machina* fashion several times at crucial
points. He offers the aid of his Algerian troops to stop
the massacre as word arrives that French troops are on the
way. The conspirators are punished and peace restored by
the timely intervention of the French.

This résumé can only suggest the multiplicity of intrigues
and elaborate staging that thrilled the first-nighters until the
final curtain at 1:00 A.M. Jean Rousseau, who reviewed
the premiere in the 3 January 1861 issue of *Le Figaro*,
began his critique somewhat hyperbolically: "Cinq cents
figures environ,-plutôt plus que moins—traversent le drame
nouveau, et l'on ne compte dans cette légion d'acteurs, que
trois cent cinquante comparses!"

Rousseau recognized the popular appeal, but was not blind
to the blatant propaganda. He gives Jean-François-Constant
Mocquard, Napoleon III's personal secretary, as co-author,
although Mocquard's name does not appear in the printed
version of the play. While no definite play is attributed
to him, the older Larousse encyclopedias note: "Il passe
pour avoir collaboré à plusieurs drames." Rousseau initially
omitted in his plot résumé the role of Papillon, an itinerant
barber in the tradition of Figaro:

> Ainsi nous avons coupé tout le rôle de Papillon, un des
> plus jolis pourtant de la pièce, qu'il égaye de perpétuels
> lazzis. . . . Aux Druzes qui lui demandent arrogamment
> ce que c'est la France, il répond de son accent le plus
> agressif:—La France? C'est les Pyramides où quarante
> siècles nous contemplent. . . . C'est Alger que nous
> avons bombardé et pris. . . . C'est Sébastopol où l'on
> vous aurait éreintés sans nous . . . voilà ce que c'est!

It is given to Ab-el-Kader, however, to play the sycophant
whose gratitude to Napoleon III is boundless. As he tries
to dissuade his Moslem brothers, he evokes the emperor's
name:

> Malheureux! . . . mais vous n'entendez donc pas, du
> côté de l'Occident, les Francs qui s'agitent dèja! . . .
> mais leur glorieux et puissant souverain qui a tout
> quitté pour protéger un peuple étranger et ressuciter
> l'Italie de ses propres mains . . . vous demandera
> compte du sang des siens . . . Oh! je le connais . . .
> il se lèvera le premier . . . il appellera la civilisation
> contre la barbarie . . . il viendra . . . il vient peut-être!
>
>   (Tableau VI, Scene viii)

Ben-Yacoub thinks the older man wants supreme power and he offers it to him while reminding him à la Corneille: "Je suis ce que tu étais en Afrique." Ab-el-Kader spurns the offer and brandishes his sword:

> Napoléon III m'a donne cette épée . . . je me sentais assez grand pour l'accepter; je me sens assez digne pour m'en servir! . . . Je prouverai au sultan de France que cette main qu'il a touchée est sienne et qu'il a un serviteur dévoué et un soldat de plus en moi.
>
> (Tableau VII, Scene vi)

In summary, Rousseau of *Le Figaro* wrote:

> Le fait est, bien que la pièce ait duré jusqu'à une heure du matin, que l'attention n'a pas langui un moment. On a suivi avec un intérêt croissant les aspects changeants de ce grand spectacle qui mêle la comédie à l'historie, le drame au ballet, les féeries de l'Opéra aux péripéties du boulevard.

There is a racial allusion which is not specifically applicable to Blacks, if one relies solely on the text. If refers to la D'Jemmala-D'Jezza, whom one would assume to be a gypsy firebrand because of her dress and manner. When first seen in Tableau I, Scene xi, Séjour describes her thus: "Elle est vêtue d'une façon bizarre; tout en elle provoque la surprise et même l'effroi." As the impending massacre draws near, she boasts that she will pass unnoticed as all of her kind look the same to those outside the group: "Les visages noirs n'ont pas d'empreintes: traits effacés, œil éteint; à vingt pas, doute; à trente, confusion et ténèbres; à cinquante, nuit" (Tableau IV, Scene i). On stage, however, she is definitely a Black. Rousseau called her "une négresse furibonde."

The only other vaguely racial allusion is to slavery, and here the slaves are Caucasians. The hero's mother was captured and sold as a slave in the early stages of the Drusian attack. Upon hearing the news Georges exclaims: "Ma mère, une Moréac, une femme noble et libre vendue comme une esclave" (Tableau VI, Scene i). There is no more comment, just this indignant outburst. Though neither he nor his parents had ever been slaves, we can only guess what the author had in mind when he put these words in the mouth of a character just months before the Civil War.

Séjour had six plays staged after *Les Massacres de la Syrie,* but his apogee had passed. He died impoverished and tubercular on 20 September 1874. Quite fittingly for a disciple of Hugo, he was working on a *Cromwell* at the time of his death, and like Hugo, his play was performed after his death.

Earlier we noted Francisque Sarcey's progressively acerbic criticism. He gave some indication of what displeased him (would that he had given more); indeed, eighteen years after his death, Séjour was still serving him as a critical *point de repère.* Sarcey's first reference to him came in a 24 June 1867 critique of *Hernani,* which, for Sarcey, had value only as an iconoclasm. Of the author he wrote: "Tout

ce qui est antithèse; soit de caractères, soit de passions; soit d'événements, il l'a patiemment et vigoureusement combiné, et il a ainsi abouti, à force d'application et de travail, à des situations aussi terribles qu'en ont jamais imaginé les d'Ennery et les Victor Séjour" (Vol. IV, pp. 1-2).

In an 16 April 1869 review of *L'Aventurière* of Augier, Sarcey admitted that he was having difficulty producing a coherent review: "Que le lecteur me pardonne . . . j'ai hier, durant quatre heures d'horloge, entendu la prose de M. Victor Séjour; je me débarbouille comme je peux" (Vol. V, p. 12). The unnamed Séjour play was not a premiere; he had none that year.

His last references to Séjour occur in a 15 February 1892 review of *Par le glaive* of Jean Richepin. If Séjour had fallen completely into oblivion, it would have been pointless to cite him, yet Sarcey does—five times. The author's name and memory must have been very much alive for the theater-going public of 1892. Richepin's play "n'est qu'un drame de Victor Séjour mis en musique par un grand virtuose." A few lines later he starts a new paragraph: "Il y a du Victor Séjour dans Richepin." Mounet-Sully *et al.* are praised for their fine acting in Act III, but the act itself "sent d'une lieue son Victor Séjour." The play's last two acts are abominable, or as Sarcey stated simply: "C'est du Victor Séjour dans sa mélodramtique horreur" (Vol. VII, pp. 265-77).

Le Fils de la nuit (Paris: Michel Lévy Frères, 1856) had its premiere 11 July 1856 at the Théâtre de la Porte-Saint-Martin. It is the play that captured the public's imagination. The plot is typical: a mother switches babies in their cribs to ensure a better life for her own. The child is predictably killed in the place of the other, and the curtain again falls to "J'ai tué mon enfant." What raised this melodrama to new heights was the appearance of a moving ship on stage. Depending on one's judgment, it was a stroke of genius or the ruination of the theater. Savard was inclined to the latter view: "Victor Séjour ne tarda à se sacrifier au *truc*; c'est même lui qui, on peut le dire, l'a inventé. Que de pages il y aurait à écrire sur la détestable influence qu'a exercée le vaisseau du *Fils de la nuit* sur la littérature contemporaine. Tous nos maux viennent de là. Le public n'écoute plus, il regarde; il faut que sans cesse les directeurs se surpassent euxmêmes" (pp. 50-51).

If Séjour, single-handed, had indeed changed the orientation of French theater, he assumes significant proportions aside from any purely literary or esthetic values.

A word about the title of this article seems appropriate. France was represented in *Les Massacres de la Syrie* as the bastion of freedom and the defender of the oppressed. Louisiana Blacks of Séjour's socio-economic background did, on occasion, settle in France to avoid racial discrimination. Even those who stayed in their native state sound French in education, culture, and loyalty to a "mother country" they had never seen. The leading historian of these

"Black Frenchmen" was Rodolphe Desdunes, who published their story in 1911 under the title of *Nos Hommes et notre historie*. He, too, was born *homme de couleur libre*, but when he died in 1928 the space on his death certificate following "Race" was filled with the word "French."[4]

NOTES

[1]See Francisque Sarcey, *Quarante Ans de théâtre*, 8 vols. (Paris: Bibliothèque des Annales, 1900-02). All further references to this work will appear in the text.

[2]L. Felix Savard, "M. Victor Séjour," *Les Chroniques Littéraires*, 2 (1862), 48. All further references to this work will appear in the text.

[3]Gulnare is also the heroine of "The Corsair" by Byron. She saves a gaiaour from death by killing a coreligionist.

[4]New Orleans Archdiocesan Cemetery Records.

FURTHER READING

Daley, T. A. "Victor Séjour." *Phylon* IV, No. 1 (First Quarter 1943): 5-16.
      Biographical and critical survey of Séjour's career.

Peterson, Bernard L. Entry on Victor Séjour. In *Early Black American Playwrights and Dramatic Writers: A Biographical Directory and Catalog of Plays, Films, and Broadcasting Scripts*, pp. 172-75. New York : Greenwood Press, 1990.
      Includes a brief biography and a descriptive catalogue of about twenty of Séjour's plays.

Additional coverage of Séjour's life and career is contained in the following source published by Gale Research: *Dictionary of Literary Biography*, Vol. 50.

Luis Valdez
1940-

INTRODUCTION

Considered the originator of modern Chicano theater, Valdez is best known as the founding director of El Teatro Campesino, a seminal grassroots theater group initially formed to convince California migrant farmworkers of the value of unionization. Valdez, who writes some works in English and others in a blend of English and Spanish, is credited with having provided momentum to the Chicano theater movement through his highly vivid style and his ability to place the Chicano experience within a universal American framework.

BIOGRAPHICAL INFORMATION

Born into a family of migrant farmworkers in Delano, California, Valdez began working in the fields at six years of age. Although his education was frequently interrupted by his family's constant travel, Valdez finished high school and subsequently attended San Jose State College. After graduating in 1964 Valdez joined the San Francisco Mime Troupe, from which he gained an appreciation of agitprop theater, which makes use of political agitation and propaganda to protest social injustice. Valdez returned to Delano in 1965 to assist César Chávez and the United Farmworkers Union in their efforts to unionize migrant workers. There Valdez organized the strikers into a performing group to dramatize the exploitation of farmworkers and to demonstrate the necessity of unionization for their financial survival. In 1967 Valdez and El Teatro Campesino began touring nationally, expanding their focus on the plight of migrant farmworkers to include the Chicanos' roots in Native American history, music, and myth. In the early 1970s Valdez's emphasis on mysticism and indigenous concerns eventually resulted in a split between El Teatro Campesino and the overall Chicano theater movement. Since the mid-1970s Valdez has become additionally involved in writing and directing for television and film productions. In 1994 he received the Aguila Azteca Award (Golden Eagle Award) from the Mexican Government. The following year he became a founding faculty member of the new California State University at Monterey Bay.

MAJOR WORKS

Valdez was credited early in his career with creating the *acto*, a short, often humorous dramatic sketch that employs the language of working-class Chicanos to present a lucid social or political message. Valdez's early actos,

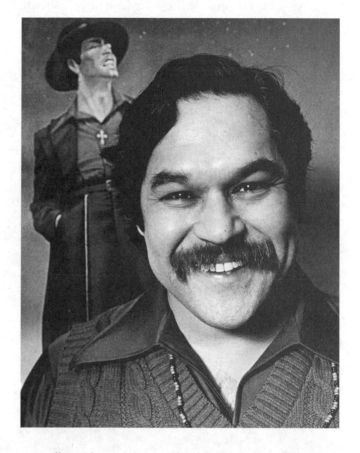

generally written or created with other members of El Teatro Campesino, often make use of humor and simple representational strategies, including signs imprinted with characters' occupations that are hung around actors' necks or masks that actors exchange to reverse their traditional roles. Valdez's plays of the late 1960s and early 1970s, including *No saco nada de la escuela, Vietnam campesino*, and *Soldado razo* (*The Chicano Soldier*), deal with such subjects as the American school system's tendency to force cultural assimilation on minorities and the overrepresentation of Chicanos in the Vietnam War. Traditional Native American and modern issues converge in *Dark Root of a Scream*, in which the death of a Chicano soldier is treated as a sacrifice to the gods, paralleling Aztec culture and history. By the mid-1970s El Teatro Campesino had become more commercially oriented. In 1978 Valdez's drama *Zoot Suit* enjoyed a highly successful run in Los Angeles. Considered the first play to draw large Mexican American audiences to a mainstream American theater production, the drama is metatheatrical and documentary in nature. In this work Valdez uses Latin American music, sections of courtroom transcripts, and quotes from newspaper reports to examine the Sleepy Lagoon murder case, in which several young Chicanos in east Los Angeles were convicted of murder and sentenced to life imprisonment based on circumstantial evidence. In subsequent works, such as his play *I Don't Have to Show You No Stinking Badges!* and *La Bamba*, a film concerning Chicano pop star Ritchie Valens, Valdez has continued to deconstruct negative stereotypes regarding Chicanos and Mexicans within a mainstream perspective that avoids exclusive minority concerns.

CRITICAL RECEPTION

Although sometimes faulted for his overly idealistic rendering of Native American culture, Valdez has been credited with providing the impetus that led to the genesis of the Chicano theater movement and with creating the now-accepted genre of Chicano theater, as based on the acto. A leader and innovator, Valdez is widely recognized as one of the few dramatists who have been able to change the way Chicanos are perceived by white America. Summarizing Valdez's achievement, John Harrop and Jorge Huerta have declared that "dedication to theatre, to his people, and to all humanity has always been the guiding spirit and sustaining force of Luis Valdez."

PRINCIPAL WORKS

PLAYS

The Theft   1961
The Shrunken Head of Pancho Villa   1963
Las dos caras del patroncito [*The Two Faces of the Boss*]   1965
La quinta temporada   1966
Los vendidos [*The Sell Outs*]   1967
La conquista de México   1968
The Militants   1969
No saco nada de la escuela   1969
Bernabé   1970
Huelguistas [*The Strikers*]   1970
Vietnam campesino   1970
Actos [with El Teatro Campesino]   1971
Dark Root of a Scream   1971
La gran carpa de los rasquachis [*The Great Tent of the Underdogs*]   1971
Soldado razo [*The Chicano Soldier*]   1971
La virgen del Tepeyac   1971
El fin del mundo   1972
Los olivos pits   1972
El baile de los gigantes   1974
Zoot Suit   1978
Bandido!   1981
Corridos   1982
I Don't Have to Show You No Stinking Badges!   1986
Zoot Suit and Other Plays   1992

SCREENPLAYS

I Am Joaquín   1969
Los vendidos   1972
Zoot Suit   1982
La Bamba   1987

TELEVISION SCRIPTS

Los vendidos   1972
*El corrido   1977
Corridos! Tales of Passion and Revolution   1987
Los mineros   1991

OTHER MAJOR WORKS

Aztlan: An Anthology of Mexican American Literature [editor; with Stan Steiner] (anthology)   1972
Pensamento Sepentino: A Chicano Approach to the Theatre of Reality (poem)   1973
Luis Valdez—Early Works: Actos, Bernabé and Pensimento Serpentino (miscellany)   1990

**This work is an adaptation of *La gran carpa de los Rasquachis.*

AUTHOR COMMENTARY

Notes on Chicano Theatre (1970)

SOURCE: "Notes on Chicano Theatre," in *Luis Valdez—Early Works: Actos, Bernabé and Pensamiento Serpentino*, Arte Publico Press, 1990, pp. 6-10.

[*In the following essay, which was written in 1970, Valdez attempts to define a uniquely Chicano theater.*]

What is Chicano theatre? It is theatre as beautiful, rasquachi, human, cosmic, broad, deep, tragic, comic, as the life of La Raza itself. At its high point Chicano theatre is religion—the huelguistas de Delano praying at the shrine of the Virgen de Guadalupe, located in the rear of an old station wagon parked across the road from DiGiorgio's camp #4; at its low point, it is a cuento or a chiste told somewhere in the recesses of the barrio, puro pedo.

Chicano theatre, then, is first a reaffirmation of LIFE. That is what all theatre is supposed to be, of course; but the limp, superficial, gringo seco productions in the "professional" American theatre (and the college and university drama departments that serve it) are so antiseptic, they are antibiotic (anti-life). The characters and life situations emerging from our little teatros are too real, too full of sudor, sangre and body smells to be boxed in. Audience participation is no cute production trick with us; it is a pre-established, pre-assumed privilege. "¡Que le suenen la campanita!"

Defining Chicano theatre is a little like defining a Chicano car. We can start with a lowriders' cool Merc or a campesino's banged-up Chevi, and describe the various paint jobs, hub caps, dents, taped windows, Virgin on the dashboard, etc. that define the car as particularly Raza. Underneath all the trimmings, however, is an unmistakable product of Detroit, an extension of General Motors. Consider now a theatre that uses the basic form, the vehicle, created by Broadway or Hollywood: that is, the "realistic" play. Actually, this type of play was created in Europe, but where French, German, and Scandinavian play-wrights went beyond realism and naturalism long ago, commercial gabacho theatre refuses to let go. It reflects a characteristic "American" hang-up on the material aspect of human existence. European theatre, by contrast, has been influenced since around 1900 by the unrealistic, formal rituals of Oriental theatre.

What does Oriental and European theatre have to do with teatro Chicano? Nothing, except that we are talking about a theatre that is particularly our own, not another imitation of the gabacho. If we consider our origins, say the theatre of the Mayans or the Aztecs, we are talking about something totally unlike the realistic play and more Chinese or Japanese in spirit. *Kabuki*, as a matter of fact, started long ago as something like our actos and evolved over two centuries into the highly exacting artform it is today; but it still contains pleberías. It evolved from and still belongs to el pueblo japonés.

In Mexico, before the coming of the white man, the greatest examples of total theatre were, of course, the human sacrifices. *El Rabinal Achi*, one of the few surviving pieces of indigenous theatre, describes the sacrifice of a courageous guerrillero, who rather than dying passively on the block is granted the opportunity to fight until he is killed. It is a tragedy, naturally, but it is all the more transcendant because of the guerrillero's identification, through sacrifice, with God. The only "set" such a drama-ritual needed was a stone block; nature took care of the rest.

But since the Conquest, Mexico's theatre, like its society, has had to imitate Europe and, in recent times, the United States. In the same vein, Chicanos in Spanish classes are frequently involved in productions of plays by Lope de Vega, Calderón de la Barca, Tirso de Molina and other classic playwrights. Nothing is wrong with this, but it does obscure the indio fountains of Chicano culture. Is Chicano theatre, in turn, to be nothing but an imitation of gabacho playwrights, with barrio productions of racist works by Eugene O'Neil and Tennessee Williams? Will Broadway produce a Chicano version of "Hello, Dolly" now that it has produced a Black one?

The nature of Chicanismo calls for a revolutionary turn in the arts as well as in society. Chicano theatre must be revolutionary in technique as well as content. It must be popular, subject to no other critics except the pueblo itself; but it must also educate the pueblo toward an appreciation of *social change*, on and off the stage.

It is particularly important for teatro Chicano to draw a distinction between what is theatre and what is reality. A demonstration with a thousand Chicanos, all carrying flags and picket signs, shouting CHICANO POWER! is not the revolution. It is theatre about the revolution. The people must act in *reality*, not on stage (which could be anywhere, even a sidewalk) in order to achieve real change. The Raza gets excited, simón, but unless the demonstration evolves into a street battle (which has not yet happened but it is possible), it is basically a lot of emotion with very little political power, as Chicanos have discovered by demonstrating, picketing and shouting before school boards, police departments and stores to no avail.

Such guerrilla theatre passing as a demonstration has its uses, of course. It is agit-prop theatre, as white radicals used to call it in the '30's: agitation and propaganda. It helps to stimulate and sustain the mass strength of a crowd. Hitler was very effective with this kind of theatre, from the swastika to the Wagneresque stadium at Nuremburg. At the other end of the political spectrum, the Huelga march to Sacramento in 1966 was pure guerrilla theatre. The red and black thunderbird flags of the UFWOC (then NFWA) and the standard of the Virgen de Guadalupe challenged the bleak sterility of Highway 99. Its emotional impact was irrefutable. Its political power was somewhat less. Governor Brown was not at the state capitol, and only one grower, Schenley Industries, signed a contract. Later contracts have been won through a brilliant balance between highly publicized events, which gained public support (marches, César's fast, visits by Reuther, Robert and Ted Kennedy, etc.), and actual hard-ass, door to door, worker to worker organizing. Like Delano, other aspects of the Chicano movement must remember what is teatro and what is reality.

But beyond the mass struggle of La Raza in the fields and barrios of America, there is an internal struggle in the very corazón of our people. That struggle, too, calls for revolutionary change. Our belief in God, the church, the social role of women, these must be subject to examination and redefinition on some kind of public forum. And that again means teatro. Not a teatro composed of actos or agit-pop, but a teatro of ritual, of music, of beauty and spiritual sensitivity. This type of theatre will require real dedication; it may, indeed, require a couple of generations of Chicanos devoted to the use of the theatre as an instrument in the evolution of our people.

The teatros in existence today reflect the most intimate understanding of everyday events in the barrios from which they have emerged. But if Aztlán is to become a reality, then we as Chicanos must not be reluctant to act nationally. To think in national terms: politically, economically and spiritually. We must destroy the deadly regionalism that keeps us apart. The concept of a national theatre for La

Raza is intimately related to our evolving nationalism in Aztlán.

Consider a *Teatro Nacional de Aztlán* that performs with the same skill and prestige as the Ballet Folklórico de Méico (not for gabachos, however, but for the Raza). Such a teatro could carry the message of La Raza into Latin America, Europe, Japan, Africa—in short, all over the world. It would draw its strength from all the small teatros in the barrios, in terms of people and their plays, songs, designs; and it would give back funds, training and augmented strength of national unity. One season the teatro members would be on tour with the Teatro Nacional; the next season they would be back in the barrio sharing their skills and experience. It would accomodate about 150 altogether, with 20-25 in the National and the rest spread out in various parts of Aztlán, working with the Campesino, the Urbano, the Mestizo, the Piojo, etc.

Above all, the national organization of teatros Chicanos would be self-supporting and independent, meaning no government grants. The corazón de la Raza cannot be revolutionized on a grant from Uncle Sam. Though many of the teatros, including El Campesino, have been born out of pre-established political groups, thus making them harbingers of that particular group's viewpoint, news and political prejudices, there is yet a need for independence for the following reasons: objectivity, artistic competence, survival. El Teatro Campesino was born in the huelga, but the very huelga would have killed it, if we had not moved sixty miles to the north of Delano. A struggle like the huelga needs every person it can get to serve its immediate goals in order to survive; the teatro, as well as the clinic, service center and newspaper, being less important at the moment of need than the survival of the union, were always losing people to the grape boycott. When it became clear to us that the UFWOC would succeed and continue to grow, we felt it was time for us to move and to begin speaking about things beyond the huelga: Vietnam, the barrio, racial discrimination, etc.

The teatros must never get away from La Raza. Without the palomilla sitting there, laughing, crying and sharing whatever is onstage, the teatros will dry up and die. If the raza will not come to the theatre, then the theatre must go to the raza.

This, in the long run, will determine the shape, style, content, spirit and form of el teatro Chicano. Pachucos, campesinos, low-riders, pintos, chavalonas, familias, cuñados, tíos, primos, Mexican-Americans, all the human essence of the barrio, is starting to appear in the mirror of our theatre. With them come the joys, sufferings, disappointments and aspirations of our gente. We challenge Chicanos to become involved in the art, the life style, the political and religious act of doing teatro.

Interview with Valdez (1988)

An interview with Luis Valdez, in *In Their Own Words: Contemporary American Playwrights*, by David Savran, Theatre Communications Group, 1988, pp. 257-71.

[*In the conversation below, Valdez discusses the development of his drama and the forces that have had an impact on his work.*]

One month into the 1965 Delano grape strike, which solidified the power of the United Farm Workers, Luis Valdez met with a group of union volunteers and devised a short comic skit to help persuade reluctant workers to join the strike. He hung signs reading *Huelgista* (striker) on two men and *Esquirol* (scab) on a third. The two *Huelgistas* starting yelling at the *Esquirol* and the audience laughed. Thus began Valdez's career as founder and director of El Teatro Campesino and author of a diverse and yet deeply interconnected collection of plays.

For two years the Teatro remained actively involved in the union's struggle, performing in meeting halls, fields and strike camps. Drawing on *commedia dell'arte* and elements of Mexican folk culture, Valdez created *actos* (acts), short comic sketches designed to raise political awareness and inspire action. ***Los Vendidos*** (***The Sellouts***, 1967), for example, attacks the stereotyping of Chicanos and government-sanctioned tokenism. A Chicano secretary from Governor Reagan's office goes to Honest Sancho's Used Mexican Lot to buy "a Mexican type" for the front office. She examines several models—a farm worker, a young *pachuco* (swaggering street kid), a *revolucionario* and finally a Mexican-American in a business suit who sings "God Bless America" and drinks dry martinis. As soon as she buys the last, he malfunctions and begins shouting *"Viva la huelga,"* while the others chase her away and divide the money.

At the same time that he was writing and performing agitprop for the Farm Workers, Valdez turned to examine his pre-Columbian heritage, the sophisticated religion and culture of the ancient Mayans. The Teatro settled in two houses in San Juan Bautista in 1971, where they farmed according to Mayan practices and Valdez developed the second of his dramatic forms, the *mito* (myth), which characteristically takes the form of a parable based on Indian ritual. For Valdez the *mito* is an attempt to integrate political activism and religious ritual—to tie "the cause of social justice" to "the cause of everything else in our universe." ***Bernabe*** (1970) is a parable about the prostitution of the land. It opposes the pure, mystical love for La Tierra (the Earth) by the mentally retarded *campesino* of the title against its simple possession by landowners and banks. At the play's end Bernabe is visited by La Luna (the Moon), dressed as a 1942 *pachuco*; La Tierra; and El Sol (the Sun), in the guise of Tonatiuh, the Aztec sun god. In a final apotheosis, the "cosmic idiot" is made whole and united with La Tierra, at last revealed to be Coatlicue, the Aztec goddess of life, death and rebirth.

In the 1970s Valdez developed a third dramatic form, the *corrido* (ballad), which, like the *mito*, is intended to claim a cultural heritage rather than inspire political revolution. The *corrido* is Valdez's reinvention of the musical, based on Mexican-American folk ballads telling tales of love, death and heroism. *Zoot Suit* (1978) is perhaps his best known *corrido* and was the first Hispanic play to reach Broadway, after a long and successful run in Los Angeles. Mixing narrative, action, song and dance, it is the story of members of a zoot suit-clad *pachuco* gang of the forties, their wrongful conviction for murder and the "Zoot Suit Riots" that followed. His 1983 piece, *Corridos,* featuring songs in Spanish and dialogue in English, has been videotaped for Public Television.

Valdez's most recent play is the comedy *I Don't Have to Show You No Stinking Badges,* which has been acclaimed in Los Angeles and San Diego. A play about the political and existential implications of acting, both in theatre and society, it takes place in a television studio in which is set the suburban southern California home of Buddy and Connie Villa, two assimilated, middle-class Chicanos, "the silent bit king and queen of Hollywood." Their son, Sonny, who has just dropped out of Harvard Law School and has returned home with his Asian-American girlfriend, tries to find work in Hollywood, but despairs at having to become one of the many "actors faking our roles to fit into the great American success story." With Pirandellian sleight of hand, Valdez uses a director to interrupt the scene (which it turns out is an episode of a new sitcom, *Badges*!) in order to debate the social function of art. "This isn't reality," Sonny protests. But the director assures him, "Frankly, reality's a big boring pain in the ass. We're in the entertainment business. Laughs, Sonny, that's more important than reality."

Although closer to mainstream comedy than mystery play, Valdez's exploration of role-playing represents more a development of than a break with the technique of his early *mitos*. Both *Bernabe* and *Badges* eschew naturalism in favor of a more theatrically bold style, the earlier play drawing upon a naive formal model and the later a sophisticated one. *Bernabe,* in keeping with the conventions of religious drama, opts for a simple, mystical ending, while *Badges* refuses the pat resolution of television sitcom by offering several alternative endings. Both examine the spiritual implications of material choices; both are celebratory despite their socially critical vision. This continuity over a fifteen-year period attests to the clarity of Valdez's intention: to put the Chicano experience on stage in all of its political, cultural and religious complexity; and to examine the interrelationship between the political and the metaphysical, between historically determined oppressive structures and man's transhistorical desire for faith and freedom.

MAY 6, 1987—LUIS VALDEZ'S OFFICE IN EL TEATRO CAMPESINO, SAN JUAN BAUTISTA, CALIFORNIA

[David Savran]: *How did you get interested in theatre?*

[Luis Valdez]: There's a story that's almost apocryphal, I've repeated it so many times now. It's nevertheless true. I got hooked on the theatre when I was six. I was born into a family of migrant farm workers and shortly after World War II we were in a cotton camp in the San Joaquin valley. The season was over, it was starting to rain, but we were still there because my dad's little Ford pickup truck had broken down and was up on blocks and there was no way for us to get out. Life was pretty meager then and we survived by fishing in a river and sharing staples like beans, rice and flour. And the bus from the local school used to come in from a place called Stratford—irony of ironies, except it was on the San Joaquin River [laughs].

I took my lunch to school in a little brown paper bag—which was a valuable commodity because there were still paper shortages in 1946. One day as school let out and the kids were rushing toward the bus, I found my bag missing and went around in a panic looking for it. The teacher saw me and said, "Are you looking for your bag?" and I said, "Yes." She said, "Come here," and she took me in the little back room and there, on a table, were some things laid out that completely changed my perception of the universe. She'd torn the bag up and placed it in water. I was horrified. But then she showed me the next bowl. It was a paste. She was making papier-mâché. A little farther down the line, she'd taken the paper and put it on a clay mold of a face of a monkey, and finally there was a finished product, unpainted but nevertheless definitely a monkey. And she said, "I'm making masks."

I was amazed, shocked in an exhilarating way, that she could do this with paper and paste. As it turned out, she was making masks for the school play. I didn't know what a play was, but she explained and said, "We're having tryouts." I came back the next week all enthused and auditioned for a part and got a leading role as a monkey. The play was about Christmas in the jungle. I was measured for a costume that was better than the clothes I was wearing at the time, certainly more colorful. The next few weeks were some of the most exciting in my short life. After seeing the stage transformed into a jungle and after all the excitement of the preparations—I doubt that it was as elaborate as my mind remembers it now—my dad got the truck fixed and a week before the show was to go on, we moved away. So I never got to be in the Christmas play.

That left an unfillable gap, a vacuum that I've been pouring myself into for the last forty-one years. From then on, it was just a question of evolution. Later I got into puppets. I was a ventriloquist, believe it or not. In 1956 when I was in high school, I became a regular on a local television program. I was still living in a *barrio* with my family, a place in San Jose called Sal Si Puedes—Get Out if You Can. It was one of those places with dirt streets and chuckholes, a terrible place. But I was on television, right? [laughs], and I wrote my own stuff and it established me in high school.

By the time I graduated, I had pretty well decided that writing was my consuming passion. Coming from my background, I didn't feel right about going to my parents and saying, "I want to be a playwright." So I started college majoring in math and physics. Then one day late in my freshman year I walked to the drama department and decided, "The hell with it, I'm going to go with this." I changed majors to English, with an emphasis on playwriting, and that's what I did for the rest of my college days.

In 1964 I wrote and directed my first full-length play, **The Shrunken Head of Pancho Villa.** People saw it and gave me a lot of encouragement. I joined the San Francisco Mime Troupe the following year, and then in '65 joined the Farm Workers Union and essentially started El Teatro Campesino. The evolution has been continuous since then, both of the company and of my styles of playwriting.

During that period, what was your most important theatre training—college, the Mime Troupe?

It's all important. It's a question of layering. I love to layer things, I think they achieve a certain richness—I'm speaking now about "the work." But life essentially evolves that way, too. Those years of studying theatre history were extremely important. I connected with a number of ancient playwrights in a very direct way. Plautus was a revelation, he spoke directly to me. I took four years of Latin so I was able to read him in Latin. There are clever turns of phrases that I grew to appreciate and, in my own way, was able almost to reproduce in Spanish. The central figure of the wily servant in classical Roman drama—Greek also—became a standard feature of my work with El Teatro Campesino. The striker was basically a wily servant. I'd also been exposed to *commedia dell'arte* through the San Francisco Mime Troupe, with its stock characters, the Brighellas, Arlecchinos and Pantalones. I saw a direct link between these *commedia* types and the types I had to work with in order to put together a Farm Workers' theatre. I chose to do an outdoor, robust theatre of types. I figured it hit the reality.

My second phase was the raw, elemental education I got, performing under the most primitive conditions in the farm labor camps and on flatbed trucks. In doing so, I dealt with the basic elements of drama: structure, language, music, movement. The first education was literary, the second practical. We used to put on stuff every week, under all kinds of circumstances: outdoors, indoors, under the threat of violence. There was a period during the grape strike in '67 when we had become an effective weapon within the Farm Workers and were considered enough of a threat that a rumor flashed across the strike camp that somebody was after me with a high-powered rifle. We went out to the labor camp anyway, but I was really sweating it. I don't think I've sweated any performance since then. It changed my perspective on what I was doing. Was this really worth it? Was it a life-and-death issue? Of course it was for me at the time, and still is. But I learned that in a very direct

and practical way. I was beaten and kicked and jailed, also in the sixties, essentially for doing theatre. I knew the kind of theatre we were doing was a political act, it was art and politics. At least I hope I wasn't being kicked for the art [laughs].

What other playwrights had a major impact on you in those days?

Brecht looms huge in my orientation. I discovered Brecht in college, from an intellectual perspective. That was really the only way—no one was doing Brecht back in 1961. When Esslin's book *Brecht: The Man and His Work*, came out in 1960, I was working in the library, so I had first dibs on all the new books. Brecht to me had been only a name. But this book opened up Brecht and I started reading all his plays and his theories, which I subscribed to immediately. I continue to use his alienation effect to this day. I don't think audiences like it too much, but I like it because it seems to me an essential feature of the experience of theatre.

Theatre should reflect an audience back on itself. You should think as well as feel. Still, there's no underestimating the power of emotional impact—I understand better now how ideas are conveyed and exchanged on a beam of emotion. I think Brecht began to discover that in his later works and integrated it. I've integrated a lot of feeling into my works, but I still love ideas. I still love communicating a concept, an abstraction. That's the mathematician in me.

How has your way of writing changed over the years?

What has changed over the years is an approach and a technique. The first few years with the Teatro Campesino were largely improvisational. I wrote outlines. I sketched out a dramatic structure, sometimes on a single page, and used that as my guide to direct the actors. Later on, I began to write very simple scripts that were sometimes born out of improvisations. During the first ten years, from '65 to '75, the collective process became more complicated and more sophisticated within the company—we were creating longer pieces, full-length pieces, but they'd take forever to complete using the collective process.

By 1975, I'd taken the collective process as far as I could. I enjoyed working with people. I didn't have to deal with the loneliness of writing. My problem was that I was so much part of the collective that I couldn't leave for even a month without the group having serious problems. By 1975 we were stable enough as a company for me to begin to take a month, two months, six months, eventually a year. I turned a corner and was ready to start writing plays again.

In 1975 I took a month off and wrote a play. We did a piece called **El Fin del Mundo** (**The End of the World**) from 1974 through 1980, a different version every year. The '75 version was a play I sat down and wrote. I started with a lot of abstract notions—the mathematician sometimes gets in the way—but eventually I plugged into characters born of my experience. Those characters are still alive for me. Someday I'll finish all of that as a play or else it will be poured into a screenplay for a "major motion picture" [laughs].

Shortly after that, in 1977, I was invited by the Mark Taper Forum to write a play for their New Theatre for Now series. We agreed on the Zoot Suit Riots as a subject. *Zoot Suit* firmly reestablished my self-identity as a playwright. Essentially I've been writing nonstop since '75. That's not to say I didn't write anything between '65 and '75. *Soldado Razo,* which is probably my most performed play around the world, was written in 1970, as was *Bernabe. The Dark Root of a Scream* was written in 1967. These are all one-acts. I used to work on them with a sense of longing, wanting more time to be able to sit down and write.

Now I'm firmly back in touch with myself as a playwright. When I begin, I allow myself at least a month of free association with notes. I can start anywhere. I can start with an abstract notion, a character . . . it's rarely dialogue or anything specific like that. More often than not, it's just an amorphous bunch of ideas, impressions and feelings. I allow myself to tumble in this ball of thoughts and impressions, knowing that I'm heading toward a play and that eventually I've got to begin dealing with character and then structure.

Because of the dearth of Hispanic playwrights—or even American playwrights, for that matter—I felt it necessary to explore the territory, to cover the range of theatre as widely as I could. Political theatre with the Farm Workers was sometimes minimal scale, a small group of workers gathered in some dusty little corner in a labor camp, and sometimes immense—huge crowds, ten thousand, fifteen thousand, with banners flying. But the political theatre extends beyond the farm worker into the whole Chicano experience. We've dealt with a lot of issues: racism, education, immigration—and that took us, again, through many circles.

We evolved three separate forms: the *acto* was the political act, the short form, fifteen minutes; the *mito* was the mythic, religious play; and the *corrido* was the ballad. I just finished a full-length video program called *Corridos.* So the form has evolved into another medium. I do political plays, musicals, historical dramas, religious dramas. We still do our religious plays at the Mission here every year. They're nurturing, they feed the spirit. Peter Brook's response when he saw our Virgin play, years ago, was that it was like something out of the Middle Ages. It's religion for many of the people who come see it, not just entertainment. And of course we've gone on to do serious plays and comedies like *I Don't Have to Show You No Stinking Badges.*

It seems that a play like **Bernabe** *aligns the* acto *and the* mito, *politics and the myth. It uses religious mysticism to point out the difference between simply owning the land and loving it. The political point is made by appeal to mystical process.*

The spiritual aspect of the political struggle has been part of the work from the beginning. Some of that is through Cesar Chavez, who is a spiritual-political leader. Some people—say, the political types—have had trouble dealing with the spiritual. They say, "It's a distortion. Religion is the opium of the masses." But it seems to me that the spiritual is very much part of everyday life. There's no way to exclude it . . . we are spirit. We're a manifestation of something, of an energy.

The whole fusion between the spiritual and the material is for me the paradox of human existence. That's why I connected with Peter Brook when he was here in '73—his question was, "How do you make the invisible visible?" To me myth is not something that's fake or not real. On the contrary, it's so real that it's just below the surface—it's the supporting structure of our everyday reality. That makes me a lot more Jungian than Freudian. And it distinguishes me, I think, from a lot of other playwrights. A lot of modern playwrights go to psychoanalysis to work out their problems. I can't stop there, that's just the beginning for me. I've had to go to the root of my own existence in order to effect my own salvation, if you will. The search for meaning took me into religion and science, and into mythology.

I had to sound out these things in myself. Someone pointed out to me the evolution a couple of years ago. *The Shrunken Head of Pancho Villa* is theatre of the absurd. One of the characters, the oldest brother, is a disembodied head, huge, oversized. He eats all of the food that the family can produce. So they stay poor. He has lice that turn out to be tiny cockroaches that grow and cover the walls. He sings "La Cucaracha" but cannot talk. And he can't move. He's just kind of there. In a metaphorical sense, that was me back in the early sixties. That's the way I felt—that I had no legs, no arms. By 1970, when I got to *Bernabe,* I was the idiot, but I'd gotten in contact with the sun and the moon and earth. Fortunately, out of these grotesque self-portraits, my characters have attained a greater and greater degree of humanity.

I've always had difficulty with naturalism in the theatre. Consequently, a lot of people have looked at my work and said, "Maybe he just can't write naturalism. His is the theatre of types, of simplistic little stick figures." What I needed was a medium in which to be able to do naturalism, so I came to film. *La Bamba* is naturalism, as well as of the spirit. There I wanted the dirt, so I got the dirt. I wanted intimate realistic scenes between two real people. I can write that stuff for the stage too, but it just doesn't interest me. The stage for me—that box, that flat floor—holds other potentials, it's a means to explore other things.

As much a ritual space as anything else.

Most definitely. It seems to me that the essence of the human being is to act, to move through space in patterns that give his life meaning. We adorn ourselves with symbolic objects that give that movement even more meaning. Then we come out with sounds. And then somewhere along the line we begin to call that reality—but it's a self-created reality. The whole of civilization is a dance. I think the theatre celebrates that.

So religion functions in your work as a connection with the past, with one's heritage and one's bond to all men.

Sounding out those elemental drums, going back into the basics. I was doing this as a Chicano but I was also doing it as someone who inhabits the twentieth century. I think we need to reconnect. The word religion means "a tying back."

The vacuum I thought I was born into turned out to be full of all kinds of mystery and power. The strange things that were going on in the *barrio*—the Mexican things, the ethnic things—seemed like superstition, but on another level there was a lot of psychic activity. There's a lot of psychic activity in Mexican culture that is actually political at times.

Zoot Suit is another extremely spiritual, political play. And it was never understood. People thought it was about juvenile delinquents and that I was putting the Pachuco on the stage just to be snide. But the young man, Henry Reyna, achieves his own liberation by coming into contact with this internal authority. The Pachuco is the Jungian self-image, the superego if you will, the power inside every individual that's greater than any human institution. The Pachuco says, "It'll take more than the U.S. Navy to beat me down," referring to the navy and marines stripping zoot suiters in the 1940s. "I don't give a fuck what you do to me, you can't take this from me. And I reassert myself, in this guise." The fact that critics couldn't accept that guise was too bad, but it doesn't change the nature of what the play's about. It deals with self-salvation. And you can follow the playwright through the story—I was also those two dudes. With *Zoot Suit* I was finally able to transcend social conditions, and the way I did it on stage was to give the Pachuco absolute power, as the master of ceremonies. He could snap his fingers and stop the action. It was a Breehtian device that allowed the plot to move forward, but psychically and symbolically, in the right way.

And Chicanos got off on it. That's why a half-million people came to see it in L.A. Because I had given a disenfranchised people their religion back. I dressed the Pachuco in the colors of Testatipoka, the Aztec god of education, the dean of the school of hard knocks. There's another god of culture, Quetzalcoatl, the feathered serpent, who's much kinder. He surfaces in *La Bamba* as the figure of Ritchie Valens. He's an artist and poet and is gentle and not at all fearful. When my audiences see *La Bamba,* they like that positive spirit. The Pachuco's a little harder to take. But these are evolutions. I use the metaphor of the serpent crawling out of its skin. There's that symbolism in

La Bamba—it's pre-Columbian, but it's also very accurate in terms of the way that I view my own life. I've crawled through many of my own dead skins.

Although **Badges** *and* **Bernabe** *are very different, in both of them the metaphysical is given a political dimension.*

I like to think there's a core that's constant. In one way, what I have to say is quite basic, quite human. In another way, it's specifically American, in a continental sense. I'm reaching back to pre-Columbian America and trying to share that. I feel and sense those rhythms within me. I'm not just a Mexican farm worker. I'm an American with roots in Mayan culture. I can resonate and unlock some of the mysteries of this land which reside in all of us. I've just been in the neighborhood a little bit longer. I'm a great believer in dreams. I've had some fantastic dreams. I dream when I'm standing up. I try to make my dreams come true.

What about the endings of your plays? **Zoot Suit***'s seems very Brechtian, a happy ending immediately called into question. Then you present three different possible futures for the characters. And* **Badges** *is similar. You present what could happen, depending on the choices the characters make.*

Multiple endings—multiple beginnings, too—have started to evolve in my work. I don't think there's any single end. I firmly believe that we exist simultaneously on seven levels—you can call them *shakras* if you're so inclined, or you can call them something else. In the Mayan sculptures, there's a vision of the universe in those ancient headdresses, in which you see the open mouths of birds with human heads coming through them, and then something else going in through the eyes and coming out again. That's a pulsating vision of the universe. It might have been born from the jungle but is, nevertheless, an accurate description of what is going on below the surface, at the nuclear level, in the way atomic particles are interacting. To me the universe is a huge, pulsating, enormously vital and *conscious* phenomenon. There is no end. There is no beginning. There's only an apparent end and an apparent beginning.

We're very emotional beings—tremendously gregarious creatures. We're very loving and caring for our mates. We're violent, there's no question about that. Tremendously cruel, intellectually cruel, unlike the animals. But even the cold-blooded murderers among us have emotion and sentiment. So it's good to end on a strong feeling. Sometimes, in the search for the right feeling, I have three or four endings.

We had an ending and beginning to *La Bamba,* which I had scripted and seemed right on paper. But our first preview audiences rejected them, so eventually we snipped them. What we had was not exactly a Brechtian turn, but it was a stepping back and looking at the fifties from the perspective of the eighties. Our audiences told us they didn't want to come back into the eighties. They wanted to stay in the fifties. I had been trying, on some level, to alleviate the pain of Ritchie Valens' death, but audiences told us, "Leave us with the pain." So that's where we left it.

Can you describe how you work as a director with your own material? When you start rehearsals, do you have a finished script?

These days, there's at least a first or second draft. I've also worked in the opposite way, with no script whatsoever. I believe in the reality of my process as a playwright, and sometimes the audience has to suffer through it, although I try not to force paying audiences to. But back in the late sixties, early seventies, our audiences didn't pay that much—in fact, many of our performances were free—so I felt I could take certain liberties. One time we were working on a new piece, on the road in L.A., and I got new ideas for some dialogue. I was talking to the actors all the way up until curtain time. During the show I was in the wings, making notes on scraps of paper and handing them to the actors as they went on stage [laughs]. And what's really ridiculous is that they did it.

Now this is not as crazy as it sounds. You can do precisely this in making a movie. You create new lines on the spot, the actor goes in front of the camera and delivers. I'm still rewriting **Badges.** This is our closing weekend coming up and I'm introducing a couple of new scenes in the second act. I feel that so far I've found only an apparent ending. The real ending is down the road someplace. I'm touring with this play across country, I want to get to New York with it, so I'm working on it.

As a director I switch gears. Writing is a solitary process—you're in there with the words and I love that. But I also love directing, getting out of myself and into other people. As a director—and this again comes from my experiences in the Farm Worker days—I have to know who I'm working with. And what they are like. If I have four actors, or a dozen actors, plus crew, my first job as a director is to get them to become one, to arouse a lot of enthusiasm.

More and more the first thing I want to establish in character development is the movement. You can't have a feeling, an emotion, without motion. You can pick up a lot from the associative school, referring back to your own experiences, but I think it's also possible to get people to laugh and cry through what they do to their bodies.

We talk a lot about the theatre of the sphere. I firmly believe that each of us exists within his or her own sphere. The actor must begin to move within it. Every part of him resolves itself in tiny spheres—a fist spinning on a wrist, joints, legs, arms. The body centers on the solar plexus and the gut, the pelvis. I insist the first element is to move your pelvis. That gets into very sexual kinds of movements and people sometimes get embarrassed. But out of them comes a lot of basic emotion. Freud is right. We are anal and sexual. Jung comes in with the idea that

we trace a sphere. Once you get into the sphere, you find your connection with Mother Earth, with the sun, with the moon, with a drop of water, with the known universe. And when you begin to inhabit your own sphere as an actor, you finally begin to stretch its limits, to encompass and envelop other people, including an entire audience. You can project yourself.

You can't get away with "acting" on film. You have to cut it so close to the bone, you have to *be*, to get down-and-dirty. It's "the Method," to be sure. So you have to make it small, intense and real. On the stage, because you have to project, things sometimes get out of whack. And you have to switch to a new mentality. This is where ritual comes in. Performance on the stage is much more like dance than anything else. Dance is real. You can't fake dance. But somehow a lot of people start acting as if they're "acting," and think they're doing it right. In fact, acting is something totally different: it's a *real act*. Which gets back to politics, in that our first theatrical acts were real political acts. That's why that dude was out there with a high-powered rifle—he wasn't seeing theatre, but a threatening political act.

Now it seems that the political dimension has become sublimated, less explicit. You're no longer writing agitprop.

There is a time and place for all forms. It's twenty years down the road. But the political impact is still there. The only difference is that I'm being asked to run for governor now, which I'm not interested in doing. My purpose is still to impact socially, culturally and politically. I'm reaffirming some things that are very important to all of us as Americans, those things that we all believe to be essential to our society. What I hope is changing is a perception about the country as a whole. And the continent as well.

I'm just trying to kick my two cents into the pot. I still want El Teatro Campesino to perform on Broadway, because I think that's a political act. El Teatro Campesino is in Hollywood, and I don't think we've compromised any social statements. We started out in '65 doing these *actos* within the context of the United Farm Workers. Twenty-two years later, my next movie may be about the grape strike. My Vietnam was at home. I refused to go to Vietnam, but I encountered all the violence I needed on the home front: people were killed by the Farm Workers' strike.

Some critics have accused you of selling out.

I used to joke, "It's impossible for us to sell out because nobody wants to buy us." That doesn't bother me in the least. There's too much to do, to be socially conscious about. In some ways, it's just people sounding me out. I don't mind people referring back to what I have been. We're all like mirrors to each other. People help to keep you on course. I've strayed very little from my pronounced intentions. In '67 when we left United Farm Workers and started our own cultural center in Del Rey, we came out with a manifesto essentially stating that we were trying to put the tools of the artist in the hands of the humblest, the working people. But not just nineteenth-century tools, not clay and straw, or spit and masking tape, or felt pens. We were talking about video, film, recording studios. Now we're beginning to work in the best facilities that the industry has to offer. What we do with them is something else.

Do you read the critics?

Sure. I love listening to the public. They're the audience, who am I to argue with them? They either got it or they didn't. The critics are part of the process. I do have some strong feelings about the nature of American criticism—I don't think that it's deeply rooted enough in a knowledge of theatre history. Very often newspapers just assign reporters, Joe Blow off the street. Perhaps it would be too much for the public to have somebody who's overly informed—is that possible?—about the theatre. There's no overriding sense of what the theatre's about in America. There's more of that sense in Europe, and a deeper appreciation for change, direction and a body of work.

In this country we are still victims of our economic system. If you make a buck, you're interesting. So obviously the only solution is to make a buck, to show that you can. That doesn't bother me, if it's attached to reaching an audience. At first, we never thought much about charging. But the poor people saw us working. They said, "We feel funny about taking this without giving you something." Our entry into the professional theatre meant that there was an audience here willing to pay.

How do you see the American theatre today?

My overwhelming impression is that theatre's not nearly as interesting as it could be, that it's been stuck in its traces for many, many years. Broadway has not moved out of the twenties from what I can see. It might be because so many of the houss on Broadway are nineteenth-century playhouses. Much of the material that I see—and I don't see nearly enough—is too anemic for my tastes. I have trouble staying awake in the theatre, believe it or not [laughs]. I mean I can barely stay awake at my own plays.

I feel that the whole question of the human enterprise is up for grabs. I don't think this country has come to terms with its racial questions, obviously. And because of that, it has not really come to terms with the cultural question of what America is. There are two vast melting pots that must eventually come together. The Hispanic, after all, is really the product of a melting pot—there's no such thing as a Latin American race. The Hispanic melting pot melds all the races of the world, like the Anglo melting pot does; so one of these days, and probably in the United States, those two are going to be poured together—probably in a play, and it could be one of my own [laughs].

There's a connection with the Indian cultures that has to be established in American life. Before we can do that,

however, we have to get beyond the national guilt over the genocide of the Indian. What's needed is expiation and forgiveness, and the only ones in a position to forgive are the Indian peoples. I'm a Yaqui Indian—Spanish blood, yes, but largely Yaqui. I'm in a position to be able to forgive white people. And why not? I think that's what we're here for, to forgive each other. Martin Luther King speaking in 1963 at the Lincoln Memorial was a beginning. It didn't reach nearly far enough. We're still wrestling with it. Deep fears, about miscegenation and the despoliation of the race, have to be dealt with. I'm here, through my work, to show that short, brown people are okay. We've got ideas, too, and we've got a song, and a dance or two. We know something about the world that we can share. I'm here to show that to other brown people who don't think very much of themselves, and there are a lot of those.

I wish there were more plays that dealt with the reality of this country. The racial issue is always just swept aside. It deserves to be swept aside only after it's been dealt with. We cannot begin to approach a real solution to our social ills—a solution like integration, for instance, or assimilation, without dealing with all our underlying feelings about each other. I'm trying to deal with my past, not just with respect to Anglos, but to blacks and Asians. I draw on the symbolism of the four roads: the black road, the white road, the red road and the yellow road. They all meet in the navel of the universe, the place where the upper road leads into the underworld—read consciousness and subconsciousness. I think that where they come home is in America.

What are your plans for the future? And goals.

I'm into a very active phase right now, as writer and director, but with writing as the base. I have a number of very central stories I want to tell—on film, on television and on the stage. I want to be working in the three media, on simultaneous projects that feed each other. I like the separation between film, television and theatre. It makes each a lot clearer for me. In theatre, there are a number of ritualistic pieces I want to do that explore the movement of bodies in space and the relation between movement and language. That sphere I can explore on film, too, or television. What film gives me is movement around the actor—I can explore from any viewpoint, any distance. But theatre's the only medium that gives me the sheer beauty, power and presence of bodies. Ritual, literally.

I've got a piece that I've been working on for many, many years, called *The Earthquake Sun,* about our time. All I can tell you is that it will be on the road one of these days. I have another play called *The Mummified Fetus.* It takes off from a real incident that happened a couple of years ago: an eighty-five-year-old woman was discovered with a mummified fetus in her womb. I have a couple of plays that the world has not seen, that we've only done here.

In television I have a number of projects. *Corridos* has begun to open up other possibilities. I talk about video as electronic theatre. I'm getting into the idea of doing theatre before cameras, but going for specifically theatrical moments as opposed to real cinematic moments. *Corridos* is an example of this. And film—I'm going after the proverbial three-picture deal. I want to make movies the way I do plays.

I hope a more workable touring network will develop in this country. The links between East and West must be solidified. I think it's great for companies to tour. We're very excited about the possibility of our company plugging into the resources of the regional theatres, as we've done with *Badges* in San Diego and at the Los Angeles Theatre Center, even with the Burt Reynolds Playhouse in Florida. We hope to be able to go from regional theatre to regional theatre all the way across the country, including New York. In that way, we'll be able to reach a national audience.

I still want to experience the dust and sweat occasionally. I'm trying to leave time open for that. This month we're going to celebrate the twenty-fifth anniversary of the United Farm Workers—we'll be back on a flatbed truck, doing some of the old *actos*. I don't want to lose any of our audience. I want worldwide audience. We had that—up until 1980 we were touring Europe and Latin America. I want to tour Asia with the Teatro Campesino. Essentially, I would like to see theatre develop the kind of mass audience—it's impossible of course—that the movies have. I wish we could generate that enthusiasm in young people and in audiences in general, get them out of their homes, away from their VCRs, to experience the theatre as the life-affirming, life-giving experience that it is.

OVERVIEWS AND GENERAL STUDIES

John Harrop and Jorge Huerta (essay date 1975)

SOURCE: "The Agitprop Pilgrimage of Luis Valdez and El Teatro Campesino," in *Theatre Quarterly*, Vol. 5, No. 17, March-May 1975, pp. 30-9.

[*In this essay, the authors trace the origins and evolution of El Teatro Campesino and Valdez's work with the group.*]

San Juan Bautista is a very ordinary, small town in central California. Its chief attraction to outsiders is the Catholic Mission—one of those churches the Spanish priests dotted along the coast of California in their eighteenth century odyssey, with cross and sword, to claim the heathen Indian for Christ. An odd place to find Peter Brook and his International Centre for Theatre Research—among the arid hills where, for the mere wages of survival, expatriate Mexicans now work the land that once belonged to their ancestors.

But here, for six weeks in the summer of 1973, Brook and his acolytes came to work with and to learn from one of the most remarkable theatre groups now working in the

United States. For San Juan Bautista is the present home of Luis Valdez and his Teatro Campesino—farmworkers' theatre—which, since it was founded in late 1965 to protest against the economic and spiritual exploitation of the Chicanos,[1] has managed to retain its popular integrity while achieving an artistic stature that has won it awards in the United States and appearances at international festivals in Europe.

Valdez, the founder and guiding spirit of El Teatro, is himself the son of a migrant farm worker, and spent his youth fruit picking around central California while gleaning sufficient education to gain entrance to the California State College. Here an earlier interest in theatre (stimulated by a kindergarten play in which masks and physical movements had compensated for the fact that Valdez couldn't speak English) manifested itself again, and he wrote and had produced two plays during his undergraduate years.

Uncertain what his future would be after graduation, Valdez happened upon a performance by the San Francisco Mime Troupe and, immediately taken by their physically direct and dynamic style, he moved to San Francisco and joined the company. Those were the heady days when the civil rights movement and the anti-war movement were gathering momentum, and street theatre such as performed by the Mime Troupe (and the Bread and Puppet Theatre in New York), was beginning to be seen as a natural tool of non-violent protest. Theatre was being 'brought back to the people' on portable stages set up in parks; with marching bands and puppet shows in the streets; and with a broad and bawdy physicality that went for the guts and the heart.

While Valdez was with the Mime Troupe, the atmosphere of protest in America reached the migrant Mexican farmworkers in central California: they went on strike against wages and conditions in the grape fields. These were Valdez' fellow Chicanos—indeed, part of his family was striking—and he came down from San Francisco to join with Cesar Chavez' United Farmworkers Union in a protest march in Delano, California.

EL TEATRO IS BORN

As a result of that experience, Valdez conceived the idea of a theatre which would support and further politicize the Mexican farmworkers in their struggle. In November 1965, with the blessing of Chavez, he held a meeting at which he broached the idea of a theatre to the striking workers. The first response was uncertain—chiefly because none of the workers had ever been to a theatre—and Valdez realized that to interest the workers he had to relate directly to their own experiences. So he had some signs made—Esquirol (scab), Huelgista (striker), Patroncito (grower) and Contratista (contractor)—and hung these around the necks of some of the workers, telling them to enact the characteristics of their signs. The results far exceeded his expectations:

> *The scab didn't want to at first, because it was a dirty word at that time, but he did so in good spirits. Then*

the two strikers started shouting at him, and everybody started cracking up. All of a sudden people started coming . . . they filled up the whole kitchen. We started changing signs around, and people started volunteering . . . imitating all kinds of things. We ran for two hours just doing that.[2]

Thus was El Teatro Campesino born.

From this beginning Valdez gathered a small group to work with each other each evening after the day's picketing. This group evolved what they called 'actos'—short scenes dealing with some specific element of the strike. The actors started with a real life incident, character or idea, and improvised around this in commedia dell'arte fashion, using no scripts or scenery. For simplicity of communication and ease of identification they kept the original idea of wearing signs around their necks to indicate the characters or attitudes bring represented. Props or costumes were used only as a basic reinforcement of character or situation. Valdez was careful not to disguise the fact that the actors were themselves strikers engaged in the same cause as the people for whom they were performing. He was also concerned not to alienate his audience by requiring any political or theatrical sophistication: the actors always appealed directly and simply to the immediate experience of the striking farmworkers.

REALITY THROUGH HUMOR

Typical of the early *actos* was **Three Grapes.** A green, a ripe, and a rotten grape come onto the stage and squat. Each wishes to be picked by a scab who has not joined the strike: but each time the scab attempts this he is driven away by a striker with a 'Huelga' (strike) sign. Finally all the grapes become rotten. The scab then realizes that the grower has lost his economic power and joins the strike. The simple lesson gets across: if a grower cannot harvest his crop he must concede to the strikers.

The *actos* always contained a great deal of physical business and broad humour. The farmworkers are a straightforward, simple, and ebullient people: they respond to largeness of style and comic situations. So Valdez used comedy for its direct appeal—and because, as he said, 'you can't do tragedy on the back of a truck.'[3] The social points came across through the comic situations and the broad but recognizable reality created by the actors:

When I speak about comic and dramatic images, I'm speaking about visions of reality. Our comic images represent the reality that he (the farmworker) sees. It's not a naturalistic representation: most of the time it's a symbolic, emblematic presentation of what the farmworker feels. But we can't be stuffy about it, so we use slapstick. Very often the slapstick is the image.[4]

A particularly powerful example of what Valdez meant by 'emblematic presentation' occurs in another early *acto* called **The Fifth Season,** where Summer is represented by an actor wearing an old shirt covered in dollar bills. To the farmworker Summer is the time when the fruit on the trees turns to money. The orchards and vineyards are heavy with clusters of dollars, there for the picking. But the dream of paradise is never realized: nor could it be in the present relationship of the workers to the growers. So the workers laugh at the image of Summer not because it is funny in itself, but because they recognize the irony of the situation—that the joke is on themselves.

A PERMANENT TOURING GROUP

For several months after its establishment, El Teatro picketed during the day and worked on the *actos* during the evening, giving weekly performances for the strikers in Delano. Then, in April 1966, Valdez and his actors joined the great march of strikers from Delano to the state capital of Sacramento, performing nightly in all the small towns on the route. This experience both honed their technique and extended their repertoire. It also gained them a wider reputation, which led to their first commercial performance at the Committee Theatre[5] in San Francisco, on 2 May 1966.

For the next year El Teatro lived in Delano, but toured Chicano population centres throughout California to raise support and funds for the continuing strike. The first national tour came in July and August 1967, when the company performed in union halls across the United States—and in the courtyard of the Senate building in Washington, at the Newport Jazz Festival, and at the Village Theatre in New York. The *Wall Street Journal* spoke of their 'provocative, lively, and entertaining theatre,'[6] and *Newsweek* of their 'ardent and sometimes grim gaiety.'[7] The *Newsweek* critic went on to say:

The young people of El Teatro are full of racial pride, social and political fervour, and . . . they know exactly what they mean. As in the old Everyman morality plays, each character has a clear identity, is caught in a sharply defined situation, and is presented with a clear choice of destinies.[8]

All of the New York critics drew parallels between the impact of El Teatro Campesino and that of the Federal Theatre and Labour Union Theatre in the 1930s, when economic and social distress had turned theatre into a powerful political weapon.

The New York tour, for which the company received an Obie,[9] established it nationally, and confirmed that this kind of theatre, though still based in and geared to the aims of the striking Chicano farmworkers, was capable of a dynamic relationship with a much broader spectrum of people. This faced Valdez with an important decision:

The strike in Delano is a beautiful cause, but it won't leave you alone . . . it's more important to leave a rehearsal and go back to the picket line. So we found we had to back away from Delano to be a theatre. Do you serve the moment by being just kind of half-assed, getting together whenever there's a chance, or do you really hone your theatre down into an effective weapon?[10]

So, in September 1967, Valdez moved the company away from Delano and its direct link with the Farmworkers' Union, and established El Centro Campesino Cultural in Del Rey, California.

The initial success of El Teatro had been based on a bitter truth: its work was rooted in the everyday facts of the farmworkers' lives. Now Valdez wished to keep this truth—the life blood of the worker—running through his theatre, but to reach out beyond the strike to deal with the life of the Chicano in more general terms of his human rights and self respect.

EXPLORING THE CHICANO IDENTITY

In coming to this expanded theatrical consciousness, Valdez was aware of several facts concerning the cultural identity of the Chicano. First the Spanish had come and deprived the Mexican Indians of their Mayan and Aztec ancestry—had colonized them, robbed them of their pride and wealth, and in return imposed upon them a Christianity which had taught them meekly to accept second-class citizenship in their own country. Later, the Spanish masters had been exchanged for American, and pressures to take on a set of Anglo values.[11]

More than this, many Chicanos living in the USA are not immigrants, but living in a land which is ancestrally theirs, and while there is no separatist movement on the part of the Chicanos in these territories, there is a strong movement to resist anglicization and to retain ethnic traditions. It was to this understanding of the true Chicano cultural and spiritual identity that Luis Valdez turned in taking El Teatro to Del Rey and establishing a Chicano cultural centre, to explore the music and political history of the Chicanos as well as the drama. The new purpose was to embrace and revive the culture of their ancestors, and to create a pride in being a Chicano.

Valdez recognized that to deal with these broader and more abstract issues in his theatre would require a greater technical sophistication on the part of the actors, who would now have to deal with and communicate ideas which, while related to, were no longer a direct part of their immediate experience. He therefore instituted a training programme for the company, on similar lines to those which many 'new' theatre groups were undertaking in the later' sixties.

There was a great deal of ensemble work—trust and sensitivity exercises—plus work upon physical movement and, above all, a sound technical base for the improvisational work which still formed the starting point of El Teatro's creative efforts. Of one of their exercises, Valdez wrote that it 'must clearly establish characters and their relation to each other. Such things as language, movement, and the strict adherence to the reality of inter-relationships are important. Disciplined clean characterizations are the objective.' Again, 'The emphasis is upon wit and quick thinking, as well as movement, characterization, and stage presence'.[12]

Thus, while clarifying and disciplining the work of the company, Valdez was concerned to retain the great ebullience, energy, and fundamental truth of their work. While becoming conscious of the need for theatrical technique, El Teatro never lost the sense of being a people's theatre, performed by and for the Chicano people—aesthetics never got in the way of direct communication.

What Valdez achieved was a strengthening of impact due to the disciplined channelling of the energies of his troupe, and a cleaner and quicker way of making the point, due to the greater clarity of the stage action. The earlier reliance upon signs hung around actor's necks gave way to more use of masks and the actor's own physicality. The use of props was subtler, and there was a more sophisticated sense of theatrical rhythm and timing. But the vivid sense of humour, the broad physical style, the energy spilling from the stage to sweep up the audience, and, at root, the sharing of fundamental truths by actor and audience, continued to be the hallmark of El Teatro Campesino.

NEW THEMES AND NEW AUDIENCES

After the move to Del Rey and subsequently (in 1969) to Fresno in the central farmland of California, the broader consciousness and capacity of El Teatro became apparent in the *actos* of that period. The earlier pieces were clearly geared towards the strike. *Three Grapes* has already been described, and other *actos* of the first period were *Huelgistas (The Strikers), Las Dos Caras del Patroncito (The Two Faces of the Boss),* and *Papellecion (Playing Games).* These *actos* were all very short, and to the immediate point. *Papellecion,* for example, has a grape grower with a sign, 'Smiling Jack', who tells his picker how much he loves his Mexican workers. As he talks, the sign changes to 'Liar', 'Gringo', 'Jackass', and finally 'Huelga', as the worker comes to see through the platitudes of the boss.

The new work looked at the Chicano in a wider social perspective. *No Saca Nada de la Escuela* dealt with the problems of young Chicanos in American schools, where the language and cultural barriers have left them at the bottom of the class, and encouraged a poor self-image and delinquency. *Los Vendidos (The Sell-Outs),* which was given a national television presentation by NBC, dealt with problems of those Chicanos who had tried to reject their backgrounds and became anglicized, or at least to call themselves 'Mexican-Americans'.

The inequities in the draft system in the United States during the Vietnam War were also dealt with by El Teatro. The play in which this was done, *Soldado Razo (The Chicano Soldier),* was concerned with the death of a Chicano soldier in Vietnam. It treated the 'macho' syndrome and the other forces which conspired to send him there, the absurdity of one brown slave being sent thousands of miles to kill other brown victims, and the total ugliness of the Vietnam circumstance. This was perhaps the first complete example of the new consciousness underlying the work of Valdez and El Teatro. While still based in the truth and uniqueness of the Chicano situation, it proclaims its relationship with the larger anti-war movement in the United States, and its brotherhood with all colonized peoples.[13]

Soldado Razo also illustrates the evolution of the company's work in production terms. The fundamental physical elements of the early *actos* are retained. There is no attempt to create an artificial physical environment. The stage is bare, with the exception of a simple curtain suspended from a pole upstage centre, and above the curtain is a huge sign—El Teatro Campesino de Aztlan. The emphasis is still upon actors, and actors who are people like their audiences. But the simple cardboard signs have now disappeared, to be replaced by fully fleshed-out characters created with broad and simple strokes.

A further element has also appeared. Symbolic figures, masked and costumed, create a universal environment within which particular characters work out their individual destinies. In *Soldado Razo,* Valdez employed Death as his narrator, a kindly-ironic skeleton in a monk's robe, whose mocking eye fell upon actors and audience alike.

A triple consciousness is now operating in El Teatro's work: a sense of a particular man in a local situation (the Chicano); a universal man in a world situation (the poor, or underprivileged, or oppressed), and those spiritual, cosmic, and mythological forces of man's primitive psyche which give him a common humanity. In a review of *Soldado Razo,* the drama critic of the *Los Angeles Times* wrote: 'Agitprop theatre? I guess so, if we need a definition, but equally close to *Everyman* and the great medieval chronicles. Something very complicated, and very simple, and very rare is going on. . . .'[14]

BRECHT FUSED WITH FOLKLORE

On another occasion, the *Los Angeles Times* spoke of the work of El Teatro Campesino as being 'a stunning mixture of Brechtian presentation and Chicano folklore,'[15] and as Valdez has himself referred to El Teatro's style as 'somewhere between Brecht and Cantinflas',[16] a brief comparison with Brecht might provide insights into Valdez' own work. The most apparent relationship is in the similarity of the early *actos* to Brecht's *Lehrstucke*. Both are short pieces with a didactic purpose in which the actors *present* characters rather than assume them. Both are geared to completely simple presentation—for Brecht in the classroom, for Valdez on the back of a truck. Both are meant to politicize an audience and inspire them to action.

But here, perhaps, any close analogy ends, for whereas Brecht's impact was geared to the intellectual and rational, based upon the dialectic of Marxism from which he also derived the structure of his pieces, Valdez' appeal is much simpler and more visceral. He has said: 'For our political and personal salvation we don't have to scurry to Marxism or Socialism. We can go to our own roots.'[17]

Certainly, Valdez wished to heighten his audience's understanding of experience, but it was an understanding to be gained with body and soul, rather than through an intellectual process. Nor was the structure of Valdez' *actos* based upon any intellectual conceit: it came wholly from the necessities of the circumstances in which the actors first worked. It had the basic appeal and technique of the earliest forms of popular theatre.

Valdez' simplicity was a response to fundamental human reactions and beliefs, while Brecht's was more calculated, disciplined, and cerebral. Brecht's choice of a parabolic form and destruction of theatrical illusion was self-conscious, whereas Valdez simply took what he found and gave it theatrical impact. Above all, Teatro Campesino eschewed the revolutionary humourlessness of Brecht's didactic pieces—it took its cause seriously, but never itself. Valdez remained close to Cantinflas while Brecht had ignored Hanswurst.

Both Brecht's *Lehrstücke* and Valdez' *actos* turned to historical circumstances, and to folklore or myth. But whereas with Brecht these were neither a part of his own sensibility nor that of the audience for which he was writing, Valdez had the advantage of finding his ideas within the spiritual ethos of the Chicano people. He could continue to makes use of contemporary experience, but go beneath that to touch common beliefs and attitudes based in the experiences of a still-believed Christian religion, and a Spanish colonial culture. Beneath this again, Valdez believed he could make a direct appeal to the Mayan and Aztec culture which was the deepest part of the Chicano spiritual identity.

NEW THEATRES, NEW FORMS

During the years from 1969 to 1971, while this broadening of El Teatro's purpose from the concentration upon Huelga to that of Raza (national identity) was taking place, and the company was moving to its present home in San Juan Bautista, it took part in the Seventh World Theatre Festival in Nancy, France, toured Mexico, and was constantly involved in tours on behalf of the farm-workers throughout the south-western United States.

In 1970 the company also made its first film, *I Am Joaquin*, based upon an epic poem by Corky Gonzales. The film won first prize at both the San Francisco and Monterey Festivals. But perhaps the most significant event in El Teatro's early history took place in May 1970, when it sponsored the first Chicano Theatre Festival in Fresno, California. Since 1968 small companies had sprung up in Chicano areas in the United States, emulating El Teatro Campesino in their attempt to politicize and raise a Chicano consciousness. Thirteen companies attended that first festival, which has been repeated in each subsequent year.

As a result of the success of these festivals, Luis Valdez has been instrumental in creating Tenaz (El Teatro Nacional de Aztlan), to establish communication between the companies, to provide a means for sharing material, and, above all, to hold workshops at which members of El

Teatro Campesino could share their skills with the newer companies which, at first, were founded upon enthusiasm and commitment, but scant theatrical ability. There are now more than 75 companies across the United States,[18] and the work they are doing, catalyzed and encouraged by El Teatro Campesino, is helping to create a Chicano consciousness, dignity, and sense of purpose.

While the Teatros spawned by El Teatro used the *acto* form originated by Valdez, he himself, after 1971, created what he called the *mito*, moving further in the direction of myth and symbolism, and relating to the great religious sense and spiritual intuition deep-seated within the Chicano self. Valdez became ever more convinced that the Chicano must grasp his indigenous heritage as the spiritual key to his existence and purpose in life.

The *mito* was a theatrical form with roots in the many-layered culture of the Chicano. It drew upon Aztec ritual, Mexican folklore, and Christian drama. The *auto sacramentale* structure was familiar to many Chicanos,[19] and Valdez used elements of this in a conjunction with the basic folk-ballad form of the Chicano—the *Corrido*, 'handed down from generation to generation . . . a living part of the Chicano's cultural heritage. Love, hate, jealousy, courage, pride—all of the universal themes of man's existence on earth are expressed in these songs.'[20]

El Teatro took some of these well known ballads and acted them out to the accompaniment of the guitar and singing, and then incorporated this into the *mito* structure. Thus the *mito* became the playing and singing of a narrative idea, which was illustrated by emblematic symbolism and ritual taken from the medieval religious drama, the whole being salted by the vigorous, earthy humour which had formed a dynamic element of the secular medieval theatre.

The *mito* was still geared to the making of direct points about the everday experience of the Chicano, while this was now seen in the much wider perspective of a total Chicano sensibility. To educate the Chicano to a fuller understanding of himself, to ennoble him in his own eyes, this was the function of the *mito*, in which Valdez was using traditional religious forms to proselytize a contemporary religion—*La Raza*.

WAKE FOR A DEAD SOLDIER

The levels of consciousness at work in the *mito* are well illustrated by the setting Valdez calls for in his play ***The Dark Root of a Scream.*** This play followed ***Soldado Razo,*** in which Valdez was moving towards his new form. The stage directions ask for:

> *a collage of myth and reality. It forms, in fact, a pyramid with the most real artifacts of barrio life at the broad base and an abstract mythical-religious peak at the top. Above these scenes (of barrio reality) some images are made of iron and the hard steel of modern civilization—guns, knives, automobile parts; others reveal a less violent, more spiritual origin—molcajetes, rebozos, crucifixes, etc. Finally, the very top of the pyramid is*

> *dominated by ancient indio images: conches, jade, the sunstone, feathered serpent heads.*[21]

The circumstances of this play are the wake for a dead Chicano soldier, killed in Vietnam, whose coffin is set at the top of the pyramid. The action concerns the response to the death of the soldier, whose name is Quetzacoatl Gonzales, from his family, three youths who were his friends, and the Catholic priest who has come to 'comfort' the family.

Moving in and out of the various levels of physical reality, the play touches upon the wasted lives of the youths, removed as they are from any sense of cultural identity; the passivity of the family who have settled for a colonized existence; and the stupidity and futility of the priest, whose fear of the Church leads him to reinforce the situation by explaining it as God's will. At the climax of the play a heartbeat is heard from the coffin and, when it is opened by the mother, feathers and Quetzacoatl's heart are discovered. This final symbolism relates to the early Aztec sacrifices to the Sun God, when the heart was torn out of a living body, and to the significance of Quetzacoatl as the redeemer of the Indian people—here still living, despite being killed by the colonizers.

In ***The Dark Root of a Scream,*** as in all his most recent plays, Valdez is attempting to reach the deepest levels of Chicano consciousness by his use of elements of Mayan and Aztec rituals, and their Christian equivalents. As was the case in all pagan societies, when the Indians of Mexico were converted to Christianity many of their rituals were simply overlaid with the new Christian sacraments. Thus, in the Mayan ritual of Quetzacoatl, the God is sacrificed and rises again, so that the analogy with Christ can readily be made.

There is also a close analogy between the Virgin of Guadalupe and the Aztec's own earth mother Tonantzin. The first appearance of the Virgin, to Juan Diego in 1531, was on the very hill which was the traditional home of Tonantzin. El Teatro Campesino has treated this idea which closely binds the Christian Chicano to his pre-Columbian ancestors, and has adapted a play, ***La Virgen del Tepeyac,***[22] from an original manuscript of the appearance to Juan Diego, written in 1531.

The play opens with the *corrido* idea—a traditional song dealing with the adoration of Tonantzin, to which new lyrics have been written. This is followed by a dramatization of the arrival of Cortez, the destruction of the old religion, and the yoking of the Indians to Christianity. One of the climactic moments, and most powerful images of the play, is the appearance of the Virgin out of a symbolic womb made up of the slaughtered bodies of the Indians. Lofted high on a platform the Virgin speaks to Juan Diego and tells him that she has come to end the injustice.

El Teatro's play deals with the true economic nature of the Spanish conquest, under its cloak of religious conversion, and, more importantly, suggests that the Chicano can discover his true roots and spiritual identity through the symbol of the Virgin of Guadalupe-cum-Tonantzin. That same mother earth from which we must all derive our inner strength, a sense of unity and universal love.

Possibly the most complete example of the structure and impact that Valdez is now seeking is to be found in *La Carpa de los Rasquachis (The Tent of the Underdogs),* of which Valdez has said, 'It's everything we have ever done, with this whole extra dimension, the spiritual.'[23] The play begins almost casually, with the members of the company coming on stage, clowning, chatting up the audience, and erecting their 'tent' backdrop—a curtain made up of potato sacks and torn burlap. This suggests a basic simplicity and poverty—but more than that, for the tent recalls those used by shows which toured small Mexican towns in the 1930s. The tent is the home of the under-privileged Rasquachi family in the play, and also houses the whole cultural history of the Chicanos. Three separate but interrelated levels of reality are thus established.

ADVOCATING 'MILITANT NON-VIOLENCE'

The play proper begins with the narrative musical choruses, which tie all the scenes together. Then a religious procession makes a formal entrance. Christ, with a halter round his neck, is led by a black-masked figure, overpainted with a white skeleton, wearing the helmet of the sixteenth-century Spanish Conquistadores. Devil-masked executioners surround the Christ-figure, who is ritualistically crucified.

The awesome silence attending this action is broken by lively mariachi rhythms, and we are swept into the life of poor Jesus Rasquachi, a Chicano farm-worker who is lured across the border to the United States by hopes of economic advancement and the collusion of corrupt customs officials and labour agents. The play follows the fortunes of his family through the typical experience of such a worker. One son becomes a dope addict, another a pusher; a brother becomes a dupe for an Anglo political machine, and is killed for his pains. Finally, a worn-out shell, Rasquachi dies on the floor of the welfare office while being forced to make belittling statements about himself in order to get the state's pittance.

The play is performed in Spanglish[24] by the company of twelve players, who change hats and props with skilled panache and act with great physical agility and comic flair. Nothing escapes El Teatro's eye as it exposes all that it believes to stand in the way of the full realization of Chicano individuality. It satirizes equally the puffed-up machismo of posturing revolutionary activists, and the corruption of the Catholic Church—here symbolized by a bishop with a dollar sign upon his mitre.

As in *The Dark Root of a Scream,* the essence of the play is an appeal for a return to a kind of atavistic spirituality. As a reviewer put it:

> El Teatro finally advocates a militant non-violence, a compassion which is not synonymous with compromise,

and a religious innocence which is not naivety. Transcendence for the Chicano cannot be attained through Catholicism, but rather through a uniting of the White Christ with the Aztec God Quetzacoatl.[25]

A scene exemplifying this idea takes place at the end of the play, when Quetzacoatl is reborn, magnificent in his Indian dress, transcending the tattered materialism around him. In his absence, there has been no peace, no hope for the Chicano. He brings an end to universal discord with a simple philosophy: you are my other self, if I do harm to you, I do harm to myself. If I love and respect you, I love and respect myself. It is this philosophy that El Teatro is now attempting to live and to propagate.

FROM SPECIFICS TO SPIRITUALITY?

Luis Valdez' move from active political involvement to a more personal and seemingly passive form of spiritual approach has brought criticism from some radical Chicano quarters. Valdez himself sees El Teatro's present orientation as a logical extension of its development from a theatre dealing with specific problems of the striking farm-workers, through the wider material problems of the Chicano minority to more fundamental human goals.

> Now our acts are the acts of human beings living and working on this earth. . . . We are still very much the political theatre, but our politics are the politics of the spirit—not of the flesh, but of the heart.[26]

In this search for spiritual rebirth, Valdez is greatly influenced by the myth of Quetzacoatl, who has appeared in all the recent plays. The God of positive force, Quetzacoatl was defeated by the God of negative force, Tezcatipoca, more than a thousand years ago. The rebirth of Quetzacoatl is due, according to the Mayan calendar, towards the end of this century, when the world will once again enter a period of peace and positive dynamic. Valdez believes the current task of El Teatro to be the bringing of people to a spiritual understanding which will prepare them for Quetzacoatl's return.[27]

This purpose informs the life-style and work of the company in its communal existence in San Juan Bautista.[28] It still 'combats poverty and oppression in the heart of the richest agricultural valley in the world,'[29] but now does this in the context of La Raza and a wider universal brotherhood. El Teatro's roots are more than ever in a Chicano reality, for the capacity for powerfully simple religious belief is as much a part of the Chicano's daily existence as the soil from which he draws his living. The same hands pray and pick grapes with equal honesty. It is to the full consciousness of this reality that El Teatro now appeals.

While discovering a soul, El Teatro Campesino has not lost its vulgar energy. While affirming man's sublimity, it still laughs at his human absurdity. The theatre remains as funky, beautiful, coarse, delicate, commonplace, and cosmic as La Raza itself. Words written by Luis Valdez in 1970 connect the past with the present, and to the future of El Teatro:

Beyond the mass struggle of La Raza in the fields and barrios of America, there is an internal struggle in the very heart of our people. That struggle too calls for revolutionary change. Our belief in God, the Church, the social role of women—these must be subject to examination and redefining on some kind of public platform. And that again means teatro. Not simply a teatro composed of actos or agit-prop, but a teatro of ritual, of music, of beauty and spiritual sensitivity. A teatro of legends and myths. A teatro of religious strength. This type of theatre will require real dedication.[30]

Such dedication to theatre, to his people, and to all humanity has always been the guiding spirit and sustaining force of Luis Valdez and El Teatro Campesino.

NOTES

[1]Chicano is the name adopted by politically conscious Mexicans living in the United States. After the Treaty of Guadalupe Hildago, in 1848, gave much of Northern Mexico to the United States, those Mexicans living in the area suddenly found themselves citizens of a new country which took no account of their culture, but set out to exploit them economically. The 'Chicano Movement' is usually dated from 1965, when Cesar Chavez began the struggle for the rights of the Mexican farm-workers in the United States.

[2]Beth Bagby, 'El Teatro Campesino: Interviews With Luis Valdez', *Tulane Drama Review*, XI, 4 (Summer 1967), pp. 74-5.

[3]Ibid., p. 77.

[4]Ibid.

[5]The Committee Theatre was one of the most famous theatres improvising political satire in the United States. It went into voluntary dissolution in 1972, when it believed all the sacred cows to be dead.

[6]*Wall Street Journal*, 24 July 1967, p. 10.

[7]*Newsweek*, 31 July 1967, p. 43.

[8]Ibid.

[9]An 'Obie' is an award made by American critics for excellence in performance at off-Broadway theatres.

[10]San Francisco Mime Troupe, *Radical Theatre Festival, San Francisco* (1969), p. 6.

[11]The Chicano name for much of the South Western United States is Aztlan, which literally means the 'Land to the North'. It is the traditional homeland of the Aztecs who came down to Central America (Mexico) from North America, and looked upon the land to the north as that of their ancestors. Aztlan comparises California, Colorado, New Mexico, Nevada, and Arizona—land which had been a part of Spanish Mexico, and was either taken by conquest or bought by the United States.

[12]Luis Valdez, 'Notes on Chicano Theater', *El Teatro*, I, 3 (February 1971), p. 11.

[13]Poorly educated, and thus unlikely to get a graduate deferment, unable to afford a smart lawyer, and too reliant upon family roots to run to Canada, the Chicano made up a larger proportion of the armed forces in Vietnam than his numbers in the community should have dictated.

[14]*Los Angeles Times*, 23 September 1971, Sec. 4, p. 1.

[15]*Los Angeles Times*, 5 July 1971, p. 6.

[16]*Radical Theatre Festival*, p. 10. Mario Morenos Cantinflas was a famous Mexican comic actor, somewhere between Chaplin and Scapin, based upon the Mexican 'pelado'. The 'pelado' (the stripped one) has to earn a day-to-day living by his wits and by dint of any number of ingenious schemes.

[17]Quoted in the *Los Angeles Sunday Times Calendar*, 11 November 1973, p. 36.

[18]Typical of these companies is El Teatro de la Esperanza, which was formed in Santa Barbara, California, in 1971. The group, initially students from the University of California, remodelled a room in the Chicano community centre to make a theatre to seat 70 people. They were immediately successful with a programme of songs and *actos* originally performed by El Teatro Campesino, and now have turned a warehouse into a Chicano community theatre seating 140 people.

[19]The Catholic religion took a firm and fervent hold upon the Mexican Indian, and religious drama became a part of the culture of the people. At the Festival of Corpus Christi at Tlaxcala in 1538, an elaborate *auto sacramentale* was performed on the sin of Adam and Eve. See M.R. Cole, 'Los Pastores', *Memoirs of the American Folklore Society*, IX (Boston, 1907), p. 9.

[20]*Los Angeles Free Press*, 24 September 1971, p. 21.

[21]*Dark Root of a Scream* in *From the Barrio: a Chicano Anthology* (San Francisco: Canfield Press, 1973), p. 79.

[22]Tepeyac was the name of the hill upon which the Virgin appeared.

[23]Quoted in the *Los Angeles Sunday Times Calendar*, 11 November 1973, p. 36.

[24]Spanglish is a mixture of Spanish and English used by Chicanos as everyday speech. This, together with the explicit physicality of their work, makes the performances of El Teatro Campesino perfectly understandable to both Chicano and no-Spanish-speaking audiences.

[25]Roger Copeland, 'Theatre in Review', *Educational Theatre Journal*, XXV, 3 (October 1973), p. 368.

[26]Quoted in the *Santa Barbara News and Review*. 17 May 1974, p. 14.

[27]There is an interesting analogy here with the revived interest in astrology among young people, and the belief that the world is entering the 'age of Aquarius' an age of peace and positive force.

[28]The company today comprises about 30 people in a family of families. Their total income from tours, donations, and rental of the film, is a little over $3,000 a month. Members of the company receive between $60 and $300 a month from the communal exchequer. This is less than the government doles out to its welfare recipients, but there is no poverty in El Teatro.

[29]Luis Valdez, 'El Teatro Campesino', *El Teatro*. Summer 1970, p. 1. No better proof could be found of El Teatro's continued involvement with the farmworkers cause than during the visit of Peter Brook's company in 1973. At this time the Teamsters Union, perhaps one of the most vicious examples of capitalistic labour in the United States, was brutalizing the Chicano workers into Leaving Cesar Chavez' union, and undoing much of what had been achieved since 1965. The combined Valdez-Brook company went back into the very fields from which El Teatro Campesino had sprung, to bring support to the farm-workers as in the early days of 'huelga'. It is also interesting to note that the theatre piece they took to the workers was not a simple *acto*, but a work on the ability of the human spirit to withstand force and violence—*The Fatties and the Shrimps*. The occasion bears witness both to the expanded spiritual concern of El Teatro and the direct relationship it has retained with its roots.

[30]Luis Valdez, 'Notes on Chicano Theatre', *El Teatro*, Summer 1970, p. 5.

Jorge A. Huerta (essay date 1982)

SOURCE: *Chicano Theater: Themes and Forms*, Bilingual Press/Editorial Bilingüe, 1982, 274 p.

[*In this essay, Huerta examines the Chicano experience depicted in four plays by Valdez*: The Shrunken Head of Pancho Villa, Bernabé, Dark Root of a Scream, *and* Zoot Suit.]

CUCARACHAS ON THE WALLS AND VENDIDOS IN THE CLOSET: *THE SHRUNKEN HEAD OF PANCHO VILLA*

Of Luis Valdez' four plays to be discussed in separate chapters of this book, **The Shrunken Head of Pancho Villa** is the most concerned with the identity of the Chicano. **Bernabé** is a contemporary myth that mingles indigenous deities with barrio characters in a search for cosmic revelation. **Dark Root of a Scream** is another modern mythical play that investigates the past and the present through a young Chicano who died in Vietnam. Finally, **Zoot Suit** recalls the Mechicanos of the 1940s and the discrimination they suffered at the hands of the media and the courts. Through each of the four plays investigates different aspects of the Chicano experience, the first focuses more on the inner workings of the family unit.

It is not surprising that Luis Valdez' first full-length play is about a Mechicano family, for each of the works he has created concerns a family in crisis. For Valdez, the family is the main source from which his dramaturgy must spring forward, searching for its identity or its purpose. It is the family that copes with the conflicts and confronts the problems generated by the society around it. That society is generally the Anglo-dominated world that remains on the periphery of his plays yet is most often responsible for the economic oppression his protagonists encounter. As with the farmworker *actos* discussed in Chapter One, the Chicano is also capable of betraying his own people, but it is ultimately the economic system that has the final power over the characters' lives.

Above all, Valdez' plays reflect a struggle for cultural survival. The initial search for identity in the first play will recur in each succeeding work, with certain character types returning in different forms. The youthful renegade, the *vato loco* or pachuco, is present in each of the plays and finds his ultimate personification as the narrator of **Zoot Suit.** While the first work sympathetically investigates the ubiquitous pachuco, it also concerns itself with the opposite type: the *vendido.* The subsequent dramas find their antagonists in other Chicano types or in those representatives of the system who continually oppress the Chicano. We will find Anglo policemen and Chicano recketeers, Catholic priests and racist judges, as Valdez depicts the forces that confront his characters.

History is also an important element in Valdez' dramaturgy, reflecting his concern with the Chicano's past as well as future. For Valdez, Chicanos must be aware of their history and must continually fight not only to preserve it but to portray it as it really was. His plays will never settle for school-book depictions of the Chicano's historical importance in this society, for those books have been written with "Manifest Destiny" in mind. Our playwright's mission is to set the record straight.

All of Valdez' plays are political. "To create art amidst this oppression," he told a tenaz Director's Conference in 1971, "is to be political."[1] His art has never strayed from its original intent of showing the Chicano vis-à-vis the family, and in so doing it has not ignored the economic realities of the barrio. His families reflect the poorer echelons of Chicano society, not because there are no middle-class Chicanos, but because the poor are the people whose condition must improve. In his portrayal of the struggle for survival, it is the playwright's concern that his characters remain "culturally pure," even as they strive for economic progress. By exposing the situation of these impoverished families, Valdez is setting up a sociopolitical comment, for we cannot ignore their condition.

Thus we have a sense of community in each of Valdez' plays. His characters are not alone in their oppression but are members of a larger family called *La Raza.* His mothers become symbolic figures as they reflect the struggles of Mechicanas in crisis: they are the all-suffering members of their communities. The homes they occupy are warm, if very humble, and are extensions of any barrio household. Audiences can look at these dwellings and say "Yes, I've been there," for they know too well the cracking walls and rusty pipes re-created on stage. The old saying *"Mi casa es su casa"* ("My house is your house") becomes a summons in Valdez' plays that calls the audience in closer, saying "Don't be afraid, I know what it's like."

The characters who populate Valdez' stage are based on his acute observations of human nature in all its complexity, and if they are sometimes distorted or stereotypical it is because the playwright feels that these extensions of reality will best suit his purpose: to show how people can change, for better or for worse. Therefore the first family Valdez writes about becomes a dream-like vision, with attitudes and actions exaggerated beyond the commonplace in order to arouse the audience's imagination and interest. At times the lesson is clear; in other instances the audience members may have to decide for themselves the significance of the symbols.

In contrast to the symbolism that pervades the action of **The Shrunken Head of Pancho Villa,** the playwright calls for a musical slide presentation to precede the action—a history lesson which recognizes the fact that many in the audience do not know the true story of Pancho Villa's death. Though the characters in the play will later discuss the fabled revolutionary's life and times, this montage of slides and music evokes impressive images that will recur in the spectators' minds as the action unfolds. "We have a history," Valdez is telling his audience, "and this is only a small part of that tradition."

After informing us that Pancho Villa was ambushed in his car in 1920, the narration adds that his body was later disinterred and decapitated. The head was never found. The prologue concludes with the following: "This is the story of a people who followed him beyond borders, beyond death."[2] This is not the story of a family, the prologue tells us, but rather the story of a people. From the beginning, then, we know that these characters are representative of many Chicanos in Valdez' analysis of his people's condition.

This play is divided into five acts, the action taking place over a period of less than three years. It is a tale of survival, as we watch the Mexican parents attempt to keep their family of Chicano children together. Characters become the focus of the action, with dialogue created to move the story forward with humor and insight. The major action of the play is the transformation of two of the brothers, Joaquín and Domingo. These two represent opposite character types for Valdez; one is a *vendido*, the other a street youth who becomes a social bandit. Like so many of the later *actos*, the play's theme is unity, exploring various Mechicano types in its search for an answer to the loss of identity that Valdez feels is bred by acculturation.

Though the family loses its father to an ignoble death and a son abandons the family to become "Americanized," the family unit does not dissolve altogether. The daughter matures to resemble her mother, marrying a man who looks like her father, and the young couple has a baby whose physical uniqueness recalls the parents' first-born, Belarmino. Belo, as he is called, is only a head; he has no body, and when Joaquín returns from prison without a head at the end of the play, Valdez hints that an alliance between the bodyless head and the headless body will bring about the solution to the family's plight. The play ends on a note of hope but cannot offer easy answers to the problems posed. It is an interesting first work that has fascinated its audiences with its symbolism and the characterizations that Valdez creates so effectively.

Valdez' dramaturgy has always displayed an individuality and eclecticism that makes his style difficult to categorize. The opening scene is juxtaposed with the musical slide prologue as the playwright introduces us to this Mechicano family. As the curtain opens to reveal the living room of what appears to be a typical barrio dwelling, a guitar plays "La cucaracha," a popular song of the Mexican Revolution, and we find Pedro, the father, snoring on the couch. After the final note is heard on the guitar, Pedro shouts "Viva Villa!" in his sleep. This is followed by "the cry of a full-grown man" in the next room and a fierce rendition of "La cucaracha" from the unseen voice. The play begins with noises because sound is very important to the playwright. Speaking of this play in 1968, Valdez called attention to the importance of noise to the Mechicano and pointed out how street hawkers in Mexico represent the sounds that we do not hear in the United States. "That's because this society doesn't allow Mexicans to make noise. We're supposed to get off the streets, and stay at las cantinas and keep our mouths shut," Valdez told participants in a Radical Theatre Festival in San Francisco.[3] The opening scene of this play was a symbolic *grito* or shout of independence for the playwright as his script leapt with an audible vengeance onto the stage, declaring it his own.

Once we have been exposed to the sight and sound of the setting—the modest home and the rather loud snoring, shouting, and singing—Cruz, the mother, enters. We immediately see this woman as more Mexicana than Chicana, for she speaks with an accent and at times confuses words in English. It is important that she be the first character to speak for she is really the backbone of the family. She is also continually concerned about her son in the next room, always telling the others to be quiet lest they should disturb his sleep. The opening scene tells us that her husband is a man who drinks and lives in the past, purporting to have ridden with Pancho Villa. Since he is not young, and the action of the play takes place "fifty years after the Mexican Revolution," he could in fact have known Villa. His wife puts up with his references to the past with the resignation of any alcoholic's spouse. Her name means "Cross" in English and is symbolic of her station, for she is the standard-bearer for the family and also has her own cross to bear.

We discover another of Cruz's crosses in the character of her youngest son, Joaquín. He represents the Chicano who has lost his Mexican identity yet is not Anglicized either. He is a street youth who we discover has been released from jail the day before and who his sister calls a "lousy pachuco." He tells the others that he had a fight with a *gavacho* (Anglo) who called him "Pancho." "I wasn't looking for no trouble," he says. "I even take Pancho at first, which was bad enough, but then he call me a lousy Pancho, and I hit the stupid vato in the mouth." He has taken the term "lousy" literally and resents the inference. Like the cockroaches that will become important symbols of this family's plight, lice identify a certain social standing and are negative images that Joaquín loathes. When his mother asks him what troubles him so much, he responds: "The gavachos."

It is Joaquín, the youngest son of this family in flux, who represents the hope of the future, recalling the early California folk hero Joaquín Murieta, who also had his troubles with the "gavacho." Our contemporary Joaquín, unable to blend into the larger society, has already been in trouble with the authorities, but we see him as a good person who is a victim of injustice. Explaining to his father how he was falsely accused, Joaquín says, "Then there at the station the placa [police] give us all matches, and the one wis the short one was guilty. They catch me red-handed! But I didn't swipe no tires." He has spent the last year in jail and has returned to find his family on welfare, awaiting the arrival of his older brother, the "war veteran."

The first act is a quick succession of scenes that keep the action flowing. There are few discussions that last longer than two pages without another character coming on or going off. The dialogue is also quickly paced. The exposition is carefully situated to make the conversations interesting, and the typical Valdezian humor abounds, with double entendres and sibling insults that remind us of our own youth. The first lengthy discussion is between Joaquín and his father and reveals the son's character as well as the father's obsession with Villa. Pedro recalls the fact that Pancho Villa bought a "Chivi" when his favorite horse died and was subsequently ambushed while driving that car. Joaquín asks if Villa ran down "a lotta gavachos" in the car, adding the image: "Squashed 'em!" Joaquín's hatred of the Anglo is constantly present, and his last remark reminds us of the act of squashing a cockroach or a louse.

The discussion about Pancho Villa fascinates our young warrior of the streets and is the first step toward transforming Joaquín into the revolutionary he will become. All the while, the women are in the kitchen preparing beans and tortillas for Belarmino, the oldest son who has only been heard grunting, belching, and shouting from the other room. He is, it seems, eating them all out of house and home, a constant consumer of the family's meager provisions. All but the mother speak disparagingly about Belarmino, yet he is accepted as another burden on the family with the resignation common in the barrio.

The discussion about Villa is interrupted by the arrival of Mingo (as Domingo is called), whose entrance is marked by a certain departure from reality. The mother has just asked "Where's Mingo?" in an absent-minded fashion, and when Joaquín says "Not home from the war yet," Mingo appears at the front door with the line: "Anybody say war?" The all-too-well timed arrival suddenly sets things ajar, beginning the transformation from social realism into fantasy. Mingo is the first *vendido* in Valdez' dramaturgy: a cold materialistic ex-Marine whose major goal is to get the family "Americanized" and out of the barrio. When he announces that he has bought a new "Chivi," the allusion to Pancho Villa's last ride cannot be ignored. The American car was the Mexican revolutionary's death trap and we wonder if it will bring about the demise of this would-be "Mexican American."

The change of style that begins with the soldier's entrance is prompted by his almost stereotypical character. Mingo is on a different level of reality in this play, and his transformation into the ultimate sellout contrasts with Joaquín's conversion into a revolutionary. Both the pachuco and the *vendido* fascinate Valdez, but it is the latter who remains outside the bounds of conventional reality. The fact that Mingo does not remember his sister's name or even that he has another brother reveals the acculturation process begun in the Marines, but the overtness of this transformation cannot be termed a subtle change of character. Domingo foreshadows another *acto* villain, for he tells his family that he is going to get rich as a farm-labor contractor, thus

combining the unsavory characteristics of both the *vendido* and the coyote.

In his "Note on Style" preceding the play, Valdez states: "The play is not intended as a 'realistic' interpretation of Chicano life . . . [but contains] realistic and surrealistic elements working together to achieve a transcendental expression of the social condition of La Raza in Los Estados Unidos." The first act constructs the realistic framework for the audience to identify with and gradually begins its transformation just as the characters evolve. We are carefully introduced to the surreal just as one would walk slowly into a cold stream rather than take a quick, shocking leap. Speaking of the *actos* in 1970, Valdez remarked: ". . . we can only stay a step ahead of our audience, and it has to be a very easy step for them to make, or they won't make it. . . ."[4] He understood that axiom when he wrote *The Shrunken Head of Pancho Villa,* and he searched for a form that would best describe his vision of *La Raza's* plight.

When the second act opens it is three months later. Once again we are confronted with loud Mexican music when the curtain rises, but there is something strange about the walls. We look more closely and discover that they are speckled with red cockroaches of various sizes. The daughter, Lupe, is standing behind her father, delousing him as he sleeps. A white lace veil covers Belarmino's head on an old sofa in the corner, and when Lupe finds something on her father's head she exclaims, "Lousy cucaracha!" This is curious, for we think she is delousing him; yet she seems to have found a cockroach in his hair and she describes it as "lousy." For Valdez and other Chicano writers, the cockroach represents *La Raza* in its indomitable spirit and ability to survive against all odds. A cockroach that is "lousy" is a metaphor for a Chicano who is infested with lice and thus a member of the poorest class.

The setting, with its cockroach-covered walls, suggests the expressionism of the early twentieth century, with exaggerated settings and properties used to emphasize the forces that overpower characters in the plays. In Valdez' dramaturgy, the symbols do not overpower as much as they serve to underline images that are recognizable to the Chicano. When the mother tells her daughter to "Go water the beans," a barrio audience will immediately know what she means. Someone who is not familiar with the Mechicano kitchen may think the daughter is going to the garden to water plants, when she is simply being asked to add water to the pot of boiling beans. A Mechicano audience knows all too well that Lupe is looking for lice and is thus aware of the juxtaposition that occurs when she pulls out a cockroach. Someone who has never experienced the process of delousing would lose the effect. The cockroach metaphor becomes increasingly important as the play develops.

After adjusting to the visual image of cockroach-covered walls, we find that Lupe resents her bodyless brother, for she has to stay home to feed him. She uncovers the head for a moment, and we see that it is the face of a 30 to 35-year-old man with deep, dark expressive eyes and a large moustache. Since he cannot talk, he communicates in grunts and howls and with those all-encompassing eyes. His head is larger than normal, a full eighteen inches in diameter. Lupe is in the midst of deriding her brother for making her feel like a slave, a *negra*, when her boyfriend Chato enters saying, "Hi *negra*." Though he uses the term endearingly, it is tantamount to "blackie," and we discover that neither of these young, dark-skinned Chicanos wants to be considered "dark." They are not aspiring to the Anglo world like Mingo, but they are representative of the many Chicano young people who are ashamed of their skin color and who respond to media images of what is beautiful. Chato tells Lupe that people are talking about her brother, claiming that he is only a head, to which she responds, "You black *negro*! You dirty Mexican!" employing racist epithets to combat his tauntings. She, we discover, cannot speak Spanish, but Chato can. Lupe becomes a transitional character caught between the pachuco and the *vendido* syndromes, neither one nor the other, searching for her identity. When she denies the fact that her brother is a head, she in effect denies her very culture.

Mingo, the aspiring farm-labor contractor, announces that they are going to buy a new house in "Prune Blossom Acres." He has previously referred to his family as "defeated" and insists that they have to leave the barrio to improve their condition. The move to the new location would constitute the ultimate rejection of his cultural heritage, Valdez is telling us, for it is symbolic of the Anglo encroachment of the land since the Southwest was taken from Mexico. What used to be an orchard where this family once worked has been converted into a typical California tract of identical houses bunched closely together. Cruz does not want to move, however, because in the barrio she feels safe from people's reactions to her oldest son. She does not realize that even there the people are talking, for she claims, "In this barrio they don't care."

MINGO: I care!

CRUZ: And the gringos?

MINGO: Whatta you mean gringos?

CRUZ: Who else live in new houses?

The playwright carefully controls the fantastic aspects of the play, exposing the fact that Belo is only a head at the close of the first act without actually revealing the visage. Belo's head sits onstage in the second act, covered by a cloth. We see his face for a moment and are very much aware of his presence. In the third act, Valdez uncovers the head and places it prominently upstage center. Having prepared his audience for this surrealistic atmosphere, the playwright is ready to add to the complexity. It is during the crucial third act that Belo first speaks. The speechless head can talk, and he warns his younger brother Joaquín not to tell anyone that he is really the head of Pancho Villa. Belo chooses Joaquín for this revelation because he recognizes him as the only hope for the family's salvation, calling his

identity a "political secret." When Joaquín enthusiastically tells his parents that Belo is really Pancho Villa, neither will believe him. Ironically, Pedro, who is continually referring to "Mi General Francisco Villa," does not accept Belo's head as that of the martyred revolutionary. The father represents the shattered hope of the Revolution, living on inebriated images of Mexico's true liberation. When the father dies, his hopes of a return to Mexico fade away with him, underlining the playwright's belief that the revolution is here and now.

Pedro is killed by a passing train, a symbol of the revolutionaries' transport in Mexico. Recalling the emotion of Pancho Villa's campaigns, Pedro had described the excitement that would greet his train, with people "climbing all over like lices." The image once again equates the poor with lice, and it is heightened by the old photographs that preceded the play—projections in black and white that caught the fervor of the moment and which the audience no doubt envisions in its mind. Though we do not see Pedro's death, the playwright calls up the sounds of the train passing and the progression from the railroad crossing bells to church bells; Belo then lets out a "sorrowful cry of death" and the scene blacks out. It is a poignant moment in a play that depends on character and language more than mournful emotions for its effect. The father's demise is soon overshadowed by the familial conflicts, for this is a play about life, not death.

Pedro's passing leaves Cruz in charge of the family, but she is helpless in the face of the poverty and dissolution of her brood. Lupe is pregnant out of wedlock, Joaquín is an ex-offender, and Mingo is slowly denying not only his heritage but his family as well. Mingo wants his brother to join the Marines, while Joaquín berates him for not being "Chicano." Joaquín tells Mingo that he can never be what he really wants, "Gavacho," which emphasizes what the Chicano is *not* rather than describing what he should be. As the play progresses, the brothers' transformations are the central issue. Mingo finally leaves the family and Joaquín becomes a "social bandit."

The transformations are bilateral, climaxed by Joaquín's arrest and Mingo's collusion with the police. When the latter arrive, Mingo tells them he is "only a boarder in this house." He helps them capture Joaquín rather than assisting his brother, who has become a Chicano Robin Hood. In helping the police, Mingo comes to embody the idea of "law and order." Joaquín has organized his friends to steal food from the supermarkets to feed the poor, offering an active, if illegal, alternative to their poverty. In contrast, Mingo hoards his food in the refrigerator, unwilling to share it with his own family. Both are exaggerated expressions of what the playwright is underscoring: extremes that have real counterparts in society.

Food is a major image in this play, first as nourishment for Belo, then as the symbol of liberation through Joaquín's supermarket forays. By the fourth act everybody is clamoring for food: Mingo hoards it; the women constantly make beans and tortillas to feed Belo; Joaquín comes home with sacks of beans and flour; and the ever-present Belo eats anything that is put into his mouth. Food becomes more than physical nourishment; it is a symbol for energy, drive, and initiative. Mingo tells his mother that instead of spending money on "the head," he is going to spend money "where it counts: on self-improvement." Yet his self-improvement is only a conversion from a family orientation to selfish egocentrism. This early version of the *vendido* finds it very easy to deny even sustenance to his family and, in effect, to his people.

The final act takes place two years after the close of the previous act. It is winter again, and the walls are crawling with larger cockroaches than before. Lupe's baby is also just a head, and both she and her husband Chato have begun to resemble her parents in appearance and dress. History, it seems, is repeating itself. Paralleling the opening of the first act, they are waiting for Joaquín to arrive, released from prison. They are also awaiting a visit from the social worker. Belo has learned to talk and has become, in his mother's words, "the man of the house." "The head of the house," his sister responds, enjoying the pun.

When the social worker arrives, we recognize him as Mingo, but when his mother runs to kiss him he tells her his name is Mr. Sunday and that though he once lived in a house very much like this one, it was "in another barrio . . . another town." Mr. Sunday now speaks some Spanish and is representative of those Mexican Americans who claim to be interested in helping "others less fortunate" while denying their own families as well as translating their names, for Domingo means Sunday in English. Mr. Sunday brings in a reformed Joaquín who is clean, well-dressed, and even taller, but who has no head. Lupe consoles her mother with: "He can still find a job in the fields. A man don't need a head to work there."

When Belo sees that muscular, headless body, he is delighted, and he asks someone to place him on top of Joaquín's shoulders. But Cruz tells her children that neither Belo nor the new baby will get this body as she leads Joaquín into another room. All go to bed, leaving Belo to tell the audience:

> . . . Sooner or later, the jefita gots to come across wis Joaquín's body. All I need is to talk sweet when she give me my beans, eh? In other words, organize her. Those people don't even believe who I am. Tha's how I wan' it. To catch 'em by surprise. So don' worry, my people, because one of this days Pancho Villa will pass among you again. Look to your mountains, your pueblos, your barrios. He will be there. Buenas noches.

Belarmino *is* the head of Pancho Villa, just as he is the hope for the future or the oppression of the present. This fantastic head represents the characters' ability to help themselves if they recognize the challenge. That challenge, in Belo's words, is to organize. As long as Cruz refuses to accept the fact that her oldest son is only a head, she must feed him beyond endurance. Her blindness is further emphasized when she sees Joaquín's headless body and refuses to combine it with Belo's head. When Belo says he has to organize her, he is speaking of La Raza as a whole, for which Cruz has become the archetype. She is more than the symbol of motherhood; she is all Mechicanos.

Belarmino represents the symbolic head of the Mechicano people as they have become under the yoke of Anglo-dominated society. The bodyless head typifies the disunity among the Mechicanos and their inability to see that their condition would change if they could get organized. It will not be through Mexican-American social workers, Chicano Robin Hoods, or even "50,000 vatos on horses and Chivis" that the Mechicano will find social justice, but in his own home. Just as Cruz refuses to accept the fact that she and her family are oppressed by the economic system around them, neither will she recognize the fact that her son is only a head. When she acknowledges the true nature of her family's condition, Valdez is telling us, she will have liberated herself from that internal colonialism that keeps the Mechicano in his subservient place.

For Valdez, the family is the hope for the future; it is the cradle of birth, maturation, death, and rebirth. The family he has dramatized in this play is also representative of the larger microcosm called the barrio. Valdez points to the barrio itself for the answers, underlining the premise that Mingo's total assimilation is a rejection of the heritage and culture of the community that nurtured him. Mr. Sunday's cold, deliberate denial of his family's basic needs paints a very negative picture of the sellout type. In contrasting the socially conscious Joaquín with Mr. Sunday, Valdez obviously favors the young warrior's determination to help his people. As a farm-labor contractor we see Mingo cheat his workers of their pay, and we also observe his selfishness in the home. But Joaquín's enthusiastic shoplifting earns him the respect of the people and the retribution of the establishment. When he returns from prison "reformed," he has no head and is therefore speechless; yet Belo knows that his mother will eventually combine the strong youthful body with the mind that is aware of its history and understands that its people are oppressed.

Given its use of fantasy and of symbols that are sometimes simplistic and sometimes obscure, *The Shrunken Head of Pancho Villa* is not easily interpreted. What is very clear, however, is Valdez' attitude toward the ubiquitous *vendido*. The playwright condemns those Chicanos who attempt to deny their culture and offers as an alternative the combination of Joaquín's youthful strength and Belo's tradition of revolution. Though the youngest son has been supposedly "rehabilitated," the playwright leaves his audience with the impression that he can still be helped. The power of the people is stronger than the institutions that attempt to suppress active resistance, Valdez tells us, and only time will reveal how long it will take for the people to put the necessary forces together.

. . . . .

A VETERANO'S MITO: *DARK ROOT OF A SCREAM*

The simple, silent procession past the dead soldier's body in the final scene of **Soldado razo** has become a wake in the living room of Quetzalcóatl Gonzales, another casualty of the war in Vietnam, in **Dark Root of a Scream.** Having participated in the collective creation of **Vietnam campesino** and **Soldado razo** as the Teatro Campesino's statements against the war, Valdez complemented and extended those *actos* with a very moving play which he terms a *"mito,"* or myth. To Valdez, the *acto* portrays the Chicano through the eyes of man, while the *mito* sees the Chicano "through the eyes of God."[5] **Dark Root of a Scream** continues where **Soldado razo** left off; it is the playwright's attempt to synthesize the earthly with the spiritual, the present with the past. The previous *acto* had begun with La Muerte's sardonic introduction, telling the audience what was going to happen and then narrating the action as it moved to its inevitable conclusion. **Dark Root of a Scream** begins with the *acto's* emotional ending, and through exposition it tells us who and what the dead soldier represented. Like the constant pull of the positive and negative forces that propel a molecule, this play moves forward as it reaches to the past, bringing the two forces together in a stunning climax.

Unlike any of the *actos*, this play depends a great deal upon its setting. The surreal interior of *The Shrunken Head of Pancho Villa* and the stylized setting of *Bernabé*[6] come together in this work to form a pyramid whose different levels represent the Chicano's progression from the earthly to the spiritual. At opposite ends of the base of the pyramid are two settings: a street scene and the interior of a living room. Rising behind these two settings is the pyramid itself, which changes as it ascends from a composition of "iron and the hard steel of modern civilization—guns, knives, automobile parts; others reveal a less violent, more spiritual origin—molcajetes [Mexican stone mortars], rebozos [shawls], crucifixes, etc."[7] These earthly objects blend into indigenous symbols as the pyramid rises, crowned with conches, jade, and feathered serpent heads. The lighting is a very important element in this production, accenting the progression from the materialistic to the transcendental as it blends from brightness at the base to darkness at the crest. Although this is not indicated in the published script, in a 1971 production of this play the lighting shifted from the street to the wake as the dialogue undulated from one side to the other.[8] Though the play can be produced without a complex lighting plan, the 1971 production benefited greatly from the spectacle.

From the beginning of this play, with its symbolic setting, the audience is aware that it is witnessing a non-realistic vision. The curtain rises on the fantastic setting and the two tableaux of characters at the base of the pyramid. Stage left is the wake, with a priest, an older woman, and a young woman. These three are entering through a curtained doorway, and they freeze as the action immediately shifts to the street scene and the three *vatos* who draw our attention. The youths are typical pachucos in their dress and demeanor, but their faces are made up to look like their nicknames: Gato (Cat), Lizard, and Conejo (Rabbit). These sobriquets echo the barrio custom of giving someone a name that fits his or her character (such as "Smiley") or physical features (such as "Negro"). The makeup and costumes of the three youths reflect their animal characteristics and recall indigenous attitudes toward their animal types. Lizard is a sexual animal, snake-like and obsessed with the physical. Gato is cunning and evil, the major antagonist in this play. Conejo is kind, softhearted, yet the wisest of the three. He is the main connection with the dead soldier whose body lies in the metal coffin at the wake, and like his sister, who we will presently meet, Conejo defends the fallen warrior.

In what is a meticulously planned and well-timed technique, the action shifts from side to side, as would a serpent—the major motif of this play about a Chicano named Quetzalcóatl, or feathered serpent. The undulating rhythm is at first slow, then builds to a point where the dialogue of the two separate scenes is melded into what seems a single conversation. This duality of scenes and dialogue is a metaphor for the redeemer-figure, Quetzalcóatl, for the feathered serpent represents the coming together of the earthly—the serpent—and the heavenly—the quetzal bird. Whereas **Bernabé** brings back the Aztec Sun God, a symbol of that people's militaristic society, this play recalls his opposite force, the kindly Quetzalcóatl, giver of life and symbol of divine transcendence over the mundane. Valdez is here discovering ancestral philosophies, and he finds a sharper focus in this play as he creates a modern *mito* that compares the god and culture hero Quetzalcóatl with a contemporary Chicano leader who was also named Quetzalcóatl. **Dark Root of a Scream** is basically a history lesson, but the premise on which it is based creates a fascinating drama.

While *The Shrunken Head of Pancho Villa* was constantly moving forward with crises and continual entrances and exits of characters, **Dark Root of a Scream** is much more dependent upon the past to move the action forward. It is the story of the dead soldier, and his past is recalled by the characters in the two scenes as they discuss his life. What could become a boring biography is kept interesting by Valdez' constant use of colorful, witty dialogue and the contrast of the two settings. The opening lines, delivered by Lizard, are: "Come on, ese, let's toke up" (p. 80), immediately identifying these other-worldly characters as contemporary *vatos*, smoking that ever-present symbol of their defiance, marijuana. Their dialogue tells us who they are and the fact that they knew the dead soldier, nicknamed Indio. We learn that Conejo's sister was Indio's girlfriend, and the scene shifts suddenly to the opposite side of the stage where the priest is saying. "That's it, easy does it, Señora Gonzales. No sense in getting hysterical about these things" (p. 80).

The priest, we discover, is not Hispanic, though he does speak Spanish when he communicates with the mother. His opening remarks establish him as somewhat cold, an outsider who feels that he knows what is best for his barrio parish. Though he speaks the language, he obviously has little understanding of the people. The first four scenes are brief encounters with the characters that establish the situation and the major objective: to mourn the dead soldier. However, the true mourners are the mother, the girlfriend, Dalia, and her brother, Conejo. The attitudes of the other three range from the indifference of the priest to the hostility of Gato. The Valdezian family in crisis is reduced to a suffering mother-figure who has lost everybody: her husband and her three sons. The first son died in World War II, the second in Korea, and the last lies in a coffin beside her. Now the mother is left with mere extensions of her son: Dalia and Dalia's brother, who was his friend. The family has, in effect, crumbled, and we find these vestiges of a once-proud people in verbal combat with the others to protect the image of the dead Chicano.

At the beginning of Scene IV, the mother finds blood dripping from the flag draped over the coffin. This discovery makes her think that her son is alive in the coffin, and she shouts "¡Mi hijo está vivo!" (My son is alive!), foreshadowing the major premise of the play: Quetzalcóatl lives. She faints from the stress of this discovery, and the action shifts quickly to the next scene on the street. In the following scene the dialogue begins to alternate between settings and characters. At first the transition is subtle. The boys are discussing another dead soldier whose body had already begun to reek of death at his funeral, and Gato remarks: "I bet Indio smells like that." Immediately the scene shifts to the wake, where the priest offers the stricken mother a cloth soaked with alcohol and says: "Here, madre, smell this" (p. 83). Though the numbering does not change to Scene VI, the focus remains on the wake rather than the street. Scene VI switches back to the street, and we continue to learn about Indio's past. Once again, in Scene VIII, the dialogue fuses, this time as if the two conversations were identical.

The boys discuss Indio's given name, and Conejo says, "Quetzalcóatl, the feathered serpent," to which the priest adds: "Quetzalcóatl Gonzales. What a name for an American soldier. I wonder what it means? The first part, of course. Everyone knows what Gonzales means" (p. 85). Conejo then answers the question as if he had been asked by one of the *vatos*. The conversations have become one now, and though the characters are separated in time and space, their discussion clarifies the differences in objectivity about the dead soldier. Scene IX illustrates the different levels of communication between the characters as Conejo and Dalia answer questions for the priest and Lizard:

PRIEST: How did Indio come to have a name like that?

CONEJO: His father name him that.

PRIEST: Oh yes, his father. How did his father—?

DALIA: He was a teacher in Mexico.

CONEJO: His name was Mixcóatl—Cloud-serpent.

PRIEST: I see. A nationalist, eh?

LIZARD: So what, man? Over here he was a wetback, a farm laborer just like everybody else.

PRIEST: A political exile, no doubt.

CONEJO: He knew a lot about Mexican history. Quetzalcóatl used to be a god for the Indians a long time ago.

LIZARD: Sure, man, the Apaches

(p. 85).

Both the priest and Lizard hold attitudes toward Indio and his culture that are bred of ignorance and insensitivity: the priest representing the Church's apathy toward indigenous cultures and the street youth indicative of another form of cultural bias. Lizard can only think of "Apaches" when the image of an Indian comes to his mind, the product of John Wayne movies and television stereotypes. Lizard's line is also an example of Valdez' juxtaposition of the serious with the sardonic, the ridiculous with the sublime. Like many immigrants to this country, Indio's father left his country an educated man, only to become another common laborer.

As the scenes evolve and the dialogue continues to undulate from one group to the other, the discussion centers around the god Quetzalcóatl, the Toltec leader named after him, and the Chicano named after both.[9] Valdez does not bother to distinguish between the myths surrounding the Toltec leader Ce Acatl Topiltzin Quetzalcóatl and the god after whom he was named, for the central theme is the parallel between the indigenous figure, whether god or man, and his contemporary incarnation. It is Valdez' intent to draw comparisons between the indigenous myth and the Chicano *mito* and his characters describe the corresponding qualities of each. Like the indigenous figure, Indio did not like war and human sacrifice and had worked to stop street violence and restore the Chicanos' pride in their heritage and culture. Indio was a contemporary leader who was drafted in the prime of his cause, a victim of the racism the priest accused him of. This juxtaposition is interesting, for the audience knows that it is the priest, not the Chicano, who is basically racist in his inability to comprehend the youth's motives for trying to help his people.

In an interesting parallel, Indio was betrayed by the priest and Mexican Americans in his parish who did not allow him to use the church hall for meetings, just as Quetzalcóatl was tricked by evil priests who caused his downfall. The legendary figure was deceived by Tezcatlipoca, who got him drunk and then forced him to see himself as he really was in a mirror. Shamed, Quetzalcóatl fled on a raft of serpents, promising to return. When Indio got drafted, he consulted with the priest about what to do. The priest tells Dalia: "He was considering fleeing the country, but he knew he'd never be able to return as a community leader." To which Gato responds in the other scene: "Big community leader." That draft notice showed him to his face who he was, "like a mirror" (p. 90). By drawing contemporary parallels to ancient themes and symbols,

Valdez succeeds in educating his audience about the past and the present. The main theme of **Soldado razo,** which attributed the soldier's basic willingness to go to war to societal pressures, is reflected here again, but the dynamics become much more complex than in the *acto.*

The *vatos* decide to go to the wake after Gato and Lizard have a scuffle. Gato is clearly the other's superior, and the emotional climax of the threatened knife fight is comically dissipated by lizard's cocky strut offstage after he has composed himself. Lizard's exit is juxtaposed with the priest's next line: "Now we will pray," as the scene shifts back to the wake and the requiem for the dead. The three youths appear at the door and clumsily enter the service. Gato sits by Dalia and attempts to get fresh with her, while the priest chants "Quetzalcóatl, your humble servant," and the others repeat "Bless him Señor" (p. 94). The service is halted when the youths repeat "Your humble *serpent*" and the priest discovers Gato's lascivious advances toward Dalia. Pandemonium breaks loose; the priest rushes out for the police with Lizard close behind him. Gato tells Conejo to try and stop him, and the intensity builds until the mother lets out a blood-chilling wail and attacks Gato. This stops Gato; then, as the mother sobs over her son's coffin, Lizard enters dressed in the priest's cassock.

Once again there is a mixture of pathos and the grotesque as Lizard tells the others that the priest is running down the streets "in his shorts" (p. 96). Suddenly he notices the mother and Dalia at the coffin; they have discovered more blood dripping onto the floor. As the boys decide who is going to open the coffin, the mother steps up to it and pulls up the lid. Conejo looks in and says, "It's . . . feathers!" Lizard reaches in and pulls out "a brilliant headdress of green feathers and a cloak of Aztec design" (p. 97). He puts these vestments on and asks:"How do I look, ese?" as drums begin to beat in the background. They all look toward the coffin, and Lizard, looking very much like an Aztec priest atop a ceremonial pyramid, reaches into the casket, pulls out something, and lifting it in his hands screams: "Indio's heart!" (p. 98). The stage directions tell us that "the heart gives out light in the descending darkness," and the play ends.

In the 1971 production mentioned above, the scrim behind the pyramid dissolved, revealing the silhouette of the mythical Quetzalcóatl in his indigenous costume, looming above everything as the heart emitted a pulsating light in Lizard's hands. Just as he had promised, Quetzalcóatl had returned. In his review of that production, Dan Sullivan asked: "Is that a dead soldier or a dead god lying under the American Flag in the funeral parlor? If a dead god, is he dead forever? If a dead soldier, need there be others?"[10]

Sullivan recognized Valdez' genius in this production and noted that his plays "seem to spring from a far more comprehensive view of life than most Americans can manage without confusion." His question reflected that complexity, for unlike **Soldado razo, Dark Root of a Scream** evoked many images and called upon its audiences

to go back and forth in time and space just as the action had. According to Valdez' *mito,* that bleeding, pulsating heart must be likened to the Sacred Heart of Jesus, which represents eternal life, not death. The light that emantes from the heart is energy; therefore it lives, and so too does Quetzalcóatl.

In the opinion of this author, **Dark Root of a Scream** remained for several years Valdez' finest dramatic achievement, but ironically it was seldom produced. The cost of an adequate production was inhibitory and the playwright also told this writer that he felt the work was not yet complete. The spectacle required is also difficult to produce and would be virtually impossible to tour to the usual barrio locations. Within a few years the war ended, causing the play to lose its topical impact. Because most Chicano theater groups attempt to produce works that speak to the immediate issues affecting the barrio, this play has not been produced since the war ceased. Still, **Dark Root of a Scream** is an excellent example of the Valdezian *mito* that addresses a current issue even as it explores ancient and universal concepts. It is a short play, yet it is such a gripping tale that it leaves its audiences immersed in its themes, engrossed by its premise.

. . . . .

THE ULTIMATE PACHUCO: *ZOOT SUIT*

For years, Luis Valdez had looked upon the professional stage as a platform Chicano theater should avoid. "Will Broadway produce a Chicano version of *Hello Dolly* now that it has produced a Black one?" he asked in 1971.[11] As a leading figure in the Alternative Theater Movement of the 1960s, Valdez viewed the Broadway stage as pure commercialism, to be avoided by any truly political theater company. Broadway was and is big business and Valdez felt at the time that neither he nor his group would benefit from any association with professional producers and Equity contracts. Nor were any offers forthcoming, given the fact that political theater has seldom been an attraction on the Great White Way. The Teatro Campesino was a frequent visitor to off-Broadway houses; it even received an Obie in 1968 for "creating a worker's theater to demonstrate the politics of survival."[12] But Broadway houses and professional costs were anathema to Valdez and his troupe in 1971.

Riding on the popular success of **La gran carpa de los rasquachis (The Great Tent of the Underdogs)** in 1974, three years after he had produced **Dark Root of a Scream,** Valdez told this author that he would never write a play again.[13] **Carpa** was a magnificent product of collective creation under Valdez' guiding genius. Both its success and the resulting notoriety caused him to pause and reconsider his creative processes. He had not written a script independently since **Dark Root of a Scream,** and he felt that the individual playwright must give way to the group process. In addition, because of the number of projects the Teatro Campesino had undertaken, he never had time to write. The group had recently purchased forty acres of land on a sloping hill overlooking the rural community of San Juan Bautista in central California. Valdez looked forward to building a complex of offices, rehearsal spaces, studios, and housing for his extended family. He was also chief administrator of a growing business that included a publishing house, record and film distribution, and the yearly tours that generated the group's major income.

But by 1976 Valdez had again grasped the playwright's pen to write a realistic play, *Fin del mundo*. . . . The author was pleased with his script, but confided that the members of his troupe, accustomed to the broad *acto-carpa* style of acting, were having trouble with the portrayals required for this realistic work. It was then that Valdez told this author that he was going to write a play about the "Zoot Suit Riots" of the early 1940s and produce it at the Mark Taper Forum in Los Angeles. "It will probably go to Broadway," he said, "because we have to spread beyond the audiences we have been reaching."[14] He now agreed that teatro had become theater for the already initiated and that the time had come to seek a larger, more varied public. Certainly, the Teatro Campesino was internationally known and the troupe had been seen by scores of people on television, but Valdez, the visionary, understood the need for a more professional attitude in Chicano theater. Continuing that conversation, he said,

> You know, I'm tired of having our group perform for some disorganized student organization that can't generate enough publicity to gather an audience . . . The Teatro was supposed to perform in some little town, and when they arrived, the people said: "We didn't know you were coming, man. . . ."

We laughed about the reality of that scene, for it had happened to many groups in different places. The Chicano Movement was grinding to a halt it seemed, lost in philosophical debates that had been parodied by teatros in such works as the Campesino's *Militants* and Teatro Mestizo's *Cuatro años de colegio* (Four Years of College).[15] The "Revolution" was over, said the critics of the Movement, when campus organizations could not decide upon a name for their group much less the direction or political stance they should take. Disorganization plagued all aspects of the Movement, including the teatros. People who were truly serious about their work in theater were often frustrated in their efforts by undisciplined aficionados to whom teatro was a thing of the moment.

Although the Teatro Campesino is a professional theater company, Valdez, as a director, realized during rehearsals for the 1976 version of *Fin del mundo* that some of his actors lacked the breadth of those exposed to a variety of acting experiences. He was ready to work with a different breed of professionally trained actors, both Chicano and Anglo. "There are a lot of talented Chicano actors and actresses in Los Angeles," Valdez remarked, "and they've never had a chance to be in a real Chicano play or movie." He knew that if his plans succeeded, the play he envisioned would be the first of its kind on either side of the continent. A professionally produced play, written, directed, and performed by Chicanos about their own struggles had never been achieved. It was a totally new direction for Valdez and was a natural step in the evolution of his Teatro and in his own commitments as a playwright and director. That 1976 conversation became a reality when *Zoot Suit* opened at the Mark Taper Forum in Los Angeles two years later.

The move to the professional stage was a conscious act for Valdez and came as no surprise to anyone who had spoken with him over the years. At an early meeting of teatro directors in 1971, he had advised the teatros to seek a professionalism that would attract the public in the same way their favorite Mexican enertainers did. By going to Hollywood and then New York, Valdez was telling other teatros: ". . . it's a career, a serious one. Not just the money—that's the base level—but a profession. . . . Playwrighting is a noble profession."[16]

Gordon Davidson, the artistic director of the Center Theatre Group in Los Angeles, had long been interested in producing theater for the Mechicano community. The Teatro Campesino performed *La gran carpa de los rasquachis* in the Group's Mark Taper Forum in 1974 and attracted a large number of Mechicanos who would otherwise never have attended this prestigious theater in Los Angeles' imposing Music Center. Special public relations efforts were conducted in the barrios of Los Angeles and busloads of students and community members ushered in a new audience for the Forum's "New Theatre for Now Series." The *Carpa* was billed as a work in progress, part of a series of new plays, and the production pleased the public and critics alike. It was Valdez' first exposure to Davidson's company as well as the Center Theater Group's first experience with a Chicano theater group and its audiences. Both sides were pleased with the result of the alliance. When Davidson decided to investigate the possibility of producing a Chicano play, he turned to Luis Valdez.

Davidson was interested in theater that reflected our society's minority cultures and had engaged anthropologist Kenneth Brecher to oversee productions of this nature. Valdez suggested a play about the zoot suiters of the 1940s, and both Davidson and Brecher responded enthusiastically.

With a grant from the Rockefeller Foundation, Valdez and members of his toupe researched the events surrounding the Sleepy Lagoon murder trial and found that "what we came up with isn't a Chicano play, like the ones we do at San Juan Bautista. It's an American play."[17] It was another form of the indigenous theater Valdez had become known for. In this case the play was native to Los Angeles rather than to Mesoamerica. By terming it an "American play," Valdez was in effect telling his prospective audiences: "We've been considered different long enough. Now it's time to see the Chicano not as separate from this society, but as an integral part of it." Los Angeles, which has the largest concentration of Mexicans outside of Mexico

City, was the perfect birthplace for a work that effectively dramatized an important episode in Mechicano history.

After months of research and writing and weeks of rehearsal and anticipation, tickets went on sale for the premiere of *Zoot Suit* in April 1978. Everyone involved in the production knew that there was great community interest in the play, but when it sold out its ten-day run in less than two days, the reality struck home: Chicanos wanted to see plays about themselves. Tickets to the performances became prized possessions as people clamored to see what *Zoot Suit* was all about. Even before opening night, the producers knew that they had struck a chord in the Chicano community that had only begun to vibrate.

The initial version of Valdez' vision of the Chicano in the 1940s was immediately hailed as a milestone in the American theater, although most of the critics agreed that the work in progress needed more developing and polishing. No matter how critical or cautious the reviewers were, however, the audiences were undaunted in their enthusiastic responses to the production. They laughed and cheered, cried and hissed, commenting upon the action as it unfolded before them. Those who had lived through the period being dramatized were moved by the representation, for they understood what it meant to be a Mechicano in this country in 1942. Audiences were divided between the subscribers—basically a white, theater-going public—and the Mechicanos—most of whom had never been to the Forum or any other legitimate theater to see a play. Many of the non-Spanish-speaking members of the audience felt left out when others laughed at the jokes in Spanish or *caló*, but they joined the cheering crowds who jumped to their feet at the end of each performance.

Something beautiful and strange was happening on that stage while Anglo and Chicano heroes and villains marched across Valdez' panorama of Los Angeles and the nation in the early 1940s. The play focused on the Sleepy Lagoon murder trial, concentrating on the leader of a group of young Chicanos who were virtually railroaded on charges of murder. As the defense lawyer says in the trial scene, "The only thing the prosecution has been able to prove beyond a shadow of a doubt is that these boys are Mexican!" The play mingled fact and fantasy, drawing on documentation and the playwright's imagination, to create a collage of events presented in the eclectic style that is Valdez' trademark. He combined elements of the *acto, corrido, carpa*, and *mito* with Living Newspaper techniques to dramatize a Chicano family in crisis.

Zoot Suit opened with the boys' release from prison and then flashed back to recall the events that had led to their imprisonment. Interwoven with this main thread of action was a developing love affair between the leader, Henry Reyna, and the Marxist Jewess who led the Defense Committee, Alice Springfield. Valdez also included other themes and unnecessary characters that tended to cloud the issues, and confusion surrounded his version of the death of the Chicano at the Sleepy Lagoon. The play seemed to grope about for an effective ending. Nonetheless, Valdez had stepped onto the professional stage with grace and confidence. The producers could not ignore the response of the public or the critics and selected the play to open the regular subscription season for a six-week run beginning the following August.

While the production was still enjoying its initial success, talk began about a Broadway production, a motion picture, a touring company, and other possible consequences of that triumph. But before any of these options could be considered, the playwright had to return to his typewriter and resolve the problems in the script. Valdez told this author, "Directing it was a breeze compared to the writing. Writing it was hell."[18] This was no longer a Chicano theater troupe leaving San Juan Bautista with a freshly typed revision and rehearsing on the road. Now there were union contracts, established runs, and opening nights that could not be avoided or postponed. Valdez could no longer substitute another *acto* if this one was not working. The pressure might have stopped a lesser man. Painfully, he rewrote and recast, while the others on the production staff revised their initial visions as the opening approached.

When tickets for the August production were about to go on sale, the newspapers began to publicize that "On July 30, 1978, the Second Zoot Suit Riot begins"—and it did. The play again sold out in record time and this prompted the Center Theater Group to begin looking for another space. "Zoot Suit fever" had hit Los Angeles once more and though the advertising campaign might have been considered offensive by some, those who understood the nomenclature appreciated the metaphor: the ad was a celebration of a people gathering to buy tickets to a play that spoke to them. Opening night again inspired a standing ovation, as would every subsequent production of the play in Los Angeles.

Valdez had trimmed the play considerably and focused more clearly on the people and events surrounding the trial. Gone were the superfluous characters and situations that had plagued the earlier version, replaced by a plot line that was clearly directed to the final scene. Changes in the casting helped create a stronger vision of the characters and newly choreographed dances and songs added to the spectacle considerably. The original set was altered to a slicker version, substituting clear plastic floors and invisible walls for the original wagon settings and barrio textures. Instead of the partial walls and movable furniture that rolled on in the first version, the designers and director chose to use stacks of newspapers as chairs, the judge's bench, and other set props. In a backyard scene, instead of taking clothes off the clothesline, the mother removes newspapers, folds them, and places them in a laundry basket.[19]

The burlap backdrop of earlier Campesino productions was replaced by a twenty-foot high blowup of the *Los Angeles Herald Examiner* carrying the headline "American Bomber Victim of Jap Raider" and a composite of other articles relating to the war abroad and the "wars" at home—the "Zoot Suit Riots." It was a Valdezian indictment of the press, which had helped create and perpetuate the racist hysteria of the period. As in the allegorical *actos*, a character named The Press continually debates the issues involved in this period of Los Angeles' history. In the trial scene, The Press becomes the prosecutor; he begins his comments to the court with, "The Press will prove beyond a shadow of a doubt—I mean the *prosecution* will prove . . ."—and the point is made.

From its opening scene, ***Zoot Suit*** is the product of all that Valdez had done before. The houselights dim, swing music of the 40s comes on, and a three-foot switchblade cuts through the huge newspaper. This is followed by the entrance of a zoot suiter, who is simply El Pachuco, the archetypal predecessor to the *vato loco* we have seen before on teatro stages. But this pachuco, dressed in his finest, strutting with a cocksure stance that seems to defy gravity, is unlike the previous types Valdez has dramatized. Like his switchblade, he is much larger than life; he makes a theatrical statement none of the critics can dismiss no matter what they think of the play.

After he surveys the spectators with a "What the hell are you looking at me for?" glance, El Pachuco tells them: "It is the secret fantasy of every *vato* to put on the zoot suit and play the part of the pachuco." This brings cheers from the contemporary *vatos* in the audience who share this fantasy. The others listen carefully as this figure from the past reveals the playwright's purpose in this "construct of fact and fantasy": to reveal a period in our history that is generally neglected in the history books.

From his opening narrative to the close of the play, El Pachuco has the audience in his grasp, commenting upon the action and occasionally stopping it like La Muerte did in ***Soldado razo*** in order to remind the audience that they are in a theater. El Pachuco is Henry Reyna's alter ego, his pachuco-half that sometimes keeps him from doing things he otherwise would, such as saying "thank you" to his lawyer. At other times he provokes Henry to do a deed he might have avoided. During a moment of intensity, when Henry yells out in anguish at his hounding subconscious, El Pachuco tells him, "*Orale pues, buey*, don't take the play so seriously!" The Pachuco's continual comments to Henry are calculated to break moments of tension with humor or skepticism. When the police are questioning Henry about his involvement in the alleged murder, The Press is behind them reading actual headlines from newspapers of the day. Quoting from a report to the grand jury, The Press refers to the zoot suiters as descendants of "bloodthirsty savages who sacrificed human beings." El Pachuco quickly interjects: "*¡Pues ponte las plumas, que ya te van a chingar!*" ("Well, put on your feathers, 'cause now they're gonna fuck you!").[20]

Valdez continually plays with his audience, poking at them with many barbs: emotional, comic, tragic, sardonic. After the climactic ending of the first act when the boys

have been found guilty of murder and sentenced to life imprisonment, all leave the stage except for El Pachuco. He surveys the audience slowly, strutting to center stage where he can capture their attention with a mere glance. With a "Whadya think of *that* shit" look, he says: "Now we're gonna take a little break . . . so you can take a leak." Moments before, the audience was suffering for the families and the obviously innocent Chicanos; now their laughter is released at this mundane yet practical suggestion.

While the first act focuses on the trial and the events leading up to it, the second act finds the boys in jail while the Defense Committee works to free them. The rather maudlin romance between Henry and Alice in the first version is here replaced by a sensitive portrayal of an imprisoned man and his only link with the outside world—Alice. She is reluctant to get emotionally involved, but nonetheless their visit ends with an embrace and a kiss that is as tentative as Henry's hopes for freedom. Eventually the boys are freed, but what might have become a happy ending is channeled into a collage of possible conclusions to Henry's story. Each character surrounding the central figure of Henry addresses the audience with different versions of what happened to him: "He married and had three children"; "He died of the tragedy of his own existence"; "He overdosed a few years later." Other possibilities are thrown at the audience, reminding it that this character from the past still lives. The play's message calls for the audience to reappraise its attitudes and secret fantasies as it leaves the theater amid contemporary versions of historical personages.

In a climactic moment, after having been stripped by a group of sailors, El Pachuco is left in a loincloth, lying on the ground. Humiliated before the audience, no longer protected by the costume that distinguishes him, El Pachuco rises slowly, regains his dignity, and walks off the stage, a reminder in his nakedness of his *indio* ancestors. It is only a moment in this epic play, but it conveys that overriding ability to survive that has been postulated in all of Valdez' works. The pachuco—the symbol of fear, mistrust, and secret fantasies of defiance—permeates the minds of those in the audience. During a scene in the prison, Henry and another character are about to get into a fight when El Pachuco stops him with: "That's exactly what the play needs right now: two Mexicans killing each other! Everybody's watching, *ese* . . . that's what they came to see." Mechicanos and Anglos alike have probably wished at some point that "those pachucos would just kill each other off." They may laugh at El Pachuco's statement, but they may also, hopefully, consider the truth behind it.

After quickly selling out its initial run at the Forum, ***Zoot Suit*** moved to a larger theater in Hollywood, the Aquarius, six weeks later. Audiences lined up to buy tickets and the Center Theater Group signed a contract with the Shubert organization to open the play in New York the following year. While the play continued to run in Los Angeles with a largely new cast, the original cast went to New York and opened the production on March 25, 1979. Pre-opening publicity heralded the first Latino play on Broadway as a major event, and relatives, friends, and teatro aficionados flew to New York for the occasion.

The audience loved the production; the New York critics did not. Sylvie Drake, who has followed Valdez' evolution closely since he first began the Teatro Campesino, was present that opening night and thought the production was at its best, fitting "neatly into the stage of the Winter Garden, with an assurance and focus refined well beyond all three of the previous L. A. versions."[21] However, her initial statement about the New York opening provides an ironic metaphor for the production:

> Smooth as El Pachuco's reet pleat, slick as the mocking feather in his broad-brimmed hat, **"Zoot Suit"** skidded onto Broadway Sunday with all the sass of a high school dropout clamoring for admission to an Ivy League college.
>
> . . . admission was not granted.[22]

Ironic, because pachucos, as we learned in *No saco nada de la escuela,* are high school dropouts, as were a majority of Chicanos until quite recently.[23] Ironic, because few Chicanos have been admitted to Ivy League colleges. And finally, ironic because the "skid" Ms. Drake refers to suggests a stop, as if that were the production's ultimate destiny. It was not. While the play was breaking records in Los Angeles and Valdez was preparing for the move to Broadway, he told this author that New York was only another step in the course the production had to take.[24] Responding to the New York critics, Valdez told an interviewer:

> The play is still an enormous success in Los Angeles; it's going to do phenomenal business throughout the Southwest and Latin America, and it's going to continue to run in the great cities of America whether the critics like it or not.[25]

Zoot Suit lasted four weeks on Broadway while the producers attempted to recruit the Hispanic and Black audiences that might not be dissuaded by the largely negative press. Publicity campaigns were conducted in Latino neighborhoods, but the appeal failed to overcome the high cost of survival on the Great White Way. Most productions greeted with the notices ***Zoot Suit*** received close in a few days, yet this pachuco of the theater held on, determined to make its mark. The major New York critics called ***Zoot Suit*** "overblown and undernourished";[26] "a great deal of loose material draped over a spindly form";[27] "simplistic . . . poorly written and atrociously directed";[28] and "bloodless rhetoric."[29] There were positive reviews as well, but in the commercial arena of skyrocketing ticket prices few productions could overcome such condemnation.

Years before the Broadway experience, Valdez had written that the teatros must never get away from La Raza. "Without the *palomía* [populace] sitting there," he said, "laughing, crying and sharing whatever is onstage, the teatros will dry up and die."[30] Although he was speaking figuratively

about the importance of reflecting the Chicano's reality, there was something prophetic in the statement. After the New York run, Valdez likened his play to the pachucos who went to the Hollywood Palladium dressed in their finest in the 1940s and were sometimes admitted, though often they were not. Today, Broadway is the Palladium of the theater world and ***Zoot Suit*** the pachuco who is not accepted. In Valdez' words: "The Pachuco himself is stripped . . . just as ***Zoot Suit*** has been stripped. But that doesn't take away its dignity. He still stands and ***Zoot Suit*** will stand."[31]

The play continued to run in Los Angeles while plans were made for a national tour and Valdez began the task of transforming a theatrical spectacle into a screenplay. The New York experience had been a challenge from the start; although the play did not fulfill the hopes of its producers and creators, it had made an impact. Like the sleekly dressed pachuco, ***Zoot Suit*** could not be ignored. Critics might laugh at its bravado, scorn its audacity, and cry for a statement they could better understand, but they could never change this child of the barrios into what they termed "good theater." As Valdez had expected, the Hispanic and Black audiences in New York understood his play perfectly. El Pachuco was as much their symbol of defiance as he was the Chicanos', for he stood before his audience and declared himself a member of this society, whether society wanted him or not. "This is a cultural stand," Valdez told an interviewer in New York, "and America has got to come to grips with it. Because we're not going to go away."[32]

That *palomía* Valdez had written about in 1971 was still enchanted with his theatrical statements, and the impact he and his troupe had made on the Chicano Movement would continue to mold the direction for other teatros. The Teatro Campesino would continue to perform in this country and abroad; ***Zoot Suit*** would pack the houses in every major center of Mechicano population. Luis Miguel Valdez, the man who had started a national theatrical movement, had gone full circle. From political street theater to cultural and spiritual revolution to professional playwright and director, Luis Valdez remained constant to his initial purpose. His theater entertained as it educated; it was didactic, yet born of a basic human spirit that had endured the criticisms of both the politicians and the aesthetes. Valdez' world encompasses more than most of his critics can comprehend. As he continues to place his characters on stages that reflect his own people, this contemporary man of the theater will prevail.

· · · · ·

A CONTEMPORARY MYTH: *BERNABÉ*

Luis Valdez first directed ***Bernabé*** in 1970, five years after the birth of the Teatro Campesino. This was the playwright's first *mito,* a term he chose to express the form and content of the play, and it ushered in a new period for the man who had formulated the *acto.* The change in terms reveals a change of thematic focus. Although the *actos* were collectively created, ***Bernabé*** is the product of Valdez' dramaturgy alone; it was his first attempt at playwrighting after the initial production of ***The Shrunken Head of Pancho Villa*** in 1963.

In 1971 Valdez discussed what he foresaw as the future of Chicano theater: "Not a teatro composed of actos or agit-prop but a teatro of ritual, of music, of beauty and spiritual sensitivity. A teatro of legends and myths."[33] Valdez described the genesis of the *acto* as taking place "through the eyes of man," while the *mito* was created "through the eyes of God."[34] Valdez, the constant seeker of truth, had begun to reach beyond the early Spanish religious theater to the ritual dramas of the Aztecs and Mayas.

For his first *mito*, Valdez chose to dramatize the transformation of a *loquito del pueblo* (village idiot) into a "child of the sun." If the *mito* was in fact written "through the eyes of God," that God was not the Judeo-Christian diety of barrio churches, but was instead the omnipotent Sun God, Huitzilopochtli, ruler of the cosmos. It was Huitzilopochtli who demanded human sacrifices, and Valdez becomes a modern interpreter of the sacred ceremonies atop the Mexica temples. Bernabé, the character for whom the play is named, is a universal symbol of innocence and purity who becomes the archetypal Chicano seeking his connection with Mother Earth, La Tierra. Bernabé is a character familiar to any barrio audience, for the people do not hide their abnormal children or adults in institutions. Although Bernabé is retarded, he commands our attention by his simplicity and honesty of purpose. As Valdez says in his introduction: "There is a central duality in the character of Bernabé: there is divinity in madness."[35]

Bernabé is a crippled farmworker, the only son of a pious, all-suffering mother who sees him as her single solace as well as her major burden. She is constantly scolding him and reminding him that he is her personal cross to bear. In the first scene, while they are walking down the barrio street under the noonday sun, the mother warns her son to avoid matters of the flesh with threats that the earth will swallow him up. She is the typical Roman Catholic *madre* who reflects a conservative theology. Her warning foreshadows the major action of the play, for Bernabé will indeed be swallowed up by the earth. Both the earth and the sun, whose heat is a constant presence, are stressed in the opening of the play, establishing the two major forces that Bernabé will later confront. The first part of the play is a realistic portrayal of barrio realities, setting the mood and establishing characters and individual objectives.

Economic survival is an important theme in the play's initial scenes. Money is the central force around which everything revolves except for Bernabé, whose only love is La Tierra. He talks to the earth as if she were another character, informing the others that he will someday marry her. To the normal characters, Bernabé's expressed desire is indicative of his mental state—he is crazy, after all. But when this realism is transformed into a fantastical vision of Bernabé's objective, the question becomes: "Who is crazy?"

Bernabé is a brief play, divided into seven scenes that lead to the transformation of the central figure. The setting is usually a stylized representation of a typical rural town, with the major action transpiring on the street. When the action shifts from outdoors to a prostitute's room, we enter Bernabé's mind and see the inner workings of his so-called distorted vision. Coaxed into an unwanted encounter with the prostitute Consuelo (literally, "solace"), Bernabé envisions his mother reprimanding him for commiting a sin. He has never had sexual relations with a woman; what would have been his loss of innocence is interrupted by his guilt and the appearance of his mother in Consuelo's garb. The two women merge in Bernabé's mind and the playwright lets the audience see the apparition. Bernabé flees from the hotel thinking he has killed his cousin in a skirmish and runs out to the fields. He hides in a hole he has dug in the earth, a mythic womb in which he has often masturbated in a symbolic copulation with La Tierra.

In this climactic scene in the fields Valdez takes us back in mythical and historical time. Bernabé's hole in the ground becomes larger than life and expands to include the audience within its protective walls. Bernabé is visited by allegorical figures that recall the Aztec gods and by figures from later periods in Mechicano history. First to appear is La Luna (The Moon), dressed as a 1940s zoot suiter, smoking a marijuana cigarette. La Luna is a detached and mythical figure whose very presence evokes a magnified vision of historical heroes. La Luna introduces Bernabé to his sister, La Tierra, who is dressed as an "Adelita," the name given to camp followers during the Mexican Revolution of 1910. The moon is a cool *vato* who speaks the language of the streets, but the earth is a revolutionary woman, aware of suffering and oppression. La Luna is Valdez' first re-creation of a mythical pachuco and foreshadows his later incarnation in ***Zoot Suit***.

La Tierra questions Bernabé's love and asks him, "Well what makes you so macho? The smell of your sweat? The work you do for the patrón? I thought you were a Chicano!" (Steiner, p. 368). According to La Tierra the true Chicano will not let himself be manipulated by oppressive forces. "Are you Chicano enough to kill?" she asks this humble *campesino*, who is slowly gaining confidence and a masculinity that he did not have before. This Adelita, this vision from the past who encompasses both an indigenous deity (La Tierra) and an archetypal heroine from recent history, is forcing Bernabé to show an independence and assertiveness that will make him whole. Bernabé's response to the question of killing is still uncertain, for he has not committed himself to the ultimate sacrifice: his life for La Tierra's love.

El Sol is pleased with Bernabé and tells him that there were once men like him who respected La Tierra. "They saw what only a loco can understand," he tells our simple hero, "that life is death and death is life." In a ceremony that recalls the Aztec sacrifices to Huitzilopochtli, Bernabé gives his heart for La Tierra and becomes a natural man no longer crippled or retarded. When Bernabé promises to love his bride "unto death," she reveals a skull mask to him and the ritual is over. The last scene once again returns the audience to "reality," the barrio street, and we discover that Bernabé has died, his body discovered buried in his hole. In the "real world" Bernabé is presumably dead, the victim of a cave-in, but in the mythical world of gods and goddesses immortality is achieved by giving one's life.

It is his willingness to die that sets Bernabé apart from sane men. The innocence of madness, coupled with his instinctive respect for La Tierra, makes him a representative peasant whose death symbolizes the transformation from innocence to wisdom. His love for La Tierra reflects the Maya respect for all things natural, a philosophy that will greatly influence Valdez' later work. Bernabé dies in the so-called real world, but lives on in his spirit. The marriage with La Tierra is ultimately consummated in a manner that recalls the duality of Maya philosophy. Valdez told a group of teatro representatives a few years later that the Maya word for the phrase "to bury a body," *mucnal*, also means "to plant a seed."[36] To the Mayas they are the same thing, for death does produce life in the natural order of things.

Bernabé is in reality Valdez' myth. In the Aztec pantheon, Coatlicue, the earth goddess/virgin mother, gives birth to Huitzilopochtli, the sun. The moon, Coyolxauhqui, is the sun's sister. Valdez' dramatization of the sun as father and the earth and moon as children thus differs from the Aztec legends. In changing the sexes and relationships of this cosmic triumvirate, the playwright creates his own *mito*, based on his interpretation of the hero/quest myth. It is as if Bernabé could not want to marry the "mother of God" since that would be too presumptuous, but he can ask for the hand of the sun god's daughter. In the Nahuatl account of the birth of Huitzilopochtli, Coatlicue is merely the vessel for the virgin birth. But in Valdez' vision La Tierra is an activist who urges Bernabé to fight and die and even kill for her.

Teatro critic Betty Diamond believes that La Tierra is at heart "just a woman who wants only to be fought over and made love to,"[37] but the symbolic copulation is more than sexual; it is a holy consummation between man and earth that Valdez sees as a metaphor for becoming one with La Tierra. El Sol tells Bernabé that his daughter has been "fucked" many times, contrasting the act of lust and the quest for power with Bernabé's sincere love and respect for La Tierra. Throughout history, the play reminds its audience, man has violated the Earth by stealing her resources and destroying her natural beauties. By telling the humble *campesino* to give his life for La Tierra, Valdez makes a rather difficult request that contrasts sharply with the *actos'* original call to "join the Union." This is what separates this *mito* from the earlier *actos*: the solution becomes symbolic, couched in allegorical figures who represent natural forces. Bernabé's struggle represents an inner tension whose battle-ground is actually in the mind

of each observer. The *acto* depends upon the sympathies of a politically aware audience, while the *mito* demands a spiritual understanding.

Valdez' script calls for anthropomorphic deities; they are not superhuman like the Greek gods but personas from barrio myths. The ubiquitous pachuco and the legendary Adelita are both figures of esteem and mystery to the people—both warriors, both misunderstood. They represent defiance against the system, whether the Anglo-dominated society of the United States or the military forces of both this country and Mexico. The Adelita echoes Pancho Villa's struggle in Valdez' first play, transporting the Chicano back in time to a real revolution. Marijuana, which was the subject of the revolutionary song "La cucaracha," the musical motif for **The Shrunken Head of Pancho Villa** represents the defiance of La Luna as he smokes a marijuana cigarette with Bernabé.

Bernabé is the first *mito* to come from Valdez' pen, but the major theme of the play will be echoed in subsequent collective works, especially **El fin del mundo.** The later play looks more closely at how man has taken advantage of the Earth and lost the innocence of earlier times. By contrasting the human family with the cosmic order, Valdez points toward the Chicanos' greater understanding of their role in history as a people with a past and a heritage of myth. No one, not even the rich and powerful, can really own La Tierra, the main character tells us, for though men take from her in time they will all return to her eternal womb. In effect, the play tells us that the "real Chicano" will fight against the landowners for La Tierra and if need be will die for her. It is, after all, a metaphor for Zapata's famous decree: "The land belongs to those that work it."

NOTES

[1]This quote is from the author's notes of a TENAZ Director's Conference in San Fernando, California, 4 September 1971. The first conference had been held the previous April in Fresno, California, following the "Second Annual Chicano Theater Festival" the previous week.

[2]This and all other quotes are from an unpublished ms. of *The Shrunken Head of Pancho Villa* in the author's collection, copyright 1976 by Luis Valdez.

[3]*Radical Theatre Festival* (San Francisco: San Francisco Mime Troupe, 1969), p. 19.

[4]Sylvie Drake, "El Teatro Campesino: Keeping the Revolution on Stage," *Performing Arts*, September 1970, pp. 58-59.

[5]Valdez, *Actos* (San Juan Bautista: Cucaracha Press, 1971), p. 5.

[6]*The Shrunken Head of Pancho Villa* is discussed in Chapter Two. Luis Valdez' first *mito*, *Bernabé*, is discussed in Chapter Six.

[7]These and all other quotes from *Dark Root of a Scream* are from Lilian Faderman and Omar Salinas, *From the Barrio* (San Francisco: Canfield Press, 1973), pp. 79-98. The setting is described on pp. 79-80.

[8]*Dark Root of a Scream* was first produced at the Inner City Cultural Center in Los Angeles as part of a "Fiesta de los Teatros" from September

16-26, 1971. This was the first time and only instance of a TENAZ production outside of San Juan Bautista, California, home base of the Teatro Campesino after 1971. This ten-day effort brought together representatives from various teatros in the organization, and it proved successful but difficult to repeat. For a review of that production, see note 18, below.

[9]For more information about the legendary and historic Quetzalcóatls, see Miguel León-Portilla's two important books: *Aztec Thought and Culture* (Norman: University of Oklahoma Press, 1963), and *Pre-Columbian Literatures of Mexico* (Norman: University of Oklahoma Press, 1969).

[10]Dan Sullivan, "Homecoming of a Dead GI," *Los Angeles Times*, 25 September 1971, II, p. 8.

[11]Luis Valdez, *Actos* (San Juan Bautista: Cucaracha Publications, 1971), p. 2.

[12]From the citation awarded the Teatro Campesino in 1968, on file in San Juan Bautista, California.

[13]From an interview with Luis Valdez in the spring of 1974 in San Juan Bautista, California.

[14]From an interview with Luis Valdez in the spring of 1976 in San Francisco, California.

[15]Teatro Mestizo is a San Diego-based group that was formed in 1969 by students at San Diego State College. In 1974, this very active troupe collectively created a critique of the Chicano student movement entitled *Cuatro años de colegio* (Four Years of College). Nick Kanellos described this three-part *acto* as "a rollicking and biting satire" in the *Latin American Theatre Review*, 9 (fall 1975), p. 83. Teatro Mestizo continues to work in San Diego with a constantly changing membership of students and community members under the leadership of Marcos Contreras and Carolina Flores.

[16]Tomás Benitel, "Facing the Issues Beyond 'Zoot Suit'," *Neworld*, 5/1 (1978), p. 37.

[17]Dan Sullivan, "Putting the Boomp into 'Zoot Suit'," *Los Angeles Times*, 16 April 1978, Calendar Section, p. 1.

[18]From an interview with Luis Valdez in October of 1978 in San Juan Bautista, California.

[19]In an interview with Eduardo Robledo, a former member of the Teatro Campesino, he recalled: "The use of newspapers as other objects came out of a summer workshop with Ron Davis in 1972. The mimetic images in 'Carpa' and 'Zoot Suit' are influenced by that workshop." San Francisco, California, March, 1979. The workshop Robledo refers to was the second annual TENAZ Summer Workshop held in San Juan Bautista, hosted by the Teatro Campesino.

[20]The exact quote comes from a report to the Los Angeles County Grand Jury of 1942 written by a Lt. Duran Ayres of the Los Angeles County Sheriff's Department. See the McWilliams Collection # 107 (Rare Books Section), folder 7, in the public affairs section of the UCLA Research Library. Reference is made to this document in Arturo Madrid-Barela, "In Search of the Authentic Pachuco: An Interpretive Essay," *Aztlán*, 4 (spring 1973), p. 34. Dr. Madrid's article is an excellent analysis of the pachuco in literature.

[21]Sylvie Drake, "Broadway Cool to 'Zoot Suit'," *Los Angeles Times*, 27 March 1979, IV, p. 1.

[22]Ibid.

[23]A look at the census reports for 1960 and 1970 reveals an improvement in the educational achievement of Spanish-surnamed people of Mexican descent, but the median is well below the national average.

[24]From an interview with Luis Valdez in October of 1978 in San Juan Bautista, California.

[25]"First Hispanic-American Show on Broadway: ZOOT SUIT," *New York Theatre Review*, 3 (May 1979), p. 23.

[26]Richard Eder, "Theatre; 'Zoot Suit,' Chicano Music-Drama," *New York Times*, 26 March 1979, Sec. C, p. 13.

[27]Ibid.

[28]Douglass Watt, "'Zoot Suit' slithers in at the Winter Garden," *New York Daily News*, 26 March 1979, p. 21.

[29]Walter Kerr, "'Zoot Suit' Loses Its Way in Bloodless Rhetoric," *New York Times*, 1 April 1979, Sec. D, p. 3.

[30]Luis Valdez, *Actos*, p. 4.

[31]"First Hispanic-American Show," p. 23.

[32]Ibid.

[33]Luis Valdez, *Actos*, p. 3.

[34]Valdez, *Actos*, p. 5.

[35]Stan Steiner and Luis Valdez, *Aztlán: An Anthology of Mexican-American Literature* (New York: Random House/Vintage, 1972), p. 364. Scene Three from *Bernabé*; appears in Spanglish in the Steiner-Valdez anthology, pp. 361-76. A complete version of this script in Spanish is published in Roberto Garza, *Contemporary Chicano Theatre* (Notre Dame: University of Notre Dame Press, 1976), pp. 30-58.

[36]From an informal discussion with Luis Valdez in the spring of 1973. Valdez was greatly influenced by the interesting treatise of Mexican anthropologist Domingo Martínez Paredez, *El Popol Vuh tiene razón* (México: Editorial Orion, 1968). In a controversial interpretation of the Maya classic, Dr. Martínez asserts that it is a scientific explanation of the creation of this planet. In reference to the word *mucnal*, Dr. Martínez states: ". . . MORIR es BAJAR, y esto es innegable, porque el cuerpo BAJA a la sepultura y a ésta se le llama MUCNAL—ENTERRAR MAIZ" (to die is to go down, and this is undeniable, because the body is lowered into the grave and this is called *mucnal*—to plant the corn. My translation), p. 153.

[37]Betty Diamond, *Brown-Eyed Children of the Sun; The Cultural Politics of El Teatro Campesino* (Ann Arbor: University Microfilms, 1977), p. 153.

Jorge Huerta (essay date 1992)

SOURCE: An introduction to *Zoot Suit and Other Plays*, by Luis Valdez, Arte Publico Press, 1992, pp. 7-20.

[*Here, Huerta surveys Valdez's career, stressing the playwright's continual questioning of notions of reality and identity.*]

It is a pleasure to introduce the reader to *Zoot Suit, Bandido!* and *I Don't Have to Show You No Stinking Badges!*, as well as to their celebrated creator, Luis Miguel Valdez. These plays have never been published before and are an important addition to the growing corpus of Valdez's writings that have been preserved for future theater artists, students, scholars and the general reader. These three plays represent only a fraction of Valdez's astounding output since he first began writing plays in college.

For some, Luis Valdez needs no introduction; for others, his name may only be associated with his more widely seen films and television programs. No other individual has made as important an impact on Chicano theater as Luis Valdez. He is widely recognized as the leading Chicano director and playwright who, as the founder of El Teatro Campesino (Farmworker's Theatre) in 1965, inspired a national movement of theater troupes dedicated to the exposure of socio-political problems within the Chicano communities of the United States. His output includes plays, poems, books, essays, films and videos, all of which deal with the Chicano and Mexican experience in the U.S. Before discussing the plays in this collection, I would like to briefly trace the director/playwright's development, placing him and these plays in their historical context.

FROM FLATBED TRUCKS TO HOLLYWOOD SOUND STAGES: THE EVOLUTION OF LUIS VALDEZ

Luis Valdez was born to migrant farmworker parents in Delano, California, on June 26, 1940, the second in a family of ten children. Although his early schooling was constantly interrupted as his family followed the crops, he managed to do well in school. By the age of twelve, he had developed an interest in puppet shows, which he would stage for neighbors and friends. While still in high school he appeared regularly on a local television program, foreshadowing the work in film and video which would later give him his widest audience. After high school, Valdez entered San Jose State College where his interest in theater fully developed.

Valdez's first full-length play, **The Shrunken Head of Pancho Villa,** was produced by San Jose State College in 1964, setting the young artist's feet firmly in the theater. Following graduation in 1964, Valdez worked with the San Francisco Mime Troupe before founding El Teatro Campesino. Valdez became the Artistic Director as well as resident playwright for this raggle-taggle troupe of striking farmworkers, creating and performing brief comedia-like sketches called *"actos"* about the need for a farmworker's union. The *acto* became the signature style for the Teatro and Valdez, inspiring many other teatros to emulate this type of broad, farcical and presentational political theater based on improvisations of socio-political issues.

Within a matter of months El Teatro Campesino was performing away from the fields, educating the general public about the farmworkers' struggle and earning revenue for the Union. By 1967 Valdez decided to leave the ranks of the union in order to focus on his theater rather than on the demands of a struggling labor organization. As a playwright, Valdez could now explore issues relevant to the Chicano beyond the fields; as a director, he could begin to develop a core of actors no longer committed to one cause and one style alone.

Although he and his troupe were working collectively from the beginning, the individual playwright in Valdez was anxious to emerge. Discussing the process of writing plays outside of the group, Valdez recalled: "I used to work on them with a sense of longing, wanting more time to be able to sit down and write." In 1967, the playwright did

sit down and write, creating what he termed a *"mito,"* or myth, that condemned the Vietnam war, titled **Dark Root of a Scream.** This contemporary myth takes place during a wake for a Chicano who died in Vietnam, an ex-community leader who should have stayed home and fought the battle in the barrio. The dead soldier becomes symbolic of all Chicanos who fought in a war that the playwright himself objected to. "I refused to go to Vietnam," Valdez said twenty years later, "but I encountered all the violence I needed on the home front: people were killed by the farmworkers' strike."

In 1968 the Teatro was awarded an Obie, off-Broadway's highest honor, and the following year Valdez and his troupe gained international exposure at the *Theatre des Nations* at Nancy, France. In 1970 Valdez wrote his second *mito*, **Bernabé.** This one act play is the tale of a *loquito del pueblo* (village idiot), Bernabé, who is in love with La Tierra (The Earth) and wants to marry her. La Tierra is portrayed as a *soldadera*, one of the women who followed and supported the troops during the Mexican Revolution of 1910.

Bernabé is a wonderfully written play that brings together myth and history, contemporary figures and historical icons. The allegorical figure of La Luna, brother to La Tierra, is portrayed as a Zoot Suiter. This is Valdez's first theatrical exploration of this 1940's Chicano renegade, foreshadowing one of his most powerful characters, El Pachuco, in **Zoot Suit. Bernabé** tells its audience that Chicanos not only have a history of struggle but *are* that struggle. Bernabé "marries" La Tierra and becomes a whole person; he symbolically represents all men who love and respect the earth.

Also in 1970, even as Valdez, the playwright, was scripting his individual statement about the Chicano and his relationship to the earth, Valdez, the director, was guiding the collective creation of an *acto* dealing with the war in Vietnam: **Soldado Razo** (**Buck Private**). **Soldado Razo** carefully explored some of the reasons young Chicanos were willing to go fight in Vietnam. Reflecting the influences of Bertholt Brecht's theories, the playwright uses the allegorical figure of La Muerte (Death) as a constant presence narrating the action, continually reminding his audience that this is theater and that the soldier's death is inevitable.

Soldado Razo complemented and expanded the earlier *mito*, **Dark Root of a Scream,** looking at the same issue but from a different viewpoint and in a distinct style. In Valdez's words, the *acto* "is the Chicano through the eyes of man," whereas the *mito* "is the Chicano through the eyes of God," exploring the Chicanos' roots in Mayan philosophy, science, religion and art. While **Soldado Razo** methodically demonstrates the eventual death of its central figure, **Dark Root of a Scream** begins after a soldier's death, exploring the cause from a mythical distance.

In 1971 the troupe moved to its permanent home base in the rural village of San Juan Bautista, California, where the Teatro established itself as a resident company. During this period Valdez began to explore the idea of adapting the traditional Mexican *corridos*, or ballads, to the stage. A singer would sing the songs and the actors would act them out, adding dialogue from the corridos' texts. Sometimes the singer/narrator would verbalize the text while the actors mimed the physical actions indicated by the song. These simple movements were stylized, enhancing the musical rhythms and adding to the unique combination of elements. The *corrido* style was to appear again, altered to suit the needs of a broader theatrical piece, *La Carpa de los Rasquachis* (*The Tent of the Underdogs*).

Developed over a period of years, *La carpa de los Rasquachis* stunned the audience at the Fourth Annual Chicano Theater Festival in San Jose, California in 1973. This production became the hallmark of the Teatro for several years, touring the United States and Europe many times to great critical acclaim. This piece is epic in scope, following a Cantinflas-like (read "Mexico's Charlie Chaplin") Mexican character from his crossing the border into the U.S. and the subsequent indignities to which he is exposed until his death.

La carpa de los Rasquachis brought together a Valdezian aesthetic that could be defined as raucous, lively street theater with deep socio-political and spiritual roots. The style combined elements of the *acto, mito* and *corrido* with an almost constant musical background as a handful of actors revealed the action in multiple roles with minimal costumes, props and set changes. This was the apogee of Valdez's "poor theater," purposely based on the early twentieth-century Mexican tent shows, otherwise known as "carpas."

In an effort to define his neo-Mayan philosophy, Valdez wrote a poem, *Pensamiento Serpentino,* in 1973. The poem describes a way of thinking that was determining the content of Valdez's evolving dramaturgy. The poem begins:

> *Teatro*
> *eres el mundo*
> *y las paredes de los*
> buildings *más grandes*
> *son* nothing but scenery.

Later in the poem Valdez describes and revives the Mayan philosophy of "In Lak Ech" which translates as "*Tú eres mi otro yo* / You are my other me." The phrase represents the following philosophy:

> Tú eres mi otro yo / You are my other me.
> Si te hago daño a ti / If I do harm to you,
> Me hago daño a mí mismo / I do harm to myself;
> Si te amo y respeto / If I love and respect you,
> Me amo y respeto yo / I love and respect myself.

In the opening lines Valdez describes Chicano theater as a reflection of the world; a universal statement about what it is to be a Chicano in the United States. Recognizing the many injustices the Chicano has suffered in this country, the poet nonetheless attempts to revive a non-violent response. Valdez creates a distinct vision of a "cosmic people" whose destiny is finally being realized as Chicanos who are capable of love rather than hate, action rather than words.

While *La carpa de los Rasquachis* continued to tour, Valdez made another crucial change in his development by writing *Zoot Suit* and co-producing it with the Center Theatre Group of Los Angeles. Once again at the vanguard, Valdez began the mainstreaming of Chicano theater, or, for some observers, "the infiltration of the regional theaters."

The director/playwright did not abandon El Teatro Campesino by getting involved with a major regional theater. The Teatro was still touring and *Zoot Suit* was co-produced by both theater organizations, thus including the Teatro in all negotiations and contracts. But this was a first step towards an individual identity that Valdez had previously rejected by working in a collective.

As advertised in the Los Angeles press, "On July 30, 1978, the Second Zoot Suit Riot begins," and it did. *Zoot Suit* played to sold-out houses for eleven months—breaking all previous records for Los Angeles theater. While the Los Angeles production continued to run, another production opened in New York on March 25, 1979, the first (and only) Chicano play to open on Broadway. Although audiences were enthusiastic, the New York critics were not, and the play was closed after a four-week run. Hurt, but undaunted, Valdez could have the satisfaction that the play continued to be the biggest hit ever in Los Angeles and a motion picture contract had been signed.

Zoot Suit marked an important turning point in Valdez's relationship with El Teatro Campesino as he began to write for actors outside the group. This experience introduced Valdez to the Hollywood Latino and non-Latino talent pool, suddenly bringing him into contact with a different breed of artist. With a large population of professionals at his disposal, Valdez's vision had to expand. No longer surrounded by sincere, but sometimes limited talent, Valdez could explore any avenue of theater he desired. The success of the Los Angeles run of *Zoot Suit* enabled our playwright/director to move more seriously into filmmaking. Valdez adapted and directed *Zoot Suit* as a motion picture in 1981.

The collaboration with a non-Hispanic theater company and subsequent move into Hollywood film making was inevitable for Valdez; the natural course for a man determined to reach as many people as possible with his message and with his art. Theater was his life's work, it was in his blood, but so was the fascinating world of film and video.

With the financial success of *Zoot Suit,* Valdez purchased an old packing house in San Juan Bautista and had it converted into a theater for the company. This new playhouse and administrative complex was inaugurated in 1981 with a production of David Belasco's 1905 melodrama *Rose of the Rancho,* adapted by Valdez. This old fashioned melodrama was an ideal play for San Juan Bautista, because it was based on actual historical figures and events that had occurred in that town in the nineteenth century. Played as a revival of the melodrama genre, the play could be taken for face value, a tongue-in-cheek taste of history replete with stereotypes and misconceptions.

The experiment with *Rose of the Rancho* served as a kind of motivation for Valdez, inspiring him to write the second play in this collection, *Bandido!* which he then directed in 1982 in the Teatro's theater. This was Valdez's personal adaptation of the melodrama genre but with a distinctly Valdezian touch as we will see later.

Valdez wrote and directed *Corridos* for the 1983 season, producing this elaboration of the earlier exercises in San Francisco's Marine's Memorial Theater, a large house that was filled to capacity for six months. The San Francisco production garnered eleven awards from the Bay Area Theater Critics Circle before moving on to residencies in San Diego and Los Angeles.

All of his interaction in Hollywood and his own sense of history inspired Valdez to write the final play in this collection, *I Don't Have to Show You No Stinking Badges!,* first produced by El Teatro Campesino and the Los Angeles Theatre Center in 1986. This production represented the beginning of yet another phase for Valdez and his company. El Teatro Campesino was no longer a full-time core of artists, living and creating collectively under Valdez's direction. Instead, the company began to contract talent only for the rehearsal and performance period. El Teatro Campesino became a producing company with Valdez at the helm as Artistic Director and writer. After great success in Los Angeles, *Badges!* was co-produced with the San Diego Repertory Theater and the Burt Reynolds Dinner Theatre in Jupiter, Florida. While the Teatro continued to produce, Valdez began to focus his efforts more on writing and directing films.

Valdez directed *La Bamba,* the sleeper hit of the summer of 1987, finally opening up the doors that had been so difficult to penetrate for so many years. "When I drove up to the studio gate," Valdez related, following the success of his film, "the guard at the gate told me that the pastries were taken to a certain door. The only other Mexican he ever saw delivered the pastries." That same year our playwright adapted and directed the earlier *Corridos* into a PBS version titled *Corridos: Tales of Passion and Revolution,* starring Linda Rondstadt and featuring himself as narrator. This production won the Peabody Award, the Pulitzer Prize of broadcasting.

Following the success of *La Bamba* and *Corridos* Valdez continued to work on other projects for television and film as he also took his position as the leading Chicano filmmaker in Hollywood. Ever the activist, Valdez helped form the Latino Writers Group, which he hoped would pressure the studios to produce films written by Latinos.

"The embryo is the screenplay," he said. "The embryo, in fact, is what is written on the page. This is where you begin to tell the difference between a stereotype and reality."

In 1991, Valdez adapted and directed *La Pastorela,* or *Shepherd's Play* for a great performances segment on PBS. This television production is based on the traditional Christmas play, which El Teatro Campesino has produced in the mission at San Juan Bautista for many years. That same year, Valdez and his wife, Lupe, co-scripted a motion picture based on the life of Frida Kahlo, for production in 1992. Plans were also underway for a revival of *Bandido!* in San Juan Bautista during the 1992 season as well as a re-mounting of *Zoot Suit* for a national tour.

Valdez's impressive career can be separated into the following four periods: Phase One, the director/playwright of the original group of farmworkers; Phase Two, a Teatro Campesino independent of the Union; Phase Three, a professional Teatro and co-productions such as *Zoot Suit;* and the current, Fourth Phase, Luis Valdez, the filmmaker alongside El Teatro Campesino, professional productions across the country and community-professional productions at home.

CUTTING THROUGH THE NEWS: *ZOOT SUIT*

Zoot Suit is the logical culmination of all that Valdez had written before, combining elements of the *acto, mito* and *corrido* in a spectacular documentary play with music. Unlike any of his previous plays or *actos,* however, *Zoot Suit* is based on historical fact, not a current crisis.

By illuminating an actual incident in the history of Chicano-Anglo relations in Los Angeles, *Zoot Suit* does not have the immediacy of an *acto* about today's headlines. The politically aware will know that the police brutality and injustices rendered in this play are still happening; others may lose the point. Most significantly, this play illuminates events that had a major impact on the Chicano community of Los Angeles during World War Ii, incidents that are carefully ignored by most high school history books.

Like the *acto,* *Zoot Suit* exposes social ills in a presentational style. It is a play that is closer to the docu-drama form, owing more to Brecht than to Odets as the action reveals the events surrounding the infamous Sleepy Lagoon Murder Trial of 1942. By employing a narrator, Valdez is discarding a totally representational style in favor of this more direct contact with his audience. El Pachuco's almost constant presence, underscoring Henry's inner thoughts and tribulations, skillfully captivates the audience and serves as a continual commentator on the action.

Just as La Muerte did in *Soldado Razo,* El Pachuco will stop the action entirely in order to make a point, telling Henry (and the audience) to listen again when the judge rules that the "zoot haircuts will be retained throughout the trial for purposes of identification . . ." It is a kind of "instant replay" that is only used once for maximum effect. Countering the figure of El Pachuco is the allegorical character of The Press which descends directly from the *acto* as well.

Like the *corrido*, there is a musical underscoring in ***Zoot Suit,*** placing the events in a historical context by employing the music of the period. El Pachuco sings some of the songs, as in a *corrido*, setting the mood through lyrics such as those that introduce the "Saturday Night Dance" in Act One, Scene Seven. While El Pachuco sings, the actors dance to the rhythms he creates, transforming from youthful fun to vengeful intensity gone wild by the end of the scene.

Some of the songs are original while others are traditional Latin or Anglo-American tunes, such as Glenn Miller's "In The Mood." Unlike the *corrido*, in which the music was played by live musicians, however, the music is pre-recorded. The choreography is also more like that of a musical comedy during the dance numbers, staged with historical authenticity to enhance the theatricality and further engage the audience.

Most importantly, this play places the Chicanos in a historical context that identifies them as "American," by showing that they, too, danced the swing as well as the mambo. Valdez is telling his audience that the Chicanos' taste for music can be as broad as anyone's. He is also revealing a cross-culturalism in the Chicanos' language, customs and myths. As Valdez so emphatically stated when this play first appeared, "this is an *American* play," attempting to dispel previous notions of separatism from the society at large. He is also reminding us that Americans populate The Americas, not just the U.S.

Valdez will not ignore his indigenous American ancestors, either, employing elements of the *mito* very subtly when the Pachuco is stripped of his zoot suit and remains covered only by an indigenous loincloth. This image suggests the sacrificial "god" of the Aztecs, stripped bare before his heart is offered to the cosmos. It is a stunning moment in the play, when the cocky Pachuco is reduced to bare nakedness in piercing contrast to his treasured "drapes." He may be naked, but he rises nobly in his bareness, dissolving into darkness. He will return, and he does.

The character of El Pachuco also represents the Aztec concept of the *"nahual,"* or other self as he comes to Henry's support during the solitary scene in prison. Henry is frightened, stripped emotionally bare in his cell and must rely on his imagination to recall the spirit of El Pachuco in order to survive. The strength he receives from his other self is determined by his ability to get in touch with his *nahual*.

The documentary form of the play is influenced by the Living Newspaper style, a documentary theater that exposed current events during the 1930's through dramatizations of those events. The use of newspapers for much of the set decoration, as well as the giant front page backdrop through which El Pachuco cuts his way at the top of the play is an effective metaphor for the all-pervading presence of the press. When Dolores Reyna hangs newspapers on the clothesline instead of actual laundry, the comment is complete.

Like most of Valdez's works, this play dramatizes a Chicano family in crisis. Henry Reyna is the central figure, but he is not alone. His *familia* is the link with the Chicano community in the audience, a continuing reminder that the Chicano *is* a community. Unlike the members of his family, however, Henry's alter-ego brings another dimension to this misunderstood figure. El Pachuco represents an inner attitude of defiance determining Henry's actions most of the time. El Pachuco is reminiscent at times of the Diablo and Diabla characters that permeated the *corridos*, motivating the characters' hapless choices as in Medieval morality plays.

El Pachuco's advice is not based on a moral choice, as in the *corridos*, but rather, on judgments of character. Mostly, El Pachuco represents the defiance against the system that identifies and determines the pachuco character. Sometimes, Henry does not take El Pachuco's advice, choosing instead to do what he thinks is right. At times, Henry has no choice, whether he listens to his alter-ego or to another part of himself, he will still get beaten. Interestingly, El Pachuco is sometimes more politically astute than the defendants themselves, allowing Henry an awareness his fellows do not have. In other instances, such as when the boys debate whether to confide in George, the boys' instincts are better for the whole and Henry must ignore El Pachuco's advice.

Now available in video, the motion picture of ***Zoot Suit*** is a vivid record of elements of the original stage production, because it was filmed in the Aquarius Theatre in Hollywood where it had played. The motion picture recreates and reconstructs the play. At times we watch the action unfolding as if we, too, are one of the hundreds sitting in the audience, watching the play; then suddenly the characters are in a realistic setting, as in a sound stage and we are enveloped in social realism. Just as the Pachuco continually reminds the audience that "this is just a play" in the stage version, the film also prompts us to remember that this is a *demonstration of actual events*, urging us to think about it as we watch the action moving back and forth between realities. ***Zoot Suit*** is also a rewriting of history, as is the central issue of the next play, ***Bandido!***

REWRITING HISTORY: *BANDIDO!*

Bandido! is an exploration and expurgation of old clichés about the early California bandits. Valdez's intent is to alter history by demonstrating his version of the exploits of one Tiburcio Vásquez, the last man to be publicly hanged in California. The play is therefore didactic like an *acto* or a docu-drama but goes beyond those forms to become a "melodrama within a play." The playwright creates a construct in which audience sees Vásquez through different eyes. Vásquez is sympathetic when observed through the playwright's eyes and a stereotype when seen through history's distorted characterization.

The key to a successful production of *Bandido!* lies in an understanding of the satiric nature within the form of the play. Valdez's introductory notes state the challenge to director and actors most clearly: "The contrast of theatrical styles between the realism of the jail and the *trompe l'oleil* of the melodrama is purely intentional and part of the theme of the play . . . their combined reality must be a metaphor—and not a facile cliché—of the Old West." The actors must therefore represent real people in the jail scenes and stereotypes of those characters and others in the melodramatic scenes.

Valdez is no stranger to stereotypes, as is illustrated in one of the playwright's most enduring *actos*, *Los vendidos* (*The Sellouts*), which he first wrote in 1967. In this very funny and popular *acto*, the playwright turns stereotyping around, making the audience reassess their attitudes about various Chicano and Mexican "types." We laugh, but also understand that the characteristics exposed are a reflection of Anglo perceptions and, yes, even sometimes our own biases as Chicanos. In both *Los vendidos* and *Bandido!* the playwright is portraying these characters *with a clear understanding that they are stereotypes.*

The characterization of Tiburcio Vásquez will vary according to the point of view of who is re-creating him on stage. If he is perceived as "real" in the jail scenes and a stereotype in the melodrama, the audience will distinguish the playwright's bias. They might also understand that their own biases come from the Hollywood stereotype of a "bandido." The actor, too, must delight in demonstrating the exaggeration, commenting upon his character even as he explores the exaggerations. This is a Brechtian acting technique, asking the actor to have an opinion about his character's actions and choices. Within the construct of the melodrama within the play, this can be effectively displayed.

Valdez clearly thinks of Vásquez as a social bandit, a gentleman who never killed anyone but who was forced into a life of crime by the Anglo invaders of his homeland. The playwright's goal here is to make Tiburcio Vásquez more than a romantic figure cloaked in evil, to present us with a reason for his actions instead of only the results.

Valdez's first play, *The Shrunken Head of Pancho Villa,* featured a young Chicano social bandit named Joaquín, symbolic of that better known *"bandido,"* Joaquín Murrieta. Labelled a pachuco by the police, Joaquín steals from the rich to give to the poor. Neither Joaquín nor Vásquez are clearly understood by the authorities, but they fascinate their communities. As Pico says to Vásquez in the second act: "You've given all of us Californios twenty years of secret vicarious revenge."

The Shrunken Head of Pancho Villa offers hope for the community through unified social action, although the fate of *Bandido!*'s central figure is predetermined by history. Valdez knows that nobody can change the inequities of the past, but offers the suggestion that the future can be altered for the better, if misrepresentations of the Chicano are altered.

It is not that Valdez is attempting to completely whitewash Vásquez, either. When the Impresario asks him, "Are you comic or tragic, a good man or a bad man?" Vásquez responds: "All of them." To which the playwright might respond: "Aren't we *all* comic and tragic, good and bad?" It is perhaps the degree of evil that fascinates our playwright here, that degree always determined by who is being asked. Thus, the opposing views of this comic, tragic, good and bad man.

Valdez's style here is reminiscent of Luigi Pirandello, the Italian playwright and novelist whose works often turn reality inside out, leaving the reader or observer to ponder the nature of reality. Again, the Impresario states the obvious when he tells Vásquez, "Reality and theater don't mix, sir," as we watch a play that is watching its own melodrama.

Above all, *Bandido!* is *theatrical*, offering the audience a delightful mixture of songs and dances that narrate the story as in the *corrido*, as well as characters that can be hissed or cheered as they would have been in the nineteenth century. Melodramas were extremely popular in Mexican theaters and *carpas* of the nineteenth and early twentieth centuries in this country, a fact that histories of U.S. theater neglect to report. In other words, the genre belongs to all of us.

What makes this play truly Valdezian, however, is the fact that it is not simply a play presenting us with villains and heroes in conflict. The conflict is the melodrama itself—the distortion the Impresario wants to present for profit. "The public will only buy tickets to savour the evil in your soul," he tells Vásquez, a truism that cannot be denied. It is more fun to watch the villain than the hero in an old fashioned melodrama. In Valdez's play, however, the villain is the Impresario, precursor to a legion of Hollywood producers. If history cannot be changed in either *Zoot Suit* or *Bandido!,* the next play looks to the future as the only hope.

SEARCHING FOR REALITY: *I DON'T HAVE TO SHOW YOU NO STINKING BADGES!*

The Valdezian questioning of reality reaches its pinnacle in *I Don't Have to Show You No Stinking Badges!* In this play the playwright presents us with a world that resembles a hall of mirrors, sometimes catching this picture, other times another view. One never knows for certain if what we are observing is real or an illusion. Instead of *Bandido!*'s "Melodrama within a play," we are now given a much more complex vision as Valdez explores the different levels of reality between the world of the stage and the realm of television. Like *Zoot Suit,* this play was written for a fully-equipped theater. Furthermore, it requires a realistic set, designed to look like a television studio setting, including video monitors hanging above the set to help the audience understand its transformation into a "live studio audience."

Badges! focuses on a middle-aged Chicano couple who have made their living as "King and Queen of the Hollywood Extras," playing non-speaking roles as maids, gardeners and the like. The couple have been very successful, having put their daughter through medical school and their son into Harvard. They have, in effect, accomplished the American Dream, with a suburban home complete with swimming pool, family room and microwave.

The major conflict arises when Sonny, alienated from the Ivy League reality, comes home from Harvard unexpectedly and announces that he has dropped-out. To make matters worse, he decides he will become a Hollywood actor. His parents, his girlfriend and the audience know his fate will be the same as his parents', playing "on the hyphen" in bit parts as thieves, drug addicts and rapists. Or will he? Like *Zoot Suit, I Don't Have to Show You No Stinking Badges!* does not give a distinct ending, but rather, leaves the solution up to the audience members to decide.

While *Zoot Suit* takes us from a presentational style to a representational style as a play, *Bandido!* explores both styles transferring from the "real" Tiburcio Vásquez to the melodramatic version: Vásquez through the eyes of Luis Valdez and Vásquez through the eyes of Hollywood and dime novels. *Badges!,* on the other hand, takes us on a much more involved journey, by remodeling the theater to look like an actual television studio with all of the paraphernalia of the medium. To add to the effect, when the action begins it begins as an actual taping in progress.

As soon as the action begins in *Badges!,* we begin to think of it as a play, performed in the style of a sit-com, not a taping, but rather, a *play*, until the final scene. This is when it becomes difficult to tell if what we are seeing is a part of Buddy and Consuelo's "sit-com," or if what we are witnessing is Sonny's "sit-com," or his "play," existing only in his mind.

Just as we saw Tiburcio Vásquez attempting to write the true version of his story, we now see Sonny Villa recreating his reality. "Is it real, or is it Memorex?" he asks, underscoring the premise of the play itself. Are we, the audience, a "live studio audience?" Are they really taping this? Did Sonny really rob a fast food restaurant? Questions mount as we watch Sonny's transformation, his angst or his drama.

What is real to Sonny is the fact that he must find himself within this society, the son of parents whose very existence has depended on portraying the marginalized "other." When Connie tells her son "I'd rather play a maid than *be* a maid," she makes a point but cannot escape the fact that maids are all she ever will play. Sonny knows that he, too, will not be given greater opportunities unless he writes and directs his own material, to his standards and not some Hollywood advertising agency's.

From melodrama-within-a-play to video-within-a-play, the playwright takes us on theatrical explorations that offer no easy solutions. The earliest *actos* offered clearly defined action: "Join the union," "Boycott grapes," etc. But what to do about distorted history or negative portrayals of Chicanos in the media? Can any of us, as Sonny Villa proposes to do, write and produce films and videos that cut through the biases of generations? Only a select few will ever have that opportunity and Luis Valdez is one of them.

Ultimately, these three plays present us with different aspects of the playwright himself. Valdez is the Pachuco of Broadway, the social bandit of the media and the brilliant student who will change the face of Hollywood portrayals of his people. He laughs at himself as much as at historians and Hollywood in these plays, exploding myths by creating others, transforming the way in which Chicanos and Chicanas view themselves within the context of this society. Each of these plays is finally about a search for identity through the playwright's quest for what is reality—past, present and future. "How can we know who we are," he continually asks, "if we do not know who we were?"

In the twenty-six years since he founded El Teatro Campesino, Luis Valdez has made an odyssey few theater artists in the United States can claim. This course could not have been predicted, yet the journey was inevitable. Yes, Valdez has gone from the fields of Delano to the migrant labor of a theater artist, to the even more complex world of Broadway and Hollywood. But he has never forgotten his roots, has never abandoned the beauty of his languages, both *Inglés* and Spanish.

Nor has he forgotten about his people's troubles and triumphs.

Valdez taught us to laugh at ourselves as we worked to improve the conditions in our barrios and in our nation. In particular, he urges us to embrace life with all of the vigor we can muster in the midst of seemingly insurmountable obstacles. May these plays inspire others to follow in his footsteps.

ZOOT SUIT

R. G. Davis and Betty Diamond (essay date 1981)

SOURCE: "*Zoot Suit*: From the Barrio to Broadway," in *Ideologies & Literature*, Vol. III, No. 15, January-March 1981, pp. 124-33.

[*In the essay below, Davis and Diamond charge that* Zoot Suit *is "a bad play, politically and aesthetically."*]

Zoot Suit, by Luis Valdez, was the first Chicano play on Broadway. Valdez chose as his subject an actual event—the

Daniel Valdez as Henry Reyna, Rose Portillo as Delia Barrios, and Edward James Olmos as El Pachuco, in the film adaptation of Zoot Suit.

Sleepy Lagoon Murder case. On August 2, 1942. José Díaz was found dead in a dirt road near Los Angeles. There were no witnesses and no murder weapon, but twenty-four Chicanos were indicted for the murder of this one boy. The Hearst papers played it up as a "Mexican crimewave," and in the trial the Chicanos involved were referred to as members of a "gang." The prosecution charged that one of the members of the gang, Henry Leyvas, was beaten by members of a rival gang at the reservoir nicknamed "Sleepy Lagoon," and that Leyvas and his gang returned armed and organized for the purpose of revenge on the rival gang. Admitted as evidence was this statement from a report written by Capt. E. Duran Ayers, Chief of Foreign Relations Bureau of the Los Angeles County Sheriff's Department:

> The biological basis is the main basis to work from. Although a wild cat and a domestic cat are of the same family, they have certain biological characteristics so different that while one may be domesticated, the other would have to be caged to be kept in captivity; and there is practically as much difference between the races of man as so aptly recognized by Rudyard Kipling when he said when writing of the Oriental. 'East is East and West is West and never the twain shall meet' which

gives us an insight into the present problem because the Indian, from Alaska to Patagonia, is evidently Oriental in background—at least he shows many of the Oriental characteristics, especially so in his utter disregard for the value of life.[1]

Ayers traces the "utter disregard for the value of life" back to the Aztec sacrifices. Of the twenty-four Chicano boys indicted, seventeen were convicted. Three were found guilty of first degree murder; two of second degree. One, asleep in his car through the whole incident, was given five years to life. All were sent to San Quentin. Two boys who had enough money for their own lawyers demanded separate trials, and their cases were dismissed for insufficient evidence. On October 4, 1944, the District Court of Appeals, in a unanimous decision, reversed the conviction of all the defendants and the case was later dismissed due to lack of evidence.

Valdez' choice of subject was thus clearly a political one. *Zoot Suit,* a docu-drama with music, focuses on the trial of Henry Reyna—the fictionalized Henry Leyvas and leader of the pachuco gang—on Reyna's relationship to his family and friends, and on the relationship of the pachuco to the Mexican-American community. The play gets its name from the exaggerated clothing that was the badge of the pachuco—high-waisted, baggy, pegged pants; square-shouldered, oversized jacket; and long, dangling key chain.

Zoot Suit began as an experimental production of the Mark Taper Forum's "New Theatre for Now" series in April, 1978. The response to the original fourteen performances was electric enough to convince Gordon Davidson, the Forum's artistic director, to move it to the theatre's main space, rework it, and have it open the Forum's twelfth season.

In October, 1978, after a successful six-week run at the Forum, *Zoot Suit* moved to the 1200-seat Aquarius Theatre in downtown L. A. where it remained until last summer. It brought in an average of $90-100,000 a week. While still playing in L. A., a modified version opened on Broadway at the Winter Garden on March 25, 1979, and closed April 29, after 17 performances, at an $800,000 loss.

It is possible the play failed on Broadway, as Valdez contends, because of racist reviewers. Even though plays can endure despite negative reviews, New York reviewers are extremely influential figures and they almost universally panned the play. Focusing on the issue of racism, however, diverts us from a far more significant issue: that *Zoot Suit,* as presented on Broadway, was in fact a bad play, politically and aesthetically.

In case anyone has any doubts about this being "Brechtian" theatre—and we mention this because the work of Valdez is constantly described as being "somewhere between Brecht and Cantinflas"—Valdez opens the play with the disclaimer, mouthed by El Pachuco, the interlocutor and Spirit of the pachuco, that the theatre by nature is a place of pretense, a place of fantasy. The docu-drama is thus undercut before the newspapers which form much of the set (symbolizing the complicity of the Hearst papers in the racist hysteria of the period) are brought on stage. And at the end of the play, Henry Reyna, released from jail, finds himself in a dilemma: shall he marry Alice Bloomfield, the Jewish Communist working for the Defense Committee which grew up around the Sleepy Lagoon case, or his faithful Chicana, Della Barrios? (With such a name, Henry's ultimate choice is predestined.) The false love story between Alice and Henry, a love which never happened in the real case, is so badly written that the progressive Alice—and in turn her politics—is laughed at.

In the thirteen years of his work with El Teatro Campesino, Valdez was conscious of his social role, and in *Zoot Suit,* many social and political issues are touched upon: the complicity of the Hearst press, the racism of the judicial and penal systems, the nature of Chicano family relationships. But rather than politicizing the events by deepening the analysis, Valdez adds musical dance numbers to keep the spirits up, leaves the barrio behind, sentimentalizes all relationships in order to make his "message" palatable and saleable, and invests his Pachuco with Indian and Existential consciousness.

It is the pachuco, the 1940's street youth, who is the central focus of the play. In addition to the pachucos who make up Henry's gang, there is the larger than life character—El Pachuco—who speaks directly to the audience, wittily introduces and interrupts the play, criticizes the action and acts as Henry Reyna's inner voice. El Pachuco is the mythic spirit of "pachuquismo." Valdez claims this existential rebellious youth is the predecessor of the Mexican-American consciousness of the early '70's Chicanismo. This mythic interpretation of the real-life pachuco is one of the central political problems of the play.

To understand where this interpretation of the pachuco comes from, it is helpful to look briefly at the history of El Teatro Campesino. When Valdez started El Teatro Campesino in 1965, he was responding to immediate material needs: the U. F. W. needed workers to leave the fields and Anglos to send money for support. So Valdez and his campesinos created "actos," agit-prop pieces to do just that. After two years, he and his teatro left Delano and the U. F. W. because he wanted to devote more time to teatro; because he wanted to deal with broader issues—Viet Nam, racism, imperialism, the situation of the urban Chicano; and because he wanted to do teatro only about Chicanos, a position clearly untenable in the multi-ethnic U. F. W., yet in keeping with the increasingly nationalist thrust of the chicano movement at that time. Accordingly, the earliest works of Campesino are peopled by campesinos, patrones, coyotes, and esquiroles, but it is not long before the figure of the pachuco appears.

At first a minor character whose "bilingualism" consists of the ability to say both "En la madre la placa" and "Fuck you," and whose money is made by "liberating" purses, the pachuco becomes, in the person of the "vato loco," the contemporary street dude, a rebel-hero who, allied with a Black Panther, "liberates" the college that has refused him admission.

Once separated from the U. F. W., Valdez' plays come more and more to treat the question of ethnic identity and national consciousness. Actos begin to be accompanied by "mitos," religious rituals and plays with metaphysical themes. The shift in theme is not as dramatic as it first appears, however, for even in his U. F. W. days Valdez spoke of Chicano identity in terms which included Aztec/Mayan and Christian religious thought, mysticism, and mythification.

Accordingly, the pachuco is, in one play, the character who is most sympathetic to the revolutionary cries of "Viva Villa" which emanate from a bodiless head with a Villa moustache and a voracious appetite for cockroaches; but in another, he appears as the unseen central character, Quetzacoatl Gonzales, a cultural nationalist and community leader, whose name and activities suggest this vato is linked to the Azted savior-god, Quetzacoatl. The pachuco is rebel/hero/savior.

In 1974, by the way, because of such mitos, Valdez came under attack for "misleading the people" and ultimately left TENAZ, an association of Chicano theatres which he helped found, because he did not accept the increasing criticism of his essentially religious solutions to material problems.

It is in the 1976 touring version of *El Fin del Mundo* that the character of the vato, played, as in *Zoot Suit,* by Daniel Valdez, is given its closest examination. The story of Raymundo Mata, while a naturalistic story of union organizing in "Burlap, California," is also encased in an obvious symbolic framework. It is the story of the "end of the world" as we know it today, and of the literal "end"—the death—of Raymundo Mata, known in the barrio as "el Mundo." In the play, although Mundo is held up as a potential model, there is a serious study of the contradictions within him and of the complications of using such a figure as hero. Mundo, the local drug dealer, arrogant, rebellious in the face of authorities, violent, sexist, egocentric, is willing to do anything for money, even disrupt the U. F. W.'s organizing. Ultimately, he learns compassion, faith, and brotherhood, but at the very moment of his apotheosis, he is killed. It is clear that as a street dude, he is useless, even harmful, to his comunity. It is only after he has harnessed his rebelliousness that he becomes useful and admirable.

In *Zoot Suit,* however, the complexities arc lost and the historical facts, distorted, in the service of mythification. El Pachuco is presented as a model, but just what does he model? In an interview with Valdez in New York City on December 30, 1978, R. G. Davis pointed out that El Pachuco is like Superfly, and that Superfly, the pimp hustler of Black exploitation films, is different from the working class Blacks moving up and buying a house in the white ghetto of Lorraine Hansbury's *Raisin in the Sun.*

The regressing Superfly is a no-work character much like *Zoot Suit*'s Pachuco. Neither one shows or demonstrated work; in fact, they secret their labor. How did they get their two hundred dollars for those threads? Such a model is not useful.

Furthermore, as Yvonne Yarbro-Bejarano and Tomás Ybarra-Frausto point out in an unpublished paper entitled "Un Análisis Crítico de *Zoot Suit* de Luis Valdez", not all pachucos were "lumpen." Some worked and "eran como pachucos de fin de semana." Thus, they continue, Valdez' portrait of El Pachuco and the pachuco gang members futhers a simplistic stereotype. (Valdez must have been somewhat aware of this criticism because he tries to avert it by having Communist Alice comment to Henry: "You're an excellent mechanic. You fix all the guy's cars. Well, at least you're not one of the lumpen proletariat." Her analysis is, at best, weak.)

The pachuco is also presented as a defender of Chicano pride and culture, as a rebel. He is meant to be seen, as we are repeatedly told, as the "home front warrior." But to what end? The only value he articulates is that he "takes no shit from anyone." True, the pachuco possesses a rebelliousness, but it is totally without direction; it is a blind lashing out. Richard A. García, a Chicano historian at UC-Irvine, argues with Valdez' interpretation of the pachuco. In a *Los Angeles Times* article, he wrote that pachucos are regarded by some as:

> The first Mexican-Americans to have consciously celebrated their bicultural heritage. This view is dangerously romantic and historically false. Indeed, *pachucos*—far from being progressive—were among the most reactionary segments of the Mexican-American community. . . . The failure to distinguish clearly between criminal behavior and authentic political action underlies current attempts to turn *pachucos* into Chicano folk heroes.[2]

Valdez' elevation of the pachuco to the status of social bandit is like Norman Mailer's encomium of subway graffiti as a grand existential assertion of "I am." There is much energy and much anger in such scrawling, but when the graffiti cover up the subway map, you get lost.

Valdez realizes that he has distorted the character of the pachuco. In the Davis interview, Valdez states that the pachuco is a creation of 1978, not of 1942; that he represents a consciousness that is present today. He also says that the pachuco does not represent an ultimate solution, but is only a phase, a symbol that change is possible, that Chicanos can do something with their lives. In *Zoot Suit,* however, the fact that the pachuco must be transformed before he can do something useful is undercut. One of the pachucos in San Quentin turns to the audience and declaims naively that he has come to a grand realization: when he gets out of jail, the thing he can do is become a union organizer (audience laughter)—or a professional baseball player (more audience laughter). The "message" is played for a laugh. Similarly, that the pachuco can become useful only when he changes and ceases to be a pachuco is contradicted by the insistence upon the mythic, i.e., static, nature of El Pachuco.

Valdez wants the figurative character and the documented imitation of Henry Reyna to carry all the weight of his own Chicanismo and Mayan Aztec mysticism. Henry is a tough blowhard, but loves his family. El Pachuco is a tough blowheard, but is beaten up by Marines and Sailors and ends up naked, except for a loincloth, on stage in a pool of light. The loin cloth is supposed to represent, if you know Campesino's mitos, the Indian under the clothes of the city dude. The image is barely understood by those of us who know, giggled at by Chicanos in the Los Angeles audience, and viewed as melodramatic and confusing in New York City. Thus the confused politics produces confused art.

The other political problems in the play are also inseparable from the aesthetic problems. When a cultural nationalist goes to Broadway to reach a "wider audience," his message, which previously gained much of its force precisely from its cultural specificity, must be diluted to be intelligible to those not a part of that culture. Valdez, in other words, had to professionalize the "rasquachiness" that gave the works of El Teatro Campesino their unique force and vigor.

According to Valdez, the major changes in *Zoot Suit* were made before the trip to Broadway, between the original version as played on the Taper's experimental stage, and the version as performed on the main stage of the Forum. It is at this juncture that the barrio disappeared from the set and the Las Vegas shiny dance floor stage emerged; the love story between Alice Bloomfield and Henry Reyna came to dominate the historical political material; and the production staff, formerly members of Campesino, was changed. (Pat Birch of *Grease* fame, for example, became principal choreographer; Thomas A. Walsh, a set designer, replaced Bob Morales; and Abe Jacob, a sound designer, was added.)

But the play was a great success in L. A. even after the professionalization and homogenization began. There is another, very slippery, issue here. The success of *Zoot Suit* in L. A. was due, in part, to the California audience—Chicano and non-Chicano—which could read the geography and personal Chicano experiences into the play, however simple the characterizations, just as Campesino's original farmworker audience could read into the agit-prop "actos" in Delano.

In Valdez' earliest works, the people on stage and the people off stage were the same. They came from the same place and their concerns were specifically those of the Huelga. Even when those concerns broadened, the effect of the actors and plays was great because the Chicano performers' persona gave an additional dimension to the plays. They were speaking the language of the audience, legitimizing its culture. So when someone on stage said "Chale, ese," the audience roared at hearing its private language in a public place; there was the laughter of recognition, of complicity.

Similarly, in Los Angeles, when El Pachuco came on stage and preened in his Zoot Suit, the largely Chicano audience went wild. In New York, however, there was an embarrased silence, perhaps a chuckle or two. As Clive Barnes wrote, "Broadway is not the street where it lives." Though Barnes' comment may have been motivated by East Coast snobbery, it has a certain validity. Take away the Chicano audience and the Chicano actors, take away the Chicano locale, and all you have left is the play itself, a play which does not hold up to critical scrutiny.

Also, once on Broadway, the play had to be changed even further to reach not merely a wider "audience," but a wider "market." Culture, politics, become part of a product that must be packaged and sold. The Shubert Organization, owners of seventeen theatres on Broadway and the producers of *Zoot Suit,* was interested in developing the newly discovered Hispanic market, a market which Hollywood has also recently discovered (*Gang, Boulevard Nights, Up in Smoke*).

The show had to be changed to fit both the white New York theatre scene, and to attract the Puerto Rican, Cuban, Dominican audience. Accordingly, it was cut and reshaped to fit what Valdez and Davidson would "work" in New York. But it is a tricky problem to reach a wider audience rather than cater to it, as one moves from local community to state and on to the national stage. "Once the Broadway machinery takes hold, other things happen," said Davidson.

The first problem was that of language. The *Wiz, Ain't Misbehavin', Eubie, Timbuctoo* are "Black" shows, but they are big musicals that attract both Blacks and whites to the theatre. But if a play is in Spanish, only the Spanish speaking will attend. Political problem: in the actos, one way in which the Good Guys were distinguished from the Bad Guys was their embrace of Chicano Spanish. We know "Miss JIM-enez" is a villain because she denies her culture and anglicizes the pronunciation of her name. However, the more *Zoot Suit* belonged to the Spanish speaking, the less it could be understood by the English speaking. And the more Chicano slang, the less it could be understood by Puerto Ricans, Cubans, and Dominicans. Thus to reach a wider audience market, the language had to change. One political point down. Spanish slang out: sentimentalized English in.

A different set of problems resulted from the marketing scheme of placing *Zoot Suit* in the Winter Garden, a large theatre which demands musical extravaganza. The play was too small for the house. In addition, the 1943 Zoot Suit riots in which white sailors and marines attacked pachucos in L. A. seemed a bit distant in this docu-drama interrupted by dance and song. The historical importance of these events was buried by flashback and flashy gimmicry. (The "minority" play most recently at the Winter Garden was *Comin' Uptown*, an all Black musical version of *A Christmas Carol*. Its politics? Scrooge is a black tap dancing slum landlord.)

Finally, problems in the play also came from Valdez' politics of cultural nationalism. He did not want Anglos to walk out,—to get his "message" to them and to sell them tickets. However, because Valdez does still experience the world as divided between "us" and "them," his ability to understand those outside his culture is limited. We get recreations of others experiences, i.e., characters from bad movies. In *Zoot Suit,* we have the heroic white liberal lawyer whose startling message is that the system works, and the feisty Jewish Communist who of course falls in love with Henry, ever true to the cheap theatrics that two who are antagonists at the beginning of a show will become lovers by its end.

Also, Valdez' cultural nationalism relies heavily on the "spirituality" that is, in his view, the inheritance of the Chicanos from their Indian past. He believes in his "mission": *Zoot Suit,* he said to R. G. Davis when asked how the play was going in L. A., "is doing what it is supposed to do, what it has to do." He has faith. He, by himself, would change Establishment theatre. Campesino would take over, though just how the takeover was to be accomplished and what would happen once it had, was vague, rather like the unfocused rebelliousness of the pachuco hero Henry Reyna. Valdez has faith, rather than a proposal. So too *Zoot Suit.*

It is not Valdez' success one criticizes, for who in the good world of the liberal left dare proclaim poverty is moral? But what *Zoot Suit* offers us is ultimately the pachuco. While the performance of Eddie Olmos on Broadway lent an alluring stature to EIP achuco, the real life pachuco was a kid, a clothes model, an image of political reaction and temporary identity rebelliousness. To select as truth only those elements one wishes to see as true, to ignore the historical reality of the central characters of a drama based on political fact, is to create a model of the Chicano as useless as the Frito Bandito.

NOTES

[1]Quoted in Armando Morales, *Ando Sangrando (I Am Bleeding): A Study of Mexican American-Police Conflict* (La Puente. California: Perspectiva Publications, 1974), p. 13.

[2]Richard A. Garcia, "Do Zoot Suiters Deserve Hoorays?", *Los Angeles Times,* August 27, 1978, Part V, p. 6.

Yolanda Broyles-González (essay date 1994)

SOURCE: "The New Professionalism: *Zoot Suit* in the mainstream," in *El Teatro Campesino: Theater in the Chicano Movement*, University of Texas Press, 1994, pp. 177-205.

[*Broyles-González recounts the development of* Zoot Suit, *assessing the relative merits of the various rewritings and restagings of the play.*]

After the 1977 staging of *Rose of the Rancho* the Teatro Campesino resumed work on *Fin del mundo* in hopes of converting it into a "hit." In the words of ensemble member (and later producer) José Delgado: "We didn't travel in 1977 specifically because we wanted to do something that was going to be a hit. We thought it was going to be *Fin del mundo*" (Delgado and Esparza interview, 8/10/1983).

As the ensemble began working on *Fin del mundo,* a parallel activity was initiated by Luis Valdez, who perhaps had a different notion of where the next "hit" would come from. Valdez (through Delgado) offered his services to the prestigious Los Angeles Mark Taper Forum; the offer *excluded* the ensemble. José Delgado recalls: "I had written a letter to Gordon Davidson suggesting the idea of maybe Luis directing *The Shrunken Head of Pancho Villa* down in Los Angeles. It didn't have to be Teatro Campesino actors. It could be L.A. talent. All he would be interested in doing would be directing it. That was the proposal that was originally sent out" (Delgado and Esparza interview, 8/10/1983). Luis Valdez's offer to work independently of the Teatro Campesino collective was certainly also in keeping with the new plan to "focus on developing individuals."

Gordon Davidson did not respond to the proposal until months later when the idea of *Zoot Suit* emerged. Delgado described the steps leading up to the *Zoot Suit* idea:

> Meanwhile what happens is that the tenth anniversary of the Mark Taper Forum was taking place that April [1977]. That's when we first met with Gordon [Davidson]. We asked him if he got the letter. He says: "Yes, I got the letter, we have to talk." We came back to San Juan; Diane [Rodríguez] and I went back down to Los Angeles to do more research. We found the files, Carey McWilliams's files at UCLA, stayed there for about three or four days, gathered as much information as we could, brought it back, showed Luis the stuff. He got all excited about it and came up with the title for this piece that he was going to write called *Zoot Suit.* . . . Gordon was very excited and interested in the idea. From there it went into the hands of the Mark Taper Forum.

> (Delgado and Esparza interview, 8/10/1983)

The plan to launch a "hit" under the auspices of the Mark Taper Forum marked the beginning of a growing division of performance interests within the Teatro Campesino company. On the one hand, there was the mainstream project *Zoot Suit,* while most ensemble members continued to work as a collective within the Rasquachi Aesthetic. Luis Valdez was individually commissioned to write the play *Zoot Suit,* while the Teatro Campesino ensemble prepared for a second European tour of *Fin del mundo.* Delgado describes the ensemble's new divided work situation: "Meanwhile as Luis was directing *Zoot Suit* in L.A. what happened to us is we came back to San Juan Bautista and started to deal with the whole problem of trying to continue the work in San Juan without Luis. That was when he handed us, basically, the company as it existed at that time. This was in 1978" (Delgado and Esparza interview, 8/10/1983).

While Luis Valdez began the work of writing *Zoot Suit* (June-Dec. 1977) under the auspices of a Rockefeller Foundation Playwright-in-Residence grant, the Teatro Campesino ensemble worked on the third version of *Fin del mundo* for touring after the European tour. In the spring of 1978 the ensemble embarked on a Southwest tour of *Fin del mundo* and then a European tour of *Carpa de los Rasquachis*. Although the ensemble was in Europe during the first ten-day run of *Zoot Suit*—"Baby Zoot" as it is known in the company—they returned in time to attend *Zoot Suit*'s second opening at the Mark Taper Forum's main season on August 17, 1978. After that the ensemble resumed its U.S. tour and returned in time to catch the *Zoot Suit* opening at the Aquarius Theater in Hollywood on December 3, 1978. Most ensemble members participated in the *Fin del mundo* tour, but a few did participate in the *Zoot Suit* project. Roberta Delgado did the initial research for the dances of the period and then acted as assistant to the choreographer in subsequent productions. In the Broadway production she also played the role of Henry Reyna's sister Lupe. Diane Rodríguez and Socorro Valdez had minor acting roles. Phillip Esparza became associate producer.

Although the ensemble's participation in the final *Zoot Suit* production was minimal, much of the play was in fact the product of the ensemble's prior collective creativity. Much of the play had been generated through the collective improvisation process by ensemble members in San Juan Bautista—prior to the Mark Taper production. Hence a play that ultimately was credited to one individual was, in fact, in large part created by the Teatro Campesino ensemble. Ensemble member Olivia Chumacero (interview, 1/19/1983) describes it in this way: "Luis Valdez has drawn from our collective work even years later. The first time that I saw the play *Zoot Suit,* 'Baby Zoot' at the Mark Taper forum, I sat there and I could tell you who the people were who had improvised the blocking and the types of scenes that Luis used. I could sit there and tell you: 'Socorro thought of that' or 'So-and-so put that together' or 'This person improvised that particular blocking.'"

Zoot Suit drew much inspiration from the work of many people. Beyond the various elements that can be traced to particular individuals, *Zoot Suit* is very much a product of the general Teatro Campesino conglomerate performance style: the Rasquachi mixture of style and performance genres—vignettes of action, song, dance, dialogue—in rapid and smooth transition, which is in turn a hallmark of the Mexican popular performance tradition. What is new is their application in a context of high-tech mainstream theater.

The extent of *Zoot Suit*'s success exceeded everyone's wildest expectations. The initial Mark Taper Forum production with a ten-day run (April 1978) sold out almost immediately. What ensued was a series of successful restagings: first a main stage production at the Taper's 1978 season, then a production at the twelve hundred-seat Aquarius Theater in Hollywood, which opened on December 3, 1978, and ran for almost ten months. The Hollywood production broke box office records for a play originating on the West Cost; the New York production (1979) was the first Chicana/o play in several decades staged on Broadway. Although *Zoot Suit* closed on Broadway after only five weeks—due to poor turnout and an unfavorable critical response—it signaled the beginning of a process that has come to be known as "mainstreaming." The desire to launch a hit in the mainstream initiated a process that ultimately transformed the Teatro Campesino ensemble entirely. One symbolic and material indicator of that transformation is the fact that the Teatro Campesino ensemble members were all laid off, for the first time in that company's history, at about the time that *Zoot Suit* opened on Broadway (spring 1979).

Before discussing the nature of the impact of the mainstreaming process on the Teatro Campesino ensemble, it is perhaps illuminating first to examine the play *Zoot Suit* and the impact of the mainstreaming process on the various productions. An examination of relations of production in the mainstream and of the impact of those relations on artistic creation is of particular relevance in any discussion of mainstreaming. From its original scripting as "Baby Zoot," to the Mark Taper main stage, to the Aquarius, and then to Broadway and film, *Zoot Suit* underwent a number of transformations. These transformations—rewritings and restagings—can be viewed as a response to changing relations of production: those conditions of artistic practice include the numerous factors and persons that influence productions, be they collaborators such as producers, investors, designers, choreographers; be they questions of physical environment such as theater size and location; be they variables of social and artistic environment. In the course of its performance life, *Zoot Suit* went through five performance sites (including the film set) and at least nine rewritings, three of them for the film version alone. It is of course not possible, or perhaps even desirable, to understand what motivated each and every change throughout the various productions. What is more relevant is a general understanding of each production, of its significance and of the principal developments and changes as *Zoot Suit* moved from its initial staging at the Mark Taper Forum to ever-larger houses in Hollywood and Broadway.

Zoot Suit's five performance sites trace a progression representing various *degrees* of mainstreaming. These sites range from the less commercial Mark Taper Forum to the highly commercial Broadway stage (the Winter Garden Theater). Houses such as the Mark Taper Forum are somewhat less subject to economic pressures of the market, for they are heavily subsidized by government and foundation grants, as well as individual arts patrons, which augment box office income. As a nonprofit theater, the Mark Taper Forum is viewed as providing a community service. The Mark Taper Forum furthermore relies economically on a large subscription audience, which buys into productions with little or no knowledge of their merit or orientation. For-profit Broadway stages, on the other hand, subsist entirely without subsidy. As such they are more susceptible to marketing pressures and mount productions first and foremost with commercial considerations in mind. As will be seen, such differences in performance sites even within the mainstream of so-called professional theater involve a different set of work conditions and place a different set of expectations or demands on productions.

What follows is an analysis of the six major **Zoot Suit** scripts, including the film version. **Zoot Suit** went through considerable changes each time it moved to a bigger performance venue. In each of those scripts the Sleepy Lagoon Murder Case took on a different configuration. **Zoot Suit** dramatizes the 1942 Sleepy Lagoon Case in which twenty-two *pachuco* youths were unjustly convicted of criminal conspiracy in connection with the death of a Chicano youth named José Díaz. In a gripping series of chronological and spatial leaps, **Zoot Suit** links the events surrounding the case, the trial, the youths' two-year imprisonment while awaiting appeal, as well as scenes from the day-to-day lives of some of the *pachuco* youth. Although the facts of the case would suggest the use of a group protagonist, Valdez created an individual protagonist in the form of Henry Reyna and his companion, the archetypal "El Pachuco." In later versions the prominence of the El Pachuco character matches that of Henry Reyna, the leader of the 38th Street gang under mass indictment for murder.

It is fitting that **Zoot Suit** should be born and premiered in Los Angeles where the infamous Sleepy Lagoon Case was initiated and tried. What led up to the trial was the pervasive racism against the Chicana/o citizenry of Los Angeles, which found its wartime outlet in the form of U.S. Marine riots brutalizing *pachucos* and other Chicanas/os in the barrio. The main story line of the play **Zoot Suit** remained constant throughout all versions: it is a story of racism and classism against Chicanas/os in 1940s Los Angeles as manifest in the Anglo system of justice and law enforcement. The role of the press and the police in sustaining that system is highlighted. Luis Valdez (1978*b*) has described the climate of those times, which fostered the mass trial of twenty-two youths for one murder, as well as the subsequent U.S. Marine riots in the barrios: "Public resentment against the zoot suiters grew, compounded by a certain 'wartime hysteria.' In 1942, as the federal government mounted extensive campaigns to encourage patriotism and spur the World War II defense efforts, those who were out of step with majority customs or who jarred cultural norms and dress codes, were often abused" (Valdez 8/13/78).

From the onset, Luis Valdez chose to mitigate the hard historical reality of racial violence by adding a fictitious love story between a white woman (Alice Springfield—later changed to Bloomfield) and Chicano protagonist Henry Reyna. This contrived love plot—the love triangle between

Alice, Henry, and his girlfriend, Della—is a highly problematical element within the play, competing with and at times even supplanting the historical realities being portrayed. It is not surprising that the Alice/Henry/Della love story had trouble fitting into the play's trajectory and underwent more revision than any other element within **Zoot Suit**. The first draft is a case in point. In it, Alice has the first and last words in the play, including a highly patronizing, trivial, and lengthy closing monologue directed at an absent Henry Reyna. Alice—one of the play's white saviors—is the most prominent speaking subject. Her prominence contrasts markedly with the shadowlike presence of Della, Henry's Chicana girlfriend, who is present only as a mute body constantly snubbed by Henry. In the final scene she is even knocked to the ground by Henry—only to bounce back inexplicably in the end as Henry's girlfriend ("she embraces him from behind and he responds").

It is significant that the first draft of **Zoot Suit** was rejected by the Mark Taper Forum, on the grounds that it was too "realistic." It was through such institutional pressure that a second **Zoot Suit** was written.

The second draft (dated 2/28/78) was the first one actually performed. It had a very limited (ten-day) run in the New Theater for Now series of the Mark Taper Forum. In this second draft, the prominence of Alice Springfield was somewhat reduced, perhaps because of the introduction of the archetypal El Pachuco character, who opens the play by slashing an overblown facsimile of the newspaper front page with his switchblade and emerging from the slit. El Pachuco, the *bato loco*, or the *cholo* (streetwise dude) had been developed in earlier Teatro Campesino *actos* and plays such as **Bernabé** and **Fin del mundo**. In **Zoot Suit** Edward James Olmos was an unforgettable presence as El Pachuco. His sensual sliding gait, his staccato speech and honeyed speaking voice were among the characteristics that gave him a distinctive personality. The first spoken words in this version of the play are in *pachuco* Caló—the *pachuco* idiom. He speaks Caló throughout the play—a language shunned by the Mexican middle-class let alone Anglos. In spite of his charismatic presence, however, the archetypal El Pachuco character is not present in many scenes. It was only in later versions of the play that his presence became central or even dominant within the play.

A second important feature of the second draft is the introduction of the villainous Press, or Reporter, character, who illustrates and personifies the key position played by the Hearst newspapers in swaying public sentiment and motivating the rioting against Chicanas/os in general and *pachuco* youth in particular. In various scenes the Press is shown telling sensationalist stories. Interspersed are the alternative versions of such stories told by El Pachuco, by Della (who relates the events at Sleepy Lagoon), and others. Hence, the antagonism between the Chicana/o community and the white establishment press constitutes a strong and effective through-line in "Baby Zoot," as this first staged version came to be known. One of the play's most memorable and striking features—illustrating the confluence of oppressive forces—is the use of the Press character as Prosecutor during the Sleepy Legoon Trial.

From the very beginning, *Zoot Suit* made generous use of music, in characteristic Teatro Campesino fashion. Frequent dance sequences, performed for the most part in nightclub scenes, are key in establishing the Chicana/o musical ambience of the 1940s. The play highlights the music of Lalo Guerrero ("Chicas Patas Boogie," "Los Chucos," "Vamos a Bailar"), who was popular in the 1940s, but it also features the Big Band sound of Harry James ("Sleepy Lagoon"), Glenn Miller ("In the Mood"), the Dorseys, and Benny Goodman—all popular among Chicanas/os of that era. Choreographed sequences also feature the various dances popular in the 1940s and the 1950s: *pachuco* versions of the mambo, *danzón*, swing, jitterbug, boogie.

"Baby Zoot" is not without its weaknesses, however. Among them is the abundance of superfluous scenes, discussions, and characters, which detracts from the play's movement instead of enhancing it. Another problem is the final scene, which dangles without any conclusion (in the earlier *Zoot Suit* the outcome of the trial, the acquittal, is revealed to us from the start). "Baby Zoot" also suffers from the excessive use of violence. As if in a diplo matic effort to balance the instances of violence against Chicanas/os by whites, Valdez punctuates the entire play with numerous instances of violence among Mexicans. For example, the two brothers, Henry and Rudy Reyna, are stopped from fighting each other by their father. Rudy and Joey fight over Bertha. At the police interrogation, Valdez has a Chicano detective (Galindo) beat up Henry Reyna. Furthermore, Rudy Reyna is shown hitting (and presumably murdering) a man with a big stick at Sleepy Lagoon. (Did he murder José Díaz?) We are, in addition, told that Henry Reyna stabbed a prison guard in San Quentin. Violence among Chicanas/os is everywhere: Henry Reyna and his cousin Ramon Gilbert almost have a fist fight. Bertha and Lupe are stopped from fighting. Henry and Rafas go at each other with switchblades. Some audience members might well have wondered whether Mexicans are not in fact a bloodthirsty lot who belong behind bars.

In the use of violence, dramatic effects took precedence over historical accuracy. In the play, for example, the switchblade plays a prominent role and we quickly associate the switchblade with *pachuco* youth. Interestingly, it is historically documented that the 38th Street Gang (or *pachucos* in general) did not carry switchblades. It is a curious historical twist that the eight surviving defendants of the Sleepy Lagoon Case filed suit in 1979 against Luis Valdez and others involved in the production after seeing *Zoot Suit* at the Mark Taper Forum. They settled out of court and, ironically, were awarded financial participation in the proceeds from the play and the movie (Trombetta 1981).

In spite of such shortcomings, *Zoot Suit* represented a rare theatrical event featuring characters and situations with which Chicanos could identify. Audience response was so enthusiastic that the initial ten-day run at the Mark Taper Forum sold out almost immediately. The instant success of that production motivated the Mark Taper Forum to open its main season that same year with an eight-week run of *Zoot Suit* (August 17-October 1). That run also met with an overwhelming response, breaking single-day sales records for the theater. Almost $18,000 in tickets were sold on the first Sunday tickets were offered for sale. Among those waiting in line were Lupe Leyvas, the real-life sister of the play's protagonist, "Henry Reyna" (Henry Leyvas), who died of a heart attack in 1971. Lupe Leyvas commented: "The truth is finally being told. I was there when they arrested my brother. I went to the police station and they said: 'You want to see your brother?' He was handcuffed to a chair, his face was bleeding and he was unconscious. They ruined him, his pride, everything about him" (Miller 1978). The day tickets went on sale Lupe Leyvas, her brother Rudy, nieces, nephews and cousins purchased 121 tickets for $879.50. The play very clearly spoke to a need in the Chicana/o community to see realistic images of its own history in the entertainment world.

As *Zoot Suit* moved on to the Mark Taper main season it underwent further changes. Speaking in general terms, the play took on more abstract effects, moving away from the strong stage realism of the earlier version. To give but one example, many elements of the stage set that were originally depicted in realistic fashion—such as the Henry Reyna home complete with plants that were watered—eventually took on an abstract quality. Real furniture, for example, was converted into the symbolic medium of newspaper bundles. As the *Zoot Suit* production continued its run, the remaining elements of a realistic stage were eventually replaced by one-dimensional planes constructed of black mylar with silver trim. That effect gave the Broadway production in particular a highly surreal dimension, a quality reinforced by the large *pachuco* shadow backdrops introduced into the set. These changes may very well reflect one of the major tensions connected with the play: the challenge of merging historical documentation and dramatic effect.

The tension between theatrics and historical narrative remained visible throughout all *Zoot Suit* productions and was a source of considerable controversy in the establishment press as well as in the Chicana/o community. Dan Sullivan of the *Los Angeles Times*, for example, had problems with the play's "construct of fact and fantasy" as announced by El Pachuco in his opening monologue. Sullivan (1978) stated: "Fiction and fact blur here, and all we know is that this is how it *felt* in the barrio. That is no small thing to know, but we would like more hard documentation." Between the two productions at the Mark Taper Forum, Valdez described his move away from realism as a move away from "documentary" and toward "dramatic narrative" ("As I go back into a rewrite, I'll make it into more of a dramatic narrative, rather than a documentary" [Benitel 1978:34]).

The new streamlined Mark Taper script remained essentially the script used in subsequent productions (at the Aquarius Theater and on Broadway) although there were some significant alterations in the actual *staging* of the script. The new script that emerged (dated July 11, 1978) greatly improved the play's flow. Cumbersome scenes (such as the long and pointless posttrial socializing at the Sleepy Lagoon Defense Committee office) and various superfluous characters (such as Ramón Gilbert and the anarcho-syndicalist Villareal) were eliminated. Although the second Mark Taper script was greatly streamlined, some critics noted a loss of passion as well. *Variety* (8/11/1978) noted that "the show has been Mark Taper-ized to the point where it no longer has any emotion, impact or soul . . . dry as a conservative newspaper that takes no sides in controversies." Similarly, another reviewer noted: "The current version is more theatrical, better constructed and technically superior. But somewhere in the re-doing a measure of fire and passion was lost. This rendition is probably more commercially acceptable but the rough, unedited original had a bite and flavor that needed no gloss to hit with a deep emotional impact" (Goldsmith 1978). Longtime Teatro Campesino supporter Sylvie Drake (1978) on the other hand wrote about the "new improved version" in the *L.A.Times*: "For whatever price it is paying in gloss and slickness, *Zoot Suit* has gained enormous size and theatricality."

Unlike previous versions, the Mark Taper main season production (and subsequent versions) does not reveal the Chicana/o youths' acquittal until the next-to-the-last scene, thereby maintaining dramatic suspense throughout. Although this version eliminates the pithy El Pachuco/Press debate scene—a scene in which El Pachuco exposes a great deal of the society's racism as well as the opportunism of the Press—that omission is made up for by a brilliant change in design: all conceivable stage furniture and props are constructed with newspaper bundles. All chairs, the judges' bench, prison cots, and other furniture are conspicuously lugged onstage, by the Reporter, a newsboy, and other characters. When Henry is interrogated, he sits on a newspaper bundle. Henry's mother removes newspaper pages from the clothesline instead of clothes. Henry's prison cell is made of newspaper handcarts wheeled in around him. These effects are tied together by the giant facsimile (with sensationalist headlines) used as a backdrop in front of which all the play's action unfolds. The Press's overpowering physical presence—in the form of newspapers—makes a palpable statement concerning its powerful role (and its close collaboration with the authorities) in the Sleepy Lagoon Case, in inciting the Marine riots, and in the lives of Chicanas/os in general.

As in previous versions, the second Mark Taper production features the press reporter doubling as prosecutor, thus underscoring the unholy alliance between the judicial system and the media. The third pillar in this alliance is law enforcement officials. This alliance is further accentuated through the doubling of Police Sergeant Smith as Court Bailiff and the tripling of Police Lieutenant Edwards as Judge Charles and Prison Guard. The complicity of press and police within an oppressive social system is stunningly illustrated by Police Lieutenant Edwards's racist press release proclaiming that Mexicans have a genetic propensity for violence dating back to their "Aztec bloodlust." It hardly comes as a surprise when the *pachucos* are convicted of murder.

The second act unfolds episodes from the *pachuco* youths' two-year imprisonment as they await the appeal, the so-called zoot suit riots in Los Angeles, and the winning of the appeal, which is juxtaposed with the victory of World War II. New as well are references to World War II and connections established between the Sleepy Lagoon case and the greater context of the war. Woven into the final scene is another unconvincing exchange between white social activist Alice Springfield and Henry Reyna. Like some earlier versions, the fourth rewriting concludes with a victory celebration scene at the Reyna home in the barrio. Yet the victory does not signify a story with a happy end. In the midst of the merriment El Pachuco interjects that trouble will resume as soon as the celebration ends. In his omniscient way, El Pachuco foreshadows the segment in the final scene in which we witness continued police harassment and racism in the barrio.

Although the play does not diminish the importance of the Sleepy Lagoon victory it does situate it within the larger context of continued oppression. The personal or individual fate of Henry Reyna becomes secondary and recedes behind a broader social panorama. At the play's conclusion, three contradictory but possible ends to his life are mentioned; they are capsule statements representing the potential success or failure of *pachuco* lives.

During its main stage run at the Mark Taper Forum, ***Zoot Suit*** broke the Taper's box office record, taking in a total of $357,843.[1] Audience enthusiasm was matched by that of the critics. The City of Los Angeles, with the exception of the *Herald-Examiner* critic, seemed swept by ***Zoot Suit*** fever. Mayor Tom Bradley even proclaimed a ***Zoot Suit*** Week (November 13-20, 1978). Interestingly the most dissenting voices were the New York City critics who came west to view the play. Their negative response was a portent.

Zoot Suit*'s success at the Mark Taper Forum inspired the producers (Center Theater Group/Mark Taper Forum) to transfer the production from the 740-seat Mark Taper Forum to the 1,200-seat Aquarius Theater in Hollywood. Although the Aquarius is owned by the Mark Taper, the move meant a departure from a heavily subsidized tax-exempt theater (nonprofit) with a subscription audience of twenty-five thousand people to a sink-or-swim commercial stage dependent wholly upon the sale of tickets ranging in price from twelve to twenty dollars. What ensued made theater history. ***Zoot Suit*** played to capacity audiences for months, setting a new Los Angeles attendance record for a play originating on the West Coast. What was—and has remained—unique about ***Zoot Suit*** is that it succeeded in attracting barrio audiences, that is, persons who do not normally attend theatrical productions, in large numbers.

For the Chicana/o community the staging of *Zoot Suit* was of particular significance because it marked the first time that a Chicana/o play with a predominantly Chicana/o cast had gained entry into a white establishment theater. More significant, there was a deep sense of satisfaction among Chicana/o audiences at seeing images on stage that to some extent critically reflected upon the Chicana/o experience in this country. *Zoot Suit* at the Mark Taper Forum in Los Angeles clearly spoke to a need in the community and the community response was enthusiastic. It should not be overlooked, however, that a great deal of the momentum behind that response was also, in part, due to the existence of a loyal Teatro Campesino following as well as to the attraction of the play's central *pachuco* figure—as one of those highly distinctive and maligned Chicana/o street dudes of the 1940s and the 1950s who organized within neighborhood clubs. El Pachuco was rehabilitated during the Chicano movement and had been reconstituted as something of a positive antihero.

Part of the play's attraction can be ascribed to the fact that the very performance site (the Mark Taper Forum) stands where a Mexican barrio stood not long ago. What is more, the historical and human events portrayed hit at the heart of the Los Angeles Chicana/o *and* Anglo communities—a rare achievement for any regional theater. And it should not be overlooked that the Chicana/o community's pride and enthusiasm stemmed in part from the fact of *Zoot Suit*'s near-subversive presence in a space commonly reserved for white elite entertainment: the Los Angeles Music Center. The play clearly possessed a magnetism for both white and nonwhite audiences that has not been equaled by any other Chicana/o production in the mainstream.

It should not be overlooked that *Zoot Suit* also opened new vistas to many Chicana/o performers. Many of the Chicana/o cast members who participated in the show had never worked in what is known as "legitimate" theater. Most had never worked in so-called professional houses. The exposure and experience they gained from the *Zoot Suit* production—and the prominence of that production in Chicana/o community consciousness—motivated many young artists to pursue a career in mainstream theater institutions, formerly considered politically or racially off-limits. The theater establishment, on the other hand, was jolted into recognizing the presence of Chicanas/os and the need to view the Chicana/o community as part of its constituency.

While *Zoot Suit* was still playing to capacity audiences in Hollywood, negotiations began between the Los Angeles producers and the Shubert Organization in New York for a Broadway production. A growing consciousness of the Chicana/o and Latina/o *market*—if not of the people themselves—was a motivating force behind the Shubert Organization's $700,000 investment in a Broadway *Zoot Suit* staging with a weekly operating budget of about $90,000.

Barbara Darwell, head of the Shubert Organization's department of sales and marketing, commented at the time: "We've been interested for some time in finding a way to develop the Hispanic market in New York. But until now we haven't had a product to induce them to come to the theater" (Lawson 1978). Bernard Jacobs (*New Yorker* 2/19/79), co-owner of the Shubert Organization, which owns twenty-two theaters, including the Winter Garden, where *Zoot Suit* was staged, indicated that the search for a "Hispanic" play had been on since *The Wiz*—Broadway's first successful staging of an all-black musical—had finally tapped the "black market." The black market had been "developed" for the first time in 1975 through the nonmessage all-black musical *The Wiz*. It opened to scathing reviews but became an audience success nonetheless. Two other black shows were running on Broadway at the same time as *Zoot Suit*: *Eubie* and *Ain't Misbehavin'*. The Broadway production of *Zoot Suit* opened on March 25, 1979, in New York City's biggest theater, the Winter Garden, while *Zoot Suit* was still running at the Aquarius in Hollywood. All of the lead actors were transferred to New York from the Hollywood production, which continued its run with new leads (Marcos Rodríguez as El Pachuco; Enrique Castillo as Henry Reyna). *Zoot Suit* on Broadway, however, was not successful. It closed a mere five weeks after it had opened, at a loss of $825,000. *Zoot Suit* in fact was the most expensive nonmusical production in Broadway history.

Although it is impossible to state with any certainty why *Zoot Suit* did not repeat its West Coast success, we can speculate about what went wrong. One of the difficulties faced by the play with each change of theater was the successively larger theater space, culminating in the huge fifteen hundred-seat Winter Garden on Broadway. The Broadway aesthetic—generated partially in response to the monstrous theater size—usually calls for a great deal of slickness or ostentatiousness. One *Washington Post* critic has described Broadway in the following way: "The style is inherently exaggeration" (Coe 1979). The Broadway *Zoot Suit* underwent some considerable changes, virtually all of them in an effort to adapt visually and acoustically to the Broadway environment. Speaking in general terms, the Broadway staging enhanced its production values, as some critics noted: "Valdez is still making changes in the New York version, highlighting the universality, making the music hotter and the costumes flashier" (Herridge 1979). The *Washington Post* critic indicated:

"The major leads of the 28-member cast . . . state that the Winter Garden production is planned to be 'more extravagant and costlier.' That may be helpful, but one recalls other regional creations fatally started up for Broadway inspection" (Coe 1979). Valdez himself commented on the increased embellishment: "We are polishing it to a great sheen" (Herridge 1979). This "great sheen" was perhaps the single greatest difference between the Broadway production and prior ones: richer costumes, heightened lighting effects, a bigger backdrop, a more pronounced symbolism in general. And although the sheen—or effects needed to adequately "fill" the cavernous Winter Garden theater—was perhaps a necessary adaptation to the Broadway environment, the embellishment in production values may well have overshadowed the play's actual substance.

The sense that the Broadway staging suffered from overproduction is the general consensus among the cast.[2] This, in fact, might have contributed, for example, to critic Richard Eder's (1979) view that the piece was "overblown and undernourished." The *New Yorker* also refers to the "grotesquely overamplified sound" (Gill 1979). Yet in spite of the play's embellishments it did maintain its basic thrust, plot, dialogue, and pace.

Like Eder, some establishment critics produced scathing reviews of the production. Yet their response to the play was triggered not by its cosmetic problems of overproduction but by other factors. Various New York critics resented the very subject matter of *Zoot Suit* because of the guilt it evidently made them feel. That sense of discomfort manifested itself in critical backlash ("We are being sermonized at, and suddenly we feel that Roots III is being directed at our guilt regions again" (Bondy 1979). One critic put it quite succinctly: "White Americans will be uneasy" (*Daily News* 3/28/1979). And who wants to attend a Broadway play that will make one feel uneasy?

The dramatic portrayal of white powerholders abusing Chicanas/os provided the cue for defensive anger and retaliation in some critics. The *Daily News* critic is a case in point. He indicated that the play was "a slanted neo-rabble-rouser, abrading ethnic emotions, presented in unnecessary hyperbole, terminal exaggerations. . . . The plot is almost totally stereotypical anti-American establishment." The same critic then told us that if we put all of the play's factualness aside and viewed it all as fiction—that is, if we performed the impossible feat of "putting aside" what the play was saying, the play's actual substance—*then* it would be a great play. In his own words: "But let's take *Zoot Suit* out of its unfairness as factual drama and see it as pure fiction: on that level it is riveting drama told with tough, bitter, and ruthless wit, performed with consummate acting and direction by a cast of virtually unknown professionals" (*Daily News* 3/28/1979).

One of the most often heard stories in connection with *Zoot Suit* (especially from Luis Valdez) was that the critics killed it in New York. In reality critical opinion was divided, with more positive reviews than negative. The positive reviews should not be overlooked, even if some very pivotal reviews—such as those in the *New York Times* and *The New Yorker*—were hostile. Interestingly, all West Coast reviews of the New York production were as positive as ever. There was clearly an East/West divide. What then did New York critics dislike about *Zoot Suit?*

Although different elements of the play were criticized in the various reviews, there are recurring statements to the effect that the play employs too many clichés, too much rhetoric; that it is simplistic, overly sentimental, and

sententious; that the characters and political arguments are too black-and-white, too cardboard. "Agitprop" is commonly used as a put-down. Critic Walter Kerr in the *New York Times* (4/1/1979) formalistically dwelled exclusively on the play's language flaws, unable to look beyond the "stale phrasings," the "bloodless rhetoric": "He [Valdez] is utterly unable to resist a cliché, possibly even to recognize one." Michael Feingold in the *Village Voice* (4/2/1979) also focused on language: "In fact, he [Valdez] is not primarily a writer, and one of the things wrong with *Zoot Suit* is that the writing gets clumsier as it gets closer to seriousness, instead of the reverse. It bogs down in platitude, which may come partly from the fact that English is not Valdez's primary language, and in overstatement. . . . the clunky sententiousness of the language offends me."

In attempting to determine what displeased the critics about *Zoot Suit* I found the *tone* of their reviews as revealing as their arguments. The tone in the negative reviews is one of hostility and defensiveness mixed with an air of condescension that is perhaps reserved only for *upstarts*—indeed *minority* upstarts and from the West Coast. In understanding the critical response, two very significant realities must be kept in mind. One is the critics' sense of self-importance as gatekeepers and self-appointed spokespeople for the east Coast Great White Way aesthetic. They reserve the right to make pronouncements on theatrical quality, to declare what is good and what is below standard. That attitude, combined with *Zoot Suit*'s tremendous publicity campaign and the buildup preceding the opening, did not sit well with many critics. We can only imagine how some critics felt when *Zoot Suit* exploded onto the New York scene with a tremendous publicity campaign ($15,000 weekly) announcing the arrival of one of the greatest plays ever—indeed a "New American Play"—to Broadway's biggest theater. Various newspapers commented on what they called the "Ballyhoo about this work." *Drama-Logue* wrote: "The big news is the advertising campaign. . . . Clothing stores are doing zoot suit windows and there are plans to have 'trendsetters' photographed wearing zoot suits of fashionable discos. NBC is doing a half-hour special on the play, and major New York banks are being asked to enlist their support in underwriting theatre tickets for students" (Cole 1979). Another critic indicated: "But I am concerned over the 'hype' surrounding the play and its author. In recent articles in major newspapers and magazines, much praise and publicity have been lavished on Valdez and *Zoot Suit*" (Otten 1979). Another critic drew a direct connection between the media hype and his "disappointment": "*Zoot Suit* is a disappointment perhaps in part because of the hype that preceded its arrival here" (le Sourd 1979).

Zoot Suit arrived with such a splash that some critics must have felt eclipsed in their roles as guardians of public opinion. The response was predictable. Various reviews were written in that "I'll show them" attitude of condescension, unfairly condemning the play lock, stock, and barrel with insufficient supporting evidence. What follow are examples of this tendency:

There is inadequate material for making organized theater of *Zoot Suit*. A porridge of dates and facts, lectures and slogans, a romance, a trial, plus showy dance numbers and incidental drama—weakly written, directed, and played—it is, more than anything else, a "living newspaper" play out of the 30's.

(Gottfried 1979)

I regret to say that it does not seem to me to be major-league theatre.

(Hughes 1979)

It's filled with Good People and Bad People. The former are Chicanos and the latter are Anglos. . . . the writing is honest, but in the hands of such incompetence it turns out phoney—verbal posturings and inflations that couldn't be worse if Valdez' intentions were sheer hack.

(Kauffmann 1979)

Zoot Suit turns out to be mediocre or worse all down the line—book, acting, production.

(Currie 1979)

The playwright's treatment is leaden, superficial and as emotionally manipulative as the cheapest agit-prop of the period. . . . not really meant for the Great White Way.

(le Sourd 1978)

Zoot Suit at the Winter Garden makes for a better fashion show than it does a play. . . . This treatment of the prosecution of Los Angeles Chicanos for the Sleepy Lagoon Murder in 1942 grinds its ax so monotonously that it can cause an Excedrin headache by the second act.

(Sharp 1979)

A simplistic show . . . Poorly written and atrociously directed. . . . *Zoot Suit* is flat and boring child's play.

(Watt 1979)

Zoot Suit . . . is a great deal of loose material draped over a spindly form.

(Eder 1979)

One critic, insensitive to how offensive expletives can be when taken out of their spoken context, even availed himself of *pachuco* or Mexican derogatory terms in reviewing *Zoot Suit:* "The characters are caricatures . . . the action is spasmodic, inconsistent . . . the staging by Luis Valdez is as *pinche* as his dramaturgy. The acting is hard to evaluate, since the writing is mostly *pendejadas*" (Simon 1979).

Some critics found the "mixture of styles" characteristic of the Teatro Campesino style (and of the Mexican oral performance tradition) distasteful, although some praised *Zoot* despite this supposed shortcoming:

Playwright Luis Valdez has tried to shape this tale as a mixture of myth, documentation and fantasy, but he never gets past the Abc's in any category.

(Kalem 1979)

The kaleidoscopic barrage of styles with which Valdez dramatizes all this may not be a masterpiece of form, but a strong emotion and elegance is somehow shaped by this barrage, and we're seeing the image and energy of a culture that's never been seen on a Broadway stage before.

(Kroll 1979)

Zoot Suit . . . is overblown and undernourished. It is a bewildering mixture of styles—realism, stylization, agitprop and plain showbiz gaudiness—that clash and undermine one another.

(Eder 1979)

The political arguments of *Zoot Suit* are presented in stilted and paper-thin terms.

(Eder 1979)

One critic, however, did see value in Valdez's Rasquachi eclecticism, indicating that the "mishmash" did "compose a theatrically vivid unity" and "stirring outcry against racial bigotry":

On the face of it, it is crude stuff. Its method harks back to the Living Newspaper of the New Deal days. It also employs certain vaudeville and sideshow techniques. There are smatterings of Brecht's "alienation effects." All these—call it a mishmash if you will—nevertheless compose a theatrically vivid unity, mounting to a stirring outcry against racial bigotry and the cruel mass stupidity which such hysteria engenders.

(Clurman 1979)

An additional source of irritation for some New York critics was the fact that a good amount of the advertising campaign targeted the Puerto Rican and Latina/o population, thereby triggering a defensive attitude of ethnic polarization in some critics, perhaps a sense that this play was not really *for them*. The *New York Times*—in a tone of indignation with racist overtones—reported on how the producers were "reaching out to the Hispanic community": "They have two Spanish-speaking people taking ticket orders on the phone, and one Spanish-speaking person in the box office. They are also paying for ads in the newspaper *El Diario* and the magazine *Nuestro* and for commercials on radio station WADO and television channels 41 and 43. The 'Anglo' advertising, meanwhile, is minimal" (Corry 1979).

Months prior to the show's opening the *New York Times* quoted Mark Taper Forum coproducer, Ken Brecher, concerning all the special preparations in advance of the Broadway *Zoot Suit* production: "No one preparing for a Broadway show has spent so much time in the South Bronx as we have. . . . We have already decided that the ushers and box-office people will be bilingual. It's very important to make these people [Latinos] feel at home in the theater" (Lawson 1978). Brecher and Phil Esparza sent out forty thousand mailers, accompanied by a personal letter, to Puerto Rican families. They visited with community organizations and enlisted their help. (The community self-help organization CHARAS, for example, formed a "Barrio Brigade" of youths to distribute promotional materials.) Through the Theater Development Fund and group sales it was possible to see *Zoot Suit* for as little as $4.50.

Another major factor contributing to the negative critical response was the East Coast/West Coast competitive posture that exists in theatrical circles as well as other institutions. The aggressive condescension cultivated particularly by members of the East Coast theater establishment toward West Coast theater was evident even among *Zoot Suit*'s *own producers*: the East Coast Shubert Organization (represented by Bernard Jacobs) and the West Coast Mark Taper Forum (represented by Gordon Davidson). A considerable East/West divide was clearly visible in their very first face-to-face meeting in New York, which culminated in Jacobs's patronizing comment: "For the West Coast, Gordon does a great job" (*New Yorker* 2/19/1979). The effort to prove one's own coast superior to the other is also manifest in territorial statements such as that by Mark Taper Forum artistic director Gordon Davidson: "New York is no longer the generator of theater in America, but the receiver" (Thompson 1979). Such a statement, trumpeted in the *New York Times* ten days before *Zoot Suit* opened—along with all the other media hype—might well have negatively predisposed the very provincial and ethnocentric New York critics toward the West Coast's *Zoot Suit.*

It is striking that the same *New York Times* launched not simply *one* scathing review of *Zoot Suit* (by Richard Eder on opening night, March 26, 1979) but *two*. The second scorched-earth review (by Walter Kerr) was published one week after the first review (April 1, 1979). The *Los Angeles Times* was quick to respond: "For this West Coast observer, however, *Zoot Suit* has, ironically, never seemed in better shape. It fits neatly into the stage of Winter Garden, with an assurance and focus refined well beyond all three of the previous L.A. versions" (Drake 1979). In an opening night review in the *Washington Post*, critic R. L. Coe (1979)—as if responding to Gordon Davidson—stated: "The Los Angeles stage, though lively enough, remains strongly New York-oriented." With characteristic colonial hubris, another New York critic prefaced his review with a reference to California as a "cultural wilderness": "Out of a monied paradise but cultural wilderness steps a character of mythic proportions" (Lewis 1979). The inane privilege of belittling the *other* coast was no doubt a factor in some critics' reviews.

Some very positive reviews (*Wall Street Journal, Variety*, the *Washington Post, Daily News, Newsweek*, to name a few) were issued as well, however. Virginia Woodruff of Channel 10 (3/25/1979), for example, praised the production lavishly: "Once in a while a play fairly exploding

with passion and vitality, one simply yet flawlessly staged, comes along." *Newsweek* published a patronizingly glowing review: "Any drama-school freshman can see *Zoot Suit*'s flaws of structure and tone, but these should not obscure the guts, flash, class, sweetness, pride, pain, humor and sheer vitality of the enterprise" (Kroll 1979). Audiences who saw the play on Broadway responded with wild cheering and standing ovations uncharacteristic of audience reaction on the Great White Way. Many critics noted this fact. *Zoot* clearly touched a chord in New York audiences, although they did not come out in the numbers needed to float the play.

As one might expect, Chicana/o critical response to *Zoot Suit* was of an entirely different order. Chicanas/os were, first of all, much more concerned about and appreciative of the play's *content*, while the New York critics took issue with the play's *form*, often indicating that the form cheapened the political thrust. (We might well wonder to what extent the play's politics caused them to take exception with the form.) Chicana/o critics and the West Coast press showed themselves in possession of a different aesthetic and social sensibility as well as different tolerance levels when it came to viewing on stage the naked realities of racism. In reference to the New York critics Luis Valdez indicated that they found fault with *Zoot Suit* because they felt it was still rebelling. That no doubt was a factor in the critics' response.

Chicana/o critical opinion, although heavily focused on content, was to some extent divided. Most Chicana/o critics shared the enthusiastic audience response of the Los Angeles and New York audiences. Critics such as Antonio Burciaga and Jorge Huerta praised the play, speaking to its historical significance—as a mainstream performance—its merits as a theatrical spectacle, and its social relevance as a document exposing an important chapter in Chicana/o history. Jorge Huerta (1982:183) discusses Valdez and *Zoot* in nothing but superlatives ("Valdez' world encompasses more than most of his critics can comprehend"). In the process, however, he fails to examine what might be considered the shortcomings of *Zoot Suit* or contradictions in the mainstreaming process. His discussion ends with an overly optimistic flourish of predictions that have failed to come true: "The Teatro Campesino would continue to perform in this country and abroad; *Zoot Suit* would pack the houses in every major center of the Mechicano population" (p. 183). In fact, the Teatro Campesino ensemble never again performed in this country or abroad. Nor did *Zoot Suit* "pack the houses in every major center of the Mechicano population."

Critics Yvonne Yarbro-Bejarano and Tomás Ybarra-Frausto, on the other hand, focus heavily on what they consider the play's numerous problems, while not commenting on what one might consider the play's virtues. Ybarra-Frausto and Yarbro-Bejarano (1980) deliver an interesting ideological analysis of *Zoot Suit,* focusing above all on the *pachuco* character. Their focus on some aspects of the play's ideological thrust, however, happens almost entirely at the level of script. The authors disregard entirely the play's theatricality, the function (ideological and other) of—for example—the music and dance sequences, other significant *performance* elements, and audience response. A disregard for the economic realities governing *all* Broadway productions, furthermore, leads them to state, contradictorily, that they do *not* at all criticize Luis Valdez for going to Broadway, yet they decry the commercialization of the piece (i.e., the heavy advertising campaign, the high price of tickets, etc.). Yet Broadway, in fact, is the quintessential commercialization of theater and going to Broadway necessarily involves working within a specific set of economic terms. The critique ends with a summons to Chicanas/os in theater: to follow the "alternative of taking nourishment from our popular roots. That way we will reclaim the mass communications media, radio, television, Hollywood and Broadway, not as individual artists, but as a popular theatrical movement" ("Ofrecemos esta crítica de la obra para continuar la discusión, para que se plantee la alternativa de volver a nutrirse de la raíz popular en contra de la imitación de Valdez. Y así vamos a recuperar los medios masivos de comunicación, la radio, la televisión, Hollywood y hasta Broadway, pero no como artistas individuales, sino como un movimiento teatral popular") (Yarbro-Bejarano and Ybarra-Frausto 1980:56).

Yarbro-Bejarano and Ybarra-Frausto put their finger on one of the chief contradictions of the mainstreaming project: the conflict between "popular roots" and "popular theatrical movement" (which are based in collectivity), and the dimension of individual ambition and success. In spite of *Zoot Suit*'s contradictions, however, there can be no doubt that as a theatrical product its merits by far surpassed those of average Broadway fare. As a play depicting a highly racist era of American history it did present an alternative reality in a theater world that ordinarily specializes in superficial entertainment glorifying the status quo.

The question remains: What are the problems Chicana/o theater faces when it becomes a Janus-faced undertaking, one face looking to the Great White Way and the other to Chicano reality and the needs of Chicana/o communities? Public response to a play will vary significantly, depending on what any given public expects from theater or Chicana/o theater. Many New York critics were overwhelmed by the historical and political reality presented in *Zoot Suit,* for example, while Chicana/o critics Yarbro-Bejarano and Ybarra-Frausto faulted what they considered the "diluted historicism" of the piece.

Most Los Angeles and New York critics—along with various Chicana/o critics—found El Pachuco (Edward James Olmos) extraordinarily impressive while Yarbro-Bejarano and Ybarra-Frausto did not comment on Olmos's extraordinary performance, or El Pachuco's function as a theatrical device. They viewed him wholly as a mythical character who they felt stood in contrast to—and eclipsed—the play's historical dimensions. Although I share their uneasiness concerning the tension between "fact and fantasy,"

between the mythical and the historical, in *Zoot Suit* I do not view the mythical El Pachuco character as competing with or supplanting the historical figure Henry Reyna. As a theatrical device, the mythical El Pachuco has a twofold function. On one level, he is Henry Reyna's doppelgänger (*cuate*), his alter ego, or super-ego, always at Reyna's side and visible and audible only to Reyna. Dramaturgically speaking, the El Pachuco/Henry relationship allows us to listen in on Henry's dialogue with himself, his *internal* struggle, without having to turn it into dreary monologues directed at the audience.

Throughout the play, El Pachuco and Reyna are seemingly at odds. They represent the dialectical unity of opposites, united in contradiction, providing the two sides of every story, two opinions on every discussion, two possible reactions to every action. At times El Pachuco utters what Henry is thinking and cannot express without editorializing; at other times he serves as the voice of historical experience repeatedly warning Henry not to expect justice in a society without justice. He goads Henry to do things he might not want to do, to think things he had not thought. He serves as a *mirror* of Henry. El Pachuco's colors—red and black—as well as his frequent associations with mirrors and smoke tie him symbolically to the Aztec deity Tezcatlipoca. He embodies the voice of wisdom, of conscience, of the school of hard knocks. The connection between Chicano and Indio is thus established. Henry Reyna and El Pachuco are not necessarily *separate* entities but a carefully construed duality within one Chicana/o youth. To view El Pachuco only as a separate mythical character and as an "evasión de lo histórico concreto" (evasion of the historically concrete) is to disregard the theatrical complementarity of El Pachuco and Henry Reyna.

El Pachuco's second important function as a theatrical device rests with his role as omniscient master of ceremonies facilitating the play's presentational mode and its many transitions. He allows us to move smoothly in and out of the past. With a snap of his fingers, a wave of his arm, or a turn of his body El Pachuco changes scenes, flips us into a courtroom, or into the Reyna home, beckons dancers onto the stage, flirts or kids with the audience—breaks through the play's dramatic climaxes, turns tragic moments into humorous ones, or injects cynicism into lighthearted moments. As a commentator *outside* the action he serves as a perpetual distancing device (what Brecht calls a *Verfremdungseffekt*), which forces us to *reflect* on the theatricality of what we are seeing, instead of allowing us to be unthinkingly *absorbed* by the action. By extension, El Pachuco's "mythical" position outside the play's particulars allows the play to give expression to many positive human dimensions of *pachuco* life: in his extravagance El Pachuco symbolizes imagination, fantasy, aspiration, defiance; he is downtrodden yet courageous and independent, a proud symbol of the barrio.

The use of *pachucos* in *Zoot Suit* opened the door to another lively controversy. Some Chicana/o critics felt that the play glorified *pachucos* and that historically speaking *pachucos* were nothing to be proud of. Richard García, a Chicano historian, published an essay in which he sought to prove that *pachucos* were a reactionary element in the Chicano community and that their cultural pride was expressed mainly through criminal violence and extravagant dress. For García *pachucos* were essentially hoodlums. The *Los Angeles Times* (García 1978) published his view: "Most pachucos ended up dead, in prison, or alcoholic. The current celebration of an underclass of dropouts and failures is damaging . . . The pachucos were lumpen—groups of chronically unemployed and often delinquent youths." García made the same mistake the Hearst press did in the 1940s: he interpreted what was a hip fashion among youth—*el tacuche* (zoot suit)—as something synonymous with gangsterism. Indeed the play *Zoot Suit* endeavors to illustrate that the attire was worn by noncriminals as well. The term *"pachuco"* came to be a generic term for "hip youth" dressed in a distinctive fashion. *Some* were organized in neighborhood clubs; others not. Some were delinquents; most were not.

El Pachuco and the play *Zoot Suit* must also be understood within the historical context of the 1970s: as part of the Chicano movement's revalorization of traditionally maligned sectors within the barrio or within Chicana/o working-class reality. Such a revalorization of the *pachuca/o*—a conscious crediting of what can be considered his or her admirable dimensions—must be seen in the general context of cultural nationalism and the Chicano Movement's intense debate concerning Chicana/o identity. That debate includes artists' responses to Octavio Paz's denigrating interpretation of *pachuquismo* in *The Labyrinth of Solitude*, a text widely read by Chicana/o intellectuals in the 1960s and the 1970s. Contrary to Paz, Valdez describes El Pachuco's positive potential: "The need to stand up and just rebel, to say no, is to provide a new possibility: it's to bring a new consciousness into being" (Orona-Córdova 1983:110). The revalorization of the *pachuco* was one of a number of redefinitions that, among other things, gave us the word *Chicana/o* in its current usage. Such redefinitions of "outsider" or "underdog" figures occurred in Chicana/o art, in Chicana/o literature, in Chicana/o theater. Indeed, much of the moving force for the new Chicana/o literature of the 1960s came from former *pachucos*: José Montoya, Raúl Salinas, Ricardo Sánchez. Being a *pachuco* during one's youth was not incompatible with developing into a responsible adult. United Farm Workers founder and president, César Chávez, was a *pachuco*. This is not to say that *pachucos* were all great kids. Nor does Valdez portray them as innocent angels. But they were not necessarily criminals either. What should not be overlooked, however, is that the heavy focus on *pachucos* in *Zoot Suit* gives the play an overbearingly masculine bent.

Yarbro-Bejarano and Ybarra-Frausto (1980) concur with García's and Ron Davis's highly negative view of *pachucos* and also deplore the fact that Valdez does not depict the *pachuco* as a productive member of the labor force.

The expectation that Valdez portray his Sleepy Lagoon characters as members of the work force is perhaps an unrealistic expectation for a play focusing primarily on these youths' *incarceration*. Valdez, however, does emphasize Henry Reyna's (and his brother's) enlistment in the armed forces—which, to this day, unfortunately represents one of the few avenues open to young Chicanos seeking "dignified" work or job training.

Zoot Suit is most problematic with regard to its gender politics and construction of the historical past. As has been shown, Valdez's gender politics and his construction of history are intertwined. Both are steeped in a dominant ideology that has traditionally assigned Chicanas/os a passive role in history. In the opening monologue of *Zoot Suit*, El Pachuco refers to the play as "a construct of fact and fantasy." That of course can be understood in any number of ways. Does it mean that all the historical facts presented are true and simply presented in an imaginative way? Or does the intermingling of fact and fantasy signify that important facts are modified or even falsified? To what end? What constitutes historical "fact" anyway? Recent theory of history teaches us that *any* writing of supposed "facts" involves a good dose of fantasy, in their selection, organization, and the rhetorical strategies by which they are conveyed. The choices Valdez made in the selection, organization, and delivery of historical fact in *Zoot Suit* are very much in need of examination.

It is where historical facts are imperceptibly altered or tailored to suit fantasy or marketing needs that the drama is at its weakest and the play's ideological thrust most questionable. The two major Anglo figures in *Zoot Suit* signal a particular orientation in the selection and organization of historical facts, that is, in the construction of Chicana/o history. Alice Bloomfield (Springfield in an earlier draft) and George Shearer (a lawyer) function as "white savior" figures such as are present in virtually all Luis Valdez productions since he decided to mainstream. In *Zoot Suit* the white saviors figure most prominently: they organize the Sleepy Lagoon Defense Committee; they visit the beleaguered "boys" in prison; they instruct the young Chicanos on how to fight the system; they profess faith in the system; they occasionally patronize the young Chicanos; and they win the case for them on appeal. Chicanas/os are not shown in a position of self-help, nor as agents in their own destiny. In *Zoot Suit*, the Chicana/o community as a whole is strikingly absent in the defense of the *pachuco* youths.

It is interesting that this was not a feature of *Zoot Suit* initially. In the first version, a Chicano movie star (the character named Ramón Gilbert) is prominent in raising support and funds for the legal appeal. This figure disappears in subsequent versions where there are, however, references to Chicanas/os helping out. By the time *Zoot Suit* appeared on Broadway and in the film version, Alice Bloomfield and George Shearer were bigger than life and references to barrio leaders and activists in defense of the *pachucos* had all but vanished.

The prominence of the white saviors constitutes a very particular kind of distortion of historical fact, or a reshaping of historical fact along specific lines. It corresponds to the dominant ideology's traditional view of Chicanas/os as passive subjects who simply let history happen. The truth of the Sleepy Lagoon case is not the story portrayed in the film *Zoot Suit*. In *fact* the Los Angeles Chicana/o community was not a peripheral element in the Sleepy Lagoon case, but the moving central force. For one thing, the role occupied by Alice Bloomfield in the movie was—in historical fact—occupied by Chicanas, namely Josefina Fierro and Luisa Moreno. Chicano historian and activist Bert N. Corona—who was also a member of the Sleepy Lagoon Defense Committee—speaks to the vital role played by these two women:

> In 1942, Josefina Fierro, as national secretary of the Congreso Nacional de los Pueblos de Habla Española, carried out two very significant actions. One was the formation of the Sleepy Lagoon Defense Committee (contrary to the distorted version in Luis Valdez's play *Zoot Suit*) which conducted the public defense of the twenty-two Mexicans who were tried for the death of one. Josefina traveled all over the nation, assisted by Luisa Moreno, to develop the broad national campaign against the racist and divisive indictments and yellow journalistic press descriptions of the Hearst Press. . . . It is to be deplored that Luis Valdez could find insufficient drama in the true facts about the Defense of the Sleepy Lagoon and *Zoot Suit* victims, that he had to rely upon Hollywood gimmicks of a fictitious melodrama between two persons [Alice Bloomfield and Henry Reyna] that never took place in order to tell his story.

(1983:16)

Although a real "Alice Bloomfield" (named Alice Greenfield McGrath) does exist, she did not occupy the savior role attributed to her in *Zoot Suit*. In reality she was a paid employee of the Sleepy Lagoon Defense Committee and was not hired until months after the very long first trial ended. Needless to say, the romantic involvement between Alice and Henry, so prominent in *Zoot Suit,* never existed. Historical fact notwithstanding, Valdez even places Alice at the play's center: "In Alice Greenfield McGrath [named Alice Bloomfield in the play and movie] we finally discovered the mainline of the play. It was her relationship to the boys" (Valdez 1978*a*).

The role of the Los Angeles Mexican American community in the defense of the Sleepy Lagoon defendants is correspondingly obscured in the film. Yet the community's role was central. One Sleepy Lagoon case attorney, George E. Shibley (1979)—after whom the *Zoot Suit* character of attorney George Shearer is patterned—in 1979 publicly stated that "*Zoot Suit* does perpetuate some seriously damaging distortions of the realities of the Sleepy Lagoon murder case." He elaborated on these serious and damaging distortions: "Chief among these distortions are the myths that the Mexican-Americans themselves had little or no part in the organization of the Sleepy Lagoon Defense Committee; that no ethnic group other than Jews came to

the aid of the 22 defendants; that the case was won almost singlehandedly by the unmarried heroine, Alice, whose Jewish identity impelled her to set up a defense committee, hire a lawyer, and then fall in love with the chief defendant, Henry Reyna." Shibley goes on to point out that Chicanas/os were "active and indispensable" in organizing the defense and that the appeal was in reality fought by a team of at least five lawyers (not one), including a lawyer retained by the Mexican Consulate.

Luis Valdez's decision to create white savior characters that eclipse the role of the Chicana/o community has considerable ideological implications. Most significant, it implies that the Chicana/o community is unwilling or unable to be an agent in history, to act on and in its own behalf. It paints a picture of Chicana/o helplessness. For help, the impotent Mexican community must turn to whites. Such highlighting of white saviors is not accidental, and this choice of characters certainly raises another question: To what extent does this distortion constitute a Valdezian attempt to ingratiate himself with the powers that be? Is it a means of making the *Zoot Suit* project more "palatable" to whites, be they producers, theater administrators, critics, or audiences? Is this the kind of concession the mainstream requires? Is it anticipatorily accommodationist on the part of Valdez? One New York critic saw in Valdez's use of white characters in dominant roles a form of "calculation." In reference to the white characters of George and Alice that critic points out that "the former [is] implicitly, the latter explicitly, Jewish . . . on the assumption, I daresay, that most of our theatergoers are Jewish and that buttering them up is good for business" (Simon 1979).

The white savior dimension of *Zoot Suit and* its male-centeredness certainly served to *weaken* the film and had a direct impact on its exploitative gender politics. As it is, the Chicana characters are largely inconsequential or shallow because they stand in Alice Bloomfield's shadow. Beyond that, Chicanas fall into the standard Teatro Campesino categories of (a) being auxiliary to males and (b) consisting of one of two types: the virgin or the whore, the long-suffering mother or the "cheap broad." Della Barrios is Henry Reyna's virginal girlfriend who puts up with everything. Bertha is her counterpoint: the woman who sleeps around. This shallow one-dimensional representation of Chicana women is of course intensified by denying recognition to Chicana historical figures such as Josefina Fierro or Luisa Moreno, and by transferring that recognition to a larger-than-life fictional white female savior. Such blatant erasure of Chicanas as historical agents is not unique to *Zoot Suit,* however. It parallels the widespread erasure of Chicanas from Chicano historiography and other forms of discourse.

The weakness of Chicana roles in *Zoot Suit* went virtually unperceived by critics. Valdez's gender politics was either altogether ignored or referred to only in passing. Chicano theater historian Jorge Huerta fleetingly indicated: "Valdez's treatment of the women has also been the concern of all the women I have talked to who saw the production" (1978). Unfortunately, Huerta did not elaborate on what women said or on the nature of Valdez's treatment of women. Teatro Campesino ensemble member Roberta Delgado—who carried out the initial research into *pachuco* dance styles of the 1940s and choreographed the dance sequences for the early *Zoot Suit*—similarly indicated that the *women's* roles were consistently questioned by Chicanas who attended the postperformance colloquia at the Mark Taper Forum: "When we were doing *Zoot Suit* we would have these symposia when we were at the Taper. They were discussions. You know, Chicana women would always ask about the women's roles" (interview, 7/21/1983). In spite of this feedback, the hegemonic and exploitative portrayal of Chicanas in *Zoot Suit*—involving active historical distortion—remained unaltered throughout all productions.

Zoot Suit's critics, however, did not focus on the ideological and political significance of a play in which Chicanas/os are portrayed as a passive entity and as people whose only hope for social change rests with the intervention of white saviors. Questions such as the portrayal of the Chicana/o community or of Chicana women were also certainly of no concern to the New York critics who panned *Zoot Suit.*

Zoot Suit closed on Broadway due to various factors largely unrelated to its good or bad points. It is of course impossible to single out only one or two reasons why *Zoot Suit* did not enjoy success in New York. Various factors have been discussed here, such as many critics' defensive reactions vis-à-vis a highly touted West Coast play, a play that furthermore exposed a chapter of racism in this country *and* that was created and performed by newcomers to the Great White Way. But the critics are not omnipotent and many plays are successful in spite of negative critical opinion. Although we can surmise that the critics kept a portion of the traditional white audience from seeing the play, Puerto Rican and black audiences do not read critics like Clive Barnes, Martin Gottfried, or Richard Eder. These are the "nontraditional" audiences *Zoot Suit* producers were hoping to attract or develop. Yet Latinas/os did not attend the production in sufficient numbers to keep the play going. The unstated but existent boundaries of segregation in this country have kept Broadway almost exclusively white, notwithstanding the handful of successful black productions. Broadway is not a space frequented by Latinos and they were understandably reticent, even after several thousand discount ticket coupons were distributed. Furthermore, *Zoot Suit* did not hold the same kind of attraction for them as it did for Chicanas/os on the West Coast.

Bernard Jacobs, *Zoot Suit* coproducer and president of the Shubert Organization, speculated as to why *Zoot Suit* did not enjoy success: "What went wrong? I would criticize the marketing, not the play. The Hispanic community didn't support it sufficiently. The community's leaders were wonderfully supportive, but the troops weren't ready yet. The first attempt is inevitably a failure. There will be a

successful Hispanic play some day. It took about 10 black plays before we got a successful one" (Lawson 1979). Of course the expectation that a Chicana/o play should appeal mainly to Puerto Ricans and not especially to white theatergoers is a curious assumption.

NOTES

[1]The previous high total of $337,512 was set by *For Colored Girls Who Have Considered Suicide When the Rainbow is Enuf* ("*Zoot Suit* Breaks Mark Taper Mark" 1978).

[2]This has repeatedly been expressed to me in conversations with cast members.

BIBLIOGRAPHY

Unpublished Sources

ORAL HISTORIES

Chumacero, Olivia. 1/19/1983. Interview. San Juan Bautista.

Delgado, José, and Phillip Esparza. 8/10/1983. Interview. San Juan Bautista.

Delgado, Roberta. 7/21/1983. Interview. San Juan Bautista and Gilroy.

OTHER UNPUBLISHED SOURCES

Woodruff, Virginia. 1979. Channel 10 Broadcast. 3/25. TS. Personal archive, Olivia Chumacero.

Published Sources

Benitel, Tomás. 1978. "Facing the Issues beyond *Zoot Suit.*" *Neworld* 4:34-38.

Bondy, Filip. 1979. "*Zoot Suit* Collapses under Its Weighty Subject Matter." *Patterson News* (3/27).

Clurman, Harold. 1979. "Theater." *The Nation* (4/21).

Coe, Richard. 1979. "City Cowboys and the West Coast Stage." *Washington Post* (3/25).

Cole, Doug. 1979. "New York, New York." *Drama Logue* (3/2-8).

Corona, Bert. 1983. "Chicano Scholars and Public Issues in the United States in the Eighties." In *History, Culture and Society: Chicano Studies*, edited by Mario García et al., pp. 11-18. Ypsilanti, Mich.: Bilingual Review Press.

Corry, John. 1979. "Broadway." *New York Times* (3/30).

Currie, Glenn. 1979. "*Zoot Suit*: Damp Cracker on Broadway." *News World* (3/29).

Drake, Sylvie. 1978. "*Zoot Suit* at the Taper." *Los Angeles Times* (8/18), part IV.

————. 1979. "Broadway Cool to *Zoot Suit.*" *Los Angeles Times* (3/27), part IV, pp. 1-2.

————. 1979. "*Zoot Suit* Keeps Chin Up Despite Negative Reviews." *Los Angeles Times* (4/8), Calendar, p. 62.

Eder, Richard. 1979. "Theater: *Zoot Suit*, Chicano Music-Drama." The *New York Times* (3/26), part C, p. 13.

Feingold, Michael. 1979. "Truth in Melodrama." The *Village Voice* (4/2), p. 89.

García, Richard. 1978. "Do Zoot Suiters Deserve Hoorays?" *Los Angeles Times* (8/27), part V.

Gill, Brendan. 1979. "Borrowings." *The New Yorker* (4/2), p. 94.

Goldsmith, Len. 1978. "*Zoot Suit*: A Piece of Los Angeles History." *Daily Signal/Daily Southeast News* (8/18).

Gottfried, Martin. 1979. "Zoot Suit." *Cue New York* (4/27). [Also in *Saturday Review* (5/26/1979).]

Herridge, Frances. 1979. "Valdez Hopes His 'Zoot' Suits the B'way Audience." *New York Post* (3/23).

Huerta, Jorge. 1978. "Tenaz Talks Teatro." *El Tecolote*, supplement, 1, no. 2.

————. 1982. *Chicano Theater: Themes and Forms*. Ypsilanti, Mich.: Bilingual Review Press.

Hughes, Catharine. 1979. "Mixed Bags." *America* (4/21).

Kalem, T. E. 1979. "Threads Bare." *Time* (4/9).

Kanellos, Nicolás, ed. 1983. *Mexican American Theater: Then and Now*. Houston: Arte Publico (appeared as issue of *Revista Chicano-Riqueña* XI/1).

Kauffmann, Stanley. 1979. "Stanley Kauffmann on Theater." *The New Republic* (4/21).

Kerr, Walter. 1979. "*Zoot Suit* Loses Its Way in Bloodless Rhetoric." The *New York Times* (4/1), part 2, pp. 3, 20.

Kroll, Jack. 1979. "Heartbeats from the Barrio." *Newsweek* (4/9), pp. 85-86.

Lawson, Carol. 1978. "*Zoot Suit* Seeks Hispanic 'Sí'." The *New York Times* (12/27).

————. 1979. "'Loose Ends' Is Title—and Situation." The *New York Times* (4/25).

le Sourd, Jacques. 1978. "Two Openings: One Sizzles, One Fizzles." *Reporter Dispatch* (4/1).

————. 1979. "Californian Drama *Zoot Suit* Tells of Chicano Oppression." *Standard Star* (3/26).

Lewis, Barbara. 1979. "*Zoot Suit*: Black Experience with Chicano Accent." *New York Amsterdam News* (4/14), p. 25.

Miller, Marjorie. 1978. "*Zoot Suit* Pulls the Nostalgic and the Curious." *Los Angeles Times* (7/31), part II, pp. 1-2.

Orona-Córdova, Roberta. 1983. "*Zoot Suit* and the Pachuco Phenomenon. An Interview with Luis Valdez." Kanellos 1983:95-111.

Otten, Ted. 1979. "*Zoot Suit* Stands on Its Own." *P.S.* (3/28).

Sharp, Christopher. 1979. N.t. *Women's Wear Daily* (3/27).

Shibley, George. 1979. "Sleepy Lagoon: The True Story." *Westword* (1/15), p. 88.

Simon, John. 1979. "West Coast Story." *New York Magazine* (4/9), p. 93.

Sullivan, Dan. 1978. "*Zoot Suit* at the Taper Forum." *Los Angeles Times* (4/24), part IV, pp. 1, 11.

Thompson, Thomas. 1979. "A Dynamo Named Gordon Davison." The *New York Times Magazine* (3/11).

Trombetta, Jim. 1981. "*Zoot Suit* and Its Real Defendants." *Los Angeles Times* (10/11), Calendar, p. 4.

Valdez, Luis. 1978a. "From a Pamphlet to a Play." *Zoot Suit* program. Mark Taper Forum.

————. 1978b. "Once Again, Meet the Zoot Suiters." *Los Angeles Times* (8/13), part V, p. 3.

Watt, Douglas. 1979. "*Zoot Suit* Slithers in at the Winter Garden." *New York Daily News* (3/26), p. 21.

Yarbro-Bejarano, Yvonne, and Tomás Ybarra-Frausto. 1980. "*Zoot Suit* y el movimiento chicano." *Plural* (April) IX-VII, no. 103:49-56.

"*Zoot Suit.*" 1978. *Variety* (8/18), p. 14.

"*Zoot Suit* Badly Tailored Truth, Good Dramatic Fit." 1979. *New York Daily News* (3/28).

Granger Babcock   (essay date 1995)

SOURCE: "Looking for a Third Space: *El Pachuco* and Chicano Nationalism in Luis Valdez's *Zoot Suit*," in *Staging Difference: Cultural Pluralism in American Theatre and Drama*, edited by Marc Maufort, Peter Lang, 1995, pp. 215-25.

[*In the following essay, Babcock focuses on the significance of the figure of the* pachuco *in* Zoot Suit.]

In *Zoot Suit: An American Play* (1978), Luis Valdez emphatically reasserts the figure of the *pachuco*, which, as Jorge Huerta, Marcos Sanchez-Tranquilino, John Tagg, and Angie Chabram-Dernersesian have all theorized, marks the limit of the first stage, or wave, of Chicano cultural nationalism. As an outgrowth of Valdez's work with *El Teatro Campesino* (The Farmworker's Theater), *Zoot Suit* also represents the culmination of what is generally recognized as the first stage of his work (1965-1978), which, not coincidentally, parallels the initial period of the Chicano Civil Rights Movement in the Southwest.

Valdez began his "professional" writing and directing career in 1965 when he founded the Teatro Campesino during the Delano Grape Strike as a way to gain support for the United Farm Workers of California (UFWOC), then under the leadership of Caesar Chavez. At this time, Valdez's writing and directing focused on what he called *actos*; collectively created, *actos* were highly improvised skits that focused on the multiple oppressions experienced by the Chicano *huelguistas* (strikers) at the hands of the growers and *esquiroles* (scabs). According to Valdez, "The *actos* were born quite matter of factly in Delano. *Nacieron hambrientos de la realidad* [They were born of the hunger for reality]. Everything and anything that pertained to the daily life, *la vida cotidiana*, of the *huelguistas*, became food for thought, material for *actos*" (*Early Works* 11; italics added).

In 1967, in an effort to form a permanent theater company and thereby expand its political base, Valdez and the Teatro Campesino left the sponsorship of the United Farm Workers. According to Jorge Huerta, "It was not an ideological difference that motivated the separation, but the need to become a full-time theater, unencumbered by the daily demands of a struggling labor union. Valdez had to ask himself if he could really accomplish his goals with a sometime troupe, or if the Teatro Campesino could become a major force in the wider spectrum of the burgeoning Chicano Movement" (61). Valdez located the theater permanently in San Juan Bautista, California. Writing in 1970, Valdez explained the decision to leave the union: "*El Teatro Campesino* was born in the *huelga* [strike], but the very *huelga* would have killed it. . . . A struggle like the *huelga* needs every person it can get to serve its immediate goals in order to survive; the teatro, as well as the clinic, service center and newspaper, being less important at the moment of need than the survival of the union, were always losing people to the grape boycott. When it became clear to us that the UFWOC would succeed and continue to grow, we felt it was time for us to move and to begin speaking about things beyond the *huelga*: Vietnam, the barrio, racial discrimination, etc" (*Early Works* 10; italics added).

In order to conceptualize Valdez's emerging political goals during the late 1960s and early 70s, Jorge Huerta has introduced the term "Mechicano" to describe the Teatro's broadening audience. As I understand the term, "Mechicano" suggests a unification, or alliance, of various subject and class positions (and therefore political interests) within the Chicano community in order to challenge Anglo-American racism. Mechicano is a fusion of the words "Chicano" and "Mexican." Although the origin of the word "Chicano" is uncertain, according to Huerta

> most observers agree that "Chicano" came from the people themselves; it is a self-definition that denies both a Mexican and an Anglo-American distinction, yet is influenced by both. In essence, Chicanos assert that they are neither Mexican nor Anglo-American, employing a term that stems from barrio realities and linguistic patterns on this side of the Mexican border [the United States]. The term has been in common usage for generations and is often employed to distinguish between the middle-class Mexican American and the working class Chicano, a delineation that separates the so-called "assimilationist" from the political activist. There are still many Americans of Mexican descent who see the term Chicano as "common" and indicative of a low-class status.

(4)

Mexican, on the other hand, Huerta defines as *los un-documentos*, Spanish-speaking, undocumented workers, or "illegal aliens," who are denied citizenship but, ironically, form a vital part of the American economy. So, following Huerta's definition, Mechicano can be understood as a working class audience that has experienced the same consequences of racism: "poverty, alienation, exploitation in wars, manipulation by government, ignorance in the schools, and injustice in the courts" (Huerta 5). Nevertheless, because of the way Valdez envisioned his audience, "Mexican" could also be understood to represent the more liberal segments of the Mexican-American middle class, especially those families with children attending college for the first time in the 1960s. Valdez called his audience "*la raza*" (the race), or "*la gente*" (the people), and

seems to have had in mind a more broad coalition of political and social interests than Huerta theorizes (*Early Works* 10; italics added). This is not to say that Huerta is wrong, but in essentializing the term mechicano as working class, he marginalizes the importance of the Chicano student movement, which was largely an effect of an emerging Mexican-American middle class whose children, under "minority" status, were now in the 1960s entering the California university system and finding themselves alienated. Valdez was trying to turn this audience into political activists; he used their alienation in an essentially Anglo system as a catalyst, not only to encourage theater but also to construct a cultural nationalism based on identity politics or difference.

Valdez's strategy, then, in politicizing, and in other cases repoliticizing, his audience was to reject "assimilationist" politics and to refigure cultural stereotypes by controlling them and by then reasserting them as positive. The plays Valdez produced directly after leaving the UFWOC—*The Shrunken Head of Pancho Villa* (1964)[1] and *Los vendidos* (*The Sellouts*; 1967) focused on characters who deny their identity in order to "blend into the allegorical melting pot" (47). According to Huerta, "By focusing on characters who deny their heritage and attempt to blend into the allegorical melting pot, [these] plays demonstrate what the Chicano should not be and indicate positive alternatives to such behavior. . . . [T]he ideal characters exhibit a political awareness that suggests an active substitution to assimilation" (47).

Another—and related—goal of the Teatro at this juncture was to foster cultural nationalism by self-representation. As Huerta puts it, the desire for self-representation was part of a "renaissance of cultural and political activity among Chicanos" during the campaign for civil rights post-1965: "[Chicanos] would no longer acquiesce to the stereotypes and racial biases that plagued all aspects of the media but would, instead, fight for dignified representation on stage and film, in print and on the air" (Huerta 2). Part of this struggle, as the term Chicano suggests, was an active and sustained rejection of Anglo modes of culture, most prominently represented by the figure of the Mexican-American "sellout," in favor of a positive rearticulation of previously racist stereotypes. In other words, to help construct a unified Chicano movement, Valdez and other cultural workers took "outlaw" figures—stereotypes that were largely the projections of Anglo-American fear and racism—and gave them a positive value by using these outlaws to define Chicano identity.

One of the outlaw figures that Valdez chose as the embodiment of Chicano identity was the *pachuco*. In fact, by 1977, when he started to write **Zoot Suit,** the *pachuco* was his pre-eminent symbol of cultural resistance and self-definition. As Huerta points out, the "renegade" was essential to Valdez's theater from the beginning: "Above all, Valdez's plays reflect a struggle for cultural survival. The initial search for identity in the first play will recur in each suceeding work, with certain character types returning in different forms. The youthful renegade, the *vato loco* [crazy dude] or *pachuco*, is present in each of the plays and finds his ultimate personification as the narrator of *Zoot Suit*" (50; italics).

Valdez viewed the *pachuco* as a Chicano archetype, as, in his words, a "Jungian self-image" (Savran 265); and as both the precursor and definition of what Valdez called "Chicano consciousness," the *pachuco* gained his value because he both rejected and was rejected by the Anglo culture that encircled and in many ways controlled Valdez's audience. His non-conformity to the values of the majority culture made him a threat, and Valdez used this threat as a strategy of what Frederic Jameson calls "fabulation" to construct solidarity through "CHICANO POWER." That is, for his Mechicano audience, the *pachuco* represented a fantasy of empowerment, a figure, for the most part, that was not determined by Anglo life; he represented, as Valdez said, "the power inside every individual that's greater than any human institution" (Savran 265); yet for most of Valdez's Mechicano audience, material transcendence of racism and poverty was difficult, if not impossible—the *pachuco* therefore created solidarity out of the hope embodied by his resistance.

Historically, the *pachuco* style, or *pachuquismo*, emerged in the early 1940s in Los Angeles and New York. The visible sign of *pachuquismo* was the *tacuche*, or zoot suit: "the padded, finger-length coat with wide lapels; the narrow-brimmed lid or hat; the draped pants with reat-pleats, ballooning to the knee then narrowing tightly at the ankle; the looping [watch] chain; the double-soled shoes . . ." (Sanchez-Tranquilino and Tagg 559). Like his fashion, the *pachuco*'s culture was, as Sanchez-Tranquilino and Tagg note, "an assemblage:" "It was a cultural *affirmation* not by nostalgic return to an imaginary originary wholeness and past, but by appropriation, transgression, reassemblage, breaking and restructuring the laws of language: in the speech of *Calo* and *pochismos*,[2] but also in the languages of the body, gesture, hair, tattoos, dress, and dance; and in the languages of space, the city, the *barrio*, the street" (559). *Pachuquismo* sought to construct a discursive space of and for its own identity; as Sanchez-Tranquilino and Tagg suggest, a "third space" assembled from but not of the *buenas garras* (fine clothes or rags) of two cultures: "a third space, between the dualities of rural and urban, Eastside and Westside, Mexican and American, and, arguably, feminine and masculine. Not pure negation. Not *mestizo*—half and half—but an even greater *mestizaje*. A new space: a new field of identity" (560).

Valdez was drawn to *pachuquismo* because, as he said to Carlos Morton in an interview in 1982, it "was the direct antecedent of what has come to be termed 'Chicano consciousness:'"

> In the 1940s *pachucos* were caught between two cultures, viewed with suspicion by both conservative Mexican-Americans and Anglos. The *pachucos* were the first to acknowledge their bicultural backgrounds and to create a subculture based on this circumstance. The Anglo establishment, caught up in its "war-time hysteria" labeled the *pachucos* "zoot suiters" after their most flamboyant fashion. They were highly visible and easy targets for the U.S. Servicemen in Los Angeles in 1942. The *pachuco* emerged as a cult figure for he was the first to take pride in the complexity of his origins, and to *resist* conformity.
>
> (Morton 75)

Further, for Valdez, the *pachuco* represented a transgression in style and in language that simultaneously revealed the limits of Anglo-American democracy and in theory projected a more utopian politics based on hybridity and inclusion. As Sanchez-Tranquilino and Tagg write, "Tragic, heroic, delinquent, or grotesque, without a clear identity or location, the *pachuco* is a scandal of civilized meaning" (559). The very visibleness of the *pachuco* style was a threat because it destablized conventional and normative cultural codes, meanings which could only be restored by outlawing the pachuco; in fact, *pachucos* attempted to subvert conventionalized meanings and modes of dress by reappropriating and subverting them, much like the culture of Gangsta' Rap does today. To quote Sanchez-Tranquilino and Tagg again: "[*Pachucos*] got into the dress codes of white male status and normality, playing with the images of an Anglo popular culture's own masculine "outsiders"—the Southern dandy, the Western gambler, the *modern* gangster. They did not negate "the very principles" of North American fashion, as [Octavio] Paz tells us, but subsumed them in their own rhythms, arenas, and exchanges . . ." (559). As Valdez writes in the prologue of *Zoot Suit,* "The *Pachuco* Style was an act in life and his language a new creation" (25; italics added).

More specifically, in *Zoot Suit* Valdez "recovers" the *pachuco* "as the proto-subject of national regeneration" in a period (the late 1970s) when the Chicano Civil Rights Movement was "entering a less militant phase" (Sanchez-Tranquilino and Tagg 558, 561). The play is a reconstruction of the Sleepy Lagoon Trial and the "Zoot Suit Riots," which took place in Los Angeles during the summers of 1942 and 1943, respectively. Briefly,[3] in August of 1942 the Los Angeles Police Department used the murder of Jose Díaz as a pretext to arrest and question over 600 Mexican-American adults and teenagers, who the police had identified as "suspected gang members." The arrests led to a mass trial in which seventeen Chicano youths were illegally convicted and imprisoned for murder. These convictions were overturned by an appellate court in 1944. As in the Chicago trial on which Richard Wright's *Native Son* in based, the racism of Los Angeles newspapers made it easier for the court to ignore "normal judicial procedures" to gain convictions (Mazon 21-2). Los Angeles newspapers also made it possible for Anglo-Americans to blame "Zoot Suiters" for the "riots" that took place between June 3 and June 13 of 1943, even though eyewitness accounts clearly showed that American military personnel were responsible for the majority of the violence and property damage. In fact, as Mauricio Mazón has argued, the term "Zoot-Suit Riots," coined by the newspapers, is a misnomer because white servicemen actually started the rioting, during which they arbitrarily attacked men wearing zoot suits and, in many cases, raped *pachucos* who were wearing zoot suits. The "war-time hysteria" made it possible for the newspapers to construct *pachucos* as traitors. As Mazón writes, "Zoot-suiters transgressed the patriotic ideals of commitment, integrity, and loyalty with noncommitment, incoherence, and defiance. They seemed to be marking time while the rest of the country intensified the war effort" (9). And as Valdez notes above, their "flamboyant fashion" made them visible symbols of transgression during a period of hyper-conformity.

It is fitting then that in **Zoot Suit** Valdez uses newspapers and the Press as omnipresent symbols of Anglo racism and brutality. One of the most important instances of this device occurs in scene nine of act one, where at the opening of the Sleepy Lagoon Trial, the Judge is wheeled in on his "throne," which is made of "newspaper bundles piled squarely on a four-wheeled hand truck." The Press also rides in with the Judge, "holding the State and Federal Flags" (52). Valdez does this to underscore the collusion between the State and the Press in the contravention of justice during the Sleepy Lagoon Trial; he also does this to draw attention to the Press's ability to define and control the symbolic and social arenas in which the *pachucos* act. As *El Pachuco* says to the Press, "The Press distorted the very meaning of the word 'zoot suit.' All it is for you guys is another way to say Mexican" (80).

Throughout the play, Valdez's characters, and in particular *El Pachuco*, oppose the Press's ability to define reality, but they are only partially successful in challenging the racism and violence created and advocated by the Press and the State. In the play's opening scene, for example, *El Pachuco* "plunges" a switchblade through a "giant facsimile" of *The Los Angeles Herald Express* (June 3, 1943). The Headline reads: "ZOOT-SUITER HORDES INVADE LOS ANGELES. US NAVY AND MARINES ARE CALLED IN" (24). As he "emerges from the slit," he "dons" his coat and that and "becomes the very image of the *Pachuco* myth:" "HE proudly, slovenly, defiantly makes his way downstage. HE stops and assumes a pachuco stance" (25; italics added). Edward James Olmos's portrayal of *El Pachuco* in the movie version of **Zoot Suit** is instructive here. As Olmos emerges from the knife cut in the newspaper, his body assumes a semi-erect, stylized slouch that he maintains throughout the play. Like his switchblade, his body becomes a phallic weapon that cuts through not only the reality constructed by the Press but also counters the realistic acting styles used by the play's other actors; Olmos's stylized performance gives *El Pachuco* a mythic dimension; his body moves in and out and between the other actors almost like a knife. His patterns of speech and movements are a direct contrast to the documentary style used by the other actors in creating the fiction of Los Angeles in the 1940s. As "HE" says, *El Pachuco*'s performance embodies "the secret fantasy of every bato [dude] in and out of the *Chicanada* [neighborhood] to put on a Zoot

Suit and play the Myth *más chucote que la chingada* [just like a motherfucker]" (26; italics added). In this context, *"Chinanada"* has a double meaning: it suggests not only the act of intercourse but also the idea of relentless verbal or physical badgering. Both meanings suggest a kind of assault which conveys the thrusting of a knife or the phallus during sexual intercourse. "Playing" the myth can then be read as a relentless style or performance that defies normal modes of conduct and/or conventional codes of dress and speech, a style that asserts its reality by calling attention to its pretense, a visible act of rebellion that is "a construct of fact and fantasy" (25). Additionally, one of the root meanings of *"Chicanada"*[4] is chicanery or trickery, which Valdez uses to suggest that the space in which *El Pachuco* acts is subversive.

To emphasize the *chicana*, or chicanery, of *El Pachuco*'s space and performance, Valdez has him break realistic theatrical conventions. As Valdez said in an interview with David Savran,

> With **Zoot Suit** I was finally able to transcend social conditions, and the way I did it on stage was to give the *Pachuco* absolute power, as the master of ceremonies. He could snap his fingers and stop the action. It was a Brechtian device that allowed the plot to move forward, but psychically and symbolically, in the right way.
>
> And Chicanos got off on it. That's why a half-million came to see it in L.A. Because I had given a disenfranchised people their religion back. I dressed the *Pachuco* in the colors of Testatipoka, the Aztec god of education, the dean of the school of hard knocks.
>
> (265; italics added)

In addition to having *El Pachuco* control the action of the play, Valdez also has him directly address the audience as well as the main character within the play. At one point, for example, when the main character, Henry Reyna, is about to kill a rival gang member, *El Pachuco* stops the action and comments, "*Qué mamada* [What luck], Hank. That's just what the play needs right now. Two more Mexicans killing each other. . . . Everybody's looking at you. . . . That's exactly what they paid to see. Think about it" (46; italics added). *El Pachuco* then snaps his fingers to resume the action, and Reyna lets his rival go.

This scene is typical of the way Valdez uses the Brechtian concept of estrangement. By having *El Pachuco* interrupt the killing, he prevents the audience from psychically participating in the murder of "two more Mexicans." As an educator, *El Pachuco* problematizes the audience's desired response by contextualizing the violence. In doing so, the stage becomes *El Pachuco*'s *chicanada*, in which he subverts the audience's ability to identify with practices and social codes that have limited the solidarity of the disenfranchised—practices such as gang warfare. Nevertheless, despite Valdez's claims to the contrary, *El Pachuco*'s power is not absolute; the master of ceremonies is unable to transcend social conditions; he cannot escape the violence of the "Zoot-Suit Riots."

At the beginning of the second act, *El Pachuco* warns the audience:

> *Watchamos* [we watch] pachucos
> los batos
> the dudes
> street-corner warriors who fought and moved
> like unknown soldiers in wars of their own
> *El Pueblo de Los* [Los Angeles] was the battle zone
> from Sleepy Lagoon to the Zoot Suit wars
> when Marines and Sailors made their scores
> stomping like Nazis on East L.A. . . .

(65; italics added)

Here *El Pachuco* outlines the action of the second act in advance and in effect prepares the audience for the violence that comes in scene six ("ZOOT SUIT RIOTS"), where he substitutes himself for one of the *pachucos* in order to face an angry mob alone: "EL PACHUCO is overpowered and stripped. . . . The PRESS and SERVICEMEN exit with pieces of EL PACHUCO's zoot suit. EL PACHUCO stands. The only item of clothing on his body is a small loincloth. . . . HE opens his arms as an Aztec conch blows, and HE slowly exits backward with powerful calm into the shadows" (81). Valdez reads this scene as *El Pachuco* saying, "'It'll take more the the the U.S. Navy to beat me down'. . . . 'I don't give a fuck what you do to me. And I reassert myself, in this guise [the zoot suit]'" (Savran 265). This scene also links *El Pachuco*'s resistance with his Aztec past, in an attempt to ground his resistance in a historical continuum that has its origins in pre-Columbian America.

Nevertheless, while Valdez's reading is accurate, I find that it is problematic because in order to preserve or model dignity, *El Pachuco* chooses to be a victim; his substitution as victim also calls attention to the actual violence endured by Mexican-Americans, which *El Pachuco* cannot alleviate or fight, even in a symbolic manner. This is not to fault Valdez, however. The play must be read historically in the context of the Chicano Civil Rights Movement. His essentialization of Chicano identity, as I suggest at the beginning of this essay, marks the limits of the first stage of Chicano cultural nationalism. At this point, resistance is figured by essentializing identity (*El Pachuco*) and by providing a usable past that empowers that identity as a political weapon. Still, as Henry Giroux has recently argued, the practices of "identity politics" that emerged in the late 1970s, with their emphasis on difference, have become ineffective because of their "modernist" conception of personal agency. That is, to use Giroux's words, "Instead of recognizing multiple, collective agents capable of both challenging existing configurations of power and offering new visions of the future, modernism constructed a politics of identity within the narrow parameters of an individualism that was fixed, unburdened by history, and free from the constraints of multiple forms of domination" (63). Again, Valdez's essentialization of Chicano identity in *Zoot Suit* was a historically necessary political act to give, as he says, "a disenfranchised people their religion back." However,

this reduction of identity ultimately produced an impasse because it marginalized lived social conditions and other possible identities.

To be fair, Valdez does try to problematize his "modernist" tendencies in the play by providing multiple endings for the character of Henry Reyna. Nevertheless, this deconstruction of identity will be ignored by most male members of the audience because they will have identified in advance with the "absolute power" of *El Pachuco*. In other words, playing the myth *más chucote que la chingada* hinders Chicana participation because the code of its resistance is "machismo," as Angie Chabram-Dernersesian comments. "Within this logic," she writes, "if Chicanas wished to receive the authorizing signature of the predominant movement discourses and figure within the record of Mexican practices of resistance in the U.S., then they had to embody themselves as male, adopt traditional family relations, and dwell only on their racial and/or ethnic oppression" (83).

Chabram-Dernersesian's critique of Chicano nationalism and Giroux's critique of identity politics are useful not only because they allow us to read **Zoot Suit** in its historical context, but also because their critiques suggest ways for us to rethink the processes of cultural nationalisms in order that we might move beyond the limited (and limiting) politics of difference. Such movement is necessary in the United States if we are to rearticulate a vision of democratic culture that moves beyond the narrow borders of identity politics, so that we might indeed discover a "third space" that addresses and transforms the shared oppressions of marginalized communities.

NOTES

[1]*The Shrunken Head of Pancho Villa* was written in 1964 when Valdez was a student at San Jose State.

[2]*Caló*; and *pochismos* are used here to denote the hybridity of the pachuco's language. According to Sanchez-Tranquilino, "Pochismos or Anglicismos are translated and Hispanicized English words taken over into southwestern interlingual slang. Caló; draws on Southwestern Spanish, regional dialect, Mexican slang, and words that have changed little in form and meaning from Spanish Gypsy slang of the fifteenth century; but it is also a language of constant innovation, kept in restrictive usage by frequent and rapid changes of content through the invention of new terms" (564).

[3]For a detailed account of the Sleepy Lagoon Trial and the Zoot-Suit Riots, see Mauricio Mazón, *The Zoot-Suit Riots: The Psychology of Symbolic Annihilation* (Austin, Texas: University of Texas Press, 1984).

[4]In the movie version of *Zoot Suit*, Valdez substitutes the word *pachucada* for *chicanada* in order to further assert *El Pachuco*'s control of meaning and social space.

Chabram-Dernersesian, Angie. "I Throw Puches for My Race, but I Don't Want to be a Man: Writing Us—*Chica-nos* (Girl, Us / *Chicanas*—into the Movement Script." Grossberger 81-95.

Giroux, Henry A. *Living Dangerously: Multiculturalism and the Politics of Difference*. New York: Peter Lang, 1993.

Grossberger, Lawrence, Cary Nelson, and Paula A. Treichler, ed. *Cultural Studies*. New York: Routledge, 1992.

Huerta, Jorge A. *Chicano Theater: Themes and Forms*. Tempe, AZ: Bilingual Press/Editorial Bilingue, 1982.

Mazón, Mauricio. *The Zoot-Suit Riots: The Psychology of Symbolic Annihilation*. Austin, TX: U of Texas P, 1984.

Morton, Carlos. "An Interview with Luis Valdez." *Latin American Theatre Review* 15.2 (Spring 1982): 73-76.

Sanchez-Tranquilino, Marcos and John Tagg. "The Pachuco's Flayed Hide: Mobility, Identity, and *Buenas Garras*." Grossberger 556-70.

Savran, David. *In Their Own Words: Contemporary American Playwrights*. New York: Theatre Communications Group, 1988.

Valdez, Luis. *Zoot Suit and Other Plays*. Houston, TX: Arte Publico, 1992.

————. *Early Works: Actos, Bernabe and Pensamiento Serpentino*. Houston, TX: Arte Publico, 1990.

FURTHER READING

Bagby, Beth. "El Teatro Campesino: Interviews with Luis Valdez." *Tulane Drama Review* 11, No. 4 (Summer 1967): 70-80.

Discussion in which Valdez speaks of his involvement in activist theater.

Brokaw, John W. Review of *Dos peones por patroncito, Los vendidos*, and *El soldado razo*. *Educational Theatre Journal* 26, No. 1 (March 1974): 108-10.

Descriptive review of the performance of three of Valdez's works theater in Mexico City. "The political power of Valdez' scripts is well documented," Brokaw asserts, "but it took a Mexican director and his actors to realize that the plays have this much esthetic power."

Drake, Sylvie. "El Teatro Campesino: Keeping the Revolution on Stage." *Performing Arts* 4, No. 9 (September 1970): 56-62.

Profile of Valdez and El Teatro Campesino. The Campesino's impact Drake observes, is "immediate and enormous, characterized by extraordinary vitality, earthy humor, and an approach so direct as to seem more primitive than it really is."

Herms, Dieter. "Luis Valdez, Chicano Dramatist: An Introduction and an Interview." In *Essays on American Drama*, ed. Hedwig Bock and Albert Wertheim, pp. 257-78. Munich: Max Hueber Verlag, 1981.

Focuses on "the genesis, on the shaping and the making of *Zoot Suit*, at a time when preparations began for taking the production to Broadway."

Kanellos, Nicolás. *Hispanic Theatre in the United States*. Houston: Arte Público Press, 1984.

Contains two essays that treat Valdez and his work: Jorge A. Huerta's "Labor Theatre, Street Theatre and Community Theatre in the Barrios, 1965-1983," and Margarita B. Melville's "Female and Male in Chicano Theatre."

Morton, Carlos. "An Interview with Luis Valdez." *Latin American Theatre Review* 15, No. 2 (Spring 1982): 73-6.

Brief discussion of Valdez's theatrical origins.

How to Use This Index

The main references

Calvino, Italo
1923–1985 .... CLC 5, 8, 11, 22, 33, 39,
73; SSC 3

list all author entries in the following Gale Literary Criticism series:

BLC = *Black Literature Criticism*
CLC = *Contemporary Literary Criticism*
CLR = *Children's Literature Review*
CMLC = *Classical and Medieval Literature Criticism*
DA = *DISCovering Authors*
DAB = *DISCovering Authors: British*
DAC = *DISCovering Authors: Canadian*
DAM = *DISCovering Authors: Modules*
        DRAM: *Dramatists Module;* *MST*: *Most-Studied Authors Module;*
        MULT: *Multicultural Authors Module;* *NOV*: *Novelists Module;*
        POET: *Poets Module;* *POP*: *Popular Fiction and Genre Authors Module*
DC = *Drama Criticism*
HLC = *Hispanic Literature Criticism*
LC = *Literature Criticism from 1400 to 1800*
NCLC = *Nineteenth-Century Literature Criticism*
PC = *Poetry Criticism*
SSC = *Short Story Criticism*
TCLC = *Twentieth-Century Literary Criticism*
WLC = *World Literature Criticism, 1500 to the Present*

The cross-references

See also CANR 23; CA 85-88;
    obituary CA116

list all author entries in the following Gale biographical and literary sources:

AAYA = *Authors & Artists for Young Adults*
AITN = *Authors in the News*
BEST = *Bestsellers*
BW = *Black Writers*
CA = *Contemporary Authors*
CAAS = *Contemporary Authors Autobiography Series*
CABS = *Contemporary Authors Bibliographical Series*
CANR = *Contemporary Authors New Revision Series*
CAP = *Contemporary Authors Permanent Series*
CDALB = *Concise Dictionary of American Literary Biography*
CDBLB = *Concise Dictionary of British Literary Biography*
DLB = *Dictionary of Literary Biography*
DLBD = *Dictionary of Literary Biography Documentary Series*
DLBY = *Dictionary of Literary Biography Yearbook*
HW = *Hispanic Writers*
JRDA = *Junior DISCovering Authors*
MAICYA = *Major Authors and Illustrators for Children and Young Adults*
MTCW = *Major 20th-Century Writers*
NNAL = *Native North American Literature*
SAAS = *Something about the Author Autobiography Series*
SATA = *Something about the Author*
YABC = *Yesterday's Authors of Books for Children*

Literary Criticism Series
Cumulative Author Index

20/1631
See Upward, Allen

A/C Cross
See Lawrence, T(homas) E(dward)

Abasiyanik, Sait Faik 1906-1954
See Sait Faik

Abbey, Edward 1927-1989 .... **CLC 36, 59**
See also CA 45-48; 128; CANR 2, 41

Abbott, Lee K(ittredge) 1947- .... **CLC 48**
See also CA 124; CANR 51; DLB 130

Abe, Kobo 1924-1993 .... **CLC
8, 22, 53, 81; DAM NOV**
See also CA 65-68; 140; CANR 24, 60; DLB
182; MTCW 1

Abelard, Peter c. 1079-c. 1142 ...... **CMLC 11**
See also DLB 115

Abell, Kjeld 1901-1961 .... **CLC 15**
See also CA 111

Abish, Walter 1931- .... **CLC 22**
See also CA 101; CANR 37; DLB 130

Abrahams, Peter (Henry) 1919- .... **CLC 4**
See also BW 1; CA 57-60; CANR 26; DLB
117; MTCW 1

Abrams, M(eyer) H(oward) 1912- .... **CLC 24**
See also CA 57-60; CANR 13, 33; DLB 67

Abse, Dannie 1923- .... **CLC
7, 29; DAB; DAM POET**
See also CA 53-56; CAAS 1; CANR 4, 46,
74; DLB 27

Achebe, (Albert) Chinua(lumogu)
1930- .... **CLC 1,
3, 5, 7, 11, 26, 51, 75; BLC 1; DA; DAB;
DAC; DAM MST, MULT, NOV; WLC**
See also AAYA 15; BW 2; CA 1-4R; CANR
6, 26, 47, 73; CLR 20; DLB 117; MAICYA;
MTCW 1; SATA 40; SATA-Brief 38

Acker, Kathy 1948-1997 .... **CLC 45, 111**
See also CA 117; 122; 162; CANR 55

Ackroyd, Peter 1949- .... **CLC 34, 52**
See also CA 123; 127; CANR 51, 74; DLB
155; INT 127

Acorn, Milton 1923- .... **CLC 15; DAC**
See also CA 103; DLB 53; INT 103

Adamov, Arthur 1908-1970 .... **CLC
4, 25; DAM DRAM**
See also CA 17-18; 25-28R; CAP 2; MTCW
1

Adams, Alice (Boyd) 1926- .... **CLC
6, 13, 46; SSC 24**
See also CA 81-84; CANR 26, 53, 75; DLBY
86; INT CANR-26; MTCW 1

Adams, Andy 1859-1935 .... **TCLC 56**
See also YABC 1

Adams, Brooks 1848-1927 .... **TCLC 80**
See also CA 123; DLB 47

Adams, Douglas (Noel) 1952- .... **CLC
27, 60; DAM POP**
See also AAYA 4; BEST 89:3; CA 106;
CANR 34, 64; DLBY 83; JRDA

Adams, Francis 1862-1893 .... **NCLC 33**

Adams, Henry (Brooks) 1838-1918 ..... **TCLC
4, 52; DA; DAB; DAC; DAM MST**
See also CA 104; 133; DLB 12, 47, 189

Adams, Richard (George) 1920- .... **CLC
4, 5, 18; DAM NOV**
See also AAYA 16; AITN 1, 2; CA 49-52;
CANR 3, 35; CLR 20; JRDA; MAICYA;
MTCW 1; SATA 7, 69

Adamson, Joy(-Friederike Victoria)
1910-1980 .... **CLC 17**
See also CA 69-72; 93-96; CANR 22;
MTCW 1; SATA 11; SATA-Obit 22

Adcock, Fleur 1934- .... **CLC 41**
See also CA 25-28R; CAAS 23; CANR 11,
34, 69; DLB 40

Addams, Charles (Samuel) 1912-1988 ... **CLC
30**
See also CA 61-64; 126; CANR 12

Addams, Jane 1860-1945 .... **TCLC 76**

Addison, Joseph 1672-1719 ....**LC 18**
See also CDBLB 1660-1789; DLB 101

Adler, Alfred (F.) 1870-1937 .... **TCLC 61**
See also CA 119; 159

Adler, C(arole) S(chwerdtfeger)
1932- .... **CLC 35**
See also AAYA 4; CA 89-92; CANR 19, 40;
JRDA; MAICYA; SAAS 15; SATA 26, 63,
102

Adler, Renata 1938- .... **CLC 8, 31**
See also CA 49-52; CANR 5, 22, 52; MTCW
1

Ady, Endre 1877-1919 .... **TCLC 11**
See also CA 107

A.E. 1867-1935 .... **TCLC 3, 10**
See also Russell, George William

Aeschylus 525B.C.-456B.C. .... **CMLC
11; DA; DAB; DAC; DAM DRAM,
MST; DC 8; WLCS**
See also DLB 176

Aesop 620(?)B.C.-564(?)B.C. .... **CMLC 24**
See also CLR 14; MAICYA; SATA 64

Affable Hawk
See MacCarthy, Sir(Charles Otto) Desmond

Africa, Ben
See Bosman, Herman Charles

Afton, Effie
See Harper, Frances Ellen Watkins

Agapida, Fray Antonio
See Irving, Washington

Agee, James (Rufus) 1909-1955 .... **TCLC
1, 19; DAM NOV**
See also AITN 1; CA 108; 148; CDALB
1941-1968; DLB 2, 26, 152

Aghill, Gordon
See Silverberg, Robert

Agnon, S(hmuel) Y(osef Halevi)
1888-1970 .... **CLC 4, 8, 14; SSC 30**
See also CA 17-18; 25-28R; CANR 60; CAP
2; MTCW 1

Agrippa von Nettesheim, Henry Cornelius
1486-1535 ....**LC 27**

Aherne, Owen
See Cassill, R(onald) V(erlin)

Ai 1947- ....**CLC 4, 14, 69**
See also CA 85-88; CAAS 13; CANR 70;
DLB 120

Aickman, Robert (Fordyce) 1914-1981 ... **CLC
57**
See also CA 5-8R; CANR 3, 72

Aiken, Conrad (Potter) 1889-1973 ..... **CLC 1,
3, 5, 10, 52; DAM NOV, POET; SSC 9**
See also CA 5-8R; 45-48; CANR 4, 60;
CDALB 1929-1941; DLB 9, 45, 102;
MTCW 1; SATA 3, 30

Aiken, Joan (Delano) 1924- .... **CLC 35**
See also AAYA 1, 25; CA 9-12R; CANR 4,
23, 34, 64; CLR 1, 19; DLB 161; JRDA;
MAICYA; MTCW 1; SAAS 1; SATA 2, 30,
73

Ainsworth, William Harrison
1805-1882 .... **NCLC 13**
See also DLB 21; SATA 24

Aitmatov, Chingiz (Torekulovich)
1928- .... **CLC 71**
See also CA 103; CANR 38; MTCW 1;
SATA 56

Akers, Floyd
See Baum, L(yman) Frank

Akhmadulina, Bella Akhatovna 1937-... **CLC
53; DAM POET**
See also CA 65-68

Akhmatova, Anna 1888-1966 .... **CLC
11, 25, 64; DAM POET; PC 2**
See also CA 19-20; 25-28R; CANR 35; CAP
1; MTCW 1

Aksakov, Sergei Timofeyvich
1791-1859 ....**NCLC 2**
See also DLB 198

Aksenov, Vassily
See Aksyonov, Vassily (Pavlovich)

Ammons, A(rchie) R(andolph) 1926-..... **CLC 2, 3, 5, 8, 9, 25, 57, 108; DAM POET; PC 16**
See also AITN 1, CA 9-12R, CANR 6, 36, 51, 73; DLB 5, 165; MTCW 1

Amo, Tauraatua i
See Adams, Henry (Brooks)

Amory, Thomas 1691(?)-1788.............**LC 48**

Anand, Mulk Raj 1905- .... **CLC 23, 93; DAM NOV**
See also CA 65-68; CANR 32, 64; MTCW 1

Anatol
See Schnitzler, Arthur

Anaximander c. 610B.C.-c. 546B.C.... **CMLC 22**

Anaya, Rudolfo A(lfonso) 1937-........... **CLC 23; DAM MULT, NOV; HLC**
See also AAYA 20; CA 45-48; CAAS 4; CANR 1, 32, 51; DLB 82, 206; HW 1; MTCW 1

Andersen, Hans Christian 1805-1875 .... **NCLC 7; DA; DAB; DAC; DAM MST, POP; SSC 6; WLC**
See also CLR 6; MAICYA; SATA 100; YABC 1

Anderson, C. Farley
See Mencken, H(enry) L(ouis); Nathan, George Jean

Anderson, Jessica (Margaret) Queale 1916- .... **CLC 37**
See also CA 9-12R; CANR 4, 62

Anderson, Jon (Victor) 1940- .... **CLC 9; DAM POET**
See also CA 25-28R; CANR 20

Anderson, Lindsay (Gordon) 1923-1994 .... **CLC 20**
See also CA 125; 128; 146

Anderson, Maxwell 1888-1959........... **TCLC 2; DAM DRAM**
See also CA 105; 152; DLB 7

Anderson, Poul (William) 1926-....... **CLC 15**
See also AAYA 5; CA 1-4R; CAAS 2; CANR 2, 15, 34, 64; DLB 8; INT CANR-15; MTCW 1; SATA 90; SATA-Brief 39

Anderson, Robert (Woodruff) 1917- ..... **CLC 23; DAM DRAM**
See also AITN 1; CA 21-24R; CANR 32; DLB 7

Anderson, Sherwood 1876-1941......... **TCLC 1, 10, 24; DA; DAB; DAC; DAM MST, NOV; SSC 1; WLC**
See also CA 104; 121; CANR 61; CDALB 1917-1929; DLB 4, 9, 86; DLBD 1; MTCW 1

Andier, Pierre
See Desnos, Robert

Andouard
See Giraudoux, (Hippolyte) Jean

Andrade, Carlos Drummond de....... **CLC 18**
See also Drummond de Andrade, Carlos

Andrade, Mario de 1893-1945 .... **TCLC 43**

Andreae, Johann V(alentin) 1586-1654.... **LC 32**
See also DLB 164

Andreas-Salome, Lou 1861-1937.... **TCLC 56**
See also DLB 66

Andress, Lesley
See Sanders, Lawrence

Andrewes, Lancelot 1555-1626 .... **LC 5**
See also DLB 151, 172

Andrews, Cicily Fairfield
See West, Rebecca

Andrews, Elton V.
See Pohl, Frederik

Andreyev, Leonid (Nikolaevich) 1871-1919 ....**TCLC 3**
See also CA 104

Andric, Ivo 1892-1975 ....**CLC 8**
See also CA 81-84; 57-60; CANR 43, 60; DLB 147; MTCW 1

Androvar
See Prado (Calvo), Pedro

Angelique, Pierre
See Bataille, Georges

Angell, Roger 1920- .... **CLC 26**
See also CA 57-60; CANR 13, 44, 70; DLB 171, 185

Angelou, Maya 1928-........................ **CLC 12, 35, 64, 77; BLC 1; DA; DAB; DAC; DAM MST, MULT, POET, POP; WLCS**
See also AAYA 7, 20; BW 2; CA 65-68; CANR 19, 42, 65; CLR 53; DLB 38; MTCW 1; SATA 49

Anna Comnena 1083-1153........... **CMLC 25**

Annensky, Innokenty (Fyodorovich) 1856-1909 .... **TCLC 14**
See also CA 110; 155

Annunzio, Gabriele d'
See D'Annunzio, Gabriele

Anodos
See Coleridge, Mary E(lizabeth)

Anon, Charles Robert
See Pessoa, Fernando (Antonio Nogueira)

Anouilh, Jean (Marie Lucien Pierre) 1910-1987 ....**CLC 1, 3, 8, 13, 40, 50; DAM DRAM; DC 8**
See also CA 17-20R; 123; CANR 32; MTCW 1

Anthony, Florence
See Ai

Anthony, John
See Ciardi, John (Anthony)

Anthony, Peter
See Shaffer, Anthony (Joshua); Shaffer, Peter (Levin)

Anthony, Piers 1934-..... **CLC 35; DAM POP**
See also AAYA 11; CA 21-24R; CANR 28, 56, 73; DLB 8; MTCW 1; SAAS 22; SATA 84

Anthony, Susan B(rownell) 1916-1991 .... **TCLC 84**
See also CA 89-92; 134

Antoine, Marc
See Proust, (Valentin-Louis-George-Eugene-) Marcel

Antoninus, Brother
See Everson, William (Oliver)

Antonioni, Michelangelo 1912- .... **CLC 20**
See also CA 73-76; CANR 45

Antschel, Paul 1920-1970
See Celan, Paul

Anwar, Chairil 1922-1949............. **TCLC 22**
See also CA 121

Apess, William 1798-1839(?) ....**NCLC 73; DAM MULT**
See also DLB 175; NNAL

Apollinaire, Guillaume 1880-1918 ...... **TCLC 3, 8, 51; DAM POET; PC 7**
See also Kostrowitzki, Wilhelm Apollinaris de

Appelfeld, Aharon 1932- ....**CLC 23, 47**
See also CA 112; 133

Apple, Max (Isaac) 1941-.............. **CLC 9, 33**
See also CA 81-84; CANR 19, 54; DLB 130

Appleman, Philip (Dean) 1926-........ **CLC 51**
See also CA 13-16R; CAAS 18; CANR 6, 29, 56

Appleton, Lawrence
See Lovecraft, H(oward) P(hillips)

Apteryx
See Eliot, T(homas) S(tearns)

Apuleius, (Lucius Madaurensis) 125(?)-175(?) ....**CMLC 1**

Aquin, Hubert 1929-1977 .... **CLC 15**
See also CA 105; DLB 53

Aragon, Louis 1897-1982.................... **CLC 3, 22; DAM NOV, POET**
See also CA 69-72; 108; CANR 28, 71; DLB 72; MTCW 1

Arany, Janos 1817-1882 .... **NCLC 34**

Aranyos, Kakay
See Mikszath, Kalman

Arbuthnot, John 1667-1735 .... **LC 1**
See also DLB 101

Archer, Herbert Winslow
See Mencken, H(enry) L(ouis)

Archer, Jeffrey (Howard) 1940- .... **CLC 28; DAM POP**
See also AAYA 16; BEST 89:3; CA 77-80; CANR 22, 52; INT CANR-22

Archer, Jules 1915- .... **CLC 12**
See also CA 9-12R; CANR 6, 69; SAAS 5; SATA 4, 85

Archer, Lee
See Ellison, Harlan (Jay)

Arden, John 1930-......................... **CLC 6, 13, 15; DAM DRAM**
See also CA 13-16R; CAAS 4; CANR 31, 65, 67; DLB 13; MTCW 1

Arenas, Reinaldo 1943-1990............... **CLC 41; DAM MULT; HLC**
See also CA 124; 128; 133; CANR 73; DLB 145; HW

Arendt, Hannah 1906-1975.........**CLC 66, 98**
See also CA 17-20R; 61-64; CANR 26, 60; MTCW 1

Aretino, Pietro 1492-1556.................**LC 12**

Arghezi, Tudor 1880-1967 .... **CLC 80**
See also Theodorescu, Ion N.

Arguedas, Jose Maria 1911-1969......... **CLC 10, 18**
See also CA 89-92; CANR 73; DLB 113; HW

Argueta, Manlio 1936-.................. **CLC 31**
See also CA 131; CANR 73; DLB 145; HW

Ariosto, Ludovico 1474-1533.............. **LC 6**

Aristides
See Epstein, Joseph

Aristophanes 450B.C.-385B.C........... **CMLC 4; DA; DAB; DAC; DAM DRAM, MST; DC 2; WLCS**
See also DLB 176

Aristotle 384B.C.-322B.C............. **CMLC 31; DA; DAB; DAC; DAM MST; WLCS**
See also DLB 176

Arlt, Roberto (Godofredo Christophersen) 1900-1942 .... **TCLC 29; DAM MULT; HLC**
See also CA 123; 131; CANR 67; HW

Armah, Ayi Kwei 1939-..................... **CLC 5, 33; BLC 1; DAM MULT, POET**
See also BW 1; CA 61-64; CANR 21, 64; DLB 117; MTCW 1

Armatrading, Joan 1950- .... **CLC 17**
See also CA 114

Arnette, Robert
See Silverberg, Robert

Arnim, Achim von (Ludwig Joachim von Arnim) 1781-1831...... **NCLC 5; SSC 29**
See also DLB 90

Arnim, Bettina von 1785-1859 .... **NCLC 38**
See also DLB 90

Arnold, Matthew 1822-1888.............. **NCLC 6, 29; DA; DAB; DAC; DAM MST, POET; PC 5; WLC**
See also CDBLB 1832-1890; DLB 32, 57

Arnold, Thomas 1795-1842........... **NCLC 18**
See also DLB 55

Arnow, Harriette (Louisa) Simpson 1908-1986 .... **CLC 2, 7, 18**
See also CA 9-12R; 118; CANR 14; DLB 6; MTCW 1; SATA 42; SATA-Obit 47

Arouet, Francois-Marie
See Voltaire

Arp, Hans
See Arp, Jean

Arp, Jean 1887-1966 .... **CLC 5**
See also CA 81-84; 25-28R; CANR 42

Arrabal
See Arrabal, Fernando

Arrabal, Fernando 1932-......**CLC 2, 9, 18, 58**
See also CA 9-12R; CANR 15

Arrick, Fran............................... **CLC 30**
See also Gaberman, Judie Angell

Artaud, Antonin (Marie Joseph) 1896-1948 ....**TCLC 3, 36; DAM DRAM**
See also CA 104; 149

Arthur, Ruth M(abel) 1905-1979 ...... **CLC 12**
See also CA 9-12R; 85-88; CANR 4; SATA 7, 26

Artsybashev, Mikhail (Petrovich) 1878-1927 .... **TCLC 31**
See also CA 170

Arundel, Honor (Morfydd) 1919-1973... **CLC 17**
See also CA 21-22; 41-44R; CAP 2; CLR 35; SATA 4; SATA-Obit 24

Arzner, Dorothy 1897-1979 .... **CLC 98**

Asch, Sholem 1880-1957................. **TCLC 3**
See also CA 105

Ash, Shalom
See Asch, Sholem

Ashbery, John (Lawrence) 1927-.... **CLC 2, 3, 4, 6, 9, 13, 15, 25, 41, 77; DAM POET**
See also CA 5-8R; CANR 9, 37, 66; DLB 5, 165; DLBY 81; INT CANR-9; MTCW 1

Ashdown, Clifford
See Freeman, R(ichard) Austin

Ashe, Gordon
See Creasey, John

Ashton-Warner, Sylvia (Constance) 1908-1984 .... **CLC 19**
See also CA 69-72; 112; CANR 29; MTCW 1

Asimov, Isaac 1920-1992 .... **CLC 1, 3, 9, 19, 26, 76, 92; DAM POP**
See also AAYA 13; BEST 90:2; CA 1-4R; 137; CANR 2, 19, 36, 60; CLR 12; DLB 8; DLBY 92; INT CANR-19; JRDA; MAICYA; MTCW 1; SATA 1, 26, 74

Assis, Joaquim Maria Machado de
See Machado de Assis, Joaquim Maria

Astley, Thea (Beatrice May) 1925-.... **CLC 41**
See also CA 65-68; CANR 11, 43

Aston, James
See White, T(erence) H(anbury)

Asturias, Miguel Angel 1899-1974 .... **CLC 3, 8, 13; DAM MULT, NOV; HLC**
See also CA 25-28; 49-52; CANR 32; CAP 2; DLB 113; HW; MTCW 1

Atares, Carlos Saura
See Saura (Atares), Carlos

Atheling, William
See Pound, Ezra (Weston Loomis)

Atheling, William, Jr.
See Blish, James (Benjamin)

Atherton, Gertrude (Franklin Horn) 1857-1948 .... **TCLC 2**
See also CA 104; 155; DLB 9, 78, 186

Atherton, Lucius
See Masters, Edgar Lee

Atkins, Jack
See Harris, Mark

Atkinson, Kate........................... **CLC 99**
See also CA 166

Attaway, William (Alexander) 1911-1986 .... **CLC 92; BLC 1; DAM MULT**
See also BW 2; CA 143; DLB 76

Atticus
See Fleming, Ian (Lancaster); Wilson, (Thomas) Woodrow

Atwood, Margaret (Eleanor) 1939-....... **CLC 2, 3, 4, 8, 13, 15, 25, 44, 84; DA; DAB; DAC; DAM MST, NOV, POET; PC 8; SSC 2; WLC**
See also AAYA 12; BEST 89:2; CA 49-52; CANR 3, 24, 33, 59; DLB 53; INT CANR-24; MTCW 1; SATA 50

Aubigny, Pierre d'
See Mencken, H(enry) L(ouis)

Aubin, Penelope 1685-1731(?) .... **LC 9**
See also DLB 39

Auchincloss, Louis (Stanton) 1917-....... **CLC 4, 6, 9, 18, 45; DAM NOV; SSC 22**
See also CA 1-4R; CANR 6, 29, 55; DLB 2; DLBY 80; INT CANR-29; MTCW 1

Auden, W(ystan) H(ugh) 1907-1973... **CLC 1, 2, 3, 4, 6, 9, 11, 14, 43; DA; DAB; DAC; DAM DRAM, MST, POET; PC 1; WLC**
See also AAYA 18; CA 9-12R; 45-48; CANR 5, 61; CDBLB 1914-1945; DLB 10, 20; MTCW 1

Audiberti, Jacques 1900-1965............. **CLC 38; DAM DRAM**
See also CA 25-28R

Audubon, John James 1785-1851 ... **NCLC 47**

Auel, Jean M(arie) 1936-................... **CLC 31, 107; DAM POP**
See also AAYA 7; BEST 90:4; CA 103; CANR 21, 64; INT CANR-21; SATA 91

Auerbach, Erich 1892-1957........... **TCLC 43**
See also CA 118; 155

Augier, Emile 1820-1889 .... **NCLC 31**
See also DLB 192

August, John
See De Voto, Bernard (Augustine)

Augustine, St. 354-430..........**CMLC 6; DAB**

Aurelius
See Bourne, Randolph S(illiman)

Aurobindo, Sri
See Ghose, Aurabinda

Austen, Jane 1775-1817 .... **NCLC 1, 13, 19, 33, 51; DA; DAB; DAC; DAM MST, NOV; WLC**
See also AAYA 19; CDBLB 1789-1832; DLB 116

Auster, Paul 1947- .... **CLC 47**
See also CA 69-72; CANR 23, 52, 75

Austin, Frank
See Faust, Frederick (Schiller)

Austin, Mary (Hunter) 1868-1934... **TCLC 25**
See also CA 109; DLB 9, 78, 206

Autran Dourado, Waldomiro
See Dourado, (Waldomiro Freitas) Autran

Averroes 1126-1198..................... **CMLC 7**
See also DLB 115

Avicenna 980-1037.................... **CMLC 16**
See also DLB 115

Avison, Margaret 1918-..................... **CLC 2, 4, 97; DAC; DAM POET**
See also CA 17-20R; DLB 53; MTCW 1

Axton, David
See Koontz, Dean R(ay)

Ayckbourn, Alan 1939- .... **CLC 5, 8, 18, 33, 74; DAB; DAM DRAM**
See also CA 21-24R; CANR 31, 59; DLB 13; MTCW 1

Aydy, Catherine
See Tennant, Emma (Christina)

Ayme, Marcel (Andre) 1902-1967 ..... **CLC 11**
See also CA 89-92; CANR 67; CLR 25; DLB 72; SATA 91

Ayrton, Michael 1921-1975 .... **CLC 7**
See also CA 5-8R; 61-64; CANR 9, 21

Azorin .... **CLC 11**
See also Martinez Ruiz, Jose

Azuela, Mariano 1873-1952 .... **TCLC 3; DAM MULT; HLC**
See also CA 104; 131; HW; MTCW 1

Baastad, Babbis Friis
See Friis-Baastad, Babbis Ellinor

Bab
See Gilbert, W(illiam) S(chwenck)

Babbis, Eleanor
See Friis-Baastad, Babbis Ellinor

Babel, Isaac
See Babel, Isaak (Emmanuilovich)

Babel, Isaak (Emmanuilovich) 1894-1941(?) .... **TCLC 2, 13; SSC 16**
See also CA 104; 155

Babits, Mihaly 1883-1941 .... **TCLC 14**
See also CA 114

Babur 1483-1530 .... **LC 18**

Bacchelli, Riccardo 1891-1985 .... **CLC 19**
See also CA 29-32R; 117

Bach, Richard (David) 1936- .... **CLC 14; DAM NOV, POP**
See also AITN 1; BEST 89:2; CA 9-12R; CANR 18; MTCW 1; SATA 13

Bachman, Richard
See King, Stephen (Edwin)

Bachmann, Ingeborg 1926-1973 .... **CLC 69**
See also CA 93-96; 45-48; CANR 69; DLB 85

Bacon, Francis 1561-1626 .... **LC 18, 32**
See also CDBLB Before 1660; DLB 151

Bacon, Roger 1214(?)-1292 .... **CMLC 14**
See also DLB 115

Bacovia, George .... **TCLC 24**
See also Vasiliu, Gheorghe

Badanes, Jerome 1937- .... **CLC 59**

Bagehot, Walter 1826-1877 .... **NCLC 10**
See also DLB 55

Bagnold, Enid 1889-1981.................... **CLC 25; DAM DRAM**
See also CA 5-8R; 103; CANR 5, 40; DLB 13, 160, 191; MAICYA; SATA 1, 25

Bagritsky, Eduard 1895-1934 .... **TCLC 60**

Bagrjana, Elisaveta
See Belcheva, Elisaveta

Bagryana, Elisaveta .... **CLC 10**
See also Belcheva, Elisaveta

Bailey, Paul 1937- .... **CLC 45**
See also CA 21-24R; CANR 16, 62; DLB 14

Baillie, Joanna 1762-1851 .... **NCLC 71**
See also DLB 93

Bainbridge, Beryl (Margaret) 1933- ...... **CLC 4, 5, 8, 10, 14, 18, 22, 62; DAM NOV**
See also CA 21-24R; CANR 24, 55, 75; DLB 14; MTCW 1

Baker, Elliott 1922- .... **CLC 8**
See also CA 45-48; CANR 2, 63

Baker, Jean H. .... **TCLC 3, 10**
See also Russell, George William

Baker, Nicholson 1957- ...**CLC 61; DAM POP**
See also CA 135; CANR 63

Baker, Ray Stannard 1870-1946 ..... **TCLC 47**
See also CA 118

Baker, Russell (Wayne) 1925- .... **CLC 31**
See also BEST 89:4; CA 57-60; CANR 11, 41, 59; MTCW 1

Bakhtin, M.
See Bakhtin, Mikhail Mikhailovich

Bakhtin, M. M.
See Bakhtin, Mikhail Mikhailovich

Bakhtin, Mikhail
See Bakhtin, Mikhail Mikhailovich

Bakhtin, Mikhail Mikhailovich 1895-1975 .... **CLC 83**
See also CA 128; 113

Bakshi, Ralph 1938(?)- .... **CLC 26**
See also CA 112; 138

Bakunin, Mikhail (Alexandrovich) 1814-1876 ....**NCLC 25, 58**

Baldwin, James (Arthur) 1924-1987... **CLC 1, 2, 3, 4, 5, 8, 13, 15, 17, 42, 50, 67, 90; BLC 1; DA; DAB; DAC; DAM MST, MULT, NOV, POP; DC 1; SSC 10, 33; WLC**
See also AAYA 4; BW 1; CA 1-4R; 124; CABS 1; CANR 3, 24; CDALB 1941-1968; DLB 2, 7, 33; DLBY 87; MTCW 1; SATA 9; SATA-Obit 54

Ballard, J(ames) G(raham) 1930- .... **CLC 3, 6, 14, 36; DAM NOV, POP; SSC 1**
See also AAYA 3; CA 5-8R; CANR 15, 39, 65; DLB 14; MTCW 1; SATA 93

Balmont, Konstantin (Dmitriyevich) 1867-1943 .... **TCLC 11**
See also CA 109; 155

Baltausis, Vincas
See Mikszath, Kalman

Balzac, Honore de 1799-1850 ....**NCLC 5, 35, 53; DA; DAB; DAC; DAM MST, NOV; SSC 5; WLC**
See also DLB 119

Bambara, Toni Cade 1939-1995 .... **CLC 19, 88; BLC 1; DA; DAC; DAM MST, MULT; WLCS**
See also AAYA 5; BW 2; CA 29-32R; 150; CANR 24, 49; DLB 38; MTCW 1

Bamdad, A.
See Shamlu, Ahmad

Banat, D. R.
See Bradbury, Ray (Douglas)

Bancroft, Laura
See Baum, L(yman) Frank

Banim, John 1798-1842................ **NCLC 13**
See also DLB 116, 158, 159

Banim, Michael 1796-1874............ **NCLC 13**
See also DLB 158, 159

Banjo, The
See Paterson, A(ndrew) B(arton)

Banks, Iain
See Banks, Iain M(enzies)

Banks, Iain M(enzies) 1954- .... **CLC 34**
See also CA 123; 128; CANR 61; DLB 194; INT 128

Banks, Lynne Reid.................... **CLC 23**
See also Reid Banks, Lynne

Banks, Russell 1940- ....**CLC 37, 72**
See also CA 65-68; CAAS 15; CANR 19, 52, 73; DLB 130

Banville, John 1945-...................... **CLC 46**
See also CA 117; 128; DLB 14; INT 128

Banville, Theodore (Faullain) de 1832-1891 ....**NCLC 9**

Baraka, Amiri 1934- ....**CLC 1, 2, 3, 5, 10, 14, 33, 115; BLC 1; DA; DAC; DAM MST, MULT, POET, POP; DC 6; PC 4; WLCS**
See also Jones, LeRoi

Barbauld, Anna Laetitia 1743-1825 ....**NCLC 50**
See also DLB 107, 109, 142, 158

Barbellion, W. N. P...................... **TCLC 24**
See also Cummings, Bruce F(rederick)

Barbera, Jack (Vincent) 1945- .... **CLC 44**
See also CA 110; CANR 45

Barbey d'Aurevilly, Jules Amedee 1808-1889 .... **NCLC 1; SSC 17**
See also DLB 119

Barbusse, Henri 1873-1935.............**TCLC 5**
See also CA 105; 154; DLB 65

Barclay, Bill
See Moorcock, Michael (John)

Barclay, William Ewert
See Moorcock, Michael (John)

Barea, Arturo 1897-1957.............. **TCLC 14**
See also CA 111

Barfoot, Joan 1946-...................... **CLC 18**
See also CA 105

Baring, Maurice 1874-1945............**TCLC 8**
See also CA 105; 168; DLB 34

Baring-Gould, Sabine 1834-1924.... **TCLC 88**
See also DLB 156, 190

Barker, Clive 1952- .... **CLC 52; DAM POP**
See also AAYA 10; BEST 90:3; CA 121; 129; CANR 71; INT 129; MTCW 1

Barker, George Granville 1913-1991 ..... **CLC 8, 48; DAM POET**
See also CA 9-12R; 135; CANR 7, 38; DLB 20; MTCW 1

Barker, Harley Granville
See Granville-Barker, Harley

Barker, Howard 1946- .... **CLC 37**
See also CA 102; DLB 13

Barker, Jane 1652-1732.....................**LC 42**

Barker, Pat(ricia) 1943- ....**CLC 32, 94**
See also CA 117; 122; CANR 50; INT 122

Barlach, Ernst 1870-1938 .... **TCLC 84**
See also DLB 56, 118

Beerbohm, Max
See Beerbohm, (Henry) Max(imilian)

Beerbohm, (Henry) Max(imilian)
1872-1956 .... **TCLC 1, 24**
See also CA 104; 154; DLB 34, 100

Beer-Hofmann, Richard 1866-1945 .... **TCLC 60**
See also CA 160; DLB 81

Begiebing, Robert J(ohn) 1946- .... **CLC 70**
See also CA 122; CANR 40

Behan, Brendan 1923-1964 .... **CLC 1, 8, 11, 15, 79; DAM DRAM**
See also CA 73-76; CANR 33; CDBLB 1945-1960; DLB 13; MTCW 1

Behn, Aphra 1640(?)-1689 .... **LC 1, 30, 42; DA; DAB; DAC; DAM DRAM, MST, NOV, POET; DC 4; PC 13; WLC**
See also DLB 39, 80, 131

Behrman, S(amuel) N(athaniel)
1893-1973 .... **CLC 40**
See also CA 13-16; 45-48; CAP 1; DLB 7, 44

Belasco, David 1853-1931 .... **TCLC 3**
See also CA 104; 168; DLB 7

Belcheva, Elisaveta 1893- .... **CLC 10**
See also Bagryana, Elisaveta

Beldone, Phil "Cheech"
See Ellison, Harlan (Jay)

Beleno
See Azuela, Mariano

Belinski, Vissarion Grigoryevich
1811-1848 ....**NCLC 5**
See also DLB 198

Belitt, Ben 1911-........................... **CLC 22**
See also CA 13-16R; CAAS 4; CANR 7; DLB 5

Bell, Gertrude (Margaret Lowthian)
1868-1926 .... **TCLC 67**
See also CA 167; DLB 174

Bell, J. Freeman
See Zangwill, Israel

Bell, James Madison 1826-1902 .... **TCLC 43; BLC 1; DAM MULT**
See also BW 1; CA 122; 124; DLB 50

Bell, Madison Smartt 1957- ...... **CLC 41, 102**
See also CA 111; CANR 28, 54, 73

Bell, Marvin (Hartley) 1937- .... **CLC 8, 31; DAM POET**
See also CA 21-24R; CAAS 14; CANR 59; DLB 5; MTCW 1

Bell, W. L. D.
See Mencken, H(enry) L(ouis)

Bellamy, Atwood C.
See Mencken, H(enry) L(ouis)

Bellamy, Edward 1850-1898............**NCLC 4**
See also DLB 12

Bellin, Edward J.
See Kuttner, Henry

Belloc, (Joseph) Hilaire (Pierre Sebastien Rene Swanton) 1870-1953.......... **TCLC 7, 18; DAM POET; PC 24**
See also CA 106; 152; DLB 19, 100, 141, 174; YABC 1

Belloc, Joseph Peter Rene Hilaire
See Belloc, (Joseph) Hilaire (Pierre Sebastien Rene Swanton)

Belloc, Joseph Pierre Hilaire
See Belloc, (Joseph) Hilaire (Pierre Sebastien Rene Swanton)

Belloc, M. A.
See Lowndes, Marie Adelaide (Belloc)

Bellow, Saul 1915- ....**CLC 1, 2, 3, 6, 8, 10, 13, 15, 25, 33, 34, 63, 79; DA; DAB; DAC; DAM MST, NOV, POP; SSC 14; WLC**
See also AITN 2; BEST 89:3; CA 5-8R; CABS 1; CANR 29, 53; CDALB 1941-1968; DLB 2, 28; DLBD 3; DLBY 82; MTCW 1

Belser, Reimond Karel Maria de 1929-
See Ruyslinck, Ward

Bely, Andrey .... **TCLC 7; PC 11**
See also Bugayev, Boris Nikolayevich

Belyi, Andrei
See Bugayev, Boris Nikolayevich

Benary, Margot
See Benary-Isbert, Margot

Benary-Isbert, Margot 1889-1979 .... **CLC 12**
See also CA 5-8R; 89-92; CANR 4, 72; CLR 12; MAICYA; SATA 2; SATA-Obit 21

Benavente (y Martinez), Jacinto
1866-1954 .... **TCLC 3; DAM DRAM, MULT**
See also CA 106; 131; HW; MTCW 1

Benchley, Peter (Bradford) 1940- .... **CLC 4, 8; DAM NOV, POP**
See also AAYA 14; AITN 2; CA 17-20R; CANR 12, 35, 66; MTCW 1; SATA 3, 89

Benchley, Robert (Charles)
1889-1945 .... **TCLC 1, 55**
See also CA 105; 153; DLB 11

Benda, Julien 1867-1956 .... **TCLC 60**
See also CA 120; 154

Benedict, Ruth (Fulton) 1887-1948 ..... **TCLC 60**
See also CA 158

Benedict, Saint c. 480-c. 547 .... **CMLC 29**

Benedikt, Michael 1935-.............. **CLC 4, 14**
See also CA 13-16R; CANR 7; DLB 5

Benet, Juan 1927-........................ **CLC 28**
See also CA 143

Benet, Stephen Vincent 1898-1943 ...... **TCLC 7; DAM POET; SSC 10**
See also CA 104; 152; DLB 4, 48, 102; DLBY 97; YABC 1

Benet, William Rose 1886-1950.......... **TCLC 28; DAM POET**
See also CA 118; 152; DLB 45

Benford, Gregory (Albert) 1941-...... **CLC 52**
See also CA 69-72; CAAS 27; CANR 12, 24, 49; DLBY 82

Bengtsson, Frans (Gunnar)
1894-1954 .... **TCLC 48**
See also CA 170

Benjamin, David
See Slavitt, David R(ytman)

Benjamin, Lois
See Gould, Lois

Benjamin, Walter 1892-1940 .... **TCLC 39**
See also CA 164

Benn, Gottfried 1886-1956.............. **TCLC 3**
See also CA 106; 153; DLB 56

Bennett, Alan 1934- .... **CLC 45, 77; DAB; DAM MST**
See also CA 103; CANR 35, 55; MTCW 1

Bennett, (Enoch) Arnold 1867-1931 .... **TCLC 5, 20**
See also CA 106; 155; CDBLB 1890-1914; DLB 10, 34, 98, 135

Bennett, Elizabeth
See Mitchell, Margaret (Munnerlyn)

Bennett, George Harold 1930-
See Bennett, Hal

Bennett, Hal...............................**CLC 5**
See also Bennett, George Harold

Bennett, Jay 1912- .... **CLC 35**
See also AAYA 10; CA 69-72; CANR 11, 42; JRDA; SAAS 4; SATA 41, 87; SATA-Brief 27

Bennett, Louise (Simone) 1919- .... **CLC 28; BLC 1; DAM MULT**
See also BW 2; CA 151; DLB 117

Benson, E(dward) F(rederic)
1867-1940 .... **TCLC 27**
See also CA 114; 157; DLB 135, 153

Benson, Jackson J. 1930-................ **CLC 34**
See also CA 25-28R; DLB 111

Benson, Sally 1900-1972................. **CLC 17**
See also CA 19-20; 37-40R; CAP 1; SATA 1, 35; SATA-Obit 27

Benson, Stella 1892-1933 .... **TCLC 17**
See also CA 117; 155; DLB 36, 162

Bentham, Jeremy 1748-1832 .... **NCLC 38**
See also DLB 107, 158

Bentley, E(dmund) C(lerihew)
1875-1956 .... **TCLC 12**
See also CA 108; DLB 70

Bentley, Eric (Russell) 1916- .... **CLC 24**
See also CA 5-8R; CANR 6, 67; INT CANR-6

Beranger, Pierre Jean de 1780-1857....**NCLC 34**

Berdyaev, Nicolas
See Berdyaev, Nikolai (Aleksandrovich)

Berdyaev, Nikolai (Aleksandrovich)
1874-1948 .... **TCLC 67**
See also CA 120; 157

Berdyayev, Nikolai (Aleksandrovich)
See Berdyaev, Nikolai (Aleksandrovich)

Berendt, John (Lawrence) 1939- ...... **CLC 86**
See also CA 146; CANR 75

Beresford, J(ohn) D(avys) 1873-1947... **TCLC 81**
See also CA 112; 155; DLB 162, 178, 197

Bergelson, David 1884-1952 .... **TCLC 81**

Berger, Colonel
See Malraux, (Georges-)Andre

Berger, John (Peter) 1926-.......... **CLC 2, 19**
See also CA 81-84; CANR 51; DLB 14

Blais, Marie-Claire 1939- .... **CLC
2, 4, 6, 13, 22; DAC; DAM MST**
See also CA 21-24R; CAAS 4; CANR 38, 75;
DLB 53; MTCW 1

Blaise, Clark 1940- .... **CLC 29**
See also AITN 2; CA 53-56; CAAS 3; CANR
5, 66; DLB 53

Blake, Fairley
See De Voto, Bernard (Augustine)

Blake, Nicholas
See Day Lewis, C(ecil)

Blake, William 1757-1827 .... **NCLC
13, 37, 57; DA; DAB; DAC; DAM
MST, POET; PC 12; WLC**
See also CDBLB 1789-1832; CLR 52; DLB
93, 163; MAICYA; SATA 30

Blasco Ibanez, Vicente 1867-1928 .... **TCLC
12; DAM NOV**
See also CA 110; 131; HW; MTCW 1

Blatty, William Peter 1928- .... **CLC
2; DAM POP**
See also CA 5-8R; CANR 9

Bleeck, Oliver
See Thomas, Ross (Elmore)

Blessing, Lee 1949- .... **CLC 54**

Blish, James (Benjamin) 1921-1975... **CLC 14**
See also CA 1-4R; 57-60; CANR 3; DLB 8;
MTCW 1; SATA 66

Bliss, Reginald
See Wells, H(erbert) G(eorge)

Blixen, Karen (Christentze Dinesen)
1885-1962
See Dinesen, Isak

Bloch, Robert (Albert) 1917-1994 ..... **CLC 33**
See also CA 5-8R; 146; CAAS 20; CANR 5;
DLB 44; INT CANR-5; SATA 12; SATA-
Obit 82

Blok, Alexander (Alexandrovich)
1880-1921 .... **TCLC 5; PC 21**
See also CA 104

Blom, Jan
See Breytenbach, Breyten

Bloom, Harold 1930- .... **CLC 24, 103**
See also CA 13-16R; CANR 39, 75; DLB 67

Bloomfield, Aurelius
See Bourne, Randolph S(illiman)

Blount, Roy (Alton), Jr. 1941- .... **CLC 38**
See also CA 53-56; CANR 10, 28, 61; INT
CANR-28; MTCW 1

Bloy, Leon 1846-1917 .... **TCLC 22**
See also CA 121; DLB 123

Blume, Judy (Sussman) 1938- .... **CLC
12, 30; DAM NOV, POP**
See also AAYA 3, 26; CA 29-32R; CANR
13, 37, 66; CLR 2, 15; DLB 52; JRDA;
MAICYA; MTCW 1; SATA 2, 31, 79

Blunden, Edmund (Charles)
1896-1974 .... **CLC 2, 56**
See also CA 17-18; 45-48; CANR 54; CAP
2; DLB 20, 100, 155; MTCW 1

Bly, Robert (Elwood) 1926- .... **CLC
1, 2, 5, 10, 15, 38; DAM POET**
See also CA 5-8R; CANR 41, 73; DLB 5;
MTCW 1

Boas, Franz 1858-1942................ **TCLC 56**
See also CA 115

Bobette
See Simenon, Georges (Jacques Christian)

Boccaccio, Giovanni 1313-1375......... **CMLC
13; SSC 10**

Bochco, Steven 1943- .... **CLC 35**
See also AAYA 11; CA 124; 138

Bodel, Jean 1167(?)-1210............. **CMLC 28**

Bodenheim, Maxwell 1892-1954..... **TCLC 44**
See also CA 110; DLB 9, 45

Bodker, Cecil 1927- .... **CLC 21**
See also CA 73-76; CANR 13, 44; CLR 23;
MAICYA; SATA 14

Boell, Heinrich (Theodor) 1917-1985 .... **CLC
2, 3, 6, 9, 11, 15, 27, 32, 72; DA; DAB;
DAC; DAM MST, NOV; SSC 23; WLC**
See also CA 21-24R; 116; CANR 24; DLB
69; DLBY 85; MTCW 1

Boerne, Alfred
See Doeblin, Alfred

Boethius 480(?)-524(?) .... **CMLC 15**
See also DLB 115

Bogan, Louise 1897-1970.................... **CLC
4, 39, 46, 93; DAM POET; PC 12**
See also CA 73-76; 25-28R; CANR 33; DLB
45, 169; MTCW 1

Bogarde, Dirk............................. **CLC 19**
See also Van Den Bogarde, Derek Jules Gas-
pard Ulric Niven

Bogosian, Eric 1953- .... **CLC 45**
See also CA 138

Bograd, Larry 1953- .... **CLC 35**
See also CA 93-96; CANR 57; SAAS 21;
SATA 33, 89

Boiardo, Matteo Maria 1441-1494........ **LC 6**

Boileau-Despreaux, Nicolas 1636-1711... **LC 3**

Bojer, Johan 1872-1959................ **TCLC 64**

Boland, Eavan (Aisling) 1944- .... **CLC
40, 67, 113; DAM POET**
See also CA 143; CANR 61; DLB 40

Boll, Heinrich
See Boell, Heinrich (Theodor)

Bolt, Lee
See Faust, Frederick (Schiller)

Bolt, Robert (Oxton) 1924-1995 .... **CLC
14; DAM DRAM**
See also CA 17-20R; 147; CANR 35, 67;
DLB 13; MTCW 1

Bombet, Louis-Alexandre-Cesar
See Stendhal

Bomkauf
See Kaufman, Bob (Garnell)

Bonaventura .... **NCLC 35**
See also DLB 90

Bond, Edward 1934- .... **CLC
4, 6, 13, 23; DAM DRAM**
See also CA 25-28R; CANR 38, 67; DLB 13;
MTCW 1

Bonham, Frank 1914-1989.............. **CLC 12**
See also AAYA 1; CA 9-12R; CANR 4, 36;
JRDA; MAICYA; SAAS 3; SATA 1, 49;
SATA-Obit 62

Bonnefoy, Yves 1923-........................**CLC
9, 15, 58; DAM MST, POET**
See also CA 85-88; CANR 33, 75; MTCW 1

Bontemps, Arna(ud Wendell)
1902-1973 .... **CLC 1,
18; BLC 1; DAM MULT, NOV, POET**
See also BW 1; CA 1-4R; 41-44R; CANR 4,
35; CLR 6; DLB 48, 51; JRDA; MAICYA;
MTCW 1; SATA 2, 44; SATA-Obit 24

Booth, Martin 1944-...................... **CLC 13**
See also CA 93-96; CAAS 2

Booth, Philip 1925- .... **CLC 23**
See also CA 5-8R; CANR 5; DLBY 82

Booth, Wayne C(layson) 1921-......... **CLC 24**
See also CA 1-4R; CAAS 5; CANR 3, 43;
DLB 67

Borchert, Wolfgang 1921-1947 ....**TCLC 5**
See also CA 104; DLB 69, 124

Borel, Petrus 1809-1859 .... **NCLC 41**

Borges, Jorge Luis 1899-1986.............. **CLC
1, 2, 3, 4, 6, 8, 9, 10, 13, 19, 44, 48, 83;
DA; DAB; DAC; DAM MST, MULT;
HLC; PC 22; SSC 4; WLC**
See also AAYA 26; CA 21-24R; CANR 19,
33, 75; DLB 113; DLBY 86; HW; MTCW
1

Borowski, Tadeusz 1922-1951.......... **TCLC 9**
See also CA 106; 154

Borrow, George (Henry) 1803-1881 ....**NCLC
9**
See also DLB 21, 55, 166

Bosman, Herman Charles 1905-1951... **TCLC
49**
See also Malan, Herman

Bosschere, Jean de 1878(?)-1953 .... **TCLC 19**
See also CA 115

Boswell, James 1740-1795.................. **LC 4;
DA; DAB; DAC; DAM MST; WLC**
See also CDBLB 1660-1789; DLB 104, 142

Bottoms, David 1949- .... **CLC 53**
See also CA 105; CANR 22; DLB 120;
DLBY 83

Boucicault, Dion 1820-1890........... **NCLC 41**

Boucolon, Maryse 1937(?)-
See Conde, Maryse

Bourget, Paul (Charles Joseph)
1852-1935 .... **TCLC 12**
See also CA 107; DLB 123

Bourjaily, Vance (Nye) 1922-........ **CLC 8, 62**
See also CA 1-4R; CAAS 1; CANR 2, 72;
DLB 2, 143

Bourne, Randolph S(illiman)
1886-1918 .... **TCLC 16**
See also CA 117; 155; DLB 63

Bova, Ben(jamin William) 1932- ...... **CLC 45**
See also AAYA 16; CA 5-8R; CAAS 18;
CANR 11, 56; CLR 3; DLBY 81; INT
CANR-11; MAICYA; MTCW 1; SATA 6,
68

Brodsky, Joseph 1940-1996 .... **CLC 4, 6, 13, 36, 100; PC 9**
See also Brodskii, Iosif; Brodsky, Iosif Alexandrovich

Brodsky, Michael (Mark) 1948- .... **CLC 19**
See also CA 102; CANR 18, 41, 58

Bromell, Henry 1947- .... **CLC 5**
See also CA 53-56; CANR 9

Bromfield, Louis (Brucker) 1896-1956 .... **TCLC 11**
See also CA 107; 155; DLB 4, 9, 86

Broner, E(sther) M(asserman) 1930- .... **CLC 19**
See also CA 17-20R; CANR 8, 25, 72; DLB 28

Bronk, William 1918- .... **CLC 10**
See also CA 89-92; CANR 23; DLB 165

Bronstein, Lev Davidovich
See Trotsky, Leon

Bronte, Anne 1820-1849 .... **NCLC 71**
See also DLB 21, 199

Bronte, Charlotte 1816-1855 .... **NCLC 3, 8, 33, 58; DA; DAB; DAC; DAM MST, NOV; WLC**
See also AAYA 17; CDBLB 1832-1890; DLB 21, 159, 199

Bronte, Emily (Jane) 1818-1848 .... **NCLC 16, 35; DA; DAB; DAC; DAM MST, NOV, POET; PC 8; WLC**
See also AAYA 17; CDBLB 1832-1890; DLB 21, 32, 199

Brooke, Frances 1724-1789 .... **LC 6, 48**
See also DLB 39, 99

Brooke, Henry 1703(?)-1783 .... **LC 1**
See also DLB 39

Brooke, Rupert (Chawner) 1887-1915 .... **TCLC 2, 7; DA; DAB; DAC; DAM MST, POET; PC 24; WLC**
See also CA 104; 132; CANR 61; CDBLB 1914-1945; DLB 19; MTCW 1

Brooke-Haven, P.
See Wodehouse, P(elham) G(renville)

Brooke-Rose, Christine 1926(?)- ...... **CLC 40**
See also CA 13-16R; CANR 58; DLB 14

Brookner, Anita 1928- .... **CLC 32, 34, 51; DAB; DAM POP**
See also CA 114; 120; CANR 37, 56; DLB 194; DLBY 87; MTCW 1

Brooks, Cleanth 1906-1994 ...**CLC 24, 86, 110**
See also CA 17-20R; 145; CANR 33, 35; DLB 63; DLBY 94; INT CANR-35; MTCW 1

Brooks, George
See Baum, L(yman) Frank

Brooks, Gwendolyn 1917- .... **CLC 1, 2, 4, 5, 15, 49; BLC 1; DA; DAC; DAM MST, MULT, POET; PC 7; WLC**
See also AAYA 20; AITN 1; BW 2; CA 1-4R; CANR 1, 27, 52, 75; CDALB 1941-1968; CLR 27; DLB 5, 76, 165; MTCW 1; SATA 6

Brooks, Mel .... **CLC 12**
See also Kaminsky, Melvin

Brooks, Peter 1938- .... **CLC 34**
See also CA 45-48; CANR 1

Brooks, Van Wyck 1886-1963 .... **CLC 29**
See also CA 1-4R; CANR 6; DLB 45, 63, 103

Brophy, Brigid (Antonia) 1929-1995 ..... **CLC 6, 11, 29, 105**
See also CA 5-8R; 149; CAAS 4; CANR 25, 53; DLB 14; MTCW 1

Brosman, Catharine Savage 1934- ......**CLC 9**
See also CA 61-64; CANR 21, 46

Brossard, Nicole 1943- ....**CLC 115**
See also CA 122; CAAS 16; DLB 53

Brother Antoninus
See Everson, William (Oliver)

The Brothers Quay
See Quay, Stephen; Quay, Timothy

Broughton, T(homas) Alan 1936- ..... **CLC 19**
See also CA 45-48; CANR 2, 23, 48

Broumas, Olga 1949- ....**CLC 10, 73**
See also CA 85-88; CANR 20, 69

Brown, Alan 1950- .... **CLC 99**
See also CA 156

Brown, Charles Brockden 1771-1810 ....**NCLC 22, 74**
See also CDALB 1640-1865; DLB 37, 59, 73

Brown, Christy 1932-1981 .... **CLC 63**
See also CA 105; 104; CANR 72; DLB 14

Brown, Claude 1937- .... **CLC 30; BLC 1; DAM MULT**
See also AAYA 7; BW 1; CA 73-76

Brown, Dee (Alexander) 1908- .... **CLC 18, 47; DAM POP**
See also CA 13-16R; CAAS 6; CANR 11, 45, 60; DLBY 80; MTCW 1; SATA 5

Brown, George
See Wertmueller, Lina

Brown, George Douglas 1869-1902 ..... **TCLC 28**
See also CA 162

Brown, George Mackay 1921-1996 .... **CLC 5, 48, 100**
See also CA 21-24R; 151; CAAS 6; CANR 12, 37, 67; DLB 14, 27, 139; MTCW 1; SATA 35

Brown, (William) Larry 1951- .... **CLC 73**
See also CA 130; 134; INT 133

Brown, Moses
See Barrett, William (Christopher)

Brown, Rita Mae 1944- .... **CLC 18, 43, 79; DAM NOV, POP**
See also CA 45-48; CANR 2, 11, 35, 62; INT CANR-11; MTCW 1

Brown, Roderick (Langmere) Haig-
See Haig-Brown, Roderick (Langmere)

Brown, Rosellen 1939- .... **CLC 32**
See also CA 77-80; CAAS 10; CANR 14, 44

Brown, Sterling Allen 1901-1989 .... **CLC 1, 23, 59; BLC 1; DAM MULT, POET**
See also BW 1; CA 85-88; 127; CANR 26, 74; DLB 48, 51, 63; MTCW 1

Brown, Will
See Ainsworth, William Harrison

Brown, William Wells 1813-1884 .... **NCLC 2; BLC 1; DAM MULT; DC 1**
See also DLB 3, 50

Browne, (Clyde) Jackson 1948(?)- .... **CLC 21**
See also CA 120

Browning, Elizabeth Barrett 1806-1861 .... **NCLC 1, 16, 61, 66; DA; DAB; DAC; DAM MST, POET; PC 6; WLC**
See also CDBLB 1832-1890; DLB 32, 199

Browning, Robert 1812-1889 .... **NCLC 19; DA; DAB; DAC; DAM MST, POET; PC 2; WLCS**
See also CDBLB 1832-1890; DLB 32, 163; YABC 1

Browning, Tod 1882-1962 .... **CLC 16**
See also CA 141; 117

Brownson, Orestes Augustus 1803-1876 .... **NCLC 50**
See also DLB 1, 59, 73

Bruccoli, Matthew J(oseph) 1931- .... **CLC 34**
See also CA 9-12R; CANR 7; DLB 103

Bruce, Lenny .... **CLC 21**
See also Schneider, Leonard Alfred

Bruin, John
See Brutus, Dennis

Brulard, Henri
See Stendhal

Brulls, Christian
See Simenon, Georges (Jacques Christian)

Brunner, John (Kilian Houston) 1934-1995 .... **CLC 8, 10; DAM POP**
See also CA 1-4R; 149; CAAS 8; CANR 2, 37; MTCW 1

Bruno, Giordano 1548-1600 ....**LC 27**

Brutus, Dennis 1924- .... **CLC 43; BLC 1; DAM MULT, POET; PC 24**
See also BW 2; CA 49-52; CAAS 14; CANR 2, 27, 42; DLB 117

Bryan, C(ourtlandt) D(ixon) B(arnes) 1936- .... **CLC 29**
See also CA 73-76; CANR 13, 68; DLB 185; INT CANR-13

Bryan, Michael
See Moore, Brian

Bryant, William Cullen 1794-1878 ...... **NCLC 6, 46; DA; DAB; DAC; DAM MST, POET; PC 20**
See also CDALB 1640-1865; DLB 3, 43, 59, 189

Bryusov, Valery Yakovlevich 1873-1924 .... **TCLC 10**
See also CA 107; 155

Buchan, John 1875-1940 .... **TCLC 41; DAB; DAM POP**
See also CA 108; 145; DLB 34, 70, 156; YABC 2

Buchanan, George 1506-1582 .... **LC 4**
See also DLB 152

Buchheim, Lothar-Guenther 1918- .....**CLC 6**
See also CA 85-88

Buchner, (Karl) Georg 1813-1837 ... **NCLC 26**

Buchwald, Art(hur) 1925- .... **CLC 33**
See also AITN 1; CA 5-8R; CANR 21, 67;
MTCW 1; SATA 10

Buck, Pearl S(ydenstricker)
1892-1973 ....**CLC 7, 11,
18; DA; DAB; DAC; DAM MST, NOV**
See also AITN 1; CA 1-4R; 41-44R; CANR
1, 34; DLB 9, 102; MTCW 1; SATA 1, 25

Buckler, Ernest 1908-1984 .... **CLC
13; DAC; DAM MST**
See also CA 11-12; 114; CAP 1; DLB 68;
SATA 47

Buckley, Vincent (Thomas) 1925-1988 ... **CLC
57**
See also CA 101

Buckley, William F(rank), Jr. 1925- ...... **CLC
7, 18, 37; DAM POP**
See also AITN 1; CA 1-4R; CANR 1, 24,
53; DLB 137; DLBY 80; INT CANR-24;
MTCW 1

Buechner, (Carl) Frederick 1926- .... **CLC
2, 4, 6, 9; DAM NOV**
See also CA 13-16R; CANR 11, 39, 64;
DLBY 80; INT CANR-11; MTCW 1

Buell, John (Edward) 1927- .... **CLC 10**
See also CA 1-4R; CANR 71; DLB 53

Buero Vallejo, Antonio 1916-.......**CLC 15, 46**
See also CA 106; CANR 24, 49, 75; HW;
MTCW 1

Bufalino, Gesualdo 1920(?)- .... **CLC 74**
See also DLB 196

Bugayev, Boris Nikolayevich
1880-1934 .... **TCLC 7; PC 11**
See also Bely, Andrey

Bukowski, Charles 1920-1994..... **CLC 2, 5, 9,
41, 82, 108; DAM NOV, POET; PC 18**
See also CA 17-20R; 144; CANR 40, 62;
DLB 5, 130, 169; MTCW 1

Bulgakov, Mikhail (Afanas'evich)
1891-1940 .... **TCLC
2, 16; DAM DRAM, NOV; SSC 18**
See also CA 105; 152

Bulgya, Alexander Alexandrovich
1901-1956 .... **TCLC 53**
See also Fadeyev, Alexander

Bullins, Ed 1935-.....................**CLC 1, 5, 7;
BLC 1; DAM DRAM, MULT; DC 6**
See also BW 2; CA 49-52; CAAS 16; CANR
24, 46, 73; DLB 7, 38; MTCW 1

**Bulwer-Lytton, Edward (George Earle
Lytton)** 1803-1873.............**NCLC 1, 45**
See also DLB 21

Bunin, Ivan Alexeyevich 1870-1953 .... **TCLC
6; SSC 5**
See also CA 104

Bunting, Basil 1900-1985.................... **CLC
10, 39, 47; DAM POET**
See also CA 53-56; 115; CANR 7; DLB 20

Bunuel, Luis 1900-1983..................... **CLC
16, 80; DAM MULT; HLC**
See also CA 101; 110; CANR 32; HW

Bunyan, John 1628-1688 .... **LC 4;
DA; DAB; DAC; DAM MST; WLC**
See also CDBLB 1660-1789; DLB 39

Burckhardt, Jacob (Christoph)
1818-1897 .... **NCLC 49**

Burford, Eleanor
See Hibbert, Eleanor Alice Burford

Burgess, Anthony .... **CLC 1, 2, 4, 5,
8, 10, 13, 15, 22, 40, 62, 81, 94; DAB**
See also Wilson, John (Anthony) Burgess

Burke, Edmund 1729(?)-1797........**LC 7, 36;
DA; DAB; DAC; DAM MST; WLC**
See also DLB 104

Burke, Kenneth (Duva) 1897-1993........ **CLC
2, 24**
See also CA 5-8R; 143; CANR 39, 74; DLB
45, 63; MTCW 1

Burke, Leda
See Garnett, David

Burke, Ralph
See Silverberg, Robert

Burke, Thomas 1886-1945 .... **TCLC 63**
See also CA 113; 155; DLB 197

Burney, Fanny 1752-1840.........**NCLC 12, 54**
See also DLB 39

Burns, Robert 1759-1796..................... **LC
3, 29, 40; DA; DAB; DAC; DAM
MST, POET; PC 6; WLC**
See also CDBLB 1789-1832; DLB 109

Burns, Tex
See L'Amour, Louis (Dearborn)

Burnshaw, Stanley 1906-.........**CLC 3, 13, 44**
See also CA 9-12R; DLB 48; DLBY 97

Burr, Anne 1937-...........................**CLC 6**
See also CA 25-28R

Burroughs, Edgar Rice 1875-1950 ...... **TCLC
2, 32; DAM NOV**
See also AAYA 11; CA 104; 132; DLB 8;
MTCW 1; SATA 41

Burroughs, William S(eward)
1914-1997 .... **CLC
1, 2, 5, 15, 22, 42, 75, 109; DA; DAB;
DAC; DAM MST, NOV, POP; WLC**
See also AITN 2; CA 9-12R; 160; CANR
20, 52; DLB 2, 8, 16, 152; DLBY 81, 97;
MTCW 1

Burton, Richard F. 1821-1890........ **NCLC 42**
See also DLB 55, 184

Busch, Frederick 1941-...... **CLC 7, 10, 18, 47**
See also CA 33-36R; CAAS 1; CANR 45, 73;
DLB 6

Bush, Ronald 1946-....................... **CLC 34**
See also CA 136

Bustos, F(rancisco)
See Borges, Jorge Luis

Bustos Domecq, H(onorio)
See Bioy Casares, Adolfo; Borges, Jorge Luis

Butler, Octavia E(stelle) 1947- .... **CLC
38; BLCS; DAM MULT, POP**
See also AAYA 18; BW 2; CA 73-76; CANR
12, 24, 38, 73; DLB 33; MTCW 1; SATA
84

Butler, Robert Olen (Jr.) 1945- .... **CLC
81; DAM POP**
See also CA 112; CANR 66; DLB 173; INT
112

Butler, Samuel 1612-1680 .... **LC 16, 43**
See also DLB 101, 126

Butler, Samuel 1835-1902 ... **TCLC 1, 33; DA;
DAB; DAC; DAM MST, NOV; WLC**
See also CA 143; CDBLB 1890-1914; DLB
18, 57, 174

Butler, Walter C.
See Faust, Frederick (Schiller)

Butor, Michel (Marie Francois) 1926- ... **CLC
1, 3, 8, 11, 15**
See also CA 9-12R; CANR 33, 66; DLB 83;
MTCW 1

Butts, Mary 1892(?)-1937 .... **TCLC 77**
See also CA 148

Buzo, Alexander (John) 1944- .... **CLC 61**
See also CA 97-100; CANR 17, 39, 69

Buzzati, Dino 1906-1972................. **CLC 36**
See also CA 160; 33-36R; DLB 177

Byars, Betsy (Cromer) 1928-........... **CLC 35**
See also AAYA 19; CA 33-36R; CANR
18, 36, 57; CLR 1, 16; DLB 52; INT
CANR-18; JRDA; MAICYA; MTCW 1;
SAAS 1; SATA 4, 46, 80

Byatt, A(ntonia) S(usan Drabble)
1936- ......**CLC 19, 65; DAM NOV, POP**
See also CA 13-16R; CANR 13, 33, 50, 75;
DLB 14, 194; MTCW 1

Byrne, David 1952-....................... **CLC 26**
See also CA 127

Byrne, John Keyes 1926-
See Leonard, Hugh

Byron, George Gordon (Noel)
1788-1824 ....**NCLC 2, 12; DA; DAB;
DAC; DAM MST, POET; PC 16; WLC**
See also CDBLB 1789-1832; DLB 96, 110

Byron, Robert 1905-1941 .... **TCLC 67**
See also CA 160; DLB 195

C. 3. 3.
See Wilde, Oscar (Fingal O'Flahertie Wills)

Caballero, Fernan 1796-1877 .... **NCLC 10**

Cabell, Branch
See Cabell, James Branch

Cabell, James Branch 1879-1958...... **TCLC 6**
See also CA 105; 152; DLB 9, 78

Cable, George Washington
1844-1925 .... **TCLC 4; SSC 4**
See also CA 104; 155; DLB 12, 74; DLBD
13

Cabral de Melo Neto, Joao 1920- .... **CLC
76; DAM MULT**
See also CA 151

Cabrera Infante, G(uillermo) 1929- ...... **CLC
5, 25, 45; DAM MULT; HLC**
See also CA 85-88; CANR 29, 65; DLB 113;
HW; MTCW 1

Cade, Toni
See Bambara, Toni Cade

Cadmus and Harmonia
See Buchan, John

Caedmon fl. 658-680 .... **CMLC 7**
See also DLB 146

Caeiro, Alberto
See Pessoa, Fernando (Antonio Nogueira)

Cage, John (Milton, Jr.) 1912-1992... **CLC 41**
See also CA 13-16R; 169; CANR 9; DLB 193; INT CANR-9

Cahan, Abraham 1860-1951 .... **TCLC 71**
See also CA 108; 154; DLB 9, 25, 28

Cain, G.
See Cabrera Infante, G(uillermo)

Cain, Guillermo
See Cabrera Infante, G(uillermo)

Cain, James M(allahan) 1892-1977....... **CLC 3, 11, 28**
See also AITN 1; CA 17-20R; 73-76; CANR 8, 34, 61; MTCW 1

Caine, Mark
See Raphael, Frederic (Michael)

Calasso, Roberto 1941- .... **CLC 81**
See also CA 143

Calderon de la Barca, Pedro 1600-1681 ... **LC 23; DC 3**

Caldwell, Erskine (Preston) 1903-1987... **CLC 1, 8, 14, 50, 60; DAM NOV; SSC 19**
See also AITN 1; CA 1-4R; 121; CAAS 1; CANR 2, 33; DLB 9, 86; MTCW 1

Caldwell, (Janet Miriam) Taylor (Holland) 1900-1985 .... **CLC 2, 28, 39; DAM NOV, POP**
See also CA 5-8R; 116; CANR 5; DLBD 17

Calhoun, John Caldwell 1782-1850.....**NCLC 15**
See also DLB 3

Calisher, Hortense 1911- .... **CLC 2, 4, 8, 38; DAM NOV; SSC 15**
See also CA 1-4R; CANR 1, 22, 67; DLB 2; INT CANR-22; MTCW 1

Callaghan, Morley Edward 1903-1990... **CLC 3, 14, 41, 65; DAC; DAM MST**
See also CA 9-12R; 132; CANR 33, 73; DLB 68; MTCW 1

Callimachus c. 305B.C.-c. 240B.C. ..... **CMLC 18**
See also DLB 176

Calvin, John 1509-1564.....................**LC 37**

Calvino, Italo 1923-1985 .... **CLC 5, 8, 11, 22, 33, 39, 73; DAM NOV; SSC 3**
See also CA 85-88; 116; CANR 23, 61; DLB 196; MTCW 1

Cameron, Carey 1952-.................... **CLC 59**
See also CA 135

Cameron, Peter 1959-..................... **CLC 44**
See also CA 125; CANR 50

Campana, Dino 1885-1932............ **TCLC 20**
See also CA 117; DLB 114

Campanella, Tommaso 1568-1639 ....**LC 32**

Campbell, John W(ood, Jr.) 1910-1971 .... **CLC 32**
See also CA 21-22; 29-32R; CANR 34; CAP 2; DLB 8; MTCW 1

Campbell, Joseph 1904-1987.......... **CLC 69**
See also AAYA 3; BEST 89:2; CA 1-4R; 124; CANR 3, 28, 61; MTCW 1

Campbell, Maria 1940-..........**CLC 85; DAC**
See also CA 102; CANR 54; NNAL

Campbell, (John) Ramsey 1946- .... **CLC 42; SSC 19**
See also CA 57-60; CANR 7; INT CANR-7

Campbell, (Ignatius) Roy (Dunnachie) 1901-1957 ....**TCLC 5**
See also CA 104; 155; DLB 20

Campbell, Thomas 1777-1844 .... **NCLC 19**
See also DLB 93; 144

Campbell, Wilfred ....**TCLC 9**
See also Campbell, William

Campbell, William 1858(?)-1918
See Campbell, Wilfred

Campion, Jane .... **CLC 95**
See also CA 138

Campos, Alvaro de
See Pessoa, Fernando (Antonio Nogueira)

Camus, Albert 1913-1960 .... **CLC 1, 2, 4, 9, 11, 14, 32, 63, 69; DA; DAB; DAC; DAM DRAM, MST, NOV; DC 2; SSC 9; WLC**
See also CA 89-92; DLB 72; MTCW 1

Canby, Vincent 1924- .... **CLC 13**
See also CA 81-84

Cancale
See Desnos, Robert

Canetti, Elias 1905-1994..................... **CLC 3, 14, 25, 75, 86**
See also CA 21-24R; 146; CANR 23, 61; DLB 85, 124; MTCW 1

Canfield, Dorothea F.
See Fisher, Dorothy (Frances) Canfield

Canfield, Dorothea Frances
See Fisher, Dorothy (Frances) Canfield

Canfield, Dorothy
See Fisher, Dorothy (Frances) Canfield

Canin, Ethan 1960-........................ **CLC 55**
See also CA 131; 135

Cannon, Curt
See Hunter, Evan

Cao, Lan 1961- ....**CLC 109**
See also CA 165

Cape, Judith
See Page, P(atricia) K(athleen)

Capek, Karel 1890-1938.................... **TCLC 6, 37; DA; DAB; DAC; DAM DRAM, MST, NOV; DC 1; WLC**
See also CA 104; 140

Capote, Truman 1924-1984.............. **CLC 1, 3, 8, 13, 19, 34, 38, 58; DA; DAB; DAC; DAM MST, NOV, POP; SSC 2; WLC**
See also CA 5-8R; 113; CANR 18, 62; CDALB 1941-1968; DLB 2, 185; DLBY 80, 84; MTCW 1; SATA 91

Capra, Frank 1897-1991 .... **CLC 16**
See also CA 61-64; 135

Caputo, Philip 1941- .... **CLC 32**
See also CA 73-76; CANR 40

Caragiale, Ion Luca 1852-1912 ...... **TCLC 76**
See also CA 157

Card, Orson Scott 1951-..................... **CLC 44, 47, 50; DAM POP**
See also AAYA 11; CA 102; CANR 27, 47, 73; INT CANR-27; MTCW 1; SATA 83

Cardenal, Ernesto 1925- .... **CLC 31; DAM MULT, POET; HLC; PC 22**
See also CA 49-52; CANR 2, 32, 66; HW; MTCW 1

Cardozo, Benjamin N(athan) 1870-1938 .... **TCLC 65**
See also CA 117; 164

Carducci, Giosue (Alessandro Giuseppe) 1835-1907 .... **TCLC 32**
See also CA 163

Carew, Thomas 1595(?)-1640 ....**LC 13**
See also DLB 126

Carey, Ernestine Gilbreth 1908-....... **CLC 17**
See also CA 5-8R; CANR 71; SATA 2

Carey, Peter 1943- .... **CLC 40, 55, 96**
See also CA 123; 127; CANR 53; INT 127; MTCW 1; SATA 94

Carleton, William 1794-1869...........**NCLC 3**
See also DLB 159

Carlisle, Henry (Coffin) 1926- .... **CLC 33**
See also CA 13-16R; CANR 15

Carlsen, Chris
See Holdstock, Robert P.

Carlson, Ron(ald F.) 1947-.............. **CLC 54**
See also CA 105; CANR 27

Carlyle, Thomas 1795-1881..............**NCLC 70; DA; DAB; DAC; DAM MST**
See also CDBLB 1789-1832; DLB 55; 144

Carman, (William) Bliss 1861-1929 .... **TCLC 7; DAC**
See also CA 104; 152; DLB 92

Carnegie, Dale 1888-1955............. **TCLC 53**

Carossa, Hans 1878-1956 .... **TCLC 48**
See also CA 170; DLB 66

Carpenter, Don(ald Richard) 1931-1995 .... **CLC 41**
See also CA 45-48; 149; CANR 1, 71

Carpenter, Edward 1844-1929....... **TCLC 88**
See also CA 163

Carpentier (y Valmont), Alejo 1904-1980 .... **CLC 8, 11, 38, 110; DAM MULT; HLC**
See also CA 65-68; 97-100; CANR 11, 70; DLB 113; HW

Carr, Caleb 1955(?)-..................... **CLC 86**
See also CA 147; CANR 73

Carr, Emily 1871-1945................. **TCLC 32**
See also CA 159; DLB 68

Carr, John Dickson 1906-1977.......... **CLC 3**
See also Fairbairn, Roger

Carr, Philippa
See Hibbert, Eleanor Alice Burford

Carr, Virginia Spencer 1929-.......... **CLC 34**
See also CA 61-64; DLB 111

Carrere, Emmanuel 1957- .... **CLC 89**

Carrier, Roch 1937- .... **CLC 13, 78; DAC; DAM MST**
See also CA 130; CANR 61; DLB 53

Carroll, James P. 1943(?)-.............. **CLC 38**
See also CA 81-84; CANR 73

Carroll, Jim 1951- .... **CLC 35**
See also AAYA 17; CA 45-48; CANR 42

Chapman, Walker
See Silverberg, Robert

Chappell, Fred (Davis) 1936-.......**CLC 40, 78**
See also CA 5-8R; CAAS 4; CANR 8, 33, 67;
DLB 6, 105

Char, Rene(-Emile) 1907-1988.............**CLC 9, 11, 14, 55; DAM POET**
See also CA 13-16R; 124; CANR 32; MTCW 1

Charby, Jay
See Ellison, Harlan (Jay)

Chardin, Pierre Teilhard de
See Teilhard de Chardin, (Marie Joseph) Pierre

Charles I 1600-1649.........................**LC 13**

Charriere, Isabelle de 1740-1805.... **NCLC 66**

Charyn, Jerome 1937-.............. **CLC 5, 8, 18**
See also CA 5-8R; CAAS 1; CANR 7, 61;
DLBY 83; MTCW 1

Chase, Mary (Coyle) 1907-1981...........**DC 1**
See also CA 77-80; 105; SATA 17; SATA-Obit 29

Chase, Mary Ellen 1887-1973............**CLC 2**
See also CA 13-16; 41-44R; CAP 1; SATA 10

Chase, Nicholas
See Hyde, Anthony

Chateaubriand, Francois Rene de
1768-1848.............................**NCLC 3**
See also DLB 119

Chatterje, Sarat Chandra 1876-1936(?)
See Chatterji, Saratchandra

Chatterji, Bankim Chandra
1838-1894..........................**NCLC 19**

Chatterji, Saratchandra...............TCLC 13
See also Chatterje, Sarat Chandra

Chatterton, Thomas 1752-1770..............**LC 3; DAM POET**
See also DLB 109

Chatwin, (Charles) Bruce 1940-1989.....**CLC 28, 57, 59; DAM POP**
See also AAYA 4; BEST 90:1; CA 85-88;
127; DLB 194

Chaucer, Daniel
See Ford, Ford Madox

Chaucer, Geoffrey 1340(?)-1400.............**LC 17; DA; DAB; DAC; DAM MST, POET; PC 19; WLCS**
See also CDBLB Before 1660; DLB 146

Chaviaras, Strates 1935-
See Haviaras, Stratis

Chayefsky, Paddy.........................CLC 23
See also Chayefsky, Sidney

Chayefsky, Sidney 1923-1981
See Chayefsky, Paddy

Chedid, Andree 1920-....................**CLC 47**
See also CA 145

Cheever, John 1912-1982....................**CLC 3, 7, 8, 11, 15, 25, 64; DA; DAB; DAC; DAM MST, NOV, POP; SSC 1; WLC**
See also CA 5-8R; 106; CABS 1; CANR 5, 27; CDALB 1941-1968; DLB 2, 102;
DLBY 80, 82; INT CANR-5; MTCW 1

Cheever, Susan 1943-.................**CLC 18, 48**
See also CA 103; CANR 27, 51; DLBY 82;
INT CANR-27

Chekhonte, Antosha
See Chekhov, Anton (Pavlovich)

Chekhov, Anton (Pavlovich)
1860-1904..............................**TCLC 3, 10, 31, 55; DA; DAB; DAC; DAM DRAM, MST; DC 9; SSC 2, 28; WLC**
See also CA 104; 124; SATA 90

Chernyshevsky, Nikolay Gavrilovich
1828-1889............................**NCLC 1**

Cherry, Carolyn Janice 1942-
See Cherryh, C. J.

Cherryh, C. J.............................CLC 35
See also Cherry, Carolyn Janice

Chesnutt, Charles W(addell)
1858-1932............................**TCLC 5, 39; BLC 1; DAM MULT; SSC 7**
See also BW 1; CA 106; 125; DLB 12, 50, 78; MTCW 1

Chester, Alfred 1929(?)-1971...........**CLC 49**
See also CA 33-36R; DLB 130

Chesterton, G(ilbert) K(eith)
1874-1936..............................**TCLC 1, 6, 64; DAM NOV, POET; SSC 1**
See also CA 104; 132; CANR 73; CDBLB 1914-1945; DLB 10, 19, 34, 70, 98, 149, 178; MTCW 1; SATA 27

Chiang, Pin-chin 1904-1986
See Ding Ling

Ch'ien Chung-shu 1910-................**CLC 22**
See also CA 130; CANR 73; MTCW 1

Child, L. Maria
See Child, Lydia Maria

Child, Lydia Maria 1802-1880.... **NCLC 6, 73**
See also DLB 1, 74; SATA 67

Child, Mrs.
See Child, Lydia Maria

Child, Philip 1898-1978..............**CLC 19, 68**
See also CA 13-14; CAP 1; SATA 47

Childers, (Robert) Erskine
1870-1922.........................**TCLC 65**
See also CA 113; 153; DLB 70

Childress, Alice 1920-1994..................**CLC 12, 15, 86, 96; BLC 1; DAM DRAM, MULT, NOV; DC 4**
See also AAYA 8; BW 2; CA 45-48; 146;
CANR 3, 27, 50, 74; CLR 14; DLB 7, 38;
JRDA; MAICYA; MTCW 1; SATA 7, 48, 81

Chin, Frank (Chew, Jr.) 1940-.............**DC 7**
See also CA 33-36R; CANR 71; DAM MULT

Chislett, (Margaret) Anne 1943-...... **CLC 34**
See also CA 151

Chitty, Thomas Willes 1926-...........**CLC 11**
See also Hinde, Thomas

Chivers, Thomas Holley 1809-1858.....**NCLC 49**
See also DLB 3

Chomette, Rene Lucien 1898-1981
See Clair, Rene

Chopin, Kate.................................TCLC 5, 14; DA; DAB; SSC 8; WLCS
See also Chopin, Katherine

Chopin, Katherine 1851-1904
See Chopin, Kate

Chretien de Troyes c. 12th cent. - ...**CMLC 10**

Christie
See Ichikawa, Kon

Christie, Agatha (Mary Clarissa)
1890-1976.................**CLC 1, 6, 8, 12, 39, 48, 110; DAB; DAC; DAM NOV**
See also AAYA 9; AITN 1, 2; CA 17-20R;
61-64; CANR 10, 37; CDBLB 1914-1945;
DLB 13, 77; MTCW 1; SATA 36

Christie, (Ann) Philippa
See Pearce, Philippa

Christine de Pizan 1365(?)-1431(?).......**LC 9**

Chubb, Elmer
See Masters, Edgar Lee

Chulkov, Mikhail Dmitrievich
1743-1792.............................**LC 2**
See also DLB 150

Churchill, Caryl 1938-......**CLC 31, 55; DC 5**
See also CA 102; CANR 22, 46; DLB 13;
MTCW 1

Churchill, Charles 1731-1764..............**LC 3**
See also DLB 109

Chute, Carolyn 1947-.....................**CLC 39**
See also CA 123

Ciardi, John (Anthony) 1916-1986........**CLC 10, 40, 44; DAM POET**
See also CA 5-8R; 118; CAAS 2; CANR 5, 33; CLR 19; DLB 5; DLBY 86; INT CANR-5; MAICYA; MTCW 1; SAAS 26; SATA 1, 65; SATA-Obit 46

Cicero, Marcus Tullius 106B.C.-43B.C..................................**CMLC 3**

Cimino, Michael 1943-...................**CLC 16**
See also CA 105

Cioran, E(mil) M. 1911-1995...........**CLC 64**
See also CA 25-28R; 149

Cisneros, Sandra 1954-......................**CLC 69; DAM MULT; HLC; SSC 32**
See also AAYA 9; CA 131; CANR 64; DLB 122, 152; HW

Cixous, Helene 1937-.....................**CLC 92**
See also CA 126; CANR 55; DLB 83;
MTCW 1

Clair, Rene.................................CLC 20
See also Chomette, Rene Lucien

Clampitt, Amy 1920-1994......**CLC 32; PC 19**
See also CA 110; 146; CANR 29; DLB 105

Clancy, Thomas L., Jr. 1947-
See Clancy, Tom

Clancy, Tom...................................CLC 45, 112; DAM NOV, POP
See also Clancy, Thomas L., Jr.

Clare, John 1793-1864.....................**NCLC 9; DAB; DAM POET; PC 23**
See also DLB 55, 96

Clarin
See Alas (y Urena), Leopoldo (Enrique Garcia)

Colman, George 1732-1794
See Glassco, John

Colt, Winchester Remington
See Hubbard, L(afayette) Ron(ald)

Colter, Cyrus 1910-........................ **CLC 58**
See also BW 1; CA 65-68; CANR 10, 66;
DLB 33

Colton, James
See Hansen, Joseph

Colum, Padraic 1881-1972............... **CLC 28**
See also CA 73-76; 33-36R; CANR 35; CLR
36; MAICYA; MTCW 1; SATA 15

Colvin, James
See Moorcock, Michael (John)

Colwin, Laurie (E.) 1944-1992............. **CLC
5, 13, 23, 84**
See also CA 89-92; 139; CANR 20, 46;
DLBY 80; MTCW 1

Comfort, Alex(ander) 1920-............... **CLC
7; DAM POP**
See also CA 1-4R; CANR 1, 45

Comfort, Montgomery
See Campbell, (John) Ramsey

Compton-Burnett, I(vy) 1884(?)-1969.... **CLC
1, 3, 10, 15, 34; DAM NOV**
See also CA 1-4R; 25-28R; CANR 4; DLB
36; MTCW 1

Comstock, Anthony 1844-1915 ...... **TCLC 13**
See also CA 110; 169

Comte, Auguste 1798-1857 .... **NCLC 54**

Conan Doyle, Arthur
See Doyle, Arthur Conan

Conde, Maryse 1937-........................ **CLC
52, 92; BLCS; DAM MULT**
See also Boucolon, Maryse

Condillac, Etienne Bonnot de 1714-1780... **LC
26**

Condon, Richard (Thomas) 1915-1996... **CLC
4, 6, 8, 10, 45, 100; DAM NOV**
See also BEST 90:3; CA 1-4R; 151; CAAS
1; CANR 2, 23; INT CANR-23; MTCW 1

Confucius 551B.C.-479B.C. .... **CMLC 19;
DA; DAB; DAC; DAM MST; WLCS**

Congreve, William 1670-1729................ **LC
5, 21; DA; DAB; DAC; DAM DRAM,
MST, POET; DC 2; WLC**
See also CDBLB 1660-1789; DLB 39, 84

Connell, Evan S(helby), Jr. 1924-......... **CLC
4, 6, 45; DAM NOV**
See also AAYA 7; CA 1-4R; CAAS 2; CANR
2, 39; DLB 2; DLBY 81; MTCW 1

Connelly, Marc(us Cook) 1890-1980 ...**CLC 7**
See also CA 85-88; 102; CANR 30; DLB 7;
DLBY 80; SATA-Obit 25

Connor, Ralph .... **TCLC 31**
See also Gordon, Charles William

Conrad, Joseph 1857-1924................ **TCLC
1, 6, 13, 25, 43, 57; DA; DAB; DAC;
DAM MST, NOV; SSC 9; WLC**
See also AAYA 26; CA 104; 131; CANR 60;
CDBLB 1890-1914; DLB 10, 34, 98, 156;
MTCW 1; SATA 27

Conrad, Robert Arnold
See Hart, Moss

Conroy, Pat
See Conroy, (Donald) Pat(rick)

Conroy, (Donald) Pat(rick) 1945-......... **CLC
30, 74; DAM NOV, POP**
See also AAYA 8; AITN 1; CA 85-88; CANR
24, 53; DLB 6; MTCW 1

Constant (de Rebecque), (Henri) Benjamin
1767-1830 ....**NCLC 6**
See also DLB 119

Conybeare, Charles Augustus
See Eliot, T(homas) S(tearns)

Cook, Michael 1933- .... **CLC 58**
See also CA 93-96; CANR 68; DLB 53

Cook, Robin 1940-........ **CLC 14; DAM POP**
See also BEST 90:2; CA 108; 111; CANR
41; INT 111

Cook, Roy
See Silverberg, Robert

Cooke, Elizabeth 1948- .... **CLC 55**
See also CA 129

Cooke, John Esten 1830-1886..........**NCLC 5**
See also DLB 3

Cooke, John Estes
See Baum, L(yman) Frank

Cooke, M. E.
See Creasey, John

Cooke, Margaret
See Creasey, John

Cook-Lynn, Elizabeth 1930-................ **CLC
93; DAM MULT**
See also CA 133; DLB 175; NNAL

Cooney, Ray .... **CLC 62**

Cooper, Douglas 1960- .... **CLC 86**

Cooper, Henry St. John
See Creasey, John

Cooper, J(oan) California .... **CLC
56; DAM MULT**
See also AAYA 12; BW 1; CA 125; CANR
55

Cooper, James Fenimore 1789-1851 ....**NCLC
1, 27, 54**
See also AAYA 22; CDALB 1640-1865;
DLB 3; SATA 19

Coover, Robert (Lowell) 1932-........**CLC 3,
7, 15, 32, 46, 87; DAM NOV; SSC 15**
See also CA 45-48; CANR 3, 37, 58; DLB 2;
DLBY 81; MTCW 1

Copeland, Stewart (Armstrong)
1952- .... **CLC 26**

Copernicus, Nicolaus 1473-1543..........**LC 45**

Coppard, A(lfred) E(dgar)
1878-1957 ....**TCLC 5; SSC 21**
See also CA 114; 167; DLB 162; YABC 1

Coppee, Francois 1842-1908 .... **TCLC 25**
See also CA 170

Coppola, Francis Ford 1939-........... **CLC 16**
See also CA 77-80; CANR 40; DLB 44

Corbiere, Tristan 1845-1875..........**NCLC 43**

Corcoran, Barbara 1911- .... **CLC 17**
See also AAYA 14; CA 21-24R; CAAS
2; CANR 11, 28, 48; CLR 50; DLB 52;
JRDA; SAAS 20; SATA 3, 77

Cordelier, Maurice
See Giraudoux, (Hippolyte) Jean

Corelli, Marie 1855-1924.............. **TCLC 51**
See also Mackay, Mary

Corman, Cid 1924- .... **CLC 9**
See also Corman, Sidney

Corman, Sidney 1924-
See Corman, Cid

Cormier, Robert (Edmund) 1925-.....**CLC 12,
30; DA; DAB; DAC; DAM MST, NOV**
See also AAYA 3, 19; CA 1-4R; CANR 5, 23;
CDALB 1968-1988; CLR 12, 55; DLB 52;
INT CANR-23; JRDA; MAICYA; MTCW
1; SATA 10, 45, 83

Corn, Alfred (DeWitt III) 1943-....... **CLC 33**
See also CA 104; CAAS 25; CANR 44; DLB
120; DLBY 80

Corneille, Pierre 1606-1684................... **LC
28; DAB; DAM MST**

Cornwell, David (John Moore) 1931- ....**CLC
9, 15; DAM POP**
See also le Carre, John

Corso, (Nunzio) Gregory 1930-..... **CLC 1, 11**
See also CA 5-8R; CANR 41; DLB 5, 16;
MTCW 1

Cortazar, Julio 1914-1984................... **CLC
2, 3, 5, 10, 13, 15, 33, 34, 92; DAM
MULT, NOV; HLC; SSC 7**
See also CA 21-24R; CANR 12, 32; DLB
113; HW; MTCW 1

CORTES, HERNAN 1484-1547..........**LC 31**

Corvinus, Jakob
See Raabe, Wilhelm (Karl)

Corwin, Cecil
See Kornbluth, C(yril) M.

Cosic, Dobrica 1921- .... **CLC 14**
See also CA 122; 138; DLB 181

Costain, Thomas B(ertram) 1885-1965... **CLC
30**
See also CA 5-8R; 25-28R; DLB 9

Costantini, Humberto 1924(?)-1987 ...**CLC 49**
See also CA 131; 122; HW

Costello, Elvis 1955-...................... **CLC 21**

Cotes, Cecil V.
See Duncan, Sara Jeannette

Cotter, Joseph Seamon Sr.
1861-1949 .... **TCLC
28; BLC 1; DAM MULT**
See also BW 1; CA 124; DLB 50

Couch, Arthur Thomas Quiller
See Quiller-Couch, SirArthur (Thomas)

Coulton, James
See Hansen, Joseph

Couperus, Louis (Marie Anne)
1863-1923 .... **TCLC 15**
See also CA 115

Coupland, Douglas 1961- .... **CLC
85; DAC; DAM POP**
See also CA 142; CANR 57

Court, Wesli
See Turco, Lewis (Putnam)

Courtenay, Bryce 1933- .... **CLC 59**
See also CA 138

Curtin, Philip
　See Lowndes, Marie Adelaide (Belloc)

Curtis, Price
　See Ellison, Harlan (Jay)

Cutrate, Joe
　See Spiegelman, Art

Cynewulf c. 770-c. 840............... **CMLC 23**

Czaczkes, Shmuel Yosef
　See Agnon, S(hmuel) Y(osef Halevi)

Dabrowska, Maria (Szumska)
　1889-1965 .... **CLC 15**
　See also CA 106

Dabydeen, David 1955-................. **CLC 34**
　See also BW 1; CA 125; CANR 56

Dacey, Philip 1939- .... **CLC 51**
　See also CA 37-40R; CAAS 17; CANR 14,
　32, 64; DLB 105

Dagerman, Stig (Halvard) 1923-1954... **TCLC**
　17
　See also CA 117; 155

Dahl, Roald 1916-1990........**CLC 1, 6, 18, 79;**
　DAB; DAC; DAM MST, NOV, POP
　See also AAYA 15; CA 1-4R; 133; CANR
　6, 32, 37, 62; CLR 1, 7, 41; DLB 139;
　JRDA; MAICYA; MTCW 1; SATA 1, 26,
　73; SATA-Obit 65

Dahlberg, Edward 1900-1977.... **CLC 1, 7, 14**
　See also CA 9-12R; 69-72; CANR 31, 62;
　DLB 48; MTCW 1

Daitch, Susan 1954- .... **CLC 103**
　See also CA 161

Dale, Colin............................... **TCLC 18**
　See also Lawrence, T(homas) E(dward)

Dale, George E.
　See Asimov, Isaac

Daly, Elizabeth 1878-1967 .... **CLC 52**
　See also CA 23-24; 25-28R; CANR 60; CAP
　2

Daly, Maureen 1921- .... **CLC 17**
　See also AAYA 5; CANR 37; JRDA;
　MAICYA; SAAS 1; SATA 2

Damas, Leon-Gontran 1912-1978..... **CLC 84**
　See also BW 1; CA 125; 73-76

Dana, Richard Henry Sr. 1787-1879 ...**NCLC**
　53

Daniel, Samuel 1562(?)-1619 ....**LC 24**
　See also DLB 62

Daniels, Brett
　See Adler, Renata

Dannay, Frederic 1905-1982............... **CLC**
　11; DAM POP
　See also Queen, Ellery

D'Annunzio, Gabriele 1863-1938 .... **TCLC**
　6, 40
　See also CA 104; 155

Danois, N. le
　See Gourmont, Remy (-Marie-Charles) de

Dante 1265-1321......**CMLC 3, 18; DA; DAB;**
　DAC; DAM MST, POET; PC 21; WLCS

d'Antibes, Germain
　See Simenon, Georges (Jacques Christian)

Danticat, Edwidge 1969- .... **CLC 94**
　See also CA 152; CANR 73

Danvers, Dennis 1947-................... **CLC 70**

Danziger, Paula 1944-.................... **CLC 21**
　See also AAYA 4; CA 112; 115; CANR 37;
　CLR 20; JRDA; MAICYA; SATA 36, 63,
　102; SATA-Brief 30

Da Ponte, Lorenzo 1749-1838........ **NCLC 50**

Dario, Ruben 1867-1916................... **TCLC**
　4; DAM MULT; HLC; PC 15
　See also CA 131; HW; MTCW 1

Darley, George 1795-1846...............**NCLC 2**
　See also DLB 96

Darrow, Clarence (Seward)
　1857-1938 .... **TCLC 81**
　See also CA 164

Darwin, Charles 1809-1882........... **NCLC 57**
　See also DLB 57, 166

Daryush, Elizabeth 1887-1977 ...... **CLC 6, 19**
　See also CA 49-52; CANR 3; DLB 20

Dasgupta, Surendranath 1887-1952 .... **TCLC**
　81
　See also CA 157

Dashwood, Edmee Elizabeth Monica de
　la Pasture 1890-1943
　See Delafield, E. M.

Daudet, (Louis Marie) Alphonse
　1840-1897 ....**NCLC 1**
　See also DLB 123

Daumal, Rene 1908-1944.............. **TCLC 14**
　See also CA 114

Davenant, William 1606-1668.............**LC 13**
　See also DLB 58, 126

Davenport, Guy (Mattison, Jr.) 1927-.... **CLC**
　6, 14, 38; SSC 16
　See also CA 33-36R; CANR 23, 73; DLB 130

Davidson, Avram 1923-1993
　See Queen, Ellery

Davidson, Donald (Grady) 1893-1968.... **CLC**
　2, 13, 19
　See also CA 5-8R; 25-28R; CANR 4; DLB
　45

Davidson, Hugh
　See Hamilton, Edmond

Davidson, John 1857-1909 .... **TCLC 24**
　See also CA 118; DLB 19

Davidson, Sara 1943-...................... **CLC 9**
　See also CA 81-84; CANR 44, 68; DLB 185

Davie, Donald (Alfred) 1922-1995 .... **CLC**
　5, 8, 10, 31
　See also CA 1-4R; 149; CAAS 3; CANR 1,
　44; DLB 27; MTCW 1

Davies, Ray(mond Douglas) 1944-.... **CLC 21**
　See also CA 116; 146

Davies, Rhys 1901-1978 .... **CLC 23**
　See also CA 9-12R; 81-84; CANR 4; DLB
　139, 191

Davies, (William) Robertson
　1913-1995 .... **CLC**
　2, 7, 13, 25, 42, 75, 91; DA; DAB; DAC;
　DAM MST, NOV, POP; WLC
　See also BEST 89:2; CA 33-36R; 150;
　CANR 17, 42; DLB 68; INT CANR-17;
　MTCW 1

Davies, W(illiam) H(enry) 1871-1940... **TCLC**
　5
　See also CA 104; DLB 19, 174

Davies, Walter C.
　See Kornbluth, C(yril) M.

Davis, Angela (Yvonne) 1944-.............. **CLC**
　77; DAM MULT
　See also BW 2; CA 57-60; CANR 10

Davis, B. Lynch
　See Bioy Casares, Adolfo; Borges, Jorge Luis

Davis, Harold Lenoir 1896-1960....... **CLC 49**
　See also CA 89-92; DLB 9

Davis, Rebecca (Blaine) Harding
　1831-1910 ....**TCLC 6**
　See also CA 104; DLB 74

Davis, Richard Harding 1864-1916..... **TCLC**
　24
　See also CA 114; DLB 12, 23, 78, 79, 189;
　DLBD 13

Davison, Frank Dalby 1893-1970 ..... **CLC 15**
　See also CA 116

Davison, Lawrence H.
　See Lawrence, D(avid) H(erbert Richards)

Davison, Peter (Hubert) 1928-......... **CLC 28**
　See also CA 9-12R; CAAS 4; CANR 3, 43;
　DLB 5

Davys, Mary 1674-1732 .... **LC 1, 46**
　See also DLB 39

Dawson, Fielding 1930-.................... **CLC 6**
　See also CA 85-88; DLB 130

Dawson, Peter
　See Faust, Frederick (Schiller)

Day, Clarence (Shepard, Jr.)
　1874-1935 .... **TCLC 25**
　See also CA 108; DLB 11

Day, Thomas 1748-1789 .... **LC 1**
　See also DLB 39; YABC 1

Day Lewis, C(ecil) 1904-1972 .... **CLC**
　1, 6, 10; DAM POET; PC 11
　See also Blake, Nicholas

Dazai Osamu 1909-1948............... **TCLC 11**
　See also Tsushima, Shuji

de Andrade, Carlos Drummond
　See Drummond de Andrade, Carlos

Deane, Norman
　See Creasey, John

de Beauvoir, Simone (Lucie Ernestine
　Marie Bertrand)
　See Beauvoir, Simone (Lucie Ernestine
　Marie Bertrand) de

de Beer, P.
　See Bosman, Herman Charles

de Brissac, Malcolm
　See Dickinson, Peter (Malcolm)

de Chardin, Pierre Teilhard
　See Teilhard de Chardin, (Marie Joseph)
　Pierre

Dee, John 1527-1608 ....**LC 20**

Deer, Sandra 1940- .... **CLC 45**

De Ferrari, Gabriella 1941- .... **CLC 65**
　See also CA 146

Dickens, Charles (John Huffam)
1812-1870 ....**NCLC 3, 8, 18, 26, 37, 50; DA; DAB; DAC; DAM MST, NOV; SSC 17; WLC**
See also AAYA 23; CDBLB 1832-1890; DLB 21, 55, 70, 159, 166; JRDA; MAICYA; SATA 15

Dickey, James (Lafayette) 1923-1997 .... **CLC 1, 2, 4, 7, 10, 15, 47, 109; DAM NOV, POET, POP**
See also AITN 1, 2; CA 9-12R; 156; CABS 2; CANR 10, 48, 61; CDALB 1968-1988; DLB 5, 193; DLBD 7; DLBY 82, 93, 96, 97; INT CANR-10; MTCW 1

Dickey, William 1928-1994 .... **CLC 3, 28**
See also CA 9-12R; 145; CANR 24; DLB 5

Dickinson, Charles 1951-................ **CLC 49**
See also CA 128

Dickinson, Emily (Elizabeth)
1830-1886 ....**NCLC 21; DA; DAB; DAC; DAM MST, POET; PC 1; WLC**
See also AAYA 22; CDALB 1865-1917; DLB 1; SATA 29

Dickinson, Peter (Malcolm) 1927- .... **CLC 12, 35**
See also AAYA 9; CA 41-44R; CANR 31, 58; CLR 29; DLB 87, 161; JRDA; MAICYA; SATA 5, 62, 95

Dickson, Carr
See Carr, John Dickson

Dickson, Carter
See Carr, John Dickson

Diderot, Denis 1713-1784 ....**LC 26**

Didion, Joan 1934-............................ **CLC 1, 3, 8, 14, 32; DAM NOV**
See also AITN 1; CA 5-8R; CANR 14, 52; CDALB 1968-1988; DLB 2, 173, 185; DLBY 81, 86; MTCW 1

Dietrich, Robert
See Hunt, E(verette) Howard, (Jr.)

Difusa, Pati
See Almodovar, Pedro

Dillard, Annie 1945-........................**CLC 9, 60, 115; DAM NOV**
See also AAYA 6; CA 49-52; CANR 3, 43, 62; DLBY 80; MTCW 1; SATA 10

Dillard, R(ichard) H(enry) W(ilde)
1937- ....**CLC 5**
See also CA 21-24R; CAAS 7; CANR 10; DLB 5

Dillon, Eilis 1920-1994 .... **CLC 17**
See also CA 9-12R; 147; CAAS 3; CANR 4, 38; CLR 26; MAICYA; SATA 2, 74; SATA-Obit 83

Dimont, Penelope
See Mortimer, Penelope (Ruth)

Dinesen, Isak .... **CLC 10, 29, 95; SSC 7**
See also Blixen, Karen (Christentze Dinesen)

Ding Ling .... **CLC 68**
See also Chiang, Pin-chin

Diphusa, Patty
See Almodovar, Pedro

Disch, Thomas M(ichael) 1940-..... **CLC 7, 36**
See also AAYA 17; CA 21-24R; CAAS 4; CANR 17, 36, 54; CLR 18; DLB 8; MAICYA; MTCW 1; SAAS 15; SATA 92

Disch, Tom
See Disch, Thomas M(ichael)

d'Isly, Georges
See Simenon, Georges (Jacques Christian)

Disraeli, Benjamin 1804-1881..... **NCLC 2, 39**
See also DLB 21, 55

Ditcum, Steve
See Crumb, R(obert)

Dixon, Paige
See Corcoran, Barbara

Dixon, Stephen 1936-.......... **CLC 52; SSC 16**
See also CA 89-92; CANR 17, 40, 54; DLB 130

Doak, Annie
See Dillard, Annie

Dobell, Sydney Thompson
1824-1874 ....**NCLC 43**
See also DLB 32

Doblin, Alfred.............................**TCLC 13**
See also Doeblin, Alfred

Dobrolyubov, Nikolai Alexandrovich
1836-1861 ....**NCLC 5**

Dobson, Austin 1840-1921 .... **TCLC 79**
See also DLB 35; 144

Dobyns, Stephen 1941- .... **CLC 37**
See also CA 45-48; CANR 2, 18

Doctorow, E(dgar) L(aurence) 1931-..... **CLC 6, 11, 15, 18, 37, 44, 65, 113; DAM NOV, POP**
See also AAYA 22; AITN 2; BEST 89:3; CA 45-48; CANR 2, 33, 51; CDALB 1968-1988; DLB 2, 28, 173; DLBY 80; MTCW 1

Dodgson, Charles Lutwidge 1832-1898
See Carroll, Lewis

Dodson, Owen (Vincent) 1914-1983 ...... **CLC 79; BLC 1; DAM MULT**
See also BW 1; CA 65-68; 110; CANR 24; DLB 76

Doeblin, Alfred 1878-1957 .... **TCLC 13**
See also Doblin, Alfred

Doerr, Harriet 1910-...................... **CLC 34**
See also CA 117; 122; CANR 47; INT 122

Domecq, H(onorio) Bustos
See Bioy Casares, Adolfo; Borges, Jorge Luis

Domini, Rey
See Lorde, Audre (Geraldine)

Dominique
See Proust, (Valentin-Louis-George-Eugene-) Marcel

Don, A
See Stephen, SirLeslie

Donaldson, Stephen R. 1947-............... **CLC 46; DAM POP**
See also CA 89-92; CANR 13, 55; INT CANR-13

Donleavy, J(ames) P(atrick) 1926- .... **CLC 1, 4, 6, 10, 45**
See also AITN 2; CA 9-12R; CANR 24, 49, 62; DLB 6, 173; INT CANR-24; MTCW 1

Donne, John 1572-1631 .... **LC 10, 24; DA; DAB; DAC; DAM MST, POET; PC 1; WLC**
See also CDBLB Before 1660; DLB 121, 151

Donnell, David 1939(?)- .... **CLC 34**

Donoghue, P. S.
See Hunt, E(verette) Howard, (Jr.)

Donoso (Yanez), Jose 1924-1996........... **CLC 4, 8, 11, 32, 99; DAM MULT; HLC**
See also CA 81-84; 155; CANR 32, 73; DLB 113; HW; MTCW 1

Donovan, John 1928-1992.............. **CLC 35**
See also AAYA 20; CA 97-100; 137; CLR 3; MAICYA; SATA 72; SATA-Brief 29

Don Roberto
See Cunninghame Graham, R(obert) B(ontine)

Doolittle, Hilda 1886-1961 .... **CLC 3, 8, 14, 31, 34, 73; DA; DAC; DAM MST, POET; PC 5; WLC**
See also H. D.

Dorfman, Ariel 1942- .... **CLC 48, 77; DAM MULT; HLC**
See also CA 124; 130; CANR 67, 70; HW; INT 130

Dorn, Edward (Merton) 1929-.....**CLC 10, 18**
See also CA 93-96; CANR 42; DLB 5; INT 93-96

Dorris, Michael (Anthony) 1945-1997 ... **CLC 109; DAM MULT, NOV**
See also AAYA 20; BEST 90:1; CA 102; 157; CANR 19, 46, 75; DLB 175; NNAL; SATA 75; SATA-Obit 94

Dorris, Michael A.
See Dorris, Michael (Anthony)

Dorsan, Luc
See Simenon, Georges (Jacques Christian)

Dorsange, Jean
See Simenon, Georges (Jacques Christian)

Dos Passos, John (Roderigo)
1896-1970 ....**CLC 1, 4, 8, 11, 15, 25, 34, 82; DA; DAB; DAC; DAM MST, NOV; WLC**
See also CA 1-4R; 29-32R; CANR 3; CDALB 1929-1941; DLB 4, 9; DLBD 1, 15; DLBY 96; MTCW 1

Dossage, Jean
See Simenon, Georges (Jacques Christian)

Dostoevsky, Fedor Mikhailovich
1821-1881 ....**NCLC 2, 7, 21, 33, 43; DA; DAB; DAC; DAM MST, NOV; SSC 2, 33; WLC**

Doughty, Charles M(ontagu)
1843-1926 .... **TCLC 27**
See also CA 115; DLB 19, 57, 174

Douglas, Ellen............................. **CLC 73**
See also Haxton, Josephine Ayres; Williamson, Ellen Douglas

Douglas, Gavin 1475(?)-1522..............**LC 20**
See also DLB 132

Douglas, George
See Brown, George Douglas

Douglas, Keith (Castellain)
1920-1944 .... TCLC 40
See also CA 160; DLB 27

Douglas, Leonard
See Bradbury, Ray (Douglas)

Douglas, Michael
See Crichton, (John) Michael

Douglas, (George) Norman
1868-1952 .... TCLC 68
See also CA 119; 157; DLB 34, 195

Douglas, William
See Brown, George Douglas

Douglass, Frederick 1817(?)-1895 .... NCLC
7, 55; BLC 1; DA; DAC; DAM
MST, MULT; WLC
See also CDALB 1640-1865; DLB 1, 43, 50,
79; SATA 29

Dourado, (Waldomiro Freitas) Autran
1926- .... CLC 23, 60
See also CA 25-28R; CANR 34

Dourado, Waldomiro Autran
See Dourado, (Waldomiro Freitas) Autran

Dove, Rita (Frances) 1952- .... CLC 50,
81; BLCS; DAM MULT, POET; PC 6
See also BW 2; CA 109; CAAS 19; CANR
27, 42, 68; DLB 120

Doveglion
See Villa, Jose Garcia

Dowell, Coleman 1925-1985 .... CLC 60
See also CA 25-28R; 117; CANR 10; DLB
130

Dowson, Ernest (Christopher)
1867-1900 .... TCLC 4
See also CA 105; 150; DLB 19, 135

Doyle, A. Conan
See Doyle, Arthur Conan

Doyle, Arthur Conan 1859-1930 .... TCLC
7; DA; DAB; DAC; DAM MST,
NOV; SSC 12; WLC
See also AAYA 14; CA 104; 122; CDBLB
1890-1914; DLB 18, 70, 156, 178; MTCW
1; SATA 24

Doyle, Conan
See Doyle, Arthur Conan

Doyle, John
See Graves, Robert (von Ranke)

Doyle, Roddy 1958(?)- .... CLC 81
See also AAYA 14; CA 143; CANR 73; DLB
194

Doyle, Sir A. Conan
See Doyle, Arthur Conan

Doyle, Sir Arthur Conan
See Doyle, Arthur Conan

Dr. A
See Asimov, Isaac; Silverstein, Alvin

Drabble, Margaret 1939- CLC
2, 3, 5, 8, 10, 22, 53; DAB; DAC;
DAM MST, NOV, POP
See also CA 13-16R; CANR 18, 35, 63;
CDBLB 1960 to Present; DLB 14, 155;
MTCW 1; SATA 48

Drapier, M. B.
See Swift, Jonathan

Drayham, James
See Mencken, H(enry) L(ouis)

Drayton, Michael 1563-1631 LC
8; DAM POET
See also DLB 121

Dreadstone, Carl
See Campbell, (John) Ramsey

Dreiser, Theodore (Herman Albert)
1871-1945 ..... TCLC 10, 18, 35, 83; DA;
DAC; DAM MST, NOV; SSC 30; WLC
See also CA 106; 132; CDALB 1865-1917;
DLB 9, 12, 102, 137; DLBD 1; MTCW 1

Drexler, Rosalyn 1926- .... CLC 2, 6
See also CA 81-84; CANR 68

Dreyer, Carl Theodor 1889-1968 ...... CLC 16
See also CA 116

Drieu la Rochelle, Pierre(-Eugene)
1893-1945 .... TCLC 21
See also CA 117; DLB 72

Drinkwater, John 1882-1937 .... TCLC 57
See also CA 109; 149; DLB 10, 19, 149

Drop Shot
See Cable, George Washington

Droste-Hulshoff, Annette Freiin von
1797-1848 .... NCLC 3
See also DLB 133

Drummond, Walter
See Silverberg, Robert

Drummond, William Henry
1854-1907 .... TCLC 25
See also CA 160; DLB 92

Drummond de Andrade, Carlos
1902-1987 .... CLC 18
See also Andrade, Carlos Drummond de

Drury, Allen (Stuart) 1918-1998 .... CLC 37
See also CA 57-60; 170; CANR 18, 52; INT
CANR-18

Dryden, John 1631-1700 LC
3, 21; DA; DAB; DAC; DAM DRAM,
MST, POET; DC 3; PC 25; WLC
See also CDBLB 1660-1789; DLB 80, 101,
131

Duberman, Martin (Bauml) 1930- ...... CLC 8
See also CA 1-4R; CANR 2, 63

Dubie, Norman (Evans) 1945- .... CLC 36
See also CA 69-72; CANR 12; DLB 120

Du Bois, W(illiam) E(dward) B(urghardt)
1868-1963 CLC
1, 2, 13, 64, 96; BLC 1; DA; DAC;
DAM MST, MULT, NOV; WLC
See also BW 1; CA 85-88; CANR 34;
CDALB 1865-1917; DLB 47, 50, 91;
MTCW 1; SATA 42

Dubus, Andre 1936- ...CLC 13, 36, 97; SSC 15
See also CA 21-24R; CANR 17; DLB 130;
INT CANR-17

Duca Minimo
See D'Annunzio, Gabriele

Ducharme, Rejean 1941- .... CLC 74
See also CA 165; DLB 60

Duclos, Charles Pinot 1704-1772 .... LC 1

Dudek, Louis 1918- .... CLC 11, 19
See also CA 45-48; CAAS 14; CANR 1; DLB
88

Duerrenmatt, Friedrich 1921-1990 CLC
1, 4, 8, 11, 15, 43, 102; DAM DRAM
See also CA 17-20R; CANR 33; DLB 69,
124; MTCW 1

Duffy, Bruce (?)- .... CLC 50

Duffy, Maureen 1933- .... CLC 37
See also CA 25-28R; CANR 33, 68; DLB 14;
MTCW 1

Dugan, Alan 1923- .... CLC 2, 6
See also CA 81-84; DLB 5

du Gard, Roger Martin
See Martin du Gard, Roger

Duhamel, Georges 1884-1966 .... CLC 8
See also CA 81-84; 25-28R; CANR 35; DLB
65; MTCW 1

Dujardin, Edouard (Emile Louis)
1861-1949 .... TCLC 13
See also CA 109; DLB 123

Dulles, John Foster 1888-1959 .... TCLC 72
See also CA 115; 149

Dumas, Alexandre (pere)
See Dumas, Alexandre (Davy de la Pailleterie)

Dumas, Alexandre (Davy de la Pailleterie)
1802-1870 .... NCLC 11; DA;
DAB; DAC; DAM MST, NOV; WLC
See also DLB 119, 192; SATA 18

Dumas, Alexandre (fils) 1824-1895 ..... NCLC
71; DC 1
See also AAYA 22; DLB 192

Dumas, Claudine
See Malzberg, Barry N(athaniel)

Dumas, Henry L. 1934-1968 .... CLC 6, 62
See also BW 1; CA 85-88; DLB 41

du Maurier, Daphne 1907-1989 CLC
6, 11, 59; DAB; DAC; DAM MST,
POP; SSC 18
See also CA 5-8R; 128; CANR 6, 55; DLB
191; MTCW 1; SATA 27; SATA-Obit 60

Dunbar, Paul Laurence 1872-1906 ...... TCLC
2, 12; BLC 1; DA; DAC; DAM MST,
MULT, POET; PC 5; SSC 8; WLC
See also BW 1; CA 104; 124; CDALB 1865-
1917; DLB 50, 54, 78; SATA 34

Dunbar, William 1460(?)-1530(?) .... LC 20
See also DLB 132, 146

Duncan, Dora Angela
See Duncan, Isadora

Duncan, Isadora 1877(?)-1927 .... TCLC 68
See also CA 118; 149

Duncan, Lois 1934- .... CLC 26
See also AAYA 4; CA 1-4R; CANR 2, 23, 36;
CLR 29; JRDA; MAICYA; SAAS 2; SATA
1, 36, 75

Duncan, Robert (Edward) 1919-1988 CLC
1, 2, 4, 7, 15, 41, 55; DAM POET; PC 2
See also CA 9-12R; 124; CANR 28, 62; DLB
5, 16, 193; MTCW 1

Duncan, Sara Jeannette 1861-1922 ..... TCLC
60
See also CA 157; DLB 92

Dunlap, William 1766-1839.............**NCLC 2**
   See also DLB 30, 37, 59

Dunn, Douglas (Eaglesham) 1942-........ **CLC 6, 40**
   See also CA 45-48; CANR 2, 33; DLB 40; MTCW 1

Dunn, Katherine (Karen) 1945- .... **CLC 71**
   See also CA 33-36R; CANR 72

Dunn, Stephen 1939- .... **CLC 36**
   See also CA 33-36R; CANR 12, 48, 53; DLB 105

Dunne, Finley Peter 1867-1936 ...... **TCLC 28**
   See also CA 108; DLB 11, 23

Dunne, John Gregory 1932- .... **CLC 28**
   See also CA 25-28R; CANR 14, 50; DLBY 80

Dunsany, Edward John Moreton Drax Plunkett 1878-1957
   See Dunsany, Lord

Dunsany, Lord .... **TCLC 2, 59**
   See also Dunsany, Edward John Moreton Drax Plunkett

du Perry, Jean
   See Simenon, Georges (Jacques Christian)

Durang, Christopher (Ferdinand) 1949- ....**CLC 27, 38**
   See also CA 105; CANR 50

Duras, Marguerite 1914-1996.............. **CLC 3, 6, 11, 20, 34, 40, 68, 100**
   See also CA 25-28R; 151; CANR 50; DLB 83; MTCW 1

Durban, (Rosa) Pam 1947- .... **CLC 39**
   See also CA 123

Durcan, Paul 1944- .... **CLC 43, 70; DAM POET**
   See also CA 134

Durkheim, Emile 1858-1917......... **TCLC 55**

Durrell, Lawrence (George) 1912-1990 .... **CLC 1, 4, 6, 8, 13, 27, 41; DAM NOV**
   See also CA 9-12R; 132; CANR 40; CD-BLB 1945-1960; DLB 15, 27; DLBY 90; MTCW 1

Durrenmatt, Friedrich
   See Duerrenmatt, Friedrich

Dutt, Toru 1856-1877 .... **NCLC 29**

Dwight, Timothy 1752-1817 .... **NCLC 13**
   See also DLB 37

Dworkin, Andrea 1946-.................. **CLC 43**
   See also CA 77-80; CAAS 21; CANR 16, 39; INT CANR-16; MTCW 1

Dwyer, Deanna
   See Koontz, Dean R(ay)

Dwyer, K. R.
   See Koontz, Dean R(ay)

Dwyer, Thomas A. 1923- ....**CLC 114**
   See also CA 115

Dye, Richard
   See De Voto, Bernard (Augustine)

Dylan, Bob 1941-.............**CLC 3, 4, 6, 12, 77**
   See also CA 41-44R; DLB 16

Eagleton, Terence (Francis) 1943-
   See Eagleton, Terry

Eagleton, Terry .... **CLC 63**
   See also Eagleton, Terence (Francis)

Early, Jack
   See Scoppettone, Sandra

East, Michael
   See West, Morris L(anglo)

Eastaway, Edward
   See Thomas, (Philip) Edward

Eastlake, William (Derry) 1917-1997... **CLC 8**
   See also CA 5-8R; 158; CAAS 1; CANR 5, 63; DLB 6; INT CANR-5

Eastman, Charles A(lexander) 1858-1939 .... **TCLC 55; DAM MULT**
   See also DLB 175; NNAL; YABC 1

Eberhart, Richard (Ghormley) 1904-.... **CLC 3, 11, 19, 56; DAM POET**
   See also CA 1-4R; CANR 2; CDALB 1941-1968; DLB 48; MTCW 1

Eberstadt, Fernanda 1960- .... **CLC 39**
   See also CA 136; CANR 69

Echegaray (y Eizaguirre), Jose (Maria Waldo) 1832-1916 ....**TCLC 4**
   See also CA 104; CANR 32; HW; MTCW 1

Echeverria, (Jose) Esteban (Antonino) 1805-1851 ....**NCLC 18**

Echo
   See Proust, (Valentin-Louis-George-Eugene-) Marcel

Eckert, Allan W. 1931-.................... **CLC 17**
   See also AAYA 18; CA 13-16R; CANR 14, 45; INT CANR-14; SAAS 21; SATA 29, 91; SATA-Brief 27

Eckhart, Meister 1260(?)-1328(?) ....**CMLC 9**
   See also DLB 115

Eckmar, F. R.
   See de Hartog, Jan

Eco, Umberto 1932- .... **CLC 28, 60; DAM NOV, POP**
   See also BEST 90:1; CA 77-80; CANR 12, 33, 55; DLB 196; MTCW 1

Eddison, E(ric) R(ucker) 1882-1945.... **TCLC 15**
   See also CA 109; 156

Eddy, Mary (Morse) Baker 1821-1910 .... **TCLC 71**
   See also CA 113

Edel, (Joseph) Leon 1907-1997 ....**CLC 29, 34**
   See also CA 1-4R; 161; CANR 1, 22; DLB 103; INT CANR-22

Eden, Emily 1797-1869 ....**NCLC 10**

Edgar, David 1948- ....**CLC 42; DAM DRAM**
   See also CA 57-60; CANR 12, 61; DLB 13; MTCW 1

Edgerton, Clyde (Carlyle) 1944- ...... **CLC 39**
   See also AAYA 17; CA 118; 134; CANR 64; INT 134

Edgeworth, Maria 1768-1849 ..... **NCLC 1, 51**
   See also DLB 116, 159, 163; SATA 21

Edmonds, Paul
   See Kuttner, Henry

Edmonds, Walter D(umaux) 1903-1998 .... **CLC 35**
   See also CA 5-8R; CANR 2; DLB 9; MAICYA; SAAS 4, SATA 1, 27, SATA-Obit 99

Edmondson, Wallace
   See Ellison, Harlan (Jay)

Edson, Russell .... **CLC 13**
   See also CA 33-36R

Edwards, Bronwen Elizabeth
   See Rose, Wendy

Edwards, G(erald) B(asil) 1899-1976 .... **CLC 25**
   See also CA 110

Edwards, Gus 1939-...................... **CLC 43**
   See also CA 108; INT 108

Edwards, Jonathan 1703-1758.............. **LC 7; DA; DAC; DAM MST**
   See also DLB 24

Efron, Marina Ivanovna Tsvetaeva
   See Tsvetaeva (Efron), Marina (Ivanovna)

Ehle, John (Marsden, Jr.) 1925-....... **CLC 27**
   See also CA 9-12R

Ehrenbourg, Ilya (Grigoryevich)
   See Ehrenburg, Ilya (Grigoryevich)

Ehrenburg, Ilya (Grigoryevich) 1891-1967 .... **CLC 18, 34, 62**
   See also CA 102; 25-28R

Ehrenburg, Ilyo (Grigoryevich)
   See Ehrenburg, Ilya (Grigoryevich)

Ehrenreich, Barbara 1941- ....**CLC 110**
   See also BEST 90:4; CA 73-76; CANR 16, 37, 62; MTCW 1

Eich, Guenter 1907-1972................ **CLC 15**
   See also CA 111; 93-96; DLB 69, 124

Eichendorff, Joseph Freiherr von 1788-1857 ....**NCLC 8**
   See also DLB 90

Eigner, Larry ....**CLC 9**
   See also Eigner, Laurence (Joel)

Eigner, Laurence (Joel) 1927-1996
   See Eigner, Larry

Einstein, Albert 1879-1955........... **TCLC 65**
   See also CA 121; 133; MTCW 1

Eiseley, Loren Corey 1907-1977 ....**CLC 7**
   See also AAYA 5; CA 1-4R; 73-76; CANR 6; DLBD 17

Eisenstadt, Jill 1963- .... **CLC 50**
   See also CA 140

Eisenstein, Sergei (Mikhailovich) 1898-1948 .... **TCLC 57**
   See also CA 114; 149

Eisner, Simon
   See Kornbluth, C(yril) M.

Ekeloef, (Bengt) Gunnar 1907-1968 ...... **CLC 27; DAM POET; PC 23**
   See also CA 123; 25-28R

Ekelof, (Bengt) Gunnar
   See Ekeloef, (Bengt) Gunnar

Ekelund, Vilhelm 1880-1949 .... **TCLC 75**

Ekwensi, C. O. D.
   See Ekwensi, Cyprian (Odiatu Duaka)

Ekwensi, Cyprian (Odiatu Duaka)
1921- ....**CLC 4; BLC 1; DAM MULT**
See also BW 2; CA 29-32R; CANR 18, 42, 74; DLB 117; MTCW 1; SATA 66

Elaine .... **TCLC 18**
See also Leverson, Ada

El Crummo
See Crumb, R(obert)

Elder, Lonne III 1931-1996 .... **DC 8**
See also BLC 1; BW 1; CA 81-84; 152; CANR 25; DAM MULT; DLB 7, 38, 44

Elia
See Lamb, Charles

Eliade, Mircea 1907-1986 .... **CLC 19**
See also CA 65-68; 119; CANR 30, 62; MTCW 1

Eliot, A. D.
See Jewett, (Theodora) Sarah Orne

Eliot, Alice
See Jewett, (Theodora) Sarah Orne

Eliot, Dan
See Silverberg, Robert

Eliot, George 1819-1880 .... **NCLC 4, 13, 23, 41, 49; DA; DAB; DAC; DAM MST, NOV; PC 20; WLC**
See also CDBLB 1832-1890; DLB 21, 35, 55

Eliot, John 1604-1690 .... **LC 5**
See also DLB 24

Eliot, T(homas) S(tearns) 1888-1965 ..... **CLC 1, 2, 3, 6, 9, 10, 13, 15, 24, 34, 41, 55, 57, 113; DA; DAB; DAC; DAM DRAM, MST, POET; PC 5; WLC**
See also CA 5-8R; 25-28R; CANR 41; CDALB 1929-1941; DLB 7, 10, 45, 63; DLBY 88; MTCW 1

Elizabeth 1866-1941 .... **TCLC 41**

Elkin, Stanley L(awrence) 1930-1995 .... **CLC 4, 6, 9, 14, 27, 51, 91; DAM NOV, POP; SSC 12**
See also CA 9-12R; 148; CANR 8, 46; DLB 2, 28; DLBY 80; INT CANR-8; MTCW 1

Elledge, Scott .... **CLC 34**

Elliot, Don
See Silverberg, Robert

Elliott, Don
See Silverberg, Robert

Elliott, George P(aul) 1918-1980 .... **CLC 2**
See also CA 1-4R; 97-100; CANR 2

Elliott, Janice 1931- .... **CLC 47**
See also CA 13-16R; CANR 8, 29; DLB 14

Elliott, Sumner Locke 1917-1991 ..... **CLC 38**
See also CA 5-8R; 134; CANR 2, 21

Elliott, William
See Bradbury, Ray (Douglas)

Ellis, A. E. .... **CLC 7**

Ellis, Alice Thomas .... **CLC 40**
See also Haycraft, Anna

Ellis, Bret Easton 1964- .... **CLC 39, 71, 117; DAM POP**
See also AAYA 2; CA 118; 123; CANR 51, 74; INT 123

Ellis, (Henry) Havelock 1859-1939 ...... **TCLC 14**
See also CA 109; 169; DLB 190

Ellis, Landon
See Ellison, Harlan (Jay)

Ellis, Trey 1962- .... **CLC 55**
See also CA 146

Ellison, Harlan (Jay) 1934- .... **CLC 1, 13, 42; DAM POP; SSC 14**
See also CA 5-8R; CANR 5, 46; DLB 8; INT CANR-5; MTCW 1

Ellison, Ralph (Waldo) 1914-1994... **CLC 1, 3, 11, 54, 86, 114; BLC 1; DA; DAB; DAC; DAM MST, MULT, NOV; SSC 26; WLC**
See also AAYA 19; BW 1; CA 9-12R; 145; CANR 24, 53; CDALB 1941-1968; DLB 2, 76; DLBY 94; MTCW 1

Ellmann, Lucy (Elizabeth) 1956-...... **CLC 61**
See also CA 128

Ellmann, Richard (David) 1918-1987 .... **CLC 50**
See also BEST 89:2; CA 1-4R; 122; CANR 2, 28, 61; DLB 103; DLBY 87; MTCW 1

Elman, Richard (Martin) 1934-1997 ..... **CLC 19**
See also CA 17-20R; 163; CAAS 3; CANR 47

Elron
See Hubbard, L(afayette) Ron(ald)

Eluard, Paul .... **TCLC 7, 41**
See also Grindel, Eugene

Elyot, Sir Thomas 1490(?)-1546 .... **LC 11**

Elytis, Odysseus 1911-1996 .... **CLC 15, 49, 100; DAM POET; PC 21**
See also CA 102; 151; MTCW 1

Emecheta, (Florence Onye) Buchi 1944- .... **CLC 14, 48; BLC 2; DAM MULT**
See also BW 2; CA 81-84; CANR 27; DLB 117; MTCW 1; SATA 66

Emerson, Mary Moody 1774-1863...... **NCLC 66**

Emerson, Ralph Waldo 1803-1882...... **NCLC 1, 38; DA; DAB; DAC; DAM MST, POET; PC 18; WLC**
See also CDALB 1640-1865; DLB 1, 59, 73

Eminescu, Mihail 1850-1889 .... **NCLC 33**

Empson, William 1906-1984................ **CLC 3, 8, 19, 33, 34**
See also CA 17-20R; 112; CANR 31, 61; DLB 20; MTCW 1

Enchi, Fumiko (Ueda) 1905-1986 ..... **CLC 31**
See also CA 129; 121

Ende, Michael (Andreas Helmuth) 1929-1995 .... **CLC 31**
See also CA 118; 124; 149; CANR 36; CLR 14; DLB 75; MAICYA; SATA 61; SATA-Brief 42; SATA-Obit 86

Endo, Shusaku 1923-1996.................. **CLC 7, 14, 19, 54, 99; DAM NOV**
See also CA 29-32R; 153; CANR 21, 54; DLB 182; MTCW 1

Engel, Marian 1933-1985 .... **CLC 36**
See also CA 25-28R; CANR 12; DLB 53; INT CANR-12

Engelhardt, Frederick
See Hubbard, L(afayette) Ron(ald)

Enright, D(ennis) J(oseph) 1920-.......... **CLC 4, 8, 31**
See also CA 1-4R; CANR 1, 42; DLB 27; SATA 25

Enzensberger, Hans Magnus 1929-... **CLC 43**
See also CA 116; 119

Ephron, Nora 1941- .... **CLC 17, 31**
See also AITN 2; CA 65-68; CANR 12, 39

Epicurus 341B.C.-270B.C. .... **CMLC 21**
See also DLB 176

Epsilon
See Betjeman, John

Epstein, Daniel Mark 1948- .... **CLC 7**
See also CA 49-52; CANR 2, 53

Epstein, Jacob 1956- .... **CLC 19**
See also CA 114

Epstein, Joseph 1937- .... **CLC 39**
See also CA 112; 119; CANR 50, 65

Epstein, Leslie 1938- .... **CLC 27**
See also CA 73-76; CAAS 12; CANR 23, 69

Equiano, Olaudah 1745(?)-1797............. **LC 16; BLC 2; DAM MULT**
See also DLB 37, 50

ER .... **TCLC 33**
See also CA 160; DLB 85

Erasmus, Desiderius 1469(?)-1536.......**LC 16**

Erdman, Paul E(mil) 1932-............. **CLC 25**
See also AITN 1; CA 61-64; CANR 13, 43

Erdrich, Louise 1954-....................... **CLC 39, 54; DAM MULT, NOV, POP**
See also AAYA 10; BEST 89:1; CA 114; CANR 41, 62; DLB 152, 175; MTCW 1; NNAL; SATA 94

Erenburg, Ilya (Grigoryevich)
See Ehrenburg, Ilya (Grigoryevich)

Erickson, Stephen Michael 1950-
See Erickson, Steve

Erickson, Steve 1950- .... **CLC 64**
See also Erickson, Stephen Michael

Ericson, Walter
See Fast, Howard (Melvin)

Eriksson, Buntel
See Bergman, (Ernst) Ingmar

Ernaux, Annie 1940- .... **CLC 88**
See also CA 147

Erskine, John 1879-1951 .... **TCLC 84**
See also CA 112; 159; DLB 9, 102

Eschenbach, Wolfram von
See Wolfram von Eschenbach

Eseki, Bruno
See Mphahlele, Ezekiel

Esenin, Sergei (Alexandrovich) 1895-1925 .... **TCLC 4**
See also CA 104

Eshleman, Clayton 1935-.................**CLC 7**
See also CA 33-36R; CAAS 6; DLB 5

Espriella, Don Manuel Alvarez
See Southey, Robert

Espriu, Salvador 1913-1985 .... **CLC 9**
See also CA 154; 115; DLB 134

Espronceda, Jose de 1808-1842 ...... **NCLC 39**

Esse, James
See Stephens, James

Esterbrook, Tom
See Hubbard, L(afayette) Ron(ald)

Estleman, Loren D. 1952- .... **CLC 48; DAM NOV, POP**
See also AAYA 27; CA 85-88; CANR 27, 74; INT CANR-27; MTCW 1

Euclid 306B.C.-283B.C. .... **CMLC 25**

Eugenides, Jeffrey 1960(?)- .... **CLC 81**
See also CA 144

Euripides c. 485B.C.-406B.C. .... **CMLC 23; DA; DAB; DAC; DAM DRAM, MST; DC 4; WLCS**
See also DLB 176

Evan, Evin
See Faust, Frederick (Schiller)

Evans, Caradoc 1878-1945 .... **TCLC 85**

Evans, Evan
See Faust, Frederick (Schiller)

Evans, Marian
See Eliot, George

Evans, Mary Ann
See Eliot, George

Evarts, Esther
See Benson, Sally

Everett, Percival L. 1956- .... **CLC 57**
See also BW 2; CA 129

Everson, R(onald) G(ilmour) 1903-... **CLC 27**
See also CA 17-20R; DLB 88

Everson, William (Oliver) 1912-1994 .... **CLC 1, 5, 14**
See also CA 9-12R; 145; CANR 20; DLB 5, 16; MTCW 1

Evtushenko, Evgenii Aleksandrovich
See Yevtushenko, Yevgeny (Alexandrovich)

Ewart, Gavin (Buchanan) 1916-1995 .... **CLC 13, 46**
See also CA 89-92; 150; CANR 17, 46; DLB 40; MTCW 1

Ewers, Hanns Heinz 1871-1943 ...... **TCLC 12**
See also CA 109; 149

Ewing, Frederick R.
See Sturgeon, Theodore (Hamilton)

Exley, Frederick (Earl) 1929-1992 .... **CLC 6, 11**
See also AITN 2; CA 81-84; 138; DLB 143; DLBY 81

Eynhardt, Guillermo
See Quiroga, Horacio (Sylvestre)

Ezekiel, Nissim 1924- .... **CLC 61**
See also CA 61-64

Ezekiel, Tish O'Dowd 1943- .... **CLC 34**
See also CA 129

Fadeyev, A.
See Bulgya, Alexander Alexandrovich

Fadeyev, Alexander .... **TCLC 53**
See also Bulgya, Alexander Alexandrovich

Fagen, Donald 1948- .... **CLC 26**

Fainzilberg, Ilya Arnoldovich 1897-1937
See Ilf, Ilya

Fair, Ronald L. 1932- .... **CLC 18**
See also BW 1; CA 69-72; CANR 25; DLB 33

Fairbairn, Roger
See Carr, John Dickson

Fairbairns, Zoe (Ann) 1948- .... **CLC 32**
See also CA 103; CANR 21

Falco, Gian
See Papini, Giovanni

Falconer, James
See Kirkup, James

Falconer, Kenneth
See Kornbluth, C(yril) M.

Falkland, Samuel
See Heijermans, Herman

Fallaci, Oriana 1930- .... **CLC 11, 110**
See also CA 77-80; CANR 15, 58; MTCW 1

Faludy, George 1913- .... **CLC 42**
See also CA 21-24R

Faludy, Gyoergy
See Faludy, George

Fanon, Frantz 1925-1961 .... **CLC 74; BLC 2; DAM MULT**
See also BW 1; CA 116; 89-92

Fanshawe, Ann 1625-1680 .... **LC 11**

Fante, John (Thomas) 1911-1983 ..... **CLC 60**
See also CA 69-72; 109; CANR 23; DLB 130; DLBY 83

Farah, Nuruddin 1945- .... **CLC 53; BLC 2; DAM MULT**
See also BW 2; CA 106; DLB 125

Fargue, Leon-Paul 1876(?)-1947 .... **TCLC 11**
See also CA 109

Farigoule, Louis
See Romains, Jules

Farina, Richard 1936(?)-1966 .... **CLC 9**
See also CA 81-84; 25-28R

Farley, Walter (Lorimer) 1915-1989 ..... **CLC 17**
See also CA 17-20R; CANR 8, 29; DLB 22; JRDA; MAICYA; SATA 2, 43

Farmer, Philip Jose 1918- .... **CLC 1, 19**
See also CA 1-4R; CANR 4, 35; DLB 8; MTCW 1; SATA 93

Farquhar, George 1677-1707 .... **LC 21; DAM DRAM**
See also DLB 84

Farrell, J(ames) G(ordon) 1935-1979 ... **CLC 6**
See also CA 73-76; 89-92; CANR 36; DLB 14; MTCW 1

Farrell, James T(homas) 1904-1979 ...... **CLC 1, 4, 8, 11, 66; SSC 28**
See also CA 5-8R; 89-92; CANR 9, 61; DLB 4, 9, 86; DLBD 2; MTCW 1

Farren, Richard J.
See Betjeman, John

Farren, Richard M.
See Betjeman, John

Fassbinder, Rainer Werner 1946-1982... **CLC 20**
See also CA 93-96; 106; CANR 31

Fast, Howard (Melvin) 1914- .... **CLC 23; DAM NOV**
See also AAYA 16; CA 1-4R; CAAS 18; CANR 1, 33, 54, 75; DLB 9; INT CANR-33; SATA 7

Faulcon, Robert
See Holdstock, Robert P.

Faulkner, William (Cuthbert) 1897-1962 .... **CLC 1, 3, 6, 8, 9, 11, 14, 18, 28, 52, 68; DA; DAB; DAC; DAM MST, NOV; SSC 1; WLC**
See also AAYA 7; CA 81-84; CANR 33; CDALB 1929-1941; DLB 9, 11, 44, 102; DLBD 2; DLBY 86, 97; MTCW 1

Fauset, Jessie Redmon 1884(?)-1961 ..... **CLC 19, 54; BLC 2; DAM MULT**
See also BW 1; CA 109; DLB 51

Faust, Frederick (Schiller) 1892-1944(?) .... **TCLC 49; DAM POP**
See also CA 108; 152

Faust, Irvin 1924- .... **CLC 8**
See also CA 33-36R; CANR 28, 67; DLB 2, 28; DLBY 80

Fawkes, Guy
See Benchley, Robert (Charles)

Fearing, Kenneth (Flexner) 1902-1961... **CLC 51**
See also CA 93-96; CANR 59; DLB 9

Fecamps, Elise
See Creasey, John

Federman, Raymond 1928- .... **CLC 6, 47**
See also CA 17-20R; CAAS 8; CANR 10, 43; DLBY 80

Federspiel, J(uerg) F. 1931- .... **CLC 42**
See also CA 146

Feiffer, Jules (Ralph) 1929- .... **CLC 2, 8, 64; DAM DRAM**
See also AAYA 3; CA 17-20R; CANR 30, 59; DLB 7, 44; INT CANR-30; MTCW 1; SATA 8, 61

Feige, Hermann Albert Otto Maximilian
See Traven, B.

Feinberg, David B. 1956-1994 .... **CLC 59**
See also CA 135; 147

Feinstein, Elaine 1930- .... **CLC 36**
See also CA 69-72; CAAS 1; CANR 31, 68; DLB 14, 40; MTCW 1

Feldman, Irving (Mordecai) 1928- ...... **CLC 7**
See also CA 1-4R; CANR 1; DLB 169

Felix-Tchicaya, Gerald
See Tchicaya, Gerald Felix

Fellini, Federico 1920-1993 .... **CLC 16, 85**
See also CA 65-68; 143; CANR 33

Felsen, Henry Gregor 1916- .... **CLC 17**
See also CA 1-4R; CANR 1; SAAS 2; SATA 1

Fenno, Jack
See Calisher, Hortense

Garner, Alan 1934- .... **CLC 17; DAB; DAM POP**
See also AAYA 18; CA 73-76; CANR 15, 64; CLR 20; DLB 161; MAICYA; MTCW 1; SATA 18, 69

Garner, Hugh 1913-1979 .... **CLC 13**
See also CA 69-72; CANR 31; DLB 68

Garnett, David 1892-1981................. **CLC 3**
See also CA 5-8R; 103; CANR 17; DLB 34

Garos, Stephanie
See Katz, Steve

Garrett, George (Palmer) 1929- .... **CLC 3, 11, 51; SSC 30**
See also CA 1-4R; CAAS 5; CANR 1, 42, 67; DLB 2, 5, 130, 152; DLBY 83

Garrick, David 1717-1779 .... **LC 15; DAM DRAM**
See also DLB 84

Garrigue, Jean 1914-1972.............. **CLC 2, 8**
See also CA 5-8R; 37-40R; CANR 20

Garrison, Frederick
See Sinclair, Upton (Beall)

Garth, Will
See Hamilton, Edmond; Kuttner, Henry

Garvey, Marcus (Moziah, Jr.) 1887-1940 .... **TCLC 41; BLC 2; DAM MULT**
See also BW 1; CA 120; 124

Gary, Romain............................. **CLC 25**
See also Kacew, Romain

Gascar, Pierre............................. **CLC 11**
See also Fournier, Pierre

Gascoyne, David (Emery) 1916-....... **CLC 45**
See also CA 65-68; CANR 10, 28, 54; DLB 20; MTCW 1

Gaskell, Elizabeth Cleghorn 1810-1865 .... **NCLC 70; DAB; DAM MST; SSC 25**
See also CDBLB 1832-1890; DLB 21, 144, 159

Gass, William H(oward) 1924-............. **CLC 1, 2, 8, 11, 15, 39; SSC 12**
See also CA 17-20R; CANR 30, 71; DLB 2; MTCW 1

Gasset, Jose Ortega y
See Ortega y Gasset, Jose

Gates, Henry Louis, Jr. 1950-............. **CLC 65; BLCS; DAM MULT**
See also BW 2; CA 109; CANR 25, 53, 75; DLB 67

Gautier, Theophile 1811-1872............ **NCLC 1, 59; DAM POET; PC 18; SSC 20**
See also DLB 119

Gawsworth, John
See Bates, H(erbert) E(rnest)

Gay, Oliver
See Gogarty, Oliver St. John

Gaye, Marvin (Penze) 1939-1984...... **CLC 26**
See also CA 112

Gebler, Carlo (Ernest) 1954- .... **CLC 39**
See also CA 119; 133

Gee, Maggie (Mary) 1948-.............. **CLC 57**
See also CA 130

Gee, Maurice (Gough) 1931-........... **CLC 29**
See also CA 97-100; CANR 67; SATA 46, 101

Gelbart, Larry (Simon) 1923-......**CLC 21, 61**
See also CA 73-76; CANR 45

Gelber, Jack 1932- ....**CLC 1, 6, 14, 79**
See also CA 1-4R; CANR 2; DLB 7

Gellhorn, Martha (Ellis) 1908-1998 ...... **CLC 14, 60**
See also CA 77-80; 164; CANR 44; DLBY 82

Genet, Jean 1910-1986...................... **CLC 1, 2, 5, 10, 14, 44, 46; DAM DRAM**
See also CA 13-16R; CANR 18; DLB 72; DLBY 86; MTCW 1

Gent, Peter 1942-.......................... **CLC 29**
See also AITN 1; CA 89-92; DLBY 82

Gentlewoman in New England, A
See Bradstreet, Anne

Gentlewoman in Those Parts, A
See Bradstreet, Anne

George, Jean Craighead 1919- .... **CLC 35**
See also AAYA 8; CA 5-8R; CANR 25; CLR 1; DLB 52; JRDA; MAICYA; SATA 2, 68

George, Stefan (Anton) 1868-1933 ...... **TCLC 2, 14**
See also CA 104

Georges, Georges Martin
See Simenon, Georges (Jacques Christian)

Gerhardi, William Alexander
See Gerhardie, William Alexander

Gerhardie, William Alexander 1895-1977 ....**CLC 5**
See also CA 25-28R; 73-76; CANR 18; DLB 36

Gerstler, Amy 1956- .... **CLC 70**
See also CA 146

Gertler, T.................................... **CLC 34**
See also CA 116; 121; INT 121

Ghalib .... **NCLC 39**
See also Ghalib, Hsadullah Khan

Ghalib, Hsadullah Khan 1797-1869
See Ghalib

Ghelderode, Michel de 1898-1962......... **CLC 6, 11; DAM DRAM**
See also CA 85-88; CANR 40

Ghiselin, Brewster 1903- .... **CLC 23**
See also CA 13-16R; CAAS 10; CANR 13

Ghose, Aurabinda 1872-1950 .... **TCLC 63**
See also CA 163

Ghose, Zulfikar 1935-.................... **CLC 42**
See also CA 65-68; CANR 67

Ghosh, Amitav 1956-.................... **CLC 44**
See also CA 147

Giacosa, Giuseppe 1847-1906 .... **TCLC 7**
See also CA 104

Gibb, Lee
See Waterhouse, Keith (Spencer)

Gibbon, Lewis Grassic................... **TCLC 4**
See also Mitchell, James Leslie

Gibbons, Kaye 1960- .... **CLC 50, 88; DAM POP**
See also CA 151; CANR 75

Gibran, Kahlil 1883-1931 .... **TCLC 1, 9; DAM POET, POP; PC 9**
See also CA 104; 150

Gibran, Khalil
See Gibran, Kahlil

Gibson, William 1914- .... **CLC 23; DA; DAB; DAC; DAM DRAM, MST**
See also CA 9-12R; CANR 9, 42, 75; DLB 7; SATA 66

Gibson, William (Ford) 1948-.............. **CLC 39, 63; DAM POP**
See also AAYA 12; CA 126; 133; CANR 52

Gide, Andre (Paul Guillaume) 1869-1951 ... **TCLC 5, 12, 36; DA; DAB; DAC; DAM MST, NOV; SSC 13; WLC**
See also CA 104; 124; DLB 65; MTCW 1

Gifford, Barry (Colby) 1946-........... **CLC 34**
See also CA 65-68; CANR 9, 30, 40

Gilbert, Frank
See De Voto, Bernard (Augustine)

Gilbert, W(illiam) S(chwenck) 1836-1911 .... **TCLC 3; DAM DRAM, POET**
See also CA 104; SATA 36

Gilbreth, Frank B., Jr. 1911-........... **CLC 17**
See also CA 9-12R; SATA 2

Gilchrist, Ellen 1935-...................... **CLC 34, 48; DAM POP; SSC 14**
See also CA 113; 116; CANR 41, 61; DLB 130; MTCW 1

Giles, Molly 1942-........................ **CLC 39**
See also CA 126

Gill, Eric 1882-1940 .... **TCLC 85**

Gill, Patrick
See Creasey, John

Gilliam, Terry (Vance) 1940-........... **CLC 21**
See also Monty Python

Gillian, Jerry
See Gilliam, Terry (Vance)

Gilliatt, Penelope (Ann Douglass) 1932-1993 .... **CLC 2, 10, 13, 53**
See also AITN 2; CA 13-16R; 141; CANR 49; DLB 14

Gilman, Charlotte (Anna) Perkins (Stetson) 1860-1935 .... **TCLC 9, 37; SSC 13**
See also CA 106; 150

Gilmour, David 1949- .... **CLC 35**
See also CA 138, 147

Gilpin, William 1724-1804........... **NCLC 30**

Gilray, J. D.
See Mencken, H(enry) L(ouis)

Gilroy, Frank D(aniel) 1925- .... **CLC 2**
See also CA 81-84; CANR 32, 64; DLB 7

Gilstrap, John 1957(?)- .... **CLC 99**
See also CA 160

Ginsberg, Allen 1926-1997................. **CLC 1, 2, 3, 4, 6, 13, 36, 69, 109; DA; DAB; DAC; DAM MST, POET; PC 4; WLC**
See also AITN 1; CA 1-4R; 157; CANR 2, 41, 63; CDALB 1941-1968; DLB 5, 16, 169; MTCW 1

Ginzburg, Natalia 1916-1991 .... **CLC 5, 11, 54, 70**
See also CA 85-88; 135; CANR 33; DLB 177; MTCW 1

Giono, Jean 1895-1970 .... **CLC 4, 11**
See also CA 45-48; 29-32R; CANR 2, 35; DLB 72; MTCW 1

Giovanni, Nikki 1943- .... **CLC 2, 4, 19, 64, 117; BLC 2; DA; DAB; DAC; DAM MST, MULT, POET; PC 19; WLCS**
See also AAYA 22; AITN 1; BW 2; CA 29-32R; CAAS 6; CANR 18, 41, 60; CLR 6; DLB 5, 41; INT CANR-18; MAICYA; MTCW 1; SATA 24

Giovene, Andrea 1904- .... **CLC 7**
See also CA 85-88

Gippius, Zinaida (Nikolayevna) 1869-1945
See Hippius, Zinaida

Giraudoux, (Hippolyte) Jean 1882-1944 ..... **TCLC 2, 7; DAM DRAM**
See also CA 104; DLB 65

Gironella, Jose Maria 1917- .... **CLC 11**
See also CA 101

Gissing, George (Robert) 1857-1903 ... **TCLC 3, 24, 47**
See also CA 105; 167; DLB 18, 135, 184

Giurlani, Aldo
See Palazzeschi, Aldo

Gladkov, Fyodor (Vasilyevich) 1883-1958 .... **TCLC 27**
See also CA 170

Glanville, Brian (Lester) 1931- .... **CLC 6**
See also CA 5-8R; CAAS 9; CANR 3, 70; DLB 15, 139; SATA 42

Glasgow, Ellen (Anderson Gholson) 1873-1945 .... **TCLC 2, 7**
See also CA 104; 164; DLB 9, 12

Glaspell, Susan 1882(?)-1948 .... **TCLC 55; DC 10**
See also CA 110; 154; DLB 7, 9, 78; YABC 2

Glassco, John 1909-1981 .... **CLC 9**
See also CA 13-16R; 102; CANR 15; DLB 68

Glasscock, Amnesia
See Steinbeck, John (Ernst)

Glasser, Ronald J. 1940(?)- .... **CLC 37**

Glassman, Joyce
See Johnson, Joyce

Glendinning, Victoria 1937- .... **CLC 50**
See also CA 120; 127; CANR 59; DLB 155

Glissant, Edouard 1928- .... **CLC 10, 68; DAM MULT**
See also CA 153

Gloag, Julian 1930- .... **CLC 40**
See also AITN 1; CA 65-68; CANR 10, 70

Glowacki, Aleksander
See Prus, Boleslaw

Gluck, Louise (Elisabeth) 1943- .... **CLC 7, 22, 44, 81; DAM POET; PC 16**
See also CA 33-36R; CANR 40, 69; DLB 5

Glyn, Elinor 1864-1943 .... **TCLC 72**
See also DLB 153

Gobineau, Joseph Arthur (Comte) de 1816-1882 .... **NCLC 17**
See also DLB 123

Godard, Jean-Luc 1930- .... **CLC 20**
See also CA 93-96

Godden, (Margaret) Rumer 1907-.... **CLC 53**
See also AAYA 6; CA 5-8R; CANR 4, 27, 36, 55; CLR 20; DLB 161; MAICYA; SAAS 12; SATA 3, 36

Godoy Alcayaga, Lucila 1889-1957
See Mistral, Gabriela

Godwin, Gail (Kathleen) 1937- .... **CLC 5, 8, 22, 31, 69; DAM POP**
See also CA 29-32R; CANR 15, 43, 69; DLB 6; INT CANR-15; MTCW 1

Godwin, William 1756-1836 .... **NCLC 14**
See also CDBLB 1789-1832; DLB 39, 104, 142, 158, 163

Goebbels, Josef
See Goebbels, (Paul) Joseph

Goebbels, (Paul) Joseph 1897-1945 ..... **TCLC 68**
See also CA 115; 148

Goebbels, Joseph Paul
See Goebbels, (Paul) Joseph

Goethe, Johann Wolfgang von 1749-1832 .... **NCLC 4, 22, 34; DA; DAB; DAC; DAM DRAM, MST, POET; PC 5; WLC**
See also DLB 94

Gogarty, Oliver St. John 1878-1957 .... **TCLC 15**
See also CA 109; 150; DLB 15, 19

Gogol, Nikolai (Vasilyevich) 1809-1852 .... **NCLC 5, 15, 31; DA; DAB; DAC; DAM DRAM, MST; DC 1; SSC 4, 29; WLC**
See also DLB 198

Goines, Donald 1937(?)-1974 .... **CLC 80; BLC 2; DAM MULT, POP**
See also AITN 1; BW 1; CA 124; 114; DLB 33

Gold, Herbert 1924- .... **CLC 4, 7, 14, 42**
See also CA 9-12R; CANR 17, 45; DLB 2; DLBY 81

Goldbarth, Albert 1948- .... **CLC 5, 38**
See also CA 53-56; CANR 6, 40; DLB 120

Goldberg, Anatol 1910-1982 .... **CLC 34**
See also CA 131; 117

Goldemberg, Isaac 1945- .... **CLC 52**
See also CA 69-72; CAAS 12; CANR 11, 32; HW

Golding, William (Gerald) 1911-1993.... **CLC 1, 2, 3, 8, 10, 17, 27, 58, 81; DA; DAB; DAC; DAM MST, NOV; WLC**
See also AAYA 5; CA 5-8R; 141; CANR 13, 33, 54; CDBLB 1945-1960; DLB 15, 100; MTCW 1

Goldman, Emma 1869-1940 .... **TCLC 13**
See also CA 110; 150

Goldman, Francisco 1954- .... **CLC 76**
See also CA 162

Goldman, William (W.) 1931- .... **CLC 1, 48**
See also CA 9-12R; CANR 29, 69; DLB 44

Goldmann, Lucien 1913-1970 .... **CLC 24**
See also CA 25-28; CAP 2

Goldoni, Carlo 1707-1793 .... **LC 4; DAM DRAM**

Goldsberry, Steven 1949- .... **CLC 34**
See also CA 131

Goldsmith, Oliver 1728-1774 .... **LC 2, 48; DA; DAB; DAC; DAM DRAM, MST, NOV, POET; DC 8; WLC**
See also CDBLB 1660-1789; DLB 39, 89, 104, 109, 142; SATA 26

Goldsmith, Peter
See Priestley, J(ohn) B(oynton)

Gombrowicz, Witold 1904-1969 .... **CLC 4, 7, 11, 49; DAM DRAM**
See also CA 19-20; 25-28R; CAP 2

Gomez de la Serna, Ramon 1888-1963... **CLC 9**
See also CA 153; 116; HW

Goncharov, Ivan Alexandrovich 1812-1891 .... **NCLC 1, 63**

Goncourt, Edmond (Louis Antoine Huot) de 1822-1896 .... **NCLC 7**
See also DLB 123

Goncourt, Jules (Alfred Huot) de 1830-1870 .... **NCLC 7**
See also DLB 123

Gontier, Fernande 19(?)- .... **CLC 50**

Gonzalez Martinez, Enrique 1871-1952 .... **TCLC 72**
See also CA 166; HW

Goodman, Paul 1911-1972 ....**CLC 1, 2, 4, 7**
See also CA 19-20; 37-40R; CANR 34; CAP 2; DLB 130; MTCW 1

Gordimer, Nadine 1923- .... **CLC 3, 5, 7, 10, 18, 33, 51, 70; DA; DAB; DAC; DAM MST, NOV; SSC 17; WLCS**
See also CA 5-8R; CANR 3, 28, 56; INT CANR-28; MTCW 1

Gordon, Adam Lindsay 1833-1870 ..... **NCLC 21**

Gordon, Caroline 1895-1981 .... **CLC 6, 13, 29, 83; SSC 15**
See also CA 11-12; 103; CANR 36; CAP 1; DLB 4, 9, 102; DLBD 17; DLBY 81; MTCW 1

Gordon, Charles William 1860-1937
See Connor, Ralph

Gordon, Mary (Catherine) 1949- .... **CLC 13, 22**
See also CA 102; CANR 44; DLB 6; DLBY 81; INT 102; MTCW 1

Gordon, N. J.
See Bosman, Herman Charles

Gordon, Sol 1923- .... **CLC 26**
See also CA 53-56; CANR 4; SATA 11

Gordone, Charles 1925-1995 .... **CLC 1, 4; DAM DRAM; DC 8**
See also BW 1; CA 93-96; 150; CANR 55; DLB 7; INT 93-96; MTCW 1

Gore, Catherine 1800-1861 .... **NCLC 65**
See also DLB 116

Gorenko, Anna Andreevna
See Akhmatova, Anna

Gorky, Maxim 1868-1936 .... **TCLC 8; DAB; SSC 28; WLC**
    See also Peshkov, Alexei Maximovich

Goryan, Sirak
    See Saroyan, William

Gosse, Edmund (William) 1849-1928... **TCLC 28**
    See also CA 117; DLB 57, 144, 184

Gotlieb, Phyllis Fay (Bloom) 1926- ... **CLC 18**
    See also CA 13-16R; CANR 7; DLB 88

Gottesman, S. D.
    See Kornbluth, C(yril) M.; Pohl, Frederik

Gottfried von Strassburg fl. c. 1210- .... **CMLC 10**
    See also DLB 138

Gould, Lois .... **CLC 4, 10**
    See also CA 77-80; CANR 29; MTCW 1

Gourmont, Remy (-Marie-Charles) de 1858-1915 .... **TCLC 17**
    See also CA 109; 150

Govier, Katherine 1948- .... **CLC 51**
    See also CA 101; CANR 18, 40

Goyen, (Charles) William 1915-1983..... **CLC 5, 8, 14, 40**
    See also AITN 2; CA 5-8R; 110; CANR 6, 71; DLB 2; DLBY 83; INT CANR-6

Goytisolo, Juan 1931- .... **CLC 5, 10, 23; DAM MULT; HLC**
    See also CA 85-88; CANR 32, 61; HW; MTCW 1

Gozzano, Guido 1883-1916 .... **PC 10**
    See also CA 154; DLB 114

Gozzi, (Conte) Carlo 1720-1806 ..... **NCLC 23**

Grabbe, Christian Dietrich 1801-1836 .... **NCLC 2**
    See also DLB 133

Grace, Patricia 1937- .... **CLC 56**

Gracian y Morales, Baltasar 1601-1658 ... **LC 15**

Gracq, Julien .... **CLC 11, 48**
    See also Poirier, Louis

Grade, Chaim 1910-1982 .... **CLC 10**
    See also CA 93-96; 107

Graduate of Oxford, A
    See Ruskin, John

Grafton, Garth
    See Duncan, Sara Jeannette

Graham, John
    See Phillips, David Graham

Graham, Jorie 1951- .... **CLC 48**
    See also CA 111; CANR 63; DLB 120

Graham, R(obert) B(ontine) Cunninghame
    See Cunninghame Graham, R(obert) B(ontine)

Graham, Robert
    See Haldeman, Joe (William)

Graham, Tom
    See Lewis, (Harry) Sinclair

Graham, W(illiam) S(ydney) 1918-1986 .... **CLC 29**
    See also CA 73-76; 118; DLB 20

Graham, Winston (Mawdsley) 1910- .... **CLC 23**
    See also CA 49-52; CANR 2, 22, 45, 66; DLB 77

Grahame, Kenneth 1859-1932 .... **TCLC 64; DAB**
    See also CA 108; 136; CLR 5; DLB 34, 141, 178; MAICYA; SATA 100; YABC 1

Grant, Skeeter
    See Spiegelman, Art

Granville-Barker, Harley 1877-1946 ... **TCLC 2; DAM DRAM**
    See also Barker, Harley Granville

Grass, Guenter (Wilhelm) 1927- .... **CLC 1, 2, 4, 6, 11, 15, 22, 32, 49, 88; DA; DAB; DAC; DAM MST, NOV; WLC**
    See also CA 13-16R; CANR 20, 75; DLB 75, 124; MTCW 1

Gratton, Thomas
    See Hulme, T(homas) E(rnest)

Grau, Shirley Ann 1929- ....**CLC 4, 9; SSC 15**
    See also CA 89-92; CANR 22, 69; DLB 2; INT CANR-22; MTCW 1

Gravel, Fern
    See Hall, James Norman

Graver, Elizabeth 1964- .... **CLC 70**
    See also CA 135; CANR 71

Graves, Richard Perceval 1945- .... **CLC 44**
    See also CA 65-68; CANR 9, 26, 51

Graves, Robert (von Ranke) 1895-1985 .... **CLC 1, 2, 6, 11, 39, 44, 45; DAB; DAC; DAM MST, POET; PC 6**
    See also CA 5-8R; 117; CANR 5, 36; CD-BLB 1914-1945; DLB 20, 100, 191; DLBD 18; DLBY 85; MTCW 1; SATA 45

Graves, Valerie
    See Bradley, Marion Zimmer

Gray, Alasdair (James) 1934- .... **CLC 41**
    See also CA 126; CANR 47, 69; DLB 194; INT 126; MTCW 1

Gray, Amlin 1946- .... **CLC 29**
    See also CA 138

Gray, Francine du Plessix 1930- .... **CLC 22; DAM NOV**
    See also BEST 90:3; CA 61-64; CAAS 2; CANR 11, 33, 75; INT CANR-11; MTCW 1

Gray, John (Henry) 1866-1934 ...... **TCLC 19**
    See also CA 119; 162

Gray, Simon (James Holliday) 1936-..... **CLC 9, 14, 36**
    See also AITN 1; CA 21-24R; CAAS 3; CANR 32, 69; DLB 13; MTCW 1

Gray, Spalding 1941- .... **CLC 49, 112; DAM POP; DC 7**
    See also CA 128; CANR 74

Gray, Thomas 1716-1771 .... **LC 4, 40; DA; DAB; DAC; DAM MST; PC 2; WLC**
    See also CDBLB 1660-1789; DLB 109

Grayson, David
    See Baker, Ray Stannard

Grayson, Richard (A.) 1951- .... **CLC 38**
    See also CA 85-88; CANR 14, 31, 57

Greeley, Andrew M(oran) 1928-........... **CLC 28; DAM POP**
    See also CA 5-8R; CAAS 7; CANR 7, 43, 69; MTCW 1

Green, Anna Katharine 1846-1935 ..... **TCLC 63**
    See also CA 112; 159; DLB 202

Green, Brian
    See Card, Orson Scott

Green, Hannah
    See Greenberg, Joanne (Goldenberg)

Green, Hannah 1927(?)-1996............. **CLC 3**
    See also CA 73-76; CANR 59

Green, Henry 1905-1973 .... **CLC 2, 13, 97**
    See also Yorke, Henry Vincent

Green, Julian (Hartridge) 1900-1998
    See Green, Julien

Green, Julien......................... **CLC 3, 11, 77**
    See also Green, Julian (Hartridge)

Green, Paul (Eliot) 1894-1981.............. **CLC 25; DAM DRAM**
    See also AITN 1; CA 5-8R; 103; CANR 3; DLB 7, 9; DLBY 81

Greenberg, Ivan 1908-1973
    See Rahv, Philip

Greenberg, Joanne (Goldenberg) 1932- .... **CLC 7, 30**
    See also AAYA 12; CA 5-8R; CANR 14, 32, 69; SATA 25

Greenberg, Richard 1959(?)-........... **CLC 57**
    See also CA 138

Greene, Bette 1934-....................... **CLC 30**
    See also AAYA 7; CA 53-56; CANR 4; CLR 2; JRDA; MAICYA; SAAS 16; SATA 8, 102

Greene, Gael .... **CLC 8**
    See also CA 13-16R; CANR 10

Greene, Graham (Henry) 1904-1991 ..... **CLC 1, 3, 6, 9, 14, 18, 27, 37, 70, 72; DA; DAB; DAC; DAM MST, NOV; SSC 29; WLC**
    See also AITN 2; CA 13-16R; 133; CANR 35, 61; CDBLB 1945-1960; DLB 13, 15, 77, 100, 162, 201; DLBY 91; MTCW 1; SATA 20

Greene, Robert 1558-1592 .... **LC 41**
    See also DLB 62, 167

Greer, Richard
    See Silverberg, Robert

Gregor, Arthur 1923- .... **CLC 9**
    See also CA 25-28R; CAAS 10; CANR 11; SATA 36

Gregor, Lee
    See Pohl, Frederik

Gregory, Isabella Augusta (Persse) 1852-1932 .... **TCLC 1**
    See also CA 104; DLB 10

Gregory, J. Dennis
    See Williams, John A(lfred)

Grendon, Stephen
    See Derleth, August (William)

Grenville, Kate 1950- .... **CLC 61**
    See also CA 118; CANR 53

Grenville, Pelham
See Wodehouse, P(elham) G(renville)

Greve, Felix Paul (Berthold Friedrich)
1879-1948
See Grove, Frederick Philip

Grey, Zane 1872-1939....**TCLC 6; DAM POP**
See also CA 104; 132; DLB 9; MTCW 1

Grieg, (Johan) Nordahl (Brun)
1902-1943 .... **TCLC 10**
See also CA 107

Grieve, C(hristopher) M(urray)
1892-1978 ..... **CLC 11, 19; DAM POET**
See also MacDiarmid, Hugh; Pteleon

Griffin, Gerald 1803-1840 ....**NCLC 7**
See also DLB 159

Griffin, John Howard 1920-1980...... **CLC 68**
See also AITN 1; CA 1-4R; 101; CANR 2

Griffin, Peter 1942-....................... **CLC 39**
See also CA 136

Griffith, D(avid Lewelyn) W(ark)
1875(?)-1948....................... **TCLC 68**
See also CA 119; 150

Griffith, Lawrence
See Griffith, D(avid Lewelyn) W(ark)

Griffiths, Trevor 1935-...............**CLC 13, 52**
See also CA 97-100; CANR 45; DLB 13

Griggs, Sutton Elbert 1872-1930(?)..... **TCLC 77**
See also CA 123; DLB 50

Grigson, Geoffrey (Edward Harvey)
1905-1985 .... **CLC 7, 39**
See also CA 25-28R; 118; CANR 20, 33;
DLB 27; MTCW 1

Grillparzer, Franz 1791-1872 ....**NCLC 1**
See also DLB 133

Grimble, Reverend Charles James
See Eliot, T(homas) S(tearns)

Grimke, Charlotte L(ottie) Forten
1837(?)-1914
See Forten, Charlotte L.

Grimm, Jacob Ludwig Karl
1785-1863 ....**NCLC 3**
See also DLB 90; MAICYA; SATA 22

Grimm, Wilhelm Karl 1786-1859 .....**NCLC 3**
See also DLB 90; MAICYA; SATA 22

Grimmelshausen, Johann Jakob Christoffel
von 1621-1676.......................... **LC 6**
See also DLB 168

Grindel, Eugene 1895-1952
See Eluard, Paul

Grisham, John 1955-..... **CLC 84; DAM POP**
See also AAYA 14; CA 138; CANR 47, 69

Grossman, David 1954 .... **CLC 67**
See also CA 138

Grossman, Vasily (Semenovich)
1905-1964 .... **CLC 41**
See also CA 124; 130; MTCW 1

Grove, Frederick Philip ....**TCLC 4**
See also Greve, Felix Paul (Berthold
Friedrich)

Grubb
See Crumb, R(obert)

Grumbach, Doris (Isaac) 1918-............ **CLC 13, 22, 64**
See also CA 5-8R; CAAS 2; CANR 9, 42, 70;
INT CANR-9

Grundtvig, Nicolai Frederik Severin
1783-1872 ....**NCLC 1**

Grunge
See Crumb, R(obert)

Grunwald, Lisa 1959-.................... **CLC 44**
See also CA 120

Guare, John 1938- .... **CLC 8, 14, 29, 67; DAM DRAM**
See also CA 73-76; CANR 21, 69; DLB 7;
MTCW 1

Gudjonsson, Halldor Kiljan 1902-1998
See Laxness, Halldor

Guenter, Erich
See Eich, Guenter

Guest, Barbara 1920- .... **CLC 34**
See also CA 25-28R; CANR 11, 44; DLB 5,
193

Guest, Judith (Ann) 1936- .... **CLC 8, 30; DAM NOV, POP**
See also AAYA 7; CA 77-80; CANR 15, 75;
INT CANR-15; MTCW 1

Guevara, Che ....**CLC 87; HLC**
See also Guevara (Serna), Ernesto

Guevara (Serna), Ernesto 1928-1967
See Guevara, Che

Guild, Nicholas M. 1944-................ **CLC 33**
See also CA 93-96

Guillemin, Jacques
See Sartre, Jean-Paul

Guillen, Jorge 1893-1984.................... **CLC 11; DAM MULT, POET**
See also CA 89-92; 112; DLB 108; HW

Guillen, Nicolas (Cristobal) 1902-1989... **CLC 48, 79; BLC 2; DAM MST, MULT, POET; HLC; PC 23**
See also BW 2; CA 116; 125; 129; HW

Guillevic, (Eugene) 1907- .... **CLC 33**
See also CA 93-96

Guillois
See Desnos, Robert

Guillois, Valentin
See Desnos, Robert

Guiney, Louise Imogen 1861-1920... **TCLC 41**
See also CA 160; DLB 54

Guiraldes, Ricardo (Guillermo)
1886-1927 .... **TCLC 39**
See also CA 131; HW; MTCW 1

Gumilev, Nikolai (Stepanovich)
1886-1921 .... **TCLC 60**
See also CA 165

Gunesekera, Romesh 1954-............. **CLC 91**
See also CA 159

Gunn, Bill....................................**CLC 5**
See also Gunn, William Harrison

Gunn, Thom(son William) 1929-.......... **CLC 3, 6, 18, 32, 81; DAM POET**
See also CA 17-20R; CANR 9, 33; CDBLB
1960 to Present; DLB 27; INT CANR-33;
MTCW 1

Gunn, William Harrison 1934(?)-1989
See Gunn, Bill

Gunnars, Kristjana 1948-............... **CLC 69**
See also CA 113; DLB 60

Gurdjieff, G(eorgei) I(vanovich)
1877(?)-1949...................... **TCLC 71**
See also CA 157

Gurganus, Allan 1947-... **CLC 70; DAM POP**
See also BEST 90:1; CA 135

Gurney, A(lbert) R(amsdell), Jr. 1930-... **CLC 32, 50, 54; DAM DRAM**
See also CA 77-80; CANR 32, 64

Gurney, Ivor (Bertie) 1890-1937 .... **TCLC 33**
See also CA 167

Gurney, Peter
See Gurney, A(lbert) R(amsdell), Jr.

Guro, Elena 1877-1913 .... **TCLC 56**

Gustafson, James M(oody) 1925- ....**CLC 100**
See also CA 25-28R; CANR 37

Gustafson, Ralph (Barker) 1909- ..... **CLC 36**
See also CA 21-24R; CANR 8, 45; DLB 88

Gut, Gom
See Simenon, Georges (Jacques Christian)

Guterson, David 1956-.................... **CLC 91**
See also CA 132; CANR 73

Guthrie, A(lfred) B(ertram), Jr.
1901-1991 .... **CLC 23**
See also CA 57-60; 134; CANR 24; DLB 6;
SATA 62; SATA-Obit 67

Guthrie, Isobel
See Grieve, C(hristopher) M(urray)

Guthrie, Woodrow Wilson 1912-1967
See Guthrie, Woody

Guthrie, Woody .... **CLC 35**
See also Guthrie, Woodrow Wilson

Guy, Rosa (Cuthbert) 1928-............ **CLC 26**
See also AAYA 4; BW 2; CA 17-20R;
CANR 14, 34; CLR 13; DLB 33; JRDA;
MAICYA; SATA 14, 62

Gwendolyn
See Bennett, (Enoch) Arnold

H. D............. **CLC 3, 8, 14, 31, 34, 73; PC 5**
See also Doolittle, Hilda

H. de V.
See Buchan, John

Haavikko, Paavo Juhani 1931- ....**CLC 18, 34**
See also CA 106

Habbema, Koos
See Heijermans, Herman

Habermas, Juergen 1929-..............**CLC 104**
See also CA 109

Habermas, Jurgen
See Habermas, Juergen

Hacker, Marilyn 1942-...................... **CLC 5, 9, 23, 72, 91; DAM POET**
See also CA 77-80; CANR 68; DLB 120

Haeckel, Ernst Heinrich (Philipp August)
1834-1919 .... **TCLC 83**
See also CA 157

Haggard, H(enry) Rider 1856-1925..... **TCLC 11**
See also CA 108; 148; DLB 70, 156, 174, 178; SATA 16

Hagiosy, L.
See Larbaud, Valery (Nicolas)

Hagiwara Sakutaro 1886-1942.......... **TCLC 60; PC 18**

Haig, Fenil
See Ford, Ford Madox

Haig-Brown, Roderick (Langmere) 1908-1976 .... **CLC 21**
See also CA 5-8R; 69-72; CANR 4, 38; CLR 31; DLB 88; MAICYA; SATA 12

Hailey, Arthur 1920- .... **CLC 5; DAM NOV, POP**
See also AITN 2; BEST 90:3; CA 1-4R; CANR 2, 36, 75; DLB 88; DLBY 82; MTCW 1

Hailey, Elizabeth Forsythe 1938-...... **CLC 40**
See also CA 93-96; CAAS 1; CANR 15, 48; INT CANR-15

Haines, John (Meade) 1924-............ **CLC 58**
See also CA 17-20R; CANR 13, 34; DLB 5

Hakluyt, Richard 1552-1616 .... **LC 31**

Haldeman, Joe (William) 1943-........ **CLC 61**
See also CA 53-56; CAAS 25; CANR 6, 70, 72; DLB 8; INT CANR-6

Haley, Alex(ander Murray Palmer) 1921-1992 ... **CLC 8, 12, 76; BLC 2; DA; DAB; DAC; DAM MST, MULT, POP**
See also AAYA 26; BW 2; CA 77-80; 136; CANR 61; DLB 38; MTCW 1

Haliburton, Thomas Chandler 1796-1865 .... **NCLC 15**
See also DLB 11, 99

Hall, Donald (Andrew, Jr.) 1928- .... **CLC 1, 13, 37, 59; DAM POET**
See also CA 5-8R; CAAS 7; CANR 2, 44, 64; DLB 5; SATA 23, 97

Hall, Frederic Sauser
See Sauser-Hall, Frederic

Hall, James
See Kuttner, Henry

Hall, James Norman 1887-1951 ..... **TCLC 23**
See also CA 123; SATA 21

Hall, Radclyffe
See Hall, (Marguerite) Radclyffe

Hall, (Marguerite) Radclyffe 1886-1943 .... **TCLC 12**
See also CA 110; 150; DLB 191

Hall, Rodney 1935- .... **CLC 51**
See also CA 109; CANR 69

Halleck, Fitz-Greene 1790-1867 ..... **NCLC 47**
See also DLB 3

Halliday, Michael
See Creasey, John

Halpern, Daniel 1945-.................... **CLC 14**
See also CA 33-36R

Hamburger, Michael (Peter Leopold) 1924- .... **CLC 5, 14**
See also CA 5-8R; CAAS 4; CANR 2, 47; DLB 27

Hamill, Pete 1935- .... **CLC 10**
See also CA 25-28R; CANR 18, 71

Hamilton, Alexander 1755(?)-1804 .....**NCLC 49**
See also DLB 37

Hamilton, Clive
See Lewis, C(live) S(taples)

Hamilton, Edmond 1904-1977 .... **CLC 1**
See also CA 1-4R; CANR 3; DLB 8

Hamilton, Eugene (Jacob) Lee
See Lee-Hamilton, Eugene (Jacob)

Hamilton, Franklin
See Silverberg, Robert

Hamilton, Gail
See Corcoran, Barbara

Hamilton, Mollie
See Kaye, M(ary) M(argaret)

Hamilton, (Anthony Walter) Patrick 1904-1962 .... **CLC 51**
See also CA 113; DLB 10

Hamilton, Virginia 1936-.................... **CLC 26; DAM MULT**
See also AAYA 2, 21; BW 2; CA 25-28R; CANR 20, 37, 73; CLR 1, 11, 40; DLB 33, 52; INT CANR-20; JRDA; MAICYA; MTCW 1; SATA 4, 56, 79

Hammett, (Samuel) Dashiell 1894-1961 .... **CLC 3, 5, 10, 19, 47; SSC 17**
See also AITN 1; CA 81-84; CANR 42; CDALB 1929-1941; DLBD 6; DLBY 96; MTCW 1

Hammon, Jupiter 1711(?)-1800(?) ......**NCLC 5; BLC 2; DAM MULT, POET; PC 16**
See also DLB 31, 50

Hammond, Keith
See Kuttner, Henry

Hamner, Earl (Henry), Jr. 1923- ...... **CLC 12**
See also AITN 2; CA 73-76; DLB 6

Hampton, Christopher (James) 1946- .... **CLC 4**
See also CA 25-28R; DLB 13; MTCW 1

Hamsun, Knut ....**TCLC 2, 14, 49**
See also Pedersen, Knut

Handke, Peter 1942-.......................... **CLC 5, 8, 10, 15, 38; DAM DRAM, NOV**
See also CA 77-80; CANR 33, 75; DLB 85, 124; MTCW 1

Hanley, James 1901-1985 ...... **CLC 3, 5, 8, 13**
See also CA 73-76; 117; CANR 36; DLB 191; MTCW 1

Hannah, Barry 1942-............ **CLC 23, 38, 90**
See also CA 108; 110; CANR 43, 68; DLB 6; INT 110; MTCW 1

Hannon, Ezra
See Hunter, Evan

Hansberry, Lorraine (Vivian) 1930-1965 .... **CLC 17, 62; BLC 2; DA; DAB; DAC; DAM DRAM, MST, MULT; DC 2**
See also AAYA 25; BW 1; CA 109; 25-28R; CABS 3; CANR 58; CDALB 1941-1968; DLB 7, 38; MTCW 1

Hansen, Joseph 1923-.................... **CLC 38**
See also CA 29-32R; CAAS 17; CANR 16, 44, 66; INT CANR-16

Hansen, Martin A(lfred) 1909-1955 .... **TCLC 32**
See also CA 167

Hanson, Kenneth O(stlin) 1922-....... **CLC 13**
See also CA 53-56; CANR 7

Hardwick, Elizabeth (Bruce) 1916-....... **CLC 13; DAM NOV**
See also CA 5-8R; CANR 3, 32, 70; DLB 6; MTCW 1

Hardy, Thomas 1840-1928....**TCLC 4, 10, 18, 32, 48, 53, 72; DA; DAB; DAC; DAM MST, NOV, POET; PC 8; SSC 2; WLC**
See also CA 104; 123; CDBLB 1890-1914; DLB 18, 19, 135; MTCW 1

Hare, David 1947-......................**CLC 29, 58**
See also CA 97-100; CANR 39; DLB 13; MTCW 1

Harewood, John
See Van Druten, John (William)

Harford, Henry
See Hudson, W(illiam) H(enry)

Hargrave, Leonie
See Disch, Thomas M(ichael)

Harjo, Joy 1951-.........**CLC 83; DAM MULT**
See also CA 114; CANR 35, 67; DLB 120, 175; NNAL

Harlan, Louis R(udolph) 1922-........ **CLC 34**
See also CA 21-24R; CANR 25, 55

Harling, Robert 1951(?)- .... **CLC 53**
See also CA 147

Harmon, William (Ruth) 1938-........ **CLC 38**
See also CA 33-36R; CANR 14, 32, 35; SATA 65

Harper, F. E. W.
See Harper, Frances Ellen Watkins

Harper, Frances E. W.
See Harper, Frances Ellen Watkins

Harper, Frances E. Watkins
See Harper, Frances Ellen Watkins

Harper, Frances Ellen
See Harper, Frances Ellen Watkins

Harper, Frances Ellen Watkins 1825-1911 .... **TCLC 14; BLC 2; DAM MULT, POET; PC 21**
See also BW 1; CA 111; 125; DLB 50

Harper, Michael S(teven) 1938- .... **CLC 7, 22**
See also BW 1; CA 33-36R; CANR 24; DLB 41

Harper, Mrs. F. E. W.
See Harper, Frances Ellen Watkins

Harris, Christie (Lucy) Irwin 1907-... **CLC 12**
See also CA 5-8R; CANR 6; CLR 47; DLB 88; JRDA; MAICYA; SAAS 10; SATA 6, 74

Harris, Frank 1856-1931 .... **TCLC 24**
See also CA 109; 150; DLB 156, 197

Harris, George Washington 1814-1869 .... **NCLC 23**
See also DLB 3, 11

Harris, Joel Chandler 1848-1908........ **TCLC 2; SSC 19**
See also CA 104; 137; CLR 49; DLB 11, 23, 42, 78, 91; MAICYA; SATA 100; YABC 1

Harris, John (Wyndham Parkes Lucas) Beynon 1903-1969
See Wyndham, John

Harris, MacDonald .... **CLC 9**
See also Heiney, Donald (William)

Harris, Mark 1922-....................... **CLC 19**
See also CA 5-8R; CAAS 3; CANR 2, 55; DLB 2; DLBY 80

Harris, (Theodore) Wilson 1921-...... **CLC 25**
See also BW 2; CA 65-68; CAAS 16; CANR 11, 27, 69; DLB 117; MTCW 1

Harrison, Elizabeth Cavanna 1909-
See Cavanna, Betty

Harrison, Harry (Max) 1925-.......... **CLC 42**
See also CA 1-4R; CANR 5, 21; DLB 8; SATA 4

Harrison, James (Thomas) 1937-......... **CLC 6, 14, 33, 66; SSC 19**
See also CA 13-16R; CANR 8, 51; DLBY 82; INT CANR-8

Harrison, Jim
See Harrison, James (Thomas)

Harrison, Kathryn 1961-................ **CLC 70**
See also CA 144; CANR 68

Harrison, Tony 1937- .... **CLC 43**
See also CA 65-68; CANR 44; DLB 40; MTCW 1

Harriss, Will(ard Irvin) 1922- .... **CLC 34**
See also CA 111

Harson, Sley
See Ellison, Harlan (Jay)

Hart, Ellis
See Ellison, Harlan (Jay)

Hart, Josephine 1942(?)-.................... **CLC 70; DAM POP**
See also CA 138; CANR 70

Hart, Moss 1904-1961...................... **CLC 66; DAM DRAM**
See also CA 109; 89-92; DLB 7

Harte, (Francis) Bret(t) 1836(?)-1902... **TCLC 1, 25; DA; DAC; DAM MST; SSC 8; WLC**
See also CA 104; 140; CDALB 1865-1917; DLB 12, 64, 74, 79, 186; SATA 26

Hartley, L(eslie) P(oles) 1895-1972........ **CLC 2, 22**
See also CA 45-48; 37-40R; CANR 33; DLB 15, 139; MTCW 1

Hartman, Geoffrey H. 1929- .... **CLC 27**
See also CA 117; 125; DLB 67

Hartmann, Sadakichi 1867-1944 .... **TCLC 73**
See also CA 157; DLB 54

Hartmann von Aue c. 1160-c. 1205 .... **CMLC 15**
See also DLB 138

Hartmann von Aue 1170-1210 ...... **CMLC 15**

Haruf, Kent 1943- .... **CLC 34**
See also CA 149

Harwood, Ronald 1934-.................... **CLC 32; DAM DRAM, MST**
See also CA 1-4R; CANR 4, 55; DLB 13

Hasegawa Tatsunosuke
See Futabatei, Shimei

Hasek, Jaroslav (Matej Frantisek) 1883-1923 .... **TCLC 4**
See also CA 104; 129; MTCW 1

Hass, Robert 1941- .... **CLC 18, 39, 99; PC 16**
See also CA 111; CANR 30, 50, 71; DLB 105; SATA 94

Hastings, Hudson
See Kuttner, Henry

Hastings, Selina .... **CLC 44**

Hathorne, John 1641-1717................. **LC 38**

Hatteras, Amelia
See Mencken, H(enry) L(ouis)

Hatteras, Owen......................... **TCLC 18**
See also Mencken, H(enry) L(ouis); Nathan, George Jean

Hauptmann, Gerhart (Johann Robert) 1862-1946 .... **TCLC 4; DAM DRAM**
See also CA 104; 153; DLB 66, 118

Havel, Vaclav 1936-.......................... **CLC 25, 58, 65; DAM DRAM; DC 6**
See also CA 104; CANR 36, 63; MTCW 1

Haviaras, Stratis .... **CLC 33**
See also Chaviaras, Strates

Hawes, Stephen 1475(?)-1523(?)..........**LC 17**
See also DLB 132

Hawkes, John (Clendennin Burne, Jr.) 1925-1998 .... **CLC 1, 2, 3, 4, 7, 9, 14, 15, 27, 49**
See also CA 1-4R; 167; CANR 2, 47, 64; DLB 2, 7; DLBY 80; MTCW 1

Hawking, S. W.
See Hawking, Stephen W(illiam)

Hawking, Stephen W(illiam) 1942-....... **CLC 63, 105**
See also AAYA 13; BEST 89:1; CA 126; 129; CANR 48

Hawkins, Anthony Hope
See Hope, Anthony

Hawthorne, Julian 1846-1934........ **TCLC 25**
See also CA 165

Hawthorne, Nathaniel 1804-1864 .... **NCLC 39; DA; DAB; DAC; DAM MST, NOV; SSC 3, 29; WLC**
See also AAYA 18; CDALB 1640-1865; DLB 1, 74; YABC 2

Haxton, Josephine Ayres 1921-
See Douglas, Ellen

Hayaseca y Eizaguirre, Jorge
See Echegaray (y Eizaguirre), Jose (Maria Waldo)

Hayashi, Fumiko 1904-1951.......... **TCLC 27**
See also CA 161; DLB 180

Haycraft, Anna
See Ellis, Alice Thomas

Hayden, Robert E(arl) 1913-1980......... **CLC 5, 9, 14, 37; BLC 2; DA; DAC; DAM MST, MULT, POET; PC 6**
See also BW 1; CA 69-72; 97-100; CABS 2; CANR 24, 75; CDALB 1941-1968; DLB 5, 76; MTCW 1; SATA 19; SATA-Obit 26

Hayford, J(oseph) E(phraim) Casely
See Casely-Hayford, J(oseph) E(phraim)

Hayman, Ronald 1932- .... **CLC 44**
See also CA 25-28R; CANR 18, 50; DLB 155

Haywood, Eliza 1693(?)-1756 ....**LC 44**
See also DLB 39

Haywood, Eliza (Fowler) 1693(?)-1756 .... **LC 1, 44**

Hazlitt, William 1778-1830 .... **NCLC 29**
See also DLB 110, 158

Hazzard, Shirley 1931- .... **CLC 18**
See also CA 9-12R; CANR 4, 70; DLBY 82; MTCW 1

Head, Bessie 1937-1986..................... **CLC 25, 67; BLC 2; DAM MULT**
See also BW 2; CA 29-32R; 119; CANR 25; DLB 117; MTCW 1

Headon, (Nicky) Topper 1956(?)- ..... **CLC 30**

Heaney, Seamus (Justin) 1939- .... **CLC 5, 7, 14, 25, 37, 74, 91; DAB; DAM POET; PC 18; WLCS**
See also CA 85-88; CANR 25, 48, 75; CD-BLB 1960 to Present; DLB 40; DLBY 95; MTCW 1

Hearn, (Patricio) Lafcadio (Tessima Carlos) 1850-1904 ....**TCLC 9**
See also CA 105; 166; DLB 12, 78, 189

Hearne, Vicki 1946- .... **CLC 56**
See also CA 139

Hearon, Shelby 1931- .... **CLC 63**
See also AITN 2; CA 25-28R; CANR 18, 48

Heat-Moon, William Least .... **CLC 29**
See also Trogdon, William (Lewis)

Hebbel, Friedrich 1813-1863 .... **NCLC 43; DAM DRAM**
See also DLB 129

Hebert, Anne 1916-.......................... **CLC 4, 13, 29; DAC; DAM MST, POET**
See also CA 85-88; CANR 69; DLB 68; MTCW 1

Hecht, Anthony (Evan) 1923-.............. **CLC 8, 13, 19; DAM POET**
See also CA 9-12R; CANR 6; DLB 5, 169

Hecht, Ben 1894-1964...................... **CLC 8**
See also CA 85-88; DLB 7, 9, 25, 26, 28, 86

Hedayat, Sadeq 1903-1951........... **TCLC 21**
See also CA 120

Hegel, Georg Wilhelm Friedrich 1770-1831 .... **NCLC 46**
See also DLB 90

Heidegger, Martin 1889-1976 .... **CLC 24**
See also CA 81-84; 65-68; CANR 34; MTCW 1

Heidenstam, (Carl Gustaf) Verner von 1859-1940 ....**TCLC 5**
See also CA 104

Heifner, Jack 1946- .... **CLC 11**
See also CA 105; CANR 47

Honig, Edwin 1919- .... **CLC 33**
   See also CA 5-8R; CAAS 8; CANR 4, 45;
   DLB 5

Hood, Hugh (John Blagdon) 1928- .... **CLC 15, 28**
   See also CA 49-52; CAAS 17; CANR 1, 33;
   DLB 53

Hood, Thomas 1799-1845 .... **NCLC 16**
   See also DLB 96

Hooker, (Peter) Jeremy 1941- .... **CLC 43**
   See also CA 77-80; CANR 22; DLB 40

hooks, bell ....**CLC 94; BLCS**
   See also Watkins, Gloria

Hope, A(lec) D(erwent) 1907- .... **CLC 3, 51**
   See also CA 21-24R; CANR 33, 74; MTCW 1

Hope, Anthony 1863-1933 .... **TCLC 83**
   See also CA 157; DLB 153, 156

Hope, Brian
   See Creasey, John

Hope, Christopher (David Tully) 1944- .... **CLC 52**
   See also CA 106; CANR 47; SATA 62

Hopkins, Gerard Manley 1844-1889 ...**NCLC 17; DA; DAB; DAC; DAM MST, POET; PC 15; WLC**
   See also CDBLB 1890-1914; DLB 35, 57

Hopkins, John (Richard) 1931-1998....**CLC 4**
   See also CA 85-88; 169

Hopkins, Pauline Elizabeth 1859-1930 .... **TCLC 28; BLC 2; DAM MULT**
   See also BW 2; CA 141; DLB 50

Hopkinson, Francis 1737-1791...........**LC 25**
   See also DLB 31

Hopley-Woolrich, Cornell George 1903-1968
   See Woolrich, Cornell

Horatio
   See Proust, (Valentin-Louis-George-Eugene-) Marcel

Horgan, Paul (George Vincent O'Shaughnessy) 1903-1995 .... **CLC 9, 53; DAM NOV**
   See also CA 13-16R; 147; CANR 9, 35; DLB 102; DLBY 85; INT CANR-9; MTCW 1; SATA 13; SATA-Obit 84

Horn, Peter
   See Kuttner, Henry

Hornem, Horace Esq.
   See Byron, George Gordon (Noel)

Horney, Karen (Clementine Theodore Danielsen) 1885-1952............ **TCLC 71**
   See also CA 114; 165

Hornung, E(rnest) W(illiam) 1866-1921 .... **TCLC 59**
   See also CA 108; 160; DLB 70

Horovitz, Israel (Arthur) 1939-............ **CLC 56; DAM DRAM**
   See also CA 33-36R; CANR 46, 59; DLB 7

Horvath, Odon von
   See Horvath, Oedoen von

Horvath, Oedoen von 1901-1938 .... **TCLC 45**
   See also Horvath, Odon von

Horwitz, Julius 1920-1986 .... **CLC 14**
   See also CA 9-12R; 119; CANR 12

Hospital, Janette Turner 1942- .... **CLC 42**
   See also CA 108; CANR 48

Hostos, E. M. de
   See Hostos (y Bonilla), Eugenio Maria de

Hostos, Eugenio M. de
   See Hostos (y Bonilla), Eugenio Maria de

Hostos, Eugenio Maria
   See Hostos (y Bonilla), Eugenio Maria de

Hostos (y Bonilla), Eugenio Maria de 1839-1903 .... **TCLC 24**
   See also CA 123; 131; HW

Houdini
   See Lovecraft, H(oward) P(hillips)

Hougan, Carolyn 1943-.................. **CLC 34**
   See also CA 139

Household, Geoffrey (Edward West) 1900-1988 .... **CLC 11**
   See also CA 77-80; 126; CANR 58; DLB 87; SATA 14; SATA-Obit 59

Housman, A(lfred) E(dward) 1859-1936 ....**TCLC 1, 10; DA; DAB; DAC; DAM MST, POET; PC 2; WLCS**
   See also CA 104; 125; DLB 19; MTCW 1

Housman, Laurence 1865-1959........**TCLC 7**
   See also CA 106; 155; DLB 10; SATA 25

Howard, Elizabeth Jane 1923-...... **CLC 7, 29**
   See also CA 5-8R; CANR 8, 62

Howard, Maureen 1930- ....**CLC 5, 14, 46**
   See also CA 53-56; CANR 31, 75; DLBY 83; INT CANR-31; MTCW 1

Howard, Richard 1929- ....**CLC 7, 10, 47**
   See also AITN 1; CA 85-88; CANR 25; DLB 5; INT CANR-25

Howard, Robert E(rvin) 1906-1936 ...**TCLC 8**
   See also CA 105; 157

Howard, Warren F.
   See Pohl, Frederik

Howe, Fanny (Quincy) 1940-........... **CLC 47**
   See also CA 117; CAAS 27; CANR 70; SATA-Brief 52

Howe, Irving 1920-1993 .... **CLC 85**
   See also CA 9-12R; 141; CANR 21, 50; DLB 67; MTCW 1

Howe, Julia Ward 1819-1910........ **TCLC 21**
   See also CA 117; DLB 1, 189

Howe, Susan 1937-....................... **CLC 72**
   See also CA 160; DLB 120

Howe, Tina 1937- .... **CLC 48**
   See also CA 109

Howell, James 1594(?)-1666 ....**LC 13**
   See also DLB 151

Howells, W. D.
   See Howells, William Dean

Howells, William D.
   See Howells, William Dean

Howells, William Dean 1837-1920 ...... **TCLC 7, 17, 41**
   See also CA 104; 134; CDALB 1865-1917; DLB 12, 64, 74, 79, 189

Howes, Barbara 1914-1996 .... **CLC 15**
   See also CA 9-12R; 151; CAAS 3; CANR 53; SATA 5

Hrabal, Bohumil 1914-1997 ....**CLC 13, 67**
   See also CA 106; 156; CAAS 12; CANR 57

Hroswitha of Gandersheim c. 935-c. 1002 .... **CMLC 29**
   See also DLB 148

Hsun, Lu
   See Lu Hsun

Hubbard, L(afayette) Ron(ald) 1911-1986 .... **CLC 43; DAM POP**
   See also CA 77-80; 118; CANR 52

Huch, Ricarda (Octavia) 1864-1947 .... **TCLC 13**
   See also CA 111; DLB 66

Huddle, David 1942- .... **CLC 49**
   See also CA 57-60; CAAS 20; DLB 130

Hudson, Jeffrey
   See Crichton, (John) Michael

Hudson, W(illiam) H(enry) 1841-1922 .... **TCLC 29**
   See also CA 115; DLB 98, 153, 174; SATA 35

Hueffer, Ford Madox
   See Ford, Ford Madox

Hughart, Barry 1934-..................... **CLC 39**
   See also CA 137

Hughes, Colin
   See Creasey, John

Hughes, David (John) 1930-............ **CLC 48**
   See also CA 116; 129; DLB 14

Hughes, Edward James
   See Hughes, Ted

Hughes, (James) Langston 1902-1967.... **CLC 1, 5, 10, 15, 35, 44, 108; BLC 2; DA; DAB; DAC; DAM DRAM, MST, MULT, POET; DC 3; PC 1; SSC 6; WLC**
   See also AAYA 12; BW 1; CA 1-4R; 25-28R; CANR 1, 34; CDALB 1929-1941; CLR 17; DLB 4, 7, 48, 51, 86; JRDA; MAICYA; MTCW 1; SATA 4, 33

Hughes, Richard (Arthur Warren) 1900-1976 ....**CLC 1, 11; DAM NOV**
   See also CA 5-8R; 65-68; CANR 4; DLB 15, 161; MTCW 1; SATA 8; SATA-Obit 25

Hughes, Ted 1930-1998 .... **CLC 2, 4, 9, 14, 37; DAB; DAC; PC 7**
   See also Hughes, Edward James

Hugo, Richard F(ranklin) 1923-1982 .... **CLC 6, 18, 32; DAM POET**
   See also CA 49-52; 108; CANR 3; DLB 5

Hugo, Victor (Marie) 1802-1885...... **NCLC 3, 10, 21; DA; DAB; DAC; DAM DRAM, MST, NOV, POET; PC 17; WLC**
   See also DLB 119, 192; SATA 47

Huidobro, Vicente
   See Huidobro Fernandez, Vicente Garcia

Huidobro Fernandez, Vicente Garcia 1893-1948 .... **TCLC 31**
   See also CA 131; HW

Hulme, Keri 1947- .... **CLC 39**
   See also CA 125; CANR 69; INT 125

Hulme, T(homas) E(rnest)
1883-1917 .... **TCLC 21**
See also CA 117; DLB 19

Hume, David 1711-1776 .... **LC 7**
See also DLB 104

Humphrey, William 1924-1997 .... **CLC 45**
See also CA 77-80; 160; CANR 68; DLB 6

Humphreys, Emyr Owen 1919-........ **CLC 47**
See also CA 5-8R; CANR 3, 24; DLB 15

Humphreys, Josephine 1945-.......**CLC 34, 57**
See also CA 121; 127; INT 127

Huneker, James Gibbons 1857-1921 ... **TCLC 65**
See also DLB 71

Hungerford, Pixie
See Brinsmead, H(esba) F(ay)

Hunt, E(verette) Howard, (Jr.) 1918-... **CLC 3**
See also AITN 1; CA 45-48; CANR 2, 47

Hunt, Kyle
See Creasey, John

Hunt, (James Henry) Leigh
1784-1859 .....**NCLC 1, 70; DAM POET**
See also DLB 96, 110, 144

Hunt, Marsha 1946-...................... **CLC 70**
See also BW 2; CA 143

Hunt, Violet 1866(?)-1942............. **TCLC 53**
See also DLB 162, 197

Hunter, E. Waldo
See Sturgeon, Theodore (Hamilton)

Hunter, Evan 1926-...**CLC 11, 31; DAM POP**
See also CA 5-8R; CANR 5, 38, 62; DLBY 82; INT CANR-5; MTCW 1; SATA 25

Hunter, Kristin (Eggleston) 1931-..... **CLC 35**
See also AITN 1; BW 1; CA 13-16R; CANR 13; CLR 3; DLB 33; INT CANR-13; MAICYA; SAAS 10; SATA 12

Hunter, Mollie 1922- .... **CLC 21**
See also McIlwraith, Maureen Mollie Hunter

Hunter, Robert (?)-1734 .... **LC 7**

Hurston, Zora Neale 1903-1960 .... **CLC 7, 30, 61; BLC 2; DA; DAC; DAM MST, MULT, NOV; SSC 4; WLCS**
See also AAYA 15; BW 1; CA 85-88; CANR 61; DLB 51, 86; MTCW 1

Huston, John (Marcellus) 1906-1987..... **CLC 20**
See also CA 73-76; 123; CANR 34; DLB 26

Hustvedt, Siri 1955- .... **CLC 76**
See also CA 137

Hutten, Ulrich von 1488-1523.............**LC 16**
See also DLB 179

Huxley, Aldous (Leonard) 1894-1963 .... **CLC 1, 3, 4, 5, 8, 11, 18, 35, 79; DA; DAB; DAC; DAM MST, NOV; WLC**
See also AAYA 11; CA 85-88; CANR 44; CDBLB 1914-1945; DLB 36, 100, 162, 195; MTCW 1; SATA 63

Huxley, T(homas) H(enry)
1825-1895 .... **NCLC 67**
See also DLB 57

Huysmans, Joris-Karl 1848-1907 .... **TCLC 7, 69**
See also CA 104; 165; DLB 123

Hwang, David Henry 1957-................. **CLC 55; DAM DRAM; DC 4**
See also CA 127; 132; INT 132

Hyde, Anthony 1946-.................... **CLC 42**
See also CA 136

Hyde, Margaret O(ldroyd) 1917-...... **CLC 21**
See also CA 1-4R; CANR 1, 36; CLR 23; JRDA; MAICYA; SAAS 8; SATA 1, 42, 76

Hynes, James 1956(?)- .... **CLC 65**
See also CA 164

Ian, Janis 1951-............................. **CLC 21**
See also CA 105

Ibanez, Vicente Blasco
See Blasco Ibanez, Vicente

Ibarguengoitia, Jorge 1928-1983 ...... **CLC 37**
See also CA 124; 113; HW

Ibsen, Henrik (Johan) 1828-1906 .... **TCLC 2, 8, 16, 37, 52; DA; DAB; DAC; DAM DRAM, MST; DC 2; WLC**
See also CA 104; 141

Ibuse, Masuji 1898-1993 .... **CLC 22**
See also CA 127; 141; DLB 180

Ichikawa, Kon 1915- .... **CLC 20**
See also CA 121

Idle, Eric 1943- .... **CLC 21**
See also Monty Python

Ignatow, David 1914-1997 ....**CLC 4, 7, 14, 40**
See also CA 9-12R; 162; CAAS 3; CANR 31, 57; DLB 5

Ihimaera, Witi 1944- .... **CLC 46**
See also CA 77-80

Ilf, Ilya.................................... **TCLC 21**
See also Fainzilberg, Ilya Arnoldovich

Illyes, Gyula 1902-1983....................**PC 16**
See also CA 114; 109

Immermann, Karl (Lebrecht)
1796-1840 .... **NCLC 4, 49**
See also DLB 133

Ince, Thomas H. 1882-1924.......... **TCLC 89**

Inchbald, Elizabeth 1753-1821....... **NCLC 62**
See also DLB 39, 89

Inclan, Ramon (Maria) del Valle
See Valle-Inclan, Ramon (Maria) del

Infante, G(uillermo) Cabrera
See Cabrera Infante, G(uillermo)

Ingalls, Rachel (Holmes) 1940- .... **CLC 42**
See also CA 123; 127

Ingamells, Reginald Charles
See Ingamells, Rex

Ingamells, Rex 1913-1955 .... **TCLC 35**
See also CA 167

Inge, William (Motter) 1913-1973 .... **CLC 1, 8, 19; DAM DRAM**
See also CA 9-12R; CDALB 1941-1968; DLB 7; MTCW 1

Ingelow, Jean 1820-1897 .... **NCLC 39**
See also DLB 35, 163; SATA 33

Ingram, Willis J.
See Harris, Mark

Innaurato, Albert (F.) 1948(?)-.....**CLC 21, 60**
See also CA 115; 122; INT 122

Innes, Michael
See Stewart, J(ohn) I(nnes) M(ackintosh)

Innis, Harold Adams 1894-1952..... **TCLC 77**
See also DLB 88

Ionesco, Eugene 1909-1994 .... **CLC 1, 4, 6, 9, 11, 15, 41, 86; DA; DAB; DAC; DAM DRAM, MST; WLC**
See also CA 9-12R; 144; CANR 55; MTCW 1; SATA 7; SATA-Obit 79

Iqbal, Muhammad 1873-1938........ **TCLC 28**

Ireland, Patrick
See O'Doherty, Brian

Iron, Ralph
See Schreiner, Olive (Emilie Albertina)

Irving, John (Winslow) 1942- .... **CLC 13, 23, 38, 112; DAM NOV, POP**
See also AAYA 8; BEST 89:3; CA 25-28R; CANR 28, 73; DLB 6; DLBY 82; MTCW 1

Irving, Washington 1783-1859...........**NCLC 2, 19; DA; DAB; DAC; DAM MST; SSC 2; WLC**
See also CDALB 1640-1865; DLB 3, 11, 30, 59, 73, 74, 186; YABC 2

Irwin, P. K.
See Page, P(atricia) K(athleen)

Isaacs, Jorge Ricardo 1837-1895 .... **NCLC 70**

Isaacs, Susan 1943- .... **CLC 32; DAM POP**
See also BEST 89:1; CA 89-92; CANR 20, 41, 65; INT CANR-20; MTCW 1

Isherwood, Christopher (William Bradshaw)
1904-1986 .... **CLC 1, 9, 11, 14, 44; DAM DRAM, NOV**
See also CA 13-16R; 117; CANR 35; DLB 15, 195; DLBY 86; MTCW 1

Ishiguro, Kazuo 1954- .... **CLC 27, 56, 59, 110; DAM NOV**
See also BEST 90:2; CA 120; CANR 49; DLB 194; MTCW 1

Ishikawa, Hakuhin
See Ishikawa, Takuboku

Ishikawa, Takuboku 1886(?)-1912 ...... **TCLC 15; DAM POET; PC 10**
See also CA 113; 153

Iskander, Fazil 1929-..................... **CLC 47**
See also CA 102

Isler, Alan (David) 1934- .... **CLC 91**
See also CA 156

Ivan IV 1530-1584 ....**LC 17**

Ivanov, Vyacheslav Ivanovich
1866-1949 .... **TCLC 33**
See also CA 122

Ivask, Ivar Vidrik 1927-1992........... **CLC 14**
See also CA 37-40R; 139; CANR 24

Ives, Morgan
See Bradley, Marion Zimmer

J. R. S.
See Gogarty, Oliver St. John

Jabran, Kahlil
See Gibran, Kahlil

Jabran, Khalil
See Gibran, Kahlil

Jackson, Daniel
   See Wingrove, David (John)

Jackson, Jesse 1908-1983................ **CLC 12**
   See also BW 1; CA 25-28R; 109; CANR 27;
   CLR 28; MAICYA; SATA 2, 29; SATA-
   Obit 48

Jackson, Laura (Riding) 1901-1991
   See Riding, Laura

Jackson, Sam
   See Trumbo, Dalton

Jackson, Sara
   See Wingrove, David (John)

Jackson, Shirley 1919-1965... **CLC 11, 60, 87;**
   DA; DAC; DAM MST; SSC 9; WLC
   See also AAYA 9; CA 1-4R; 25-28R; CANR
   4, 52; CDALB 1941-1968; DLB 6; SATA 2

Jacob, (Cyprien-)Max 1876-1944 ..... **TCLC 6**
   See also CA 104

Jacobs, Harriet A(nn) 1813(?)-1897 .... **NCLC 67**

Jacobs, Jim 1942- .... **CLC 12**
   See also CA 97-100; INT 97-100

Jacobs, W(illiam) W(ymark)
   1863-1943 .... **TCLC 22**
   See also CA 121; 167; DLB 135

Jacobsen, Jens Peter 1847-1885 ..... **NCLC 34**

Jacobsen, Josephine 1908-........ **CLC 48, 102**
   See also CA 33-36R; CAAS 18; CANR 23,
   48

Jacobson, Dan 1929- .... **CLC 4, 14**
   See also CA 1-4R; CANR 2, 25, 66; DLB 14;
   MTCW 1

Jacqueline
   See Carpentier (y Valmont), Alejo

Jagger, Mick 1944-........................ **CLC 17**

Jahiz, al- c. 780-c. 869 .... **CMLC 25**

Jakes, John (William) 1932-................ **CLC 29; DAM NOV, POP**
   See also BEST 89:4; CA 57-60; CANR 10,
   43, 66; DLBY 83; INT CANR-10; MTCW
   1; SATA 62

James, Andrew
   See Kirkup, James

James, C(yril) L(ionel) R(obert)
   1901-1989 ....**CLC 33; BLCS**
   See also BW 2; CA 117; 125; 128; CANR 62;
   DLB 125; MTCW 1

James, Daniel (Lewis) 1911-1988
   See Santiago, Danny

James, Dynely
   See Mayne, William (James Carter)

James, Henry Sr. 1811-1882.......... **NCLC 53**

James, Henry 1843-1916 .... **TCLC 2, 11, 24, 40, 47, 64; DA; DAB; DAC; DAM MST, NOV; SSC 8, 32; WLC**
   See also CA 104; 132; CDALB 1865-1917;
   DLB 12, 71, 74, 189; DLBD 13; MTCW 1

James, M. R.
   See James, Montague (Rhodes)

James, Montague (Rhodes)
   1862-1936 ....**TCLC 6; SSC 16**
   See also CA 104; DLB 201

James, P. D. 1920-.................... **CLC 18, 46**
   See also White, Phyllis Dorothy James

James, Philip
   See Moorcock, Michael (John)

James, William 1842-1910 ....**TCLC 15, 32**
   See also CA 109

James I 1394-1437 ....**LC 20**

Jameson, Anna 1794-1860 .... **NCLC 43**
   See also DLB 99, 166

Jami, Nur al-Din 'Abd al-Rahman
   1414-1492 .... **LC 9**

Jammes, Francis 1868-1938 .... **TCLC 75**

Jandl, Ernst 1925- .... **CLC 34**

Janowitz, Tama 1957-.... **CLC 43; DAM POP**
   See also CA 106; CANR 52

Japrisot, Sebastien 1931-................ **CLC 90**

Jarrell, Randall 1914-1965.................. **CLC 1, 2, 6, 9, 13, 49; DAM POET**
   See also CA 5-8R; 25-28R; CABS 2; CANR
   6, 34; CDALB 1941-1968; CLR 6; DLB
   48, 52; MAICYA; MTCW 1; SATA 7

Jarry, Alfred 1873-1907 .... **TCLC 2, 14; DAM DRAM; SSC 20**
   See also CA 104; 153; DLB 192

Jarvis, E. K.
   See Bloch, Robert (Albert); Ellison, Harlan
   (Jay); Silverberg, Robert

Jeake, Samuel, Jr.
   See Aiken, Conrad (Potter)

Jean Paul 1763-1825 ....**NCLC 7**

Jefferies, (John) Richard 1848-1887....**NCLC 47**
   See also DLB 98, 141; SATA 16

Jeffers, (John) Robinson 1887-1962 ...... **CLC 2, 3, 11, 15, 54; DA; DAC; DAM MST, POET; PC 17; WLC**
   See also CA 85-88; CANR 35; CDALB
   1917-1929; DLB 45; MTCW 1

Jefferson, Janet
   See Mencken, H(enry) L(ouis)

Jefferson, Thomas 1743-1826 .... **NCLC 11**
   See also CDALB 1640-1865; DLB 31

Jeffrey, Francis 1773-1850 .... **NCLC 33**
   See also DLB 107

Jelakowitch, Ivan
   See Heijermans, Herman

Jellicoe, (Patricia) Ann 1927- .... **CLC 27**
   See also CA 85-88; DLB 13

Jen, Gish .... **CLC 70**
   See also Jen, Lillian

Jen, Lillian 1956(?)-
   See Jen, Gish

Jenkins, (John) Robin 1912-............ **CLC 52**
   See also CA 1-4R; CANR 1; DLB 14

Jennings, Elizabeth (Joan) 1926-... **CLC 5, 14**
   See also CA 61-64; CAAS 5; CANR 8, 39,
   66; DLB 27; MTCW 1; SATA 66

Jennings, Waylon 1937- .... **CLC 21**

Jensen, Johannes V. 1873-1950 ...... **TCLC 41**
   See also CA 170

Jensen, Laura (Linnea) 1948-.......... **CLC 37**
   See also CA 103

Jerome, Jerome K(lapka) 1859-1927... **TCLC 23**
   See also CA 119; DLB 10, 34, 135

Jerrold, Douglas William 1803-1857 ...**NCLC 2**
   See also DLB 158, 159

Jewett, (Theodora) Sarah Orne
   1849-1909 ....**TCLC 1, 22; SSC 6**
   See also CA 108; 127; CANR 71; DLB 12,
   74; SATA 15

Jewsbury, Geraldine (Endsor)
   1812-1880 .... **NCLC 22**
   See also DLB 21

Jhabvala, Ruth Prawer 1927-.............. **CLC 4, 8, 29, 94; DAB; DAM NOV**
   See also CA 1-4R; CANR 2, 29, 51, 74; DLB
   139, 194; INT CANR-29; MTCW 1

Jibran, Kahlil
   See Gibran, Kahlil

Jibran, Khalil
   See Gibran, Kahlil

Jiles, Paulette 1943- ....**CLC 13, 58**
   See also CA 101; CANR 70

Jimenez (Mantecon), Juan Ramon
   1881-1958 .... **TCLC 4; DAM MULT, POET; HLC; PC 7**
   See also CA 104; 131; CANR 74; DLB 134;
   HW; MTCW 1

Jimenez, Ramon
   See Jimenez (Mantecon), Juan Ramon

Jimenez Mantecon, Juan
   See Jimenez (Mantecon), Juan Ramon

Jin, Ha 1956-...........................**CLC 109**
   See also CA 152

Joel, Billy................................. **CLC 26**
   See also Joel, William Martin

Joel, William Martin 1949-
   See Joel, Billy

John, Saint 7th cent. - .... **CMLC 27**

John of the Cross, St. 1542-1591 ....**LC 18**

Johnson, B(ryan) S(tanley William)
   1933-1973 ....**CLC 6, 9**
   See also CA 9-12R; 53-56; CANR 9; DLB
   14, 40

Johnson, Benj. F. of Boo
   See Riley, James Whitcomb

Johnson, Benjamin F. of Boo
   See Riley, James Whitcomb

Johnson, Charles (Richard) 1948- .... **CLC 7, 51, 65; BLC 2; DAM MULT**
   See also BW 2; CA 116; CAAS 18; CANR
   42, 66; DLB 33

Johnson, Denis 1949-..................... **CLC 52**
   See also CA 117; 121; CANR 71; DLB 120

Johnson, Diane 1934- ....**CLC 5, 13, 48**
   See also CA 41-44R; CANR 17, 40, 62;
   DLBY 80; INT CANR-17; MTCW 1

Johnson, Eyvind (Olof Verner)
   1900-1976 .... **CLC 14**
   See also CA 73-76; 69-72; CANR 34

Johnson, J. R.
   See James, C(yril) L(ionel) R(obert)

Keynes, John Maynard 1883-1946 ...**TCLC 64**
See also CA 114; 162, 163; DLBD 10

Khanshendel, Chiron
See Rose, Wendy

Khayyam, Omar 1048-1131 .... **CMLC 11; DAM POET; PC 8**

Kherdian, David 1931- ....**CLC 6, 9**
See also CA 21-24R; CAAS 2; CANR 39;
CLR 24; JRDA; MAICYA; SATA 16, 74

Khlebnikov, Velimir .... **TCLC 20**
See also Khlebnikov, Viktor Vladimirovich

Khlebnikov, Viktor Vladimirovich 1885-1922
See Khlebnikov, Velimir

Khodasevich, Vladislav (Felitsianovich)
1886-1939 .... **TCLC 15**
See also CA 115

Kielland, Alexander Lange
1849-1906 ....**TCLC 5**
See also CA 104

Kiely, Benedict 1919-.................**CLC 23, 43**
See also CA 1-4R; CANR 2; DLB 15

Kienzle, William X(avier) 1928-............ **CLC 25; DAM POP**
See also CA 93-96; CAAS 1; CANR 9, 31,
59; INT CANR-31; MTCW 1

Kierkegaard, Soren 1813-1855 ...... **NCLC 34**

Killens, John Oliver 1916-1987 .... **CLC 10**
See also BW 2; CA 77-80; 123; CAAS 2;
CANR 26; DLB 33

Killigrew, Anne 1660-1685 .... **LC 4**
See also DLB 131

Kim
See Simenon, Georges (Jacques Christian)

Kincaid, Jamaica 1949-...................... **CLC 43, 68; BLC 2; DAM MULT, NOV**
See also AAYA 13; BW 2; CA 125; CANR
47, 59; DLB 157

King, Francis (Henry) 1923- .... **CLC 8, 53; DAM NOV**
See also CA 1-4R; CANR 1, 33; DLB 15,
139; MTCW 1

King, Kennedy
See Brown, George Douglas

King, Martin Luther, Jr. 1929-1968 ...... **CLC 83; BLC 2; DA; DAB; DAC; DAM MST, MULT; WLCS**
See also BW 2; CA 25-28; CANR 27, 44;
CAP 2; MTCW 1; SATA 14

King, Stephen (Edwin) 1947-...... **CLC 12, 26, 37, 61, 113; DAM NOV, POP; SSC 17**
See also AAYA 1, 17; BEST 90:1; CA 61-64;
CANR 1, 30, 52; DLB 143; DLBY 80;
JRDA; MTCW 1; SATA 9, 55

King, Steve
See King, Stephen (Edwin)

King, Thomas 1943-........................ **CLC 89; DAC; DAM MULT**
See also CA 144; DLB 175; NNAL; SATA 96

Kingman, Lee............................. **CLC 17**
See also Natti, (Mary) Lee

Kingsley, Charles 1819-1875 .... **NCLC 35**
See also DLB 21, 32, 163, 190; YABC 2

Kingsley, Sidney 1906-1995............. **CLC 44**
See also CA 85-88; 147; DLB 7

Kingsolver, Barbara 1955-................. **CLC 55, 81; DAM POP**
See also AAYA 15; CA 129; 134; CANR 60;
INT 134

Kingston, Maxine (Ting Ting) Hong
1940- .... **CLC 12, 19, 58; DAM MULT, NOV; WLCS**
See also AAYA 8; CA 69-72; CANR 13, 38,
74; DLB 173; DLBY 80; INT CANR-13;
MTCW 1; SATA 53

Kinnell, Galway 1927- ...**CLC 1, 2, 3, 5, 13, 29**
See also CA 9-12R; CANR 10, 34, 66; DLB
5; DLBY 87; INT CANR-34; MTCW 1

Kinsella, Thomas 1928-............... **CLC 4, 19**
See also CA 17-20R; CANR 15; DLB 27;
MTCW 1

Kinsella, W(illiam) P(atrick) 1935-....... **CLC 27, 43; DAC; DAM NOV, POP**
See also AAYA 7; CA 97-100; CAAS 7;
CANR 21, 35, 66, 75; INT CANR-21;
MTCW 1

Kipling, (Joseph) Rudyard
1865-1936 .... **TCLC 8, 17; DA; DAB; DAC; DAM MST, POET; PC 3; SSC 5; WLC**
See also CA 105; 120; CANR 33; CDBLB
1890-1914; CLR 39; DLB 19, 34, 141, 156;
MAICYA; MTCW 1; SATA 100; YABC 2

Kirkup, James 1918-........................**CLC 1**
See also CA 1-4R; CAAS 4; CANR 2; DLB
27; SATA 12

Kirkwood, James 1930(?)-1989..........**CLC 9**
See also AITN 2; CA 1-4R; 128; CANR 6, 40

Kirshner, Sidney
See Kingsley, Sidney

Kis, Danilo 1935-1989................... **CLC 57**
See also CA 109; 118; 129; CANR 61; DLB
181; MTCW 1

Kivi, Aleksis 1834-1872................ **NCLC 30**

Kizer, Carolyn (Ashley) 1925-.............. **CLC 15, 39, 80; DAM POET**
See also CA 65-68; CAAS 5; CANR 24, 70;
DLB 5, 169

Klabund 1890-1928..................... **TCLC 44**
See also CA 162; DLB 66

Klappert, Peter 1942- .... **CLC 57**
See also CA 33-36R; DLB 5

Klein, A(braham) M(oses) 1909-1972.... **CLC 19; DAB; DAC; DAM MST**
See also CA 101; 37-40R; DLB 68

Klein, Norma 1938-1989 .... **CLC 30**
See also AAYA 2; CA 41-44R; 128; CANR
15, 37; CLR 2, 19; INT CANR-15; JRDA;
MAICYA; SAAS 1; SATA 7, 57

Klein, T(heodore) E(ibon) D(onald)
1947- .... **CLC 34**
See also CA 119; CANR 44, 75

Kleist, Heinrich von 1777-1811 .... **NCLC 2, 37; DAM DRAM; SSC 22**
See also DLB 90

Klima, Ivan 1931-.........**CLC 56; DAM NOV**
See also CA 25-28R; CANR 17, 50

Klimentov, Andrei Platonovich 1899-1951
See Platonov, Andrei

Klinger, Friedrich Maximilian von
1752-1831 ....**NCLC 1**
See also DLB 94

Klingsor the Magician
See Hartmann, Sadakichi

Klopstock, Friedrich Gottlieb
1724-1803 .... **NCLC 11**
See also DLB 97

Knapp, Caroline 1959-................... **CLC 99**
See also CA 154

Knebel, Fletcher 1911-1993............. **CLC 14**
See also AITN 1; CA 1-4R; 140; CAAS 3;
CANR 1, 36; SATA 36; SATA-Obit 75

Knickerbocker, Diedrich
See Irving, Washington

Knight, Etheridge 1931-1991.............. **CLC 40; BLC 2; DAM POET; PC 14**
See also BW 1; CA 21-24R; 133; CANR 23;
DLB 41

Knight, Sarah Kemble 1666-1727.........**LC 7**
See also DLB 24, 200

Knister, Raymond 1899-1932 .... **TCLC 56**
See also DLB 68

Knowles, John 1926- .... **CLC 1, 4, 10, 26; DA; DAC; DAM MST, NOV**
See also AAYA 10; CA 17-20R; CANR 40,
74; CDALB 1968-1988; DLB 6; MTCW 1;
SATA 8, 89

Knox, Calvin M.
See Silverberg, Robert

Knox, John c. 1505-1572 ....**LC 37**
See also DLB 132

Knye, Cassandra
See Disch, Thomas M(ichael)

Koch, C(hristopher) J(ohn) 1932-..... **CLC 42**
See also CA 127

Koch, Christopher
See Koch, C(hristopher) J(ohn)

Koch, Kenneth 1925-...................... **CLC 5, 8, 44; DAM POET**
See also CA 1-4R; CANR 6, 36, 57; DLB 5;
INT CANR-36; SATA 65

Kochanowski, Jan 1530-1584 ....**LC 10**

Kock, Charles Paul de 1794-1871 ... **NCLC 16**

Koda Shigeyuki 1867-1947
See Rohan, Koda

Koestler, Arthur 1905-1983................. **CLC 1, 3, 6, 8, 15, 33**
See also CA 1-4R; 109; CANR 1, 33; CD-
BLB 1945-1960; DLBY 83; MTCW 1

Kogawa, Joy Nozomi 1935-................ **CLC 78; DAC; DAM MST, MULT**
See also CA 101; CANR 19, 62; SATA 99

Kohout, Pavel 1928-...................... **CLC 13**
See also CA 45-48; CANR 3

Koizumi, Yakumo
See Hearn, (Patricio) Lafcadio (Tessima Carlos)

Kolmar, Gertrud 1894-1943 .... **TCLC 40**
See also CA 167

Komunyakaa, Yusef 1947- CLC
  86, 94; BLCS
    See also CA 147; DLB 120

Konrad, George
    See Konrad, Gyoergy

Konrad, Gyoergy 1933- ....CLC 4, 10, 73
    See also CA 85-88

Konwicki, Tadeusz 1926-... CLC 8, 28, 54, 117
    See also CA 101; CAAS 9; CANR 39, 59;
    MTCW 1

Koontz, Dean R(ay) 1945- CLC
  78; DAM NOV, POP
    See also AAYA 9; BEST 89:3, 90:2; CA 108;
    CANR 19, 36, 52; MTCW 1; SATA 92

Kopernik, Mikolaj
    See Copernicus, Nicolaus

Kopit, Arthur (Lee) 1937- CLC
  1, 18, 33; DAM DRAM
    See also AITN 1; CA 81-84; CABS 3; DLB
    7; MTCW 1

Kops, Bernard 1926- ....CLC 4
    See also CA 5-8R; DLB 13

Kornbluth, C(yril) M. 1923-1958......TCLC 8
    See also CA 105; 160; DLB 8

Korolenko, V. G.
    See Korolenko, Vladimir Galaktionovich

Korolenko, Vladimir
    See Korolenko, Vladimir Galaktionovich

Korolenko, Vladimir G.
    See Korolenko, Vladimir Galaktionovich

Korolenko, Vladimir Galaktionovich
    1853-1921 .... TCLC 22
    See also CA 121

Korzybski, Alfred (Habdank Skarbek)
    1879-1950 .... TCLC 61
    See also CA 123; 160

Kosinski, Jerzy (Nikodem) 1933-1991 ... CLC
  1, 2, 3, 6, 10, 15, 53, 70; DAM NOV
    See also CA 17-20R; 134; CANR 9, 46; DLB
    2; DLBY 82; MTCW 1

Kostelanetz, Richard (Cory) 1940- ... CLC 28
    See also CA 13-16R; CAAS 8; CANR 38

Kostrowitzki, Wilhelm Apollinaris
    de 1880-1918
    See Apollinaire, Guillaume

Kotlowitz, Robert 1924- ....CLC 4
    See also CA 33-36R; CANR 36

Kotzebue, August (Friedrich Ferdinand) von
    1761-1819 .... NCLC 25
    See also DLB 94

Kotzwinkle, William 1938- ......CLC 5, 14, 35
    See also CA 45-48; CANR 3, 44; CLR 6;
    DLB 173; MAICYA; SATA 24, 70

Kowna, Stancy
    See Szymborska, Wislawa

Kozol, Jonathan 1936- .... CLC 17
    See also CA 61-64; CANR 16, 45

Kozoll, Michael 1940(?)- .... CLC 35

Kramer, Kathryn 19(?)- .... CLC 34

Kramer, Larry 1935-........................ CLC
  42; DAM POP; DC 8
    See also CA 124; 126; CANR 60

Krasicki, Ignacy 1735-1801.............NCLC 8

Krasinski, Zygmunt 1812-1859........NCLC 4

Kraus, Karl 1874-1936..................TCLC 5
    See also CA 104; DLB 118

Kreve (Mickevicius), Vincas
    1882-1954 .... TCLC 27
    See also CA 170

Kristeva, Julia 1941- .... CLC 77
    See also CA 154

Kristofferson, Kris 1936-................ CLC 26
    See also CA 104

Krizanc, John 1956-...................... CLC 57

Krleza, Miroslav 1893-1981 ....CLC 8, 114
    See also CA 97-100; 105; CANR 50; DLB
    147

Kroetsch, Robert 1927-...................... CLC
  5, 23, 57; DAC; DAM POET
    See also CA 17-20R; CANR 8, 38; DLB 53;
    MTCW 1

Kroetz, Franz
    See Kroetz, Franz Xaver

Kroetz, Franz Xaver 1946- .... CLC 41
    See also CA 130

Kroker, Arthur (W.) 1945-.............. CLC 77
    See also CA 161

Kropotkin, Peter (Aleksieevich)
    1842-1921 .... TCLC 36
    See also CA 119

Krotkov, Yuri 1917- .... CLC 19
    See also CA 102

Krumb
    See Crumb, R(obert)

Krumgold, Joseph (Quincy)
    1908-1980 .... CLC 12
    See also CA 9-12R; 101; CANR 7;
    MAICYA; SATA 1, 48; SATA-Obit 23

Krumwitz
    See Crumb, R(obert)

Krutch, Joseph Wood 1893-1970...... CLC 24
    See also CA 1-4R; 25-28R; CANR 4; DLB
    63

Krutzch, Gus
    See Eliot, T(homas) S(tearns)

Krylov, Ivan Andreevich 1768(?)-
    1844 ....NCLC 1
    See also DLB 150

Kubin, Alfred (Leopold Isidor)
    1877-1959 .... TCLC 23
    See also CA 112; 149; DLB 81

Kubrick, Stanley 1928- .... CLC 16
    See also CA 81-84; CANR 33; DLB 26

Kumin, Maxine (Winokur) 1925- CLC
  5, 13, 28; DAM POET; PC 15
    See also AITN 2; CA 1-4R; CAAS 8; CANR
    1, 21, 69; DLB 5; MTCW 1; SATA 12

Kundera, Milan 1929- ....CLC 4, 9,
  19, 32, 68, 115; DAM NOV; SSC 24
    See also AAYA 2; CA 85-88; CANR 19, 52,
    74; MTCW 1

Kunene, Mazisi (Raymond) 1930- .... CLC 85
    See also BW 1; CA 125; DLB 117

Kunitz, Stanley (Jasspon) 1905-........... CLC
  6, 11, 14; PC 19
    See also CA 41-44R; CANR 26, 57; DLB 48;
    INT CANR-26; MTCW 1

Kunze, Reiner 1933-...................... CLC 10
    See also CA 93-96; DLB 75

Kuprin, Aleksandr Ivanovich
    1870-1938 .... TCLC 5
    See also CA 104

Kureishi, Hanif 1954(?)-................ CLC 64
    See also CA 139; DLB 194

Kurosawa, Akira 1910-1998................ CLC
  16; DAM MULT
    See also AAYA 11; CA 101; 170; CANR 46

Kushner, Tony 1957(?)-...................... CLC
  81; DAM DRAM; DC 10
    See also CA 144; CANR 74

Kuttner, Henry 1915-1958 .... TCLC 10
    See also Vance, Jack

Kuzma, Greg 1944-........................CLC 7
    See also CA 33-36R; CANR 70

Kuzmin, Mikhail 1872(?)-1936 ...... TCLC 40
    See also CA 170

Kyd, Thomas 1558-1594...................... LC
  22; DAM DRAM; DC 3
    See also DLB 62

Kyprianos, Iossif
    See Samarakis, Antonis

La Bruyere, Jean de 1645-1696...........LC 17

Lacan, Jacques (Marie Emile)
    1901-1981 .... CLC 75
    See also CA 121; 104

Laclos, Pierre Ambroise Francois Choderlos
    de 1741-1803 ....NCLC 4

La Colere, Francois
    See Aragon, Louis

Lacolere, Francois
    See Aragon, Louis

La Deshabilleuse
    See Simenon, Georges (Jacques Christian)

Lady Gregory
    See Gregory, Isabella Augusta (Persse)

Lady of Quality, A
    See Bagnold, Enid

La Fayette, Marie (Madelaine Pioche de la
    Vergne Comtes 1634-1693............ LC 2

Lafayette, Rene
    See Hubbard, L(afayette) Ron(ald)

Laforgue, Jules 1860-1887 ....NCLC
  5, 53; PC 14; SSC 20

Lagerkvist, Paer (Fabian) 1891-1974 CLC
  7, 10, 13, 54; DAM DRAM, NOV
    See also Lagerkvist, Par

Lagerkvist, Par .... SSC 12
    See also Lagerkvist, Paer (Fabian)

Lagerloef, Selma (Ottiliana Lovisa)
    1858-1940 .... TCLC 4, 36
    See also Lagerlof, Selma (Ottiliana Lovisa)

Lagerlof, Selma (Ottiliana Lovisa)
    See Lagerloef, Selma (Ottiliana Lovisa)

Layton, Irving (Peter) 1912-................ **CLC 2, 15; DAC; DAM MST, POET**
See also CA 1-4R; CANR 2, 33, 43, 66; DLB 88; MTCW 1

Lazarus, Emma 1849-1887 .... **NCLC 8**

Lazarus, Felix
See Cable, George Washington

Lazarus, Henry
See Slavitt, David R(ytman)

Lea, Joan
See Neufeld, John (Arthur)

Leacock, Stephen (Butler) 1869-1944 ... **TCLC 2; DAC; DAM MST**
See also CA 104; 141; DLB 92

Lear, Edward 1812-1888 .... **NCLC 3**
See also CLR 1; DLB 32, 163, 166; MAICYA; SATA 18, 100

Lear, Norman (Milton) 1922- .... **CLC 12**
See also CA 73-76

Leautaud, Paul 1872-1956 .... **TCLC 83**
See also DLB 65

Leavis, F(rank) R(aymond) 1895-1978 ... **CLC 24**
See also CA 21-24R; 77-80; CANR 44; MTCW 1

Leavitt, David 1961- ...... **CLC 34; DAM POP**
See also CA 116; 122; CANR 50, 62; DLB 130; INT 122

Leblanc, Maurice (Marie Emile) 1864-1941 .... **TCLC 49**
See also CA 110

Lebowitz, Fran(ces Ann) 1951(?)-......... **CLC 11, 36**
See also CA 81-84; CANR 14, 60, 70; INT CANR-14; MTCW 1

Lebrecht, Peter
See Tieck, (Johann) Ludwig

le Carre, John................ **CLC 3, 5, 9, 15, 28**
See also Cornwell, David (John Moore)

Le Clezio, J(ean) M(arie) G(ustave) 1940- .... **CLC 31**
See also CA 116; 128; DLB 83

Leconte de Lisle, Charles-Marie-Rene 1818-1894 .... **NCLC 29**

Le Coq, Monsieur
See Simenon, Georges (Jacques Christian)

Leduc, Violette 1907-1972 .... **CLC 22**
See also CA 13-14; 33-36R; CANR 69; CAP 1

Ledwidge, Francis 1887(?)-1917 ..... **TCLC 23**
See also CA 123; DLB 20

Lee, Andrea 1953- .... **CLC 36; BLC 2; DAM MULT**
See also BW 1; CA 125

Lee, Andrew
See Auchincloss, Louis (Stanton)

Lee, Chang-rae 1965- .... **CLC 91**
See also CA 148

Lee, Don L. .... **CLC 2**
See also Madhubuti, Haki R.

Lee, George W(ashington) 1894-1976 .... **CLC 52; BLC 2; DAM MULT**
See also BW 1; CA 125; DLB 51

Lee, (Nelle) Harper 1926-....**CLC 12, 60; DA; DAB; DAC; DAM MST, NOV; WLC**
See also AAYA 13; CA 13-16R; CANR 51; CDALB 1941-1968; DLB 6; MTCW 1; SATA 11

Lee, Helen Elaine 1959(?)- .... **CLC 86**
See also CA 148

Lee, Julian
See Latham, Jean Lee

Lee, Larry
See Lee, Lawrence

Lee, Laurie 1914-1997 .... **CLC 90; DAB; DAM POP**
See also CA 77-80; 158; CANR 33, 73; DLB 27; MTCW 1

Lee, Lawrence 1941-1990 .... **CLC 34**
See also CA 131; CANR 43

Lee, Li-Young 1957-......................... **PC 24**
See also CA 153; DLB 165

Lee, Manfred B(ennington) 1905-1971 ... **CLC 11**
See also Queen, Ellery

Lee, Shelton Jackson 1957(?)-............ **CLC 105; BLCS; DAM MULT**
See also Lee, Spike

Lee, Spike
See Lee, Shelton Jackson

Lee, Stan 1922- .... **CLC 17**
See also AAYA 5; CA 108; 111; INT 111

Lee, Tanith 1947-........................... **CLC 46**
See also AAYA 15; CA 37-40R; CANR 53; SATA 8, 88

Lee, Vernon....................**TCLC 5; SSC 33**
See also Paget, Violet

Lee, William
See Burroughs, William S(eward)

Lee, Willy
See Burroughs, William S(eward)

Lee-Hamilton, Eugene (Jacob) 1845-1907 .... **TCLC 22**
See also CA 117

Leet, Judith 1935-........................ **CLC 11**

Le Fanu, Joseph Sheridan 1814-1873 ... **NCLC 9, 58; DAM POP; SSC 14**
See also DLB 21, 70, 159, 178

Leffland, Ella 1931- .... **CLC 19**
See also CA 29-32R; CANR 35; DLBY 84; INT CANR-35; SATA 65

Leger, Alexis
See Leger, (Marie-Rene Auguste) Alexis Saint-Leger

Leger, (Marie-Rene Auguste) Alexis Saint-Leger 1887-1975 .... **CLC 4, 11, 46; DAM POET; PC 23**
See also CA 13-16R; 61-64; CANR 43; MTCW 1

Leger, Saintleger
See Leger, (Marie-Rene Auguste) Alexis Saint-Leger

Le Guin, Ursula K(roeber) 1929- .... **CLC 8, 13, 22, 45, 71; DAB; DAC; DAM MST, POP; SSC 12**
See also AAYA 9, 27; AITN 1; CA 21-24R; CANR 9, 32, 52, 74; CDALB 1968-1988; CLR 3, 28; DLB 8, 52; INT CANR-32; JRDA; MAICYA; MTCW 1; SATA 4, 52, 99

Lehmann, Rosamond (Nina) 1901-1990 .... **CLC 5**
See also CA 77-80; 131; CANR 8, 73; DLB 15

Leiber, Fritz (Reuter, Jr.) 1910-1992 ..... **CLC 25**
See also CA 45-48; 139; CANR 2, 40; DLB 8; MTCW 1; SATA 45; SATA-Obit 73

Leibniz, Gottfried Wilhelm von 1646-1716 .... **LC 35**
See also DLB 168

Leimbach, Martha 1963-
See Leimbach, Marti

Leimbach, Marti .... **CLC 65**
See also Leimbach, Martha

Leino, Eino .... **TCLC 24**
See also Loennbohm, Armas Eino Leopold

Leiris, Michel (Julien) 1901-1990 ..... **CLC 61**
See also CA 119; 128; 132

Leithauser, Brad 1953- .... **CLC 27**
See also CA 107; CANR 27; DLB 120

Lelchuk, Alan 1938-....................... **CLC 5**
See also CA 45-48; CAAS 20; CANR 1, 70

Lem, Stanislaw 1921- ....**CLC 8, 15, 40**
See also CA 105; CAAS 1; CANR 32; MTCW 1

Lemann, Nancy 1956-.................... **CLC 39**
See also CA 118; 136

Lemonnier, (Antoine Louis) Camille 1844-1913 .... **TCLC 22**
See also CA 121

Lenau, Nikolaus 1802-1850........... **NCLC 16**

L'Engle, Madeleine (Camp Franklin) 1918- .... **CLC 12; DAM POP**
See also AAYA 1; AITN 2; CA 1-4R; CANR 3, 21, 39, 66; CLR 1, 14; DLB 52; JRDA; MAICYA; MTCW 1; SAAS 15; SATA 1, 27, 75

Lengyel, Jozsef 1896-1975 .... **CLC 7**
See also CA 85-88; 57-60; CANR 71

Lenin 1870-1924
See Lenin, V. I.

Lenin, V. I. .... **TCLC 67**
See also Lenin

Lennon, John (Ono) 1940-1980....**CLC 12, 35**
See also CA 102

Lennox, Charlotte Ramsay 1729(?)-1804...................... **NCLC 23**
See also DLB 39

Lentricchia, Frank (Jr.) 1940- .... **CLC 34**
See also CA 25-28R; CANR 19

Lenz, Siegfried 1926-.......... **CLC 27; SSC 33**
See also CA 89-92; DLB 75

Leonard, Elmore (John, Jr.) 1925-........ **CLC 28, 34, 71; DAM POP**
See also AAYA 22; AITN 1; BEST 89:1, 90:4; CA 81-84; CANR 12, 28, 53; DLB 173; INT CANR-28; MTCW 1

Leonard, Hugh .... **CLC 19**
See also Byrne, John Keyes

Leonov, Leonid (Maximovich) 1899-1994 ....**CLC 92; DAM NOV**
See also CA 129; CANR 74; MTCW 1

Leopardi, (Conte) Giacomo 1798-1837 .... **NCLC 22**

Le Reveler
See Artaud, Antonin (Marie Joseph)

Lerman, Eleanor 1952- .... **CLC 9**
See also CA 85-88; CANR 69

Lerman, Rhoda 1936-................... **CLC 56**
See also CA 49-52; CANR 70

Lermontov, Mikhail Yuryevich 1814-1841 .... **NCLC 47; PC 18**
See also DLB 205

Leroux, Gaston 1868-1927............ **TCLC 25**
See also CA 108; 136; CANR 69; SATA 65

Lesage, Alain-Rene 1668-1747 ....**LC 2, 28**

Leskov, Nikolai (Semyonovich) 1831-1895 .... **NCLC 25**

Lessing, Doris (May) 1919- .... **CLC 1, 2, 3, 6, 10, 15, 22, 40, 94; DA; DAB; DAC; DAM MST, NOV; SSC 6; WLCS**
See also CA 9-12R; CAAS 14; CANR 33, 54; CDBLB 1960 to Present; DLB 15, 139; DLBY 85; MTCW 1

Lessing, Gotthold Ephraim 1729-1781 ... **LC 8**
See also DLB 97

Lester, Richard 1932- .... **CLC 20**

Lever, Charles (James) 1806-1872... **NCLC 23**
See also DLB 21

Leverson, Ada 1865(?)-1936(?) ...... **TCLC 18**
See also Elaine

Levertov, Denise 1923-1997........ **CLC 1, 2, 3, 5, 8, 15, 28, 66; DAM POET; PC 11**
See also CA 1-4R; 163; CAAS 19; CANR 3, 29, 50; DLB 5, 165; INT CANR-29; MTCW 1

Levi, Jonathan............................ **CLC 76**

Levi, Peter (Chad Tigar) 1931- .... **CLC 41**
See also CA 5-8R; CANR 34; DLB 40

Levi, Primo 1919-1987... **CLC 37, 50; SSC 12**
See also CA 13-16R; 122; CANR 12, 33, 61, 70; DLB 177; MTCW 1

Levin, Ira 1929- ....**CLC 3, 6; DAM POP**
See also CA 21-24R; CANR 17, 44, 74; MTCW 1; SATA 66

Levin, Meyer 1905-1981... **CLC 7; DAM POP**
See also AITN 1; CA 9-12R; 104; CANR 15; DLB 9, 28; DLBY 81; SATA 21; SATA-Obit 27

Levine, Norman 1924- .... **CLC 54**
See also CA 73-76; CAAS 23; CANR 14, 70; DLB 88

Levine, Philip 1928- .... **CLC 2, 4, 5, 9, 14, 33; DAM POET; PC 22**
See also CA 9-12R; CANR 9, 37, 52; DLB 5

Levinson, Deirdre 1931-................. **CLC 49**
See also CA 73-76; CANR 70

Levi-Strauss, Claude 1908-............. **CLC 38**
See also CA 1-4R; CANR 6, 32, 57; MTCW 1

Levitin, Sonia (Wolff) 1934- .... **CLC 17**
See also AAYA 13; CA 29-32R; CANR 14, 32; CLR 53; JRDA; MAICYA; SAAS 2; SATA 4, 68

Levon, O. U.
See Kesey, Ken (Elton)

Levy, Amy 1861-1889 .... **NCLC 59**
See also DLB 156

Lewes, George Henry 1817-1878.... **NCLC 25**
See also DLB 55, 144

Lewis, Alun 1915-1944................... **TCLC 3**
See also CA 104; DLB 20, 162

Lewis, C. Day
See Day Lewis, C(ecil)

Lewis, C(live) S(taples) 1898-1963 .... **CLC 1, 3, 6, 14, 27; DA; DAB; DAC; DAM MST, NOV, POP; WLC**
See also AAYA 3; CA 81-84; CANR 33, 71; CDBLB 1945-1960; CLR 3, 27; DLB 15, 100, 160; JRDA; MAICYA; MTCW 1; SATA 13, 100

Lewis, Janet 1899- .... **CLC 41**
See also Winters, Janet Lewis

Lewis, Matthew Gregory 1775-1818.... **NCLC 11, 62**
See also DLB 39, 158, 178

Lewis, (Harry) Sinclair 1885-1951...... **TCLC 4, 13, 23, 39; DA; DAB; DAC; DAM MST, NOV; WLC**
See also CA 104; 133; CDALB 1917-1929; DLB 9, 102; DLBD 1; MTCW 1

Lewis, (Percy) Wyndham 1882(?)-1957 .... **TCLC 2, 9**
See also CA 104; 157; DLB 15

Lewisohn, Ludwig 1883-1955 .... **TCLC 19**
See also CA 107; DLB 4, 9, 28, 102

Lewton, Val 1904-1951................. **TCLC 76**

Leyner, Mark 1956- .... **CLC 92**
See also CA 110; CANR 28, 53

Lezama Lima, Jose 1910-1976 .... **CLC 4, 10, 101; DAM MULT**
See also CA 77-80; CANR 71; DLB 113; HW

L'Heureux, John (Clarke) 1934- ...... **CLC 52**
See also CA 13-16R; CANR 23, 45

Liddell, C. H.
See Kuttner, Henry

Lie, Jonas (Lauritz Idemil) 1833-1908(?)........................**TCLC 5**
See also CA 115

Lieber, Joel 1937-1971 .... **CLC 6**
See also CA 73-76; 29-32R

Lieber, Stanley Martin
See Lee, Stan

Lieberman, Laurence (James) 1935- ..... **CLC 4, 36**
See also CA 17-20R; CANR 8, 36

Lieh Tzu fl. 7th cent. B.C.-5th cent. B.C.................................. **CMLC 27**

Lieksman, Anders
See Haavikko, Paavo Juhani

Li Fei-kan 1904-
See Pa Chin

Lifton, Robert Jay 1926- .... **CLC 67**
See also CA 17-20R; CANR 27; INT CANR-27; SATA 66

Lightfoot, Gordon 1938- .... **CLC 26**
See also CA 109

Lightman, Alan P(aige) 1948-.......... **CLC 81**
See also CA 141; CANR 63

Ligotti, Thomas (Robert) 1953- .... **CLC 44; SSC 16**
See also CA 123; CANR 49

Li Ho 791-817................................**PC 13**

Liliencron, (Friedrich Adolf Axel) Detlev von 1844-1909 .... **TCLC 18**
See also CA 117

Lilly, William 1602-1681 ....**LC 27**

Lima, Jose Lezama
See Lezama Lima, Jose

Lima Barreto, Afonso Henrique de 1881-1922 .... **TCLC 23**
See also CA 117

Limonov, Edward 1944-................. **CLC 67**
See also CA 137

Lin, Frank
See Atherton, Gertrude (Franklin Horn)

Lincoln, Abraham 1809-1865 .... **NCLC 18**

Lind, Jakov....................**CLC 1, 2, 4, 27, 82**
See also Landwirth, Heinz

Lindbergh, Anne (Spencer) Morrow 1906- ....**CLC 82; DAM NOV**
See also CA 17-20R; CANR 16, 73; MTCW 1; SATA 33

Lindsay, David 1878-1945............. **TCLC 15**
See also CA 113

Lindsay, (Nicholas) Vachel 1879-1931 .... **TCLC 17; DA; DAC; DAM MST, POET; PC 23; WLC**
See also CA 114; 135; CDALB 1865-1917; DLB 54; SATA 40

Linke-Poot
See Doeblin, Alfred

Linney, Romulus 1930- .... **CLC 51**
See also CA 1-4R; CANR 40, 44

Linton, Eliza Lynn 1822-1898........ **NCLC 41**
See also DLB 18

Li Po 701-763 .... **CMLC 2**

Lipsius, Justus 1547-1606.................**LC 16**

Lipsyte, Robert (Michael) 1938-........... **CLC 21; DA; DAC; DAM MST, NOV**
See also AAYA 7; CA 17-20R; CANR 8, 57; CLR 23; JRDA; MAICYA; SATA 5, 68

Lish, Gordon (Jay) 1934-..... **CLC 45; SSC 18**
See also CA 113; 117; DLB 130; INT 117

Lispector, Clarice 1925(?)-1977........ **CLC 43**
See also CA 139; 116; CANR 71; DLB 113

Littell, Robert 1935(?)- .... **CLC 42**
See also CA 109; 112; CANR 64

Little, Malcolm 1925-1965
See Malcolm X

Littlewit, Humphrey Gent.
See Lovecraft, H(oward) P(hillips)

Litwos
See Sienkiewicz, Henryk (Adam Alexander Pius)

Liu, E 1857-1909 .... **TCLC 15**
See also CA 115

Lively, Penelope (Margaret) 1933- .... **CLC 32, 50; DAM NOV**
See also CA 41-44R; CANR 29, 67; CLR 7; DLB 14, 161; JRDA; MAICYA; MTCW 1; SATA 7, 60, 101

Livesay, Dorothy (Kathleen) 1909- .... **CLC 4, 15, 79; DAC; DAM MST, POET**
See also AITN 2; CA 25-28R; CAAS 8; CANR 36, 67; DLB 68; MTCW 1

Livy c. 59B.C.-c. 17 .... **CMLC 11**

Lizardi, Jose Joaquin Fernandez de 1776-1827 .... **NCLC 30**

Llewellyn, Richard
See Llewellyn Lloyd, Richard Dafydd Vivian

Llewellyn Lloyd, Richard Dafydd Vivian 1906-1983 .... **CLC 7, 80**
See also Llewellyn, Richard

Llosa, (Jorge) Mario (Pedro) Vargas
See Vargas Llosa, (Jorge) Mario (Pedro)

Lloyd, Manda
See Mander, (Mary) Jane

Lloyd Webber, Andrew 1948-
See Webber, Andrew Lloyd

Llull, Ramon c. 1235-c. 1316 .... **CMLC 12**

Lobb, Ebenezer
See Upward, Allen

Locke, Alain (Le Roy) 1886-1954 .... **TCLC 43; BLCS**
See also BW 1; CA 106; 124; DLB 51

Locke, John 1632-1704 .... **LC 7, 35**
See also DLB 101

Locke-Elliott, Sumner
See Elliott, Sumner Locke

Lockhart, John Gibson 1794-1854 ....**NCLC 6**
See also DLB 110, 116, 144

Lodge, David (John) 1935- .... **CLC 36; DAM POP**
See also BEST 90:1; CA 17-20R; CANR 19, 53; DLB 14, 194; INT CANR-19; MTCW 1

Lodge, Thomas 1558-1625 .... **LC 41**

Lodge, Thomas 1558-1625 .... **LC 41**
See also DLB 172

Loennbohm, Armas Eino Leopold 1878-1926
See Leino, Eino

Loewinsohn, Ron(ald William) 1937- .... **CLC 52**
See also CA 25-28R; CANR 71

Logan, Jake
See Smith, Martin Cruz

Logan, John (Burton) 1923-1987 ....**CLC 5**
See also CA 77-80; 124; CANR 45; DLB 5

Lo Kuan-chung 1330(?)-1400(?) ....**LC 12**

Lombard, Nap
See Johnson, Pamela Hansford

London, Jack... **TCLC 9, 15, 39; SSC 4; WLC**
See also London, John Griffith

London, John Griffith 1876-1916
See London, Jack

Long, Emmett
See Leonard, Elmore (John, Jr.)

Longbaugh, Harry
See Goldman, William (W.)

Longfellow, Henry Wadsworth 1807-1882 ....**NCLC 2, 45; DA; DAB; DAC; DAM MST, POET; WLCS**
See also CDALB 1640-1865; DLB 1, 59; SATA 19

Longinus c. 1st cent. - .... **CMLC 27**
See also DLB 176

Longley, Michael 1939- .... **CLC 29**
See also CA 102; DLB 40

Longus fl. c. 2nd cent. - .... **CMLC 7**

Longway, A. Hugh
See Lang, Andrew

Lonnrot, Elias 1802-1884 .... **NCLC 53**

Lopate, Phillip 1943- .... **CLC 29**
See also CA 97-100; DLBY 80; INT 97-100

Lopez Portillo (y Pacheco), Jose 1920- .... **CLC 46**
See also CA 129; HW

Lopez y Fuentes, Gregorio 1897(?)-1966 .... **CLC 32**
See also CA 131; HW

Lorca, Federico Garcia
See Garcia Lorca, Federico

Lord, Bette Bao 1938- .... **CLC 23**
See also BEST 90:3; CA 107; CANR 41; INT 107; SATA 58

Lord Auch
See Bataille, Georges

Lord Byron
See Byron, George Gordon (Noel)

Lorde, Audre (Geraldine) 1934-1992 ..... **CLC 18, 71; BLC 2; DAM MULT, POET; PC 12**
See also BW 1; CA 25-28R; 142; CANR 16, 26, 46; DLB 41; MTCW 1

Lord Houghton
See Milnes, Richard Monckton

Lord Jeffrey
See Jeffrey, Francis

Lorenzini, Carlo 1826-1890
See Collodi, Carlo

Lorenzo, Heberto Padilla
See Padilla (Lorenzo), Heberto

Loris
See Hofmannsthal, Hugo von

Loti, Pierre .... **TCLC 11**
See also Viaud, (Louis Marie) Julien

Louie, David Wong 1954- .... **CLC 70**
See also CA 139

Louis, Father M.
See Merton, Thomas

Lovecraft, H(oward) P(hillips) 1890-1937 .... **TCLC 4, 22; DAM POP; SSC 3**
See also AAYA 14; CA 104; 133; MTCW 1

Lovelace, Earl 1935- .... **CLC 51**
See also BW 2; CA 77-80; CANR 41, 72; DLB 125; MTCW 1

Lovelace, Richard 1618-1657 ....**LC 24**
See also DLB 131

Lowell, Amy 1874-1925 .... **TCLC 1, 8; DAM POET; PC 13**
See also CA 104; 151; DLB 54, 140

Lowell, James Russell 1819-1891 ......**NCLC 2**
See also CDALB 1640-1865; DLB 1, 11, 64, 79, 189

Lowell, Robert (Traill Spence, Jr.) 1917-1977 .... **CLC 1, 2, 3, 4, 5, 8, 9, 11, 15, 37; DA; DAB; DAC; DAM MST, NOV; PC 3; WLC**
See also CA 9-12R; 73-76; CABS 2; CANR 26, 60; DLB 5, 169; MTCW 1

Lowndes, Marie Adelaide (Belloc) 1868-1947 .... **TCLC 12**
See also CA 107; DLB 70

Lowry, (Clarence) Malcolm 1909-1957 ....**TCLC 6, 40; SSC 31**
See also CA 105; 131; CANR 62; CDBLB 1945-1960; DLB 15; MTCW 1

Lowry, Mina Gertrude 1882-1966
See Loy, Mina

Loxsmith, John
See Brunner, John (Kilian Houston)

Loy, Mina ....**CLC 28; DAM POET; PC 16**
See also Lowry, Mina Gertrude

Loyson-Bridet
See Schwob, Marcel (Mayer Andre)

Lucas, Craig 1951- .... **CLC 64**
See also CA 137; CANR 71

Lucas, E(dward) V(errall) 1868-1938 .... **TCLC 73**
See also DLB 98, 149, 153; SATA 20

Lucas, George 1944- .... **CLC 16**
See also AAYA 1, 23; CA 77-80; CANR 30; SATA 56

Lucas, Hans
See Godard, Jean-Luc

Lucas, Victoria
See Plath, Sylvia

Ludlam, Charles 1943-1987 ....**CLC 46, 50**
See also CA 85-88; 122; CANR 72

Ludlum, Robert 1927- .... **CLC 22, 43; DAM NOV, POP**
See also AAYA 10; BEST 89:1, 90:3; CA 33-36R; CANR 25, 41, 68; DLBY 82; MTCW 1

Ludwig, Ken .... **CLC 60**

Ludwig, Otto 1813-1865 ....**NCLC 4**
See also DLB 129

Lugones, Leopoldo 1874-1938 .... **TCLC 15**
See also CA 116; 131; HW

Lu Hsun 1881-1936 ....**TCLC 3; SSC 20**
See also Shu-Jen, Chou

Lukacs, George .... **CLC 24**
  See also Lukacs, Gyorgy (Szegeny von)

Lukacs, Gyorgy (Szegeny von) 1885-1971
  See Lukacs, George

Luke, Peter (Ambrose Cyprian)
  1919-1995 .... **CLC 38**
  See also CA 81-84; 147; CANR 72; DLB 13

Lunar, Dennis
  See Mungo, Raymond

Lurie, Alison 1926- ....**CLC 4, 5, 18, 39**
  See also CA 1-4R; CANR 2, 17, 50; DLB 2;
  MTCW 1; SATA 46

Lustig, Arnost 1926-...................... **CLC 56**
  See also AAYA 3; CA 69-72; CANR 47;
  SATA 56

Luther, Martin 1483-1546...............**LC 9, 37**
  See also DLB 179

Luxemburg, Rosa 1870(?)-1919 ..... **TCLC 63**
  See also CA 118

Luzi, Mario 1914-........................ **CLC 13**
  See also CA 61-64; CANR 9, 70; DLB 128

Lyly, John 1554(?)-1606 .... **LC 41; DAM DRAM; DC 7**
  See also DLB 62, 167

L'Ymagier
  See Gourmont, Remy (-Marie-Charles) de

Lynch, B. Suarez
  See Bioy Casares, Adolfo; Borges, Jorge Luis

Lynch, David (K.) 1946- .... **CLC 66**
  See also CA 124; 129

Lynch, James
  See Andreyev, Leonid (Nikolaevich)

Lynch Davis, B.
  See Bioy Casares, Adolfo; Borges, Jorge Luis

Lyndsay, Sir David 1490-1555 ....**LC 20**

Lynn, Kenneth S(chuyler) 1923- ...... **CLC 50**
  See also CA 1-4R; CANR 3, 27, 65

Lynx
  See West, Rebecca

Lyons, Marcus
  See Blish, James (Benjamin)

Lyre, Pinchbeck
  See Sassoon, Siegfried (Lorraine)

Lytle, Andrew (Nelson) 1902-1995 .... **CLC 22**
  See also CA 9-12R; 150; CANR 70; DLB 6;
  DLBY 95

Lyttelton, George 1709-1773 ....**LC 10**

Maas, Peter 1929-........................ **CLC 29**
  See also CA 93-96; INT 93-96

Macaulay, Rose 1881-1958......... **TCLC 7, 44**
  See also CA 104; DLB 36

Macaulay, Thomas Babington
  1800-1859 .... **NCLC 42**
  See also CDBLB 1832-1890; DLB 32, 55

MacBeth, George (Mann) 1932-1992..... **CLC 2, 5, 9**
  See also CA 25-28R; 136; CANR 61, 66;
  DLB 40; MTCW 1; SATA 4; SATA-Obit 70

MacCaig, Norman (Alexander) 1910-.... **CLC 36; DAB; DAM POET**
  See also CA 9-12R; CANR 3, 34; DLB 27

MacCarthy, Sir(Charles Otto) Desmond
  1877-1952 .... **TCLC 36**
  See also CA 167

MacDiarmid, Hugh........................ **CLC 2, 4, 11, 19, 63; PC 9**
  See also Grieve, C(hristopher) M(urray)

MacDonald, Anson
  See Heinlein, Robert A(nson)

Macdonald, Cynthia 1928-..........**CLC 13, 19**
  See also CA 49-52; CANR 4, 44; DLB 105

MacDonald, George 1824-1905 ....**TCLC 9**
  See also CA 106; 137; DLB 18, 163, 178;
  MAICYA; SATA 33, 100

Macdonald, John
  See Millar, Kenneth

MacDonald, John D(ann) 1916-1986 ..... **CLC 3, 27, 44; DAM NOV, POP**
  See also CA 1-4R; 121; CANR 1, 19, 60;
  DLB 8; DLBY 86; MTCW 1

Macdonald, John Ross
  See Millar, Kenneth

Macdonald, Ross ....**CLC 1, 2, 3, 14, 34, 41**
  See also Millar, Kenneth

MacDougal, John
  See Blish, James (Benjamin)

MacEwen, Gwendolyn (Margaret)
  1941-1987 ....**CLC 13, 55**
  See also CA 9-12R; 124; CANR 7, 22; DLB
  53; SATA 50; SATA-Obit 55

Macha, Karel Hynek 1810-1846..... **NCLC 46**

Machado (y Ruiz), Antonio
  1875-1939 ....**TCLC 3**
  See also CA 104; DLB 108

Machado de Assis, Joaquim Maria
  1839-1908 .....**TCLC 10; BLC 2; SSC 24**
  See also CA 107; 153

Machen, Arthur ....**TCLC 4; SSC 20**
  See also Jones, Arthur Llewellyn

Machiavelli, Niccolo 1469-1527.......**LC 8, 36; DA; DAB; DAC; DAM MST; WLCS**

MacInnes, Colin 1914-1976.......... **CLC 4, 23**
  See also CA 69-72; 65-68; CANR 21; DLB
  14; MTCW 1

MacInnes, Helen (Clark) 1907-1985...... **CLC 27, 39; DAM POP**
  See also CA 1-4R; 117; CANR 1, 28, 58;
  DLB 87; MTCW 1; SATA 22; SATA-Obit
  44

Mackay, Mary 1855-1924
  See Corelli, Marie

Mackenzie, Compton (Edward Montague)
  1883-1972 .... **CLC 18**
  See also CA 21-22; 37-40R; CAP 2; DLB 34,
  100

Mackenzie, Henry 1745-1831 .... **NCLC 41**
  See also DLB 39

Mackintosh, Elizabeth 1896(?)-1952
  See Tey, Josephine

MacLaren, James
  See Grieve, C(hristopher) M(urray)

Mac Laverty, Bernard 1942- .... **CLC 31**
  See also CA 116; 118; CANR 43; INT 118

MacLean, Alistair (Stuart)
  1922(?)-1987............................ **CLC 3, 13, 50, 63; DAM POP**
  See also CA 57-60; 121; CANR 28, 61;
  MTCW 1; SATA 23; SATA-Obit 50

Maclean, Norman (Fitzroy) 1902-1990... **CLC 78; DAM POP; SSC 13**
  See also CA 102; 132; CANR 49

MacLeish, Archibald 1892-1982.......... **CLC 3, 8, 14, 68; DAM POET**
  See also CA 9-12R; 106; CANR 33, 63; DLB
  4, 7, 45; DLBY 82; MTCW 1

MacLennan, (John) Hugh 1907-1990 .... **CLC 2, 14, 92; DAC; DAM MST**
  See also CA 5-8R; 142; CANR 33; DLB 68;
  MTCW 1

MacLeod, Alistair 1936-..................... **CLC 56; DAC; DAM MST**
  See also CA 123; DLB 60

Macleod, Fiona
  See Sharp, William

MacNeice, (Frederick) Louis
  1907-1963 .... **CLC 1, 4, 10, 53; DAB; DAM POET**
  See also CA 85-88; CANR 61; DLB 10, 20;
  MTCW 1

MacNeill, Dand
  See Fraser, George MacDonald

Macpherson, James 1736-1796 ....**LC 29**
  See also Ossian

Macpherson, (Jean) Jay 1931-......... **CLC 14**
  See also CA 5-8R; DLB 53

MacShane, Frank 1927-................. **CLC 39**
  See also CA 9-12R; CANR 3, 33; DLB 111

Macumber, Mari
  See Sandoz, Mari(e Susette)

Madach, Imre 1823-1864.............. **NCLC 19**

Madden, (Jerry) David 1933- .... **CLC 5, 15**
  See also CA 1-4R; CAAS 3; CANR 4, 45;
  DLB 6; MTCW 1

Maddern, Al(an)
  See Ellison, Harlan (Jay)

Madhubuti, Haki R. 1942-............... **CLC 6, 73; BLC 2; DAM MULT, POET; PC 5**
  See also Lee, Don L.

Maepenn, Hugh
  See Kuttner, Henry

Maepenn, K. H.
  See Kuttner, Henry

Maeterlinck, Maurice 1862-1949........ **TCLC 3; DAM DRAM**
  See also CA 104; 136; DLB 192; SATA 66

Maginn, William 1794-1842 ....**NCLC 8**
  See also DLB 110, 159

Mahapatra, Jayanta 1928-.................. **CLC 33; DAM MULT**
  See also CA 73-76; CAAS 9; CANR 15, 33,
  66

Mahfouz, Naguib (Abdel Aziz Al-Sabilgi)
  1911(?)-
  See Mahfuz, Najib

Mahfuz, Najib ....CLC **52, 55**
  See also Mahfouz, Naguib (Abdel Aziz
  Al-Sabilgi)

Mavor, Osborne Henry 1888-1951
See Bridie, James

Maxwell, William (Keepers, Jr.)
1908- .... **CLC 19**
See also CA 93-96; CANR 54; DLBY 80;
INT 93-96

May, Elaine 1932-......................... **CLC 16**
See also CA 124; 142; DLB 44

Mayakovski, Vladimir (Vladimirovich)
1893-1930 .... **TCLC 4, 18**
See also CA 104; 158

Mayhew, Henry 1812-1887 .... **NCLC 31**
See also DLB 18, 55, 190

Mayle, Peter 1939(?)- .... **CLC 89**
See also CA 139; CANR 64

Maynard, Joyce 1953- .... **CLC 23**
See also CA 111; 129; CANR 64

Mayne, William (James Carter)
1928- .... **CLC 12**
See also AAYA 20; CA 9-12R; CANR 37;
CLR 25; JRDA; MAICYA; SAAS 11;
SATA 6, 68

Mayo, Jim
See L'Amour, Louis (Dearborn)

Maysles, Albert 1926-..................... **CLC 16**
See also CA 29-32R

Maysles, David 1932-...................... **CLC 16**

Mazer, Norma Fox 1931-................. **CLC 26**
See also AAYA 5; CA 69-72; CANR 12, 32,
66; CLR 23; JRDA; MAICYA; SAAS 1;
SATA 24, 67

Mazzini, Guiseppe 1805-1872 .... **NCLC 34**

McAuley, James Phillip 1917-1976 ... **CLC 45**
See also CA 97-100

McBain, Ed
See Hunter, Evan

McBrien, William Augustine 1930-... **CLC 44**
See also CA 107

McCaffrey, Anne (Inez) 1926- .... **CLC
17; DAM NOV, POP**
See also AAYA 6; AITN 2; BEST 89:2; CA
25-28R; CANR 15, 35, 55; CLR 49; DLB
8; JRDA; MAICYA; MTCW 1; SAAS 11;
SATA 8, 70

McCall, Nathan 1955(?)-................ **CLC 86**
See also CA 146

McCann, Arthur
See Campbell, John W(ood, Jr.)

McCann, Edson
See Pohl, Frederik

McCarthy, Charles, Jr. 1933-
See McCarthy, Cormac

McCarthy, Cormac 1933-................... **CLC
4, 57, 59, 101**
See also McCarthy, Charles, Jr.

McCarthy, Mary (Therese) 1912-1989... **CLC
1, 3, 5, 14, 24, 39, 59; SSC 24**
See also CA 5-8R; 129; CANR 16, 50, 64;
DLB 2; DLBY 81; INT CANR-16; MTCW
1

McCartney, (James) Paul 1942- ...**CLC 12, 35**
See also CA 146

McCauley, Stephen (D.) 1955- .... **CLC 50**
See also CA 141

McClure, Michael (Thomas) 1932- .... **CLC
6, 10**
See also CA 21-24R; CANR 17, 46; DLB 16

McCorkle, Jill (Collins) 1958-......... **CLC 51**
See also CA 121; DLBY 87

McCourt, Frank 1930-..................**CLC 109**
See also CA 157

McCourt, James 1941-.....................**CLC 5**
See also CA 57-60

McCoy, Horace (Stanley) 1897-1955 ... **TCLC
28**
See also CA 108; 155; DLB 9

McCrae, John 1872-1918.............. **TCLC 12**
See also CA 109; DLB 92

McCreigh, James
See Pohl, Frederik

McCullers, (Lula) Carson (Smith)
1917-1967 .... **CLC
1, 4, 10, 12, 48, 100; DA; DAB; DAC;
DAM MST, NOV; SSC 9, 24; WLC**
See also AAYA 21; CA 5-8R; 25-28R; CABS
1, 3; CANR 18; CDALB 1941-1968; DLB
2, 7, 173; MTCW 1; SATA 27

McCulloch, John Tyler
See Burroughs, Edgar Rice

McCullough, Colleen 1938(?)- .... **CLC
27, 107; DAM NOV, POP**
See also CA 81-84; CANR 17, 46, 67;
MTCW 1

McDermott, Alice 1953- .... **CLC 90**
See also CA 109; CANR 40

McElroy, Joseph 1930-................ **CLC 5, 47**
See also CA 17-20R

McEwan, Ian (Russell) 1948-............... **CLC
13, 66; DAM NOV**
See also BEST 90:4; CA 61-64; CANR 14,
41, 69; DLB 14, 194; MTCW 1

McFadden, David 1940- .... **CLC 48**
See also CA 104; DLB 60; INT 104

McFarland, Dennis 1950- .... **CLC 65**
See also CA 165

McGahern, John 1934- .... **CLC
5, 9, 48; SSC 17**
See also CA 17-20R; CANR 29, 68; DLB 14;
MTCW 1

McGinley, Patrick (Anthony) 1937- ...**CLC 41**
See also CA 120; 127; CANR 56; INT 127

McGinley, Phyllis 1905-1978 .... **CLC 14**
See also CA 9-12R; 77-80; CANR 19; DLB
11, 48; SATA 2, 44; SATA-Obit 24

McGinniss, Joe 1942- .... **CLC 32**
See also AITN 2; BEST 89:2; CA 25-28R;
CANR 26, 70; DLB 185; INT CANR-26

McGivern, Maureen Daly
See Daly, Maureen

McGrath, Patrick 1950- .... **CLC 55**
See also CA 136; CANR 65

McGrath, Thomas (Matthew)
1916-1990 ..... **CLC 28, 59; DAM POET**
See also CA 9-12R; 132; CANR 6, 33;
MTCW 1; SATA 41; SATA-Obit 66

McGuane, Thomas (Francis III) 1939-... **CLC
3, 7, 18, 45**
See also AITN 2; CA 49-52; CANR 5, 24, 49;
DLB 2; DLBY 80; INT CANR-24; MTCW
1

McGuckian, Medbh 1950- .... **CLC
48; DAM POET**
See also CA 143; DLB 40

McHale, Tom 1942(?)-1982 ....**CLC 3, 5**
See also AITN 1; CA 77-80; 106

McIlvanney, William 1936-............. **CLC 42**
See also CA 25-28R; CANR 61; DLB 14

McIlwraith, Maureen Mollie Hunter
See Hunter, Mollie

McInerney, Jay 1955-....................... **CLC
34, 112; DAM POP**
See also AAYA 18; CA 116; 123; CANR 45,
68; INT 123

McIntyre, Vonda N(eel) 1948-.......... **CLC 18**
See also CA 81-84; CANR 17, 34, 69;
MTCW 1

McKay, Claude .... **TCLC
7, 41; BLC 3; DAB; PC 2**
See also McKay, Festus Claudius

McKay, Festus Claudius 1889-1948
See McKay, Claude

McKuen, Rod 1933-.....................**CLC 1, 3**
See also AITN 1; CA 41-44R; CANR 40

McLoughlin, R. B.
See Mencken, H(enry) L(ouis)

McLuhan, (Herbert) Marshall
1911-1980 ....**CLC 37, 83**
See also CA 9-12R; 102; CANR 12, 34, 61;
DLB 88; INT CANR-12; MTCW 1

McMillan, Terry (L.) 1951-........**CLC 50, 61,
112; BLCS; DAM MULT, NOV, POP**
See also AAYA 21; BW 2; CA 140; CANR
60

McMurtry, Larry (Jeff) 1936- .... **CLC
2, 3, 7, 11, 27, 44; DAM NOV, POP**
See also AAYA 15; AITN 2; BEST 89:2; CA
5-8R; CANR 19, 43, 64; CDALB 1968-
1988; DLB 2, 143; DLBY 80, 87; MTCW
1

McNally, T. M. 1961-..................... **CLC 82**

McNally, Terrence 1939- .... **CLC
4, 7, 41, 91; DAM DRAM**
See also CA 45-48; CANR 2, 56; DLB 7

McNamer, Deirdre 1950-............... **CLC 70**

McNeile, Herman Cyril 1888-1937
See Sapper

McNickle, (William) D'Arcy
1904-1977 ....**CLC 89; DAM MULT**
Scc also CA 9-12R; 85-88; CANR 5, 45;
DLB 175; NNAL; SATA-Obit 22

McPhee, John (Angus) 1931-........... **CLC 36**
See also BEST 90:1; CA 65-68; CANR 20,
46, 64, 69; DLB 185; MTCW 1

McPherson, James Alan 1943-............. **CLC
19, 77; BLCS**
See also BW 1; CA 25-28R; CAAS 17;
CANR 24, 74; DLB 38; MTCW 1

McPherson, William (Alexander)
1933- .... **CLC 34**
See also CA 69-72; CANR 28; INT
CANR-28

Mead, George Herbert 1873-1958... **TCLC 89**

Mead, Margaret 1901-1978............ **CLC 37**
See also AITN 1; CA 1-4R; 81-84; CANR 4;
MTCW 1; SATA-Obit 20

Meaker, Marijane (Agnes) 1927-
See Kerr, M. E.

Medoff, Mark (Howard) 1940- .... **CLC
6, 23; DAM DRAM**
See also AITN 1; CA 53-56; CANR 5; DLB
7; INT CANR-5

Medvedev, P. N.
See Bakhtin, Mikhail Mikhailovich

Meged, Aharon
See Megged, Aharon

Meged, Aron
See Megged, Aharon

Megged, Aharon 1920-.................... **CLC 9**
See also CA 49-52; CAAS 13; CANR 1

Mehta, Ved (Parkash) 1934-........... **CLC 37**
See also CA 1-4R; CANR 2, 23, 69; MTCW
1

Melanter
See Blackmore, R(ichard) D(oddridge)

Melies, Georges 1861-1938........... **TCLC 81**

Melikow, Loris
See Hofmannsthal, Hugo von

Melmoth, Sebastian
See Wilde, Oscar (Fingal O'Flahertie Wills)

Meltzer, Milton 1915-.................... **CLC 26**
See also AAYA 8; CA 13-16R; CANR 38;
CLR 13; DLB 61; JRDA; MAICYA; SAAS
1; SATA 1, 50, 80

Melville, Herman 1819-1891 .... **NCLC
3, 12, 29, 45, 49; DA; DAB; DAC; DAM
MST, NOV; SSC 1, 17; WLC**
See also AAYA 25; CDALB 1640-1865;
DLB 3, 74; SATA 59

Menander c. 342B.C.-c. 292B.C. .... **CMLC
9; DAM DRAM; DC 3**
See also DLB 176

Mencken, H(enry) L(ouis) 1880-1956... **TCLC
13**
See also CA 105; 125; CDALB 1917-1929;
DLB 11, 29, 63, 137; MTCW 1

Mendelsohn, Jane 1965(?)- .... **CLC 99**
See also CA 154

Mercer, David 1928-1980.................... **CLC
5; DAM DRAM**
See also CA 9-12R; 102; CANR 23; DLB 13;
MTCW 1

Merchant, Paul
See Ellison, Harlan (Jay)

Meredith, George 1828-1909 .... **TCLC
17, 43; DAM POET**
See also CA 117; 153; CDBLB 1832-1890;
DLB 18, 35, 57, 159

Meredith, William (Morris) 1919- .... **CLC
4, 13, 22, 55; DAM POET**
See also CA 9-12R; CAAS 14; CANR 6, 40;
DLB 5

Merezhkovsky, Dmitry Sergeyevich
1865-1941 .... **TCLC 29**
See also CA 169

Merimee, Prosper 1803-1870............. **NCLC
6, 65; SSC 7**
See also DLB 119, 192

Merkin, Daphne 1954-.................... **CLC 44**
See also CA 123

Merlin, Arthur
See Blish, James (Benjamin)

Merrill, James (Ingram) 1926-1995 ...... **CLC
2, 3, 6, 8, 13, 18, 34, 91; DAM POET**
See also CA 13-16R; 147; CANR 10, 49, 63;
DLB 5, 165; DLBY 85; INT CANR-10;
MTCW 1

Merriman, Alex
See Silverberg, Robert

Merriman, Brian 1747-1805.......... **NCLC 70**

Merritt, E. B.
See Waddington, Miriam

Merton, Thomas 1915-1968 .... **CLC
1, 3, 11, 34, 83; PC 10**
See also CA 5-8R; 25-28R; CANR 22, 53;
DLB 48; DLBY 81; MTCW 1

Merwin, W(illiam) S(tanley) 1927- .... **CLC 1,
2, 3, 5, 8, 13, 18, 45, 88; DAM POET**
See also CA 13-16R; CANR 15, 51; DLB 5,
169; INT CANR-15; MTCW 1

Metcalf, John 1938- .... **CLC 37**
See also CA 113; DLB 60

Metcalf, Suzanne
See Baum, L(yman) Frank

Mew, Charlotte (Mary) 1870-1928....**TCLC 8**
See also CA 105; DLB 19, 135

Mewshaw, Michael 1943- .... **CLC 9**
See also CA 53-56; CANR 7, 47; DLBY 80

Meyer, June
See Jordan, June

Meyer, Lynn
See Slavitt, David R(ytman)

Meyer-Meyrink, Gustav 1868-1932
See Meyrink, Gustav

Meyers, Jeffrey 1939- .... **CLC 39**
See also CA 73-76; CANR 54; DLB 111

**Meynell, Alice (Christina Gertrude
Thompson)** 1847-1922 ....**TCLC 6**
See also CA 104; DLB 19, 98

Meyrink, Gustav .... **TCLC 21**
See also Meyer-Meyrink, Gustav

Michaels, Leonard 1933- ...**CLC 6, 25; SSC 16**
See also CA 61-64; CANR 21, 62; DLB 130;
MTCW 1

Michaux, Henri 1899-1984.......... **CLC 8, 19**
See also CA 85-88; 114

Micheaux, Oscar 1884-1951 .... **TCLC 76**
See also DLB 50

Michelangelo 1475-1564.................... **LC 12**

Michelet, Jules 1798-1874............. **NCLC 31**

Michels, Robert 1876-1936 .... **TCLC 88**

Michener, James A(lbert) 1907(?)-
1997 .... **CLC
1, 5, 11, 29, 60, 109; DAM NOV, POP**
See also AAYA 27; AITN 1; BEST 90:1;
CA 5-8R; 161; CANR 21, 45, 68; DLB 6;
MTCW 1

Mickiewicz, Adam 1798-1855 ....**NCLC 3**

Middleton, Christopher 1926- .... **CLC 13**
See also CA 13-16R; CANR 29, 54; DLB 40

Middleton, Richard (Barham)
1882-1911 .... **TCLC 56**
See also DLB 156

Middleton, Stanley 1919-............. **CLC 7, 38**
See also CA 25-28R; CAAS 23; CANR 21,
46; DLB 14

Middleton, Thomas 1580-1627................ **LC
33; DAM DRAM, MST; DC 5**
See also DLB 58

Migueis, Jose Rodrigues 1901-......... **CLC 10**

Mikszath, Kalman 1847-1910 .... **TCLC 31**
See also CA 170

Miles, Jack................................**CLC 100**

Miles, Josephine (Louise) 1911-1985 ..... **CLC
1, 2, 14, 34, 39; DAM POET**
See also CA 1-4R; 116; CANR 2, 55; DLB
48

Militant
See Sandburg, Carl (August)

Mill, John Stuart 1806-1873......**NCLC 11, 58**
See also CDBLB 1832-1890; DLB 55, 190

Millar, Kenneth 1915-1983 .... **CLC
14; DAM POP**
See also Macdonald, Ross

Millay, E. Vincent
See Millay, Edna St. Vincent

Millay, Edna St. Vincent 1892-1950 .... **TCLC
4, 49; DA; DAB; DAC; DAM MST,
POET; PC 6**
See also CA 104; 130; CDALB 1917-1929;
DLB 45; MTCW 1

Miller, Arthur 1915-...................... **CLC 1,
2, 6, 10, 15, 26, 47, 78; DA; DAB; DAC;
DAM DRAM, MST; DC 1; WLC**
See also AAYA 15; AITN 1; CA 1-4R; CABS
3; CANR 2, 30, 54; CDALB 1941-1968;
DLB 7; MTCW 1

Miller, Henry (Valentine) 1891-1980 ..... **CLC
1, 2, 4, 9, 14, 43, 84; DA; DAB; DAC;
DAM MST, NOV; WLC**
See also CA 9-12R; 97-100; CANR 33, 64;
CDALB 1929-1941; DLB 4, 9; DLBY 80;
MTCW 1

Miller, Jason 1939(?)- .... **CLC 2**
See also AITN 1; CA 73-76; DLB 7

Miller, Sue 1943- .... **CLC 44; DAM POP**
See also BEST 90:3; CA 139; CANR 59;
DLB 143

Miller, Walter M(ichael, Jr.) 1923- .... **CLC
4, 30**
See also CA 85-88; DLB 8

Millett, Kate 1934-........................ **CLC 67**
See also AITN 1; CA 73-76; CANR 32, 53;
MTCW 1

Millhauser, Steven (Lewis) 1943-.......... **CLC 21, 54, 109**
See also CA 110; 111; CANR 63; DLB 2; INT 111

Millin, Sarah Gertrude 1889-1968.... **CLC 49**
See also CA 102; 93-96

Milne, A(lan) A(lexander) 1882-1956... **TCLC 6, 88; DAB; DAC; DAM MST**
See also CA 104; 133; CLR 1, 26; DLB 10, 77, 100, 160; MAICYA; MTCW 1; SATA 100; YABC 1

Milner, Ron(ald) 1938-...................... **CLC 56; BLC 3; DAM MULT**
See also AITN 1; BW 1; CA 73-76; CANR 24; DLB 38; MTCW 1

Milnes, Richard Monckton 1809-1885 .... **NCLC 61**
See also DLB 32, 184

Milosz, Czeslaw 1911-........ **CLC 5, 11, 22, 31, 56, 82; DAM MST, POET; PC 8; WLCS**
See also CA 81-84; CANR 23, 51; MTCW 1

Milton, John 1608-1674 .... **LC 9, 43; DA; DAB; DAC; DAM MST, POET; PC 19; WLC**
See also CDBLB 1660-1789; DLB 131, 151

Min, Anchee 1957-......................... **CLC 86**
See also CA 146

Minehaha, Cornelius
See Wedekind, (Benjamin) Frank(lin)

Miner, Valerie 1947-...................... **CLC 40**
See also CA 97-100; CANR 59

Minimo, Duca
See D'Annunzio, Gabriele

Minot, Susan 1956- .... **CLC 44**
See also CA 134

Minus, Ed 1938-........................... **CLC 39**

Miranda, Javier
See Bioy Casares, Adolfo

Mirbeau, Octave 1848-1917 .... **TCLC 55**
See also DLB 123, 192

Miro (Ferrer), Gabriel (Francisco Victor) 1879-1930 .... **TCLC 5**
See also CA 104

Mishima, Yukio 1925-1970 .... **CLC 2, 4, 6, 9, 27; DC 1; SSC 4**
See also Hiraoka, Kimitake

Mistral, Frederic 1830-1914 .... **TCLC 51**
See also CA 122

Mistral, Gabriela................. **TCLC 2; HLC**
See also Godoy Alcayaga, Lucila

Mistry, Rohinton 1952-.......... **CLC 71; DAC**
See also CA 141

Mitchell, Clyde
See Ellison, Harlan (Jay); Silverberg, Robert

Mitchell, James Leslie 1901-1935
See Gibbon, Lewis Grassic

Mitchell, Joni 1943- .... **CLC 12**
See also CA 112

Mitchell, Joseph (Quincy) 1908-1996 .... **CLC 98**
See also CA 77-80; 152; CANR 69; DLB 185; DLBY 96

Mitchell, Margaret (Munnerlyn) 1900-1949 ...**TCLC 11; DAM NOV, POP**
See also AAYA 23; CA 109; 125; CANR 55; DLB 9; MTCW 1

Mitchell, Peggy
See Mitchell, Margaret (Munnerlyn)

Mitchell, S(ilas) Weir 1829-1914 .... **TCLC 36**
See also CA 165; DLB 202

Mitchell, W(illiam) O(rmond) 1914-1998 ... **CLC 25; DAC; DAM MST**
See also CA 77-80; 165; CANR 15, 43; DLB 88

Mitchell, William 1879-1936 .... **TCLC 81**

Mitford, Mary Russell 1787-1855.....**NCLC 4**
See also DLB 110, 116

Mitford, Nancy 1904-1973 .... **CLC 44**
See also CA 9-12R; DLB 191

Miyamoto, Yuriko 1899-1951 .... **TCLC 37**
See also CA 170; DLB 180

Miyazawa, Kenji 1896-1933 .... **TCLC 76**
See also CA 157

Mizoguchi, Kenji 1898-1956.......... **TCLC 72**
See also CA 167

Mo, Timothy (Peter) 1950(?)- .... **CLC 46**
See also CA 117; DLB 194; MTCW 1

Modarressi, Taghi (M.) 1931- .... **CLC 44**
See also CA 121; 134; INT 134

Modiano, Patrick (Jean) 1945-......... **CLC 18**
See also CA 85-88; CANR 17, 40; DLB 83

Moerck, Paal
See Roelvaag, O(le) E(dvart)

Mofolo, Thomas (Mokopu) 1875(?)-1948.......................... **TCLC 22; BLC 3; DAM MULT**
See also CA 121; 153

Mohr, Nicholasa 1938-...................... **CLC 12; DAM MULT; HLC**
See also AAYA 8; CA 49-52; CANR 1, 32, 64; CLR 22; DLB 145; HW; JRDA; SAAS 8; SATA 8, 97

Mojtabai, A(nn) G(race) 1938- .... **CLC 5, 9, 15, 29**
See also CA 85-88

Moliere 1622-1673 ....**LC 10, 28; DA; DAB; DAC; DAM DRAM, MST; WLC**

Molin, Charles
See Mayne, William (James Carter)

Molnar, Ferenc 1878-1952 .... **TCLC 20; DAM DRAM**
See also CA 109; 153

Momaday, N(avarre) Scott 1934- ...... **CLC 2, 19, 85, 95; DA; DAB; DAC; DAM MST, MULT, NOV, POP; PC 25; WLCS**
See also AAYA 11; CA 25-28R; CANR 14, 34, 68; DLB 143, 175; INT CANR-14; MTCW 1; NNAL; SATA 48; SATA-Brief 30

Monette, Paul 1945-1995 .... **CLC 82**
See also CA 139; 147

Monroe, Harriet 1860-1936........... **TCLC 12**
See also CA 109; DLB 54, 91

Monroe, Lyle
See Heinlein, Robert A(nson)

Montagu, Elizabeth 1720-1800 ....**NCLC 7**

Montagu, Mary (Pierrepont) Wortley 1689-1762 .... **LC 9; PC 16**
See also DLB 95, 101

Montagu, W. H.
See Coleridge, Samuel Taylor

Montague, John (Patrick) 1929-... **CLC 13, 46**
See also CA 9-12R; CANR 9, 69; DLB 40; MTCW 1

Montaigne, Michel (Eyquem) de 1533-1592 .... **LC 8; DA; DAB; DAC; DAM MST; WLC**

Montale, Eugenio 1896-1981 .... **CLC 7, 9, 18; PC 13**
See also CA 17-20R; 104; CANR 30; DLB 114; MTCW 1

Montesquieu, Charles-Louis de Secondat 1689-1755 .... **LC 7**

Montgomery, (Robert) Bruce 1921-1978
See Crispin, Edmund

Montgomery, L(ucy) M(aud) 1874-1942 .... **TCLC 51; DAC; DAM MST**
See also AAYA 12; CA 108; 137; CLR 8; DLB 92; DLBD 14; JRDA; MAICYA; SATA 100; YABC 1

Montgomery, Marion H., Jr. 1925- .....**CLC 7**
See also AITN 1; CA 1-4R; CANR 3, 48; DLB 6

Montgomery, Max
See Davenport, Guy (Mattison, Jr.)

Montherlant, Henry (Milon) de 1896-1972 ......**CLC 8, 19; DAM DRAM**
See also CA 85-88; 37-40R; DLB 72; MTCW 1

Monty Python
See Chapman, Graham; Cleese, John (Marwood); Gilliam, Terry (Vance); Idle, Eric; Jones, Terence Graham Parry; Palin, Michael (Edward)

Moodie, Susanna (Strickland) 1803-1885 .... **NCLC 14**
See also DLB 99

Mooney, Edward 1951-
See Mooney, Ted

Mooney, Ted................................ **CLC 25**
See also Mooney, Edward

Moorcock, Michael (John) 1939-.......... **CLC 5, 27, 58**
See also AAYA 26; CA 45-48; CAAS 5; CANR 2, 17, 38, 64; DLB 14; MTCW 1; SATA 93

Moore, Brian 1921-...............**CLC 1, 3, 5, 7, 8, 19, 32, 90; DAB; DAC; DAM MST**
See also CA 1-4R; CANR 1, 25, 42, 63; MTCW 1

Moore, Edward
See Muir, Edwin

Moore, G. E. 1873-1958 .... **TCLC 89**

Moore, George Augustus 1852-1933.... **TCLC 7; SSC 19**
See also CA 104; DLB 10, 18, 57, 135

Moore, Lorrie.................... **CLC 39, 45, 68**
See also Moore, Marie Lorena

Nichol, B(arrie) P(hillip) 1944-1988 ...**CLC 18**
See also CA 53-56; DLB 53; SATA 66

Nichols, John (Treadwell) 1940- .... **CLC 38**
See also CA 9-12R; CAAS 2; CANR 6, 70;
DLBY 82

Nichols, Leigh
See Koontz, Dean R(ay)

Nichols, Peter (Richard) 1927-............. **CLC
5, 36, 65**
See also CA 104; CANR 33; DLB 13;
MTCW 1

Nicolas, F. R. E.
See Freeling, Nicolas

Niedecker, Lorine 1903-1970............... **CLC
10, 42; DAM POET**
See also CA 25-28; CAP 2; DLB 48

Nietzsche, Friedrich (Wilhelm)
1844-1900 .... **TCLC 10, 18, 55**
See also CA 107; 121; DLB 129

Nievo, Ippolito 1831-1861 .... **NCLC 22**

Nightingale, Anne Redmon 1943-
See Redmon, Anne

Nightingale, Florence 1820-1910 .... **TCLC 85**
See also DLB 166

Nik. T. O.
See Annensky, Innokenty (Fyodorovich)

Nin, Anais 1903-1977................ **CLC 1, 4, 8,
11, 14, 60; DAM NOV, POP; SSC 10**
See also AITN 2; CA 13-16R; 69-72; CANR
22, 53; DLB 2, 4, 152; MTCW 1

Nishida, Kitaro 1870-1945 .... **TCLC 83**

Nishiwaki, Junzaburo 1894-1982.........**PC 15**
See also CA 107

Nissenson, Hugh 1933-................... **CLC 4, 9**
See also CA 17-20R; CANR 27; DLB 28

Niven, Larry .... **CLC 8**
See also Niven, Laurence Van Cott

Niven, Laurence Van Cott 1938-
See Niven, Larry

Nixon, Agnes Eckhardt 1927-.......... **CLC 21**
See also CA 110

Nizan, Paul 1905-1940 .... **TCLC 40**
See also CA 161; DLB 72

Nkosi, Lewis 1936-............................ **CLC
45; BLC 3; DAM MULT**
See also BW 1; CA 65-68; CANR 27; DLB
157

Nodier, (Jean) Charles (Emmanuel)
1780-1844 .... **NCLC 19**
See also DLB 119

Noguchi, Yone 1875-1947 .... **TCLC 80**

Nolan, Christopher 1965- .... **CLC 58**
See also CA 111

Noon, Jeff 1957- .... **CLC 91**
See also CA 148

Norden, Charles
See Durrell, Lawrence (George)

Nordhoff, Charles (Bernard)
1887-1947 .... **TCLC 23**
See also CA 108; DLB 9; SATA 23

Norfolk, Lawrence 1963-................ **CLC 76**
See also CA 144

Norman, Marsha 1947-..................... **CLC
28; DAM DRAM; DC 8**
See also CA 105; CABS 3; CANR 41; DLBY
84

Normyx
See Douglas, (George) Norman

Norris, Frank 1870-1902 .... **SSC 28**
See also Norris, (Benjamin) Frank(lin, Jr.)

Norris, (Benjamin) Frank(lin, Jr.)
1870-1902 .... **TCLC 24**
See also Norris, Frank

Norris, Leslie 1921-...................... **CLC 14**
See also CA 11-12; CANR 14; CAP 1; DLB
27

North, Andrew
See Norton, Andre

North, Anthony
See Koontz, Dean R(ay)

North, Captain George
See Stevenson, Robert Louis (Balfour)

North, Milou
See Erdrich, Louise

Northrup, B. A.
See Hubbard, L(afayette) Ron(ald)

North Staffs
See Hulme, T(homas) E(rnest)

Norton, Alice Mary
See Norton, Andre

Norton, Andre 1912- .... **CLC 12**
See also Norton, Alice Mary

Norton, Caroline 1808-1877 .... **NCLC 47**
See also DLB 21, 159, 199

Norway, Nevil Shute 1899-1960
See Shute, Nevil

Norwid, Cyprian Kamil 1821-1883 ..... **NCLC
17**

Nosille, Nabrah
See Ellison, Harlan (Jay)

Nossack, Hans Erich 1901-1978 .... **CLC 6**
See also CA 93-96; 85-88; DLB 69

Nostradamus 1503-1566.................... **LC 27**

Nosu, Chuji
See Ozu, Yasujiro

Notenburg, Eleanora (Genrikhovna) von
See Guro, Elena

Nova, Craig 1945-...................... **CLC 7, 31**
See also CA 45-48; CANR 2, 53

Novak, Joseph
See Kosinski, Jerzy (Nikodem)

Novalis 1772-1801....................... **NCLC 13**
See also DLB 90

Novis, Emile
See Weil, Simone (Adolphine)

Nowlan, Alden (Albert) 1933-1983........ **CLC
15; DAC; DAM MST**
See also CA 9-12R; CANR 5; DLB 53

Noyes, Alfred 1880-1958................**TCLC 7**
See also CA 104; DLB 20

Nunn, Kem .... **CLC 34**
See also CA 159

Nye, Robert 1939-.... **CLC 13, 42; DAM NOV**
See also CA 33-36R; CANR 29, 67; DLB 14;
MTCW 1; SATA 6

Nyro, Laura 1947- .... **CLC 17**

Oates, Joyce Carol 1938-......**CLC 1, 2, 3, 6, 9,
11, 15, 19, 33, 52, 108; DA; DAB; DAC;
DAM MST, NOV, POP; SSC 6; WLC**
See also AAYA 15; AITN 1; BEST 89:2; CA
5-8R; CANR 25, 45, 74; CDALB 1968-
1988; DLB 2, 5, 130; DLBY 81; INT
CANR-25; MTCW 1

O'Brien, Darcy 1939-1998 .... **CLC 11**
See also CA 21-24R; 167; CANR 8, 59

O'Brien, E. G.
See Clarke, Arthur C(harles)

O'Brien, Edna 1936- .... **CLC 3, 5, 8,
13, 36, 65, 116; DAM NOV; SSC 10**
See also CA 1-4R; CANR 6, 41, 65; CDBLB
1960 to Present; DLB 14; MTCW 1

O'Brien, Fitz-James 1828-1862...... **NCLC 21**
See also DLB 74

O'Brien, Flann .... **CLC 1, 4, 5, 7, 10, 47**
See also O Nuallain, Brian

O'Brien, Richard 1942- .... **CLC 17**
See also CA 124

O'Brien, (William) Tim(othy) 1946-...... **CLC
7, 19, 40, 103; DAM POP**
See also AAYA 16; CA 85-88; CANR 40, 58;
DLB 152; DLBD 9; DLBY 80

Obstfelder, Sigbjoern 1866-1900 .... **TCLC 23**
See also CA 123

O'Casey, Sean 1880-1964 .... **CLC
1, 5, 9, 11, 15, 88; DAB; DAC; DAM
DRAM, MST; WLCS**
See also CA 89-92; CANR 62; CDBLB
1914-1945; DLB 10; MTCW 1

O'Cathasaigh, Sean
See O'Casey, Sean

Ochs, Phil 1940-1976..................... **CLC 17**
See also CA 65-68

O'Connor, Edwin (Greene) 1918-1968... **CLC
14**
See also CA 93-96; 25-28R

O'Connor, (Mary) Flannery
1925-1964 ....**CLC 1, 2, 3, 6,
10, 13, 15, 21, 66, 104; DA; DAB; DAC;
DAM MST, NOV; SSC 1, 23; WLC**
See also AAYA 7; CA 1-4R; CANR 3, 41;
CDALB 1941-1968; DLB 2, 152; DLBD
12; DLBY 80; MTCW 1

O'Connor, Frank...............**CLC 23; SSC 5**
See also O'Donovan, Michael John

O'Dell, Scott 1898-1989 .... **CLC 30**
See also AAYA 3; CA 61-64; 129; CANR 12,
30; CLR 1, 16; DLB 52; JRDA; MAICYA;
SATA 12, 60

Odets, Clifford 1906-1963................... **CLC
2, 28, 98; DAM DRAM; DC 6**
See also CA 85-88; CANR 62; DLB 7, 26;
MTCW 1

O'Doherty, Brian 1934- .... **CLC 76**
See also CA 105

O'Donnell, K. M.
See Malzberg, Barry N(athaniel)

O'Donnell, Lawrence
See Kuttner, Henry

O'Donovan, Michael John 1903-1966 ... CLC 14
See also O'Connor, Frank

Oe, Kenzaburo 1935-......................... CLC 10, 36, 86; DAM NOV; SSC 20
See also CA 97-100; CANR 36, 50, 74; DLB 182; DLBY 94; MTCW 1

O'Faolain, Julia 1932- ......CLC 6, 19, 47, 108
See also CA 81-84; CAAS 2; CANR 12, 61; DLB 14; MTCW 1

O'Faolain, Sean 1900-1991 .... CLC 1, 7, 14, 32, 70; SSC 13
See also CA 61-64; 134; CANR 12, 66; DLB 15, 162; MTCW 1

O'Flaherty, Liam 1896-1984 .... CLC 5, 34; SSC 6
See also CA 101; 113; CANR 35; DLB 36, 162; DLBY 84; MTCW 1

Ogilvy, Gavin
See Barrie, J(ames) M(atthew)

O'Grady, Standish (James) 1846-1928 ....TCLC 5
See also CA 104; 157

O'Grady, Timothy 1951-................. CLC 59
See also CA 138

O'Hara, Frank 1926-1966 .... CLC 2, 5, 13, 78; DAM POET
See also CA 9-12R; 25-28R; CANR 33; DLB 5, 16, 193; MTCW 1

O'Hara, John (Henry) 1905-1970......... CLC 1, 2, 3, 6, 11, 42; DAM NOV; SSC 15
See also CA 5-8R; 25-28R; CANR 31, 60; CDALB 1929-1941; DLB 9, 86; DLBD 2; MTCW 1

O Hehir, Diana 1922-..................... CLC 41
See also CA 93-96

Okigbo, Christopher (Ifenayichukwu) 1932-1967 ....CLC 25, 84; BLC 3; DAM MULT, POET; PC 7
See also BW 1; CA 77-80; CANR 74; DLB 125; MTCW 1

Okri, Ben 1959-........................... CLC 87
See also BW 2; CA 130; 138; CANR 65; DLB 157; INT 138

Olds, Sharon 1942- .... CLC 32, 39, 85; DAM POET; PC 22
See also CA 101; CANR 18, 41, 66; DLB 120

Oldstyle, Jonathan
See Irving, Washington

Olesha, Yuri (Karlovich) 1899-1960....CLC 8
See also CA 85-88

Oliphant, Laurence 1829(?)-1888 ... NCLC 47
See also DLB 18, 166

Oliphant, Margaret (Oliphant Wilson) 1828-1897 .... NCLC 11, 61; SSC 25
See also DLB 18, 159, 190

Oliver, Mary 1935-............... CLC 19, 34, 98
See also CA 21-24R; CANR 9, 43; DLB 5, 193

Olivier, Laurence (Kerr) 1907-1989 ...CLC 20
See also CA 111; 150; 129

Olsen, Tillie 1912-............... CLC 4, 13, 114; DA; DAB; DAC; DAM MST; SSC 11
See also CA 1-4R; CANR 1, 43, 74; DLB 28; DLBY 80; MTCW 1

Olson, Charles (John) 1910-1970....... CLC 1, 2, 5, 6, 9, 11, 29; DAM POET; PC 19
See also CA 13-16; 25-28R; CABS 2; CANR 35, 61; CAP 1; DLB 5, 16, 193; MTCW 1

Olson, Toby 1937-......................... CLC 28
See also CA 65-68; CANR 9, 31

Olyesha, Yuri
See Olesha, Yuri (Karlovich)

Ondaatje, (Philip) Michael 1943- .... CLC 14, 29, 51, 76; DAB; DAC; DAM MST
See also CA 77-80; CANR 42, 74; DLB 60

Oneal, Elizabeth 1934-
See Oneal, Zibby

Oneal, Zibby .... CLC 30
See also Oneal, Elizabeth

O'Neill, Eugene (Gladstone) 1888-1953 .... TCLC 1, 6, 27, 49; DA; DAB; DAC; DAM DRAM, MST; WLC
See also AITN 1; CA 110; 132; CDALB 1929-1941; DLB 7; MTCW 1

Onetti, Juan Carlos 1909-1994............. CLC 7, 10; DAM MULT, NOV; SSC 23
See also CA 85-88; 145; CANR 32, 63; DLB 113; HW; MTCW 1

O Nuallain, Brian 1911-1966
See O'Brien, Flann

Ophuls, Max 1902-1957 .... TCLC 79
See also CA 113

Opie, Amelia 1769-1853 .... NCLC 65
See also DLB 116, 159

Oppen, George 1908-1984 ....CLC 7, 13, 34
See also CA 13-16R; 113; CANR 8; DLB 5, 165

Oppenheim, E(dward) Phillips 1866-1946 .... TCLC 45
See also CA 111; DLB 70

Opuls, Max
See Ophuls, Max

Origen c. 185-c. 254................... CMLC 19

Orlovitz, Gil 1918-1973.................. CLC 22
See also CA 77-80; 45-48; DLB 2, 5

Orris
See Ingelow, Jean

Ortega y Gasset, Jose 1883-1955 .... TCLC 9; DAM MULT; HLC
See also CA 106; 130; HW; MTCW 1

Ortese, Anna Maria 1914- .... CLC 89
See also DLB 177

Ortiz, Simon J(oseph) 1941-................ CLC 45; DAM MULT, POET; PC 17
See also CA 134; CANR 69; DLB 120, 175; NNAL

Orton, Joe .... CLC 4, 13, 43; DC 3
See also Orton, John Kingsley

Orton, John Kingsley 1933-1967
See Orton, Joe

Orwell, George .... TCLC 2, 6, 15, 31, 51; DAB; WLC
See also Blair, Eric (Arthur)

Osborne, David
See Silverberg, Robert

Osborne, George
See Silverberg, Robert

Osborne, John (James) 1929-1994 .... CLC 1, 2, 5, 11, 45; DA; DAB; DAC; DAM DRAM, MST; WLC
See also CA 13-16R; 147; CANR 21, 56; CDBLB 1945-1960; DLB 13; MTCW 1

Osborne, Lawrence 1958-............... CLC 50

Oshima, Nagisa 1932-................... CLC 20
See also CA 116; 121

Oskison, John Milton 1874-1947 .... TCLC 35; DAM MULT
See also CA 144; DLB 175; NNAL

Ossian c. 3rd cent. -.................... CMLC 28
See also Macpherson, James

Ossoli, Sarah Margaret (Fuller marchesa d') 1810-1850
See Fuller, Margaret

Ostrovsky, Alexander 1823-1886........NCLC 30, 57

Otero, Blas de 1916-1979................ CLC 11
See also CA 89-92; DLB 134

Otto, Rudolf 1869-1937................ TCLC 85

Otto, Whitney 1955-...................... CLC 70
See also CA 140

Ouida .... TCLC 43
See also De La Ramee, (Marie) Louise

Ousmane, Sembene 1923-..... CLC 66; BLC 3
See also BW 1; CA 117; 125; MTCW 1

Ovid 43B.C.-18(?)......................... CMLC 7; DAM POET; PC 2

Owen, Hugh
See Faust, Frederick (Schiller)

Owen, Wilfred (Edward Salter) 1893-1918 ....TCLC 5, 27; DA; DAB; DAC; DAM MST, POET; PC 19; WLC
See also CA 104; 141; CDBLB 1914-1945; DLB 20

Owens, Rochelle 1936-.....................CLC 8
See also CA 17-20R; CAAS 2; CANR 39

Oz, Amos 1939-............................ CLC 5, 8, 11, 27, 33, 54; DAM NOV
See also CA 53-56; CANR 27, 47, 65; MTCW 1

Ozick, Cynthia 1928-........................CLC 3, 7, 28, 62; DAM NOV, POP; SSC 15
See also BEST 90:1; CA 17-20R; CANR 23, 58; DLB 28, 152; DLBY 82; INT CANR-23; MTCW 1

Ozu, Yasujiro 1903-1963 .... CLC 16
See also CA 112

Pacheco, C.
See Pessoa, Fernando (Antonio Nogueira)

Pa Chin................................... CLC 18
See also Li Fei-kan

Pack, Robert 1929- .... CLC 13
See also CA 1-4R; CANR 3, 44; DLB 5

Padgett, Lewis
See Kuttner, Henry

Padilla (Lorenzo), Heberto 1932- ..... CLC 38
See also AITN 1; CA 123; 131; HW

Rexroth, Kenneth 1905-1982 ...... **CLC 1, 2, 6, 11, 22, 49, 112; DAM POET; PC 20**
See also CA 5-8R; 107; CANR 14, 34, 63; CDALB 1941-1968; DLB 16, 48, 165; DLBY 82; INT CANR-14; MTCW 1

Reyes, Alfonso 1889-1959 .... **TCLC 33**
See also CA 131; HW

Reyes y Basoalto, Ricardo Eliecer Neftali
See Neruda, Pablo

Reymont, Wladyslaw (Stanislaw) 1868(?)-1925 .... **TCLC 5**
See also CA 104

Reynolds, Jonathan 1942-............ **CLC 6, 38**
See also CA 65-68; CANR 28

Reynolds, Joshua 1723-1792 .... **LC 15**
See also DLB 104

Reynolds, Michael Shane 1937- .... **CLC 44**
See also CA 65-68; CANR 9

Reznikoff, Charles 1894-1976............ **CLC 9**
See also CA 33-36; 61-64; CAP 2; DLB 28, 45

Rezzori (d'Arezzo), Gregor von 1914-1998 .... **CLC 25**
See also CA 122; 136; 167

Rhine, Richard
See Silverstein, Alvin

Rhodes, Eugene Manlove 1869-1934 ... **TCLC 53**

Rhodius, Apollonius c. 3rd cent. B.C.-............................... **CMLC 28**
See also DLB 176

R'hoone
See Balzac, Honore de

Rhys, Jean 1890(?)-1979.................. **CLC 2, 4, 6, 14, 19, 51; DAM NOV; SSC 21**
See also CA 25-28R; 85-88; CANR 35, 62; CDBLB 1945-1960; DLB 36, 117, 162; MTCW 1

Ribeiro, Darcy 1922-1997 .... **CLC 34**
See also CA 33-36R; 156

Ribeiro, Joao Ubaldo (Osorio Pimentel) 1941- ....**CLC 10, 67**
See also CA 81-84

Ribman, Ronald (Burt) 1932-............ **CLC 7**
See also CA 21-24R; CANR 46

Ricci, Nino 1959-.......................... **CLC 70**
See also CA 137

Rice, Anne 1941- .... **CLC 41; DAM POP**
See also AAYA 9; BEST 89:2; CA 65-68; CANR 12, 36, 53, 74

Rice, Elmer (Leopold) 1892-1967 .... **CLC 7, 49; DAM DRAM**
See also CA 21-22; 25-28R; CAP 2; DLB 4, 7; MTCW 1

Rice, Tim(othy Miles Bindon) 1944- ...**CLC 21**
See also CA 103; CANR 46

Rich, Adrienne (Cecile) 1929-..... **CLC 3, 6, 7, 11, 18, 36, 73, 76; DAM POET; PC 5**
See also CA 9-12R; CANR 20, 53, 74; DLB 5, 67; MTCW 1

Rich, Barbara
See Graves, Robert (von Ranke)

Rich, Robert
See Trumbo, Dalton

Richard, Keith........................... **CLC 17**
See also Richards, Keith

Richards, David Adams 1950- .... **CLC 59; DAC**
See also CA 93-96; CANR 60; DLB 53

Richards, I(vor) A(rmstrong) 1893-1979 ....**CLC 14, 24**
See also CA 41-44R; 89-92; CANR 34, 74; DLB 27

Richards, Keith 1943-
See Richard, Keith

Richardson, Anne
See Roiphe, Anne (Richardson)

Richardson, Dorothy Miller 1873-1957 ....**TCLC 3**
See also CA 104; DLB 36

Richardson, Ethel Florence (Lindesay) 1870-1946
See Richardson, Henry Handel

Richardson, Henry Handel........**TCLC 4**
See also Richardson, Ethel Florence (Lindesay)

Richardson, John 1796-1852 ....**NCLC 55; DAC**
See also DLB 99

Richardson, Samuel 1689-1761 .... **LC 1, 44; DA; DAB; DAC; DAM MST, NOV; WLC**
See also CDBLB 1660-1789; DLB 39

Richler, Mordecai 1931-............ **CLC 3, 5, 9, 13, 18, 46, 70; DAC; DAM MST, NOV**
See also AITN 1; CA 65-68; CANR 31, 62; CLR 17; DLB 53; MAICYA; MTCW 1; SATA 44, 98; SATA-Brief 27

Richter, Conrad (Michael) 1890-1968.... **CLC 30**
See also AAYA 21; CA 5-8R; 25-28R; CANR 23; DLB 9; MTCW 1; SATA 3

Ricostranza, Tom
See Ellis, Trey

Riddell, Charlotte 1832-1906......... **TCLC 40**
See also CA 165; DLB 156

Riding, Laura...........................**CLC 3, 7**
See also Jackson, Laura (Riding)

Riefenstahl, Berta Helene Amalia 1902-
See Riefenstahl, Leni

Riefenstahl, Leni .... **CLC 16**
See also Riefenstahl, Berta Helene Amalia

Riffe, Ernest
See Bergman, (Ernst) Ingmar

Riggs, (Rolla) Lynn 1899-1954........... **TCLC 56; DAM MULT**
See also CA 144; DLB 175; NNAL

Riis, Jacob A(ugust) 1849-1914 ...... **TCLC 80**
See also CA 113; 168; DLB 23

Riley, James Whitcomb 1849-1916 ..... **TCLC 51; DAM POET**
See also CA 118; 137; MAICYA; SATA 17

Riley, Tex
See Creasey, John

Rilke, Rainer Maria 1875-1926.......... **TCLC 1, 6, 19; DAM POET; PC 2**
See also CA 104; 132; CANR 62; DLB 81; MTCW 1

Rimbaud, (Jean Nicolas) Arthur 1854-1891 ....**NCLC 4, 35; DA; DAB; DAC; DAM MST, POET; PC 3; WLC**

Rinehart, Mary Roberts 1876-1958..... **TCLC 52**
See also CA 108; 166

Ringmaster, The
See Mencken, H(enry) L(ouis)

Ringwood, Gwen(dolyn Margaret) Pharis 1910-1984 .... **CLC 48**
See also CA 148; 112; DLB 88

Rio, Michel 19(?)- .... **CLC 43**

Ritsos, Giannes
See Ritsos, Yannis

Ritsos, Yannis 1909-1990.........**CLC 6, 13, 31**
See also CA 77-80; 133; CANR 39, 61; MTCW 1

Ritter, Erika 1948(?)- .... **CLC 52**

Rivera, Jose Eustasio 1889-1928 .... **TCLC 35**
See also CA 162; HW

Rivers, Conrad Kent 1933-1968.........**CLC 1**
See also BW 1; CA 85-88; DLB 41

Rivers, Elfrida
See Bradley, Marion Zimmer

Riverside, John
See Heinlein, Robert A(nson)

Rizal, Jose 1861-1896 .... **NCLC 27**

Roa Bastos, Augusto (Antonio) 1917-.... **CLC 45; DAM MULT; HLC**
See also CA 131; DLB 113; HW

Robbe-Grillet, Alain 1922-.................. **CLC 1, 2, 4, 6, 8, 10, 14, 43**
See also CA 9-12R; CANR 33, 65; DLB 83; MTCW 1

Robbins, Harold 1916-1997................. **CLC 5; DAM NOV**
See also CA 73-76; 162; CANR 26, 54; MTCW 1

Robbins, Thomas Eugene 1936-
See Robbins, Tom

Robbins, Tom ....**CLC 9, 32, 64**
See also Robbins, Thomas Eugene

Robbins, Trina 1938-.................... **CLC 21**
See also CA 128

Roberts, Charles G(eorge) D(ouglas) 1860-1943 ....**TCLC 8**
See also CA 105; CLR 33; DLB 92; SATA 88; SATA-Brief 29

Roberts, Elizabeth Madox 1886-1941 .... **TCLC 68**
See also CA 111; 166; DLB 9, 54, 102; SATA 33; SATA-Brief 27

Roberts, Kate 1891-1985 .... **CLC 15**
See also CA 107; 116

Roberts, Keith (John Kingston) 1935- .... **CLC 14**
See also CA 25-28R; CANR 46

Roberts, Kenneth (Lewis) 1885-1957... **TCLC 23**
See also CA 109; DLB 9

Roberts, Michele (B.) 1949-.............. **CLC 48**
See also CA 115; CANR 58

Robertson, Ellis
See Ellison, Harlan (Jay); Silverberg, Robert

Robertson, Thomas William
1829-1871 .... **NCLC 35; DAM DRAM**

Robeson, Kenneth
See Dent, Lester

Robinson, Edwin Arlington
1869-1935 ....**TCLC 5;**
DA; DAC; DAM MST, POET; PC 1
See also CA 104; 133; CDALB 1865-1917;
DLB 54; MTCW 1

Robinson, Henry Crabb 1775-1867..... **NCLC 15**
See also DLB 107

Robinson, Jill 1936- .... **CLC 10**
See also CA 102; INT 102

Robinson, Kim Stanley 1952- .... **CLC 34**
See also AAYA 26; CA 126

Robinson, Lloyd
See Silverberg, Robert

Robinson, Marilynne 1944-.............. **CLC 25**
See also CA 116

Robinson, Smokey .... **CLC 21**
See also Robinson, William, Jr.

Robinson, William, Jr. 1940-
See Robinson, Smokey

Robison, Mary 1949-.................**CLC 42, 98**
See also CA 113; 116; DLB 130; INT 116

Rod, Edouard 1857-1910.............. **TCLC 52**

Roddenberry, Eugene Wesley 1921-1991
See Roddenberry, Gene

Roddenberry, Gene....................... **CLC 17**
See also Roddenberry, Eugene Wesley

Rodgers, Mary 1931-..................... **CLC 12**
See also CA 49-52; CANR 8, 55; CLR 20;
INT CANR-8; JRDA; MAICYA; SATA 8

Rodgers, W(illiam) R(obert)
1909-1969 ....**CLC 7**
See also CA 85-88; DLB 20

Rodman, Eric
See Silverberg, Robert

Rodman, Howard 1920(?)-1985 .... **CLC 65**
See also CA 118

Rodman, Maia
See Wojciechowska, Maia (Teresa)

Rodriguez, Claudio 1934-.............. **CLC 10**
See also DLB 134

Roelvaag, O(le) E(dvart) 1876-1931 .... **TCLC 17**
See also CA 117; 171; DLB 9

Roethke, Theodore (Huebner)
1908-1963 ....**CLC 1, 3, 8, 11, 19, 46, 101; DAM POET; PC 15**
See also CA 81-84; CABS 2; CDALB 1941-
1968; DLB 5; MTCW 1

Rogers, Samuel 1763-1855 .... **NCLC 69**
See also DLB 93

Rogers, Thomas Hunton 1927- .... **CLC 57**
See also CA 89-92; INT 89-92

Rogers, Will(iam Penn Adair)
1879-1935 .... **TCLC 8, 71; DAM MULT**
See also CA 105; 144; DLB 11; NNAL

Rogin, Gilbert 1929-...................... **CLC 18**
See also CA 65-68; CANR 15

Rohan, Koda .... **TCLC 22**
See also Koda Shigeyuki

Rohlfs, Anna Katharine Green
See Green, Anna Katharine

Rohmer, Eric............................. **CLC 16**
See also Scherer, Jean-Marie Maurice

Rohmer, Sax............................. **TCLC 28**
See also Ward, Arthur Henry Sarsfield

Roiphe, Anne (Richardson) 1935-....**CLC 3, 9**
See also CA 89-92; CANR 45, 73; DLBY 80;
INT 89-92

Rojas, Fernando de 1465-1541............**LC 23**

Rolfe, Frederick (William Serafino Austin Lewis Mary) 1860-1913......... **TCLC 12**
See also CA 107; DLB 34, 156

Rolland, Romain 1866-1944 .... **TCLC 23**
See also CA 118; DLB 65

Rolle, Richard c. 1300-c. 1349...... **CMLC 21**
See also DLB 146

Rolvaag, O(le) E(dvart)
See Roelvaag, O(le) E(dvart)

Romain Arnaud, Saint
See Aragon, Louis

Romains, Jules 1885-1972.................**CLC 7**
See also CA 85-88; CANR 34; DLB 65;
MTCW 1

Romero, Jose Ruben 1890-1952 ..... **TCLC 14**
See also CA 114; 131; HW

Ronsard, Pierre de 1524-1585.... **LC 6; PC 11**

Rooke, Leon 1934-....**CLC 25, 34; DAM POP**
See also CA 25-28R; CANR 23, 53

Roosevelt, Theodore 1858-1919...... **TCLC 69**
See also CA 115; 170; DLB 47, 186

Roper, William 1498-1578 ....**LC 10**

Roquelaure, A. N.
See Rice, Anne

Rosa, Joao Guimaraes 1908-1967..... **CLC 23**
See also CA 89-92; DLB 113

Rose, Wendy 1948- .... **CLC 85; DAM MULT; PC 13**
See also CA 53-56; CANR 5, 51; DLB 175;
NNAL; SATA 12

Rosen, R. D.
See Rosen, Richard (Dean)

Rosen, Richard (Dean) 1949-.......... **CLC 39**
See also CA 77-80; CANR 62; INT
CANR-30

Rosenberg, Isaac 1890-1918 .... **TCLC 12**
See also CA 107; DLB 20

Rosenblatt, Joe .... **CLC 15**
See also Rosenblatt, Joseph

Rosenblatt, Joseph 1933-
See Rosenblatt, Joe

Rosenfeld, Samuel
See Tzara, Tristan

Rosenstock, Sami
See Tzara, Tristan

Rosenstock, Samuel
See Tzara, Tristan

Rosenthal, M(acha) L(ouis) 1917-1996... **CLC 28**
See also CA 1-4R; 152; CAAS 6; CANR 4,
51; DLB 5; SATA 59

Ross, Barnaby
See Dannay, Frederic

Ross, Bernard L.
See Follett, Ken(neth Martin)

Ross, J. H.
See Lawrence, T(homas) E(dward)

Ross, John Hume
See Lawrence, T(homas) E(dward)

Ross, Martin
See Martin, Violet Florence

Ross, (James) Sinclair 1908-................ **CLC 13; DAC; DAM MST; SSC 24**
See also CA 73-76; DLB 88

Rossetti, Christina (Georgina)
1830-1894 ...**NCLC 2, 50, 66; DA; DAB;**
DAC; DAM MST, POET; PC 7; WLC
See also DLB 35, 163; MAICYA; SATA 20

Rossetti, Dante Gabriel 1828-1882...... **NCLC 4; DA; DAB; DAC; DAM MST, POET; WLC**
See also CDBLB 1832-1890; DLB 35

Rossner, Judith (Perelman) 1935-......... **CLC 6, 9, 29**
See also AITN 2; BEST 90:3; CA 17-20R;
CANR 18, 51, 73; DLB 6; INT CANR-18;
MTCW 1

Rostand, Edmond (Eugene Alexis)
1868-1918 .... **TCLC 6, 37; DA;**
DAB; DAC; DAM DRAM, MST; DC 10
See also CA 104; 126; DLB 192; MTCW 1

Roth, Henry 1906-1995 ...... **CLC 2, 6, 11, 104**
See also CA 11-12; 149; CANR 38, 63; CAP
1; DLB 28; MTCW 1

Roth, Philip (Milton) 1933- ...**CLC 1, 2, 3, 4, 6, 9, 15, 22, 31, 47, 66, 86; DA; DAB; DAC;**
DAM MST, NOV, POP; SSC 26; WLC
See also BEST 90:3; CA 1-4R; CANR 1, 22,
36, 55; CDALB 1968-1988; DLB 2, 28,
173; DLBY 82; MTCW 1

Rothenberg, Jerome 1931-........... **CLC 6, 57**
See also CA 45-48; CANR 1; DLB 5, 193

Roumain, Jacques (Jean Baptiste)
1907-1944 .... **TCLC 19; BLC 3; DAM MULT**
See also BW 1; CA 117; 125

Rourke, Constance (Mayfield)
1885-1941 .... **TCLC 12**
See also CA 107; YABC 1

Rousseau, Jean-Baptiste 1671-1741 ...... **LC 9**

Rousseau, Jean-Jacques 1712-1778.....**LC 14, 36; DA; DAB; DAC; DAM MST; WLC**

Roussel, Raymond 1877-1933 .... **TCLC 20**
See also CA 117

Rovit, Earl (Herbert) 1927-.............. **CLC 7**
See also CA 5-8R; CANR 12

Salisbury, John
See Caute, (John) David

Salter, James 1925- ....CLC 7, 52, 59
See also CA 73-76; DLB 130

Saltus, Edgar (Everton) 1855-1921 ...TCLC 8
See also CA 105; DLB 202

Saltykov, Mikhail Evgrafovich
1826-1889 .... NCLC 16

Samarakis, Antonis 1919-.................CLC 5
See also CA 25-28R; CAAS 16; CANR 36

Sanchez, Florencio 1875-1910........ TCLC 37
See also CA 153; HW

Sanchez, Luis Rafael 1936- .... CLC 23
See also CA 128; DLB 145; HW

Sanchez, Sonia 1934-......................... CLC
5, 116; BLC 3; DAM MULT; PC 9
See also BW 2; CA 33-36R; CANR 24, 49,
74; CLR 18; DLB 41; DLBD 8; MAICYA;
MTCW 1; SATA 22

Sand, George 1804-1876................... NCLC
2, 42, 57; DA; DAB; DAC; DAM
MST, NOV; WLC
See also DLB 119, 192

Sandburg, Carl (August) 1878-1967...... CLC
1, 4, 10, 15, 35; DA; DAB; DAC; DAM
MST, POET; PC 2; WLC
See also AAYA 24; CA 5-8R; 25-28R;
CANR 35; CDALB 1865-1917; DLB 17,
54; MAICYA; MTCW 1; SATA 8

Sandburg, Charles
See Sandburg, Carl (August)

Sandburg, Charles A.
See Sandburg, Carl (August)

Sanders, (James) Ed(ward) 1939-..... CLC 53
See also CA 13-16R; CAAS 21; CANR 13,
44; DLB 16

Sanders, Lawrence 1920-1998 CLC
41; DAM POP
See also BEST 89:4; CA 81-84; 165; CANR
33, 62; MTCW 1

Sanders, Noah
See Blount, Roy (Alton), Jr.

Sanders, Winston P.
See Anderson, Poul (William)

Sandoz, Mari(e Susette) 1896-1966... CLC 28
See also CA 1-4R; 25-28R; CANR 17, 64;
DLB 9; MTCW 1; SATA 5

Saner, Reg(inald Anthony) 1931-........CLC 9
See also CA 65-68

Sannazaro, Jacopo 1456(?)-1530 .... LC 8

Sansom, William 1912-1976 CLC
2, 6; DAM NOV; SSC 21
See also CA 5-8R; 65-68; CANR 42; DLB
139; MTCW 1

Santayana, George 1863-1952 .... TCLC 40
See also CA 115; DLB 54, 71; DLBD 13

Santiago, Danny.......................... CLC 33
See also James, Daniel (Lewis)

Santmyer, Helen Hoover 1895-1986 ...CLC 33
See also CA 1-4R; 118; CANR 15, 33; DLBY
84; MTCW 1

Santoka, Taneda 1882-1940 .... TCLC 72

Santos, Bienvenido N(uqui) 1911-1996... CLC
22; DAM MULT
See also CA 101; 151; CANR 19, 46

Sapper .... TCLC 44
See also McNeile, Herman Cyril

Sapphire
See Sapphire, Brenda

Sapphire, Brenda 1950- .... CLC 99

Sappho fl. 6th cent. B.C.- .... CMLC
3; DAM POET; PC 5
See also DLB 176

Sarduy, Severo 1937-1993............. CLC 6, 97
See also CA 89-92; 142; CANR 58; DLB
113; HW

Sargeson, Frank 1903-1982............. CLC 31
See also CA 25-28R; 106; CANR 38

Sarmiento, Felix Ruben Garcia
See Dario, Ruben

Saro-Wiwa, Ken(ule Beeson)
1941-1995 ....CLC 114
See also BW 2; CA 142; 150; CANR 60;
DLB 157

Saroyan, William 1908-1981 .... CLC 1,
8, 10, 29, 34, 56; DA; DAB; DAC; DAM
DRAM, MST, NOV; SSC 21; WLC
See also CA 5-8R; 103; CANR 30; DLB 7, 9,
86; DLBY 81; MTCW 1; SATA 23; SATA-
Obit 24

Sarraute, Nathalie 1900- CLC
1, 2, 4, 8, 10, 31, 80
See also CA 9-12R; CANR 23, 66; DLB 83;
MTCW 1

Sarton, (Eleanor) May 1912-1995......... CLC
4, 14, 49, 91; DAM POET
See also CA 1-4R; 149; CANR 1, 34, 55;
DLB 48; DLBY 81; INT CANR-34;
MTCW 1; SATA 36; SATA-Obit 86

Sartre, Jean-Paul 1905-1980 CLC
1, 4, 7, 9, 13, 18, 24, 44, 50, 52; DA;
DAB; DAC; DAM DRAM, MST,
NOV; DC 3; SSC 32; WLC
See also CA 9-12R; 97-100; CANR 21; DLB
72; MTCW 1

Sassoon, Siegfried (Lorraine)
1886-1967 .... CLC 36;
DAB; DAM MST, NOV, POET; PC 12
See also CA 104; 25-28R; CANR 36; DLB
20, 191; DLBD 18; MTCW 1

Satterfield, Charles
See Pohl, Frederik

Saul, John (W. III) 1942-.................... CLC
46; DAM NOV, POP
See also AAYA 10; BEST 90:4; CA 81-84;
CANR 16, 40; SATA 98

Saunders, Caleb
See Heinlein, Robert A(nson)

Saura (Atares), Carlos 1932-........... CLC 20
See also CA 114; 131; HW

Sauser-Hall, Frederic 1887-1961 ...... CLC 18
See also Cendrars, Blaise

Saussure, Ferdinand de 1857-1913 ..... TCLC
49

Savage, Catharine
See Brosman, Catharine Savage

Savage, Thomas 1915- .... CLC 40
See also CA 126; 132; CAAS 15; INT 132

Savan, Glenn 19(?)-...................... CLC 50

Sayers, Dorothy L(eigh) 1893-1957..... TCLC
2, 15; DAM POP
See also CA 104; 119; CANR 60; CDBLB
1914-1945; DLB 10, 36, 77, 100; MTCW
1

Sayers, Valerie 1952-..................... CLC 50
See also CA 134; CANR 61

Sayles, John (Thomas) 1950-....CLC 7, 10, 14
See also CA 57-60; CANR 41; DLB 44

Scammell, Michael 1935-................. CLC 34
See also CA 156

Scannell, Vernon 1922- .... CLC 49
See also CA 5-8R; CANR 8, 24, 57; DLB 27;
SATA 59

Scarlett, Susan
See Streatfeild, (Mary) Noel

Scarron
See Mikszath, Kalman

Schaeffer, Susan Fromberg 1941-......... CLC
6, 11, 22
See also CA 49-52; CANR 18, 65; DLB 28;
MTCW 1; SATA 22

Schary, Jill
See Robinson, Jill

Schell, Jonathan 1943-.................... CLC 35
See also CA 73-76; CANR 12

Schelling, Friedrich Wilhelm Joseph von
1775-1854 .... NCLC 30
See also DLB 90

Schendel, Arthur van 1874-1946 .... TCLC 56

Scherer, Jean-Marie Maurice 1920-
See Rohmer, Eric

Schevill, James (Erwin) 1920-...........CLC 7
See also CA 5-8R; CAAS 12

Schiller, Friedrich 1759-1805.............NCLC
39, 69; DAM DRAM
See also DLB 94

Schisgal, Murray (Joseph) 1926-........CLC 6
See also CA 21-24R; CANR 48

Schlee, Ann 1934-......................... CLC 35
See also CA 101; CANR 29; SATA 44;
SATA-Brief 36

Schlegel, August Wilhelm von
1767-1845 .... NCLC 15
See also DLB 94

Schlegel, Friedrich 1772-1829........ NCLC 45
See also DLB 90

Schlegel, Johann Elias (von)
1719(?)-1749............................LC 5

Schlesinger, Arthur M(eier), Jr.
1917- .... CLC 84
See also AITN 1; CA 1-4R; CANR 1, 28, 58;
DLB 17; INT CANR-28; MTCW 1; SATA
61

Schmidt, Arno (Otto) 1914-1979 ...... CLC 56
See also CA 128; 109; DLB 69

Schmitz, Aron Hector 1861-1928
See Svevo, Italo

Schnackenberg, Gjertrud 1953-........ CLC 40
See also CA 116; DLB 120

Schneider, Leonard Alfred 1925-1966
See Bruce, Lenny

Schnitzler, Arthur 1862-1931 .... **TCLC 4; SSC 15**
See also CA 104; DLB 81, 118

Schoenberg, Arnold 1874-1951 ...... **TCLC 75**
See also CA 109

Schonberg, Arnold
See Schoenberg, Arnold

Schopenhauer, Arthur 1788-1860 ... **NCLC 51**
See also DLB 90

Schor, Sandra (M.) 1932(?)-1990 ...... **CLC 65**
See also CA 132

Schorer, Mark 1908-1977 .... **CLC 9**
See also CA 5-8R; 73-76; CANR 7; DLB 103

Schrader, Paul (Joseph) 1946- .... **CLC 26**
See also CA 37-40R; CANR 41; DLB 44

Schreiner, Olive (Emilie Albertina) 1855-1920 .... **TCLC 9**
See also CA 105; 154; DLB 18, 156, 190

Schulberg, Budd (Wilson) 1914- ... **CLC 7, 48**
See also CA 25-28R; CANR 19; DLB 6, 26, 28; DLBY 81

Schulz, Bruno 1892-1942 .... **TCLC 5, 51; SSC 13**
See also CA 115; 123

Schulz, Charles M(onroe) 1922- .... **CLC 12**
See also CA 9-12R; CANR 6; INT CANR-6; SATA 10

Schumacher, E(rnst) F(riedrich) 1911-1977 .... **CLC 80**
See also CA 81-84; 73-76; CANR 34

Schuyler, James Marcus 1923-1991 .... **CLC 5, 23; DAM POET**
See also CA 101; 134; DLB 5, 169; INT 101

Schwartz, Delmore (David) 1913-1966 ... **CLC 2, 4, 10, 45, 87; PC 8**
See also CA 17-18; 25-28R; CANR 35; CAP 2; DLB 28, 48; MTCW 1

Schwartz, Ernst
See Ozu, Yasujiro

Schwartz, John Burnham 1965- .... **CLC 59**
See also CA 132

Schwartz, Lynne Sharon 1939- .... **CLC 31**
See also CA 103; CANR 44

Schwartz, Muriel A.
See Eliot, T(homas) S(tearns)

Schwarz-Bart, Andre 1928- .... **CLC 2, 4**
See also CA 89-92

Schwarz-Bart, Simone 1938- ... **CLC 7; BLCS**
See also BW 2; CA 97-100

Schwob, Marcel (Mayer Andre) 1867-1905 .... **TCLC 20**
See also CA 117; 168; DLB 123

Sciascia, Leonardo 1921-1989 .... **CLC 8, 9, 41**
See also CA 85-88; 130; CANR 35; DLB 177; MTCW 1

Scoppettone, Sandra 1936- .... **CLC 26**
See also AAYA 11; CA 5-8R; CANR 41, 73; SATA 9, 92

Scorsese, Martin 1942- .... **CLC 20, 89**
See also CA 110; 114; CANR 46

Scotland, Jay
See Jakes, John (William)

Scott, Duncan Campbell 1862-1947 .... **TCLC 6; DAC**
See also CA 104; 153; DLB 92

Scott, Evelyn 1893-1963 .... **CLC 43**
See also CA 104; 112; CANR 64; DLB 9, 48

Scott, F(rancis) R(eginald) 1899-1985 .... **CLC 22**
See also CA 101; 114; DLB 88; INT 101

Scott, Frank
See Scott, F(rancis) R(eginald)

Scott, Joanna 1960- .... **CLC 50**
See also CA 126; CANR 53

Scott, Paul (Mark) 1920-1978 .... **CLC 9, 60**
See also CA 81-84; 77-80; CANR 33; DLB 14; MTCW 1

Scott, Sarah 1723-1795 .... **LC 44**
See also DLB 39

Scott, Walter 1771-1832 .... **NCLC 15, 69; DA; DAB; DAC; DAM MST, NOV, POET; PC 13; SSC 32; WLC**
See also AAYA 22; CDBLB 1789-1832; DLB 93, 107, 116, 144, 159; YABC 2

Scribe, (Augustin) Eugene 1791-1861 .... **NCLC 16; DAM DRAM; DC 5**
See also DLB 192

Scrum, R.
See Crumb, R(obert)

Scudery, Madeleine de 1607-1701 .... **LC 2**

Scum
See Crumb, R(obert)

Scumbag, Little Bobby
See Crumb, R(obert)

Seabrook, John
See Hubbard, L(afayette) Ron(ald)

Sealy, I. Allan 1951- .... **CLC 55**

Search, Alexander
See Pessoa, Fernando (Antonio Nogueira)

Sebastian, Lee
See Silverberg, Robert

Sebastian Owl
See Thompson, Hunter S(tockton)

Sebestyen, Ouida 1924- .... **CLC 30**
See also AAYA 8; CA 107; CANR 40; CLR 17; JRDA; MAICYA; SAAS 10; SATA 39

Secundus, H. Scriblerus
See Fielding, Henry

Sedges, John
See Buck, Pearl S(ydenstricker)

Sedgwick, Catharine Maria 1789-1867 .... **NCLC 19**
See also DLB 1, 74

Seelye, John (Douglas) 1931- .... **CLC 7**
See also CA 97-100; CANR 70; INT 97-100

Seferiades, Giorgos Stylianou 1900-1971
See Seferis, George

Seferis, George .... **CLC 5, 11**
See also Seferiades, Giorgos Stylianou

Segal, Erich (Wolf) 1937- .... **CLC 3, 10; DAM POP**
See also BEST 89:1; CA 25-28R; CANR 20, 36, 65, DLBY 86; INT CANR 20; MTCW 1

Seger, Bob 1945- .... **CLC 35**

Seghers, Anna .... **CLC 7**
See also Radvanyi, Netty

Seidel, Frederick (Lewis) 1936- .... **CLC 18**
See also CA 13-16R; CANR 8; DLBY 84

Seifert, Jaroslav 1901-1986 .... **CLC 34, 44, 93**
See also CA 127; MTCW 1

Sei Shonagon c. 966-1017(?) .... **CMLC 6**

Sejour, Victor 1817-1874 .... **DC 10**
See also DLB 50

Sejour Marcou et Ferrand, Juan Victor
See Sejour, Victor

Selby, Hubert, Jr. 1928- .... **CLC 1, 2, 4, 8; SSC 20**
See also CA 13-16R; CANR 33; DLB 2

Selzer, Richard 1928- .... **CLC 74**
See also CA 65-68; CANR 14

Sembene, Ousmane
See Ousmane, Sembene

Senancour, Etienne Pivert de 1770-1846 .... **NCLC 16**
See also DLB 119

Sender, Ramon (Jose) 1902-1982 .... **CLC 8; DAM MULT; HLC**
See also CA 5-8R; 105; CANR 8; HW; MTCW 1

Seneca, Lucius Annaeus 4B.C.-65 ...... **CMLC 6; DAM DRAM; DC 5**

Senghor, Leopold Sedar 1906- .... **CLC 54; BLC 3; DAM MULT, POET; PC 25**
See also BW 2; CA 116; 125; CANR 47, 74; MTCW 1

Serling, (Edward) Rod(man) 1924-1975 .... **CLC 30**
See also AAYA 14; AITN 1; CA 162; 57-60; DLB 26

Serna, Ramon Gomez de la
See Gomez de la Serna, Ramon

Serpieres
See Guillevic, (Eugene)

Service, Robert
See Service, Robert W(illiam)

Service, Robert W(illiam) 1874(?)-1958 .... **TCLC 15; DA; DAC; DAM MST, POET; WLC**
See also Service, Robert

Seth, Vikram 1952- .... **CLC 43, 90; DAM MULT**
See also CA 121; 127; CANR 50, 74; DLB 120; INT 127

Seton, Cynthia Propper 1926-1982 ... **CLC 27**
See also CA 5-8R; 108; CANR 7

Seton, Ernest (Evan) Thompson 1860-1946 .... **TCLC 31**
See also CA 109; DLB 92; DLBD 13; JRDA; SATA 18

Seton-Thompson, Ernest
See Seton, Ernest (Evan) Thompson

Settle, Mary Lee 1918-................CLC 19, 61
    See also CA 89-92; CAAS 1; CANR 44; DLB
    6; INT 89-92

Seuphor, Michel
    See Arp, Jean

**Sevigne, Marie (de Rabutin-Chantal)
    Marquise de** 1626-1696.............LC 11

Sewall, Samuel 1652-1730.................LC 38
    See also DLB 24

Sexton, Anne (Harvey) 1928-1974 CLC
    2, 4, 6, 8, 10, 15, 53; DA; DAB; DAC;
    DAM MST, POET; PC 2; WLC
    See also CA 1-4R; 53-56; CABS 2; CANR
    3, 36; CDALB 1941-1968; DLB 5, 169;
    MTCW 1; SATA 10

Shaara, Michael (Joseph, Jr.)
    1929-1988 .... CLC 15; DAM POP
    See also AITN 1; CA 102; 125; CANR 52;
    DLBY 83

Shackleton, C. C.
    See Aldiss, Brian W(ilson)

Shacochis, Bob............................ CLC 39
    See also Shacochis, Robert G.

Shacochis, Robert G. 1951-
    See Shacochis, Bob

Shaffer, Anthony (Joshua) 1926- CLC
    19; DAM DRAM
    See also CA 110; 116; DLB 13

Shaffer, Peter (Levin) 1926- ....CLC 5, 14, 18,
    37, 60; DAB; DAM DRAM, MST; DC 7
    See also CA 25-28R; CANR 25, 47, 74; CD-
    BLB 1960 to Present; DLB 13; MTCW 1

Shakey, Bernard
    See Young, Neil

Shalamov, Varlam (Tikhonovich)
    1907(?)-1982........................ CLC 18
    See also CA 129; 105

Shamlu, Ahmad 1925- .... CLC 10

Shammas, Anton 1951-.................. CLC 55

Shange, Ntozake 1948-...... CLC 8, 25, 38, 74;
    BLC 3; DAM DRAM, MULT; DC 3
    See also AAYA 9; BW 2; CA 85-88; CABS
    3; CANR 27, 48, 74; DLB 38; MTCW 1

Shanley, John Patrick 1950-........... CLC 75
    See also CA 128; 133

Shapcott, Thomas W(illiam) 1935- ... CLC 38
    See also CA 69-72; CANR 49

Shapiro, Jane .... CLC 76

Shapiro, Karl (Jay) 1913-................... CLC
    4, 8, 15, 53; PC 25
    See also CA 1-4R; CAAS 6; CANR 1, 36, 66;
    DLB 48; MTCW 1

Sharp, William 1855-1905 .... TCLC 39
    See also CA 160; DLB 156

Sharpe, Thomas Ridley 1928-
    See Sharpe, Tom

Sharpe, Tom............................... CLC 36
    See also Sharpe, Thomas Ridley

Shaw, Bernard............................TCLC 45
    See also Shaw, George Bernard

Shaw, G. Bernard
    See Shaw, George Bernard

Shaw, George Bernard 1856-1950 ...... TCLC
    3, 9, 21; DA; DAB; DAC; DAM
    DRAM, MST; WLC
    See also Shaw, Bernard

Shaw, Henry Wheeler 1818-1885.... NCLC 15
    See also DLB 11

Shaw, Irwin 1913-1984 CLC
    7, 23, 34; DAM DRAM, POP
    See also AITN 1; CA 13-16R; 112; CANR
    21; CDALB 1941-1968; DLB 6, 102;
    DLBY 84; MTCW 1

Shaw, Robert 1927-1978..................CLC 5
    See also AITN 1; CA 1-4R; 81-84; CANR 4;
    DLB 13, 14

Shaw, T. E.
    See Lawrence, T(homas) E(dward)

Shawn, Wallace 1943-.................... CLC 41
    See also CA 112

Shea, Lisa 1953-......................... CLC 86
    See also CA 147

Sheed, Wilfrid (John Joseph) 1930- CLC
    2, 4, 10, 53
    See also CA 65-68; CANR 30, 66; DLB 6;
    MTCW 1

Sheldon, Alice Hastings Bradley 1915(?)-1987
    See Tiptree, James, Jr.

Sheldon, John
    See Bloch, Robert (Albert)

Shelley, Mary Wollstonecraft (Godwin)
    1797-1851 .... NCLC 14, 59; DA;
    DAB; DAC; DAM MST, NOV; WLC
    See also AAYA 20; CDBLB 1789-1832;
    DLB 110, 116, 159, 178; SATA 29

Shelley, Percy Bysshe 1792-1822 ....NCLC
    18; DA; DAB; DAC; DAM MST,
    POET; PC 14; WLC
    See also CDBLB 1789-1832; DLB 96, 110,
    158

Shepard, Jim 1956-...................... CLC 36
    See also CA 137; CANR 59; SATA 90

Shepard, Lucius 1947-................... CLC 34
    See also CA 128; 141

Shepard, Sam 1943-...................... CLC 4,
    6, 17, 34, 41, 44; DAM DRAM; DC 5
    See also AAYA 1; CA 69-72; CABS 3;
    CANR 22; DLB 7; MTCW 1

Shepherd, Michael
    See Ludlum, Robert

Sherburne, Zoa (Morin) 1912-......... CLC 30
    See also AAYA 13; CA 1-4R; CANR 3, 37;
    MAICYA; SAAS 18; SATA 3

Sheridan, Frances 1724-1766 .... LC 7
    See also DLB 39, 84

Sheridan, Richard Brinsley
    1751-1816 .... NCLC 5; DA; DAB;
    DAC; DAM DRAM, MST; DC 1; WLC
    See also CDBLB 1660-1789; DLB 89

Sherman, Jonathan Marc.............. CLC 55

Sherman, Martin 1941(?)- .... CLC 19
    See also CA 116; 123

Sherwin, Judith Johnson 1936-..... CLC 7, 15
    See also CA 25-28R; CANR 34

Sherwood, Frances 1940- .... CLC 81
    See also CA 146

Sherwood, Robert E(mmet)
    1896-1955 .... TCLC 3; DAM DRAM
    See also CA 104; 153; DLB 7, 26

Shestov, Lev 1866-1938................ TCLC 56

Shevchenko, Taras 1814-1861........ NCLC 54

Shiel, M(atthew) P(hipps) 1865-1947... TCLC
    8
    See also Holmes, Gordon

Shields, Carol 1935- ....CLC 91, 113; DAC
    See also CA 81-84; CANR 51, 74

Shields, David 1956-..................... CLC 97
    See also CA 124; CANR 48

Shiga, Naoya 1883-1971 ...... CLC 33; SSC 23
    See also CA 101; 33-36R; DLB 180

Shikibu, Murasaki c. 978-c. 1014 .... CMLC 1

Shilts, Randy 1951-1994................ CLC 85
    See also AAYA 19; CA 115; 127; 144; CANR
    45; INT 127

Shimazaki, Haruki 1872-1943
    See Shimazaki Toson

Shimazaki Toson 1872-1943 .... TCLC 5
    See also Shimazaki, Haruki

Sholokhov, Mikhail (Aleksandrovich)
    1905-1984 .... CLC 7, 15
    See also CA 101; 112; MTCW 1; SATA-Obit
    36

Shone, Patric
    See Hanley, James

Shreve, Susan Richards 1939- .... CLC 23
    See also CA 49-52; CAAS 5; CANR 5, 38,
    69; MAICYA; SATA 46, 95; SATA-Brief
    41

Shue, Larry 1946-1985..................... CLC
    52; DAM DRAM
    See also CA 145; 117

Shu-Jen, Chou 1881-1936
    See Lu Hsun

Shulman, Alix Kates 1932- .... CLC 2, 10
    See also CA 29-32R; CANR 43; SATA 7

Shuster, Joe 1914-....................... CLC 21

Shute, Nevil............................... CLC 30
    See also Norway, Nevil Shute

Shuttle, Penelope (Diane) 1947- ....CLC 7
    See also CA 93-96; CANR 39; DLB 14, 40

Sidney, Mary 1561-1621............... LC 19, 39

Sidney, Sir Philip 1554-1586.........LC 19, 39;
    DA; DAB; DAC; DAM MST, POET
    See also CDBLB Before 1660; DLB 167

Siegel, Jerome 1914-1996 .... CLC 21
    See also CA 116; 169; 151

Siegel, Jerry
    See Siegel, Jerome

Sienkiewicz, Henryk (Adam Alexander Pius)
    1846-1916 ....TCLC 3
    See also CA 104; 134

Sierra, Gregorio Martinez
    See Martinez Sierra, Gregorio

Sierra, Maria (de la O'LeJarraga) Martinez
    See Martinez Sierra, Maria (de la O'LeJar-
    raga)

Sigal, Clancy 1926- ....CLC 7
    See also CA 1-4R

Sigourney, Lydia Howard (Huntley)
1791-1865 .... **NCLC 21**
See also DLB 1, 42, 73

Siguenza y Gongora, Carlos de
1645-1700 .... **LC 8**

Sigurjonsson, Johann 1880-1919 .... **TCLC 27**
See also CA 170

Sikelianos, Angelos 1884-1951 .... **TCLC 39**

Silkin, Jon 1930- .... **CLC 2, 6, 43**
See also CA 5-8R; CAAS 5; DLB 27

Silko, Leslie (Marmon) 1948- .... **CLC
23, 74, 114; DA; DAC; DAM MST,
MULT, POP; WLCS**
See also AAYA 14; CA 115; 122; CANR 45,
65; DLB 143, 175; NNAL

Sillanpaa, Frans Eemil 1888-1964 .... **CLC 19**
See also CA 129; 93-96; MTCW 1

Sillitoe, Alan 1928- ...... **CLC 1, 3, 6, 10, 19, 57**
See also AITN 1; CA 9-12R; CAAS 2; CANR
8, 26, 55; CDBLB 1960 to Present; DLB
14, 139; MTCW 1; SATA 61

Silone, Ignazio 1900-1978 .... **CLC 4**
See also CA 25-28; 81-84; CANR 34; CAP
2; MTCW 1

Silver, Joan Micklin 1935- .... **CLC 20**
See also CA 114; 121; INT 121

Silver, Nicholas
See Faust, Frederick (Schiller)

Silverberg, Robert 1935- ... **CLC 7; DAM POP**
See also AAYA 24; CA 1-4R; CAAS 3;
CANR 1, 20, 36; DLB 8; INT CANR-20;
MAICYA; MTCW 1; SATA 13, 91

Silverstein, Alvin 1933- .... **CLC 17**
See also CA 49-52; CANR 2; CLR 25;
JRDA; MAICYA; SATA 8, 69

Silverstein, Virginia B(arbara Opshelor)
1937- .... **CLC 17**
See also CA 49-52; CANR 2; CLR 25;
JRDA; MAICYA; SATA 8, 69

Sim, Georges
See Simenon, Georges (Jacques Christian)

Simak, Clifford D(onald) 1904-1988 ..... **CLC
1, 55**
See also CA 1-4R; 125; CANR 1, 35; DLB 8;
MTCW 1; SATA-Obit 56

Simenon, Georges (Jacques Christian)
1903-1989 .... **CLC
1, 2, 3, 8, 18, 47; DAM POP**
See also CA 85-88; 129; CANR 35; DLB 72;
DLBY 89; MTCW 1

Simic, Charles 1938- .... **CLC
6, 9, 22, 49, 68; DAM POET**
See also CA 29-32R; CAAS 4; CANR 12, 33,
52, 61; DLB 105

Simmel, Georg 1858-1918 .... **TCLC 64**
See also CA 157

Simmons, Charles (Paul) 1924- .... **CLC 57**
See also CA 89-92; INT 89-92

Simmons, Dan 1948- ..... **CLC 44; DAM POP**
See also AAYA 16; CA 138; CANR 53

Simmons, James (Stewart Alexander)
1933- .... **CLC 43**
See also CA 105; CAAS 21; DLB 40

Simms, William Gilmore 1806-1870 .... **NCLC
3**
See also DLB 3, 30, 59, 73

Simon, Carly 1945- .... **CLC 26**
See also CA 105

Simon, Claude 1913-1984 .... **CLC
4, 9, 15, 39; DAM NOV**
See also CA 89-92; CANR 33; DLB 83;
MTCW 1

Simon, (Marvin) Neil 1927- .... **CLC
6, 11, 31, 39, 70; DAM DRAM**
See also AITN 1; CA 21-24R; CANR 26, 54;
DLB 7; MTCW 1

Simon, Paul (Frederick) 1941(?)- ..... **CLC 17**
See also CA 116; 153

Simonon, Paul 1956(?)- .... **CLC 30**

Simpson, Harriette
See Arnow, Harriette (Louisa) Simpson

Simpson, Louis (Aston Marantz)
1923- .... **CLC 4, 7, 9, 32; DAM POET**
See also CA 1-4R; CAAS 4; CANR 1, 61;
DLB 5; MTCW 1

Simpson, Mona (Elizabeth) 1957- ..... **CLC 44**
See also CA 122; 135; CANR 68

Simpson, N(orman) F(rederick)
1919- .... **CLC 29**
See also CA 13-16R; DLB 13

Sinclair, Andrew (Annandale) 1935- ..... **CLC
2, 14**
See also CA 9-12R; CAAS 5; CANR 14, 38;
DLB 14; MTCW 1

Sinclair, Emil
See Hesse, Hermann

Sinclair, Iain 1943- .... **CLC 76**
See also CA 132

Sinclair, Iain MacGregor
See Sinclair, Iain

Sinclair, Irene
See Griffith, D(avid Lewelyn) W(ark)

Sinclair, Mary Amelia St. Clair 1865(?)-1946
See Sinclair, May

Sinclair, May 1863-1946 .... **TCLC 3, 11**
See also Sinclair, Mary Amelia St. Clair

Sinclair, Roy
See Griffith, D(avid Lewelyn) W(ark)

Sinclair, Upton (Beall) 1878-1968 .... **CLC
1, 11, 15, 63; DA; DAB; DAC; DAM
MST, NOV; WLC**
See also CA 5-8R; 25-28R; CANR 7;
CDALB 1929-1941; DLB 9; INT CANR-7;
MTCW 1; SATA 9

Singer, Isaac
See Singer, Isaac Bashevis

Singer, Isaac Bashevis 1904-1991 .... **CLC 1,
3, 6, 9, 11, 15, 23, 38, 69, 111; DA; DAB;
DAC; DAM MST, NOV; SSC 3; WLC**
See also AITN 1, 2; CA 1-4R; 134; CANR
1, 39; CDALB 1941-1968; CLR 1; DLB
6, 28, 52; DLBY 91; JRDA; MAICYA;
MTCW 1; SATA 3, 27; SATA-Obit 68

Singer, Israel Joshua 1893-1944 ..... **TCLC 33**
See also CA 169

Singh, Khushwant 1915- .... **CLC 11**
See also CA 9-12R; CAAS 9; CANR 6

Singleton, Ann
See Benedict, Ruth (Fulton)

Sinjohn, John
See Galsworthy, John

Sinyavsky, Andrei (Donatevich)
1925-1997 .... **CLC 8**
See also CA 85-88; 159

Sirin, V.
See Nabokov, Vladimir (Vladimirovich)

Sissman, L(ouis) E(dward) 1928-1976 ... **CLC
9, 18**
See also CA 21-24R; 65-68; CANR 13; DLB
5

Sisson, C(harles) H(ubert) 1914- .... **CLC 8**
See also CA 1-4R; CAAS 3; CANR 3, 48;
DLB 27

Sitwell, Dame Edith 1887-1964 .... **CLC
2, 9, 67; DAM POET; PC 3**
See also CA 9-12R; CANR 35; CDBLB
1945-1960; DLB 20; MTCW 1

Siwaarmill, H. P.
See Sharp, William

Sjoewall, Maj 1935- .... **CLC 7**
See also CA 65-68; CANR 73

Sjowall, Maj
See Sjoewall, Maj

Skelton, John 1463-1529 .... **PC 25**

Skelton, Robin 1925-1997 .... **CLC 13**
See also AITN 2; CA 5-8R; 160; CAAS 5;
CANR 28; DLB 27, 53

Skolimowski, Jerzy 1938- .... **CLC 20**
See also CA 128

Skram, Amalie (Bertha) 1847-1905 ..... **TCLC
25**
See also CA 165

Skvorecky, Josef (Vaclav) 1924- .... **CLC
15, 39, 69; DAC; DAM NOV**
See also CA 61-64; CAAS 1; CANR 10, 34,
63; MTCW 1

Slade, Bernard .... **CLC 11, 46**
See also Newbound, Bernard Slade

Slaughter, Carolyn 1946- .... **CLC 56**
See also CA 85-88

Slaughter, Frank G(ill) 1908- .... **CLC 29**
See also AITN 2; CA 5-8R; CANR 5; INT
CANR-5

Slavitt, David R(ytman) 1935- ...... **CLC 5, 14**
See also CA 21-24R; CAAS 3; CANR 41;
DLB 5, 6

Slesinger, Tess 1905-1945 .... **TCLC 10**
See also CA 107; DLB 102

Slessor, Kenneth 1901-1971 .... **CLC 14**
See also CA 102; 89-92

Slowacki, Juliusz 1809-1849 .... **NCLC 15**

Smart, Christopher 1722-1771 .... **LC
3; DAM POET; PC 13**
See also DLB 109

Smart, Elizabeth 1913-1986 .... **CLC 54**
See also CA 81-84; 118; DLB 88

Smiley, Jane (Graves) 1949- .... **CLC
53, 76; DAM POP**
See also CA 104; CANR 30, 50, 74; INT
CANR-30

Smith, A(rthur) J(ames) M(arshall)
1902-1980 .... **CLC 15; DAC**
See also CA 1-4R; 102; CANR 4; DLB 88

Smith, Adam 1723-1790.................... **LC 36**
See also DLB 104

Smith, Alexander 1829-1867 .... **NCLC 59**
See also DLB 32, 55

Smith, Anna Deavere 1950- .... **CLC 86**
See also CA 133

Smith, Betty (Wehner) 1896-1972..... **CLC 19**
See also CA 5-8R; 33-36R; DLBY 82; SATA 6

Smith, Charlotte (Turner)
1749-1806 .... **NCLC 23**
See also DLB 39, 109

Smith, Clark Ashton 1893-1961 .... **CLC 43**
See also CA 143

Smith, Dave .... **CLC 22, 42**
See also Smith, David (Jeddie)

Smith, David (Jeddie) 1942-
See Smith, Dave

Smith, Florence Margaret 1902-1971
See Smith, Stevie

Smith, Iain Crichton 1928-1998 .... **CLC 64**
See also CA 21-24R; 171; DLB 40, 139

Smith, John 1580(?)-1631 .... **LC 9**
See also DLB 24, 30

Smith, Johnston
See Crane, Stephen (Townley)

Smith, Joseph, Jr. 1805-1844......... **NCLC 53**

Smith, Lee 1944- .... **CLC 25, 73**
See also CA 114; 119; CANR 46; DLB 143; DLBY 83; INT 119

Smith, Martin
See Smith, Martin Cruz

Smith, Martin Cruz 1942- .... **CLC 25; DAM MULT, POP**
See also BEST 89:4; CA 85-88; CANR 6, 23, 43, 65; INT CANR-23; NNAL

Smith, Mary-Ann Tirone 1944-....... **CLC 39**
See also CA 118; 136

Smith, Patti 1946-...................... **CLC 12**
See also CA 93-96; CANR 63

Smith, Pauline (Urmson) 1882-1959.... **TCLC 25**

Smith, Rosamond
See Oates, Joyce Carol

Smith, Sheila Kaye
See Kaye-Smith, Sheila

Smith, Stevie .... **CLC 3, 8, 25, 44; PC 12**
See also Smith, Florence Margaret

Smith, Wilbur (Addison) 1933-........ **CLC 33**
See also CA 13-16R; CANR 7, 46, 66; MTCW 1

Smith, William Jay 1918- .... **CLC 6**
See also CA 5-8R; CANR 44; DLB 5; MAICYA; SAAS 22; SATA 2, 68

Smith, Woodrow Wilson
See Kuttner, Henry

Smolenskin, Peretz 1842-1885 .... **NCLC 30**

Smollett, Tobias (George) 1721-1771 .... **LC 2, 46**
See also CDBLB 1660-1789; DLB 39, 104

Snodgrass, W(illiam) D(e Witt) 1926-.... **CLC 2, 6, 10, 18, 68; DAM POET**
See also CA 1-4R; CANR 6, 36, 65; DLB 5; MTCW 1

Snow, C(harles) P(ercy) 1905-1980 .... **CLC 1, 4, 6, 9, 13, 19; DAM NOV**
See also CA 5-8R; 101; CANR 28; CD-BLB 1945-1960; DLB 15, 77; DLBD 17; MTCW 1

Snow, Frances Compton
See Adams, Henry (Brooks)

Snyder, Gary (Sherman) 1930- .... **CLC 1, 2, 5, 9, 32; DAM POET; PC 21**
See also CA 17-20R; CANR 30, 60; DLB 5, 16, 165

Snyder, Zilpha Keatley 1927- .... **CLC 17**
See also AAYA 15; CA 9-12R; CANR 38; CLR 31; JRDA; MAICYA; SAAS 2; SATA 1, 28, 75

Soares, Bernardo
See Pessoa, Fernando (Antonio Nogueira)

Sobh, A.
See Shamlu, Ahmad

Sobol, Joshua .... **CLC 60**

Socrates 469B.C.-399B.C. .... **CMLC 27**

Soderberg, Hjalmar 1869-1941 ...... **TCLC 39**

Sodergran, Edith (Irene)
See Soedergran, Edith (Irene)

Soedergran, Edith (Irene) 1892-1923... **TCLC 31**

Softly, Edgar
See Lovecraft, H(oward) P(hillips)

Softly, Edward
See Lovecraft, H(oward) P(hillips)

Sokolov, Raymond 1941-.................. **CLC 7**
See also CA 85-88

Solo, Jay
See Ellison, Harlan (Jay)

Sologub, Fyodor.......................... **TCLC 9**
See also Teternikov, Fyodor Kuzmich

Solomons, Ikey Esquir
See Thackeray, William Makepeace

Solomos, Dionysios 1798-1857 .... **NCLC 15**

Solwoska, Mara
See French, Marilyn

Solzhenitsyn, Aleksandr I(sayevich)
1918- .... **CLC 1, 2, 4, 7, 9, 10, 18, 26, 34, 78; DA; DAB; DAC; DAM MST, NOV; SSC 32; WLC**
See also AITN 1; CA 69-72; CANR 40, 65; MTCW 1

Somers, Jane
See Lessing, Doris (May)

Somerville, Edith 1858-1949 .... **TCLC 51**
See also DLB 135

Somerville & Ross
See Martin, Violet Florence; Somerville, Edith

Sommer, Scott 1951-...................... **CLC 25**
See also CA 106

Sondheim, Stephen (Joshua) 1930- .... **CLC 30, 39; DAM DRAM**
See also AAYA 11; CA 103; CANR 47, 68

Song, Cathy 1955- .... **PC 21**
See also CA 154; DLB 169

Sontag, Susan 1933-......................... **CLC 1, 2, 10, 13, 31, 105; DAM POP**
See also CA 17-20R; CANR 25, 51, 74; DLB 2, 67; MTCW 1

Sophocles 496(?)B.C.-406(?)B.C. .... **CMLC 2; DA; DAB; DAC; DAM DRAM, MST; DC 1; WLCS**
See also DLB 176

Sordello 1189-1269 .... **CMLC 15**

Sorel, Julia
See Drexler, Rosalyn

Sorrentino, Gilbert 1929-.................. **CLC 3, 7, 14, 22, 40**
See also CA 77-80; CANR 14, 33; DLB 5, 173; DLBY 80; INT CANR-14

Soto, Gary 1952-............................ **CLC 32, 80; DAM MULT; HLC**
See also AAYA 10; CA 119; 125; CANR 50, 74; CLR 38; DLB 82; HW; INT 125; JRDA; SATA 80

Soupault, Philippe 1897-1990 .... **CLC 68**
See also CA 116; 147; 131

Souster, (Holmes) Raymond 1921-........ **CLC 5, 14; DAC; DAM POET**
See also CA 13-16R; CAAS 14; CANR 13, 29, 53; DLB 88; SATA 63

Southern, Terry 1924(?)-1995............ **CLC 7**
See also CA 1-4R; 150; CANR 1, 55; DLB 2

Southey, Robert 1774-1843 .... **NCLC 8**
See also DLB 93, 107, 142; SATA 54

Southworth, Emma Dorothy Eliza Nevitte
1819-1899 .... **NCLC 26**

Souza, Ernest
See Scott, Evelyn

Soyinka, Wole 1934-............... **CLC 3, 5, 14, 36, 44; BLC 3; DA; DAB; DAC; DAM DRAM, MST, MULT; DC 2; WLC**
See also BW 2; CA 13-16R; CANR 27, 39; DLB 125; MTCW 1

Spackman, W(illiam) M(ode)
1905-1990 .... **CLC 46**
See also CA 81-84; 132

Spacks, Barry (Bernard) 1931-........ **CLC 14**
See also CA 154; CANR 33; DLB 105

Spanidou, Irini 1946-.................... **CLC 44**

Spark, Muriel (Sarah) 1918- .... **CLC 2, 3, 5, 8, 13, 18, 40, 94; DAB; DAC; DAM MST, NOV; SSC 10**
See also CA 5-8R; CANR 12, 36; CDBLB 1945-1960; DLB 15, 139; INT CANR-12; MTCW 1

Spaulding, Douglas
See Bradbury, Ray (Douglas)

Spaulding, Leonard
See Bradbury, Ray (Douglas)

Spence, J. A. D.
See Eliot, T(homas) S(tearns)

Spencer, Elizabeth 1921- .... **CLC 22**
See also CA 13-16R; CANR 32, 65; DLB 6;
MTCW 1; SATA 14

Spencer, Leonard G.
See Silverberg, Robert

Spencer, Scott 1945-...................... **CLC 30**
See also CA 113; CANR 51; DLBY 86

Spender, Stephen (Harold) 1909-1995 ... **CLC**
1, 2, 5, 10, 41, 91; DAM POET
See also CA 9-12R; 149; CANR 31, 54; CD-
BLB 1945-1960; DLB 20; MTCW 1

Spengler, Oswald (Arnold Gottfried)
1880-1936 .... **TCLC 25**
See also CA 118

Spenser, Edmund 1552(?)-1599 .... **LC**
5, 39; DA; DAB; DAC; DAM MST,
POET; PC 8; WLC
See also CDBLB Before 1660; DLB 167

Spicer, Jack 1925-1965...................... **CLC**
8, 18, 72; DAM POET
See also CA 85-88; DLB 5, 16, 193

Spiegelman, Art 1948- .... **CLC 76**
See also AAYA 10; CA 125; CANR 41, 55,
74

Spielberg, Peter 1929-......................**CLC 6**
See also CA 5-8R; CANR 4, 48; DLBY 81

Spielberg, Steven 1947-.................. **CLC 20**
See also AAYA 8, 24; CA 77-80; CANR 32;
SATA 32

Spillane, Frank Morrison 1918-
See Spillane, Mickey

Spillane, Mickey........................ **CLC 3, 13**
See also Spillane, Frank Morrison

Spinoza, Benedictus de 1632-1677 .... **LC 9**

Spinrad, Norman (Richard) 1940-.... **CLC 46**
See also CA 37-40R; CAAS 19; CANR 20;
DLB 8; INT CANR-20

Spitteler, Carl (Friedrich Georg)
1845-1924 .... **TCLC 12**
See also CA 109; DLB 129

Spivack, Kathleen (Romola Drucker)
1938- ....**CLC 6**
See also CA 49-52

Spoto, Donald 1941-...................... **CLC 39**
See also CA 65-68; CANR 11, 57

Springsteen, Bruce (F.) 1949- .... **CLC 17**
See also CA 111

Spurling, Hilary 1940-.................... **CLC 34**
See also CA 104; CANR 25, 52

Spyker, John Howland
See Elman, Richard (Martin)

Squires, (James) Radcliffe 1917-1993 .... **CLC**
51
See also CA 1-4R; 140; CANR 6, 21

Srivastava, Dhanpat Rai 1880(?)-1936
See Premchand

Stacy, Donald
See Pohl, Frederik

Stael, Germaine de 1766-1817
See Stael-Holstein, Anne Louise Germaine
Necker Baronn

Stael-Holstein, Anne Louise Germaine
Necker Baronn 1766-1817 ....**NCLC 3**
See also Stael, Germaine de

Stafford, Jean 1915-1979.................... **CLC**
4, 7, 19, 68; SSC 26
See also CA 1-4R; 85-88; CANR 3, 65; DLB
2, 173; MTCW 1; SATA-Obit 22

Stafford, William (Edgar) 1914-1993 .... **CLC**
4, 7, 29; DAM POET
See also CA 5-8R; 142; CAAS 3; CANR 5,
22; DLB 5; INT CANR-22

Stagnelius, Eric Johan 1793-1823 ... **NCLC 61**

Staines, Trevor
See Brunner, John (Kilian Houston)

Stairs, Gordon
See Austin, Mary (Hunter)

Stannard, Martin 1947- .... **CLC 44**
See also CA 142; DLB 155

Stanton, Elizabeth Cady 1815-1902 .... **TCLC**
73
See also CA 171; DLB 79

Stanton, Maura 1946-......................**CLC 9**
See also CA 89-92; CANR 15; DLB 120

Stanton, Schuyler
See Baum, L(yman) Frank

Stapledon, (William) Olaf 1886-1950... **TCLC**
22
See also CA 111; 162; DLB 15

Starbuck, George (Edwin) 1931-1996.... **CLC**
53; DAM POET
See also CA 21-24R; 153; CANR 23

Stark, Richard
See Westlake, Donald E(dwin)

Staunton, Schuyler
See Baum, L(yman) Frank

Stead, Christina (Ellen) 1902-1983 .... **CLC**
2, 5, 8, 32, 80
See also CA 13-16R; 109; CANR 33, 40;
MTCW 1

Stead, William Thomas 1849-1912...... **TCLC**
48
See also CA 167

Steele, Richard 1672-1729 ....**LC 18**
See also CDBLB 1660-1789; DLB 84, 101

Steele, Timothy (Reid) 1948- .... **CLC 45**
See also CA 93-96; CANR 16, 50; DLB 120

Steffens, (Joseph) Lincoln 1866-1936... **TCLC**
20
See also CA 117

Stegner, Wallace (Earle) 1909-1993....... **CLC**
9, 49, 81; DAM NOV; SSC 27
See also AITN 1; BEST 90:3; CA 1-4R; 141;
CAAS 9; CANR 1, 21, 46; DLB 9; DLBY
93; MTCW 1

Stein, Gertrude 1874-1946................ **TCLC**
1, 6, 28, 48; DA; DAB; DAC; DAM
MST, NOV, POET; PC 18; WLC
See also CA 104; 132; CDALB 1917-1929;
DLB 4, 54, 86; DLBD 15; MTCW 1

Steinbeck, John (Ernst) 1902-1968 .... **CLC 1,**
5, 9, 13, 21, 34, 45, 75; DA; DAB; DAC;
DAM DRAM, MST, NOV; SSC 11; WLC
See also AAYA 12; CA 1-4R; 25-28R;
CANR 1, 35; CDALB 1929-1941; DLB 7,
9; DLBD 2; MTCW 1; SATA 9

Steinem, Gloria 1934-.................... **CLC 63**
See also CA 53-56; CANR 28, 51; MTCW 1

Steiner, George 1929- ....**CLC 24; DAM NOV**
See also CA 73-76; CANR 31, 67; DLB 67;
MTCW 1; SATA 62

Steiner, K. Leslie
See Delany, Samuel R(ay, Jr.)

Steiner, Rudolf 1861-1925............. **TCLC 13**
See also CA 107

Stendhal 1783-1842........................**NCLC**
23, 46; DA; DAB; DAC; DAM MST,
NOV; SSC 27; WLC
See also DLB 119

Stephen, Adeline Virginia
See Woolf, (Adeline) Virginia

Stephen, SirLeslie 1832-1904........ **TCLC 23**
See also CA 123; DLB 57, 144, 190

Stephen, Sir Leslie
See Stephen, SirLeslie

Stephen, Virginia
See Woolf, (Adeline) Virginia

Stephens, James 1882(?)-1950 .... **TCLC 4**
See also CA 104; DLB 19, 153, 162

Stephens, Reed
See Donaldson, Stephen R.

Steptoe, Lydia
See Barnes, Djuna

Sterchi, Beat 1949-........................ **CLC 65**

Sterling, Brett
See Bradbury, Ray (Douglas); Hamilton, Edmond

Sterling, Bruce 1954-...................... **CLC 72**
See also CA 119; CANR 44

Sterling, George 1869-1926........... **TCLC 20**
See also CA 117; 165; DLB 54

Stern, Gerald 1925-................. **CLC 40, 100**
See also CA 81-84; CANR 28; DLB 105

Stern, Richard (Gustave) 1928- .... **CLC 4, 39**
See also CA 1-4R; CANR 1, 25, 52; DLBY
87; INT CANR-25

Sternberg, Josef von 1894-1969 .... **CLC 20**
See also CA 81-84

Sterne, Laurence 1713-1768.... **LC 2, 48; DA;**
DAB; DAC; DAM MST, NOV; WLC
See also CDBLB 1660-1789; DLB 39

Sternheim, (William Adolf) Carl
1878-1942 ....**TCLC 8**
See also CA 105; DLB 56, 118

Stevens, Mark 1951-...................... **CLC 34**
See also CA 122

Stevens, Wallace 1879-1955.............. **TCLC**
3, 12, 45; DA; DAB; DAC; DAM
MST, POET; PC 6; WLC
See also CA 104; 124; CDALB 1929-1941;
DLB 54; MTCW 1

Stevenson, Anne (Katharine) 1933-....... **CLC 7, 33**
See also CA 17-20R; CAAS 9; CANR 9, 33; DLB 40; MTCW 1

Stevenson, Robert Louis (Balfour) 1850-1894 ...**NCLC 5, 14, 63; DA; DAB; DAC; DAM MST, NOV; SSC 11; WLC**
See also AAYA 24; CDBLB 1890-1914; CLR 10, 11; DLB 18, 57, 141, 156, 174; DLBD 13; JRDA; MAICYA; SATA 100; YABC 2

Stewart, J(ohn) I(nnes) M(ackintosh) 1906-1994 ....**CLC 7, 14, 32**
See also CA 85-88; 147; CAAS 3; CANR 47; MTCW 1

Stewart, Mary (Florence Elinor) 1916-... **CLC 7, 35, 117; DAB**
See also CA 1-4R; CANR 1, 59; SATA 12

Stewart, Mary Rainbow
See Stewart, Mary (Florence Elinor)

Stifle, June
See Campbell, Maria

Stifter, Adalbert 1805-1868 ....**NCLC 41; SSC 28**
See also DLB 133

Still, James 1906-..........................**CLC 49**
See also CA 65-68; CAAS 17; CANR 10, 26; DLB 9, SATA 29

Sting 1951-
See Sumner, Gordon Matthew

Stirling, Arthur
See Sinclair, Upton (Beall)

Stitt, Milan 1941-.........................**CLC 29**
See also CA 69-72

Stockton, Francis Richard 1834-1902
See Stockton, Frank R.

Stockton, Frank R. ....**TCLC 47**
See also Stockton, Francis Richard

Stoddard, Charles
See Kuttner, Henry

Stoker, Abraham 1847-1912
See Stoker, Bram

Stoker, Bram 1847-1912...................**TCLC 8; DAB; WLC**
See also Stoker, Abraham

Stolz, Mary (Slattery) 1920-............**CLC 12**
See also AAYA 8; AITN 1; CA 5-8R; CANR 13, 41; JRDA; MAICYA; SAAS 3; SATA 10, 71

Stone, Irving 1903-1989 ...**CLC 7; DAM POP**
See also AITN 1; CA 1-4R; 129; CAAS 3; CANR 1, 23; INT CANR-23; MTCW 1; SATA 3; SATA-Obit 64

Stone, Oliver (William) 1946-..........**CLC 73**
See also AAYA 15; CA 110; CANR 55

Stone, Robert (Anthony) 1937-............**CLC 5, 23, 42**
See also CA 85-88; CANR 23, 66; DLB 152; INT CANR-23; MTCW 1

Stone, Zachary
See Follett, Ken(neth Martin)

Stoppard, Tom 1937-.........................**CLC 1, 3, 4, 5, 8, 15, 29, 34, 63, 91; DA; DAB; DAC; DAM DRAM, MST; DC 6; WLC**
See also CA 81-84; CANR 39, 67; CD-BLB 1960 to Present; DLB 13; DLBY 85; MTCW 1

Storey, David (Malcolm) 1933- ....**CLC 2, 4, 5, 8; DAM DRAM**
See also CA 81-84; CANR 36; DLB 13, 14; MTCW 1

Storm, Hyemeyohsts 1935- ....**CLC 3; DAM MULT**
See also CA 81-84; CANR 45; NNAL

Storm, Theodor 1817-1888 ....**SSC 27**

Storm, (Hans) Theodor (Woldsen) 1817-1888 ....**NCLC 1; SSC 27**
See also DLB 129

Storni, Alfonsina 1892-1938 ....**TCLC 5; DAM MULT; HLC**
See also CA 104; 131; HW

Stoughton, William 1631-1701............**LC 38**
See also DLB 24

Stout, Rex (Todhunter) 1886-1975 ......**CLC 3**
See also AITN 2; CA 61-64; CANR 71

Stow, (Julian) Randolph 1935-.....**CLC 23, 48**
See also CA 13-16R; CANR 33; MTCW 1

Stowe, Harriet (Elizabeth) Beecher 1811-1896 ....**NCLC 3, 50; DA; DAB; DAC; DAM MST, NOV; WLC**
See also CDALB 1865-1917; DLB 1, 12, 42, 74, 189; JRDA; MAICYA; YABC 1

Strachey, (Giles) Lytton 1880-1932 .....**TCLC 12**
See also CA 110; DLB 149; DLBD 10

Strand, Mark 1934- ....**CLC 6, 18, 41, 71; DAM POET**
See also CA 21-24R; CANR 40, 65; DLB 5; SATA 41

Straub, Peter (Francis) 1943- ....**CLC 28, 107; DAM POP**
See also BEST 89:1; CA 85-88; CANR 28, 65; DLBY 84; MTCW 1

Strauss, Botho 1944- ....**CLC 22**
See also CA 157; DLB 124

Streatfeild, (Mary) Noel 1895(?)-1986.... **CLC 21**
See also CA 81-84; 120; CANR 31; CLR 17; DLB 160; MAICYA; SATA 20; SATA-Obit 48

Stribling, T(homas) S(igismund) 1881-1965 ....**CLC 23**
See also CA 107; DLB 9

Strindberg, (Johan) August 1849-1912 .... **TCLC 1, 8, 21, 47; DA; DAB; DAC; DAM DRAM, MST; WLC**
See also CA 104; 135

Stringer, Arthur 1874-1950...........**TCLC 37**
See also CA 161; DLB 92

Stringer, David
See Roberts, Keith (John Kingston)

Stroheim, Erich von 1885-1957 ......**TCLC 71**

Strugatskii, Arkadii (Natanovich) 1925-1991 ....**CLC 27**
See also CA 106; 135

Strugatskii, Boris (Natanovich) 1933- ....**CLC 27**
See also CA 106

Strummer, Joe 1953(?)-.................**CLC 30**

Stuart, Don A.
See Campbell, John W(ood, Jr.)

Stuart, Ian
See MacLean, Alistair (Stuart)

Stuart, Jesse (Hilton) 1906-1984...........**CLC 1, 8, 11, 14, 34; SSC 31**
See also CA 5-8R; 112; CANR 31; DLB 9, 48, 102; DLBY 84; SATA 2; SATA-Obit 36

Sturgeon, Theodore (Hamilton) 1918-1985 ....**CLC 22, 39**
See also Queen, Ellery

Sturges, Preston 1898-1959 ....**TCLC 48**
See also CA 114; 149; DLB 26

Styron, William 1925-................**CLC 1, 3, 5, 11, 15, 60; DAM NOV, POP; SSC 25**
See also BEST 90:4; CA 5-8R; CANR 6, 33, 74; CDALB 1968-1988; DLB 2, 143; DLBY 80; INT CANR-6; MTCW 1

Su, Chien 1884-1918
See Su Man-shu

Suarez Lynch, B.
See Bioy Casares, Adolfo; Borges, Jorge Luis

Suckow, Ruth 1892-1960 ....**SSC 18**
See also CA 113; DLB 9, 102

Sudermann, Hermann 1857-1928... **TCLC 15**
See also CA 107; DLB 118

Sue, Eugene 1804-1857 ....**NCLC 1**
See also DLB 119

Sueskind, Patrick 1949- ....**CLC 44**
See also Suskind, Patrick

Sukenick, Ronald 1932- ....**CLC 3, 4, 6, 48**
See also CA 25-28R; CAAS 8; CANR 32; DLB 173; DLBY 81

Suknaski, Andrew 1942- ....**CLC 19**
See also CA 101; DLB 53

Sullivan, Vernon
See Vian, Boris

Sully Prudhomme 1839-1907........**TCLC 31**

Su Man-shu.............................**TCLC 24**
See also Su, Chien

Summerforest, Ivy B.
See Kirkup, James

Summers, Andrew James 1942-....... **CLC 26**

Summers, Andy
See Summers, Andrew James

Summers, Hollis (Spurgeon, Jr.) 1916- ....**CLC 10**
See also CA 5-8R; CANR 3; DLB 6

Summers, (Alphonsus Joseph-Mary Augustus) Montague 1880-1948 ....**TCLC 16**
See also CA 118; 163

Sumner, Gordon Matthew..............**CLC 26**
See also Sting

Surtees, Robert Smith 1803-1864 ... **NCLC 14**
See also DLB 21

Susann, Jacqueline 1921-1974 .... **CLC 3**
See also AITN 1; CA 65-68; 53-56; MTCW 1

Su Shih 1036-1101 .... **CMLC 15**

Suskind, Patrick
See Sueskind, Patrick

Sutcliff, Rosemary 1920-1992 .... **CLC 26; DAB; DAC; DAM MST, POP**
See also AAYA 10; CA 5-8R; 139; CANR 37; CLR 1, 37; JRDA; MAICYA; SATA 6, 44, 78; SATA-Obit 73

Sutro, Alfred 1863-1933 .... **TCLC 6**
See also CA 105; DLB 10

Sutton, Henry
See Slavitt, David R(ytman)

Svevo, Italo 1861-1928 ... **TCLC 2, 35; SSC 25**
See also Schmitz, Aron Hector

Swados, Elizabeth (A.) 1951-........... **CLC 12**
See also CA 97-100; CANR 49; INT 97-100

Swados, Harvey 1920-1972 .... **CLC 5**
See also CA 5-8R; 37-40R; CANR 6; DLB 2

Swan, Gladys 1934-...................... **CLC 69**
See also CA 101; CANR 17, 39

Swarthout, Glendon (Fred) 1918-1992 ... **CLC 35**
See also CA 1-4R; 139; CANR 1, 47; SATA 26

Sweet, Sarah C.
See Jewett, (Theodora) Sarah Orne

Swenson, May 1919-1989 .... **CLC 4, 14, 61, 106; DA; DAB; DAC; DAM MST, POET; PC 14**
See also CA 5-8R; 130; CANR 36, 61; DLB 5; MTCW 1; SATA 15

Swift, Augustus
See Lovecraft, H(oward) P(hillips)

Swift, Graham (Colin) 1949- .... **CLC 41, 88**
See also CA 117; 122; CANR 46, 71; DLB 194

Swift, Jonathan 1667-1745.................... **LC 1, 42; DA; DAB; DAC; DAM MST, NOV, POET; PC 9; WLC**
See also CDBLB 1660-1789; CLR 53; DLB 39, 95, 101; SATA 19

Swinburne, Algernon Charles 1837-1909 ....**TCLC 8, 36; DA; DAB; DAC; DAM MST, POET; PC 24; WLC**
See also CA 105; 140; CDBLB 1832-1890; DLB 35, 57

Swinfen, Ann.............................. **CLC 34**

Swinnerton, Frank Arthur 1884-1982 ... **CLC 31**
See also CA 108; DLB 34

Swithen, John
See King, Stephen (Edwin)

Sylvia
See Ashton-Warner, Sylvia (Constance)

Symmes, Robert Edward
See Duncan, Robert (Edward)

Symonds, John Addington 1840-1893 .... **NCLC 34**
See also DLB 57, 144

Symons, Arthur 1865-1945 .... **TCLC 11**
See also CA 107; DLB 19, 57, 149

Symons, Julian (Gustave) 1912-1994..... **CLC 2, 14, 32**
See also CA 49-52; 147; CAAS 3; CANR 3, 33, 59; DLB 87, 155; DLBY 92; MTCW 1

Synge, (Edmund) J(ohn) M(illington) 1871-1909 .... **TCLC 6, 37; DAM DRAM; DC 2**
See also CA 104; 141; CDBLB 1890-1914; DLB 10, 19

Syruc, J.
See Milosz, Czeslaw

Szirtes, George 1948-..................... **CLC 46**
See also CA 109; CANR 27, 61

Szymborska, Wislawa 1923-............ **CLC 99**
See also CA 154; DLBY 96

T. O., Nik
See Annensky, Innokenty (Fyodorovich)

Tabori, George 1914-..................... **CLC 19**
See also CA 49-52; CANR 4, 69

Tagore, Rabindranath 1861-1941 .... **TCLC 3, 53; DAM DRAM, POET; PC 8**
See also CA 104; 120; MTCW 1

Taine, Hippolyte Adolphe 1828-1893 ... **NCLC 15**

Talese, Gay 1932- .... **CLC 37**
See also AITN 1; CA 1-4R; CANR 9, 58; DLB 185; INT CANR-9; MTCW 1

Tallent, Elizabeth (Ann) 1954-......... **CLC 45**
See also CA 117; CANR 72; DLB 130

Tally, Ted 1952-........................... **CLC 42**
See also CA 120; 124; INT 124

Talvik, Heiti 1904-1947 .... **TCLC 87**

Tamayo y Baus, Manuel 1829-1898 ... **NCLC 1**

Tammsaare, A(nton) H(ansen) 1878-1940 .... **TCLC 27**
See also CA 164

Tam'si, Tchicaya U
See Tchicaya, Gerald Felix

Tan, Amy (Ruth) 1952- .... **CLC 59; DAM MULT, NOV, POP**
See also AAYA 9; BEST 89:3; CA 136; CANR 54; DLB 173; SATA 75

Tandem, Felix
See Spitteler, Carl (Friedrich Georg)

Tanizaki, Jun'ichiro 1886-1965............ **CLC 8, 14, 28; SSC 21**
See also CA 93-96; 25-28R; DLB 180

Tanner, William
See Amis, Kingsley (William)

Tao Lao
See Storni, Alfonsina

Tarassoff, Lev
See Troyat, Henri

Tarbell, Ida M(inerva) 1857-1944 ... **TCLC 40**
See also CA 122; DLB 47

Tarkington, (Newton) Booth 1869-1946 .... **TCLC 9**
See also CA 110; 143; DLB 9, 102; SATA 17

Tarkovsky, Andrei (Arsenyevich) 1932-1986 .... **CLC 75**
See also CA 127

Tartt, Donna 1964(?)- .... **CLC 76**
See also CA 142

Tasso, Torquato 1544-1595 .... **LC 5**

Tate, (John Orley) Allen 1899-1979....... **CLC 2, 4, 6, 9, 11, 14, 24**
See also CA 5-8R; 85-88; CANR 32; DLB 4, 45, 63; DLBD 17; MTCW 1

Tate, Ellalice
See Hibbert, Eleanor Alice Burford

Tate, James (Vincent) 1943- ...... **CLC 2, 6, 25**
See also CA 21-24R; CANR 29, 57; DLB 5, 169

Tavel, Ronald 1940- .... **CLC 6**
See also CA 21-24R; CANR 33

Taylor, C(ecil) P(hilip) 1929-1981 ..... **CLC 27**
See also CA 25-28R; 105; CANR 47

Taylor, Edward 1642(?)-1729............. **LC 11; DA; DAB; DAC; DAM MST, POET**
See also DLB 24

Taylor, Eleanor Ross 1920- .... **CLC 5**
See also CA 81-84; CANR 70

Taylor, Elizabeth 1912-1975 ...... **CLC 2, 4, 29**
See also CA 13-16R; CANR 9, 70; DLB 139; MTCW 1; SATA 13

Taylor, Frederick Winslow 1856-1915 .... **TCLC 76**

Taylor, Henry (Splawn) 1942-.......... **CLC 44**
See also CA 33-36R; CAAS 7; CANR 31; DLB 5

Taylor, Kamala (Purnaiya) 1924-
See Markandaya, Kamala

Taylor, Mildred D. .... CLC 21
See also AAYA 10; BW 1; CA 85-88; CANR 25; CLR 9; DLB 52; JRDA; MAICYA; SAAS 5; SATA 15, 70

Taylor, Peter (Hillsman) 1917-1994....... **CLC 1, 4, 18, 37, 44, 50, 71; SSC 10**
See also CA 13-16R; 147; CANR 9, 50; DLBY 81, 94; INT CANR-9; MTCW 1

Taylor, Robert Lewis 1912-1998....... **CLC 14**
See also CA 1-4R; 170; CANR 3, 64; SATA 10

Tchekhov, Anton
See Chekhov, Anton (Pavlovich)

Tchicaya, Gerald Felix 1931-1988....**CLC 101**
See also CA 129; 125

Tchicaya U Tam'si
See Tchicaya, Gerald Felix

Teasdale, Sara 1884-1933 .... **TCLC 4**
See also CA 104; 163; DLB 45; SATA 32

Tegner, Esaias 1782-1846................**NCLC 2**

Teilhard de Chardin, (Marie Joseph) Pierre 1881-1955 ....**TCLC 9**
See also CA 105

Temple, Ann
See Mortimer, Penelope (Ruth)

Tennant, Emma (Christina) 1937- .... **CLC 13, 52**
See also CA 65-68; CAAS 9; CANR 10, 38, 59; DLB 14

Tenneshaw, S. M.
See Silverberg, Robert

Tennyson, Alfred 1809-1892.............NCLC 30, 65; DA; DAB; DAC; DAM MST, POET; PC 6; WLC
See also CDBLB 1832-1890; DLB 32

Teran, Lisa St. Aubin de ....CLC 36
See also St. Aubin de Teran, Lisa

Terence 195(?)B.C.-159B.C...............CMLC 14; DC 7

Teresa de Jesus, St. 1515-1582.............LC 18

Terkel, Louis 1912-
See Terkel, Studs

Terkel, Studs...............................CLC 38
See also Terkel, Louis

Terry, C. V.
See Slaughter, Frank G(ill)

Terry, Megan 1932-.......................CLC 19
See also CA 77-80; CABS 3; CANR 43; DLB 7

Tertullian c. 155-c. 245 ....CMLC 29

Tertz, Abram
See Sinyavsky, Andrei (Donatevich)

Tesich, Steve 1943(?)-1996 ....CLC 40, 69
See also CA 105; 152; DLBY 83

Tesla, Nikola 1856-1943 ....TCLC 88

Teternikov, Fyodor Kuzmich 1863-1927
See Sologub, Fyodor

Tevis, Walter 1928-1984 ....CLC 42
See also CA 113

Tey, Josephine ....TCLC 14
See also Mackintosh, Elizabeth

Thackeray, William Makepeace 1811-1863 ....NCLC 5, 14, 22, 43; DA; DAB; DAC; DAM MST, NOV; WLC
See also CDBLB 1832-1890; DLB 21, 55, 159, 163; SATA 23

Thakura, Ravindranatha
See Tagore, Rabindranath

Tharoor, Shashi 1956-....................CLC 70
See also CA 141

Thelwell, Michael Miles 1939- ....CLC 22
See also BW 2; CA 101

Theobald, Lewis, Jr.
See Lovecraft, H(oward) P(hillips)

Theodorescu, Ion N. 1880-1967
See Arghezi, Tudor

Theriault, Yves 1915-1983 ....CLC 79; DAC; DAM MST
See also CA 102; DLB 88

Theroux, Alexander (Louis) 1939-........CLC 2, 25
See also CA 85-88; CANR 20, 63

Theroux, Paul (Edward) 1941- ....CLC 5, 8, 11, 15, 28, 46; DAM POP
See also BEST 89:4; CA 33-36R; CANR 20, 45, 74; DLB 2; MTCW 1; SATA 44

Thesen, Sharon 1946-....................CLC 56
See also CA 163

Thevenin, Denis
See Duhamel, Georges

Thibault, Jacques Anatole Francois 1844-1924
See France, Anatole

Thiele, Colin (Milton) 1920-............CLC 17
See also CA 29-32R; CANR 12, 28, 53; CLR 27; MAICYA; SAAS 2; SATA 14, 72

Thomas, Audrey (Callahan) 1935-........CLC 7, 13, 37, 107; SSC 20
See also AITN 2; CA 21-24R; CAAS 19; CANR 36, 58; DLB 60; MTCW 1

Thomas, D(onald) M(ichael) 1935- ....CLC 13, 22, 31
See also CA 61-64; CAAS 11; CANR 17, 45, 75; CDBLB 1960 to Present; DLB 40; INT CANR-17; MTCW 1

Thomas, Dylan (Marlais) 1914-1953 ... TCLC 1, 8, 45; DA; DAB; DAC; DAM DRAM, MST, POET; PC 2; SSC 3; WLC
See also CA 104; 120; CANR 65; CDBLB 1945-1960; DLB 13, 20, 139; MTCW 1; SATA 60

Thomas, (Philip) Edward 1878-1917 ... TCLC 10; DAM POET
See also CA 106; 153; DLB 19

Thomas, Joyce Carol 1938-.............CLC 35
See also AAYA 12; BW 2; CA 113; 116; CANR 48; CLR 19; DLB 33; INT 116; JRDA; MAICYA; MTCW 1; SAAS 7; SATA 40, 78

Thomas, Lewis 1913-1993...............CLC 35
See also CA 85-88; 143; CANR 38, 60; MTCW 1

Thomas, M. Carey 1857-1935........TCLC 89

Thomas, Paul
See Mann, (Paul) Thomas

Thomas, Piri 1928- ....CLC 17
See also CA 73-76; HW

Thomas, R(onald) S(tuart) 1913-..........CLC 6, 13, 48; DAB; DAM POET
See also CA 89-92; CAAS 4; CANR 30; CD-BLB 1960 to Present; DLB 27; MTCW 1

Thomas, Ross (Elmore) 1926-1995.... CLC 39
See also CA 33-36R; 150; CANR 22, 63

Thompson, Francis Clegg
See Mencken, H(enry) L(ouis)

Thompson, Francis Joseph 1859-1907 ....TCLC 4
See also CA 104; CDBLB 1890-1914; DLB 19

Thompson, Hunter S(tockton) 1939-..... CLC 9, 17, 40, 104; DAM POP
See also BEST 89:1; CA 17-20R; CANR 23, 46, 74; DLB 185; MTCW 1

Thompson, James Myers
See Thompson, Jim (Myers)

Thompson, Jim (Myers) 1906-1977(?) ... CLC 69
See also CA 140

Thompson, Judith ....CLC 39

Thomson, James 1700-1748 ....LC 16, 29, 40; DAM POET
See also DLB 95

Thomson, James 1834-1882 ....NCLC 18; DAM POET
See also DLB 35

Thoreau, Henry David 1817-1862.......NCLC 7, 21, 61; DA; DAB; DAC; DAM MST; WLC
See also CDALB 1640-1865; DLB 1

Thornton, Hall
See Silverberg, Robert

Thucydides c. 455B.C.-399B.C...... CMLC 17
See also DLB 176

Thurber, James (Grover) 1894-1961 ..... CLC 5, 11, 25; DA; DAB; DAC; DAM DRAM, MST, NOV; SSC 1
See also CA 73-76; CANR 17, 39; CDALB 1929-1941; DLB 4, 11, 22, 102; MAICYA; MTCW 1; SATA 13

Thurman, Wallace (Henry) 1902-1934 ....TCLC 6; BLC 3; DAM MULT
See also BW 1; CA 104; 124; DLB 51

Ticheburn, Cheviot
See Ainsworth, William Harrison

Tieck, (Johann) Ludwig 1773-1853.....NCLC 5, 46; SSC 31
See also DLB 90

Tiger, Derry
See Ellison, Harlan (Jay)

Tilghman, Christopher 1948(?)-.......CLC 65
See also CA 159

Tillinghast, Richard (Williford) 1940- ....CLC 29
See also CA 29-32R; CAAS 23; CANR 26, 51

Timrod, Henry 1828-1867.............NCLC 25
See also DLB 3

Tindall, Gillian (Elizabeth) 1938- ....CLC 7
See also CA 21-24R; CANR 11, 65

Tiptree, James, Jr. ....CLC 48, 50
See also Sheldon, Alice Hastings Bradley

Titmarsh, Michael Angelo
See Thackeray, William Makepeace

Tocqueville, Alexis (Charles Henri Maurice Clerel, Comte) de 1805-1859 ....NCLC 7, 63

Tolkien, J(ohn) R(onald) R(euel) 1892-1973 ....CLC 1, 2, 3, 8, 12, 38; DA; DAB; DAC; DAM MST, NOV, POP; WLC
See also AAYA 10; AITN 1; CA 17-18; 45-48; CANR 36; CAP 2; CDBLB 1914-1945; DLB 15, 160; JRDA; MAICYA; MTCW 1; SATA 2, 32, 100; SATA-Obit 24

Toller, Ernst 1893-1939...............TCLC 10
See also CA 107; DLB 124

Tolson, M. B.
See Tolson, Melvin B(eaunorus)

Tolson, Melvin B(eaunorus) 1898(?)-1966 ....CLC 36, 105; BLC 3; DAM MULT, POET
See also BW 1; CA 124; 89-92; DLB 48, 76

Tolstoi, Aleksei Nikolaevich
See Tolstoy, Alexey Nikolaevich

Tolstoy, Alexey Nikolaevich 1882-1945 ....TCLC 18
See also CA 107; 158

Tolstoy, Count Leo
See Tolstoy, Leo (Nikolaevich)

Tolstoy, Leo (Nikolaevich) 1828-1910... **TCLC 4, 11, 17, 28, 44, 79; DA; DAB; DAC; DAM MST, NOV; SSC 9, 30; WLC**
See also CA 104; 123; SATA 26

Tomasi di Lampedusa, Giuseppe 1896-1957
See Lampedusa, Giuseppe (Tomasi) di

Tomlin, Lily .... **CLC 17**
See also Tomlin, Mary Jean

Tomlin, Mary Jean 1939(?)-
See Tomlin, Lily

Tomlinson, (Alfred) Charles 1927-........ **CLC 2, 4, 6, 13, 45; DAM POET; PC 17**
See also CA 5-8R; CANR 33; DLB 40

Tomlinson, H(enry) M(ajor) 1873-1958 .... **TCLC 71**
See also CA 118; 161; DLB 36, 100, 195

Tonson, Jacob
See Bennett, (Enoch) Arnold

Toole, John Kennedy 1937-1969 ... **CLC 19, 64**
See also CA 104; DLBY 81

Toomer, Jean 1894-1967...................... **CLC 1, 4, 13, 22; BLC 3; DAM MULT; PC 7; SSC 1; WLCS**
See also BW 1; CA 85-88; CDALB 1917-1929; DLB 45, 51; MTCW 1

Torley, Luke
See Blish, James (Benjamin)

Tornimparte, Alessandra
See Ginzburg, Natalia

Torre, Raoul della
See Mencken, H(enry) L(ouis)

Torrey, E(dwin) Fuller 1937-........... **CLC 34**
See also CA 119; CANR 71

Torsvan, Ben Traven
See Traven, B.

Torsvan, Benno Traven
See Traven, B.

Torsvan, Berick Traven
See Traven, B.

Torsvan, Berwick Traven
See Traven, B.

Torsvan, Bruno Traven
See Traven, B.

Torsvan, Traven
See Traven, B.

Tournier, Michel (Edouard) 1924- .... **CLC 6, 23, 36, 95**
See also CA 49-52; CANR 3, 36, 74; DLB 83; MTCW 1; SATA 23

Tournimparte, Alessandra
See Ginzburg, Natalia

Towers, Ivar
See Kornbluth, C(yril) M.

Towne, Robert (Burton) 1936(?)-...... **CLC 87**
See also CA 108; DLB 44

Townsend, Sue .... **CLC 61**
See also Townsend, Susan Elaine

Townsend, Susan Elaine 1946-
See Townsend, Sue

Townshend, Peter (Dennis Blandford) 1945- ....**CLC 17, 42**
See also CA 107

Tozzi, Federigo 1883-1920 .... **TCLC 31**
See also CA 160

Traill, Catharine Parr 1802-1899 ... **NCLC 31**
See also DLB 99

Trakl, Georg 1887-1914 .... **TCLC 5; PC 20**
See also CA 104; 165

Transtroemer, Tomas (Goesta) 1931-..... **CLC 52, 65; DAM POET**
See also CA 117; 129; CAAS 17

Transtromer, Tomas Gosta
See Transtroemer, Tomas (Goesta)

Traven, B. (?)-1969 .... **CLC 8, 11**
See also CA 19-20; 25-28R; CAP 2; DLB 9, 56; MTCW 1

Treitel, Jonathan 1959- .... **CLC 70**

Tremain, Rose 1943-..................... **CLC 42**
See also CA 97-100; CANR 44; DLB 14

Tremblay, Michel 1942- .... **CLC 29, 102; DAC; DAM MST**
See also CA 116; 128; DLB 60; MTCW 1

Trevanian .... **CLC 29**
See also Whitaker, Rod(ney)

Trevor, Glen
See Hilton, James

Trevor, William 1928-...................... **CLC 7, 9, 14, 25, 71, 116; SSC 21**
See also Cox, William Trevor

Trifonov, Yuri (Valentinovich) 1925-1981 .... **CLC 45**
See also CA 126; 103; MTCW 1

Trilling, Lionel 1905-1975........**CLC 9, 11, 24**
See also CA 9-12R; 61-64; CANR 10; DLB 28, 63; INT CANR-10; MTCW 1

Trimball, W. H.
See Mencken, H(enry) L(ouis)

Tristan
See Gomez de la Serna, Ramon

Tristram
See Housman, A(lfred) E(dward)

Trogdon, William (Lewis) 1939-
See Heat-Moon, William Least

Trollope, Anthony 1815-1882 ....**NCLC 6, 33; DA; DAB; DAC; DAM MST, NOV; SSC 28; WLC**
See also CDBLB 1832-1890; DLB 21, 57, 159; SATA 22

Trollope, Frances 1779-1863 .... **NCLC 30**
See also DLB 21, 166

Trotsky, Leon 1879-1940 .... **TCLC 22**
See also CA 118; 167

Trotter (Cockburn), Catharine 1679-1749 .... **LC 8**
See also DLB 84

Trout, Kilgore
See Farmer, Philip Jose

Trow, George W. S. 1943- .... **CLC 52**
See also CA 126

Troyat, Henri 1911-..................... **CLC 23**
See also CA 45-48; CANR 2, 33, 67; MTCW 1

Trudeau, G(arretson) B(eekman) 1948-
See Trudeau, Garry B.

Trudeau, Garry B. .... **CLC 12**
See also Trudeau, G(arretson) B(eekman)

Truffaut, Francois 1932-1984 .... **CLC 20, 101**
See also CA 81-84; 113; CANR 34

Trumbo, Dalton 1905-1976 .... **CLC 19**
See also CA 21-24R; 69-72; CANR 10; DLB 26

Trumbull, John 1750-1831............ **NCLC 30**
See also DLB 31

Trundlett, Helen B.
See Eliot, T(homas) S(tearns)

Tryon, Thomas 1926-1991 .... **CLC 3, 11; DAM POP**
See also AITN 1; CA 29-32R; 135; CANR 32; MTCW 1

Tryon, Tom
See Tryon, Thomas

Ts'ao Hsueh-ch'in 1715(?)-1763 .... **LC 1**

Tsushima, Shuji 1909-1948
See Dazai Osamu

Tsvetaeva (Efron), Marina (Ivanovna) 1892-1941 ....**TCLC 7, 35; PC 14**
See also CA 104; 128; CANR 73; MTCW 1

Tuck, Lily 1938-......................... **CLC 70**
See also CA 139

Tu Fu 712-770................................ **PC 9**
See also DAM MULT

Tunis, John R(oberts) 1889-1975 ...... **CLC 12**
See also CA 61-64; CANR 62; DLB 22, 171; JRDA; MAICYA; SATA 37; SATA-Brief 30

Tuohy, Frank............................. **CLC 37**
See also Tuohy, John Francis

Tuohy, John Francis 1925-
See Tuohy, Frank

Turco, Lewis (Putnam) 1934- ......**CLC 11, 63**
See also CA 13-16R; CAAS 22; CANR 24, 51; DLBY 84

Turgenev, Ivan 1818-1883.................**NCLC 21; DA; DAB; DAC; DAM MST, NOV; DC 7; SSC 7; WLC**

Turgot, Anne-Robert-Jacques 1727-1781 ....**LC 26**

Turner, Frederick 1943- .... **CLC 48**
See also CA 73-76; CAAS 10; CANR 12, 30, 56; DLB 40

Tutu, Desmond M(pilo) 1931-.............. **CLC 80; BLC 3; DAM MULT**
See also BW 1; CA 125; CANR 67

Tutuola, Amos 1920-1997 .... **CLC 5, 14, 29; BLC 3; DAM MULT**
See also BW 2; CA 9-12R; 159; CANR 27, 66; DLB 125; MTCW 1

Twain, Mark .... **TCLC 6, 12, 19, 36, 48, 59; SSC 6, 26; WLC**
See also Clemens, Samuel Langhorne

Tyler, Anne 1941- ....**CLC 7, 11, 18, 28, 44, 59, 103; DAM NOV, POP**
See also AAYA 18; BEST 89:1; CA 9-12R; CANR 11, 33, 53; DLB 6, 143; DLBY 82; MTCW 1; SATA 7, 90

Tyler, Royall 1757-1826..................NCLC 3
See also DLB 37

Tynan, Katharine 1861-1931 ....TCLC 3
See also CA 104; 167; DLB 153

Tyutchev, Fyodor 1803-1873 .... NCLC 34

Tzara, Tristan 1896-1963 CLC
47; DAM POET
See also CA 153; 89-92

Uhry, Alfred 1936-............................CLC
55; DAM DRAM, POP
See also CA 127; 133; INT 133

Ulf, Haerved
See Strindberg, (Johan) August

Ulf, Harved
See Strindberg, (Johan) August

Ulibarri, Sabine R(eyes) 1919-.............CLC
83; DAM MULT
See also CA 131; DLB 82; HW

Unamuno (y Jugo), Miguel de
1864-1936 .... TCLC 2,
9; DAM MULT, NOV; HLC; SSC 11
See also CA 104; 131; DLB 108; HW;
MTCW 1

Undercliffe, Errol
See Campbell, (John) Ramsey

Underwood, Miles
See Glassco, John

Undset, Sigrid 1882-1949.........TCLC 3; DA;
DAB; DAC; DAM MST, NOV; WLC
See also CA 104; 129; MTCW 1

Ungaretti, Giuseppe 1888-1970............ CLC
7, 11, 15
See also CA 19-20; 25-28R; CAP 2; DLB 114

Unger, Douglas 1952- .... CLC 34
See also CA 130

Unsworth, Barry (Forster) 1930-...... CLC 76
See also CA 25-28R; CANR 30, 54; DLB 194

Updike, John (Hoyer) 1932-................ CLC
1, 2, 3, 5, 7, 9, 13, 15, 23, 34, 43, 70;
DA; DAB; DAC; DAM MST, NOV,
POET, POP; SSC 13, 27; WLC
See also CA 1-4R; CABS 1; CANR 4, 33, 51;
CDALB 1968-1988; DLB 2, 5, 143; DLBD
3; DLBY 80, 82, 97; MTCW 1

Upshaw, Margaret Mitchell
See Mitchell, Margaret (Munnerlyn)

Upton, Mark
See Sanders, Lawrence

Upward, Allen 1863-1926............. TCLC 85
See also CA 117; DLB 36

Urdang, Constance (Henriette)
1922- .... CLC 47
See also CA 21-24R; CANR 9, 24

Uriel, Henry
See Faust, Frederick (Schiller)

Uris, Leon (Marcus) 1924-.................. CLC
7, 32; DAM NOV, POP
See also AITN 1, 2; BEST 89:2; CA 1-4R;
CANR 1, 40, 65; MTCW 1; SATA 49

Urmuz
See Codrescu, Andrei

Urquhart, Jane 1949- .... CLC 90; DAC
See also CA 113; CANR 32, 68

Ustinov, Peter (Alexander) 1921-........CLC 1
See also AITN 1; CA 13-16R; CANR 25, 51;
DLB 13

U Tam'si, Gerald Felix Tchicaya
See Tchicaya, Gerald Felix

U Tam'si, Tchicaya
See Tchicaya, Gerald Felix

Vachss, Andrew (Henry) 1942- ....CLC 106
See also CA 118; CANR 44

Vachss, Andrew H.
See Vachss, Andrew (Henry)

Vaculik, Ludvik 1926- ....CLC 7
See also CA 53-56; CANR 72

Vaihinger, Hans 1852-1933 .... TCLC 71
See also CA 116; 166

Valdez, Luis (Miguel) 1940- CLC
84; DAM MULT; DC 10; HLC
See also CA 101; CANR 32; DLB 122; HW

Valenzuela, Luisa 1938- CLC
31, 104; DAM MULT; SSC 14
See also CA 101; CANR 32, 65; DLB 113;
HW

Valera y Alcala-Galiano, Juan
1824-1905 .... TCLC 10
See also CA 106

Valery, (Ambroise) Paul (Toussaint Jules)
1871-1945 .... TCLC
4, 15; DAM POET; PC 9
See also CA 104; 122; MTCW 1

Valle-Inclan, Ramon (Maria) del
1866-1936 .... TCLC
5; DAM MULT; HLC
See also CA 106; 153; DLB 134

Vallejo, Antonio Buero
See Buero Vallejo, Antonio

Vallejo, Cesar (Abraham) 1892-1938... TCLC
3, 56; DAM MULT; HLC
See also CA 105; 153; HW

Valles, Jules 1832-1885 .... NCLC 71
See also DLB 123

Vallette, Marguerite Eymery
See Rachilde

Valle Y Pena, Ramon del
See Valle-Inclan, Ramon (Maria) del

Van Ash, Cay 1918-....................... CLC 34

Vanbrugh, Sir John 1664-1726 LC
21; DAM DRAM
See also DLB 80

Van Campen, Karl
See Campbell, John W(ood, Jr.)

Vance, Gerald
See Silverberg, Robert

Vance, Jack................................. CLC 35
See also Kuttner, Henry; Vance, John Holbrook

Vance, John Holbrook 1916-
See Queen, Ellery; Vance, Jack

Van Den Bogarde, Derek Jules Gaspard
Ulric Niven 1921-
See Bogarde, Dirk

Vandenburgh, Jane....................... CLC 59
See also CA 168

Vanderhaeghe, Guy 1951-............... CLC 41
See also CA 113; CANR 72

van der Post, Laurens (Jan) 1906-1996... CLC
5
See also CA 5-8R; 155; CANR 35

van de Wetering, Janwillem 1931-.... CLC 47
See also CA 49-52; CANR 4, 62

Van Dine, S. S. .... TCLC 23
See also Wright, Willard Huntington

Van Doren, Carl (Clinton) 1885-1950... TCLC
18
See also CA 111; 168

Van Doren, Mark 1894-1972 .... CLC 6, 10
See also CA 1-4R; 37-40R; CANR 3; DLB
45; MTCW 1

Van Druten, John (William)
1901-1957 ....TCLC 2
See also CA 104; 161; DLB 10

Van Duyn, Mona (Jane) 1921- CLC
3, 7, 63, 116; DAM POET
See also CA 9-12R; CANR 7, 38, 60; DLB 5

Van Dyne, Edith
See Baum, L(yman) Frank

van Itallie, Jean-Claude 1936-...........CLC 3
See also CA 45-48; CAAS 2; CANR 1, 48;
DLB 7

van Ostaijen, Paul 1896-1928 .... TCLC 33
See also CA 163

Van Peebles, Melvin 1932- CLC
2, 20; DAM MULT
See also BW 2; CA 85-88; CANR 27, 67

Vansittart, Peter 1920-................... CLC 42
See also CA 1-4R; CANR 3, 49

Van Vechten, Carl 1880-1964 .... CLC 33
See also CA 89-92; DLB 4, 9, 51

Van Vogt, A(lfred) E(lton) 1912- ....CLC 1
See also CA 21-24R; CANR 28; DLB 8;
SATA 14

Varda, Agnes 1928-....................... CLC 16
See also CA 116; 122

Vargas Llosa, (Jorge) Mario (Pedro)
1936- .... CLC 3,
6, 9, 10, 15, 31, 42, 85; DA; DAB; DAC;
DAM MST, MULT, NOV; HLC
See also CA 73-76; CANR 18, 32, 42, 67;
DLB 145; HW; MTCW 1

Vasiliu, Gheorghe 1881-1957
See Bacovia, George

Vassa, Gustavus
See Equiano, Olaudah

Vassilikos, Vassilis 1933- ....CLC 4, 8
See also CA 81-84; CANR 75

Vaughan, Henry 1621-1695...............LC 27
See also DLB 131

Vaughn, Stephanie....................... CLC 62

Vazov, Ivan (Minchov) 1850-1921... TCLC 25
See also CA 121; 167; DLB 147

Veblen, Thorstein B(unde)
1857-1929 .... TCLC 31
See also CA 115; 165

Vega, Lope de 1562-1635 ....LC 23

Venison, Alfred
See Pound, Ezra (Weston Loomis)

Verdi, Marie de
See Mencken, H(enry) L(ouis)

Verdu, Matilde
See Cela, Camilo Jose

Verga, Giovanni (Carmelo)
1840-1922 ....TCLC 3; SSC 21
See also CA 104; 123

Vergil 70B.C.-19B.C. .... CMLC 9; DA; DAB;
DAC; DAM MST, POET; PC 12; WLCS

Verhaeren, Emile (Adolphe Gustave)
1855-1916 .... TCLC 12
See also CA 109

Verlaine, Paul (Marie) 1844-1896 .... NCLC
2, 51; DAM POET; PC 2

Verne, Jules (Gabriel) 1828-1905........ TCLC
6, 52
See also AAYA 16; CA 110; 131; DLB 123;
JRDA; MAICYA; SATA 21

Very, Jones 1813-1880 ....NCLC 9
See also DLB 1

Vesaas, Tarjei 1897-1970 .... CLC 48
See also CA 29-32R

Vialis, Gaston
See Simenon, Georges (Jacques Christian)

Vian, Boris 1920-1959....................TCLC 9
See also CA 106; 164; DLB 72

Viaud, (Louis Marie) Julien 1850-1923
See Loti, Pierre

Vicar, Henry
See Felsen, Henry Gregor

Vicker, Angus
See Felsen, Henry Gregor

Vidal, Gore 1925- ....CLC 2, 4,
6, 8, 10, 22, 33, 72; DAM NOV, POP
See also AITN 1; BEST 90:2; CA 5-8R;
CANR 13, 45, 65; DLB 6, 152; INT
CANR-13; MTCW 1

Viereck, Peter (Robert Edwin) 1916-... CLC 4
See also CA 1-4R; CANR 1, 47; DLB 5

Vigny, Alfred (Victor) de 1797-1863 .... NCLC
7; DAM POET
See also DLB 119, 192

Vilakazi, Benedict Wallet 1906-1947 ... TCLC
37
See also CA 168

Villa, Jose Garcia 1904-1997 .... PC 22
See also CA 25-28R; CANR 12

Villaurrutia, Xavier 1903-1950 ...... TCLC 80
See also HW

Villiers de l'Isle Adam, Jean Marie
Mathias Philippe Auguste, Comte de
1838-1889 .... NCLC 3; SSC 14
See also DLB 123

Villon, Francois 1431-1463(?) ....PC 13

Vinci, Leonardo da 1452-1519 ....LC 12

Vine, Barbara............................ CLC 50
See also Rendell, Ruth (Barbara)

Vinge, Joan (Carol) D(ennison) 1948-.... CLC
30; SSC 24
See also CA 93-96; CANR 72; SATA 36

Violis, G.
See Simenon, Georges (Jacques Christian)

Virgil
See Vergil

Visconti, Luchino 1906-1976 .... CLC 16
See also CA 81-84; 65-68; CANR 39

Vittorini, Elio 1908-1966 .... CLC 6, 9, 14
See also CA 133; 25-28R

Vivekananda, Swami 1863-1902..... TCLC 88

Vizenor, Gerald Robert 1934-.............. CLC
103; DAM MULT
See also CA 13-16R; CAAS 22; CANR 5, 21,
44, 67; DLB 175; NNAL

Vizinczey, Stephen 1933- .... CLC 40
See also CA 128; INT 128

Vliet, R(ussell) G(ordon) 1929-1984 ...CLC 22
See also CA 37-40R; 112; CANR 18

Vogau, Boris Andreyevich 1894-1937(?)
See Pilnyak, Boris

Vogel, Paula A(nne) 1951- .... CLC 76
See also CA 108

Voigt, Cynthia 1942-..................... CLC 30
See also AAYA 3; CA 106; CANR 18, 37,
40; CLR 13, 48; INT CANR-18; JRDA;
MAICYA; SATA 48, 79; SATA-Brief 33

Voigt, Ellen Bryant 1943- .... CLC 54
See also CA 69-72; CANR 11, 29, 55; DLB
120

Voinovich, Vladimir (Nikolaevich)
1932- ....CLC 10, 49
See also CA 81-84; CAAS 12; CANR 33, 67;
MTCW 1

Vollmann, William T. 1959- CLC
89; DAM NOV, POP
See also CA 134; CANR 67

Voloshinov, V. N.
See Bakhtin, Mikhail Mikhailovich

Voltaire 1694-1778 ...LC 14; DA; DAB; DAC;
DAM DRAM, MST; SSC 12; WLC

von Aschendrof, BaronIgnatz
See Ford, Ford Madox

von Daeniken, Erich 1935-.............. CLC 30
See also AITN 1; CA 37-40R; CANR 17, 44

von Daniken, Erich
See von Daeniken, Erich

von Heidenstam, (Carl Gustaf) Verner
See Heidenstam, (Carl Gustaf) Verner von

von Heyse, Paul (Johann Ludwig)
See Heyse, Paul (Johann Ludwig von)

von Hofmannsthal, Hugo
See Hofmannsthal, Hugo von

von Horvath, Odon
See Horvath, Oedoen von

von Horvath, Oedoen
See Horvath, Oedoen von

von Liliencron, (Friedrich Adolf Axel) Detlev
See Liliencron, (Friedrich Adolf Axel) Detlev
von

Vonnegut, Kurt, Jr. 1922-....CLC 1, 2, 3, 4, 5,
8, 12, 22, 40, 60, 111; DA; DAB; DAC;
DAM MST, NOV, POP; SSC 8; WLC
See also AAYA 6; AITN 1; BEST 90:4; CA
1-4R; CANR 1, 25, 49, 75; CDALB 1968-
1988; DLB 2, 8, 152; DLBD 3; DLBY 80;
MTCW 1

Von Rachen, Kurt
See Hubbard, L(afayette) Ron(ald)

von Rezzori (d'Arezzo), Gregor
See Rezzori (d'Arezzo), Gregor von

von Sternberg, Josef
See Sternberg, Josef von

Vorster, Gordon 1924- .... CLC 34
See also CA 133

Vosce, Trudie
See Ozick, Cynthia

Voznesensky, Andrei (Andreievich)
1933- .... CLC 1, 15, 57; DAM POET
See also CA 89-92; CANR 37; MTCW 1

Waddington, Miriam 1917-............. CLC 28
See also CA 21-24R; CANR 12, 30; DLB 68

Wagman, Fredrica 1937-...................CLC 7
See also CA 97-100; INT 97-100

Wagner, Linda W.
See Wagner-Martin, Linda (C.)

Wagner, Linda Welshimer
See Wagner-Martin, Linda (C.)

Wagner, Richard 1813-1883............NCLC 9
See also DLB 129

Wagner-Martin, Linda (C.) 1936- .... CLC 50
See also CA 159

Wagoner, David (Russell) 1926- CLC
3, 5, 15
See also CA 1-4R; CAAS 3; CANR 2, 71;
DLB 5; SATA 14

Wah, Fred(erick James) 1939-......... CLC 44
See also CA 107; 141; DLB 60

Wahloo, Per 1926-1975 ....CLC 7
See also CA 61-64; CANR 73

Wahloo, Peter
See Wahloo, Per

Wain, John (Barrington) 1925-1994...... CLC
2, 11, 15, 46
See also CA 5-8R; 145; CAAS 4; CANR 23,
54; CDBLB 1960 to Present; DLB 15, 27,
139, 155; MTCW 1

Wajda, Andrzej 1926-.................... CLC 16
See also CA 102

Wakefield, Dan 1932- ....CLC 7
See also CA 21-24R; CAAS 7

Wakoski, Diane 1937-...................... CLC
2, 4, 7, 9, 11, 40; DAM POET; PC 15
See also CA 13-16R; CAAS 1; CANR 9, 60;
DLB 5; INT CANR-9

Wakoski-Sherbell, Diane
See Wakoski, Diane

Walcott, Derek (Alton) 1930-.............. CLC
2, 4, 9, 14, 25, 42, 67, 76; BLC 3; DAB;
DAC; DAM MST, MULT, POET; DC 7
See also BW 2; CA 89-92; CANR 26, 47, 75;
DLB 117; DLBY 81; MTCW 1

Waldman, Anne (Lesley) 1945-..........CLC 7
See also CA 37-40R; CAAS 17; CANR 34,
69; DLB 16

Waldo, E. Hunter
See Sturgeon, Theodore (Hamilton)

Waldo, Edward Hamilton
See Sturgeon, Theodore (Hamilton)

Weber, Lenora Mattingly 1895-1971 ..... **CLC 12**
See also CA 19-20; 29-32R; CAP 1; SATA 2; SATA-Obit 26

Weber, Max 1864-1920 .... **TCLC 69**
See also CA 109

Webster, John 1579(?)-1634(?) .... **LC 33; DA; DAB; DAC; DAM DRAM, MST; DC 2; WLC**
See also CDBLB Before 1660; DLB 58

Webster, Noah 1758-1843 .... **NCLC 30**

Wedekind, (Benjamin) Frank(lin) 1864-1918 .... **TCLC 7; DAM DRAM**
See also CA 104; 153; DLB 118

Weidman, Jerome 1913-1998............. **CLC 7**
See also AITN 2; CA 1-4R; 171; CANR 1; DLB 28

Weil, Simone (Adolphine) 1909-1943... **TCLC 23**
See also CA 117; 159

Weininger, Otto 1880-1903 .... **TCLC 84**

Weinstein, Nathan
See West, Nathanael

Weinstein, Nathan von Wallenstein
See West, Nathanael

Weir, Peter (Lindsay) 1944- .... **CLC 20**
See also CA 113; 123

Weiss, Peter (Ulrich) 1916-1982 .... **CLC 3, 15, 51; DAM DRAM**
See also CA 45-48; 106; CANR 3; DLB 69, 124

Weiss, Theodore (Russell) 1916-........... **CLC 3, 8, 14**
See also CA 9-12R; CAAS 2; CANR 46; DLB 5

Welch, (Maurice) Denton 1915-1948 ... **TCLC 22**
See also CA 121; 148

Welch, James 1940-......................... **CLC 6, 14, 52; DAM MULT, POP**
See also CA 85-88; CANR 42, 66; DLB 175; NNAL

Weldon, Fay 1931-.......................... **CLC 6, 9, 11, 19, 36, 59; DAM POP**
See also CA 21-24R; CANR 16, 46, 63; CDBLB 1960 to Present; DLB 14, 194; INT CANR-16; MTCW 1

Wellek, Rene 1903-1995 .... **CLC 28**
See also CA 5-8R; 150; CAAS 7; CANR 8; DLB 63; INT CANR-8

Weller, Michael 1942-................CLC 10, 53
See also CA 85-88

Weller, Paul 1958-.......................... **CLC 26**

Wellershoff, Dieter 1925-................ **CLC 46**
See also CA 89-92; CANR 16, 37

Welles, (George) Orson 1915-1985........ **CLC 20, 80**
See also CA 93-96; 117

Wellman, John McDowell 1945-
See Wellman, Mac

Wellman, Mac 1945- .... **CLC 65**
See also Wellman, John McDowell; Wellman, John McDowell

Wellman, Manly Wade 1903-1986 .... **CLC 49**
See also CA 1-4R; 118; CANR 6, 16, 44; SATA 6; SATA-Obit 47

Wells, Carolyn 1869(?)-1942......... **TCLC 35**
See also CA 113; DLB 11

Wells, H(erbert) G(eorge) 1866-1946... **TCLC 6, 12, 19; DA; DAB; DAC; DAM MST, NOV; SSC 6; WLC**
See also AAYA 18; CA 110; 121; CDBLB 1914-1945; DLB 34, 70, 156, 178; MTCW 1; SATA 20

Wells, Rosemary 1943-................... **CLC 12**
See also AAYA 13; CA 85-88; CANR 48; CLR 16; MAICYA; SAAS 1; SATA 18, 69

Welty, Eudora 1909-......................... **CLC 1, 2, 5, 14, 22, 33, 105; DA; DAB; DAC; DAM MST, NOV; SSC 1, 27; WLC**
See also CA 9-12R; CABS 1; CANR 32, 65; CDALB 1941-1968; DLB 2, 102, 143; DLBD 12; DLBY 87; MTCW 1

Wen I-to 1899-1946..................... **TCLC 28**

Wentworth, Robert
See Hamilton, Edmond

Werfel, Franz (Viktor) 1890-1945.....**TCLC 8**
See also CA 104; 161; DLB 81, 124

Wergeland, Henrik Arnold 1808-1845 ....NCLC 5

Wersba, Barbara 1932-................... **CLC 30**
See also AAYA 2; CA 29-32R; CANR 16, 38; CLR 3; DLB 52; JRDA; MAICYA; SAAS 2; SATA 1, 58

Wertmueller, Lina 1928- .... **CLC 16**
See also CA 97-100; CANR 39

Wescott, Glenway 1901-1987........... **CLC 13**
See also CA 13-16R; 121; CANR 23, 70; DLB 4, 9, 102

Wesker, Arnold 1932-........................ **CLC 3, 5, 42; DAB; DAM DRAM**
See also CA 1-4R; CAAS 7; CANR 1, 33; CDBLB 1960 to Present; DLB 13; MTCW 1

Wesley, Richard (Errol) 1945- ....CLC 7
See also BW 1; CA 57-60; CANR 27; DLB 38

Wessel, Johan Herman 1742-1785 .... **LC 7**

West, Anthony (Panther) 1914-1987 ..... **CLC 50**
See also CA 45-48; 124; CANR 3, 19; DLB 15

West, C. P.
See Wodehouse, P(elham) G(renville)

West, (Mary) Jessamyn 1902-1984........ **CLC 7, 17**
See also CA 9-12R; 112; CANR 27; DLB 6; DLBY 84; MTCW 1; SATA-Obit 37

West, Morris L(anglo) 1916- .... **CLC 6, 33**
See also CA 5-8R; CANR 24, 49, 64; MTCW 1

West, Nathanael 1903-1940............... **TCLC 1, 14, 44; SSC 16**
See also CA 104; 125; CDALB 1929-1941; DLB 4, 9, 28; MTCW 1

West, Owen
See Koontz, Dean R(ay)

West, Paul 1930-.....................CLC 7, 14, 96
See also CA 13-16R; CAAS 7; CANR 22, 53; DLB 14; INT CANR-22

West, Rebecca 1892-1983 .....CLC 7, 9, 31, 50
See also CA 5-8R; 109; CANR 19; DLB 36; DLBY 83; MTCW 1

Westall, Robert (Atkinson) 1929-1993 ... **CLC 17**
See also AAYA 12; CA 69-72; 141; CANR 18, 68; CLR 13; JRDA; MAICYA; SAAS 2; SATA 23, 69; SATA-Obit 75

Westermarck, Edward 1862-1939... **TCLC 87**

Westlake, Donald E(dwin) 1933- .... **CLC 7, 33; DAM POP**
See also CA 17-20R; CAAS 13; CANR 16, 44, 65; INT CANR-16

Westmacott, Mary
See Christie, Agatha (Mary Clarissa)

Weston, Allen
See Norton, Andre

Wetcheek, J. L.
See Feuchtwanger, Lion

Wetering, Janwillem van de
See van de Wetering, Janwillem

Wetherald, Agnes Ethelwyn 1857-1940 .... **TCLC 81**
See also DLB 99

Wetherell, Elizabeth
See Warner, Susan (Bogert)

Whale, James 1889-1957 .... **TCLC 63**

Whalen, Philip 1923-................... **CLC 6, 29**
See also CA 9-12R; CANR 5, 39; DLB 16

Wharton, Edith (Newbold Jones) 1862-1937 .... **TCLC 3, 9, 27, 53; DA; DAB; DAC; DAM MST, NOV; SSC 6; WLC**
See also AAYA 25; CA 104; 132; CDALB 1865-1917; DLB 4, 9, 12, 78, 189; DLBD 13; MTCW 1

Wharton, James
See Mencken, H(enry) L(ouis)

Wharton, William (a pseudonym) .... **CLC 18, 37**
See also CA 93-96; DLBY 80; INT 93-96

Wheatley (Peters), Phillis 1754(?)-1784.... **LC 3; BLC 3; DA; DAC; DAM MST, MULT, POET; PC 3; WLC**
See also CDALB 1640-1865; DLB 31, 50

Wheelock, John Hall 1886-1978 .... **CLC 14**
See also CA 13-16R; 77-80; CANR 14; DLB 45

White, E(lwyn) B(rooks) 1899-1985 ...... **CLC 10, 34, 39; DAM POP**
See also AITN 2; CA 13-16R; 116; CANR 16, 37; CLR 1, 21; DLB 11, 22; MAICYA; MTCW 1; SATA 2, 29, 100; SATA-Obit 44

White, Edmund (Valentine III) 1940- .... **CLC 27, 110; DAM POP**
See also AAYA 7; CA 45-48; CANR 3, 19, 36, 62; MTCW 1

White, Patrick (Victor Martindale) 1912-1990 ....CLC 3, 4, 5, 7, 9, 18, 65, 69
See also CA 81-84; 132; CANR 43; MTCW 1

White, Phyllis Dorothy James 1920-
See James, P. D.

White, T(erence) H(anbury)
1906-1964 .... **CLC 30**
See also AAYA 22; CA 73-76; CANR 37;
DLB 160; JRDA; MAICYA; SATA 12

White, Terence de Vere 1912-1994 .... **CLC 49**
See also CA 49-52; 145; CANR 3

White, Walter F(rancis) 1893-1955 ..... **TCLC 15**
See also White, Walter

White, William Hale 1831-1913
See Rutherford, Mark

Whitehead, E(dward) A(nthony)
1933- .... **CLC 5**
See also CA 65-68; CANR 58

Whitemore, Hugh (John) 1936-........ **CLC 37**
See also CA 132; INT 132

Whitman, Sarah Helen (Power)
1803-1878 .... **NCLC 19**
See also DLB 1

Whitman, Walt(er) 1819-1892 .... **NCLC 4, 31; DA; DAB; DAC; DAM MST, POET; PC 3; WLC**
See also CDALB 1640-1865; DLB 3, 64;
SATA 20

Whitney, Phyllis A(yame) 1903- .... **CLC 42; DAM POP**
See also AITN 2; BEST 90:3; CA 1-4R;
CANR 3, 25, 38, 60; JRDA; MAICYA;
SATA 1, 30

Whittemore, (Edward) Reed (Jr.)
1919- .... **CLC 4**
See also CA 9-12R; CAAS 8; CANR 4; DLB 5

Whittier, John Greenleaf 1807-1892 .... **NCLC 8, 59**
See also DLB 1

Whittlebot, Hernia
See Coward, Noel (Peirce)

Wicker, Thomas Grey 1926-
See Wicker, Tom

Wicker, Tom .... **CLC 7**
See also Wicker, Thomas Grey

Wideman, John Edgar 1941-.............. **CLC 5, 34, 36, 67; BLC 3; DAM MULT**
See also BW 2; CA 85-88; CANR 14, 42, 67;
DLB 33, 143

Wiebe, Rudy (Henry) 1934- .... **CLC 6, 11, 14; DAC; DAM MST**
See also CA 37-40R; CANR 42, 67; DLB 60

Wieland, Christoph Martin
1733-1813 .... **NCLC 17**
See also DLB 97

Wiene, Robert 1881-1938 .... **TCLC 56**

Wieners, John 1934-........................ **CLC 7**
See also CA 13-16R; DLB 16

Wiesel, Elie(zer) 1928- .... **CLC 3, 5, 11, 37; DA; DAB; DAC; DAM MST, NOV; WLCS**
See also AAYA 7; AITN 1; CA 5-8R; CAAS 4; CANR 8, 40, 65; DLB 83; DLBY 87; INT CANR-8; MTCW 1; SATA 56

Wiggins, Marianne 1947- .... **CLC 57**
See also BEST 89:3; CA 130; CANR 60

Wight, James Alfred 1916-1995
See Herriot, James

Wilbur, Richard (Purdy) 1921-............ **CLC 3, 6, 9, 14, 53, 110; DA; DAB; DAC; DAM MST, POET**
See also CA 1-4R; CABS 2; CANR 2, 29;
DLB 5, 169; INT CANR-29; MTCW 1;
SATA 9

Wild, Peter 1940-......................... **CLC 14**
See also CA 37-40R; DLB 5

Wilde, Oscar (Fingal O'Flahertie Wills)
1854(?)-1900......................... **TCLC 1, 8, 23, 41; DA; DAB; DAC; DAM DRAM, MST, NOV; SSC 11; WLC**
See also CA 104; 119; CDBLB 1890-1914;
DLB 10, 19, 34, 57, 141, 156, 190; SATA 24

Wilder, Billy .... **CLC 20**
See also Wilder, Samuel

Wilder, Samuel 1906-
See Wilder, Billy

Wilder, Thornton (Niven) 1897-1975..... **CLC 1, 5, 6, 10, 15, 35, 82; DA; DAB; DAC; DAM DRAM, MST, NOV; DC 1; WLC**
See also AITN 2; CA 13-16R; 61-64; CANR 40; DLB 4, 7, 9; DLBY 97; MTCW 1

Wilding, Michael 1942-................... **CLC 73**
See also CA 104; CANR 24, 49

Wiley, Richard 1944-..................... **CLC 44**
See also CA 121; 129; CANR 71

Wilhelm, Kate .... **CLC 7**
See also Wilhelm, Katie Gertrude

Wilhelm, Katie Gertrude 1928-
See Wilhelm, Kate

Wilkins, Mary
See Freeman, Mary Eleanor Wilkins

Willard, Nancy 1936- .... **CLC 7, 37**
See also CA 89-92; CANR 10, 39, 68; CLR 5; DLB 5, 52; MAICYA; MTCW 1; SATA 37, 71; SATA-Brief 30

Williams, Ben Ames 1889-1953 ...... **TCLC 89**
See also DLB 102

Williams, C(harles) K(enneth) 1936-..... **CLC 33, 56; DAM POET**
See also CA 37-40R; CAAS 26; CANR 57;
DLB 5

Williams, Charles
See Collier, James L(incoln)

Williams, Charles (Walter Stansby)
1886-1945 .... **TCLC 1, 11**
See also CA 104; 163; DLB 100, 153

Williams, (George) Emlyn 1905-1987 .... **CLC 15; DAM DRAM**
See also CA 104; 123; CANR 36; DLB 10, 77; MTCW 1

Williams, Hank 1923-1953............ **TCLC 81**

Williams, Hugo 1942- .... **CLC 42**
See also CA 17-20R; CANR 45; DLB 40

Williams, J. Walker
See Wodehouse, P(elham) G(renville)

Williams, John A(lfred) 1925- .... **CLC 5, 13; BLC 3; DAM MULT**
See also BW 2; CA 53-56; CAAS 3; CANR 6, 26, 51; DLB 2, 33; INT CANR-6

Williams, Jonathan (Chamberlain)
1929- .... **CLC 13**
See also CA 9-12R; CAAS 12; CANR 8; DLB 5

Williams, Joy 1944-....................... **CLC 31**
See also CA 41-44R; CANR 22, 48

Williams, Norman 1952- .... **CLC 39**
See also CA 118

Williams, Sherley Anne 1944-.............. **CLC 89; BLC 3; DAM MULT, POET**
See also BW 2; CA 73-76; CANR 25; DLB 41; INT CANR-25; SATA 78

Williams, Shirley
See Williams, Sherley Anne

Williams, Tennessee 1911-1983 .... **CLC 1, 2, 5, 7, 8, 11, 15, 19, 30, 39, 45, 71, 111; DA; DAB; DAC; DAM DRAM, MST; DC 4; WLC**
See also AITN 1, 2; CA 5-8R; 108; CABS 3; CANR 31; CDALB 1941-1968; DLB 7; DLBD 4; DLBY 83; MTCW 1

Williams, Thomas (Alonzo) 1926-1990... **CLC 14**
See also CA 1-4R; 132; CANR 2

Williams, William C.
See Williams, William Carlos

Williams, William Carlos 1883-1963 ..... **CLC 1, 2, 5, 9, 13, 22, 42, 67; DA; DAB; DAC; DAM MST, POET; PC 7; SSC 31**
See also CA 89-92; CANR 34; CDALB 1917-1929; DLB 4, 16, 54, 86; MTCW 1

Williamson, David (Keith) 1942- ...... **CLC 56**
See also CA 103; CANR 41

Williamson, Ellen Douglas 1905-1984
See Douglas, Ellen

Williamson, Jack......................... **CLC 29**
See also Williamson, John Stewart

Williamson, John Stewart 1908-
See Williamson, Jack

Willie, Frederick
See Lovecraft, H(oward) P(hillips)

Willingham, Calder (Baynard, Jr.)
1922-1995 .... **CLC 5, 51**
See also CA 5-8R; 147; CANR 3; DLB 2, 44; MTCW 1

Willis, Charles
See Clarke, Arthur C(harles)

Willy
See Colette, (Sidonie-Gabrielle)

Willy, Colette
See Colette, (Sidonie-Gabrielle)

Wilson, A(ndrew) N(orman) 1950- ... **CLC 33**
See also CA 112; 122; DLB 14, 155, 194

Wilson, Angus (Frank Johnstone)
1913-1991 ... **CLC 2, 3, 5, 25, 34; SSC 21**
See also CA 5-8R; 134; CANR 21; DLB 15, 139, 155; MTCW 1

Wilson, August 1945- ....CLC 39,
50, 63; BLC 3; DA; DAB; DAC; DAM
DRAM, MST, MULT; DC 2; WLCS
See also AAYA 16; BW 2; CA 115; 122;
CANR 42, 54; MTCW 1

Wilson, Brian 1942- .... CLC 12

Wilson, Colin 1931-.................... CLC 3, 14
See also CA 1-4R; CAAS 5; CANR 1, 22, 33;
DLB 14, 194; MTCW 1

Wilson, Dirk
See Pohl, Frederik

Wilson, Edmund 1895-1972 CLC
1, 2, 3, 8, 24
See also CA 1-4R; 37-40R; CANR 1, 46;
DLB 63; MTCW 1

Wilson, Ethel Davis (Bryant)
1888(?)-1980............................ CLC
13; DAC; DAM POET
See also CA 102; DLB 68; MTCW 1

Wilson, John 1785-1854 ....NCLC 5

Wilson, John (Anthony) Burgess 1917-1993
See Burgess, Anthony

Wilson, Lanford 1937-...................... CLC
7, 14, 36; DAM DRAM
See also CA 17-20R; CABS 3; CANR 45;
DLB 7

Wilson, Robert M. 1944- ....CLC 7, 9
See also CA 49-52; CANR 2, 41; MTCW 1

Wilson, Robert McLiam 1964-......... CLC 59
See also CA 132

Wilson, Sloan 1920- .... CLC 32
See also CA 1-4R; CANR 1, 44

Wilson, Snoo 1948- .... CLC 33
See also CA 69-72

Wilson, William S(mith) 1932-......... CLC 49
See also CA 81-84

Wilson, (Thomas) Woodrow
1856-1924 .... TCLC 79
See also CA 166; DLB 47

Winchilsea, Anne (Kingsmill) Finch
Counte 1661-1720
See Finch, Anne

Windham, Basil
See Wodehouse, P(elham) G(renville)

Wingrove, David (John) 1954-......... CLC 68
See also CA 133

Wintergreen, Jane
See Duncan, Sara Jeannette

Winters, Janet Lewis..................... CLC 41
See also Lewis, Janet

Winters, (Arthur) Yvor 1900-1968........ CLC
4, 8, 32
See also CA 11-12; 25-28R; CAP 1; DLB 48;
MTCW 1

Winterson, Jeanette 1959- CLC
64; DAM POP
See also CA 136; CANR 58

Winthrop, John 1588-1649 ....LC 31
See also DLB 24, 30

Wiseman, Frederick 1930-............. CLC 20
See also CA 159

Wister, Owen 1860-1938............... TCLC 21
See also CA 108; 162; DLB 9, 78, 186; SATA
62

Witkacy
See Witkiewicz, Stanislaw Ignacy

Witkiewicz, Stanislaw Ignacy
1885-1939 ....TCLC 8
See also CA 105; 162

Wittgenstein, Ludwig (Josef Johann)
1889-1951 .... TCLC 59
See also CA 113; 164

Wittig, Monique 1935(?)- .... CLC 22
See also CA 116; 135; DLB 83

Wittlin, Jozef 1896-1976................. CLC 25
See also CA 49-52; 65-68; CANR 3

Wodehouse, P(elham) G(renville)
1881-1975 ....CLC 1, 2, 5,
10, 22; DAB; DAC; DAM NOV; SSC 2
See also AITN 2; CA 45-48; 57-60; CANR
3, 33; CDBLB 1914-1945; DLB 34, 162;
MTCW 1; SATA 22

Woiwode, L.
See Woiwode, Larry (Alfred)

Woiwode, Larry (Alfred) 1941-..... CLC 6, 10
See also CA 73-76; CANR 16; DLB 6; INT
CANR-16

Wojciechowska, Maia (Teresa)
1927- .... CLC 26
See also AAYA 8; CA 9-12R; CANR 4, 41;
CLR 1; JRDA; MAICYA; SAAS 1; SATA
1, 28, 83

Wolf, Christa 1929-.............. CLC 14, 29, 58
See also CA 85-88; CANR 45; DLB 75;
MTCW 1

Wolfe, Gene (Rodman) 1931- CLC
25; DAM POP
See also CA 57-60; CAAS 9; CANR 6, 32,
60; DLB 8

Wolfe, George C. 1954-.........CLC 49; BLCS
See also CA 149

Wolfe, Thomas (Clayton) 1900-1938 ... TCLC
4, 13, 29, 61; DA; DAB; DAC; DAM
MST, NOV; SSC 33; WLC
See also CA 104; 132; CDALB 1929-1941;
DLB 9, 102; DLBD 2, 16; DLBY 85, 97;
MTCW 1

Wolfe, Thomas Kennerly, Jr. 1930-
See Wolfe, Tom

Wolfe, Tom ....CLC 1, 2, 9, 15, 35, 51
See also Wolfe, Thomas Kennerly, Jr.

Wolff, Geoffrey (Ansell) 1937-......... CLC 41
See also CA 29-32R; CANR 29, 43

Wolff, Sonia
See Levitin, Sonia (Wolff)

Wolff, Tobias (Jonathan Ansell) 1945-... CLC
39, 64
See also AAYA 16; BEST 90:2; CA 114; 117;
CAAS 22; CANR 54; DLB 130; INT 117

Wolfram von Eschenbach c. 1170-c.
1220 ....CMLC 5
See also DLB 138

Wolitzer, Hilma 1930-.................... CLC 17
See also CA 65-68; CANR 18, 40; INT
CANR-18; SATA 31

Wollstonecraft, Mary 1759-1797 .... LC 5
See also CDBLB 1789-1832; DLB 39, 104,
158

Wonder, Stevie............................ CLC 12
See also Morris, Steveland Judkins

Wong, Jade Snow 1922- .... CLC 17
See also CA 109

Woodberry, George Edward
1855-1930 .... TCLC 73
See also CA 165; DLB 71, 103

Woodcott, Keith
See Brunner, John (Kilian Houston)

Woodruff, Robert W.
See Mencken, H(enry) L(ouis)

Woolf, (Adeline) Virginia 1882-1941 ... TCLC
1, 5, 20, 43, 56; DA; DAB; DAC; DAM
MST, NOV; SSC 7; WLC
See also CA 104; 130; CANR 64; CDBLB
1914-1945; DLB 36, 100, 162; DLBD 10;
MTCW 1

Woolf, Virginia Adeline
See Woolf, (Adeline) Virginia

Woollcott, Alexander (Humphreys)
1887-1943 ....TCLC 5
See also CA 105; 161; DLB 29

Woolrich, Cornell 1903-1968........... CLC 77
See also Hopley-Woolrich, Cornell George

Wordsworth, Dorothy 1771-1855 ... NCLC 25
See also DLB 107

Wordsworth, William 1770-1850........NCLC
12, 38; DA; DAB; DAC; DAM MST,
POET; PC 4; WLC
See also CDBLB 1789-1832; DLB 93, 107

Wouk, Herman 1915- CLC
1, 9, 38; DAM NOV, POP
See also CA 5-8R; CANR 6, 33, 67; DLBY
82; INT CANR-6; MTCW 1

Wright, Charles (Penzel, Jr.) 1935-....... CLC
6, 13, 28
See also CA 29-32R; CAAS 7; CANR 23, 36,
62; DLB 165; DLBY 82; MTCW 1

Wright, Charles Stevenson 1932- CLC
49; BLC 3; DAM MULT, POET
See also BW 1; CA 9-12R; CANR 26; DLB
33

Wright, Frances 1795-1852 .... NCLC 74
See also DLB 73

Wright, Jack R.
See Harris, Mark

Wright, James (Arlington) 1927-1980 ... CLC
3, 5, 10, 28; DAM POET
See also AITN 2; CA 49-52; 97-100; CANR
4, 34, 64; DLB 5, 169; MTCW 1

Wright, Judith (Arandell) 1915-........... CLC
11, 53; PC 14
See also CA 13-16R; CANR 31; MTCW 1;
SATA 14

Wright, L(aurali) R. 1939-............. CLC 44
See also CA 138

Drama Criticism
Cumulative Nationality Index

Drama Criticism
Cumulative Title Index

Title Index

Title Index

Title Index

Title Index